2011
Scholarship
Handbook

2011
Scholarship Handbook

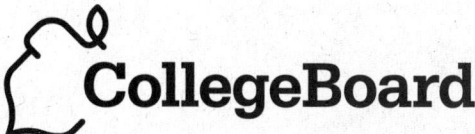

Fourteenth Edition

The College Board, New York

The College Board

The College Board is a not-for-profit membership association whose mission is to connect students to college success and opportunity. Founded in 1900, the College Board is composed of more than 5,700 schools, colleges, universities and other educational organizations. Each year, the College Board serves seven million students and their parents, 23,000 high schools, and 3,800 colleges through major programs and services in college readiness, college admission, guidance, assessment, financial aid and enrollment. Among its widely recognized programs are the SAT®, the PSAT/NMSQT®, the Advanced Placement Program® (AP®), SpringBoard® and ACCUPLACER®. The College Board is committed to the principles of excellence and equity, and that commitment is embodied in all of its programs, services, activities and concerns.

For further information, visit www.collegeboard.com.

Editorial inquiries concerning this book should be directed to College Planning Services, The College Board, 45 Columbus Avenue, New York, NY 10023-6992; or telephone 212-713-8000.

Copies of this book are available from your local bookseller or may be ordered from College Board Publications, P.O. Box 8670, Reston, VA 20195. The book may also be ordered online through the College Board Store at www.collegeboard.com. The price is $28.99.

Contents

Preface vii

How to Use This Book 1

Understanding Financial Aid 5

Finding and Applying for Scholarships 11

Sources of Information About State Grant Programs 18

Glossary 21

Eligibility Indexes

Corporate/Employer 27
Disabilities 27
Field of Study/Intended Career 27
Gender 48
International Student 49
Military Participation 49
Minority Status 51
National/Ethnic Background 55
Organization/Civic Affiliation 55
Religious Affiliation 57
Returning Adult 58
State of Residence 58
Study Abroad 71

Scholarships 73

Internships 525

Loans 573

Sponsor Index 589

Program Index 597

Contents

Preface

How to Use This Book

Understanding Financial Aid

Finding and Applying for Scholarships

Sources of Information About State Grant
Programs

Glossary

Eligibility Indexes

Scholarships

Internships

Loans

Sponsor Index

Program Index

Preface

Searching for scholarships has often been described as looking for a needle in a haystack. There are thousands of award programs available, but the typical student can expect to qualify for only a small number of them. This book is designed to point you toward programs that match your own personal and academic qualifications.

Compiled within this book are detailed descriptions of national and state-level award programs for undergraduate students. Most are available to all under-graduates, but some are restricted to entering freshmen, and others are only for continuing students — sophomores, juniors or seniors. Most awards are only available to U.S. citizens or permanent residents, but some are also available to students in other countries who plan to come to the United States for college.

The award program descriptions are based on information provided by the sponsors themselves, in response to the College Board's Annual Survey of Financial Aid Programs, conducted in the spring of 2010. A staff of editors verified the facts for every award program. While every effort was made to ensure that the information is correct and up to date, we urge you to confirm facts, especially deadline information, with the programs themselves. The award programs' websites are the best sources for current information.

We'd like to thank those who worked so hard to bring the *Scholarship Handbook 2011* to press: Data was compiled and edited by editors Rachel Mason, Rachel Korowitz, Elizabeth Blue and Jennifer Donato under the direction of project manager Andy Costello. Finally, we would like to thank the team of programmers and composers at Content Data Solutions, Inc., who converted the database into readable pages.

Tom Vanderberg
Senior Editor, College Planning Services

Michael Polizzi
Assistant Editor, College Planning Services

How to Use This Book

You may be tempted to go directly to the program descriptions and start browsing, but to get the most out of this book, start by reading the information and advice in the opening pages. They'll help you get a realistic perspective on financial aid and give you useful guidelines for understanding and taking advantage of your college funding options.

Your next step should be to complete the "Personal Characteristics Checklist" on page 13. This will help you think about all the ways you might qualify for scholarships and give you an idea of where you might start looking for awards you can apply for.

Using the eligibility indexes

After your checklist is complete, use the eligibility indexes beginning on page 27 to find the award programs that correspond to your qualifications. You can also use the scholarship search program on www.collegeboard.com. This user-friendly program enables you to search with more criteria and with much greater speed than is possible with print indexes.

Please keep in mind that the eligibility indexes show programs for which *one* of the criteria is covered by the index. Most of these programs have additional requirements, such as financial need (as demonstrated on the FAFSA or CSS/Financial Aid PROFILE®), standardized test scores or GPA.

Corporate/Employer: Listed here are the many companies and businesses that offer scholarships to employees and/or employees' family members. You should check out any company that employs a member of your immediate family.

Disabilities: This category covers students with hearing or visual impairments, physical handicaps or learning disabilities.

Field of Study/Intended Career: This category, by far the longest, identifies broad major and career areas. If you don't see your specific area of interest, look for a more general area into which it might fit. In many cases, these awards require applicants to be already enrolled in college and to have declared a major in the relevant field.

KNOW THE LINGO

You'll find sidebars like this throughout the first part of this book highlighting and defining key terms. There's also a comprehensive glossary beginning on page 21.

Gender: Although the vast majority of awards are not gender-specific, there are more than 95 awards in this book exclusively for women, and more than 20 for men only.

International Students: Most awards in this book are available only to U.S. citizens or permanent residents. The programs in this category, however, are open to students from outside the United States.

Military Participation: Many of the awards in this category are for the children, descendants or spouses of members of the military, including the Reserves and National Guard, going back as far as the Civil War.

Minority Status: There are eight groups within this category, representing a wide range of awards.

National/Ethnic Background: The national/ethnic groups in this category are determined by the sponsoring organizations that responded to our annual survey.

Organization/Civic Affiliation: Many membership organizations and civic associations have generous higher education funding programs that are available for their members and/or their members' dependents or relatives. Check to see if any apply to your family.

Religious Affiliation: The 10 denominations in this category represent a broad range but, like the national/ethnic category, are determined by the respondents to our annual survey.

Returning Adult: This category includes awards for undergraduate, graduate and nondegree study. The age qualification varies, but most often is for students 25 years or older.

State of Residence: Each state has several award programs exclusively for state residents. Be sure to examine closely all those listed under your state.

Study Abroad: While most award programs for study abroad are for graduate students, a few are geared for undergraduates, and you will find them listed here.

What's in the program descriptions?

The scholarship programs in this book are organized alphabetically by sponsor within three sections.

The scholarships section covers public and private scholarships and research grants for undergraduates. To be included, a scholarship program must grant at least $250 for the purpose of financing some aspect of higher education: tuition and fees, research, study abroad, travel expenses or other educational endeavors.

KEEP IN MIND

This book does not describe local award programs that are restricted to a single community or school. For information about local programs for which you might qualify, talk to your school counselor or contact your local chamber of commerce.

Also not included in this are scholarships offered by colleges to their own students. For these "inside" awards, you should consult the financial aid offices at the colleges you are considering. Detailed financial aid information for more than 3,000 colleges can also be found in the College Board book *Getting Financial Aid 2011.*

PLANNING AHEAD

Even if you qualify for a scholarship, you won't get it if you don't **apply on time**! Use the **planning worksheet on page 17** to keep track of deadlines, application requirements and notification dates for the programs you've selected.

The internships section covers public and private internships, providing opportunities either to earn money for education or to gain academic credit. To be included, paid internships must pay at least $100 per week and provide a viable path toward a future career. (The General Motors internship is an example of this; the Oscar Mayer Wienermobile is not.)

The loans section covers public and private education loan programs. Many have loan forgiveness options, usually in exchange for public or community service for a certain period of time.

Each program description contains all of the information provided by the sponsor and verified for accuracy by a staff of editors at the College Board. A typical description includes:

Type of award: Whether the award is a scholarship, grant, internship or loan; and whether it's renewable.

Intended use: Tells you the range and limitations of the award, such as level of study, full time or part time, at what kind of institution, and whether in the United States or abroad.

Eligibility: Indicates the characteristics you must have to be considered for an award — for example, U.S. citizenship, specific state of residence, disability, membership in a particular organization or minority status.

Basis for selection: May include major or career interest; personal qualities such as seriousness of purpose, high academic achievement or depth of character; or financial need.

Application requirements: Outlines what you must provide in support of your application, such as recommendations, essay, transcript, interview, proof of eligibility, a résumé or references.

Additional information: Gives you any facts or requirements not covered in the categories above — for example, which test scores to submit, GPA required, whether a particular type of student is given special consideration, when application forms are available, etc.

Amount of award: A single figure generally means the standard amount, but may indicate the maximum of a range of amounts. If a program awards different amounts, the range is provided.

Number of awards: Tells you how many awards are granted by the sponsor.

Number of applicants: Tells you how many students applied the previous year.

Application deadline: The date by which your application must be submitted; some scholarships have two deadlines for considering applications. Note: This information was obtained in spring 2010. Deadlines may have passed or changed. Check the sponsor's website for current deadlines.

Notification begins: The earliest date that an award notification is sent; in some cases, all go out on the same date; in others, notification is on a rolling basis. If there are two application deadlines, there are usually two notification dates.

GOOD TO KNOW

In addition to the eligibility indexes preceding the scholarship descriptions, there are two general indexes in the back of the book that list award programs by sponsor name and program name.

KNOW THE LINGO

Academic internship — An internship where you are not paid for your work, but rather earn college credit.

Paid internship — An internship where you are paid for your work.

Total amount awarded: Tells you how much money is disbursed in the current award year, including renewable awards.

Contact: Gives you all available information on where to get application forms and further information. Where the contact name and address are identical for several different scholarship programs sponsored by the same organization, this information will appear at the end of the last scholarship in that group.

While some descriptions don't include all these details because they were either not applicable or not supplied by the sponsor, in every case all essential information is provided. Readers are urged to verify all information (the sponsor's website is the best source) before submitting applications.

Understanding Financial Aid

You shouldn't count on "outside scholarships" and summer internships like the ones in this book to pay for college. Rather, you should treat them as one possible source of aid, along with federal student aid and the scholarships and work-study jobs offered by colleges. In fact, outside scholarships account for only 8 percent of total student financial aid each year.

In order to get the most out of this book, you should first understand how to apply for the other 92 percent of total aid.

What Is Financial Aid?

Financial aid is money given or loaned to you to help you pay for college. Different forms have different rules. The vast majority of aid comes from the federal government, and most of it consists of loans that you must pay back. However, some aid does not require repayment — which makes it the best kind.

If you qualify for financial aid, your college will put together an aid "package," usually with different types of aid bundled together. Most students qualify for some form of financial aid, so it makes sense to apply for it.

You'll apply for financial aid either at the same time or soon after you apply for admission. You may have to fill out more than one application. At the very least you will fill out the FAFSA, or federal government form, available on the Web at www.fafsa.ed.gov. You may also fill out another form, the CSS/Financial Aid PROFILE, which many colleges require. Some colleges and state aid agencies require their own financial aid forms, too. The colleges to which you apply will use the forms to figure out what your family can afford to pay and what your "need" is — that is, the difference between what you can pay and what the college actually costs. If the school wants you as a student but sees that you can't handle the whole bill, it will make you a financial aid offer to help you meet your need. If you accept, that financial aid package is your award.

KNOW THE LINGO

Merit aid — Aid awarded on the basis of academics, character or talent.

Need-based aid — Aid awarded on the basis of a family's inability to pay the full cost of attending a particular college.

Non-need-based aid — Aid awarded on some basis other than need or merit, such as grants with eligibility requirements related to field of study or state residence.

You will need to apply for financial aid every year that you are in college, mainly because your family's financial situation changes yearly. As a result, your financial aid package will probably be somewhat different from year to year.

Financial aid is a helping hand, not a free pass. In the United States, everyone has a right to a free public school education, but not to a free college education. The federal government and most colleges agree that students and their parents are the ones most responsible for paying for college. "The primary responsibility of paying for the student's education lies with the student and his or her parents," says Forrest M. Stuart, the director of financial aid at Furman University in Greenville, S.C. "Financial aid comes in to fill that gap, if you will, between what they can afford and what the college costs."

Types of Aid

Financial aid may come in many forms. However, all forms can be grouped into two major categories: gift aid and self-help aid.

Gift Aid

Gift aid is free money, money that you don't have to pay back or work for. Naturally, this is the kind of aid most people want. It can take the form of grants or scholarships.

The terms "grant" and "scholarship" are often used interchangeably to mean free money. But here's the difference: A grant is usually given only on the basis of need, or your family's inability to pay the full cost of college. Scholarships are usually awarded only to those who have "merit," such as proven ability in academics, the arts or athletics. Once you're in college, you may have to maintain a minimum GPA or take certain courses to continue receiving a scholarship.

Self-Help Aid

Self-help aid is money that requires a contribution from you. That can mean paying back the money (if the aid is a loan) or working for the money (if the aid is a work-study job).

The most common form of self-help aid is a loan. A loan is money that you have to pay back with interest. In light of that, you might not consider this aid at all. But it is — a loan means you don't have to pay the full price of college all at once: You can stretch the payments over time, as you would when buying a house or a car. Furthermore, some student loans are subsidized by the federal government, which means you don't have to pay the interest that comes due while you're in college.

Subsidized loans, which are awarded based on need and administered by the college, are the best kind. But you can also take out unsubsidized student loans and parent loans, which are not packaged by most colleges. However, be careful not to take on more debt than necessary. No matter what kind of loan you take out, you will have to pay it back.

GOOD TO KNOW

For a more thorough explanation of student financial aid, read the College Board book *Getting Financial Aid 2011*, or read the articles in the "Pay for College" section of www.collegeboard.com.

Another form of self-help is work-study. This is financial aid in the form of a job. Since you earn the money through your work, this too may not seem like aid. But it is, because the federal work-study program pays most of your wages. And work-study jobs are usually available right on campus, with limits on your hours so that you won't be unduly distracted from studying.

Who Gets Aid?

Grants and loans are not just for the poorest of the poor, nor are scholarships only for the smartest of the smart. The truth about who gets financial aid is somewhat different from what many people think.

Those Who Need It

Most financial aid is based on need, not merit. There is money for merit, but most colleges in the United States focus their financial aid packages on meeting financial need.

However, there is a lot of confusion about what "need" means. "A lot of people think that they either have to be on welfare or Social Security — really poor — to get financial aid, and that's not correct," says Mary San Agustin, director of financial aid and scholarships at Palomar College in San Marcos, Calif. On the other hand, some rich families mistakenly think they are needy because their high living expenses leave them little money for college. "It's this expectation of, I pay my taxes, so my kid should be entitled to some federal financial aid regardless of how much money I make," says San Agustin.

Need simply means that your family can't afford to pay the full cost of a particular college. The *amount* of your need will vary from college to college, because it depends on the cost of attending an individual college. Whether your family has need is determined not by whether you think you are rich or poor, but by the financial aid forms you fill out.

Those Who Don't

Despite the overall emphasis on need, many colleges do give away money on the basis of merit. They do this to attract the students they want most, and they may award this money even if it is more than the student needs. However, in many cases, the student both needs the money and has earned it on the basis of merit.

Don't think that only geniuses get merit aid. At many colleges a B average can put you in the running for merit money. Sometimes a separate application for merit aid is required to put you into consideration; sometimes your application for admission is enough. In either case, don't count yourself out by not applying; apply and let the college decide.

Grants are sometimes awarded based on neither need nor merit. For example, you may get a grant if you are in a certain field of study, are a resident of the state, or are a student from the same town as the college.

KNOW THE LINGO

EFC (Expected Family Contribution) — How much money a family is expected to pay for college, based on the family's ability to pay.

Need — The difference between your EFC and the cost of attending a particular college you've chosen. Financial aid is designed to meet your need, not your EFC.

Gap — The difference (if any) between the financial aid you need and the amount offered by a particular college.

Part-Time Students

Some kinds of aid are only available to students enrolled in college full time — usually 12 or more credit hours of courses per semester. But part-time students are eligible for some financial aid. For example, federal loan programs require only that students be enrolled at least half time. Also, some employers offer tuition reimbursement benefits to students who work full time and go to college part time.

Where the Money Comes From

Financial aid comes from three basic sources: governments (both federal and state), colleges and outside benefactors.

From the Government

The lion's share of total financial aid awarded to undergraduates comes from the federal government. Fully 69 percent of all such aid is sent from Washington. The largest chunk of that consists of federal loans, which total $83.9 billion a year and represent 45 percent of all student aid. The loans take multiple shapes. Perkins loans are subsidized, with the lowest interest rate of any education loan. Stafford loans may be subsidized or unsubsidized. Both Perkins and Stafford loans are for students, but parents may take out a PLUS loan, which is not subsidized, to help pay for their children's education.

The federal government also funds several grants: the Pell Grant, the Supplemental Educational Opportunity Grant (SEOG), the Academic Competitiveness Grant and the SMART Grant. The Pell and SEOG grants are strictly need based, while the last two are based on both need and academic criteria. The government also funds the federal work-study program.

A much smaller piece of the financial aid pie (7 percent) comes from individual state governments. This is available in the form of grants, scholarships and loans. Most of this aid is for use only at colleges within the state, though a few states offer "portable" aid, which state residents can take with them to a college in another state.

From the College

A great deal of financial aid comes from individual colleges, using their own "institutional" funds. In fact, colleges award nearly half of all grants. Many, though not all, award merit scholarships as well as need-based grants. They may also offer on-campus job opportunities and loans.

Private colleges give more financial aid than public ones, but their tuition is usually higher as well. Public colleges award less aid, but taxpayer support keeps their tuition lower.

Outside Grants and Scholarships

Outside grants and scholarships come from sources other than the government or the college. These sources may include corporations like Coca-Cola or community groups like the Elks Club. Some are well known, such as National Merit Scholarship Corporation, but altogether they are the smallest piece of the financial aid pie: Only 8 percent of all student aid comes from outside sources. Pursue them, but don't expect them to outweigh the other aid you will get.

Bear in mind also that an outside scholarship is unlikely to expand the total aid you receive. If a college has already "met your full need" — that is, offered an aid package that covers the entire difference between what the college costs and what your family is expected to pay — it will not add an outside scholarship to that aid package. Rather, it will use your scholarship to substitute for some other piece of aid in the package. Think of your financial aid package as a barrel: When the barrel is full, no more can be added unless something is taken away. The last thing colleges will take away is whatever sum of money your family is expected to contribute.

How Outside Awards Can Help

Even though outside scholarships rarely decrease the amount that your family is expected to pay out of pocket, it's still very worthwhile to pursue them. Why? Simply put, they expand your options for where you can go to college.

At some colleges, the first things taken away from a full-need package to make room for an outside scholarship are loans. Since that reduces the total amount you will have to pay back later, it makes that college more affordable. (Colleges vary in their policies on how they adjust packages for outside scholarships; you should call or e-mail the financial aid offices at the colleges you're considering to learn about their policies.)

There are also colleges that can't afford to offer every admitted student a financial aid package that meets the student's full need. If, for example, your need is $25,000 at a particular university, and the university's aid office can only offer you a combined total of $23,000 in grants, scholarships, work-study and subsidized federal loans, then there is a $2,000 "gap" in your aid package. Outside scholarships can help fill that gap.

Finally, there may be colleges where you don't have any financial need. For example, if your family's expected contribution to your college costs is $10,000, a state university that costs $10,000 a year to attend couldn't offer you any need-based aid. An outside merit scholarship, in this case, could decrease what your family pays below their expected contribution.

FINANCIAL AID APPLICATION CALENDAR

SOPHOMORE/JUNIOR YEARS

- Talk to your parents about college costs. Have realistic expectations, but understand how financial aid can expand your options.
- Take the PSAT/NMSQT® in October of each year. If you take it as a junior and meet other requirements, you will be entered into National Merit Scholarship Corporation competitions.
- Think about colleges you might want to apply to. If possible, visit some campuses in the spring of your junior year.
- Take the SAT® in the spring of your junior year.
- If you have a job, do your taxes each year (ask your parents for help). Knowing about tax forms and documents will be helpful when you have to fill out financial aid applications.
- Think about taking SAT Subject Tests™ near the end of courses in the subject areas you are studying.

SENIOR YEAR

SEPTEMBER
- Create a list of colleges you want to apply to. Start a checklist of their financial aid requirements and deadlines.
- If you're thinking about applying Early Decision to a college, ask whether it offers an early estimate of financial aid eligibility, and if so, what forms are required to receive one.
- Begin searching for outside scholarship programs available to seniors. Ask your school counselor about local scholarships offered by groups and businesses in your community.

OCTOBER
- Ask your school counselor if there will be a family financial aid night at your school or elsewhere in your area this fall. If there is, be sure to attend; the event may be your single best source of information.
- Use the online calculators at **www.collegeboard.com** to estimate your family's Expected Family Contribution (EFC).
- If you need to fill out the CSS/Financial Aid PROFILE, you can do so on the PROFILE Online Web site starting Oct. 1.

NOVEMBER
- Finalize the list of colleges that you'll apply to regular decision. Make sure you have all the financial aid forms you need.
- Starting Nov. 1, you can visit the FAFSA on the Web and get a sense of how the site works and what the application will ask for. But remember, you can't file the FAFSA until Jan. 1.

DECEMBER
- You and your parents should save all end-of-year pay stubs for the year. You can use these to estimate income on aid forms.
- Apply for scholarships in time to meet application deadlines.
- Get PINs for the FAFSA for both yourself and one of your parents from **www.pin.ed.gov**.

JANUARY
- You can file the FAFSA starting Jan. 1.
- If any colleges you're applying to have a financial aid priority date of Feb. 1, fill out the FAFSA (and PROFILE, if necessary) using estimated income information from your end-of-year pay stubs and last year's tax returns.
- Submit any other financial aid forms that may be required. Keep copies.

FEBRUARY
- If you didn't file the FAFSA and other aid forms in January, do so now, using drafts of your family's income tax returns.
- Check your federal Student Aid Report (SAR) when you receive it, and correct it if necessary.
- You and your parents should consider filing your income tax returns early this year. Some colleges will request copies of your family's returns before finalizing offers.

MARCH
- If necessary, write to colleges alerting them to special circumstances that affect your family's ability to pay for college.
- As you begin to receive letters of acceptance, check with aid offices to see if additional documentation (such as tax forms) must be submitted.

APRIL
- Compare your financial aid award letters using the online tools at **www.collegeboard.com**.
- Write, e-mail or call the colleges that have offered you aid if you have any questions about the packages they've offered you.
- If you don't get enough aid to be able to attend a college, consider your options, which include appealing the award.

MAY
- Be sure to accept the aid package from the college you want to attend by May 1.
- Be sure also to let other schools know you won't be attending.
- Plan now how you will cover your family's out-of-pocket expenses.
- Apply for loans if necessary.

Finding and Applying for Scholarships

While you're researching and applying for colleges, you should also use this book to find scholarships that you qualify for and apply for them. In this chapter you'll find advice, as well as a calendar and worksheets to help keep you on track.

When to Start Looking

It's never too early to start looking for scholarships. There are several programs that are open only to high school freshmen and sophomores, and some that are open only to juniors. There are other programs where you begin the work of applying up to a year before the final determination is made. For example, National Merit Scholarship Corporation competitions begin when students take the PSAT/NMSQT® in October of their junior year, and the competitions proceed in several rounds until fall of their senior year. If you're already a senior, though, don't despair — there are plenty of programs for entering freshmen that you can apply for during your senior year.

No matter what grade level you're in, the best time of the year to research programs is in the summer or early fall. That way you can be sure to find programs before their deadlines have passed, and with enough advance time to prepare a complete, competitive application. Remember that many scholarship programs require you to submit an essay as part of your application, and essays take time to write. Many programs also require recommendations; as a general rule, you should ask for recommendations at least four weeks in advance, and preferably more. Some programs even require you to perform additional academic work outside of school, such as writing a research paper or competing in a science fair.

You should let your school counselor know as early as possible that you're interested in applying for scholarships. He or she can help you think about your strengths as a student, which will make it easier to narrow down your scholarship search. Your counselor will also be able to recommend some programs you should apply for. (See "Thinking Locally" on page 14.)

Playing Catch-Up

If it's already the middle of your senior year, you've probably missed a lot of opportunities to apply for scholarships with October, November and December deadlines. But don't give up yet; there are plenty of scholarships with January, February and March deadlines.

The key to playing catch-up is to start working now, today. Find scholarships where the deadline hasn't passed. Get applications from the sponsors' websites. Talk to your school counselor immediately. The longer you wait, the less likely you are to win any awards.

The good news: Since you're already far into the college application process, you're now a pro at describing yourself to admission committees and scholarship review boards. You also have personal essays, academic writing samples and teacher recommendations ready to go.

Choosing Where to Apply

There are so many scholarships, grants, fellowships, internships, fee waivers, work-study jobs and low-interest loans available for college-level study that just looking at the options can be daunting. (This book alone describes 2,100 national and state-level programs.) Fortunately, there are some easy ways to narrow the field of potential programs down to the ones where you have a good chance of winning an award.

The personal characteristics checklist on the next page highlights some of the common eligibility criteria for scholarship programs. You're not likely to find a scholarship that's targeted to every one of your characteristics, but you can use your answers on the checklist as a starting point for finding programs. The eligibility indexes on pages 27 to 71 will help you quickly match your characteristics to programs.

You'll probably find a few scholarship programs that match your characteristics. If you find a lot, you should consider narrowing your search — applying for scholarships is a lot of work! It's far better to send in four high-quality applications to programs that closely match your characteristics and interests than to send 16 hurried applications to a wide variety of programs.

PLANNING AHEAD

If you haven't already started looking for scholarships, start now. Today. Use this book to find a program you qualify for, and make a note of its application deadline and requirements. Then go to the program's website and download an application.

PERSONAL CHARACTERISTICS
CHECKLIST

Are you **male** or **female**?

What is your **state of residence**?

Do you have a **learning or physical disability**? Many scholarships are offered to those who are disabled in any way, but some are for those with a specific disability.

Military service is the basis of many scholarships. Many of these awards are not just for those who have worn a uniform, but also for their spouses and children, or even descendants of a veteran. Talk to your family about its military history (was Grandpa in the Korean War?) Be sure to find out what branch of the military your family members served in, and, if possible, which unit(s) they served in.

List any family history of military service here:

You'll find scholarships for students with **minority status**, (e.g., African American, Alaska Native), and also for students with a particular **nationality or ethnic background** (e.g., Chinese, Greek).

If you belong to a minority, list it here:

List your ethnic and/or national origin(s) here:

What, if any, is your **religious affiliation**?

Are you an **international student** (a citizen of a foreign country, including Canada, seeking to study in the United States)?

The largest category of scholarships and internships is for students planning to study a particular college major (e.g., math, English, a foreign language) or prepare for a particular career (e.g., law, education, aviation). Even if you are "undecided" at this point, you should list all the **majors/careers** you are leaning toward.

☐ Do you want to **study abroad**? There are scholarships to help you pay for it — check here to remind yourself to seek them out.

"Returning adult" refers to students who have been out of high school a year or more before entering college. If that's you, look for scholarships designed to encourage your pursuit.

Years out of high school:

Your age:

Do you or any members of your family belong to a **national or local organization** or **civic association** (e.g., Kiwanis, Rotary, Elks Club)? Many such groups offer scholarships to members and/or their families. List here any that apply:

Employers and corporations often offer scholarship benefits to employees and/or their families. List the companies that you or someone in your family works for here:

Narrowing Your Search

If you're having trouble narrowing down your scholarship search, consider the following:

How many applicants are there each year? Some of the better-known programs (such as the Coca-Cola Scholars Program) see hundreds of applicants for every award they give out! It can't hurt to apply for these programs, but you shouldn't invest so much effort in applying for them that you miss out on smaller programs where your chances may be better.

Is this really for me? If you couldn't get through *Atlas Shrugged* the first time, don't force yourself to read it and write an essay on its philosophical meaning for the Ayn Rand Institute contest — even if you're a great English student. Focus instead on programs that appeal to you or sound like fun.

Can I live with the strings attached? Many scholarship and internship programs have service requirements. Most notably, the Reserve Officers Training Corps (ROTC) program requires cadets to become military reserve officers upon graduation. And some summer internships will require you to move to another city.

KEEP IN MIND

Don't let your scholarship search overshadow your other responsibilities and application requirements. You still need to do well in school, get your college applications in on time, and submit the FAFSA and other financial aid forms by your colleges' priority dates.

Thinking Locally

This book contains national and statewide financial aid programs offered by government agencies, charitable foundations and major corporations. But there are also thousands of small scholarship programs offered on a local level by civic clubs, parishes, memorial foundations and small businesses.

In many cases, these programs award just a few hundred dollars — enough to buy a semester's worth of textbooks. But since they are offered on a local level, your chances of receiving an award are much higher than they are for the big national competitions. So it pays to look for local scholarships.

Your school counselor may have files of local scholarship programs. There may even be a scholarship designated for graduates of your high school — you'll never know until you ask. You should also check with employers (either your parents' or your own); your church, temple or mosque; and any civic clubs that your family members are involved in.

Avoiding Scholarship Scams

The Federal Trade Commission (FTC) developed Project $cholar$cam to alert students and families about potential scams and how to recognize them. Here are the FTC's seven basic warning signs:

- "This scholarship is guaranteed or your money back."
- "You can't get this information anywhere else."
- "May I have your credit card/bank account number to hold this scholarship?"
- "We'll do all the work for you."

- "The scholarship will cost some money."
- "You've been selected by a national foundation to receive a scholarship."
- "You're a finalist" in a competition you never entered.

Remember that no one can guarantee that you'll receive a grant or scholarship, and that you will have to do the work of submitting applications to be considered. Don't pay money for a service without a written document saying what you'll get for your money and what the company's refund policies are. And never, ever give your credit card number, Social Security number or bank account information to someone who called you unsolicited.

Applying for Scholarships

This may mean not only filling out a form but also compiling supporting documents, such as transcripts, recommendations and an essay. Or you might need to provide evidence of leadership, patriotism, depth of character, desire to serve, or financial need. Get to know the requirements of each scholarship as early as possible so you can do any necessary extra work on time.

A few pointers to remember:

Apply early! Apply as early as possible to scholarship programs. If you can, do it in the fall of your senior year, even if the deadlines aren't until February or March. Very often, scholarship programs will have awarded all their funds for the year on a first-come, first-served basis before their stated deadline.

Follow directions. Read instructions carefully and do what they say. Scholarship programs receive hundreds and even thousands of applications. Don't lose out because of failure to submit a typewritten essay versus a handwritten one if required, or to provide appropriate recommendations. If you have a question about your eligibility for a particular scholarship or how to complete the application, contact the scholarship sponsors.

Be organized. It's a good idea to create a separate file for each scholarship and sort them by their due dates. Track application deadlines and requirements. Store in one place the different supporting documents you may need, such as transcripts, standardized test scores and letters of recommendation.

Check your work. Proofread your applications for spelling or grammar errors, fill in all blanks and make sure your handwriting is legible.

Keep copies of everything. If application materials get lost, having copies on file will make it easier to resend the application quickly.

Reapply. Some programs only offer money for the first year of college, but others must be renewed each subsequent year.

SCHOLARSHIP APPLICATION PLANNER

	PROGRAM 1	PROGRAM 2	PROGRAM 3
PROGRAM/SPONSOR	National Merit Scholarship	Young Epidemiology Scholars	First Bank
ELIGIBILITY REQUIREMENTS	Academic merit	Academic merit	Need, local residency
TYPE OF AWARD	Scholarship	Scholarship	Internship
AMOUNT OF AWARD	$2,500	$1,000 or more	$2,500
CAN BE USED FOR	Tuition/fees	Any expense	Any expense
CAN BE USED AT	First-choice college	Any college	In-state colleges
DEADLINE	Oct. 1 (give essay to English teacher for review)	Feb. 1	April 1
FORMS REQUIRED	NMSC application	Web form	Application (includes need analysis)
TEST SCORES REQUIRED	PSAT/NMSQT (already took), SAT (by December)	None	SAT
ESSAY OR ACADEMIC SAMPLE	Personal statement, academic transcript	Essay, research project	None required
RECOMMENDATIONS	Principal	None	One teacher (Mr. Filmer), Local branch manager
NOTIFICATION BEGINS	March	Not sure	May 15
REQUIREMENTS TO KEEP AFTER FRESHMAN YEAR	One-time payment only	One-time payment only	Based on performance during internship

For a blank version of this worksheet that you can photocopy for your own use, see the next page.

SCHOLARSHIP APPLICATION PLANNER

	PROGRAM 1	PROGRAM 2	PROGRAM 3
PROGRAM/SPONSOR			
ELIGIBILITY REQUIREMENTS			
TYPE OF AWARD			
AMOUNT OF AWARD			
CAN BE USED FOR			
CAN BE USED AT			
DEADLINE			
FORMS REQUIRED			
TEST SCORES REQUIRED			
ESSAY OR ACADEMIC SAMPLE			
RECOMMENDATIONS			
NOTIFICATION BEGINS			
REQUIREMENTS TO KEEP AFTER FRESHMAN YEAR			

Sources of Information About State Grant Programs

Alabama
Alabama Commission on
 Higher Education
P.O. Box 302000
Montgomery, AL 36130-2000
334-242-1998
www.ache.state.al.us

Alaska
Alaska Commission on
 Postsecondary Education
P.O. Box 110505
Juneau, AK 99811-0505
800-441-2962
www.state.ak.us/acpe

Arizona
Arizona Department of Education
1535 West Jefferson Street
Phoenix, AZ 85007
800-352-4558
www.ade.state.az.us

Arkansas
Arkansas Department of Higher
 Education
114 East Capitol Avenue
Little Rock, AR 72201
501-371-2000
www.adhe.edu

California
California Student Aid Commission
P.O. Box 419026
Rancho Cordova, CA 95741-9026
888-224-7268
www.csac.ca.gov

Colorado
Colorado Department of Education
201 East Colfax Avenue
Denver, CO 80203-1799
303-866-6600
www.cde.state.co.us

Connecticut
Connecticut Department of Higher
 Education
61 Woodland Street
Hartford, CT 06105-2326
860-947-1800
www.ctdhe.org

Delaware
Delaware Higher Education
 Commission
Carvel State Office Building, 5th floor
820 North French Street
Wilmington, DE 19801-3509
800-292-7935
www.doe.state.de.us/high-ed

District of Columbia
Office of the State Superintendent
 of Education
810 First Street, NE, 9th Floor
Washington, DC 20002
202-727-6436
www.seo.dc.gov

Florida
Florida Department of Education
Office of Student Financial Aid
1940 North Monroe Street, Suite 70
Tallahassee, FL 32303-4759
888-827-2004
www.floridastudentfinancialaid.org

Georgia
Georgia Student Finance Commission
2082 East Exchange Place
Tucker, GA 30084
800-505-4732
www.gsfc.org

Hawaii
Hawaii State Department
 of Education
P.O. Box 2360
Honolulu, HI 96804
808-586-3230
www.doe.k12.hi.us

Idaho
Idaho State Department of Education
650 West State Street
P.O. Box 83720
Boise, ID 83720-0027
800-432-4601
www.sde.idaho.gov

Illinois
Illinois Student Assistance
 Commission
1755 Lake Cook Road
Deerfield, IL 60015-5209
800-899-4722
www.collegezone.com

Indiana
State Student Assistance
 Commission of Indiana
W462 Indiana Government
 Center South
402 West Washington Street
Indianapolis, IN 46204
317-232-2350
www.in.gov/ssaci

Iowa
Iowa College Student
 Aid Commission
200 10th Street, Fourth Floor
Des Moines, IA 50309-3609
877-272-4456
www.iowacollegeaid.org

Kansas
Kansas Board of Regents
1000 SW Jackson Street, Suite 520
Topeka, KS 66612-1368
785-296-3421
www.kansasregents.org

Kentucky
KHEAA Student Aid Branch
P.O. Box 798
Frankfort, KY 40602
800-928-8926
www.kheaa.com

Louisiana

Louisiana Office of Student
  Financial Assistance
P.O. Box 91202
Baton Rouge, LA 70821-9202
800-259-5626
www.osfa.state.la.us

Maine

Finance Authority of Maine
Education Assistance Division
P.O. Box 949
5 Community Drive
Augusta, ME 04332
800-228-3734
www.famemaine.com

Maryland

Maryland Higher Education
  Commission
Office of Student Financial
  Assistance
839 Bestgate Road, Suite 400
Annapolis, MD 21401
800-974-0203
www.mhec.state.md.us

Massachusetts

Massachusetts Board of Higher
  Education
Office of Student Financial
  Assistance
454 Broadway, Suite 200
Revere, MA 02151-3034
617-727-9420
www.osfa.mass.edu

Michigan

Michigan Higher Education
  Assistance Authority
Office of Scholarships and Grants
P.O. Box 30462
Lansing, MI 48909-7962
888-447-2687
www.michigan.gov/mistudentaid

Minnesota

Minnesota Office of Higher Education
1450 Energy Park Drive, Suite 350
St. Paul, MN 55108-5227
800-657-3866
www.ohe.state.mn.us

Mississippi

Mississippi Office of Student
  Financial Aid
3825 Ridgewood Road
Jackson, MS 39211-6453
800-327-2980
www.ihl.state.ms.us/financialaid

Missouri

Missouri Department of
  Higher Education
3515 Amazonas Drive
Jefferson City, MO 65109-5717
800-473-6757
www.dhe.mo.gov

Montana

Montana Board of Regents
P.O. Box 203201
2500 Broadway Street
Helena, MT 59620-3201
406-444-6570
www.mus.edu

Nebraska

Nebraska Coordination Commission
  for Postsecondary Education
P.O. Box 95005
Lincoln, NE 68509-5005
402-471-2847
www.ccpe.state.ne.us

Nevada

Nevada Department of Education
700 East Fifth Street
Carson City, NV 89701
775-687-9220
www.doe.nv.gov

New Hampshire

New Hampshire Postsecondary
  Education Commission
3 Barrell Court, Suite 300
Concord, NH 03301-8543
603-271-2555
www.nh.gov/postsecondary

New Jersey

New Jersey Higher Education
  Student Assistance Authority
P.O. Box 540
Trenton, NJ 08625
800-792-8670
www.hesaa.org

New Mexico

New Mexico Higher Education
  Department
2048 Galisteo Street
Santa Fe, NM 87505
505-476-8400
www.hed.state.nm.us

New York

New York State Higher Education
  Services Corporation
99 Washington Avenue
Albany, NY 12255
888-697-4372
www.hesc.state.ny.us

North Carolina

North Carolina State Education
  Assistance Authority
P.O. Box 14103
Research Triangle Park, NC 27709
919-549-8614
www.ncseaa.edu

North Dakota

North Dakota University System
10th Floor, State Capitol
600 East Boulevard Ave, Dept. 215
Bismarck, ND 58505-0230
701-328-2960
www.ndus.nodak.edu

Ohio

Ohio Board of Regents
30 East Broad Street, 36th Floor
Columbus, OH 43215-3414
614-466-6000
www.regents.ohio.gov

Oklahoma

Oklahoma State Regents for
  Higher Education
Tuition Aid Grant Program
655 Research Parkway, Suite 200
Oklahoma City, OK 73104
405-225-9100
www.okhighered.org

Oregon

Oregon Student Assistance
  Commission
1500 Valley River Drive, Suite 100
Eugene, OR 97401
800-452-8807
www.osac.state.or.us

Pennsylvania

Pennsylvania Higher Education
  Assistance Agency
1200 North Seventh Street
Harrisburg, PA 17102-1444
800-233-0557
www.pheaa.org

Puerto Rico

Departmento de Educacion
P.O. Box 190759
San Juan, PR 00919-0759
787-759-2000
www.de.gobierno.pr

Rhode Island

Rhode Island Higher Education
  Assistance Authority
560 Jefferson Boulevard, Suite 100
Warwick, RI 02886
401-736-1100
www.riheaa.org

South Carolina

South Carolina Commission on
  Higher Education
1333 Main Street, Suite 200
Columbia, SC 29201
803-737-2260
www.che.sc.gov

South Dakota

South Dakota Department
  of Education
Office of Finance and Management
700 Governors Drive
Pierre, SD 57501
605-773-3134
www.doe.sd.gov/stateaid

Tennessee

Tennessee Student Assistance
  Corporation
404 James Robertson Parkway,
Suite 1510, Parkway Towers
Nashville, TN 37243-0820
800-342-1663
www.state.tn.us/tsac

Texas

Texas Higher Education
  Coordinating Board
Division of Student Services
P.O. Box 12788, Capital Station
Austin, TX 78711
800-242-3062
www.hhloans.com

Utah

Utah Higher Education
  Assistance Authority
Board of Regents Building,
  The Gateway
60 South 400 West
Salt Lake City, UT 84101-1284
877-336-7378
www.uheaa.org

Vermont

Vermont Student Assistance
  Corporation
P.O. Box 999
Winooski, VT 05404
800-798-8722
www.vsac.org

Virginia

State Council of Higher Education
  for Virginia
James Monroe Building
101 North 14th Street
Richmond, VA 23219
804-225-2600
www.schev.edu

Washington

Washington Higher Education
  Coordination Board
917 Lakeridge Way
P.O. Box 43430
Olympia, WA 98504-3430
360-753-7800
www.hecb.wa.gov

West Virginia

West Virginia Higher Education Policy
  Commission
Central Office, Higher Education
  Grant Program
1018 Kanawha Boulevard East,
  Suite 700
Charleston, WV 25301-2800
304-558-4614
www.hepc.wvnet.edu

Wisconsin

Wisconsin Higher Educational
  Aids Board
P. O. Box 7885
Madison, WI 53707
608-267-2206
www.heab.state.wi.us

Wyoming

Wyoming Department of Education
2300 Capitol Avenue
Hathaway Building, Second Floor
Cheyenne, WY 82002-0050
307-777-7690
www.k12.wy.us

Guam

University of Guam
Student Financial Aid Office
UOG Station
Mangilao, GU 96923
671-735-2284
www.uog.edu

Virgin Islands

Financial Aid Office, Virgin Islands
  Board of Education
P.O. Box 11900
St. Thomas, VI 00801
340-774-4546

Glossary

ACT. A college admission test given at test centers in the United States and other countries on specified dates. Please visit the organization's website for further information.

Award letter. A means of notifying admitted students of the financial aid being offered by the college or university. The award letter provides information on the types and amounts of aid offered, students' responsibilities and the conditions that govern the awards. Generally, the award letter gives students the opportunity to accept or decline the aid offered, and a deadline by which to respond.

College Scholarship Service (CSS). *See* CSS/Financial Aid PROFILE®.

Competition. An award based upon superior performance in relation to others in the competition. This book lists competitions based upon artistic talent, writing ability and other demonstrable talents.

Cooperative education (co-op). A career-oriented program in which students alternate between class attendance and employment in business, industry or government. Co-op students usually receive both academic credit and payment for their work. Under a cooperative plan, five years are normally required for completion of a bachelor's degree, but graduates have the advantage of about a year's practical work experience in addition to their studies.

CSS code. A four-digit College Board number that students use to designate colleges or scholarship programs to receive their CSS/Financial Aid PROFILE information. A complete list of all CSS codes can be viewed at the CSS/Financial Aid PROFILE section on collegeboard.com.

CSS/Financial Aid PROFILE®. A Web-based application service offered by the College Board and used by some colleges, universities and private scholarship programs to award their private financial aid funds. Students register for and complete the PROFILE on collegeboard.com. PROFILE provides a customized application for each registrant, based on the student's registration information and the requirements of the colleges and programs to which she or he is applying. The PROFILE is not a federal form and may not be used to apply for federal student aid.

Curriculum Vitae (CV). A type of résumé, from the Latin for "the course of one's life." Typically, a CV is used by applicants for fellowships or grants, or jobs in higher education, the sciences, or in a research capacity. The CV is typically longer than a résumé, and provides details about papers published, research conducted and more.

Dependent student. For federal financial aid purposes, the status that includes students who are under the age of 24; attend an undergraduate program; are not married; do not have children of their own; are not orphans, or wards of the court, veterans of the active-duty armed services; or certified as homeless. The term is used to define eligibility for certain financial aid programs, regardless of whether the student lives with a parent, receives financial support from a parent, or is claimed on a parents' tax returns. If a student is defined as a dependent, parental financial information must be supplied on the Free Application for Federal Student Aid (FAFSA) and institutional aid applications.

Dependents. Generally speaking, people who are dependent upon others (parents, relatives, a spouse) for food, clothing, shelter and other basics. For purposes of getting federal financial aid, students must meet strict criteria in order to be defined as dependents; in the view of federal aid programs, the family is the primary source of support for college. College students may have dependents (children dependent on them), and this too is taken into account by the federal government. Federal forms ask a series of questions about age, marital status, etc., to determine whether applicants are dependent on others or independent.

Direct Loan Program. *See* Federal Direct Loan Program.

Expected Family Contribution (EFC). The total amount students and their families are expected to pay toward college costs from their income and assets for one academic year.

FAFSA. *See* Free Application for Federal Student Aid.

Federal code number. A six-digit number that identifies a specific college to which students want their Free Application for Federal Student Aid form submitted. Also known as the Title IV number.

Federal Direct Loan Program. A program that allows participating schools to administer subsidized and unsubsidized Stafford and PLUS loans directly to student and parent borrowers. Direct loans have mostly the same terms and conditions as FFELP loans. Funds for these programs are provided by the federal government.

Federal Family Education Loan Program (FFELP). The subsidized and unsubsidized Federal Stafford Loan, PLUS Loan and Federal Loan Consolidation programs. Funds for these programs are provided by lenders, and the loans are guaranteed by the federal government.

Federal Parent Loan for Undergraduate Students (PLUS). A program that permits parents of undergraduate students to borrow up to the full cost of education, less any other financial aid the student may have received.

Federal Pell Grant Program. A federally sponsored and administered program that provides need-based grants to undergraduate students. Eligibility for Pell Grants is based on a student's expected family contribution, the total cost of attendance at the college, and whether the student is attending the college full time or part time.

Federal Perkins Loan Program. A federally funded campus-based program that provides low-interest loans, based on need, for undergraduate study. The combined cumulative total of loan funds available to an individual for undergraduate and graduate education is $40,000. Repayment need not begin until completion of the student's education, and may be deferred for limited periods of service in the military, Peace Corps or

approved comparable organizations. The total debt may be forgiven by the federal government if the recipient enters a career of service as a public health nurse, law enforcement officer, public school teacher or social worker.

Federal Stafford Loan. A program that allows students to borrow money for education expenses from banks and other lending institutions (and sometimes from the colleges themselves). Subsidized Stafford loans are offered by colleges based on need. The federal government pays the interest on subsidized loans while the borrower is in college. Unsubsidized Stafford loans are non-need based; anyone may apply for one, regardless of their ability to pay for college. The interest on unsubsidized loans begins accumulating immediately. For both programs, the amounts that may be borrowed depend on the student's year in school.

Federal student aid. A number of programs sponsored by the federal government that award students loans, grants or work-study jobs for the purpose of meeting their financial need. To receive any federal student aid, a student must demonstrate financial need by filing the Free Application for Federal Student Aid, be enrolled in college at least half time, and meet certain other eligibility requirements.

Federal Supplemental Educational Opportunity Grant Program (SEOG). A federal campus-based program that provides need-based grants for undergraduate study. Each college is given a certain total amount of SEOG money each year to distribute among its financial aid applicants, and each determines the amount to which the student is entitled.

Federal Work-Study Program. A campus-based financial aid program that allows students to meet some of their financial need by working on or off campus while attending school. The wages earned are used to help pay the student's education costs for the academic year. Job opportunities vary from campus to campus. The time commitment for a work-study job is usually between 10 and 15 hours each week.

Financial aid. Money awarded to students to help them pay for college. Financial aid comes in the form of gifts (scholarships and grants) and self-help aid (loans and work-study opportunities). Most aid is awarded on the basis of financial need, but some awards are non-need-based. Both need-based and non-need-based aid may be offered on the additional basis of merit.

Financial aid award letter. *See* award letter.

Financial aid package. The total financial aid offered to a student by a college, including all loans, grants, scholarships and work-study opportunities.

Financial Aid PROFILE. *See* CSS/Financial Aid PROFILE.

Financial need. The difference between the total cost of attending a college and a student's expected family contribution (EFC). Financial aid grants, loans and work-study will be offered by each college to fill the student's need.

Free Application for Federal Student Aid (FAFSA). A form completed by all applicants for federal student aid. The FAFSA is available on the Web at www.fafsa.ed.gov. In many states, completion of the FAFSA is also sufficient to establish eligibility for state-sponsored aid programs. There is no charge to students for completing the FAFSA. The FAFSA may be filed any time after Jan. 1 of the year for which one is seeking aid (e.g., after Jan. 1, 2011, for the academic year 2011-12).

Full-time status. Enrollment at a college or university for 12 or more credit hours per semester. Students must be enrolled full time to qualify for the maximum award available to them from federal grant programs.

General Educational Development (GED). A series of tests that individuals who did not complete high school may take through their state education system to qualify for a high school equivalency certificate.

Gift. Financial aid in the form of scholarships or grants that do not have to be repaid.

Grade Point Average (GPA). A system used by many schools for evaluating the overall scholastic performance of students. Grade

points are determined by first multiplying the number of hours given for a course by the numerical value of the grade and then dividing the sum of all grade points by the total number of hours carried. The most common system of numerical values for grades is A = 4, B = 3, C = 2, D = 1, and E or F = 0.

Grant. A financial aid award that is given to a student and does not have to be paid back. The terms "grant" and "scholarship" are often used interchangeably to refer to gift aid, but often grants are awarded solely on the basis of financial need, while scholarships may require the student to demonstrate merit.

Half-time status. Enrollment at a college or university for at least six credit hours per semester, but less than the 12 credit hours required to qualify as full time. Students must be enrolled at least half time to qualify for federal student aid loan programs.

High school transcript. A formal document that shows all classes taken and grades earned in high school. It needs to be sent from the school to the scholarship sponsor, not from the applicant.

Independent student. For federal financial aid purposes, the status that generally includes students who are either 24 years old, married, a veteran or an orphan, a ward of the court, certified as homeless or have legal dependents (not including spouse). Independent students do not need to provide parental information to be considered for federal financial aid programs. However, private institutions may require independent students to provide parental information on their institutional forms in order to be considered for nonfederal sources of funding.

Internship. Any short-term, supervised work, usually related to a student's major, for which academic credit is earned. The work can be full or part time, on or off campus, paid or unpaid. Some majors require the student to complete an internship.

Loan. Money lent with interest for a specified period of time. This book includes several loan programs; some forgive the loan in exchange for public service, such as teaching in a rural area.

Major. The subject area in which students concentrate during their undergraduate study. At most colleges, students take a third to a half of their courses in the major; the rest of their course work is devoted to core requirements and electives. In liberal arts majors, students generally take a third of their courses in their chosen field, which they usually must choose by the beginning of their junior year. In career-related programs, such as nursing or engineering, students may take up to half of their courses in their major.

Merit aid. Financial aid awarded on the basis of academic qualifications, artistic or athletic talent, leadership qualities or similar qualities. Most merit aid comes in the form of scholarships. Merit aid may be non-need based, or the merit criteria may be in addition to a requirement that the student demonstrate financial need.

National Science and Mathematics Access to Retain Talent (SMART) Grant. A federal grant program for Pell Grant recipients who are in their third or fourth year of undergraduate study, have declared a major in the sciences, mathematics, engineering, technology or certain foreign languages, and have maintained a GPA of at least 3.0 in that major. The maximum annual award is $4,000, in addition to the student's Pell Grant.

Need-based aid. Financial aid (scholarships, grants, loans or work-study opportunities) given to students who have demonstrated financial need, calculated by subtracting the student's expected family contribution from a college's total cost of attendance. The largest source of need-based aid is the federal government, but colleges, states and private foundations also award need-based aid to eligible students.

Nomination. Being named as a candidate for an award or scholarship. Some scholarship programs require that a teacher or principal nominate students as applicants, and do not invite applications from students.

Non-need-based aid. Financial aid awarded without regard to the student's demonstrated ability to pay for college. Unsubsidized loans and scholarships awarded solely on the basis of merit are both non-need based. Some financial aid sponsors also offer non-need-based grants that are not tied to merit, but rather to other qualities, such as state of residence or participation in ROTC.

Outside resources. Student financial aid granted by a source other than the college that the college must take into account when assembling an aid package. Examples of common outside resources include scholarships from private foundations, employer tuition assistance and veterans' educational benefits.

Parents' contribution. The amount a student's parents are expected to pay toward college costs from their income and assets. It is derived from need analysis of the parents' overall financial situation. The parents' contribution and the student's contribution together constitute the total expected family contribution (EFC).

Part-time status. Enrollment at a college or university for 11 or fewer credit hours per semester.

Pell Grant. *See* Federal Pell Grant Program.

Perkins Loan. *See* Federal Perkins Loan Program.

Permanent resident. A non-U.S. citizen who has been given permission to make his or her permanent home in the United States. All permanent residents hold a "green card," and all holders of a green card are permanent residents. Permanent residents are eligible for numerous award programs.

PLUS Loan. *See* Federal Parent Loan for Undergraduate Students.

Portfolio. A physical collection of a student's work that demonstrates their skills and accomplishments. Portfolios may be physical or electronic. There are academic portfolios that include student-written papers and projects, and also portfolios that include created objects — art, photography, fashion illustrations and more. Some scholarship programs request a portfolio.

Priority date. The date by which applications for financial aid must be received to be given the strongest possible consideration. The college will consider the financial need of applicants who make the priority date before any other applicants. Qualified applicants who do not make the priority date are considered on a first-come, first-served basis, and are only offered financial aid if (and to the extent that) the college still has sufficient money left over after all the offers it has made.

PROFILE. *See* CSS/Financial Aid PROFILE.

PSAT/NMSQT® (Preliminary SAT/ National Merit Scholarship Qualifying Test). A preparatory tool for the SAT that is administered by high schools to sophomores and juniors each year in October. The PSAT/NMSQT serves as the qualifying test for scholarships awarded by the National Merit Scholarship Corporation.

Renewable. A scholarship or loan that can be renewed after the first award. Typically students have to apply annually in order to receive the funds after the first year.

Renewal FAFSA. A simplified reapplication form for continuing students. The Renewal FAFSA allows the student to update the financial information and other items that have changed from the prior year's FAFSA, rather than completing the entire FAFSA for each award year.

Reserve Officers' Training Corps (ROTC). Programs conducted by certain colleges in cooperation with the United States Air Force, Army and Navy reserves. Participating students may receive a merit scholarship while they are in college, and will enter the reserves of their service branch as an officer upon graduation. Navy ROTC includes the Marine Corps. (The Coast Guard and Merchant Marine do not sponsor ROTC programs.) Local recruiting offices of the services themselves can supply detailed information about these programs, as can participating colleges.

Residency requirements. The minimum amount of time a student is required to have lived in a particular state or community in order to be eligible for scholarship, internship or loan programs offered to such residents.

Can also refer to the minimum amount of time a student is required to have lived in a state to be eligible for in-state tuition at a public college or university.

SAR. *See* Student Aid Report.

SAT®. A college entrance exam, that tests critical reading, writing and mathematics skills, given on specified dates throughout the year at test centers in the United States and other countries. The SAT is used by most colleges and sponsors of financial aid programs.

SAT Subject Tests™. Admission tests in specific subjects that are given at test centers in the United States and other countries on specified dates throughout the year. The tests are used by colleges for help in both evaluating applicants for admission and determining course placement and exemption of enrolled first-year students.

Scholarship. A type of financial aid that doesn't have to be repaid. Grants are often based on financial need. Scholarships may be based on need, on need combined with merit, or solely on the basis of merit or some other qualification, such as minority status.

Section 529 plans. State-sponsored college savings programs commonly referred to as "529 plans" after the section of the Internal Revenue Code that provides the plan's tax breaks. There are two kinds: Section 529 college savings plans and Section 529 prepaid tuition plans.

Self-help aid. Student financial aid, such as loans and jobs, that requires repayment or employment.

SEOG. *See* Federal Supplemental Educational Opportunity Grant Program.

SMART Grant. *See* National Science and Mathematics Access to Retain Talent Grant.

Stafford Loan. *See* Federal Stafford Loan.

Student Aid Report (SAR). A report produced by the U.S. Department of Education and sent to students in response to their having filed the Free Application for Federal Student Aid (FAFSA). The SAR contains information the student provided on the FAFSA as well as the federally calculated expected family contribution.

Student expense budget. A calculation of the annual cost of attending college that is used to determine your financial need. Student expense budgets usually include tuition and fees, books and supplies, room and board, personal expenses and transportation. Sometimes additional expenses are included for students with special education needs, students who have a disability, or students who are married or have children.

Student's contribution. The amount you are expected to pay toward college costs from your income and assets. The amount is derived from need analysis of your resources. Your contribution and your parents' contribution together add up to the total expected family contribution.

Subsidized Federal Stafford Loan. *See* Federal Stafford Loan.

Subsidized loan. A loan awarded to a student on the basis of financial need. The federal government or the state awarding the loan pays the borrower's interest while the student is in college at least half time, thereby subsidizing the loan.

Supplemental Educational Opportunity Grant. *See* Federal Supplemental Educational Opportunity Grant Program.

Tuition. The price of instruction at a college. Tuition may be charged per term or per credit hour.

Undergraduate. A college student in the freshman, sophomore, junior or senior year of study, as opposed to a graduate student who has earned an undergraduate degree and is pursuing a master's, doctoral or professional degree.

Unmet need. The difference between a specific student's total available resources and the total cost for the student's attendance at a specific institution.

Unsubsidized Federal Stafford Loan. *See* Federal Stafford Loan.

Unsubsidized loan. An education loan that is non-need based and therefore not subsidized by the federal government; the borrower is responsible for accrued interest throughout the life of the loan.

Verification. A procedure whereby a school checks the information that the student reported on the FAFSA, usually by requesting a copy of the tax returns filed by the student and, if applicable, the student's spouse and parent(s). Colleges are required by federal regulations to verify a minimum percentage of financial aid applications.

William D. Ford Federal Direct Loan Program. *See* Federal Direct Loan Program.

Work-Study. An arrangement by which a student combines employment and college study. The employment may be an integral part of the academic program (as in cooperative education and internships) or simply a means of paying for college (as in the need-based Federal Work-Study Program).

Eligibility Indexes

Corporate/ Employer

Aviation industry, 79
Federal/U.S. Government, 238
Footwear/Leather Industry, 495
Wal-Mart Stores, Inc., 514
West Pharmaceutical Services, Inc., 516

Disabilities

Hearing impaired

AG Bell College Scholarship Awards, 85
New York State Readers Aid Program, 397
Scholarship for People with Disabilities, 226
Sertoma Scholarships for Students Who are Hard of Hearing or Deaf, 436
Students With Disabilities Endowed Scholarship Honoring Elizabeth Daley Jeffords, 510
Texas Tuition Exemption for Blind or Deaf Students, 485
Virginia Rehabilitative Services College Program, 513
Wisconsin Hearing & Visually Handicapped Student Grant, 521
Yellow Ribbon Scholarship, 493

Learning disabled

Anne Ford and Allegra Ford Scholarship, 359
Challenge Met Scholarship, 162
Marion Huber Learning Through Listening Award, 425
North Carolina Vocational Rehabilitation Award, 392
Students With Disabilities Endowed Scholarship Honoring Elizabeth Daley Jeffords, 510
The Tommy Tranchin Award, 228
Virginia Rehabilitative Services College Program, 513

Physically challenged

National ChairScholars Scholarship, 215
New Mexico Teacher's Loan-for-Service, 581

North Carolina Vocational Rehabilitation Award, 392
RehabGYM Scholarship, 509
Scholarship for People with Disabilities, 226
Students With Disabilities Endowed Scholarship Honoring Elizabeth Daley Jeffords, 510
The Tommy Tranchin Award, 228
Virginia Rehabilitative Services College Program, 513
Yellow Ribbon Scholarship, 493

Visually impaired

Alabama Scholarship for Dependents of Blind Parents, 471
Arthur and Helen Copeland Scholarship for Females, 500
Arthur E. Copeland Scholarship, 500
Charles and Melva T. Owen Memorial Scholarship, 362
Charles E. Leonard Memorial Scholarship, 507
Christian Record Services Scholarship, 217
Christine H. Eidie Memorial Scholarship, 318
Computer Science Scholarship, 362
Delta Gamma Foundation Florence Margaret Harvey Memorial Scholarship, 98
E.U. Parker Memorial Scholarship, 362
Ferdinand Torres Scholarship, 98
Floyd Qualls Memorial Scholarship, 94
Hank LeBonne Scholarship, 363
Hermione Grant Calhoun Scholarship, 363
Howard Brown Rickard Scholarship, 363
Jeannette C. Eyerly Memorial Scholarship, 363
Kenneth Jernigan Memorial Scholarship, 364
Kuchler-Killian Memorial Scholarship, 364
Lighthouse College-Bound Award, 319
Lighthouse Undergraduate Award, 319
Mary P. Oenslager Scholastic Achievement Award, 426
National Federation of the Blind Educator of Tomorrow Award, 364
National Federation of the Blind Scholarships, 364
New York State Readers Aid Program, 397
Paul and Helen Ruckes Scholarship, 98

R.L. Gillette Scholarship, 98
Rudolph Dillman Memorial Scholarship, 98
Scholarship for People with Disabilities, 226
Students With Disabilities Endowed Scholarship Honoring Elizabeth Daley Jeffords, 510
Texas Tuition Exemption for Blind or Deaf Students, 485
Virginia Rehabilitative Services College Program, 513
Wisconsin Hearing & Visually Handicapped Student Grant, 521
Yellow Ribbon Scholarship, 493

Field of Study/ Intended Career

Agricultural science, business, and natural resources conservation

Abbie Sargent Memorial Scholarship, 73
American Chemical Society Scholars Program, 90
American Society for Enology and Viticulture Scholarship Program, 170
AMHI Educational Scholarships, 157
AMHI van Schaik Dressage Scholarship, 158
Amtrol Scholarship, 99
Annie's Homegrown Sustainable Agriculture Scholarships, 180
Arboriculture Internship, 547
Arthur K. Gilkey Memorial/William Putnam/Bedayn Research Grants, 88
A.T. Anderson Memorial Scholarship, 104
A.W. "Winn" Brindle Memorial Education Loan, 573
Award in Desert Studies, 244
Ball Horticultural Company Scholarship, 95
Baroid Scholarship, 99
California Farm Bureau Scholarship, 208
Cargill Scholarship Program, 498
Caroline Thorn Kissel Summer Environmental Studies Scholarship, 244
Carville M. Akehurst Memorial Scholarship, 284

Field of Study/Intended Career: Agricultural science, business, and natural resources conservation

Eligibility Indexes

Charles (Tommy) Thomas Memorial Scholarship, 158
Core Scholarship, 360
Dairy Student Recognition Program, 360
Decommissioning, Decontamination and Reutilization Scholarship, 159
Disney Theme Parks & Resorts Professional Internships, 569
DMI Milk Marketing Scholarships, 360
Donald A. Williams Soil Conservation Scholarship, 463
Dr. W. Wes Eckenfelder Jr. Scholarship, 206
Earl Dedman Memorial Scholarship, 95
Ed Markham International Scholarship, 95
EPA National Network for Environmental Management Studies Fellowship, 503
Field Botany Scholarships, 244
Filoli Center Garden Internships and Apprenticeships, 538
Fran Johnson Non-Traditional Scholarship, 96
Garden Club of America Summer Environmental Awards, 245
GCA Internship in Garden History and Design, 539
Global Change Education Program, 554
Good Eats Scholarship Fund, 260
Grange Denise Scholarship, 386
Great Lakes Colleges Association/Associated Colleges of the Midwest Oak Ridge Science Semester, 554
Greater Research Opportunities Undergraduate Student Fellowships, 504
Harold Bettinger Memorial Scholarship, 96
Healthy Waters Institute of the Freshwater Trust, 407
Horticultural Research Institute Spring Meadow Scholarship, 285
Iager Dairy Scholarship, 360
Iowa Farm Bureau Federation Scholarship, 297
Jacob Van Namen Marketing Scholarship, 96
James Bridenbaugh Memorial Scholarship, 96
J.K. Rathmell, Jr. Memorial Scholarship for Work/Study Abroad, 97
Katharine M. Grosscup Scholarship, 245
Klussendorf Scholarship, 360
Leonard Bettinger Memorial Vocational Scholarship, 97
Limi Boosters National Educational Grant, 391
Lindbergh Grant, 215

Louisiana Rockefeller Wildlife Scholarship, 320
The Loy McCandless Marks Scholarship, 245
Marshall E. McCullough Undergraduate Scholarship, 361
Masonic Range Science Scholarship, 440
Minority Scholarship Program, 206
Morris Arboretum Education Internship, 547
Morris Arboretum Horticulture Internship, 547
MTA Doug Slifka Memorial Scholarship, 341
Muggets Scholarship, 285
NASA Space Grant South Carolina Undergraduate Student Research Fellowship, 352
NASA Space Grant Teacher Education Scholarship, 353
National Dairy Shrine Kildee Scholarship, 361
National Oceanic and Atmospheric Administration Hollings Undergraduate Scholarship, 555
NEHA/AAS Scholarship, 362
NPFDA Scholarship, 368
Oregon Dungeness Crab Commission, 410
Oregon Foundation for Blacktail Deer Outdoor & Wildlife Scholarship, 410
ORISE Department of Energy Community College Institute, 555
ORISE Higher Education Research Experiences at Oak Ridge National Laboratory for Students, 555
ORISE Professional Internship Program for National Energy Technology Laboratory, 556
ORISE Research Participation Program at the U.S. Army Center for Health Promotion and Preventive Medicine, 556
ORISE Student Environmental Management Participation at the U.S. Army Environmental Center, 556
ORISE Student Research at the Centers for Disease Control and Prevention/Agency for Toxic Substances and Disease Registry, 557
Part-Time Horticultural Internship, 568
Phipps Conservatory and Botanical Gardens Internships, 560
Plant Propagation Internship, 547
Plant Protection Internship, 547
Rain Bird Intelligent Use of Water Company Scholarship, 315
Rose and Flower Garden Internship, 548
Savannah River Site Professional Internship Program, 557
SCA Conservation Internships, 564

Science Undergraduate Laboratory Internships, 558
Siegel Service Technology Scholarships, 432
Siemens Competition in Math, Science and Technology, 437
Smithsonian Environmental Research Center Internship Program, 561
Smithsonian Minority Internship, 562
Society of Exploration Geophysicists Scholarship, 441
South Dakota Ardell Bjugstad Scholarship, 468
Southern Nursery Organization Sidney B. Meadows Scholarship, 469
Southface Internship, 563
Student Research at the U.S. Army Edgewood Chemical Biological Center, 567
Thomas M. Stetson Scholarship, 99
Timothy S. and Palmer W. Bigelow Scholarship, 285
Truman D. Picard Scholarship, 296
Tyson Foods Intern Program, 566
Urban Forestry Internship, 548
U.S. Department of Homeland Security Scholarship and Fellowship Program, 558
U.S. National Arboretum Summer Internship, 568
USDA/1890 National Scholars Program, 502
Water Companies (NJ Chapter) Scholarship, 357
Year-Long Horticultural Internship, 568

Architecture and design

AIA New Jersey Scholarship Foundation, 106
AIA/AAF Minority/Disadvantaged Scholarship, 105
Alfred T. Granger Student Art Fund, 507
Arboriculture Internship, 547
ASHRAE Region IV Benny Bootle Scholarship, 172
Award in Desert Studies, 244
Bechtel Foundation Scholarship, 452
Bechtel Group Foundation Scholarship, 373
BIA San Diego Scholarship, 206
Carville M. Akehurst Memorial Scholarship, 284
CBC Scholarship, 221
Center for Architecture Design Scholarship, 213
Community Scholarship Fund, 255
Courtland Paul Scholarship, 314
Dallas Architectural Foundation - Humphries/HKS Scholarship, 226
Dallas Architectural Foundation - Swank Travelling Fellowship, 227
David T. Woolsey Scholarship, 315
Disney Theme Parks & Resorts Professional Internships, 569
The EDSA Minority Scholarship, 315

Eleanor Allwork Scholarship, 213
Elizabeth Dow Ltd. Internships, 530
Filoli Center Garden Internships and Apprenticeships, 538
Florence Lemcke Memorial Scholarship, 152
Fontainebleau Prize, 214
Gabriel Prize, 519
GCA Internship in Garden History and Design, 539
GCSAA Scholars Competition, 235
GCSAA Student Essay Contest, 235
Homestead Capital Housing Scholarship, 407
Honeywell International Inc. Scholarship, 458
Horticultural Research Institute Spring Meadow Scholarship, 285
Howard Brown Rickard Scholarship, 363
International Furnishings and Design Association Educational Foundation Leaders Commemorative Scholarship, 295
International Furnishings and Design Association Student Member Scholarships, 295
J.K. Rathmell, Jr. Memorial Scholarship for Work/Study Abroad, 97
Joel Polsky Academic Achievement Award, 174
Landscape Forms Design for People Scholarship, 315
The Loy McCandless Marks Scholarship, 245
Muggets Scholarship, 285
Multicultural Undergraduate Summer Internships at the Getty Center, 541
NASA Space Grant Wisconsin Consortium Undergraduate Research Program, 354
National Association of Women in Construction Founders' Scholarship, 358
Northrop Grumman Corporate Scholarship, 375
Part-Time Horticultural Internship, 568
Part-Time Student Scholarship, 295
PBS&J Corporate Scholarship, 375
Peridian International Inc./Rae L. Price FASLA Scholarship, 315
Phipps Conservatory and Botanical Gardens Internships, 560
Plumbing-Heating-Cooling Contractors - National Association Educational Foundation Scholarship, 420
Rain Bird Intelligent Use of Water Company Scholarship, 315
Raymond F. Cain Scholarship Fund, 270
The Scotts Company Scholars Program, 536
Southface Internship, 563

Steven G. King Play Environments Scholarship, 316
Summer Internship Program, 531
Timothy S. and Palmer W. Bigelow Scholarship, 285
Urban Forestry Internship, 548
Women in Architecture Scholarship, 197
Yale R. Burge Competition, 175
Year-Long Horticultural Internship, 568

Area and ethnic studies

Adele Filene Student Presenter Grant, 224
AFSCMA/UNCF Union Scholars Program, 527
Blossom Kalama Evans Memorial Scholarship, 253
Elie Wiesel Prize in Ethics, 233
Harriet Irsay Scholarship, 106
Hispanic Division Huntington Fellowship, 544
Jennifer C. Groot Fellowship, 90
Jerry Clark Memorial Scholarship, 95
Joseph S. Adams Scholarship, 439
King Olav V Norwegian-American Heritage Fund, 465
Kosciuszko Foundation Year Abroad Program, 312
Smithsonian Native American Internship, 562
U.S. Department of Education Fulbright-Hays Project Abroad Scholarship for Programs in China, 225

Arts, visual and performing

Abe Voron Scholarship, 204
Adele Filene Student Presenter Grant, 224
Alexander M. Tanger Scholarship, 204
Alfred T. Granger Student Art Fund, 507
American Conservatory Theater Production Internships, 526
American Legion Maryland Auxiliary Scholarship, 125
American Legion Music Scholarship, 120
American Legion Press Club of New Jersey and Post 170--Arthur Dehardt Memorial Scholarship, 146
Anna K. Meredith Fund Scholarship, 473
Anthropology Internship Program, 527
Applied Arts Internships, 530
Artistic and Administrative Internships, 526
Arts & Business Council of New York Internship, 528
Arts Policy Internship, 528

Associated Press/APTRA-Clete Roberts Memorial Journalism Scholarship, 181
Audria M. Edwards Scholarship Fund, 414
BB&T Charitable Scholarship Program, 276
Bernard B. Jacobs Internship Program, 552
BMI Student Composer Awards, 203
Broadcast News Grants, 188
Carole Fielding Video Grant, 501
Carole Simpson Scholarship, 356, 424
The CBC Spouses Performing Arts Scholarship Program, 220
The CBC Spouses Visual Arts Scholarship, 220
Center for Architecture Design Scholarship, 213
Charles & Lucille King Family Foundation Scholarships, 215
Clare Brett Smith Scholarship, 473
The Cloisters Summer Internship Program, 545
College Television Awards, 73
Community Scholarship Fund, 255
Computer Science Scholarship, 362
CRT Internship Program, 533
David L. Stashower Scholarship, 318
Davidson Fellows Scholarship, 229
Department of Commerce Internship for Postsecondary Students, 554
Doris & Clarence Glick Classical Music Scholarship, 256
Ed Bradley Scholarship, 424
Elizabeth A. Sackler Museum Educational Trust, 473
Elizabeth Dow Ltd. Internships, 530
The Elizabeth Greenshields Grant, 233
Endowment Fund For Education (EFFE), 202
ESPN Internship, 536
Essence Summer Internship, 537
Esther Kanagawa Memorial Art Scholarship, 258
Eugene Bennet Visual Arts Scholarship, 406
Eugenia Vellner Fischer Award for the Performing Arts, 335
Fashion Group International of Portland Scholarship, 406
Fisher Broadcasting Company Scholarship for Minorities, 240
Florence Lemcke Memorial Scholarship, 152
Fox Internship, 538
The Fred Rogers Memorial Scholarship, 73
GCA Internship in Garden History and Design, 539
The George Foreman Tribute to Lyndon B. Johnson Scholarship, 424
Gerrit R. Ludwig Scholarship, 260
Government and Public Affairs Internship, 528
Guggenheim Museum Internship, 563

Harriet Irsay Scholarship, 106

Harry & Lorraine Ausprich Endowed
Scholarship for the Arts, 417

Hearst Journalism Award, 519

Helen J. Sioussat/Fay Wells
Scholarship, 204

Hon Chew Hee Scholarship Fund, 262

International Furnishings and Design
Association Educational Foundation
Leaders Commemorative
Scholarship, 295

International Incentive Awards, 474

Janet Jackson Rhythm Nation
Scholarships, 499

Japanese American Music Scholarship
Competition, 305

John Lennon Scholarships, 203

Jules Maidoff Scholarship, 474

Kathryn Dettman Memorial
Journalism Scholarship, 196

Ken Kashiwahara Scholarship, 424

Kennedy Library Archival
Internship, 542

KIMT Weather/News Internships, 544

Laheenae Rebecca Hart Gay
Scholarship, 266

Lee A. Lyman Memorial Music
Scholarship, 508

Lele Cassin Scholarship, 474

Leonard M. Perryman
Communications Scholarship for
Ethnic Minority Students, 498

Local Arts Agency Services
Intern, 529

Lou and Carole Prato Sports
Reporting Scholarship, 425

Maryland Distinguished Scholar:
Talent in the Arts, 325

MCC Theater Internships, 545

McNamara Family Creative Arts
Project Grant, 278

Membership Internship, 529

Morton Gould Young Composer
Awards, 188

Multicultural Undergraduate Summer
Internships at the Getty Center, 541

Museum Coca-Cola Internship, 551

Museum of Modern Art
Internship, 548

NABJ Internships, 550

NAMTA Foundation Visual Arts
Major Scholarship, 355

National Guild of Piano Teachers
$200 Scholarship, 91

National Museum of the American
Indian Internship, 551

National Press Photographers
Foundation Television News
Scholarship, 369

NBA Internship Program, 551

New York American Legion Press
Association Scholarship, 140

Nissan Community College Transfer
Scholarship, 278

ORISE Student Research at the
Centers for Disease Control and
Prevention/Agency for Toxic
Substances and Disease
Registry, 557

peermusic Latin Scholarship, 203

Peggy Guggenheim Internship, 563

Performing Arts Fellowships, 186

Pete Carpenter Fellowship, 531

Pete Wilson Journalism
Scholarship, 425

PGA Tour Diversity Intern
Program, 560

PGSF Annual Scholarship
Competition, 423

Presidents' $2,500 Scholarships, 425

Press Club of Houston
Scholarship, 422

Princess Grace Award for Dance, 422

Princess Grace Award For Film, 422

Princess Grace Award For
Playwriting, 422

Princess Grace Award For
Theater, 423

Private-Sector Initiatives
Internship, 529

Ray Yoshida Kauai Fine Arts
Scholarship, 270

Research Services Internship, 530

Richard Eaton Foundation Award, 205

Richie Gregory Fund, 270

R.L. Gillette Scholarship, 98

Roosevelt Archival Internships, 538

Rudolf Nissim Prize, 188

Ruth Clark Furniture Design
Scholarship, 296

SACI Consortium Scholarship, 474

Scholarships for Children of SACI
Alumni, 474

Scholastic Art Portfolio Gold
Award, 86

Scholastic Art Portfolio Silver
Award, 86

Scholastic Photography Portfolio Gold
Award, 86

Scholastic Photography Portfolio
Silver Award, 86

Scholastic Writing Portfolio Gold
Award, 86

Sculpture Society Scholarship, 371

Seattle Professional Chapter
Scholarship, 197

Six-Month Internship, 546

Smithsonian Minority Internship, 562

Sony Credited Internship, 563

Southern California Council Endowed
Internship, 552

Southface Internship, 563

Spoleto Festival Apprenticeship
Program, 564

Stanfield and D'Orlando Art
Scholarship, 497

Stella Blum Student Research
Grant, 224

Student Internship Program, 525

Summer Internship Program, 546

Time Inc. Internship Program, 565

Two Ten Footwear Design
Scholarship, 495

Two Year Community College BEA
Award, 205

United States Holocaust Memorial
Museum Internship, 566

Vermont Alliance for Arts Education
(VAEE) Scholarship, 510

Virgin Islands Music Scholarship, 511

Virginia Museum of Fine Arts
Fellowship, 513

Vision Award, 205

Walter S. Patterson Scholarship, 205

Web Challenge Contest, 476

Wolf Trap Foundation for the
Performing Arts Internship, 570

Worldstudio AIGA Scholarship, 523

Biological and biomedical sciences

American Foundation for Aging
Research Fellowship, 97

American Legion Maryland Auxiliary
Scholarship, 125

Brill Family Scholarship, 453

Endowment Fund For Education
(EFFE), 202

Lindbergh Grant, 215

Biological and physical sciences

Adler Science and Math
Scholarship, 124

Aerospace Undergraduate Research
Scholarship Program, 353

AFCEA General Emmett Paige
Scholarship, 183

AFCEA General John A. Wickham
Scholarship, 184

AFCEA ROTC Scholarship, 184

AFCEA Scholarship for Working
Professionals, 184

AIAA Foundation Undergraduate
Scholarship, 105

American Chemical Society Scholars
Program, 90

American Foundation for Aging
Research Fellowship, 97

American Legion Maryland Auxiliary
Scholarship, 125

American Meteorological Society
Undergraduate Scholarships, 156

American Meteorological
Society/Industry Minority
Scholarship, 156

Amtrol Scholarship, 99

Angelo S. Bisesti Scholarship, 158

ANS Undergraduate Scholarships, 158

Arthur and Doreen Parrett
Scholarship, 187

Arthur K. Gilkey Memorial/William
Putnam/Bedayn Research
Grants, 88

ASNE Scholarship, 175

A.T. Anderson Memorial
Scholarship, 104

Award in Desert Studies, 244

Baroid Scholarship, 99

Barry M. Goldwater Scholarship, 201

Batttelle Collegiate Scholarship, 373

Burlington Northern Santa Fe Foundation Scholarship, 104

Cargill Scholarship Program, 498

Castle & Cooke Mililani Technology Park Scholarship Fund, 254

Charles and Annette Hill Scholarship, 121

Charles (Tommy) Thomas Memorial Scholarship, 158

Chevron Internship Program, 532

Cooperative Internship Programs, 535

Davidson Fellows Scholarship, 229

Delaware Space Grant Undergraduate Research Internship, 549

Delaware Space Grant Undergraduate Tuition Scholarship, 344

Delayed Education Scholarship for Women, 159

Department of Commerce Internship for Postsecondary Students, 554

Disabled War Veterans Scholarship, 184

Distance Learning/Online Scholarship, 185

DOE Pre-Service Teacher Internships, 554

Dr. W. Wes Eckenfelder Jr. Scholarship, 206

DuPont Co-ops, 535

DuPont Internships, 535

Earl & Patricia Armstrong Scholarship, 498

Endowment Fund For Education (EFFE), 202

The Entomological Foundation BioQuip Undergraduate Scholarship, 234

Explorers Club Youth Activity Fund, 238

Extrusion Division/Lew Erwin Memorial Scholarship, 448

Father James B. Macelwane Annual Award, 157

Field Botany Scholarships, 244

Filoli Center Garden Internships and Apprenticeships, 538

Fleming/Blaszcak Scholarship, 448

Francis M. Peacock Native Bird Habitat Scholarship, 245

Freshman Undergraduate Scholarship Program, 157

Garden Club of America Summer Environmental Awards, 245

Gary J. Miller Undergraduate Prizes for Cancer and Cancer-Related Biomedical Research, 88

GCA Internship in Garden History and Design, 539

Genentech, Inc. Internship Program, 539

George A. Hall/Harold F. Mayfield Award, 520

Global Change Education Program, 554

Great Lakes Colleges Association/Associated Colleges of the Midwest Oak Ridge Science Semester, 554

Great Minds in Stem Scholars Program, 251

Greater Research Opportunities Undergraduate Student Fellowships, 504

Gulf Coast Hurricane Scholarships, 449

Healthy Waters Institute of the Freshwater Trust, 407

Henry Broughton, K2AE Memorial Scholarship, 164

Highmark Scholarship, 417

Hoffman-La Roche Inc. Student Internship, 540

Horizons Scholarship, 522

Howard Brown Rickard Scholarship, 363

Hubertus W.V. Wellems Scholarship for Male Students, 342

Intel International Science and Engineering Fair, 440

Intel Science Talent Search, 440

Internship and Co-op Program, 530

Internship Program for Laboratory Technology, 555

Jacob Van Namen Marketing Scholarship, 96

Jennifer Ritzmann Scholarship for Studies in Tropical Biology, 224

John and Muriel Landis Scholarship, 159

John R. Lamarsh Scholarship, 159

Joseph R. Dietrich Scholarship, 159

K. K. Wang Scholarship, 449

Kathleen S. Anderson Award, 323

Kathryn D. Sullivan Science and Engineering Fellowship, 351

KIMT Weather/News Internships, 544

Louisiana Rockefeller Wildlife Scholarship, 320

The Loy McCandless Marks Scholarship, 245

Marathon Oil Corporation College Scholarship, 277

Marine Corps Sgt. Jeannette L. Winters Memorial Scholarship, 185

MESBEC Scholarships, 212

Microbiology Undergraduate Research Fellowship (MURF), 170

Microscopy Society of America Undergraduate Research Scholarship, 332

Microsoft General Scholarship, 332

Minority Scholarship Program, 206

Morris Arboretum Education Internship, 547

MSGC Undergraduate Underrepresented Minority Fellowship Program, 346

MTA Doug Slifka Memorial Scholarship, 341

Nancy Lorraine Jensen Memorial Scholarship, 466

NASA Academy Internship, 550

NASA Connecticut Space Grant Undergraduate Fellowship, 343

NASA District of Columbia Undergraduate Scholarship, 344

NASA Hawaii Undergraduate Student Research Program, 549

NASA Idaho Space Grant Undergraduate Scholarship, 345

NASA Minnesota Space Grant Consortium Wide Scholarship, 347

NASA Missouri State Space Grant Undergraduate Scholarship, 347

NASA Ohio Space Grant Junior/Senior Scholarship Program, 350

NASA Pennsylvania Space Grant Sylvia Stein Memorial Scholarship, 350

NASA Rocky Mountain Space Grant Consortium Undergraduate Scholarship, 351

NASA Space Grant Arizona Undergraduate Research Internship, 549

NASA Space Grant Georgia Fellowship Program, 344

NASA Space Grant Hawaii Undergraduate Fellowship, 344

NASA Space Grant Kentucky Undergraduate Scholarship, 345

NASA Space Grant Maine Consortium Annual Scholarship and Fellowship Program, 346

NASA Space Grant Michigan Undergraduate Fellowship, 346

NASA Space Grant Montana Undergraduate Scholarship Program, 347

NASA Space Grant Nevada Undergraduate Scholarship, 348

NASA Space Grant New Mexico Undergraduate Scholarship, 348

NASA Space Grant North Dakota Consortium Lillian Goettler Scholarship, 349

NASA Space Grant North Dakota Undergraduate Scholarship, 349

NASA Space Grant Oregon Undergraduate Scholarship, 350

NASA Space Grant Rhode Island Undergraduate Research Scholarship, 350

NASA Space Grant South Carolina Undergraduate Student Research Fellowship, 352

NASA Space Grant Teacher Education Scholarship, 353

NASA Space Grant Texas Columbia Crew Memorial Undergraduate Scholarships, 352

NASA Space Grant Undergraduate Scholarship, 343

NASA Space Grant Vermont Consortium Undergraduate Scholarships, 352

NASA Space Grant Virginia Community College Scholarship, 353

NASA Space Grant Wisconsin Consortium Undergraduate Research Program, 354

NASA Space Grant Wisconsin Consortium Undergraduate Scholarship, 354

NASA West Virginia Space Grant Undergraduate Research Fellowship, 353

National Oceanic and Atmospheric Administration Hollings Undergraduate Scholarship, 555

Nick Van Pernis Scholarship, 268

North Carolina Student Loans for Health/Science/Mathematics, 582

Operations and Power Division Scholarship, 160

Oregon Foundation for Blacktail Deer Outdoor & Wildlife Scholarship, 410

ORISE Department of Energy Community College Institute, 555

ORISE Higher Education Research Experiences at Oak Ridge National Laboratory for Students, 555

ORISE Nuclear Regulatory Commission Historically Black Colleges and Universities Student Research Participation, 556

ORISE Professional Internship Program for National Energy Technology Laboratory, 556

ORISE Research Participation Program at the U.S. Army Center for Health Promotion and Preventive Medicine, 556

ORISE Student Environmental Management Participation at the U.S. Army Environmental Center, 556

ORISE Student Research - National Center for Toxicological Research, 557

ORISE Student Research at the Centers for Disease Control and Prevention/Agency for Toxic Substances and Disease Registry, 557

ORISE Student Research Participation at the U.S. Army Medical Research Institute of Chemical Defense, 557

ORISE Student Research Participation at U.S. Army Research Laboratory, 557

Pacific Gas and Electric Summer Intern Program, 559

Part-Time Horticultural Internship, 568

Paul A. Stewart Award, 520

Paul and Helen Ruckes Scholarship, 98

Payzer Scholarship, 238

Pearl I. Young Scholarship, 349

Phipps Conservatory and Botanical Gardens Internships, 560

Pittsburgh Local Section Scholarship, 160

Pittsburgh Scholarship, 449

Plant Propagation Internship, 547

Plant Protection Internship, 547

Plasma Physics National Undergraduate Fellowship Program, 560

Plastics Pioneers Scholarships, 449

Procter & Gamble Scholarship, 278

Raymond DiSalvo Scholarship, 160

RCMI Technical/Trade School Scholarship, 428

Research Experiences for Undergraduates - Maria Mitchell Observatory, 552

Research Experiences for Undergraduates in Systematics and Evolutionary Biology, 527

Research Experiences for Undergraduates in the Physical Sciences, 527

Robert G. Lacy Scholarship, 160

Robert Noyce Scholarship Program, 418

Robert T. (Bob) Liner Scholarship, 160

Rocky Mountain Coal Mining Institute Scholarship, 428

Savannah River Site Professional Internship Program, 557

SCA Conservation Internships, 564

Scholarship for Minority Undergraduate Physics Majors, 161

Science Undergraduate Laboratory Internships, 558

SciTech Scholarship, 416

SEG Foundation Scholarship, 441

Shuichi, Katsu and Itsuyo Suga Scholarship, 272

Siemens Competition in Math, Science and Technology, 437

Smithsonian Environmental Research Center Internship Program, 561

Smithsonian Minority Internship, 562

Society of Exploration Geophysicists Scholarship, 441

Society of Physics Students Leadership Scholarship, 448

Society of Physics Students Summer Internship Program, 562

Society of Plastics Engineers General Scholarships, 450

SPIE Educational Scholarship in Optical Science and Engineering, 470

Stan Beck Fellowship, 235

STEM Scholarship, 352

Student Research at the U.S. Army Edgewood Chemical Biological Center, 567

Student Research Participation at the Federal Bureau of Investigation, 558

Summer Undergraduate Scholarship, 351

Technical Minority Scholarship, 524

Tennessee Student Assistance Corporation/Math And Science Teachers Loan Forgiveness Program, 584

Thermoforming Division Memorial Scholarships, 450

Thermoset Division/James I. MacKenzie Memorial Scholarship, 450

Thomas J. Bardos Science Education Awards for Undergraduate Students, 89

Thomas M. Stetson Scholarship, 99

Toshiba/NSTA ExploraVision Award, 371

Tyson Foods Intern Program, 566

Undergraduate Research Fellowship (URF), 171

Undergraduate Research Scholarship, 348

Undergraduate Scholarship Program, 349

Undergraduate Summer Fellowships in Engineering and Science, 550

Urban Forestry Internship, 548

U.S. Department of Homeland Security Scholarship and Fellowship Program, 558

U.S. Department of State Internship, 567

U.S. National Arboretum Summer Internship, 568

U.S. Steel NSBE Academic Scholarship, 376

USDA/1890 National Scholars Program, 502

VADM Samuel L. Gravely Jr. USN (Ret.) Memorial Scholarship, 186

Vogt Radiochemistry Scholarship, 161

Water Companies (NJ Chapter) Scholarship, 357

West Virginia Engineering, Science, and Technology Scholarship, 517

Western Plastics Pioneers Scholarship, 450

William E. "Buck" Bragunier Scholarship for Outstanding Leadership, 186

William James & Dorothy Bading Lanquist Fund, 274

William R. Goldfarb Memorial Scholarship, 168

Yasme Foundation Scholarship, 168

Year-Long Horticultural Internship, 568

Young Epidemiology Scholars Student Competition, 218

Zeller Summer Scholarship in Medicinal Botany, 245

Business/management/administration

Academic Scholarship for High School Seniors and GED Graduates, 370

Academic Scholarship for Undergraduate Students, 370

Accuracy in Media Internships, 525

Actuarial Diversity Scholarships, 74

Actuary of Tomorrow Stuart A. Robertson Memorial Scholarship, 74

Advertising Internship, 531

AFSCMA/UNCF Union Scholars Program, 527

AICP Heartland Chapter Scholarship, 198

AICP Scholarship, 199

Alexander Harris Scholarship, 487

Allstate Internships, 525

Alpha Beta Gamma National Scholarship, 87

American Express Scholarship Competition, 100

American Express Travel Scholarship, 487

American Hotel & Lodging Educational Foundation Incoming Freshman Scholarship Competition, 101

American Legion Maryland Auxiliary Scholarship, 125

American Legion Press Club of New Jersey and Post 170--Arthur Dehardt Memorial Scholarship, 146

American Society of International Law Internships, 528

A.O. Smith Water Heaters Scholarship, 419

Applied Arts Internships, 530

Artistic and Administrative Internships, 526

Arts & Business Council of New York Internship, 528

Arts Action Fund Internship, 528

Arts Policy Internship, 528

Aspiring Sports Journalist Internship, 564

BB&T Charitable Scholarship Program, 276

Bern Laxer Memorial Scholarship, 301

Bernard B. Jacobs Internship Program, 552

Best Teen Chef Culinary Scholarship Competition, 187

BIA San Diego Scholarship, 206

Bob Zappatelli Memorial Scholarship, 301

Boeing Internships, 532

Bradford White Scholarship, 419

Burlington Northern Santa Fe Foundation Scholarship, 104

Business Achievement Awards, 249

Business Reporting Intern Program, 534

Canada Scholarship, 488

Candon, Todd, & Seabolt Scholarship Fund, 254

C.A.R. Scholarship, 207

Cargill Scholarship Program, 498

CBC Scholarship, 221

Charles and Annette Hill Scholarship, 121

Chefs of Louisiana Cookery Scholarship, 301

Chevron Internship Program, 532

CIA Undergraduate Scholarship Program, 214

CITE Scholarship, 223

Citizens for Global Solutions Internship, 533

Congressional Institute Internships, 533

Connecticut Scholarship, 488

Construction Trades Scholarship, 358

Contiki Vacations Scholarship, 488

Cooperative Internship Programs, 535

CRT Internship Program, 533

Dairy Student Recognition Program, 360

Dave Herren Memorial Scholarship, 488

David J. Hallissey Memorial Internship, 565

David L. Stashower Scholarship, 318

Delta Faucet Company Scholarship, 419

Denver Rescue Mission Center for Mission Studies Internships, 534

Department of Commerce Internship for Postsecondary Students, 554

Disney Theme Parks & Resorts Professional Internships, 569

Dr. Alvin and Monica Saake Scholarship, 256

DuPont Co-ops, 535

DuPont Internships, 535

Earl G. Graves Scholarship, 342

Ecolab Scholarship Competition, 101

Economic Research Division Project Internships, 532

Ed Markham International Scholarship, 95

Elizabeth Dow Ltd. Internships, 530

Entergy Jumpstart Co-ops and Internships, 536

EPA National Network for Environmental Management Studies Fellowship, 503

ESPN Internship, 536

Essence Summer Internship, 537

Finance Undergraduate Internships, 568

Financial Women International Scholarship, 259

Fisher Broadcasting Company Scholarship for Minorities, 240

Florida Power & Light Internship Program, 538

Florida Scholarship, 489

Foodservice Communicators Scholarship, 294

Ford Motor Company/American Indian College Fund Corporate Scholars Program, 102

Fox Internship, 538

GE Business/Engineering Scholarship for Minority Students, 316

Genentech, Inc. Internship Program, 539

General Scholarship, 219

George M. Brooker Collegiate Scholarship for Minorities, 293

George Mason Business Scholarship Fund, 259

Georgia-Pacific Internship and Co-op Programs, 539

Government and Public Affairs Internship, 528

Guggenheim Museum Internship, 563

Harold Bettinger Memorial Scholarship, 96

Harriet Irsay Scholarship, 106

Hawaii Chuck Yim Gee Scholarship, 489

Hawaii Society of Certified Public Accountants Scholarship Fund, 261

Henry A. Zuberano Scholarship, 261

Hoffman-La Roche Inc. Student Internship, 540

Homestead Capital Housing Scholarship, 407

Horizons Scholarship, 522

House Member Internships, 567

HSBC-North America Scholarship Program, 277

Hudner Medal of Honor Scholarship, 237

The Hyatt Hotels Fund for Minority Lodging Management Students Competition, 101

IBM Co-op and Intern Program, 540

IEHA Educational Foundation Scholarship, 294

Inn at Blackberry Farm Scholarship, 302

INROADS Internship, 541

Internship and Co-op Program, 530

ISFA Education Foundation College Scholarship, 293

Jacob Van Namen Marketing Scholarship, 96

James A. Turner, Jr. Memorial Scholarship, 178

James E. Webb Internship Program for Minority Undergraduate Seniors and Graduate Students in Business and Public Administration, 562

Jedidiah Zabrosky Scholarship, 508

Jennifer Curtis Byler Scholarship Fund for the Study of Public Affairs, 377

John Deere Student Training Programs, 542

John F. Kennedy Scholars Award, 329

John Joseph Moakley Democratic Internship, 545

John Wiley and Sons, Inc. Internship Program, 543

Johnson Controls Co-op and Internship Programs, 543

J.W. Saxe Memorial Prize for Public Service, 543

Kathy LeTarte Scholarship, 489

Kennedy Center Arts Management Internship, 542

KIMT Weather/News Internships, 544

Kittredge Coddington Memorial Scholarship, 508

Lagrant Scholarships, 314

LaMacchia Family Scholarship, 489

Letitia B. Carter Scholarship, 427

Local Arts Agency Services Intern, 529

Lou and Carole Prato Sports Reporting Scholarship, 425

Louis and Fannie Sager Memorial Scholarship, 372

Louis Carr Summer Internship, 544

Maine Innkeepers Association Scholarship, 321

Marathon Oil Corporation College Scholarship, 277

Marcia S. Harris Legacy Fund Scholarship, 427

Mark J. Smith Scholarship, 219

Marketing and Communications Internship, 529

Marketing Internship Scholarship, 295

Marriott Scholars Program, 275

Massachusetts Scholarship, 490

MassMutual Multicultural College Scholarship, 277

Mayflower Tours Patrick Murphy Internship, 565

MCC Theater Internships, 545

Meetings and Events/Executive Office Internship, 529

Membership Internship, 529

MESBEC Scholarships, 212

Michigan Scholarship, 490

Morgan Stanley Scholars Program, 102

Multicultural Arts Management Internship Program, 531

Multicultural Undergraduate Summer Internships at the Getty Center, 541

Museum Coca-Cola Internship, 551

Museum of Modern Art Internship, 548

NABA National Scholarship Program, 356

NAMTA Foundation Visual Arts Major Scholarship, 355

NASA Space Grant Wisconsin Consortium Undergraduate Research Program, 354

National Association of Women in Construction Founders' Scholarship, 358

National Society of Accountants Scholarship, 372

National Tour Association State Scholarship, 490

NBA Internship Program, 551

NCR Summer Internships, 552

NEEBC Scholarship, 380

New Horizons Rene Campbell Memorial Scholarship, 490

New Jersey Scholarship, 491

New York Scholarship, 491

Nissan Community College Transfer Scholarship, 278

Northern California Chapter - Richard Epping Scholarship, 491

OCA/Verizon Foundation College Scholarship, 397

Ohio Scholarship, 491

Oracle Scholars Internship Program, 566

Oscar and Rosetta Fish Fund, 269

Owens Corning Internships, 559

Pacific Gas and Electric Summer Intern Program, 559

Pacific Northwest Chapter/William Hunt Scholarship, 492

Pat & Jim Host Scholarship, 492

PGA Tour Diversity Intern Program, 560

PHCC Educational Foundation Need-Based Scholarship, 420

Philip and Alice Angell Eastern Star Scholarship, 509

Plumbing-Heating-Cooling Contractors - National Association Educational Foundation Scholarship, 420

Princess Cruises Scholarship, 492

Private-Sector Initiatives Internship, 529

ProStart National Certificate of Achievement Scholarship, 370

PRSA-Hawaii/Roy Leffingwell Public Relations Scholarship, 270

Public Relations Internship, 545

Quebec Scholarship, 492

Research Services Internship, 530

Rhode Island State Government Internship Program, 561

Ritchie-Jennings Memorial Scholarship, 74

Savannah River Site Professional Internship Program, 557

Scarlett Family Foundation Scholarship, 434

Scholarship for Minority Accounting Students, 106

Seattle Professional Chapter Scholarship, 197

Shirley McKown Scholarship Fund, 272

Sony Credited Internship, 563

Southern California Council Endowed Internship, 552

Southface Internship, 563

Spoleto Festival Apprenticeship Program, 564

Stan and Leone Pollard Scholarship, 493

Stanley H. Stearman Award, 372

Staples Summer Internship Program, 564

Summer Internship Program, 531, 546

Summer Research Diversity Fellowships in Law and Social Sciences for Undergraduate Students, 526

Texas Fifth-Year Accounting Student Scholarship Program, 483

Thomas R. Pickering Foreign Affairs Fellowship, 523

Time Inc. Internship Program, 565

Travelers Foundation, 103

Tribal Business Management Scholarship, 212

Trimmer Education Foundation Student Scholarships, 195

Tri-State Surveying & Photogrammetry Kris M. Kunze Scholarship, 93

Tyson Foods Intern Program, 566

UBS/PaineWebber Scholarships, 499

Undergraduate Summer Internship, 537

U.S. Department of Education Fulbright-Hays Project Abroad Scholarship for Programs in China, 225

U.S. Department of State Internship, 567

U.S. National Arboretum Summer Internship, 568

U.S. Senate Member Internships, 566

Utah Keith Griffall Scholarship, 493

Verizon Corporate Scholarship, 376

Washington Crossing Foundation Scholarship, 514

Water Companies (NJ Chapter) Scholarship, 357

Wayne G. Failor Scholarship, 418

Wells Fargo Scholarship, 279

William R. Goldfarb Memorial Scholarship, 168

Wilma D. Hoyal/Maxine Chilton Memorial Scholarship, 109

Wolf Trap Foundation for the Performing Arts Internship, 570

Women's Sports Foundation Internship, 571

Wooddy Scholarship, 74

Yellow Ribbon Scholarship, 493

Communications

AAJA Texas Student Scholarship, 189

Accuracy in Media Internships, 525

AdOhio Advertising Internship, 558

Advertising Internship, 531

Allison E. Fisher Scholarship, 356

American Legion Press Club of New Jersey and Post 170--Arthur Dehardt Memorial Scholarship, 146

American Society of International Law Internships, 528

Aspiring Sports Journalist Internship, 564

Associated Press/APTRA-Clete Roberts Memorial Journalism Scholarship, 181

BIA San Diego Scholarship, 206

Bob Baxter Scholarship, 368

Bob East Scholarship Fund, 368
Boston Globe Summer Internship, 532
Broadcast News Grants, 188
Business Reporting Intern
    Program, 534
Carole Simpson Scholarship, 356, 424
CCNMA Scholarship, 213
Charles & Lucille King Family
    Foundation Scholarships, 215
Charles Clarke Cordle Memorial
    Scholarship, 162
Charles N. Fisher Memorial
    Scholarship, 163
CITE Scholarship, 223
Citizens for Global Solutions
    Internship, 533
College Photographer of the Year
    Competition, 369
Congressional Institute
    Internships, 533
David L. Stashower Scholarship, 318
Delaware Space Grant Undergraduate
    Tuition Scholarship, 344
Department of Commerce Internship
    for Postsecondary Students, 554
Dr. James L. Lawson Memorial
    Scholarship, 163
Ed Bradley Scholarship, 424
Edward J. Nell Memorial
    Scholarship, 424
Edward Payson and Bernice Pi'ilani
    Irwin Scholarship Trust Fund, 257
Endowment Fund For Education
    (EFFE), 202
Entertainment Weekly Internship
    Program, 536
EPA National Network for
    Environmental Management Studies
    Fellowship, 503
ESPN Internship, 536
Essence Summer Internship, 537
Fifth Floor Restaurant
    Scholarship, 302
Fisher Broadcasting Company
    Scholarship for Minorities, 240
Foodservice Communicators
    Scholarship, 294
Fox Internship, 538
Fred R. McDaniel Memorial
    Scholarship, 164
The George Foreman Tribute to
    Lyndon B. Johnson
    Scholarship, 424
Guggenheim Museum Internship, 563
Harold K. Douthit Scholarship, 398
Harriet Irsay Scholarship, 106
Hearst Journalism Award, 519
House Member Internships, 567
HSBC-North America Scholarship
    Program, 277
INROADS Internship, 541
International Radio and Television
    Society Foundation Summer
    Fellowship Program, 541
Irving W. Cook WA0CGS
    Scholarship, 165

Jackson Foundation Journalism
    Scholarship, 408
Janet Jackson Rhythm Nation
    Scholarships, 499
Jerry Clark Memorial Scholarship, 95
Jimi Lott Scholarship, 369
John Wiley and Sons, Inc. Internship
    Program, 543
Kathryn Dettman Memorial
    Journalism Scholarship, 196
Ken Kashiwahara Scholarship, 424
Kennedy Library Archival
    Internship, 542
KIMT Weather/News Internships, 544
L. Phil Wicker Scholarship, 165
Lagrant Scholarships, 314
Larry Whiteside Scholarship, 356
Leonard M. Perryman
    Communications Scholarship for
    Ethnic Minority Students, 498
Local Arts Agency Services
    Intern, 529
Lou and Carole Prato Sports
    Reporting Scholarship, 425
Louis Carr Summer Internship, 544
Marketing and Communications
    Internship, 529
Marshall E. McCullough
    Undergraduate Scholarship, 361
McNamara Family Creative Arts
    Project Grant, 278
Meetings and Events/Executive Office
    Internship, 529
Mississippi Scholarship, 166
Mother Jones Ben Bagdikian
    Fellowship Program, 548
Multicultural Advertising Intern
    Program, 525
Multicultural Undergraduate Summer
    Internships at the Getty Center, 541
Multimedia Intern Program, 534
Museum Coca-Cola Internship, 551
NABJ Internships, 550
NASA Space Grant Arizona
    Undergraduate Research
    Internship, 549
National Press Photographers
    Foundation Still and Multimedia
    Scholarship, 369
National Press Photographers
    Foundation Television News
    Scholarship, 369
National Speakers Association
    Scholarship, 377
NEMAL Electronics Scholarship, 166
The New Republic Internship, 553
New York American Legion Press
    Association Scholarship, 140
New York Times James Reston
    Reporting Fellowships, 554
New York Women in Communications
    Foundation Scholarship, 389
Newhouse Foundation
    Scholarship, 550
News Copy Editing Intern
    Program, 534

Nissan Community College Transfer
    Scholarship, 278
Ohio Newspaper Association
    Publications/Public Relations
    Internship, 558
Ohio Newspapers Minority
    Scholarship, 399
Ohio Newspapers Women's
    Scholarship, 399
ORISE Student Research at the
    Centers for Disease Control and
    Prevention/Agency for Toxic
    Substances and Disease
    Registry, 557
Owens Corning Internships, 559
Pacific Gas and Electric Summer
    Intern Program, 559
Paul and Helen L. Grauer
    Scholarship, 167
Pete Wilson Journalism
    Scholarship, 425
PGA Tour Diversity Intern
    Program, 560
PGSF Annual Scholarship
    Competition, 423
PHD Amateur Radio Association
    Scholarship, 167
Presidents' $2,500 Scholarships, 425
Press Club of Houston
    Scholarship, 422
Print & Online News Grants, 188
PRSA-Hawaii/Roy Leffingwell Public
    Relations Scholarship, 270
Public Relations Internship, 545
Pulliam Journalism Fellowship, 540
Random House Summer Internship
    Program, 560
Reid Blackburn Scholarship, 369
SCA Conservation Internships, 564
Scholastic Writing Portfolio Gold
    Award, 86
Seattle Professional Chapter
    Scholarship, 197
Shirley McKown Scholarship
    Fund, 272
Simon and Schuster Summer
    Internship Program, 561
Sony Credited Internship, 563
Sports Copy Editing Intern
    Program, 535
Sports Illustrated Scholarship, 356
Stanford Chen Internship Grant, 189
Staples Summer Internship
    Program, 564
Thomas R. Pickering Foreign Affairs
    Fellowship, 523
Time Inc. Internship Program, 565
United States Holocaust Memorial
    Museum Internship, 566
University Journalism
    Scholarship, 399
U.S. Department of State
    Internship, 567
U.S. Senate Member Internships, 566
Visual Task Force (VTF)
    Scholarship, 357

The Wall Street Journal Asia Internship, 569
The Wall Street Journal Europe Internship, 569
The Wall Street Journal Journalism Internship, 569
Water Companies (NJ Chapter) Scholarship, 357
Women's Sports Foundation Internship, 571
World Security Institute Internship, 571

Computer and information sciences

Aerospace Undergraduate Research Scholarship Program, 353
AFCEA General Emmett Paige Scholarship, 183
AFCEA General John A. Wickham Scholarship, 184
AFCEA ROTC Scholarship, 184
AFCEA Scholarship for Working Professionals, 184
Albert E. Wischmeyer Memorial Scholarship Award, 441
Allstate Internships, 525
Alpha Beta Gamma National Scholarship, 87
Arthur and Gladys Cervenka Scholarship, 441
A.T. Anderson Memorial Scholarship, 104
Batttelle Collegiate Scholarship, 373
BMW/SAE Engineering Scholarships, 430
Boeing Internships, 532
Boston Scientific Scholarship, 453
Burlington Northern Santa Fe Foundation Scholarship, 104
Cargill Scholarship Program, 498
Castle & Cooke Mililani Technology Park Scholarship Fund, 254
The CBC Spouses Cheerios Brand Health Initiative Scholarship, 220
Chapter 17 St. Louis Scholarship, 442
Chapter 6 - Fairfield County Scholarship, 443
Chevron Corporation Scholarships, 454
Chevron Internship Program, 532
Chrysler Foundation Scholarship, 454
CIA Undergraduate Scholarship Program, 214
CITE Scholarship, 223
Citizens for Global Solutions Internship, 533
Clinton J. Helton Manufacturing Scholarship Award, 444
Computer Science Scholarship, 362
Connie and Robert T. Gunter Scholarship, 444
Cooperative Internship Programs, 535
Davidson Fellows Scholarship, 229
Delaware Space Grant Undergraduate Research Internship, 549
Dell Inc. Scholarship, 455

Denver Rescue Mission Center for Mission Studies Internships, 534
Department of Commerce Internship for Postsecondary Students, 554
Disabled War Veterans Scholarship, 184
Disney Theme Parks & Resorts Professional Internships, 569
Distance Learning/Online Scholarship, 185
DPMA/PC Scholarship, 228
E. Wayne Kay Community College Scholarship, 445
E. Wayne Kay Co-op Scholarship, 445
Economic Research Division Project Internships, 532
Engineering/Technology Achievement Awards, 249
Entergy Jumpstart Co-ops and Internships, 536
EPA National Network for Environmental Management Studies Fellowship, 503
ESPN Internship, 536
Florida Power & Light Internship Program, 538
Ford Motor Company/American Indian College Fund Corporate Scholars Program, 102
Future Leaders of Manufacturing Scholarships, 446
Genentech, Inc. Internship Program, 539
Giuliano Mazzetti Scholarship, 446
Global Change Education Program, 554
Goldman, Sachs and Co. Scholarship, 458
Google Hispanic College Fund Scholarship Program, 275
Great Lakes Colleges Association/Associated Colleges of the Midwest Oak Ridge Science Semester, 554
Great Minds in Stem Scholars Program, 251
Greater Research Opportunities Undergraduate Student Fellowships, 504
Hoffman-La Roche Inc. Student Internship, 540
Honeywell International Inc. Scholarship, 458
Horizons Scholarship, 522
IBM Co-op and Intern Program, 540
IBM Corporation Scholarship, 458
INROADS Internship, 541
Internship and Co-op Program, 530
Internship Program for Laboratory Technology, 555
ITT Scholarship, 458
John Deere Student Training Programs, 542
John Wiley and Sons, Inc. Internship Program, 543
Kawasaki-McGaha Scholarship Fund, 265

Lehman Scholarship, 459
Marble-Boyle Award, 198
Marine Corps Sgt. Jeannette L. Winters Memorial Scholarship, 185
MESBEC Scholarships, 212
Microsoft Corporation Scholarships, 461
Microsoft General Scholarship, 332
Morgan Stanley Scholars Program, 102
NASA Rocky Mountain Space Grant Consortium Undergraduate Scholarship, 351
NASA Space Grant Georgia Fellowship Program, 344
NASA Space Grant Montana Undergraduate Scholarship Program, 347
NASA Space Grant Nevada Undergraduate Scholarship, 348
NASA Space Grant New Mexico Undergraduate Scholarship, 348
NASA Space Grant North Dakota Undergraduate Scholarship, 349
NASA Space Grant Teacher Education Scholarship, 353
NASA Space Grant Texas Columbia Crew Memorial Undergraduate Scholarships, 352
NASA Space Grant Virginia Community College Scholarship, 353
National Oceanic and Atmospheric Administration Hollings Undergraduate Scholarship, 555
National Security Agency Stokes Educational Scholarship Program, 372
National Society of Black Engineers Golden Torch Awards, 374
NBA Internship Program, 551
NCR Summer Internships, 552
Northrop Grumman Corporate Scholarship, 375
Northrop Grumman Corporation Scholarship, 462
Oracle Scholars Internship Program, 566
ORISE Department of Energy Community College Institute, 555
ORISE Higher Education Research Experiences at Oak Ridge National Laboratory for Students, 555
ORISE Nuclear Regulatory Commission Historically Black Colleges and Universities Student Research Participation, 556
ORISE Professional Internship Program for National Energy Technology Laboratory, 556
ORISE Student Environmental Management Participation at the U.S. Army Environmental Center, 556
ORISE Student Research - National Center for Toxicological Research, 557

ORISE Student Research Participation at U.S. Army Research Laboratory, 557
Owens Corning Internships, 559
Pacific Gas and Electric Summer Intern Program, 559
Paul and Helen Ruckes Scholarship, 98
Pearl I. Young Scholarship, 349
PGA Tour Diversity Intern Program, 560
PHD Amateur Radio Association Scholarship, 167
Plasma Physics National Undergraduate Fellowship Program, 560
Procter & Gamble Scholarship, 278
Product Development Summer Internship Program, 559
Robert Noyce Scholarship Program, 418
Rockwell Automation Scholarships, 463
Rodney E. Powell Memorial Scholarship, 391
Roosevelt Archival Internships, 538
SAE Detroit Section Technical Scholarship, 431
Savannah River Site Professional Internship Program, 557
Science Undergraduate Laboratory Internships, 558
SciTech Scholarship, 416
Shuichi, Katsu and Itsuyo Suga Scholarship, 272
Siemens Competition in Math, Science and Technology, 437
Sony Credited Internship, 563
Staples Summer Internship Program, 564
STEM Scholarship, 352
Student Merit Scholarships, 79
Student Research at the U.S. Army Edgewood Chemical Biological Center, 567
Technical Minority Scholarship, 524
Time Inc. Internship Program, 565
Travelers Foundation, 103
Tyson Foods Intern Program, 566
Undergraduate Research Scholarship, 348
Undergraduate Summer Fellowships in Engineering and Science, 550
Undergraduate Summer Internship, 537
U.S. Department of Homeland Security Scholarship and Fellowship Program, 558
U.S. Department of State Internship, 567
U.S. Steel NSBE Academic Scholarship, 376
VADM Samuel L. Gravely Jr. USN (Ret.) Memorial Scholarship, 186
Verizon Corporate Scholarship, 376

Vice Admiral Jerry O. Tuttle, USN (Ret.) and Mrs. Barbara A. Tuttle Science and Technology Scholarship, 186
Wal-Mart Stores Inc. Corporate Scholarship, 376
Washington Internships for Students of Engineering, 570
Water Companies (NJ Chapter) Scholarship, 357
Web Challenge Contest, 476
Wells Fargo Scholarship, 279
West Virginia Engineering, Science, and Technology Scholarship, 517
William E. "Buck" Bragunier Scholarship for Outstanding Leadership, 186
William R. Goldfarb Memorial Scholarship, 168
World Security Institute Internship, 571

Education

AFCEA General Emmett Paige Scholarship, 183
AFCEA General John A. Wickham Scholarship, 184
AFCEA ROTC Scholarship, 184
Alaska Teacher Education Loan, 573
Alma White-Delta Kappa Gamma Scholarship, 253
Alpha Delta Kappa/Harriet Simmons Scholarship, 403
American Legion Maryland Auxiliary Scholarship, 125
Applied Arts Internships, 530
Arthur Patch McKinlay Scholarship, 90
Assumption Program of Loans for Education (APLE), 574
Averyl Elaine Keriakedes Memorial Scholarship, 134
Burlington Northern Santa Fe Foundation Scholarship, 104
C. J. Davidson Scholarship, 480
California Child Development Grant Program, 209
California Teachers Association Martin Luther King, Jr., Memorial Scholarship, 210
Christa McAuliffe Memorial Scholarship, 136
Christa McAuliffe Teacher Incentive Program, 575
Colorado Supplemental Leveraging Educational Assistance Partnership (SLEAP), 218
Community Scholarship Fund, 255
Connecticut Minority Teacher Incentive Grant, 222
Critical Needs Alternative Route Teacher Loan/Scholarship, 578
Critical Teacher Shortage Student Loan Forgiveness Program, 576
CRT Internship Program, 533
CTA Scholarship for Dependent Children, 211

CTA Scholarships for Members, 211
Cushman School Internship, 533
David Family Scholarship, 406
Delta Gamma Foundation Florence Margaret Harvey Memorial Scholarship, 98
Developmental Disability Scholastic Achievement Scholarship, 202
Disabled War Veterans Scholarship, 184
Distance Learning/Online Scholarship, 185
DMI Milk Marketing Scholarships, 360
DOE Pre-Service Teacher Internships, 554
Dr. Alfred C. Fones Scholarship, 76
Dr. Hannah K. Vuolo Memorial Scholarship, 140
Dr. Hans & Clara Zimmerman Foundation Education Scholarship, 256
Early Childhood Development Scholarship, 310
Education Achievement Awards, 249
Educational Aide Exemption, 481
Eight and Forty Lung and Respiratory Nursing Scholarship Fund, 132
Erman W. Taylor Memorial Scholarship, 129
The Fred Rogers Memorial Scholarship, 73
Future Teachers Scholarship, 400
Gates Millennium Scholars Program, 498
Georgia Promise Teacher Scholarship, 576
Golden Apple Scholars of Illinois Program, 248
Government and Public Affairs Internship, 528
Grow Your Own Teacher Scholarship Program, 287
Guggenheim Museum Internship, 563
Harriet Hoffman Memorial Scholarship, 119
Harriet Irsay Scholarship, 106
Highmark Scholarship, 417
Hokuli'a Foundation Scholarship Fund, 262
Idaho Education Incentive Loan Forgiveness Program, 577
Illinois Future Teacher Corps, 290
Indiana Minority Teacher & Special Education Services Scholarship, 471
Iowa Farm Bureau Federation Scholarship, 297
Isemoto Contracting Co., Ltd. Scholarship Fund, 263
Jack A. & Marilyn MacAllister Foundation, 102
James Carlson Memorial Scholarship, 408
Jedidiah Zabrosky Scholarship, 508
Kansas Teacher Service Scholarship, 308

Eligibility Indexes

Kentucky Teacher Scholarship, 310
L. Gordon Bittle Memorial
    Scholarship for SCTA, 211
Latin Honor Society Scholarship, 367
Lillian and Samuel Sutton Education
    Scholarship, 342
Lindbergh Grant, 215
Marine Corps Sgt. Jeannette L.
    Winters Memorial Scholarship, 185
Maureen V. O'Donnell/Eunice C.
    Kraft Teacher Training
    Scholarships, 90
MESBEC Scholarships, 212
MG Eugene C. Renzi/ManTech
    International Corporation
    Scholarship for Math and Science
    Teachers, 185
Minority Teachers of Illinois
    Scholarship, 290
Mississippi Nursing Education
    Loan/Scholarship, 579
Mississippi William Winter Teacher
    Scholar Loan Program, 579
Missouri Minority Teaching
    Scholarship, 338
Morris Arboretum Education
    Internship, 547
Museum Coca-Cola Internship, 551
NASA Pennsylvania Space Grant
    Sylvia Stein Memorial
    Scholarship, 350
NASA Space Grant Arizona
    Undergraduate Research
    Internship, 549
NASA Space Grant Georgia
    Fellowship Program, 344
NASA Space Grant Kentucky
    Undergraduate Scholarship, 345
NASA Space Grant Teacher Education
    Scholarship, 353
National Federation of the Blind
    Educator of Tomorrow Award, 364
National Junior Classical League
    Scholarship, 367
National Oceanic and Atmospheric
    Administration Hollings
    Undergraduate Scholarship, 555
Native American Leadership in
    Education Scholarship, 212
New Mexico Teacher's
    Loan-for-Service, 581
Nick Van Pernis Scholarship, 268
OCA/Verizon Foundation College
    Scholarship, 397
PAGE Foundation Scholarships, 423
Peggy Guggenheim Internship, 563
Philip and Alice Angell Eastern Star
    Scholarship, 509
Presbyterian Student Opportunity
    Scholarship, 421
Robert Noyce Scholarship
    Program, 418
Ron Bright Scholarship, 271
Roosevelt Archival Internships, 538
Rudolph Dillman Memorial
    Scholarship, 98
SCA Conservation Internships, 564

Smithsonian Environmental Research
    Center Internship Program, 561
South Carolina Teacher Loans, 583
South Dakota Annis I. Fowler/Kaden
    Scholarship, 468
South Dakota Haines Memorial
    Scholarship, 468
Special Education Teacher Tuition
    Waiver, 291
Special Education Teaching
    Scholarships, 117
STEM Teacher Scholarships, 185
Teacher Assistant Scholarship
    Fund, 395
Teacher Quest Scholarship
    Program, 206
Tennessee Minority Teaching Fellows
    Program, 584
Tennessee Student Assistance
    Corporation/Math And Science
    Teachers Loan Forgiveness
    Program, 584
Tennessee Teaching Scholars
    Program, 584
United Health Foundation
    Scholarship, 103
U.S. Department of Education
    Fulbright-Hays Project Abroad
    Scholarship for Programs in
    China, 225
U.S. National Arboretum Summer
    Internship, 568
Utah Career Teaching
    Scholarship/T.H. Bell Teaching
    Incentive Loan, 586
Weisman Scholarship, 223
West Virginia Underwood-Smith
    Teacher Scholarship, 518
Wilma D. Hoyal/Maxine Chilton
    Memorial Scholarship, 109
Wisconsin Minority Teacher Loan
    Program, 587
Workforce Incentive Program, 580

Engineering and engineering technology

ACEC Scholarship, 94
ACSM Fellows Scholarship, 91
Ada I. Pressman Memorial
    Scholarship, 451
Admiral Grace Murray Hopper
    Scholarship, 451
Aerospace Undergraduate Research
    Scholarship Program, 353
AFCEA General Emmett Paige
    Scholarship, 183
AFCEA General John A. Wickham
    Scholarship, 184
AFCEA ROTC Scholarship, 184
AFCEA Scholarship for Working
    Professionals, 184
AGC Education and Research
    Undergraduate Scholarship, 195
Agnes Malakate Kezios
    Scholarship, 191
AIAA Foundation Undergraduate
    Scholarship, 105

Albert E. Wischmeyer Memorial
    Scholarship Award, 441
Allen J. Baldwin Scholarship, 191
Alwin B. Newton Scholarship, 172
American Chemical Society Scholars
    Program, 90
American Council of Engineering
    Companies of Oregon
    Scholarship, 403
American Electric Power
    Scholarship, 192
American Meteorological Society
    Undergraduate Scholarships, 156
American Meteorological
    Society/Industry Minority
    Scholarship, 156
Amtrol Scholarship, 99
Angelo S. Bisesti Scholarship, 158
Anne Maureen Whitney Barrow
    Memorial, 452
ANS Undergraduate Scholarships, 158
A.O. Smith Water Heaters
    Scholarship, 419
Arizona Chapter Vertical Flight
    Engineering Scholarship, 100
ARRL Earl I. Anderson
    Scholarship, 162
Arthur and Doreen Parrett
    Scholarship, 187
Arthur and Gladys Cervenka
    Scholarship, 441
ASDSO Undergraduate
    Scholarship, 199
ASHRAE General Scholarships, 172
ASHRAE Memorial Scholarship, 172
ASHRAE Region IV Benny Bootle
    Scholarship, 172
ASHRAE Region VIII
    Scholarship, 173
ASM Outstanding Scholars
    Awards, 189
ASME Auxiliary Student Loan
    Fund, 574
ASME Auxiliary/FIRST Clarke
    Scholarship, 192
The ASME Foundation Hanley
    Scholarship, 192
ASME Foundation Scholarships, 192
ASME Power Division
    Scholarship, 192
ASME Student Loan Program, 574
ASNE Scholarship, 175
A.T. Anderson Memorial
    Scholarship, 104
Aviation Maintenance Technician
    Scholarship Award, 274
B. K. Krenzer Re-entry
    Scholarship, 452
Baker Hughes Scholarship, 452
Baroid Scholarship, 99
Barry K. Wendt Commitment Award
    and Scholarship, 377
Barry M. Goldwater Scholarship, 201
Batttelle Collegiate Scholarship, 373
Bechtel Foundation Scholarship, 452
Bechtel Group Foundation
    Scholarship, 373

Berna Lou Cartwright Scholarship, 191
Berntsen International Scholarship in Surveying Technology, 92
Bertha Lamme Memorial Scholarship, 453
BIA San Diego Scholarship, 206
B.J. Harrod Scholarships, 453
BMW/SAE Engineering Scholarships, 430
Boeing Internships, 532
Boston Scientific Scholarship, 453
BP Corporate Scholarship, 373
Bradford White Scholarship, 419
Brill Family Scholarship, 453
Bud Glover Memorial Scholarship, 80
Burlington Northern Santa Fe Foundation Scholarship, 104
Cady McDonnell Memorial Scholarship, 92
California Farm Bureau Scholarship, 208
Cargill Scholarship Program, 498
Castle & Cooke Mililani Technology Park Scholarship Fund, 254
Caterpillar Corporate Scholarship, 373
Caterpillar Inc. Scholarship, 454
Caterpillar Scholars Award, 442
CBC Scholarship, 221
The CBC Spouses Cheerios Brand Health Initiative Scholarship, 220
Center for Architecture Design Scholarship, 213
Central New Mexico Scholarship, 454
Chapter 17 St. Louis Scholarship, 442
Chapter 198 - Downriver Detroit Scholarship, 442
Chapter 4 - Lawrence A. Wacker Memorial Scholarship, 442
Chapter 52 - Wichita Scholarship, 443
Chapter 56 - Fort Wayne Scholarship, 443
Chapter 6 - Fairfield County Scholarship, 443
Chapter 67 - Phoenix Scholarship, 443
Charles and Annette Hill Scholarship, 121
Charles B. Scharp Scholarship, 191
Chevron Corporation Scholarships, 454
Chevron Internship Program, 532
Chrysler Foundation Scholarship, 454
CIA Undergraduate Scholarship Program, 214
CITE Scholarship, 223
The Clarence & Josephine Myers Scholarship, 443
Clinton J. Helton Manufacturing Scholarship Award, 444
Computer Science Scholarship, 362
Connie and Robert T. Gunter Scholarship, 444
Cooperative Internship Programs, 535
Cummins Inc. Corporate Scholarship, 373
Cummins Scholarship, 455

D. Fred and Mariam L. Bovie Scholarship, 176
David Alan Quick Scholarship, 237
David Arver Memorial Scholarship, 80
David J. Fitzmaurice Scholarship, 299
Decommissioning, Decontamination and Reutilization Scholarship, 159
DEED Student Research Grants, 161
Delaware Space Grant Undergraduate Tuition Scholarship, 344
Delayed Education Scholarship for Women, 159
Dell Inc. Scholarship, 455
Delta Faucet Company Scholarship, 419
Department of Commerce Internship for Postsecondary Students, 554
Detroit Chapter One - Founding Chapter Scholarship Award, 444
Disabled War Veterans Scholarship, 184
Disney Theme Parks & Resorts Professional Internships, 569
Distance Learning/Online Scholarship, 185
Dorothy Lemke Howarth Scholarships, 455
Dorothy M. & Earl S. Hoffman Scholarships, 455
Dorothy P. Morris Scholarship, 456
Dr. W. Wes Eckenfelder Jr. Scholarship, 206
Duane Hanson Scholarship, 173
DuPont Company Scholarship, 456
DuPont Co-ops, 535
DuPont Internships, 535
Dutch and Ginger Arver Scholarship, 80
E. Wayne Kay Co-op Scholarship, 445
E. Wayne Kay High School Scholarship, 445
E. Wayne Kay Scholarship, 445
Edmond A. Metzger Scholarship, 164
Edward D. Hendrickson/SAE Engineering Scholarship, 430
Edward J. Brady Memorial Scholarship, 177
Edward J. Dulis Scholarship, 189
Edward S. Roth Manufacturing Engineering, 446
Electronics for Imaging Scholarship, 456
Elizabeth McLean Memorial Scholarship, 456
Ellison Onizuka Memorial Scholarship, 258
Engineering Scholarship Program, 481
Engineering Technology Scholarships, 173
Engineering/Technology Achievement Awards, 249
Engineers Foundation of Ohio Scholarships, 234
Entergy Jumpstart Co-ops and Internships, 536

Eugene C. Figg Jr. Civil Engineering Scholarship, 171
Exelon Scholarship, 456
Extrusion Division/Lew Erwin Memorial Scholarship, 448
ExxonMobil Corporate Scholarship, 374
Father James B. Macelwane Annual Award, 157
Field Aviation Co. Inc. Scholarship, 81
Fleming/Blaszcak Scholarship, 448
Florida Power & Light Internship Program, 538
Ford Motor Company Scholarship, 457
Ford Motor Company/American Indian College Fund Corporate Scholars Program, 102
Frank and Dorothy Miller ASME Auxiliary Scholarships, 193
Frank M. Coda Scholarship, 173
Fred M. Young, Sr./SAE Engineering Scholarship, 430
Freeman Fellowship, 171
Freshman Undergraduate Scholarship Program, 157
Fulfilling the Legacy Scholarship, 374
Future Leaders of Manufacturing Scholarships, 446
F.W. "Beich" Beichley Scholarship, 193
Garland Duncan Scholarships, 193
Garmin Scholarship, 81
Gary J. Miller Undergraduate Prizes for Cancer and Cancer-Related Biomedical Research, 88
Gates Millennium Scholars Program, 498
GE Business/Engineering Scholarship for Minority Students, 316
Genentech, Inc. Internship Program, 539
General Electric Foundation Scholarship, 457
General Electric Women's Network Scholarship, 457
General Motors Foundation Scholarships, 457
Geography Students Internship, 551
George A. Roberts Scholarships, 190
Georgia-Pacific Internship and Co-op Programs, 539
Giuliano Mazzetti Scholarship, 446
Global Change Education Program, 554
Goldman, Sachs and Co. Scholarship, 458
Google Hispanic College Fund Scholarship Program, 275
Great Lakes Colleges Association/Associated Colleges of the Midwest Oak Ridge Science Semester, 554
Great Minds in Stem Scholars Program, 251

Greater Research Opportunities Undergraduate Student Fellowships, 504

Gulf Coast Hurricane Scholarships, 449

Hansen Scholarship, 237

Henry Adams Scholarship, 174

Henry Broughton, K2AE Memorial Scholarship, 164

Hoffman-La Roche Inc. Student Internship, 540

Homestead Capital Housing Scholarship, 407

Honeywell Avionics Scholarship, 81

Honeywell International Inc. Scholarship, 458

Horizons Scholarship, 522

Howard Brown Rickard Scholarship, 363

HSBC-North America Scholarship Program, 277

Hubertus W.V. Wellems Scholarship for Male Students, 342

IBM Co-op and Intern Program, 540

IBM Corporation Scholarship, 458

Industrial Automation Engineering College Scholarships, 188

INROADS Internship, 541

Intel International Science and Engineering Fair, 440

International Gas Turbine Institute (IGTI) Scholarship, 193

International Studies Scholarship, 374

Internship and Co-op Program, 530

Internship Program for Laboratory Technology, 555

Isemoto Contracting Co., Ltd. Scholarship Fund, 263

ITT Scholarship, 458

Ivy Parker Memorial Scholarship, 459

J. Richard Mehalick Scholarship, 174

James L. Allhands Essay Competition, 195

Jeffrey Alan Scoggins Memorial Scholarship, 408

Jere W. Thompson, Jr. Scholarship Fund, 227

Jill S. Tietjen P.E. Scholarship, 459

John & Elsa Gracik Scholarships, 193

John and Muriel Landis Scholarship, 159

John Deere Student Training Programs, 542

John M. Haniak Scholarship, 190

John R. Lamarsh Scholarship, 159

Johnny Davis Memorial Scholarship, 81

Johnson Controls Co-op and Internship Programs, 543

Joseph R. Dietrich Scholarship, 159

Judith Resnik Memorial Scholarship, 459

K. K. Wang Scholarship, 449

Kathryn D. Sullivan Science and Engineering Fellowship, 351

Kenneth Andrew Roe Mechanical Engineering Scholarship, 194

L-3 Avionics Systems Scholarship, 81

Lee Tarbox Memorial Scholarship, 82

Lehman Scholarship, 459

Lillian Moller Gilbreth Scholarship, 460

Lockheed Martin Aeronautics Company Scholarships, 460

Lockheed Martin Corporate Scholarship, 374

Lockheed Martin Foundation Scholarships, 460

Lowell Gaylor Memorial Scholarship, 82

Lucile B. Kaufman Women's Scholarship, 446

Lucille & Charles A. Wert Scholarship, 190

Lydia I. Pickup Memorial Scholarship, 460

Maine Metal Products Association Scholarship, 322

Maine Society of Professional Engineers Scholarship Program, 322

Marathon Oil Corporation College Scholarship, 277

Marine Corps Sgt. Jeannette L. Winters Memorial Scholarship, 185

Mary V. Munger Scholarship, 461

MassMutual Multicultural College Scholarship, 277

MASWE Scholarships, 461

Matsuo Bridge Company Ltd of Japan Scholarship, 178

Melvin R. Green Scholarships, 194

Meridith Thoms Memorial Scholarships, 461

MESBEC Scholarships, 212

Michigan Society of Professional Engineers Scholarships for High School Seniors, 331

Microscopy Society of America Undergraduate Research Scholarship, 332

Microsoft Corporation Scholarships, 461

Microsoft General Scholarship, 332

Mid-Continent Instrument Scholarship, 82

Minority Scholarship Program, 206

MSGC Undergraduate Underrepresented Minority Fellowship Program, 346

Myrtle and Earl Walker Scholarship, 446

Nancy Lorraine Jensen Memorial Scholarship, 466

NASA Academy Internship, 550

NASA Connecticut Space Grant Undergraduate Fellowship, 343

NASA District of Columbia Undergraduate Scholarship, 344

NASA Hawaii Undergraduate Student Research Program, 549

NASA Idaho Space Grant Undergraduate Scholarship, 345

NASA Minnesota Space Grant Consortium Wide Scholarship, 347

NASA Missouri State Space Grant Undergraduate Scholarship, 347

NASA Ohio Space Grant Junior/Senior Scholarship Program, 350

NASA Pennsylvania Space Grant Sylvia Stein Memorial Scholarship, 350

NASA Rocky Mountain Space Grant Consortium Undergraduate Scholarship, 351

NASA Space Grant Arizona Undergraduate Research Internship, 549

NASA Space Grant Georgia Fellowship Program, 344

NASA Space Grant Hawaii Undergraduate Fellowship, 344

NASA Space Grant Illinois Undergraduate Scholarship, 345

NASA Space Grant Kentucky Undergraduate Scholarship, 345

NASA Space Grant Maine Consortium Annual Scholarship and Fellowship Program, 346

NASA Space Grant Michigan Undergraduate Fellowship, 346

NASA Space Grant Montana Undergraduate Scholarship Program, 347

NASA Space Grant Nevada Undergraduate Scholarship, 348

NASA Space Grant New Mexico Undergraduate Scholarship, 348

NASA Space Grant North Dakota Consortium Lillian Goettler Scholarship, 349

NASA Space Grant North Dakota Undergraduate Scholarship, 349

NASA Space Grant Oregon Undergraduate Scholarship, 350

NASA Space Grant Rhode Island Undergraduate Research Scholarship, 350

NASA Space Grant South Carolina Undergraduate Student Research Fellowship, 352

NASA Space Grant Teacher Education Scholarship, 353

NASA Space Grant Texas Columbia Crew Memorial Undergraduate Scholarships, 352

NASA Space Grant Undergraduate Scholarship, 343

NASA Space Grant Vermont Consortium Undergraduate Scholarships, 352

NASA Space Grant Virginia Community College Scholarship, 353

NASA Space Grant Wisconsin Consortium Undergraduate Research Program, 354

NASA Space Grant Wisconsin Consortium Undergraduate Scholarship, 354
NASA West Virginia Space Grant Undergraduate Research Fellowship, 353
National Association of Women in Construction Founders' Scholarship, 358
National Oceanic and Atmospheric Administration Hollings Undergraduate Scholarship, 555
National Security Agency Stokes Educational Scholarship Program, 372
National Society of Black Engineers Golden Torch Awards, 374
NCR Summer Internships, 552
New Jersey Scholarship, 462
Nissan Community College Transfer Scholarship, 278
North Central Region Scholarship, 447
Northrop Grumman Corporate Scholarship, 375
Northrop Grumman Corporation Scholarship, 462
NSBE Fellows Scholarship, 375
OCA/Verizon Foundation College Scholarship, 397
Oklahoma Engineering Foundation Scholarship, 399
Olive Lynn Salembier Re-entry Scholarship, 462
Operations and Power Division Scholarship, 160
Oracle Scholars Internship Program, 566
ORISE Department of Energy Community College Institute, 555
ORISE Higher Education Research Experiences at Oak Ridge National Laboratory for Students, 555
ORISE Nuclear Regulatory Commission Historically Black Colleges and Universities Student Research Participation, 556
ORISE Professional Internship Program for National Energy Technology Laboratory, 556
ORISE Research Participation Program at the U.S. Army Center for Health Promotion and Preventive Medicine, 556
ORISE Student Environmental Management Participation at the U.S. Army Environmental Center, 556
ORISE Student Research Participation at U.S. Army Research Laboratory, 557
Owens Corning Internships, 559
Pacific Gas and Electric Summer Intern Program, 559
Past Presidents Scholarship, 179
Past Presidents Scholarships, 462

Paul and Helen Ruckes Scholarship, 98
Payzer Scholarship, 238
PBS&J Corporate Scholarship, 375
Pearl I. Young Scholarship, 349
PHCC Educational Foundation Need-Based Scholarship, 420
PHD Amateur Radio Association Scholarship, 167
Phoenix Section Scholarship, 463
Pittsburgh Local Section Scholarship, 160
Pittsburgh Scholarship, 449
Plane & Pilot Magazine/Garmin Scholarship, 82
Plasma Physics National Undergraduate Fellowship Program, 560
Plastics Pioneers Scholarships, 449
Plumbing-Heating-Cooling Contractors - National Association Educational Foundation Scholarship, 420
Procter & Gamble Scholarship, 278
Rain Bird Intelligent Use of Water Company Scholarship, 315
Ralph K. Hillquist Honorary SAE Scholarship, 431
Raymond DiSalvo Scholarship, 160
RCMI Technical/Trade School Scholarship, 428
Reuben Trane Scholarship, 174
Robert G. Lacy Scholarship, 160
Robert Noyce Scholarship Program, 418
Robert T. (Bob) Liner Scholarship, 160
Rockwell Automation Scholarships, 463
Rocky Mountain Coal Mining Institute Scholarship, 428
Rodney E. Powell Memorial Scholarship, 391
RWMA Scholarship, 180
SAE Detroit Section Technical Scholarship, 431
SAE Long-Term Member Sponsored Scholarship, 431
SAE Women Engineers Committee Scholarship, 431
SAE/David Hermance Hybird Technologies Scholarship, 431
Samuel Fletcher Tapman ASCE Student Chapter Scholarship, 171
Savannah River Site Professional Internship Program, 557
Scholarship Educational Assistance Program, 354
Science Undergraduate Laboratory Internships, 558
Siemens Competition in Math, Science and Technology, 437
SME Education Foundation Family Scholarship, 447
Society of Plastics Engineers General Scholarships, 450
Southface Internship, 563

The SPE Foundation Blow Molding Division Memorial Scholarships, 450
Spence Reese Scholarship, 204
SPIE Educational Scholarship in Optical Science and Engineering, 470
STEM Scholarship, 352
Stephen T. Kugle Scholarship, 194
Student Research at the U.S. Army Edgewood Chemical Biological Center, 567
Summer Internship Program, 531
Summer Undergraduate Scholarship, 351
Susan Miszkowitz Memorial Scholarship, 463
Sylvia W. Farny Scholarship, 191
Tau Beta Pi/SAE Engineering Scholarship, 432
Technical Minority Scholarship, 524
Thermoforming Division Memorial Scholarships, 450
Thermoset Division/James I. MacKenzie Memorial Scholarship, 450
Thomas J. Bardos Science Education Awards for Undergraduate Students, 89
TMC/SAE Donald D. Dawson Technical Scholarship, 432
Toyota Corporate Scholarship, 376
Travelers Foundation, 103
Tyson Foods Intern Program, 566
Undergraduate Research Scholarship, 348
Undergraduate Scholarship Program, 349
Undergraduate Summer Fellowships in Engineering and Science, 550
U.S. Department of Homeland Security Scholarship and Fellowship Program, 558
U.S. Steel NSBE Academic Scholarship, 376
VADM Samuel L. Gravely Jr. USN (Ret.) Memorial Scholarship, 186
Verizon Corporate Scholarship, 376
Vertical Flight Foundation Scholarship, 100
Vice Admiral Jerry O. Tuttle, USN (Ret.) and Mrs. Barbara A. Tuttle Science and Technology Scholarship, 186
Wal-Mart Stores Inc. Corporate Scholarship, 376
Walt Bartram Memorial Education Award (Region 12 and Chapter 119), 447
Washington Internships for Students of Engineering, 570
Water Companies (NJ Chapter) Scholarship, 357
Wells Fargo Scholarship, 279
West Virginia Engineering, Science, and Technology Scholarship, 517

Western Plastics Pioneers
Scholarship, 450
William E. "Buck" Bragunier
Scholarship for Outstanding
Leadership, 186
William E. Weisel Scholarship, 447
William J. and Marijane E. Adams, Jr.
Scholarship, 194
William Park Woodside Founder's
Scholarship, 190
William R. Goldfarb Memorial
Scholarship, 168
Willis F. Thompson Memorial
Scholarship, 195
Willis H. Carrier Scholarship, 174
Women in Architecture
Scholarship, 197
Yanmar/SAE Scholarship, 432
Yasme Foundation Scholarship, 168
Y.C. Yang Civil Engineering
Scholarship, 172

English and literature

Ahmad-Sehar Saleha Ahmad and
Abrahim Ekramullah Zafar
Foundation, 403
Arthur Patch McKinlay
Scholarship, 90
Artistic and Administrative
Internships, 526
Aspiring Sports Journalist
Internship, 564
Davidson Fellows Scholarship, 229
Florence Lemcke Memorial
Scholarship, 152
Gerrit R. Ludwig Scholarship, 260
Janet Jackson Rhythm Nation
Scholarships, 499
Kennedy Library Archival
Internship, 542
Latin Honor Society Scholarship, 367
Maureen V. O'Donnell/Eunice C.
Kraft Teacher Training
Scholarships, 90
National Junior Classical League
Scholarship, 367
Public Relations Internship, 545
R.L. Gillette Scholarship, 98
Scholastic Writing Portfolio Gold
Award, 86
Signet Classic Student Scholarship
Essay Contest, 414
United States Holocaust Memorial
Museum Internship, 566

Foreign languages

AFCEA ROTC Scholarship, 184
Alpha Mu Gamma Scholarships, 87
CIA Undergraduate Scholarship
Program, 214
Intelligence Scholarships, 185
Italian Language Scholarship, 464
Joseph S. Adams Scholarship, 439
Sorrento Lingue Scholarship, 465
Thomas R. Pickering Foreign Affairs
Fellowship, 523

United States Holocaust Memorial
Museum Internship, 566
U.S. Department of Education
Fulbright-Hays Project Abroad
Scholarship for Programs in
China, 225
U.S. Department of State
Internship, 567
Workforce Incentive Program, 580

Health professions and allied services

ADHA Institute General
Scholarships, 75
ADHA Institute Merit
Scholarships, 75
ADHA Institute Part-Time
Scholarship, 75
AFPE Gateway to Research
Scholarships, 97
Aiea General Hospital Association
Scholarship, 253
Allan Eldin & Agnes Sutorik Geiger
Scholarship Fund, 253
Allman Medical Scholarships, 335
Aloha Scholarship, 131
AMBUCS Scholars-Scholarship for
Therapists, 88
American Legion Arizona Auxiliary
Health Care Occupation
Scholarship, 108
American Legion Arizona Auxiliary
Nurses' Scholarship, 109
American Legion Idaho Auxiliary
Nurse's Scholarship, 116
American Legion Maryland Auxiliary
Scholarship, 125
American Legion Ohio Auxiliary Past
President's Parley Nurse's
Scholarship, 143
American Legion Oregon Auxiliary
Department Nurses
Scholarship, 144
American Legion Puerto Rico
Auxiliary Nursing
Scholarships, 146
American Legion South Dakota
Auxiliary Nurse's Scholarship, 147
American Legion Texas Auxiliary
Medical Scholarship, 149
American Legion Wisconsin Auxiliary
Past Presidents Parley
Scholarship, 155
American Legion Wyoming Auxiliary
Past Presidents' Parley
Scholarship, 156
Arthur and Doreen Parrett
Scholarship, 187
A.T. Anderson Memorial
Scholarship, 104
Athletic Trainers' Entry Level
Scholarship, 358
Bachelor's Scholarships, 402
Behavioral Sciences Student
Fellowship, 236
Bertha P. Singer Scholarship, 405
Black Nurses Scholarship, 358

Burlington Northern Santa Fe
Foundation Scholarship, 104
Cadbury Community Outreach
Scholarships, 75
California Farm Bureau
Scholarship, 208
Caroline Kark Scholarship, 386
The CBC Spouses Cheerios Brand
Health Initiative Scholarship, 220
Champlain Valley Kennel Club
Scholarship, 507
Charles W. Riley Fire and Emergency
Medical Services Tuition
Reimbursement Program, 324
Chester Haddan Scholarship
Program, 412
Clark-Phelps Scholarship, 405
CLN Scholarships, 223
Colgate "Bright Smiles, Bright
Futures" Minority Scholarships, 76
Colon Furr Scholarship, 141
Cora Aguda Manayan Fund, 255
Crest Oral-B Dental Hygiene
Scholarship, 76
The Cynthia E. Morgan Memorial
Scholarship Fund, 226
Cystic Fibrosis Student
Traineeship, 226
Dairy Student Recognition
Program, 360
Dan McKeever Scholarship
Program, 412
David Family Scholarship, 406
Delaware Nursing Incentive
Program, 575
Delta Gamma Foundation Florence
Margaret Harvey Memorial
Scholarship, 98
Denver Rescue Mission Center for
Mission Studies Internships, 534
Department of Commerce Internship
for Postsecondary Students, 554
Developmental Disability Scholastic
Achievement Scholarship, 202
Dr. Alfred C. Fones Scholarship, 76
Dr. Alvin and Monica Saake
Scholarship, 256
Dr. Hans and Clara Zimmerman
Foundation Health Scholarship, 257
Dr. Harold Hillenbrand
Scholarship, 76
Earl & Patricia Armstrong
Scholarship, 498
Eight and Forty Lung and Respiratory
Nursing Scholarship Fund, 132
The Filipino Nurses' Organization of
Hawaii Scholarship, 259
Foundation Student Scholarship, 242
Four-Year Nursing Scholarship, 429
Gary J. Miller Undergraduate Prizes
for Cancer and Cancer-Related
Biomedical Research, 88
Gates Millennium Scholars
Program, 498
Genentech, Inc. Internship
Program, 539

Global Change Education Program, 554

Goldman Family Fund: New Leader Scholarship, 323

Great Lakes Colleges Association/Associated Colleges of the Midwest Oak Ridge Science Semester, 554

The Grotto Scholarships, 475

Hannaford Internships, 539

Hawaii Pacific Gerontological Society Nursing Scholarship Fund, 260

Health Career Scholarship, 296

Highmark Scholarship, 417

Hoffman-La Roche Inc. Student Internship, 540

Hokuli'a Foundation Scholarship Fund, 262

Howard Brown Rickard Scholarship, 363

Hu-Friedy/Esther Wilkins Instrument Scholarships, 77

Idaho Education Incentive Loan Forgiveness Program, 577

Indiana Minority Teacher & Special Education Services Scholarship, 471

Indiana Nursing Scholarship, 472

INROADS Internship, 541

Iowa Farm Bureau Federation Scholarship, 297

Irene E. Newman Scholarship, 77

Isemoto Contracting Co., Ltd. Scholarship Fund, 263

Jimmy A. Young Memorial Education Recognition Award, 169

John and Geraldine Hobble Licensed Practical Nursing Scholarship, 121

John Dawe Dental Education Fund, 263

John Deere Student Training Programs, 542

Johnson & Johnson Scholarships, 77

Juliette A. Southard/Oral-B Laboratories Scholarship, 94

June Gill Nursing Scholarship, 387

Kansas Nursing Service Scholarship, 308

Karla Girts Memorial Community Outreach Scholarship, 77

Ken Chagnon Scholarship, 413

Laura N. Dowsett Fund, 267

Laurence R. Foster Memorial Scholarship, 409

Lindbergh Grant, 215

Margaret E. Swanson Scholarship, 77

Margaret Jones Memorial Nursing Scholarship, 267

Margarite McAlpin Nurse's Scholarship, 152

Margo Ballard and Vivian Meinecke Memorial Scholarship, 339

Mary Marshall Nursing LPN Scholarship, 512

Mary Virginia Macrea Memorial Scholarship, 120

Maryland Tuition Reduction for Non-Resident Nursing Students, 327

Massachusetts Gilbert Matching Student Grant, 328

McFarland Charitable Foundation Scholarship, 252

M.D. "Jack" Murphy Memorial Nurses Training Fund, 130

Medical Career Scholarships, 127

Medical Technologists Student Scholarship, 156

MESBEC Scholarships, 212

Mississippi Health Care Professions Loan/Scholarship, 579

Mississippi Nursing Education Loan/Scholarship, 579

Missouri League for Nursing Scholarship, 339

Morton B. Duggan, Jr. Memorial Education Recognition Award, 169

NASA District of Columbia Undergraduate Scholarship, 344

NASA Space Grant Maine Consortium Annual Scholarship and Fellowship Program, 346

NASA Space Grant Wisconsin Consortium Undergraduate Research Program, 354

National Amateur Baseball Federation Scholarship, 355

National Health Service Corps Scholarship, 503

National Student Nurses Association Scholarship, 243

NBRC/AMP Robert M. Lawrence, MD Education Recognition Award, 170

NBRC/AMP William W. Burgin, Jr. MD Education Recognition Award, 170

NEEBC Scholarship, 380

NEHA/AAS Scholarship, 362

New Mexico Allied Health Student Loan-for-Service Program, 580

New Mexico Nursing Student Loan-for-Service, 581

Nick Van Pernis Scholarship, 268

North Carolina Nurse Scholars Program, 582

North Carolina Student Loans for Health/Science/Mathematics, 582

Nuclear Medicine Student Fellowship Award, 439

Nurse Gift Tuition Scholarships, 134

Nurse Practioner Nurse Midwife Scholarship, 512

Ohio Nurse Education Assistance Loan Program, 582

OMNE/Nursing Leaders of Maine Scholarship, 402

ORISE Higher Education Research Experiences at Oak Ridge National Laboratory for Students, 555

ORISE Nuclear Regulatory Commission Historically Black Colleges and Universities Student Research Participation, 556

ORISE Research Participation Program at the U.S. Army Center for Health Promotion and Preventive Medicine, 556

ORISE Student Research - National Center for Toxicological Research, 557

ORISE Student Research at the Centers for Disease Control and Prevention/Agency for Toxic Substances and Disease Registry, 557

ORISE Student Research Participation at the U.S. Army Medical Research Institute of Chemical Defense, 557

ORISE Student Research Participation at U.S. Army Research Laboratory, 557

Past President's Parley Health Care Scholarship, 128

Past President's Parley Nurse's Scholarship, 112

Past President's Parley Nurses Scholarship, 115

Past President's Parley Nurses' Scholarship, 136, 138 , 139

Past Presidents' Parley Nursing Scholarship, 111

Past President's Parley Nursing Scholarship, 113, 119

Past President's Parley Scholarship, 110, 126 , 131 , 142

Past President's Parley Scholarship for Nurses, 140

Past President's Parley Student Scholarship in Medical Field, 141

Patrick and Judith McHugh Scholarship, 509

Paul Cole Scholarship, 439

Paulina L. Sorg Scholarship, 269

Practical Nursing Scholarship, 135

Presbyterian Student Opportunity Scholarship, 421

President's Parley Nursing Scholarship, 124

Raymond K. Conley Memorial Scholarship, 137

Rich Meiers Health Administration Fund, 270

Robanna Fund, 271

ROTC/Navy Nurse Corps Scholarship Program, 504

Rudolph Dillman Memorial Scholarship, 98

SciTech Scholarship, 416

Siemens Competition in Math, Science and Technology, 437

Sigma Phi Alpha Undergraduate Scholarship, 78

Spence Reese Scholarship, 204

Student Merit Scholarships, 79

Student Nurse Scholarship, 117

Student Research Participation at the Federal Bureau of Investigation, 558
Texas Scholarships for Nursing Students, 485
Thomas J. Bardos Science Education Awards for Undergraduate Students, 89
Thz Fo Farm Fund, 272
Tyson Foods Intern Program, 566
United Health Foundation Scholarship, 103
Walter and Marie Schmidt Scholarship, 412
Wild Bill Fogle Memorial Scholarship, 412
William R. Goldfarb Memorial Scholarship, 168
Wilma Motley Memorial California Merit Scholarship, 78
Workforce Incentive Program, 580
Young Epidemiology Scholars Student Competition, 218

Home economics

Academic Scholarship for High School Seniors and GED Graduates, 370
Academic Scholarship for Undergraduate Students, 370
American Chemical Society Scholars Program, 90
American Society for Enology and Viticulture Scholarship Program, 170
Bern Laxer Memorial Scholarship, 301
Bob Zappatelli Memorial Scholarship, 301
Chefs of Louisiana Cookery Scholarship, 301
Christian Wolffer Scholarship, 301
Clat Triplette Scholarship, 302
The Cynthia E. Morgan Memorial Scholarship Fund, 226
Dairy Student Recognition Program, 360
Deseo at the Westin Scholarship, 302
DMI Milk Marketing Scholarships, 360
Fifth Floor Restaurant Scholarship, 302
Foodservice Communicators Scholarship, 294
Graduate, Baccalaureate or Coordinated Program Scholarships, 94
Iager Dairy Scholarship, 360
Inn at Blackberry Farm Scholarship, 302
Institute of Food Technologists Freshman Scholarship, 292
Institute of Food Technologists Junior/Senior Scholarship, 292
Institute of Food Technologists Sophomore Scholarship, 293
Klussendorf Scholarship, 360

Marcia S. Harris Legacy Fund Scholarship, 427
National Dairy Shrine Kildee Scholarship, 361
New Mexico Allied Health Student Loan-for-Service Program, 580
NPFDA Scholarship, 368
The Peter Cameron/Housewares Charity Foundation Scholarship, 303
Peter Kump Memorial Scholarship, 303
ProStart National Certificate of Achievement Scholarship, 370
The Publican Scholarship, 303
Tyson Foods Intern Program, 566
USDA/1890 National Scholars Program, 502

Law

Alphonso Deal Scholarship, 359
American Society of International Law Internships, 528
BB&T Charitable Scholarship Program, 276
Congressional Institute Internships, 533
Dairy Student Recognition Program, 360
EPA National Network for Environmental Management Studies Fellowship, 503
Genentech, Inc. Internship Program, 539
Goldman Family Fund: New Leader Scholarship, 323
Horizons Scholarship, 522
Howard Brown Rickard Scholarship, 363
Johnson Controls Co-op and Internship Programs, 543
NASA Space Grant Wisconsin Consortium Undergraduate Research Program, 354
Sony Credited Internship, 563
Spence Reese Scholarship, 204
Summer Research Diversity Fellowships in Law and Social Sciences for Undergraduate Students, 526
Tyson Foods Intern Program, 566
U.S. Senate Member Internships, 566
Water Companies (NJ Chapter) Scholarship, 357

Liberal arts and interdisciplinary studies

AFSCMA/UNCF Union Scholars Program, 527
Charles L. Hebner Memorial Scholarship, 230
Community Scholarship Fund, 255
CRT Internship Program, 533
Feminism & Leadership Internship, 537
Harriet Irsay Scholarship, 106

Multicultural Undergraduate Summer Internships at the Getty Center, 541
National Federation of the Blind Scholarships, 364
National Junior Classical League Scholarship, 367
Pulliam Journalism Fellowship, 540
Sid Richardson Scholarship, 437
Summer Research Diversity Fellowships in Law and Social Sciences for Undergraduate Students, 526
Wisconsin Indian Student Assistance Grant, 521
Women's Sports Foundation Internship, 571

Library science

ALISE Bohdan S. Wynar Research Paper Competition, 196
ALISE Research Grant, 196
ALISE/Dialog Methodology Paper Competition, 197
American Society of International Law Internships, 528
Gates Millennium Scholars Program, 498
Guggenheim Museum Internship, 563
Hispanic Division Huntington Fellowship, 544
Kennedy Library Archival Internship, 542
Museum Coca-Cola Internship, 551
Roosevelt Archival Internships, 538

Mathematics

Actuarial Diversity Scholarships, 74
Actuary of Tomorrow Stuart A. Robertson Memorial Scholarship, 74
Adler Science and Math Scholarship, 124
Aerospace Undergraduate Research Scholarship Program, 353
AFCEA General Emmett Paige Scholarship, 183
AFCEA General John A. Wickham Scholarship, 184
AFCEA ROTC Scholarship, 184
AFCEA Scholarship for Working Professionals, 184
AIAA Foundation Undergraduate Scholarship, 105
AICP Heartland Chapter Scholarship, 198
AICP Scholarship, 199
Allstate Internships, 525
A.T. Anderson Memorial Scholarship, 104
Barry M. Goldwater Scholarship, 201
Batttelle Collegiate Scholarship, 373
Boeing Internships, 532
Burlington Northern Santa Fe Foundation Scholarship, 104
CITE Scholarship, 223
Davidson Fellows Scholarship, 229

Delaware Space Grant Undergraduate Research Internship, 549
Department of Commerce Internship for Postsecondary Students, 554
Disabled War Veterans Scholarship, 184
Distance Learning/Online Scholarship, 185
DOE Pre-Service Teacher Internships, 554
Economic Research Division Project Internships, 532
ESPN Internship, 536
Gates Millennium Scholars Program, 498
Global Change Education Program, 554
Great Lakes Colleges Association/Associated Colleges of the Midwest Oak Ridge Science Semester, 554
Great Minds in Stem Scholars Program, 251
Greater Research Opportunities Undergraduate Student Fellowships, 504
Horizons Scholarship, 522
Hubertus W.V. Wellems Scholarship for Male Students, 342
Intel Science Talent Search, 440
Kathryn D. Sullivan Science and Engineering Fellowship, 351
Lockheed Martin Corporate Scholarship, 374
Marine Corps Sgt. Jeannette L. Winters Memorial Scholarship, 185
MassMutual Multicultural College Scholarship, 277
MESBEC Scholarships, 212
Microsoft General Scholarship, 332
MSGC Undergraduate Underrepresented Minority Fellowship Program, 346
NASA Academy Internship, 550
NASA District of Columbia Undergraduate Scholarship, 344
NASA Hawaii Undergraduate Student Research Program, 549
NASA Idaho Space Grant Undergraduate Scholarship, 345
NASA Minnesota Space Grant Consortium Wide Scholarship, 347
NASA Missouri State Space Grant Undergraduate Scholarship, 347
NASA Ohio Space Grant Junior/Senior Scholarship Program, 350
NASA Pennsylvania Space Grant Sylvia Stein Memorial Scholarship, 350
NASA Rocky Mountain Space Grant Consortium Undergraduate Scholarship, 351
NASA Space Grant Michigan Undergraduate Fellowship, 346
NASA Space Grant Nevada Undergraduate Scholarship, 348

NASA Space Grant New Mexico Undergraduate Scholarship, 348
NASA Space Grant North Dakota Consortium Lillian Goettler Scholarship, 349
NASA Space Grant North Dakota Undergraduate Scholarship, 349
NASA Space Grant Oregon Undergraduate Scholarship, 350
NASA Space Grant South Carolina Undergraduate Student Research Fellowship, 352
NASA Space Grant Teacher Education Scholarship, 353
NASA Space Grant Texas Columbia Crew Memorial Undergraduate Scholarships, 352
NASA Space Grant Vermont Consortium Undergraduate Scholarships, 352
NASA Space Grant Virginia Community College Scholarship, 353
NASA West Virginia Space Grant Undergraduate Research Fellowship, 353
National Oceanic and Atmospheric Administration Hollings Undergraduate Scholarship, 555
National Society of Black Engineers Golden Torch Awards, 374
North Carolina Student Loans for Health/Science/Mathematics, 582
ORISE Department of Energy Community College Institute, 555
ORISE Higher Education Research Experiences at Oak Ridge National Laboratory for Students, 555
ORISE Nuclear Regulatory Commission Historically Black Colleges and Universities Student Research Participation, 556
ORISE Professional Internship Program for National Energy Technology Laboratory, 556
ORISE Student Research - National Center for Toxicological Research, 557
Payzer Scholarship, 238
Pearl I. Young Scholarship, 349
Plasma Physics National Undergraduate Fellowship Program, 560
Procter & Gamble Scholarship, 278
Robert Noyce Scholarship Program, 418
Savannah River Site Professional Internship Program, 557
Science Undergraduate Laboratory Internships, 558
SEG Foundation Scholarship, 441
Shuichi, Katsu and Itsuyo Suga Scholarship, 272
Siemens Competition in Math, Science and Technology, 437
Smithsonian Environmental Research Center Internship Program, 561

STEM Scholarship, 352
Student Research at the U.S. Army Edgewood Chemical Biological Center, 567
Tennessee Student Assistance Corporation/Math And Science Teachers Loan Forgiveness Program, 584
Travelers Foundation, 103
Undergraduate Research Scholarship, 348
U.S. Department of Homeland Security Scholarship and Fellowship Program, 558
U.S. Steel NSBE Academic Scholarship, 376
VADM Samuel L. Gravely Jr. USN (Ret.) Memorial Scholarship, 186
William E. "Buck" Bragunier Scholarship for Outstanding Leadership, 186
Young Epidemiology Scholars Student Competition, 218

Military science

Disabled War Veterans Scholarship, 184
Four-Year Nursing Scholarship, 429
Four-Year Scholarship, 429
Hudner Medal of Honor Scholarship, 237
World Security Institute Internship, 571

Mortuary science

American Board of Funeral Service Education National Scholarship, 89

Philosophy, religion, and theology

Calvin Coolidge Memorial Foundation Scholarship, 507
Davidson Fellows Scholarship, 229
Denver Rescue Mission Center for Mission Studies Internships, 534
Leonard M. Perryman Communications Scholarship for Ethnic Minority Students, 498
Presbyterian Student Opportunity Scholarship, 421

Protective services

Alphonso Deal Scholarship, 359
Calvin Coolidge Memorial Foundation Scholarship, 507
Captain James J. Regan Memorial Scholarship, 317
Charles W. Riley Fire and Emergency Medical Services Tuition Reimbursement Program, 324
NC Sheriff's Association Criminal Justice Scholarship, 393
Neil Hamilton Memorial Scholarship, 409
Ritchie-Jennings Memorial Scholarship, 74

Sheryl A. Horak Law Enforcement
  Explorer Scholarship, 318
Summer Research Diversity
  Fellowships in Law and Social
  Sciences for Undergraduate
  Students, 526

Social sciences and history

Adele Filene Student Presenter
  Grant, 224
AFCEA ROTC Scholarship, 184
AFSCMA/UNCF Union Scholars
  Program, 527
AICP Heartland Chapter
  Scholarship, 198
AICP Scholarship, 199
American Society of International
  Law Internships, 528
Anne U. White Fund, 198
Anthropology Internship
  Program, 527
Arts Action Fund Internship, 528
Averyl Elaine Keriakedes Memorial
  Scholarship, 134
BB&T Charitable Scholarship
  Program, 276
Behavioral Sciences Student
  Fellowship, 236
Calvin Coolidge Memorial
  Foundation Scholarship, 507
Center for Architecture Design
  Scholarship, 213
Charles L. Hebner Memorial
  Scholarship, 230
Chevron Internship Program, 532
CIA Undergraduate Scholarship
  Program, 214
Citizens for Global Solutions
  Internship, 533
The Cloisters Summer Internship
  Program, 545
Community Scholarship Fund, 255
Congressional Institute
  Internships, 533
Darrel Hess Community College
  Geography Scholarship, 198
Delaware Space Grant Undergraduate
  Research Internship, 549
Delaware Space Grant Undergraduate
  Tuition Scholarship, 344
Denver Rescue Mission Center for
  Mission Studies Internships, 534
Developmental Disability Scholastic
  Achievement Scholarship, 202
Donald Riebhoff Memorial
  Scholarship, 163
Economic Research Division Project
  Internships, 532
Elie Wiesel Prize in Ethics, 233
Feminism & Leadership
  Internship, 537
Finance Undergraduate
  Internships, 568
Geography Students Internship, 551
Global Change Education
  Program, 554

Goldman Family Fund: New Leader
  Scholarship, 323
Government and Public Affairs
  Internship, 528
Greater Research Opportunities
  Undergraduate Student
  Fellowships, 504
Harriet Irsay Scholarship, 106
Henry A. Zuberano Scholarship, 261
Hokuli'a Foundation Scholarship
  Fund, 262
Homestead Capital Housing
  Scholarship, 407
Horizons Scholarship, 522
House Member Internships, 567
HSBC-North America Scholarship
  Program, 277
Intelligence Scholarships, 185
Iowa Farm Bureau Federation
  Scholarship, 297
Jennifer C. Groot Fellowship, 90
Jerry Clark Memorial Scholarship, 95
John F. Kennedy Scholars Award, 329
John Joseph Moakely Democratic
  Internship, 545
Kawasaki-McGaha Scholarship
  Fund, 265
Kennedy Library Archival
  Internship, 542
Marble-Boyle Award, 198
MassMutual Multicultural College
  Scholarship, 277
The Merchants Exhange Scholarship
  Fund, 330
Mississippi Health Care Professions
  Loan/Scholarship, 579
Mother Jones Ben Bagdikian
  Fellowship Program, 548
NASA District of Columbia
  Undergraduate Scholarship, 344
NASA Space Grant Hawaii
  Undergraduate Fellowship, 344
National Oceanic and Atmospheric
  Administration Hollings
  Undergraduate Scholarship, 555
National Peace Essay Contest, 500
North Carolina Student Loans for
  Health/Science/Mathematics, 582
ORISE Student Environmental
  Management Participation at the
  U.S. Army Environmental
  Center, 556
ORISE Student Research at the
  Centers for Disease Control and
  Prevention/Agency for Toxic
  Substances and Disease
  Registry, 557
Pacific Gas and Electric Summer
  Intern Program, 559
Patrick and Judith McHugh
  Scholarship, 509
Presbyterian Student Opportunity
  Scholarship, 421
Public Relations Internship, 545
Rain Bird Intelligent Use of Water
  Company Scholarship, 315

Rhode Island State Government
  Internship Program, 561
Roosevelt Archival Internships, 538
SCA Conservation Internships, 564
Senior Scholarship, 314
Six-Month Internship, 546
Smithsonian Minority Internship, 562
Southface Internship, 563
Spence Reese Scholarship, 204
Stella Blum Student Research
  Grant, 224
Summer Internship Program, 531
Summer Research Diversity
  Fellowships in Law and Social
  Sciences for Undergraduate
  Students, 526
Thomas R. Pickering Foreign Affairs
  Fellowship, 523
Tribal Business Management
  Scholarship, 212
UBS/PaineWebber Scholarships, 499
Undergraduate Summer
  Internship, 537
United States Holocaust Memorial
  Museum Internship, 566
U.S. Department of Homeland
  Security Scholarship and
  Fellowship Program, 558
U.S. Department of State
  Internship, 567
U.S. Senate Member Internships, 566
Washington Crossing Foundation
  Scholarship, 514
Wells Fargo Scholarship, 279
Wilma D. Hoyal/Maxine Chilton
  Memorial Scholarship, 109
Women in Architecture
  Scholarship, 197
World Security Institute
  Internship, 571
Young Epidemiology Scholars Student
  Competition, 218

Trade and industry

AAGS Joseph F. Dracup Scholarship
  Award, 91
Academic Scholarship for High
  School Seniors and GED
  Graduates, 370
Academic Scholarship for
  Undergraduate Students, 370
ACSM Fellows Scholarship, 91
AFCEA ROTC Scholarship, 184
AGC Education and Research
  Undergraduate Scholarship, 195
AGC of Maine Scholarship
  Program, 196
Air Traffic Control Full-Time
  Employee Student Scholarship, 79
Airgas-Jerry Baker Scholarship, 175
Airgas-Terry Jarvis Memorial
  Scholarship, 176
AIWF Culinary Scholarship, 507
A.J. Spielman Scholarship, 487
Alaska Airlines Scholarship, 487
Albert E. Wischmeyer Memorial
  Scholarship Award, 441

Alexander Harris Scholarship, 487
Alice Glaisyer Warfield Memorial
    Scholarship, 493
Alwin B. Newton Scholarship, 172
American Express Travel
    Scholarship, 487
American Welding Society District
    Scholarship Program, 176
A.O. Smith Water Heaters
    Scholarship, 419
AOPA Air Safety
    Foundation/McAllister Memorial
    Scholarship, 83
Arizona Chapter Vertical Flight
    Engineering Scholarship, 100
Arizona Scholarship, 488
Arsham Amirikian Engineering
    Scholarship, 176
ASHRAE General Scholarships, 172
ASHRAE Memorial Scholarship, 172
ASHRAE Region IV Benny Bootle
    Scholarship, 172
ASHRAE Region VIII
    Scholarship, 173
Automotive Educational Fund
    Scholarship, 199
Bern Laxer Memorial
    Scholarship, 301
Berntsen International Scholarship in
    Surveying, 91
Berntsen International Scholarship in
    Surveying Technology, 92
Best Teen Chef Culinary Scholarship
    Competition, 187
BIA San Diego Scholarship, 206
Bob Zappatelli Memorial
    Scholarship, 301
Boeing Internships, 532
Bradford White Scholarship, 419
Buckingham Memorial
    Scholarship, 80
Bud Glover Memorial Scholarship, 80
Cady McDonnell Memorial
    Scholarship, 92
Canada Scholarship, 488
Caterpillar Scholars Award, 442
CBC Scholarship, 221
Chapter 17 St. Louis Scholarship, 442
Chapter 198 - Downriver Detroit
    Scholarship, 442
Chapter 4 - Lawrence A. Wacker
    Memorial Scholarship, 442
Chapter 6 - Fairfield County
    Scholarship, 443
Chapter 67 - Phoenix Scholarship, 443
Charles Clarke Cordle Memorial
    Scholarship, 162
Charles N. Fisher Memorial
    Scholarship, 163
Charlotte Woods Memorial
    Scholarship, 494
Chefs of Louisiana Cookery
    Scholarship, 301
Christian Wolffer Scholarship, 301

The Clarence & Josephine Myers
    Scholarship, 443
Clat Triplette Scholarship, 302
Clinton J. Helton Manufacturing
    Scholarship Award, 444
Connecticut Scholarship, 488
Connie and Robert T. Gunter
    Scholarship, 444
Construction Trades Scholarship, 358
Contiki Vacations Scholarship, 488
Cooperative Internship Programs, 535
D. Fred and Mariam L. Bovie
    Scholarship, 176
D. Fred and Mariam L. Bovie
    Technical Scholarship, 176
Dairy Student Recognition
    Program, 360
Dave Herren Memorial
    Scholarship, 488
David Arver Memorial
    Scholarship, 80
David J. Hallissey Memorial
    Internship, 565
DEED Student Research Grants, 161
Delta Faucet Company
    Scholarship, 419
Denny Lydic Scholarship, 494
Deseo at the Westin Scholarship, 302
Detroit Chapter One - Founding
    Chapter Scholarship Award, 444
Directors Scholarship, 444
Disney Theme Parks & Resorts
    Professional Internships, 569
Donald and Shirley Hastings National
    Scholarship, 177
Donald Burnside Memorial
    Scholarship, 180
Donald F. Hastings Scholarship, 177
Dr. James L. Lawson Memorial
    Scholarship, 163
Duane Hanson Scholarship, 173
Dutch and Ginger Arver
    Scholarship, 80
E. Wayne Kay Community College
    Scholarship, 445
E. Wayne Kay Co-op Scholarship, 445
E. Wayne Kay High School
    Scholarship, 445
E. Wayne Kay Scholarship, 445
Edward J. Brady Memorial
    Scholarship, 177
Edward S. Roth Manufacturing
    Engineering, 177
Engineering Technology
    Scholarships, 173
Field Aviation Co. Inc.
    Scholarship, 81
Fifth Floor Restaurant
    Scholarship, 302
Florida Scholarship, 489
Foodservice Communicators
    Scholarship, 294
Ford Motor Company
    Scholarship, 457
Frank M. Coda Scholarship, 173
Fred R. McDaniel Memorial
    Scholarship, 164

Future Leaders of Manufacturing
    Scholarships, 446
Gabe A. Hartl Scholarship, 80
Garmin Scholarship, 81
General Motors Foundation
    Scholarships, 457
George Reinke Scholarship, 489
Ginger and Fred Deines Canada
    Scholarship, 494
Ginger and Fred Deines Mexico
    Scholarship, 494
Giuliano Mazzetti Scholarship, 446
Good Eats Scholarship Fund, 260
Hansen Scholarship, 237
Hawaii Chuck Yim Gee
    Scholarship, 489
Henry Adams Scholarship, 174
Honeywell Avionics Scholarship, 81
Honeywell International Inc.
    Scholarship, 458
Hooper Memorial Scholarship, 494
Howard E. and Wilma J. Adkins
    Memorial Scholarship, 177
H.P. "Bud" Milligan Aviation
    Scholarship, 237
Hudner Medal of Honor
    Scholarship, 237
Iager Dairy Scholarship, 360
Inn at Blackberry Farm
    Scholarship, 302
INROADS Internship, 541
Irving W. Cook WA0CGS
    Scholarship, 165
J. Richard Mehalick Scholarship, 174
Jack R. Barckhoff Welding
    Management Scholarship, 178
James A. Turner, Jr. Memorial
    Scholarship, 178
James L. Allhands Essay
    Competition, 195
John C. Lincoln Memorial
    Scholarship, 178
Johnny Davis Memorial
    Scholarship, 81
Johnson Controls Co-op and
    Internship Programs, 543
Kathy LeTarte Scholarship, 489
Klussendorf Scholarship, 360
Kurt W. Schneider Memorial
    Scholarship Fund, 266
L. Phil Wicker Scholarship, 165
L-3 Avionics Systems Scholarship, 81
La Toque Scholarship in Wine
    Studies, 302
LaMacchia Family Scholarship, 489
Lee Tarbox Memorial Scholarship, 82
Lindbergh Grant, 215
Lowell Gaylor Memorial
    Scholarship, 82
Lucile B. Kaufman Women's
    Scholarship, 446
Maine Innkeepers Association
    Scholarship, 321
Maine Metal Products Association
    Scholarship, 322
ManageFirst Program
    Scholarship, 370

Marcia S. Harris Legacy Fund
Scholarship, 427
Marine Corps Sgt. Jeannette L.
Winters Memorial Scholarship, 185
Marriott Scholars Program, 275
Mary Macey Scholarship, 522
Massachusetts Scholarship, 490
Matsuo Bridge Company Ltd of Japan
Scholarship, 178
Mayflower Tours Patrick Murphy
Internship, 565
Michigan Scholarship, 490
Mid-Continent Instrument
Scholarship, 82
Miller Electric Manufacturing
Company Ivic Scholarship, 179
Miller Electric Mfg. Co.
Scholarship, 179
Mississippi Scholarship, 166
Monte R. Mitchell Global
Scholarship, 82
Museum Coca-Cola Internship, 551
Myrtle and Earl Walker
Scholarship, 446
NASA Space Grant Virginia
Community College
Scholarship, 353
National Association of Women in
Construction Founders'
Scholarship, 358
National Dairy Shrine Kildee
Scholarship, 361
National Tour Association State
Scholarship, 490
NEMAL Electronics Scholarship, 166
Nettie Dracup Memorial
Scholarship, 92
New Horizons Rene Campbell
Memorial Scholarship, 490
New Jersey Scholarship, 491
New York Scholarship, 491
North Carolina State Board of
Refrigeration Examiners
Scholarship, 392
North Central Region
Scholarship, 447
Northern California Chapter - Richard
Epping Scholarship, 491
NSPS Board of Governors
Scholarship, 93
NSPS Scholarships, 93
OCA/Verizon Foundation College
Scholarship, 397
Ohio Scholarship, 491
Pacific Northwest Chapter/William
Hunt Scholarship, 492
Past Presidents Scholarship, 179
Pat & Jim Host Scholarship, 492
Paul and Helen L. Grauer
Scholarship, 167
Payzer Scholarship, 238
The Peter Cameron/Housewares
Charity Foundation
Scholarship, 303
Peter Kump Memorial
Scholarship, 303

PGSF Annual Scholarship
Competition, 423
PHCC Educational Foundation
Need-Based Scholarship, 420
Plane & Pilot Magazine/Garmin
Scholarship, 82
Plumbing-Heating-Cooling
Contractors - National Association
Educational Foundation
Scholarship, 420
Poggio Scholarship, 303
Praxair International Scholarship, 179
Princess Cruises Scholarship, 492
Professional Land Surveyors of
Oregon Scholarship, 411
ProStart National Certificate of
Achievement Scholarship, 370
The Publican Scholarship, 303
Puckemin Inn Scholarship, 303
Quebec Scholarship, 492
Reuben Trane Scholarship, 174
Richard Lee Vernon Aviation
Scholarship, 238
Robert L. Peaslee-Detroit Brazing and
Soldering Division Scholarship, 179
Rockwell Automation
Scholarships, 463
Rodney E. Powell Memorial
Scholarship, 391
Russ Casey Scholarship, 322
RWMA Scholarship, 180
Schonstedt Scholarships in
Surveying, 93
Siegel Service Technology
Scholarships, 432
SME Education Foundation Family
Scholarship, 447
Southern California Chapter - Pleasant
Holidays Scholarship, 492
Spencer's Scholarship, 304
Stan and Leone Pollard
Scholarship, 493
Studio at the Montage Resort & Spa
Scholarship, 304
Texas Transportation Scholarship, 494
Trimmer Education Foundation
Student Scholarships, 195
Tri-State Surveying &
Photogrammetry Kris M. Kunze
Scholarship, 93
Tyson Foods Intern Program, 566
Utah Keith Griffall Scholarship, 493
Vertical Flight Foundation
Scholarship, 100
Vicki Willder Scholarship Fund, 273
Walt Bartram Memorial Education
Award (Region 12 and Chapter
119), 447
William A. and Ann M. Brothers
Scholarship, 180
William B. Howell Memorial
Scholarship, 180
William E. Weisel Scholarship, 447
Willis H. Carrier Scholarship, 174
Yellow Ribbon Scholarship, 493
Zov's Bistro Scholarship, 304

Gender

Female

Ada I. Pressman Memorial
Scholarship, 451
Admiral Grace Murray Hopper
Scholarship, 451
Ahmad-Sehar Saleha Ahmad and
Abrahim Ekramullah Zafar
Foundation, 403
Allman Medical Scholarships, 335
Alumnae Panhellenic Association
Women's Scholarship, 87
American Legion Kentucky Auxiliary
Mary Barrett Marshall
Scholarship, 122
American Legion Maryland Auxiliary
Scholarship, 125
American Legion Michigan Auxiliary
Memorial Scholarship, 127
Anne Maureen Whitney Barrow
Memorial, 452
Averyl Elaine Keriakedes Memorial
Scholarship, 134
B. K. Krenzer Re-entry
Scholarship, 452
Baker Hughes Scholarship, 452
Bechtel Foundation Scholarship, 452
Bertha Lamme Memorial
Scholarship, 453
B.J. Harrod Scholarships, 453
Boston Scientific Scholarship, 453
Brill Family Scholarship, 453
Cady McDonnell Memorial
Scholarship, 92
California's Junior Miss
Competition, 208
Caterpillar Inc. Scholarship, 454
Central New Mexico Scholarship, 454
Chevron Corporation
Scholarships, 454
Chrysler Foundation Scholarship, 454
Cummins Scholarship, 455
Delayed Education Scholarship for
Women, 159
Dell Inc. Scholarship, 455
Dorothy Campbell Memorial
Scholarship, 406
Dorothy Lemke Howarth
Scholarships, 455
Dorothy M. & Earl S. Hoffman
Scholarships, 455
Dorothy P. Morris Scholarship, 456
DuPont Company Scholarship, 456
Electronics for Imaging
Scholarship, 456
Elizabeth A. Sackler Museum
Educational Trust, 473
Elizabeth McLean Memorial
Scholarship, 456
Eugenia Vellner Fischer Award for the
Performing Arts, 335
Exelon Scholarship, 456
Financial Women International
Scholarship, 259

Ford Motor Company
  Scholarship, 457
General Electric Foundation
  Scholarship, 457
General Electric Women's Network
  Scholarship, 457
General Motors Foundation
  Scholarships, 457
Girl Scout Achievement Award, 133
Goldman, Sachs and Co.
  Scholarship, 458
Grace S. High Memorial Child
  Welfare Scholarship Fund, 138
The Grotto Scholarships, 475
Hermione Grant Calhoun
  Scholarship, 363
Honeywell International Inc.
  Scholarship, 458
Horizons Scholarship, 522
IBM Corporation Scholarship, 458
Ida M. Pope Memorial
  Scholarship, 263
ITT Scholarship, 458
Ivy Parker Memorial Scholarship, 459
Jean Fitzgerald Scholarship Fund, 263
Jeanette Rankin Foundation
  Scholarship, 306
Jill S. Tietjen P.E. Scholarship, 459
Judith Resnik Memorial
  Scholarship, 459
Junior Miss Scholarship, 88
Ka'iulani Home for Girls Trust
  Scholarship, 264
Lehman Scholarship, 459
Lillian Moller Gilbreth
  Scholarship, 460
Lillie Lois Ford Girls'
  Scholarship, 130
Lockheed Martin Aeronautics
  Company Scholarships, 460
Lockheed Martin Foundation
  Scholarships, 460
Lucile B. Kaufman Women's
  Scholarship, 446
Lydia I. Pickup Memorial
  Scholarship, 460
Margot Karle Scholarship Fund, 199
Mary Barrett Marshall Student Loan
  Fund, 573
Mary V. Munger Scholarship, 461
MASWE Scholarships, 461
Meridith Thoms Memorial
  Scholarships, 461
Microsoft Corporation
  Scholarships, 461
Miss America Competition
  Awards, 336
Nancy Lorraine Jensen Memorial
  Scholarship, 466
NASA Space Grant North Dakota
  Consortium Lillian Goettler
  Scholarship, 349
New Jersey Scholarship, 462
Northrop Grumman Corporation
  Scholarship, 462
Olive Lynn Salembier Re-entry
  Scholarship, 462

Past President's Parley Nursing
  Scholarship, 119
Past President's Parley
  Scholarship, 110
Past Presidents Scholarships, 462
Pearl I. Young Scholarship, 349
R.L. Gillette Scholarship, 98
Rockwell Automation
  Scholarships, 463
SAE Women Engineers Committee
  Scholarship, 431
Shannon Scholarship, 495
Society of Daughters of United States
  Army Scholarship Program, 440
Sports Illustrated Scholarship, 356
Student Aid Foundation Loan, 583
Supreme Guardian Council,
  International Order of Job's
  Daughters Scholarship, 475
Susan Burdett Scholarship, 152
Susan Miszkowitz Memorial
  Scholarship, 463
Susie Holmes Memorial
  Scholarship, 475
Top 10 College Women
  Competition, 248
Women in Architecture
  Scholarship, 197
Women's Western Golf Foundation
  Scholarship, 523

Male

American Legion Eagle Scout of the
  Year, 132, 150
American Legion Maryland Boys
  State Scholarship, 124
American Legion New Hampshire
  Boys State Scholarship, 136
American Legion Wisconsin Eagle
  Scout of the Year Scholarship, 153
Arthur M. and Berdena King Eagle
  Scout Scholarship, 377
Boy Scout of the Year
  Scholarship, 119
Chester M. Vernon Memorial Eagle
  Scout Scholarship, 366
Dr. Click Cowger Scholarship, 121
Dr. Dan J. and Patricia S. Pickard
  Scholarship, 227
Eagle Scout of the Year, 114
Eagle Scout of the Year
  Scholarship, 148
Frank D. Visceglia Memorial
  Scholarship, 204
Frank L. Weil Memorial Eagle Scout
  Scholarship, 366
Hall/McElwain Merit
  Scholarship, 361
Hubertus W.V. Wellems Scholarship
  for Male Students, 342
John A. High Child Welfare
  Scholarship, 137
John McKee Scholarship, 329
Lillie Lois Ford Boys'
  Scholarship, 130
NESA Academic Scholarships, 361
Spence Reese Scholarship, 204

International Student

Actuarial Diversity Scholarships, 74
Adele Filene Student Presenter
  Grant, 224
Allison E. Fisher Scholarship, 356
Automotive Educational Fund
  Scholarship, 199
Business Reporting Intern
  Program, 534
Carole Simpson Scholarship, 356
David J. Hallissey Memorial
  Internship, 565
Eleanor Allwork Scholarship, 213
Hannaford Internships, 539
Multimedia Intern Program, 534
Museum of Modern Art
  Internship, 548
Newhouse Foundation
  Scholarship, 550
News Copy Editing Intern
  Program, 534
School Art Scholarships, 286
Six-Month Internship, 546
Southface Internship, 563
Sports Copy Editing Intern
  Program, 535
Stella Blum Student Research
  Grant, 224
Summer Internship Program, 546
Toyota Motor Sales U.S.A., Inc.
  Scholarship, 278
United States Holocaust Memorial
  Museum Internship, 566
Wolf Trap Foundation for the
  Performing Arts Internship, 570

Military Participation

Air Force

Air Force Aid Society Education
  Grant, 79
Air Force Sergeants Association
  Scholarship, Airmen Memorial
  Foundation, and Chief Master
  Sergeants of the Air Force
  Scholarship Programs, 78
Commander's Scholarship Fund, 129
Darlene Hooley for Oregon Veterans
  Scholarship, 405
Erman W. Taylor Memorial
  Scholarship, 129
Helping Heroes Grant, 477
Katherine F. Gruber Scholarship
  Program, 202
Lillie Lois Ford Boys'
  Scholarship, 130
Lillie Lois Ford Girls'
  Scholarship, 130

Maria C. Jackson-General George A.
White Scholarship, 409
Matthews/Swift Educational Trust -
Military Dependants, 312
M.D. "Jack" Murphy Memorial
Nurses Training Fund, 130
Military Dependents Scholarship
Program, 183
Minnesota GI Bill, 334
MOAA Interest-Free Loan and Grant
Program, 578
New Jersey War Orphans Tuition
Assistance Program, 381
North Carolina Scholarships for
Children of War Veterans, 392
Operation Enduring Freedom and
Operation Iraqi Freedom
Scholarship, 509
West Virginia War Orphans
Educational Assistance, 517

Army

Commander's Scholarship Fund, 129
Darlene Hooley for Oregon Veterans
Scholarship, 405
Erman W. Taylor Memorial
Scholarship, 129
Helping Heroes Grant, 477
Katherine F. Gruber Scholarship
Program, 202
Lillie Lois Ford Boys'
Scholarship, 130
Lillie Lois Ford Girls'
Scholarship, 130
Maria C. Jackson-General George A.
White Scholarship, 409
Maryland Edward T. Conroy
Memorial Scholarship Program, 326
Matthews/Swift Educational Trust -
Military Dependants, 312
M.D. "Jack" Murphy Memorial
Nurses Training Fund, 130
MG James Ursano Scholarship
Program, 187
Military Dependents Scholarship
Program, 183
Minnesota GI Bill, 334
MOAA Interest-Free Loan and Grant
Program, 578
Montgomery GI Bill (MGIB), 501
New Jersey War Orphans Tuition
Assistance Program, 381
North Carolina Scholarships for
Children of War Veterans, 392
Operation Enduring Freedom and
Operation Iraqi Freedom
Scholarship, 509
Selected Reserve Montgomery GI
Bill, 501
West Virginia War Orphans
Educational Assistance, 517

Coast Guard

Commander's Scholarship Fund, 129
Darlene Hooley for Oregon Veterans
Scholarship, 405

Erman W. Taylor Memorial
Scholarship, 129
Katherine F. Gruber Scholarship
Program, 202
Lillie Lois Ford Boys'
Scholarship, 130
Lillie Lois Ford Girls'
Scholarship, 130
Maria C. Jackson-General George A.
White Scholarship, 409
Matthews/Swift Educational Trust -
Military Dependants, 312
M.D. "Jack" Murphy Memorial
Nurses Training Fund, 130
Military Dependents Scholarship
Program, 183
Minnesota GI Bill, 334
MOAA Interest-Free Loan and Grant
Program, 578
New Jersey War Orphans Tuition
Assistance Program, 381
North Carolina Scholarships for
Children of War Veterans, 392
Operation Enduring Freedom and
Operation Iraqi Freedom
Scholarship, 509
West Virginia War Orphans
Educational Assistance, 517

Marines

Commander's Scholarship Fund, 129
Darlene Hooley for Oregon Veterans
Scholarship, 405
Erman W. Taylor Memorial
Scholarship, 129
First Marine Division Association
Scholarship, 239
Gold Star Scholarship Program, 378
Helping Heroes Grant, 477
Katherine F. Gruber Scholarship
Program, 202
Lillie Lois Ford Boys'
Scholarship, 130
Lillie Lois Ford Girls'
Scholarship, 130
Maria C. Jackson-General George A.
White Scholarship, 409
Marine Corps Scholarship, 324
Marine Corps Sgt. Jeannette L.
Winters Memorial Scholarship, 185
Matthews/Swift Educational Trust -
Military Dependants, 312
M.D. "Jack" Murphy Memorial
Nurses Training Fund, 130
Memorial Scholarship Fund, 486
Military Dependents Scholarship
Program, 183
Minnesota GI Bill, 334
MOAA Interest-Free Loan and Grant
Program, 578
New Jersey War Orphans Tuition
Assistance Program, 381
North Carolina Scholarships for
Children of War Veterans, 392
Operation Enduring Freedom and
Operation Iraqi Freedom
Scholarship, 509

Second Marine Division Association
Scholarship Fund, 435
Vice Admiral E.P. Travers Loan, 579
West Virginia War Orphans
Educational Assistance, 517

Navy

Commander's Scholarship Fund, 129
Darlene Hooley for Oregon Veterans
Scholarship, 405
Erman W. Taylor Memorial
Scholarship, 129
Gold Star Scholarship Program, 378
Helping Heroes Grant, 477
Katherine F. Gruber Scholarship
Program, 202
Lillie Lois Ford Boys'
Scholarship, 130
Lillie Lois Ford Girls'
Scholarship, 130
Maria C. Jackson-General George A.
White Scholarship, 409
Matthews/Swift Educational Trust -
Military Dependants, 312
M.D. "Jack" Murphy Memorial
Nurses Training Fund, 130
Memorial Scholarship Fund, 486
Military Dependents Scholarship
Program, 183
Minnesota GI Bill, 334
MOAA Interest-Free Loan and Grant
Program, 578
Navy Supply Corps Foundation
Scholarship, 378
New Jersey War Orphans Tuition
Assistance Program, 381
North Carolina Scholarships for
Children of War Veterans, 392
Operation Enduring Freedom and
Operation Iraqi Freedom
Scholarship, 509
Seabee Memorial Scholarship, 434
Vice Admiral E.P. Travers Loan, 579
West Virginia War Orphans
Educational Assistance, 517

Reserves/National Guard

Alabama National Guard Educational
Assistance Program, 83
Darlene Hooley for Oregon Veterans
Scholarship, 405
Helping Heroes Grant, 477
Illinois National Guard Grant, 290
Indiana National Guard Supplemental
Grant, 472
Iowa National Guard Educational
Assistance Program, 297
Matthews/Swift Educational Trust -
Military Dependants, 312
Military Dependents Scholarship
Program, 183
Minnesota GI Bill, 334
MOAA Interest-Free Loan and Grant
Program, 578
National Guard Educational
Assistance Program, 309
National Guard Tuition Waiver, 401

New Jersey War Orphans Tuition Assistance Program, 381

Ohio National Guard Scholarship Program, 398

Operation Enduring Freedom and Operation Iraqi Freedom Scholarship, 509

Selected Reserve Montgomery GI Bill, 501

Texas National Guard Tuition Assistance Program, 484

West Virginia War Orphans Educational Assistance, 517

Minority Status

African American

Actuarial Diversity Scholarships, 74

AFSCMA/UNCF Union Scholars Program, 527

American Chemical Society Scholars Program, 90

American Meteorological Society/Industry Minority Scholarship, 156

Batttelle Collegiate Scholarship, 373

BB&T Charitable Scholarship Program, 276

Bechtel Group Foundation Scholarship, 373

Black Nurses Scholarship, 358

The BlackNews.com Scholarship Essay Contest, 202

BP Corporate Scholarship, 373

California Teachers Association Martin Luther King, Jr., Memorial Scholarship, 210

Caterpillar Corporate Scholarship, 373

CITE Scholarship, 223

Colgate "Bright Smiles, Bright Futures" Minority Scholarships, 76

Connecticut Minority Teacher Incentive Grant, 222

Cummins Inc. Corporate Scholarship, 373

Dr. Dan J. and Patricia S. Pickard Scholarship, 227

The EDSA Minority Scholarship, 315

Education and Leadership Development Program, 300

ExxonMobil Corporate Scholarship, 374

Fisher Broadcasting Company Scholarship for Minorities, 240

Gates Millennium Scholars Program, 498

GE Business/Engineering Scholarship for Minority Students, 316

George M. Brooker Collegiate Scholarship for Minorities, 293

Herbert Lehman Educational Fund, 343

Historically Black Colleges and Minority Institutions Scholarships, 203

The Hyatt Hotels Fund for Minority Lodging Management Students Competition, 101

Indiana Minority Teacher & Special Education Services Scholarship, 471

INROADS Internship, 541

International Studies Scholarship, 374

James E. Webb Internship Program for Minority Undergraduate Seniors and Graduate Students in Business and Public Administration, 562

Jimmy A. Young Memorial Education Recognition Award, 169

Kansas Ethnic Minority Scholarship, 307

Lagrant Scholarships, 314

Larry Whiteside Scholarship, 356

Leonard M. Perryman Communications Scholarship for Ethnic Minority Students, 498

Lockheed Martin Corporate Scholarship, 374

Louis Carr Summer Internship, 544

Marathon Oil Corporation College Scholarship, 277

MassMutual Multicultural College Scholarship, 277

The Mayor's Chesapeake Energy Scholarship, 228

Microbiology Undergraduate Research Fellowship (MURF), 170

Mildred Towle Scholarship for African-Americans, 268

Minority Scholarship Program, 206

Minority Teachers of Illinois Scholarship, 290

Missouri Minority Teaching Scholarship, 338

MSGC Undergraduate Underrepresented Minority Fellowship Program, 346

Multicultural Advertising Intern Program, 525

Multicultural Undergraduate Summer Internships at the Getty Center, 541

NABA National Scholarship Program, 356

NABJ Internships, 550

NAFEO (National Association for Equal Opportunity in Higher Education) Scholarships, 105

National Achievement Scholarships, 367

National Society of Black Engineers Leroy Callendar PCI Award Program, 375

Northrop Grumman Corporate Scholarship, 375

Ohio Newspapers Minority Scholarship, 399

PBS&J Corporate Scholarship, 375

Preservation Fellows Program, 565

Ron Brown Scholar Program, 211

Rosewood Family Scholarship Program, 242

Sachs Foundation Undergraduate Grant, 430

Scholarship for Minority Accounting Students, 106

Scholarship for Minority Undergraduate Physics Majors, 161

Sports Illustrated Scholarship, 356

Teacher Quest Scholarship Program, 206

Technical Minority Scholarship, 524

Tennessee Minority Teaching Fellows Program, 584

Toyota Corporate Scholarship, 376

U.S. Steel NSBE Academic Scholarship, 376

Verizon Corporate Scholarship, 376

Visual Task Force (VTF) Scholarship, 357

Wal-Mart Stores Inc. Corporate Scholarship, 376

Weisman Scholarship, 223

Wisconsin Minority Teacher Loan Program, 587

Wisconsin Minority Undergraduate Retention Grant, 521

Alaskan native

Actuarial Diversity Scholarships, 74

AFSCMA/UNCF Union Scholars Program, 527

American Meteorological Society/Industry Minority Scholarship, 156

A.T. Anderson Memorial Scholarship, 104

Burlington Northern Santa Fe Foundation Scholarship, 104

California Teachers Association Martin Luther King, Jr., Memorial Scholarship, 210

Connecticut Minority Teacher Incentive Grant, 222

The EDSA Minority Scholarship, 315

Education and Leadership Development Program, 300

Fisher Broadcasting Company Scholarship for Minorities, 240

Ford Motor Company/American Indian College Fund Corporate Scholars Program, 102

Foundation Scholarship, 102

Gates Millennium Scholars Program, 498

GE Business/Engineering Scholarship for Minority Students, 316

George M. Brooker Collegiate Scholarship for Minorities, 293

The Hyatt Hotels Fund for Minority Lodging Management Students Competition, 101

INROADS Internship, 541

Jack A. & Marilyn MacAllister Foundation, 102

James E. Webb Internship Program for Minority Undergraduate Seniors and Graduate Students in Business and Public Administration, 562
Jimmy A. Young Memorial Education Recognition Award, 169
Kansas Ethnic Minority Scholarship, 307
Lagrant Scholarships, 314
Leonard M. Perryman Communications Scholarship for Ethnic Minority Students, 498
Marathon Oil Corporation College Scholarship, 277
The Mayor's Chesapeake Energy Scholarship, 228
MESBEC Scholarships, 212
Microbiology Undergraduate Research Fellowship (MURF), 170
Minority Scholarship Program, 206
Minority Teachers of Illinois Scholarship, 290
Missouri Minority Teaching Scholarship, 338
Morgan Stanley Scholars Program, 102
NABA National Scholarship Program, 356
Native American Education Grant, 421
Nissan North America, Inc. Scholarship, 102
Preservation Fellows Program, 565
Rosewood Family Scholarship Program, 242
Scholarship for Minority Accounting Students, 106
Smithsonian Native American Internship, 562
Sovereign Nations Scholarship Fund, 103
Teacher Quest Scholarship Program, 206
Technical Minority Scholarship, 524
Tennessee Minority Teaching Fellows Program, 584
Travelers Foundation, 103
Tribal Business Management Scholarship, 212
Truman D. Picard Scholarship, 296
United Health Foundation Scholarship, 103
Weisman Scholarship, 223

American Indian

Actuarial Diversity Scholarships, 74
AFSCMA/UNCF Union Scholars Program, 527
American Chemical Society Scholars Program, 90
American Meteorological Society/Industry Minority Scholarship, 156
A.T. Anderson Memorial Scholarship, 104
Austin Family Scholarship Endowment, 101

Burlington Northern Santa Fe Foundation Scholarship, 104
California Teachers Association Martin Luther King, Jr., Memorial Scholarship, 210
Choctaw Nation Higher Education Program, 216
Colgate "Bright Smiles, Bright Futures" Minority Scholarships, 76
Connecticut Minority Teacher Incentive Grant, 222
The EDSA Minority Scholarship, 315
Education and Leadership Development Program, 300
Fisher Broadcasting Company Scholarship for Minorities, 240
Ford Motor Company/American Indian College Fund Corporate Scholars Program, 102
Foundation Scholarship, 102
Gates Millennium Scholars Program, 498
GE Business/Engineering Scholarship for Minority Students, 316
George M. Brooker Collegiate Scholarship for Minorities, 293
Higher Education Grant Program, 207
Hopi BIA Higher Education Grant, 279
Hopi Education Award, 279
Hopi Tribal Priority Award, 279
The Hyatt Hotels Fund for Minority Lodging Management Students Competition, 101
INROADS Internship, 541
Jack A. & Marilyn MacAllister Foundation, 102
James E. Webb Internship Program for Minority Undergraduate Seniors and Graduate Students in Business and Public Administration, 562
Jimmy A. Young Memorial Education Recognition Award, 169
Kansas Ethnic Minority Scholarship, 307
Lagrant Scholarships, 314
Leonard M. Perryman Communications Scholarship for Ethnic Minority Students, 498
Marathon Oil Corporation College Scholarship, 277
The Mayor's Chesapeake Energy Scholarship, 228
Menominee Adult Vocational Training Grant, 330
Menominee Higher Education Grant, 330
MESBEC Scholarships, 212
Microbiology Undergraduate Research Fellowship (MURF), 170
Minnesota Indian Scholarship Program, 334
Minority Scholarship Program, 206
Minority Teachers of Illinois Scholarship, 290
Missouri Minority Teaching Scholarship, 338

Morgan Stanley Scholars Program, 102
MSGC Undergraduate Underrepresented Minority Fellowship Program, 346
Multicultural Advertising Intern Program, 525
Multicultural Undergraduate Summer Internships at the Getty Center, 541
NABA National Scholarship Program, 356
Native American Education Grant, 421
Native American Leadership in Education Scholarship, 212
New York State Native American Student Aid Program, 389
Nissan North America, Inc. Scholarship, 102
North American Indian Scholarship, 296
North Dakota Indian Scholarship Program, 395
Northern Cheyenne Higher Education Program, 396
Ohio Newspapers Minority Scholarship, 399
Osage Tribal Education Committee Award, 207
Osage Tribal Education Scholarship, 413
Preservation Fellows Program, 565
Rosewood Family Scholarship Program, 242
Scholarship for Minority Accounting Students, 106
Scholarship for Minority Undergraduate Physics Majors, 161
Seneca Nation Higher Education Program, 436
Shoshone Tribal Scholarship, 436
Silver Eagle Indian Scholarship, 136
Smithsonian Native American Internship, 562
South Dakota Ardell Bjugstad Scholarship, 468
Sovereign Nations Scholarship Fund, 103
Teacher Quest Scholarship Program, 206
Technical Minority Scholarship, 524
Tennessee Minority Teaching Fellows Program, 584
Travelers Foundation, 103
Tribal Business Management Scholarship, 212
Truman D. Picard Scholarship, 296
United Health Foundation Scholarship, 103
Weisman Scholarship, 223
Wisconsin Indian Student Assistance Grant, 521
Wisconsin Minority Teacher Loan Program, 587
Wisconsin Minority Undergraduate Retention Grant, 521

Asian American

AFSCMA/UNCF Union Scholars
Program, 527
American Meteorological
Society/Industry Minority
Scholarship, 156
California Teachers Association
Martin Luther King, Jr., Memorial
Scholarship, 210
Colgate "Bright Smiles, Bright
Futures" Minority Scholarships, 76
Connecticut Minority Teacher
Incentive Grant, 222
The EDSA Minority Scholarship, 315
Education and Leadership
Development Program, 300
Fisher Broadcasting Company
Scholarship for Minorities, 240
Gates Millennium Scholars
Program, 498
GE Business/Engineering Scholarship
for Minority Students, 316
George M. Brooker Collegiate
Scholarship for Minorities, 293
The Hyatt Hotels Fund for Minority
Lodging Management Students
Competition, 101
Indian American Scholarship, 501
INROADS Internship, 541
James E. Webb Internship Program for
Minority Undergraduate Seniors
and Graduate Students in Business
and Public Administration, 562
Jimmy A. Young Memorial Education
Recognition Award, 169
Kansas Ethnic Minority
Scholarship, 307
Leonard M. Perryman
Communications Scholarship for
Ethnic Minority Students, 498
MassMutual Multicultural College
Scholarship, 277
The Mayor's Chesapeake Energy
Scholarship, 228
Minority Scholarship Program, 206
Minority Teachers of Illinois
Scholarship, 290
Missouri Minority Teaching
Scholarship, 338
Multicultural Advertising Intern
Program, 525
Multicultural Undergraduate Summer
Internships at the Getty Center, 541
NABA National Scholarship
Program, 356
OCA-AXA Achievement
Scholarships, 397
OCA/UPS Foundation Gold Mountain
College Scholarship, 397
OCA/Verizon Foundation College
Scholarship, 397
Ohio Newspapers Minority
Scholarship, 399
Preservation Fellows Program, 565
Rosewood Family Scholarship
Program, 242

Scholarship for Minority Accounting
Students, 106
Teacher Quest Scholarship
Program, 206
Technical Minority Scholarship, 524
Tennessee Minority Teaching Fellows
Program, 584
Weisman Scholarship, 223
Wisconsin Minority Teacher Loan
Program, 587
Wisconsin Minority Undergraduate
Retention Grant, 521

Hispanic American

Actuarial Diversity Scholarships, 74
AFSCMA/UNCF Union Scholars
Program, 527
American Chemical Society Scholars
Program, 90
American Meteorological
Society/Industry Minority
Scholarship, 156
Atrisco Heritage Foundation
Scholarship, 276
California Teachers Association
Martin Luther King, Jr., Memorial
Scholarship, 210
CCNMA Scholarship, 213
Colgate "Bright Smiles, Bright
Futures" Minority Scholarships, 76
Connecticut Minority Teacher
Incentive Grant, 222
The EDSA Minority Scholarship, 315
Education and Leadership
Development Program, 300
Fisher Broadcasting Company
Scholarship for Minorities, 240
Gates Millennium Scholars
Program, 498
GE Business/Engineering Scholarship
for Minority Students, 316
General College Scholarship, 276
George M. Brooker Collegiate
Scholarship for Minorities, 293
Google Hispanic College Fund
Scholarship Program, 275
HACU (Hispanic Association of
Colleges and Universities)
Scholarships, 104
HCF Scholarship Program, 275
Hispanic Heritage Youth Awards
Program, 276
HSBC-North America Scholarship
Program, 277
The Hyatt Hotels Fund for Minority
Lodging Management Students
Competition, 101
Indiana Minority Teacher & Special
Education Services
Scholarship, 471
INROADS Internship, 541
James E. Webb Internship Program for
Minority Undergraduate Seniors
and Graduate Students in Business
and Public Administration, 562
Jimmy A. Young Memorial Education
Recognition Award, 169

Jose Marti Scholarship Challenge
Grant Fund, 241
Kansas Ethnic Minority
Scholarship, 307
Lagrant Scholarships, 314
Latin American Educational
Scholarship, 316
Latino Diamante Scholarship
Fund, 393
Leonard M. Perryman
Communications Scholarship for
Ethnic Minority Students, 498
Los Padres Foundation College
Tuition Assistance Program, 319
LULAC National Scholarship Fund
Honors Awards, 317
LULAC National Scholarship Fund
National Scholastic Achievement
Awards, 317
LULAC National Scholarshp Fund
General Awards, 317
Macy's College Scholarship
Program, 277
Marathon Oil Corporation College
Scholarship, 277
Marriott Scholars Program, 275
MassMutual Multicultural College
Scholarship, 277
The Mayor's Chesapeake Energy
Scholarship, 228
McNamara Family Creative Arts
Project Grant, 278
Microbiology Undergraduate
Research Fellowship (MURF), 170
Minority Scholarship Program, 206
Minority Teachers of Illinois
Scholarship, 290
Missouri Minority Teaching
Scholarship, 338
MSGC Undergraduate
Underrepresented Minority
Fellowship Program, 346
Multicultural Advertising Intern
Program, 525
Multicultural Undergraduate Summer
Internships at the Getty Center, 541
NABA National Scholarship
Program, 356
Nissan Community College Transfer
Scholarship, 278
Ohio Newspapers Minority
Scholarship, 399
Preservation Fellows Program, 565
Procter & Gamble Scholarship, 278
Rosewood Family Scholarship
Program, 242
Scholarship for Minority Accounting
Students, 106
Scholarship for Minority
Undergraduate Physics Majors, 161
Second Chance Program, 319
Teacher Quest Scholarship
Program, 206
Technical Minority Scholarship, 524
Tennessee Minority Teaching Fellows
Program, 584

Eligibility Indexes

Toyota Motor Sales U.S.A., Inc.
Scholarship, 278
Wal-Mart Stores, Inc. High School
Scholarship, 278
Weisman Scholarship, 223
Wells Fargo Scholarship, 279
Wisconsin Minority Teacher Loan
Program, 587
Wisconsin Minority Undergraduate
Retention Grant, 521

Mexican American

Actuarial Diversity Scholarships, 74
AFSCMA/UNCF Union Scholars
Program, 527
American Chemical Society Scholars
Program, 90
American Meteorological
Society/Industry Minority
Scholarship, 156
Atrisco Heritage Foundation
Scholarship, 276
California Teachers Association
Martin Luther King, Jr., Memorial
Scholarship, 210
CCNMA Scholarship, 213
Colgate "Bright Smiles, Bright
Futures" Minority Scholarships, 76
Connecticut Minority Teacher
Incentive Grant, 222
The EDSA Minority Scholarship, 315
Education and Leadership
Development Program, 300
Fisher Broadcasting Company
Scholarship for Minorities, 240
Fleming/Blaszcak Scholarship, 448
Gates Millennium Scholars
Program, 498
GE Business/Engineering Scholarship
for Minority Students, 316
General College Scholarship, 276
George M. Brooker Collegiate
Scholarship for Minorities, 293
HACU (Hispanic Association of
Colleges and Universities)
Scholarships, 104
HSBC-North America Scholarship
Program, 277
The Hyatt Hotels Fund for Minority
Lodging Management Students
Competition, 101
Indiana Minority Teacher & Special
Education Services
Scholarship, 471
INROADS Internship, 541
James E. Webb Internship Program for
Minority Undergraduate Seniors
and Graduate Students in Business
and Public Administration, 562
Jimmy A. Young Memorial Education
Recognition Award, 169
Jose Marti Scholarship Challenge
Grant Fund, 241
Kansas Ethnic Minority
Scholarship, 307
Lagrant Scholarships, 314

Latin American Educational
Scholarship, 316
Leonard M. Perryman
Communications Scholarship for
Ethnic Minority Students, 498
Los Padres Foundation College
Tuition Assistance Program, 319
LULAC National Scholarship Fund
Honors Awards, 317
LULAC National Scholarshp Fund
General Awards, 317
Macy's College Scholarship
Program, 277
Marriott Scholars Program, 275
MassMutual Multicultural College
Scholarship, 277
The Mayor's Chesapeake Energy
Scholarship, 228
McNamara Family Creative Arts
Project Grant, 278
Microbiology Undergraduate
Research Fellowship (MURF), 170
Minority Scholarship Program, 206
Minority Teachers of Illinois
Scholarship, 290
Missouri Minority Teaching
Scholarship, 338
Multicultural Advertising Intern
Program, 525
Multicultural Undergraduate Summer
Internships at the Getty Center, 541
NABA National Scholarship
Program, 356
Nissan Community College Transfer
Scholarship, 278
Preservation Fellows Program, 565
Procter & Gamble Scholarship, 278
Rosewood Family Scholarship
Program, 242
Scholarship for Minority Accounting
Students, 106
Scholarship for Minority
Undergraduate Physics Majors, 161
Second Chance Program, 319
Teacher Quest Scholarship
Program, 206
Technical Minority Scholarship, 524
Toyota Motor Sales U.S.A., Inc.
Scholarship, 278
Wal-Mart Stores, Inc. High School
Scholarship, 278
Weisman Scholarship, 223
Wells Fargo Scholarship, 279
Wisconsin Minority Teacher Loan
Program, 587
Wisconsin Minority Undergraduate
Retention Grant, 521

Native Hawaiian/Pacific Islander

Actuarial Diversity Scholarships, 74
AFSCMA/UNCF Union Scholars
Program, 527
Blossom Kalama Evans Memorial
Scholarship, 253

California Teachers Association
Martin Luther King, Jr., Memorial
Scholarship, 210
Connecticut Minority Teacher
Incentive Grant, 222
The EDSA Minority Scholarship, 315
Fisher Broadcasting Company
Scholarship for Minorities, 240
Gates Millennium Scholars
Program, 498
GE Business/Engineering Scholarship
for Minority Students, 316
The Hyatt Hotels Fund for Minority
Lodging Management Students
Competition, 101
Ida M. Pope Memorial
Scholarship, 263
James E. Webb Internship Program for
Minority Undergraduate Seniors
and Graduate Students in Business
and Public Administration, 562
Jimmy A. Young Memorial Education
Recognition Award, 169
Ka'iulani Home for Girls Trust
Scholarship, 264
Lagrant Scholarships, 314
Leonard M. Perryman
Communications Scholarship for
Ethnic Minority Students, 498
Marathon Oil Corporation College
Scholarship, 277
MassMutual Multicultural College
Scholarship, 277
The Mayor's Chesapeake Energy
Scholarship, 228
Microbiology Undergraduate
Research Fellowship (MURF), 170
Minority Scholarship Program, 206
MSGC Undergraduate
Underrepresented Minority
Fellowship Program, 346
Multicultural Advertising Intern
Program, 525
Multicultural Undergraduate Summer
Internships at the Getty Center, 541
OCA-AXA Achievement
Scholarships, 397
OCA/UPS Foundation Gold Mountain
College Scholarship, 397
Office of Hawaiian Affairs Scholarship
Fund, 268
Preservation Fellows Program, 565
Rosemary & Nellie Ebrie Fund, 271
Rosewood Family Scholarship
Program, 242
Scholarship for Minority Accounting
Students, 106
Technical Minority Scholarship, 524
Tennessee Minority Teaching Fellows
Program, 584
Weisman Scholarship, 223

Puerto Rican

Actuarial Diversity Scholarships, 74
AFSCMA/UNCF Union Scholars
Program, 527

American Chemical Society Scholars Program, 90

American Meteorological Society/Industry Minority Scholarship, 156

Atrisco Heritage Foundation Scholarship, 276

California Teachers Association Martin Luther King, Jr., Memorial Scholarship, 210

CCNMA Scholarship, 213

Colgate "Bright Smiles, Bright Futures" Minority Scholarships, 76

Connecticut Minority Teacher Incentive Grant, 222

The EDSA Minority Scholarship, 315

Education and Leadership Development Program, 300

Fisher Broadcasting Company Scholarship for Minorities, 240

Gates Millennium Scholars Program, 498

GE Business/Engineering Scholarship for Minority Students, 316

General College Scholarship, 276

George M. Brooker Collegiate Scholarship for Minorities, 293

HACU (Hispanic Association of Colleges and Universities) Scholarships, 104

HSBC-North America Scholarship Program, 277

The Hyatt Hotels Fund for Minority Lodging Management Students Competition, 101

Indiana Minority Teacher & Special Education Services Scholarship, 471

INROADS Internship, 541

James E. Webb Internship Program for Minority Undergraduate Seniors and Graduate Students in Business and Public Administration, 562

Jimmy A. Young Memorial Education Recognition Award, 169

Jose Marti Scholarship Challenge Grant Fund, 241

Kansas Ethnic Minority Scholarship, 307

Lagrant Scholarships, 314

Latin American Educational Scholarship, 316

Leonard M. Perryman Communications Scholarship for Ethnic Minority Students, 498

Los Padres Foundation College Tuition Assistance Program, 319

LULAC National Scholarship Fund Honors Awards, 317

LULAC National Scholarshp Fund General Awards, 317

Macy's College Scholarship Program, 277

Marriott Scholars Program, 275

MassMutual Multicultural College Scholarship, 277

The Mayor's Chesapeake Energy Scholarship, 228

McNamara Family Creative Arts Project Grant, 278

Microbiology Undergraduate Research Fellowship (MURF), 170

Minority Scholarship Program, 206

Minority Teachers of Illinois Scholarship, 290

Missouri Minority Teaching Scholarship, 338

Multicultural Advertising Intern Program, 525

Multicultural Undergraduate Summer Internships at the Getty Center, 541

NABA National Scholarship Program, 356

Nissan Community College Transfer Scholarship, 278

Preservation Fellows Program, 565

Procter & Gamble Scholarship, 278

Rosewood Family Scholarship Program, 242

Scholarship for Minority Accounting Students, 106

Scholarship for Minority Undergraduate Physics Majors, 161

Scholarships for Students of Puerto Rican Descent, 275

Second Chance Program, 319

Teacher Quest Scholarship Program, 206

Technical Minority Scholarship, 524

Toyota Motor Sales U.S.A., Inc. Scholarship, 278

Wal-Mart Stores, Inc. High School Scholarship, 278

Weisman Scholarship, 223

Wells Fargo Scholarship, 279

Wisconsin Minority Teacher Loan Program, 587

Wisconsin Minority Undergraduate Retention Grant, 521

National/ethnic background

Armenian

Performing Arts Fellowships, 186

Chinese

Thz Fo Farm Fund, 272

Italian

Alphonse A. Miele Scholarship, 496

Charles Evans Scholarship, 464

College Scholarship Program, 219

Emanuele and Emilia Inglese Memorial Scholarship, 365

General Scholarship, 464

Henry Salvatori Scholarship, 464

Italian Catholic Federation Scholarship, 299

Italian Language Scholarship, 464

Jospeh L. Bracone Memorial Scholarship, 464

Major Don S. Gentile Scholarship, 496

National Leadership Grant, 465

Sorrento Lingue Scholarship, 465

Theodore Mazza Scholarship, 496

William C. Davini Scholarship, 496

Japanese

Eizo & Toyo Sakumoto Trust Scholarship, 257

Japanese American General Scholarship, 305

Japanese American Music Scholarship Competition, 305

Ventura County Japanese-American Citizens League Scholarships, 506

Jewish

Jewish War Veterans of the United States of America Bernard Rotberg Memorial Scholarship, 306

Jewish War Veterans of the United States of America JWV Grant, 306

Louis S. Silvey Grant, 307

Polish

Massachusetts Federation of Polish Women's Clubs Scholarships, 313

The Polish American Club of North Jersey Scholarships, 313

The Polish National Alliance of Brooklyn, USA, Inc. Scholarships, 313

Swiss

Sonia Streuli Maguire Outstanding Scholastic Achievement Award, 476

Swiss Benevolent Society Medicus Student Exchange, 476

Swiss Benevolent Society Pellegrini Scholarship, 476

Welsh

Undergraduate Scholarship, 516

Welsh Heritage Scholarship, 516

Organization/civic affiliation

American Legion

Albert M. Lappin Scholarship, 120

Albert T. Marcoux Memorial Scholarship, 136

American Legion Alabama Oratorical Contest, 106

American Legion Alabama Scholarship, 107

American Legion Alaska Oratorical
   Contest, 107
American Legion Arizona Oratorical
   Contest, 108
American Legion Arkansas Oratorical
   Contest, 109
American Legion Arkansas
   Scholarship, 109
American Legion Family
   Scholarship, 118
American Legion Florida General
   Scholarship, 114
American Legion Idaho
   Scholarships, 115
American Legion Illinois
   Scholarships, 116
American Legion Massachusetts
   General and Nursing
   Scholarships, 125
American Legion Minnesota
   Legionnaire Insurance Trust
   Scholarship, 127
American Legion Nebraska Oratorical
   Contest, 133
American Legion New York
   Oratorical Contest, 140
American Legion Ohio
   Scholarships, 143
American Legion Press Club of New
   Jersey and Post 170--Arthur
   Dehardt Memorial Scholarship, 146
American Legion Washington
   Scholarships, 151
American Legion Western District
   Postsecondary Scholarship, 107
American Legion Wyoming E.A.
   Blackmore Memorial
   Scholarship, 155
Charles and Annette Hill
   Scholarship, 121
Charles L. Bacon Memorial
   Scholarship, 129
Children and Youth Scholarships, 123
Department of New Hampshire
   Scholarship, 137
Department Oratorical Awards, 143
Department Vocational
   Scholarship, 137
Dr. Hannah K. Vuolo Memorial
   Scholarship, 140
Eagle Scout of the Year, 114
Edgar J. Boschult Memorial
   Scholarship, 134
Hugh A. Smith Scholarship, 121
James V. Day Scholarship, 123
Joseph J. Frank Scholarship, 129
Joseph P. Gavenonis Scholarship, 145
Lawrence Luterman Memorial
   Scholarships, 139
Maynard Jensen American Legion
   Memorial Scholarship, 134
The Minnesota American Legion
   Memorial Scholarship, 128
New York American Legion Press
   Association Scholarship, 140
Rosedale Post 346 Scholarship, 121

Samsung American Legion
   Scholarship, 133
Schneider-Emanuel American Legion
   Scholarships, 154
Stutz Memorial Scholarship, 139
Ted and Nora Anderson
   Scholarship, 122

American Legion Auxiliary

Aloha Scholarship, 131
American Legion Alabama Auxiliary
   Scholarship, 107
American Legion Alaska Auxiliary
   Scholarship, 108
American Legion Alaska Auxiliary
   Western District Scholarship, 108
American Legion Arizona Auxiliary
   Health Care Occupation
   Scholarship, 108
American Legion Arizona Auxiliary
   Nurses' Scholarship, 109
American Legion Arkansas Auxiliary
   Scholarships, 110
American Legion Auxiliary National
   President's Scholarship, 132
American Legion California Auxiliary
   General Scholarships, 111
American Legion Florida Auxiliary
   Memorial Scholarship, 114
American Legion Florida Auxiliary
   Scholarships, 114
American Legion Georgia Auxiliary
   Scholarship, 115
American Legion Kentucky Auxiliary
   Mary Barrett Marshall
   Scholarship, 122
American Legion Minnesota Auxiliary
   Department Scholarship, 128
American Legion Ohio Auxiliary Past
   President's Parley Nurse's
   Scholarship, 143
American Legion Ohio Auxiliary
   Scholarship, 143
American Legion Rhode Island
   Auxiliary Book Award, 146
American Legion South Carolina
   Auxiliary Scholarship, 147
American Legion South Dakota
   Auxiliary Nurse's Scholarship, 147
American Legion South Dakota
   Auxiliary Scholarships, 147
American Legion Wisconsin Auxiliary
   Department President's
   Scholarship, 154
American Legion Wisconsin Auxiliary
   H.S. and Angeline Lewis
   Scholarships, 154
American Legion Wisconsin Auxiliary
   Merit and Memorial
   Scholarship, 154
American Legion Wisconsin Auxiliary
   Past Presidents Parley
   Scholarship, 155
Anna Gear Junior Scholarship, 151
Continuing or Re-entry Student
   Scholarship, 111

Della Van Deuren Memorial
   Scholarship, 155
Department President's
   Scholarship, 112
Department President's Scholarship
   for Junior Auxiliary Members, 112
Dr. Kate Waller Barrett Grant, 151
Edna M. Barcus Memorial
   Scholarship and Hoosier
   Scholarship, 118
Girl Scout Achievement Award, 133
Grace S. High Memorial Child
   Welfare Scholarship Fund, 138
Laura Blackburn Memorial
   Scholarship, 123
Mary Barrett Marshall Student Loan
   Fund, 573
Memorial Education Grant, 113
Nannie W. Norfleet Scholarship, 142
National President's Scholarship, 144
Past Department Presidents' Junior
   Scholarship, 111
Past President's Parley Education
   Grant, 113
Past President's Parley Health Care
   Scholarship, 128
Past President's Parley Nurse's
   Scholarship, 112
Past President's Parley Nurses
   Scholarship, 115
Past Presidents' Parley Nursing
   Scholarship, 111
Past President's Parley Nursing
   Scholarship, 113, 119
Past President's Parley
   Scholarship, 142
Ruby Paul Campaign Fund
   Scholarship, 135
Scholarship for College or
   Vocational, 148
Spirit of Youth Scholarship, 144
Spirit of Youth Scholarship for Junior
   Members, 133
Thelma Foster Junior American
   Legion Auxiliary Members
   Scholarship, 148
Thelma Foster Senior American
   Legion Auxiliary Member
   Scholarship, 148
Wilma D. Hoyal/Maxine Chilton
   Memorial Scholarship, 109

American Legion, Boys State

American Legion Maryland Boys
   State Scholarship, 124
American Legion New Hampshire
   Boys State Scholarship, 136
Lillie Lois Ford Boys'
   Scholarship, 130

American Legion/Boys Scouts of America

American Legion Wisconsin Eagle
   Scout of the Year Scholarship, 153

ASTA Arizona Chapter

Arizona Chapter Dependent Scholarship, 487

Boy Scouts of America

American Legion Illinois Boy Scout Scholarship, 116

Boy Scouts of America, Eagle Scouts

American Legion Eagle Scout of the Year, 132, 150
Boy Scout of the Year Scholarship, 119
Eagle Scout of the Year Scholarship, 148

Harness Racing Industry

Harness Tracks of America Scholarship Fund, 252

International Union of EESMF Workers, AFL-CIO

Bruce van Ess Scholarship, 299
David J. Fitzmaurice Scholarship, 299
James B. Carey Scholarship, 299
Sal Ingrassia Scholarship, 300
Willie Rudd Scholarship, 300

Jaycees

Thomas Wood Baldridge Scholarship, 305

Knights of Columbus

Matthews/Swift Educational Trust - Military Dependants, 312
Matthews/Swift Educational Trust - Police/Firefighters, 312
Pro Deo/Pro Patria Scholarship, 312

Lambda Alpha

Senior Scholarship, 314

Learning for Life

Captain James J. Regan Memorial Scholarship, 317
Sheryl A. Horak Law Enforcement Explorer Scholarship, 318

National Art Materials Trade Association

NAMTA Educational Scholarship, 355
NAMTA Foundation Visual Arts Major Scholarship, 355

National Society of Black Engineers

Batttelle Collegiate Scholarship, 373
Bechtel Group Foundation Scholarship, 373
BP Corporate Scholarship, 373
Caterpillar Corporate Scholarship, 373
Cummins Inc. Corporate Scholarship, 373
ExxonMobil Corporate Scholarship, 374
Fulfilling the Legacy Scholarship, 374
International Studies Scholarship, 374
Lockheed Martin Corporate Scholarship, 374
National Society of Black Engineers Golden Torch Awards, 374
National Society of Black Engineers Leroy Callendar PCI Award Program, 375
Northrop Grumman Corporate Scholarship, 375
NSBE Fellows Scholarship, 375
PBS&J Corporate Scholarship, 375
Toyota Corporate Scholarship, 376
U.S. Steel NSBE Academic Scholarship, 376
Verizon Corporate Scholarship, 376
Wal-Mart Stores Inc. Corporate Scholarship, 376

Native Daughters of the Golden West

Native Daughters of the Golden West Scholarship, 378

New York State Grange

June Gill Nursing Scholarship, 387

Polish National Alliance of Brooklyn

The Polish National Alliance of Brooklyn, USA, Inc. Scholarships, 313

Reserve Officers Training Corps (ROTC)

Kansas ROTC Service Scholarship, 308

Screen Actor's Guild

John L. Dales Standard Scholarship, 434

Service Employees International Union

Charles Hardy Memorial Scholarship, 436

Society of Physics Students

Society of Physics Students Summer Internship Program, 562

Society of Women Engineers

Goldman, Sachs and Co. Scholarship, 458

Sons of Norway

Astrid G. Cates Scholarship Fund and Myrtle Beinhauer Scholarship, 465
Nancy Lorraine Jensen Memorial Scholarship, 466

Transportation Clubs International

Charlotte Woods Memorial Scholarship, 494

United Food and Commerical Workers

United Food and Commercial Workers International Union Scholarship Program, 497

United Transportation Union

United Transportation Union Insurance Association Scholarship, 501

Religious Affiliation

Eastern Orthodox

Boy and Girl Scouts Scholarship, 233

Episcopal

Shannon Scholarship, 495

Jewish

Chester M. Vernon Memorial Eagle Scout Scholarship, 366
Frank L. Weil Memorial Eagle Scout Scholarship, 366
Jewish Vocational Service Scholarship Fund, 306
JFCS Scholarship Fund, 577
Taglit-Birthright Israel Gift, 477

Lutheran

Developmental Disability Scholastic Achievement Scholarship, 202

Presbyterian

National Presbyterian Scholarship, 421
Presbyterian Student Opportunity Scholarship, 421
Presbyterian Undergraduate and Graduate Loan, 583
Samuel Robinson Award, 421

Roman Catholic

Italian Catholic Federation Scholarship, 299

Matthews/Swift Educational Trust - Military Dependants, 312
Matthews/Swift Educational Trust - Police/Firefighters, 312
Pro Deo/Pro Patria Scholarship, 312

Unitarian Universalist

Stanfield and D'Orlando Art Scholarship, 497

United Methodist

Leonard M. Perryman Communications Scholarship for Ethnic Minority Students, 498
United Methodist Loan Program, 585
United Methodist Scholarships, 497

Returning Adult

Adrienne Alix Scholarship, 138
Air Traffic Control Full-Time Employee Student Scholarship, 79
A.J. Spielman Scholarship, 487
American Legion Alaska Auxiliary Western District Scholarship, 108
B. K. Krenzer Re-entry Scholarship, 452
Charles R. Ford Scholarship, 305
Connecticut Tuition Waiver for Senior Citizens, 222
Delayed Education Scholarship for Women, 159
Eight and Forty Lung and Respiratory Nursing Scholarship Fund, 132
Fran Johnson Non-Traditional Scholarship, 96
GEICO Life Scholarship, 249
George Reinke Scholarship, 489
New York State Veterans Tuition Award, 389
Olive Lynn Salembier Re-entry Scholarship, 462
Second Effort Scholarship, 183
Senior Citizen, 65 or Older, Free Tuition for Up to 6 Credit Hours, 482
Slovenian Women's Union Scholarship For Returning Adults, 438
Stan and Leone Pollard Scholarship, 493
Undergraduate Research Scholarship, 348
West Virginia Higher Education Adult Part-time Student (HEAPS) Grant Program, 517
Workforce Improvement Grant, 183

State of Residence

Aerospace Undergraduate Research Scholarship Program, 353

Airgas-Jerry Baker Scholarship, 175
Alabama Junior/Community College Athletic Scholarship, 84
American Ex-Prisoner of War, Peter Connacher Memorial Scholarship, 403
American Federation of State, County, and Municipal Employees (AFSCME) Oregon Council #75, 404
American Legion Wyoming Auxiliary Past Presidents' Parley Scholarship, 156
American Restaurant Scholarship, 301
Associated Press/APTRA-Clete Roberts Memorial Journalism Scholarship, 181
A.W. Bodine Sunkist Memorial Scholarship, 475
The CBC Spouses Education Scholarship, 220
CHESLA Loan Program, 575
CITE Scholarship, 223
The Cynthia E. Morgan Memorial Scholarship Fund, 226
D. Fred and Mariam L. Bovie Technical Scholarship, 176
Dolphin Scholarship, 232
Fifth Floor Restaurant Scholarship, 302
Franklin Lindsay Student Aid Loan, 576
G.I. Dependents' Scholarship Program, 84
Grant Program for Dependents of Correctional Officers, 289
Grant Program for Dependents of Police or Fire Officers, 289
Herschel C. Price Educational Scholarship, 274
Homestead Capital Housing Scholarship, 407
Institutional Scholarship Waivers, 84
J. Richard Mehalick Scholarship, 174
The Kaj Christensen Scholarship for Vocational Training, 396
Katharine M. Grosscup Scholarship, 245
Kathryn D. Sullivan Science and Engineering Fellowship, 351
LaMacchia Family Scholarship, 489
Legacy of Hope, 473
Lighthouse College-Bound Award, 319
Lighthouse Undergraduate Award, 319
Louisiana Memorial Scholarship, 165
Maine State Society of Washington, DC, Foundation Scholarship Program, 323
Maryland Tuition Reduction for Non-Resident Nursing Students, 327
Minnesota Student Educational Loan Fund (SELF), 578
MTA Doug Slifka Memorial Scholarship, 341

NASA Ohio Space Grant Junior/Senior Scholarship Program, 350
NASA Pennsylvania Space Grant Sylvia Stein Memorial Scholarship, 350
NASA Space Grant Kentucky Undergraduate Scholarship, 345
NASA Space Grant Maine Consortium Annual Scholarship and Fellowship Program, 346
NASA Space Grant Michigan Undergraduate Fellowship, 346
NASA Space Grant Montana Undergraduate Scholarship Program, 347
NASA Space Grant Nevada Undergraduate Scholarship, 348
NASA Space Grant New Mexico Undergraduate Scholarship, 348
NASA Space Grant North Dakota Consortium Lillian Goettler Scholarship, 349
NASA Space Grant North Dakota Undergraduate Scholarship, 349
NASA Space Grant Rhode Island Undergraduate Research Scholarship, 350
NASA Space Grant South Carolina Undergraduate Student Research Fellowship, 352
NASA Space Grant Virginia Community College Scholarship, 353
NASA West Virginia Space Grant Undergraduate Research Fellowship, 353
NCR Summer Internships, 552
New Jersey Class Loan Program, 580
New Jersey STARS II, 382
New Mexico Competitive Scholarships, 384
New York Women in Communications Foundation Scholarship, 389
Oracle Scholars Internship Program, 566
The Ouimet Scholarship, 243
Pearl I. Young Scholarship, 349
Pittsburgh Local Section Scholarship, 160
Poggio Scholarship, 303
Preservation Fellows Program, 565
Press Club of Houston Scholarship, 422
The Publican Scholarship, 303
Richard F. Brentano Memorial Scholarship, 411
Roger W. Emmons Memorial Scholarship, 411
Rosewood Family Scholarship Program, 242
Stan and Leone Pollard Scholarship, 493
Studio at the Montage Resort & Spa Scholarship, 304
Summer Undergraduate Scholarship, 351

Undergraduate Research
Scholarship, 348
Undergraduate Scholarship
Program, 349
Wilma Motley Memorial California
Merit Scholarship, 78
Women in Architecture
Scholarship, 197
Year-Long Horticultural
Internship, 568
Zov's Bistro Scholarship, 304

Alabama

Alabama National Guard Educational
Assistance Program, 83
Alabama Scholarship for Dependents
of Blind Parents, 471
Alabama Student Assistance
Program, 83
Alabama Student Grant Program, 83
American Legion Alabama Auxiliary
Scholarship, 107
American Legion Alabama Oratorical
Contest, 106
American Legion Alabama
Scholarship, 107
Charles Clarke Cordle Memorial
Scholarship, 162
Gulf Coast Hurricane
Scholarships, 449
NASA Space Grant Undergraduate
Scholarship, 343
Police/Firefighters' Survivors
Educational Assistance Program, 84
Robert C. Byrd Honors
Scholarship, 84
Southern Nursery Organization Sidney
B. Meadows Scholarship, 469

Alaska

ACEC Scholarship, 94
Alaska Family Education Loan, 573
Alaska Teacher Education Loan, 573
American Legion Alaska Auxiliary
Scholarship, 108
American Legion Alaska Auxiliary
Western District Scholarship, 108
American Legion Alaska Oratorical
Contest, 107
American Legion Western District
Postsecondary Scholarship, 107
A.W. "Winn" Brindle Memorial
Education Loan, 573
Cady McDonnell Memorial
Scholarship, 92
Carl N. & Margaret Karcher
Founders' Scholarship, 212
Clark-Phelps Scholarship, 405
Mary Lou Brown Scholarship, 166
The Merchants Exhange Scholarship
Fund, 330
Pacific Northwest Chapter/William
Hunt Scholarship, 492

Arizona

All-Arizona Academic Team, 181

American Legion Arizona Auxiliary
Health Care Occupation
Scholarship, 108
American Legion Arizona Auxiliary
Nurses' Scholarship, 109
American Legion Arizona Oratorical
Contest, 108
Arizona Chapter Dependent
Scholarship, 487
Arizona Scholarship, 488
Arizona Tuition Scholarships for
Children/Spouses of Slain Public
Servants, 181
Burlington Northern Santa Fe
Foundation Scholarship, 104
Cady McDonnell Memorial
Scholarship, 92
Carl N. & Margaret Karcher
Founders' Scholarship, 212
Chapter 67 - Phoenix Scholarship, 443
Charles N. Fisher Memorial
Scholarship, 163
Deseo at the Westin Scholarship, 302
High Honors Endorsement Tuition
Scholarship, 182
Horatio Alger Arizona
Scholarship, 280
Italian Catholic Federation
Scholarship, 299
NASA Space Grant Arizona
Undergraduate Research
Internship, 549
Phoenix Section Scholarship, 463
RCMI Technical/Trade School
Scholarship, 428
Rocky Mountain Coal Mining
Institute Scholarship, 428
United Health Foundation
Scholarship, 103
Walt Bartram Memorial Education
Award (Region 12 and Chapter
119), 447
Wilma D. Hoyal/Maxine Chilton
Memorial Scholarship, 109

Arkansas

Academic Challenge Scholarship, 182
American Legion Arkansas Auxiliary
Scholarships, 110
American Legion Arkansas Oratorical
Contest, 109
American Legion Arkansas
Scholarship, 109
ASHRAE Region VIII
Scholarship, 173
Fred R. McDaniel Memorial
Scholarship, 164
Governor's Scholars Program, 182
Law Enforcement Officers'
Dependents Scholarship, 182
Military Dependents Scholarship
Program, 183
Second Effort Scholarship, 183
Southern Nursery Organization Sidney
B. Meadows Scholarship, 469
Workforce Improvement Grant, 183

California

American Legion California Auxiliary
General Scholarships, 111
American Legion California
Oratorical Contest, 110
Assumption Program of Loans for
Education (APLE), 574
Bay Area Council Scholarship
Program, 201
BIA San Diego Scholarship, 206
Burlington Northern Santa Fe
Foundation Scholarship, 104
Cady McDonnell Memorial
Scholarship, 92
Cal Grant A & B Entitlement Award
Program, 209
Cal Grant A and B Competitive
Awards, 209
Cal Grant C Award, 209
California Child Development Grant
Program, 209
California Farm Bureau
Scholarship, 208
California Masonic Foundation
Scholarship, 208
California Robert C. Byrd Honors
Scholarship, 210
California Teachers Association
Martin Luther King, Jr., Memorial
Scholarship, 210
California's Junior Miss
Competition, 208
C.A.R. Scholarship, 207
Carl N. & Margaret Karcher
Founders' Scholarship, 212
Charles Hardy Memorial
Scholarship, 436
Charles N. Fisher Memorial
Scholarship, 163
Continuing or Re-entry Student
Scholarship, 111
CTA Scholarship for Dependent
Children, 211
CTA Scholarships for Members, 211
Epilepsy Foundation of San Diego
County Scholarship, 236
Fashion Group International of
Portland Scholarship, 406
Goldman Family Fund: New Leader
Scholarship, 323
Grange Insurance Scholarship, 251
Horatio Alger California Scholarship
Program, 280
HSBC-North America Scholarship
Program, 277
Italian Catholic Federation
Scholarship, 299
Jewish Vocational Service Scholarship
Fund, 306
JFCS Scholarship Fund, 577
L. Gordon Bittle Memorial
Scholarship for SCTA, 211
Law Enforcement Personnel
Dependents (LEPD) Grant
Program, 210
Marin Education Undergraduate
Scholarships, 324

The Merchants Exhange Scholarship
Fund, 330
Muggets Scholarship, 285
Native Daughters of the Golden West
Scholarship, 378
Northern California Chapter - Richard
Epping Scholarship, 491
Past Department Presidents' Junior
Scholarship, 111
Past Presidents' Parley Nursing
Scholarship, 111
Pete Wilson Journalism
Scholarship, 425
Southern California Council Endowed
Internship, 552
Toyota Motor Sales U.S.A., Inc.
Scholarship, 278
Ventura County Japanese-American
Citizens League Scholarships, 506
Walt Bartram Memorial Education
Award (Region 12 and Chapter
119), 447
William E. "Buck" Bragunier
Scholarship for Outstanding
Leadership, 186
William J. and Marijane E. Adams, Jr.
Scholarship, 194
Wilma Motley Memorial California
Merit Scholarship, 78

Colorado

Burlington Northern Santa Fe
Foundation Scholarship, 104
Cady McDonnell Memorial
Scholarship, 92
Carl N. & Margaret Karcher
Founders' Scholarship, 212
Clinton J. Helton Manufacturing
Scholarship Award, 444
Colorado Masons Scholarship, 219
Colorado Student Grant, 218
Colorado Supplemental Leveraging
Educational Assistance Partnership
(SLEAP), 218
Colorado Work-Study Program, 218
Department President's
Scholarship, 112
Department President's Scholarship
for Junior Auxiliary Members, 112
General Scholarship, 219
Grange Insurance Scholarship, 251
Greenhouse Scholars, 251
Latin American Educational
Scholarship, 316
Legacy of Hope, 473
Mark J. Smith Scholarship, 219
National High School Oratorical
Contest, 112
Past President's Parley Nurse's
Scholarship, 112
RCMI Technical/Trade School
Scholarship, 428
Rocky Mountain Coal Mining
Institute Scholarship, 428
Sachs Foundation Undergraduate
Grant, 430

Connecticut

CBC Scholarship, 221
CLN Scholarships, 223
College Scholarship Program, 219
Connecticut Aid for Public College
Students, 221
Connecticut Aid to Dependents of
Deceased/POW/MIA Veterans, 221
Connecticut Capitol Scholarship
Program, 221
Connecticut Independent College
Student Grant, 222
Connecticut Minority Teacher
Incentive Grant, 222
Connecticut Robert C. Byrd Honors
Scholarship, 222
Connecticut Scholarship, 488
Connecticut Tuition Waiver for Senior
Citizens, 222
Connecticut Tuition Waiver for
Veterans, 222
Connecticut Tuition Waiver for
Vietnam MIA/POW
Dependents, 223
Dr. James L. Lawson Memorial
Scholarship, 163
Japanese American General
Scholarship, 305
Massachusetts MASSgrant
Program, 328
Moody's Mega Math "M3"
Challenge, 341
National High School Oratorical
Contest, 112
NEBHE's Tuition Break Regional
Student Program, 380
New England FEMARA
Scholarship, 166
Sonia Streuli Maguire Outstanding
Scholastic Achievement Award, 476
Swiss Benevolent Society Pellegrini
Scholarship, 476
Timothy S. and Palmer W. Bigelow
Scholarship, 285
Weisman Scholarship, 223
Yankee Clipper Contest Club, Inc.
Youth Scholarship, 168

Delaware

B. Bradford Barnes Scholarship, 230
Charles L. Hebner Memorial
Scholarship, 230
Christa McAuliffe Teacher Incentive
Program, 575
College Scholarship Program, 219
Delaware Nursing Incentive
Program, 575
Delaware Scholarship Incentive
Program, 230
Diamond State Scholarship, 230
Educational Benefits for Children of
Deceased Veterans and Others, 231
Herman M. Holloway, Sr. Memorial
Scholarship, 231
Horatio Alger Delaware Scholarship
Program, 280

Moody's Mega Math "M3"
Challenge, 341
Past President's Parley Nursing
Scholarship, 113
Robert C. Byrd Honors
Scholarship, 231
Sonia Streuli Maguire Outstanding
Scholastic Achievement Award, 476
Swiss Benevolent Society Pellegrini
Scholarship, 476
Undergraduate Scholarship, 516

District of Columbia

Alumnae Panhellenic Association
Women's Scholarship, 87
College Scholarship Program, 219
DC Adoption Scholarship, 232
DC Tuition Assistance Grant Program
(DCTAG), 232
District of Columbia Leveraging
Educational Assistance Partnership
Program, 232
Horatio Alger District of Columbia,
Maryland and Virginia Scholarship
Program, 281
HSBC-North America Scholarship
Program, 277
Massachusetts MASSgrant
Program, 328
Moody's Mega Math "M3"
Challenge, 341
National High School Oratorical
Contest, 113

Florida

Access to Better Learning and
Education (ABLE) Grant
Program, 240
American Legion Florida Auxiliary
Memorial Scholarship, 114
American Legion Florida Auxiliary
Scholarships, 114
American Legion Florida General
Scholarship, 114
ARRL Earl I. Anderson
Scholarship, 162
Bern Laxer Memorial
Scholarship, 301
Bob East Scholarship Fund, 368
Critical Teacher Shortage Student
Loan Forgiveness Program, 576
Eagle Scout of the Year, 114
Florida Academic Scholars
Award, 240
Florida Gold Seal Vocational Scholars
Award, 240
Florida Medallion Scholars
Award, 241
Florida Scholarship, 489
Florida Student Assistance Grant
Program, 241
Florida Work Experience
Program, 538
Gulf Coast Hurricane
Scholarships, 449
High School Oratorical Contest, 114

HSBC-North America Scholarship Program, 277
Jose Marti Scholarship Challenge Grant Fund, 241
Mary McLeod Bethune Scholarship, 241
Moody's Mega Math "M3" Challenge, 341
Robert C. Byrd Honors Scholarship Program, 241
Salute to Education Scholarship, 433
Scholarships for Children and Spouses of Deceased or Disabled Veterans and Servicemembers, 242
Southern Nursery Organization Sidney B. Meadows Scholarship, 469
William L. Boyd, IV, Florida Resident Access Grant Program, 242

Georgia

Accel Program Grant, 246
American Legion Georgia Auxiliary Scholarship, 115
ASHRAE Region IV Benny Bootle Scholarship, 172
Charles Clarke Cordle Memorial Scholarship, 162
Eugene "Gene" Sallee, W4YFR Memorial Scholarship, 164
Georgia Hope Grant - GED Recipient, 246
Georgia Hope Grant - Public Technical Institution, 246
Georgia Hope Scholarship - Private Institution, 246
Georgia Hope Scholarship - Public College or University, 247
Georgia Law Enforcement Personnel Dependents Grant, 247
Georgia LEAP Grant, 247
Georgia Promise Teacher Scholarship, 576
Georgia Robert C. Byrd Scholarship, 247
Georgia Tuition Equalization Grant, 247
Horatio Alger Georgia Scholarship Program, 281
Moody's Mega Math "M3" Challenge, 341
NASA Space Grant Georgia Fellowship Program, 344
PAGE Foundation Scholarships, 423
Past President's Parley Nurses Scholarship, 115
Southern Nursery Organization Sidney B. Meadows Scholarship, 469
Student Aid Foundation Loan, 583
Web Challenge Contest, 476

Hawaii

ABC Stores Jumpstart Scholarship, 252
Aiea General Hospital Association Scholarship, 253
Allan Eldin & Agnes Sutorik Geiger Scholarship Fund, 253

Alma White-Delta Kappa Gamma Scholarship, 253
American Legion Oratorical Contest, 115
Bal Dasa Scholarship Fund, 253
Blossom Kalama Evans Memorial Scholarship, 253
Cady McDonnell Memorial Scholarship, 92
Camille C. Chidiac Fund, 254
Candon, Todd, & Seabolt Scholarship Fund, 254
Carl N. & Margaret Karcher Founders' Scholarship, 212
Castle & Cooke Mililani Technology Park Scholarship Fund, 254
Castle & Cooke W. Y. Yim Scholarship Fund, 254
Cayetano Foundation Scholarship, 255
Community Scholarship Fund, 255
Cora Aguda Manayan Fund, 255
David L. Irons Memorial Scholarship Fund, 255
David T. Woolsey Scholarship, 315
Dolly Ching Scholarship Fund, 255
Doris & Clarence Glick Classical Music Scholarship, 256
Dr. Alvin and Monica Saake Scholarship, 256
Dr. and Mrs. Moon Park Scholarship, 256
Dr. Hans & Clara Zimmerman Foundation Education Scholarship, 256
Dr. Hans and Clara Zimmerman Foundation Health Scholarship, 257
Eastside & Northshore Kauai Scholarship Fund, 257
Edward Payson and Bernice Pi'ilani Irwin Scholarship Trust Fund, 257
E.E. Black Scholarship, 257
Eizo & Toyo Sakumoto Trust Scholarship, 257
Elena Albano "Maka'alohilohi" Scholarship Fund, 258
Ellison Onizuka Memorial Scholarship, 258
Esther Kanagawa Memorial Art Scholarship, 258
F. Koehnen Ltd. Scholarship Fund, 258
The Filipino Nurses' Organization of Hawaii Scholarship, 259
Financial Women International Scholarship, 259
Fletcher & Fritzi Hoffmann Education Fund, 259
Friends of Hawaii Public Housing Scholarship, 259
George Mason Business Scholarship Fund, 259
Gerrit R. Ludwig Scholarship, 260
Good Eats Scholarship Fund, 260
Grace Pacific Outstanding Scholars Fund, 260
Guy Marshall Scholarship Fund, 260

Hawaii Chuck Yim Gee Scholarship, 489
Hawaii Pacific Gerontological Society Nursing Scholarship Fund, 260
Hawaii Pizza Hut Scholarship Fund, 261
Hawaii Society of Certified Public Accountants Scholarship Fund, 261
Henry A. Zuberano Scholarship, 261
Herbert & Ollie Brook Fund, 261
Hideko & Zenzo Matsuyama Scholarship Fund, 262
Hilo Chinese School Scholarship, 262
Hokuli'a Foundation Scholarship Fund, 262
Hon Chew Hee Scholarship Fund, 262
Ho'omaka Hou Scholarship, 262
Ian Doane Smith Scholarship Fund, 262
Ida M. Pope Memorial Scholarship, 263
Isemoto Contracting Co., Ltd. Scholarship Fund, 263
Jean Fitzgerald Scholarship Fund, 263
John Dawe Dental Education Fund, 263
Joseph & Alice Duarte Memorial Fund, 263
Ka'a'awa Community Fund, 264
Kahala Nui Residents Scholarship Fund, 264
Kahiau Scholarship Fund, 264
Ka'iulani Home for Girls Trust Scholarship, 264
Kapolei Community & Business Scholarship, 264
Kawasaki-McGaha Scholarship Fund, 265
Kazuma and Ichiko Hisanaga Scholarship Fund, 265
King Kekaulike High School Scholarship, 265
K.M. Hatano Scholarship, 265
Kohala Ditch Education Fund, 266
Koloa Scholarship, 266
Korean University Club Scholarship Fund, 266
Kurt W. Schneider Memorial Scholarship Fund, 266
Laheenae Rebecca Hart Gay Scholarship, 266
Laura N. Dowsett Fund, 267
Laura Rowe Burdick Scholarship Fund, 267
Margaret Jones Memorial Nursing Scholarship, 267
Marion Maccarrell Scott Scholarship, 267
Mary Josephine Bloder Scholarship, 268
Mildred Towle Scholarship - Study Abroad, 268
Mildred Towle Scholarship for African-Americans, 268
NASA Hawaii Undergraduate Student Research Program, 549

NASA Space Grant Hawaii Undergraduate Fellowship, 344
Nick Van Pernis Scholarship, 268
Oscar and Rosetta Fish Fund, 269
Paulina L. Sorg Scholarship, 269
Perry & Sally Sorenson Scholarship for Dependents of Hospitality Workers, 269
Perry & Sally Sorenson Scholarship for Foster Youth, 269
Peter Papworth Scholarship, 269
PRSA-Hawaii/Roy Leffingwell Public Relations Scholarship, 270
Ray Yoshida Kauai Fine Arts Scholarship, 270
Raymond F. Cain Scholarship Fund, 270
Rich Meiers Health Administration Fund, 270
Richie Gregory Fund, 270
Robanna Fund, 271
Ron Bright Scholarship, 271
Rosemary & Nellie Ebrie Fund, 271
Safeway Foundation Hawaii Scholarship Fund, 271
Senator Richard M. & Dr. Ruth Matsuura Scholarship Fund, 271
Shirley McKown Scholarship Fund, 272
Shuichi, Katsu and Itsuyo Suga Scholarship, 272
Takehiko Hasegawa Academic Scholarship, 272
Thz Fo Farm Fund, 272
Tommy Lee Memorial Scholarship Fund, 272
The Tongan Cultural Society Scholarship, 273
Toraji & Toki Yoshinaga Scholarship, 273
Vicki Willder Scholarship Fund, 273
Walter H. Kupau Memorial Fund, 273
Will J. Henderson Scholarship Fund in Hawaii, 273
William J. and Marijane E. Adams, Jr. Scholarship, 194
William James & Dorothy Bading Lanquist Fund, 274

Idaho

American Legion Idaho Auxiliary Nurse's Scholarship, 116
American Legion Idaho Scholarships, 115
Bank of the Cascades Scholarship, 404
Cady McDonnell Memorial Scholarship, 92
Carl N. & Margaret Karcher Founders' Scholarship, 212
Earl Dedman Memorial Scholarship, 95
Fashion Group International of Portland Scholarship, 406
Grange Insurance Scholarship, 251
Grow Your Own Teacher Scholarship Program, 287
Horatio Alger Idaho Scholarship Program, 281
Idaho Education Incentive Loan Forgiveness Program, 577
Idaho Governor's Cup Scholarship, 287
Idaho Minority/"At-Risk" Scholarship, 287
Idaho Robert C. Byrd Scholarship, 288
Mary Lou Brown Scholarship, 166
The Merchants Exhange Scholarship Fund, 330
Oratorical Contest, 115
Pacific Northwest Chapter/William Hunt Scholarship, 492
Robert R. Lee Promise Category A Scholarship, 288
Robert R. Lee Promise Category B Scholarship, 288
Treacy Company Scholarship, 495

Illinois

Ada Mucklestone Memorial Scholarship, 117
American Legion Illinois Boy Scout Scholarship, 116
American Legion Illinois Oratorical Contest, 116
American Legion Illinois Scholarships, 116
Americanism Essay Contest Scholarship, 110
ARRL Earl I. Anderson Scholarship, 162
Bonus Incentive Grant (BIG), 289
Chicago FM Club Scholarship, 163
Chicago Scholars Program, 216
David Arver Memorial Scholarship, 80
Edmond A. Metzger Scholarship, 164
Golden Apple Scholars of Illinois Program, 248
Horatio Alger Illinois Scholarship Program, 281
HSBC-North America Scholarship Program, 277
Illinois Future Teacher Corps, 290
Illinois General Assembly Legislative Scholarships, 289
Illinois National Guard Grant, 290
Illinois Veteran Grant (IVG) Program, 290
Italian Catholic Federation Scholarship, 299
Marie Sheehe Trade School Scholarship, 117
McFarland Charitable Foundation Scholarship, 252
Midwest Student Exchange Program, 332
Mildred R. Knoles Opportunity Scholarship, 117
Minority Teachers of Illinois Scholarship, 290
Monetary Award Program (MAP), 291
Robert C. Byrd Honors Scholarship Program, 291
Silas Purnell Illinois Incentive for Access, 291
Six Meter Club of Chicago Scholarship, 167
Special Education Teacher Tuition Waiver, 291
Special Education Teaching Scholarships, 117
Student Nurse Scholarship, 117
Student-to-Student (STS) Program, 292

Indiana

American Legion Americanism and Government Test, 118
American Legion Family Scholarship, 118
American Legion Indiana Oratorical Contest, 118
American Legion Legacy Scholarship, 132
ARRL Earl I. Anderson Scholarship, 162
Chapter 56 - Fort Wayne Scholarship, 443
Chicago FM Club Scholarship, 163
The Clarence & Josephine Myers Scholarship, 443
David Arver Memorial Scholarship, 80
Edmond A. Metzger Scholarship, 164
Edna M. Barcus Memorial Scholarship and Hoosier Scholarship, 118
Frank O'Bannon Grant, 471
Indiana Minority Teacher & Special Education Services Scholarship, 471
Indiana National Guard Supplemental Grant, 472
Indiana Nursing Scholarship, 472
Indiana Robert C. Byrd Honors Scholarship, 472
Indiana Twenty-First Century Scholars Program, 472
John W. Anderson Foundation Scholarship, 499
Midwest Student Exchange Program, 332
Past President's Parley Nursing Scholarship, 119
Young Survivor Scholarship, 89

Iowa

AICP Heartland Chapter Scholarship, 198
All Iowa Opportunity Scholarship, 297
American Legion Iowa Oratorical Contest, 119
Boy Scout of the Year Scholarship, 119
David Arver Memorial Scholarship, 80
Department of Iowa Scholarships, 119

Governor Terry E. Branstad Iowa State Fair Scholarship, 297
Harriet Hoffman Memorial Scholarship, 119
Horatio Alger Ak-Sar-Ben Scholarship Program, 280
Iowa Farm Bureau Federation Scholarship, 297
Iowa Grant, 297
Iowa National Guard Educational Assistance Program, 297
Iowa Robert C. Byrd Honor Scholarship, 298
Iowa Tuition Grant, 298
Iowa Vocational-Technical Tuition Grant, 298
Mary Virginia Macrea Memorial Scholarship, 120
North Central Region Scholarship, 447
Past President's Scholarship, 120
Paul and Helen L. Grauer Scholarship, 167
PHD Amateur Radio Association Scholarship, 167
Robert D. Blue Scholarship, 298

Kansas

AICP Heartland Chapter Scholarship, 198
Albert M. Lappin Scholarship, 120
American Legion Kansas Auxiliary Department Scholarships, 122
American Legion Music Scholarship, 120
American Legion Oratorical Contest, 120
Burlington Northern Santa Fe Foundation Scholarship, 104
Chapter 52 - Wichita Scholarship, 443
Charles and Annette Hill Scholarship, 121
David Arver Memorial Scholarship, 80
Dr. Click Cowger Scholarship, 121
Hugh A. Smith Scholarship, 121
Irving W. Cook WA0CGS Scholarship, 165
John and Geraldine Hobble Licensed Practical Nursing Scholarship, 121
Kansas Comprehensive Grant, 307
Kansas Ethnic Minority Scholarship, 307
Kansas Nursing Service Scholarship, 308
Kansas ROTC Service Scholarship, 308
Kansas State Scholarship, 308
Kansas Teacher Service Scholarship, 308
Kansas Vocational Education Scholarship, 309
Midwest Student Exchange Program, 332
National Guard Educational Assistance Program, 309

Paul and Helen L. Grauer Scholarship, 167
PHD Amateur Radio Association Scholarship, 167
Rosedale Post 346 Scholarship, 121
Ted and Nora Anderson Scholarship, 122
Travelers Foundation, 103

Kentucky

American Legion Department Oratorical Awards, 122
American Legion Kentucky Auxiliary Mary Barrett Marshall Scholarship, 122
Early Childhood Development Scholarship, 310
Go Higher Grant, 310
Kentucky College Access Program Grant (CAP), 310
Kentucky Educational Excellence Scholarship (KEES), 310
Kentucky Teacher Scholarship, 310
Kentucky Tuition Grant, 311
Kentucky Work-Study Program, 543
Laura Blackburn Memorial Scholarship, 123
Mary Barrett Marshall Student Loan Fund, 573
Mary Jo Young Scholarship, 311
Pat & Jim Host Scholarship, 492
Robert C. Byrd Honors Scholarship, 311
Southern Nursery Organization Sidney B. Meadows Scholarship, 469

Louisiana

ASHRAE Region VIII Scholarship, 173
Chefs of Louisiana Cookery Scholarship, 301
Fred R. McDaniel Memorial Scholarship, 164
Gulf Coast Hurricane Scholarships, 449
Horatio Alger Louisiana Scholarship Program, 282
Louisiana Go Grants, 320
Louisiana Rockefeller Wildlife Scholarship, 320
Louisiana Taylor Opportunity Program for Students (TOPS) Award, 320
Louisiana Veterans Affairs Educational Assistance for Dependent Children, 320
Louisiana Veterans Affairs Educational Assistance for Surviving Spouse, 320
Robert C. Byrd Honors Scholarship, 321
Southern Nursery Organization Sidney B. Meadows Scholarship, 469

Maine

AGC of Maine Scholarship Program, 196
American Legion Maine Auxiliary Scholarship, 124
Children and Youth Scholarships, 123
College Scholarship Program, 219
Daniel E. Lambert Memorial Scholarship, 123
Dr. James L. Lawson Memorial Scholarship, 163
James V. Day Scholarship, 123
The Joel Abromson Memorial Scholarship, 236
Maine Innkeepers Association Scholarship, 321
The Maine Loan, 577
Maine Metal Products Association Scholarship, 322
Maine Robert C. Byrd Honors Scholarship, 239
Maine Society of Professional Engineers Scholarship Program, 322
Maine Veterans Services Dependents Educational Benefits, 321
Massachusetts MASSgrant Program, 328
Moody's Mega Math "M3" Challenge, 341
NEBHE's Tuition Break Regional Student Program, 380
New England FEMARA Scholarship, 166
OMNE/Nursing Leaders of Maine Scholarship, 402
President's Parley Nursing Scholarship, 124
Russ Casey Scholarship, 322
Senator George J. Mitchell Scholarship, 435
Timothy S. and Palmer W. Bigelow Scholarship, 285
Yankee Clipper Contest Club, Inc. Youth Scholarship, 168

Maryland

Adler Science and Math Scholarship, 124
American Legion Maryland Auxiliary Scholarship, 125
American Legion Maryland Boys State Scholarship, 124
American Legion Maryland Oratorical Contest, 124
American Legion Maryland Scholarship, 124
Carville M. Akehurst Memorial Scholarship, 284
Charles W. Riley Fire and Emergency Medical Services Tuition Reimbursement Program, 324
College Scholarship Program, 219
The Cynthia E. Morgan Memorial Scholarship Fund, 226

Howard P. Rawlings Guaranteed
Access Grant, 324
Letitia B. Carter Scholarship, 427
Marcia S. Harris Legacy Fund
Scholarship, 427
Maryland Delegate Scholarship, 325
Maryland Distinguished Scholar:
Achievement, 325
Maryland Distinguished Scholar:
National Merit and National
Achievement Finalists, 325
Maryland Distinguished Scholar:
Talent in the Arts, 325
Maryland Educational Assistance
Grant, 326
Maryland Jack F. Tolbert Memorial
Grant, 326
Maryland Part-Time Grant
Program, 327
Maryland Senatorial Scholarship, 327
Moody's Mega Math "M3"
Challenge, 341
Past President's Parley
Scholarship, 110
Southern Nursery Organization Sidney
B. Meadows Scholarship, 469
Tuition Waiver for Foster Care
Recipients, 327
Undergraduate Scholarship, 516

Massachusetts

American Legion Massachusetts
Auxiliary Scholarship, 126
American Legion Massachusetts
General and Nursing
Scholarships, 125
College Scholarship Program, 219
Department of Massachusetts
Oratorical Contest, 125
Dr. James L. Lawson Memorial
Scholarship, 163
John F. Kennedy Scholars Award, 329
John Joseph Moakely Democratic
Internship, 545
Massachusetts Christian A. Herter
Memorial Scholarship Program, 328
Massachusetts Gilbert Matching
Student Grant, 328
Massachusetts MASSgrant
Program, 328
Massachusetts No Interest Loan, 577
Massachusetts Public Service Grant
Program, 328
Massachusetts Robert C. Byrd Honors
Scholarship, 329
Massachusetts Scholarship, 490
Moody's Mega Math "M3"
Challenge, 341
NEBHE's Tuition Break Regional
Student Program, 380
New England FEMARA
Scholarship, 166
Past President's Parley
Scholarship, 126
Paul Tsongas Scholarship
Program, 328

PHCC Auxiliary of Massachusetts
Scholarship, 420
Timothy S. and Palmer W. Bigelow
Scholarship, 285
Yankee Clipper Contest Club, Inc.
Youth Scholarship, 168

Michigan

American Legion Michigan Auxiliary
Memorial Scholarship, 127
American Legion Michigan Oratorical
Contest, 126
ARRL Earl I. Anderson
Scholarship, 162
Children of Veterans Tuition
Grant, 330
David Arver Memorial
Scholarship, 80
Guy M. Wilson Scholarship, 126
Kathy LeTarte Scholarship, 489
Medical Career Scholarships, 127
Michigan Competitive
Scholarship, 330
Michigan Robert C. Byrd Honors
Scholarship, 331
Michigan Scholarship, 490
Michigan Society of Professional
Engineers Scholarships for High
School Seniors, 331
Michigan Tuition Grant, 331
Midwest Student Exchange
Program, 332
MSGC Undergraduate
Underrepresented Minority
Fellowship Program, 346
National President's Scholarship, 127
North Central Region
Scholarship, 447
Tuition Incentive Program, 331
William D. & Jewell W. Brewer
Scholarship Trusts, 126
Young Survivor Scholarship, 89
Zachary Taylor Stevens Memorial
Scholarship, 169

Minnesota

AICP Heartland Chapter
Scholarship, 198
American Legion Minnesota Auxiliary
Department Scholarship, 128
American Legion Minnesota
Legionnaire Insurance Trust
Scholarship, 127
American Legion Minnesota
Oratorical Contest, 127
Burlington Northern Santa Fe
Foundation Scholarship, 104
David Arver Memorial
Scholarship, 80
Horatio Alger Minnesota Scholarship
Program, 282
Midwest Student Exchange
Program, 332
Minnesota Achieve Scholarship, 334
The Minnesota American Legion
Memorial Scholarship, 128

Minnesota Educational Assistance for
Surviving Spouse or
Dependent, 333
Minnesota Educational Assistance for
Veterans, 334
Minnesota GI Bill, 334
Minnesota Indian Scholarship
Program, 334
Minnesota Post-Secondary Child Care
Grant, 335
Minnesota Public Safety Officers
Survivors Program, 335
Minnesota State Grant Program, 335
Minnesota Work-Study Program, 546
North Central Region
Scholarship, 447
Past President's Parley Health Care
Scholarship, 128
Scholarship for People with
Disabilities, 226
Travelers Foundation, 103

Mississippi

American Legion Mississippi
Auxiliary Scholarship, 128
Critical Needs Alternative Route
Teacher Loan/Scholarship, 578
Fred R. McDaniel Memorial
Scholarship, 164
Gulf Coast Hurricane
Scholarships, 449
Leveraging Educational Assistance
Partnership Program (LEAP), 336
Mississippi Eminent Scholars
Grant, 336
Mississippi Health Care Professions
Loan/Scholarship, 579
Mississippi Higher Education
Legislative Plan, 336
Mississippi Nursing Education
Loan/Scholarship, 579
Mississippi Scholarship, 166
Mississippi Tuition Assistance
Grant, 337
Mississippi William Winter Teacher
Scholar Loan Program, 579
Nissan Scholarship, 337
Southern Nursery Organization Sidney
B. Meadows Scholarship, 469

Missouri

Access Missouri Financial Assistance
Program, 337
AICP Heartland Chapter
Scholarship, 198
American Legion Missouri Auxiliary
Scholarship, 131
Chapter 52 - Wichita Scholarship, 443
Charles L. Bacon Memorial
Scholarship, 129
Commander's Scholarship Fund, 129
David Arver Memorial
Scholarship, 80
Erman W. Taylor Memorial
Scholarship, 129
Horatio Alger Missouri Scholarship
Program, 282

Joseph J. Frank Scholarship, 129
Lillie Lois Ford Boys'
    Scholarship, 130
Lillie Lois Ford Girls'
    Scholarship, 130
Margo Ballard and Vivian Meinecke
    Memorial Scholarship, 339
Marguerite Ross Barnett Memorial
    Scholarship, 338
M.D. "Jack" Murphy Memorial
    Nurses Training Fund, 130
Midwest Student Exchange
    Program, 332
Missouri Department of Higher
    Education Vietnam Veteran's
    Survivor Grant Program, 338
Missouri Higher Education "Bright
    Flight" Academic Scholarship, 338
Missouri League for Nursing
    Scholarship, 339
Missouri Minority Teaching
    Scholarship, 338
Missouri Public Safety Officer or
    Employee's Child Survivor
    Grant, 339
Missouri Robert C. Byrd Honors
    Scholarship, 337
NASA Missouri State Space Grant
    Undergraduate Scholarship, 347
Past President's Parley
    Scholarship, 131
Paul and Helen L. Grauer
    Scholarship, 167
PHD Amateur Radio Association
    Scholarship, 167
Shane Dean Voyles Memorial
    Scholarship, 130
Southern Nursery Organization Sidney
    B. Meadows Scholarship, 469

Montana

Aloha Scholarship, 131
American Legion Montana Auxiliary
    Scholarships (1), 131
American Legion Montana Auxiliary
    Scholarships (2), 131
Burlington Northern Santa Fe
    Foundation Scholarship, 104
Cady McDonnell Memorial
    Scholarship, 92
Earl Dedman Memorial
    Scholarship, 95
Governor's High School Merit
    Scholarship, 339
Governor's Merit-at-Large
    Scholarship, 340
Governor's Need Based
    Scholarship, 340
Horatio Alger Montana Scholarship
    Program, 282
Legacy of Hope, 473
Mary Lou Brown Scholarship, 166
The Merchants Exhange Scholarship
    Fund, 330
Montana Higher Education Grant, 340
Montana Tuition Fee Waiver for
    Veterans, 340

Montana University System
    Community College Honor
    Scholarship, 340
Montana University System Honor
    Scholarship, 341
Pacific Northwest Chapter/William
    Hunt Scholarship, 492
RCMI Technical/Trade School
    Scholarship, 428
Rocky Mountain Coal Mining
    Institute Scholarship, 428
Siegel Service Technology
    Scholarships, 432
Travelers Foundation, 103
Treacy Company Scholarship, 495

Nebraska

AICP Heartland Chapter
    Scholarship, 198
American Legion Nebraska Oratorical
    Contest, 133
American Legion Nebraska
    President's Scholarship, 134
Averyl Elaine Keriakedes Memorial
    Scholarship, 134
David Arver Memorial
    Scholarship, 80
Edgar J. Boschult Memorial
    Scholarship, 134
Horatio Alger Ak-Sar-Ben Scholarship
    Program, 280
Junior Member Scholarship, 134
Maynard Jensen American Legion
    Memorial Scholarship, 134
Midwest Student Exchange
    Program, 332
Nebraska Robert C. Byrd Honors
    Scholarship, 379
Nebraska State Grant, 379
North Central Region
    Scholarship, 447
Nurse Gift Tuition Scholarships, 134
Paul and Helen L. Grauer
    Scholarship, 167
PHD Amateur Radio Association
    Scholarship, 167
Practical Nursing Scholarship, 135
Richard W. Bendicksen Memorial
    Scholarship, 167
Roberta Marie Stretch Memorial
    Scholarship, 135
Ruby Paul Campaign Fund
    Scholarship, 135
Student Aid Grant or Vocational
    Technical Scholarship, 135

Nevada

ABC Stores Jumpstart
    Scholarship, 252
American Legion Nevada Oratorical
    Contest, 135
Cady McDonnell Memorial
    Scholarship, 92
Carl N. & Margaret Karcher
    Founders' Scholarship, 212
HSBC-North America Scholarship
    Program, 277

Italian Catholic Federation
    Scholarship, 299
Nevada Robert C. Byrd Honors
    Scholarship, 379
Nevada Student Incentive Grant, 380
Past President's Parley Nurses'
    Scholarship, 136
President's Scholarship, 136
Silver Eagle Indian Scholarship, 136
William J. and Marijane E. Adams, Jr.
    Scholarship, 194

New Hampshire

Abbie Sargent Memorial
    Scholarship, 73
Adrienne Alix Scholarship, 138
Albert T. Marcoux Memorial
    Scholarship, 136
American Legion New Hampshire
    Boys State Scholarship, 136
American Legion New Hampshire
    Oratorical Contest, 136
Christa McAuliffe Memorial
    Scholarship, 136
College Scholarship Program, 219
Department of New Hampshire
    Scholarship, 137
Department Vocational
    Scholarship, 137
Dr. James L. Lawson Memorial
    Scholarship, 163
Elsie B. Brown Scholarship Fund, 138
Grace S. High Memorial Child
    Welfare Scholarship Fund, 138
John A. High Child Welfare
    Scholarship, 137
Leaf Loan Program, 580
Marion J. Bagley Scholarship, 138
Massachusetts MASSgrant
    Program, 328
Moody's Mega Math "M3"
    Challenge, 341
NEBHE's Tuition Break Regional
    Student Program, 380
New England FEMARA
    Scholarship, 166
New Hampshire Incentive
    Program, 380
New Hampshire Scholarship for
    Orphans of Veterans, 381
Past President's Parley Nurses'
    Scholarship, 138
Raymond K. Conley Memorial
    Scholarship, 137
Timothy S. and Palmer W. Bigelow
    Scholarship, 285
Workforce Incentive Program, 580
Yankee Clipper Contest Club, Inc.
    Youth Scholarship, 168

New Jersey

AIA New Jersey Scholarship
    Foundation, 106
Alexander Harris Scholarship, 487
American Legion New Jersey
    Auxiliary Department
    Scholarships, 139

American Legion New Jersey
Oratorical Contest, 139
American Legion Press Club of New
Jersey and Post 170--Arthur
Dehardt Memorial Scholarship, 146
Caroline Thorn Kissel Summer
Environmental Studies
Scholarship, 244
Claire Oliphant Memorial
Scholarship, 139
College Scholarship Program, 219
Dana Christmas Scholarship for
Heroism, 382
Frank D. Visceglia Memorial
Scholarship, 204
Japanese American General
Scholarship, 305
Law Enforcement Officer Memorial
Scholarship, 382
Lawrence Luterman Memorial
Scholarships, 139
The L.B. Cebik, W4RNL, and Jean
Cebik, N4TZP, Memorial
Scholarship, 165
Los Padres Foundation College
Tuition Assistance Program, 319
Moody's Mega Math "M3"
Challenge, 341
New Jeresy Student Tuition Assistance
Reward Scholarship
(NJSTARS), 382
New Jersey Educational Opportunity
Fund Grant, 381
New Jersey Edward J. Bloustein
Distinguished Scholars, 382
New Jersey POW/MIA Tuition Benefit
Program, 381
New Jersey Scholarship, 462, 491
New Jersey STARS II, 382
New Jersey Tuition Aid Grants
(TAG), 383
New Jersey Urban Scholars, 383
New Jersey War Orphans Tuition
Assistance Program, 381
New Jersey World Trade Center
Scholarship, 383
Part-Time Tuition Aid Grant for
County Colleges, 383
Past President's Parley Nurses'
Scholarship, 139
Second Chance Program, 319
Sonia Streuli Maguire Outstanding
Scholastic Achievement Award, 476
Stutz Memorial Scholarship, 139
Swiss Benevolent Society Pellegrini
Scholarship, 476
Undergraduate Scholarship, 516
Water Companies (NJ Chapter)
Scholarship, 357
Yankee Clipper Contest Club, Inc.
Youth Scholarship, 168

New Mexico

Albuquerque ARC/Toby Cross
Scholarship, 162
Burlington Northern Santa Fe
Foundation Scholarship, 104

Cady McDonnell Memorial
Scholarship, 92
Carl N. & Margaret Karcher
Founders' Scholarship, 212
Central New Mexico Scholarship, 454
Fred R. McDaniel Memorial
Scholarship, 164
National President's Scholarship, 140
New Mexico Allied Health Student
Loan-for-Service Program, 580
New Mexico Legislative Endowment
Program, 384
New Mexico Legislative Lottery
Scholarship, 384
New Mexico Nursing Student
Loan-for-Service, 581
New Mexico Scholars Program, 384
New Mexico Student Choice
Grant, 385
New Mexico Student Incentive
Grant, 385
New Mexico Teacher's
Loan-for-Service, 581
New Mexico Vietnam Veteran's
Scholarship, 385
New Mexico Work-Study
Program, 553
Past President's Parley Scholarship for
Nurses, 140
RCMI Technical/Trade School
Scholarship, 428
Rocky Mountain Coal Mining
Institute Scholarship, 428
Walt Bartram Memorial Education
Award (Region 12 and Chapter
119), 447

New York

Albert E. Wischmeyer Memorial
Scholarship Award, 441
Alexander Harris Scholarship, 487
American Legion New York Auxiliary
Scholarship, 141
American Legion New York
Oratorical Contest, 140
Caroline Kark Scholarship, 386
Christian Wolffer Scholarship, 301
City University SEEK/College
Discovery Program, 387
College Scholarship Program, 219
Dr. James L. Lawson Memorial
Scholarship, 163
Eleanor Allwork Scholarship, 213
Flight 587 Memorial
Scholarships, 387
Grange Denise Scholarship, 386
Grange Student Loan Fund, 581
Grange Susan W. Freestone Education
Award, 386
Henry Broughton, K2AE Memorial
Scholarship, 164
HSBC-North America Scholarship
Program, 277
Japanese American General
Scholarship, 305
June Gill Nursing Scholarship, 387

Los Padres Foundation College
Tuition Assistance Program, 319
MCC Theater Internships, 545
Military Service Recognition
Scholarship (MSRS), 387
Moody's Mega Math "M3"
Challenge, 341
New York American Legion Press
Association Scholarship, 140
New York Scholarship, 491
New York State Aid for Part-time
Study Program, 388
New York State Arthur O. Eve Higher
Education Opportunity Program
(HEOP), 385
New York State Memorial Scholarship
for Families of Deceased
Police/Volunteer Firefighters/Peace
Officers and Emergency Medical
Service Workers, 388
New York State Native American
Student Aid Program, 389
New York State Readers Aid
Program, 397
New York State Regents Awards for
Children of Deceased and Disabled
Veterans, 388
New York State Robert C. Byrd
Federal Honors Scholarship, 386
New York State Scholarships for
Academic Excellence, 386
New York State Tuition Assistance
Program, 388
New York State Veterans Tuition
Award, 389
Northern California DX Foundation
Scholarship, 166
Past President's Parley Student
Scholarship in Medical Field, 141
Peter F. Vallone Academic
Scholarship, 217
Second Chance Program, 319
Sonia Streuli Maguire Outstanding
Scholastic Achievement Award, 476
Swiss Benevolent Society Pellegrini
Scholarship, 476
Yankee Clipper Contest Club, Inc.
Youth Scholarship, 168

North Carolina

American Legion Oratorical
Contest, 141
ASHRAE Region IV Benny Bootle
Scholarship, 172
Colon Furr Scholarship, 141
Community College Grant &
Loan, 581
The Dayton Amateur Radio
Association Scholarships, 163
GlaxoSmithKline Opportunity
Scholarship, 392
Golden LEAF Scholars Program -
Two-Year Colleges, 393
Golden LEAF Scholarship - Four-Year
University Program, 393
Jagannathan Scholarship, 393
L. Phil Wicker Scholarship, 165

Latino Diamante Scholarship Fund, 393

Maya Angelou/Vivian Baxter Scholarship, 499

Moody's Mega Math "M3" Challenge, 341

Nannie W. Norfleet Scholarship, 142

NC Sheriff's Association Criminal Justice Scholarship, 393

New Horizons Rene Campbell Memorial Scholarship, 490

North Carolina Aubrey Lee Brooks Scholarship, 394

North Carolina Community Colleges Wachovia Technical Scholarship, 391

North Carolina Legislative Tuition Grant, 394

North Carolina Nurse Scholars Program, 582

North Carolina Scholarships for Children of War Veterans, 392

North Carolina State Board of Refrigeration Examiners Scholarship, 392

North Carolina Student Incentive Grant, 394

North Carolina Student Loans for Health/Science/Mathematics, 582

North Carolina Vocational Rehabilitation Award, 392

Rodney E. Powell Memorial Scholarship, 391

Southern Nursery Organization Sidney B. Meadows Scholarship, 469

State Contractual Scholarship Fund, 394

Teacher Assistant Scholarship Fund, 395

North Dakota

AICP Heartland Chapter Scholarship, 198

American Legion North Dakota Auxiliary Scholarships, 142

American Legion North Dakota Oratorical Contest, 142

Burlington Northern Santa Fe Foundation Scholarship, 104

David Arver Memorial Scholarship, 80

Hattie Tedrow Memorial Fund Scholarship, 142

Horatio Alger North Dakota Scholarship Program, 283

Midwest Student Exchange Program, 332

North Central Region Scholarship, 447

North Dakota Indian Scholarship Program, 395

North Dakota Scholars Program, 395

North Dakota State Student Incentive Grant, 395

Past President's Parley Scholarship, 142

RCMI Technical/Trade School Scholarship, 428

Rocky Mountain Coal Mining Institute Scholarship, 428

South Dakota Ardell Bjugstad Scholarship, 468

Treacy Company Scholarship, 495

Ohio

AdOhio Advertising Internship, 558

American Legion Ohio Auxiliary Past President's Parley Nurse's Scholarship, 143

American Legion Ohio Auxiliary Scholarship, 143

David L. Stashower Scholarship, 318

Department Oratorical Awards, 143

Engineers Foundation of Ohio Scholarships, 234

Harold K. Douthit Scholarship, 398

NEMAL Electronics Scholarship, 166

NMIA Ohio Scholarship Program, 390

Ohio College Opportunity Grant, 397

Ohio National Guard Scholarship Program, 398

Ohio Newspaper Association Publications/Public Relations Internship, 558

Ohio Newspapers Minority Scholarship, 399

Ohio Newspapers Women's Scholarship, 399

Ohio Nurse Education Assistance Loan Program, 582

Ohio Safety Officers College Memorial Fund, 398

Ohio Scholarship, 491

Ohio War Orphans Scholarship, 398

University Journalism Scholarship, 399

Zachary Taylor Stevens Memorial Scholarship, 169

Oklahoma

Academic Scholars Program, 400

ASHRAE Region VIII Scholarship, 173

Austin Family Scholarship Endowment, 101

Burlington Northern Santa Fe Foundation Scholarship, 104

Carl N. & Margaret Karcher Founders' Scholarship, 212

Chapter 52 - Wichita Scholarship, 443

Fred R. McDaniel Memorial Scholarship, 164

Future Teachers Scholarship, 400

Heartland Scholarship Fund, 400

Independent Living Act (Department of Human Services Tuition Waiver), 400

National Guard Tuition Waiver, 401

Oklahoma Engineering Foundation Scholarship, 399

Oklahoma Tuition Aid Grant, 401

Oklahoma's Promise - Oklahoma Higher Learning Access Program, 401

Regional University Baccalaureate Scholarship, 401

Robert C. Byrd Honors Scholarship Program, 400

Southern Nursery Organization Sidney B. Meadows Scholarship, 469

Tom and Judith Comstock Scholarship, 168

Oregon

Ahmad-Sehar Saleha Ahmad and Abrahim Ekramullah Zafar Foundation, 403

Albina Fuel Company Scholarship, 403

Allcott/Hunt Share It Now II Scholarship, 403

Alpha Delta Kappa/Harriet Simmons Scholarship, 403

American Council of Engineering Companies of Oregon Scholarship, 403

American Legion Auxiliary Department of Oregon Scholarship, 144

American Legion Department Oratorical Contest, 144

American Legion Oregon Auxiliary Department Nurses Scholarship, 144

Audria M. Edwards Scholarship Fund, 414

Bandon Submarine Cable Council Scholarship, 404

Bank of the Cascades Scholarship, 404

Ben Selling Scholarship, 404

Benjamin Franklin/Edith Green Scholarship, 404

Bertha P. Singer Scholarship, 405

Bob Hasson Memorial Scholarship Fund Essay, 402

Burlington Northern Santa Fe Foundation Scholarship, 104

Cady McDonnell Memorial Scholarship, 92

Carl N. & Margaret Karcher Founders' Scholarship, 212

Chafee Education and Training Scholarship, 405

Clark-Phelps Scholarship, 405

Darfur Humanitarian Essay, 405

Darlene Hooley for Oregon Veterans Scholarship, 405

David Family Scholarship, 406

Dorothy Campbell Memorial Scholarship, 406

DPMA/PC Scholarship, 228

Earl Dedman Memorial Scholarship, 95

Eugene Bennet Visual Arts Scholarship, 406

Fashion Group International of Portland Scholarship, 406

Eligibility Indexes

Ford Opportunity Program, 406
Ford Scholars Program, 407
Frank Stenzel M.D. and Kathryn Stenzel II Scholarship, 407
Glenn Jackson Scholars, 407
Grange Insurance Scholarship, 251
Healthy Waters Institute of the Freshwater Trust, 407
Homestead Capital Housing Scholarship, 407
Ida M. Crawford Scholarship, 408
Jackson Foundation Journalism Scholarship, 408
James Carlson Memorial Scholarship, 408
Jeffrey Alan Scoggins Memorial Scholarship, 408
Jerome B. Steinbach Scholarship, 409
Jose D. Garcia Migrant Education Scholarship, 409
Laurence R. Foster Memorial Scholarship, 409
Maria C. Jackson-General George A. White Scholarship, 409
Mary Lou Brown Scholarship, 166
The Merchants Exhange Scholarship Fund, 330
NASA Space Grant Oregon Undergraduate Scholarship, 350
National President's Scholarship, 144
Neil Hamilton Memorial Scholarship, 409
Oregon Dungeness Crab Commission, 410
Oregon Foundation for Blacktail Deer Outdoor & Wildlife Scholarship, 410
Oregon Occupational Safety and Health Division Workers Memorial Scholarship, 410
Oregon Robert C. Byrd Honors Scholarship, 410
Oregon Scholarship Fund Community College Student Award Programs, 410
Pacific Northwest Chapter/William Hunt Scholarship, 492
Professional Land Surveyors of Oregon Scholarship, 411
Spirit of Youth Scholarship, 144
Teamsters Clyde C. Crosby/Joseph M. Edgar Memorial Scholarship, 411
Teamsters Council #37 Federal Credit Union Scholarship, 411
Teamsters Local 305 Scholarship, 412
Walter and Marie Schmidt Scholarship, 412

Pennsylvania

American Legion High School Oratorical Contest, 145
Chafee Education and Training Grant (ETG) Program, 415
College Scholarship Program, 219
Dr. & Mrs. Arthur William Phillips Scholarship, 417
Gaining Early Awareness and Readiness for Undergraduate Programs (GEAR UP) Scholarship, 415
Horatio Alger Franklin Scholarship, 281
Horatio Alger Pennsylvania Scholarship Program, 283
James Hughes Memorial Scholarship Fund, 417
John McKee Scholarship, 329
Joseph P. Gavenonis Scholarship, 145
Massachusetts MASSgrant Program, 328
Moody's Mega Math "M3" Challenge, 341
NASA Academy Internship, 550
Partnership for Access to Higher Education (PATH), 415
Pennsylvania Robert C. Byrd Honors Scholarship, 415
Pennsylvania State Grant Program, 415
Pennsylvania Work-Study Program, 416
Pittsburgh Scholarship, 449
Postsecondary Educational Gratuity Program, 416
Rainbow Scholarship, 422
Robert Noyce Scholarship Program, 418
Robert W. Valimont Endowment Fund Scholarship, 145
Scholarship for Children of Deceased or Totally Disabled Veterans, 145
Scholarship for Children of Living Veterans, 145
SciTech Scholarship, 416
Shannon Scholarship, 495
Sonia Streuli Maguire Outstanding Scholastic Achievement Award, 476
Swiss Benevolent Society Pellegrini Scholarship, 476
Technology Scholarship, 416
Undergraduate Scholarship, 516
Washington Crossing Foundation Scholarship, 514
Wayne G. Failor Scholarship, 418
West Virginia Higher Education Grant, 518
Yankee Clipper Contest Club, Inc. Youth Scholarship, 168
You've Got a Friend in Pennsylvania Scholarship, 169

Puerto Rico

American Legion Puerto Rico Auxiliary Nursing Scholarships, 146
Second Chance Program, 319

Rhode Island

American Legion Rhode Island Auxiliary Book Award, 146
American Legion Rhode Island Oratorical Contest, 146
College Bound Fund Academic Promise Scholarship, 427
College Scholarship Program, 219
Dr. James L. Lawson Memorial Scholarship, 163
Massachusetts MASSgrant Program, 328
Moody's Mega Math "M3" Challenge, 341
NEBHE's Tuition Break Regional Student Program, 380
New England FEMARA Scholarship, 166
Rhode Island State Government Internship Program, 561
Rhode Island State Grant, 427
Timothy S. and Palmer W. Bigelow Scholarship, 285
Yankee Clipper Contest Club, Inc. Youth Scholarship, 168

South Carolina

American Legion South Carolina Auxiliary Scholarship, 147
American Legion South Carolina Department Oratorical Contest, 147
ASHRAE Region IV Benny Bootle Scholarship, 172
C.G. Fuller Foundation Scholarship, 215
Charleston Women in International Trade Scholarship, 216
Dayco Scholarship Program, 466
James F. Byrnes Scholarship, 304
L. Phil Wicker Scholarship, 165
LIFE Scholarship Program, 466
Lighthouse College-Bound Award, 319
Lottery Tuition Assistance Program, 466
Moody's Mega Math "M3" Challenge, 341
Palmetto Fellows Scholarship Program, 467
South Carolina HOPE Scholarships, 467
South Carolina Need-Based Grants Program, 467
South Carolina Teacher Loans, 583
South Carolina Tuition Grants, 467
Southern Nursery Organization Sidney B. Meadows Scholarship, 469

South Dakota

AICP Heartland Chapter Scholarship, 198
American Legion South Dakota Auxiliary Nurse's Scholarship, 147
American Legion South Dakota Auxiliary Scholarships, 147
American Legion South Dakota Educational Loan, 574
American Legion South Dakota Oratorical Contest, 147
Burlington Northern Santa Fe Foundation Scholarship, 104

David Arver Memorial
Scholarship, 80
Horatio Alger South Dakota
Scholarship Program, 283
North Central Region
Scholarship, 447
Scholarship for College or
Vocational, 148
South Dakota Annis I. Fowler/Kaden
Scholarship, 468
South Dakota Ardell Bjugstad
Scholarship, 468
South Dakota Haines Memorial
Scholarship, 468
South Dakota Marlin R. Scarborough
Memorial Scholarship, 468
South Dakota Opportunity Scholarship
Program, 469
South Dakota Robert C. Byrd Honors
Scholarship, 469
Thelma Foster Junior American
Legion Auxiliary Members
Scholarship, 148
Thelma Foster Senior American
Legion Auxiliary Member
Scholarship, 148

Tennessee

American Legion Tennessee
Oratorical Contest, 148
Dual Enrollment Grant, 477
Eagle Scout of the Year
Scholarship, 148
Helping Heroes Grant, 477
Hope Foster Child Tuition Grant, 477
HOPE-Aspire Award, 477
Hope-General Assembly Merit
Scholarship, 478
Internship Program for Laboratory
Technology, 555
Scarlett Family Foundation
Scholarship, 434
Southern Nursery Organization Sidney
B. Meadows Scholarship, 469
Tennessee Dependent Children
Scholarship Program, 478
Tennessee HOPE Access Grant, 478
Tennessee HOPE Scholarship, 478
Tennessee Minority Teaching Fellows
Program, 584
Tennessee Ned McWherter Scholars
Program, 479
Tennessee Robert C. Byrd Honors
Scholarship Program, 479
Tennessee Student Assistance Award
Program, 479
Tennessee Student Assistance
Corporation/Math And Science
Teachers Loan Forgiveness
Program, 584
Tennessee Teaching Scholars
Program, 584
Vara Gray Scholarship Fund, 149
Wilder-Naifeh Technical Skills
Grant, 479

Texas

American Legion Texas Auxiliary
General Education Scholarship, 149
American Legion Texas Auxiliary
Medical Scholarship, 149
Area Go Texan Scholarships, 286
ASHRAE Region VIII
Scholarship, 173
Blue Bell Scholarship, 480
C. J. Davidson Scholarship, 480
Carl N. & Margaret Karcher
Founders' Scholarship, 212
College Access Loan (CAL), 584
Concurrent Enrollment Waiver
(Enrollment in Two Texas
Community Colleges), 481
Dallas Architectural Foundation -
Humphries/HKS Scholarship, 226
Dallas Architectural Foundation -
Swank Travelling Fellowship, 227
Dr. Dan J. and Patricia S. Pickard
Scholarship, 227
Dr. Don and Rose Marie Benton
Scholarship, 227
Educational Aide Exemption, 481
Engineering Scholarship Program, 481
Exemption for Peace Officers
Disabled in the Line of Duty, 482
Exemption for the Surviving Spouse
and Dependent Children of Certain
Deceased Public Servants
(Employees), 482
FFA Scholarships, 481
Fred R. McDaniel Memorial
Scholarship, 164
The George Foreman Tribute to
Lyndon B. Johnson
Scholarship, 424
Gulf Coast Hurricane
Scholarships, 449
Horatio Alger Texas Ft. Worth
Scholarship Program, 283
Horatio Alger Texas Scholarship
Program, 284
Houston Livestock Show and Rodeo
Scholarships, 480
HSBC-North America Scholarship
Program, 277
Jere W. Thompson, Jr. Scholarship
Fund, 227
The Mayor's Chesapeake Energy
Scholarship, 228
Metropolitan Scholarships, 286
Opportunity Scholarship, 286
Peters Scholarship, 228
RCMI Technical/Trade School
Scholarship, 428
Reduction in Tuition Charges for
Students Taking 15 or More
Semester Credit Hours Per
Term, 482
Robert C. Byrd Honors
Scholarship, 482
Rocky Mountain Coal Mining
Institute Scholarship, 428
School Art Scholarships, 286

Southern Nursery Organization Sidney
B. Meadows Scholarship, 469
TANF (Temporary Assistance to
Needy Families) Exemption, 483
Texas 4-H Opportunity
Scholarships, 479
Texas Early High School Graduation
Scholarship, 483
Texas Farm Bureau Scholarship, 480
Texas Fifth-Year Accounting Student
Scholarship Program, 483
Texas Foster Care Students
Exemption, 483
Texas Good Neighbor
Scholarship, 483
TEXAS Grant (Toward Excellence,
Access, and Success), 483
Texas Hazlewood Act Tuition
Exemption: Veterans, 484
Texas Highest Ranking High School
Graduate Tuition Exemption, 484
Texas Legion Oratorical Contest, 149
Texas National Guard Tuition
Assistance Program, 484
Texas Public Educational Grant, 484
Texas Scholarships for Nursing
Students, 485
Texas Tuition Exemption for Blind or
Deaf Students, 485
Tom and Judith Comstock
Scholarship, 168
The Tommy Tranchin Award, 228
Toyota Motor Sales U.S.A., Inc.
Scholarship, 278
Tuition Equalization Grant
(TEG), 485
Tuition Exemption for Children of
Disabled or Deceased Firefighters,
Peace Officers, Game Wardens, and
Employees of Correctional
Institutions, 485
Tuition Exemption for Children of
U.S. Military POW/MIAs from
Texas, 485
Tuition Rebate for Certain
Undergraduates, 486

U.S. Territories

National Co-op Scholarship, 359

Utah

American Legion Utah Auxiliary
National President's
Scholarship, 150
Cady McDonnell Memorial
Scholarship, 92
Carl N. & Margaret Karcher
Founders' Scholarship, 212
Horatio Alger Utah Scholarship
Program, 284
Leveraging Educational Assistance
Partnership (LEAP), 505
RCMI Technical/Trade School
Scholarship, 428
Rocky Mountain Coal Mining
Institute Scholarship, 428
UHEAA Grant, 505

Utah Career Teaching
Scholarship/T.H. Bell Teaching
Incentive Loan, 586
Utah Centennial Opportunity Program
for Education (UCOPE), 505
Utah Keith Griffall Scholarship, 493
Utah Robert C. Byrd Honors
Scholarship, 506

Vermont

AIWF Culinary Scholarship, 507
Alfred T. Granger Student Art
Fund, 507
American Legion Eagle Scout of the
Year, 150
American Legion Vermont
Scholarship, 150
Calvin Coolidge Memorial
Foundation Scholarship, 507
Champlain Valley Kennel Club
Scholarship, 507
Charles E. Leonard Memorial
Scholarship, 507
Chittenden Bank Scholarship, 508
College Scholarship Program, 219
Dr. James L. Lawson Memorial
Scholarship, 163
Emily Lester Vermont Opportunity
Scholarship, 508
Jedidiah Zabrosky Scholarship, 508
Kittredge Coddington Memorial
Scholarship, 508
Lee A. Lyman Memorial Music
Scholarship, 508
Lighthouse College-Bound
Award, 319
Massachusetts MASSgrant
Program, 328
Moody's Mega Math "M3"
Challenge, 341
NASA Space Grant Vermont
Consortium Undergraduate
Scholarships, 352
National High School Oratorical
Contest, 150
NEBHE's Tuition Break Regional
Student Program, 380
New England FEMARA
Scholarship, 166
Operation Enduring Freedom and
Operation Iraqi Freedom
Scholarship, 509
Patrick and Judith McHugh
Scholarship, 509
Philip and Alice Angell Eastern Star
Scholarship, 509
RehabGYM Scholarship, 509
Samara Foundation of Vermont
Scholarship, 510
Students With Disabilities Endowed
Scholarship Honoring Elizabeth
Daley Jeffords, 510
Timothy S. and Palmer W. Bigelow
Scholarship, 285
Vermont Alliance for Arts Education
(VAEE) Scholarship, 510

Vermont Golf Association
Scholarship, 506
Vermont Incentive Grant, 510
Vermont John H. Chafee Education
and Training Scholarship, 510
Vermont Non-Degree Program, 511
Vermont Part-Time Grant, 511
Yankee Clipper Contest Club, Inc.
Youth Scholarship, 168

Virgin Islands

Virgin Islands Leveraging Educational
Assistance Partnership
Program, 511
Virgin Islands Music Scholarship, 511
Virgin Islands Territorial Grants/Loans
Program, 586

Virginia

American Legion Virginia Oratorical
Contest, 151
Anna Gear Junior Scholarship, 151
Carville M. Akehurst Memorial
Scholarship, 284
Dr. Kate Waller Barrett Grant, 151
HSBC-North America Scholarship
Program, 277
L. Phil Wicker Scholarship, 165
Lighthouse College-Bound
Award, 319
Mary Marshall Nursing LPN
Scholarship, 512
Moody's Mega Math "M3"
Challenge, 341
Nurse Pracitioner Nurse Midwife
Scholarship, 512
Southern Nursery Organization Sidney
B. Meadows Scholarship, 469
Virginia Academic Common
Market, 471
Virginia Lee-Jackson Scholarship, 512
Virginia Museum of Fine Arts
Fellowship, 513
Virginia Rehabilitative Services
College Program, 513
Virginia Robert C. Byrd Honors
Scholarship, 512
Virginia Tuition Assistance Grant, 471

Washington

Albina Fuel Company
Scholarship, 403
American Legion Department
Oratorical Contest, 151
American Legion Washington
Auxiliary Scholarships, 152
American Legion Washington
Scholarships, 151
Arthur and Doreen Parrett
Scholarship, 187
Audria M. Edwards Scholarship
Fund, 414
Burlington Northern Santa Fe
Foundation Scholarship, 104
Cady McDonnell Memorial
Scholarship, 92

Carl N. & Margaret Karcher
Founders' Scholarship, 212
DPMA/PC Scholarship, 228
Earl Dedman Memorial
Scholarship, 95
Edmund F. Maxwell Foundation
Scholarship, 233
Fashion Group International of
Portland Scholarship, 406
Florence Lemcke Memorial
Scholarship, 152
Fred G. Zahn Foundation
Scholarship, 243
Grange Insurance Scholarship, 251
Margarite McAlpin Nurse's
Scholarship, 152
Mary Lou Brown Scholarship, 166
The Merchants Exhange Scholarship
Fund, 330
National Co-op Scholarship, 359
Pacific Northwest Chapter/William
Hunt Scholarship, 492
Seattle Jaycees Scholarship, 435
Seattle Professional Chapter
Scholarship, 197
Susan Burdett Scholarship, 152
Travelers Foundation, 103
Washington State American Indian
Endowed Scholarship, 515
Washington State Need Grant, 515
Washington State Scholars
Program, 515
Washington State Scholarship
Program, 515

West Virginia

American Legion West Virginia
Auxiliary Scholarship, 153
American Legion West Virginia
Oratorical Contest, 153
Carville M. Akehurst Memorial
Scholarship, 284
Greater Kanawha Valley Scholarship
Program, 251
L. Phil Wicker Scholarship, 165
Lighthouse College-Bound
Award, 319
Moody's Mega Math "M3"
Challenge, 341
PROMISE Scholarship, 517
Southern Nursery Organization Sidney
B. Meadows Scholarship, 469
West Virginia Engineering, Science,
and Technology Scholarship, 517
West Virginia Higher Education Adult
Part-time Student (HEAPS) Grant
Program, 517
West Virginia Higher Education
Grant, 518
West Virginia Robert C. Byrd Honors
Scholarship, 518
West Virginia Underwood-Smith
Teacher Scholarship, 518
West Virginia War Orphans
Educational Assistance, 517
William F. Johnson Memorial
Scholarship, 153

Zachary Taylor Stevens Memorial
   Scholarship, 169

Wisconsin

American Legion Wisconsin Auxiliary
   Department President's
   Scholarship, 154
American Legion Wisconsin Auxiliary
   H.S. and Angeline Lewis
   Scholarships, 154
American Legion Wisconsin Auxiliary
   Merit and Memorial
   Scholarship, 154
American Legion Wisconsin Auxiliary
   Past Presidents Parley
   Scholarship, 155
American Legion Wisconsin Eagle
   Scout of the Year Scholarship, 153
Chapter 4 - Lawrence A. Wacker
   Memorial Scholarship, 442
Chicago FM Club Scholarship, 163
David Arver Memorial
   Scholarship, 80
Della Van Deuren Memorial
   Scholarship, 155
Edmond A. Metzger Scholarship, 164
Hudner Medal of Honor
   Scholarship, 237
Midwest Student Exchange
   Program, 332
North Central Region
   Scholarship, 447
Oratorical Contest Scholarships, 153
Schneider-Emanuel American Legion
   Scholarships, 154
Wisconsin Academic Excellence
   Scholarship, 521
Wisconsin Hearing & Visually
   Handicapped Student Grant, 521
Wisconsin Higher Education
   Grant, 521
Wisconsin Indian Student Assistance
   Grant, 521
Wisconsin Minority Teacher Loan
   Program, 587
Wisconsin Minority Undergraduate
   Retention Grant, 521
Wisconsin Talent Incentive Program
   Grant, 522
Wisconsin Tuition Grant, 522
Wisconsin Veterans Affairs Personal
   Loan Program, 586
Wisconsin Veterans Affairs Retraining
   Grant, 520
Wisconsin Veterans Education GI Bill
   Tuition Remission Program, 520

Wyoming

American Legion Wyoming E.A.
   Blackmore Memorial
   Scholarship, 155
American Legion Wyoming Oratorical
   Contest, 155
Cady McDonnell Memorial
   Scholarship, 92
Davis-Roberts Scholarship, 229

Earl Dedman Memorial
   Scholarship, 95
Grange Insurance Scholarship, 251
Horatio Alger Wyoming Scholarship
   Program, 284
The Merchants Exhange Scholarship
   Fund, 330
RCMI Technical/Trade School
   Scholarship, 428
Rocky Mountain Coal Mining
   Institute Scholarship, 428

Study Abroad

Academic-Year Ambassadorial
   Scholarship, 428
Anna K. Meredith Fund
   Scholarship, 473
Clare Brett Smith Scholarship, 473
Elizabeth A. Sackler Museum
   Educational Trust, 473
HACU (Hispanic Association of
   Colleges and Universities)
   Scholarships, 104
International Incentive Awards, 474
International Semester
   Scholarship, 104
Jules Maidoff Scholarship, 474
Kosciuszko Foundation Year Abroad
   Program, 312
Lele Cassin Scholarship, 474
NAFEO (National Association for
   Equal Opportunity in Higher
   Education) Scholarships, 105
SACI Consortium Scholarship, 474
Scholarships for Children of SACI
   Alumni, 474
Swiss Benevolent Society Medicus
   Student Exchange, 476

Scholarships

1199 SEIU Benefit Funds

Joseph Tauber Scholarship

Type of award: Scholarship, renewable.
Intended use: For full-time undergraduate or non-degree study at accredited vocational, 2-year or 4-year institution in or outside United States.
Basis for selection: Applicant must demonstrate financial need.
Application requirements: Transcript, proof of eligibility. CSS profile.
Additional information: Must be receiving family coverage (Wage or Eligibility Class One) through benefit fund. Apply for pre-screening by deadline date; applications sent to qualified candidates. Visit Website for updates. Must apply for renewal.

Amount of award:	$750-$6,000
Number of awards:	2,000
Number of applicants:	5,000
Application deadline:	January 30
Notification begins:	November 1
Total amount awarded:	$4,500,000

Contact:
1199 SEIU Child Care Funds Joseph Tauber Scholarship Program
330 West 42nd Street, 18th Floor
New York, NY 10036-6977
Phone: 646-473-8999
Fax: 646-473-6949
Web: www.1199seiubenefits.org

Abbie Sargent Memorial Scholarship Fund

Abbie Sargent Memorial Scholarship

Type of award: Scholarship, renewable.
Intended use: For undergraduate or graduate study at postsecondary institution.
Eligibility: Applicant must be residing in New Hampshire.
Basis for selection: Major/career interest in agriculture. Applicant must demonstrate financial need, high academic achievement and depth of character.
Application requirements: Recommendations, essay, transcript. Recent photo.
Additional information: Recipient may attend out-of-state university. Send SASE for application or download from Website. Number of awards varies.

Amount of award:	$400-$1,000
Number of applicants:	17
Application deadline:	March 15
Notification begins:	June 1

Contact:
Abbie Sargent Memorial Scholarship
Attn: Melanie Phelps, Treasurer
295 Sheep Davis Road
Concord, NH 03301
Phone: 603-224-1934
Web: www.nhfarmbureau.org

Academy of Television Arts & Sciences Foundation

College Television Awards

Type of award: Scholarship.
Intended use: For full-time undergraduate or graduate study in United States.
Basis for selection: Competition/talent/interest in visual arts, based on excellence of submitted film/video. Major/career interest in radio/television/film.
Application requirements: Submit online: video, 45-second promo, JPEG image optional. Signed faculty form.
Additional information: Award for student producer of video, digital, and film work in the following categories: animation, children's, comedy, commercial, documentary, drama, interactive media, magazine, music (best composition), music (best use), narrative series (includes webisodes), and newscast. Piece must have been produced during the calendar year, while registered in school, and related to either a class or school group. Seymour Bricker Humanitarian Award of $4,000 is presented to the first or second place winner whose work best represents a humanitarian concern. Best directing award is presented for outstanding direction for a documentary, drama, comedy, or series. Application deadline in mid-January; apply online. Visit Website for additional details.

Amount of award:	$500-$2,000
Number of awards:	24
Number of applicants:	600

Contact:
Academy of Television Arts & Sciences Foundation
College Television Awards
5220 Lankershim Boulevard
North Hollywood, CA 91601-3109
Phone: 818-754-2800
Fax: 818-761-2827
Web: www.emmysfoundation.org

The Fred Rogers Memorial Scholarship

Type of award: Scholarship.
Intended use: For undergraduate or graduate study at accredited postsecondary institution.
Basis for selection: Major/career interest in education, early childhood; film/video; music or radio/television/film.
Application requirements: Recommendations. Project plan and budget.

Additional information: Applicant must have ultimate goal of working in children's media and must have studied or have experience in at least two of the following fields: early childhood education, child development/child psychology, film/television production, music, or animation. Download application from Website.

Amount of award:	$10,000
Number of awards:	3
Number of applicants:	100
Application deadline:	February 26
Total amount awarded:	$10,000

Contact:
Academy of Television Arts & Sciences Foundation
Attn: Michele Fowble
5220 Lankershim Boulevard
North Hollywood, CA 91601-3109
Phone: 818-754-2802
Web: www.emmysfoundation.org

ACFE Foundation

Ritchie-Jennings Memorial Scholarship

Type of award: Scholarship.
Intended use: For full-time undergraduate or graduate study at accredited 4-year institution.
Basis for selection: Major/career interest in criminal justice/law enforcement; accounting; business or finance/banking.
Application requirements: Recommendations, essay, transcript.
Additional information: Award includes one-year ACFE Student Associate membership. Notifications of award begins in end of April. Visit Website for additional information.

Amount of award:	$1,000
Number of awards:	30
Number of applicants:	150
Application deadline:	January 15
Total amount awarded:	$30,000

Contact:
ACFE Foundation Scholarships Program Coordinator
The Gregor Building
716 West Avenue
Austin, TX 78701-2727
Phone: 800-245-3321
Fax: 512-478-9297
Web: www.acfe.com/membership/students.asp

The Actuarial Foundation

Actuarial Diversity Scholarships

Type of award: Scholarship, renewable.
Intended use: For full-time undergraduate or graduate study at accredited 2-year, 4-year or graduate institution.
Eligibility: Applicant must be Alaskan native, African American, Mexican American, Hispanic American, Puerto Rican, American Indian or Native Hawaiian/Pacific Islander. Applicant must be U.S. citizen, permanent resident or international student.

Basis for selection: Major/career interest in insurance/actuarial science or mathematics. Applicant must demonstrate high academic achievement.
Application requirements: Recommendations, essay, transcript, proof of eligibility. SAT/ACT scores.
Additional information: Must have at least one birth parent who is Black/African American, Hispanic, or Native American. Applicant must be admitted to institution offering actuarial science program or courses that will prepare student for actuarial career. Minimum 3.0 GPA. Minimum 28 ACT math score or 600 SAT math score. International students must have F1 visa. Visit Website for application, deadline, and more information.

Amount of award:	$1,000-$5,000
Number of awards:	29
Notification begins:	June 15
Total amount awarded:	$62,000

Contact:
The Actuarial Foundation
Minority Scholarship Coordinator
475 North Martingale Road, Suite 600
Schaumburg, IL 60173-2226
Phone: 847-706-3501
Fax: 847-706-3599
Web: www.actuarialfoundation.org/programs/actuarial/scholarships.shtml

Actuary of Tomorrow Stuart A. Robertson Memorial Scholarship

Type of award: Scholarship.
Intended use: For full-time sophomore, junior or senior study at accredited 4-year institution in United States.
Basis for selection: Major/career interest in accounting; mathematics or statistics. Applicant must demonstrate high academic achievement.
Application requirements: Recommendations, essay, transcript.
Additional information: Minimum 3.0 GPA. Must have successfully completed two actuarial exams. Must pursue course of study leading to career in actuarial science. Visit Website for essay topic and application.

Amount of award:	$7,500
Number of awards:	1
Application deadline:	June 1
Notification begins:	August 1
Total amount awarded:	$7,500

Contact:
The Actuarial Foundation
Attn: Actuary of Tomorrow Scholarship
475 N. Martingale Road, Suite 600
Schaumburg, IL 60173-2226
Phone: 847-706-3535
Fax: 847-706-3599
Web: www.actuarialfoundation.org/programs/actuarial/scholarships.shtml

Wooddy Scholarship

Type of award: Scholarship.
Intended use: For full-time senior study at 4-year institution.
Eligibility: Applicant must be U.S. citizen or permanent resident.
Basis for selection: Major/career interest in insurance/actuarial science. Applicant must demonstrate high academic achievement and leadership.

Application requirements: Recommendations, essay, transcript, nomination by professor.

Additional information: Applicant must have passed at least one actuarial examination and must rank in the top quarter of class. Application is available on Website. Immediate relatives of members of the Board of Trustees of the Actuarial Foundation or boards of affiliated organizations are not eligible to apply. Limit one application per school.

Amount of award:	$2,000
Number of awards:	12
Application deadline:	June 24
Total amount awarded:	$24,000

Contact:
The Actuarial Foundation
Attn: John Culver Wooddy Scholarship
475 N. Martingale Road, Suite 600
Schaumburg, IL 60173-2226
Phone: 847-706-3535
Fax: 847-706-3599
Web: www.actuarialfoundation.org/programs/actuarial/scholarships.shtml

ADHA Institute for Oral Health

ADHA Institute General Scholarships

Type of award: Scholarship, renewable.

Intended use: For full-time undergraduate certificate, sophomore, junior, senior or graduate study at accredited postsecondary institution in United States.

Basis for selection: Major/career interest in dental hygiene. Applicant must demonstrate financial need and high academic achievement.

Application requirements: Recommendations, essay. FAFSA.

Additional information: Download application from Website. Minimum 3.0 GPA. Applicants must have completed at least one year in dental hygiene program; may apply during first year. Applicant must be member of ADHA or Student ADHA. Graduate students must hold active dental hygiene license. Number of awards varies based on funding. Applicants may only apply for one ADHA scholarship, but those not selected may be eligible for other general scholarships.

Amount of award:	$1,500
Application deadline:	February 1

Contact:
ADHA Institute for Oral Health
Scholarship Award Program
444 N. Michigan Ave., Suite 3400
Chicago, IL 60611-3980
Phone: 312-440-8900
Fax: 312-467-1806
Web: www.adha.org/institute

ADHA Institute Merit Scholarships

Type of award: Scholarship.

Intended use: For full-time undergraduate certificate, sophomore, junior, senior or graduate study at accredited 2-year, 4-year or graduate institution in United States.

Basis for selection: Major/career interest in dental hygiene. Applicant must demonstrate high academic achievement.

Application requirements: Recommendations, essay.

Additional information: Must have completed one year of dental hygiene curriculum by award year; may apply during first year. Must be active ADHA or Student ADHA member with minimum 3.0 dental hygiene GPA. Graduate applicants must have active dental hygiene license. Download application from Website. Number of awards varies. Applicants may apply for only one ADHA scholarship, but those not selected may be eligible for general scholarship.

Application deadline:	February 1

Contact:
ADHA Institute for Oral Health
Scholarship Award Program
444 N. Michigan Avenue, Suite 3400
Chicago, IL 60611-3980
Phone: 312-440-8900
Fax: 312-467-1806
Web: www.adha.org/institute

ADHA Institute Part-Time Scholarship

Type of award: Scholarship, renewable.

Intended use: For half-time undergraduate or graduate study at accredited 2-year, 4-year or graduate institution in United States.

Basis for selection: Major/career interest in dental hygiene. Applicant must demonstrate financial need and high academic achievement.

Application requirements: Recommendations, essay. FAFSA.

Additional information: Applicant must be member of ADHA or Student ADHA and have completed a minimum of one year in dental hygiene program; may apply during first year. Minimum 3.5 GPA in dental hygiene. Graduate students must hold active dental hygiene license. Visit Website for application. Applicants may apply for only one ADHA scholarship, but those not selected may be eligible for general scholarship.

Amount of award:	$1,500
Number of awards:	1
Application deadline:	February 1

Contact:
ADHA Institute for Oral Health
Scholarship Award Program
444 N. Michigan Avenue, Suite 3400
Chicago, IL 60611-3980
Phone: 800-735-4916
Fax: 312-467-1806
Web: www.adha.org/institute

Cadbury Community Outreach Scholarships

Type of award: Scholarship.

Intended use: For full-time undergraduate certificate, sophomore, junior or senior study at accredited 2-year or 4-year institution in United States.

Basis for selection: Major/career interest in dental hygiene. Applicant must demonstrate financial need, high academic achievement and service orientation.

Application requirements: Recommendations, essay. FAFSA. Additional essay required.

Additional information: Must have completed one year of dental hygiene curriculum by award year; may apply during first year. Must be active ADHA or Student ADHA member with minimum 3.0 dental hygiene GPA. Must display commitment to improving community's oral health. Download application from Website. Applicants may apply for only one

ADHA scholarship, but those not selected may be eligible for general scholarship.

Amount of award: $1,500
Number of awards: 5
Application deadline: February 1
Contact:
ADHA Institute for Oral Health
Scholarship Award Program
444 N. Michigan Avenue, Suite 3400
Chicago, IL 60611-3980
Phone: 312-440-8900
Fax: 312-467-1806
Web: www.adha.org/institute

Colgate "Bright Smiles, Bright Futures" Minority Scholarships

Type of award: Scholarship, renewable.
Intended use: For full-time undergraduate certificate, sophomore, junior or senior study in United States.
Eligibility: Applicant must be Asian American, African American, Mexican American, Hispanic American, Puerto Rican or American Indian.
Basis for selection: Major/career interest in dental hygiene. Applicant must demonstrate financial need and high academic achievement.
Application requirements: Recommendations, essay. FAFSA.
Additional information: Applicant must be member of ADHA or Student ADHA. Men considered a minority in this field and encouraged to apply. Applicant must have completed at least one year of certificate-level dental hygiene program; may apply during first year. Minimum 3.0 dental hygiene GPA. Download application from Website. Applicants may only apply for one ADHA scholarship, but those not selected may be eligible for general scholarship.

Amount of award: $1,250
Number of awards: 2
Application deadline: February 1
Contact:
ADHA Institute for Oral Health
Scholarship Award Program
444 N. Michigan Ave., Suite 3400
Chicago, IL 60611-3980
Phone: 312-440-8900
Fax: 312-467-1806
Web: www.adha.org/institute

Crest Oral-B Dental Hygiene Scholarship

Type of award: Scholarship.
Intended use: For full-time sophomore, junior or senior study at accredited 4-year institution in United States.
Basis for selection: Major/career interest in dental hygiene. Applicant must demonstrate financial need, high academic achievement and seriousness of purpose.
Application requirements: Recommendations, essay. FAFSA.
Additional information: Applicant must have completed minimum one year dental hygiene curriculum; may apply during first year. Minimum 3.5 GPA in dental hygiene. Must demonstrate intent to encourage professional excellence and scholarship, promote quality research, and support dental hygiene through public and private education. Must be member of ADHA or Student ADHA. Download application from Website. Applicants may only apply for one ADHA scholarship, but those not selected may be eligible for general scholarship.

Amount of award: $1,000
Number of awards: 2
Application deadline: February 1
Contact:
ADHA Institute for Oral Health
Scholarship Award Program
444 N. Michigan Ave., Suite 3400
Chicago, IL 60611-3980
Phone: 312-440-8900
Fax: 312-467-1806
Web: www.adha.org/institute

Dr. Alfred C. Fones Scholarship

Type of award: Scholarship.
Intended use: For full-time undergraduate or graduate study at accredited 4-year or graduate institution in United States.
Basis for selection: Major/career interest in dental hygiene or education. Applicant must demonstrate financial need and high academic achievement.
Application requirements: Recommendations, essay. FAFSA. Additional essay for graduate degree-level applicants.
Additional information: Applicant must intend to become dental hygiene educator. Must have completed one year of dental hygiene curriculum by award year; may apply during first year. Must be active ADHA or Student ADHA member with minimum 3.0 dental hygiene GPA. Graduate applicants must have active dental hygiene license. Download application from Website. Applicants may apply for only one ADHA scholarship, but those not selected may be eligible for general scholarship.

Amount of award: $1,500
Number of awards: 1
Application deadline: February 1
Contact:
ADHA Institute for Oral Health
Scholarship Award Program
444 N. Michigan Avenue, Suite 3400
Chicago 60611-3980
Phone: 312-440-8900
Fax: 312-467-1806
Web: www.adha.org/institute

Dr. Harold Hillenbrand Scholarship

Type of award: Scholarship, renewable.
Intended use: For full-time undergraduate certificate, sophomore, junior, senior or graduate study at accredited 2-year, 4-year or graduate institution in United States.
Basis for selection: Major/career interest in dental hygiene. Applicant must demonstrate financial need and high academic achievement.
Application requirements: Recommendations, essay. FAFSA.
Additional information: Applicant must have completed minimum one year of dental hygiene program, have outstanding clinical performance, and minimum 3.5 GPA in dental hygiene; may apply during first year. Applicant must be member of ADHA or Student ADHA. Graduate students must hold active dental hygiene license. Visit Website for application. Applicants may apply for only one ADHA scholarship, but those not selected may be eligible for general scholarship.

Amount of award: $1,500
Number of awards: 1
Application deadline: February 1

Contact:
ADHA Institute for Oral Health
Scholarship Award Program
444 N. Michigan Avenue, Suite 3400
Chicago, IL 60611-3980
Phone: 312-440-8900
Fax: 312-467-1806
Web: www.adha.org/institute

Hu-Friedy/Esther Wilkins Instrument Scholarships

Type of award: Scholarship.
Intended use: For full-time undergraduate certificate, sophomore, junior or senior study at accredited 2-year or 4-year institution in United States.
Basis for selection: Major/career interest in dental hygiene. Applicant must demonstrate financial need and high academic achievement.
Application requirements: Recommendations, essay. FAFSA.
Additional information: Must have completed one year of dental hygiene curriculum by award year; may apply during first year. Must be active ADHA or Student ADHA member with minimum 3.0 dental hygiene GPA. Download application from Website. Award given as $1,000 worth of Hu-Friedy dental hygiene instruments. Applicants may apply for only one ADHA scholarship, but those not selected may be eligible for general scholarship.

Amount of award:	$1,000
Application deadline:	February 1

Contact:
ADHA Institute for Oral Health
Scholarship Award Program
444 N. Michigan Avenue, Suite 3400
Chicago, IL 60611-3980
Phone: 312-440-8900
Fax: 312-467-1806
Web: www.adha.org/institute

Irene E. Newman Scholarship

Type of award: Scholarship.
Intended use: For full-time undergraduate or graduate study at accredited 4-year or graduate institution in United States.
Basis for selection: Major/career interest in dental hygiene or public health. Applicant must demonstrate financial need and high academic achievement.
Application requirements: Recommendations, essay. FAFSA. Additional essay for graduate degree-level applicants.
Additional information: Must demonstrate strong potential in public health or community dental health. Must have completed at least one year of dental hygiene curriculum by award year; may apply during first year. Graduate applicants must have active dental hygiene license. Must be ADHA or Student ADHA member with minimum 3.0 dental hygiene GPA. Download application from Website. Applicants may apply for only one ADHA scholarship, but those not selected may be eligible for general scholarship.

Amount of award:	$1,500
Number of awards:	1
Application deadline:	February 1

Johnson & Johnson Scholarships

Type of award: Scholarship.
Intended use: For full-time undergraduate certificate, sophomore, junior or senior study at accredited 2-year or 4-year institution in United States.
Basis for selection: Major/career interest in dental hygiene. Applicant must demonstrate financial need and high academic achievement.
Application requirements: Recommendations, essay. FAFSA.
Additional information: Must have completed one year of dental hygiene curriculum by award year; may apply during first year. Must be active ADHA or Student ADHA member with minimum 3.5 dental hygiene GPA. Visit Website for application. Applicants may apply for only one ADHA scholarship, but those not selected may be eligible for general scholarship.

Amount of award:	$1,000
Number of awards:	5
Application deadline:	February 1
Total amount awarded:	$7,500

Contact:
ADHA Institute for Oral Health
Scholarship Award Program
444 N. Michigan Avenue, Suite 3400
Chicago, IL 60611-3980
Phone: 312-440-8900
Fax: 312-467-1806
Web: www.adha.org/institute

Karla Girts Memorial Community Outreach Scholarship

Type of award: Scholarship.
Intended use: For full-time sophomore, junior or senior study at accredited 2-year or 4-year institution in United States.
Basis for selection: Major/career interest in dental hygiene.
Application requirements: Essay.
Additional information: Applicants must display a commitment to improving oral health within the geriatric population. Minimum 3.0 GPA. Must be student member of American Dental Hygienist's Association (ADHA). Must have documented financial need of at least $1,500. Visit Website for application and more information.

Amount of award:	$2,000
Number of awards:	2
Application deadline:	February 1

Contact:
ADHA Institute for Oral Health
Scholarship Award Program
444 N. Michigan Avenue, Suite 3400
Chicago, IL 60611-3980
Phone: 312-440-8900
Fax: 312-467-1806
Web: www.adha.org/institute

Margaret E. Swanson Scholarship

Type of award: Scholarship.

Intended use: For full-time undergraduate certificate or sophomore study at accredited 2-year institution in United States.
Basis for selection: Major/career interest in dental hygiene. Applicant must demonstrate financial need, high academic achievement and leadership.
Application requirements: Recommendations, essay. FAFSA.
Additional information: Minimum 3.0 GPA in dental hygiene. Must be member of ADHA or Student ADHA, and have completed a minimum of one year in dental hygiene program; may apply during first year. Visit Website for application. Applicants may apply for only one ADHA scholarship, but those not selected may be eligible for general scholarship.

Amount of award:	$1,500
Number of awards:	1
Application deadline:	February 1

Contact:
ADHA Institute for Oral Health
Scholarship Award Program
444 N. Michigan Avenue, Suite 3400
Chicago, IL 60611-3980
Phone: 312-440-8900
Fax: 312-467-1806
Web: www.adha.org/institute

Sigma Phi Alpha Undergraduate Scholarship

Type of award: Scholarship.
Intended use: For full-time undergraduate certificate, sophomore, junior or senior study at accredited 2-year or 4-year institution in United States. Designated institutions: Schools with active chapter of Sigma Phi Alpha Dental Hygiene Honor Society.
Basis for selection: Major/career interest in dental hygiene. Applicant must demonstrate financial need and high academic achievement.
Application requirements: Recommendations, essay. FAFSA.
Additional information: Must be member of Sigma Phi Alpha. Minimum 3.5 GPA in dental hygiene. Must be member of ADHA or Student ADHA. Must have completed at least one year of dental hygiene program. Visit Website for application. Applicants may apply for only one ADHA scholarship, but those not selected may be eligible for general scholarship.

Amount of award:	$1,000
Number of awards:	1
Application deadline:	February 1

Contact:
ADHA Institute for Oral Health
Scholarship Award Program
444 N. Michigan Avenue, Suite 3400
Chicago, IL 60611-3980
Phone: 312-440-8900
Fax: 312-467-1806
Web: www.adha.org/institute

Wilma Motley Memorial California Merit Scholarship

Type of award: Scholarship.
Intended use: For full-time undergraduate certificate, sophomore, junior or senior study at accredited 2-year or 4-year institution in United States.
Eligibility: Applicant must be residing in California or.

Basis for selection: Major/career interest in dental hygiene. Applicant must demonstrate high academic achievement and leadership.
Application requirements: Recommendations, essay.
Additional information: Must have completed one year of dental hygiene curriculum by award year; may apply during first year. Must be active ADHA or Student ADHA member with minimum 3.5 dental hygiene GPA. Download application from Website. Applicants may apply for only one ADHA scholarship, but those not selected may be eligible for general scholarship.

Amount of award:	$1,000
Number of awards:	2
Application deadline:	February 1
Total amount awarded:	$2,000

Contact:
ADHA Institute for Oral Health
Scholarship Award Program
444 N. Michigan Avenue, Suite 3400
Chicago, IL 60611-3980
Phone: 312-440-8900
Fax: 312-467-1806
Web: www.adha.org/institute

AFSA Scholarship Programs

Air Force Sergeants Association Scholarship, Airmen Memorial Foundation, and Chief Master Sergeants of the Air Force Scholarship Programs

Type of award: Scholarship.
Intended use: For full-time undergraduate study at accredited postsecondary institution in United States.
Eligibility: Applicant must be single, no older than 23. Applicant must be dependent of active service person or veteran in the Air Force. May be dependent of retired member as well. Dependents of members of the Air National Guard or Air Force Reserve also eligible.
Basis for selection: Applicant must demonstrate high academic achievement, depth of character and leadership.
Application requirements: Recommendations, essay, transcript, proof of eligibility.
Additional information: Applicant must be under 23 years of age as of August 1 of award year. Applications available November 1 to March 31. Amount of award varies. See Website for application and eligibility requirements.

Amount of award:	$1,000-$3,000
Number of awards:	44
Number of applicants:	154
Application deadline:	March 31
Notification begins:	July 1
Total amount awarded:	$70,500

Contact:
AFSA Scholarship Programs
Attn: Daniyel Artis, Scholarship Coordinator
P.O. Box 50
Temple Hills, MD 20757-0050
Phone: 800-638-0594 ext. 230
Fax: 301-899-3500 ext. 230
Web: www.hqafsa.org

AHIMA Foundation

Student Merit Scholarships

Type of award: Scholarship.
Intended use: For full-time undergraduate or graduate study at accredited 2-year, 4-year or graduate institution.
Basis for selection: Major/career interest in information systems; health services administration or health-related professions. Applicant must demonstrate high academic achievement.
Application requirements: Recommendations, transcript. Enrollment verification form.
Additional information: Applicant must be member of AHIMA and enrolled in CAHIIM-accredited health information administration or health information technology program. Minimum 3.0 GPA. Award is $1,000 for students at two-year schools, $1,200 for students at four-year schools, and $2,500 for graduate students. Apply online.

Amount of award:	$1,000-$2,500
Number of awards:	64
Number of applicants:	155
Application deadline:	April 30
Notification begins:	June 15
Total amount awarded:	$86,500

Contact:
AHIMA Foundation
233 North Michigan Avenue, 21st Floor
Chicago, IL 60601-5800
Phone: 312-233-1131
Web: www.ahimafoundation.org

Air Force Aid Society

Air Force Aid Society Education Grant

Type of award: Scholarship.
Intended use: For full-time undergraduate study at accredited vocational, 2-year or 4-year institution in or outside United States.
Eligibility: Applicant must be spouse of active service person or deceased veteran who serves or served in the Air Force. Applicant may also be dependent child of active, retired or deceased Air Force service member. Veteran status alone not eligible. Sponsoring member must be active duty, retired Reserve with 20-plus qualifying years, retired Air Force with 20-plus years active duty service, or deceased while on active duty or in retired status. Dependent children of Title 32 AGR performing full-time active duty service are also eligible.
Basis for selection: Applicant must demonstrate financial need.
Application requirements: Proof of eligibility.
Additional information: Minimum 2.0 GPA.

Amount of award:	$2,000
Number of awards:	3,000
Number of applicants:	5,000
Application deadline:	March 11
Notification begins:	June 1
Total amount awarded:	$6,000,000

Contact:
Air Force Aid Society
Education Assistance Department
241 18th Street South, Suite 202
Arlington, VA 22202
Phone: 800-429-9475
Web: www.afas.org

Air Force/ROTC

Minority School Scholarships

Type of award: Scholarship.
Intended use: For undergraduate study at accredited 4-year institution in United States. Designated institutions: Historically black colleges/universities.
Eligibility: Applicant must be at least 17, no older than 26. Applicant must be U.S. citizen.
Basis for selection: Applicant must demonstrate high academic achievement and depth of character.
Application requirements: Interview, transcript.
Additional information: Must maintain 2.5 GPA in college. Scholarship is Type 2: tuition is capped at $18,000 per year plus $900 per year for books. Must pass the AFOQ Test and the AFROTC Physical Fitness Test. Must pass physical examination and be certified as commission-qualified. Visit www.afrotc.com for full list of moral and other scholarship requirements for Air Force ROTC. Contact local ROTC recruiter for more information.

Amount of award:	Full tuition

Contact:
AFROTC Admissions
551 E. Maxwell Blvd.
Maxwell AFB, AL 36112-5917
Phone: 866-423-7682
Web: www.afrotc.com

Air Traffic Control Association, Inc.

Air Traffic Control Full-Time Employee Student Scholarship

Type of award: Scholarship.
Intended use: For freshman, sophomore, junior, graduate or non-degree study at accredited postsecondary institution.
Eligibility: Applicant or parent must be employed by Aviation industry. Applicant must be returning adult student.
Basis for selection: Major/career interest in aviation. Applicant must demonstrate financial need.
Application requirements: Recommendations, essay, transcript.
Additional information: Applicant must work full-time in aviation-related field and be enrolled in coursework designed to enhance air traffic control or aviation skills. Must have minimum 30 semester or 45 quarter hours still to be completed before graduation. Award amount determined by ATCA Scholarship Program Board of Directors. Visit Website for application.

Number of awards: 1
Application deadline: May 1
Contact:
Air Traffic Control Association, Inc.
Attn: Scholarship Fund
1101 King Street, Suite 300
Alexandria, VA 22314
Phone: 703-299-2430
Fax: 703-299-2437
Web: www.atca.org

Buckingham Memorial Scholarship

Type of award: Scholarship, renewable.
Intended use: For freshman, sophomore, junior or graduate study at accredited 4-year or graduate institution in United States.
Eligibility: Applicant must be U.S. citizen.
Basis for selection: Major/career interest in aviation. Applicant must demonstrate financial need.
Application requirements: Recommendations, essay, transcript.
Additional information: Must be child of a person serving, or having served, as an air traffic control specialist. Must have minimum of 30 semester or 45 quarter hours to be completed before graduation. Number of awards varies based on funding.
Application deadline: May 1
Contact:
Air Traffic Control Association, Inc.
Attn: Scholarship Fund
1101 King Street, Suite 300
Alexandria, VA 22314
Phone: 703-299-2430
Fax: 703-299-2437
Web: www.atca.org

Gabe A. Hartl Scholarship

Type of award: Scholarship.
Intended use: For freshman, sophomore or junior study at 2-year or 4-year institution. Designated institutions: FAA-approved institutions.
Basis for selection: Major/career interest in aviation. Applicant must demonstrate financial need.
Application requirements: Recommendations, essay, transcript.
Additional information: Must have minimum of 30 semester or 45 quarter hours to be completed before graduation. Must be enrolled in air traffic control curriculum. Number of awards varies based on funding.
Application deadline: May 1
Contact:
Air Traffic Control Association, Inc.
Attn: Scholarship Fund
1101 King Street, Suite 300
Alexandria, VA 22314
Phone: 703-299-2430
Fax: 703-299-2437
Web: www.atca.org

Aircraft Electronics Association Educational Foundation

Bud Glover Memorial Scholarship

Type of award: Scholarship, renewable.
Intended use: For full-time undergraduate study at accredited vocational, 2-year or 4-year institution.
Basis for selection: Major/career interest in aviation; aviation repair or electronics. Applicant must demonstrate depth of character and seriousness of purpose.
Application requirements: Recommendations, essay, transcript, proof of eligibility.
Additional information: Minimum 2.5 GPA. Awards are announced at AEA Annual Convention and Trade Show each spring. Visit Website for more information.
Amount of award: $1,000
Number of awards: 1
Application deadline: February 15
Notification begins: April 1
Contact:
Aircraft Electronics Association Educational Foundation
3570 NE Ralph Powell Road
Lee's Summit, MO 64064
Phone: 816-347-8400
Fax: 816-347-8405
Web: www.aea.net/educationalfoundation

David Arver Memorial Scholarship

Type of award: Scholarship, renewable.
Intended use: For full-time undergraduate study at accredited vocational or 2-year institution.
Eligibility: Applicant must be residing in Wisconsin, Michigan, Iowa, South Dakota, Minnesota, Kansas, Indiana, Nebraska, Illinois, North Dakota or Missouri.
Basis for selection: Major/career interest in aviation; aviation repair or electronics. Applicant must demonstrate depth of character and seriousness of purpose.
Application requirements: Recommendations, essay, transcript, proof of eligibility.
Additional information: Minimum 2.5 GPA. Awards are announced at AEA Annual Convention and Trade Show each spring. Visit Website for more information.
Amount of award: $1,000
Number of awards: 1
Application deadline: February 15
Notification begins: April 1
Total amount awarded: $1,000
Contact:
Aircraft Electronics Association Educational Foundation
3570 NE Ralph Powell Road
Lee's Summit, MO 64064
Phone: 816-347-8400
Fax: 816-347-8405
Web: www.aea.net/educationalfoundation

Dutch and Ginger Arver Scholarship

Type of award: Scholarship, renewable.
Intended use: For full-time undergraduate study at accredited vocational, 2-year or 4-year institution.

Basis for selection: Major/career interest in aviation; electronics or aviation repair. Applicant must demonstrate depth of character and seriousness of purpose.
Application requirements: Recommendations, essay, transcript, proof of eligibility.
Additional information: Minimum 2.5 GPA. Awards are announced at AEA Annual Convention and Trade Show each spring. Visit Website for more information.

Amount of award:	$1,000
Number of awards:	1
Application deadline:	February 15
Notification begins:	April 1
Total amount awarded:	$1,000

Contact:
Aircraft Electronics Association Educational Foundation
3570 NE Ralph Powell Road
Lee's Summit, MO 64064
Phone: 816-347-8400
Fax: 816-347-8405
Web: www.aea.net/educationalfoundation

Field Aviation Co. Inc. Scholarship

Type of award: Scholarship, renewable.
Intended use: For full-time undergraduate study at accredited vocational, 2-year or 4-year institution.
Basis for selection: Major/career interest in aviation; aviation repair or electronics. Applicant must demonstrate depth of character and seriousness of purpose.
Application requirements: Recommendations, essay, transcript, proof of eligibility.
Additional information: Minimum 2.5 GPA. Awards are announced at AEA Annual Convention and Trade Show each spring. Visit Website for more information.

Amount of award:	$1,000
Number of awards:	1
Application deadline:	February 15
Notification begins:	April 1

Contact:
Aircraft Electronics Association Educational Foundation
3570 NE Ralph Powell Road
Lee's Summit, MO 64064
Phone: 816-347-8400
Fax: 816-347-8405
Web: www.aea.net/educationalfoundation

Garmin Scholarship

Type of award: Scholarship, renewable.
Intended use: For full-time undergraduate study at accredited vocational, 2-year or 4-year institution.
Basis for selection: Major/career interest in aviation; aviation repair or electronics. Applicant must demonstrate depth of character and seriousness of purpose.
Application requirements: Recommendations, essay, transcript, proof of eligibility.
Additional information: Minimum 2.5 GPA. Awards are announced at AEA Annual Convention and Trade Show each spring. For more information, visit Website.

Amount of award:	$2,000
Number of awards:	1
Application deadline:	February 15
Notification begins:	April 1
Total amount awarded:	$2,000

Contact:
Aircraft Electronics Association Educational Foundation
3570 NE Ralph Powell Road
Lee's Summit, MO 64064
Phone: 816-347-8400
Fax: 816-347-8405
Web: www.aea.net/educationalfoundation

Honeywell Avionics Scholarship

Type of award: Scholarship, renewable.
Intended use: For full-time undergraduate study at accredited vocational, 2-year or 4-year institution.
Basis for selection: Major/career interest in aviation; aviation repair or electronics.
Application requirements: Recommendations, essay, transcript, proof of eligibility.
Additional information: Minimum 2.5 GPA. Awards are announced at AEA Annual Convention and Trade Show each spring. Visit Website for additional information.

Amount of award:	$1,000
Number of awards:	1
Application deadline:	February 15
Notification begins:	April 1
Total amount awarded:	$1,000

Contact:
Aircraft Electronics Association Educational Foundation
3570 NE Ralph Powell Road
Lee's Summit, MO 64064
Phone: 816-347-8400
Fax: 816-347-8405
Web: www.aea.net/educationalfoundation

Johnny Davis Memorial Scholarship

Type of award: Scholarship, renewable.
Intended use: For full-time undergraduate study at accredited vocational, 2-year or 4-year institution.
Basis for selection: Major/career interest in aviation; aviation repair or electronics. Applicant must demonstrate depth of character and seriousness of purpose.
Application requirements: Recommendations, essay, transcript, proof of eligibility.
Additional information: Minimum 2.5 GPA. Awards are announced at AEA Annual Convention and Trade Show each spring. Visit Website for additional information.

Amount of award:	$1,000
Number of awards:	1
Application deadline:	February 15
Notification begins:	April 1
Total amount awarded:	$1,000

Contact:
Aircraft Electronics Association Educational Foundation
3570 NE Ralph Powell Road
Lee's Summit, MO 64064
Phone: 816-347-8400
Fax: 816-347-8405
Web: www.aea.net/educationalfoundation

L-3 Avionics Systems Scholarship

Type of award: Scholarship, renewable.
Intended use: For full-time undergraduate study at accredited vocational, 2-year or 4-year institution.
Basis for selection: Major/career interest in aviation; aviation repair or electronics. Applicant must demonstrate depth of character and seriousness of purpose.

Application requirements: Recommendations, essay, transcript, proof of eligibility.

Additional information: Applicant may be high school senior. Minimum 2.5 GPA. Awards are announced at AEA Annual Convention and Trade Show each spring. Visit Website for more information.

Amount of award:	$2,500
Number of awards:	1
Application deadline:	February 15
Notification begins:	April 1
Total amount awarded:	$2,500

Contact:
Aircraft Electronics Association Educational Foundation
3570 NE Ralph Powell Road
Lee's Summit, MO 64064
Phone: 816-347-8400
Fax: 816-347-8405
Web: www.aea.net/educationalfoundation

Lee Tarbox Memorial Scholarship

Type of award: Scholarship, renewable.

Intended use: For full-time undergraduate study at accredited vocational, 2-year or 4-year institution.

Basis for selection: Major/career interest in aviation; aviation repair or electronics. Applicant must demonstrate depth of character and seriousness of purpose.

Application requirements: Recommendations, essay, transcript, proof of eligibility.

Additional information: Minimum 2.5 GPA. Awards are announced at AEA Annual Convention and Trade Show each spring. Visit Website for additional information.

Amount of award:	$2,500
Number of awards:	1
Application deadline:	February 15
Notification begins:	April 1
Total amount awarded:	$2,500

Contact:
Aircraft Electronics Association Educational Foundation
3570 NE Ralph Powell Road
Lee's Summit, MO 64064
Phone: 816-347-8400
Fax: 816-347-8405
Web: www.aea.net/educationalfoundation

Lowell Gaylor Memorial Scholarship

Type of award: Scholarship, renewable.

Intended use: For full-time undergraduate study at accredited vocational, 2-year or 4-year institution.

Basis for selection: Major/career interest in aviation; aviation repair or electronics. Applicant must demonstrate depth of character and seriousness of purpose.

Application requirements: Recommendations, essay, transcript, proof of eligibility.

Additional information: Minimum 2.5 GPA. Awards are announced at AEA Annual Convention and Trade Show each spring. Visit Website for more information.

Amount of award:	$1,000
Number of awards:	1
Application deadline:	February 15
Notification begins:	April 1

Contact:
Aircraft Electronics Association Educational Foundation
3570 NE Ralph Powell Road
Lee's Summit, MO 64064
Phone: 816-347-8400
Fax: 816-347-8405
Web: www.aea.net/educationalfoundation

Mid-Continent Instrument Scholarship

Type of award: Scholarship, renewable.

Intended use: For full-time undergraduate study at accredited vocational, 2-year or 4-year institution.

Basis for selection: Major/career interest in aviation; electronics or aviation repair. Applicant must demonstrate depth of character and seriousness of purpose.

Application requirements: Recommendations, essay, transcript, proof of eligibility.

Additional information: Minimum 2.5 GPA. Awards are announced at AEA Annual Convention and Trade Show each spring. Visit Website for more information.

Amount of award:	$1,000
Number of awards:	1
Application deadline:	February 15
Notification begins:	April 1
Total amount awarded:	$1,000

Contact:
Aircraft Electronics Association Educational Foundation
3570 NE Ralph Powell Road
Lee's Summit, MO 64064
Phone: 816-347-8400
Fax: 816-347-8405
Web: www.aea.net/educationalfoundation

Monte R. Mitchell Global Scholarship

Type of award: Scholarship, renewable.

Intended use: For full-time undergraduate study at accredited postsecondary institution in or outside United States.
Designated institutions: Institutions with aviation maintenance technology, avionics, or aviation repair programs located in Europe or the United States.

Eligibility: Applicant must be U.S. citizen or European citizen.

Basis for selection: Major/career interest in aviation.
Applicant must demonstrate depth of character and seriousness of purpose.

Application requirements: Essay, transcript.

Additional information: Applicant must have finished secondary school. Minimum 2.5 GPA. Scholarship given by Mid-Continent Instruments Company. Awards are announced at AEA Annual Convention and Trade Show each spring.

Amount of award:	$1,000
Number of awards:	1
Application deadline:	February 15
Notification begins:	April 1

Contact:
Aircraft Electronics Association
3570 NE Ralph Powell Road
Lee's Summit, MO 64064
Phone: 816-347-8400
Fax: 816-347-8405
Web: www.aea.net/educationalfoundation

Plane & Pilot Magazine/Garmin Scholarship

Type of award: Scholarship, renewable.
Intended use: For full-time undergraduate study at accredited vocational institution.
Basis for selection: Major/career interest in aviation; aviation repair or electronics. Applicant must demonstrate depth of character and seriousness of purpose.
Application requirements: Recommendations, essay, transcript, proof of eligibility.
Additional information: Available to students in avionics or aircraft repair programs. Minimum 2.5 GPA. Awards are announced at AEA Annual Convention and Trade Show each spring. Visit Website for additional information.

Amount of award:	$2,000
Number of awards:	1
Application deadline:	February 15
Notification begins:	April 1
Total amount awarded:	$2,000

Contact:
Aircraft Electronics Association Educational Foundation
3570 NE Ralph Powell Road
Lee's Summit, MO 64064
Phone: 816-347-8400
Fax: 816-347-8405
Web: www.aea.net/educationalfoundation

Aircraft Owners and Pilots Association (AOPA)

AOPA Air Safety Foundation/ McAllister Memorial Scholarship

Type of award: Scholarship.
Intended use: For full-time junior or senior study at accredited 4-year institution in United States.
Eligibility: Applicant must be U.S. citizen.
Basis for selection: Major/career interest in aviation. Applicant must demonstrate financial need and high academic achievement.
Application requirements: Essay, transcript.
Additional information: Applicant must be enrolled in non-engineering aviation program. Minimum 3.25 GPA. Application available online. Must submit original and seven copies of entire application packet.

Amount of award:	$1,000
Number of awards:	1
Application deadline:	March 31
Notification begins:	July 1

Contact:
Dr. Mark Sherman
Farmingdale State College, 107 Lupton Hall
2350 Broadhollow Road
Farmingdale, NY 11735
Phone: 301-695-2000
Fax: 301-695-2375
Web: www.aopa.org/asf/about/scholarship/mcallister.html

Alabama Commission on Higher Education

Alabama National Guard Educational Assistance Program

Type of award: Scholarship, renewable.
Intended use: For undergraduate or graduate study at postsecondary institution. Designated institutions: Public institutions in Alabama.
Eligibility: Applicant must be U.S. citizen residing in Alabama. Applicant must be in military service in the Reserves/National Guard. Must be active member in good standing with federally recognized unit of Alabama National Guard.
Application requirements: Proof of eligibility.
Additional information: Award to be used for tuition, books, fees, and supplies (minus any federal veterans benefits). Applications available from Alabama National Guard units. Funds are limited; apply early.

Amount of award:	$25-$1,000
Number of applicants:	759
Total amount awarded:	$476,691

Contact:
Phone: 334-242-2273
Fax: 334-242-2269
Web: www.ache.state.al.us

Alabama Student Assistance Program

Type of award: Scholarship, renewable.
Intended use: For full-time undergraduate study. Designated institutions: Eligible Alabama institutions.
Eligibility: Applicant must be residing in Alabama.
Basis for selection: Applicant must demonstrate financial need.
Application requirements: Proof of eligibility. FAFSA.
Additional information: Students urged to apply early.

Amount of award:	$300-$5,000
Number of applicants:	11,520

Contact:
Applications available at college financial aid office.
Phone: 334-242-2273
Fax: 334-242-2269
Web: www.ache.state.al.us

Alabama Student Grant Program

Type of award: Scholarship, renewable.
Intended use: For undergraduate study at 2-year or 4-year institution. Designated institutions: Amridge University, Birmingham-Southern College, Concordia College, Faulkner University, Huntingdon College, Judson College, Miles College, Oakwood College, Samford University, Spring Hill College, Stillman College, United States Sports Academy, University of Mobile.
Eligibility: Applicant must be residing in Alabama.
Application requirements: Proof of eligibility.

Amount of award:	$1,200
Number of applicants:	7,312
Application deadline:	February 15, September 15

Contact:
Contact financial aid office of participating colleges.
Phone: 334-242-2273
Fax: 334-242-2269
Web: www.ache.state.al.us

Police/Firefighters' Survivors Educational Assistance Program

Type of award: Scholarship, renewable.
Intended use: For undergraduate study at vocational, 2-year or 4-year institution.
Eligibility: Applicant must be residing in Alabama. Applicant's parent must have been killed or disabled in work-related accident as firefighter or police officer.
Application requirements: Proof of eligibility.
Additional information: Grant covers full tuition, mandatory fees, books, and supplies. Also available to eligible spouses.

Amount of award:	Full tuition
Number of applicants:	17

Contact:
Alabama Commission on Higher Education
P.O. Box 302000
Montgomery, AL 36130-2000
Phone: 334-242-2273
Fax: 334-242-2269
Web: www.ache.state.al.us

Alabama Department of Education

Robert C. Byrd Honors Scholarship

Type of award: Scholarship, renewable.
Intended use: For full-time undergraduate study at 2-year or 4-year institution in United States.
Eligibility: Applicant must be high school senior. Applicant must be U.S. citizen residing in Alabama.
Basis for selection: Applicant must demonstrate high academic achievement.
Application requirements: Nomination by high school guidance counselor. SAT/ACT scores.
Additional information: Contact high school guidance office or principal for information. Scholarship renewable up to four years if qualifications met. Number of scholarships varies. Visit Website for details.

Amount of award:	$1,500
Number of applicants:	140
Application deadline:	March 5

Contact:
Alabama State Department of Education
Robert C. Byrd Honors Scholarship
50 North Ripley Street, Box 302101
Montgomery, AL 36104
Web: www.alsde.edu

Alabama Department of Postsecondary Education

Alabama Junior/Community College Athletic Scholarship

Type of award: Scholarship, renewable.
Intended use: For full-time freshman or sophomore study at 2-year institution.
Eligibility: Applicant must be U.S. citizen or permanent resident.
Basis for selection: Competition/talent/interest in athletics/sports, based on athletic ability determined through tryouts.
Additional information: Renewal dependent on continued athletic participation. Contact individual institutions for specific requirements. Number of awards available varies by sport.

Amount of award:	Full tuition

Contact:
Department of Postsecondary Education
P.O. Box 302130
Montgomery, AL 36130-2130
Phone: 334-293-4557
Fax: 334-293-4559
Web: www.accs.cc

Institutional Scholarship Waivers

Type of award: Scholarship, renewable.
Intended use: For freshman or sophomore study at accredited 2-year institution.
Eligibility: Applicant must be U.S. citizen or permanent resident.
Basis for selection: Applicant must demonstrate high academic achievement.
Additional information: Focus of scholarship is determined by each institution. Application deadlines printed on application forms. Award may be renewed if student demonstrates academic excellence. Contact individual institutions for scholarship/waiver requirements. Number of awards varies.

Amount of award:	$350

Contact:
Department of Postsecondary Education
P.O. Box 302130
Montgomery, AL 36130-2130
Phone: 334-293-4557
Fax: 334-293-4559
Web: www.accs.cc

Alabama Department of Veterans Affairs

G.I. Dependents' Scholarship Program

Type of award: Scholarship, renewable.
Intended use: For undergraduate or graduate study at postsecondary institution. Designated institutions: Alabama public institutions.
Eligibility: Applicant must be dependent of disabled veteran, deceased veteran or POW/MIA; or spouse of disabled veteran, deceased veteran or POW/MIA. Veteran must have served for at

least 90 days continuous active federal duty, be rated with at least a 20% service connected disability and must have resided in the state of Alabama for at least one year prior to enlistment or be rated with a 100% service connected disability and be a permanent resident of the State of Alabama for at least 5 years immediately prior to application for program.

Application requirements: Proof of eligibility.

Additional information: Children of veterans must submit application before their 26th birthday. Spouses of veterans have no age limit, but must not be remarried. Award for five academic years for children and three academic years for spouses (or part-time equivalent); covers tuition, textbooks, and laboratory fees. Unlimited number of awards available; no application deadline.

Amount of award:	Full tuition
Number of applicants:	2,417
Total amount awarded:	$15,827,191

Contact:
Alabama Department of Veterans Affairs
P.O. Box 1509
Montgomery, AL 36102-1509
Phone: 334-242-5077
Fax: 334-242-5102
Web: www.va.alabama.gov/scholarship.htm

Alcoa Foundation

Alcoa Foundation Sons and Daughters Scholarship Program

Type of award: Scholarship, renewable.

Intended use: For full-time undergraduate study at accredited vocational, 2-year or 4-year institution in United States.

Eligibility: Applicant must be high school senior.

Basis for selection: Applicant must demonstrate high academic achievement, depth of character, leadership and service orientation.

Application requirements: Recommendations, essay, transcript, proof of eligibility. SAT/ACT scores (if attending four-year institution), school profile.

Additional information: Parent must be employed by Alcoa Inc. Four-year award renewable for three years. Two-year award renewable for one year. Deadline in January; see Website for details.

Amount of award:	$1,500
Number of awards:	100
Number of applicants:	150
Total amount awarded:	$54,000

Contact:
Alcoa Foundation Sons and Daughters Scholarship Program
P.O. Box 4030
Iowa City, IA 52243-4030
Phone: 800-525-6932
Fax: 319-337-1204
Web: www.act.org/alcoafoundation

Alexander Graham Bell Association for the Deaf and Hard of Hearing

AG Bell College Scholarship Awards

Type of award: Scholarship.

Intended use: For full-time undergraduate or graduate study at accredited 2-year, 4-year or graduate institution in or outside United States.

Eligibility: Applicant must be hearing impaired.

Basis for selection: Applicant must demonstrate high academic achievement.

Application requirements: Recommendations, essay, transcript, proof of eligibility. Recent audiogram or MAPping report.

Additional information: Applicant must have bilateral hearing loss in the moderate to profound range, diagnosed before age seven. Must use speech as primary form of communication, and be accepted or enrolled in mainstream college/university. Number of awards granted varies. Visit Website for application deadline.

Amount of award:	$1,000-$10,000
Number of applicants:	348
Total amount awarded:	$80,000

Contact:
AG Bell College Scholarship Program
3417 Volta Place, NW
Washington, DC 20007-2778
Phone: 202-337-5220
Web: www.agbell.org

Alexia Foundation

Alexia Foundation Grant and Scholarship

Type of award: Scholarship.

Intended use: For full-time undergraduate or graduate study in or outside United States or Canada. Designated institutions: Syracuse University London Program.

Basis for selection: Competition/talent/interest in photography.

Application requirements: Essay. Resume, portfolio of 10 to 20 photographs.

Additional information: Grand prize of full tuition scholarship to study photojournalism during fall semester at Syracuse University in London, plus $1,000 grant for completion of photo-story proposal. Additional awards will be given. Students who have completed more than three internships or who have a year of full-time professional experience are not eligible. Application must be submitted online.

Amount of award:	$2,100-$16,300
Number of awards:	10
Application deadline:	February 1

Contact:
David Sutherland
S.I. Newhouse School of Communications
215 University Place
Syracuse, NY 13244-2100
Phone: 315-446-1144
Web: www.alexiafoundation.org

Alliance for Young Artists and Writers

Scholastic Art Portfolio Gold Award

Type of award: Scholarship.
Intended use: For undergraduate study at postsecondary institution.
Eligibility: Applicant must be high school senior.
Basis for selection: Competition/talent/interest in visual arts, based on originality, level of technical proficiency, and emergence of personal style or vision. Major/career interest in arts, general.
Application requirements: Portfolio, recommendations. Signed registration form. Portfolio must contain eight works.
Additional information: Deadline varies. Contact sponsor or visit Website for more information.

Amount of award:	$10,000
Number of awards:	6
Total amount awarded:	$50,000

Contact:
Alliance for Young Artists & Writers
The Scholastic Art & Writing Awards
557 Broadway
New York, NY 10012
Phone: 212-343-6100
Fax: 212-389-3939
Web: www.artandwriting.org

Scholastic Art Portfolio Silver Award

Type of award: Scholarship.
Intended use: For undergraduate study at postsecondary institution.
Eligibility: Applicant must be high school senior.
Basis for selection: Competition/talent/interest in visual arts, based on originality, level of technical proficiency, and emergence of personal style or vision. Major/career interest in arts, general.
Application requirements: Portfolio, recommendations. Signed registration form. Portfolio must contain eight works.
Additional information: Students nominated for scholarships offered by participating higher education institutions. Deadline varies. Contact sponsor or visit Website for more information.

Number of awards:	6

Contact:
Alliance for Young Artists & Writers
The Scholastic Art & Writing Awards
557 Broadway
New York, NY 10012
Phone: 212-343-6100
Fax: 212-389-3939
Web: www.artandwriting.org

Scholastic Photography Portfolio Gold Award

Type of award: Scholarship.
Intended use: For undergraduate study at postsecondary institution.
Eligibility: Applicant must be high school senior.
Basis for selection: Competition/talent/interest in photography, based on originality, level of technical proficiency, and emergence of personal style or vision. Major/career interest in arts, general.
Application requirements: Portfolio, recommendations. Signed registration form. Portfolio must contain eight works in form of prints.
Additional information: Deadline varies. Contact sponsor or visit Website for more information.

Amount of award:	$10,000
Number of awards:	2
Total amount awarded:	$20,000

Contact:
Alliance for Young Artists & Writers
The Scholastic Art & Writing Awards
557 Broadway
New York, NY 10012
Phone: 212-343-6100
Fax: 212-389-3939
Web: www.artandwriting.org

Scholastic Photography Portfolio Silver Award

Type of award: Scholarship.
Intended use: For undergraduate study at postsecondary institution.
Eligibility: Applicant must be high school senior.
Basis for selection: Competition/talent/interest in photography, based on originality, level of technical proficiency, and emergence of personal style or vision. Major/career interest in arts, general.
Application requirements: Portfolio, recommendations. Portfolio must contain eight works in form of prints. Signed registration form.
Additional information: Students nominated for scholarships offered by participating higher education institutions. Deadline varies. Contact sponsor or visit Website for more information.

Number of awards:	2

Contact:
Alliance for Young Artists & Writers
The Scholastic Art & Writing Awards
557 Broadway
New York, NY 10012
Phone: 212-343-6100
Fax: 212-389-3939
Web: www.artandwriting.org

Scholastic Writing Portfolio Gold Award

Type of award: Scholarship.
Intended use: For undergraduate study at postsecondary institution.
Eligibility: Applicant must be high school senior.
Basis for selection: Competition/talent/interest in writing/journalism, based on originality, level of technical proficiency, and emergence of personal voice or style. Major/career interest in English; journalism; literature or theater arts.

Application requirements: Portfolio, recommendations, essay. Portfolio must contain three to eight works of narratives, individual poems, or dramatic scripts demonstrating diversity and talent. Excerpts from longer works permitted. Entry form must be signed by student's parent and teacher, counselor, or principal.

Additional information: Deadline varies. Application fee varies by location and may be waived. Contact sponsor or visit Website for more information.

Amount of award:	$10,000
Number of awards:	4
Total amount awarded:	$50,000

Contact:
Alliance for Young Artists & Writers
The Scholastic Art & Writing Awards
557 Broadway
New York, NY 10012
Phone: 212-343-6100
Fax: 212-389-3939
Web: www.artandwriting.org

Alpha Beta Gamma International Business Honor Society

Alpha Beta Gamma National Scholarship

Type of award: Scholarship.

Intended use: For full-time junior or senior study at accredited 4-year institution. Designated institutions: Participating four-year colleges.

Basis for selection: Major/career interest in business; business, international; business/management/administration; accounting or computer/information sciences. Applicant must demonstrate high academic achievement and leadership.

Application requirements: Recommendations. Copy of ABG diploma.

Additional information: Must be initiated member of Alpha Beta Gamma. Awarded to enrollees of two-year schools who have been accepted at four-year schools to pursue baccalaureate degree in business or related professions. Some colleges have minimum GPA requirement. Amount of award varies by institution.

Amount of award:	$500-$8,100
Number of awards:	300
Number of applicants:	400
Total amount awarded:	$600,000

Contact:
Alpha Beta Gamma Scholarship Committee
75 Grasslands Road
Valhalla, NY 10595
Web: www.abg.org

Alpha Mu Gamma, the National Collegiate Foreign Language Honor Society

Alpha Mu Gamma Scholarships

Type of award: Scholarship.

Intended use: For full-time undergraduate, graduate or postgraduate study at 2-year, 4-year or graduate institution.

Basis for selection: Major/career interest in foreign languages. Applicant must demonstrate high academic achievement and seriousness of purpose.

Application requirements: Recommendations, essay, transcript. Photocopy of applicant's AMG full member certificate.

Additional information: Applicant must be full member of Alpha Mu Gamma. Three $1,000 awards granted for study of any foreign language; one $400 award for study of Esperanto or Spanish. May apply unlimited number of times. National office will not send out applications; forms must be requested from advisor of local AMG chapter.

Amount of award:	$400-$1,000
Number of awards:	4
Number of applicants:	25
Application deadline:	February 1
Notification begins:	April 1
Total amount awarded:	$3,400

Contact:
Advisor of local Alpha Mu Gamma chapter.
Web: www.lacitycollege.edu/academic/honor/amg/homepage.html

Alumnae Panhellenic Association of Washington, D.C.

Alumnae Panhellenic Association Women's Scholarship

Type of award: Scholarship, renewable.

Intended use: For sophomore, junior, senior or graduate study at 4-year or graduate institution.

Eligibility: Applicant must be female. Applicant must be residing in District of Columbia.

Basis for selection: Based on sorority involvement. Applicant must demonstrate high academic achievement and service orientation.

Application requirements: Recommendations, essay, transcript.

Additional information: Applicant must be member in good standing of sorority of National Panhellenic Conference and live or attend school in Washington, D.C., metro area. Send email for application request.

Amount of award:	$650
Number of awards:	3
Number of applicants:	21
Application deadline:	March 15
Notification begins:	April 10
Total amount awarded:	$1,950

AMBUCS

AMBUCS Scholars-Scholarship for Therapists

Type of award: Scholarship.
Intended use: For full-time junior, senior or master's study at accredited 4-year or graduate institution in United States. Designated institutions: Schools with programs accredited by appropriate health therapy association.
Eligibility: Applicant must be U.S. citizen.
Basis for selection: Major/career interest in occupational therapy; physical therapy or speech pathology/audiology. Applicant must demonstrate financial need, depth of character and service orientation.
Additional information: Award amount typically maximum $1,500, but one additional two-year award of $6,000 offered. Students must apply online; no paper applications accepted. Applicants may print online enrollment certificate. Additional documentation, including prior year's 1040 tax form, requested if applicant is selected as semifinalist.

Amount of award:	$500-$6,000
Number of applicants:	1,823
Application deadline:	April 15
Notification begins:	June 20
Total amount awarded:	$139,675

Contact:
AMBUCS Resource Center
P.O. Box 5127
High Point, NC 27262
Phone: 336-852-0052
Fax: 336-852-6830
Web: www.ambucs.org

America's Junior Miss, Inc.

Junior Miss Scholarship

Type of award: Scholarship.
Intended use: For undergraduate or graduate study.
Eligibility: Applicant must be single, female, high school junior or senior. Applicant must be U.S. citizen.
Basis for selection: Competition/talent/interest in poise/talent/fitness, based on scholastic evaluation, skill in creative and performing arts, physical fitness, presence and composure, and panel interview.
Additional information: Must compete in state of legal residence. State winners expected to compete at higher levels. Must never have been married or pregnant. Only high school seniors can compete in finals but students are encouraged to begin application process during sophomore year. Scholarship funds can be used for undergraduate work or deferred for graduate and professional studies. Visit Website for application deadline information, as it varies from state to state.

Amount of award:	$100-$50,000
Number of applicants:	6,000

Contact:
America's Junior Miss
Contestant Inquiry
751 Government Street
Mobile, AL 36602
Phone: 800-256-5435
Fax: 251-431-0063
Web: www.ajm.org

American Alpine Club

Arthur K. Gilkey Memorial/William Putnam/Bedayn Research Grants

Type of award: Research grant.
Intended use: For undergraduate or graduate study.
Basis for selection: Major/career interest in science, general; biology; environmental science; forestry or atmospheric sciences/meteorology.
Application requirements: Research proposal. Curriculum vitae with biographical information.
Additional information: Research proposals evaluated on scientific or technical quality and contribution to scientific endeavor germane to mountain regions. Applications available from Website; must be submitted via email. Number of awards varies.

Amount of award:	$200-$1,000
Number of applicants:	18
Application deadline:	March 1
Notification begins:	May 1
Total amount awarded:	$10,000

Contact:
American Alpine Club
710 Tenth Street
Suite 100
Golden, CO 80401
Phone: 303-384-0110
Fax: 303-384-0111
Web: www.americanalpineclub.org/grants

American Association for Cancer Research

Gary J. Miller Undergraduate Prizes for Cancer and Cancer-Related Biomedical Research

Type of award: Scholarship.
Intended use: For full-time undergraduate or graduate study at 4-year institution.
Basis for selection: Competition/talent/interest in science project. Major/career interest in biochemistry; biology; chemistry; pharmacy/pharmaceutics/pharmacology; microbiology; engineering, chemical; epidemiology; oncology or science, general. Applicant must demonstrate high academic achievement.
Additional information: Applicants compete in the annual Undergraduate Student Caucus and Poster Competition, where applicants exhibit a scientific poster concerning cancer or

cancer-related biomedical research. First prize receives $1,500 in funding to support cost of participation in the next AACR Annual Meeting. Second place receives $300; third place receives $200. All applicants receive complimentary registration to the AACR Annual Meeting, where the competition takes place. Application deadline and Abstract submission deadlines in late March. Visit Website for dates and details.

Amount of award:	$200-$1,500
Number of awards:	3

Contact:
American Association for Cancer Research
615 Chestnut Street, 17th Floor
Philadelphia, PA 19106-4404
Phone: 215-440-9300
Fax: 215-440-9412
Web: www.aacr.org/ScienceEducation

Thomas J. Bardos Science Education Awards for Undergraduate Students

Type of award: Research grant.
Intended use: For full-time junior study at 4-year institution.
Basis for selection: Major/career interest in biochemistry; biology; chemistry; pharmacy/pharmaceutics/pharmacology; microbiology; engineering, chemical; epidemiology; oncology or science, general.
Application requirements: Recommendations, essay.
Additional information: Two-year award consists of $1,500 per year for travel expenses and registration fee waiver for AACR annual meeting. Selection based on qualifications and interest in research, mentor references, and selection committee's evaluation of potential professional benefit. Applicants not yet committed to cancer research welcome; those studying molecular biology and genetics or pathology also eligible. Awardees must attend scientific sessions at AACR meeting for at least four days and participate in required activities. Must submit two comprehensive reports each year. Contact AACR or visit Website for more information. Application deadline in early December.

Amount of award:	$3,000
Number of awards:	10

Contact:
American Association for Cancer Research
615 Chestnut Street, 17th Floor
Philadelphia, PA 19106-4404
Phone: 215-440-9300
Fax: 215-440-9412
Web: www.aacr.org/BardosAward

American Board of Funeral Service Education

American Board of Funeral Service Education National Scholarship

Type of award: Scholarship.
Intended use: For full-time undergraduate study at 2-year or 4-year institution in United States.
Eligibility: Applicant must be U.S. citizen or permanent resident.
Basis for selection: Major/career interest in mortuary science. Applicant must demonstrate financial need, high academic achievement, depth of character, leadership and seriousness of purpose.
Application requirements: Recommendations, essay.
Additional information: Student must have completed at least one semester (or quarter) of study in funeral service or mortuary science at an education program accredited by American Board of Funeral Service Education. Visit Website for more information and application. Extracurricular activities are considered for eligibility.

Amount of award:	$250-$2,500
Number of awards:	30
Number of applicants:	100
Application deadline:	March 1, September 1
Notification begins:	May 1, November 1
Total amount awarded:	$25,000

Contact:
American Board of Funeral Service Education
Attn: Scholarship Committee
3414 Ashland, Suite G
St. Joseph, MO 64506
Phone: 816-233-3747
Fax: 816-233-3793
Web: www.abfse.org

American Cancer Society Great Lakes Division Foundation

Young Survivor Scholarship

Type of award: Scholarship.
Intended use: For full-time undergraduate study at accredited 2-year or 4-year institution in United States. Designated institutions: Michigan or Indiana institutions.
Eligibility: Applicant must be no older than 20, high school senior. Applicant must be U.S. citizen residing in Michigan or Indiana.
Basis for selection: Applicant must demonstrate financial need, depth of character, leadership and service orientation.
Application requirements: Recommendations, essay, transcript, proof of eligibility. FAFSA. Letter from doctor verifying diagnosis.
Additional information: Applicant must be cancer survivor, carry 12 or more credit hours a minimum of a 2.0 GPA.

Amount of award:	$2,500
Number of applicants:	103
Application deadline:	April 16
Total amount awarded:	$25,000

Contact:
American Cancer Society Great Lakes Division Foundation
Young Survivor Scholarship Program
1755 Abbey Road
East Lansing, MI 48823
Phone: 800-723-0360
Fax: 517-664-1497
Web: www.cancer.org/scholarships

American Center of Oriental Research

Jennifer C. Groot Fellowship

Type of award: Research grant.
Intended use: For undergraduate or graduate study at 4-year or graduate institution.
Eligibility: Applicant must be U.S. citizen or Canadian citizen.
Basis for selection: Major/career interest in archaeology; Middle Eastern studies; ancient Near Eastern studies or ethnic/cultural studies.
Application requirements: Proof of acceptance on archaeological fieldwork in Jordan.
Additional information: Applicant must be accepted as staff member on archaeological project in Jordan with ASOR/CAP affiliation. Award used only for travel to project site in Jordan.

Amount of award:	$1,800
Number of awards:	2
Number of applicants:	15
Application deadline:	February 1
Notification begins:	April 15
Total amount awarded:	$4,500

Contact:
American Center of Oriental Research
Fellowship Committee
656 Beacon Street
Boston, MA 02215-2010
Phone: 617-353-6571
Fax: 617-353-6575
Web: www.bu.edu/acor

American Chemical Society

American Chemical Society Scholars Program

Type of award: Scholarship, renewable.
Intended use: For full-time undergraduate study at accredited 2-year or 4-year institution in United States.
Eligibility: Applicant must be African American, Mexican American, Hispanic American, Puerto Rican or American Indian. Applicant must be U.S. citizen or permanent resident.
Basis for selection: Major/career interest in chemistry; biochemistry; engineering, chemical; materials science; environmental science; forensics or food science/technology. Applicant must demonstrate financial need, high academic achievement, leadership, seriousness of purpose and service orientation.
Application requirements: Recommendations, transcript. SAR. ACT/SAT scores (for high school applicants).
Additional information: Other chemically-related majors also eligible. Minimum 3.0 GPA. Must be planning career in chemical sciences (pre-med and pharmacy programs not eligible).

Amount of award:	$1,000-$5,000
Number of awards:	100
Number of applicants:	670
Application deadline:	March 1
Notification begins:	May 31
Total amount awarded:	$900,000

Contact:
ACS Scholars Program
1155 16th Street, NW
Washington, DC 20036
Phone: 800-227-5558 ext. 6250
Fax: 202-872-4361
Web: www.chemistry.org/scholars

American Classical League

Arthur Patch McKinlay Scholarship

Type of award: Scholarship.
Intended use: For non-degree study.
Basis for selection: Major/career interest in classics or education. Applicant must demonstrate financial need.
Application requirements: Recommendations. Study program proposal, including budget.
Additional information: Must be current member of American Classical League and for three years preceding application. Must be planning to teach classics in elementary or secondary school in upcoming school year. May apply for independent study program funding or support to attend American Classical League Institute for first time. Number of awards varies year to year.

Amount of award:	$1,500
Number of applicants:	20
Application deadline:	January 15

Contact:
American Classical League Scholarship Awards
Miami University
422 Wells Mill Drive
Oxford, OH 45056
Phone: 513-529-7741
Fax: 513-529-7742
Web: www.aclclassics.org

Maureen V. O'Donnell/Eunice C. Kraft Teacher Training Scholarships

Type of award: Scholarship.
Intended use: For junior, senior or graduate study at 4-year or graduate institution.
Basis for selection: Major/career interest in education or classics.
Application requirements: Recommendations.
Additional information: Must be member of ACL. Must be training for certification to teach Latin and have completed a substantial number of these courses. Must wait at least three years before reapplying. Number of awards varies.

Amount of award:	$1,000
Number of applicants:	13
Application deadline:	December 1

Contact:
The American Classical League
Miami University
422 Wells Mill Drive
Oxford, OH 45056
Phone: 513-529-7741
Fax: 513-529-7742
Web: www.aclclassics.org

American College of Musicians

National Guild of Piano Teachers $200 Scholarship

Type of award: Scholarship.
Intended use: For undergraduate, graduate or non-degree study.
Basis for selection: Major/career interest in music.
Application requirements: Nomination by piano teacher, who must be member of National Guild of Piano Teachers. Copies of ten inner report cards and stubs.
Additional information: Award to be used for piano study. Student must have been national winner for ten years, Paderewski Medal winner, and Guild High School Diploma recipient.

Amount of award:	$200
Number of awards:	150
Application deadline:	September 15
Notification begins:	October 1

Contact:
American College of Musicians
Scholarship Committee
P.O. Box 1807
Austin, TX 78767-1807
Phone: 512-478-5775
Web: www.pianoguild.com

National Guild of Piano Teachers Composition Contest

Type of award: Scholarship.
Intended use: For undergraduate, graduate or non-degree study.
Basis for selection: Competition/talent/interest in music performance/composition, based on composition for solo keyboard and keyboard ensemble.
Application requirements: Manuscript of composition.
Additional information: Teacher must be member of National Guild of Piano Teachers. Compositions rated on imagination, originality, and skill. Entry fees vary according to classification of student and length of composition. See Website for specific details.

Amount of award:	$50-$150
Number of awards:	14
Application deadline:	November 8

Contact:
American College of Musicians
P.O. Box 1807
Austin, TX 78767-1807
Phone: 512-478-5775
Web: www.pianoguild.com

American Congress on Surveying and Mapping

AAGS Joseph F. Dracup Scholarship Award

Type of award: Scholarship, renewable.
Intended use: For undergraduate study at 4-year institution.
Basis for selection: Major/career interest in surveying/mapping. Applicant must demonstrate high academic achievement and seriousness of purpose.
Application requirements: Recommendations, essay, transcript, proof of eligibility.
Additional information: Applicant must be member of American Congress on Surveying and Mapping. Preference will be given to applicants with significant focus on geodetic surveying. Visit Website for deadlines and additional information.

Amount of award:	$2,000
Number of awards:	1
Number of applicants:	36
Total amount awarded:	$2,000

Contact:
American Congress on Surveying and Mapping
6 Montgomery Village Avenue
Suite 403
Gaithersburg, MD 20879
Phone: 240-632-9716 ext. 113
Fax: 240-632-1321
Web: www.acsm.net

ACSM Fellows Scholarship

Type of award: Scholarship.
Intended use: For junior or senior study at 4-year institution.
Basis for selection: Major/career interest in surveying/mapping or cartography.
Additional information: Applicant must be an ACSM member and be student in one of ACSM disciplines: surveying, mapping, geographic land sciences, or cartography. Visit Website for deadlines and additional information.

Amount of award:	$2,000
Number of awards:	1
Number of applicants:	20
Notification begins:	January 1
Total amount awarded:	$2,000

Contact:
American Congress on Surveying & Mapping
6 Montgomery Village Avenue
Suite 403
Gaithersburg, MD 20879
Phone: 240-632-9716 ext. 113
Fax: 240-632-1321
Web: www.acsm.net

Berntsen International Scholarship in Surveying

Type of award: Scholarship, renewable.
Intended use: For undergraduate study at 4-year institution.
Basis for selection: Major/career interest in surveying/mapping. Applicant must demonstrate high academic achievement and seriousness of purpose.

Application requirements: Recommendations, essay, transcript, proof of eligibility.
Additional information: Applicant must be member of ACSM. Open to students in surveying or closely related programs such as geomatics or surveying engineering. Degree of financial need will be used, if necessary, to break ties after the primary criteria have been considered. Funded by Berntsen International Inc. of Madison, Wisconsin. Visit Website for deadlines and additional information.

Amount of award:	$1,500
Number of awards:	1
Number of applicants:	36
Total amount awarded:	$1,500

Contact:
American Congress on Surveying and Mapping
6 Montgomery Village Avenue
Suite 403
Gaithersburg, MD 20879
Phone: 240-632-9716 ext. 113
Fax: 240-632-1321
Web: www.acsm.net

Berntsen International Scholarship in Surveying Technology

Type of award: Scholarship, renewable.
Intended use: For undergraduate certificate study at 2-year institution.
Basis for selection: Major/career interest in surveying/mapping or cartography. Applicant must demonstrate high academic achievement and seriousness of purpose.
Application requirements: Recommendations, essay, transcript, proof of eligibility.
Additional information: Applicant must be member of ACSM. Funded by Berntsen International Inc. of Madison, Wisconsin. Visit Website for deadlines and additional information.

Amount of award:	$500
Number of awards:	1
Number of applicants:	15
Total amount awarded:	$500

Contact:
American Congress on Surveying and Mapping
6 Montgomery Village Avenue
Suite 403
Gaithersburg, MD 20879
Phone: 240-632-9716 ext. 113
Fax: 240-632-1321
Web: www.acsm.net

Cady McDonnell Memorial Scholarship

Type of award: Scholarship, renewable.
Intended use: For undergraduate study at 2-year or 4-year institution.
Eligibility: Applicant must be female. Applicant must be residing in Utah, Alaska, Washington, Arizona, Nevada, Wyoming, California, Montana, Oregon, New Mexico, Idaho, Colorado or Hawaii.
Basis for selection: Major/career interest in surveying/mapping or cartography. Applicant must demonstrate high academic achievement and seriousness of purpose.
Application requirements: Recommendations, essay, transcript, proof of eligibility. Proof of legal home residence.
Additional information: Applicant must be member of American Congress on Surveying and Mapping. Degree of

financial need will be used, if necessary, to break ties after the primary criteria have been considered. Visit Website for deadlines and additional information.

Amount of award:	$1,000
Number of awards:	1
Number of applicants:	10
Total amount awarded:	$1,000

Contact:
American Congress on Surveying and Mapping
6 Montgomery Village Avenue
Suite 403
Gaithersburg, MD 20879
Phone: 240-632-9716 ext. 113
Fax: 240-632-1321
Web: www.acsm.net

The Lowell H. and Dorothy Loving Undergraduate Scholarship

Type of award: Scholarship.
Intended use: For junior or senior study at accredited postsecondary institution.
Application requirements: Recommendations, essay, transcript.
Additional information: Applicant must be ACSM member and take courses in land surveying, geometric geodesy, photogrammetry/remote sensing or analysis, and design of spatial measurement. Visit Website for deadlines and additional information.

Amount of award:	$2,500
Number of awards:	1
Number of applicants:	8
Total amount awarded:	$2,500

Contact:
American Congress on Surveying and Mapping
6 Montgomery Village Avenue
Suite 403
Gaithersburg, MD 20879
Phone: 240-632-9716 ext. 113
Fax: 240-632-1321
Web: www.acsm.net

Nettie Dracup Memorial Scholarship

Type of award: Scholarship, renewable.
Intended use: For undergraduate study at accredited 4-year institution.
Eligibility: Applicant must be U.S. citizen.
Basis for selection: Major/career interest in surveying/mapping. Applicant must demonstrate high academic achievement and seriousness of purpose.
Application requirements: Recommendations, essay, transcript, proof of eligibility.
Additional information: Applicant must be member of American Congress on Surveying and Mapping and enrolled in geodetic surveying program. Degree of financial need will be used, if necessary, to break ties after primary criteria have been considered. Visit Website for deadlines and additional information.

Amount of award:	$2,000
Number of awards:	2
Number of applicants:	13
Total amount awarded:	$4,000

Contact:
American Congress on Surveying and Mapping
6 Montgomery Village Avenue
Suite 403
Gaithersburg, MD 20879
Phone: 240-632-9716 ext. 113
Fax: 240-632-1321
Web: www.acsm.net

NSPS Board of Governors Scholarship

Type of award: Scholarship, renewable.
Intended use: For junior study at 4-year institution.
Basis for selection: Major/career interest in surveying/mapping. Applicant must demonstrate high academic achievement and seriousness of purpose.
Application requirements: Recommendations, essay, transcript, proof of eligibility.
Additional information: Applicant must be member of American Congress on Surveying and Mapping. Minimum 3.0 GPA. Degree of financial need will be used, if necessary, to break ties after the primary criteria have been considered. Visit Website for deadlines and additional information.

Amount of award:	$1,000
Number of awards:	1
Number of applicants:	15
Total amount awarded:	$1,000

Contact:
American Congress on Surveying and Mapping
6 Montgomery Village Avenue
Suite 403
Gaithersburg, MD 20879
Phone: 240-632-9716 ext. 113
Fax: 240-632-1321
Web: www.acsm.net

NSPS Scholarships

Type of award: Scholarship, renewable.
Intended use: For full-time undergraduate study at 4-year institution.
Basis for selection: Major/career interest in surveying/mapping. Applicant must demonstrate high academic achievement and seriousness of purpose.
Application requirements: Recommendations, essay, transcript, proof of eligibility.
Additional information: Applicant must be member of American Congress on Surveying and Mapping. Degree of financial need will be used, if necessary, to break ties after the primary criteria have been considered. Awarded by National Society of Professional Surveyors. Visit Website for deadlines and additional information.

Amount of award:	$1,000
Number of awards:	2
Number of applicants:	12
Total amount awarded:	$2,000

Contact:
American Congress on Surveying and Mapping
6 Montgomery Village Avenue
Suite 403
Gaithersburg, MD 20879
Phone: 240-632-9716 ext. 113
Fax: 240-632-1321
Web: www.acsm.net

Schonstedt Scholarships in Surveying

Type of award: Scholarship, renewable.
Intended use: For undergraduate study at 4-year institution.
Basis for selection: Major/career interest in surveying/mapping. Applicant must demonstrate high academic achievement and seriousness of purpose.
Application requirements: Recommendations, essay, transcript, proof of eligibility.
Additional information: Applicant must be member of American Congress on Surveying and Mapping. Preference given to applicants with junior or senior standing. Degree of financial need will be used, if necessary, to break ties after primary criteria have been considered. Funded by Schonstedt Instrument Company of Kearneysville, West Virginia. Schonstedt donates magnetic locator to surveying program at each recipient's school. Visit Website for deadlines and additional information.

Amount of award:	$1,500
Number of awards:	1
Number of applicants:	16
Total amount awarded:	$1,500

Contact:
American Congress on Surveying and Mapping
6 Montgomery Village Avenue
Suite 403
Gaithersburg, MD 20879
Phone: 240-632-9716 ext. 113
Fax: 240-632-1321
Web: www.acsm.net

Tri-State Surveying & Photogrammetry Kris M. Kunze Scholarship

Type of award: Scholarship.
Intended use: For undergraduate study at postsecondary institution.
Basis for selection: Major/career interest in business; business/management/administration or surveying/mapping.
Additional information: Applicant must be ACSM member. First priority: licensed professional land surveyors or certified photogrammetrists taking college business administration or management courses. Second priority: certified land survey interns taking college business administration or management courses. Third priority: full-time students in two or four-year surveying and mapping degree programs taking business administration or management courses. Visit Website for deadlines and additional information.

Amount of award:	$1,000
Number of awards:	1
Number of applicants:	12
Total amount awarded:	$1,000

Contact:
ACSM
6 Montgomery Village Avenue
Suite 403
Gaithersburg, MD 20879
Phone: 240-632-9716 ext. 113
Fax: 240-632-1321
Web: www.acsm.net

Scholarships

American Council of Engineering Companies

ACEC Scholarship

Type of award: Scholarship, renewable.
Intended use: For junior, senior, master's or doctoral study at postsecondary institution. Designated institutions: ABET-accredited engineering programs.
Eligibility: Applicant must be U.S. citizen residing in Alaska.
Basis for selection: Major/career interest in engineering. Applicant must demonstrate seriousness of purpose.
Application requirements: Recommendations, essay, transcript, nomination by Council Member Organization.
Additional information: Submit application through respective state member organization.

Amount of award:	$5,000-$10,000
Number of awards:	4
Number of applicants:	18
Total amount awarded:	$22,500

Contact:
American Council of Engineering Companies
1015 15th Street, NW
8th Floor
Washington, DC 20005-2605
Phone: 202-347-7474
Fax: 202-898-0068
Web: www.acec.org/awards/scholarships.cfm

American Council of the Blind

Floyd Qualls Memorial Scholarship

Type of award: Scholarship, renewable.
Intended use: For full-time undergraduate or graduate study at accredited postsecondary institution in United States.
Eligibility: Applicant must be visually impaired.
Basis for selection: Applicant must demonstrate high academic achievement, depth of character and leadership.
Application requirements: Interview, recommendations, essay, transcript, proof of eligibility.
Additional information: Applicant must be legally blind in both eyes. One award each for an entering freshman, other undergraduate, graduate, and vocational student, plus one discretionary award.

Amount of award:	$2,500
Number of awards:	5
Number of applicants:	200
Application deadline:	March 1
Notification begins:	May 15
Total amount awarded:	$12,500

Contact:
American Council of the Blind
2200 Wilson Boulevard
Suite 650
Arlington, VA 22201
Phone: 202-467-5081
Fax: 703-465-5085
Web: www.acb.org

American Dental Assistants Association

Juliette A. Southard/Oral-B Laboratories Scholarship

Type of award: Scholarship.
Intended use: For undergraduate study.
Basis for selection: Major/career interest in dental assistant. Applicant must demonstrate high academic achievement.
Application requirements: Recommendations, essay, transcript, proof of eligibility.
Additional information: Scholarships open to high school graduates and GED certificate holders. Must be ADAA member. Applicants must be enrolled in dental assisting program or be taking courses applicable to furthering career in dental assisting. Visit Website for application. All forms must be submitted via email.

Amount of award:	$750
Number of awards:	10
Number of applicants:	30
Application deadline:	March 1
Total amount awarded:	$7,500

Contact:
American Dental Assistants Association
35 East Wacker Drive
Suite 1730
Chicago, IL 60601-2211
Phone: 312-541-1550
Fax: 312-541-1496
Web: www.dentalassistant.org

American Dietetic Association Foundation

Graduate, Baccalaureate or Coordinated Program Scholarships

Type of award: Scholarship, renewable.
Intended use: For full-time junior, senior or graduate study at accredited 4-year or graduate institution. Designated institutions: CADE-accredited/approved dietetics education programs.
Eligibility: Applicant must be U.S. citizen or permanent resident.
Basis for selection: Major/career interest in dietetics/nutrition. Applicant must demonstrate high academic achievement and seriousness of purpose.
Application requirements: Recommendations, proof of eligibility. GPA documentation signed by academic advisor.
Additional information: Applicant must be a member of the American Dietetic Association. Number and amount of awards varies. To be eligible, applicant must be enrolled in the approved program a minimum of four months during the academic year. Minority status considered. Must demonstrate or show promise of being a valuable, contributing member of the profession. See Website for more information and application.

Amount of award: $800-$4,500
Number of awards: 220
Number of applicants: 540
Application deadline: February 15
Notification begins: July 1
Total amount awarded: $250,000
Contact:
American Dietetic Association
Education Programs
120 South Riverside Plaza, Suite 2000
Chicago, IL 60606-6995
Phone: 800-877-1600 ext. 5400
Web: www.eatright.org/students/careers/aid.aspx

American Federation of State, County and Municipal Employees

AFSCME Family Scholarship

Type of award: Scholarship, renewable.
Intended use: For full-time undergraduate study at accredited 4-year institution.
Eligibility: Applicant must be high school senior.
Application requirements: Recommendations, essay, transcript, proof of eligibility. SAT or ACT scores.
Additional information: Scholarships open to children and financially dependent grandchildren of active or retired AFSCME members.
Amount of award: $2,000
Number of awards: 10
Number of applicants: 650
Application deadline: December 31
Notification begins: March 31
Total amount awarded: $20,000
Contact:
AFSCME Family Scholarship Program
Attn: Education Department
1625 L Street, NW
Washington, DC 20036
Phone: 202-429-1250
Web: www.afscme.org

Jerry Clark Memorial Scholarship

Type of award: Scholarship, renewable.
Intended use: For full-time junior study at accredited 4-year institution.
Basis for selection: Major/career interest in political science/government; sociology; communications or ethnic/cultural studies.
Application requirements: Transcript, proof of eligibility.
Additional information: Scholarships open to children and financially dependent grandchildren of AFSCME members. Applicant must be a current college sophomore. Winners given opportunity to intern at International Union headquarters in Political Action department. Minimum 2.5 GPA.
Amount of award: $5,000
Number of awards: 2
Number of applicants: 30
Application deadline: April 30
Notification begins: August 1
Total amount awarded: $10,000

Contact:
Jerry Clark Memorial Scholarship Program
AFSCME, AFL-CIO, Attn: Education Department
1625 L Street, NW
Washington, DC 20036
Phone: 202-429-1250
Web: www.afscme.org

American Floral Endowment

Ball Horticultural Company Scholarship

Type of award: Scholarship.
Intended use: For junior or senior study at accredited 4-year institution in United States or Canada.
Eligibility: Applicant must be U.S. citizen, permanent resident or Canadian citizen/resident.
Basis for selection: Major/career interest in horticulture.
Application requirements: Recommendations, transcript.
Additional information: Intended for students pursuing career in commercial floriculture. Minimum 3.0 GPA. Submit transcript and letters of recommendation via e-mail.
Amount of award: $500-$2,000
Application deadline: May 1
Notification begins: January 1
Contact:
American Floral Endowment
Attn: AFE Scholarship Applications
1601 Duke Street
Alexandria, VA 22314
Phone: 703-838-5211
Fax: 703-838-5212
Web: www.endowment.org

Earl Dedman Memorial Scholarship

Type of award: Scholarship.
Intended use: For full-time sophomore, junior or senior study at accredited 4-year institution in United States or Canada.
Eligibility: Applicant must be U.S. citizen, permanent resident or Canadian citizen. Applicant must be residing in Wyoming, Oregon, Montana, Idaho or Washington.
Basis for selection: Major/career interest in horticulture.
Application requirements: Recommendations, transcript.
Additional information: Minimum 3.0 GPA. Career interest in becoming a greenhouse grower required. To apply for this scholarship, applicant must have interest in greenhouse production and potted plants. Applicant must be from the Northwestern area of the U.S. Number and amount of scholarships vary.
Amount of award: $500-$2,000
Application deadline: May 1
Notification begins: January 1
Contact:
American Floral Endowment
1601 Duke Street
Alexandria, VA 22314
Phone: 703-838-5211
Fax: 703-838-5212
Web: www.endowment.org

Ed Markham International Scholarship

Type of award: Scholarship.
Intended use: For sophomore, junior, senior or graduate study at accredited 2-year, 4-year or graduate institution in United States or Canada.
Eligibility: Applicant must be U.S. citizen, permanent resident or Canadian citizen.
Basis for selection: Major/career interest in horticulture or marketing. Applicant must demonstrate financial need and high academic achievement.
Application requirements: Recommendations, transcript.
Additional information: Minimum 3.0 GPA. Must have interest in studying horticulture marketing through international travel. Number and amount of awards vary.

Amount of award:	$500-$2,000
Application deadline:	May 1
Notification begins:	January 1

Contact:
American Floral Endowment
1601 Duke Street
Alexandria, VA 22314
Phone: 703-838-5211
Fax: 703-838-5212
Web: www.endowment.org

Fran Johnson Non-Traditional Scholarship

Type of award: Scholarship.
Intended use: For full-time undergraduate or graduate study at accredited 4-year or graduate institution in United States or Canada.
Eligibility: Applicant must be returning adult student. Applicant must be U.S. citizen, permanent resident or Canadian citizen.
Basis for selection: Major/career interest in horticulture. Applicant must demonstrate financial need and high academic achievement.
Application requirements: Recommendations, transcript.
Additional information: Specific interest in bedding plants or floral crops required. Must be re-entering school after a minimum five-year absence. Number and amount of awards vary.

Amount of award:	$500-$2,000
Application deadline:	May 1
Notification begins:	January 1

Contact:
American Floral Endowment
1601 Duke Street
Alexandria, VA 22314
Phone: 703-838-5211
Fax: 703-838-5212
Web: www.endowment.org

Harold Bettinger Memorial Scholarship

Type of award: Scholarship.
Intended use: For full-time sophomore, junior or senior study at accredited 4-year institution in United States or Canada.
Eligibility: Applicant must be U.S. citizen, permanent resident or Canadian citizen.

Basis for selection: Major/career interest in horticulture; business or marketing. Applicant must demonstrate financial need and high academic achievement.
Application requirements: Recommendations, transcript.
Additional information: Minimum 3.0 GPA. To apply for this scholarship, applicant's major or minor must be in business and/or marketing with intent to apply it to a horticulture-related business. Amount of award varies.

Amount of award:	$500-$2,000
Number of awards:	1
Application deadline:	May 1
Notification begins:	January 1

Contact:
American Floral Endowment
1601 Duke Street
Alexandria, VA 22314
Phone: 703-838-5211
Fax: 703-838-5212
Web: www.endowment.org

Jacob Van Namen Marketing Scholarship

Type of award: Scholarship.
Intended use: For sophomore, junior or senior study at accredited 2-year or 4-year institution in United States or Canada.
Eligibility: Applicant must be U.S. citizen, permanent resident or Canadian citizen/resident.
Basis for selection: Major/career interest in horticulture; agribusiness; marketing; botany or agriculture. Applicant must demonstrate financial need and high academic achievement.
Application requirements: Recommendations, transcript.
Additional information: Minimum 3.0 GPA. Applicant must have interest in agribusiness marketing and distribution of floral products. Number and amount of awards vary.

Amount of award:	$500-$2,000
Application deadline:	May 1
Notification begins:	January 1

Contact:
American Floral Endowment
1601 Duke Street
Alexandria, VA 22314
Phone: 703-838-5211
Fax: 703-838-5212
Web: www.endowment.org

James Bridenbaugh Memorial Scholarship

Type of award: Scholarship.
Intended use: For sophomore, junior or senior study at accredited postsecondary institution.
Eligibility: Applicant must be U.S. citizen, permanent resident or Canadian citizen/resident.
Basis for selection: Major/career interest in horticulture.
Application requirements: Recommendations, transcript.
Additional information: For students pursuing career in floral design and marketing of fresh flowers and plants. Minimum 3.0 GPA. E-mail is preferred method for submitting transcripts and letters of recommendation.

Amount of award:	$500-$2,000
Application deadline:	May 1
Notification begins:	January 1

Contact:
American Floral Endowment
Attn: AFE Scholarship Applications
1601 Duke Street
Alexandria, VA 22314
Phone: 703-838-5211
Fax: 703-838-5212
Web: www.endowment.org

J.K. Rathmell, Jr. Memorial Scholarship for Work/Study Abroad

Type of award: Scholarship.
Intended use: For full-time junior, senior or graduate study at accredited 4-year or graduate institution outside United States.
Eligibility: Applicant must be U.S. citizen, permanent resident or Canadian citizen.
Basis for selection: Competition/talent/interest in study abroad. Major/career interest in horticulture or landscape architecture. Applicant must demonstrate financial need, high academic achievement, depth of character and seriousness of purpose.
Application requirements: Recommendations, transcript. Letter of invitation from host institution abroad.
Additional information: Minimum 3.0 GPA. Applicants must plan work/study abroad and submit specific plan for such. Preference given to those planning to work or study for six months or longer. Must have interest in floriculture, ornamental horticulture, or landscape architecture. Number and amount of awards vary.

Amount of award:	$500-$2,000
Application deadline:	May 1
Notification begins:	January 1

Contact:
American Floral Endowment
1601 Duke Street
Alexandria, VA 22314
Phone: 703-838-5211
Fax: 703-838-5212
Web: www.endowment.org

Leonard Bettinger Memorial Vocational Scholarship

Type of award: Scholarship.
Intended use: For full-time undergraduate certificate, freshman, sophomore or non-degree study at accredited vocational or 2-year institution in United States or Canada.
Eligibility: Applicant must be U.S. citizen, permanent resident or Canadian citizen.
Basis for selection: Major/career interest in horticulture. Applicant must demonstrate financial need and high academic achievement.
Application requirements: Recommendations, transcript.
Additional information: Minimum 3.0 GPA. Must intend to become floriculture grower or greenhouse manager. Number and amount of awards vary.

Amount of award:	$500-$2,000
Application deadline:	May 1
Notification begins:	January 1

Contact:
American Floral Endowment
1601 Duke Street
Alexandria, VA 22314
Phone: 703-838-5211
Fax: 703-838-5212
Web: www.endowment.org

American Foundation for Aging Research

American Foundation for Aging Research Fellowship

Type of award: Research grant, renewable.
Intended use: For full-time undergraduate, master's, doctoral or first professional study in United States.
Basis for selection: Major/career interest in biochemistry or biomedical. Applicant must demonstrate high academic achievement.
Application requirements: Recommendations, transcript, proof of eligibility, research proposal.
Additional information: Applicants must be actively involved or planning active involvement in specific biomedical or biochemical research project in field of aging. AFAR areas of interest: cellular biology, immunobiology, cancer, neurobiology, biochemistry, molecular biophysics, genomics, and proteomics. Sociology, psychology, and health-related research (e.g., physical therapy/exercise physiology) not currently funded. Those granted awards utilize modern and innovative approaches/technologies. Also applicable toward Ph.D., MD, DVM, and DDS degrees. Number of awards varies. Call sponsor for information regarding deadline. Applicants must complete online pre-application in order to qualify for full application. Notification begins one month after paperwork is received.

Amount of award:	$500-$2,000
Number of awards:	12
Number of applicants:	50
Total amount awarded:	$13,500

Contact:
American Foundation for Aging Research
North Carolina State University
Biochem. Dept., Campus Box 7622
Raleigh, NC 27695-7622
Phone: 919-515-5679
Fax: 919-515-2047
Web: www.agingresearchfoundation.org

American Foundation for Pharmaceutical Education

AFPE Gateway to Research Scholarships

Type of award: Research grant.
Intended use: For sophomore, junior, senior or first professional study at accredited 4-year or graduate institution.
Eligibility: Applicant must be U.S. citizen or permanent resident.
Basis for selection: Major/career interest in pharmacy/pharmaceutics/pharmacology.
Application requirements: Recommendations, essay, transcript, research proposal, nomination by faculty member sponsoring research. Copy of faculty member's curriculum vitae.
Additional information: Award intended to encourage students to undertake mentored research experience and to

consider pursuing Ph.D. in pharmaceutical science. At least $4,000 is provided as a student stipend for a research project done over full calendar year. Up to $1,000 may be used by sponsoring faculty member in direct support of research effort. One award reserved for Black or Hispanic student.

Amount of award:	$5,000
Number of awards:	15
Number of applicants:	57
Application deadline:	January 22
Notification begins:	April 16
Total amount awarded:	$75,000

Contact:
American Foundation for Pharmaceutical Education
One Church Street, Suite 202
Rockville, MD 20850
Phone: 301-738-2160
Fax: 301-738-2161
Web: www.afpenet.org

American Foundation for the Blind

Delta Gamma Foundation Florence Margaret Harvey Memorial Scholarship

Type of award: Scholarship.
Intended use: For undergraduate or graduate study at accredited postsecondary institution in United States.
Eligibility: Applicant must be visually impaired. Applicant must be U.S. citizen.
Basis for selection: Major/career interest in education, special or rehabilitation/therapeutic services.
Application requirements: Recommendations, essay, transcript, proof of eligibility.
Additional information: Applicant must be legally blind and studying in field of rehabilitation and/or education of blind or visually impaired persons.

Amount of award:	$1,000
Number of awards:	1
Application deadline:	March 31
Total amount awarded:	$1,000

Contact:
American Foundation for the Blind Scholarship Committee
Attn: Dawn Bodrogi
11 Penn Plaza, Suite 300
New York, NY 10001
Phone: 212-502-7661
Web: www.afb.org/scholarships.asp

Ferdinand Torres Scholarship

Type of award: Scholarship.
Intended use: For full-time undergraduate or graduate study at postsecondary institution in United States.
Eligibility: Applicant must be visually impaired. Applicant must be U.S. citizen or permanent resident.
Basis for selection: Applicant must demonstrate financial need.
Application requirements: Recommendations, essay, transcript, proof of eligibility. Student Aid Report (SAR).

Additional information: Applicant must be legally blind. Preference given to residents of New York City metropolitan area and new immigrants to the United States.

Amount of award:	$2,500
Number of awards:	1
Application deadline:	March 31

Contact:
American Foundation for the Blind Scholarship Committee
Attn: Dawn Bodrogi
11 Penn Plaza, Suite 300
New York, NY 10001
Phone: 212-502-7661
Web: www.afb.org/scholarships.asp

Paul and Helen Ruckes Scholarship

Type of award: Scholarship, renewable.
Intended use: For full-time undergraduate or graduate study at accredited postsecondary institution in United States.
Eligibility: Applicant must be visually impaired. Applicant must be U.S. citizen.
Basis for selection: Major/career interest in engineering; computer/information sciences; physical sciences or life sciences.
Application requirements: Recommendations, essay, transcript, proof of eligibility.
Additional information: Applicant must be legally blind.

Amount of award:	$1,000
Number of awards:	1
Application deadline:	March 31
Total amount awarded:	$1,000

Contact:
American Foundation for the Blind Scholarship Committee
Attn: Dawn Bodrogi
11 Penn Plaza, Suite 300
New York, NY 10001
Phone: 212-502-7661
Web: www.afb.org/scholarships.asp

R.L. Gillette Scholarship

Type of award: Scholarship, renewable.
Intended use: For full-time undergraduate study at accredited 4-year institution in United States.
Eligibility: Applicant must be visually impaired. Applicant must be female. Applicant must be U.S. citizen.
Basis for selection: Major/career interest in literature or music.
Application requirements: Recommendations, essay, transcript, proof of eligibility. Creative writing sample or performance tape/CD not to exceed 30 minutes.
Additional information: Applicant must be legally blind.

Amount of award:	$1,000
Number of awards:	2
Application deadline:	March 31
Total amount awarded:	$2,000

Contact:
American Foundation for the Blind Scholarship Committee
Attn: Dawn Bodrogi
11 Penn Plaza, Suite 300
New York, NY 10001
Phone: 212-502-7661
Web: www.afb.org/scholarships.asp

Rudolph Dillman Memorial Scholarship

Type of award: Scholarship.

Intended use: For full-time undergraduate or graduate study at accredited postsecondary institution in United States.
Eligibility: Applicant must be visually impaired. Applicant must be U.S. citizen.
Basis for selection: Major/career interest in education, special or rehabilitation/therapeutic services.
Application requirements: Recommendations, essay, transcript, proof of eligibility. SAR (financial need applicants only).
Additional information: Applicant must be legally blind and studying in field of rehabilitation and/or education of blind or visually impaired persons. One scholarship specifically for student who submits evidence of economic need.

Amount of award:	$2,500
Number of awards:	4
Application deadline:	March 31
Total amount awarded:	$10,000

Contact:
American Foundation for the Blind Scholarship Committee
Attn: Dawn Bodrogi
11 Penn Plaza, Suite 300
New York, NY 10001
Phone: 212-502-7661
Web: www.afb.org/scholarships.asp

American Ground Water Trust

Amtrol Scholarship

Type of award: Scholarship.
Intended use: For full-time freshman study at 4-year institution.
Eligibility: Applicant must be high school senior. Applicant must be U.S. citizen or permanent resident.
Basis for selection: Major/career interest in geology/earth sciences; engineering, environmental; environmental science; natural resources/conservation or hydrology. Applicant must demonstrate high academic achievement, leadership, seriousness of purpose and service orientation.
Application requirements: Recommendations, essay, transcript. Description of completed high school science project involving ground water resources or of non-school work experience related to environment and natural resources.
Additional information: Applicant must be entering field related to ground water, e.g., geology, hydrology, environmental science, or hydrogeology. Minimum 3.0 GPA required. Visit Website for application procedure and forms.

Amount of award:	$1,000
Number of awards:	1
Number of applicants:	1
Application deadline:	June 1
Notification begins:	August 15

Contact:
American Ground Water Trust Scholarship
50 Pleasant Street, Suite 2
Concord, NH 03301-4073
Phone: 603-228-5444
Fax: 603-228-6557
Web: www.agwt.org

Baroid Scholarship

Type of award: Scholarship.

Intended use: For full-time freshman study at accredited 4-year institution.
Eligibility: Applicant must be high school senior. Applicant must be U.S. citizen or permanent resident.
Basis for selection: Major/career interest in engineering, environmental; geology/earth sciences; environmental science or natural resources/conservation. Applicant must demonstrate high academic achievement, leadership, seriousness of purpose and service orientation.
Application requirements: Recommendations, essay, transcript. Description of previously completed high school science project involving ground water resources or of non-school work experience related to environment and natural resources.
Additional information: Must be entering field related to ground water, e.g., hydrology or hydrogeology. Minimum 3.0 GPA. Visit Website for application procedure and forms.

Amount of award:	$2,000
Number of awards:	1
Number of applicants:	1
Application deadline:	June 1
Notification begins:	August 15

Contact:
American Ground Water Trust Scholarship
50 Pleasant Street, Suite 2
Concord, NH 03301-4073
Phone: 603-228-5444
Fax: 603-228-6557
Web: www.agwt.org

Thomas M. Stetson Scholarship

Type of award: Scholarship.
Intended use: For full-time undergraduate study at accredited 4-year institution in United States. Designated institutions: Colleges and universities located west of the Mississippi River.
Eligibility: Applicant must be high school senior. Applicant must be U.S. citizen or permanent resident.
Basis for selection: Major/career interest in environmental science; natural resources/conservation or science, general. Applicant must demonstrate high academic achievement.
Application requirements: Recommendations, essay.
Additional information: Applicant must intend to pursue career in ground water related field. Minimum 3.0 GPA. Visit Website for application procedure and forms.

Amount of award:	$1,500
Number of awards:	1
Application deadline:	June 1
Notification begins:	August 15
Total amount awarded:	$1,500

Contact:
American Ground Water Trust
50 Pleasant Street
Concord, NH 03301
Phone: 603-228-5444
Fax: 603-228-6557
Web: www.agwt.org

American Helicopter Society

Arizona Chapter Vertical Flight Engineering Scholarship

Type of award: Scholarship.
Intended use: For full-time undergraduate or graduate study. Designated institutions: Schools of engineering in Arizona.
Basis for selection: Major/career interest in aviation or engineering. Applicant must demonstrate high academic achievement.
Application requirements: Recommendations, transcript. Resume.
Additional information: Award for students who demonstrate an interest in pursuing engineering careers in the fixed wing, rotorcraft, or VTOL aircraft industry. Recipients also receive one-year membership in AHS.

Amount of award:	$1,500-$2,500
Number of awards:	1
Application deadline:	October 10
Notification begins:	November 26

Contact:
Ms. Pam Howard
The Boeing Company
Mail Stop M530-B111, 5000 East McDowell Road
Mesa, AZ 85215-9797
Phone: 480-891-5475
Web: www.vtol.org

Vertical Flight Foundation Scholarship

Type of award: Scholarship.
Intended use: For full-time junior, senior, master's or doctoral study at accredited postsecondary institution.
Basis for selection: Major/career interest in aerospace; aviation or engineering. Applicant must demonstrate high academic achievement, depth of character and seriousness of purpose.
Application requirements: Recommendations, essay, transcript.
Additional information: Must demonstrate career interest in vertical flight engineering industry. Minimum 3.0 GPA required, 3.5 recommended. Number of awards varies based on funding.

Amount of award:	$1,000-$4,000
Number of awards:	13
Number of applicants:	64
Application deadline:	February 1
Notification begins:	April 15
Total amount awarded:	$32,000

Contact:
The Vertical Flight Foundation
217 North Washington Street
Alexandria, VA 22314-2538
Phone: 703-684-6777
Fax: 703-739-9279
Web: www.vtol.org

American Hellenic Educational Progressive Association Educational Foundation

AHEPA Educational Foundation Scholarships

Type of award: Scholarship.
Intended use: For full-time undergraduate or graduate study at accredited postsecondary institution.
Basis for selection: Applicant must demonstrate high academic achievement and service orientation.
Application requirements: Recommendations, transcript. Photo, financial information (when applicable).
Additional information: Applicant must be of Greek descent, or member/child of member (in good standing) of AHEPA, Daughters of Penelope, Sons of Pericles, or Maids of Athena. Minimum 3.0 GPA. High school seniors eligible to apply. Visit Website for details and application.

Amount of award:	$2,000
Application deadline:	March 31

Contact:
AHEPA Educational Foundation
1909 Q Street N.W., Suite 500
Washington, DC 20009-1007
Phone: 202-232-6300
Fax: 202-232-2140
Web: www.ahepa.org

American Hotel & Lodging Educational Foundation

American Express Scholarship Competition

Type of award: Scholarship, renewable.
Intended use: For undergraduate study at accredited 2-year or 4-year institution.
Basis for selection: Major/career interest in hotel/restaurant management or hospitality administration/management.
Application requirements: Essay, transcript.
Additional information: Must work at hotel 20 hours a week and have 12 months of hotel experience. Hotel must be member of American Hotel & Lodging Association. Dependents of hotel employees may also apply. Award must be used in hospitality management degree program. Visit Website to download application or apply online.

Amount of award:	$500-$2,000
Number of applicants:	27
Application deadline:	May 1
Notification begins:	July 15
Total amount awarded:	$15,000

Contact:
American Hotel & Lodging Educational Foundation
1201 New York Avenue, NW
Suite 600
Washington, DC 20005-3931
Phone: 202-289-3100
Fax: 202-289-3199
Web: www.ahlef.org

American Hotel & Lodging Educational Foundation Incoming Freshman Scholarship Competition

Type of award: Scholarship.
Intended use: For full-time freshman study at 2-year or 4-year institution.
Eligibility: Applicant must be U.S. citizen or permanent resident.
Basis for selection: Major/career interest in hotel/restaurant management or hospitality administration/management.
Additional information: Award must be used in hospitality management program. Minimum 2.0 GPA. $1,000 awards go to Associate majors, $2,000 to Baccalaureate majors. Preference will be given to high school graduates of the Lodging Management Program (LMP). Visit Website to download application or apply online.

Amount of award:	$1,000-$2,000
Number of applicants:	118
Application deadline:	May 1
Notification begins:	July 15
Total amount awarded:	$21,000

Contact:
American Hotel & Lodging Educational Foundation
1201 New York Avenue, NW
Suite 600
Washington, DC 20005-3931
Phone: 202-289-3100
Fax: 202-289-3199
Web: www.ahlef.org

Ecolab Scholarship Competition

Type of award: Scholarship.
Intended use: For full-time undergraduate study at 2-year or 4-year institution in United States.
Basis for selection: Major/career interest in hotel/restaurant management or hospitality administration/management.
Application requirements: Essay, transcript.
Additional information: Award must be used in hospitality management program. Applicant must maintain minimum 12 credit hours. Visit Website to download application or apply online.

Amount of award:	$1,000-$2,000
Number of applicants:	566
Application deadline:	May 1
Notification begins:	July 15
Total amount awarded:	$17,000

Contact:
American Hotel & Lodging Educational Foundation
1201 New York Avenue, NW
Suite 600
Washington, DC 20005-3931
Phone: 202-289-3100
Fax: 202-289-3199
Web: www.ahlef.org

The Hyatt Hotels Fund for Minority Lodging Management Students Competition

Type of award: Scholarship, renewable.
Intended use: For sophomore, junior or senior study at 4-year institution.
Eligibility: Applicant must be Alaskan native, Asian American, African American, Mexican American, Hispanic American, Puerto Rican, American Indian or Native Hawaiian/Pacific Islander. Applicant must be U.S. citizen or permanent resident.
Basis for selection: Major/career interest in hotel/restaurant management or hospitality administration/management.
Application requirements: Recommendations, essay, transcript.
Additional information: Award must be used in hospitality management program. Must be enrolled in at least 12 credit hours for upcoming fall and spring semesters, or just fall semester if graduating in December. Visit Website to download application or apply online.

Amount of award:	$2,000
Number of awards:	10
Number of applicants:	107
Application deadline:	May 1
Notification begins:	July 15
Total amount awarded:	$34,000

Contact:
American Hotel & Lodging Educational Foundation
1201 New York Avenue, NW
Suite 600
Washington, DC 20005
Phone: 202-289-3100
Fax: 202-289-3199
Web: www.ahlef.org

American Indian College Fund

Austin Family Scholarship Endowment

Type of award: Scholarship, renewable.
Intended use: For full-time sophomore, junior or senior study at 4-year institution in United States. Designated institutions: University of Oklahoma (OU) or Southeastern Oklahoma State University (SOSU).
Eligibility: Applicant must be American Indian. Applicant must be U.S. citizen residing in Oklahoma.
Basis for selection: Applicant must demonstrate financial need.
Application requirements: Essay, proof of eligibility. Recent photo.
Additional information: Minimum 2.5 GPA. Must be a member or descendant of a tribe in Oklahoma.

Amount of award:	$1,000
Number of awards:	5
Number of applicants:	316
Application deadline:	May 31
Total amount awarded:	$9,000

Contact:
American Indian College Fund
Austin Family Scholarship Endowment
8333 Greenwood Blvd
Denver, CO 80221
Phone: 800-776-3863
Web: www.collegefund.org

Ford Motor Company/American Indian College Fund Corporate Scholars Program

Type of award: Scholarship, renewable.
Intended use: For full-time sophomore, junior or senior study at 4-year institution. Designated institutions: Participating colleges and universities.
Eligibility: Applicant must be Alaskan native or American Indian. Must have proof of tribal enrollment or ancestry. Applicant must be U.S. citizen.
Basis for selection: Major/career interest in computer/information sciences; engineering, electrical/electronic; accounting; finance/banking; information systems; marketing or business. Applicant must demonstrate financial need, high academic achievement, depth of character and leadership.
Application requirements: Recommendations, essay, transcript, proof of eligibility. Small color photo.
Additional information: Student must demonstrate leadership and commitment to the American Indian community and be attending a participating college or university. Award is up to $10,000 based on financial need. Minimum 3.0 GPA.

Amount of award:	$10,000
Number of awards:	5
Number of applicants:	316
Application deadline:	May 31
Notification begins:	September 30
Total amount awarded:	$50,000

Contact:
American Indian College Fund
Corporate Scholars Program
8333 Greenwood Blvd
Denver, CO 80221
Phone: 800-776-3863
Fax: 303-426-1200
Web: www.collegefund.org

Foundation Scholarship

Type of award: Scholarship, renewable.
Intended use: For full-time undergraduate study in United States.
Eligibility: Applicant must be Alaskan native or American Indian. Applicant must be U.S. citizen.
Basis for selection: Applicant must demonstrate financial need.
Application requirements: Essay, proof of eligibility. Recent photo.
Additional information: Minimum 2.5 GPA. Applicant must be a resident of California or be a member or descendant of a California-based tribe.

Amount of award:	$3,000
Number of awards:	4
Application deadline:	May 31

Contact:
American Indian College Fund
Foundation Scholarship
8333 Greenwood Blvd.
Denver, CO 80221
Phone: 800-776-3863
Web: www.collegefund.org

Jack A. & Marilyn MacAllister Foundation

Type of award: Scholarship, renewable.
Intended use: For full-time undergraduate study in United States. Designated institutions: University of Nebraska-Omaha.
Eligibility: Applicant must be Alaskan native or American Indian. Applicant must be U.S. citizen.
Basis for selection: Major/career interest in education. Applicant must demonstrate financial need.
Application requirements: Essay, proof of eligibility. Recent photo.
Additional information: Minimum 2.5 GPA. Applicant must have graduated or transferred from a tribal college.

Amount of award:	$2,000
Number of awards:	1
Application deadline:	May 31

Contact:
American Indian College Fund
Jack A. & Marilyn MacAllister Foundation
8333 Greenwood Blvd.
Denver, CO 80221
Phone: 800-776-3863
Web: www.collegefund.org

Morgan Stanley Scholars Program

Type of award: Scholarship, renewable.
Intended use: For full-time undergraduate study at 4-year institution.
Eligibility: Applicant must be Alaskan native or American Indian. Applicant must be U.S. citizen.
Basis for selection: Major/career interest in business; finance/banking; information systems; marketing or accounting. Applicant must demonstrate high academic achievement.
Application requirements: Recommendations, essay, transcript, proof of eligibility. Fall class schedule (when available), small color photograph. Personal Statement describing background and career/academic goals. Two essays, maximum 500 words each, on the topics: 1) How do you perceive yourself as a leader in your school and community? And 2) How will your education help the Native American community?
Additional information: Minimum 3.2 GPA.

Amount of award:	$10,000
Number of awards:	5
Number of applicants:	316
Application deadline:	May 31
Notification begins:	September 30
Total amount awarded:	$50,000

Contact:
American Indian College Fund
8333 Greenwood Blvd.
Denver, CO 80221
Phone: 800-776-3863
Web: www.collegefund.org

Nissan North America, Inc. Scholarship

Type of award: Scholarship, renewable.
Intended use: For full-time undergraduate study at 4-year institution.
Eligibility: Applicant must be Alaskan native or American Indian. Applicant must be U.S. citizen.
Basis for selection: Applicant must demonstrate high academic achievement and leadership.
Application requirements: Recommendations, essay, transcript, proof of eligibility. Two short essays, fall class schedule (when available), and small color photograph.
Additional information: Minimum 2.5 GPA. For use at mainstream institution, not tribal college. Must have proof of American Indian/Alaskan Native enrollment or descent.

Amount of award:	$5,000
Number of awards:	5
Number of applicants:	316
Application deadline:	May 31
Notification begins:	September 30
Total amount awarded:	$25,000

Contact:
American Indian College Fund
8333 Greenwood Blvd.
Denver, CO 80221
Phone: 800-776-3863
Web: www.collegefund.org

Sovereign Nations Scholarship Fund

Type of award: Scholarship.
Intended use: For full-time undergraduate study at 4-year or graduate institution.
Eligibility: Applicant must be Alaskan native or American Indian. Applicant must be U.S. citizen.
Basis for selection: Applicant must demonstrate financial need and high academic achievement.
Application requirements: Recommendations, essay, transcript, proof of eligibility. Two short essays, fall class schedule (when available), and small color photograph, proof of American Indian or Alaskan Native tribal enrollment or ancestry.
Additional information: Minimum 3.0 GPA. Must commit to working for tribe or Indian organization upon completion of degree. For use at mainstream institution, not tribal college.

Amount of award:	$2,000
Number of awards:	13
Number of applicants:	316
Application deadline:	May 31
Notification begins:	September 30
Total amount awarded:	$9,000

Contact:
American Indian College Fund
8333 Greenwood Blvd.
Denver, CO 80221
Phone: 800-776-3863
Web: www.collegefund.org

Travelers Foundation

Type of award: Scholarship.
Intended use: For full-time undergraduate study in United States. Designated institutions: Mainstream colleges/universities in St.Paul-Minneapolis, MN; Seattle, WA; Spokane, WA; or Kansas City, KS.
Eligibility: Applicant must be Alaskan native or American Indian. Applicant must be U.S. citizen residing in Minnesota, Montana, Kansas or Washington.
Basis for selection: Major/career interest in accounting; business; computer/information sciences; engineering or mathematics. Applicant must demonstrate financial need and high academic achievement.
Application requirements: Essay, proof of eligibility. Recent photo.
Additional information: Minimum 2.5 GPA. May also major in computer technology. Applicant must commit to leadership development by attending a two-day Travelers career day.

Amount of award:	$2,500
Number of awards:	2
Number of applicants:	316
Application deadline:	May 31
Total amount awarded:	$5,000

Contact:
American Indian College Fund
Travelers Foundation
8333 Greenwood Blvd.
Denver, CO 80221
Phone: 800-776-3863
Web: www.collegefund.org

United Health Foundation Scholarship

Type of award: Scholarship, renewable.
Intended use: For full-time undergraduate study at 4-year institution. Designated institutions: Mainstream colleges/universities in Arizona.
Eligibility: Applicant must be Alaskan native or American Indian. Applicant must be U.S. citizen residing in Arizona.
Basis for selection: Major/career interest in health-related professions; health education; health sciences or health services administration. Applicant must demonstrate financial need and high academic achievement.
Application requirements: Recommendations, essay, transcript, proof of eligibility. Two short essays, fall class schedule (when available), and small color photograph. Proof of American Indian/Alaskan Native tribal enrollment or ancestry.
Additional information: Minimum 3.0 GPA. Preference is given to tribal college graduates who are transferring.

Amount of award:	$5,000
Number of awards:	4
Number of applicants:	316
Application deadline:	May 31
Notification begins:	September 30
Total amount awarded:	$20,000

Contact:
American Indian College Fund
8333 Greenwood Blvd.
Denver, CO 80221
Phone: 800-776-3863
Web: www.collegefund.org

American Indian Science & Engineering Society

A.T. Anderson Memorial Scholarship

Type of award: Scholarship.
Intended use: For full-time undergraduate or graduate study at accredited 2-year, 4-year or graduate institution in United States.
Eligibility: Applicant must be Alaskan native or American Indian. Must be member of American Indian tribe or be at least 1/4 American Indian/Alaskan Native blood.
Basis for selection: Major/career interest in science, general; engineering; medicine; natural resources/conservation; mathematics; physical sciences or technology. Applicant must demonstrate depth of character, leadership, seriousness of purpose and service orientation.
Application requirements: Recommendations, essay, transcript, proof of eligibility. Resume.
Additional information: Must be AISES member. Minimum 3.0 GPA. Undergraduate student award $1,000; graduate student award $2,000. Membership and scholarship applications available on Website.

Amount of award:	$1,000-$2,000
Application deadline:	June 15
Notification begins:	October 1

Contact:
AISES Scholarships
P.O. Box 9828
Albuquerque, NM 87119-9828
Phone: 505-765-1052
Fax: 505-765-5608
Web: www.aises.org

Burlington Northern Santa Fe Foundation Scholarship

Type of award: Scholarship, renewable.
Intended use: For full-time undergraduate study at accredited 4-year institution in United States.
Eligibility: Applicant must be Alaskan native or American Indian. Must be member of American Indian tribe or be at least 1/4 American Indian/Alaskan Native blood. Applicant must be high school senior. Applicant must be U.S. citizen residing in South Dakota, Minnesota, Washington, Kansas, Arizona, Oklahoma, California, Oregon, Montana, New Mexico, Colorado or North Dakota.
Basis for selection: Major/career interest in science, general; engineering; mathematics; physical sciences; medicine; natural sciences; business; health services administration; technology or education. Applicant must demonstrate financial need, depth of character, leadership, seriousness of purpose and service orientation.
Application requirements: Recommendations, essay, transcript, proof of eligibility. Resume.
Additional information: Applicant must be AISES member. Minimum 2.0 GPA. Award is renewable for four years (eight semesters) or until degree obtained, whichever comes first, assuming eligibility maintained. Membership and scholarship applications available on Website.

Amount of award:	$2,500
Number of awards:	5
Application deadline:	April 15
Notification begins:	October 1

Contact:
AISES Scholarships
P.O. Box 9828
Albuquerque, NM 87119-9828
Phone: 505-765-1052
Fax: 505-765-5608
Web: www.aises.org

American Institute For Foreign Study

HACU (Hispanic Association of Colleges and Universities) Scholarships

Type of award: Scholarship.
Intended use: For undergraduate study in Australia, Austria, Brazil, China, Costa Rica, Czech Republic, England, France, Germany, India, Ireland, Italy, New Zealand, Peru, Russia, South Africa, Spain. Designated institutions: HACU member institutions.
Eligibility: Applicant must be Mexican American, Hispanic American or Puerto Rican.
Basis for selection: Competition/talent/interest in study abroad. Applicant must demonstrate high academic achievement and leadership.
Application requirements: Recommendations, essay, transcript. Disciplinary clearance.
Additional information: Scholarship intended for use at AIFS programs. Applicant must be involved in multicultural/international activities. Deadlines are March 1 for summer, April 15 for fall, and October 1 for spring. Award amount is up to half of the AIFS all-inclusive program fee for summer and semester programs.

Number of awards:	3
Number of applicants:	15
Application deadline:	March 1, April 15
Notification begins:	April 1, May 15
Total amount awarded:	$25,000

Contact:
AIFS College Division
9 West Broad Street
Stamford, CT 06902-3788
Phone: 800-727-2437
Fax: 203-399-5597
Web: www.aifsabroad.com

International Semester Scholarship

Type of award: Scholarship.
Intended use: For undergraduate study in Australia, Austria, Brazil, China, Costa Rica, Czech Republic, England, France, Germany, India, Ireland, Italy, New Zealand, Peru, Russia, South Africa, Spain. Designated institutions: AIFS programs.
Basis for selection: Competition/talent/interest in study abroad. Applicant must demonstrate high academic achievement and leadership.
Application requirements: Recommendations, essay, transcript. Disciplinary clearance.

Additional information: Minimum 3.0 GPA. Must be involved in multicultural/international activities. Award amount is $500 for summer and $1,000 for semester program. Number of awards available is 40 for fall semester, 40 for spring semester, and 50 for summer. Application deadlines are March 1 for summer, April 15 for fall, and October 1 for spring.

Amount of award:	$500-$1,000
Number of awards:	130
Number of applicants:	580
Application deadline:	October 1, April 15
Notification begins:	November 1, May 15
Total amount awarded:	$105,000

Contact:
AIFS College Division
9 West Broad Street
Stamford, CT 06902-3788
Phone: 800-727-2437
Fax: 203-399-5597
Web: www.aifsabroad.com

NAFEO (National Association for Equal Opportunity in Higher Education) Scholarships

Type of award: Scholarship.
Intended use: For undergraduate study in Australia, Austria, China, Costa Rica, Czech Republic, England, France, India, Ireland, Italy, New Zealand, Russia, South Africa, Spain. Designated institutions: HCBUs or PBIs.
Eligibility: Applicant must be African American.
Basis for selection: Competition/talent/interest in study abroad. Applicant must demonstrate high academic achievement and leadership.
Application requirements: Recommendations, essay, transcript. Disciplinary clearance.
Additional information: Scholarship intended for use at AIFS programs. Applicant must be involved in multicultural/international activities. Deadlines are April 15 for fall and October 1 for spring. Award amount is up to half of the AIFS all-inclusive program fee for summer and semester programs.

Number of awards:	2
Application deadline:	April 15, October 1
Notification begins:	May 15, November 1

Contact:
AIFS College Division
9 West Broad Street
Stamford, CT 06902-3788
Phone: 800-727-2437
Fax: 203-399-5597
Web: www.aifsabroad.com

American Institute of Aeronautics and Astronautics

AIAA Foundation Undergraduate Scholarship

Type of award: Scholarship, renewable.
Intended use: For full-time sophomore, junior or senior study at accredited 4-year institution in United States.

Basis for selection: Major/career interest in aerospace; engineering; mathematics or science, general. Applicant must demonstrate high academic achievement.
Application requirements: Recommendations, essay, transcript.
Additional information: Minimum 3.3 GPA. Must be AIAA member to apply. Not open to members of any AIAA national committees or subcommittees. Applicants must reapply for renewal.

Amount of award:	$2,000-$2,500
Number of awards:	30
Number of applicants:	110
Application deadline:	January 31
Notification begins:	June 15
Total amount awarded:	$61,000

Contact:
AIAA Student Programs
1801 Alexander Bell Drive
Suite 500
Reston, VA 20191-4344
Phone: 703-264-7500
Web: www.aiaa.org/students

American Institute of Architects

AIA/AAF Minority/Disadvantaged Scholarship

Type of award: Scholarship, renewable.
Intended use: For full-time freshman or sophomore study in United States. Designated institutions: NAAB-accredited institutions.
Eligibility: Applicant must be U.S. citizen or permanent resident.
Basis for selection: Major/career interest in architecture. Applicant must demonstrate financial need.
Application requirements: Recommendations, essay, transcript, proof of eligibility, nomination by high school guidance counselor, architect, or other individual who can speak to student's aptitude for architecture. Statement of disadvantaged circumstances, drawing.
Additional information: Check Website for deadline. Open to high school seniors and college freshmen who plan to enter programs leading to professional degree in architecture. Students who have completed full year of undergraduate course work not eligible. Renewable up to two years.

Amount of award:	$500-$2,500
Number of awards:	20
Number of applicants:	120

Contact:
The American Institute of Architects
1735 New York Avenue, NW
Washington, DC 20006-5292
Phone: 202-626-7417
Fax: 202-626-7420
Web: www.aia.org/education/AIAS075223

American Institute of Architects New Jersey

AIA New Jersey Scholarship Foundation

Type of award: Scholarship, renewable.
Intended use: For full-time sophomore, junior, senior, master's or first professional study at accredited postsecondary institution. Designated institutions: Architectural schools.
Eligibility: Applicant must be residing in New Jersey.
Basis for selection: Major/career interest in architecture. Applicant must demonstrate financial need, high academic achievement, depth of character and seriousness of purpose.
Application requirements: $5 application fee. Portfolio, essay, transcript. FAFSA.
Additional information: Non-New Jersey residents attending architecture school in New Jersey also eligible.

Amount of award:	$2,500-$5,000
Number of awards:	5
Number of applicants:	35
Application deadline:	June 1
Notification begins:	August 1
Total amount awarded:	$7,000

Contact:
AIA New Jersey Scholarship Foundation, Inc.
c/o Robert Zaccone
212 White Avenue
Old Tappan, NJ 07675
Phone: 609-393-5690
Fax: 609-393-9891
Web: www.aia-nj.org/about/scholarship.shtml

American Institute of Certified Public Accountants

Scholarship for Minority Accounting Students

Type of award: Scholarship, renewable.
Intended use: For full-time undergraduate or graduate study at postsecondary institution.
Eligibility: Applicant must be Alaskan native, Asian American, African American, Mexican American, Hispanic American, Puerto Rican, American Indian or Native Hawaiian/Pacific Islander. Applicant must be U.S. citizen or permanent resident.
Basis for selection: Major/career interest in accounting. Applicant must demonstrate high academic achievement, leadership and seriousness of purpose.
Application requirements: Recommendations, essay, transcript, proof of eligibility. Strategy plan for obtaining CPA, list of honors/activities/work experience.
Additional information: Applicants must have completed at least 30 semester hours or equivalent of college work, with at least six hours in accounting. Minimum 3.3 GPA. Undergraduate applicants must have declared accounting majors. Graduate applicants must be pursuing master's in accounting, taxation, finance, or other related field.

Amount of award:	$1,500-$3,000
Number of awards:	130
Application deadline:	March 15
Notification begins:	August 1
Total amount awarded:	$390,000

Contact:
Center for Scholarship Administration
Minority Scholarships Program
4320 Wade Hampton Boulevard, Suite G
Taylors, SC 29687
Phone: 864-268-3363
Web: www.aicpa.org/members/div/career/mini/smas.htm

American Institute of Polish Culture

Harriet Irsay Scholarship

Type of award: Scholarship.
Intended use: For full-time undergraduate or graduate study.
Eligibility: Applicant must be U.S. citizen or permanent resident.
Basis for selection: Major/career interest in communications; education; film/video; history; humanities/liberal arts; international relations; journalism; polish language/studies or public relations. Applicant must demonstrate high academic achievement.
Application requirements: $10 application fee. Recommendations, essay, transcript. Detailed resume, 700-word article on any subject about Poland.
Additional information: Send SASE with application request or download from Website. Check Website for deadline. Preference given to American students of Polish heritage.

Amount of award:	$1,000
Number of awards:	15
Number of applicants:	60
Total amount awarded:	$14,000

Contact:
The American Institute of Polish Culture Scholarship Applications
1440 79th Street Causeway
Suite 117
Miami, FL 33141-3555
Phone: 305-864-2349
Fax: 305-865-5150
Web: www.ampolinstitute.org

American Legion Alabama

American Legion Alabama Oratorical Contest

Type of award: Scholarship.
Intended use: For undergraduate study at postsecondary institution.
Eligibility: Applicant or parent must be member/participant of American Legion. Applicant must be enrolled in high school. Applicant must be U.S. citizen residing in Alabama.
Basis for selection: Competition/talent/interest in oratory/debate, based on language style, voice, diction, delivery,

originality, logic, breadth of knowledge, application of knowledge about topic, and skill in selecting examples and analogies.

Application requirements: Proof of eligibility.

Additional information: First place, $5,000; second place, $3,000; third place, $2,000. State finals held in March. Send business-size SASE for application.

Amount of award:	$2,000-$5,000
Number of awards:	3
Total amount awarded:	$10,000

Contact:
The American Legion, Department of Alabama
P.O. Box 1069
Montgomery, AL 36101-1069
Phone: 334-262-6638
Web: www.americanlegionalabama.org

American Legion Alabama Scholarship

Type of award: Scholarship, renewable.

Intended use: For undergraduate study at postsecondary institution.

Eligibility: Applicant or parent must be member/participant of American Legion. Applicant must be U.S. citizen or permanent resident residing in Alabama. Applicant must be descendant of veteran; or dependent of veteran during Korean War, Persian Gulf War, WW I, WW II or Vietnam.

Application requirements: Recommendations, transcript, proof of eligibility. SAT/ACT scores.

Additional information: Four-year scholarships at Alabama colleges. Send business-size SASE for application.

Amount of award:	$850
Number of awards:	130
Application deadline:	April 1
Total amount awarded:	$110,500

Contact:
The American Legion, Department of Alabama
P.O. Box 1069
Montgomery, AL 36101-1069
Phone: 334-262-6638
Web: www.americanlegionalabama.org

American Legion Alabama Auxiliary

American Legion Alabama Auxiliary Scholarship

Type of award: Scholarship, renewable.

Intended use: For undergraduate study at postsecondary institution. Designated institutions: Alabama state-supported colleges.

Eligibility: Applicant or parent must be member/participant of American Legion Auxiliary. Applicant must be U.S. citizen or permanent resident residing in Alabama. Applicant must be descendant of veteran; or dependent of veteran during Grenada conflict, Korean War, Lebanon conflict, Panama conflict, Persian Gulf War, WW I, WW II or Vietnam.

Application requirements: Proof of eligibility.

Additional information: Four-year scholarships at Alabama colleges. Previous one-year scholarship recipients can reapply.

Grandchildren of veterans also eligible. Send SASE for application.

Amount of award:	$850
Number of awards:	40
Application deadline:	April 1
Total amount awarded:	$34,000

Contact:
American Legion Auxiliary, Department of Alabama
120 North Jackson Street
Montgomery, AL 36104
Phone: 334-262-1176

American Legion Alaska

American Legion Alaska Oratorical Contest

Type of award: Scholarship.

Intended use: For undergraduate study at postsecondary institution.

Eligibility: Applicant or parent must be member/participant of American Legion. Applicant must be enrolled in high school. Applicant must be U.S. citizen or permanent resident residing in Alaska.

Basis for selection: Competition/talent/interest in oratory/debate, based on language style, voice, diction, delivery, originality, logic, breadth of knowledge, application of knowledge about topic, and skill in selecting examples and analogies.

Application requirements: Proof of eligibility.

Additional information: Awards: First place, $3,000; second place, $2,000; third and fourth place, $1,000. Must be high school student attending Alaska accredited institution. Must participate in local speech contests. Contest begins in November.

Amount of award:	$1,000-$3,000
Number of awards:	4
Total amount awarded:	$7,000

Contact:
American Legion, Department of Alaska
Department Adjutant
1550 Charter Circle
Anchorage, AK 99508
Phone: 907-278-8598
Fax: 907-278-0041
Web: www.alaskalegion.org

American Legion Western District Postsecondary Scholarship

Type of award: Scholarship.

Intended use: For undergraduate study at vocational, 2-year or 4-year institution.

Eligibility: Applicant or parent must be member/participant of American Legion. Applicant must be high school senior. Applicant must be residing in Alaska.

Basis for selection: Applicant must demonstrate financial need, seriousness of purpose and service orientation.

Application requirements: Recommendations, essay, transcript.

Additional information: Minimum 2.0 GPA.

Amount of award:	$750
Application deadline:	February 15

Contact:
American Legion Western District Postsecondary Scholarship
Attn: Jim Scott
1124 Holmes Road
North Pole, AK 99705
Phone: 907-488-5310
Web: www.alaskalegion.org

American Legion Alaska Auxiliary

American Legion Alaska Auxiliary Scholarship

Type of award: Scholarship.
Intended use: For freshman study at postsecondary institution.
Eligibility: Applicant or parent must be member/participant of American Legion Auxiliary. Applicant must be at least 17, no older than 24, high school senior. Applicant must be U.S. citizen or permanent resident residing in Alaska. Applicant must be dependent of veteran during Grenada conflict, Korean War, Lebanon conflict, Panama conflict, Persian Gulf War, WW I, WW II or Vietnam.
Application requirements: Proof of eligibility.
Additional information: Scholarship to apply toward tuition, matriculation, laboratory, or similar fees. Must not have attended institution of higher education.

Amount of award:	$1,500
Application deadline:	March 15

Contact:
American Legion Auxiliary, Department of Alaska
1392 6th Avenue
Fairbanks, AK 99701
Web: www.alaskalegionauxiliary.org

American Legion Alaska Auxiliary Western District Scholarship

Type of award: Scholarship.
Intended use: For undergraduate study at accredited vocational, 2-year, 4-year or graduate institution.
Eligibility: Applicant or parent must be member/participant of American Legion Auxiliary. Applicant must be returning adult student. Applicant must be residing in Alaska.
Additional information: For continuing education students who are furthering their education to enhance work skills for entry or re-entry into the work field.

Amount of award:	$1,000
Application deadline:	March 15

Contact:
American Legion Auxiliary, Department of Alaska
1392 6th Avenue
Fairbanks, AK 99701
Web: www.alaskalegionauxiliary.org

American Legion Arizona

American Legion Arizona Oratorical Contest

Type of award: Scholarship.
Intended use: For undergraduate study at postsecondary institution.
Eligibility: Applicant or parent must be member/participant of American Legion. Applicant must be enrolled in high school. Applicant must be U.S. citizen or permanent resident residing in Arizona.
Basis for selection: Competition/talent/interest in oratory/debate, based on language style, voice, diction, delivery, originality, logic, breadth of knowledge, application of knowledge about topic, and skill in selecting examples and analogies.
Additional information: Awards: First place, $1,500; second place, $800; third place, $500. For students enrolled in accredited Arizona high schools.

Amount of award:	$500-$1,500
Number of awards:	3
Application deadline:	January 15
Total amount awarded:	$2,800

Contact:
American Legion Arizona, Oratorical Contest
4701 North 19th Avenue, Suite 200
Phoenix, AZ 85015-3727
Phone: 602-264-7706
Fax: 602-264-0029
Web: www.azlegion.org

American Legion Arizona Auxiliary

American Legion Arizona Auxiliary Health Care Occupation Scholarship

Type of award: Scholarship.
Intended use: For undergraduate or post-bachelor's certificate study at accredited vocational, 2-year or 4-year institution. Designated institutions: Arizona tax-supported institutions.
Eligibility: Applicant or parent must be member/participant of American Legion Auxiliary. Applicant must be U.S. citizen residing in Arizona.
Basis for selection: Major/career interest in health-related professions; health sciences or physical therapy. Applicant must demonstrate financial need, high academic achievement, depth of character and seriousness of purpose.
Application requirements: Recommendations, essay, transcript. Photograph of self.
Additional information: Must be resident of Arizona at least one year. Preference given to immediate family members of veterans.

Amount of award:	$500
Application deadline:	May 15

Contact:
American Legion Auxiliary, Department of Arizona
4701 North 19th Avenue, Suite 100
Phoenix, AZ 85015-3727
Phone: 602-241-1080
Fax: 602-604-9640
Web: www.azlegion.org/LadiesAuxiliary.htm

American Legion Arizona Auxiliary Nurses' Scholarship

Type of award: Scholarship.
Intended use: For sophomore study. Designated institutions: Arizona institutions.
Eligibility: Applicant or parent must be member/participant of American Legion Auxiliary. Applicant must be U.S. citizen residing in Arizona.
Basis for selection: Major/career interest in nursing.
Application requirements: Recommendations, essay, transcript. Photograph of self.
Additional information: Must be pursuing RN degree. Must be Arizona resident for at least one year. Preference given to immediate family members of veterans.

Amount of award:	$600
Application deadline:	May 15

Contact:
American Legion Auxiliary, Department of Arizona
4701 North 19th Avenue, Suite 100
Phoenix, AZ 85015-3727
Phone: 602-241-1080
Fax: 602-604-9640
Web: www.azlegion.org/LadiesAuxiliary.htm

Wilma D. Hoyal/Maxine Chilton Memorial Scholarship

Type of award: Scholarship.
Intended use: For full-time sophomore, junior or senior study. Designated institutions: University of Arizona, Arizona State University, Northern Arizona University.
Eligibility: Applicant or parent must be member/participant of American Legion Auxiliary. Applicant must be U.S. citizen residing in Arizona.
Basis for selection: Major/career interest in political science/government; education, special or public administration/service. Applicant must demonstrate financial need, high academic achievement, depth of character and seriousness of purpose.
Application requirements: Recommendations, transcript. Resume.
Additional information: For second-year or upper-division full-time students. Three $1,000 awards payable to three designated institutions in Arizona. Applicant must be state resident at least one year. Preference given to immediate family members of veterans.

Amount of award:	$3,000
Number of awards:	3
Application deadline:	May 15

Contact:
American Legion Auxiliary, Department of Arizona
4701 North 19th Avenue, Suite 100
Phoenix, AZ 85015-3727
Phone: 602-241-1080
Fax: 602-604-9640
Web: www.azlegion.org/LadiesAuxiliary.htm

American Legion Arkansas

American Legion Arkansas Oratorical Contest

Type of award: Scholarship.
Intended use: For undergraduate study at postsecondary institution.
Eligibility: Applicant or parent must be member/participant of American Legion. Applicant must be high school sophomore, junior or senior. Applicant must be U.S. citizen or permanent resident residing in Arkansas.
Basis for selection: Competition/talent/interest in oratory/debate, based on language style, voice, diction, delivery, originality, logic, breadth of knowledge, application of knowledge about topic, and skill in selecting examples and analogies.
Application requirements: Proof of eligibility.
Additional information: Oratorical Contest, State Division: first place, $2,000; second place, $1,500; third place, $1,000. Must apply to local Post.

Amount of award:	$1,000-$2,000
Number of awards:	3
Application deadline:	December 1
Total amount awarded:	$4,500

Contact:
American Legion Arkansas
Department Adjutant
P.O. Box 3280
Little Rock, AR 72203
Phone: 501-375-1104
Fax: 501-375-4236
Web: www.arklegion.homestead.com

American Legion Arkansas Scholarship

Type of award: Scholarship.
Intended use: For undergraduate study at postsecondary institution.
Eligibility: Applicant or parent must be member/participant of American Legion. Applicant must be residing in Arkansas.
Application requirements: Proof of eligibility.
Additional information: Four scholarships: amount to be determined. Must be child, grandchild, or great-grandchild of American Legion member.

Number of awards:	4
Application deadline:	December 1

Contact:
American Legion Arkansas
Department Adjutant
P.O. Box 3280
Little Rock, AR 72203
Phone: 501-375-1104
Fax: 501-375-4236
Web: www.arklegion.homestead.com

Scholarships

109

American Legion Arkansas Auxiliary

American Legion Arkansas Auxiliary Scholarships

Type of award: Scholarship.
Intended use: For undergraduate study at postsecondary institution.
Eligibility: Applicant or parent must be member/participant of American Legion Auxiliary. Applicant must be high school senior. Applicant must be U.S. citizen residing in Arkansas. Applicant must be descendant of veteran; or dependent of veteran during Grenada conflict, Korean War, Lebanon conflict, Panama conflict, Persian Gulf War, WW I, WW II or Vietnam.
Basis for selection: Applicant must demonstrate financial need, high academic achievement, depth of character, leadership and patriotism.
Application requirements: Recommendations, essay, transcript, proof of eligibility. SAT/ACT scores.
Additional information: Academic Scholarship: one $500; Nurse Scholarship: one $500. Awards paid half first semester, half second semester. Student must be Arkansas resident attending Arkansas school. Include name of high school and SASE with application request.

Amount of award:	$500
Number of awards:	2
Application deadline:	March 1
Total amount awarded:	$1,000

Contact:
American Legion Auxiliary, Department of Arkansas
Department Secretary
1415 West 7th St.
Little Rock, AR 72201
Phone: 501-374-5836
Web: www.arklegion.homestead.com/ArkAux.html

American Legion Auxiliary, Department of Illinois

Americanism Essay Contest Scholarship

Type of award: Scholarship.
Intended use: For undergraduate study at postsecondary institution.
Eligibility: Applicant must be enrolled in high school. Applicant must be residing in Illinois.
Application requirements: 500-word essay on selected topic.
Additional information: Award amount depends on placement and grade level. Open to students grade 7-12 enrolled at accredited Illinois junior high and high schools. Deadline is first Friday in February. Submit essay to local American Legion Post, Auxiliary Unit, or Sons of American Legion Squadron.

Amount of award:	$100-$1,200

Contact:
American Legion Auxiliary, Department of Illinois
P.O. Box 1426
Bloomington, IL 61702-1426
Web: www.illegion.org

American Legion Auxiliary, Department of Maryland

Past President's Parley Scholarship

Type of award: Scholarship.
Intended use: For undergraduate study at 2-year or 4-year institution.
Eligibility: Applicant must be female, at least 16, no older than 22. Applicant must be residing in Maryland. Must be daughter/step-daughter, granddaughter/step-granddaughter, great-granddaughter/step-great-granddaughter of ex-servicewoman or ex-serviceman.
Basis for selection: Major/career interest in nursing. Applicant must demonstrate financial need.
Application requirements: Recommendations.
Additional information: For RN degree only.

Amount of award:	$2,000
Number of awards:	1
Application deadline:	May 1
Total amount awarded:	$2,000

Contact:
American Legion Auxiliary, Department of Maryland
Chairman, Past President's Parley Scholarship
1589 Sulphur Spring Road, Suite 105
Baltimore, MD 21227
Phone: 410-242-9519
Fax: 410-242-9553
Web: www.alamd.org

American Legion California

American Legion California Oratorical Contest

Type of award: Scholarship.
Intended use: For undergraduate study at postsecondary institution.
Eligibility: Applicant must be enrolled in high school. Applicant must be U.S. citizen or permanent resident residing in California.
Basis for selection: Competition/talent/interest in oratory/debate, based on language style, voice, diction, delivery, originality, logic, breadth of knowledge, application of knowledge about topic, and skill in selecting examples and analogies.
Additional information: Students selected by schools to participate in district contests, followed by area and departmental finals. Awards: First place, $1,200; second place, $1,000; third to sixth place, $700 each. Contact local Post for entry.

Amount of award:	$700-$1,200
Number of awards:	6
Total amount awarded:	$5,000

Contact:
American Legion California
401 Van Ness Avenue, Room 117
San Francisco, CA 94102-4587
Phone: 415-431-2400
Fax: 415-255-1571
Web: www.calegion.org

American Legion California Auxiliary

American Legion California Auxiliary General Scholarships

Type of award: Scholarship.
Intended use: For freshman study at postsecondary institution. Designated institutions: California colleges and universities.
Eligibility: Applicant or parent must be member/participant of American Legion Auxiliary. Applicant must be high school senior. Applicant must be residing in California. Applicant must be dependent of active service person or veteran during Grenada conflict, Korean War, Lebanon conflict, Panama conflict, Persian Gulf War, WW I, WW II or Vietnam.
Basis for selection: Applicant must demonstrate financial need.
Application requirements: Recommendations, transcript, proof of eligibility. Cover letter.
Additional information: Annual scholarships: One $2,000 (payable at $1,000 per year); four $1,000; three $500. Must be high school senior or graduate who has not been able to begin college due to illness or financial circumstances. See Website for application. Applications must be submitted to local Unit.

Amount of award:	$500-$2,000
Number of awards:	8
Application deadline:	March 16
Total amount awarded:	$7,500

Contact:
American Legion Auxiliary, Department of California
War Memorial Building
401 Van Ness Avenue, Room 113
San Francisco, CA 94102-4586
Phone: 415-861-5092
Fax: 415-861-8365
Web: www.calegionaux.org

Continuing or Re-entry Student Scholarship

Type of award: Scholarship.
Intended use: For undergraduate study at postsecondary institution. Designated institutions: California colleges and universities.
Eligibility: Applicant or parent must be member/participant of American Legion Auxiliary. Applicant must be residing in California. Applicant must be veteran; or dependent of active service person or veteran during Grenada conflict, Korean War, Lebanon conflict, Panama conflict, Persian Gulf War, WW I, WW II or Vietnam.
Application requirements: Recommendations, transcript. Cover letter, photo of self.
Additional information: Three $1,000 and two $500 scholarships for continuing or re-entering college students. See

Website for application. Applications must be submitted to local Unit.

Amount of award:	$500-$1,000
Number of awards:	5
Application deadline:	March 16
Total amount awarded:	$4,000

Contact:
American Legion Auxiliary, Department of California
War Memorial Building
401 Van Ness Avenue, Room 113
San Francisco, CA 94102-4586
Phone: 415-861-5092
Fax: 415-861-8365
Web: www.calegionaux.org

Past Department Presidents' Junior Scholarship

Type of award: Scholarship.
Intended use: For freshman study at postsecondary institution. Designated institutions: California colleges and universities.
Eligibility: Applicant or parent must be member/participant of American Legion Auxiliary. Applicant must be high school senior. Applicant must be residing in California. Applicant must be descendant of veteran; or dependent of veteran during Grenada conflict, Korean War, Lebanon conflict, Panama conflict, Persian Gulf War, WW I, WW II or Vietnam. Applicant must have consecutive membership as Junior for three years.
Basis for selection: Applicant must demonstrate high academic achievement and service orientation.
Application requirements: Recommendations, essay, proof of eligibility.
Additional information: Must have Junior membership for three consecutive years. Applications must be submitted to the Unit in which the Junior holds membership. See Website for application.
Contact:
American Legion Auxiliary, Department of California
War Memorial Building
401 Van Ness Avenue, Room 113
San Francisco, CA 94102-4586
Phone: 415-861-5092
Fax: 415-861-8365
Web: www.calegionaux.org

Past Presidents' Parley Nursing Scholarship

Type of award: Scholarship.
Intended use: For undergraduate study at accredited postsecondary institution. Designated institutions: California colleges and universities awarding LPN and RN degrees.
Eligibility: Applicant or parent must be member/participant of American Legion Auxiliary. Applicant must be residing in California. Applicant must be in military service or veteran; or dependent of veteran; or spouse of veteran or deceased veteran during Grenada conflict, Korean War, Lebanon conflict, Panama conflict, Persian Gulf War, WW I, WW II or Vietnam.
Basis for selection: Major/career interest in nursing. Applicant must demonstrate financial need.
Application requirements: Recommendations, transcript, proof of eligibility.
Additional information: Applicant must be entering or continuing student in a nursing program. See Website for application. Applications must be submitted to local Unit by the first Friday in April.

Number of awards: 1
Application deadline: April 3
Total amount awarded: $2,000

Contact:
American Legion Auxiliary, Department of California
War Memorial Building
401 Van Ness Avenue, Room 113
San Francisco, CA 94102-4586
Phone: 415-861-5092
Fax: 415-861-8365
Web: www.calegionaux.org

American Legion Colorado

National High School Oratorical Contest

Type of award: Scholarship.
Intended use: For undergraduate study at postsecondary institution.
Eligibility: Applicant must be enrolled in high school. Applicant must be residing in Colorado.
Basis for selection: Competition/talent/interest in oratory/ debate, based on language style, voice, diction, delivery, originality, logic, breadth of knowledge, application of knowledge about topic, and skill in selecting examples and analogies.
Additional information: Awards: First place, $2,500; second place, $2,000; third place, $1,500; fourth to twelfth place, $500. Apply at local Post.

Amount of award: $500-$2,500
Number of awards: 12
Total amount awarded: $10,500

Contact:
American Legion, Department of Colorado
7465 East First Avenue, Suite D
Denver, CO 80230
Web: www.coloradolegion.org

American Legion Colorado Auxiliary

Department President's Scholarship

Type of award: Scholarship.
Intended use: For undergraduate study at postsecondary institution.
Eligibility: Applicant or parent must be member/participant of American Legion Auxiliary. Applicant must be high school senior. Applicant must be residing in Colorado. Applicant must be dependent of veteran during Grenada conflict, Korean War, Lebanon conflict, Panama conflict, Persian Gulf War, WW I, WW II or Vietnam.
Additional information: One $1,000 award and two $500 awards.

Amount of award: $500-$1,000
Number of awards: 3
Application deadline: April 4
Total amount awarded: $2,000

Contact:
American Legion Auxiliary, Department of Colorado
7465 East First Avenue, Suite D
Denver, CO 80230

Department President's Scholarship for Junior Auxiliary Members

Type of award: Scholarship.
Intended use: For undergraduate study at postsecondary institution.
Eligibility: Applicant or parent must be member/participant of American Legion Auxiliary. Applicant must be high school senior. Applicant must be residing in Colorado. Applicant must be Colorado Junior Auxiliary member.

Amount of award: $1,000
Number of awards: 1
Application deadline: March 12
Total amount awarded: $1,000

Contact:
American Legion Auxiliary, Department of Colorado
7465 East First Avenue, Suite D
Denver, CO 80230

Past President's Parley Nurse's Scholarship

Type of award: Scholarship.
Intended use: For undergraduate study at accredited 2-year or 4-year institution.
Eligibility: Applicant or parent must be member/participant of American Legion Auxiliary. Applicant must be residing in Colorado. Applicant must be veteran; or dependent of veteran; or spouse of veteran during Grenada conflict, Korean War, Lebanon conflict, Panama conflict, Persian Gulf War, WW I, WW II or Vietnam.
Basis for selection: Major/career interest in nursing.
Additional information: Number and amount of awards vary.

Amount of award: $500-$1,000
Application deadline: April 15

Contact:
American Legion Auxiliary, Department of Colorado
7465 East First Avenue, Suite D
Denver, CO 80230

American Legion Connecticut

National High School Oratorical Contest

Type of award: Scholarship.
Intended use: For undergraduate study at postsecondary institution.
Eligibility: Applicant must be no older than 19, enrolled in high school. Applicant must be residing in Connecticut.
Basis for selection: Competition/talent/interest in oratory/ debate, based on language style, voice, diction, delivery, originality, logic, breadth of knowledge, application of knowledge about topic, and skill in selecting examples and analogies.
Additional information: Awards: First place, $3,000; second- $2,000; third to seventh place, $1,000; all in Savings Bonds.

Contest open only to students attending Connecticut high schools. Contact high school for more information.

Amount of award:	$1,000-$3,000
Number of awards:	7
Total amount awarded:	$10,000

Contact:
American Legion, Department of Connecticut
Department Oratorical Chairman
P.O. Box 208
Rocky Hill, CT 06067-0208
Phone: 860-721-5942
Web: www.ct.legion.org

American Legion Connecticut Auxiliary

Memorial Education Grant

Type of award: Scholarship.
Intended use: For undergraduate study at vocational, 2-year or 4-year institution.
Eligibility: Applicant or parent must be member/participant of American Legion Auxiliary. Applicant must be at least 16, no older than 23.
Basis for selection: Applicant must demonstrate financial need.
Application requirements: Recommendations, essay, transcript, proof of eligibility.
Additional information: Half of grants awarded to child/ grandchild of Connecticut AL/ALA member or to a member of Connecticut ALA/Sons of the AL. No residency requirement. Other half awarded to child of Connecticut resident veteran.

Amount of award:	$500
Number of awards:	4
Application deadline:	March 1
Total amount awarded:	$2,000

Contact:
American Legion Auxiliary, Department of Connecticut
P.O. Box 266
Rocky Hill, CT 06067-0266
Phone: 860-721-5945
Fax: 860-721-5828
Web: www.ct.legion.org/auxiliary.htm

Past President's Parley Education Grant

Type of award: Scholarship, renewable.
Intended use: For undergraduate study at vocational, 2-year or 4-year institution.
Eligibility: Applicant or parent must be member/participant of American Legion Auxiliary. Applicant must be at least 16, no older than 23.
Basis for selection: Applicant must demonstrate financial need.
Application requirements: Recommendations, essay, transcript, proof of eligibility.
Additional information: Preference given to child or grandchild of ex-servicewoman who is a CT American Legion or American Legion Auxiliary member of at least three years or who was a member for the three years prior to her death. Second preference to child or grandchild of CT American Legion, American Legion Auxiliary, or Sons of American

Legion member of at least three years, or who was a member for three years prior to death.

Amount of award:	$500
Number of awards:	4
Application deadline:	March 1
Total amount awarded:	$2,000

Contact:
American Legion Auxiliary, Department of Connecticut
P.O. Box 266
Rocky Hill, CT 06067-0266
Phone: 860-721-5945
Fax: 860-721-5828
Web: www.ct.legion.org/auxiliary.htm

American Legion Delaware Auxiliary

Past President's Parley Nursing Scholarship

Type of award: Scholarship.
Intended use: For undergraduate study at postsecondary institution.
Eligibility: Applicant or parent must be member/participant of American Legion Auxiliary. Applicant must be residing in Delaware. Applicant must be dependent of veteran.
Basis for selection: Major/career interest in nursing.

Amount of award:	$300
Number of awards:	1
Application deadline:	February 28
Total amount awarded:	$300

Contact:
American Legion Auxiliary, Department of Delaware
P.O. Box 157
Seaford, DE 19973

American Legion District of Columbia

National High School Oratorical Contest

Type of award: Scholarship.
Intended use: For undergraduate study at postsecondary institution.
Eligibility: Applicant must be no older than 20, enrolled in high school. Applicant must be U.S. citizen or permanent resident residing in District of Columbia.
Basis for selection: Competition/talent/interest in oratory/ debate, based on language style, voice, diction, delivery, originality, logic, breadth of knowledge, application of knowledge about topic, and skill in selecting examples and analogies.
Application requirements: Proof of eligibility.
Additional information: Awards: First place, $800; second place, $500; third place, $200; fourth place, $100. All awards in U.S. Savings Bonds.

Amount of award: $100-$800
Number of awards: 4
Total amount awarded: $1,600
Contact:
The American Legion, Department of DC
3408 Wisconsin Avenue NW, Suite 218
Washington, DC 20016
Phone: 202-362-9151
Fax: 202-362-9152
Web: www.legiondc.org

American Legion Florida

American Legion Florida General Scholarship

Type of award: Scholarship.
Intended use: For undergraduate study at accredited postsecondary institution in United States.
Eligibility: Applicant or parent must be member/participant of American Legion. Applicant must be high school senior. Applicant must be residing in Florida. Must be child, grandchild, great-grandchild, or legally adopted child of member in good standing of American Legion Florida, or of a deceased U.S. veteran who would have been eligible for membership.
Application requirements: Proof of eligibility.
Additional information: Scholarships: First place, $2,500; second place, $1,500; third place, $1,000; fourth to seventh place, $500.
Amount of award: $500-$2,500
Number of awards: 7
Application deadline: March 1
Total amount awarded: $7,000
Contact:
American Legion Florida, Department Headquarters
P.O. Box 547859
Orlando, FL 32854-7859
Phone: 407-295-2631 ext. 222
Web: www.floridalegion.org

Eagle Scout of the Year

Type of award: Scholarship.
Intended use: For undergraduate study at accredited postsecondary institution in United States.
Eligibility: Applicant or parent must be member/participant of American Legion. Applicant must be male, enrolled in high school. Applicant must be residing in Florida. Applicant must be registered, active member of Boy Scout Troop, Varsity Scout Team, or Venturing Crew chartered to an American Legion Post, Auxiliary Unit, or Sons of American Legion Squadron; or be a registered, active member of a Boy Scout Troop, Varsity Scout Team, or Venturing Crew and be a son or grandson of American Legion member.
Application requirements: Proof of eligibility.
Additional information: Awards: First place, $2,500; second place, $1,500; third place, $1,000; fourth place, $500. Must have earned Eagle Award and religious emblem.
Amount of award: $500-$2,500
Number of awards: 4
Application deadline: March 1
Total amount awarded: $5,500

Contact:
American Legion Florida, Department Headquarters
P.O. Box 547859
Orlando, FL 32854-7859
Phone: 407-295-2631 ext. 222
Web: www.floridalegion.org

High School Oratorical Contest

Type of award: Scholarship.
Intended use: For undergraduate study at postsecondary institution.
Eligibility: Applicant must be enrolled in high school. Applicant must be residing in Florida.
Basis for selection: Competition/talent/interest in oratory/debate, based on language style, voice, diction, delivery, originality, logic, breadth of knowledge, application of knowledge about topic, and skill in selecting examples and analogies.
Additional information: Awards: First place, $2,500; second place, $1,500; third place, $1,000; fourth to sixth place, $500.
Amount of award: $500-$2,500
Number of awards: 6
Application deadline: December 1
Total amount awarded: $6,500
Contact:
American Legion Florida, Department Headquarters
P.O. Box 547859
Orlando, FL 32854-7859
Phone: 407-295-2631 ext. 222
Web: www.floridalegion.org

American Legion Florida Auxiliary

American Legion Florida Auxiliary Memorial Scholarship

Type of award: Scholarship, renewable.
Intended use: For full-time undergraduate study at vocational, 2-year or 4-year institution.
Eligibility: Applicant or parent must be member/participant of American Legion Auxiliary. Applicant must be residing in Florida. Must be members or daughter/granddaughter of member with at least three years' membership in FL unit.
Application requirements: Recommendations, essay, transcript, proof of eligibility. Income tax forms.
Additional information: Up to $1,000 for junior colleges and vocational schools; $2,000 for four-year university. Must maintain minimum 2.5 GPA. Send application request by January 1.
Amount of award: $1,000-$2,000
Contact:
American Legion Auxiliary, Department of Florida
Department Secretary
P.O. Box 547917
Orlando, FL 32854-7917
Fax: 407-299-6522
Web: www.alafl.org

American Legion Florida Auxiliary Scholarships

Type of award: Scholarship, renewable.
Intended use: For undergraduate study at vocational, 2-year or 4-year institution.
Eligibility: Applicant or parent must be member/participant of American Legion Auxiliary. Applicant must be residing in Florida. Must be child or stepchild of honorably discharged U.S. military veteran and sponsored by local Auxiliary Unit.
Application requirements: Recommendations, essay, transcript, proof of eligibility. Income tax forms.
Additional information: Up to $1000 for junior colleges and vocational schools; $2,000 for four-year university. Must maintain minimum 2.5 GPA. Send application request by January 1.
   Amount of award: $1,000-$2,000
Contact:
American Legion Auxiliary, Department of Florida
Department Secretary
P.O. Box 547917
Orlando, FL 32854-7917
Fax: 407-299-6522
Web: www.alafl.org

American Legion Georgia Auxiliary

American Legion Georgia Auxiliary Scholarship

Type of award: Scholarship.
Intended use: For undergraduate study at postsecondary institution.
Eligibility: Applicant or parent must be member/participant of American Legion Auxiliary. Applicant must be high school senior. Applicant must be residing in Georgia. Applicant must be dependent of veteran or deceased veteran. Must be sponsored by local Auxiliary Unit.
Additional information: Information and application materials available through local American Legion Auxiliary Unit.
   Amount of award: $1,000
   Number of awards: 4
   Total amount awarded: $4,000
Contact:
American Legion Georgia Auxiliary, Department Headquarters
3035 Mt. Zion Road
Stockbridge, GA 30281-4101
Web: www.galegion.org/auxiliary.htm

Past President's Parley Nurses Scholarship

Type of award: Scholarship.
Intended use: For undergraduate study at 2-year or 4-year institution.
Eligibility: Applicant or parent must be member/participant of American Legion Auxiliary. Applicant must be residing in Georgia. Applicant must be dependent of veteran or deceased veteran. Must be sponsored by local Auxiliary Unit.
Basis for selection: Major/career interest in nursing.

Application requirements: Proof of eligibility.
Additional information: Amount and number of scholarships determined by available funds.
Contact:
American Legion Georgia Auxiliary, Department Headquarters
3035 Mt. Zion Road
Stockbridge, GA 30281-4101
Web: www.galegion.org/auxiliary.htm

American Legion Hawaii

American Legion Oratorical Contest

Type of award: Scholarship.
Intended use: For undergraduate study at postsecondary institution.
Eligibility: Applicant must be enrolled in high school. Applicant must be residing in Hawaii.
Basis for selection: Competition/talent/interest in oratory/debate, based on language style, voice, diction, delivery, originality, logic, breadth of knowledge, application of knowledge about topic, and skill in selecting examples and analogies.
Additional information: Awards: first place, $1000; second place, $500; third place, $100; fourth place, $50. Contest normally held in February.
   Amount of award: $50-$1,000
   Number of awards: 4
   Total amount awarded: $1,650
Contact:
American Legion Hawaii, Department Headquarters
612 McCully Street
Honolulu, HI 96826
Phone: 808-946-6383
Fax: 808-947-3957
Web: www.50legion.org

American Legion Idaho

American Legion Idaho Scholarships

Type of award: Scholarship.
Intended use: For undergraduate study at postsecondary institution.
Eligibility: Applicant or parent must be member/participant of American Legion. Applicant must be residing in Idaho.
Application requirements: Proof of eligibility.
Additional information: Grandchildren of American Legion members and children and grandchildren of American Legion Auxiliary members in Idaho also eligible. Scholarships determined annually. See Website for more information.
   Application deadline: July 1
Contact:
American Legion Idaho, Department Headquarters
901 Warren Street
Boise, ID 83706
Phone: 208-342-7061
Fax: 208-342-1964
Web: idlegion.home.mindspring.com/

Scholarships

Oratorical Contest

Type of award: Scholarship.

Intended use: For undergraduate study at postsecondary institution.

Eligibility: Applicant must be enrolled in high school. Applicant must be residing in Idaho.

Basis for selection: Competition/talent/interest in oratory/ debate, based on language style, voice, diction, delivery, originality, logic, breadth of knowledge, application of knowledge about topic, and skill in selecting examples and analogies.

Additional information: Awards: First place, $750; second place, $500; third place, $250; fourth place, $100. Visit Website for more information.

Amount of award:	$100-$750
Number of awards:	4
Total amount awarded:	$1,600

Contact:
American Legion Idaho, Department Headquarters
901 Warren Street
Boise, ID 83706
Phone: 208-342-7061
Fax: 208-342-1964
Web: idlegion.home.mindspring.com/

American Legion Idaho Auxiliary

American Legion Idaho Auxiliary Nurse's Scholarship

Type of award: Scholarship.

Intended use: For undergraduate study at 2-year or 4-year institution.

Eligibility: Applicant must be residing in Idaho. Applicant must be veteran; or dependent of veteran.

Basis for selection: Major/career interest in nursing.

Additional information: Applicant must be Idaho resident five years prior to application. Grandchildren of veterans also eligible. Submit application to local Auxiliary Unit.

Amount of award:	$1,000
Application deadline:	May 15

Contact:
American Legion Idaho Auxiliary, Department Headquarters
905 Warren Street
Boise, ID 83706-3825
Phone: 208-342-7066
Fax: 208-342-7066

American Legion Illinois

American Legion Illinois Boy Scout Scholarship

Type of award: Scholarship.

Intended use: For undergraduate study at postsecondary institution.

Eligibility: Applicant or parent must be member/participant of Boy Scouts of America. Applicant must be high school senior. Applicant must be residing in Illinois.

Basis for selection: Competition/talent/interest in writing/ journalism.

Application requirements: Proof of eligibility. 500-word essay on American Legion, Americanism, and Boy Scout programs.

Additional information: Boy Scout Scholarship: $700. Runner-up awards: $200. Contact American Legion Department of Illinois, Post, County, District, or Division for application.

Amount of award:	$200-$700
Application deadline:	April 30

Contact:
American Legion, Department of Illinois
C/O Boy Scout Committee
P.O. Box 2910
Bloomington, IL 61702-2910
Web: www.illegion.org

American Legion Illinois Oratorical Contest

Type of award: Scholarship.

Intended use: For undergraduate study at vocational, 2-year or 4-year institution.

Eligibility: Applicant must be enrolled in high school. Applicant must be U.S. citizen or permanent resident residing in Illinois.

Basis for selection: Competition/talent/interest in oratory/ debate, based on language style, voice, diction, delivery, originality, logic, breadth of knowledge, application of knowledge about topic, and skill in selecting examples and analogies.

Application requirements: Proof of eligibility.

Additional information: Contest begins in January and starts at Post level, continuing to District level, to Division level, to Department level, and ending in National Competition. Awards: First place, $2,000; second place, $1,500; third place, $1,200; fourth and fifth place, $1,000. Applications available in the fall. Contact local Post or Department Headquarters.

Amount of award:	$1,000-$2,000

Contact:
American Legion, Department of Illinois
P.O. Box 2910
Bloomington, IL 61702-2910
Web: www.illegion.org

American Legion Illinois Scholarships

Type of award: Scholarship.

Intended use: For undergraduate study at accredited vocational, 2-year or 4-year institution.

Eligibility: Applicant or parent must be member/participant of American Legion. Applicant must be high school senior. Applicant must be residing in Illinois.

Basis for selection: Applicant must demonstrate financial need and high academic achievement.

Application requirements: Proof of eligibility.

Additional information: Grandchildren of American Legion members also eligible. Applications available after December 15.

Amount of award:	$1,000
Number of awards:	20
Application deadline:	March 15
Total amount awarded:	$20,000

Contact:
American Legion, Department of Illinois
P.O. Box 2910
Bloomington, IL 61702
Phone: 309-663-0361
Web: www.illegion.org

American Legion Illinois Auxiliary

Ada Mucklestone Memorial Scholarship

Type of award: Scholarship.
Intended use: For undergraduate study at postsecondary institution.
Eligibility: Applicant must be high school senior. Applicant must be residing in Illinois. Applicant must be descendant of veteran; or dependent of veteran during Grenada conflict, Korean War, Lebanon conflict, Panama conflict, Persian Gulf War, WW I, WW II or Vietnam.
Basis for selection: Applicant must demonstrate financial need, high academic achievement, depth of character and leadership.
Application requirements: Recommendations, essay, transcript, proof of eligibility. Copy of parents' most recent federal income tax return.
Additional information: Must be a resident of Illinois or a member in good standing of The American Legion Family, Department of Illinois. Awards: First place, $1,200; second place, $1,000; several $800. Nursing majors not eligible. Unit sponsorship required. Contact local Unit for application.

Amount of award: $800-$1,200
Application deadline: March 15
Contact:
American Legion Auxiliary, Department of Illinois
P.O. Box 1426
Bloomington, IL 61702-1426
Phone: 309-663-9366
Web: www.illegion.org/auxiliary

Marie Sheehe Trade School Scholarship

Type of award: Scholarship.
Intended use: For undergraduate study at vocational institution.
Eligibility: Applicant must be residing in Illinois. Applicant must be descendant of veteran; or dependent of veteran during Grenada conflict, Korean War, Lebanon conflict, Panama conflict, Persian Gulf War, WW I, WW II or Vietnam.
Basis for selection: Applicant must demonstrate financial need, high academic achievement, depth of character and leadership.
Application requirements: Recommendations, essay, transcript, proof of eligibility. Copy of parents' most recent federal income tax return.
Additional information: Must be Illinois resident or member in good standing of American Legion Family, Department of Illinois. Unit sponsorship required. Contact local Unit for application.

Amount of award: $800
Number of awards: 1
Application deadline: March 15
Total amount awarded: $800
Contact:
American Legion Auxiliary, Department of Illinois
P.O. Box 1426
Bloomington, IL 61702-1426
Phone: 309-663-9366
Web: www.illegion.org/auxiliary

Mildred R. Knoles Opportunity Scholarship

Type of award: Scholarship.
Intended use: For sophomore, junior or senior study at postsecondary institution.
Eligibility: Applicant must be residing in Illinois. Applicant must be veteran or descendant of veteran; or dependent of veteran during Grenada conflict, Korean War, Lebanon conflict, Panama conflict, Persian Gulf War, WW I, WW II or Vietnam.
Basis for selection: Applicant must demonstrate financial need, high academic achievement, depth of character and leadership.
Application requirements: Recommendations, essay, transcript, proof of eligibility. Copy of most recent federal income tax return.
Additional information: Must be resident of Illinois or member in good standing of the American Legion Family, Department of Illinois. Awards: one $1,200; several $800. Unit sponsorship required. Contact local Unit for application.

Amount of award: $800-$1,200
Application deadline: March 15
Contact:
American Legion Auxiliary, Department of Illinois
P.O. Box 1426
Bloomington, IL 61702-1426
Phone: 309-663-9366
Web: www.illegion.org/auxiliary

Special Education Teaching Scholarships

Type of award: Scholarship.
Intended use: For sophomore or junior study at 4-year institution.
Eligibility: Applicant must be residing in Illinois. Applicant must be veteran or descendant of veteran; or dependent of veteran during Grenada conflict, Korean War, Lebanon conflict, Panama conflict, Persian Gulf War, WW I, WW II or Vietnam.
Basis for selection: Major/career interest in education, special. Applicant must demonstrate financial need.
Application requirements: Proof of eligibility.
Additional information: Unit sponsorship required. Contact local Unit for application.

Amount of award: $1,000
Application deadline: March 15
Total amount awarded: $1,000
Contact:
American Legion Auxiliary, Department of Illinois
P.O. Box 1426
Bloomington, IL 61702-1426
Phone: 309-663-9366
Web: www.illegion.org/auxiliary

Scholarships

Student Nurse Scholarship

Type of award: Scholarship.
Intended use: For undergraduate study at 2-year or 4-year institution.
Eligibility: Applicant must be residing in Illinois.
Basis for selection: Major/career interest in nursing.
Application requirements: Proof of eligibility.
Additional information: Unit sponsorship required. Contact local Unit for application.

Amount of award:	$1,000
Number of awards:	1
Application deadline:	April 10
Total amount awarded:	$1,000

Contact:
American Legion Auxiliary, Department of Illinois
P.O. Box 1426
Bloomington, IL 61702-1426
Phone: 309-663-9366
Web: www.illegion.org/auxiliary

American Legion Indiana

American Legion Americanism and Government Test

Type of award: Scholarship.
Intended use: For undergraduate study at postsecondary institution.
Eligibility: Applicant must be high school sophomore, junior or senior. Applicant must be residing in Indiana.
Additional information: Six state winners chosen annually (one male, one female in each grade). Test given during American Education Week in November. Visit Website for local chairperson's contact information.

Amount of award:	$1,000
Number of awards:	6
Total amount awarded:	$6,000

Contact:
American Legion Indiana, Department Headquarters
Americanism Office
777 North Meridian Street
Indianapolis, IN 46204
Phone: 317-630-1264
Web: www.indlegion.org

American Legion Family Scholarship

Type of award: Scholarship.
Intended use: For undergraduate study at accredited vocational, 2-year or 4-year institution in United States.
Eligibility: Applicant or parent must be member/participant of American Legion. Applicant must be residing in Indiana. Applicant must be child or grandchild of current or deceased member of The American Legion Indiana, American Legion Indiana Auxiliary, or Sons of The American Legion.
Application requirements: Essay, transcript, proof of eligibility.
Additional information: Three awards of approximately $700-$1,000 each.

Amount of award:	$700-$1,000
Number of awards:	3
Application deadline:	April 1

Contact:
American Legion Indiana, Department Headquarters
Americanism Office
777 North Meridian Street
Indianapolis, IN 46204
Phone: 317-630-1264
Web: www.indlegion.org

American Legion Indiana Oratorical Contest

Type of award: Scholarship.
Intended use: For undergraduate study at postsecondary institution.
Eligibility: Applicant must be enrolled in high school. Applicant must be residing in Indiana.
Basis for selection: Competition/talent/interest in oratory/ debate, based on language style, voice, diction, delivery, originality, logic, breadth of knowledge, application of knowledge about topic, and skill in selecting examples and analogies.
Application requirements: Proof of eligibility.
Additional information: State awards: First place, $3,400; second to fourth place, $1,000. Zone awards: four winners receive $800 each; 7 participants receive $200 each. Must participate in local contests.

Amount of award:	$200-$3,400
Number of awards:	15
Application deadline:	December 1
Total amount awarded:	$11,000

Contact:
American Legion Indiana, Department Headquarters
Americanism Office
777 North Meridian Street
Indianapolis, IN 46204
Phone: 317-630-1264
Web: www.indlegion.org

American Legion Indiana Auxiliary

Edna M. Barcus Memorial Scholarship and Hoosier Scholarship

Type of award: Scholarship.
Intended use: For undergraduate study at postsecondary institution. Designated institutions: Indiana institutions.
Eligibility: Applicant or parent must be member/participant of American Legion Auxiliary. Applicant must be residing in Indiana. Applicant must be dependent of veteran.
Basis for selection: Applicant must demonstrate high academic achievement.
Application requirements: Send SASE for application.

Amount of award:	$500
Application deadline:	April 1

Contact:
American Legion Auxiliary, Department of Indiana
Department Secretary
777 North Meridian Street, Room 107
Indianapolis, IN 46204
Phone: 317-630-1390
Fax: 317-630-1277
Web: www.amlegauxin.org/

Past President's Parley Nursing Scholarship

Type of award: Scholarship.
Intended use: For undergraduate study.
Eligibility: Applicant or parent must be member/participant of American Legion Auxiliary. Applicant must be female. Applicant must be residing in Indiana.
Basis for selection: Major/career interest in nursing.
Application requirements: Send SASE for application.
  Amount of award: $500
  Application deadline: April 1
  Total amount awarded: $500
Contact:
American Legion Auxiliary, Department of Indiana
Department Secretary
777 North Meridian Street, Room 107
Indianapolis, IN 46204
Phone: 317-630-1390
Fax: 317-630-1277
Web: www.amlegauxin.org/

American Legion Iowa

American Legion Iowa Oratorical Contest

Type of award: Scholarship.
Intended use: For undergraduate study at postsecondary institution.
Eligibility: Applicant must be enrolled in high school. Applicant must be U.S. citizen or permanent resident residing in Iowa.
Basis for selection: Competition/talent/interest in oratory/debate, based on language style, voice, diction, delivery, originality, logic, breadth of knowledge, application of knowledge about topic, and skill in selecting examples and analogies.
Application requirements: Proof of eligibility.
Additional information: Awards: First place, $2,000; second place, $1,500; third place, $1000. Must enter Oratorical Contest at local level in September.
  Amount of award: $1,000-$2,000
  Number of awards: 3
  Total amount awarded: $4,500
Contact:
American Legion Iowa, Department Headquarters
720 Lyon Street
Des Moines, IA 50309
Phone: 515-282-5068
Fax: 515-282-7583
Web: www.ialegion.org

Boy Scout of the Year Scholarship

Type of award: Scholarship.
Intended use: For undergraduate study at postsecondary institution.
Eligibility: Applicant or parent must be member/participant of Boy Scouts of America, Eagle Scouts. Applicant must be male, at least 15. Applicant must be residing in Iowa. Must be registered, active member of Boy Scout Troop, Varsity Scout Team, or Venturing Crew chartered to American Legion Post, Auxiliary Unit, or Sons of American Legion Squadron; or be a registered, active member of Boy Scout Troop, Varsity Scout Team, or Venturing Crew and the son or grandson of an American Legion or Sons of American Legion member.
Basis for selection: Applicant must demonstrate service orientation.
Application requirements: Recommendations, transcript, proof of eligibility.
Additional information: Awards: First place, $2,000; second place, $1,500; third place, $1,000. Awarded on recommendation of Boy Scout Committee to Boy Scout who demonstrates outstanding service to religious institution, school, and community. Must have received Eagle Scout Award.
  Amount of award: $1,000-$2,000
  Number of awards: 3
  Application deadline: February 1
  Total amount awarded: $4,500
Contact:
American Legion Iowa, Department Headquarters
720 Lyon Street
Des Moines, IA 50309
Phone: 515-282-5068
Fax: 515-282-7583
Web: www.ialegion.org

American Legion Iowa Auxiliary

Department of Iowa Scholarships

Type of award: Scholarship.
Intended use: For undergraduate study at postsecondary institution. Designated institutions: Eligible Iowa postsecondary institutions.
Eligibility: Applicant must be residing in Iowa. Applicant must be veteran or descendant of veteran; or dependent of veteran or deceased veteran; or spouse of veteran or deceased veteran.
Application requirements: Recommendations, essay, transcript, proof of eligibility. Photo of self.
  Amount of award: $300
  Number of awards: 10
  Application deadline: June 1
  Total amount awarded: $3,000
Contact:
American Legion Auxiliary, Department of Iowa
720 Lyon Street
Des Moines, IA 50309
Phone: 515-282-7987
Fax: 515-282-7583
Web: www.ialegion.org/ala

Scholarships

119

Harriet Hoffman Memorial Scholarship

Type of award: Scholarship.
Intended use: For undergraduate study at postsecondary institution. Designated institutions: Eligible Iowa postsecondary institutions.
Eligibility: Applicant must be residing in Iowa. Applicant must be veteran or descendant of veteran; or dependent of veteran or deceased veteran; or spouse of veteran or deceased veteran.
Basis for selection: Major/career interest in education or education, teacher.
Application requirements: Recommendations, essay, transcript, proof of eligibility. Photo of self.

Amount of award:	$400
Number of awards:	1
Application deadline:	June 1
Total amount awarded:	$400

Contact:
American Legion Auxiliary, Department of Iowa
720 Lyon Street
Des Moines, IA 50309
Phone: 515-282-7987
Fax: 515-282-7583
Web: www.ialegion.org/ala

Mary Virginia Macrea Memorial Scholarship

Type of award: Scholarship.
Intended use: For undergraduate study at postsecondary institution. Designated institutions: Eligible Iowa postsecondary institutions.
Eligibility: Applicant must be residing in Iowa. Applicant must be veteran or descendant of veteran; or dependent of veteran or deceased veteran; or spouse of veteran or deceased veteran.
Basis for selection: Major/career interest in nursing.
Application requirements: Recommendations, essay, transcript, proof of eligibility. Photo of self.

Amount of award:	$400
Number of awards:	1
Application deadline:	June 1
Total amount awarded:	$400

Contact:
American Legion Auxiliary, Department of Iowa
720 Lyon Street
Des Moines, IA 50309
Phone: 515-282-7987
Fax: 515-282-7583
Web: www.ialegion.org/ala

Past President's Scholarship

Type of award: Scholarship.
Intended use: For undergraduate study at postsecondary institution.
Eligibility: Applicant must be residing in Iowa. Applicant must be veteran or descendant of veteran; or dependent of veteran or deceased veteran; or spouse of veteran or deceased veteran.
Application requirements: Recommendations, essay, transcript, proof of eligibility. Photo of self.
Additional information: Amount of award varies.

Application deadline:	June 1

Contact:
American Legion Iowa Auxiliary
720 Lyon Street
Des Moines, IA 50309
Phone: 515-282-7987
Fax: 515-282-7583
Web: www.ialegion.org/ala

American Legion Kansas

Albert M. Lappin Scholarship

Type of award: Scholarship.
Intended use: For freshman, sophomore or junior study at accredited vocational, 2-year or 4-year institution. Designated institutions: Eligible colleges, universities, and trade schools in Kansas.
Eligibility: Applicant or parent must be member/participant of American Legion. Applicant must be residing in Kansas. Must be child of member of American Legion Kansas or American Legion Kansas Auxiliary whose parent has been a member for the past three years; or be a child of deceased member of either organization whose dues were paid-up at time of death.
Application requirements: Recommendations, essay, transcript, proof of eligibility. Income tax forms. Photo of self.

Amount of award:	$1,000
Number of awards:	1
Total amount awarded:	$1,000

Contact:
American Legion Kansas
1314 Southwest Topeka Boulevard
Topeka, KS 66612-1886
Phone: 785-232-9315
Web: www.ksamlegion.org

American Legion Music Scholarship

Type of award: Scholarship.
Intended use: For freshman, sophomore or junior study at accredited vocational, 2-year or 4-year institution. Designated institutions: Eligible Kansas colleges and universities.
Eligibility: Applicant must be residing in Kansas.
Basis for selection: Major/career interest in music. Applicant must demonstrate financial need.
Application requirements: Recommendations, transcript, proof of eligibility. Income tax forms. Photo of self.

Amount of award:	$1,000
Number of awards:	1
Total amount awarded:	$1,000

Contact:
American Legion Kansas
1314 Southwest Topeka Boulevard
Topeka, KS 66612-1886
Phone: 785-232-9315
Web: www.ksamlegion.org

American Legion Oratorical Contest

Type of award: Scholarship.
Intended use: For undergraduate study at postsecondary institution.
Eligibility: Applicant must be enrolled in high school. Applicant must be residing in Kansas.
Basis for selection: Competition/talent/interest in oratory/debate, based on language style, voice, diction, delivery,

originality, logic, breadth of knowledge, application of knowledge about topic, and skill in selecting examples and analogies.

Additional information: Awards: First place prize of $1,500 provided by National Organization; second place, $500; third place, $250, fourth place, $150. Additional awards: $1,500 first place award provided by Emporia State University Foundation; second place, $500; third place, $250; fourth place, $150 (renewable up to 4 years; must qualify for admission and attend Emporia State University).

Amount of award:	$150-$1,500

Contact:
American Legion Kansas
1314 Southwest Topeka Boulevard
Topeka, KS 66612-1886
Phone: 785-232-9315
Web: www.ksamlegion.org

Charles and Annette Hill Scholarship

Type of award: Scholarship.
Intended use: For freshman, sophomore or junior study at postsecondary institution.
Eligibility: Applicant or parent must be member/participant of American Legion. Applicant must be residing in Kansas. Must be descendent of member of American Legion Kansas who has been a member for the past three years; or be descendent of deceased member whose dues were paid-up at time of death.
Basis for selection: Major/career interest in science, general; engineering or business/management/administration. Applicant must demonstrate high academic achievement.
Application requirements: Recommendations, essay, transcript, proof of eligibility. Income tax forms. Photo of self.
Additional information: Minimum 3.0 GPA.

Amount of award:	$1,000
Number of awards:	1
Application deadline:	February 15
Total amount awarded:	$1,000

Contact:
American Legion Kansas
1314 Southwest Topeka Blvd.
Topeka, KS 66612-1886
Phone: 785-232-9315
Web: www.ksamlegion.org

Dr. Click Cowger Scholarship

Type of award: Scholarship.
Intended use: For freshman, sophomore or junior study at accredited vocational, 2-year or 4-year institution. Designated institutions: Eligible Kansas colleges, universities, and trade schools.
Eligibility: Applicant must be male. Applicant must be residing in Kansas.
Basis for selection: Competition/talent/interest in athletics/sports.
Application requirements: Recommendations, essay, transcript, proof of eligibility. Income tax forms.
Additional information: For current players or those who have played in Kansas American Legion Baseball.

Amount of award:	$500
Number of awards:	1
Application deadline:	July 15
Total amount awarded:	$500

Contact:
American Legion Kansas
1314 Southwest Topeka Boulevard
Topeka, KS 66612-1886
Phone: 785-232-9315
Web: www.ksamlegion.org

Hugh A. Smith Scholarship

Type of award: Scholarship.
Intended use: For freshman, sophomore or junior study at accredited vocational, 2-year or 4-year institution. Designated institutions: Eligible Kansas colleges, universities, and trade schools.
Eligibility: Applicant or parent must be member/participant of American Legion. Applicant must be residing in Kansas. Applicant must be dependent of veteran or deceased veteran. Must be child of member of American Legion Kansas or American Legion Kansas Auxiliary whose parent has been a member for the past three years; or be a child of deceased member of either organization whose dues were paid-up at time of death.
Application requirements: Recommendations, essay, transcript, proof of eligibility. Income tax forms. Photo of self.

Amount of award:	$500
Number of awards:	1
Total amount awarded:	$500

Contact:
American Legion Kansas
1314 Southwest Topeka Boulevard
Topeka, KS 66612-1886
Phone: 785-232-9315
Web: www.ksamlegion.org

John and Geraldine Hobble Licensed Practical Nursing Scholarship

Type of award: Scholarship.
Intended use: For freshman study at accredited postsecondary institution. Designated institutions: Kansas accredited schools that award LPN diplomas.
Eligibility: Applicant must be at least 18. Applicant must be residing in Kansas.
Basis for selection: Major/career interest in nursing. Applicant must demonstrate financial need.
Application requirements: Proof of eligibility.

Amount of award:	$300
Number of awards:	1
Total amount awarded:	$300

Contact:
American Legion Kansas
1314 Southwest Topeka Boulevard
Topeka, KS 66612-1886
Phone: 785-232-9315
Web: www.ksamlegion.org

Rosedale Post 346 Scholarship

Type of award: Scholarship.
Intended use: For freshman, sophomore or junior study at vocational, 2-year or 4-year institution.
Eligibility: Applicant or parent must be member/participant of American Legion. Applicant must be residing in Kansas. Applicant must be dependent of veteran or deceased veteran. Must be child of member of American Legion Kansas or American Legion Kansas Auxiliary whose parent has been a

member for the past three years; or be a child of deceased member of either organization whose dues were paid-up at time of death.

Application requirements: Recommendations, essay, transcript, proof of eligibility. Income tax forms. Photo of self.

Amount of award:	$1,500
Number of awards:	2
Total amount awarded:	$3,000

Contact:
American Legion Kansas
1314 Southwest Topeka Blvd.
Topeka, KS 66612-1886
Phone: 785-232-9315
Web: www.ksamlegion.org

Ted and Nora Anderson Scholarship

Type of award: Scholarship.
Intended use: For freshman, sophomore or junior study at accredited vocational, 2-year or 4-year institution. Designated institutions: Eligible colleges, universities, and trade schools in Kansas.
Eligibility: Applicant or parent must be member/participant of American Legion. Applicant must be residing in Kansas. Applicant must be dependent of veteran or deceased veteran. Must be child of member of American Legion Kansas or American Legion Kansas Auxiliary whose parent has been a member for the past three years; or be a child of deceased member of either organization whose dues were paid-up at time of death.
Application requirements: Recommendations, essay, transcript, proof of eligibility. Photo of self.

Amount of award:	$500
Number of awards:	4
Application deadline:	February 15
Total amount awarded:	$2,000

Contact:
American Legion Kansas
1314 Southwest Topeka Boulevard
Topeka, KS 66612-1886
Phone: 785-232-9315
Web: www.ksamlegion.org

American Legion Kansas Auxiliary

American Legion Kansas Auxiliary Department Scholarships

Type of award: Scholarship.
Intended use: For freshman study at postsecondary institution. Designated institutions: Kansas institutions.
Eligibility: Applicant must be residing in Kansas. Applicant must be dependent of veteran; or spouse of veteran or deceased veteran.
Additional information: Eight 2-year scholarships of $500, payable at $250 per year for two years. Applicants must be entering college for the first time. Spouses of deceased veterans must not be remarried.

Amount of award:	$500
Number of awards:	8
Application deadline:	April 1
Total amount awarded:	$4,000

Contact:
American Legion Kansas Auxiliary
Department Secretary
1314 Southwest Topeka Boulevard
Topeka, KS 66612-1886
Phone: 785-232-1396
Web: www.kslegionaux.org

American Legion Kentucky

American Legion Department Oratorical Awards

Type of award: Scholarship.
Intended use: For undergraduate study at postsecondary institution.
Eligibility: Applicant must be enrolled in high school. Applicant must be residing in Kentucky.
Basis for selection: Competition/talent/interest in oratory/ debate, based on language style, voice, diction, delivery, originality, logic, breadth of knowledge, application of knowledge about topic, and skill in selecting examples and analogies.
Additional information: Awards: First place, $1,000; second place, $800; third place, $600; and 11 $100 awards for District winners. Must be Kentucky Department Oratorical Contest participant.

Amount of award:	$100-$1,000
Number of awards:	14
Total amount awarded:	$3,500

Contact:
American Legion Kentucky, Department Headquarters
P.O. Box 2123
Louisville, KY 40201
Phone: 502-587-1414
Fax: 502-587-6356
Web: www.kylegion.org

American Legion Kentucky Auxiliary

American Legion Kentucky Auxiliary Mary Barrett Marshall Scholarship

Type of award: Scholarship.
Intended use: For undergraduate study at vocational, 2-year or 4-year institution. Designated institutions: Eligible postsecondary institutions in Kentucky.
Eligibility: Applicant or parent must be member/participant of American Legion Auxiliary. Applicant must be female. Applicant must be residing in Kentucky. Applicant must be descendant of veteran; or dependent of veteran; or spouse of veteran or deceased veteran during Grenada conflict, Korean War, Lebanon conflict, Panama conflict, Persian Gulf War, WW I, WW II or Vietnam.
Application requirements: Proof of eligibility. SASE.

Amount of award:	$1,000
Number of awards:	1
Application deadline:	April 1
Total amount awarded:	$1,000

Contact:
American Legion Auxiliary, Department of Kentucky
Chairman Lois Smith
812 Madison Street
Rockport, IN 47635
Phone: 812-649-2163
Web: www.kyamlegionaux.org

Laura Blackburn Memorial Scholarship

Type of award: Scholarship.
Intended use: For undergraduate study at postsecondary institution.
Eligibility: Applicant or parent must be member/participant of American Legion Auxiliary. Applicant must be high school senior. Applicant must be residing in Kentucky. Applicant must be descendant of veteran; or dependent of veteran during Grenada conflict, Korean War, Lebanon conflict, Panama conflict, Persian Gulf War, WW I, WW II or Vietnam.
Application requirements: Proof of eligibility.

Amount of award:	$1,000
Number of awards:	1
Application deadline:	March 31
Total amount awarded:	$1,000

Contact:
American Legion Auxiliary, Department of Kentucky
Attn: Artie Eakins
3649 Rockhouse Road
Robards, KY 42452
Phone: 270-521-7183
Web: www.kyamlegionaux.org

American Legion Maine

Children and Youth Scholarships

Type of award: Scholarship.
Intended use: For undergraduate study at accredited postsecondary institution.
Eligibility: Applicant or parent must be member/participant of American Legion. Applicant must be high school senior. Applicant must be residing in Maine.
Basis for selection: Applicant must demonstrate financial need and depth of character.
Application requirements: Recommendations, transcript.
Additional information: High school seniors, college students, and veterans eligible.

Amount of award:	$500
Number of awards:	7
Number of applicants:	300
Application deadline:	May 1
Total amount awarded:	$3,500

Contact:
American Legion Maine
Department Adjutant, State Headquarters
P.O. Box 900
Waterville, ME 04903-0900
Phone: 207-873-3229
Fax: 207-872-0501
Web: www.mainelegion.org

Daniel E. Lambert Memorial Scholarship

Type of award: Scholarship.
Intended use: For undergraduate study at accredited vocational, 2-year or 4-year institution.
Eligibility: Applicant must be high school senior. Applicant must be U.S. citizen residing in Maine. Applicant must be descendant of veteran; or dependent of veteran.
Basis for selection: Applicant must demonstrate financial need and depth of character.
Application requirements: Recommendations, proof of eligibility.
Additional information: Must be child or grandchild of veteran.

Amount of award:	$1,000
Number of awards:	1
Application deadline:	May 1
Total amount awarded:	$1,000

Contact:
American Legion Maine
Department Adjutant, State Headquarters
P.O. Box 900
Waterville, ME 04903-0900
Phone: 207-873-3229
Fax: 207-872-0501
Web: www.mainelegion.org

James V. Day Scholarship

Type of award: Scholarship.
Intended use: For undergraduate study at vocational, 2-year or 4-year institution.
Eligibility: Applicant or parent must be member/participant of American Legion. Applicant must be high school senior. Applicant must be U.S. citizen residing in Maine.
Basis for selection: Applicant must demonstrate financial need, high academic achievement and depth of character.
Application requirements: Recommendations, essay, proof of eligibility.
Additional information: Must be in top half of graduating class. Grandchildren of current American Legion Post in Maine also eligible.

Amount of award:	$500
Number of awards:	2
Application deadline:	May 1
Total amount awarded:	$1,000

Contact:
American Legion Maine
Department Adjutant, State Headquarters
P.O. Box 900
Waterville, ME 04903-0900
Phone: 207-873-3229
Fax: 207-872-0501
Web: www.mainelegion.org

American Legion Maine Auxiliary

American Legion Maine Auxiliary Scholarship

Type of award: Scholarship.
Intended use: For undergraduate study at vocational, 2-year or 4-year institution.
Eligibility: Applicant must be high school senior. Applicant must be residing in Maine. Applicant must be dependent of veteran.
Basis for selection: Applicant must demonstrate financial need.
Application requirements: Send SASE with application request.

Amount of award:	$300
Number of awards:	2
Application deadline:	April 5
Total amount awarded:	$600

Contact:
American Legion Auxiliary, Department of Maine
Department Secretary
886B Kennedy Memorial Drive
Oakland, ME 04963

President's Parley Nursing Scholarship

Type of award: Scholarship.
Intended use: For undergraduate study.
Eligibility: Applicant must be residing in Maine. Applicant must be descendant of veteran; or dependent of veteran during WW I or WW II.
Basis for selection: Major/career interest in nursing.
Application requirements: Proof of eligibility.
Additional information: Must be graduate of accredited high school.

Amount of award:	$300
Number of awards:	1
Application deadline:	April 5
Total amount awarded:	$300

Contact:
American Legion Auxiliary, Department of Maine
Department Secretary
886B Kennedy Memorial Dr
Oakland, ME 04963

American Legion Maryland

Adler Science and Math Scholarship

Type of award: Scholarship.
Intended use: For undergraduate study at postsecondary institution.
Eligibility: Applicant must be at least 16, no older than 19. Applicant must be residing in Maryland. Applicant must be dependent of veteran.
Basis for selection: Major/career interest in science, general or mathematics.

Amount of award:	$500
Number of awards:	1
Application deadline:	March 31
Total amount awarded:	$500

Contact:
American Legion Maryland
Attn: Department Adjutant
The War Memorial Building, 101 N Gay St.
Baltimore, MD 21202
Phone: 410-752-1405
Web: www.mdlegion.org

American Legion Maryland Boys State Scholarship

Type of award: Scholarship.
Intended use: For undergraduate study at postsecondary institution.
Eligibility: Applicant or parent must be member/participant of American Legion, Boys State. Applicant must be male, at least 16, no older than 19. Applicant must be residing in Maryland.
Additional information: Applicant must be Maryland Boys State graduate.

Amount of award:	$500
Number of awards:	5
Application deadline:	May 1
Total amount awarded:	$2,500

Contact:
American Legion Maryland
Attn: Department Adjutant
The War Memorial Building, 101 N Gay St.
Baltimore, MD 21202-1405
Phone: 410-752-1405
Web: www.mdlegion.org

American Legion Maryland Oratorical Contest

Type of award: Scholarship.
Intended use: For undergraduate study at postsecondary institution.
Eligibility: Applicant must be at least 16, no older than 19. Applicant must be U.S. citizen or permanent resident residing in Maryland.
Basis for selection: Competition/talent/interest in oratory/debate, based on language style, voice, diction, delivery, originality, logic, breadth of knowledge, application of knowledge about topic, and skill in selecting examples and analogies.
Additional information: Awards: First place, $2,500; second place, $1,000; third through seventh place, $500 each. Must be an American Legion Oratorical Contest Department winner. Apply to nearest American Legion Post.

Amount of award:	$500-$2,500
Number of awards:	7
Application deadline:	October 1
Total amount awarded:	$6,000

Contact:
American Legion Maryland
Attn: Department Adjutant
The War Memorial Building, 101 N Gay St.
Baltimore, MD 21202-1405
Phone: 410-752-1405
Web: www.mdlegion.org

American Legion Maryland Scholarship

Type of award: Scholarship.
Intended use: For undergraduate study at postsecondary institution.
Eligibility: Applicant must be at least 16, no older than 19. Applicant must be residing in Maryland. Applicant must be dependent of veteran.
Application requirements: Transcript.
Additional information: Applicant must not have reached 20th birthday by January 1 of calendar year application is filed.

Amount of award:	$500
Number of awards:	11
Application deadline:	March 31
Total amount awarded:	$5,500

Contact:
American Legion Maryland
Attn: Department Adjutant
The War Memorial Building, 101 N Gay St.
Baltimore, MD 21202-1405
Phone: 410-752-1405
Web: www.mdlegion.org

American Legion Maryland Auxiliary

American Legion Maryland Auxiliary Scholarship

Type of award: Scholarship.
Intended use: For undergraduate study at 2-year or 4-year institution.
Eligibility: Applicant must be female, high school senior. Applicant must be residing in Maryland. Applicant must be dependent of veteran.
Basis for selection: Major/career interest in arts, general; biomedical; business; education; health-related professions; health sciences; physical therapy; physician assistant; public administration/service or science, general.
Additional information: Other medical majors eligible. Nursing students not eligible.

Amount of award:	$2,000
Number of awards:	1
Application deadline:	May 1
Total amount awarded:	$2,000

Contact:
American Legion Auxiliary, Department of Maryland
Department Secretary
1589 Sulphur Spring Road, Suite 105
Baltimore, MD 21227
Phone: 410-242-9519
Fax: 410-242-9553
Web: www.alamd.org

American Legion Massachusetts

American Legion Massachusetts General and Nursing Scholarships

Type of award: Scholarship.
Intended use: For freshman study at 2-year or 4-year institution.
Eligibility: Applicant or parent must be member/participant of American Legion. Applicant must be residing in Massachusetts. Applicant must be descendant of veteran; or dependent of veteran.
Application requirements: Recommendations, transcript, proof of eligibility.
Additional information: Grandchildren of American Legion Department of Massachusetts members also eligible. General Scholarships: Nine $1,000 awards; ten $500 awards. Nursing Scholarship: One $1,000 award.

Amount of award:	$500-$1,000
Number of awards:	20
Application deadline:	April 1
Total amount awarded:	$15,000

Contact:
American Legion Massachusetts
Department Adjutant
State House, Room 546-2
Boston, MA 02133-1044
Web: www.masslegion.org

Department of Massachusetts Oratorical Contest

Type of award: Scholarship.
Intended use: For undergraduate study at postsecondary institution.
Eligibility: Applicant must be no older than 19. Applicant must be residing in Massachusetts.
Basis for selection: Competition/talent/interest in oratory/debate, based on language style, voice, diction, delivery, originality, logic, breadth of knowledge, application of knowledge about topic, and skill in selecting examples and analogies.
Application requirements: Proof of eligibility.
Additional information: Awards: First place, $1,000; second place, $800; third place, $700; fourth place, $600.

Amount of award:	$600-$1,000
Number of awards:	4
Application deadline:	December 15
Total amount awarded:	$3,100

Contact:
American Legion Massachusetts
Department Oratorical Chair
State House, Room 546-2
Boston, MA 02133-1044
Web: www.masslegion.org

American Legion Massachusetts Auxiliary

American Legion Massachusetts Auxiliary Scholarship

Type of award: Scholarship.
Intended use: For undergraduate study at vocational, 2-year or 4-year institution.
Eligibility: Applicant must be at least 16, no older than 22. Applicant must be residing in Massachusetts. Applicant must be descendant of veteran; or dependent of veteran or deceased veteran during Grenada conflict, Korean War, Lebanon conflict, Panama conflict, Persian Gulf War, WW I, WW II or Vietnam.
Additional information: One $750 award; ten $200 awards.

Amount of award:	$200-$750
Number of awards:	11
Application deadline:	March 1
Total amount awarded:	$2,750

Contact:
American Legion Auxiliary, Department of Massachusetts
Department Secretary
State House, Room 546-2
Boston, MA 02133-1044
Web: www.masslegion-aux.org

Past President's Parley Scholarship

Type of award: Scholarship.
Intended use: For undergraduate study at postsecondary institution.
Eligibility: Applicant must be residing in Massachusetts. Applicant must be dependent of veteran or deceased veteran.
Basis for selection: Major/career interest in nursing.
Additional information: Must be child of living or deceased veteran not eligible for Federal or Commonwealth scholarships.

Amount of award:	$200
Number of awards:	1
Application deadline:	March 1
Total amount awarded:	$200

Contact:
American Legion Massachusetts Auxiliary
Department Secretary
State House, Room 546-2
Boston, MA 02133-1044
Web: www.masslegion-aux.org

American Legion Michigan

American Legion Michigan Oratorical Contest

Type of award: Scholarship.
Intended use: For undergraduate study at postsecondary institution.
Eligibility: Applicant must be enrolled in high school. Applicant must be U.S. citizen or permanent resident residing in Michigan.
Basis for selection: Competition/talent/interest in oratory/debate, based on ability to deliver an 8- to 10-minute speech on the U.S. Constitution.

Additional information: Awards: $1,500, $1,000, $800. Local contest in early February. Must be finalist in Zone Oratorical Contest. Contact local American Legion Post for more information.

Amount of award:	$800-$1,500
Number of awards:	3
Total amount awarded:	$3,300

Contact:
Deanna Clark American Legion Michigan
212 North Verlinden Avenue
Ste A
Lansing, MI 48915
Phone: 517-371-4720 ext. 11
Fax: 517-371-2401
Web: www.michiganlegion.org

Guy M. Wilson Scholarship

Type of award: Scholarship.
Intended use: For undergraduate study at 2-year or 4-year institution. Designated institutions: Michigan institutions.
Eligibility: Applicant must be enrolled in high school. Applicant must be residing in Michigan. Applicant must be descendant of veteran; or dependent of veteran or deceased veteran.
Basis for selection: Applicant must demonstrate financial need.
Application requirements: Transcript, proof of eligibility.
Additional information: Minimum 2.5 GPA. Application should be filed at local American Legion Post. Deadline in mid-January.

Amount of award:	$500

Contact:
Deanna Clark American Legion Michigan
212 North Verlinden Avenue
Ste A
Lansing, MI 48915
Phone: 517-371-4720 ext. 11
Fax: 517-371-2401
Web: www.michiganlegion.org

William D. & Jewell W. Brewer Scholarship Trusts

Type of award: Scholarship.
Intended use: For undergraduate study at 2-year or 4-year institution.
Eligibility: Applicant must be residing in Michigan. Applicant must be descendant of veteran; or dependent of veteran or deceased veteran.
Basis for selection: Applicant must demonstrate financial need.
Application requirements: Transcript, proof of eligibility.
Additional information: Minimum 2.5 GPA. Application should be filed at local American Legion Post. Deadline in mid-January.

Amount of award:	$500

Contact:
Deanna Clark American Legion Michigan
212 North Verlinden Avenue
Ste A
Lansing, MI 48915
Phone: 517-371-4720 ext. 11
Fax: 517-371-2401
Web: www.michiganlegion.org

American Legion Michigan Auxiliary

American Legion Michigan Auxiliary Memorial Scholarship

Type of award: Scholarship, renewable.
Intended use: For undergraduate study at postsecondary institution. Designated institutions: Michigan institutions.
Eligibility: Applicant must be female, at least 16, no older than 21. Applicant must be residing in Michigan. Applicant must be descendant of veteran; or dependent of veteran or deceased veteran during Grenada conflict, Korean War, Lebanon conflict, Panama conflict, Persian Gulf War, WW I, WW II or Vietnam. Applicant must be daughter, granddaughter, or great-granddaughter of honorably discharged or deceased veteran.
Basis for selection: Applicant must demonstrate financial need and high academic achievement.
Application requirements: Recommendations, transcript, proof of eligibility. FAFSA or copy of parents' income tax forms.
Additional information: Must be Michigan resident for at least one year. Visit Website for details and application.

    Amount of award: $500
    Application deadline: March 15
Contact:
American Legion Auxiliary, Department of Michigan
212 North Verlinden Avenue
Lansing, MI 48915
Phone: 517-267-8809 ext. 22
Fax: 517-371-2401
Web: www.michalaux.org

Medical Career Scholarships

Type of award: Scholarship.
Intended use: For freshman study at postsecondary institution. Designated institutions: Michigan institutions.
Eligibility: Applicant must be high school senior. Applicant must be residing in Michigan. Applicant must be descendant of veteran; or dependent of veteran or deceased veteran; or spouse of veteran or deceased veteran during Grenada conflict, Korean War, Lebanon conflict, Panama conflict, Persian Gulf War, WW I, WW II or Vietnam. Applicant must be child, grandchild, great-grandchild, wife, or spouse of honorably discharged or deceased veteran.
Basis for selection: Major/career interest in nursing; physical therapy or respiratory therapy. Applicant must demonstrate financial need and high academic achievement.
Application requirements: Recommendations, transcript, proof of eligibility. FAFSA or copy of income tax form.
Additional information: For first-year training of men and women for the position of registered nurse, licensed practical nurse, physical therapist, or respiratory therapist. Applications available after November 15. Visit Website for details and application.

    Amount of award: $500
    Application deadline: March 15
    Total amount awarded: $10,500

Contact:
American Legion Auxiliary, Department of Michigan
212 North Verlinden Avenue
Lansing, MI 48915
Phone: 517-267-8809 ext. 22
Fax: 517-371-2401
Web: www.michalaux.org

National President's Scholarship

Type of award: Scholarship.
Intended use: For undergraduate study at postsecondary institution.
Eligibility: Applicant must be high school senior. Applicant must be residing in Michigan. Applicant must be descendant of veteran; or dependent of veteran during Grenada conflict, Korean War, Middle East War, Lebanon conflict, Panama conflict, Persian Gulf War, WW I, WW II or Vietnam.
Application requirements: Applicant must have completed 50 hours of community service during high school.

    Amount of award: $1,000-$2,500
    Number of awards: 1
    Application deadline: March 1
Contact:
American Legion Auxiliary, Department of Michigan
212 North Verlinden Avenue
Lansing, MI 48915
Phone: 517-267-8809 ext. 22
Fax: 517-371-2401
Web: www.michalaux.org

American Legion Minnesota

American Legion Minnesota Legionnaire Insurance Trust Scholarship

Type of award: Scholarship.
Intended use: For undergraduate study at accredited vocational, 2-year or 4-year institution. Designated institutions: Minnesota colleges and universities and institutions in neighboring states with reciprocating agreements.
Eligibility: Applicant or parent must be member/participant of American Legion. Applicant must be U.S. citizen residing in Minnesota. Applicant must be veteran or descendant of veteran; or dependent of veteran.
Basis for selection: Applicant must demonstrate financial need and high academic achievement.
Application requirements: Recommendations, essay, transcript, proof of eligibility.

    Amount of award: $500
    Number of awards: 3
    Application deadline: April 1
    Total amount awarded: $1,500

Contact:
American Legion Minnesota
Education Committee
20 West 12th Street, Room 300A
St. Paul, MN 55155-2000
Phone: 651-291-1800
Web: www.mnlegion.org

Scholarships

American Legion Minnesota Oratorical Contest

Type of award: Scholarship.
Intended use: For undergraduate study at accredited postsecondary institution.
Eligibility: Applicant must be enrolled in high school. Applicant must be U.S. citizen or permanent resident residing in Minnesota.
Basis for selection: Competition/talent/interest in oratory/debate, based on language style, voice, diction, delivery, originality, logic, breadth of knowledge, application of knowledge about topic, and skill in selecting examples and analogies.
Additional information: Awards: First place, $1,200; second place, $900; third place, $700; fourth place, $500.

Amount of award:	$500-$1,200
Number of awards:	4
Application deadline:	December 15
Total amount awarded:	$3,300

Contact:
American Legion Minnesota
Education Committee
20 West 12th Street, Room 300A
St. Paul, MN 55155-2000
Phone: 866-259-9163
Web: www.mnlegion.org

The Minnesota American Legion Memorial Scholarship

Type of award: Scholarship.
Intended use: For undergraduate study at accredited postsecondary institution. Designated institutions: Minnesota colleges and universities and institutions in neighboring states with reciprocating agreement.
Eligibility: Applicant or parent must be member/participant of American Legion. Applicant must be residing in Minnesota.
Basis for selection: Applicant must demonstrate financial need.
Application requirements: Recommendations, essay, transcript, proof of eligibility.
Additional information: Grandchildren of American Legion or American Legion Auxiliary members also eligible.

Amount of award:	$500
Number of awards:	6
Application deadline:	April 1
Total amount awarded:	$3,000

Contact:
American Legion Minnesota
Education Committee
20 West 12th Street, Room 300A
St. Paul, MN 55155-2000
Phone: 866-259-9163
Web: www.mnlegion.org

American Legion Minnesota Auxiliary

American Legion Minnesota Auxiliary Department Scholarship

Type of award: Scholarship.
Intended use: For undergraduate study at accredited postsecondary institution.
Eligibility: Applicant or parent must be member/participant of American Legion Auxiliary. Applicant must be residing in Minnesota. Applicant must be descendant of veteran; or dependent of veteran.

Amount of award:	$1,000
Number of awards:	7
Application deadline:	March 15
Total amount awarded:	$7,000

Contact:
American Legion Auxiliary, Department of Minnesota
State Veterans Service Building
20 W 12th Street, Room 314
St. Paul, MN 55155-2069
Phone: 651-224-7634
Fax: 651-224-5243
Web: www.mnala.org

Past President's Parley Health Care Scholarship

Type of award: Scholarship.
Intended use: For undergraduate study at accredited postsecondary institution.
Eligibility: Applicant or parent must be member/participant of American Legion Auxiliary. Applicant must be residing in Minnesota.
Basis for selection: Major/career interest in health-related professions.

Amount of award:	$1,000
Number of awards:	10
Application deadline:	March 15
Total amount awarded:	$10,000

Contact:
American Legion Auxiliary, Department of Minnesota
State Veterans Service Building
20 W. 12th Street, Room 314
St. Paul, MN 55155-2069
Phone: 651-224-7634
Fax: 651-224-5243
Web: www.mnala.org

American Legion Mississippi Auxiliary

American Legion Mississippi Auxiliary Scholarship

Type of award: Scholarship.
Intended use: For undergraduate study at accredited postsecondary institution.

Eligibility: Applicant must be high school senior. Applicant must be residing in Mississippi. Applicant must be descendant of veteran; or dependent of veteran during Korean War, Lebanon conflict, Panama conflict, Persian Gulf War, WW I, WW II or Vietnam.
Basis for selection: Applicant must demonstrate financial need.

Amount of award:	$500
Number of awards:	1
Application deadline:	March 1
Total amount awarded:	$500

Contact:
American Legion Mississippi Auxiliary, Department Headquarters
P.O. Box 1382
Jackson, MS 39215-1382
Phone: 601-353-3681
Fax: 601-353-3682
Web: www.missala.com

American Legion Missouri

Charles L. Bacon Memorial Scholarship

Type of award: Scholarship.
Intended use: For full-time undergraduate study at accredited 2-year or 4-year institution.
Eligibility: Applicant or parent must be member/participant of American Legion. Applicant must be single, no older than 20. Applicant must be U.S. citizen residing in Missouri. Applicants must be current member of American Legion, American Legion Auxiliary or the Sons of the American Legion, or descendent of any member.
Basis for selection: Applicant must demonstrate financial need.

Amount of award:	$500
Number of awards:	2
Application deadline:	April 20
Notification begins:	July 1
Total amount awarded:	$1,000

Contact:
American Legion Missouri
Attn: Education and Scholarship Committee
P.O. Box 179
Jefferson City, MO 65102-0179
Phone: 660-627-4713
Web: www.missourilegion.org

Commander's Scholarship Fund

Type of award: Scholarship.
Intended use: For undergraduate study at postsecondary institution. Designated institutions: Vocational/technical colleges or universities in Missouri.
Eligibility: Applicant must be residing in Missouri. Applicant must be veteran who served in the Army, Air Force, Marines, Navy or Coast Guard. Applicant must have served in one of the U.S. Armed Forces branches for a minimum of 90 days and received honorable discharge.
Application requirements: Proof of eligibility. Letter of acceptance from college or university.
Additional information: Membership in The American Legion not required.

Amount of award:	$1,000
Number of awards:	2
Application deadline:	April 20
Total amount awarded:	$2,000

Contact:
American Legion Missouri
Attn: Education and Scholarship Committee
P.O. Box 179
Jefferson City, MO 65102-0179
Phone: 660-627-4713
Web: www.missourilegion.org

Erman W. Taylor Memorial Scholarship

Type of award: Scholarship.
Intended use: For full-time undergraduate study at accredited 2-year or 4-year institution.
Eligibility: Applicant must be single, no older than 20. Applicant must be U.S. citizen residing in Missouri. Applicant must be descendant of veteran who served in the Army, Air Force, Marines, Navy or Coast Guard. Must be child, grandchild, or great-grandchild of veteran who served 90 or more days of active duty in the Army, Navy, Air Force, Marines, or Coast Guard and has an honorable discharge.
Basis for selection: Major/career interest in education.
Application requirements: Copy of discharge certificate for veteran parent, grandparent; essay of 500 words or less on selected topic.

Amount of award:	$500
Number of awards:	2
Application deadline:	April 20
Notification begins:	July 1
Total amount awarded:	$1,000

Contact:
American Legion Missouri
Attn: Education and Scholarship Committee
P.O. Box 179
Jefferson City, MO 65102-0179
Phone: 660-627-4713
Web: www.missourilegion.org

Joseph J. Frank Scholarship

Type of award: Scholarship.
Intended use: For full-time freshman study at accredited postsecondary institution.
Eligibility: Applicant or parent must be member/participant of American Legion. Applicant must be single, no older than 20. Applicant must be residing in Missouri. Applicant must be veteran or descendant of veteran; or dependent of veteran.
Application requirements: Proof of eligibility.
Additional information: Must be member or descendent of member of American Legion, American Legion Auxiliary, or Sons of the American Legion. Applicant must have attended a full session of The American Legion Boys State or Auxiliary Girls State program.

Amount of award:	$500
Number of awards:	5
Application deadline:	April 20
Total amount awarded:	$2,500

Contact:
American Legion Missouri
Attn: Education and Scholarship Committee
P.O. Box 179
Jefferson City, MO 65102-0179
Phone: 660-627-4713
Web: www.missourilegion.org

Lillie Lois Ford Boys' Scholarship

Type of award: Scholarship.
Intended use: For full-time undergraduate study at accredited postsecondary institution.
Eligibility: Applicant or parent must be member/participant of American Legion, Boys State. Applicant must be single, male, no older than 20. Applicant must be residing in Missouri. Applicant must be descendant of veteran who served in the Army, Air Force, Marines, Navy or Coast Guard. Must be child, grandchild, or great-grandchild of veteran who served at least 90 days active duty in Army, Navy, Air Force, Marines, or Coast Guard, and was honorably discharged.
Basis for selection: Applicant must demonstrate financial need.
Application requirements: Proof of eligibility.
Additional information: Must have attended complete session of American Legion Boys State or American Legion Department of Missouri Cadet Patrol Academy.

Amount of award:	$1,000
Number of awards:	1
Application deadline:	April 20
Notification begins:	July 1
Total amount awarded:	$1,000

Contact:
American Legion Missouri
Attn: Education and Scholarship Committee
P.O. Box 179
Jefferson City, MO 65102-0179
Phone: 660-627-4713
Web: www.missourilegion.org

Lillie Lois Ford Girls' Scholarship

Type of award: Scholarship.
Intended use: For full-time undergraduate study at accredited postsecondary institution.
Eligibility: Applicant must be single, female, no older than 20. Applicant must be residing in Missouri. Applicant must be descendant of veteran who served in the Army, Air Force, Marines, Navy or Coast Guard. Must be child, grandchild, or great-grandchild of veteran who served at least 90 days active duty in Army, Navy, Air Force, Marines, or Coast Guard, and was honorably discharged.
Basis for selection: Applicant must demonstrate financial need.
Application requirements: Proof of eligibility.
Additional information: Must have attended complete session of American Legion Auxiliary Girls State or American Legion Department of Missouri Cadet Patrol Academy.

Amount of award:	$1,000
Number of awards:	1
Application deadline:	April 20
Notification begins:	July 1
Total amount awarded:	$1,000

Contact:
American Legion Missouri
Attn: Education and Scholarship Committee
P.O. Box 179
Jefferson City, MO 65102
Phone: 660-627-4713
Web: www.missourilegion.org

M.D. "Jack" Murphy Memorial Nurses Training Fund

Type of award: Scholarship, renewable.
Intended use: For full-time undergraduate study at 2-year or 4-year institution.
Eligibility: Applicant must be single, no older than 20. Applicant must be residing in Missouri. Applicant must be descendant of veteran who served in the Army, Air Force, Marines, Navy or Coast Guard. Must be child, grandchild, or great-grandchild of veteran who served at least 90 days active duty in Army, Navy, Air Force, Marines, or Coast Guard, and was honorably discharged.
Basis for selection: Major/career interest in nursing. Applicant must demonstrate financial need.
Application requirements: Proof of eligibility.
Additional information: Available to students training to be registered nurses. Applicant must have graduated in top 40% of high school class or have minimum "C" or equivalent standing from last college semester prior to applying for award.

Amount of award:	$750
Number of awards:	1
Application deadline:	April 20
Total amount awarded:	$750

Contact:
American Legion Missouri
Attn: Education and Scholarship Committee
P.O. Box 179
Jefferson City, MO 65102-0179
Phone: 660-627-4713
Web: www.missourilegion.org

Shane Dean Voyles Memorial Scholarship

Type of award: Scholarship.
Intended use: For full-time freshman study at accredited postsecondary institution.
Eligibility: Applicant must be high school senior. Applicant must be residing in Missouri.
Basis for selection: Applicant must demonstrate high academic achievement, leadership and service orientation.
Application requirements: Nomination by high school.
Additional information: Each school in Missouri may nominate one student for the award. Nominee selected based on leadership, athletic, and scholastic abilities.

Amount of award:	$500
Number of awards:	1
Application deadline:	April 20
Total amount awarded:	$500

Contact:
American Legion Missouri
Attn: Education and Scholarship Committee
P.O. Box 179
Jefferson City, MO 65102-0179
Phone: 660-627-4713
Web: www.missourilegion.org

American Legion Missouri Auxiliary

American Legion Missouri Auxiliary Scholarship

Type of award: Scholarship.
Intended use: For undergraduate study at postsecondary institution.
Eligibility: Applicant must be high school senior. Applicant must be residing in Missouri. Applicant must be descendant of veteran; or dependent of veteran during Korean War, Lebanon conflict, Panama conflict, Persian Gulf War, WW I, WW II or Vietnam.
Additional information: Applicant must not have previously attended institution of higher learning.

Amount of award:	$500
Number of awards:	2
Application deadline:	March 1
Total amount awarded:	$1,000

Contact:
American Legion Missouri Auxiliary
Department Secretary
600 Ellis Blvd.
Jefferson City, MO 65101-2204
Phone: 573-636-9133
Fax: 573-635-3467

Past President's Parley Scholarship

Type of award: Scholarship.
Intended use: For undergraduate study at 2-year or 4-year institution.
Eligibility: Applicant must be residing in Missouri. Applicant must be descendant of veteran; or dependent of veteran.
Basis for selection: Major/career interest in nursing.
Application requirements: Recommendations.
Additional information: Applicant must not have previously attended institution of higher learning.

Amount of award:	$500
Number of awards:	2
Application deadline:	March 1

Contact:
American Legion Missouri Auxiliary
Department Secretary
600 Ellis Blvd
Jefferson City, MO 65101-2204
Phone: 573-636-9133
Fax: 573-635-3467

American Legion Montana Auxiliary

Aloha Scholarship

Type of award: Scholarship.
Intended use: For freshman study at postsecondary institution.
Designated institutions: Accredited nursing schools.
Eligibility: Applicant or parent must be member/participant of American Legion Auxiliary. Applicant must be residing in Montana.

Basis for selection: Major/career interest in nursing.
Application requirements: Recommendations, proof of eligibility.
Additional information: Grandchildren of Auxiliary members also eligible.

Amount of award:	$400
Number of awards:	1
Application deadline:	April 1

Contact:
American Legion Montana Auxiliary
Department Secretary
P.O. Box 40
Townsend, MT 59644
Phone: 406-266-4566
Fax: 406-980-0376
Web: www.mtlegion.org/auxiliary

American Legion Montana Auxiliary Scholarships (1)

Type of award: Scholarship.
Intended use: For undergraduate study at postsecondary institution.
Eligibility: Applicant must be high school senior. Applicant must be residing in Montana. Applicant must be dependent of veteran.
Application requirements: Essay, proof of eligibility.
Additional information: Applicant must be high school senior or graduate who has not attended college. Must be state resident for at least two years.

Amount of award:	$500
Number of awards:	2
Application deadline:	April 1
Total amount awarded:	$1,000

Contact:
American Legion Montana Auxiliary
Department Secretary
P.O. Box 40
Townsend, MT 59644
Phone: 406-266-4566
Fax: 406-266-4566
Web: www.mtlegion.org/auxiliary

American Legion Montana Auxiliary Scholarships (2)

Type of award: Scholarship.
Intended use: For junior study at postsecondary institution.
Eligibility: Applicant must be residing in Montana. Applicant must be dependent of veteran.
Application requirements: Proof of eligibility. Essay stating interest in issues relating to children and youth.
Additional information: Must have completed sophomore year in college and be going into field relating to children and youth.

Amount of award:	$500
Number of awards:	2
Application deadline:	June 1
Total amount awarded:	$1,000

Contact:
American Legion Montana Auxiliary
Department Secretary
P.O. Box 40
Townsend, MT 59644
Phone: 406-266-4566
Fax: 406-266-4566
Web: www.mtlegion.org/auxiliary

Scholarships

American Legion National Headquarters

American Legion Auxiliary National President's Scholarship

Type of award: Scholarship.
Intended use: For undergraduate study at postsecondary institution.
Eligibility: Applicant or parent must be member/participant of American Legion Auxiliary. Applicant must be high school senior. Applicant must be dependent of veteran during Grenada conflict, Korean War, Lebanon conflict, Panama conflict, Persian Gulf War, WW I, WW II or Vietnam.
Basis for selection: Applicant must demonstrate financial need, high academic achievement, depth of character, leadership and patriotism.
Additional information: Scholarships: five-$2,500; five-$2,000; five-$1,000; awarded annually. Applications available online, from Unit President of Auxiliary in local community, from Department Secretary, or from National Headquarters. See Website for details.

Amount of award:	$1,000-$2,500
Number of awards:	15
Application deadline:	March 1
Total amount awarded:	$27,500

Contact:
American Legion Auxiliary
8945 North Meridian Street
Indianapolis, IN 46260-1189
Phone: 317-569-4500
Web: www.legion-aux.org

American Legion Eagle Scout of the Year

Type of award: Scholarship.
Intended use: For undergraduate study at accredited postsecondary institution in United States.
Eligibility: Applicant or parent must be member/participant of Boy Scouts of America, Eagle Scouts. Applicant must be male, enrolled in high school. Applicant must be U.S. citizen.
Basis for selection: Applicant must demonstrate depth of character and service orientation.
Application requirements: Recommendations, transcript, proof of eligibility.
Additional information: Applicant must be registered, active member of Boy Scout Troop, Varsity Scout Team or Venturing Crew AND either chartered to American Legion Post/Auxiliary Unit OR son or grandson of American Legion or Auxiliary member. Awards: One $10,000 Eagle Scout of the Year; three runners-up get $2,500. Scholarships available upon graduation from accredited high school and must be used within four years of graduation date. Request application from State Department Headquarters.

Amount of award:	$2,500-$10,000
Number of awards:	4
Total amount awarded:	$17,500

Contact:
American Legion National Headquarters
Eagle Scout of the Year
P.O. Box 1055
Indianapolis, IN 46206-1055
Phone: 317-630-1249
Web: www.legion.org

American Legion Legacy Scholarship

Type of award: Scholarship, renewable.
Intended use: For undergraduate study at postsecondary institution in United States.
Eligibility: Applicant must be high school senior. Applicant must be residing in Indiana. Applicant must be child (dependent, legally adopted, or from a spouse of prior marriage) of active duty personnel of the U.S. military or National Guard or military reservists who were federalized and died on active duty on or after September 11, 2001.
Application requirements: Transcript, proof of eligibility.
Additional information: Amount and number of awards vary. Previous scholarship recipients may reapply. Visit Website for details.

Application deadline:	April 15

Contact:
American Legion National Headquarters
Education Programs Chair
P.O. Box 1055
Indianapolis, IN 46206-1055
Web: www.legion.org

American Legion National High School Oratorical Contest

Type of award: Scholarship.
Intended use: For undergraduate study at postsecondary institution.
Eligibility: Applicant must be enrolled in high school. Applicant must be U.S. citizen or permanent resident.
Basis for selection: Competition/talent/interest in oratory/debate, based on language style, voice, diction, delivery, originality, logic, breadth of knowledge, application of knowledge about topic, and skill in selecting examples and analogies.
Additional information: Awards: State winners participating in regional level win $1,500; second-round participants not advancing to national finals receive additional $1,500. Finalists win $18,000 (first place), $16,000 (runner-up), and $14,000 (third place). Obtain oratorical contest rules from local Legion Post or state Department Headquarters.

Amount of award:	$1,500-$18,000
Number of awards:	54

Contact:
American Legion National Headquarters
Education Programs Chair
P.O. Box 1055
Indianapolis, IN 46206-1055
Web: www.legion.org

Eight and Forty Lung and Respiratory Nursing Scholarship Fund

Type of award: Scholarship.

Intended use: For undergraduate, graduate or non-degree study.
Eligibility: Applicant must be returning adult student.
Basis for selection: Major/career interest in health education; health services administration or nursing.
Application requirements: Proof of eligibility.
Additional information: Applicant must be registered nurse. Program assists registered nurses with advanced preparation for positions in supervision, administration, or teaching. On completion of education, must have full-time employment prospects related to pediatric lung and respiratory control in hospitals, clinics, or health departments. Contact Eight and Forty Scholarship Chairman or the American Legion Education Program for application.

Amount of award:	$3,000
Application deadline:	May 15
Notification begins:	July 1
Total amount awarded:	$3,000

Contact:
American Legion National Headquarters
Eight and Forty Scholarships
P.O. Box 1055
Indianapolis, IN 46206-1055
Web: www.legion.org

Girl Scout Achievement Award

Type of award: Scholarship.
Intended use: For freshman study at postsecondary institution.
Eligibility: Applicant or parent must be member/participant of American Legion Auxiliary. Applicant must be female, enrolled in high school.
Additional information: Applicant must be a Gold Award recipient and in 11th grade or higher. Must be an active member of religious institution and have received religious emblem. Must have demonstrated practical citizenship in church, school, scouting, and community. See Website for details.

Amount of award:	$1,000
Number of awards:	1
Application deadline:	February 11
Total amount awarded:	$1,000

Contact:
American Legion Auxiliary
8945 North Meridian Street
Indianapolis, IN 46260
Phone: 317-569-4500
Web: www.legion-aux.org

Samsung American Legion Scholarship

Type of award: Scholarship.
Intended use: For undergraduate study at postsecondary institution in United States.
Eligibility: Applicant or parent must be member/participant of American Legion. Applicant must be high school junior. Applicant must be descendant of veteran; or dependent of veteran. Applicant must have completed American Legion Boys State or Girls State program.
Basis for selection: Applicant must demonstrate financial need, high academic achievement and service orientation.
Application requirements: Essay, proof of eligibility.
Additional information: Amount and number of awards vary. In 2007, 10 $20,000 and 90 $1,000 scholarships awarded. Visit Website for details.

Contact:
American Legion National Headquarters
Education Programs Chair
P.O. Box 1055
Indianapolis, IN 46206-1055
Web: www.legion.org

Spirit of Youth Scholarship for Junior Members

Type of award: Scholarship.
Intended use: For undergraduate study at postsecondary institution.
Eligibility: Applicant or parent must be member/participant of American Legion Auxiliary. Applicant must be high school senior. Applicant must be U.S. citizen.
Basis for selection: Applicant must demonstrate financial need, high academic achievement, depth of character, leadership and patriotism.
Application requirements: Proof of eligibility.
Additional information: Must be Junior member of three years' standing, holding current membership card. Applications available online, from Unit President of Auxiliary in local community, from Department Secretary, or from National Headquarters. See Website for details.

Amount of award:	$1,000
Number of awards:	5
Application deadline:	March 1
Total amount awarded:	$5,000

Contact:
American Legion Auxiliary
8945 North Meridian Street
Indianapolis, IN 46260
Phone: 317-569-4500
Web: www.legion-aux.org

American Legion Nebraska

American Legion Nebraska Oratorical Contest

Type of award: Scholarship.
Intended use: For undergraduate study at postsecondary institution.
Eligibility: Applicant or parent must be member/participant of American Legion. Applicant must be enrolled in high school. Applicant must be residing in Nebraska.
Basis for selection: Competition/talent/interest in oratory/debate, based on language style, voice, diction, delivery, originality, logic, breadth of knowledge, application of knowledge about topic, and skill in selecting examples and analogies.
Application requirements: Proof of eligibility.
Additional information: Awards: First place, $1,000; second place, $600; third place, $400; fourth place, $200, plus one $100 award for first place in each District upon participation in area contest. Contact local American Legion post for more information.

Amount of award:	$100-$1,000
Application deadline:	November 1

133

Contact:
American Legion Nebraska, Department Headquarters
P.O. Box 5205
Lincoln, NE 68505-0205
Phone: 402-464-6338
Web: www.ne.legion.org

Edgar J. Boschult Memorial Scholarship

Type of award: Scholarship.
Intended use: For full-time undergraduate study. Designated institutions: University of Nebraska.
Eligibility: Applicant or parent must be member/participant of American Legion. Applicant must be residing in Nebraska.
Basis for selection: Applicant must demonstrate financial need and high academic achievement.
Additional information: Must be student at University of Nebraska with high academic and ROTC standing, or military veteran attending University of Nebraska with financial need and acceptable scholastic standing.

Amount of award:	$500
Number of awards:	4
Application deadline:	March 1

Contact:
American Legion Nebraska, Department Headquarters
P.O. Box 5205
Lincoln, NE 68505-0205
Phone: 402-464-6338
Web: www.ne.legion.org

Maynard Jensen American Legion Memorial Scholarship

Type of award: Scholarship.
Intended use: For full-time undergraduate study at vocational, 2-year or 4-year institution. Designated institutions: Nebraska institutions.
Eligibility: Applicant or parent must be member/participant of American Legion. Applicant must be residing in Nebraska. Applicant must be descendant of veteran; or dependent of veteran, deceased veteran or POW/MIA.
Basis for selection: Applicant must demonstrate financial need and high academic achievement.

Amount of award:	$500
Number of awards:	10
Application deadline:	March 1
Total amount awarded:	$5,000

Contact:
American Legion Nebraska, Department Headquarters
P.O. Box 5205
Lincoln, NE 68505-0205
Phone: 402-464-6338
Web: www.ne.legion.org

American Legion Nebraska Auxiliary

American Legion Nebraska President's Scholarship

Type of award: Scholarship.

Intended use: For undergraduate study at postsecondary institution.
Eligibility: Applicant must be residing in Nebraska.
Additional information: Given to Nebraska's entry for National President's Scholarship in event applicant does not win same.

Amount of award:	$200

Contact:
American Legion Nebraska Auxiliary, Department Headquarters
P.O. Box 5227
Lincoln, NE 68505-0227
Web: www.nebraskalegionaux.net

Averyl Elaine Keriakedes Memorial Scholarship

Type of award: Scholarship.
Intended use: For undergraduate study. Designated institutions: University of Nebraska-Lincoln.
Eligibility: Applicant must be female. Applicant must be residing in Nebraska. Applicant must be descendant of veteran; or dependent of veteran; or spouse of veteran.
Basis for selection: Major/career interest in education or social/behavioral sciences.
Application requirements: Recommendations, transcript, proof of eligibility.
Additional information: Applicant must plan to teach middle or junior high school social studies.

Amount of award:	$500
Number of awards:	1
Total amount awarded:	$500

Contact:
American Legion Nebraska Auxiliary, Department Headquarters
P.O. Box 5227
Lincoln, NE 68505-0227
Web: www.nebraskalegionaux.net

Junior Member Scholarship

Type of award: Scholarship.
Intended use: For undergraduate study at postsecondary institution.
Eligibility: Applicant must be residing in Nebraska.
Additional information: Given to Nebraska's entry for Spirit of Youth Scholarship for Junior member, in event applicant does not win same.

Amount of award:	$200

Contact:
American Legion Nebraska Auxiliary
Department Education Chairman
P.O. Box 5227
Lincoln, NE 68505-0227
Web: www.nebraskalegionaux.net

Nurse Gift Tuition Scholarships

Type of award: Scholarship.
Intended use: For undergraduate study.
Eligibility: Applicant must be residing in Nebraska. Applicant must be descendant of veteran; or dependent of veteran; or spouse of veteran.
Basis for selection: Major/career interest in nursing. Applicant must demonstrate financial need.
Application requirements: Recommendations, essay, transcript, proof of eligibility.
Additional information: Awards given as funds permit.

Amount of award:	$200-$400

Contact:
American Legion Nebraska Auxiliary, Department Headquarters
P.O. Box 5227
Lincoln, NE 68505-0227
Web: www.nebraskalegionaux.net

Practical Nursing Scholarship

Type of award: Scholarship.
Intended use: For undergraduate study at 2-year or 4-year institution. Designated institutions: Schools of practical nursing.
Eligibility: Applicant must be residing in Nebraska. Applicant must be veteran or descendant of veteran; or dependent of veteran; or spouse of veteran.
Basis for selection: Major/career interest in nursing. Applicant must demonstrate financial need.
Application requirements: Recommendations, transcript, proof of eligibility.
Additional information: Must be Nebraska resident for at least three years, be accepted at school of practical nursing, and be veteran-connected.
  Amount of award: $300
Contact:
American Legion Nebraska Auxiliary, Department Headquarters
P.O. Box 5227
Lincoln, NE 68505-0227
Web: www.nebraskalegionaux.net

Roberta Marie Stretch Memorial Scholarship

Type of award: Scholarship.
Intended use: For undergraduate or master's study at 4-year institution.
Eligibility: Applicant must be residing in Nebraska. Applicant must be descendant of veteran; or dependent of veteran; or spouse of veteran.
Application requirements: Recommendations, transcript, proof of eligibility.
Additional information: Preference given to former Nebraska Girls State citizens.
  Amount of award: $400
Contact:
American Legion Nebraska Auxiliary, Department Headquarters
P.O. Box 5227
Lincoln, NE 68505-0227
Web: www.nebraskalegionaux.net

Ruby Paul Campaign Fund Scholarship

Type of award: Scholarship.
Intended use: For freshman study at accredited 2-year or 4-year institution.
Eligibility: Applicant or parent must be member/participant of American Legion Auxiliary. Applicant must be high school senior. Applicant must be residing in Nebraska. Must be Legion member, ALA member, Sons of the American Legion member of two years' standing, or child, grandchild, or great-grandchild of American Legion or ALA member of two years' standing.
Basis for selection: Applicant must demonstrate high academic achievement.
Application requirements: Recommendations, essay, transcript, proof of eligibility.
Additional information: Award varies with availability of funds. Applicant must be state resident for three years. Must have maintained "B" or better during last two semesters of high school. Must be accepted for fall term at college or university. Scholarships exclude applicants enrolled in nursing.
  Amount of award: $100-$300
  Application deadline: April 1
Contact:
American Legion Nebraska Auxiliary, Department Headquarters
P.O. Box 5227
Lincoln, NE 68505
Web: www.nebraskalegionaux.net

Student Aid Grant or Vocational Technical Scholarship

Type of award: Scholarship.
Intended use: For undergraduate study at vocational or 2-year institution in United States.
Eligibility: Applicant must be residing in Nebraska. Applicant must be descendant of veteran; or dependent of veteran; or spouse of veteran.
Application requirements: Recommendations, transcript, proof of eligibility.
  Amount of award: $200-$300
  Application deadline: April 1
Contact:
American Legion Nebraska Auxiliary, Department Headquarters
P.O. Box 5227
Lincoln, NE 68505-0227
Web: www.nebraskalegionaux.net

American Legion Nevada

American Legion Nevada Oratorical Contest

Type of award: Scholarship.
Intended use: For undergraduate study at postsecondary institution.
Eligibility: Applicant must be enrolled in high school. Applicant must be U.S. citizen or permanent resident residing in Nevada.
Basis for selection: Competition/talent/interest in oratory/debate, based on language style, voice, diction, delivery, originality, logic, breadth of knowledge, application of knowledge about topic, and skill in selecting examples and analogies.
Additional information: Awards: First place, $500; second place, $300; third place, $200; all in promissory notes.
  Amount of award: $200-$500
  Number of awards: 3
  Application deadline: January 15
  Total amount awarded: $1,000
Contact:
American Legion Nevada Oratorical Contest
737 Veterans Memorial Drive
Las Vegas, NV 89101
Web: www.nvlegion.org

American Legion Nevada Auxiliary

Past President's Parley Nurses' Scholarship

Type of award: Scholarship.
Intended use: For junior study at postsecondary institution.
Eligibility: Applicant must be residing in Nevada. Applicant must be veteran; or dependent of veteran.
Basis for selection: Major/career interest in nursing.
Additional information: $150 for each university. Applicant must have completed first two years of training.
   Amount of award: $150
Contact:
American Legion Nevada Auxiliary
Past President Parley Chair Nancy Michalski
1025 Twin Berry Ct
Henderson, NV 89002

President's Scholarship

Type of award: Scholarship.
Intended use: For undergraduate study at postsecondary institution.
Eligibility: Applicant must be residing in Nevada.
Additional information: President's Scholarship: $300 for winner of Department competition.
   Amount of award: $300
   Number of awards: 1
Contact:
American Legion Nevada Auxiliary, Department Secretary
4030 Bobolink Cir.
Reno, NV 89508

Silver Eagle Indian Scholarship

Type of award: Scholarship.
Intended use: For undergraduate study at postsecondary institution.
Eligibility: Applicant must be American Indian. Applicant must be U.S. citizen residing in Nevada. Applicant must be child or grandchild of American Indian veteran.
   Amount of award: $200
Contact:
American Legion Nevada Auxiliary, Department Secretary
4030 Bobolink Cir.
Reno, NV 89508

American Legion New Hampshire

Albert T. Marcoux Memorial Scholarship

Type of award: Scholarship.
Intended use: For freshman study at accredited postsecondary institution.
Eligibility: Applicant or parent must be member/participant of American Legion. Applicant must be residing in New Hampshire. Must be child of living or deceased New Hampshire American Legion or New Hampshire American Legion Auxiliary member.
Basis for selection: Applicant must demonstrate high academic achievement.
Application requirements: Recommendations, essay, transcript, proof of eligibility. Resume.
Additional information: Must be graduate of New Hampshire high school and state resident for three years.
   Amount of award: $2,000
   Number of awards: 1
   Application deadline: May 1
   Total amount awarded: $2,000
Contact:
American Legion New Hampshire
State House Annex
25 Capitol Street, Room 431
Concord, NH 03301-6312
Phone: 603-271-2211
Web: www.nhlegion.org

American Legion New Hampshire Boys State Scholarship

Type of award: Scholarship.
Intended use: For undergraduate study at postsecondary institution.
Eligibility: Applicant or parent must be member/participant of American Legion, Boys State. Applicant must be male. Applicant must be residing in New Hampshire.
Additional information: Award given to participants of Boys State during Boys State graduation. Award amount varies. Apply during Boys State session.
Contact:
American Legion New Hampshire
State House Annex
25 Capitol Street, Room 431
Concord, NH 03301-6312
Phone: 603-271-2211
Web: www.nhlegion.org

American Legion New Hampshire Oratorical Contest

Type of award: Scholarship.
Intended use: For undergraduate study at postsecondary institution.
Eligibility: Applicant must be enrolled in high school. Applicant must be residing in New Hampshire.
Basis for selection: Competition/talent/interest in oratory/debate, based on language style, voice, diction, delivery, originality, logic, breadth of knowledge, application of knowledge about topic, and skill in selecting examples and analogies.
Application requirements: Proof of eligibility.
Additional information: Awards: First place, $1,000; second place, $750; third place, $500; fourth place, $250; and four $100 awards.
   Amount of award: $100-$1,000
   Number of awards: 8
   Total amount awarded: $2,900
Contact:
American Legion New Hampshire
State House Annex
25 Capitol Street, Room 431
Concord, NH 03301-6312
Phone: 603-271-2211
Web: www.nhlegion.org

Christa McAuliffe Memorial Scholarship

Type of award: Scholarship.
Intended use: For freshman study at accredited 4-year institution.
Eligibility: Applicant must be residing in New Hampshire.
Basis for selection: Major/career interest in education. Applicant must demonstrate high academic achievement.
Application requirements: Recommendations, essay, transcript. Resume.
Additional information: Must be high school student or recent graduate of New Hampshire school entering first year of higher education; state resident for at least three years.

Amount of award:	$2,000
Number of awards:	1
Application deadline:	May 1
Total amount awarded:	$2,000

Contact:
American Legion New Hampshire
State House Annex
25 Capitol Street, Room 431
Concord, NH 03301-6312
Phone: 603-271-2211
Web: www.nhlegion.org

Department of New Hampshire Scholarship

Type of award: Scholarship.
Intended use: For freshman study at accredited 4-year institution.
Eligibility: Applicant or parent must be member/participant of American Legion. Applicant must be enrolled in high school. Applicant must be residing in New Hampshire.
Basis for selection: Applicant must demonstrate high academic achievement.
Application requirements: Recommendations, essay, transcript. Resume.
Additional information: Must be high school student or graduate from New Hampshire school entering first year of higher education; state resident for at least three years.

Amount of award:	$2,000
Number of awards:	2
Application deadline:	May 1
Total amount awarded:	$4,000

Contact:
American Legion New Hampshire
State House Annex
25 Capitol Street, Room 431
Concord, NH 03301-6312
Phone: 603-271-2211
Web: www.nhlegion.org

Department Vocational Scholarship

Type of award: Scholarship.
Intended use: For freshman study at vocational or 2-year institution.
Eligibility: Applicant or parent must be member/participant of American Legion. Applicant must be enrolled in high school. Applicant must be residing in New Hampshire.
Basis for selection: Applicant must demonstrate high academic achievement.
Application requirements: Recommendations, essay, transcript, proof of eligibility.

Additional information: Must be high school student or graduate from New Hampshire school entering first year of higher education in specific vocation; state resident for at least three years.

Amount of award:	$2,000
Number of awards:	1
Total amount awarded:	$2,000

Contact:
American Legion New Hampshire
State House Annex
25 Capitol Street, Room 431
Concord, NH 03301-6312
Phone: 603-271-2211
Web: www.nhlegion.org

John A. High Child Welfare Scholarship

Type of award: Scholarship.
Intended use: For freshman study at postsecondary institution.
Eligibility: Applicant must be male, high school senior. Applicant must be residing in New Hampshire.
Basis for selection: Applicant must demonstrate financial need, high academic achievement, depth of character and patriotism.
Application requirements: Recommendations, essay, transcript.
Additional information: Parent must be member of American Legion New Hampshire or American Legion New Hampshire Auxiliary for three consecutive years.

Amount of award:	$2,000
Number of awards:	1
Application deadline:	May 1
Total amount awarded:	$2,000

Contact:
American Legion New Hampshire
State House Annex
25 Capitol Street, Room 431
Concord, NH 03301-6312
Phone: 603-271-2211
Web: www.nhlegion.org

Raymond K. Conley Memorial Scholarship

Type of award: Scholarship.
Intended use: For freshman study at vocational, 2-year or 4-year institution.
Eligibility: Applicant must be high school senior. Applicant must be residing in New Hampshire.
Basis for selection: Major/career interest in rehabilitation/therapeutic services.
Application requirements: Recommendations, essay, transcript.
Additional information: Three-year state residency required. Must have at least a 'B' average.

Amount of award:	$2,000
Number of awards:	1
Application deadline:	May 1
Total amount awarded:	$2,000

Contact:
American Legion New Hampshire
State House Annex
25 Capitol Street, Room 431
Concord, NH 03301-6312
Phone: 603-271-2211
Web: www.nhlegion.org

American Legion New Hampshire Auxiliary

Adrienne Alix Scholarship

Type of award: Scholarship.
Intended use: For undergraduate study at postsecondary institution.
Eligibility: Applicant must be returning adult student. Applicant must be residing in New Hampshire.
Application requirements: Recommendations, essay.
Additional information: Must be one of the following: Re-entering work force or upgrading skills; displaced from work force; or recently honorably discharged from military. Scholarship must be used for a refresher course or to advance applicant's knowledge of techniques needed in today's work force.

Amount of award:	$1,000
Number of awards:	1
Application deadline:	May 1
Total amount awarded:	$1,000

Contact:
American Legion New Hampshire Auxiliary
Department Secretary
25 Capitol Street, Room 432
Concord, NH 03301-6312
Web: www.nhlegion.org

Elsie B. Brown Scholarship Fund

Type of award: Scholarship.
Intended use: For freshman study at postsecondary institution.
Eligibility: Applicant must be residing in New Hampshire. Applicant must be dependent of deceased veteran.
Application requirements: Recommendations, essay, transcript.

Amount of award:	$150
Number of awards:	1
Application deadline:	May 1
Total amount awarded:	$150

Contact:
American Legion New Hampshire Auxiliary
Department Secretary
25 Capitol Street, Room 432
Concord, NH 03301-6312
Web: www.nhlegion.org

Grace S. High Memorial Child Welfare Scholarship Fund

Type of award: Scholarship.
Intended use: For undergraduate study at postsecondary institution.
Eligibility: Applicant or parent must be member/participant of American Legion Auxiliary. Applicant must be female, high school senior. Applicant must be residing in New Hampshire. Parent must be member of American Legion New Hampshire or American Legion New Hampshire Auxiliary for at least three years. Daughters of deceased veterans also eligible.
Basis for selection: Applicant must demonstrate financial need.
Application requirements: Recommendations, essay, transcript, proof of eligibility.
Additional information: Applicant must be high school graduate and daughter of Legion or Auxiliary member.

Amount of award:	$300
Number of awards:	2
Application deadline:	May 1
Total amount awarded:	$600

Contact:
American Legion Auxiliary, Department of New Hampshire
Department Secretary
25 Capitol Street, Room 432
Concord, NH 03301-6312
Web: www.nhlegion.org

Marion J. Bagley Scholarship

Type of award: Scholarship.
Intended use: For undergraduate study at accredited postsecondary institution.
Eligibility: Applicant must be residing in New Hampshire.
Application requirements: Recommendations, essay, transcript.
Additional information: Applicant must be high school graduate (or equivalent) or attending school of higher learning.

Amount of award:	$1,000
Number of awards:	1
Application deadline:	May 1
Total amount awarded:	$1,000

Contact:
American Legion Auxiliary, Department of New Hampshire
Department Secretary
25 Capitol Street, Room 432
Concord, NH 03301-6312
Web: www.nhlegion.org

Past President's Parley Nurses' Scholarship

Type of award: Scholarship.
Intended use: For undergraduate study at postsecondary institution.
Eligibility: Applicant must be residing in New Hampshire.
Basis for selection: Major/career interest in nursing. Applicant must demonstrate financial need.
Application requirements: Recommendations, essay, transcript.
Additional information: Applicant must be high school graduate. Children of veteran given preference. One award to Registered Nurse study and one to Licensed Practical Nurse study.

Amount of award:	$300-$400
Number of awards:	2
Application deadline:	May 1

Contact:
American Legion Auxiliary, Department of New Hampshire
Department Secretary
25 Capitol Street, Room 432
Concord, NH 03301-6312
Web: www.nhlegion.org

American Legion New Jersey

American Legion New Jersey Oratorical Contest

Type of award: Scholarship.
Intended use: For undergraduate study at postsecondary institution.
Eligibility: Applicant must be enrolled in high school. Applicant must be residing in New Jersey.
Basis for selection: Competition/talent/interest in oratory/debate, based on language style, voice, diction, delivery, originality, logic, breadth of knowledge, application of knowledge about topic, and skill in selecting examples and analogies.
Application requirements: Proof of eligibility.
Additional information: Awards: First place, $4,000; second place, $2,500; third place, $2,000; fourth place, $1000; fifth place, $1000. See high school counselor for application.

Amount of award:	$1,000-$4,000
Number of awards:	5
Total amount awarded:	$10,500

Contact:
American Legion New Jersey
135 West Hanover Street
Trenton, NJ 08618
Phone: 609-695-5418
Web: www.njamericanlegion.org

Lawrence Luterman Memorial Scholarships

Type of award: Scholarship.
Intended use: For undergraduate study at 4-year institution.
Eligibility: Applicant or parent must be member/participant of American Legion. Applicant must be high school senior. Applicant must be residing in New Jersey. Applicant must be natural or adopted descendant of member of American Legion, Department of New Jersey.
Additional information: Two $4,000 ($1,000/year) awards; three $2,000 awards; two $1,000 awards. Contact local Post for application.

Amount of award:	$1,000-$4,000
Number of awards:	7
Application deadline:	February 15
Total amount awarded:	$16,000

Contact:
American Legion New Jersey
Department Adjutant
135 West Hanover Street
Trenton, NJ 08618
Phone: 609-695-5418
Web: www.njamericanlegion.org

Stutz Memorial Scholarship

Type of award: Scholarship.
Intended use: For undergraduate study at 4-year institution.
Eligibility: Applicant or parent must be member/participant of American Legion. Applicant must be high school senior. Applicant must be residing in New Jersey. Applicant must be natural or adopted child of American Legion, Department of

New Jersey member, or of a deceased member if parent was member at time of death.
Additional information: Award is $4,000 ($1,000/year for four years). Contact local Post for application.

Amount of award:	$4,000
Number of awards:	1
Application deadline:	February 15
Total amount awarded:	$4,000

Contact:
American Legion, Department of New Jersey
Department Adjutant
135 West Hanover Street
Trenton, NJ 08618
Phone: 609-695-5418
Web: www.njamericanlegion.org

American Legion New Jersey Auxiliary

American Legion New Jersey Auxiliary Department Scholarships

Type of award: Scholarship.
Intended use: For freshman study at 2-year or 4-year institution.
Eligibility: Applicant must be high school senior. Applicant must be residing in New Jersey. Must be child or grandchild of honorably discharged veteran of U.S. Armed Forces.
Additional information: Several awards offered. Amount and number of awards vary. Must be New Jersey resident for at least two years.

Application deadline:	April 15

Contact:
American Legion Auxiliary, Department of New Jersey
Department Secretary
1540 Kuser Road, Suite A-8
Hamilton, NJ 08619
Phone: 609-581-9580
Fax: 609-581-8429

Claire Oliphant Memorial Scholarship

Type of award: Scholarship.
Intended use: For freshman study at 2-year or 4-year institution.
Eligibility: Applicant must be high school senior. Applicant must be residing in New Jersey. Must be child of honorably discharged veteran of U.S. Armed Forces.
Additional information: Must be New Jersey resident for at least two years. Rules and applications distributed to all New Jersey high school guidance departments.

Amount of award:	$1,800
Number of awards:	1
Application deadline:	April 15
Total amount awarded:	$1,800

Contact:
American Legion Auxiliary, Department of New Jersey
Department Secretary
1540 Kuser Road, Suite A-8
Hamilton, NJ 08619
Phone: 609-581-9580
Fax: 609-581-8429

Past President's Parley Nurses' Scholarship

Type of award: Scholarship.
Intended use: For freshman study at 2-year or 4-year institution.
Eligibility: Applicant must be high school senior. Applicant must be residing in New Jersey. Must be child or grandchild of honorably discharged veteran of U.S. Armed Forces.
Basis for selection: Major/career interest in nursing.
Additional information: Applicant must be enrolled in nursing program. Must be New Jersey resident for at least two years. Award amount varies.
   Application deadline: April 15
Contact:
American Legion Auxiliary, Department of New Jersey
Department Secretary
1540 Kuser Road, Suite A-8
Hamilton, NJ 08619
Phone: 609-581-9580
Fax: 609-581-8429

American Legion New Mexico Auxiliary

National President's Scholarship

Type of award: Scholarship.
Intended use: For undergraduate study at postsecondary institution.
Eligibility: Applicant must be residing in New Mexico.
Additional information: Awarded to Department winner of National President's Scholarship, if she does not win in Division. If she does, it will be given to second place winner in Department.
   Amount of award: $150
   Number of awards: 1
   Application deadline: April 1
   Total amount awarded: $150
Contact:
American Legion New Mexico Auxiliary
Attn: National President's Scholarship
1215 Mountain Road, NE
Albuquerque, NM 87102
Phone: 505-242-9918

Past President's Parley Scholarship for Nurses

Type of award: Scholarship.
Intended use: For undergraduate study at postsecondary institution.
Eligibility: Applicant must be residing in New Mexico.
Basis for selection: Major/career interest in health-related professions; nursing or medicine.
Application requirements: Copy of school registration and letter of request for assistance.
   Application deadline: May 1

Contact:
American Legion Auxiliary, Department of New Mexico
Attn: Nurses Scholarship
1215 Mountain Road, NE
Albuquerque, NM 87102
Phone: 505-242-9918

American Legion New York

American Legion New York Oratorical Contest

Type of award: Scholarship.
Intended use: For undergraduate study at postsecondary institution.
Eligibility: Applicant or parent must be member/participant of American Legion. Applicant must be no older than 20, enrolled in high school. Applicant must be residing in New York.
Basis for selection: Competition/talent/interest in oratory/debate, based on language style, voice, diction, delivery, originality, logic, breadth of knowledge, application of knowledge about topic, and skill in selecting examples and analogies.
Application requirements: Proof of eligibility.
Additional information: Awards: First place, $6,000; second place, $4,000; third place, $2,500; fourth and fifth place, $2,000. Scholarship payments are made directly to student's college and are awarded over a four-year period. Contact local Post for more information.
   Amount of award: $2,000-$6,000
   Number of awards: 5
   Total amount awarded: $16,500
Contact:
American Legion, Department of New York
Department Adjutant
112 State Street, Suite 1300
Albany, NY 12207
Phone: 518-463-2215
Web: www.ny.legion.org

Dr. Hannah K. Vuolo Memorial Scholarship

Type of award: Scholarship.
Intended use: For freshman study at accredited 2-year or 4-year institution.
Eligibility: Applicant or parent must be member/participant of American Legion. Applicant must be no older than 20, high school senior. Applicant must be descendant of veteran.
Basis for selection: Major/career interest in education, teacher.
Additional information: Applicant must be natural or adopted direct descendant of member or deceased member of American Legion, Department of New York.
   Amount of award: $1,000
   Number of awards: 1
   Application deadline: May 1
   Total amount awarded: $1,000
Contact:
American Legion, Department of New York
Department Adjutant
112 State Street, Suite 1300
Albany, NY 12207
Phone: 518-463-2215
Web: www.ny.legion.org

New York American Legion Press Association Scholarship

Type of award: Scholarship.
Intended use: For full-time undergraduate study at accredited 4-year institution.
Eligibility: Applicant or parent must be member/participant of American Legion. Applicant must be residing in New York.
Basis for selection: Major/career interest in communications; journalism; graphic arts/design; film/video or radio/television/film.
Additional information: Applicant must be child of New York Legion or Auxiliary member; Sons of American Legion or American Legion Auxiliary Junior member; or graduate of New York American Legion Boys State or Girls State.

Amount of award:	$1,000
Number of awards:	1
Application deadline:	April 15

Contact:
New York American Legion Press Association
Scholarship Chairman
P.O. Box 650
East Aurora, NY 14052
Web: www.ny.legion.org

American Legion New York Auxiliary

American Legion New York Auxiliary Scholarship

Type of award: Scholarship.
Intended use: For undergraduate study at postsecondary institution.
Eligibility: Applicant must be U.S. citizen residing in New York. Applicant must be descendant of veteran; or dependent of veteran or deceased veteran during Grenada conflict, Korean War, Lebanon conflict, Panama conflict, Persian Gulf War, WW I, WW II or Vietnam.
Basis for selection: Applicant must demonstrate financial need, high academic achievement, depth of character, leadership and patriotism.
Additional information: May use other scholarships. Visit Website for application.

Amount of award:	$1,000
Number of awards:	1
Total amount awarded:	$1,000

Contact:
American Legion New York Auxiliary
112 State Street, Suite 1310
Albany, NY 12207-0003
Web: www.deptny.org

Past President's Parley Student Scholarship in Medical Field

Type of award: Scholarship.
Intended use: For undergraduate study at 2-year or 4-year institution.
Eligibility: Applicant must be no older than 19, high school senior. Applicant must be U.S. citizen residing in New York. Applicant must be descendant of veteran; or dependent of veteran during Grenada conflict, Korean War, Lebanon conflict, Panama conflict, Persian Gulf War, WW I, WW II or Vietnam.
Basis for selection: Major/career interest in health-related professions. Applicant must demonstrate financial need, high academic achievement, depth of character, leadership and patriotism.
Additional information: Visit Website for application.

Amount of award:	$1,500
Number of awards:	3

Contact:
American Legion New York Auxiliary
112 State Street, Suite 1310
Albany, NY 12207-0003
Phone: 518-463-1162
Web: www.deptny.org

American Legion North Carolina

American Legion Oratorical Contest

Type of award: Scholarship.
Intended use: For undergraduate study at postsecondary institution.
Eligibility: Applicant must be enrolled in high school. Applicant must be U.S. citizen or permanent resident residing in North Carolina.
Basis for selection: Competition/talent/interest in oratory/debate, based on language style, voice, diction, delivery, originality, logic, breadth of knowledge, application of knowledge about topic, and skill in selecting examples and analogies.
Additional information: Awards: First place, $2,000; second place, $750; third, fourth, and fifth place, $500. Visit Website for more information.

Amount of award:	$500-$2,000
Number of awards:	5
Total amount awarded:	$4,250

Contact:
American Legion North Carolina
Oratorical Contest
P.O. Box 26657
Raleigh, NC 27611-6657
Web: www.nclegion.org

Colon Furr Scholarship

Type of award: Scholarship.
Intended use: For undergraduate study at 2-year or 4-year institution. Designated institutions: North Carolina schools granting LPN or RN degree.
Eligibility: Applicant must be residing in North Carolina.
Basis for selection: Major/career interest in nursing.
Application requirements: Nomination by North Carolina American Legion Post.
Additional information: Applicant must be accepted or enrolled in a one-year LPN program or a two, three, or four-year RN program. Contact local Post for application.

Amount of award:	$600
Number of awards:	1
Total amount awarded:	$600

Contact:
American Legion North Carolina
P.O. Box 26657
Raleigh, NC 27611-6657
Web: www.nclegion.org

American Legion North Carolina Auxiliary

Nannie W. Norfleet Scholarship

Type of award: Scholarship.
Intended use: For undergraduate study at postsecondary institution.
Eligibility: Applicant or parent must be member/participant of American Legion Auxiliary. Applicant must be high school senior. Applicant must be residing in North Carolina.
Basis for selection: Applicant must demonstrate financial need.
Additional information: Preference given to children of American Legion Auxiliary members.

Amount of award:	$1,000
Number of awards:	1
Application deadline:	March 15
Total amount awarded:	$1,000

Contact:
American Legion North Carolina Auxiliary, Department Headquarters
P.O. Box 25726
Raleigh, NC 27611
Phone: 919-832-4051
Web: www.nclegion.org/auxil.htm

American Legion North Dakota

American Legion North Dakota Oratorical Contest

Type of award: Scholarship.
Intended use: For undergraduate study at postsecondary institution.
Eligibility: Applicant must be high school freshman, sophomore, junior or senior. Applicant must be residing in North Dakota.
Basis for selection: Competition/talent/interest in oratory/debate, based on language style, voice, diction, delivery, originality, logic, breadth of knowledge, application of knowledge about topic, and skill in selecting examples and analogies.
Application requirements: Proof of eligibility. For application, contact local American Legion Post or Department Headquarters after start of school year.
Additional information: State awards: First place, $400; second place, $300; third place, $200; fourth place, $100; East and West Divisional Contests: First place, $300; second place, $200; and 10 District Contests: First place, $300; second place, $200; third place, $100. Local contests begin in the fall.

Amount of award:	$100-$400

Contact:
American Legion North Dakota, Department Headquarters
P.O. Box 2666
Fargo, ND 58108-2666
Phone: 701-293-3120
Fax: 701-293-9951
Web: www.ndlegion.org

Hattie Tedrow Memorial Fund Scholarship

Type of award: Scholarship.
Intended use: For undergraduate study at vocational, 2-year or 4-year institution.
Eligibility: Applicant must be high school senior. Applicant must be residing in North Dakota. Applicant must be descendant of veteran; or dependent of veteran.
Basis for selection: Applicant must demonstrate high academic achievement.
Application requirements: Essay, proof of eligibility. SASE.
Additional information: Number and amount of awards based on availability of funds.

Amount of award:	$2,000
Application deadline:	April 15

Contact:
American Legion North Dakota
Hattie Tedrow Memorial Fund Scholarship
P.O. Box 1055
Indianapolis, IN 46206
Phone: 701-293-3120
Fax: 701-293-9951
Web: www.ndlegion.org

American Legion North Dakota Auxiliary

American Legion North Dakota Auxiliary Scholarships

Type of award: Scholarship.
Intended use: For undergraduate study at postsecondary institution. Designated institutions: North Dakota institutions.
Eligibility: Applicant must be residing in North Dakota.
Basis for selection: Applicant must demonstrate financial need.
Additional information: Obtain application from local American Legion Auxiliary Unit.

Amount of award:	$500
Number of awards:	4
Application deadline:	January 15

Contact:
American Legion North Dakota Auxiliary
Department Education Chairman
P.O. Box 1060
Jamestown, ND 58402-1060
Phone: 701-253-5992
Web: www.ndlegion.org

Past President's Parley Scholarship

Type of award: Scholarship.

Intended use: For undergraduate study at 2-year or 4-year institution. Designated institutions: North Dakota hospital and nursing schools.
Eligibility: Applicant or parent must be member/participant of American Legion Auxiliary. Applicant must be residing in North Dakota.
Basis for selection: Major/career interest in nursing.
Additional information: Children, grandchildren or great-grandchildren of American Legion or Auxiliary member in good standing. Must be graduate of North Dakota high school. Apply to local American Legion Auxiliary Unit.

   Amount of award: $350
   Application deadline: May 15
Contact:
American Legion Auxiliary, Department of North Dakota
Chair of Dept. Parley Scholarship Committee
P.O. Box 1060
Jamestown, ND 58402-1060
Phone: 701-872-3865
Web: www.ndlegion.org

American Legion Ohio

American Legion Ohio Scholarships

Type of award: Scholarship.
Intended use: For undergraduate study at postsecondary institution.
Eligibility: Applicant or parent must be member/participant of American Legion. For Legion members; direct descendants of Legionnaires in good standing; direct descendants of deceased Legionnaires; spouses or children of deceased U.S. military persons who died on active duty or of injuries received on active duty.
Additional information: Number and amount of awards vary. Contact sponsor or visit Website for more information.

   Amount of award: $1,500
   Application deadline: April 15
Contact:
American Legion, Department of Ohio
Department Scholarship Committee
P.O. Box 8007
Delaware, OH 43015-8007
Web: www.ohiolegion.com

Department Oratorical Awards

Type of award: Scholarship.
Intended use: For undergraduate study at postsecondary institution.
Eligibility: Applicant or parent must be member/participant of American Legion. Applicant must be enrolled in high school. Applicant must be residing in Ohio.
Basis for selection: Competition/talent/interest in oratory/ debate, based on language style, voice, diction, delivery, originality, logic, breadth of knowledge, application of knowledge about topic, and skill in selecting examples and analogies.
Additional information: Awards: First place, $2,000; second place, $1000; third place, $600; fourth place, $400.

   Amount of award: $400-$2,000
   Number of awards: 4
   Total amount awarded: $4,000

Contact:
American Legion Ohio
Department Scholarship Committee
P.O. Box 8007
Delaware, OH 43015-8007
Phone: 740-362-7478
Fax: 740-362-1429
Web: www.ohiolegion.com

American Legion Ohio Auxiliary

American Legion Ohio Auxiliary Past President's Parley Nurse's Scholarship

Type of award: Scholarship.
Intended use: For undergraduate study at 2-year or 4-year institution.
Eligibility: Applicant or parent must be member/participant of American Legion Auxiliary. Applicant must be residing in Ohio. Applicant must be descendant of veteran; or dependent of veteran; or spouse of veteran.
Basis for selection: Major/career interest in nursing.
Additional information: Awards: 15 $300 and two $750 scholarships.

   Amount of award: $300-$750
   Number of awards: 17
   Application deadline: May 1
   Total amount awarded: $6,000
Contact:
American Legion Ohio Auxiliary
Department Secretary
P.O. Box 2760
Zanesville, OH 43702-2760
Phone: 740-452-8245
Fax: 740-452-2620

American Legion Ohio Auxiliary Scholarship

Type of award: Scholarship.
Intended use: For freshman study at postsecondary institution.
Eligibility: Applicant or parent must be member/participant of American Legion Auxiliary. Applicant must be high school senior. Applicant must be residing in Ohio. Applicant must be descendant of veteran; or dependent of veteran or deceased veteran during Grenada conflict, Korean War, Lebanon conflict, Persian Gulf War, WW I, WW II or Vietnam.
Additional information: Awards: one $1,500 and one $1,000.

   Amount of award: $1,000-$1,500
   Number of awards: 2
   Application deadline: March 1
   Total amount awarded: $2,500
Contact:
American Legion Ohio Auxiliary
Department Secretary
P.O. Box 2760
Zanesville, OH 43702-2760
Phone: 740-452-8245
Fax: 740-452-2620

Scholarships

American Legion Oregon

American Legion Department Oratorical Contest

Type of award: Scholarship.
Intended use: For undergraduate study at postsecondary institution.
Eligibility: Applicant must be enrolled in high school. Applicant must be U.S. citizen or permanent resident residing in Oregon.
Basis for selection: Competition/talent/interest in oratory/ debate, based on language style, voice, diction, delivery, originality, logic, breadth of knowledge, application of knowledge about topic, and skill in selecting examples and analogies.
Application requirements: Proof of eligibility.
Additional information: Awards: First place, $500; second place, $400; third place, $300; fourth place, $200. Applications available at local high schools.

Amount of award:	$200-$500
Number of awards:	4
Application deadline:	December 1
Total amount awarded:	$1,400

Contact:
American Legion Oregon
P.O. Box 1730
Wilsonville, OR 97070-1730
Phone: 503-685-5006
Fax: 503-685-5008

American Legion Oregon Auxiliary

American Legion Auxiliary Department of Oregon Scholarship

Type of award: Scholarship.
Intended use: For undergraduate study at postsecondary institution.
Eligibility: Applicant must be residing in Oregon. Applicant must be dependent of veteran or deceased veteran; or spouse of disabled veteran or deceased veteran.

Amount of award:	$1,000
Number of awards:	1
Application deadline:	March 10
Total amount awarded:	$1,000

Contact:
American Legion Auxiliary, Department of Oregon
Chariman of Education
P.O. Box 1730
Wilsonville, OR 97070-1730

American Legion Oregon Auxiliary Department Nurses Scholarship

Type of award: Scholarship.
Intended use: For undergraduate study at accredited 2-year or 4-year institution.

Eligibility: Applicant must be residing in Oregon. Applicant must be dependent of disabled veteran or deceased veteran; or spouse of disabled veteran or deceased veteran.
Basis for selection: Major/career interest in nursing. Applicant must demonstrate financial need, high academic achievement, depth of character, seriousness of purpose and service orientation.
Application requirements: Proof of eligibility.

Amount of award:	$1,500
Number of awards:	1
Application deadline:	May 15
Total amount awarded:	$1,500

Contact:
American Legion Auxiliary, Department of Oregon
Chairman of Education
P.O. Box 1730
Wilsonville, OR 97070-1730

National President's Scholarship

Type of award: Scholarship.
Intended use: For undergraduate study at postsecondary institution.
Eligibility: Applicant or parent must be member/participant of American Legion Auxiliary. Applicant must be high school senior. Applicant must be residing in Oregon. Applicant must be dependent of veteran during Grenada conflict, Korean War, Lebanon conflict, Panama conflict, Persian Gulf War, WW I, WW II or Vietnam.
Additional information: Three awards in each division of American Legion Auxiliary: First place, $2,500; second place, $2,000; and third place, $1,000.

Amount of award:	$1,000-$2,500
Number of awards:	15
Application deadline:	March 1

Contact:
American Legion Auxiliary, Department of Oregon
Chairman of Education
P.O. Box 1730
Wilsonville, OR 97070-1730

Spirit of Youth Scholarship

Type of award: Scholarship.
Intended use: For undergraduate study at accredited vocational, 2-year or 4-year institution.
Eligibility: Applicant or parent must be member/participant of American Legion Auxiliary. Applicant must be residing in Oregon. Applicant must be dependent of deceased veteran; or spouse of disabled veteran or deceased veteran.
Additional information: Must be Junior member of The American Legion Auxiliary for past three years and hold current membership.

Amount of award:	$1,000
Application deadline:	March 1

Contact:
American Legion Auxiliary, Department of Oregon
Chairman of Education
P.O. Box 1730
Wilsonville, OR 97070-1730

American Legion Pennsylvania

American Legion High School Oratorical Contest

Type of award: Scholarship.
Intended use: For undergraduate study at postsecondary institution.
Eligibility: Applicant must be enrolled in high school. Applicant must be U.S. citizen or permanent resident residing in Pennsylvania.
Basis for selection: Competition/talent/interest in oratory/debate, based on language style, voice, diction, delivery, originality, logic, breadth of knowledge, application of knowledge about topic, and skill in selecting examples and analogies.
Additional information: Awards: First place, $7,500; second place, $5,000; third place, $4,000. Contact local American Legion Post for details and application.

Amount of award:	$4,000-$7,500
Number of awards:	3
Application deadline:	January 1
Total amount awarded:	$16,500

Contact:
American Legion Pennsylvania
Scholarship Secretary
P.O. Box 2324
Harrisburg, PA 17105-2324
Phone: 717-730-9100
Web: www.pa-legion.com

Joseph P. Gavenonis Scholarship

Type of award: Scholarship, renewable.
Intended use: For full-time undergraduate study at 4-year institution.
Eligibility: Applicant or parent must be member/participant of American Legion. Applicant must be high school senior. Applicant must be residing in Pennsylvania. Applicant must be child of living member in good standing of Pennsylvania American Legion, or child of deceased Pennsylvania American Legion member.
Basis for selection: Applicant must demonstrate financial need.
Application requirements: Transcript, proof of eligibility.
Additional information: Award is $1,000 per year for four years; renewal based on grades. Minimum GPA 2.5.

Amount of award:	$1,000
Number of awards:	1
Application deadline:	May 30
Total amount awarded:	$4,000

Contact:
American Legion Pennsylvania
Dept. Adjutant, Attn: Scholarship Secretary
P.O. Box 2324
Harrisburg, PA 17105-2324
Phone: 717-730-9100
Web: www.pa-legion.com

Robert W. Valimont Endowment Fund Scholarship

Type of award: Scholarship, renewable.

Intended use: For full-time undergraduate study at vocational or 2-year institution.
Eligibility: Applicant must be residing in Pennsylvania. Applicant must be dependent of active service person, veteran or deceased veteran.
Basis for selection: Applicant must demonstrate financial need.
Application requirements: Proof of eligibility.
Additional information: Parent must be member of American Legion, Pennsylvania. Award is $600 for first year; must reapply for second year. Minimum 2.5 GPA.

Amount of award:	$600
Application deadline:	May 30
Total amount awarded:	$600

Contact:
American Legion Pennsylvania
Dept. Adjutant, Attn: Scholarship Secretary
P.O. Box 2324
Harrisburg, PA 17105-2324
Phone: 717-730-9100
Web: www.pa-legion.com

American Legion Pennsylvania Auxiliary

Scholarship for Children of Deceased or Totally Disabled Veterans

Type of award: Scholarship.
Intended use: For undergraduate study at postsecondary institution.
Eligibility: Applicant must be high school senior. Applicant must be residing in Pennsylvania. Applicant must be dependent of disabled veteran or deceased veteran.
Basis for selection: Applicant must demonstrate financial need.
Additional information: Award is $600 per year for four years.

Amount of award:	$2,400
Number of awards:	1
Application deadline:	March 15
Total amount awarded:	$2,400

Contact:
American Legion Auxiliary, Department of Pennsylvania
Department Education Chairman
P.O. Box 1285
Camp Hill, PA 17105
Phone: 717-763-7545

Scholarship for Children of Living Veterans

Type of award: Scholarship.
Intended use: For undergraduate study at postsecondary institution.
Eligibility: Applicant must be high school senior. Applicant must be residing in Pennsylvania. Applicant must be dependent of veteran.
Basis for selection: Applicant must demonstrate financial need.
Additional information: Award: $600 per year for four years.

Amount of award: $2,400
Number of awards: 1
Application deadline: March 15
Total amount awarded: $2,400
Contact:
American Legion Auxiliary, Department of Pennsylvania
Department Education Chairman
P.O. Box 1285
Camp Hill, PA 17105
Phone: 717-763-7545

American Legion Press Club of New Jersey

American Legion Press Club of New Jersey and Post 170--Arthur Dehardt Memorial Scholarship

Type of award: Scholarship.
Intended use: For freshman study at accredited 4-year institution.
Eligibility: Applicant or parent must be member/participant of American Legion. Applicant must be residing in New Jersey. Applicant must be child or grandchild of current member of New Jersey American Legion or Auxiliary, including Sons of American Legion and Auxiliary Juniors. Graduates from either American Legion New Jersey Boys State or Auxiliary Girls State programs also eligible.
Basis for selection: Major/career interest in communications; computer graphics; journalism or public relations.
Application requirements: Essay, proof of eligibility.
Amount of award: $500
Number of awards: 2
Application deadline: July 15
Total amount awarded: $1,000
Contact:
American Legion Press Club of New Jersey
Jack W. Kuepfer, Education Chairman
68 Merrill Road
Clifton, NJ 07012-1622
Phone: 973-473-5176
Web: www.njamericanlegion.org

American Legion Puerto Rico Auxiliary

American Legion Puerto Rico Auxiliary Nursing Scholarships

Type of award: Scholarship.
Intended use: For undergraduate study at 2-year or 4-year institution. Designated institutions: Eligible institutions in Puerto Rico.
Eligibility: Applicant must be residing in Puerto Rico.
Basis for selection: Major/career interest in nursing.
Application requirements: Interview.
Additional information: Two $250 awards for two consecutive years.

Amount of award: $250
Number of awards: 2
Application deadline: March 15
Contact:
American Legion Auxiliary, Department of Puerto Rico
Education Chairman
P.O. Box 11424
Caparra Heights Station, PR 00922-1424

American Legion Rhode Island

American Legion Rhode Island Oratorical Contest

Type of award: Scholarship.
Eligibility: Applicant must be enrolled in high school. Applicant must be U.S. citizen or permanent resident residing in Rhode Island.
Basis for selection: Competition/talent/interest in oratory/debate, based on language style, voice, diction, delivery, originality, logic, breadth of knowledge, application of knowledge about topic, and skill in selecting examples and analogies.
Additional information: Awards: First place, $500; second place, $250; third place, $100; fourth place, $50.
Amount of award: $50-$500
Number of awards: 4
Total amount awarded: $900
Contact:
American Legion of Rhode Island, Oratorical Contest
1005 Charles Street
North Providence, RI 02904
Web: www.ri.legion.org

American Legion Rhode Island Auxiliary

American Legion Rhode Island Auxiliary Book Award

Type of award: Scholarship.
Intended use: For undergraduate study at postsecondary institution.
Eligibility: Applicant or parent must be member/participant of American Legion Auxiliary. Applicant must be residing in Rhode Island. Applicant must be descendant of veteran; or dependent of veteran.
Additional information: Award: $500. Must be child or grandchild of veteran.
Amount of award: $500
Number of awards: 1
Application deadline: April 1
Total amount awarded: $500
Contact:
American Legion Auxiliary, Department of Rhode Island
Department Secretary
815 Sandy Lane #18
Warwick, RI 02889

American Legion South Carolina

American Legion South Carolina Department Oratorical Contest

Type of award: Scholarship.
Intended use: For undergraduate study at postsecondary institution.
Eligibility: Applicant must be enrolled in high school. Applicant must be residing in South Carolina.
Basis for selection: Competition/talent/interest in oratory/debate, based on language style, voice, diction, delivery, originality, logic, breadth of knowledge, application of knowledge about topic, and skill in selecting examples and analogies.
Additional information: Awards: First place, $3,500; second place, $2,000; third and fourth place, $500. Distributed over four-year period. Zone Contest winners: four $100 awards.

Amount of award:	$100-$3,500
Number of awards:	8
Application deadline:	January 31
Total amount awarded:	$6,900

Contact:
American Legion South Carolina, Department Adjutant
P.O. Box 3309
Irmo, SC 29063
Phone: 803-612-1171
Fax: 803-213-9902
Web: www.scarolinalegion.org

American Legion South Carolina Auxiliary

American Legion South Carolina Auxiliary Scholarship

Type of award: Scholarship.
Intended use: For undergraduate study at postsecondary institution.
Eligibility: Applicant or parent must be member/participant of American Legion Auxiliary. Applicant must be high school senior. Applicant must be residing in South Carolina. Must be American Legion Auxiliary junior or senior member with at least three consecutive years' membership at time of application. Must have current membership card.

Amount of award:	$500
Number of awards:	2
Application deadline:	April 15
Total amount awarded:	$1,000

Contact:
American Legion Auxiliary, Department of South Carolina
Department Secretary
1200 Main Street, Suite 400-B
Columbia, SC 29201
Phone: 803-799-6695
Fax: 803-799-7907

American Legion South Dakota

American Legion South Dakota Oratorical Contest

Type of award: Scholarship.
Intended use: For undergraduate study at postsecondary institution.
Eligibility: Applicant must be enrolled in high school. Applicant must be residing in South Dakota.
Basis for selection: Competition/talent/interest in oratory/debate, based on language style, voice, diction, delivery, originality, logic, breadth of knowledge, application of knowledge about topic, and skill in selecting examples and analogies.
Application requirements: Proof of eligibility.
Additional information: Awards: First place, $1,000; second place, $500; third place, $300; fourth and fifth place, $100. Redeemable within five years of date of award.

Amount of award:	$100-$1,000
Number of awards:	5
Total amount awarded:	$2,000

Contact:
American Legion, Department of South Dakota
Department Adjutant
P.O. Box 67
Watertown, SD 57201-0067
Phone: 605-886-3604

American Legion South Dakota Auxiliary

American Legion South Dakota Auxiliary Nurse's Scholarship

Type of award: Scholarship.
Intended use: For undergraduate study at postsecondary institution.
Eligibility: Applicant or parent must be member/participant of American Legion Auxiliary. Applicant must be at least 16, no older than 22. Applicant must be residing in South Dakota. Applicant must be dependent of veteran.
Basis for selection: Major/career interest in nursing.

Amount of award:	$500
Number of awards:	2
Application deadline:	March 1
Total amount awarded:	$1,000

Contact:
American Legion South Dakota Auxiliary
Patricia Coyle, Department Secretary
P.O. Box 117
Huron, SD 57350-0117
Phone: 605-353-1793

American Legion South Dakota Auxiliary Scholarships

Type of award: Scholarship.

Intended use: For undergraduate study at vocational, 2-year or 4-year institution.

Eligibility: Applicant or parent must be member/participant of American Legion Auxiliary. Applicant must be at least 16, no older than 22. Applicant must be residing in South Dakota. Applicant must be dependent of veteran.

Additional information: College scholarships: two $500; vocational scholarships: two $500.

Amount of award:	$500
Number of awards:	4
Application deadline:	March 1
Total amount awarded:	$2,000

Contact:
American Legion South Dakota Auxiliary
Patricia Coyle, Department Secretary
P.O. Box 117
Huron, SD 57350-0117
Phone: 605-353-1793

Scholarship for College or Vocational

Type of award: Scholarship.

Intended use: For undergraduate study at vocational, 2-year or 4-year institution.

Eligibility: Applicant or parent must be member/participant of American Legion Auxiliary. Applicant must be residing in South Dakota. Applicant must have been senior South Dakota American Legion Auxiliary member for three consecutive years including current year.

Amount of award:	$400
Number of awards:	1
Application deadline:	March 1
Total amount awarded:	$400

Contact:
American Legion South Dakota Auxiliary
Patricia Coyle, Department Secretary
P.O. Box 117
Huron, SD 57350-0117
Phone: 605-353-1793

Thelma Foster Junior American Legion Auxiliary Members Scholarship

Type of award: Scholarship.

Intended use: For undergraduate study at postsecondary institution.

Eligibility: Applicant or parent must be member/participant of American Legion Auxiliary. Applicant must be residing in South Dakota. Must be Junior American Legion member for at least three years, including current year.

Additional information: Must be high school senior or graduate of accredited high school.

Amount of award:	$300
Number of awards:	1
Application deadline:	March 1

Contact:
American Legion South Dakota Auxiliary
Patricia Coyle, Dept. Secretary
P.O. Box 117
Huron, SD 57350-0117
Phone: 605-353-1793

Thelma Foster Senior American Legion Auxiliary Member Scholarship

Type of award: Scholarship.

Intended use: For undergraduate study at postsecondary institution.

Eligibility: Applicant or parent must be member/participant of American Legion Auxiliary. Applicant must be residing in South Dakota. Must be senior South Dakota American Legion Auxiliary member for past three years, including current year.

Amount of award:	$300
Number of awards:	1
Application deadline:	March 1
Total amount awarded:	$300

Contact:
American Legion South Dakota Auxiliary
Patricia Coyle, Department Secretary
P.O. Box 117
Huron, SD 57350-0117
Phone: 605-353-1793

American Legion Tennessee

American Legion Tennessee Oratorical Contest

Type of award: Scholarship, renewable.

Intended use: For undergraduate study at vocational, 2-year or 4-year institution in United States.

Eligibility: Applicant must be enrolled in high school. Applicant must be residing in Tennessee.

Basis for selection: Competition/talent/interest in oratory/ debate, based on language style, voice, diction, delivery, originality, logic, breadth of knowledge, application of knowledge about topic, and skill in selecting examples and analogies.

Application requirements: Proof of eligibility.

Additional information: Awards: First place, $3,000; second place, $2,000; third place, $1,000. First place winner eligible to enter National Contest. National winner receives $18,000 scholarship. Enter contest through local high school participating in Tennessee Oratorical Contest.

Amount of award:	$1,000-$3,000
Number of awards:	3
Application deadline:	January 1
Total amount awarded:	$6,000

Contact:
American Legion Tennessee
215 Rosa L Parks Avenue
Nashville, TN 37203-3583
Phone: 615-254-0568
Web: www.tennesseelegion.org

Eagle Scout of the Year Scholarship

Type of award: Scholarship.

Intended use: For undergraduate study at postsecondary institution in United States.

Eligibility: Applicant or parent must be member/participant of Boy Scouts of America, Eagle Scouts. Applicant must be male, at least 15, no older than 18, enrolled in high school. Applicant must be residing in Tennessee.

Scholarships

Application requirements: Nomination by Tennessee American Legion.

Additional information: Must be registered, active member of Boy Scout Troop, Varsity Scout Team, or Venturing Crew and either chartered to an American Legion Post, Auxiliary Unit or Sons of American Legion Squadron, or be son or grandson of American Legion or American Legion Auxiliary member.

Amount of award:	$1,500
Number of awards:	1
Application deadline:	January 1
Total amount awarded:	$1,500

Contact:
American Legion Tennessee
215 Rosa L Parks Avenue
Nashville, TN 37203-3583
Phone: 615-254-0568
Web: www.tennesseelegion.org

American Legion Tennessee Auxiliary

Vara Gray Scholarship Fund

Type of award: Scholarship.
Intended use: For undergraduate study at vocational, 2-year or 4-year institution.
Eligibility: Applicant must be high school senior. Applicant must be residing in Tennessee. Applicant must be dependent of veteran.
Application requirements: Recommendations, essay, nomination by local American Legion Auxiliary Unit.

Amount of award:	$500
Number of awards:	3
Application deadline:	March 1
Total amount awarded:	$1,500

Contact:
American Legion Tennessee Auxiliary, Department Headquarters
104 Point East Drive
Nashville, TN 37216
Phone: 615-226-8648
Fax: 615-226-8649

American Legion Texas

Texas Legion Oratorical Contest

Type of award: Scholarship.
Intended use: For undergraduate study at postsecondary institution.
Eligibility: Applicant must be no older than 18, enrolled in high school. Applicant must be residing in Texas.
Basis for selection: Competition/talent/interest in oratory/debate, based on language style, voice, diction, delivery, originality, logic, breadth of knowledge, application of knowledge about topic, and skill in selecting examples and analogies. Applicant must demonstrate patriotism.
Application requirements: Proof of eligibility.
Additional information: Awards: First place, $2,000; second place, $1,500; third place, $1,000; fourth place, $500. First place winner eligible to enter national contest.

Amount of award:	$500-$2,000
Number of awards:	4
Application deadline:	August 31
Total amount awarded:	$5,000

Contact:
American Legion, Department of Texas
Oratorical Contest
P.O. Box 140527
Austin, TX 78714-0527
Phone: 512-472-4138
Fax: 512-472-0603
Web: www.txlegion.org

American Legion Texas Auxiliary

American Legion Texas Auxiliary General Education Scholarship

Type of award: Scholarship.
Intended use: For undergraduate study at postsecondary institution.
Eligibility: Applicant must be residing in Texas. Applicant must be descendant of veteran; or dependent of veteran during Grenada conflict, Korean War, Lebanon conflict, Panama conflict, Persian Gulf War, WW I, WW II or Vietnam.
Basis for selection: Applicant must demonstrate financial need and depth of character.
Application requirements: Recommendations, transcript. Resume listing statements of financial support from all their sources not listed on the application, extracurricular activities, and honors and awards received.
Additional information: Obtain application from local Unit. Unit sponsorship required.

Amount of award:	$500
Application deadline:	April 1

Contact:
American Legion Auxiliary, Department of Texas
P.O. Box 140407
Austin, TX 78721-0407
Phone: 512-476-7278
Web: www.alatexas.org

American Legion Texas Auxiliary Medical Scholarship

Type of award: Scholarship.
Intended use: For undergraduate study at postsecondary institution.
Eligibility: Applicant must be residing in Texas. Applicant must be descendant of veteran; or dependent of veteran during Grenada conflict, Korean War, Lebanon conflict, Panama conflict, Persian Gulf War, WW I, WW II or Vietnam.
Basis for selection: Major/career interest in nursing; health sciences; health-related professions or medical assistant. Applicant must demonstrate depth of character and seriousness of purpose.
Application requirements: Recommendations.
Additional information: Obtain application from local Unit. Unit sponsorship required.

Amount of award:	$500
Application deadline:	June 1

Scholarships

Contact:
American Legion Auxiliary, Department of Texas
P.O. Box 140407
Austin, TX 78721-0407
Phone: 512-476-7278
Web: www.alatexas.org

American Legion Utah Auxiliary

American Legion Utah Auxiliary National President's Scholarship

Type of award: Scholarship.
Intended use: For undergraduate study at postsecondary institution.
Eligibility: Applicant must be high school senior. Applicant must be residing in Utah. Applicant must be descendant of veteran; or dependent of veteran during Grenada conflict, Korean War, Lebanon conflict, Panama conflict, Persian Gulf War, WW I, WW II or Vietnam.

Amount of award:	$1,500
Number of awards:	1
Application deadline:	February 15
Total amount awarded:	$1,500

Contact:
American Legion Utah Auxiliary
Department Secretary
P.O. Box 148000
Salt Lake City, UT 84114-8000
Phone: 801-539-1015
Fax: 801-521-9191
Web: www.legion-aux.org

American Legion Vermont

American Legion Eagle Scout of the Year

Type of award: Scholarship.
Intended use: For undergraduate study.
Eligibility: Applicant or parent must be member/participant of Boy Scouts of America, Eagle Scouts. Applicant must be male, at least 15, no older than 18, enrolled in high school. Applicant must be residing in Vermont.
Application requirements: Recommendations.
Additional information: Must be registered, active member of Boy Scout Troop, Varsity Scout Troop, or Explorer Post. Awarded for outstanding service to school and community. Applicant must have received Eagle Scout Award.

Amount of award:	$1,000
Number of awards:	1
Application deadline:	March 1
Total amount awarded:	$1,000

Contact:
American Legion of Vermont
Education and Scholarship Committee
P.O. Box 192
Montpelier, VT 05601
Phone: 802-223-0318
Web: www.legionvthq.com

American Legion Vermont Scholarship

Type of award: Scholarship.
Intended use: For undergraduate study at postsecondary institution.
Eligibility: Applicant must be high school senior. Applicant must be U.S. citizen or permanent resident residing in Vermont.
Application requirements: Recommendations, transcript.
Additional information: Awards: Charles Barber, one $1,000 award; Ray Greenwood, one $1,500 award and ten $500 awards. Applicant must be senior at Vermont secondary school; senior from adjacent state whose parents are legal Vermont residents; or senior from adjacent state attending Vermont school.

Amount of award:	$500-$1,500
Number of awards:	12
Application deadline:	April 1
Total amount awarded:	$7,500

Contact:
American Legion of Vermont
Education and Scholarship Committee
P.O. Box 192
Montpelier, VT 05601
Phone: 802-223-0318
Fax: 802-223-7131
Web: www.legionvthq.com

National High School Oratorical Contest

Type of award: Scholarship.
Intended use: For undergraduate study at postsecondary institution.
Eligibility: Applicant must be enrolled in high school. Applicant must be U.S. citizen or permanent resident residing in Vermont.
Basis for selection: Competition/talent/interest in oratory/debate, based on language style, voice, diction, delivery, originality, logic, breadth of knowledge, application of knowledge about topic, and skill in selecting examples and analogies.
Additional information: No application required. Selection based on prepared oration. Request rules by January 1.

Amount of award:	$2,000
Number of awards:	1
Total amount awarded:	$2,000

Contact:
American Legion of Vermont
Education and Scholarship Committee
P.O. Box 192
Montpelier, VT 05601-0396
Phone: 802-223-0318
Web: www.legionvthq.com

American Legion Virginia

American Legion Virginia Oratorical Contest

Type of award: Scholarship.
Intended use: For undergraduate study at postsecondary institution.
Eligibility: Applicant must be enrolled in high school. Applicant must be residing in Virginia.
Basis for selection: Competition/talent/interest in oratory/debate, based on language style, voice, diction, delivery, originality, logic, breadth of knowledge, application of knowledge about topic, and skill in selecting examples and analogies.
Application requirements: Proof of eligibility.
Additional information: Awards: First place, $1,100; second place, $600; third place, $600.

Amount of award:	$600-$1,100
Number of awards:	3
Application deadline:	December 1
Total amount awarded:	$2,300

Contact:
American Legion Virginia
Department Adjutant
1708 Commonwealth Ave.
Richmond, VA 23230
Phone: 804-353-6606
Fax: 804-358-1940
Web: www.valegion.org

American Legion Virginia Auxiliary

Anna Gear Junior Scholarship

Type of award: Scholarship.
Intended use: For undergraduate study at postsecondary institution.
Eligibility: Applicant or parent must be member/participant of American Legion Auxiliary. Applicant must be high school senior. Applicant must be residing in Virginia. Must be Junior member of American Legion Auxiliary for three years.

Amount of award:	$1,000
Number of awards:	1
Application deadline:	April 1
Total amount awarded:	$1,000

Contact:
American Legion Auxiliary, Department of Virginia
Education Chairman
1708 Commonwealth Avenue
Richmond, VA 23230
Phone: 804-355-6410
Web: www.valegion.org

Dr. Kate Waller Barrett Grant

Type of award: Scholarship.
Intended use: For undergraduate study at accredited vocational, 2-year or 4-year institution.
Eligibility: Applicant or parent must be member/participant of American Legion Auxiliary. Applicant must be high school senior. Applicant must be residing in Virginia. Applicant must be dependent of veteran.
Basis for selection: Applicant must demonstrate financial need.

Amount of award:	$1,000
Number of awards:	1
Application deadline:	March 15
Total amount awarded:	$1,000

Contact:
American Legion Auxiliary, Department of Virginia
Education Chairman
1708 Commonwealth Avenue
Richmond, VA 23230
Phone: 804-355-6410
Web: www.valegion.org

American Legion Washington

American Legion Department Oratorical Contest

Type of award: Scholarship.
Intended use: For undergraduate study at postsecondary institution.
Eligibility: Applicant must be enrolled in high school. Applicant must be residing in Washington.
Basis for selection: Competition/talent/interest in oratory/debate, based on language style, voice, diction, delivery, originality, logic, breadth of knowledge, application of knowledge about topic, and skill in selecting examples and analogies.
Additional information: Student participates in Post, District, Area, and Department contests.

Total amount awarded:	$7,800

Contact:
American Legion Washington
Chairman, Department of Child Welfare
P.O. Box 3917
Lacey, WA 98509-3917
Phone: 360-491-4373
Fax: 360-491-7442
Web: www.walegion.org

American Legion Washington Scholarships

Type of award: Scholarship.
Intended use: For undergraduate study at accredited vocational, 2-year or 4-year institution. Designated institutions: Eligible institutions in Washington State.
Eligibility: Applicant or parent must be member/participant of American Legion. Applicant must be high school senior. Applicant must be residing in Washington. Must be child of living or deceased Washington Legionnaire or Auxiliary member.
Basis for selection: Applicant must demonstrate financial need.
Application requirements: Recommendations.
Additional information: One $2,500 award and one $1,500 award.

Amount of award:	$1,500-$2,500
Number of awards:	2
Application deadline:	April 1
Total amount awarded:	$4,000

Contact:
American Legion Washington
Chairman, Department of Child Welfare
P.O. Box 3917
Lacey, WA 98509-3917
Phone: 360-491-4373
Fax: 360-491-7442
Web: www.walegion.org

American Legion Washington Auxiliary

American Legion Washington Auxiliary Scholarships

Type of award: Scholarship.
Intended use: For undergraduate study at postsecondary institution.
Eligibility: Applicant must be residing in Washington. Applicant must be dependent of disabled veteran or deceased veteran.
Basis for selection: Applicant must demonstrate financial need.
Application requirements: Recommendations, essay, transcript, proof of eligibility.
Additional information: Must be high school senior or high school graduate who has not attended institution of higher learning. Must submit application to Unit chairman.

Amount of award:	$300
Number of awards:	2
Application deadline:	March 15
Total amount awarded:	$600

Contact:
American Legion Washington Auxiliary
P.O. Box 5867
Lacey, WA 98509-5867
Phone: 360-456-5995
Fax: 360-491-7442
Web: www.walegion-aux.org

Florence Lemcke Memorial Scholarship

Type of award: Scholarship.
Intended use: For undergraduate study at 2-year or 4-year institution.
Eligibility: Applicant must be residing in Washington. Applicant must be dependent of veteran or deceased veteran.
Basis for selection: Major/career interest in arts, general; art/art history; architecture; dance; literature; music or theater arts. Applicant must demonstrate financial need and depth of character.
Application requirements: Recommendations, essay, transcript, proof of eligibility.
Additional information: For use in field of fine arts.

Amount of award:	$300
Number of awards:	1
Application deadline:	March 15
Total amount awarded:	$300

Contact:
American Legion Washington Auxiliary
P.O. Box 5867
Lacey, WA 98509-5867
Phone: 360-456-5995
Fax: 360-491-7442
Web: www.walegion-aux.org

Margarite McAlpin Nurse's Scholarship

Type of award: Scholarship.
Intended use: For undergraduate or graduate study at postsecondary institution.
Eligibility: Applicant must be residing in Washington. Applicant must be dependent of disabled veteran or deceased veteran. Grandchildren of deceased or disabled veterans also eligible.
Basis for selection: Major/career interest in nursing. Applicant must demonstrate financial need, high academic achievement and depth of character.
Application requirements: Recommendations, essay, transcript, proof of eligibility.
Additional information: Must submit application to local Unit chairman.

Amount of award:	$300
Number of awards:	1
Application deadline:	March 15
Total amount awarded:	$300

Contact:
American Legion Washington Auxiliary
P.O. Box 5867
Lacey, WA 98509-5867
Phone: 360-456-5995
Fax: 360-491-7442
Web: www.walegion-aux.org

Susan Burdett Scholarship

Type of award: Scholarship.
Intended use: For undergraduate study at postsecondary institution.
Eligibility: Applicant must be female. Applicant must be residing in Washington. Applicant must be dependent of disabled veteran or deceased veteran. Grandchildren of deceased or disabled veterans also eligible.
Basis for selection: Applicant must demonstrate financial need, high academic achievement, depth of character and leadership.
Application requirements: Recommendations, essay, transcript, proof of eligibility.
Additional information: Applicant must be former Evergreen Girls State Citizen (WA). Must submit application to local Unit chairman.

Amount of award:	$300
Number of awards:	1
Application deadline:	March 15
Total amount awarded:	$300

Contact:
American Legion Washington Auxiliary
Education Scholarships
P.O. Box 5867
Lacey, WA 98509-5867
Phone: 360-456-5995
Fax: 360-491-7442
Web: www.walegion-aux.org

American Legion West Virginia

American Legion West Virginia Oratorical Contest

Type of award: Scholarship.
Intended use: For undergraduate study at postsecondary institution.
Eligibility: Applicant must be enrolled in high school. Applicant must be residing in West Virginia.
Basis for selection: Competition/talent/interest in oratory/debate, based on language style, voice, diction, delivery, originality, logic, breadth of knowledge, application of knowledge about topic, and skill in selecting examples and analogies.
Additional information: Nine district awards of $200; three section awards of $300. State winner receives $500 and four-year scholarship to West Virginia University or other state college under control of Board of Regents. Contest is held in January and February. Information may be obtained from local high school or American Legion Post.
   Amount of award: $200-$500
Contact:
American Legion West Virginia
State Adjutant
2016 Kanawha Blvd. E, Box 3191
Charleston, WV 25332-3191
Phone: 304-343-7591
Fax: 304-343-7592
Web: www.wvlegion.org

William F. Johnson Memorial Scholarship

Type of award: Scholarship.
Intended use: For full-time freshman study at postsecondary institution.
Eligibility: Applicant must be residing in West Virginia.
Application requirements: Essay, transcript. Must submit copy of transcript from first college semester to receive award.
Additional information: First place winner: $1,000; second place: $500, to be presented to recipients before start of second semester.
   Amount of award: $500-$1,000
   Number of awards: 1
   Application deadline: May 15
   Total amount awarded: $1,000
Contact:
American Legion, Department of West Virginia
State Adjutant
2016 Kanawha Blvd. E, Box 3191
Charleston, WV 25332-3191
Phone: 304-343-7591
Fax: 304-343-7592
Web: www.wvlegion.org

American Legion West Virginia Auxiliary

American Legion West Virginia Auxiliary Scholarship

Type of award: Scholarship.
Intended use: For undergraduate study at postsecondary institution. Designated institutions: West Virginia institutions.
Eligibility: Applicant must be no older than 22. Applicant must be residing in West Virginia. Applicant must be dependent of veteran.
Application requirements: Proof of eligibility.
   Number of awards: 4
   Application deadline: March 1
Contact:
American Legion West Virginia Auxiliary
Secretary/Treasurer Mary Rose Yoho
RR 1 Box 144A
Proctor, WV 26055-9616
Phone: 304-455-3449

American Legion Wisconsin

American Legion Wisconsin Eagle Scout of the Year Scholarship

Type of award: Scholarship.
Intended use: For undergraduate study at postsecondary institution.
Eligibility: Applicant or parent must be member/participant of American Legion/Boys Scouts of America. Applicant must be male, high school senior. Applicant must be residing in Wisconsin.
Basis for selection: Applicant must demonstrate high academic achievement.
Additional information: Applicant must be Boy Scout, Varsity Scout or Explorer. Applicant's group must be sponsored by Legion, Auxiliary, or Sons of American Legion, applicant's father or grandfather must be Legion or Auxiliary member.
   Amount of award: $1,000
   Number of awards: 1
   Application deadline: March 1
   Total amount awarded: $1,000
Contact:
American Legion Wisconsin
Program Secretary
P.O. Box 388
Portage, WI 53901
Phone: 608-745-1090
Fax: 608-745-0179
Web: www.wilegion.org

Oratorical Contest Scholarships

Type of award: Scholarship.
Intended use: For undergraduate study at postsecondary institution.
Eligibility: Applicant must be enrolled in high school. Applicant must be residing in Wisconsin.

Basis for selection: Competition/talent/interest in oratory/ debate, based on language style, voice, diction, delivery, originality, logic, breadth of knowledge, application of knowledge about topic, and skill in selecting examples and analogies.

Additional information: Awards: State winner, $2,000; three regional awards of $1,000 each; regional participants win $600 each.

Amount of award:	$600-$2,000

Contact:
American Legion, Department of Wisconsin
Program Secretary
P.O. Box 388
Portage, WI 53901
Phone: 608-745-1090
Fax: 608-745-0179
Web: www.wilegion.org

Schneider-Emanuel American Legion Scholarships

Type of award: Scholarship.

Intended use: For undergraduate study at 4-year institution in United States.

Eligibility: Applicant or parent must be member/participant of American Legion. Applicant must be residing in Wisconsin. Applicant must be veteran; or dependent of veteran. Must be current member or child/grandchild of current member of American Legion, Auxiliary/Junior Auxiliary, or Sons of the American Legion, and have membership card at time of application.

Basis for selection: Applicant must demonstrate financial need, high academic achievement and depth of character.

Application requirements: Recommendations, transcript. ACT scores.

Amount of award:	$1,000
Number of awards:	3
Application deadline:	March 1
Total amount awarded:	$3,000

Contact:
American Legion, Department of Wisconsin
Program Secretary
P.O. Box 388
Portage, WI 53901
Phone: 608-745-1090
Fax: 608-745-0179
Web: www.wilegion.org

American Legion Wisconsin Auxiliary

American Legion Wisconsin Auxiliary Department President's Scholarship

Type of award: Scholarship.

Intended use: For undergraduate study at accredited postsecondary institution.

Eligibility: Applicant or parent must be member/participant of American Legion Auxiliary. Applicant must be residing in Wisconsin. Applicant must be descendant of veteran; or dependent of veteran; or spouse of veteran or deceased veteran. Mother of applicant or applicant must be Auxiliary member.

Grandchildren and great-grandchildren of veterans eligible if Auxiliary members.

Basis for selection: Applicant must demonstrate financial need.

Application requirements: Recommendations, essay, transcript, proof of eligibility.

Additional information: Minimum 3.5 GPA.

Amount of award:	$1,000
Number of awards:	3
Application deadline:	March 15
Total amount awarded:	$3,000

Contact:
American Legion Wisconsin Auxiliary
Department Secretary
P.O. Box 140
Portage, WI 53901-0140
Phone: 608-745-0124
Fax: 608-745-1947
Web: www.amlegionauxwi.org

American Legion Wisconsin Auxiliary H.S. and Angeline Lewis Scholarships

Type of award: Scholarship.

Intended use: For undergraduate or graduate study at accredited postsecondary institution.

Eligibility: Applicant or parent must be member/participant of American Legion Auxiliary. Applicant must be residing in Wisconsin. Applicant must be descendant of veteran; or dependent of veteran; or spouse of veteran or deceased veteran. Grandchildren and great-grandchildren of veterans eligible if members of Auxiliary.

Basis for selection: Applicant must demonstrate financial need.

Application requirements: Recommendations, essay, transcript, proof of eligibility.

Additional information: Minimum 3.5 GPA. One award for graduate study; five awards for undergraduate study.

Amount of award:	$1,000
Number of awards:	6
Application deadline:	March 15
Total amount awarded:	$6,000

Contact:
American Legion Wisconsin Auxiliary
Department Secretary
P.O. Box 140
Portage, WI 53901-0140
Phone: 608-745-0124
Fax: 608-745-1947
Web: www.amlegionauxwi.org

American Legion Wisconsin Auxiliary Merit and Memorial Scholarship

Type of award: Scholarship.

Intended use: For undergraduate study.

Eligibility: Applicant or parent must be member/participant of American Legion Auxiliary. Applicant must be residing in Wisconsin. Applicant must be descendant of veteran; or dependent of veteran; or spouse of veteran or deceased veteran. Grandchildren and great-grandchildren of veterans eligible if members of Auxiliary.

Basis for selection: Applicant must demonstrate financial need.

Application requirements: Recommendations, essay, transcript, proof of eligibility.
Additional information: Minimum 3.5 GPA.

Amount of award:	$1,000
Number of awards:	7
Application deadline:	March 15
Total amount awarded:	$7,000

Contact:
American Legion Wisconsin Auxiliary
Department Secretary
P.O. Box 140
Portage, WI 53901-0140
Phone: 608-745-0124
Fax: 608-745-1947
Web: www.amlegionauxwi.org

American Legion Wisconsin Auxiliary Past Presidents Parley Scholarship

Type of award: Scholarship.
Intended use: For undergraduate study at accredited vocational, 2-year or 4-year institution.
Eligibility: Applicant or parent must be member/participant of American Legion Auxiliary. Applicant must be residing in Wisconsin. Applicant must be descendant of veteran; or dependent of veteran or deceased veteran; or spouse of veteran or deceased veteran. Grandchild or great-grandchild of veteran eligible if Auxiliary member.
Basis for selection: Major/career interest in nursing. Applicant must demonstrate financial need.
Application requirements: Recommendations, essay, transcript, proof of eligibility.
Additional information: Minimum 3.5 GPA. Must be in or accepted to accredited school of nursing, accredited hospital, or university registered nursing program. Hospital, university, or technical school program acceptable.

Amount of award:	$1,200
Number of awards:	5
Application deadline:	March 15
Total amount awarded:	$6,000

Contact:
American Legion Wisconsin Auxiliary
Department Secretary
P.O. Box 140
Portage, WI 53901-0140
Phone: 608-745-0124
Fax: 608-745-1947
Web: www.amlegionauxwi.org

Della Van Deuren Memorial Scholarship

Type of award: Scholarship.
Intended use: For undergraduate study.
Eligibility: Applicant or parent must be member/participant of American Legion Auxiliary. Applicant must be residing in Wisconsin. Applicant must be descendant of veteran; or dependent of veteran; or spouse of veteran or deceased veteran. Applicant's mother or applicant must be member of American Legion Auxiliary. Grandchildren and great-grandchildren of veterans are eligible if they are members of American Legion Auxiliary.
Basis for selection: Applicant must demonstrate financial need.

Application requirements: Recommendations, essay, transcript, proof of eligibility.
Additional information: Minimum 3.5 GPA. Applicant's school need not be in Wisconsin.

Amount of award:	$1,000
Number of awards:	2
Application deadline:	March 15
Total amount awarded:	$2,000

Contact:
American Legion Wisconsin Auxiliary
Department Secretary
P.O. Box 140
Portage, WI 53901-0140
Phone: 608-745-0124
Fax: 608-745-1947
Web: www.amlegionauxwi.org

American Legion Wyoming

American Legion Wyoming E.A. Blackmore Memorial Scholarship

Type of award: Scholarship.
Intended use: For undergraduate study at postsecondary institution.
Eligibility: Applicant or parent must be member/participant of American Legion. Applicant must be residing in Wyoming. Must be child or grandchild of American Legion member in good standing, or child or grandchild of deceased American Legion member who was in good standing.
Basis for selection: Applicant must demonstrate financial need and high academic achievement.
Application requirements: Recommendations, transcript, proof of eligibility. Resume. Photo of self.
Additional information: Must rank in upper 20 percent of high school class.

Amount of award:	$1,000
Number of awards:	1
Application deadline:	May 15
Total amount awarded:	$1,000

Contact:
American Legion Wyoming
Department Adjutant
1320 Hugur Ave.
Cheyenne, WY 82001
Phone: 307-634-3035
Fax: 307-635-7093
Web: www.wylegion.org

American Legion Wyoming Oratorical Contest

Type of award: Scholarship.
Intended use: For undergraduate study at postsecondary institution.
Eligibility: Applicant must be enrolled in high school. Applicant must be U.S. citizen or permanent resident residing in Wyoming.
Basis for selection: Competition/talent/interest in oratory/debate, based on language style, voice, diction, delivery, originality, logic, breadth of knowledge, application of knowledge about topic, and skill in selecting examples and analogies.
Application requirements: Proof of eligibility.

Additional information: Award: First place, $500.

Amount of award:	$500
Number of awards:	1
Total amount awarded:	$500

Contact:
American Legion Wyoming
Department Adjutant
1320 Hugur Ave.
Cheyenne, WY 82001
Phone: 307-634-3035
Web: www.wylegion.org

American Legion Wyoming Auxiliary

American Legion Wyoming Auxiliary Past Presidents' Parley Scholarship

Type of award: Scholarship, renewable.
Intended use: For undergraduate study at 2-year or 4-year institution. Designated institutions: University of Wyoming or one of Wyoming community colleges.
Eligibility: Preference given to nursing students who are children of veterans.
Basis for selection: Major/career interest in health-related professions; medicine; nursing; occupational therapy; pharmacy/pharmaceutics/pharmacology; physical therapy; respiratory therapy or speech pathology/audiology. Applicant must demonstrate financial need and high academic achievement.
Application requirements: Recommendations.
Additional information: Must have completed one year or two semesters of study. Minimum 3.0 GPA. Preference given to Wyoming residents.

Amount of award:	$300
Number of awards:	1
Application deadline:	June 1
Total amount awarded:	$600

Contact:
American Legion Wyoming Auxiliary
Department Secretary
P.O. Box 2198
Gillette, WY 82717-2198
Phone: 307-686-7137

American Medical Technologists

Medical Technologists Student Scholarship

Type of award: Scholarship.
Intended use: For full-time undergraduate or graduate study at accredited postsecondary institution in United States.
Eligibility: Applicant must be U.S. citizen or permanent resident.
Basis for selection: Major/career interest in medical assistant; dental assistant or health services administration. Applicant must demonstrate financial need.

Application requirements: Recommendations, essay, transcript. List of school activities.
Additional information: Scholarship is available only to high school graduates studying to become one of the following: medical assistant, dental assistant, medical administrative specialist, medical technologist, medical laboratory technician, medical laboratory assistant, or phlebotomy technician.

Amount of award:	$500
Number of awards:	5
Number of applicants:	76
Application deadline:	April 1
Total amount awarded:	$2,500

Contact:
American Medical Technologists
10700 West Higgins Road, Suite 150
Rosemont, IL 60018
Phone: 847-823-5169
Fax: 847-823-0458
Web: www.amt1.com

American Meteorological Society

American Meteorological Society Undergraduate Scholarships

Type of award: Scholarship.
Intended use: For full-time senior study at accredited 4-year institution in United States.
Eligibility: Applicant must be U.S. citizen or permanent resident.
Basis for selection: Major/career interest in atmospheric sciences/meteorology; oceanography/marine studies or hydrology. Applicant must demonstrate high academic achievement and seriousness of purpose.
Application requirements: Recommendations, essay, transcript, proof of eligibility.
Additional information: Minimum 3.25 GPA. Marine biology majors not eligible. Visit Website for more information and to download application. Number and amount of scholarships vary. Applicants must demonstrate financial need to be eligible for the Schroeder Scholarship. The Murphy Scholarship is awarded to students who, through curricular or extracurricular activities, have shown interest in weather forecasting or in the value and utilization of forecasts. The Glahn Scholarship is for a student who has shown strong interest in statistical meteorology. The Crow Scholarship is for a student who has shown strong interest in applied meteorology. Number and amount of awards varies.

Application deadline:	February 6
Notification begins:	May 1

Contact:
American Meteorological Society
Fellowship/Scholarship Program
45 Beacon Street
Boston, MA 02108-3693
Phone: 617-227-2425
Fax: 617-742-8718
Web: www.ametsoc.org

American Meteorological Society/ Industry Minority Scholarship

Type of award: Scholarship.
Intended use: For full-time freshman study at accredited 4-year institution in United States.
Eligibility: Applicant must be Alaskan native, Asian American, African American, Mexican American, Hispanic American, Puerto Rican or American Indian. Applicant must be high school senior. Applicant must be U.S. citizen or permanent resident.
Basis for selection: Major/career interest in atmospheric sciences/meteorology; oceanography/marine studies or hydrology.
Application requirements: Recommendations, essay, transcript. SAT or ACT scores.
Additional information: Minimum 3.0 GPA. Award is $3,000 per year for freshman and sophomore years. Award is for minority students who have traditionally been underrepresented in the sciences, especially Hispanic, Native American, and African-American students. Marine biology majors ineligible. Number of awards varies. Visit Website to download application.

Amount of award:	$6,000
Number of applicants:	40
Application deadline:	February 6
Notification begins:	May 1
Total amount awarded:	$3,000

Contact:
American Meteorological Society
Fellowship/Scholarship Program
45 Beacon Street
Boston, MA 02108-3693
Phone: 617-227-2425
Fax: 617-742-8718
Web: www.ametsoc.org

Father James B. Macelwane Annual Award

Type of award: Scholarship.
Intended use: For undergraduate study.
Eligibility: Applicant must be U.S. citizen or permanent resident.
Basis for selection: Major/career interest in atmospheric sciences/meteorology; oceanography/marine studies or hydrology.
Application requirements: Essay, transcript, proof of eligibility. Original paper plus three photocopies. Letter of application including contact information and stating paper's title and name of university where paper was written. Letter from university faculty stating author was undergraduate when paper was written and indicating elements of paper that are original contributions by the student. Abstract of maximum 250 words describing paper.
Additional information: Award intended to stimulate interest in meteorology among college students through submission of original papers concerned with some phase of atmospheric sciences. Student must have been undergraduate when paper was written. Submissions from women, minorities and disabled students who are traditionally underrepresented in atmospheric and related oceanic and hydrologic sciences encouraged. No more than two students from any one institution may enter papers in any one contest. Visit Website for application and additional information.

Amount of award:	$1,000
Number of awards:	1
Application deadline:	June 11
Total amount awarded:	$1,000

Contact:
American Meteorological Society
Macelwane Award
45 Beacon Street
Boston, MA 02108-3693
Phone: 617-227-2425
Fax: 617-742-8718
Web: www.ametsoc.org

Freshman Undergraduate Scholarship Program

Type of award: Scholarship, renewable.
Intended use: For full-time freshman study at accredited 4-year institution in United States.
Eligibility: Applicant must be high school senior. Applicant must be U.S. citizen or permanent resident.
Basis for selection: Major/career interest in atmospheric sciences/meteorology; oceanography/marine studies or hydrology. Applicant must demonstrate high academic achievement.
Application requirements: Recommendations, essay, transcript. SAT/ACT scores.
Additional information: Scholarships are renewable for the sophomore year, providing recipient plans to continue studies in the AMS-related sciences. Minimum 3.0 GPA. Award is $2,500 each for freshman and sophomore years.

Amount of award:	$2,500
Number of awards:	14
Number of applicants:	159
Application deadline:	February 6
Notification begins:	May 1

Contact:
American Meteorological Society
Fellowship/Scholarship Program
45 Beacon Street
Boston, MA 02108-3693
Phone: 617-227-2425
Fax: 617-742-8718
Web: www.ametsoc.org

American Morgan Horse Institute

AMHI Educational Scholarships

Type of award: Scholarship.
Intended use: For undergraduate or non-degree study at vocational, 2-year or 4-year institution.
Eligibility: Applicant must be high school senior.
Basis for selection: Major/career interest in equestrian/equine studies. Applicant must demonstrate financial need, depth of character, leadership, seriousness of purpose and service orientation.
Application requirements: Recommendations, essay, transcript. List of horse-related activities, photo.
Additional information: Applicant must demonstrate achievement with registered Morgan horses. Award amount varies based on funding. Send SASE or visit Website for application.

Number of awards:	5
Number of applicants:	45
Application deadline:	March 1
Notification begins:	June 15
Total amount awarded:	$15,000

Contact:
AMHI Scholarships
P.O. Box 837
Shelburne, VT 05482-0837
Web: www.morganhorseinstitute.com

AMHI van Schaik Dressage Scholarship

Type of award: Scholarship.
Intended use: For non-degree study.
Basis for selection: Major/career interest in dressage or equestrian/equine studies. Applicant must demonstrate seriousness of purpose.
Application requirements: Recommendations, essay.
Additional information: Must be dressage rider using a registered Morgan horse and interested in advancing from lower levels of dressage to Fourth Level and above. Preference given to applicants who have competed their Morgan at First Level Test 4 or above and scored 60 percent or higher at recognized competition. Visit Website for application.

Amount of award:	$1,000
Number of awards:	1
Number of applicants:	2
Application deadline:	November 30
Notification begins:	March 31
Total amount awarded:	$1,000

Contact:
AMHI Scholarship
Attn: AMHI van Schaik Dressage Scholarship
P.O. Box 837
Shelburne, VT 05482-0837
Web: www.morganhorseinstitute.com

American Museum of Natural History

Young Naturalist Awards

Type of award: Scholarship, renewable.
Intended use: For freshman study.
Basis for selection: Competition/talent/interest in science project.
Application requirements: Essay. Original artwork/photographs.
Additional information: For students grades 7-12 in the U.S and Canada to plan and conduct scientific investigations and report them in an illustrated essay. Children of Alcoa Corporation or American Museum of Natural History employees or consultants are ineligible. Two winners per grade level receive the following: 7th grade, $500; 8th grade, $750; 9th grade, $1,000; 10th grade, $1,500; 11th grade, $2,000; 12th grade, $2,500. Also trip to New York City for award ceremony and tour of the museum. Up to 36 additional finalists receive $50 prize.

Amount of award:	$50-$2,500
Number of awards:	48
Application deadline:	March 1
Notification begins:	March 22

Contact:
Young Naturalist Awards Administrator
American Museum of Natural History
Central Park West at 79th Street
New York, NY 10024-5192
Phone: 212-496-3498
Web: www.amnh.org/nationalcenter/youngnaturalistawards

American Nuclear Society

Angelo S. Bisesti Scholarship

Type of award: Scholarship.
Intended use: For full-time junior or senior study at 4-year institution in United States.
Eligibility: Applicant must be U.S. citizen or permanent resident.
Basis for selection: Major/career interest in nuclear science or engineering, nuclear.
Additional information: Applicant must be at least entering junior enrolled in program leading to degree in nuclear science, nuclear engineering, or nuclear-related field and pursuing a career in the field of commercial nuclear power. Visit Website for application.

Amount of award:	$2,000
Number of awards:	1
Application deadline:	February 1
Total amount awarded:	$2,000

Contact:
American Nuclear Society
555 North Kensington Avenue
La Grange Park, IL 60526
Phone: 708-352-6611
Fax: 708-352-0499
Web: www.ans.org

ANS Undergraduate Scholarships

Type of award: Scholarship.
Intended use: For sophomore, junior or senior study at accredited 4-year institution in United States.
Eligibility: Applicant must be U.S. citizen or permanent resident.
Basis for selection: Major/career interest in nuclear science or engineering, nuclear.
Additional information: Maximum of four scholarships for entering sophomores in study leading to degree in nuclear science, nuclear engineering, or nuclear-related field; maximum of 21 scholarships for students who will be entering junior or senior year.

Amount of award:	$2,000
Application deadline:	February 1

Contact:
American Nuclear Society
555 North Kensington Avenue
La Grange Park, IL 60526
Phone: 708-352-6611
Fax: 708-352-0499
Web: www.ans.org

Charles (Tommy) Thomas Memorial Scholarship

Type of award: Scholarship.

Intended use: For full-time junior or senior study at accredited 4-year institution in United States.
Eligibility: Applicant must be U.S. citizen or permanent resident.
Basis for selection: Major/career interest in nuclear science; environmental science; ecology or natural resources/conservation.
Additional information: Applicant must be pursuing degree in discipline related to environmental aspects of nuclear science or nuclear engineering. See Website for application and requirements.

Amount of award:	$2,000
Number of awards:	1
Application deadline:	February 1

Contact:
American Nuclear Society
555 North Kensington Avenue
La Grange Park, IL 60526
Phone: 708-352-6611
Fax: 708-352-0499
Web: www.ans.org

Decommissioning, Decontamination and Reutilization Scholarship

Type of award: Scholarship.
Intended use: For junior or senior study at accredited 4-year institution in United States.
Eligibility: Applicant must be U.S. citizen or permanent resident.
Basis for selection: Major/career interest in engineering, nuclear; environmental science or engineering, environmental.
Additional information: Applicant must be enrolled in curriculum of engineering or science associated with decommissioning/decontamination of nuclear facilities, management/characterization of nuclear waste, or restoration of environment. If awarded scholarship, student must join ANS and designate DDR Division as one professional division. Awardee must also provide support to DDR Division at next ANS meeting after receiving award (funding provided for travel to meeting but does not include food and lodging).

Amount of award:	$2,000
Number of awards:	1
Application deadline:	February 1

Contact:
American Nuclear Society
555 North Kensington Avenue
La Grange Park, IL 60526
Phone: 708-352-6611
Fax: 708-352-0499
Web: www.ans.org

Delayed Education Scholarship for Women

Type of award: Scholarship.
Intended use: For undergraduate study at accredited 4-year institution in United States.
Eligibility: Applicant must be female, returning adult student. Applicant must be U.S. citizen or permanent resident.
Basis for selection: Major/career interest in nuclear science or engineering, nuclear. Applicant must demonstrate financial need and high academic achievement.
Additional information: Must be a mature woman whose undergraduate studies in nuclear science, nuclear engineering, or a nuclear-related field have been delayed for at least a year. Visit Website for application and requirements.

Amount of award:	$4,000
Number of awards:	1
Application deadline:	February 1

Contact:
American Nuclear Society
555 North Kensington Avenue
La Grange Park, IL 60526
Phone: 708-352-6611
Fax: 708-352-0499
Web: www.ans.org

John and Muriel Landis Scholarship

Type of award: Scholarship.
Intended use: For undergraduate or graduate study at 4-year or graduate institution in United States.
Eligibility: Applicant must be U.S. citizen or permanent resident.
Basis for selection: Major/career interest in nuclear science or engineering, nuclear. Applicant must demonstrate financial need.
Additional information: Awarded to students with greater than average financial need. Consideration given to conditions or experiences that render student disadvantaged (poor high school/undergraduate preparation, etc.). Applicants should be planning career in nuclear science or nuclear engineering. Qualified high school seniors eligible to apply. Visit Website for application and requirements.

Amount of award:	$4,000
Number of awards:	8
Application deadline:	February 1

Contact:
American Nuclear Society
555 North Kensington Avenue
La Grange Park, IL 60526
Phone: 708-352-6611
Fax: 708-352-0499
Web: www.ans.org

John R. Lamarsh Scholarship

Type of award: Scholarship.
Intended use: For full-time junior or senior study at accredited 4-year institution in United States.
Eligibility: Applicant must be U.S. citizen or permanent resident.
Basis for selection: Major/career interest in nuclear science or engineering, nuclear.
Additional information: Applicant must be at least an entering junior enrolled in program leading to degree in nuclear science or nuclear engineering. See Website for application and requirements.

Amount of award:	$2,000
Number of awards:	1
Application deadline:	February 1

Contact:
American Nuclear Society
555 North Kensington Avenue
La Grange Park, IL 60526
Phone: 708-352-6611
Fax: 708-352-0499
Web: www.ans.org

Joseph R. Dietrich Scholarship

Type of award: Scholarship.
Intended use: For full-time junior or senior study at 4-year institution in United States.

Eligibility: Applicant must be U.S. citizen or permanent resident.
Basis for selection: Major/career interest in nuclear science; engineering, nuclear; chemistry or physics.
Additional information: Applicant must be at least an entering junior enrolled in program leading to degree in nuclear science, nuclear engineering, or nuclear-related field. See Website for application and requirements.

Amount of award:	$2,000
Number of awards:	1
Application deadline:	February 1

Contact:
American Nuclear Society
555 North Kensington Avenue
La Grange Park, IL 60526
Phone: 708-352-6611
Fax: 708-352-0499
Web: www.ans.org

Operations and Power Division Scholarship

Type of award: Scholarship.
Intended use: For full-time junior or senior study at 4-year institution.
Eligibility: Applicant must be U.S. citizen or permanent resident.
Basis for selection: Major/career interest in nuclear science or engineering, nuclear.
Additional information: Applicant must be at least an entering junior enrolled in a program leading to a degree in nuclear science or nuclear engineering. Application available online.

Amount of award:	$2,500
Number of awards:	1
Application deadline:	February 1

Contact:
American Nuclear Society
555 North Kensington Avenue
La Grange Park, IL 60526
Phone: 708-352-6611
Fax: 708-352-0499
Web: www.ans.org

Pittsburgh Local Section Scholarship

Type of award: Scholarship.
Intended use: For full-time junior, senior or graduate study at accredited 4-year or graduate institution in United States.
Basis for selection: Major/career interest in nuclear science or engineering, nuclear.
Application requirements: Transcript.
Additional information: Applicant must either attend school in Western Pennsylvania or have some affiliation with the region. Awards are $2,000 for undergraduates and $3,500 for graduate students. See Website for application and requirements.

Amount of award:	$2,000-$3,500
Number of awards:	2
Application deadline:	February 1

Contact:
American Nuclear Society
555 North Kensington Avenue
La Grange Park, IL 60526
Phone: 708-352-6611
Fax: 708-352-0499
Web: www.ans.org

Raymond DiSalvo Scholarship

Type of award: Scholarship.
Intended use: For full-time junior or senior study at 4-year institution in United States.
Eligibility: Applicant must be U.S. citizen or permanent resident.
Basis for selection: Major/career interest in nuclear science or engineering, nuclear.
Additional information: Applicant must be at least an entering junior enrolled in program leading to degree in nuclear science or nuclear engineering. Application available online.

Amount of award:	$2,000
Number of awards:	1
Application deadline:	February 1

Contact:
American Nuclear Society
555 North Kensington Avenue
La Grange Park, IL 60526
Phone: 708-352-6611
Fax: 708-352-0499
Web: www.ans.org

Robert G. Lacy Scholarship

Type of award: Scholarship.
Intended use: For full-time junior or senior study at 4-year institution in United States.
Eligibility: Applicant must be U.S. citizen or permanent resident.
Basis for selection: Major/career interest in nuclear science or engineering, nuclear.
Application requirements: Recommendations, transcript, proof of eligibility.
Additional information: Applicant must be at least an entering junior enrolled in a program leading to a degree in nuclear science or nuclear engineering. Application available online.

Amount of award:	$2,000
Number of awards:	1
Application deadline:	February 1
Notification begins:	May 9

Contact:
American Nuclear Society
555 North Kensington Avenue
La Grange Park, IL 60526
Phone: 708-352-6611
Fax: 708-352-0499
Web: www.ans.org

Robert T. (Bob) Liner Scholarship

Type of award: Scholarship.
Intended use: For full-time junior or senior study at 4-year institution in United States.
Eligibility: Applicant must be U.S. citizen or permanent resident.
Basis for selection: Major/career interest in nuclear science or engineering, nuclear. Applicant must demonstrate depth of character, leadership, seriousness of purpose and service orientation.
Additional information: Applicant must be at least an entering junior enrolled in a program leading to a degree in nuclear science or nuclear engineering. Application available online.

Amount of award:	$2,000
Number of awards:	1
Application deadline:	February 1

Contact:
American Nuclear Society
555 North Kensington Avenue
La Grange Park, IL 60526
Phone: 708-352-6611
Fax: 708-352-0499
Web: www.ans.org

Vogt Radiochemistry Scholarship

Type of award: Scholarship.
Intended use: For full-time undergraduate or graduate study at accredited 4-year or graduate institution.
Eligibility: Applicant must be U.S. citizen or permanent resident.
Basis for selection: Major/career interest in chemistry or nuclear science.
Additional information: Applicants must be enrolled in or proposing to undertake research in radioanalytical chemistry, analytical chemistry, or analytical applications of nuclear science. Awards are $2,000 for undergraduates and $3,000 for graduate students. See Website for application and requirements.

Amount of award:	$2,000-$3,000
Number of awards:	1
Application deadline:	February 1
Notification begins:	May 9

Contact:
American Nuclear Society
555 North Kensington Avenue
La Grange Park, IL 60526
Phone: 708-352-6611
Fax: 708-352-0499
Web: www.ans.org

American Physical Society

Scholarship for Minority Undergraduate Physics Majors

Type of award: Scholarship, renewable.
Intended use: For full-time freshman, sophomore or junior study at 2-year or 4-year institution in United States. Designated institutions: Institutions with physics departments or provisions for procurement of physics degrees.
Eligibility: Applicant must be African American, Mexican American, Hispanic American, Puerto Rican or American Indian. Applicant must be U.S. citizen or permanent resident.
Basis for selection: Major/career interest in physics. Applicant must demonstrate high academic achievement.
Application requirements: Recommendations, essay, transcript, proof of eligibility. ACT/SAT scores.
Additional information: Must be high school senior or college freshman or sophomore to apply. Applications available early November. Visit Website for more information.

Amount of award:	$2,000-$3,000
Number of awards:	25
Number of applicants:	100
Application deadline:	February 5
Notification begins:	May 15
Total amount awarded:	$70,000

Contact:
American Physical Society
Minority Undergraduate Physics Scholarship
One Physics Ellipse
College Park, MD 20740
Phone: 301-209-3232
Fax: 301-209-0865
Web: www.aps.org/programs/minorities/honors/scholarship/

American Public Power Association

DEED Student Research Grants

Type of award: Research grant.
Intended use: For undergraduate or graduate study at accredited 2-year or 4-year institution in United States or Canada.
Eligibility: Applicant must be U.S. citizen.
Basis for selection: Major/career interest in electronics; engineering, electrical/electronic or engineering, mechanical.
Application requirements: Transcript.
Additional information: Applicants must complete energy-related research project and be sponsored by DEED member utility.

Amount of award:	$4,000
Number of awards:	10
Number of applicants:	26
Application deadline:	February 15, October 15
Notification begins:	April 1, November 1
Total amount awarded:	$40,000

Contact:
American Public Power Association
Attn: DEED Administrator
1875 Connecticut Avenue, NW, Suite 1200
Washington, DC 20009-5715
Phone: 202-467-2960
Fax: 202-467-2910
Web: www.appanet.org

American Quarter Horse Foundation

American Quarter Horse Foundation Scholarships

Type of award: Scholarship, renewable.
Intended use: For full-time undergraduate or first professional study in United States or Canada.
Eligibility: Applicant must be at least 17.
Basis for selection: Applicant must demonstrate financial need and high academic achievement.
Application requirements: Recommendations, transcript, proof of eligibility. Financial tax forms.
Additional information: Number of scholarships vary. Applicants must be current members of the American Quarter Horse Youth Association or American Quarter Horse Association, and must exhibit strong involvement. Visit Website for requirements, deadline, and scholarship criteria.

Scholarships

Amount of award:	$500-$25,000
Number of awards:	130
Number of applicants:	150
Application deadline:	December 1
Notification begins:	May 1
Total amount awarded:	$320,000

Contact:
American Quarter Horse Foundation
Scholarship Office
2601 I-40 East
Amarillo, TX 79104
Phone: 806-378-5040
Fax: 806-376-1005
Web: www.aqha.com/foundation

American Radio Relay League (ARRL) Foundation, Inc.

Albuquerque ARC/Toby Cross Scholarship

Type of award: Scholarship.
Intended use: For undergraduate study at accredited 4-year institution in United States.
Eligibility: Applicant must be residing in New Mexico.
Basis for selection: Competition/talent/interest in amateur radio.
Application requirements: Essay, transcript. One-page essay on role amateur radio has played in applicant's life.
Additional information: Must hold valid FCC amateur radio license. High school seniors are eligible to apply. Application may be obtained on Website, but no electronic submissions accepted.

Amount of award:	$500
Number of awards:	1
Application deadline:	February 1

Contact:
The ARRL Foundation, Inc. Scholarship Program
225 Main Street
Newington, CT 06111
Phone: 860-594-0397
Fax: 860-594-0259
Web: www.arrlf.org

ARRL Earl I. Anderson Scholarship

Type of award: Scholarship.
Intended use: For undergraduate or graduate study at accredited postsecondary institution.
Eligibility: Applicant must be residing in Michigan, Indiana, Illinois or Florida.
Basis for selection: Competition/talent/interest in amateur radio. Major/career interest in engineering, electrical/electronic.
Application requirements: Transcript.
Additional information: Must be amateur radio operator holding any class license. Must be ARRL member. Major may be in other related technical field. Must be attending classes in Illinois, Indiana, Michigan, or Florida. High school seniors eligible to apply. Application may be obtained on Website, but no electronic submissions accepted.

Amount of award:	$1,250
Number of awards:	3
Application deadline:	February 1

Contact:
The ARRL Foundation, Inc. Scholarship Program
225 Main Street
Newington, CT 06111
Phone: 860-594-0397
Fax: 860-594-0259
Web: www.arrlf.org

ARRL Scholarship Honoring Barry Goldwater, K7UGA

Type of award: Scholarship.
Intended use: For undergraduate or graduate study at accredited 4-year or graduate institution.
Basis for selection: Competition/talent/interest in amateur radio.
Application requirements: Transcript.
Additional information: Must be amateur radio operator with novice class license or higher. High school seniors are eligible to apply. Application may be obtained on Website, but no electronic submissions accepted.

Amount of award:	$5,000
Number of awards:	1
Application deadline:	February 1
Total amount awarded:	$5,000

Contact:
The ARRL Foundation, Inc. Scholarship Program
225 Main Street
Newington, CT 06111
Phone: 860-594-0397
Fax: 860-594-0259
Web: www.arrlf.org

Challenge Met Scholarship

Type of award: Scholarship.
Intended use: For undergraduate study at accredited vocational, 2-year or 4-year institution.
Eligibility: Applicant must be learning disabled.
Basis for selection: Competition/talent/interest in amateur radio.
Application requirements: Transcript.
Additional information: Must be amateur radio operator holding any class license. Preference given to those with documented learning disabilities who put forth effort regardless of resulting grades. High school seniors are eligible to apply. Application may be obtained on Website, but no electronic submissions accepted. Number of awards varies.

Amount of award:	$500
Application deadline:	February 1

Contact:
The ARRL Foundation, Inc. Scholarship Program
225 Main Street
Newington, CT 06111
Phone: 860-594-0347
Fax: 860-594-0259
Web: www.arrlf.org

Charles Clarke Cordle Memorial Scholarship

Type of award: Scholarship.

Intended use: For undergraduate or graduate study at postsecondary institution in United States. Designated institutions: Institutions in Alabama or Georgia.
Eligibility: Applicant must be residing in Alabama or Georgia.
Basis for selection: Competition/talent/interest in amateur radio. Major/career interest in electronics or communications.
Application requirements: Transcript.
Additional information: Minimum 2.5 GPA. Must hold active amateur radio license. Preference to students of majors listed or other related fields. High school seniors are eligible to apply. Application may be obtained from Website, but no electronic submissions accepted.

Amount of award:	$1,000
Number of awards:	1
Application deadline:	February 1
Total amount awarded:	$1,000

Contact:
The ARRL Foundation, Inc. Scholarship Program
225 Main Street
Newington, CT 06111
Phone: 860-594-0397
Fax: 860-594-0259
Web: www.arrlf.org

Charles N. Fisher Memorial Scholarship

Type of award: Scholarship.
Intended use: For undergraduate or graduate study at accredited postsecondary institution in United States.
Eligibility: Applicant must be residing in California or Arizona.
Basis for selection: Competition/talent/interest in amateur radio. Major/career interest in communications or electronics.
Application requirements: Transcript.
Additional information: Must hold active amateur radio license. Major may be in other fields related to those listed. California candidates must reside in Los Angeles, Orange County, San Diego, or Santa Barbara. High school seniors eligible to apply. Application may be obtained on Website, but no electronic submissions accepted.

Amount of award:	$1,000
Number of awards:	1
Application deadline:	February 1
Total amount awarded:	$1,000

Contact:
The ARRL Foundation, Inc. Scholarship Program
225 Main Street
Newington, CT 06111
Phone: 860-594-0397
Fax: 860-594-0259
Web: www.arrlf.org

Chicago FM Club Scholarship

Type of award: Scholarship.
Intended use: For undergraduate study at accredited vocational, 2-year or 4-year institution in United States.
Eligibility: Applicant must be U.S. citizen residing in Wisconsin, Indiana or Illinois.
Basis for selection: Competition/talent/interest in amateur radio.
Application requirements: Transcript.
Additional information: Student also eligible if within three months of becoming U.S. citizen. Must be amateur radio operator with technician class license or higher. Number of awards varies. High school seniors eligible to apply. Application

may be obtained on Website, but no electronic submissions accepted.

Amount of award:	$500
Application deadline:	February 1

Contact:
The ARRL Foundation, Inc. Scholarship Program
225 Main Street
Newington, CT 06111
Phone: 860-594-0397
Fax: 860-594-0259
Web: www.arrlf.org

The Dayton Amateur Radio Association Scholarships

Type of award: Scholarship.
Intended use: For undergraduate study at accredited 4-year institution.
Eligibility: Applicant must be residing in North Carolina.
Basis for selection: Competition/talent/interest in amateur radio.
Application requirements: Transcript.
Additional information: Must be amateur radio operator holding any class license. High school seniors are eligible to apply. Application may be obtained on Website, but no electronic submissions accepted.

Amount of award:	$1,000
Number of awards:	4
Application deadline:	February 1

Contact:
The ARRL Foundation, Inc. Scholarship Program
225 Main Street
Newington, CT 06111
Phone: 860-594-0347
Fax: 860-594-0259
Web: www.arrlf.org

Donald Riebhoff Memorial Scholarship

Type of award: Scholarship.
Intended use: For undergraduate or graduate study at accredited 4-year or graduate institution.
Basis for selection: Competition/talent/interest in amateur radio. Major/career interest in international relations.
Application requirements: Transcript.
Additional information: Must be amateur radio operator with technician class license or higher. Must be ARRL member. High school seniors are eligible to apply. Application may be obtained on Website, but no electronic submissions accepted.

Amount of award:	$1,000
Number of awards:	1
Application deadline:	February 1

Contact:
The ARRL Foundation, Inc. Scholarship Program
225 Main Street
Newington, CT 06111
Phone: 860-594-0397
Fax: 860-594-0259
Web: www.arrlf.org

Dr. James L. Lawson Memorial Scholarship

Type of award: Scholarship.

Intended use: For undergraduate or graduate study at 4-year or graduate institution in United States. Designated institutions: Any institution in New England or New York.
Eligibility: Applicant must be residing in Vermont, Connecticut, New York, New Hampshire, Maine, Massachusetts or Rhode Island.
Basis for selection: Competition/talent/interest in amateur radio. Major/career interest in communications or electronics.
Application requirements: Transcript.
Additional information: Must be amateur radio operator holding general class license or higher. Major may be in other fields related to those listed. High school seniors eligible to apply. Application may be obtained on Website, but no electronic submissions accepted.

Amount of award:	$500
Number of awards:	1
Application deadline:	February 1
Total amount awarded:	$500

Contact:
The ARRL Foundation, Inc. Scholarship Program
225 Main Street
Newington, CT 06111
Phone: 860-594-0397
Fax: 860-594-0259
Web: www.arrlf.org

Edmond A. Metzger Scholarship

Type of award: Scholarship.
Intended use: For undergraduate, graduate or non-degree study at 4-year or graduate institution in United States. Designated institutions: Schools in ARRL Central Division (Illinois, Indiana, Wisconsin).
Eligibility: Applicant must be residing in Wisconsin, Indiana or Illinois.
Basis for selection: Competition/talent/interest in amateur radio. Major/career interest in engineering, electrical/electronic.
Application requirements: Transcript.
Additional information: Must be amateur radio operator with novice class license or higher. Must be American Radio Relay League member. High school seniors eligible to apply. Application may be obtained on Website, but no electronic submissions accepted.

Amount of award:	$500
Number of awards:	1
Application deadline:	February 1
Total amount awarded:	$500

Contact:
The ARRL Foundation, Inc. Scholarship Program
225 Main Street
Newington, CT 06111
Phone: 860-594-0397
Fax: 860-594-0259
Web: www.arrlf.org

Eugene "Gene" Sallee, W4YFR Memorial Scholarship

Type of award: Scholarship.
Intended use: For undergraduate or graduate study at accredited postsecondary institution in United States.
Eligibility: Applicant must be residing in Georgia.
Basis for selection: Competition/talent/interest in amateur radio. Applicant must demonstrate high academic achievement.
Application requirements: Transcript.
Additional information: Must be amateur radio operator with technician plus or higher class license. Minimum 3.0 GPA.

High school seniors are eligible to apply. Application may be obtained on Website, but no electronic submissions accepted.

Amount of award:	$500
Number of awards:	1
Application deadline:	February 1
Total amount awarded:	$500

Contact:
The ARRL Foundation, Inc. Scholarship Program
225 Main Street
Newington, CT 06111
Phone: 860-594-0397
Fax: 860-594-0259
Web: www.arrlf.org

Fred R. McDaniel Memorial Scholarship

Type of award: Scholarship.
Intended use: For undergraduate or graduate study at 4-year or graduate institution in United States. Designated institutions: Any colleges or universities in FCC fifth call district (Texas, Oklahoma, Arkansas, Louisiana, Mississippi, New Mexico).
Eligibility: Applicant must be residing in Oklahoma, Texas, Mississippi, Arkansas, New Mexico or Louisiana.
Basis for selection: Competition/talent/interest in amateur radio. Major/career interest in electronics or communications. Applicant must demonstrate high academic achievement.
Application requirements: Transcript.
Additional information: Preference for students with minimum 3.0 GPA. Must be amateur radio operator holding general class license or higher. Major may be in other fields related to those listed. High school students eligible to apply. Application may be obtained from Website, but no electronic submissions accepted.

Amount of award:	$500
Number of awards:	1
Application deadline:	February 1
Total amount awarded:	$500

Contact:
The ARRL Foundation, Inc. Scholarship Program
225 Main Street
Newington, CT 06111
Phone: 860-594-0397
Fax: 860-594-0259
Web: www.arrlf.org

General Fund Scholarship

Type of award: Scholarship.
Intended use: For undergraduate or graduate study at postsecondary institution.
Basis for selection: Competition/talent/interest in amateur radio.
Application requirements: Transcript.
Additional information: Must hold active amateur radio license. Number of awards varies. High school seniors eligible to apply. Application may be obtained on Website, but no electronic submissions accepted.

Amount of award:	$2,000
Application deadline:	February 1

Contact:
The ARRL Foundation, Inc. Scholarship Program
225 Main Street
Newington, CT 06111
Phone: 860-594-0397
Fax: 860-594-0259
Web: www.arrlf.org

Henry Broughton, K2AE Memorial Scholarship

Type of award: Scholarship.
Intended use: For undergraduate or graduate study at accredited 4-year or graduate institution.
Eligibility: Applicant must be residing in New York.
Basis for selection: Competition/talent/interest in amateur radio. Major/career interest in engineering or science, general.
Application requirements: Transcript.
Additional information: Applicant must live within 70-mile radius of Schenectady, NY. Must be amateur radio operator with general class license. Major may be in other fields similar to those listed. High school seniors are eligible to apply. May offer additional awards if funding permits. Application may be obtained on Website, but no electronic submissions accepted.

  Amount of award: $1,000
  Number of awards: 1
  Application deadline: February 1

Contact:
The ARRL Foundation, Inc. Scholarship Program
225 Main Street
Newington, CT 06111
Phone: 860-594-0397
Fax: 860-594-0259
Web: www.arrlf.org

Irving W. Cook WA0CGS Scholarship

Type of award: Scholarship.
Intended use: For undergraduate or graduate study at postsecondary institution in United States.
Eligibility: Applicant must be residing in Kansas.
Basis for selection: Competition/talent/interest in amateur radio. Major/career interest in communications or electronics.
Application requirements: Transcript.
Additional information: Must hold active amateur radio license. Major may be in other fields related to those listed. High schools seniors eligible to apply. Application may be obtained on Website, but no electronic submissions accepted.

  Amount of award: $1,000
  Number of awards: 1
  Application deadline: February 1
  Total amount awarded: $1,000

Contact:
The ARRL Foundation, Inc. Scholarship Program
225 Main Street
Newington, CT 06111
Phone: 860-594-0397
Fax: 860-594-0259
Web: www.arrlf.org

The K2TEO Martin J. Green, Sr. Memorial Scholarship

Type of award: Scholarship.
Intended use: For undergraduate or graduate study at postsecondary institution.
Basis for selection: Competition/talent/interest in amateur radio.
Application requirements: Transcript.
Additional information: Must be amateur radio operator with general class license or higher. Preference given to student from family of ham operators. High school seniors are eligible to

apply. Application may be obtained on Website, but no electronic submissions accepted.

  Amount of award: $1,000
  Number of awards: 1
  Application deadline: February 1
  Total amount awarded: $1,000

Contact:
The ARRL Foundation, Inc. Scholarship Program
225 Main Street
Newington, CT 06111
Phone: 860-594-0397
Fax: 860-594-0259
Web: www.arrlf.org

L. Phil Wicker Scholarship

Type of award: Scholarship.
Intended use: For undergraduate, graduate or non-degree study at 4-year or graduate institution in United States. Designated institutions: Schools in ARRL Roanoke Division (NC, SC, VA, WV).
Eligibility: Applicant must be residing in Virginia, West Virginia, North Carolina or South Carolina.
Basis for selection: Competition/talent/interest in amateur radio. Major/career interest in communications or electronics.
Application requirements: Transcript.
Additional information: Must be amateur radio operator holding general class license. Major may be in other fields related to those listed. High school seniors eligible to apply. Application may be obtained on Website, but no electronic submissions accepted.

  Amount of award: $1,000
  Number of awards: 1
  Application deadline: February 1
  Total amount awarded: $1,000

Contact:
The ARRL Foundation, Inc. Scholarship Program
225 Main Street
Newington, CT 06111
Phone: 860-594-0397
Fax: 860-594-0259
Web: www.arrlf.org

The L.B. Cebik, W4RNL, and Jean Cebik, N4TZP, Memorial Scholarship

Type of award: Scholarship.
Intended use: For undergraduate study at 4-year institution.
Eligibility: Applicant must be residing in New Jersey.
Basis for selection: Competition/talent/interest in amateur radio.
Application requirements: Transcript.
Additional information: Must be amateur radio operator holding technician class license or higher. High school seniors are eligible to apply. Application may be obtained on Website, but no electronic submissions accepted.

  Amount of award: $1,000
  Number of awards: 1
  Application deadline: February 1

Contact:
The ARRL Foundation, Inc. Scholarship Program
225 Main Street
Newington, CT 06111
Phone: 860-594-0397
Fax: 860-594-0259
Web: www.arrlf.org

Louisiana Memorial Scholarship

Type of award: Scholarship.
Intended use: For undergraduate study at 4-year or graduate institution.
Basis for selection: Competition/talent/interest in amateur radio. Applicant must demonstrate high academic achievement.
Application requirements: Transcript.
Additional information: Must be resident of or student in Louisiana. Minimum 3.0 GPA. Must be amateur radio operator holding technician class license or higher. High school seniors eligible to apply. Application may be obtained on Website, but no electronic submissions accepted.

   Amount of award: $750
   Number of awards: 1
   Application deadline: February 1
Contact:
The ARRL Foundation, Inc. Scholarship Program
225 Main Street
Newington, CT 06111
Phone: 860-594-0397
Fax: 860-594-0259
Web: www.arrlf.org

Mary Lou Brown Scholarship

Type of award: Scholarship.
Intended use: For undergraduate or graduate study at 4-year or graduate institution in United States.
Eligibility: Applicant must be residing in Oregon, Montana, Alaska, Idaho or Washington.
Basis for selection: Competition/talent/interest in amateur radio. Applicant must demonstrate high academic achievement.
Application requirements: Transcript.
Additional information: Minimum 3.0 GPA and demonstrated interest in promoting Amateur Radio Service. Must be amateur radio operator with general class license. Number of awards varies based on funding. High school seniors eligible to apply. Application may be obtained on Website, but no electronic submissions accepted.

   Amount of award: $2,500
   Application deadline: February 1
Contact:
The ARRL Foundation, Inc. Scholarship Program
225 Main Street
Newington, CT 06111
Phone: 860-594-0397
Fax: 860-594-0259
Web: www.arrlf.org

Mississippi Scholarship

Type of award: Scholarship.
Intended use: For undergraduate or graduate study at 4-year or graduate institution in United States. Designated institutions: Schools in Mississippi.
Eligibility: Applicant must be no older than 30. Applicant must be residing in Mississippi.
Basis for selection: Competition/talent/interest in amateur radio. Major/career interest in communications or electronics.
Application requirements: Transcript.
Additional information: Must hold active amateur radio license. Major may be in other fields related to those listed. High school seniors eligible to apply. Application may be obtained on Website, but no electronic submissions accepted.

   Amount of award: $500
   Number of awards: 1
   Application deadline: February 1
   Total amount awarded: $500
Contact:
The ARRL Foundation, Inc. Scholarship Program
225 Main Street
Newington, CT 06111
Phone: 860-594-0397
Fax: 860-594-0259
Web: www.arrlf.org

NEMAL Electronics Scholarship

Type of award: Scholarship.
Intended use: For undergraduate study at accredited 4-year institution.
Eligibility: Applicant must be residing in Ohio.
Basis for selection: Competition/talent/interest in amateur radio. Major/career interest in electronics or communications. Applicant must demonstrate financial need, high academic achievement and service orientation.
Application requirements: Transcript.
Additional information: Major may be in other fields related to those listed. Minimum 3.0 GPA. Must be amateur radio operator holding general class license or higher. Preference given to applicants residing in southeastern U.S. High school seniors eligible to apply. Application may be obtained on Website, but no electronic submissions accepted.

   Amount of award: $1,000
   Number of awards: 1
   Application deadline: February 1
Contact:
The ARRL Foundation, Inc. Scholarship Program
225 Main Street
Newington, CT 06111
Phone: 860-594-0397
Fax: 860-594-0259
Web: www.arrlf.org

New England FEMARA Scholarship

Type of award: Scholarship.
Intended use: For undergraduate, graduate or non-degree study at postsecondary institution.
Eligibility: Applicant must be residing in Vermont, Connecticut, New Hampshire, Maine, Massachusetts or Rhode Island.
Basis for selection: Competition/talent/interest in amateur radio.
Application requirements: Transcript.
Additional information: Must be amateur radio operator holding technical class license or higher. Number of awards varies based on funding. High school seniors eligible to apply. Application may be obtained on Website, but no electronic submissions accepted.

   Amount of award: $1,000
   Application deadline: February 1
Contact:
The ARRL Foundation, Inc. Scholarship Program
225 Main Street
Newington, CT 06111
Phone: 860-594-0397
Fax: 860-594-0259
Web: www.arrlf.org

Northern California DX Foundation Scholarship

Type of award: Scholarship.
Intended use: For undergraduate study at accredited vocational, 2-year or 4-year institution in United States.
Eligibility: Applicant must be residing in New York.
Basis for selection: Competition/talent/interest in amateur radio.
Application requirements: Transcript.
Additional information: Must be amateur radio operator holding technician class license or higher. Applicant must demonstrate interest and activity in DXing. High school seniors eligible to apply. Application may be obtained on Website, but no electronic submissions accepted.

Amount of award:	$1,500
Number of awards:	2
Application deadline:	February 1
Total amount awarded:	$3,000

Contact:
The ARRL Foundation, Inc. Scholarship Program
225 Main Street
Newington, CT 06111
Phone: 860-594-0397
Fax: 860-594-0259
Web: www.arrlf.org

Paul and Helen L. Grauer Scholarship

Type of award: Scholarship.
Intended use: For undergraduate or graduate study at 4-year or graduate institution in United States. Designated institutions: Schools in Midwest Division (Iowa, Kansas, Missouri, Nebraska).
Eligibility: Applicant must be residing in Iowa, Nebraska, Kansas or Missouri.
Basis for selection: Competition/talent/interest in amateur radio. Major/career interest in communications or electronics.
Application requirements: Transcript.
Additional information: Must be amateur radio operator with novice class license or higher. Major may be in other fields related to those listed. High school seniors are eligible to apply. Application may be obtained on Website, but no electronic submissions accepted.

Amount of award:	$1,000
Number of awards:	1
Application deadline:	February 1
Total amount awarded:	$1,000

Contact:
The ARRL Foundation, Inc. Scholarship Program
225 Main Street
Newington, CT 06111
Phone: 860-594-0397
Fax: 860-594-0259
Web: www.arrlf.org

PHD Amateur Radio Association Scholarship

Type of award: Scholarship.
Intended use: For undergraduate, graduate or non-degree study at postsecondary institution in United States.
Eligibility: Applicant must be residing in Iowa, Nebraska, Kansas or Missouri.

Basis for selection: Competition/talent/interest in amateur radio. Major/career interest in journalism; computer/information sciences or engineering, electrical/electronic.
Application requirements: Transcript.
Additional information: Must hold active amateur radio license. May be child of deceased radio amateur. High school seniors eligible to apply. Application may be obtained on Website, but no electronic submissions accepted.

Amount of award:	$1,000
Number of awards:	1
Application deadline:	February 1
Total amount awarded:	$1,000

Contact:
The ARRL Foundation, Inc. Scholarship Program
225 Main Street
Newington, CT 06111
Phone: 860-594-0397
Fax: 860-594-0259
Web: www.arrlf.org

Richard W. Bendicksen Memorial Scholarship

Type of award: Scholarship.
Intended use: For undergraduate study at 4-year institution.
Eligibility: Applicant must be residing in Nebraska.
Basis for selection: Competition/talent/interest in amateur radio.
Application requirements: Transcript.
Additional information: Must hold active amateur radio license. High school seniors eligible to apply. Application may be obtained on Website, but no electronic submissions accepted.

Amount of award:	$1,000
Number of awards:	1
Application deadline:	February 1

Contact:
The ARRL Foundation, Inc. Scholarship Program
225 Main Street
Newington, CT 06111
Phone: 860-594-0397
Fax: 860-594-0259
Web: www.arrlf.org

Seth Horen, K1LOM Memorial Scholarship

Type of award: Scholarship.
Intended use: For undergraduate study at 4-year institution.
Basis for selection: Competition/talent/interest in amateur radio.
Application requirements: Transcript.
Additional information: Must hold active amateur radio license. High school seniors eligible to apply. Application may be obtained on Website, but no electronic submissions accepted.

Amount of award:	$500
Number of awards:	1
Application deadline:	February 1

Contact:
The ARRL Foundation, Inc. Scholarship Program
225 Main Street
Newington, CT 06111
Phone: 860-594-0397
Fax: 860-594-0259
Web: www.arrlf.org

Six Meter Club of Chicago Scholarship

Type of award: Scholarship.
Intended use: For undergraduate study at postsecondary institution in United States. Designated institutions: Schools in Illinois.
Eligibility: Applicant must be residing in Illinois.
Basis for selection: Competition/talent/interest in amateur radio.
Application requirements: Transcript.
Additional information: Must hold active amateur radio license. Award open to remaining ARRL Central Division states (IN and WI) if no qualified IL student identified. High school seniors eligible to apply. Application may be obtained on Website, but no electronic submissions accepted.

Amount of award:	$500
Number of awards:	1
Application deadline:	February 1
Total amount awarded:	$500

Contact:
The ARRL Foundation, Inc. Scholarship Program
225 Main Street
Newington, CT 06111
Phone: 860-594-0397
Fax: 860-594-0259
Web: www.arrlf.org

Tom and Judith Comstock Scholarship

Type of award: Scholarship.
Intended use: For undergraduate study at 2-year or 4-year institution in United States.
Eligibility: Applicant must be high school senior. Applicant must be residing in Oklahoma or Texas.
Basis for selection: Competition/talent/interest in amateur radio.
Application requirements: Transcript.
Additional information: Must hold active amateur radio license. Application may be obtained on Website, but no electronic submissions accepted.

Amount of award:	$2,000
Number of awards:	1
Application deadline:	February 1
Total amount awarded:	$2,000

Contact:
The ARRL Foundation, Inc. Scholarship Program
225 Main Street
Newington, CT 06111
Phone: 860-594-0397
Fax: 860-594-0259
Web: www.arrlf.org

William R. Goldfarb Memorial Scholarship

Type of award: Scholarship, renewable.
Intended use: For undergraduate study at accredited 4-year institution.
Eligibility: Applicant must be high school senior.
Basis for selection: Competition/talent/interest in amateur radio. Major/career interest in business; engineering; science, general; computer/information sciences; medicine or nursing. Applicant must demonstrate financial need.

Application requirements: Recommendations, transcript. FAFSA or Student Aid Report.
Additional information: Must hold active amateur radio license. Award amount varies based on applicant's qualifications, need, and other funding; $10,000 is the minimum award. Application may be obtained on Website, but no electronic submissions accepted.

Amount of award:	$10,000
Number of awards:	1
Application deadline:	February 1

Contact:
The ARRL Foundation, Inc. Scholarship Program
225 Main Street
Newington, CT 06111
Phone: 860-594-0397
Fax: 860-594-0259
Web: www.arrlf.org

Yankee Clipper Contest Club, Inc. Youth Scholarship

Type of award: Scholarship.
Intended use: For undergraduate study at accredited 2-year or 4-year institution.
Eligibility: Applicant must be residing in Vermont, New York, Maine, Pennsylvania, Massachusetts, Connecticut, New Hampshire, New Jersey or Rhode Island.
Basis for selection: Competition/talent/interest in amateur radio.
Application requirements: Transcript.
Additional information: Must be amateur radio operator holding general class license or higher. Must be resident of or college/university student in area within 175-mile radius of YCCC Center in Erving, MA. This includes MA; RI; CT; Long Island, NY; and some of VT, NH, ME, PA, and NJ. High school seniors are eligible to apply. Application may be obtained on Website, but no electronic submissions accepted.

Amount of award:	$1,000
Number of awards:	1
Application deadline:	February 1

Contact:
The ARRL Foundation, Inc. Scholarship Program
225 Main Street
Newington, CT 06111
Phone: 860-594-0397
Fax: 860-594-0259
Web: www.arrlf.org

Yasme Foundation Scholarship

Type of award: Scholarship, renewable.
Intended use: For undergraduate study at accredited 4-year institution.
Basis for selection: Competition/talent/interest in amateur radio. Major/career interest in science, general or engineering. Applicant must demonstrate high academic achievement and service orientation.
Application requirements: Transcript.
Additional information: Must hold active amateur radio license. Two awards renewable up to three years based on transcript review. Preference given to high school applicants in top five to ten percent of class or college students in top ten percent of class. Participation in local amateur radio club and community service strongly preferred. Application may be obtained on Website, but no electronic submissions accepted.

Amount of award: $2,000
Number of awards: 5
Application deadline: February 1
Contact:
The ARRL Foundation, Inc. Scholarship Program
225 Main Street
Newington, CT 06111
Phone: 860-594-0397
Fax: 860-594-0259
Web: www.arrlf.org

You've Got a Friend in Pennsylvania Scholarship

Type of award: Scholarship.
Intended use: For undergraduate, graduate or non-degree study at postsecondary institution.
Eligibility: Applicant must be residing in Pennsylvania.
Basis for selection: Competition/talent/interest in amateur radio.
Application requirements: Transcript.
Additional information: Must be amateur radio operator with general class license. Must be member of American Radio Relay League. High school seniors eligible to apply. Application may be obtained from Website, but no electronic submissions accepted.

Amount of award: $2,000
Number of awards: 1
Application deadline: February 1
Total amount awarded: $2,000
Contact:
The ARRL Foundation, Inc. Scholarship Program
225 Main Street
Newington, CT 06111
Phone: 860-594-0397
Fax: 860-594-0259
Web: www.arrlf.org

Zachary Taylor Stevens Memorial Scholarship

Type of award: Scholarship.
Intended use: For undergraduate study at accredited vocational, 2-year or 4-year institution.
Eligibility: Applicant must be residing in Michigan, Ohio or West Virginia.
Basis for selection: Competition/talent/interest in amateur radio.
Application requirements: Transcript.
Additional information: Must be amateur radio operator holding technician class license or higher. Preference given to residents of Michigan, Ohio, and West Virginia. High school seniors eligible to apply. Application may be obtained on Website, but no electronic submissions accepted.

Amount of award: $750
Number of awards: 1
Application deadline: February 1
Contact:
The ARRL Foundation, Inc. Scholarship Program
225 Main Street
Newington, CT 06111
Phone: 860-594-0397
Fax: 860-594-0259
Web: www.arrlf.org

American Respiratory Care Foundation

Jimmy A. Young Memorial Education Recognition Award

Type of award: Scholarship, renewable.
Intended use: For undergraduate study at accredited postsecondary institution.
Eligibility: Applicant must be Alaskan native, Asian American, African American, Mexican American, Hispanic American, Puerto Rican, American Indian or Native Hawaiian/Pacific Islander.
Basis for selection: Competition/talent/interest in research paper. Major/career interest in respiratory therapy. Applicant must demonstrate high academic achievement.
Application requirements: Recommendations, transcript, proof of eligibility, nomination by school or program representative. Student may initiate request for sponsorship in absence of nomination. Original referenced paper on some aspect of respiratory care.
Additional information: Minimum 3.0 GPA. Award includes airfare, one night lodging, and registration for AARC International Respiratory Congress. Application available on Website. Application must be notarized.

Amount of award: $1,000
Number of awards: 1
Application deadline: June 15
Total amount awarded: $1,000
Contact:
American Respiratory Care Foundation
Attn: Education Recognition Award
9425 N. MacArthur Blvd., Suite 100
Irving, TX 75063-4706
Phone: 972-243-2272
Fax: 972-484-2720
Web: www.arcfoundation.org/awards

Morton B. Duggan, Jr. Memorial Education Recognition Award

Type of award: Scholarship, renewable.
Intended use: For undergraduate study at accredited postsecondary institution.
Basis for selection: Competition/talent/interest in research paper. Major/career interest in respiratory therapy. Applicant must demonstrate high academic achievement.
Application requirements: Recommendations, transcript, proof of eligibility. Research paper on some aspect of respiratory care.
Additional information: Applicants accepted from all states, but preference given to applicants from Georgia and South Carolina. Minimum 3.0 GPA. Award includes airfare, one night lodging, and registration for the AARC International Respiratory Congress. Application available on Website. Application must be notarized.

Amount of award: $1,000
Number of awards: 1
Application deadline: June 15

Contact:
American Respiratory Care Foundation
Attn: Education Recogniton Award
9425 N. MacArthur Blvd., Suite 100
Irving, TX 75063-4706
Phone: 972-243-2272
Fax: 972-484-2720
Web: www.arcfoundation.org/awards

NBRC/AMP Robert M. Lawrence, MD Education Recognition Award

Type of award: Scholarship.
Intended use: For junior or senior study at accredited 4-year institution.
Basis for selection: Competition/talent/interest in research paper. Major/career interest in respiratory therapy. Applicant must demonstrate high academic achievement.
Application requirements: Recommendations, essay, transcript, proof of eligibility. Original referenced paper on some aspect of respiratory care.
Additional information: Minimum 3.0 GPA. Award includes airfare, one night lodging, and registration for AARC International Respiratory Congress. Application available on Website. Application must be notarized.
- **Amount of award:** $2,500
- **Number of awards:** 1
- **Application deadline:** June 15

Contact:
American Respiratory Care Foundation
Attn: Education Recognition Award
9425 N. MacArthur Blvd., Suite 100
Irving, TX 75063-4706
Phone: 972-243-2272
Fax: 972-484-2720
Web: www.arcfoundation.org/awards

NBRC/AMP William W. Burgin, Jr. MD Education Recognition Award

Type of award: Scholarship.
Intended use: For sophomore study at accredited 2-year institution.
Basis for selection: Competition/talent/interest in research paper. Major/career interest in respiratory therapy. Applicant must demonstrate high academic achievement.
Application requirements: Recommendations, essay, transcript, proof of eligibility, nomination by school or educational program. Original referenced paper on some aspect of respiratory care.
Additional information: Must be student in respiratory therapy associate's degree program. Minimum 3.0 GPA. Award includes one night lodging and registration for AARC International Respiratory Congress. Application available on Website. Application must be notarized.
- **Amount of award:** $2,500
- **Number of awards:** 1
- **Application deadline:** June 15

Contact:
American Respiratory Care Foundation
Attn: Education Recognition Award
9425 N. MacArthur Blvd., Suite 100
Irving, TX 75063-4706
Phone: 972-243-2272
Fax: 972-484-2720
Web: www.arcfoundation.org/awards

American Society for Enology and Viticulture

American Society for Enology and Viticulture Scholarship Program

Type of award: Scholarship, renewable.
Intended use: For full-time junior, senior or graduate study at accredited 4-year or graduate institution.
Eligibility: Applicant must be U.S. citizen, permanent resident or resident of Canada or Mexico.
Basis for selection: Major/career interest in agriculture; food science/technology or horticulture. Applicant must demonstrate financial need and high academic achievement.
Application requirements: Recommendations, essay, transcript. Student questionnaire, list of planned courses for upcoming year.
Additional information: Minimum 3.0 GPA for undergraduates, 3.2 GPA for graduate students. Applicants must be enrolled in major or graduate program emphasizing enology or viticulture, or in curriculum emphasizing science basic to wine and grape industry. Awards vary.
- **Number of applicants:** 20
- **Application deadline:** March 1

Contact:
ASEV Scholarship Committee
P.O. Box 1855
Davis, CA 95617-1855
Phone: 530-753-3142
Fax: 530-753-3318
Web: www.asev.org/scholarship-program

American Society for Microbiology

Microbiology Undergraduate Research Fellowship (MURF)

Type of award: Research grant.
Intended use: For full-time undergraduate study in United States. Designated institutions: R-01 host institutions.
Eligibility: Applicant must be Alaskan native, African American, Mexican American, Hispanic American, Puerto Rican, American Indian or Native Hawaiian/Pacific Islander. Applicant must be U.S. citizen or permanent resident.
Basis for selection: Major/career interest in microbiology. Applicant must demonstrate high academic achievement, leadership and seriousness of purpose.
Application requirements: Recommendations, transcript. Personal statement.
Additional information: Applicant must demonstrate ability to pursue graduate career (Ph.D.) in microbiology. Program provides opportunity for historically excluded and underrepresented students at non-research intensive institutions to conduct summer research with an ASM member at pre-selected R-01 host institution for 10 to 12 weeks and present research results at ASM General Meeting and at Annual Biomedical Research Conference for Minority Students (if abstract is accepted). Fellowship offers up to $3,500 stipend, up to $1,000 for student lodging at host institution, up to $500 for

travel, and up to $1,000 to attend ASM General Meeting (if abstract is accepted). Number of awards varies. See Website for application and more details.

Amount of award:	$6,000
Number of applicants:	36
Application deadline:	February 1
Notification begins:	April 15

Contact:
American Society for Microbiology
ASM MURF
1752 N Street, NW
Washington, DC 20036
Phone: 202-942-9283
Fax: 202-942-9329
Web: www.asm.org/students

Undergraduate Research Fellowship (URF)

Type of award: Research grant.
Intended use: For full-time undergraduate study in United States.
Eligibility: Applicant must be U.S. citizen or permanent resident.
Basis for selection: Major/career interest in microbiology. Applicant must demonstrate high academic achievement and seriousness of purpose.
Application requirements: Recommendations, transcript.
Additional information: Applicant must demonstrate strong interest in pursuing graduate career (Ph.D. or M.D./Ph.D.) in microbiology. Students conduct research for 10-12 weeks in summer and present results at ASM General Meeting the following year. Fellowship offers up to $4,000 stipend and up to $1,000 to travel to ASM General Meeting (if abstract is accepted). Applicant must have ASM member at home institution willing to serve as faculty mentor. Students may not receive financial support for research from other scientific organizations during fellowship. Faculty member's department chair or dean must endorse research project. Number of awards varies. See Website for application.

Amount of award:	$5,000
Number of applicants:	81
Application deadline:	February 1
Notification begins:	April 15

Contact:
American Society for Microbiology
ASM Undergraduate Research Fellowship Program
1752 N Street, NW
Washington, DC 20036
Phone: 202-942-9283
Fax: 202-942-9329
Web: www.asm.org/students

American Society of Civil Engineers

Eugene C. Figg Jr. Civil Engineering Scholarship

Type of award: Scholarship.
Intended use: For junior or senior study.
Eligibility: Applicant must be U.S. citizen.

Basis for selection: Major/career interest in engineering, civil. Applicant must demonstrate financial need, high academic achievement and leadership.
Application requirements: Recommendations, essay, transcript. One-page resume, detailed financial plan.
Additional information: Must be American Society of Civil Engineers member in good standing, be enrolled in ABET-accredited program, and have passion for bridges. Recipient eligible to interview for internship opportunity with Figg Engineering Group.

Amount of award:	$3,000
Number of awards:	1
Application deadline:	February 9
Notification begins:	April 1
Total amount awarded:	$3,000

Contact:
American Society of Civil Engineers
Attn: Student Services
1801 Alexander Bell Drive
Reston, VA 20191-4400
Phone: 800-548-2723 ext. 6106
Fax: 703-295-6222
Web: www.asce.org

Freeman Fellowship

Type of award: Research grant.
Intended use: For undergraduate or graduate study.
Basis for selection: Major/career interest in engineering, civil.
Application requirements: Recommendations, essay, transcript, research proposal. One- to two-page resume. Detailed financial statement indicating how fellowship will finance applicant's research. Statement from institution where research will be conducted.
Additional information: Applicant must be American Society of Civil Engineers member in good standing. Grants are made toward expenses for experiments, observations, and compilations to discover new and accurate data that will be useful in engineering. Grant may be in form of prize for most useful paper relating to science/art of hydraulic construction. Travel scholarships available to ASCE members under 45, in recognition of achievement or promise. Visit Website for application and more information.

Amount of award:	$2,000-$5,000
Application deadline:	February 9
Notification begins:	April 1

Contact:
American Society of Civil Engineers
Attn: Student Services
1801 Alexander Bell Drive
Reston, VA 20191-4440
Phone: 800-548-2723 ext. 6106
Fax: 703-295-6222
Web: www.asce.org

Samuel Fletcher Tapman ASCE Student Chapter Scholarship

Type of award: Scholarship, renewable.
Intended use: For undergraduate study at accredited postsecondary institution.
Basis for selection: Major/career interest in engineering, civil. Applicant must demonstrate financial need, high academic achievement and leadership.
Application requirements: Recommendations, essay, transcript. One-page resume, detailed annual budget.

Additional information: Applicant must be enrolled in ABET-accredited program and be member in good standing of local American Society of Civil Engineers student chapter and national society. Membership applications may be submitted with scholarship application. One submission per student chapter. Visit Website for application and more information.

Amount of award:	$2,500
Number of awards:	12
Application deadline:	February 9
Notification begins:	April 1

Contact:
American Society of Civil Engineers
Attn: Student Services
1801 Alexander Bell Drive
Reston, VA 20191-4440
Phone: 800-548-2723 ext. 6106
Fax: 703-295-6222
Web: www.asce.org

Y.C. Yang Civil Engineering Scholarship

Type of award: Scholarship.
Intended use: For junior or senior study.
Basis for selection: Major/career interest in engineering, civil or engineering, structural. Applicant must demonstrate financial need, high academic achievement and leadership.
Application requirements: Recommendations, essay, transcript. One-page resume, detailed financial plan.
Additional information: Must be student at ABET-accredited institution, an ASCE student member in good standing, and have interest in structural engineering. Visit Website for deadline.

Amount of award:	$3,000
Number of awards:	2
Application deadline:	February 9
Notification begins:	April 1

Contact:
American Society of Civil Engineers
Attn: Student Services
1801 Alexander Bell Drive
Reston, VA 20191-4400
Phone: 800-548-2723 ext. 6106
Fax: 703-295-6222
Web: www.asce.org

American Society of Heating, Refrigerating, and Air-Conditioning Engineers, Inc.

Alwin B. Newton Scholarship

Type of award: Scholarship.
Intended use: For full-time undergraduate study at accredited 4-year institution in or outside United States. Designated institutions: Schools with ABET-accredited programs.
Basis for selection: Major/career interest in engineering or air conditioning/heating/refrigeration technology. Applicant must demonstrate financial need, high academic achievement, depth of character and leadership.
Application requirements: Recommendations, transcript.

Additional information: For engineering students considering service to heating/ventilation/air-conditioning (HVAC) and/or refrigeration profession. Minimum 3.0 GPA.

Amount of award:	$3,000
Number of awards:	1
Application deadline:	December 1

Contact:
ASHRAE, Inc. - Scholarship Administrator
1791 Tullie Circle, NE
Atlanta, GA 30329-2305
Phone: 404-636-8400
Fax: 404-321-5478
Web: www.ashrae.org/students/page/1271

ASHRAE General Scholarships

Type of award: Scholarship.
Intended use: For full-time undergraduate study at accredited 4-year institution in or outside United States. Designated institutions: Schools with ABET-accredited programs.
Basis for selection: Major/career interest in engineering or air conditioning/heating/refrigeration technology. Applicant must demonstrate financial need, high academic achievement, depth of character and leadership.
Application requirements: Recommendations, transcript.
Additional information: For engineering students considering service to heating/ventilation/air-conditioning (HVAC) and/or refrigeration profession. Minimum 3.0 GPA.

Amount of award:	$3,000
Number of awards:	2
Application deadline:	December 1

Contact:
ASHRAE, Inc. - Scholarship Administrator
1791 Tullie Circle, NE
Atlanta, GA 30329-2305
Phone: 404-636-8400
Fax: 404-321-5478
Web: www.ashrae.org/students/page/1271

ASHRAE Memorial Scholarship

Type of award: Scholarship.
Intended use: For full-time undergraduate study at accredited 4-year institution in or outside United States. Designated institutions: Schools with ABET-accredited programs.
Basis for selection: Major/career interest in engineering or air conditioning/heating/refrigeration technology. Applicant must demonstrate financial need, high academic achievement, depth of character and leadership.
Application requirements: Recommendations, transcript.
Additional information: For engineering students considering service to heating/ventilation/air-conditioning (HVAC) and/or refrigeration profession. Minimum 3.0 GPA.

Amount of award:	$3,000
Number of awards:	1
Application deadline:	December 1

Contact:
ASHRAE, Inc. - Scholarship Administrator
1791 Tullie Circle, NE
Atlanta, GA 30329-2305
Phone: 404-636-8400
Fax: 404-321-5478
Web: www.ashrae.org/students/page/1271

ASHRAE Region IV Benny Bootle Scholarship

Type of award: Scholarship.

Intended use: For full-time undergraduate study at accredited 4-year institution. Designated institutions: Schools with NAAB or ABET-accredited program located within the geographic boundaries of ASHRAE's Region IV (North Carolina, South Carolina, Georgia).
Eligibility: Applicant must be residing in North Carolina, Georgia or South Carolina.
Basis for selection: Major/career interest in air conditioning/heating/refrigeration technology; architecture or engineering. Applicant must demonstrate financial need, high academic achievement, depth of character and leadership.
Application requirements: Recommendations, transcript.
Additional information: Minimum 3.0 GPA. For engineering or architecture students considering service to heating/ventilation/air-conditioning (HVAC) and/or refrigeration profession. Visit www.abet.org and www.naab.org for list of ABET- and NAAB-accredited programs within Region IV.

Amount of award:	$3,000
Number of awards:	1
Application deadline:	December 1

Contact:
ASHRAE, Inc. - Scholarship Administrator
1791 Tullie Circle, NE
Atlanta, GA 30329-2305
Phone: 404-636-8400
Fax: 404-321-5478
Web: www.ashrae.org/students/page/1271

ASHRAE Region VIII Scholarship

Type of award: Scholarship.
Intended use: For full-time undergraduate study in or outside United States. Designated institutions: Schools with ABET-accredited programs located within the geographic boundaries of ASHRAE's Region VIII (Arkansas, Oklahoma, Mexico, and parts of Louisiana and Texas).
Eligibility: Applicant must be residing in Oklahoma, Texas, Arkansas or Louisiana.
Basis for selection: Major/career interest in engineering or air conditioning/heating/refrigeration technology. Applicant must demonstrate financial need, high academic achievement, depth of character and leadership.
Application requirements: Recommendations, transcript.
Additional information: Minimum 3.0 GPA. For engineering students considering service to heating/ventilation/air-conditioning (HVAC) and/or refrigeration profession. Contact ASHRAE for information regarding Region VIII. Visit www.abet.org for ABET-accredited programs within the region.

Amount of award:	$3,000
Number of awards:	1
Application deadline:	December 1

Contact:
ASHRAE, Inc. - Scholarship Administrator
1791 Tullie Circle, NE
Atlanta, GA 30329-2305
Phone: 404-636-8400
Fax: 404-321-5478
Web: www.ashrae.org/students/page/1271

Duane Hanson Scholarship

Type of award: Scholarship.
Intended use: For full-time undergraduate study at accredited 4-year institution in or outside United States. Designated institutions: Schools with ABET-accredited programs.
Basis for selection: Major/career interest in engineering or air conditioning/heating/refrigeration technology. Applicant must

demonstrate financial need, high academic achievement, depth of character and leadership.
Application requirements: Recommendations, transcript.
Additional information: For engineering students considering service to heating/ventilation/air-conditioning (HVAC) and/or refrigeration profession. Minimum 3.0 GPA.

Amount of award:	$3,000
Number of awards:	1
Application deadline:	December 1

Contact:
ASHRAE, Inc. - Scholarship Administrator
1791 Tullie Circle, NE
Atlanta, GA 30329-2305
Phone: 404-636-8400
Fax: 404-321-5478
Web: www.ashrae.org/students/page/1271

Engineering Technology Scholarships

Type of award: Scholarship.
Intended use: For full-time undergraduate study at accredited 2-year or 4-year institution. Designated institutions: Schools with ABET-accredited engineering technology programs.
Basis for selection: Major/career interest in engineering or air conditioning/heating/refrigeration technology. Applicant must demonstrate financial need, high academic achievement, depth of character and leadership.
Application requirements: Recommendations, transcript.
Additional information: For students pursuing bachelor's degree in engineering technology and intending to pursue career in heating/ventilation/air-conditioning (HVAC) and/or refrigeration profession. Minimum 3.0 GPA.

Amount of award:	$3,000
Number of awards:	3
Application deadline:	May 1

Contact:
ASHRAE, Inc. - Scholarship Administrator
1791 Tullie Circle, NE
Atlanta, GA 30329-2305
Phone: 404-636-8400
Fax: 404-321-5478
Web: www.ashrae.org/students/page/1271

Frank M. Coda Scholarship

Type of award: Scholarship.
Intended use: For full-time undergraduate study at accredited 4-year institution in or outside United States. Designated institutions: Schools with ABET-accredited programs.
Basis for selection: Major/career interest in engineering or air conditioning/heating/refrigeration technology. Applicant must demonstrate financial need, high academic achievement, depth of character and leadership.
Application requirements: Recommendations, transcript.
Additional information: For engineering students considering service to heating/ventilation/air-conditioning (HVAC) and/or refrigeration profession. Minimum 3.0 GPA.

Amount of award:	$5,000
Number of awards:	1
Application deadline:	December 1

Contact:
ASHRAE, Inc. - Scholarship Administrator
1791 Tullie Circle, NE
Atlanta, GA 30329-2305
Phone: 404-636-8400
Fax: 404-321-5478
Web: www.ashrae.org/students/page/1271

Henry Adams Scholarship

Type of award: Scholarship.
Intended use: For full-time undergraduate study at accredited 4-year institution in or outside United States. Designated institutions: Schools with ABET-accredited programs.
Basis for selection: Major/career interest in engineering or air conditioning/heating/refrigeration technology. Applicant must demonstrate financial need, high academic achievement, depth of character and leadership.
Application requirements: Recommendations, transcript.
Additional information: For engineering students considering service to heating/ventilation/air-conditioning (HVAC) and/or refrigeration profession. Minimum 3.0 GPA.

Amount of award:	$3,000
Number of awards:	1
Application deadline:	December 1

Contact:
ASHRAE, Inc. - Scholarship Administrator
1791 Tullie Circle, NE
Atlanta, GA 30329-2305
Phone: 404-636-8400
Fax: 404-321-5478
Web: www.ashrae.org/students/page/1271

J. Richard Mehalick Scholarship

Type of award: Scholarship.
Intended use: For full-time undergraduate study at accredited 4-year institution in United States. Designated institutions: University of Pittsburgh.
Basis for selection: Major/career interest in engineering, mechanical or air conditioning/heating/refrigeration technology. Applicant must demonstrate financial need, high academic achievement, depth of character and leadership.
Application requirements: Recommendations, transcript.
Additional information: Must have minimum 3.0 GPA. For mechanical engineering students considering service to heating/ventilation/air-conditioning (HVAC) and/or refrigeration profession.

Amount of award:	$3,000
Number of awards:	1
Application deadline:	December 1

Contact:
ASHRAE, Inc. - Scholarship Administrator
1791 Tullie Circle, NE
Atlanta, GA 30329
Phone: 404-636-8400
Fax: 404-321-5478
Web: www.ashrae.org/students/page/1271

Reuben Trane Scholarship

Type of award: Scholarship.
Intended use: For full-time junior or senior study at accredited 4-year institution in or outside United States. Designated institutions: Schools with ABET-accredited programs.
Basis for selection: Major/career interest in air conditioning/heating/refrigeration technology or engineering. Applicant must demonstrate financial need, high academic achievement, depth of character and leadership.
Application requirements: Recommendations, transcript.
Additional information: Minimum 3.0 GPA. Award is for two years; $5,000 given at beginning of student's junior and senior years. Must be considering service to heating/ventilation/air-conditioning (HVAC) and/or refrigeration profession.

Amount of award:	$10,000
Application deadline:	December 1

Contact:
ASHRAE, Inc. - Scholarship Administrator
1791 Tullie Circle, NE
Atlanta, GA 30329-2305
Phone: 404-636-8400
Fax: 404-321-5478
Web: www.ashrae.org/students/page/1271

Willis H. Carrier Scholarship

Type of award: Scholarship.
Intended use: For full-time undergraduate study at accredited 4-year institution in or outside United States. Designated institutions: ABET-accredited institutions.
Basis for selection: Major/career interest in engineering or air conditioning/heating/refrigeration technology. Applicant must demonstrate financial need, high academic achievement, depth of character and leadership.
Application requirements: Recommendations, transcript.
Additional information: For engineering students considering service to heating/ventilation/air-conditioning (HVAC) and/or refrigeration profession. Minimum 3.0 GPA.

Amount of award:	$10,000
Number of awards:	2
Application deadline:	December 1

Contact:
ASHRAE, Inc. - Scholarship Administrator
1791 Tullie Circle, NE
Atlanta, GA 30329-2305
Phone: 404-636-8400
Fax: 404-321-5478
Web: www.ashrae.org/students/page/1271

American Society of Interior Designers Foundation, Inc.

Joel Polsky Academic Achievement Award

Type of award: Scholarship.
Intended use: For undergraduate or graduate study at postsecondary institution.
Basis for selection: Competition/talent/interest in research paper, based on content, breadth of material, comprehensive coverage of topic, innovative subject matter, bibliography, and references. Major/career interest in interior design.
Application requirements: Photo.
Additional information: Award to recognize outstanding interior design research or thesis project addressing topics such as educational research, behavioral science, business practice, design process, theory, or other technical subjects.

Amount of award:	$1,000
Number of awards:	1
Application deadline:	March 1

Contact:
American Society of Interior Designers Foundation, Inc.
Joel Polsky Academic Achievement Award
608 Massachusetts Avenue, NE
Washington, DC 20002-6006
Phone: 202-546-3480
Fax: 202-546-3240
Web: www.asid.org/asidfoundation/
Foundation+Scholarships+and+Awards.htm

Yale R. Burge Competition

Type of award: Scholarship.
Intended use: For senior study at postsecondary institution.
Basis for selection: Competition/talent/interest in visual arts, based on presentation, design and planning, and conceptual creativity. Major/career interest in interior design.
Application requirements: Portfolio. Eight to twelve portfolio components submitted as slides, PowerPoint presentation, or HTML. Photo.
Additional information: Open to all interior design students in their final year of at least three-year undergraduate program. Visit Website for application and more information.

Amount of award:	$750
Number of awards:	1
Application deadline:	March 1

Contact:
ASID Foundation, Inc.
Yale R. Burge Competition
608 Massachusetts Avenue, NE
Washington, DC 20002-6006
Phone: 202-546-3480
Fax: 202-546-3240
Web: www.asid.org/asidfoundation/
Foundation+Scholarships+and+Awards.htm

American Society of Naval Engineers

ASNE Scholarship

Type of award: Scholarship, renewable.
Intended use: For full-time senior or graduate study at accredited 4-year or graduate institution.
Eligibility: Applicant must be U.S. citizen.
Basis for selection: Major/career interest in engineering; engineering, civil; engineering, electrical/electronic; engineering, environmental; engineering, marine; engineering, mechanical; engineering, nuclear; engineering, structural or physical sciences. Applicant must demonstrate high academic achievement and seriousness of purpose.
Application requirements: Recommendations, essay, transcript.
Additional information: Graduate applicants must be members of American Society of Naval Engineers. Applicants' major/career interests may also include naval architecture, aeronautical and ocean engineering, or other programs leading to careers with relevant military and civilian organizations. Financial need may be considered. Award also includes one-year honorary student membership to Society.

Amount of award:	$3,000-$4,000
Number of awards:	21
Number of applicants:	100
Application deadline:	February 15
Notification begins:	May 1
Total amount awarded:	$72,000

Contact:
American Society of Naval Engineers
1452 Duke Street
Alexandria, VA 22314-3458
Phone: 703-836-6727
Fax: 703-836-7491
Web: www.navalengineers.org

American Water Ski Educational Foundation

American Water Ski Educational Foundation Scholarship

Type of award: Scholarship, renewable.
Intended use: For full-time sophomore, junior or senior study at 2-year or 4-year institution.
Eligibility: Applicant must be U.S. citizen.
Basis for selection: Applicant must demonstrate financial need, high academic achievement, depth of character, leadership and seriousness of purpose.
Application requirements: Recommendations, essay, transcript. College freshmen should include both college and high school transcripts. Visit Website for current essay topic.
Additional information: Must be member of USA Water Ski Association.

Amount of award:	$1,500-$3,000
Number of awards:	6
Number of applicants:	10
Application deadline:	March 1
Notification begins:	September 1
Total amount awarded:	$11,000

Contact:
American Water Ski Educational Foundation
1251 Holy Cow Road
Polk City, FL 33868-8200
Phone: 863-324-2472
Fax: 863-324-3996
Web: www.waterskihalloffame.com

American Welding Society Foundation, Inc.

Airgas-Jerry Baker Scholarship

Type of award: Scholarship, renewable.
Intended use: For full-time undergraduate study at postsecondary institution.
Eligibility: Applicant must be at least 18. Applicant must be U.S. citizen or Canadian citizen.
Basis for selection: Major/career interest in welding.
Application requirements: Essay.
Additional information: Applicants must have minimum 2.8 overall GPA with 3.0 GPA in engineering courses. Priority

given to individuals residing or attending school in Alabama, Georgia, or Florida. Applicant must show interest in welding engineering or welding engineering technology.

Amount of award:	$2,500
Number of awards:	1
Number of applicants:	5
Application deadline:	February 15
Notification begins:	April 1
Total amount awarded:	$2,500

Contact:
American Welding Society Foundation, Inc.
Att: Scholarships
550 Northwest LeJeune Road
Miami, FL 33126
Phone: 800-443-9353 ext. 461
Web: www.aws.org/foundation/scholarships

Airgas-Terry Jarvis Memorial Scholarship

Type of award: Scholarship.
Intended use: For full-time sophomore, junior or senior study at 4-year institution in United States or Canada.
Eligibility: Applicant must be at least 18. Applicant must be U.S. citizen or Canadian citizen.
Basis for selection: Major/career interest in welding.
Application requirements: Recommendations, essay, transcript, proof of eligibility.
Additional information: Must have interest in pursuing a minimum four-year degree in welding engineering or welding engineering technology. Minimum 2.8 GPA overall, with 3.0 GPA in engineering courses. Priority given to residents of Florida, Alabama, and Georgia. Applicant does not have to be a member of the American Welding Society.

Amount of award:	$2,500
Number of awards:	1
Number of applicants:	5
Application deadline:	February 15
Notification begins:	April 1
Total amount awarded:	$2,500

Contact:
American Welding Society Foundation, Inc.
Attn: Scholarships
550 Northwest LeJeune Road
Miami, FL 33126
Phone: 800-443-9353
Web: www.aws.org/foundation/scholarships

American Welding Society District Scholarship Program

Type of award: Scholarship.
Intended use: For undergraduate study at accredited vocational, 2-year or 4-year institution in United States.
Eligibility: Applicant must be U.S. citizen.
Basis for selection: Major/career interest in welding. Applicant must demonstrate financial need, high academic achievement, depth of character, leadership and seriousness of purpose.
Application requirements: Recommendations, transcript, proof of eligibility. Personal statement, biography, and photo.

Amount of award:	$200-$2,000
Number of awards:	150
Number of applicants:	270
Application deadline:	March 1
Notification begins:	July 1
Total amount awarded:	$165,000

Contact:
American Welding Society Foundation, Inc.
Attn: Scholarships
550 Northwest LeJeune Road
Miami, FL 33126
Phone: 800-443-9353
Web: www.aws.org/foundation/scholarships

Arsham Amirikian Engineering Scholarship

Type of award: Scholarship, renewable.
Intended use: For undergraduate study at accredited 4-year institution.
Eligibility: Applicant must be at least 18. Applicant must be U.S. citizen.
Basis for selection: Major/career interest in welding. Applicant must demonstrate financial need.
Additional information: Minimum 3.0 GPA. Must show interest in pursuing career in the application of the art of welding in civil and structural engineering.

Amount of award:	$2,500
Number of awards:	1
Number of applicants:	12
Application deadline:	February 15
Notification begins:	April 1
Total amount awarded:	$2,500

Contact:
American Welding Society Foundation, Inc.
Att: Scholarships
550 Northwest LeJeune Road
Miami, FL 33126
Phone: 800-443-9353
Web: www.aws.org/foundation/scholarships

D. Fred and Mariam L. Bovie Scholarship

Type of award: Scholarship, renewable.
Intended use: For full-time at 4-year institution. Designated institutions: The Ohio State University.
Eligibility: Applicant must be U.S. citizen.
Basis for selection: Major/career interest in welding or engineering, electrical/electronic.
Application requirements: Recommendations, essay, transcript, proof of eligibility. Statement of Unmet Financial Need.
Additional information: Award may be renewed for a maximum of four years. Membership in the American Welding Society is not required. Electrical engineering candidates will be considered if there are no qualified welding engineering candidates.

Amount of award:	$3,000
Number of awards:	1
Number of applicants:	4
Application deadline:	February 15

Contact:
American Welding Society Foundation, Inc.
Attn: Scholarships
550 Northwest LeJeune Road
Miami, FL 33126
Phone: 800-443-9353
Web: www.aws.org/foundation/scholarships

D. Fred and Mariam L. Bovie Technical Scholarship

Type of award: Scholarship, renewable.
Intended use: For undergraduate study at postsecondary institution.
Basis for selection: Major/career interest in welding. Applicant must demonstrate financial need.
Application requirements: Recommendations, essay, transcript, proof of eligibility. Statement of Unmet Financial Need.
Additional information: Minimum 2.8 GPA. Applicant must be pursuing an associate's degree in welding, with a minimum of a two-year program. Award may be renewed for a maximum of four years. Membership in the American Welding Society is not required.

Amount of award:	$2,000
Number of awards:	1
Number of applicants:	1
Application deadline:	February 15
Total amount awarded:	$2,000

Contact:
AWS Foundation, Inc.
Attn: Scholarships
550 Northwest LeJeune Road
Miami, FL 33126
Phone: 800-443-9353 ext. 250
Fax: 305-443-7559
Web: www.aws.org/foundation/scholarships

Donald and Shirley Hastings National Scholarship

Type of award: Scholarship, renewable.
Intended use: For undergraduate study at 4-year institution in United States.
Eligibility: Applicant must be at least 18. Applicant must be U.S. citizen.
Basis for selection: Major/career interest in welding. Applicant must demonstrate financial need.
Additional information: Minimum 2.5 GPA. Must show interest in welding engineering or welding engineering technology. Priority given to Iowa, Ohio, or California residents.

Amount of award:	$2,500
Number of awards:	1
Number of applicants:	12
Application deadline:	February 15
Notification begins:	April 1
Total amount awarded:	$2,500

Contact:
American Welding Society Foundation, Inc.
Att: Scholarships
550 Northwest LeJeune Road
Miami, FL 33126
Phone: 800-443-9353
Web: www.aws.org/foundation/scholarships

Donald F. Hastings Scholarship

Type of award: Scholarship, renewable.
Intended use: For sophomore, junior or senior study at 4-year institution in United States.
Eligibility: Applicant must be at least 18. Applicant must be U.S. citizen.

Basis for selection: Major/career interest in welding. Applicant must demonstrate financial need and seriousness of purpose.
Application requirements: Recommendations, transcript, proof of eligibility.
Additional information: Priority given to residents of Ohio and California. Minimum 2.5 GPA.

Amount of award:	$2,500
Number of awards:	1
Number of applicants:	13
Application deadline:	February 15
Notification begins:	April 1
Total amount awarded:	$2,500

Contact:
American Welding Society Foundation, Inc.
Attn: Scholarships
550 Northwest LeJeune Road
Miami, FL 33126
Phone: 800-443-9353
Web: www.aws.org/foundation/scholarships

Edward J. Brady Memorial Scholarship

Type of award: Scholarship, renewable.
Intended use: For sophomore, junior or senior study at 4-year institution.
Eligibility: Applicant must be at least 18. Applicant must be U.S. citizen or Canadian citizen.
Basis for selection: Major/career interest in welding or engineering. Applicant must demonstrate financial need and seriousness of purpose.
Application requirements: Recommendations, essay, transcript, proof of eligibility. Proposed curriculum; brief biography; proof of hands-on welding experience.
Additional information: Interest in pursuing minimum four-year degree in welding engineering or welding engineering technology. Minimum 2.5 GPA.

Amount of award:	$2,500
Number of awards:	1
Number of applicants:	8
Application deadline:	February 15
Notification begins:	April 1
Total amount awarded:	$2,500

Contact:
American Welding Society Foundation, Inc.
Attn: Scholarships
550 Northwest LeJeune Road
Miami, FL 33126
Phone: 800-443-9353
Web: www.aws.org/foundation/scholarships

Howard E. and Wilma J. Adkins Memorial Scholarship

Type of award: Scholarship, renewable.
Intended use: For full-time junior or senior study at 4-year institution.
Eligibility: Applicant must be at least 18. Applicant must be U.S. citizen.
Basis for selection: Major/career interest in welding. Applicant must demonstrate high academic achievement and seriousness of purpose.
Application requirements: Recommendations, transcript, proof of eligibility.
Additional information: Applicant should have interest in pursuing four-year degree in welding engineering or welding

engineering technology. Priority given to residents of Kentucky and Wisconsin. Minimum 3.2 GPA in engineering, scientific, and technical subjects; minimum overall 2.8 GPA.

Amount of award:	$2,500
Number of awards:	1
Number of applicants:	17
Application deadline:	February 15
Notification begins:	April 1
Total amount awarded:	$2,500

Contact:
American Welding Society Foundation Inc.
Attn: Scholarships
550 Northwest LeJeune Road
Miami, FL 33126
Phone: 800-443-9353
Web: www.aws.org/foundation/scholarships

Jack R. Barckhoff Welding Management Scholarship

Type of award: Scholarship.
Intended use: For junior study at 4-year institution.
Designated institutions: Ohio State University.
Eligibility: Applicant must be U.S. citizen.
Basis for selection: Major/career interest in welding. Applicant must demonstrate high academic achievement.
Application requirements: 300-to-500-word essay.
Additional information: Minimum 2.5 GPA.

Amount of award:	$2,500
Number of awards:	2
Number of applicants:	5
Application deadline:	February 15
Notification begins:	April 1
Total amount awarded:	$5,000

Contact:
American Welding Society Foundation
Att: Scholarships
550 Northwest LeJeune Road
Miami, FL 33126
Phone: 800-443-9353
Web: www.aws.org/foundation/scholarships

James A. Turner, Jr. Memorial Scholarship

Type of award: Scholarship, renewable.
Intended use: For full-time sophomore, junior or senior study at accredited 4-year institution.
Eligibility: Applicant must be at least 18. Applicant must be U.S. citizen.
Basis for selection: Major/career interest in welding or business/management/administration. Applicant must demonstrate financial need and seriousness of purpose.
Application requirements: Recommendations, transcript, proof of eligibility. Verification of employment, brief biography, financial aid report, proposed curriculum.
Additional information: Must have interest in pursuing management career in welding. Must work minimum ten hours per week at welding store.

Amount of award:	$3,500
Number of awards:	1
Application deadline:	February 15
Notification begins:	April 1
Total amount awarded:	$3,500

Contact:
American Welding Society Foundation, Inc.
Attn: Scholarships
550 Northwest LeJeune Road
Miami, FL 33126
Phone: 800-443-9353
Web: www.aws.org/foundation/scholarships

John C. Lincoln Memorial Scholarship

Type of award: Scholarship, renewable.
Intended use: For sophomore, junior or senior study at 4-year institution.
Eligibility: Applicant must be at least 18. Applicant must be U.S. citizen.
Basis for selection: Major/career interest in welding. Applicant must demonstrate financial need and seriousness of purpose.
Application requirements: Recommendations, transcript, proof of eligibility.
Additional information: Minimum 2.5 GPA. Priority will be given to those individuals residing or attending school in Ohio or Arizona.

Amount of award:	$3,500
Number of awards:	1
Number of applicants:	14
Application deadline:	February 15
Notification begins:	April 1
Total amount awarded:	$3,500

Contact:
American Welding Society Foundation, Inc.
Attn: Scholarships
550 Northwest LeJeune Road
Miami, FL 33126
Phone: 800-443-9353
Web: www.aws.org/foundation/scholarships

Matsuo Bridge Company Ltd of Japan Scholarship

Type of award: Scholarship.
Intended use: For junior, senior or graduate study at accredited 4-year or graduate institution in United States.
Eligibility: Applicant must be at least 18.
Basis for selection: Major/career interest in welding or engineering, civil.
Application requirements: Recommendations, transcript, proof of eligibility.
Additional information: For students interested in pursuing career in civil engineering, welding engineering, or welding engineering technology. Priority given to applicants residing in California, Texas, Oregon, or Washington. Applicant does not have to be member of American Welding Society but must agree to participate in AWS Foundation or Matsuo Bridge Company sponsored publicity. Minimum 3.0 GPA.

Amount of award:	$2,500
Number of awards:	1
Number of applicants:	7
Application deadline:	February 15
Notification begins:	April 1
Total amount awarded:	$2,500

Contact:
American Welding Society Foundation, Inc.
Attn: Scholarships
550 Northwest LeJeune Road
Miami, FL 33126
Phone: 800-443-9353
Web: www.aws.org/foundation/scholarships

Miller Electric Manufacturing Company Ivic Scholarship

Type of award: Scholarship, renewable.
Intended use: For undergraduate study at accredited vocational, 2-year or 4-year institution in United States.
Eligibility: Applicant must be U.S. citizen.
Basis for selection: Major/career interest in welding. Applicant must demonstrate depth of character, leadership and seriousness of purpose.
Additional information: Competition based on AWS National Welding Trials and World Skills Competition.

Amount of award:	$10,000
Number of awards:	1

Contact:
American Welding Society Foundation, Inc.
Attn: Scholarships
550 Northwest LeJeune Road
Miami, FL 33126
Phone: 800-443-9353
Web: www.aws.org/foundation/scholarships

Miller Electric Mfg. Co. Scholarship

Type of award: Scholarship, renewable.
Intended use: For senior study at 4-year institution.
Eligibility: Applicant must be at least 18. Applicant must be U.S. citizen.
Basis for selection: Major/career interest in welding.
Additional information: Applicant must show interest in welding engineering or welding engineering technology, and have work experience in the welding equipment field. Applicant must have minimum 3.0 GPA.

Amount of award:	$3,000
Number of awards:	2
Number of applicants:	13
Application deadline:	February 15
Notification begins:	April 1
Total amount awarded:	$6,000

Contact:
American Welding Society Foundation, Inc.
Att: Scholarships
550 Northwest LeJeune Road
Miami, FL 33126
Phone: 800-443-9353
Web: www.aws.org/foundation/scholarships

Past Presidents Scholarship

Type of award: Scholarship.
Intended use: For junior, senior, master's or doctoral study at 4-year or graduate institution.
Basis for selection: Major/career interest in welding or engineering. Applicant must demonstrate financial need.
Application requirements: Essay. Essay should be 300-500 words.

Amount of award:	$2,500
Number of awards:	1
Number of applicants:	5
Application deadline:	February 15
Notification begins:	April 1
Total amount awarded:	$2,500

Contact:
American Welding Society Foundation, Inc.
Att: Scholarships
550 Northwest LeJeune Road
Miami, FL 33126
Phone: 800-443-9353
Web: www.aws.org/foundation/scholarships

Praxair International Scholarship

Type of award: Scholarship, renewable.
Intended use: For full-time sophomore, junior or senior study at 4-year institution.
Eligibility: Applicant must be at least 18. Applicant must be U.S. citizen or Canadian citizen.
Basis for selection: Major/career interest in welding. Applicant must demonstrate financial need, leadership and service orientation.
Application requirements: Recommendations, transcript, proof of eligibility.
Additional information: Applicant must have interest in pursuing minimum four-year degree in welding engineering or welding engineering technology. Minimum 2.5 GPA.

Amount of award:	$2,500
Number of awards:	1
Number of applicants:	17
Application deadline:	February 15
Notification begins:	April 1
Total amount awarded:	$2,500

Contact:
American Welding Society Foundation, Inc.
Att: Praxair Scholarship
550 Northwest LeJeune Road
Miami, FL 33126
Phone: 800-443-9353
Web: www.aws.org/foundation/scholarships

Robert L. Peaslee-Detroit Brazing and Soldering Division Scholarship

Type of award: Scholarship, renewable.
Intended use: For junior or senior study at 4-year institution.
Eligibility: Applicant must be at least 18. Applicant must be U.S. citizen.
Basis for selection: Major/career interest in welding.
Application requirements: Recommendations, essay, transcript.
Additional information: Applicant must have 3.0 GPA in engineering courses. Must show interest in pursuing degree in welding engineering or welding technology with emphasis on brazing and soldering application.

Amount of award:	$2,500
Number of awards:	1
Number of applicants:	3
Application deadline:	February 15
Notification begins:	April 1
Total amount awarded:	$2,500

Scholarships

Contact:
American Welding Society Foundation, Inc.
Att: Scholarships
550 Northwest LeJeune Road
Miami, FL 33126
Phone: 800-443-9353
Web: www.aws.org/foundation/scholarships

RWMA Scholarship

Type of award: Scholarship.
Intended use: For full-time junior study at 4-year institution.
Eligibility: Applicant must be U.S. citizen or Canadian citizens.
Basis for selection: Major/career interest in welding or engineering. Applicant must demonstrate high academic achievement.
Application requirements: 500-word-or-less essay.
Additional information: Minimum 3.0 GPA.

Amount of award:	$2,500
Number of awards:	1
Number of applicants:	4
Application deadline:	February 15
Notification begins:	April 1

Contact:
American Welding Society Foundation, Inc.
Att: Scholarships
550 Northwest LeJeune Road
Miami, FL 33126
Phone: 800-443-9353
Web: www.aws.org/foundation/scholarships

William A. and Ann M. Brothers Scholarship

Type of award: Scholarship, renewable.
Intended use: For full-time undergraduate study at accredited 4-year institution.
Eligibility: Applicant must be at least 18. Applicant must be U.S. citizen.
Basis for selection: Major/career interest in welding. Applicant must demonstrate financial need.
Additional information: Applicant must have minimum 2.5 GPA. Priority will be given to those individuals residing or attending schools in Ohio.

Amount of award:	$3,500
Number of awards:	1
Number of applicants:	12
Application deadline:	February 15
Notification begins:	April 1
Total amount awarded:	$3,500

Contact:
American Welding Society Foundation
Att: Scholarships
550 Northwest LeJeune Road
Miami, FL 33126
Phone: 800-443-9353 ext. 461
Web: www.aws.org/foundation/scholarships

William B. Howell Memorial Scholarship

Type of award: Scholarship, renewable.
Intended use: For full-time undergraduate study at accredited 4-year institution in United States.
Eligibility: Applicant must be at least 18. Applicant must be U.S. citizen.

Basis for selection: Major/career interest in welding.
Applicant must demonstrate financial need.
Application requirements: Recommendations, transcript, proof of eligibility.
Additional information: Minimum 2.5 GPA required. Priority given to residents of Florida, Michigan, and Ohio. Applicant does not have to be a member of the American Welding Society.

Amount of award:	$2,500
Number of awards:	1
Number of applicants:	14
Application deadline:	February 15
Notification begins:	April 1
Total amount awarded:	$2,500

Contact:
American Welding Society Foundation, Inc.
Attn: Scholarships
550 Northwest LeJeune Road
Miami, FL 33126
Phone: 800-443-9353
Web: www.aws.org

Annie's Homegrown

Annie's Homegrown Sustainable Agriculture Scholarships

Type of award: Scholarship.
Intended use: For full-time undergraduate or graduate study in United States.
Basis for selection: Major/career interest in agriculture. Applicant must demonstrate high academic achievement.
Application requirements: Recommendations, essay, transcript.
Additional information: Award amount varies. Application and more information available on Website.

Number of awards:	8
Number of applicants:	100
Application deadline:	October 31
Notification begins:	March 1
Total amount awarded:	$50,000

Contact:
Annie's Homegrown Scholarship
564 Gateway Drive
Napa, CA 94558
Web: www.annies.com/sustainable_agriculture_scholarship

AOPA Air Safety Foundation

Donald Burnside Memorial Scholarship

Type of award: Scholarship.
Intended use: For junior or senior study at 4-year institution.
Eligibility: Applicant must be U.S. citizen.
Basis for selection: Major/career interest in aviation. Applicant must demonstrate financial need.
Application requirements: Essay, transcript.

Additional information: Minimum 3.25 GPA. Must be enrolled in a baccalaureate level, non-engineering aviation degree program at a four-year institution. Application available on Website. Submit original plus seven copies of application packet.

Amount of award:	$1,000
Number of awards:	1
Application deadline:	March 31
Notification begins:	July 1

Contact:
Dr. Mark Sherman, Chair and Flight Center Director
Farmingdale State College, 107 Lupton Hall
2350 Broadhollow Road
Farmingdale, NY 11735
Phone: 301-695-2000
Fax: 301-695-2375
Web: www.aopa.org/asf/about/scholarship/burnside.html

AP Los Angeles

Associated Press/APTRA-Clete Roberts Memorial Journalism Scholarship

Type of award: Scholarship.
Intended use: For sophomore, junior, senior or graduate study at 4-year or graduate institution in United States. Designated institutions: Colleges and universities in California, Nevada, Hawaii, Arizona, New Mexico, Idaho, Washington, Colorado, Utah, Montana, Wyoming and Alaska.
Basis for selection: Major/career interest in journalism or radio/television/film. Applicant must demonstrate financial need, high academic achievement and seriousness of purpose.
Application requirements: Essay. May submit examples of broadcast-related work.
Additional information: Open to students pursuing career in broadcast journalism. Applications must be typed and mailed; no e-mailed or faxed submissions accepted. Application deadline in December; see Website for exact date and more information.

Amount of award:	$1,500
Number of awards:	1
Notification begins:	January 1
Total amount awarded:	$6,000

Contact:
AP Los Angeles
Jeff Wilson
221 S. Figueroa St., Suite 300
Los Angeles, CA 90012
Web: www.aptra.com

Appaloosa Youth Foundation

Appaloosa Youth Foundation Educational Scholarships

Type of award: Scholarship, renewable.

Intended use: For full-time undergraduate or graduate study at accredited postsecondary institution in United States.
Eligibility: Applicant must be U.S. citizen or permanent resident.
Basis for selection: Applicant must demonstrate high academic achievement, leadership and service orientation.
Application requirements: Recommendations, essay, transcript, proof of eligibility. Photo, SAT/ACT scores.
Additional information: Applicant must be member of Appaloosa Horse Club or Appaloosa Youth Association. Must be involved in the Appaloosa industry and have general knowledge and accomplishments in horsemanship. One scholarship requires intent to pursue equine-related studies. GPA of 3.5 for one scholarship, GPA of 2.5 for other scholarships.

Amount of award:	$1,000-$2,000
Number of awards:	7
Application deadline:	June 1
Notification begins:	July 15

Contact:
Appaloosa Youth Foundation Scholarship Committee
2720 Pullman Road
Moscow, ID 83843
Phone: 208-882-5578 ext. 264
Fax: 208-882-8150
Web: www.appaloosa.com

Arizona Board of Regents

All-Arizona Academic Team

Type of award: Scholarship.
Intended use: For undergraduate study at postsecondary institution. Designated institutions: Arizona State University, Northern Arizona University, University of Arizona.
Eligibility: Applicant must be U.S. citizen or permanent resident residing in Arizona.
Application requirements: Proof of eligibility, nomination by Arizona community college.
Additional information: Award includes stipend between $500 and $1,000. Application deadline in late fall.

Amount of award:	Full tuition
Number of awards:	70

Contact:
Arizona Board of Regents
2020 North Central Avenue
Suite 230
Phoenix, AZ 85004-4593
Phone: 602-229-2500
Fax: 602-229-2555
Web: www.azregents.edu

Arizona Tuition Scholarships for Children/Spouses of Slain Public Servants

Type of award: Scholarship, renewable.
Intended use: For undergraduate study at accredited postsecondary institution. Designated institutions: Arizona State University, Northern Arizona University, University of Arizona.
Eligibility: Applicant must be U.S. citizen or permanent resident residing in Arizona. Applicant's parent must have been killed or disabled in work-related accident as firefighter, police officer or public safety officer.

Application requirements: Proof of eligibility.
Additional information: Applicant whose spouse was killed in work-related accident as Arizona firefighter, peace officer, or emergency paramedic also eligible. Students must meet university admissions criteria and maintain satisfactory academic progress to renew. Scholarship may also cover summer courses.

    Amount of award: Full tuition
Contact:
Arizona Board of Regents
2020 North Central Avenue
Suite 230
Phoenix, AZ 85004-4593
Phone: 602-229-2500
Fax: 602-229-2555
Web: www.azregents.edu

High Honors Endorsement Tuition Scholarship

Type of award: Scholarship, renewable.
Intended use: For undergraduate study at accredited postsecondary institution. Designated institutions: Arizona State University, Northern Arizona University, University of Arizona.
Eligibility: Applicant must be U.S. citizen or permanent resident residing in Arizona.
Basis for selection: Applicant must demonstrate high academic achievement.
Application requirements: Proof of eligibility, nomination by Arizona public high school.
Additional information: Minimum 3.5 GPA. Must complete 16 Core Competency courses with a B or better and exceed standards of all three Arizona Instrument Measuring Standards tests. Application deadline in early spring.

    Amount of award: Full tuition
Contact:
Arizona Board of Regents
2020 North Central Avenue
Suite 230
Phoenix, AZ 85004-4593
Phone: 602-229-2500
Fax: 602-229-2555
Web: www.azregents.edu

Arkansas Department of Higher Education

Academic Challenge Scholarship

Type of award: Scholarship, renewable.
Intended use: For full-time undergraduate study at postsecondary institution. Designated institutions: Approved Arkansas colleges and universities.
Eligibility: Applicant must be high school senior. Applicant must be U.S. citizen or permanent resident residing in Arkansas.
Basis for selection: Applicant must demonstrate financial need.
Application requirements: Transcript. ACT scores and FAFSA.
Additional information: Award is renewable up to four years, provided student maintains minimum 2.5 GPA and at least 30 credit hours per academic year. Applications available online or from the Department of Higher Education.

Amount of award: $2,500-$5,000
Application deadline: June 1
Contact:
Arkansas Department of Higher Education
114 East Capitol Avenue
Little Rock, AR 72201-3818
Phone: 501-371-2000
Web: www.adhe.edu

Governor's Scholars Program

Type of award: Scholarship, renewable.
Intended use: For full-time undergraduate study at postsecondary institution. Designated institutions: Approved Arkansas colleges and universities.
Eligibility: Applicant must be high school senior. Applicant must be U.S. citizen or permanent resident residing in Arkansas.
Basis for selection: Applicant must demonstrate high academic achievement and leadership.
Additional information: Governor's Distinguished Scholars must have at least 32 ACT or 1410 SAT and minimum 3.5 GPA or have been selected as National Merit or National Achievement Finalist. Governor's Distinguished Scholars receive award equal to tuition, fees, room, and board up to $10,000 per year. One Governor's Scholarship award per county given to applicants who do not meet Governor's Distinguished Scholars criteria. Governor's Scholars must have minimum 3.5 GPA or 27 ACT or 1220 SAT and receive award of $4,000. Awards renewable up to four years if Distinguished Scholars maintain minimum 3.25 GPA and Governor's Scholars maintain minimum 3.0 GPA and at least 30 credit hours per year. Visit Website for more information.

    Amount of award: $4,000-$10,000
    Number of awards: 375
    Application deadline: February 1
Contact:
Arkansas Department of Higher Education
Attn: Governor's Scholars Program
114 East Capitol Avenue
Little Rock, AR 72201-3818
Phone: 501-371-2000
Web: www.adhe.edu

Law Enforcement Officers' Dependents Scholarship

Type of award: Scholarship, renewable.
Intended use: For undergraduate study at accredited vocational, 2-year or 4-year institution in United States. Designated institutions: Public schools in Arkansas.
Eligibility: Applicant must be U.S. citizen or permanent resident residing in Arkansas.
Application requirements: Proof of eligibility.
Additional information: Applicant must be dependent or spouse of one of the following who was killed or permanently disabled in line of duty: law enforcement officer; firefighter; sheriff; constable; game warden; certain state highway, forestry, correction, or park employees; EMT; Department of Community Punishment employee. Dependent child applicant may be no older than 23; no age restriction for spouse, but must not be remarried. Award is for tuition, fees, and room and is for up to eight semesters. Must maintain 2.0 GPA. Visit Website for more information and application.

    Amount of award: Full tuition
    Application deadline: June 1, November 1

Contact:
Arkansas Department of Higher Education
114 East Capitol Avenue
Little Rock, AR 72201-3818
Phone: 501-371-2000
Web: www.adhe.edu

Military Dependents Scholarship Program

Type of award: Scholarship, renewable.
Intended use: For full-time undergraduate study at vocational, 2-year or 4-year institution in United States. Designated institutions: Public schools in Arkansas.
Eligibility: Applicant must be U.S. citizen or permanent resident residing in Arkansas. Applicant must be dependent of disabled veteran or POW/MIA; or spouse of disabled veteran or POW/MIA who served in the Army, Air Force, Marines, Navy, Coast Guard or Reserves/National Guard. Parent/spouse may also have been killed in action or killed on ordinance delivery. All incidents must have occurred while on active duty after 1/1/60. Parent/spouse must be AR resident or must have been at time of enlistment. Dependent must have been born, adopted, or in legal custody of veteran under whom he/she is applying.
Application requirements: Proof of eligibility.
Additional information: Award for tuition, fees, room, and board. Renewable up to four years. Must maintain 2.0 GPA. Visit Website for more information and application.
>   **Amount of award:**   Full tuition
>   **Application deadline:**   June 1, November 1

Contact:
Arkansas Department of Higher Education
Attn: Military Dependents Scholarship Program
114 East Capitol Avenue
Little Rock, AR 72201-3818
Phone: 501-371-2000
Web: www.adhe.edu

Second Effort Scholarship

Type of award: Scholarship, renewable.
Intended use: For undergraduate study at postsecondary institution.
Eligibility: Applicant must be at least 18, returning adult student. Applicant must be U.S. citizen or permanent resident residing in Arkansas.
Basis for selection: Applicant must demonstrate high academic achievement.
Additional information: Applicant must not have graduated from high school. Must have scored in top ten on GED test in previous calendar year. Students do not apply for this award; top ten scorers are contacted directly by Arkansas Department of Higher Education. Award renewable up to four years (or equivalent if student is enrolled part-time), provided student maintains minimum 2.5 GPA.
>   **Amount of award:** $1,000
>   **Number of awards:**   10

Contact:
Arkansas Department of Higher Education
114 East Capitol Avenue
Little Rock, AR 72201-3818
Phone: 501-371-2000
Web: www.adhe.edu

Workforce Improvement Grant

Type of award: Scholarship.

Intended use: For undergraduate study at postsecondary institution. Designated institutions: Not-for-profit institutions in AR.
Eligibility: Applicant must be at least 24, returning adult student. Applicant must be U.S. citizen or permanent resident residing in Arkansas.
Basis for selection: Applicant must demonstrate financial need.
Application requirements: FAFSA.
Additional information: Must be Arkansas resident at least six months before applying. Students enrolled part time will have grants prorated. Must have unmet need after any Pell Grant awarded. Application deadline determined by each institution for its students. Students apply by completing FAFSA. Must have graduated high school or have GED.
>   **Amount of award:** $2,000

Contact:
Arkansas Department of Higher Education
144 East Capitol Avenue
Little Rock, AR 72201
Phone: 501-371-2000
Web: www.adhe.edu

Armed Forces Communications and Electronics Association

AFCEA General Emmett Paige Scholarship

Type of award: Scholarship.
Intended use: For full-time sophomore, junior or senior study at accredited 4-year institution in United States.
Eligibility: Applicant must be U.S. citizen. Applicant must be in military service or veteran; or dependent of active service person or veteran; or spouse of active service person or veteran.
Basis for selection: Major/career interest in aerospace; computer/information sciences; engineering, chemical; physics; mathematics; engineering, electrical/electronic; education; technology or information systems. Applicant must demonstrate high academic achievement, depth of character, leadership, patriotism, seriousness of purpose and service orientation.
Application requirements: Recommendations, transcript, proof of eligibility. Copy of discharge form DD214, certificate of service, or facsimile of applicant's current DOD or Coast Guard identification card.
Additional information: Veterans enrolled as freshmen eligible to apply, but all other applicants must be in at least their sophomore year. Must have minimum 3.0 GPA. Majors directly related to support of U.S. intelligence enterprises or national security with relevance to the mission of AFCEA also eligible. Visit Website for application and deadline.
>   **Amount of award:** $2,000
>   **Number of awards:**   10
>   **Application deadline:**   March 1
>   **Notification begins:**   June 1
>   **Total amount awarded:** $20,000

Contact:
AFCEA Educational Foundation
Attn: Mr. Fred H. Rainbow
4400 Fair Lakes Court
Fairfax, VA 22033-3899
Phone: 703-631-6149
Fax: 703-631-4693
Web: www.afcea.org/scholarships

AFCEA General John A. Wickham Scholarship

Type of award: Scholarship.
Intended use: For full-time junior or senior study at accredited 4-year institution in United States.
Eligibility: Applicant must be U.S. citizen.
Basis for selection: Major/career interest in aerospace; engineering, computer; computer/information sciences; physics; mathematics; engineering, electrical/electronic; engineering, chemical; education; technology or information systems. Applicant must demonstrate high academic achievement, depth of character, leadership, patriotism, seriousness of purpose and service orientation.
Application requirements: Recommendations, transcript.
Additional information: Majors directly related to support of U.S. intelligence enterprises or national security with relevance to mission of AFCEA also eligible. Minimum 3.5 GPA. Visit Website for application and deadline.

Amount of award:	$2,000
Number of awards:	12
Application deadline:	May 1
Notification begins:	June 1
Total amount awarded:	$30,000

Contact:
AFCEA Educational Foundation
Attn: Mr. Fred H. Rainbow
4400 Fair Lakes Court
Fairfax, VA 22033-3899
Phone: 800-336-4583 ext. 6149
Fax: 703-631-4693
Web: www.afcea.org/scholarships

AFCEA ROTC Scholarship

Type of award: Scholarship.
Intended use: For full-time sophomore or junior study at accredited 4-year institution in United States.
Eligibility: Applicant must be U.S. citizen.
Basis for selection: Major/career interest in aerospace; engineering; computer/information sciences; education; physics; mathematics; technology; electronics; foreign languages or international studies. Applicant must demonstrate financial need, high academic achievement, depth of character, leadership, patriotism, seriousness of purpose and service orientation.
Application requirements: Recommendations, transcript, nomination by professor of military science, naval science, aerospace studies, or designated commanding officer.
Additional information: Applicant must be enrolled in ROTC. Majors directly related to support of U.S. national security enterprises with relevance to mission of AFCEA also eligible.

Amount of award:	$2,000
Number of awards:	50
Application deadline:	March 1
Notification begins:	June 1
Total amount awarded:	$112,000

Contact:
Armed Forces Communications and Electronics Association
Mr. Fred H. Rainbow
4400 Fair Lakes Court
Fairfax, VA 22033-3899
Phone: 703-631-6149
Fax: 703-631-4693
Web: www.afcea.org/scholarships

AFCEA Scholarship for Working Professionals

Type of award: Scholarship.
Intended use: For half-time sophomore, junior, senior or graduate study at accredited 2-year, 4-year or graduate institution in United States.
Eligibility: Applicant must be U.S. citizen.
Basis for selection: Major/career interest in engineering, electrical/electronic; aerospace; engineering, computer; information systems; physics; mathematics or engineering, chemical. Applicant must demonstrate high academic achievement.
Application requirements: Recommendations, transcript, proof of eligibility.
Additional information: Scholarship awarded to part-time students pursuing eligible undergraduate or graduate program while currently employed in science or technology disciplines related to AFCEA. Undergraduate students must be enrolled in at least two classes per semester with major in science or technology degree program. Graduate students must have completed at least two postgraduate-level classes before deadline. Minimum 3.0 GPA required.

Amount of award:	$2,000
Number of awards:	2
Application deadline:	September 1

Contact:
Armed Forces Communications and Electronics Association
Mr. Fred H. Rainbow
4400 Fair Lakes Court
Fairfax, VA 22033-3899
Phone: 703-631-6149
Fax: 703-631-4693
Web: www.afcea.org/scholarships

Disabled War Veterans Scholarship

Type of award: Scholarship, renewable.
Intended use: For undergraduate study at accredited 2-year or 4-year institution in United States.
Eligibility: Applicant must be in military service or disabled while on active duty during Middle East War. Must be disabled because of wounds received during service in Enduring Freedom -- Afghanistan or Iraqi Freedom Operations.
Basis for selection: Major/career interest in aerospace; computer/information sciences; education; engineering, computer; engineering, electrical/electronic; information systems; mathematics; military science; physics or technology. Applicant must demonstrate financial need, high academic achievement and leadership.
Application requirements: Recommendations, transcript.
Additional information: Students of accredited distance-learning programs also eligible. Majors directly related to the support of U.S. intelligence or national security enterprises with relevance to the mission of AFCEA also eligible. Visit Website for application and deadline.

Amount of award:	$2,500
Number of awards:	6

Contact:
AFCEA Educational Foundation
Attn: Mr. Fred H. Rainbow
440 Fair Lakes Court
Fairfax, VA 22033
Phone: 703-631-6149
Fax: 703-631-4693
Web: www.afcea.org/scholarships

Distance Learning/Online Scholarship

Type of award: Scholarship.
Intended use: For full-time junior, senior or graduate study at accredited 4-year or graduate institution in United States.
Eligibility: Applicant must be U.S. citizen.
Basis for selection: Major/career interest in mathematics; physics; engineering, electrical/electronic; engineering, chemical; computer/information sciences; aerospace; education or technology. Applicant must demonstrate high academic achievement.
Application requirements: Recommendations, transcript.
Additional information: Must be pursuing degree by means of distance-learning or online program. Majors directly related to support of U.S. intelligence enterprises or national security with relevance to mission of AFCEA also eligible. Undergraduate applicants must have completed two semesters of calculus. Graduate applicants must have completed at least one full semester of work and be enrolled full-time at time of application.

Amount of award:	$2,000
Number of awards:	2
Application deadline:	June 1
Total amount awarded:	$2,000

Contact:
AFCEA Educational Foundation
Attn: Mr. Fred H. Rainbow
4400 Fair Lakes Court
Fairfax, VA 22033-3899
Phone: 703-631-6149
Fax: 703-631-4693
Web: www.afcea.org/scholarships

Intelligence Scholarships

Type of award: Scholarship, renewable.
Intended use: For full-time junior, senior or graduate study at accredited 4-year or graduate institution in United States.
Eligibility: Applicant must be U.S. citizen.
Basis for selection: Major/career interest in international relations or foreign languages. Applicant must demonstrate financial need, high academic achievement and leadership.
Application requirements: Recommendations, transcript.
Additional information: Minimum 3.0 GPA. Must be majoring in field directly related to support of U.S. intelligence or homeland security enterprises. Visit Website for deadline and application.

Amount of award:	$2,250-$5,000
Number of awards:	6

Contact:
AFCEA Educational Foundation
Attn: Mr. Fred H. Rainbow
4400 Fair Lakes Court
Fairfax, VA 22033
Phone: 703-631-6149
Fax: 703-631-4693
Web: www.afcea.org/scholarships

Marine Corps Sgt. Jeannette L. Winters Memorial Scholarship

Type of award: Scholarship.
Intended use: For sophomore, junior or senior study at accredited 4-year institution in United States.
Eligibility: Applicant must be in military service or veteran in the Marines.
Basis for selection: Major/career interest in aerospace; computer/information sciences; mathematics; engineering, chemical; physics; engineering, electrical/electronic; technology; electronics; education or information systems. Applicant must demonstrate high academic achievement, depth of character, leadership, patriotism, seriousness of purpose and service orientation.
Application requirements: Recommendations, transcript, proof of eligibility. Copy of Certificate of Service, Discharge Form DD214, or facsimile of a current Department of Defense Identification Card.
Additional information: Minimum 3.0 GPA. Visit Website for application.

Amount of award:	$2,000
Number of awards:	1
Application deadline:	September 1
Notification begins:	October 15
Total amount awarded:	$2,000

Contact:
AFCEA Educational Foundation
Attn: Mr. Fred H. Rainbow
4400 Fair Lakes Court
Fairfax, VA 22033-3899
Phone: 800-336-4583 ext. 6149
Fax: 703-631-4693
Web: www.afcea.org/scholarships

MG Eugene C. Renzi/ManTech International Corporation Scholarship for Math and Science Teachers

Type of award: Scholarship, renewable.
Intended use: For full-time sophomore, junior or senior study at accredited postsecondary institution in United States.
Eligibility: Applicant must be U.S. citizen.
Basis for selection: Major/career interest in education. Applicant must demonstrate high academic achievement.
Application requirements: Recommendations, transcript.
Additional information: Award for students who intend to teach science, mathematics, or information technology at a U.S. middle or secondary school. Graduate students must be enrolled in at least two (semester-equivalent) classes. Minimum 3.0 GPA. Application available online.

Amount of award:	$2,500
Number of awards:	2
Number of applicants:	1
Application deadline:	June 1
Total amount awarded:	$2,500

Contact:
AFCEA Educational Foundation
Mr. Fred H. Rainbow
4400 Fair Lakes Court
Fairfax, VA 22033-3899
Phone: 703-631-6149
Fax: 703-631-4693
Web: www.afcea.org/scholarships

STEM Teacher Scholarships

Type of award: Scholarship.
Intended use: For full-time junior, senior or graduate study at accredited postsecondary institution in United States.
Eligibility: Applicant must be U.S. citizen.
Basis for selection: Major/career interest in education. Applicant must demonstrate high academic achievement.
Application requirements: Recommendations, transcript.
Additional information: Minimum 3.0 GPA. Intended for students pursuing an education degree for the purpose of teaching science, technology, engineering or mathematics at a U.S. middle or secondary school. Each graduating recipient receives a $1,000 AFCEA Science Teaching Tools grant per year for 3 years, on the condition they remain teaching a STEM subject.

Amount of award:	$5,000
Number of awards:	35
Application deadline:	June 10

Contact:
AFCEA Educational Foundation
Mr. Fred H. Rainbow
4400 Fair Lakes Court
Fairfax, VA 22033-3899
Phone: 703-631-6149
Fax: 703-631-4693
Web: www.afcea.org/scholarships

VADM Samuel L. Gravely Jr. USN (Ret.) Memorial Scholarship

Type of award: Scholarship.
Intended use: For junior or senior study at accredited 2-year or 4-year institution in United States. Designated institutions: Historically black colleges and universities.
Basis for selection: Major/career interest in aerospace; engineering, electrical/electronic; engineering, computer; information systems; computer/information sciences; physics or mathematics. Applicant must demonstrate financial need, high academic achievement and leadership.
Application requirements: Recommendations, transcript.
Additional information: Distance-learning or online programs affiliated with HCBUs are eligible. Majors directly related to the support of U.S. intelligence or homeland security enterprises with relevance to the mission of AFCEA are also eligible. Special consideration given to military enlisted candidates/military veterans.

Amount of award:	$5,000
Number of awards:	2
Application deadline:	September 1

Contact:
AFCEA Educational Foundation
Mr. Fred H. Rainbow
4400 Fair Lakes Court
Fairfax, VA 22033-3899
Phone: 703-631-6149
Fax: 703-631-4693
Web: www.afcea.org/scholarships

Vice Admiral Jerry O. Tuttle, USN (Ret.) and Mrs. Barbara A. Tuttle Science and Technology Scholarship

Type of award: Scholarship.
Intended use: For full-time junior or senior study at accredited postsecondary institution in United States.

Eligibility: Applicant must be U.S. citizen.
Basis for selection: Major/career interest in computer/information sciences; engineering, computer; technology; information systems or engineering, electrical/electronic.
Application requirements: Recommendations, transcript.
Additional information: Priority consideration given to military enlisted candidates. Visit Website for deadline.

Amount of award:	$2,000
Number of awards:	2
Application deadline:	November 15

Contact:
AFCEA Educational Foundation
Attn: Mr. Fred H. Rainbow
4400 Fair Lakes Court
Fairfax, VA 22033-3899
Phone: 703-631-6149
Fax: 703-631-4693
Web: www.afcea.org/scholarships

William E. "Buck" Bragunier Scholarship for Outstanding Leadership

Type of award: Scholarship.
Intended use: For full-time junior or senior study at accredited 4-year institution. Designated institutions: Colleges or universities in the greater San Diego, California geographical area.
Eligibility: Applicant must be U.S. citizen residing in California.
Basis for selection: Major/career interest in aerospace; computer/information sciences; engineering, chemical; engineering, electrical/electronic; information systems; mathematics; physics or technology. Applicant must demonstrate leadership.
Application requirements: Recommendations, transcript.
Additional information: Minimum 3.5 GPA. Applicants qualified for General Wickham Scholarship are eligible. Distance learning programs not eligible. Majors directly related to the support of U.S. intelligence enterprises or national security with relevance to the mission of AFCEA will also be eligible.

Amount of award:	$2,000
Number of awards:	2
Application deadline:	May 1
Notification begins:	June 1

Contact:
AFCEA Educational Foundation
Attn: Mr. Fred H. Rainbow
4400 Fair Lakes Court
Fairfax, VA 22033
Phone: 800-336-4583 ext. 6149
Fax: 703-631-4693
Web: www.afcea.org/scholarships

Armenian General Benevolent Union (AGBU)

Performing Arts Fellowships

Type of award: Scholarship, renewable.
Intended use: For full-time undergraduate or graduate study in United States or Canada.

Eligibility: Applicant must be Armenian. Applicant must be institutions worldwide except for those located in Armenia.
Basis for selection: Competition/talent/interest in performing arts. Major/career interest in performing arts. Applicant must demonstrate financial need, high academic achievement and service orientation.
Application requirements: Recommendations, transcript. Resume, one passport-size photograph, enrollment verification/ acceptance letter, bursar's receipt, financial award letter, most recent federal tax return (U.S. applicants only), CD of or link to most current recording (if applicable).
Additional information: Minimum 3.5 GPA. Number of awards varies based on funding. Visit Website for application.

Amount of award:	$1,000-$5,000
Number of applicants:	40
Application deadline:	May 15
Notification begins:	August 31
Total amount awarded:	$72,000

Contact:
Armenian General Benevolent Union
Attn: Scholarship Program
55 E. 59th Street, 7th Floor
New York, NY 10022-1112
Phone: 212-319-6383
Fax: 212-319-6507
Web: www.agbu.org

ARMY Emergency Relief

MG James Ursano Scholarship Program

Type of award: Scholarship, renewable.
Intended use: For full-time undergraduate study at accredited postsecondary institution.
Eligibility: Applicant must be single, no older than 22. Applicant must be dependent of active service person, veteran or deceased veteran who serves or served in the Army.
Basis for selection: Applicant must demonstrate financial need, high academic achievement and leadership.
Application requirements: Transcript, proof of eligibility. Student Aid Report (SAR).
Additional information: Applicant must be registered in DEERS. Must maintain 2.0 GPA. Number of awards varies. Application may be downloaded from Website.

Amount of award:	$500-$3,500
Number of applicants:	6,700
Application deadline:	March 1
Notification begins:	May 25
Total amount awarded:	$10,000,000

Contact:
ARMY Emergency Relief
MG James Ursano Scholarship Program
200 Stovall Street
Alexandria, VA 22332-0600
Phone: 703-428-0035
Fax: 703-325-7183
Web: www.aerhq.org

The Art Institutes

Best Teen Chef Culinary Scholarship Competition

Type of award: Scholarship.
Intended use: For undergraduate study at 2-year or 4-year institution in United States. Designated institutions: Art Institute schools offering culinary arts programs.
Eligibility: Applicant must be high school senior. Applicant must be U.S. citizen, Canadian citizen (excluding Quebec).
Basis for selection: Competition/talent/interest in culinary arts, based on meal preparation ability and originality. Major/career interest in culinary arts or hotel/restaurant management.
Application requirements: Essay, transcript. Recipe.
Additional information: Award amount varies depending on placement in competition. First-place winner will compete in national event slated for May. Minimum high school GPA of 2.0. Visit Website for deadline and application.

Number of applicants:	265

Contact:
The Art Institutes
210 Sixth Avenue, 33rd Floor
Pittsburgh, PA 15222-2603
Phone: 888-624-0300
Fax: 412-562-1732
Web: www.artinstitutes.edu/btc

Arthur and Doreen Parrett Scholarship Trust Fund

Arthur and Doreen Parrett Scholarship

Type of award: Scholarship, renewable.
Intended use: For full-time sophomore, junior, senior, master's, doctoral or first professional study at accredited postsecondary institution.
Eligibility: Applicant must be residing in Washington.
Basis for selection: Major/career interest in science, general; engineering; dentistry or medicine. Applicant must demonstrate financial need and high academic achievement.
Application requirements: Recommendations, transcript.
Additional information: Applicants must have completed first year of college. Include SASE with inquiries, and information will be forwarded.

Amount of award:	$2,500-$3,600
Number of awards:	10
Number of applicants:	50
Application deadline:	January 31

Contact:
Arthur and Doreen Parrett Scholarship Trust Fund
c/o U.S. Bank - Trust Dept.
1420 5th Avenue, Suite 2100
Seattle, WA 98101

The ASCAP Foundation

Morton Gould Young Composer Awards

Type of award: Scholarship, renewable.
Intended use: For non-degree study.
Eligibility: Applicant must be no older than 29.
Basis for selection: Competition/talent/interest in music performance/composition. Major/career interest in music.
Application requirements: Reproduction of original score, biographical and educational information, list of compositions to date, SASE, CD of composition (if available).
Additional information: Number of awards varies. Applicant must not have reached 30th birthday by January 1 and may submit only one composition. International applicants must have student visa.

Amount of award:	$750-$2,500
Number of applicants:	680
Application deadline:	March 1
Notification begins:	April 1
Total amount awarded:	$45,000

Contact:
ASCAP Foundation Morton Gould Young Composer Awards
c/o Frances Richard
One Lincoln Plaza
New York, NY 10023
Phone: 212-621-6329
Web: www.ascapfoundation.org

Rudolf Nissim Prize

Type of award: Scholarship.
Intended use: For non-degree study.
Basis for selection: Competition/talent/interest in music performance/composition. Major/career interest in music.
Application requirements: Bound copy of score of one original concert work, composer biography, SASE.
Additional information: Award for work requiring a conductor that has not been performed professionally. Applicant must be concert composer member of ASCAP. Visit Website for specific application requirements and details.

Amount of award:	$5,000
Number of awards:	1
Number of applicants:	230
Application deadline:	November 15
Notification begins:	January 15
Total amount awarded:	$5,000

Contact:
Frances Richard
c/o The ASCAP Foundation/Rudolf Nissim Prize
One Lincoln Plaza
New York, NY 10023
Phone: 212-621-6329
Web: www.ascapfoundation.org

ASCO Numatics

Industrial Automation Engineering College Scholarships

Type of award: Scholarship.

Intended use: For full-time junior, senior or graduate study at accredited 4-year or graduate institution in United States.
Eligibility: Applicant must be U.S. citizen or permanent resident.
Basis for selection: Major/career interest in engineering; engineering, electrical/electronic or engineering, mechanical. Applicant must demonstrate high academic achievement and leadership.
Additional information: For students planning to pursue careers in industrial automation-related disciplines. Engineering department of winner's college also receives $1,000 grant. Minimum 3.2 GPA. Asco Numatics employees and their families are ineligible. Application details and forms available on Website.

Amount of award:	$5,000
Number of awards:	2
Application deadline:	June 30
Total amount awarded:	$10,000

Contact:
ASCO Numatics
50 Hanover Road
Florham Park, NJ 07932
Phone: 973-966-2000
Fax: 973-966-2628
Web: www.asconumatics.com/scholarship

Asian American Journalists Association

Broadcast News Grants

Type of award: Scholarship.
Intended use: For full-time undergraduate study at 4-year institution.
Eligibility: Applicant must be at least 18.
Basis for selection: Major/career interest in journalism or radio/television/film. Applicant must demonstrate financial need.
Application requirements: Recommendations, essay. Resume, proof of age, statement of financial need, and internship verification. Submit original plus three copies of all materials.
Additional information: Applicant must have already secured summer broadcast internship at TV or radio network. Application may be downloaded from Website. AAJA membership encouraged for all applicants and required for awardees. Recent college graduates also eligible.

Amount of award:	$1,000-$2,500
Number of awards:	2
Application deadline:	April 23

Contact:
Asian American Journalists Association
Broadcast News Grants
1182 Market Street, Suite 320
San Francisco, CA 94102
Phone: 415-346-2051 ext. 102
Fax: 415-346-6343
Web: www.aaja.org

Print & Online News Grants

Type of award: Scholarship.
Intended use: For full-time undergraduate study.
Eligibility: Applicant must be at least 18.

Basis for selection: Major/career interest in journalism. Applicant must demonstrate financial need and seriousness of purpose.

Application requirements: Recommendations, essay. Resume, proof of age, statement of financial need, and internship verification. Submit original plus three copies of all material.

Additional information: Applicant may also be recent college graduate. Must have already secured summer internship at print or online company before applying. Must be committed to AAJA's mission. Application may be downloaded from Website. AAJA membership encouraged for all applicants and required for selected interns.

Amount of award:	$1,000-$1,500
Number of awards:	4
Application deadline:	April 23

Contact:
Asian American Journalists Association
Print & Online News Grants
1182 Market Street, Suite 320
San Francisco, CA 94102
Phone: 415-346-2051 ext. 102
Fax: 415-346-6343
Web: www.aaja.org

Stanford Chen Internship Grant

Type of award: Scholarship.
Intended use: For junior, senior or graduate study at 4-year or graduate institution.
Basis for selection: Major/career interest in journalism. Applicant must demonstrate financial need and seriousness of purpose.
Application requirements: Recommendations, essay. Resume, statement of financial need, and internship verification. Original plus three copies of all application materials.
Additional information: Applicant must have already secured internship with small- to medium-size media company (print companies with daily circulation under 100,000 and broadcast markets smaller than top 50). Application may be downloaded from Website. AAJA membership is encouraged for all applicants and required for selected recipients.

Amount of award:	$1,750
Number of awards:	1
Application deadline:	April 23
Total amount awarded:	$1,750

Contact:
Asian American Journalists Association
Stanford Chen Internship Grant
1182 Market Street, Suite 320
San Francisco, CA 94102
Phone: 415-346-2051 ext. 102
Fax: 415-346-6343
Web: www.aaja.org

Asian American Journalists Association, Texas Chapter

AAJA Texas Student Scholarship

Type of award: Scholarship.
Intended use: For undergraduate or graduate study.

Basis for selection: Major/career interest in journalism. Applicant must demonstrate high academic achievement and seriousness of purpose.
Application requirements: Recommendations, essay, transcript. Resume, work samples.
Additional information: Applicant must be resident of or attending school in Texas, Arkansas, Louisiana, Oklahoma, or New Mexico. Must display awareness of Asian-American issues. Visit Website for application.

Amount of award:	$1,000
Number of awards:	1
Application deadline:	May 31
Notification begins:	June 30
Total amount awarded:	$1,000

Contact:
Scott Nishimura Fort Worth Star-Telegram
P.O. Box 1870
Fort Worth, TX 76101
Phone: 817-390-7808
Web: www.aajatexas.org

ASM Materials Education Foundation

ASM Outstanding Scholars Awards

Type of award: Scholarship, renewable.
Intended use: For full-time sophomore, junior or senior study at accredited 4-year institution in or outside United States.
Basis for selection: Major/career interest in engineering, materials or materials science. Applicant must demonstrate high academic achievement.
Application requirements: Recommendations, essay, transcript. Photograph. Resume optional.
Additional information: May also major in metallurgy or related science or engineering disciplines if applicant demonstrates strong interest in materials science. Must be student member of Material Advantage. International student members may apply. Visit Website for application and full details.

Amount of award:	$2,000
Number of awards:	3
Number of applicants:	100
Application deadline:	May 1
Notification begins:	July 15
Total amount awarded:	$6,000

Contact:
ASM Materials Education Foundation
Scholarship Program
9639 Kinsman Road
Materials Park, OH 44073-0002
Phone: 440-338-5151
Fax: 440-338-4634
Web: www.asmfoundation.org

Edward J. Dulis Scholarship

Type of award: Scholarship, renewable.
Intended use: For junior or senior study at accredited 4-year institution in United States or Canada.
Basis for selection: Major/career interest in engineering, materials or materials science. Applicant must demonstrate financial need and high academic achievement.

Application requirements: Recommendations, essay, transcript. Photograph. Resume optional.
Additional information: Applicant may also major in metallurgy or related science or engineering field if interested in materials science. Must be student member of Material Advantage. Visit Website for application and full details.

Amount of award:	$1,500
Number of awards:	1
Application deadline:	May 1
Notification begins:	July 15

Contact:
ASM Materials Education Foundation
Scholarship Program
9639 Kingman Road
Materials Park, OH 44073-0002
Phone: 440-338-5151
Fax: 440-338-4634
Web: www.asmfoundation.org

George A. Roberts Scholarships

Type of award: Scholarship, renewable.
Intended use: For junior or senior study at accredited 4-year institution in United States or Canada.
Basis for selection: Major/career interest in engineering, materials or materials science. Applicant must demonstrate financial need and high academic achievement.
Application requirements: Recommendations, essay, transcript. Photograph, resume optional.
Additional information: Applicant may also major in metallurgy or related science or engineering field if interested in materials science. Must be student member of Material Advantage. Visit Website for application and full details.

Amount of award:	$6,000
Number of awards:	7
Application deadline:	May 1
Notification begins:	July 15
Total amount awarded:	$42,000

Contact:
ASM Materials Education Foundation
Scholarship Program
9639 Kinsman Road
Materials Park, OH 44073-0002
Phone: 440-338-5151
Fax: 440-338-4634
Web: www.asmfoundation.org

John M. Haniak Scholarship

Type of award: Scholarship, renewable.
Intended use: For junior or senior study at accredited 4-year institution in United States or Canada.
Basis for selection: Major/career interest in engineering, materials or materials science. Applicant must demonstrate financial need and high academic achievement.
Application requirements: Recommendations, essay, transcript. Photograph. Resume optional.
Additional information: Applicant may also major in metallurgy or related science or engineering field if interested in materials science. Must be student member of Material Advantage. Visit Website for application and full details.

Amount of award:	$1,500
Number of awards:	1
Application deadline:	May 1
Notification begins:	July 15

Contact:
ASM Materials Education Foundation
Scholarship Program
9639 Kingman Road
Materials Park, OH 44073-0002
Phone: 440-338-5151
Fax: 440-338-4634
Web: www.asmfoundation.org

Lucille & Charles A. Wert Scholarship

Type of award: Scholarship, renewable.
Intended use: For junior or senior study at accredited 4-year institution in United States or Canada.
Basis for selection: Major/career interest in engineering, materials or materials science. Applicant must demonstrate financial need and high academic achievement.
Application requirements: Recommendations, essay, transcript. Photograph, resume optional.
Additional information: Applicant may also major in metallurgy or related science or engineering field if interested in materials science. Must be student member of Material Advantage. Scholarship provides recipient with one-year full tuition up to $10,000. Visit Website for application and full details.

Amount of award:	$10,000
Number of awards:	1
Application deadline:	May 1
Notification begins:	July 15

Contact:
ASM Materials Education Foundation
Scholarship Program
9639 Kingman Road
Materials Park, OH 44073-0002
Phone: 440-338-5151
Fax: 440-338-4634
Web: www.asmfoundation.org

William Park Woodside Founder's Scholarship

Type of award: Scholarship, renewable.
Intended use: For junior or senior study at accredited 4-year institution in United States or Canada.
Basis for selection: Major/career interest in engineering, materials or materials science. Applicant must demonstrate financial need and high academic achievement.
Application requirements: Recommendations, essay, transcript. Photograph. Resume optional.
Additional information: May also have major in metallurgy or related science or engineering discipline if applicant demonstrates strong interest in materials science. Must be Material Advantage student member. Scholarship provides recipient with one-year full tuition, up to $10,000. Visit Website for application and full details.

Amount of award:	$10,000
Number of awards:	1
Application deadline:	May 1
Notification begins:	July 15
Total amount awarded:	$10,000

Contact:
ASM Materials Education Foundation
Scholarship Program
9639 Kinsman Road
Materials Park, OH 44073-0002
Phone: 440-338-5151
Fax: 440-338-4634
Web: www.asmfoundation.org

ASME Auxiliary, Inc.

Agnes Malakate Kezios Scholarship

Type of award: Scholarship.
Intended use: For senior study at 4-year institution in United States. Designated institutions: Schools with ABET-accredited mechanical engineering programs.
Eligibility: Applicant must be U.S. citizen.
Basis for selection: Major/career interest in engineering, mechanical. Applicant must demonstrate financial need, high academic achievement and depth of character.
Application requirements: Recommendations, transcript.
Additional information: For student in final year of undergraduate program in mechanical engineering. American Society of Mechanical Engineers participation preferred. Download application from Website or send SASE or e-mail to request application.

Amount of award:	$2,000
Number of awards:	1
Application deadline:	March 15

Contact:
Sara Sahay
ASME Auxiliary - Undergraduate Scholarships
170 East Opel Drive
Glastonbury, CT 06033
Web: www.asme.org/Education/College/FinancialAid/

Allen J. Baldwin Scholarship

Type of award: Scholarship.
Intended use: For senior study at 4-year institution in United States. Designated institutions: Schools with ABET-accredited mechanical engineering programs.
Eligibility: Applicant must be U.S. citizen.
Basis for selection: Major/career interest in engineering, mechanical. Applicant must demonstrate financial need, high academic achievement and depth of character.
Application requirements: Recommendations, transcript.
Additional information: For student in final year of undergraduate study in mechanical engineering. American Society of Mechanical Engineers participation preferred. Download application from Website or send SASE or e-mail to request application.

Amount of award:	$2,000
Number of awards:	1
Application deadline:	March 15

Contact:
Sara Sahay
ASME Auxiliary - Undergraduate Scholarships
170 East Opel Drive
Glastonbury, CT 06033
Web: www.asme.org/Education/College/FinancialAid/

Berna Lou Cartwright Scholarship

Type of award: Scholarship.
Intended use: For senior study at 4-year institution in United States. Designated institutions: Schools with ABET-accredited mechanical engineering programs.
Eligibility: Applicant must be U.S. citizen.
Basis for selection: Major/career interest in engineering, mechanical. Applicant must demonstrate financial need, high academic achievement and depth of character.
Application requirements: Recommendations, transcript.
Additional information: For student in final year of undergraduate program in mechanical engineering. American Society of Mechanical Engineers participation preferred. Download application from Website or send SASE or email to request application.

Amount of award:	$2,000
Number of awards:	1
Application deadline:	March 15

Contact:
Sara Sahay
ASME Auxiliary - Undergraduate Scholarships
170 East Opel Drive
Glastonbury, CT 06033
Web: www.asme.org/Education/College/FinancialAid/

Charles B. Scharp Scholarship

Type of award: Scholarship.
Intended use: For senior study at 4-year institution in United States. Designated institutions: Schools with ABET-accredited mechanical engineering programs.
Eligibility: Applicant must be U.S. citizen.
Basis for selection: Major/career interest in engineering, mechanical. Applicant must demonstrate financial need, high academic achievement and depth of character.
Application requirements: Recommendations, transcript.
Additional information: For student in final year of undergraduate program in mechanical engineering. ASME participation preferred. Download application from Website or send SASE or email to request application.

Amount of award:	$2,000
Number of awards:	1
Application deadline:	March 15

Contact:
Sara Sahay
ASME Auxiliary - Undergraduate Scholarships
170 East Opel Drive
Glastonbury, CT 06033
Web: www.asme.org/Education/College/FinancialAid/

Sylvia W. Farny Scholarship

Type of award: Scholarship.
Intended use: For senior study at 4-year institution in United States. Designated institutions: Schools with ABET-accredited mechanical engineering programs.
Eligibility: Applicant must be U.S. citizen.
Basis for selection: Major/career interest in engineering, mechanical. Applicant must demonstrate financial need, high academic achievement and depth of character.
Application requirements: Recommendations, transcript.
Additional information: For student in final year of undergraduate study in mechanical engineering. American Society of Mechanical Engineers participation preferred. Download application from Website or send SASE or email to request application.

Amount of award:	$2,000
Number of awards:	1
Application deadline:	March 15

Contact:
Sara Sahay
ASME Auxiliary - Undergraduate Scholarships
170 East Opel Drive
Glastonbury, CT 06033
Web: www.asme.org/Education/College/FinancialAid/

ASME Foundation

American Electric Power Scholarship

Type of award: Scholarship.
Intended use: For junior or senior study at accredited 4-year institution. Designated institutions: Schools with ABET-accredited programs.
Basis for selection: Major/career interest in engineering, mechanical. Applicant must demonstrate high academic achievement.
Application requirements: Recommendations, essay, transcript.
Additional information: Applicant must be American Society of Mechanical Engineers student member in good standing. Preference given to students interested in power engineering or who reside or attend school in American Electric Power service area of Arkansas, Indiana, Kentucky, Louisiana, Michigan, Ohio, Oklahoma, Tennessee, Texas, Virginia, and West Virginia. Apply online.

Amount of award:	$2,500
Number of awards:	1
Application deadline:	March 15
Notification begins:	June 15

Contact:
ASME
Attn: Beth Lefever
Three Park Avenue, 22nd Floor
New York, NY 10016-5990
Phone: 800-843-2763
Web: www.asme.org/education/college/financialaid

ASME Auxiliary/FIRST Clarke Scholarship

Type of award: Scholarship.
Intended use: For full-time freshman study at accredited 4-year institution. Designated institutions: Schools with ABET-accredited programs.
Eligibility: Applicant must be high school senior.
Basis for selection: Major/career interest in engineering, mechanical. Applicant must demonstrate financial need, high academic achievement and leadership.
Application requirements: Transcript, nomination by ASME member, ASME Auxiliary member, or student member active with FIRST. Financial data worksheet.
Additional information: Applicant must be active on FIRST team. One nomination per member. Applicant may also enroll in mechanical engineering technology program. Recipient announced at FIRST National Championship. Visit Website for more information and to download forms.

Amount of award:	$5,000
Number of awards:	5
Application deadline:	March 15

Contact:
ASME
Attn: RuthAnn Bigley
Three Park Avenue, 22nd Floor
New York, NY 10016-5990
Phone: 212-591-7650
Fax: 212-591-7739
Web: www.asme.org/education/college/financialaid

The ASME Foundation Hanley Scholarship

Type of award: Scholarship.
Intended use: For sophomore, junior or senior study at accredited 4-year institution. Designated institutions: Schools with ABET-accredited programs.
Basis for selection: Major/career interest in engineering, mechanical. Applicant must demonstrate financial need and high academic achievement.
Application requirements: Recommendations, essay, transcript.
Additional information: Must be American Society of Mechanical Engineers student member in good standing. Apply online.

Amount of award:	$2,500
Number of awards:	1
Application deadline:	March 15
Notification begins:	June 15

Contact:
ASME
Attn: Beth Lefever
Three Park Avenue, 22nd Floor
New York, NY 10016-5990
Phone: 800-843-2763
Web: www.asme.org/education/college/financialaid

ASME Foundation Scholarships

Type of award: Scholarship.
Intended use: For sophomore, junior or senior study at accredited 4-year institution. Designated institutions: Schools with ABET-accredited programs.
Basis for selection: Major/career interest in engineering, mechanical. Applicant must demonstrate high academic achievement.
Application requirements: Recommendations, essay, transcript.
Additional information: Applicant must be student member of American Society of Mechanical Engineers. Apply online.

Amount of award:	$1,500
Number of awards:	17
Application deadline:	March 15
Notification begins:	June 15

Contact:
ASME
Attn: Beth Lefever
Three Park Avenue, 22nd Floor
New York, NY 10016-5990
Phone: 800-843-2763
Web: www.asme.org/education/college/financialaid

ASME Power Division Scholarship

Type of award: Scholarship.

Intended use: For sophomore, junior or senior study at accredited 4-year institution. Designated institutions: Schools with ABET-accredited programs.

Basis for selection: Major/career interest in engineering, mechanical. Applicant must demonstrate financial need and high academic achievement.

Application requirements: Recommendations, essay, transcript.

Additional information: Applicant must be American Society of Mechanical Engineers student member in good standing and demonstrate special interest in area of fuels, combustion, or the power industry. Apply online.

Amount of award:	$2,700
Number of awards:	1
Application deadline:	March 15
Notification begins:	June 15

Contact:
ASME
Attn: Beth Lefever
Three Park Avenue, 22nd Floor
New York, NY 10016-5990
Phone: 800-843-2763
Web: www.asme.org/education/college/financialaid

Frank and Dorothy Miller ASME Auxiliary Scholarships

Type of award: Scholarship.

Intended use: For full-time sophomore, junior or senior study at accredited 4-year institution in United States. Designated institutions: Schools with ABET-accredited programs.

Eligibility: Applicant must be U.S. citizen, permanent resident or resident of Canada or Mexico.

Basis for selection: Major/career interest in engineering, mechanical. Applicant must demonstrate depth of character and leadership.

Application requirements: Recommendations, essay, transcript.

Additional information: Applicant must be student member of American Society of Mechanical Engineers. Apply online.

Amount of award:	$2,000
Number of awards:	2
Application deadline:	March 15
Notification begins:	June 15

Contact:
ASME
Attn: Beth Lefever
Three Park Avenue, 22nd Floor
New York, NY 10016-5990
Phone: 800-843-2763
Web: www.asme.org/education/college/financialaid

F.W. "Beich" Beichley Scholarship

Type of award: Scholarship.

Intended use: For junior or senior study at accredited 4-year institution in United States. Designated institutions: Schools with ABET-accredited programs.

Basis for selection: Major/career interest in engineering, mechanical. Applicant must demonstrate financial need, high academic achievement, depth of character and leadership.

Application requirements: Recommendations, essay, transcript.

Additional information: Applicant must be member of American Society of Mechanical Engineers. Apply online.

Amount of award:	$2,500
Number of awards:	1
Application deadline:	March 15
Notification begins:	June 15

Contact:
ASME
Attn: Beth Lefever
Three Park Avenue, 22nd Floor
New York, NY 10016-5990
Phone: 800-843-2763
Web: www.asme.org/education/college/financialaid

Garland Duncan Scholarships

Type of award: Scholarship.

Intended use: For junior or senior study at accredited 4-year institution. Designated institutions: Schools with ABET-accredited programs.

Basis for selection: Major/career interest in engineering, mechanical. Applicant must demonstrate financial need, high academic achievement and leadership.

Application requirements: Recommendations, essay, transcript.

Additional information: Applicant must be member of American Society of Mechanical Engineers. Apply online.

Amount of award:	$4,500
Number of awards:	2
Application deadline:	March 15
Notification begins:	June 15

Contact:
ASME
Attn: Beth Lefever
Three Park Avenue, 22nd Floor
New York, NY 10016-5990
Phone: 800-843-2763
Web: www.asme.org/education/college/financialaid

International Gas Turbine Institute (IGTI) Scholarship

Type of award: Scholarship.

Intended use: For sophomore, junior, senior or graduate study at accredited 4-year or graduate institution.

Basis for selection: Major/career interest in aerospace or engineering, mechanical. Applicant must demonstrate high academic achievement.

Application requirements: Recommendations, essay, transcript.

Additional information: Applicant must be American Society of Mechanical Engineers student member in good standing at the time of application. Applicants must be enrolled in baccalaureate or graduate program in their respective country. Preference given to students with work experience or research ties to gas turbine industry.

Amount of award:	$4,000
Number of awards:	1
Application deadline:	March 15
Notification begins:	June 15

Contact:
ASME
Attn: Beth Lefever
Three Park Avenue, 22nd Floor
New York, NY 10016-5990
Phone: 800-843-2763
Web: www.asme.org/education/college/financialaid

John & Elsa Gracik Scholarships

Type of award: Scholarship.
Intended use: For sophomore, junior or senior study at accredited 4-year institution in United States. Designated institutions: Schools with ABET-accredited programs.
Eligibility: Applicant must be U.S. citizen.
Basis for selection: Major/career interest in engineering, mechanical. Applicant must demonstrate financial need, high academic achievement, depth of character and leadership.
Application requirements: Recommendations, essay, transcript.
Additional information: Applicant must be member of American Society of Mechanical Engineers. Apply online.

Amount of award:	$1,600
Number of awards:	18
Application deadline:	March 15
Notification begins:	June 15

Contact:
ASME
Attn: Beth Lefever
Three Park Avenue, 22nd Floor
New York, NY 10016-5990
Phone: 800-843-2763
Web: www.asme.org/education/college/financialaid

Kenneth Andrew Roe Mechanical Engineering Scholarship

Type of award: Scholarship.
Intended use: For junior or senior study at accredited 4-year institution in United States. Designated institutions: Schools with ABET-accredited programs or equivalent.
Eligibility: Applicant must be U.S. citizen, permanent resident or resident of Canada or Mexico.
Basis for selection: Major/career interest in engineering, mechanical. Applicant must demonstrate high academic achievement, depth of character and leadership.
Application requirements: Recommendations, essay, transcript.
Additional information: Applicant must be member of American Society of Mechanical Engineers. Apply online.

Amount of award:	$10,000
Number of awards:	1
Application deadline:	March 15
Notification begins:	June 15

Contact:
ASME
Attn: Beth Lefever
Three Park Avenue, 22nd Floor
New York, NY 10016-5990
Phone: 800-843-2763
Web: www.asme.org/education/college/financialaid

Melvin R. Green Scholarships

Type of award: Scholarship.
Intended use: For junior or senior study at accredited 4-year institution. Designated institutions: Schools with ABET-accredited programs.
Basis for selection: Major/career interest in engineering, mechanical. Applicant must demonstrate financial need, high academic achievement and leadership.
Application requirements: Recommendations, essay, transcript.
Additional information: Applicant must be student member of American Society of Mechanical Engineers. Apply online.

Amount of award:	$4,000
Number of awards:	2
Application deadline:	March 15
Notification begins:	June 15

Contact:
ASME
Attn: Beth Lefever
Three Park Avenue, 22nd Floor
New York, NY 10016-5990
Phone: 800-843-2763
Web: www.asme.org/education/college/financialaid

Stephen T. Kugle Scholarship

Type of award: Scholarship.
Intended use: For junior or senior study at 4-year institution in United States. Designated institutions: Public colleges or universities in District E (Arizona, Arkansas, Colorado, Louisiana, New Mexico, Oklahoma, Texas, Utah, and Wyoming).
Eligibility: Applicant must be U.S. citizen.
Basis for selection: Major/career interest in engineering, mechanical.
Application requirements: Recommendations, essay, transcript.
Additional information: Applicant must be American Society of Mechanical Engineers student member in good standing and U.S. citizen by birth. Minimum 3.0 GPA. Students from University of Texas at Arlington not eligible. Apply online.

Amount of award:	$2,500
Number of awards:	1
Application deadline:	March 15
Notification begins:	June 15

Contact:
ASME
Attn: Beth Lefever
Three Park Avenue, 22nd Floor
New York, NY 10016-5990
Phone: 800-843-2763
Web: www.asme.org/education/college/financialaid

William J. and Marijane E. Adams, Jr. Scholarship

Type of award: Scholarship.
Intended use: For sophomore, junior or senior study at accredited 4-year institution in United States. Designated institutions: Schools with ABET-accredited programs in California, Nevada, and Hawaii.
Eligibility: Applicant must be residing in California, Hawaii or Nevada.
Basis for selection: Major/career interest in engineering, mechanical. Applicant must demonstrate financial need and high academic achievement.
Application requirements: Recommendations, essay, transcript.
Additional information: Minimum 2.5 GPA. Applicant must be member of American Society of Mechanical Engineers. Award designated for student with special interest in product development and design. Apply online.

Amount of award:	$3,500
Number of awards:	1
Application deadline:	March 15
Notification begins:	June 15

Contact:
ASME
Attn: Beth Lefever
Three Park Avenue, 22nd Floor
New York, NY 10016-5990
Phone: 800-843-2763
Web: www.asme.org/education/college/financialaid

Willis F. Thompson Memorial Scholarship

Type of award: Scholarship.
Intended use: For sophomore, junior, senior or graduate study at accredited 4-year institution. Designated institutions: Schools with ABET-accredited programs.
Basis for selection: Major/career interest in engineering, mechanical. Applicant must demonstrate high academic achievement.
Application requirements: Recommendations, essay, transcript.
Additional information: Applicant must be American Society of Mechanical Engineers student member in good standing. Preference given to students who demonstrate interest in advancing field of power generation. Apply online.

Amount of award:	$5,000
Number of awards:	3
Application deadline:	March 15
Notification begins:	June 15

Contact:
ASME
Attn: Beth Lefever
Three Park Avenue, 22nd Floor
New York, NY 10016-5990
Phone: 800-843-2763
Web: www.asme.org/education/college/financialaid

Associated Builders and Contractors, Inc.

Trimmer Education Foundation Student Scholarships

Type of award: Scholarship, renewable.
Intended use: For sophomore, junior or senior study at 2-year or 4-year institution.
Basis for selection: Major/career interest in construction management or construction. Applicant must demonstrate financial need and high academic achievement.
Application requirements: Recommendations, transcript. Resume, photocopy of first page of Student Aid Report.
Additional information: Minimum 3.0 GPA in major; minimum 2.85 GPA overall. Must be current member of Associated Builders and Contractors student chapter or employed by ABC member firm. Architecture and most engineering students excluded. Number of awards varies based on funding.

Amount of award:	$5,000
Number of applicants:	45
Application deadline:	May 21
Notification begins:	June 15
Total amount awarded:	$60,000

Contact:
Associated Buliders and Contractors
Attn: John Strock
4250 North Fairfax Drive, 9th Floor
Arlington, VA 22203-1607
Phone: 703-812-2000
Web: www.abc.org

Associated General Contractors Education and Research Foundation

AGC Education and Research Undergraduate Scholarship

Type of award: Scholarship, renewable.
Intended use: For full-time sophomore or junior study at accredited 4-year institution.
Eligibility: Applicant must be U.S. citizen or permanent resident.
Basis for selection: Major/career interest in engineering, civil; engineering, construction or construction.
Application requirements: Recommendations, transcript.
Additional information: Must be enrolled in or planning to enroll in an ABET- or ACCE- accredited full-time, four- or five-year university program of construction or civil engineering. Applications are available July 1 from AGC office or Website. Seniors with one full academic year of coursework remaining are eligible.

Amount of award:	$2,500-$7,500
Number of awards:	50
Number of applicants:	55
Application deadline:	November 1
Notification begins:	February 1
Total amount awarded:	$350,000

Contact:
Association of General Contractors Education and Research Foundation
Attn: Floretta Slade, Director of Programs
2300 Wilson Boulevard, Suite 400
Arlington, VA 22201
Phone: 703-837-5342
Fax: 703-837-5451
Web: www.agcfoundation.org

James L. Allhands Essay Competition

Type of award: Scholarship, renewable.
Intended use: For full-time senior study at accredited 4-year institution. Designated institutions: ABET- or ACCE-accredited universities with construction or construction-related engineering programs.
Basis for selection: Competition/talent/interest in research paper, based on advancement of technological, educational, or vocational expertise in the construction industry. Major/career interest in engineering, civil; engineering, construction or construction.
Application requirements: Essay abstract, letter from faculty sponsor.
Additional information: First prize is $1,000, plus all-expenses-paid trip to AGC convention; winner's faculty sponsor

receives $500 and all-expenses-paid trip to convention. Second prize is $500. Third prize is $300. Application material must be emailed. Only five submittals from each college/university are accepted. See Website for essay topic and guidelines.

Amount of award:	$300-$1,000
Number of awards:	3
Number of applicants:	50
Application deadline:	November 1
Notification begins:	February 1
Total amount awarded:	$2,300

Contact:
AGC Education and Research Foundation
Attn: Floretta Slade Director of Programs
2300 Wilson Boulevard, Suite 400
Arlington, VA 22201
Phone: 703-837-5342
Fax: 703-837-5451
Web: www.agcfoundation.org

Associated General Contractors of Maine Education Foundation

AGC of Maine Scholarship Program

Type of award: Scholarship.
Intended use: For full-time undergraduate study at accredited postsecondary institution in United States. Designated institutions: Schools in Maine.
Eligibility: Applicant must be U.S. citizen residing in Maine.
Basis for selection: Major/career interest in construction. Applicant must demonstrate financial need and high academic achievement.
Application requirements: Interview, recommendations, essay, transcript.
Additional information: Number of awards varies. Application deadline at end of March; check Website for exact date.

Amount of award:	$1,500-$3,000
Number of applicants:	30
Total amount awarded:	$24,000

Contact:
AGC of Maine
P.O. Box 5519
Augusta, ME 04332-5519
Phone: 207-622-4741
Web: www.agcmaine.org

Associated Press

Kathryn Dettman Memorial Journalism Scholarship

Type of award: Scholarship.
Intended use: For sophomore, junior, senior or graduate study at 4-year or graduate institution in United States. Designated institutions: Colleges and universities in California, Nevada, Hawaii, Arizona, New Mexico, Idaho, Washington, Colorado, Utah, Montana, Wyoming and Alaska.

Basis for selection: Competition/talent/interest in writing/journalism. Major/career interest in journalism or radio/television/film. Applicant must demonstrate financial need, high academic achievement and seriousness of purpose.
Application requirements: Essay. May submit examples of broadcast-related work.
Additional information: Open to students pursuing career in broadcast journalism. Applications must be typed and mailed; no e-mailed or faxed submissions accepted. Application deadline in December; see Website for exact date and more information.

Amount of award:	$1,500
Number of awards:	1
Total amount awarded:	$1,500

Contact:
AP Los Angeles
Jeff Wilson
221 S. Figueroa St., Suite 300
Los Angeles, CA 90012
Web: www.aptra.com

Association for Library and Information Science Education

ALISE Bohdan S. Wynar Research Paper Competition

Type of award: Scholarship.
Intended use: For undergraduate or graduate study.
Basis for selection: Competition/talent/interest in research paper, based on any aspect of library and information science using any methodology. Major/career interest in library science.
Application requirements: Paper must not exceed 35 double-spaced pages with one-inch margins and 12-point font. Two title pages, one with and one without author name(s) and institution.
Additional information: Research papers prepared by joint investigators eligible; at least one author must be member of Association for Library and Information Science Education. Winners expected to present papers at ALISE Annual Conference. Can submit only one paper per competition and may not submit same paper to other ALISE competitions. Paper cannot have been published, though may be accepted for publication. Papers completed in pursuit of master's and doctoral degrees not eligible, though data and spinoffs from such papers are eligible, as are papers generated through other grants and funding. Visit Website for detailed explanation of requirements.

Amount of award:	$2,500
Number of awards:	2
Number of applicants:	12
Application deadline:	July 15
Notification begins:	October 1
Total amount awarded:	$5,000

Contact:
ALISE
65 E. Wacker Place, Suite 1900
Chicago, IL 60601-7246
Phone: 312-795-0996
Fax: 312-419-8950
Web: www.alise.org

ALISE Research Grant

Type of award: Research grant.
Intended use: For non-degree study.
Basis for selection: Major/career interest in library science. Applicant must demonstrate high academic achievement.
Application requirements: Research proposal.
Additional information: Must be member of Association for Library and Information Science Education. Proposal must not exceed 20 double-spaced pages. Award to support research broadly related to education for library and information science. Visit Website for detailed explanation of proposal requirements. More than one grant may be awarded; however, total amount of funding for all grants not to exceed $5,000. Award cannot be used to support doctoral dissertation. Awardee(s) must present preliminary report at ALISE Annual Conference.

Amount of award:	$5,000
Application deadline:	October 1
Total amount awarded:	$5,000

Contact:
ALISE
65 E. Wacker Place, Suite 1900
Chicago, IL 60601-7246
Phone: 312-795-0996
Fax: 312-419-8950
Web: www.alise.org

ALISE/Dialog Methodology Paper Competition

Type of award: Scholarship.
Intended use: For undergraduate or graduate study.
Basis for selection: Competition/talent/interest in research paper, based on description and discussion of a research method or technique. Major/career interest in library science.
Application requirements: Paper must not exceed 25 double-spaced pages with one-inch margins and 12-point font. Two title pages, one with and one without author name and institution. 200-word abstract.
Additional information: Papers prepared by joint authors eligible; at least one author must be member of Association for Library and Information Science Education. Papers completed in pursuit of master's or doctoral degrees are eligible, as are papers generated as result of research grant or other source of funding. Papers that stress findings are ineligible. Winners expected to present papers at ALISE Annual Conference. May submit only one paper per competition and may not submit same paper to multiple ALISE competitions.

Amount of award:	$500
Number of awards:	1
Number of applicants:	10
Application deadline:	July 15
Notification begins:	October 1
Total amount awarded:	$500

Contact:
ALISE
65 E. Wacker Place, Suite 1900
Chicago, IL 60601-7246
Phone: 312-795-0996
Fax: 312-419-8950
Web: www.alise.org

Association for Women in Architecture Foundation

Women in Architecture Scholarship

Type of award: Scholarship, renewable.
Intended use: For full-time sophomore, junior, senior or graduate study at 4-year or graduate institution.
Eligibility: Applicant must be female.
Basis for selection: Major/career interest in architecture; interior design; landscape architecture; urban planning; engineering, structural; engineering, civil; engineering, electrical/electronic or engineering, mechanical. Applicant must demonstrate high academic achievement.
Application requirements: Portfolio, recommendations, essay, transcript. SASE.
Additional information: Must be California resident or attending accredited California school to qualify. Students may also be studying in the following majors: land planning, environmental design, architectural rendering and illustrating. Must have completed minimum of 18 units in major by application due date. Applications may be downloaded from Website. Applications due in mid-May; see Website for exact date.

Amount of award:	$1,000
Number of awards:	5
Application deadline:	May 15
Total amount awarded:	$6,000

Contact:
Association for Women in Architecture Foundation
AWAF Scholarship
22815 Frampton Avenue
Torrance, CA 90501-5034
Phone: 310-534-8466
Fax: 310-257-6885
Web: www.awa-la.org/scholarships.php

Association for Women in Communications

Seattle Professional Chapter Scholarship

Type of award: Scholarship.
Intended use: For junior, senior or graduate study at accredited 4-year or graduate institution in United States. Designated institutions: Washington state colleges.
Eligibility: Applicant must be residing in Washington.
Basis for selection: Major/career interest in communications; journalism; radio/television/film; film/video; graphic arts/design; advertising; public relations or marketing. Applicant must demonstrate financial need and high academic achievement.
Application requirements: Transcript. Cover letter, resume, two work samples.
Additional information: Additional majors may include multimedia design, photography, or technical communication. Applicant may be at community or junior college but must be accepted to four-year college where scholarship will be used. Graduate students will be considered if not in final year. Selection based on demonstrated excellence in communications and positive contributions to communications on campus or in

community. Application deadline in April; check Website for exact date.

Amount of award:	$1,000-$2,000
Number of awards:	2
Application deadline:	April 30
Total amount awarded:	$3,000

Contact:
AWC Seattle Professional Chapter
Attn: Scholarship Chair
P.O. Box 472
Mountlake Terrace, WA 98043
Phone: 206-654-2929
Web: www.seattleawc.org

Association of American Geographers

Anne U. White Fund

Type of award: Research grant, renewable.
Intended use: For non-degree study.
Basis for selection: Major/career interest in geography.
Application requirements: Research proposal.
Additional information: Fund enables Association of American Geographers member to engage in useful field study jointly with his/her partner. Must have been member for at least two years at time of application. Report summarizing results and documenting expenses underwritten by grant must be submitted within 12 months of receiving award.

Amount of award:	$1,500
Number of awards:	2
Application deadline:	December 31
Notification begins:	March 1

Contact:
Association of American Geographers
Attn: Anne U. White Fund
1710 16th Street, NW
Washington, DC 20009-3198
Phone: 202-234-1450
Fax: 202-234-2744
Web: www.aag.org/grantsawards/

Darrel Hess Community College Geography Scholarship

Type of award: Scholarship, renewable.
Intended use: For at 2-year institution in United States.
Basis for selection: Major/career interest in geography. Applicant must demonstrate financial need and high academic achievement.
Application requirements: Recommendations, essay, transcript.
Additional information: Applicants eligible if currently enrolled in a US community college, junior college, city college, or similar two-year educational institution at the time of submission of application. Applicant must have completed at least two transfer courses in geography and plan to transfer to a four-year institution as a geography major during the coming academic year. AAG membership strongly encouraged, but not required.

Amount of award:	$1,000
Number of awards:	2
Application deadline:	December 31

Contact:
Association of American Geographers
1710 16th Street NW
Washington, DC 20009-3198
Phone: 202-234-1450
Fax: 202-234-2744
Web: www.aag.org/grantsawards

Marble-Boyle Award

Type of award: Scholarship, renewable.
Intended use: For full-time senior study at accredited postsecondary institution in United States or Canada.
Basis for selection: Major/career interest in computer/information sciences or geography.
Application requirements: Recommendations, essay, transcript. Cover letter.
Additional information: Applicant must demonstrate reasonable intent to embark upon a career or further education that will make use of joint geographic science and computer science knowledge. AAG membership strongly encouraged, but not required. Award consists of $700 cash prize and $200 credit for books published by the ESRI Press. ESRI will provide priority consideration to awardees interested in participating in ESRI Summer Intern Program. Awardees also eligible to compete for an additional research fellowship award offered biannually by MicroGIS Foundation for Spatial Analysis (MFSA).

Amount of award:	$700
Number of awards:	3
Application deadline:	October 15

Contact:
Association of American Geographers
1710 16th Street NW
Washington, DC 20009-3198
Phone: 202-234-1450
Fax: 202-234-2744
Web: www.aag.org/grantsawards

The Association of Insurance Compliance Professionals

AICP Heartland Chapter Scholarship

Type of award: Scholarship, renewable.
Intended use: For full-time undergraduate or graduate study at postsecondary institution.
Eligibility: Applicant must be residing in Iowa, South Dakota, Minnesota, Nebraska, Kansas, North Dakota or Missouri.
Basis for selection: Major/career interest in accounting; business; business/management/administration; economics; finance/banking; mathematics or statistics.
Application requirements: Recommendations, transcript. Resume, short narrative describing current and future interest to pursue education/career in the insurance field.
Additional information: Must be a Heartland member in good standing; a spouse (including domestic partner or civil union partner), son, daughter, grandson, granddaughter (including step or custodial) of a Heartland member in good standing; or be sponsored by current Heartland AICP member in good standing. Minimum 2.75 GPA. Applicants with major/

career interest in risk management also eligible. Graduate students working towards an MBA in insurance, risk management, or mathematics, with an actuarial emphasis, are also eligible. Mathematics majors' studies should have emphasis in actuarial science.

Amount of award:	$500
Number of awards:	1
Application deadline:	April 1
Notification begins:	May 15
Total amount awarded:	$500

Contact:
Bob Boyce
Minnesota Department Chamber of Commerce
85 7th Place East #500
Saint Paul, MN 55101
Phone: 651-296-0139
Web: www.aicp.net

AICP Scholarship

Type of award: Scholarship, renewable.
Intended use: For full-time sophomore, junior, senior or master's study.
Basis for selection: Major/career interest in business; business/management/administration; economics; finance/banking; insurance/actuarial science; mathematics or statistics.
Application requirements: Recommendations, transcript. Resume, short narrative describing current and future interest to pursue education/career in the insurance field.
Additional information: Minimum 2.75 GPA. Applicant must be at least a second-semester sophomore. Applicants with major/career interest in risk management also eligible.

Amount of award:	$1,000
Number of awards:	3
Number of applicants:	12
Application deadline:	June 1
Notification begins:	July 1
Total amount awarded:	$3,000

Contact:
Association of Insurance Compliance Professionals
12100 Sunset Hills Road, Suite 130
Reston, VA 20190
Phone: 703-234-4074
Fax: 703-435-4390
Web: www.aicp.net

Association of State Dam Safety Officials

ASDSO Undergraduate Scholarship

Type of award: Scholarship.
Intended use: For full-time senior study in United States.
Eligibility: Applicant must be U.S. citizen.
Basis for selection: Major/career interest in engineering, civil. Applicant must demonstrate financial need and high academic achievement.
Application requirements: Recommendations, essay, transcript.
Additional information: Must be planning to pursue career in dams or dam safety. Minimum 2.5 GPA.

Amount of award:	$5,000
Number of awards:	2
Number of applicants:	60
Application deadline:	March 31
Notification begins:	June 1
Total amount awarded:	$10,000

Contact:
Association of State Dam Safety Officials
450 Old Vine Street, 2nd Floor
Lexington, KY 40507
Phone: 859-257-5140
Fax: 859-323-1958
Web: www.damsafety.org

Astraea Lesbian Foundation for Justice

Margot Karle Scholarship Fund

Type of award: Scholarship.
Intended use: For full-time undergraduate study at 2-year or 4-year institution in United States. Designated institutions: City University of New York (CUNY) schools.
Eligibility: Applicant must be female. Applicant must be U.S. citizen or permanent resident.
Basis for selection: Applicant must demonstrate financial need and service orientation.
Application requirements: Recommendations, essay, transcript.
Additional information: Transwomen may apply. Award for high degree of community involvement in working for social, racial, economic, political, and/or environmental justice. Visit Website for more information and deadline.

Amount of award:	$1,000
Number of awards:	1
Total amount awarded:	$1,000

Contact:
Astraea Lesbian Foundation for Justice
Attn: Margot Karle Scholarship
116 East 16th Street, 7th Floor
New York, NY 10003
Phone: 212-529-8021
Fax: 212-982-3321
Web: www.astraeafoundation.org

Automotive Hall of Fame

Automotive Educational Fund Scholarship

Type of award: Scholarship, renewable.
Intended use: For full-time undergraduate study at accredited 2-year, 4-year or graduate institution in United States.
Eligibility: Applicant must be U.S. citizen, permanent resident or international student.
Basis for selection: Major/career interest in automotive technology.
Application requirements: Recommendations, transcript, proof of eligibility. High school seniors must have proof of acceptance to postsecondary institution.

Additional information: Applicant must have interest in pursuing career in the automotive industry. SASE for application, or download from Website. All required materials must be submitted with application to be considered. Only award recipients will be notified. Minimum 3.0 GPA. High school seniors may also apply.

Amount of award:	$500-$2,000
Number of awards:	20
Application deadline:	June 1
Notification begins:	July 31

Contact:
Automotive Hall of Fame
21400 Oakwood Blvd.
Dearborn, MI 48124-4078
Phone: 313-240-4000
Fax: 313-240-8641
Web: www.automotivehalloffame.org

AXA Achievement Scholarship

AXA Achievement Scholarship in Association with U.S. News & World Report

Type of award: Scholarship.
Intended use: For full-time undergraduate study at accredited 2-year or 4-year institution in United States.
Eligibility: Applicant must be high school senior. Applicant must be U.S. citizen.
Application requirements: Recommendations.
Additional information: Fifty-two students, to be known as AXA Achievers, will be selected to receive $10,000 scholarships, one from each state, the District of Columbia and Puerto Rico. From among the state recipients, ten students will be named national AXA Achievers. They will be selected to receive national awards at $15,000 each for a total of $25,000 per national recipient. Must demonstrate achievement in a non-academic activity or project. Consideration will also be given to other extracurricular activities in school and community, work experience, and the applicant's academic record over the past four years. Visit Website for more information and application. Questions about the application process may be directed to Scholarship America's toll-free number or by e-mail to axaachievement@scholarshipamerica.org.

Amount of award:	$10,000-$25,000
Number of awards:	52
Application deadline:	December 15
Notification begins:	March 15
Total amount awarded:	$670,000

Contact:
AXA Achievement Scholarship
Scholarship Management Services
One Scholarship Way
Saint Peter, MN 56082
Phone: 800-537-4180
Web: www.axa-achievement.com

Ayn Rand Institute

Atlas Shrugged Essay Contest

Type of award: Scholarship.
Intended use: For undergraduate study.
Basis for selection: Competition/talent/interest in writing/journalism, based on an outstanding grasp of the philosophic meaning of "Atlas Shrugged."
Application requirements: Essay between 800 and 1,600 words, typewritten and double-spaced.
Additional information: Student must be enrolled in full-time college degree program or 12th grade at time of entry. See Website for rules, guidelines, and topic questions.

Amount of award:	$50-$10,000
Number of awards:	49
Number of applicants:	1,917
Application deadline:	September 17
Notification begins:	November 27
Total amount awarded:	$24,000

Contact:
The Ayn Rand Institute
Atlas Shrugged Essay Contest
P.O. Box 57044
Irvine, CA 92619-7044
Phone: 949-222-6550
Fax: 949-222-6558
Web: www.aynrand.org/contests

The Fountainhead Essay Contest

Type of award: Scholarship.
Intended use: For undergraduate study.
Eligibility: Applicant must be high school junior or senior.
Basis for selection: Competition/talent/interest in writing/journalism, based on an outstanding grasp of the philosophic meaning of "The Fountainhead."
Application requirements: Essay between 800 and 1,600 words, typewritten and double-spaced.
Additional information: Rules, guidelines, and topic questions on Website.

Amount of award:	$50-$10,000
Number of awards:	236
Number of applicants:	5,399
Application deadline:	April 26
Notification begins:	July 26
Total amount awarded:	$43,250

Contact:
Ayn Rand Institute
"The Fountainhead" Essay Contest
P.O. Box 57044
Irvine, CA 92619-7044
Phone: 949-222-6550
Fax: 949-222-6558
Web: www.aynrand.org/contests

"Anthem" Essay Contest

Type of award: Scholarship.
Intended use: For undergraduate study.
Eligibility: Applicant must be high school freshman or sophomore.
Basis for selection: Competition/talent/interest in writing/journalism, based on outstanding grasp of the philosophic meaning of "Anthem."

Application requirements: Essay between 600 and 1,200 words, typewritten and double-spaced.

Additional information: Eighth-grade students may also apply. Rules, guidelines, and topic questions on Website.

Amount of award:	$30-$2,000
Number of awards:	236
Number of applicants:	13,420
Application deadline:	March 20
Notification begins:	July 26
Total amount awarded:	$14,000

Contact:
Ayn Rand Institute
"Anthem" Essay Contest
P.O. Box 57044
Irvine, CA 92619-7044
Phone: 949-222-6550
Fax: 949-222-6558
Web: www.aynrand.org/contests

Barry M. Goldwater Scholarship and Excellence In Education Foundation

Barry M. Goldwater Scholarship

Type of award: Scholarship, renewable.

Intended use: For full-time junior or senior study at accredited 4-year institution in United States.

Eligibility: Applicant must be U.S. citizen, permanent resident or U.S. national.

Basis for selection: Major/career interest in engineering; mathematics or natural sciences. Applicant must demonstrate high academic achievement and seriousness of purpose.

Application requirements: Recommendations, essay, transcript, nomination by Goldwater faculty representative. Permanent resident nominees must include letter of intent to obtain U.S. citizenship and photocopy of Permanent Resident Card.

Additional information: Bulletin of information, nomination materials, application, and list of faculty representatives available on Website. Applicants must be legal residents of state in which they are candidates. Residents of District of Columbia, Puerto Rico, Guam, American Samoa, Virgin Islands, and Commonwealth of Northern Mariana Islands also eligible. Must have minimum 3.0 GPA and rank in top 25 percent of class. Application deadline in late January; check Website for exact date.

Amount of award:	$7,500
Number of awards:	300
Number of applicants:	1,097
Application deadline:	January 31
Notification begins:	March 31
Total amount awarded:	$2,407,500

Contact:
Barry M. Goldwater Scholarship and Excellence in Education Foundation
6225 Brandon Avenue
Suite 315
Springfield, VA 22150-2519
Phone: 703-756-6012
Fax: 703-756-6015
Web: www.act.org/goldwater

Bay Area Family of Funds

Bay Area Council Scholarship Program

Type of award: Scholarship.

Intended use: For full-time undergraduate study at accredited 4-year institution in United States.

Eligibility: Applicant must be high school senior. Applicant must be U.S. citizen or permanent resident residing in California.

Basis for selection: Applicant must demonstrate financial need, high academic achievement, leadership and service orientation.

Application requirements: Interview, recommendations, essay, transcript. FAFSA; SAR; copy of financial aid letter; photo.

Additional information: Available to current high school seniors who reside in underserved neighborhoods within the nine-county Bay Area, neighborhoods determined by census to be at 80% of Area Median Income or below. Visit Website for more information and application.

Amount of award:	$5,000
Number of awards:	20
Number of applicants:	10
Application deadline:	March 23
Total amount awarded:	$125,000

Contact:
Bay Area Council Scholarship Program
Bay Area Family of Funds
201 California Street, Suite 1450
CA 94111
Phone: 415-946-8717
Fax: 415-981-6408
Web: www.bayareafamilyoffunds.org

Best Buy

Best Buy @15 Scholarship Program

Type of award: Scholarship.

Intended use: For full-time undergraduate study at accredited postsecondary institution in United States.

Eligibility: Applicant must be enrolled in high school. Applicant must be U.S. citizen, permanent resident or resident of Puerto Rico.

Basis for selection: Applicant must demonstrate high academic achievement and service orientation.

Additional information: Apply online. See Website for more information.

Amount of award:	$1,000
Number of awards:	1,000
Application deadline:	February 15

Contact:
Web: www.bestbuyinc.com/community_relations/

Bethesda Lutheran Communities

Developmental Disability Scholastic Achievement Scholarship

Type of award: Scholarship.
Intended use: For full-time junior or senior study at accredited 4-year institution in United States.
Eligibility: Applicant must be Lutheran.
Basis for selection: Major/career interest in social work; education; psychology; mental health/therapy; education, special; education, early childhood; education, teacher; speech pathology/audiology; occupational therapy or health-related professions. Applicant must demonstrate high academic achievement, seriousness of purpose and service orientation.
Application requirements: Recommendations, essay, transcript, proof of eligibility.
Additional information: Preference given to those interested in working with persons with mental retardation. Minimum 3.0 GPA.

Amount of award:	$3,000
Number of awards:	2
Number of applicants:	6
Application deadline:	April 15
Notification begins:	June 1
Total amount awarded:	$6,000

Contact:
Bethesda Lutheran Communities
Coordinator, Outreach Programs
600 Hoffmann Drive
Watertown, WI 53094
Phone: 800-369-4636 ext. 4449
Fax: 920-262-6513
Web: www.bethesdalutherancommunities.org

BioCommunications Association, Inc.

Endowment Fund For Education (EFFE)

Type of award: Scholarship.
Intended use: For full-time sophomore, junior, senior or graduate study at accredited vocational or 4-year institution.
Basis for selection: Major/career interest in arts, general; biomedical; communications or science, general.
Application requirements: Portfolio, recommendations, essay, transcript, proof of eligibility.
Additional information: For students pursuing careers in scientific/biomedical visual communications and scientific/biomedical photography.

Amount of award:	$500
Number of awards:	1
Application deadline:	April 30
Notification begins:	June 1
Total amount awarded:	$1,000

Contact:
BioCommunications Association, Inc.
220 Southwind Lane
Hillsborough, NC 27278-7907
Phone: 919-245-0906
Fax: 919-245-0906
Web: www.bca.org

BlackNews.com

The BlackNews.com Scholarship Essay Contest

Type of award: Scholarship.
Intended use: For undergraduate or graduate study at vocational, 2-year or 4-year institution in United States.
Eligibility: Applicant must be African American. Applicant must be U.S. citizen or permanent resident.
Basis for selection: Competition/talent/interest in writing/journalism, based on quality, uniqueness and creativity of content in essay.
Application requirements: 500-word essay.
Additional information: One award per season. Must submit essay via e-mail in body of message. Visit Website for more information.

Amount of award:	$500
Number of awards:	4
Number of applicants:	200,000
Total amount awarded:	$2,000

Contact:
Diversity City Media
750-Q Cross Pointe Road
Columbus, OH 43230
Web: www.blacknews.com/news/scholarship.shtml

Blinded Veterans Association

Katherine F. Gruber Scholarship Program

Type of award: Scholarship, renewable.
Intended use: For full-time undergraduate or graduate study at accredited postsecondary institution in United States.
Eligibility: Applicant must be U.S. citizen. Applicant must be dependent of disabled veteran; or spouse of disabled veteran who served in the Army, Air Force, Marines, Navy or Coast Guard.
Application requirements: Recommendations, essay, transcript.
Additional information: Dependent children and spouses of blinded U.S. Armed Forces veterans are eligible, as well as blinded active duty members of the U.S. Armed Forces. Veteran must meet definition of blindness used by Blinded Veterans Association; blindness may be service-connected or non-service-connected. Katherine Gruber scholarships are awarded for one year only. The number of scholarships a recipient may receive under this program is limited to four.

Amount of award:	$2,000
Number of awards:	6
Number of applicants:	15
Application deadline:	April 16
Notification begins:	January 1
Total amount awarded:	$12,000

Contact:
Katherine F. Gruber Scholarship Program
Blinded Veterans Association
477 H Street NW
Washington, DC 20001-2694
Phone: 202-371-8880
Fax: 202-371-8258
Web: www.bva.org

BMI Foundation, Inc.

BMI Student Composer Awards

Type of award: Scholarship.
Intended use: For undergraduate or graduate study at accredited postsecondary institution.
Eligibility: Applicant must be no older than 27. Applicant must be citizen of a Western hemisphere country.
Basis for selection: Competition/talent/interest in music performance/composition, based on composition of classical music. Major/career interest in music.
Application requirements: Manuscript/recording of score, which must be submitted under a pseudonym. SASE.
Additional information: Application deadline in early February. Check Website for exact date and application. Must be enrolled in accredited public, private, or parochial secondary schools; accredited colleges or conservatories of music; or engaged in private study of music with recognized and established teachers (other than relatives).

Amount of award:	$500-$5,000
Notification begins:	May 1
Total amount awarded:	$20,000

Contact:
Ralph N. Jackson
BMI Student Composer Awards
320 W. 57th Street
New York, NY 10019
Web: www.bmifoundation.org

John Lennon Scholarships

Type of award: Scholarship.
Intended use: For undergraduate or graduate study.
Eligibility: Applicant must be at least 15, no older than 24.
Basis for selection: Competition/talent/interest in music performance/composition, based on best song of any genre with original music and lyrics. Major/career interest in music or performing arts.
Application requirements: Music and lyrics of original song, CD and three typed lyric sheets.
Additional information: Current students and alumnae at select schools may apply directly to Foundation; others must contact the National Association for Music Education chapter advisor at their college. Visit Website for application and more information.

Amount of award:	$5,000-$10,000
Number of awards:	3
Total amount awarded:	$20,000

Contact:
BMI Foundation, Inc.
John Lennon Scholarship Competition
320 W. 57th Street
New York, NY 10019
Web: www.bmifoundation.org

peermusic Latin Scholarship

Type of award: Scholarship.
Intended use: For undergraduate or graduate study at postsecondary institution in United States.
Eligibility: Applicant must be at least 16, no older than 24.
Basis for selection: Competition/talent/interest in music performance/composition, based on best song or instrumental work in any Latin genre with original music and lyrics. Major/career interest in music.
Application requirements: CD of original song and three typed lyric sheets. Should not include name of student or school.
Additional information: Application deadline in early February. Check Website for exact date and application.

Amount of award:	$5,000
Number of awards:	1

Contact:
BMI Foundation, Inc.
Porfirio Piña/peermusic Latin Scholarship
320 W. 57th St.
New York, NY 10019
Web: www.bmifoundation.org

Boeing Company

Historically Black Colleges and Minority Institutions Scholarships

Type of award: Scholarship.
Intended use: For undergraduate study at 4-year institution in United States. Designated institutions: Atlanta Consortium (Morehouse and Spelman colleges and Clark Atlanta University), Alabama A&M University, California Polytechnic State University, California State University (Fullerton, Long Beach, Los Angeles, Northridge), Central State University, Florida A&M University, Howard University, Morgan State University, New Mexico State University, North Carolina A&T State University, Prairie View A&M University, Southern University, Tennessee State University, Tuskegee University, University of Hawaii, University of Puerto Rico-Mayaguez.
Eligibility: Applicant must be African American.
Additional information: Contact college adviser for application and more information.
Contact:
Web: www.boeing.com/educationrelations/scholarships/index.html

Boy Scouts of America Patriots' Path Council

Frank D. Visceglia Memorial Scholarship

Type of award: Scholarship, renewable.
Intended use: For full-time freshman study at accredited 4-year institution.
Eligibility: Applicant must be male, high school senior. Applicant must be U.S. citizen or permanent resident residing in New Jersey.
Additional information: Applicant must be an Eagle Scout. Preference given to Scouts whose service projects relate to the environment or economy. Application available online.

Amount of award:	$1,000
Number of awards:	1
Number of applicants:	20
Application deadline:	June 1
Notification begins:	August 1
Total amount awarded:	$1,000

Contact:
The Frank D. Visceglia Memorial Scholarship Program
Attn: Dennis Kohl
222 Columbia Turnpike
Florham Park, NJ 07932
Phone: 973-765-9322
Fax: 973-765-9142
Web: www.advancement.ppbsa.org/scholarship.htm

Boys and Girls Clubs of Greater San Diego

Spence Reese Scholarship

Type of award: Scholarship, renewable.
Intended use: For full-time undergraduate study at accredited 4-year institution in United States.
Eligibility: Applicant must be male, high school senior.
Basis for selection: Major/career interest in engineering; law; medicine or political science/government. Applicant must demonstrate financial need and high academic achievement.
Application requirements: Recommendations, transcript. SAT/ACT scores, college acceptance letter.
Additional information: One award in each of four eligible majors. Award is renewable for four years of study. Application available on Website.

Amount of award:	$4,000
Number of awards:	4
Number of applicants:	40
Application deadline:	April 1
Notification begins:	May 7
Total amount awarded:	$32,000

Contact:
Boys and Girls Clubs of Greater San Diego
Attn: Jeff Miller
115 West Woodward Avenue
Escondido, CA 92025-2638
Web: www.sdyouth.org/scholarships.htm

Broadcast Education Association

Abe Voron Scholarship

Type of award: Scholarship.
Intended use: For full-time junior, senior or graduate study at 4-year or graduate institution. Designated institutions: BEA Institutional Member schools.
Basis for selection: Major/career interest in radio/television/film. Applicant must demonstrate high academic achievement, depth of character and seriousness of purpose.
Application requirements: Recommendations, essay, transcript.
Additional information: Award intended for study in radio only. Should be able to show evidence of potential to be outstanding electronic media professional. Application available from campus faculty or online.

Amount of award:	$5,000
Number of awards:	1
Number of applicants:	85
Application deadline:	October 12
Notification begins:	November 30
Total amount awarded:	$5,000

Contact:
Broadcast Education Association (BEA)
1771 N Street, N.W.
Washington, DC 20036-2891
Phone: 202-429-3935
Web: www.beaweb.org

Alexander M. Tanger Scholarship

Type of award: Scholarship.
Intended use: For full-time junior, senior or graduate study at 4-year or graduate institution in United States. Designated institutions: BEA Institutional Member schools.
Basis for selection: Major/career interest in radio/television/film. Applicant must demonstrate high academic achievement, depth of character and seriousness of purpose.
Application requirements: Recommendations, essay, transcript.
Additional information: Must show evidence of potential in electronic media. Application available from campus faculty or on Website.

Amount of award:	$5,000
Number of awards:	1
Number of applicants:	85
Application deadline:	October 12
Notification begins:	November 30
Total amount awarded:	$5,000

Contact:
Broadcast Education Association (BEA)
1771 N Street, N.W.
Washington, DC 20036-2891
Phone: 202-429-3935
Web: www.beaweb.org

Helen J. Sioussat/Fay Wells Scholarship

Type of award: Scholarship.
Intended use: For full-time junior, senior or graduate study at 4-year or graduate institution. Designated institutions: BEA Institutional Member schools.

Basis for selection: Major/career interest in radio/television/film. Applicant must demonstrate high academic achievement, depth of character and seriousness of purpose.
Application requirements: Recommendations, essay, transcript.
Additional information: Should be able to show evidence of potential in electronic media. Application available from campus faculty or on Website.

Amount of award:	$1,250
Number of awards:	2
Number of applicants:	85
Application deadline:	October 12
Notification begins:	November 30
Total amount awarded:	$2,500

Contact:
Broadcast Education Association (BEA)
1771 N Street, N.W.
Washington, DC 20036-2891
Phone: 202-429-3935
Web: www.beaweb.org

Richard Eaton Foundation Award

Type of award: Scholarship.
Intended use: For full-time junior, senior or graduate study at 4-year or graduate institution. Designated institutions: BEA Institutional Member schools.
Basis for selection: Major/career interest in radio/television/film. Applicant must demonstrate high academic achievement, depth of character and seriousness of purpose.
Application requirements: Recommendations, essay, transcript.

Amount of award:	$2,000
Number of awards:	1
Number of applicants:	85
Application deadline:	October 12
Notification begins:	November 30

Contact:
Broadcast Education Association (BEA)
1771 N Street, NW
Washington, DC 20036-2891
Phone: 202.429.3935
Web: www.beaweb.org

Two Year Community College BEA Award

Type of award: Scholarship.
Intended use: For full-time undergraduate study at 2-year or 4-year institution. Designated institutions: BEA Institutional Member schools.
Basis for selection: Major/career interest in radio/television/film. Applicant must demonstrate high academic achievement, depth of character and seriousness of purpose.
Application requirements: Recommendations, essay, transcript.
Additional information: Scholarship for use at two-year community college, or, if applicant has already graduated from BEA two-year campus, can be used at four-year school. Should show evidence of potential in electronic media. Application available from campus faculty or on Website.

Amount of award:	$1,500
Number of awards:	2
Number of applicants:	85
Application deadline:	October 12
Notification begins:	November 30
Total amount awarded:	$3,000

Contact:
Broadcast Education Association (BEA)
1771 N Street, N.W.
Washington, DC 20036-2891
Phone: 202-429-3935
Web: www.beaweb.org

Vision Award

Type of award: Scholarship.
Intended use: For full-time junior, senior or graduate study at 4-year or graduate institution. Designated institutions: BEA Institutional Member schools.
Basis for selection: Major/career interest in radio/television/film. Applicant must demonstrate high academic achievement, depth of character and seriousness of purpose.
Application requirements: Recommendations, essay, transcript.
Additional information: Must show evidence of potential in electronic media. Application available from campus faculty or on Website.

Amount of award:	$1,500
Number of awards:	1
Number of applicants:	85
Application deadline:	October 12
Notification begins:	November 30
Total amount awarded:	$1,500

Contact:
Broadcast Education Association (BEA)
1771 N Street, N.W.
Washington, DC 20036-2891
Phone: 202-429-3935
Web: www.beaweb.org

Walter S. Patterson Scholarship

Type of award: Scholarship.
Intended use: For full-time junior, senior or graduate study at 4-year or graduate institution. Designated institutions: BEA Institutional Member schools.
Basis for selection: Major/career interest in radio/television/film. Applicant must demonstrate high academic achievement, depth of character and seriousness of purpose.
Application requirements: Recommendations, essay, transcript.
Additional information: Award intended for study in radio only. Should be able to show evidence of potential in electronic media. Application available from campus faculty or on Website.

Amount of award:	$2,750
Number of awards:	2
Number of applicants:	85
Application deadline:	October 12
Notification begins:	November 30
Total amount awarded:	$4,500

Contact:
Broadcast Education Association (BEA)
1771 N Street, N.W.
Washington, DC 20036-2891
Phone: 202-429-3935
Web: www.beaweb.org

Brown and Caldwell

Dr. W. Wes Eckenfelder Jr. Scholarship

Type of award: Scholarship.
Intended use: For full-time junior, senior or graduate study at accredited 4-year or graduate institution in United States.
Eligibility: Applicant must be U.S. citizen or permanent resident.
Basis for selection: Major/career interest in engineering, civil; engineering, chemical; engineering, environmental; environmental science; biology; ecology or environmental science. Applicant must demonstrate high academic achievement and seriousness of purpose.
Application requirements: Recommendations, essay, transcript. Resume.
Additional information: Minimum 3.0 GPA. Visit Website for additional information.

Amount of award:	$3,000
Number of awards:	1
Number of applicants:	150
Application deadline:	March 1
Notification begins:	April 1
Total amount awarded:	$3,000

Contact:
Brown and Caldwell
Attn: HR/Scholarship Program
P.O. Box 8045
Walnut Creek, CA 94596
Phone: 800-727-2224
Web: www.brownandcaldwell.com/_Index_scholarships.htm

Minority Scholarship Program

Type of award: Scholarship.
Intended use: For full-time junior study at accredited 4-year institution in United States.
Eligibility: Applicant must be Alaskan native, Asian American, African American, Mexican American, Hispanic American, Puerto Rican, American Indian or Native Hawaiian/Pacific Islander. Applicant must be U.S. citizen or permanent resident.
Basis for selection: Major/career interest in engineering, civil; engineering, chemical; engineering, environmental; environmental science; biology; ecology or geology/earth sciences.
Application requirements: Recommendations, essay, transcript. Resume.
Additional information: Award includes optional paid summer internship at Brown and Caldwell office. Minimum cumulative 3.0 GPA.

Amount of award:	$3,000
Number of awards:	5
Number of applicants:	50
Application deadline:	March 31
Notification begins:	April 30
Total amount awarded:	$12,000

Contact:
Brown and Caldwell
Attn: HR/Scholarship Program
P.O. Box 8045
Walnut Creek, CA 94596
Phone: 800-727-2224
Web: www.brownandcaldwell.com/_Index_scholarships.htm

Brown Foundation

Teacher Quest Scholarship Program

Type of award: Scholarship, renewable.
Intended use: For junior or senior study at accredited 4-year institution.
Eligibility: Applicant must be Alaskan native, Asian American, African American, Mexican American, Hispanic American, Puerto Rican or American Indian.
Basis for selection: Major/career interest in education or education, teacher. Applicant must demonstrate high academic achievement and leadership.
Application requirements: Recommendations.
Additional information: Minimum 3.0 GPA. Visit Website for application.

Amount of award:	$2,000
Number of awards:	5
Number of applicants:	45
Application deadline:	March 20
Notification begins:	May 1
Total amount awarded:	$10,000

Contact:
Brown Foundation Scholarship Committee
1515 SE Monroe
Topeka, KS 66615
Phone: 785-235-3939
Fax: 785-235-1001
Web: www.brownvboard.org/foundation/scholarships/teacherquest

Building Industry Association

BIA San Diego Scholarship

Type of award: Scholarship.
Intended use: For full-time sophomore, junior or senior study at postsecondary institution.
Eligibility: Applicant must be residing in California.
Basis for selection: Major/career interest in engineering, civil; real estate; construction; finance/banking; landscape architecture; engineering, construction; advertising; accounting; architecture or engineering, structural. Applicant must demonstrate financial need, high academic achievement and seriousness of purpose.
Application requirements: Interview, essay, proof of eligibility.
Additional information: For residents of San Diego who have either graduated from a San Diego County high school or are attending college in Sand Diego and are interested in careers in the building industry. Also open to students pursuing major/career as developer, contractor, soils engineer, designer, land planner, framer, plumber, electrician, or other related profession. Number of awards varies. See Website for application and deadline.

Amount of award:	$500-$1,000

Contact:
Building Industry Association of San Diego
c/o Nancy Diamond
9201 Spectrum Center Blvd., Suite 110
San Diego, CA 92123
Phone: 858-450-1221
Web: www.biasandiego.org

Bureau of Indian Affairs-Oklahoma Area Education Office

Osage Tribal Education Committee Award

Type of award: Scholarship.
Intended use: For undergraduate or graduate study at accredited postsecondary institution in United States.
Eligibility: Applicant must be American Indian. Must be member of Osage Tribe.
Application requirements: Transcript, proof of eligibility.
Additional information: Minimum 2.0 GPA. Part-time students funded at half rate. Application deadlines: July 1 for fall semester, December 31 for spring, and May 1 for summer (funds permitting). Contact Oklahoma Area Education Office for application and additional information.

Number of applicants:	204
Application deadline:	July 1, December 31

Contact:
Burea of Indian Affairs - Oklahoma Area Education Office
200 N.W. 4th Street
Suite 4049
Oklahoma City, OK 73102
Phone: 405-605-6051 ext. 304

Bureau of Indian Education

Higher Education Grant Program

Type of award: Scholarship, renewable.
Intended use: For full-time undergraduate study at accredited 2-year or 4-year institution in United States.
Eligibility: Applicant must be American Indian. Member or at least one-quarter degree descendent of member of federally recognized tribe.
Basis for selection: Applicant must demonstrate financial need.
Application requirements: Proof of eligibility.
Additional information: Contacts or inquiries for these funds should be directed to the tribe or prospective Education Line Office relative to the person's tribal headquarters. The Higher Education scholarships are not awarded through the D.C. offices. Award amount based on student's financial need. No application deadline.

Number of awards:	12,000
Total amount awarded:	$25,000,000

Contact:
Bureau of Indian Education
Division of Post Secondary Education
215 Dean A McGee, Suite 610
Oklahoma City, OK 73102
Phone: 405-605-6001
Fax: 405-605-6010
Web: www.bie.edu

Butler Manufacturing Company Foundation

Butler Manufacturing Company Foundation Scholarship

Type of award: Scholarship, renewable.
Intended use: For full-time undergraduate study at accredited 4-year institution.
Eligibility: Applicant must be high school senior.
Basis for selection: Applicant must demonstrate financial need, high academic achievement, depth of character, leadership and service orientation.
Application requirements: Recommendations, essay, transcript. SAT/ACT scores, financial report.
Additional information: Applicant's parent must be employed by Butler Buildings or BlueScope Steel Americas Group. Contact human resources office at workplace for information and application. Renewable up to four years.

Amount of award:	$3,000
Number of awards:	8
Number of applicants:	46
Application deadline:	February 15
Notification begins:	April 30
Total amount awarded:	$24,000

Contact:
Butler Manufacturing Company Foundation
P.O. Box 419917
Kansas City, MO 64141-6917
Phone: 816-968-3208
Fax: 816-627-8993

California Association of Realtors Scholarship Foundation

C.A.R. Scholarship

Type of award: Scholarship, renewable.
Intended use: For undergraduate or graduate study at 2-year or 4-year institution. Designated institutions: California colleges/universities.
Eligibility: Applicant must be U.S. citizen residing in California.
Basis for selection: Major/career interest in real estate. Applicant must demonstrate financial need.
Application requirements: Recommendations, essay, transcript, proof of eligibility. Photocopy of valid CA driver's license or ID card.

Additional information: Must be California resident of at least one year before applying. Awarded to all eligible applicants. Students attending two-year colleges receive $2,000; four-year college/university students receive $4,000. Applications deadlines are in May, September, and December, with notification about six weeks later. May receive one award per year, maximum two years. Minimum 2.6 GPA. Must have completed minimum 12 college-level course units within last four years; at least two courses in real estate or real-estate related. Must be enrolled in one real estate course at the time of submission of application. Visit Website for application, exact deadlines, and other information.

Amount of award:	$2,000-$4,000
Number of applicants:	20
Total amount awarded:	$18,600

Contact:
California Association of Realtors Scholarship Foundation
525 South Virgil Avenue
Los Angeles, CA 90020
Phone: 213-739-8243
Fax: 213-739-7286
Web: www.car.org/aboutus

California Farm Bureau Federation

California Farm Bureau Scholarship

Type of award: Scholarship, renewable.
Intended use: For full-time undergraduate study at accredited 4-year institution. Designated institutions: Colleges/universities in California.
Eligibility: Applicant must be U.S. citizen residing in California.
Basis for selection: Major/career interest in agriculture; agribusiness; engineering, agricultural or veterinary medicine. Applicant must demonstrate high academic achievement, leadership and seriousness of purpose.
Application requirements: Recommendations, transcript.
Additional information: Visit Website for application. Must be preparing for career in agricultural industry.

Amount of award:	$1,500-$5,000
Number of applicants:	148
Application deadline:	March 1
Notification begins:	June 1
Total amount awarded:	$158,750

Contact:
California Farm Bureau Scholarship Foundation
2300 River Plaza Drive
Sacramento, CA 95833
Phone: 916-561-5500
Web: www.cfbf.com/programs/scholar

California Masonic Foundation

California Masonic Foundation Scholarship

Type of award: Scholarship, renewable.

Intended use: For full-time undergraduate study at accredited 2-year or 4-year institution.
Eligibility: Applicant must be high school senior. Applicant must be U.S. citizen residing in California.
Basis for selection: Applicant must demonstrate financial need and high academic achievement.
Application requirements: Essay.
Additional information: Minimum 3.0 GPA. Must have been California resident for at least one year. While not required, some preference is given to applicants with Masonic relatives. Visit Website for more information and application.

Amount of award:	$2,500-$10,000
Number of awards:	50
Number of applicants:	4,000
Application deadline:	February 15
Notification begins:	May 1
Total amount awarded:	$1,200,000

Contact:
California Masonic Foundation
1111 California Street
San Francisco, CA 94108-2284
Web: www.freemason.org

California's Junior Miss

California's Junior Miss Competition

Type of award: Scholarship.
Intended use: For undergraduate study at accredited 2-year or 4-year institution in United States.
Eligibility: Applicant must be single, female, high school junior. Applicant must be U.S. citizen residing in California.
Basis for selection: Competition/talent/interest in poise/talent/fitness. Applicant must demonstrate high academic achievement.
Additional information: Local competitions held from January to May; state competition held in first half of August. Awards not limited to state Junior Miss finalists; winners of various judged categories also receive awards. Winner of state-level Junior Miss program will receive $10,000; other prizes of varying amounts may be awarded on local level. Participants must never have been pregnant. Minimum 3.0 GPA. Check Website for details.

Amount of award:	$500-$10,000
Number of awards:	20
Number of applicants:	280
Application deadline:	January 1
Notification begins:	May 15
Total amount awarded:	$30,000

Contact:
California's Junior Miss
P.O. Box 27191
Bakersfield, CA 93303
Web: www.ajm.org

California Student Aid Commission

Cal Grant A & B Entitlement Award Program

Type of award: Scholarship, renewable.
Intended use: For undergraduate study at postsecondary institution. Designated institutions: Qualifying California postsecondary schools.
Eligibility: Applicant must be high school senior. Applicant must be U.S. citizen or permanent resident residing in California.
Basis for selection: Applicant must demonstrate financial need and high academic achievement.
Application requirements: FAFSA, GPA verification form.
Additional information: Applicants who graduated in the last year also eligible. Awards given to all eligible applicants. Minimum 3.0 GPA for Cal Grant A; minimum 2.0 GPA for Cal Grant B. Cal Grant A provides tuition and fees. Cal Grant B awards up to $1,551 the first year and $1,551 plus tuition and fees for years two through four. Visit Website or contact CSAC for more details.

Amount of award:	$1,551-$7,788
Number of applicants:	192,270
Application deadline:	March 2
Notification begins:	March 31
Total amount awarded:	$678,300,000

Contact:
California Student Aid Commission
Student Support Services Branch
P.O. Box 419027
Rancho Cordova, CA 95741-9027
Phone: 888-224-7268
Fax: 916-464-8002
Web: www.calgrants.org

Cal Grant A and B Competitive Awards

Type of award: Scholarship, renewable.
Intended use: For undergraduate study at postsecondary institution. Designated institutions: Qualifying California postsecondary schools.
Eligibility: Applicant must be U.S. citizen or permanent resident residing in California.
Basis for selection: Applicant must demonstrate financial need and high academic achievement.
Application requirements: FAFSA, GPA verification form.
Additional information: Minimum 3.0 GPA for Cal Grant A; minimum 2.0 GPA for Cal Grant B. Cal Grant A pays tuition and fees. Cal Grant B awards up to $1,551 first year and $1,551 plus tuition and fees for years two through four. Students with no available GPA can submit SAT, ACT, or GED scores. Visit Website or contact CSAC for more details.

Amount of award:	$1,551-$7,788
Number of awards:	22,500
Number of applicants:	62,295
Application deadline:	March 2, September 2
Notification begins:	April 30, October 31
Total amount awarded:	$129,400,000

Contact:
California Student Aid Commission
Student Support Services Branch
P.O. Box 419027
Rancho Cordova, CA 95741-9027
Phone: 888-224-7268
Fax: 916-464-8002
Web: www.calgrants.org

Cal Grant C Award

Type of award: Scholarship, renewable.
Intended use: For undergraduate study at vocational or 2-year institution. Designated institutions: Qualifying California postsecondary institutions.
Eligibility: Applicant must be U.S. citizen or permanent resident residing in California.
Basis for selection: Applicant must demonstrate financial need.
Application requirements: FAFSA, GPA verification form.
Additional information: Funding is available for up to two years, and vocational program must be at least four months in length. Visit Website or contact CSAC for more details.

Amount of award:	$576-$2,592
Number of awards:	15,000
Number of applicants:	15,875
Application deadline:	March 2
Notification begins:	May 30
Total amount awarded:	$9,200,000

Contact:
California Student Aid Commission
Student Support Services Branch
P.O. Box 419027
Rancho Cordova, CA 95741-9027
Phone: 888-224-7268
Fax: 916-464-8002
Web: www.calgrants.org

California Chafee Grant Program

Type of award: Scholarship, renewable.
Intended use: For undergraduate or graduate study at accredited postsecondary institution.
Eligibility: Applicant must be no older than 21.
Basis for selection: Applicant must demonstrate financial need.
Application requirements: FAFSA.
Additional information: Must be current or former foster youth from any state attending a California college or current foster youth from California attending any college. Must have been eligible for foster care between 16th and 18th birthdays. Must not have reached 22nd birthday by July 1st of award year. Must be enrolled at least half time in course of study lasting at least one year. Renewable through 23rd birthday. Apply early.

Amount of award:	$5,000
Number of awards:	3,400
Number of applicants:	6,028
Application deadline:	September 30
Notification begins:	August 1
Total amount awarded:	$13,000,000

Contact:
California Student Aid Commission
Attn: Specialized Programs Operations Branch
P.O. Box 419029
Rancho Cordova, CA 95741-9029
Phone: 888-224-7268
Fax: 916-464-7977
Web: www.chafee.csac.ca.gov

California Child Development Grant Program

Type of award: Scholarship.
Intended use: For undergraduate study at accredited 2-year or 4-year institution. Designated institutions: California postsecondary institutions.
Eligibility: Applicant must be U.S. citizen or permanent resident residing in California.
Basis for selection: Major/career interest in education, early childhood. Applicant must demonstrate financial need.
Application requirements: Recommendations, nomination by postsecondary institution or employing agency. FAFSA.
Additional information: Recipients attending two-year institutions receive up to $1,000 annually; those attending four-year institutions receive up to $2,000 annually. Recipients must maintain at least half-time enrollment in approved course of study leading to Child Development Permit in one of following levels: Teacher, Site Supervisor, Master Teacher, or Program Director. Must maintain satisfactory academic progress, meet federal Selective Service filing requirements, and commit to one year of full-time employment in licensed child care center for every year they receive the grant. Deadlines and notification dates vary. Visit Website for application and more information.

Amount of award:	$1,000-$2,000
Number of awards:	100
Number of applicants:	650
Total amount awarded:	$300,000

Contact:
California Student Aid Commission
Attn: Specialized Programs -- Child Dvlpmnt
P.O. Box 419029
Rancho Cordova, CA 95741-9029
Phone: 888-224-7268 opt. 3
Fax: 916-464-7977
Web: www.csac.ca.gov

California Robert C. Byrd Honors Scholarship

Type of award: Scholarship, renewable.
Intended use: For full-time undergraduate study at accredited postsecondary institution in United States.
Eligibility: Applicant must be high school senior. Applicant must be U.S. citizen or permanent resident residing in California.
Basis for selection: Applicant must demonstrate high academic achievement.
Application requirements: Nomination by high school.
Additional information: Current high school students should contact high school guidance counselor for application instructions. GED students may apply directly to the Commission. Renewable up to four years.

Amount of award:	$1,500
Number of awards:	800
Number of applicants:	1,900
Application deadline:	May 1
Notification begins:	June 1
Total amount awarded:	$1,200,000

Contact:
California Student Aid Commission
Attn: Robert C. Byrd Honors Scholarship
P.O. Box 419029
Rancho Cordova, CA 95741-9029
Phone: 888-224-7268
Fax: 916-464-7977
Web: www.csac.ca.gov

Law Enforcement Personnel Dependents (LEPD) Grant Program

Type of award: Scholarship, renewable.
Intended use: For undergraduate study at accredited 2-year or 4-year institution. Designated institutions: California postsecondary institutions.
Eligibility: Applicant must be U.S. citizen residing in California. Applicant's parent must have been killed or disabled in work-related accident as firefighter, police officer or public safety officer.
Basis for selection: Applicant must demonstrate financial need.
Application requirements: SAR, birth certificate (not required for spouse), death certificate, findings of Workers' Compensation Appeals Board.
Additional information: Applicant must be dependent or spouse of California peace or law enforcement officer, officer or employee of Department of Corrections or Department of Youth Authority in California, or California firefighter, who was killed or 100 percent disabled in performance of duty. Number of awards varies.

Amount of award:	$100-$11,259

Contact:
California Student Aid Commission
Specialized Programs
P.O. Box 419029
Rancho Cordova, CA 95741-9029
Phone: 888-224-7268 opt. 3
Fax: 916-464-7977
Web: www.csac.ca.gov

California Teachers Association

California Teachers Association Martin Luther King, Jr., Memorial Scholarship

Type of award: Scholarship.
Intended use: For undergraduate or graduate study at accredited postsecondary institution.
Eligibility: Applicant must be Alaskan native, Asian American, African American, Mexican American, Hispanic American, Puerto Rican, American Indian or Native Hawaiian/Pacific Islander. Applicant must be residing in California.
Basis for selection: Major/career interest in education; education, early childhood; education, special or education, teacher. Applicant must demonstrate financial need.
Application requirements: Recommendations, essay, transcript, proof of eligibility.
Additional information: Must be active California Teachers Association (CTA) member, active Student CTA member, or dependent child of an active, retired, or deceased CTA member. Amount of award and number of awards varies. To receive funds, must show proof of registration in approved credential or degree program. Must pursue teaching-related career in public education. Application must be typed and mailed. Check Website for deadline and additional information.

Contact:
CTA Scholarship Committee Human Rights Department
c/o Janeya Collins
P.O. Box 921
Burlingame, CA 94011-0921
Phone: 650-552-5446
Fax: 650-552-5001
Web: www.cta.org

CTA Scholarship for Dependent Children

Type of award: Scholarship, renewable.
Intended use: For full-time undergraduate or graduate study at accredited postsecondary institution.
Eligibility: Applicant must be residing in California.
Basis for selection: Major/career interest in education. Applicant must demonstrate high academic achievement, depth of character, leadership, seriousness of purpose and service orientation.
Application requirements: Recommendations, essay, transcript, proof of eligibility.
Additional information: Applicant must be dependent child of active, retired, or deceased member of California Teachers Association. Minimum 3.5 high school GPA. Awards based on overall achievement in four categories: 1) involvement in and sensitivity to human, social, and civic issues; 2) characteristics such as responsibility, reliability, and integrity; 3) academic and vocational potential; and 4) special and personal achievements. One scholarship set aside for student attending continuation high school. Application deadline between end of January and beginning of February; visit Website for exact date and the most current information. Number of awards varies.
  Amount of award: $2,000-$5,000
Contact:
CTA Scholarship Committee Human Rights Department
c/o Janeya Collins
P.O. Box 921
Burlingame, CA 94011-0921
Phone: 650-552-5446
Fax: 650-552-5001
Web: www.cta.org

CTA Scholarships for Members

Type of award: Scholarship, renewable.
Intended use: For undergraduate or graduate study at accredited postsecondary institution.
Eligibility: Applicant must be residing in California.
Basis for selection: Major/career interest in education; education, early childhood; education, special or education, teacher. Applicant must demonstrate high academic achievement, depth of character, leadership, seriousness of purpose and service orientation.
Application requirements: Recommendations, essay, transcript, proof of eligibility.
Additional information: Scholarships awarded based on overall achievement in four categories: 1) involvement in and sensitivity to human, social, and civic issues; 2) characteristics such as responsibility, reliability, and integrity; 3) academic and vocational potential; and 4) special and personal achievements. Applicant must be active member of California Teachers Association (including members working on emergency credential). Application deadline is between end of January and beginning of February; visit Website for exact date and the most up-to-date information. Number of awards varies.
  Amount of award: $2,000-$5,000

Contact:
CTA Scholarship Committee Human Rights Department
c/o Janeya Collins
P.O. Box 921
Burlingame, CA 94011-0921
Phone: 650-552-5446
Fax: 650-552-5001
Web: www.cta.org

L. Gordon Bittle Memorial Scholarship for SCTA

Type of award: Scholarship, renewable.
Intended use: For full-time undergraduate, graduate or non-degree study at accredited postsecondary institution.
Eligibility: Applicant must be residing in California.
Basis for selection: Major/career interest in education; education, early childhood; education, special or education, teacher. Applicant must demonstrate high academic achievement, depth of character and service orientation.
Application requirements: Recommendations, essay, transcript.
Additional information: Applicant must be active member of Student CTA. Minimum 3.5 high school GPA. Must pursue career in public education. Not available to CTA members currently working in schools. May be enrolled in teacher credential program. Application deadline is between end of January and beginning of February; visit Website for exact date and more information.
  Amount of award: $3,000
  Number of awards: 3
  Total amount awarded: $7,500
Contact:
CTA Scholarship Committee Human Rights Department
c/o Janeya Collins
P.O. Box 921
Burlingame, CA 94011-0921
Phone: 650-552-5446
Fax: 650-552-5001
Web: www.cta.org

CAP Charitable Foundation

Ron Brown Scholar Program

Type of award: Scholarship, renewable.
Intended use: For full-time undergraduate study at accredited 4-year institution in United States.
Eligibility: Applicant must be African American. Applicant must be high school senior. Applicant must be U.S. citizen or permanent resident.
Basis for selection: Applicant must demonstrate financial need, high academic achievement, depth of character, leadership, seriousness of purpose and service orientation.
Application requirements: Recommendations, essay, transcript.
Additional information: In addition to financial assistance, scholars get other benefits: summer internships, career guidance, placement opportunities, mentors, and leadership training. Scholarships may be used to pursue any academic discipline. Award is $10,000 per year for four years. Earlier deadline is for those who wish to have their information forwarded to select colleges and scholarship programs.

Amount of award:	$40,000
Number of awards:	10
Number of applicants:	10,400
Application deadline:	November 1, January 9
Notification begins:	April 1
Total amount awarded:	$480,000

Contact:
Ron Brown Scholar Program
1160 Pepsi Place, Suite 206
Charlottesville, VA 22901
Phone: 434-964-1588
Fax: 434-964-1589
Web: www.ronbrown.org

Carl's Jr. Restaurants

Carl N. & Margaret Karcher Founders' Scholarship

Type of award: Scholarship.
Intended use: For full-time freshman study at accredited vocational, 2-year or 4-year institution.
Eligibility: Applicant must be no older than 21, high school senior. Applicant must be residing in Utah, Texas, Alaska, Washington, Arizona, Nevada, Oklahoma, California, Oregon, Idaho, New Mexico, Colorado or Hawaii.
Application requirements: Transcript.
Additional information: High school graduates also eligible. Employees, affiliates, and franchisees of Carl Karcher Enterprises, Inc., Scholarship America, affiliated agencies and their immediate families are ineligible. Application available on Website.

Amount of award:	$1,000
Number of awards:	60
Number of applicants:	5,000
Application deadline:	February 1
Total amount awarded:	$60,000

Contact:
Carl N. & Margaret Karcher Founders' Scholarship
c/o Scholarship America
One Scholarship Way, PO Box 297
St. Peter, MN 56082
Phone: 507-931-1682
Web: www.carlsjr.com/promotions

Catching the Dream

MESBEC Scholarships

Type of award: Scholarship, renewable.
Intended use: For full-time undergraduate or graduate study at accredited postsecondary institution in United States.
Eligibility: Applicant must be Alaskan native or American Indian. Must be at least one-quarter Native American and enrolled member of federally recognized, state recognized, or terminated tribe. Applicant must be U.S. citizen or permanent resident.
Basis for selection: Major/career interest in mathematics; engineering; science, general; business; education; computer/information sciences; health sciences or medicine. Applicant must demonstrate high academic achievement, depth of

character, leadership, seriousness of purpose and service orientation.
Application requirements: Recommendations, essay, transcript, proof of eligibility.
Additional information: Deadlines are March 15 for summer funding, April 15 for fall, September 15 for spring.

Amount of award:	$500-$5,000
Number of awards:	180
Number of applicants:	150
Application deadline:	April 15, September 15
Total amount awarded:	$300,000

Contact:
Catching the Dream
8200 Mountain Road NE
Suite 203
Albuquerque, NM 87110
Phone: 505-262-2351
Fax: 505-262-0534
Web: www.catchingthedream.org

Native American Leadership in Education Scholarship

Type of award: Scholarship, renewable.
Intended use: For full-time undergraduate or graduate study at accredited postsecondary institution in United States.
Eligibility: Applicant must be American Indian. Must be at least one-quarter Native American and enrolled member of federally recognized, state recognized, or terminated tribe. Applicant must be U.S. citizen or permanent resident.
Basis for selection: Major/career interest in education. Applicant must demonstrate high academic achievement, depth of character, leadership, seriousness of purpose and service orientation.
Application requirements: Recommendations, essay, transcript, proof of eligibility.
Additional information: Deadlines are March 15 for summer funding, April 15 for fall, September 15 for spring.

Amount of award:	$500-$5,000
Number of awards:	30
Number of applicants:	40
Application deadline:	April 15, September 15
Total amount awarded:	$100,000

Contact:
Catching the Dream
8200 Mountain Road NE
Suite 203
Albuquerque, NM 87110
Phone: 505-262-2351
Fax: 505-262-0534
Web: www.catchingthedream.org

Tribal Business Management Scholarship

Type of award: Scholarship, renewable.
Intended use: For full-time undergraduate, graduate or postgraduate study at accredited postsecondary institution in United States.
Eligibility: Applicant must be Alaskan native or American Indian. Must be at least one-quarter Native American and enrolled member of federally recognized, state recognized, or terminated tribe. Applicant must be U.S. citizen or permanent resident.
Basis for selection: Major/career interest in business; economics; finance/banking; hotel/restaurant management; accounting; marketing or business/management/administration.

Applicant must demonstrate high academic achievement, depth of character, leadership, seriousness of purpose and service orientation.
Application requirements: Recommendations, essay, transcript, proof of eligibility.
Additional information: Scholarships are for fields of study directly related to tribal business development and management. Application deadlines are March 15 for summer semester, April 15 for fall semester, September 15 for spring semester.

Amount of award:	$500-$5,000
Number of awards:	15
Number of applicants:	30
Application deadline:	April 15, September 15
Total amount awarded:	$50,000

Contact:
Catching the Dream
8200 Mountain Road NE
Suite 203
Albuquerque, NM 87110
Phone: 505-262-2351
Fax: 505-262-0534
Web: www.catchingthedream.org

Catholic Aid Association

Post-High School Tuition Scholarship

Type of award: Scholarship.
Intended use: For full-time freshman or sophomore study at accredited vocational, 2-year or 4-year institution in United States.
Basis for selection: Applicant must demonstrate leadership and service orientation.
Application requirements: Essay, proof of eligibility.
Additional information: Must have been member of Catholic Aid Association for two years prior to application deadline. Award is $300 awards for students attending non-Catholic schools and $500 for those attending Catholic colleges. Visit Website for application. Number of awards varies.

Amount of award:	$300-$500
Number of awards:	486
Number of applicants:	565
Application deadline:	February 15
Notification begins:	April 1
Total amount awarded:	$162,600

Contact:
Catholic Aid Association Scholarship Program
3499 Lexington Avenue North
St. Paul, MN 55126
Phone: 651-490-0170
Web: www.catholicaid.org

CCNMA

CCNMA Scholarship

Type of award: Scholarship, renewable.
Intended use: For full-time undergraduate or graduate study at accredited postsecondary institution.

Eligibility: Applicant must be Mexican American, Hispanic American or Puerto Rican.
Basis for selection: Competition/talent/interest in writing/journalism. Major/career interest in journalism. Applicant must demonstrate financial need, high academic achievement, seriousness of purpose and service orientation.
Application requirements: Interview, recommendations, essay, transcript. Proof of full-time enrollment. Samples of work: newspaper clips, photographs, audio or television tapes.
Additional information: Must be a Latino resident of California attending school in or out of state, or nonresident attending school in California.

Amount of award:	$500-$2,000
Number of awards:	6
Number of applicants:	100
Application deadline:	April 1
Notification begins:	June 1
Total amount awarded:	$8,000

Contact:
CCNMA
727 W. 27th Street
Room 201
Los Angeles, CA 90007-3212
Phone: 213-819-0075
Fax: 213-743-1838
Web: www.ccnma.org

Center for Architecture

Center for Architecture Design Scholarship

Type of award: Scholarship.
Intended use: For undergraduate or graduate study. Designated institutions: Schools in New York State.
Basis for selection: Major/career interest in architecture; design; engineering, civil; landscape architecture or urban planning. Applicant must demonstrate financial need and high academic achievement.
Application requirements: Portfolio, recommendations, nomination by Dean of school. Cover page with full contact information, SASE optional.
Additional information: Visit Website for deadline information. Single or multiple awards up to $2,500.

Amount of award:	$2,500
Number of applicants:	22
Application deadline:	March 15
Notification begins:	May 10
Total amount awarded:	$2,500

Contact:
Center for Architecture Foundation
Attn: Design Scholarship
536 LaGuardia Place
New York, NY 10012
Phone: 212-358-6133
Web: www.cfafoundation.org/cfadesign

Eleanor Allwork Scholarship

Type of award: Scholarship.
Intended use: For graduate study at accredited postsecondary institution. Designated institutions: NAAB-accredited schools in the State of New York.

Eligibility: Applicant must be U.S. citizen, permanent resident or international student residing in New York.

Basis for selection: Major/career interest in architecture. Applicant must demonstrate financial need and high academic achievement.

Application requirements: Portfolio, recommendations, nomination by Dean of architecture school. Cover page with full contact information. SASE optional.

Additional information: Visit Website for deadline information. Single or multiple awards up to $10,000. Graduate students eligible if from a different undergraduate background and currently completing their first architectural degree.

Amount of award:	$10,000
Number of awards:	3
Number of applicants:	23
Application deadline:	March 15
Notification begins:	May 31
Total amount awarded:	$18,000

Contact:
Center for Architecture Foundation
Attn: Eleanor Allwork Scholarship
536 LaGuardia Place
New York, NY 10012
Phone: 212-358-6133
Web: www.cfafoundation.org/allwork

Fontainebleau Prize

Type of award: Scholarship.

Intended use: For senior or graduate study. Designated institutions: Ecole des Beaux Ars Summer Program at the Ecoles d'Art Americaines.

Basis for selection: Competition/talent/interest in study abroad. Major/career interest in architecture.

Application requirements: Recommendations, essay. Resume, portfolio.

Additional information: Recent graduates may apply. Tuition includes lodging, school-sponsored trips to Paris and Strasbourg, and meals five days each week (breakfast, lunch, and dinner). Visit www.fountainebleau.org to learn more. Programs are in English; knowledge of French is not required. All components of applications must be submitted both electronically as PDFs and in hard-copy form.

Amount of award:	$4,500
Number of awards:	1
Application deadline:	March 15
Notification begins:	April 30

Contact:
Center for Architecture
Fontainebleau Prize
536 LaGuardia Place
New York, NY 10012
Phone: 212-358-6133
Web: www.cfafoundation.org/fontainebleau

Center for Education Solutions

A. Patrick Charnon Memorial Scholarship

Type of award: Scholarship.

Intended use: For full-time undergraduate study at accredited 4-year institution in United States.

Basis for selection: Applicant must demonstrate service orientation.

Application requirements: Recommendations, essay, transcript.

Additional information: Must demonstrate commitment to building communities, tolerance, compassion, and respect for all people. Number of applicants limited to 250; first 250 complete applications received will be considered. Non-traditional students may apply. See Website for application or send SASE to address below. Relatives of selection committee ineligible for award. Applications must be mailed.

Amount of award:	$1,500
Number of awards:	1
Number of applicants:	250
Application deadline:	March 31
Total amount awarded:	$1,500

Contact:
A. Patrick Charnon Memorial Scholarship
The Center for Education Solutions
P.O. Box 208
San Francisco, CA 94104-0208
Phone: 925-934-7304
Web: www.cesresources.org/charnon.html

Central Intelligence Agency

CIA Undergraduate Scholarship Program

Type of award: Scholarship, renewable.

Intended use: For full-time freshman, sophomore or junior study at accredited 4-year institution in United States.

Eligibility: Applicant must be at least 18. Applicant must be U.S. citizen.

Basis for selection: Major/career interest in engineering; computer/information sciences; foreign languages; international relations; human resources or finance/banking. Applicant must demonstrate financial need, high academic achievement, depth of character, patriotism and seriousness of purpose.

Application requirements: Recommendations, transcript. SAT/ACT scores, resume, FAFSA or SAR.

Additional information: Applicant may have wide range of majors in addition to those listed. High school applicants must be 18 by April 1 of senior year. Minimum 3.0 GPA; 1000 SAT, or 21 ACT required. Household income must not exceed $70,000 for family of four or $80,000 for family of five or more. Scholars work at CIA offices in Washington, D.C. metro area during summer breaks and receive annual salary in addition to up to $18,000 per school year for tuition, fees, books, and supplies. Must commit to employment with Agency after college graduation for period 1.5 times length of scholarship. Number of awards varies. Apply online. Deadline in October; check site for exact date.

Amount of award:	$18,000

Contact:
Phone: 800-368-3886
Web: www.cia.gov

C.G. Fuller Foundation c/o Bank of America

C.G. Fuller Foundation Scholarship

Type of award: Scholarship, renewable.
Intended use: For full-time undergraduate study at 4-year institution. Designated institutions: Colleges and universities in South Carolina.
Eligibility: Applicant must be high school senior. Applicant must be residing in South Carolina.
Basis for selection: Applicant must demonstrate financial need, high academic achievement and leadership.
Application requirements: Transcript. Financial statement, recent photograph, copy of parents' most recent 1040 tax return, SAT scores.
Additional information: Contact Bank of America office for application; submit to financial aid office of college or university you plan to attend. Minimum 3.0 GPA and 1100 SAT. Number of awards varies with changes in funding. Parents' adjusted gross income must be $60,000 or less. Award is $1,000 per semester, renewable for four years.

Amount of award:	$1,000
Number of awards:	12
Number of applicants:	100
Application deadline:	April 1
Notification begins:	August 1

Contact:
C.G. Fuller Foundation Scholarship c/o Bank of America
#SC3-240-04-17
P.O. Box 448
Columbia, SC 29202-0448

ChairScholars Foundation, Inc.

National ChairScholars Scholarship

Type of award: Scholarship, renewable.
Intended use: For full-time freshman or sophomore study at postsecondary institution.
Eligibility: Applicant must be physically challenged. Applicant must be no older than 21. Applicant must be U.S. citizen or permanent resident.
Basis for selection: Applicant must demonstrate financial need and service orientation.
Application requirements: Recommendations, essay, transcript. Photograph, parent's IRS Form 1040 from last year, SAT and ACT scores.
Additional information: Applicant must have a major physical challenge but does not have to be confined to a wheelchair. Applicant must be unable to attend college without financial aid; no household income above $85,000. Applicant must have at least a B+ average. If applicant has obtained any other scholarships already, he or she must inform ChairScholars. Award is renewable up to four years, for maximum $20,000.

Amount of award:	$3,000-$5,000
Number of awards:	10
Number of applicants:	150
Application deadline:	February 15
Notification begins:	March 27
Total amount awarded:	$293,000

Contact:
ChairScholars Foundation, Inc.
16101 Carencia Lane
Odessa, FL 33556
Phone: 813-926-0544
Fax: 813-920-7661
Web: www.chairscholars.org

Charles & Lucille King Family Foundation, Inc.

Charles & Lucille King Family Foundation Scholarships

Type of award: Scholarship, renewable.
Intended use: For full-time junior or senior study at accredited 4-year institution in United States.
Basis for selection: Major/career interest in communications or radio/television/film.
Application requirements: Recommendations, transcript. Personal statement. Application form with financial information.
Additional information: Download application from Website.

Amount of award:	$3,500
Number of applicants:	93
Application deadline:	April 15
Total amount awarded:	$84,250

Contact:
Charles & Lucille King Family Foundation, Inc.
1212 Avenue of the Americas
7th Floor
New York, NY 10036
Phone: 212-682-2913
Fax: 212-949-0728
Web: www.kingfoundation.org

The Charles A. and Anne Morrow Lindbergh Foundation

Lindbergh Grant

Type of award: Research grant.
Intended use: For undergraduate or non-degree study at postsecondary institution.
Basis for selection: Major/career interest in agriculture; aviation; biomedical; education; environmental science; health sciences or natural resources/conservation.
Application requirements: Research proposal.
Additional information: Applicant research or educational project should address balance between technological advancement and environmental preservation. Citizens of all countries are eligible. Deadline is second Thursday in June.

Amount of award: $1,000-$10,580
Number of awards: 10
Number of applicants: 200
Notification begins: April 15
Contact:
The Charles A. and Anne Morrow Lindbergh Foundation
2150 Third Avenue North
Suite 310
Anoka, MN 55303-2200
Phone: 763-576-1596
Fax: 763-576-1664
Web: www.lindberghfoundation.org

Charleston Women in International Trade

Charleston Women in International Trade Scholarship

Type of award: Scholarship.
Intended use: For undergraduate study at accredited postsecondary institution in United States.
Eligibility: Applicant must be U.S. citizen residing in South Carolina.
Basis for selection: Applicant must demonstrate financial need and seriousness of purpose.
Application requirements: Recommendations, transcript, proof of eligibility. Two-page (minimum length), double-spaced essay explaining the importance of international trade and state your goals for working in the international business environment. Must also explain why you believe you should be awarded this scholarship. Listing of courses/work experience relevant to interest in international trade; extracurricular activities, civic and community involvement. List of relevant courses/work experience. Financial aid/tuition information.
Additional information: Applicant must be pursuing degree specific to international trade or related course of study. To apply, complete application on Website.

Amount of award: $3,000
Number of awards: 2
Application deadline: February 28
Total amount awarded: $6,000
Contact:
Dayna M. Jordan, CWIT Awards Chairperson
P.O. Box 31258
Charleston, SC 29417
Phone: 843-266-4974
Web: www.cwitsc.org

Chicago Scholars Foundation

Chicago Scholars Program

Type of award: Scholarship, renewable.
Intended use: For freshman study at postsecondary institution.
Eligibility: Applicant must be high school junior. Applicant must be residing in Illinois.
Basis for selection: Applicant must demonstrate financial need, high academic achievement and service orientation.

Application requirements: Recommendations, essay, transcript.
Additional information: Applicant must live or go to high school within Chicago city limits. Award provides five years' support, including a year of college prep, a $5,000 merit scholarship, summer programming, and internship opportunities. Visit Website for more information.

Amount of award: $1,250-$5,000
Number of awards: 50
Number of applicants: 131
Application deadline: January 31
Notification begins: May 1
Total amount awarded: $224,283
Contact:
Chicago Scholars Foundation
55 E. Jackson Boulevard
Suite 1010
Chicago, IL 60604
Phone: 312-784-3300
Fax: 312-784-3301
Web: www.chicagoscholars.org

Choctaw Nation of Oklahoma

Choctaw Nation Higher Education Program

Type of award: Scholarship, renewable.
Intended use: For undergraduate or graduate study at accredited 2-year, 4-year or graduate institution in United States.
Eligibility: Applicant must be American Indian. Must be enrolled member of Choctaw Tribe and have Certificate of Degree of Indian Blood (CDIB) and tribal membership card.
Application requirements: Transcript. Proof of Choctaw descent. FAFSA. School enrollment verification via submission of class schedule.
Additional information: Program made up of two awards: a grant and a scholarship. The $1,600 grant is based on financial need. The $2,000 scholarship is for applicants with minimum 2.5 GPA. Grant will assist with any unmet need up to award amount. Must reapply for renewal. Number of awards varies. May only receive either grant or scholarship.

Amount of award: $1,600-$2,000
Number of applicants: 5,000
Application deadline: October 1, March 15
Notification begins: July 15
Contact:
Choctaw Nation of Oklahoma
Higher Education Department
P.O. Box 1210
Durant, OK 74702-1210
Phone: 800-522-6170
Fax: 580-924-1267
Web: www.choctawnation.com

Christian Record Services

Christian Record Services Scholarship

Type of award: Scholarship, renewable.
Intended use: For full-time undergraduate study at postsecondary institution in United States.
Eligibility: Applicant must be visually impaired.
Basis for selection: Applicant must demonstrate financial need and high academic achievement.
Application requirements: Recommendations. Photo and bio.
Additional information: Applicants must be totally or legally blind. Awardees must reapply yearly.

Amount of award:	$500
Number of awards:	10
Number of applicants:	67
Application deadline:	April 1
Notification begins:	May 15
Total amount awarded:	$5,000

Contact:
Christian Record Services
4444 South 52 Street
Lincoln, NE 68516
Phone: 402-488-0981
Fax: 402-488-7582
Web: www.christianrecord.org

City University of New York

Peter F. Vallone Academic Scholarship

Type of award: Scholarship, renewable.
Intended use: For full-time undergraduate study. Designated institutions: CUNY branches.
Eligibility: Applicant must be residing in New York.
Application requirements: FAFSA.
Additional information: Students are considered as part of the admissions process; no separate application. Applicants must have a B average or better and have successfully completed at least 12 College Preparatory Initiative (Regents level) year-long courses. Must graduate from New York City high school. Award amount varies yearly.

Amount of award:	$650
Number of awards:	7,500
Number of applicants:	13,000
Notification begins:	August 1
Total amount awarded:	$7,500,000

Contact:
City University of New York Office of Financial Aid
1114 Avenue of the Americas, FL15
New York, NY 10036
Phone: 212-290-5600
Web: www.cuny.edu/admissions/financial-aid/grants-scholarships/nyc-grants.html

The Coca-Cola Foundation

Coca-Cola All-State Community Colleges Academic Team Scholarship

Type of award: Scholarship.
Intended use: For undergraduate study at 2-year institution in United States. Designated institutions: Community colleges.
Eligibility: Applicant must be U.S. citizen or permanent resident.
Basis for selection: Applicant must demonstrate high academic achievement, depth of character and service orientation.
Application requirements: Nomination by college at which student is enrolled or is planning to enroll.
Additional information: Applicant/nominee must have done community service within past 12 months. Minimum 3.5 GPA for all coursework completed in last five years. Minimum 30 credit hours at community college in past five years. Must be planning to enroll in at least two courses during next term. Children and grandchildren of Coca-Cola employees not eligible. Program administered by Phi Theta Kappa Honor Society. Award notification begins in March. Visit Website for college credit requirements and nomination information.

Amount of award:	$1,000-$2,000
Number of awards:	370
Number of applicants:	1,600
Application deadline:	December 1
Total amount awarded:	$500,000

Contact:
Scholarship Programs Department
Phi Theta Kappa Honor Society
1625 Eastover Drive
Jackson, MS 39211
Phone: 800-306-2653 or 601-984-3539
Fax: 601-984-3546
Web: www.coca-colascholars.org or www.ptk.org/schol/aaat/announce.htm

Coca-Cola Scholars Program

Type of award: Scholarship, renewable.
Intended use: For full-time undergraduate study at accredited 4-year institution in United States.
Eligibility: Applicant must be high school senior. Applicant must be U.S. citizen or permanent resident.
Basis for selection: Applicant must demonstrate high academic achievement, depth of character, leadership, seriousness of purpose and service orientation.
Additional information: Applicant may also be temporary resident in legalization program, refugee, asylee, Cuban/Haitian entrant, or Humanitarian Parole. Must be attending high school in United States or territories. Minimum 3.0 GPA required at the end of junior year high school. Award is for four years, $2,500 or $5,000 per year. Notification begins November 30 for semifinalists; end of February for finalists. Children and grandchildren of Coca-Cola employees not eligible.

Amount of award:	$10,000-$20,000
Number of awards:	250
Number of applicants:	75,000
Application deadline:	October 31
Notification begins:	November 30
Total amount awarded:	$3,000,000

Contact:
Coca-Cola Scholars Foundation
Four Year Award for Seniors
P.O. Box 442
Atlanta, GA 30301-0442
Phone: 800-306-2653
Web: www.coca-colascholars.org

The College Board

Young Epidemiology Scholars Student Competition

Type of award: Scholarship.
Intended use: For undergraduate study at 4-year institution in United States.
Eligibility: Applicant must be high school junior or senior. Applicant must be U.S. citizen or permanent resident.
Basis for selection: Major/career interest in epidemiology; sociology; health sciences or mathematics.
Application requirements: An individual research project that applies epidemiological principles to health-related area.
Additional information: See Website for online registration and more information.

Amount of award:	$1,000-$50,000
Number of awards:	120
Number of applicants:	561
Application deadline:	February 1
Notification begins:	March 31
Total amount awarded:	$456,000

Contact:
The College Board
YES Program
11955 Democracy Drive, Suite 300
Reston, VA 20190
Phone: 800-626-9795
Fax: 703-935-7727
Web: www.collegeboard.com/yes

Colorado Commission on Higher Education

Colorado Student Grant

Type of award: Scholarship.
Intended use: For undergraduate study at postsecondary institution. Designated institutions: Eligible Colorado institutions.
Eligibility: Applicant must be residing in Colorado.
Basis for selection: Applicant must demonstrate financial need.
Application requirements: FAFSA.
Additional information: Contact college financial aid office or visit Website for additional information. International students must be working toward becoming permanent resident of U.S.

Amount of award:	$850-$5,000
Total amount awarded:	$68,237,460

Contact:
Colorado Commission on Higher Education
1560 Broadway
Suite 1600
Denver, CO 80202
Phone: 303-866-2723
Web: highered.colorado.gov

Colorado Supplemental Leveraging Educational Assistance Partnership (SLEAP)

Type of award: Scholarship.
Intended use: For undergraduate study at accredited postsecondary institution. Designated institutions: Four-year institutions in Colorado with CCHE-authorized teacher licensure programs or institutions with post-baccalaureate licensing programs.
Eligibility: Applicant must be residing in Colorado.
Basis for selection: Major/career interest in education. Applicant must demonstrate financial need.
Application requirements: FAFSA.
Additional information: Applicant must be student teaching during award year. Contact college financial aid office for information and application. International students must be working toward becoming permanent resident of U.S.

Amount of award:	$5,000
Total amount awarded:	$954,909

Contact:
Colorado Commission on Higher Education
1560 Broadway
Suite 1600
Denver, CO 80202
Phone: 303-866-2723
Web: highered.colorado.gov

Colorado Work-Study Program

Type of award: Scholarship.
Intended use: For undergraduate study at postsecondary institution. Designated institutions: Eligible post-secondary institutions in Colorado.
Eligibility: Applicant must be residing in Colorado.
Additional information: Part-time employment program for students who need work experience or who can prove financial need. International students must be working toward becoming permanent resident of U.S. Amount of award cannot exceed need. Institutions must award 70% of work-study allocations to students with documented need; remaining 30% may be awarded to students without need. Contact college financial aid office or visit Website for additional information.

Total amount awarded:	$18,061,358

Contact:
Colorado Commission on Higher Education
1560 Broadway
Suite 1600
Denver, CO 80202
Phone: 303-866-2723
Web: highered.colorado.gov

Colorado Masons Benevolent Fund Association

Colorado Masons Scholarship

Type of award: Scholarship, renewable.
Intended use: For full-time undergraduate study at accredited vocational, 2-year or 4-year institution. Designated institutions: Institutions of higher learning in Colorado.
Eligibility: Applicant must be high school senior. Applicant must be residing in Colorado.
Basis for selection: Applicant must demonstrate financial need, high academic achievement and depth of character.
Additional information: Applicant must be graduating senior at public high school in Colorado and attending an institution of higher learning in Colorado. Scholarship is renewable for up to four years. Contact high school counselor for application details. Do not contact association directly.

Amount of award:	$7,000
Number of awards:	15
Number of applicants:	456
Application deadline:	March 7
Total amount awarded:	$279,000

Contact:
Tom J. Cox, PGM Scholarship Administrator
2445 So. Quebec St.
Denver, CO 80231
Phone: 303-290-8544
Web: www.coloradofreemasons.org

Colorado Society of CPAs Educational Foundation

General Scholarship

Type of award: Scholarship, renewable.
Intended use: For junior, senior or graduate study at accredited 4-year or graduate institution in United States. Designated institutions: Colorado colleges/universities with accredited accounting programs.
Eligibility: Applicant must be residing in Colorado.
Basis for selection: Major/career interest in accounting. Applicant must demonstrate high academic achievement.
Application requirements: Essay, transcript.
Additional information: Must have completed eight semester hours in accounting. Must be at least half-time student. Minimum 3.0 GPA. International students must have work visa. Visit Website for application.

Amount of award:	$2,500
Application deadline:	June 15, November 15

Contact:
CSCPA
7979 East Tufts Avenue
Suite 1000
Denver, CO 80237-2847
Phone: 800-523-9082 or 303-773-2877
Web: www.cocpa.org/student-center/scholarships.html

Mark J. Smith Scholarship

Type of award: Scholarship.
Intended use: For junior, senior or graduate study at accredited 4-year or graduate institution in United States. Designated institutions: Colorado colleges and universities with accredited accounting programs.
Eligibility: Applicant must be residing in Colorado.
Basis for selection: Major/career interest in accounting. Applicant must demonstrate financial need and high academic achievement.
Application requirements: Essay, transcript.
Additional information: Must be student from single-parent household. Must have completed eight semester hours in accounting. Must be at least half-time student. Minimum 3.0 GPA. International students must have work visa. Visit Website for application and deadline.

Amount of award:	$2,500
Number of awards:	1

Contact:
CSCPA
7979 East Tufts Avenue
Suite 1000
Denver, CO 80237-2847
Phone: 800-523-9082 or 303-773-2877
Web: www.cocpa.org/student-center/scholarships.html

Columbus Citizens Foundation

College Scholarship Program

Type of award: Scholarship, renewable.
Intended use: For full-time undergraduate study at accredited 4-year institution in United States or Canada.
Eligibility: Applicant must be high school senior. Applicant must be Italian. Applicant must be residing in Vermont, New York, Maine, Delaware, Maryland, Pennsylvania, Massachusetts, District of Columbia, Connecticut, New Hampshire, New Jersey or Rhode Island.
Basis for selection: Applicant must demonstrate financial need, high academic achievement and service orientation.
Application requirements: $25 application fee. Interview, recommendations, essay, transcript. Parent/guardian's most recent state and federal income tax returns, family tree.
Additional information: Minimum 3.25 GPA. Family's taxable income must not exceed $25,000 per household dependent. Applicants who reach semifinalist round must travel to New York City for interview at own expense. Applications available on Website in first week of December each year; deadline is in February or March. Number and amount of awards varies.

Application deadline:	February 1
Notification begins:	May 1

Contact:
Columbus Citizens Foundation College Scholarship Program
8 East 69th Street
New York, NY 10021-4906
Phone: 212-249-9923
Fax: 212-517-7619
Web: www.columbuscitizensfd.org

Congressional Black Caucus Foundation, Inc.

The CBC Spouses Cheerios Brand Health Initiative Scholarship

Type of award: Scholarship, renewable.
Intended use: For full-time undergraduate study at accredited 4-year institution.
Eligibility: Applicant must be U.S. citizen or permanent resident.
Basis for selection: Major/career interest in engineering; health-related professions; medicine or technology. Applicant must demonstrate financial need and service orientation.
Application requirements: Recommendations, essay, transcript, proof of eligibility. Resume, recent photo, copy of Student Aid Report (SAR).
Additional information: Minimum 2.5 GPA. Applicant must reside or attend school in congressional district represented by Congressional Black Caucus (CBC) Member. For more information about CBC districts, go to www.house.gov and enter ZIP Code. Award amount set annually. Submit application materials to CBC Member's Local Scholarship Selection Committee.
   Application deadline: June 1
Contact:
Congressional Black Caucus Foundation
1720 Massachusetts Avenue, NW
Washington, DC 20036
Phone: 202-263-2800
Fax: 202-775-0773
Web: www.cbcfinc.org

The CBC Spouses Education Scholarship

Type of award: Scholarship, renewable.
Intended use: For full-time undergraduate or graduate study at accredited 4-year or graduate institution in United States.
Eligibility: Applicant must be U.S. citizen or permanent resident.
Basis for selection: Applicant must demonstrate financial need and service orientation.
Application requirements: Recommendations, essay, transcript. Resume, recent photo, copy of Student Aid Report (SAR).
Additional information: Applicant must have minimum 2.5 GPA and reside or attend school in congressional district represented by Black Caucus member. For more information about CBC districts, go to www.house.gov and enter ZIP Code. Selection made at district level. Award amount varies. Submit application materials to CBC Member's Local Scholarship Selection Committee.
   Application deadline: June 1
Contact:
Congressional Black Caucus Foundation
1720 Massachusetts Avenue, NW
Washington, DC 20036
Phone: 202-263-2800
Fax: 202-775-0773
Web: www.cbcfinc.org

The CBC Spouses Performing Arts Scholarship Program

Type of award: Scholarship, renewable.
Intended use: For full-time undergraduate study at accredited 4-year institution.
Basis for selection: Major/career interest in performing arts. Applicant must demonstrate financial need and service orientation.
Application requirements: Recommendations, essay, transcript, proof of eligibility. Resume, recent photograph, copy of Student Aid Report (SAR), two-minute performance sample recorded on CD or DVD.
Additional information: Minimum 2.5 GPA. Check Website for application and details.
   Application deadline: April 30
Contact:
Congressional Black Caucus Foundation
1720 Massachusetts Avenue, NW
Washington, DC 20036
Phone: 202-263-2800
Fax: 202-775-0773
Web: www.cbcfinc.org

The CBC Spouses Visual Arts Scholarship

Type of award: Scholarship.
Intended use: For undergraduate study at 4-year institution in United States.
Basis for selection: Major/career interest in arts, general. Applicant must demonstrate financial need and service orientation.
Application requirements: Recommendations, essay, transcript. Recent photo of applicant, resume, copy of Student Aid Report (SAR), up to five artwork samples on CD. High school seniors must submit college acceptance letter.
Additional information: Minimum 2.5 GPA. Check Website for application and details.
   Application deadline: April 30
Contact:
Congressional Black Caucus Foundation
1720 Massachusetts Avenue, NW
Washington, DC 20036
Phone: 202-263-2800
Fax: 202-775-0773
Web: www.cbcfinc.org

Congressional Hispanic Caucus Institute

Congressional Hispanic Caucus Institute Scholarship Awards

Type of award: Scholarship.
Intended use: For full-time undergraduate or graduate study at 2-year, 4-year or graduate institution.
Eligibility: Applicant must be U.S. citizen or permanent resident.
Basis for selection: Applicant must demonstrate financial need, leadership and service orientation.

Application requirements: Recommendations, essay. Resume, SAR.
Additional information: Community college students receive $1,000; students enrolled at four-year colleges or universities receive $2,500; students enrolled in graduate programs receive $5,000. Apply online.

Amount of award:	$1,000-$5,000
Number of awards:	100
Application deadline:	April 16

Contact:
Congressional Hispanic Caucus Institute
911 2nd Street NE
Washington, DC 20002
Phone: 202-543-1771
Fax: 202-546-2143
Web: www.chci.org/scholarships

Connecticut Building Congress, Inc.

CBC Scholarship

Type of award: Scholarship, renewable.
Intended use: For undergraduate or master's study at 2-year or 4-year institution in United States.
Eligibility: Applicant must be high school senior. Applicant must be residing in Connecticut.
Basis for selection: Major/career interest in engineering, construction; architecture; construction management; surveying/mapping or construction. Applicant must demonstrate financial need and high academic achievement.
Application requirements: Essay, transcript. Student Aid Report or FAFSA.
Additional information: Must be involved in extracurricular activities and exhibit potential. Applicant may attend school outside of Connecticut. Number of awards and amount at discretion of Board of Directors. Renewable based on academic performance and available funds.

Amount of award:	$500-$2,000
Number of awards:	3
Number of applicants:	60
Application deadline:	March 31
Notification begins:	May 1
Total amount awarded:	$2,500

Contact:
Connecticut Building Congress
P.O. Box 743
Enfield, CT 06083
Phone: 860-228-1387
Web: www.cbc-ct.org/pages/scholarship.htm

Connecticut Department of Higher Education

Connecticut Aid for Public College Students

Type of award: Scholarship, renewable.

Intended use: For undergraduate study at 2-year or 4-year institution. Designated institutions: Connecticut public colleges and universities.
Eligibility: Applicant must be U.S. citizen residing in Connecticut.
Basis for selection: Applicant must demonstrate financial need.
Application requirements: FAFSA.
Additional information: Awards up to amount of unmet financial need, determined by the college. Deadline based on financial aid deadline. Apply at financial aid office at Connecticut public college.

Number of awards:	18,000
Total amount awarded:	$30,208,469

Contact:
Contact school's financial aid office, or:
Connecticut Department of Higher Education
61 Woodland Street
Hartford, CT 06105-2391
Phone: 800-842-0229
Fax: 860-947-1311
Web: www.ctdhe.org

Connecticut Aid to Dependents of Deceased/POW/MIA Veterans

Type of award: Scholarship.
Intended use: For undergraduate or graduate study. Designated institutions: Connecticut public colleges and universities.
Eligibility: Applicant must be U.S. citizen residing in Connecticut. Applicant must be dependent of deceased veteran or POW/MIA; or spouse of deceased veteran or POW/MIA. Death must be service related. Parent/spouse must have been Connecticut resident prior to enlistment.
Application requirements: Proof of eligibility.
Additional information: Visit Website for more information.

Amount of award:	Full tuition
Number of awards:	8
Number of applicants:	2
Total amount awarded:	$800

Contact:
Contact financial aid office of Connecticut public college, or:
Connecticut Department of Higher Education
61 Woodland Street
Hartford, CT 06105-2391
Phone: 800-842-0229
Fax: 860-947-1310
Web: www.ctdhe.org

Connecticut Capitol Scholarship Program

Type of award: Scholarship, renewable.
Intended use: For undergraduate study at 2-year or 4-year institution. Designated institutions: Connecticut colleges and universities; eligible institutions in Maine, Massachusetts, New Hampshire, Pennsylvania, Rhode Island, Vermont, and Washington, D.C.
Eligibility: Applicant must be high school senior. Applicant must be U.S. citizen or permanent resident residing in Connecticut.
Basis for selection: Applicant must demonstrate financial need and high academic achievement.
Application requirements: FAFSA.
Additional information: Must rank in top 20 percent of class, or have minimum 1800 SAT score or minimum 27 ACT score.

May be used at institutions in Connecticut or at institutions in states with reciprocity agreements with Connecticut.

Amount of award:	$500-$3,000
Number of awards:	5,654
Number of applicants:	4,840
Application deadline:	February 15
Total amount awarded:	$9,590,754

Contact:
High school guidance office for application, or:
Connecticut Department of Higher Education
61 Woodlawn St.
Hartford, CT 06105-2391
Phone: 800-842-0229
Fax: 860-947-1311
Web: www.ctdhe.org

Connecticut Independent College Student Grant

Type of award: Scholarship, renewable.
Intended use: For undergraduate study in United States. Designated institutions: Private institutions in Connecticut.
Eligibility: Applicant must be U.S. citizen residing in Connecticut.
Basis for selection: Applicant must demonstrate financial need.
Application requirements: FAFSA and any other financial aid forms required by the college.
Additional information: Award based on financial need. Deadline determined by financial aid deadline at each college.

Amount of award:	$8,341
Number of awards:	5,800
Total amount awarded:	$23,913,860

Contact:
Contact school's financial office, or:
Connecticut Department of Higher Education
61 Woodland Street
Hartford, CT 06105-2391
Phone: 800-842-0229
Fax: 860-947-1311
Web: www.ctdhe.org

Connecticut Minority Teacher Incentive Grant

Type of award: Scholarship.
Intended use: For full-time junior or senior study. Designated institutions: Eligible Connecticut colleges and universities.
Eligibility: Applicant must be Alaskan native, Asian American, African American, Mexican American, Hispanic American, Puerto Rican, American Indian or Native Hawaiian/Pacific Islander. Applicant must be residing in Connecticut.
Basis for selection: Major/career interest in education; education, special or education, teacher.
Application requirements: Nomination by college or university's Education Dean, or other appropriate official.
Additional information: Must be enrolled in Connecticut college or university teacher preparation program. Grants up to $5,000/year for two years; loan reimbursement of $2,500/year for up to four years of teaching in Connecticut public school. Visit Website for more information.

Amount of award:	$2,500-$5,000
Number of awards:	71
Number of applicants:	78
Application deadline:	October 1
Total amount awarded:	$286,225

Contact:
Minority Teaching Incentive Grant/Weisman Scholarship Program
Connecticut Department of Higher Education
61 Woodland Street
Hartford, CT 06105-2326
Phone: 860-947-1857
Fax: 860-947-1838
Web: www.ctdhe.org

Connecticut Robert C. Byrd Honors Scholarship

Type of award: Scholarship, renewable.
Intended use: For full-time undergraduate study.
Eligibility: Applicant must be high school senior. Applicant must be U.S. citizen or permanent resident residing in Connecticut.
Basis for selection: Applicant must demonstrate high academic achievement.
Additional information: Applicant must rank in top two percent of high school graduating class; have minimum 2100 SAT score, or minimum 32 ACT score. File applications through high school guidance office.

Amount of award:	$1,500
Number of awards:	331
Number of applicants:	1,000
Application deadline:	April 1
Total amount awarded:	$464,750

Contact:
Connecticut Department of Higher Education
61 Woodland Street
Hartford, CT 06105-2391
Phone: 800-842-0229
Fax: 860-947-1838
Web: www.ctdhe.org

Connecticut Tuition Waiver for Senior Citizens

Type of award: Scholarship.
Intended use: For undergraduate study at 2-year or 4-year institution. Designated institutions: Connecticut public colleges and universities.
Eligibility: Applicant must be returning adult student. Applicant must be U.S. citizen residing in Connecticut.
Application requirements: Proof of eligibility.
Additional information: Waivers approved on space available basis. Apply through financial aid office of institution.

Amount of award:	Full tuition

Contact:
Financial aid office of Connecticut public colleges, or:
Connecticut Department of Higher Education
61 Woodland St.
Hartford, CT 06105-2391
Phone: 800-842-0229
Fax: 860-947-1310
Web: www.ctdhe.org

Connecticut Tuition Waiver for Veterans

Type of award: Scholarship, renewable.
Intended use: For undergraduate or graduate study. Designated institutions: Connecticut public colleges and universities.
Eligibility: Applicant must be U.S. citizen residing in Connecticut. Applicant must be veteran. Must have been

Connecticut resident at time of enlistment. Active members of Connecticut Army or Air National Guard also eligible.
Application requirements: Proof of eligibility.
Additional information: Visit Website for more information.

    Amount of award: Full tuition
Contact:
Financial aid office of Connecticut public colleges, or:
Connecticut Department of Higher Education
61 Woodland St.
Hartford, CT 06105-2326
Phone: 800-842-0229
Fax: 860-947-1310
Web: www.ctdhe.org

Connecticut Tuition Waiver for Vietnam MIA/POW Dependents

Type of award: Scholarship.
Intended use: For undergraduate study. Designated institutions: Connecticut public colleges and universities.
Eligibility: Applicant must be U.S. citizen residing in Connecticut. Applicant must be dependent of POW/MIA; or spouse of POW/MIA. Open to spouse or dependent of veteran who is POW/MIA after January 1, 1960.
Application requirements: Proof of eligibility.
Additional information: Apply at financial aid office of institution. Awarded through Connecticut public colleges. Visit Website for more information.

    Amount of award: Full tuition
Contact:
Financial aid office at Connecticut public college, or:
Connecticut Department of Higher Education
61 Woodland St.
Hartford, CT 06105-2326
Phone: 800-842-0229
Fax: 860-947-1310
Web: www.ctdhe.org

Weisman Scholarship

Type of award: Scholarship, renewable.
Intended use: For full-time junior or senior study. Designated institutions: Eligible Connecticut colleges and universities.
Eligibility: Applicant must be Alaskan native, Asian American, African American, Mexican American, Hispanic American, Puerto Rican, American Indian or Native Hawaiian/Pacific Islander. Applicant must be residing in Connecticut.
Basis for selection: Major/career interest in education or education, teacher.
Application requirements: Nomination by college or university's Education Dean, or appropriate official.
Additional information: Must be enrolled in Connecticut teacher preparation program and intend to teach math or science in middle or high school. Loan reimbursement up to $2,500 per year for up to four years of teaching science or math in Connecticut public middle or high school. Visit Website for more information.

Amount of award:	$2,500-$5,000
Number of awards:	2
Number of applicants:	38
Application deadline:	October 1
Total amount awarded:	$17,500

Contact:
Connecticut Department of Higher Education
61 Woodland Street
Hartford, CT 06105-2326
Phone: 800-842-0229
Fax: 860-947-1838
Web: www.ctdhe.org

Connecticut League for Nursing

CLN Scholarships

Type of award: Scholarship.
Intended use: For sophomore, senior or graduate study at accredited 2-year or 4-year institution. Designated institutions: CLN supporting member programs in Connecticut.
Eligibility: Applicant must be U.S. citizen residing in Connecticut.
Basis for selection: Major/career interest in nursing. Applicant must demonstrate financial need and high academic achievement.
Application requirements: Recommendations, transcript.
Additional information: At least one undergraduate and one graduate award given. Applicants must have 18 credits in nursing courses to be eligible for graduate scholarship; undergraduates must have completed one year of two-year program or three years of four-year program; RN students must be entering senior year in upper-division BSN program. Application deadline in October; check Website for exact date.

Amount of award:	$1,000-$1,500
Number of applicants:	22
Notification begins:	October 31
Total amount awarded:	$9,000

Contact:
Connecticut League for Nursing
51 N. Main Street
Suite 3D
Southington, CT 06489
Phone: 860-276-9621
Fax: 860-276-8798
Web: www.ctleaguefornursing.org/scholarships.html

Consortium of Information and Telecommunication Executives

CITE Scholarship

Type of award: Scholarship.
Intended use: For full-time undergraduate study at accredited 4-year institution in United States.
Eligibility: Applicant must be African American. Applicant must be high school senior. Applicant must be U.S. citizen.
Basis for selection: Major/career interest in accounting; advertising; business; communications; computer/information sciences; engineering, electrical/electronic; engineering, industrial; finance/banking; marketing or mathematics.

Applicant must demonstrate financial need and high academic achievement.

Application requirements: Recommendations, essay, transcript. College acceptance letter, proof of parents' income.

Additional information: Minimum 3.0 GPA. Applicant must reside in area where there is a CITE chapter. Family income must be $75,000 or less. Recipient must attend a scholarship event to accept award. Deadline in spring; see Website for date and details.

Amount of award:	$3,000
Number of awards:	1
Total amount awarded:	$3,000

Contact:
Web: www.forcite.org

Costume Society of America

Adele Filene Student Presenter Grant

Type of award: Scholarship.

Intended use: For undergraduate or graduate study in United States.

Eligibility: Applicant must be U.S. citizen or international student.

Basis for selection: Major/career interest in ethnic/cultural studies; art/art history; arts, general; history or fashion/fashion design/modeling.

Application requirements: Two faculty recommendations, budget.

Additional information: Award only for those who have paper or research poster accepted for presentation at the national meeting. Award is for travel expenses to the meeting. Must be student member of Costume Society of America. Major/career interests may include apparel design, historic costume, and fashion merchandising.

Amount of award:	$500
Number of awards:	3
Application deadline:	March 1

Contact:
Costume Society of America National Office
390 Amwell Road, Suite 402
Hillsborough, NJ 08844
Phone: 800-CSA-9447 or 908-359-1471
Fax: 908-450-1118
Web: www.costumesocietyamerica.com/GrantsAwards/
adelefilene.html

Stella Blum Student Research Grant

Type of award: Research grant.

Intended use: For undergraduate or graduate study at vocational, 2-year, 4-year or graduate institution in United States.

Eligibility: Applicant must be U.S. citizen, permanent resident or international student.

Basis for selection: Major/career interest in art/art history; arts, general; history; museum studies or performing arts.

Application requirements: Recommendations, transcript. References and written proposal researching North American costumes. The proposal should be typed, double-spaced, no more than 1,000 words.

Additional information: Must be member of Costume Society of America researching a North American costume

topic as part of degree requirement. Award is $2,000 for research and $500 for expenses to present at national meeting.

Amount of award:	$2,500
Number of awards:	1
Application deadline:	May 1
Notification begins:	August 1
Total amount awarded:	$2,500

Contact:
Costume Society of America
390 Amwell Road, Suite 402
Hillsborough, NJ 08844
Phone: 800-CSA-9447 or 908-359-1471
Fax: 908-450-1118
Web: www.costumesocietyamerica.com/GrantsAwards/
stellablum.html

Council on International Educational Exchange

CIEE International Study Programs (CIEE-ISP) Scholarships

Type of award: Scholarship.

Intended use: For full-time undergraduate study at accredited 4-year institution. Designated institutions: CIEE Member or CIEE Academic Consortium Member institutions.

Basis for selection: Competition/talent/interest in study abroad. Applicant must demonstrate financial need and high academic achievement.

Application requirements: Essay, transcript.

Additional information: Available to CIEE Study Center program applicants only. Program application is used in consideration of scholarship applicants. Visit Website for details and application.

Amount of award:	$1,000-$2,000
Application deadline:	April 1, November 1
Notification begins:	May 1, December 1

Contact:
CIEE
Attn: Scholarship Committee
300 Fore Street
Portland, ME 04101
Phone: 800-40-STUDY
Fax: 207-221-1456
Web: www.ciee.org/study/scholarships.aspx

Jennifer Ritzmann Scholarship for Studies in Tropical Biology

Type of award: Scholarship.

Intended use: For full-time undergraduate study at accredited 4-year institution. Designated institutions: CIEE Study Center program in Monteverde, Costa Rica.

Basis for selection: Major/career interest in biology. Applicant must demonstrate financial need and high academic achievement.

Application requirements: Essay, transcript.

Additional information: Award is for students applying to the Monteverde, Costa Rica semester program only. Visit Website for more information.

Amount of award: $1,000
Number of awards: 2
Application deadline: April 1, November 1
Notification begins: May 1, December 1
Contact:
CIEE
Attn: Scholarship Committee
300 Fore Street
Portland, ME 04101
Phone: 800-40-STUDY
Fax: 207-221-1456
Web: www.ciee.org/study/scholarships.aspx

John E. Bowman Travel Grants

Type of award: Scholarship.
Intended use: For full-time undergraduate study at accredited 4-year institution. Designated institutions: CIEE Member or CIEE Academic Consortium member institutions.
Basis for selection: Competition/talent/interest in study abroad. Applicant must demonstrate financial need and high academic achievement.
Application requirements: Essay, transcript.
Additional information: Applicant must participate in CIEE study abroad program in Africa, Asia, Eastern Europe, or Latin America. Visit Website for details and application.
Amount of award: $1,000
Application deadline: April 1, November 1
Notification begins: May 1, December 1
Contact:
CIEE Attn: Scholarship Committee
Attn: Scholarship Committee
300 Fore Street
Portland, ME 04101
Phone: 800-40-STUDY
Fax: 207-221-1456
Web: www.ciee.org/study/scholarships.aspx

Peter Wollitzer Scholarships for Study in Asia

Type of award: Scholarship.
Intended use: For full-time undergraduate study at accredited 4-year institution. Designated institutions: CIEE Academic Consortium Board Member institutions: Columbia University; Indiana University; Oberlin College; Oregon State University; Pacific Lutheran University; Princeton University; Purdue University; Reed College; University of Nevada, Las Vegas; University of North Carolina, Charlotte; University of Tulsa.
Basis for selection: Competition/talent/interest in study abroad. Applicant must demonstrate financial need and high academic achievement.
Application requirements: Essay, transcript.
Additional information: Applicant must participate in a CIEE Study Center program in Asia (includes Cambodia, China, India, Japan, Korea, Taiwan, Thailand, and Vietnam). Award is $500 for summer program, $2,000 for spring and fall semesters.
Amount of award: $500-$2,000
Number of awards: 4
Application deadline: April 1, November 1
Notification begins: May 1, December 1

Contact:
CIEE Attn: Scholarship Committee
Attn: Scholarship Committee
300 Fore Street
Portland, ME 04101
Phone: 800-40-STUDY
Fax: 207-221-1456
Web: www.ciee.org/study/scholarships.aspx

Robert B. Bailey Scholarship

Type of award: Scholarship.
Intended use: For full-time undergraduate or graduate study at accredited 4-year institution. Designated institutions: CIEE Member or CIEE Academic Consortium member institutions.
Basis for selection: Competition/talent/interest in study abroad. Applicant must demonstrate financial need and high academic achievement.
Application requirements: Essay, transcript.
Additional information: Available to CIEE Study Center applicants only. Must be self-identified as belonging to underrepresented group. Program application is used in consideration of scholarship applicants. Visit Website for details and application.
Amount of award: $500-$1,500
Application deadline: April 1, November 1
Notification begins: May 1, December 1
Contact:
CIEE
Attn: Scholarship Committee
300 Fore Street
Portland, ME 04101
Phone: 800-40-STUDY
Fax: 207-221-1456
Web: www.ciee.org/study/scholarships.aspx

U.S. Department of Education Fulbright-Hays Project Abroad Scholarship for Programs in China

Type of award: Scholarship.
Intended use: For junior, senior, graduate or postgraduate study at postsecondary institution. Designated institutions: CIEE Study Centers at Peking University (Beijing), Nanjing University, East China Normal University (Shanghai), and National Chengchi University (Taipei).
Eligibility: Applicant must be U.S. citizen or permanent resident.
Basis for selection: Major/career interest in Asian studies; foreign languages; education or public administration/service. Applicant must demonstrate financial need and high academic achievement.
Application requirements: Essay, transcript, proof of eligibility.
Additional information: Must be applicant for CIEE programs in Beijing, Shanghai, Nanjing, or Taipei. Must plan to pursue advanced study or career related to China in the areas of academia or public affairs. Must have completed two years, or equivalent, of college-level Mandarin Chinese. Program application taken into consideration for scholarship. Visit Website for details and application.
Amount of award: $1,000-$8,000
Application deadline: April 1, November 1
Notification begins: May 1, December 1

Contact:
CIEE Attn: Scholarship Committee
Attn: Scholarship Committee
300 Fore Street
Portland, ME 04101
Phone: 800-40-STUDY
Fax: 207-221-1456
Web: www.ciee.org/study/scholarships.aspx

Courage Center

Scholarship for People with Disabilities

Type of award: Scholarship.
Intended use: For full-time undergraduate study at accredited vocational, 2-year or 4-year institution.
Eligibility: Applicant must be visually impaired, hearing impaired or physically challenged. Applicant must be U.S. citizen residing in Minnesota.
Basis for selection: Applicant must demonstrate financial need.
Application requirements: Interview, essay.
Additional information: If not Minnesota resident, student must be participant in Courage Center services.

Amount of award:	$500-$1,000
Number of awards:	20
Number of applicants:	20
Application deadline:	May 31
Notification begins:	July 31
Total amount awarded:	$12,000

Contact:
Courage Center Vocational Services
3915 Golden Valley Road
Minneapolis, MN 55422
Phone: 763-520-0553
Fax: 763-520-0577
Web: www.couragecenter.org/ContentPages/Resources.aspx

The Cynthia E. Morgan Memorial Scholarship Fund

The Cynthia E. Morgan Memorial Scholarship Fund

Type of award: Scholarship.
Intended use: For undergraduate or graduate study at accredited vocational, 2-year or 4-year institution. Designated institutions: Maryland vocational school, college, or university.
Eligibility: Applicant must be high school junior or senior. Applicant must be or Maryland.
Basis for selection: Major/career interest in medicine; nursing; pharmacy/pharmaceutics/pharmacology; dietetics/nutrition; occupational therapy; physical therapy; physician assistant or speech pathology/audiology. Applicant must demonstrate financial need and high academic achievement.
Application requirements: Essay, transcript, proof of eligibility.

Additional information: Must be first person in immediate family to attend college. Must be entering or planning on entering medical or medical-related field.

Amount of award:	$1,000
Application deadline:	February 25
Notification begins:	March 15

Contact:
The Cynthia E. Morgan Memorial Scholarship Fund
5516 Maudes Way
White Marsh, MD 21162
Web: www.cemsfund.com

Cystic Fibrosis Foundation

Cystic Fibrosis Student Traineeship

Type of award: Research grant, renewable.
Intended use: For full-time senior, master's or doctoral study at accredited 4-year or graduate institution in United States.
Basis for selection: Major/career interest in medical specialties/research.
Application requirements: Recommendations, research proposal.
Additional information: Trainees must work with faculty sponsor on research project related to cystic fibrosis. Applications accepted throughout the year, but should be submitted at least two months prior to anticipated start date of project.

Amount of award:	$1,500

Contact:
Cystic Fibrosis Foundation
Office of Grants Management
6931 Arlington Road
Bethesda, MD 20814
Phone: 301-951-4422
Fax: 301-841-2605

The Dallas Foundation

Dallas Architectural Foundation - Humphries/HKS Scholarship

Type of award: Scholarship, renewable.
Intended use: For undergraduate study at 4-year institution in or outside United States.
Eligibility: Applicant must be high school senior. Applicant must be U.S. citizen residing in Texas.
Basis for selection: Major/career interest in architecture.
Application requirements: Portfolio, recommendations, essay, transcript, nomination by dean of architecture school.
Additional information: Applicant must be resident of Dallas-Fort Worth metroplex and enrolled in Skyline High School Architecture Cluster. Visit Website for application.

Amount of award:	$2,000
Number of awards:	1
Application deadline:	March 31
Total amount awarded:	$2,000

Contact:
The Dallas Architectural Foundation
1909 Woodall Rodgers Freeway
Suite 100
Dallas, TX 75201
Phone: 214-742-3242
Web: www.dallasfoundation.org

Dallas Architectural Foundation - Swank Travelling Fellowship

Type of award: Scholarship.
Intended use: For senior or graduate study at accredited postsecondary institution.
Eligibility: Applicant must be U.S. citizen residing in Texas.
Basis for selection: Major/career interest in architecture.
Application requirements: Portfolio, recommendations, essay, transcript. Resume, budget statement.
Additional information: Applicant must be permanent resident of the Dallas-Fort Worth area. Fellowship established to assist architecture students or recent graduates in broadening their architectural knowledge through travel. Funds must be used for travel and study costs, and within the same calendar year. Recipient must agree to present program of results to the Dallas Architectural Foundation board. Visit Website for application.

Amount of award:	$2,000
Number of awards:	1
Number of applicants:	5
Application deadline:	March 31
Total amount awarded:	$2,000

Contact:
Dallas Architectural Foundation
1909 Woodall Rodgers Freeway
Suite 100
Dallas, TX 75201
Phone: 214-742-3242
Web: www.dallasfoundation.org

Dr. Dan J. and Patricia S. Pickard Scholarship

Type of award: Scholarship, renewable.
Intended use: For freshman study at 2-year or 4-year institution.
Eligibility: Applicant must be African American. Applicant must be male. Applicant must be residing in Texas.
Basis for selection: Applicant must demonstrate financial need and service orientation.
Application requirements: Recommendations, essay, transcript. FAFSA or SAR.
Additional information: Must be graduating from high school in Dallas County. Minimum 2.5 GPA. Visit Website for application.

Amount of award:	$1,000
Application deadline:	April 1

Contact:
The Dallas Foundation
900 Jackson Street, Suite 705
Dallas, TX 75202
Phone: 214-741-9898, ext. 109
Web: www.dallasfoundation.org

Dr. Don and Rose Marie Benton Scholarship

Type of award: Scholarship, renewable.

Intended use: For undergraduate or graduate study at accredited postsecondary institution in United States.
Eligibility: Applicant must be residing in Texas.
Application requirements: Nomination by member of the Scholarship Committee at Trinity River Mission.
Additional information: Award amount varies; maximum is $1,500. Number of awards varies. Applicant or parent must be affiliated with Trinity River Mission. Must reside in Dallas county.

Amount of award:	$1,500
Number of awards:	3
Number of applicants:	7
Application deadline:	April 1
Notification begins:	May 1
Total amount awarded:	$4,500

Contact:
Trinity River Mission
Attn: Ms. Dolores Sosa Green
2060 Singleton Blvd., Suite 104
Dallas, TX 75212
Phone: 214-744-5648
Web: www.dallasfoundation.org

Hirsch Family Scholarship

Type of award: Scholarship.
Intended use: For freshman study at accredited vocational, 2-year or 4-year institution in United States.
Eligibility: Applicant must be high school senior.
Basis for selection: Applicant must demonstrate high academic achievement.
Application requirements: Recommendations, essay, transcript. List of extracurricular activities, community service, and work experience; FAFSA.
Additional information: Applicant must be the dependent child of an active employee of Eagle Materials, Performance Chemicals and Ingredients, Martin Fletcher, Hadlock Plastics, Highlander Partners and any of their majority-owned subsidiaries. Past recipients are encouraged to apply each year.

Amount of award:	$2,000-$10,000
Application deadline:	March 15
Notification begins:	May 1

Contact:
The Dallas Foundation
900 Jackson Street, Suite 705
Dallas, TX 75202
Phone: 214-741-9898, Ext. 109
Web: www.dallasfoundation.org

Jere W. Thompson, Jr. Scholarship Fund

Type of award: Scholarship, renewable.
Intended use: For full-time junior or senior study at accredited 4-year institution in United States. Designated institutions: Texas institutions.
Eligibility: Applicant must be U.S. citizen or permanent resident residing in Texas.
Basis for selection: Major/career interest in engineering, civil or engineering, construction. Applicant must demonstrate financial need and seriousness of purpose.
Application requirements: Recommendations, essay, transcript, proof of eligibility. FAFSA or SAR.
Additional information: Applicant must be college sophomore. Award amount varies; maximum is $2,000 per semester, renewable for three additional semesters if student maintains 2.5 GPA. Recipients will be given opportunity for

paid internship with one of scholarship's sponsors between junior and senior year. Preference may be given to residents of Collin, Dallas, Denton, or Tarrant counties. Visit Website for program profile and application.

Amount of award:	$2,000
Number of awards:	1
Number of applicants:	3
Application deadline:	April 1
Total amount awarded:	$4,000

Contact:
The Dallas Foundation
Attn: Rachel Lasseter
900 Jackson Street, Suite 705
Dallas, TX 75202
Phone: 214-741-9898 ext. 109
Web: www.dallasfoundation.org

The Mayor's Chesapeake Energy Scholarship

Type of award: Scholarship, renewable.
Intended use: For undergraduate study at accredited vocational, 2-year or 4-year institution.
Eligibility: Applicant must be Alaskan native, Asian American, African American, Mexican American, Hispanic American, Puerto Rican, American Indian or Native Hawaiian/Pacific Islander. Applicant must be high school senior. Applicant must be U.S. citizen or permanent resident residing in Texas.
Basis for selection: Applicant must demonstrate high academic achievement and service orientation.
Application requirements: Recommendations, essay, transcript. FAFSA or SAR.
Additional information: Must be a graduating senior of eligible high schools in Dallas Independent School District. Must be active member of Education is Freedom (EIF Dallas). Must be female or member of minority group. Minimum 3.0 GPA. Must have taken SAT or ACT. Children and grandchildren of Chesapeake Energy employees not eligible. Visit Website for application.

Application deadline:	April 15

Contact:
The Dallas Foundation
900 Jackson Street, Suite 705
Dallas, TX 75202
Phone: 214-741-9898, ext. 109 214-741-9898
Web: www.dallasfoundation.org

Peters Scholarship

Type of award: Scholarship.
Intended use: For undergraduate study at accredited 2-year or 4-year institution in United States.
Eligibility: Applicant must be residing in Texas.
Basis for selection: Applicant must demonstrate financial need, high academic achievement and service orientation.
Application requirements: Recommendations, essay, transcript. FAFSA.
Additional information: Minimum 3.0 GPA. Must be working full- or part-time to contribute to cost of education. Must be a resident of Dallas and/or Collin County. Renewable if student maintains 12-hour or more courseload and a 3.0 GPA. Award varies; up to $2,500.

Application deadline:	March 31

Contact:
The Dallas Foundation
900 Jackson Street, Suite 705
Dallas, TX 75202
Phone: 214-741-9898
Web: www.dallasfoundation.org

The Tommy Tranchin Award

Type of award: Scholarship.
Intended use: For non-degree study at postsecondary institution.
Eligibility: Applicant must be physically challenged or learning disabled. Applicant must be high school freshman, sophomore, junior or senior. Applicant must be residing in Texas.
Application requirements: Recommendations, essay. Description and budget for proposed activity.
Additional information: Award for student with physical, emotional, or intellectual disability who wants to participate in an activity that furthers development in an area in which he/she excels or shows promise. Must be high school student in North Texas. Award is up to $1,500. Visit Website for application.

Application deadline:	March 5

Contact:
The Dallas Foundation
900 Jackson Street, Suite 705
Dallas, TX 75202
Phone: 214-741-9898, ext. 109
Web: www.dallasfoundation.org

Data Processing Management Association/ Portland Chapter

DPMA/PC Scholarship

Type of award: Scholarship, renewable.
Intended use: For undergraduate study in United States. Designated institutions: Institutions in Oregon or Washington.
Eligibility: Applicant must be high school senior. Applicant must be residing in Oregon or Washington.
Basis for selection: Major/career interest in computer/information sciences. Applicant must demonstrate financial need, high academic achievement and seriousness of purpose.
Application requirements: Recommendations, transcript. List and description of past and current IT-related activities, and of IT career goals. Explanation of reasons for applying for scholarship.
Additional information: Applicants must graduate from high school in Oregon or Clark County in Washington. Renewable for $500 each year if awardee maintains a minimum "B" GPA and remains in a technology-related program. Check Website for application deadline.

Amount of award:	$1,000
Number of awards:	1
Number of applicants:	17
Application deadline:	May 7
Notification begins:	May 31
Total amount awarded:	$2,500

Contact:
DPMA/PC Scholarship
Attn: Scholarship Chair
P.O. Box 443
Portland, OR 97207
Web: www.dpmapc.com/scholarship.htm

Datatel Scholars Foundation

Datatel Scholars Foundation Scholarship

Type of award: Scholarship.
Intended use: For undergraduate, graduate or non-degree study at accredited postsecondary institution. Designated institutions: Datatel client colleges/universities.
Basis for selection: Applicant must demonstrate high academic achievement.
Application requirements: Essay.
Additional information: Visit Website for application, requirements, evalution details, and deadline.
Contact:
Datatel Scholars Foundation
4375 Fair Lakes Court
Fairfax, VA 22033
Phone: 800-486-4332
Web: www.datatelscholars.org

Daughters of Union Veterans of the Civil War 1861-1865

Grand Army of the Republic Living Memorial Scholarship

Type of award: Scholarship.
Intended use: For sophomore, junior or senior study at accredited 4-year institution in United States.
Eligibility: Applicant must be descendant of veteran during Civil War. Must be lineal descendant of Union Veteran of Civil War.
Basis for selection: Applicant must demonstrate depth of character, leadership, patriotism, seriousness of purpose and service orientation.
Application requirements: Transcript. Two letters of reference, ancestor's military record.
Additional information: Must be of good moral character and have firm belief in US Government. Must have satisfactory scholastic standing. Request for information and application honored only with SASE. Number of awards varies.

Amount of award:	$200-$500
Application deadline:	April 30
Notification begins:	August 30
Total amount awarded:	$1,500

Contact:
Daughters of Union Veterans of the Civil War 1861-1865
P.O. Box 211
Springfield, IL 62704-0211

Davidson Institute

Davidson Fellows Scholarship

Type of award: Scholarship.
Intended use: For undergraduate study at accredited postsecondary institution in United States.
Eligibility: Applicant must be U.S. citizen or permanent resident.
Basis for selection: Major/career interest in literature; music; philosophy; mathematics; science, general or technology.
Application requirements: Three nominator forms, three copies of a 15-minute DVD or VHS videotape. Signed statement of commitment that, if named a Davidson Fellow, the applicant and a parent or guardian will attend the award reception in Washington, D.C.
Additional information: Applicants awarded for accomplishment that is recognized as significant by experts in that field and has a positive contribution to society. Applicant must be under the age of 18 as of October 1 of the year of application. Applications are accepted in the following categories: science, technology, mathematics, music, literature, philosophy, and "outside the box." Work may be exceptionally creative application of existing knowledge, new idea with high impact, innovative solution with broad-range implications, important advancement that can be replicated and built upon, interdisciplinary discovery, prodigious performance, or another demonstration of extraordinary accomplishment. Application deadline is first Wednesday in March.

Amount of award:	$10,000-$50,000
Number of awards:	20
Notification begins:	July 1
Total amount awarded:	$460,000

Contact:
Davidson Institute for Talent Development
9665 Gateway Drive
Suite B
Reno, NV 89521
Phone: 775-852-3483 ext. 423
Fax: 775-852-2184
Web: www.davidsongifted.org/fellows

Davis-Roberts Scholarship Fund

Davis-Roberts Scholarship

Type of award: Scholarship, renewable.
Intended use: For full-time undergraduate study at 2-year or 4-year institution.
Eligibility: Applicant must be U.S. citizen residing in Wyoming.
Basis for selection: Applicant must demonstrate financial need.
Application requirements: Recommendations, essay, transcript. Applicant's photograph.
Additional information: Applicant must be member of Job's Daughters or DeMolay.

Amount of award:	$300-$1,000
Number of awards:	10
Number of applicants:	12
Application deadline:	June 15
Notification begins:	August 31
Total amount awarded:	$4,000

Contact:
Davis-Roberts Scholarship Fund
c/o Gary D. Skillern
P.O. Box 20645
Cheyenne, WY 82003
Phone: 307-632-0491

Delaware Higher Education Commission

B. Bradford Barnes Scholarship

Type of award: Scholarship, renewable.
Intended use: For full-time freshman study at 4-year institution. Designated institutions: University of Delaware.
Eligibility: Applicant must be high school senior. Applicant must be U.S. citizen or permanent resident residing in Delaware.
Basis for selection: Applicant must demonstrate high academic achievement.
Application requirements: Essay, transcript. FAFSA.
Additional information: Must rank in top 25 percent of high school class. Combined score of 1800 on the SAT. Awards full tuition, fees, room, board, and books. Visit Website for deadline.

Amount of award:	Full tuition
Number of awards:	1
Number of applicants:	35

Contact:
Delaware Higher Education Commission
820 North French Street
Wilmington, DE 19801
Phone: 302-577-5240
Fax: 302-577-6765
Web: www.doe.k12.de.us/programs/dhec/how_to_apply/financial_aid

Charles L. Hebner Memorial Scholarship

Type of award: Scholarship, renewable.
Intended use: For full-time undergraduate study at 4-year institution. Designated institutions: University of Delaware, Delaware State University.
Eligibility: Applicant must be high school senior. Applicant must be U.S. citizen or permanent resident residing in Delaware.
Basis for selection: Major/career interest in humanities/liberal arts; social/behavioral sciences or political science/government. Applicant must demonstrate high academic achievement.
Application requirements: Essay, transcript. FAFSA.
Additional information: Applicant must rank in top half of graduating class. Minimum combined score of 1350 on SAT. Preference given to political science majors. Award covers tuition, fees, room, board, and books. Visit Website for deadline information.

Amount of award:	Full tuition
Number of awards:	2
Number of applicants:	65

Contact:
Delaware Higher Education Commission
820 North French Street
Wilmington, DE 19801
Phone: 302-577-5240
Fax: 302-577-6765
Web: www.doe.k12.de.us/programs/dhec/how_to_apply/financial_aid

Delaware Scholarship Incentive Program

Type of award: Scholarship.
Intended use: For full-time undergraduate study at accredited 2-year or 4-year institution. Designated institutions: Nonprofit, regionally accredited institutions in Delaware or Pennsylvania.
Eligibility: Applicant must be U.S. citizen or permanent resident residing in Delaware.
Basis for selection: Applicant must demonstrate financial need.
Application requirements: Transcript. FAFSA.
Additional information: Minimum 2.5 GPA. Full-time undergraduate and graduate students whose majors are not offered at a Delaware public college will be considered. Visit Website for deadline.

Amount of award:	$700-$2,200
Number of awards:	1,670
Number of applicants:	11,000
Total amount awarded:	$1,455,000

Contact:
Delaware Higher Education Commission
820 North French Street
Wilmington, DE 19801
Phone: 302-577-5240
Fax: 302-577-6765
Web: www.doe.k12.de.us/programs/dhec/how_to_apply/financial_aid

Diamond State Scholarship

Type of award: Scholarship, renewable.
Intended use: For full-time freshman study at accredited vocational, 2-year or 4-year institution in United States. Designated institutions: Nonprofit, regionally accredited institutions.
Eligibility: Applicant must be high school senior. Applicant must be U.S. citizen or permanent resident residing in Delaware.
Basis for selection: Applicant must demonstrate high academic achievement.
Application requirements: Essay, transcript. SAT scores.
Additional information: Must rank in top 25 percent of high school class. Minimum combined score of 1800 on SAT. Visit Website for deadline.

Amount of award:	$1,250
Number of awards:	12
Number of applicants:	174
Total amount awarded:	$35,000

Contact:
Delaware Higher Education Commission
820 North French Street
Wilmington, DE 19801
Phone: 302-577-5240
Fax: 302-577-6765
Web: www.doe.k12.de.us/programs/dhec/how_to_apply/
financial_aid

Educational Benefits for Children of Deceased Veterans and Others

Type of award: Scholarship, renewable.
Intended use: For undergraduate study at postsecondary institution.
Eligibility: Applicant must be at least 16, no older than 24. Applicant must be U.S. citizen or permanent resident residing in Delaware.
Additional information: Must live in Delaware for at least three years before applying. Must apply at least four weeks before classes begin. Award prorated when major not available at a Delaware public college. Award for maximum of four years. Must be child of one of the following: member of armed forces whose death was service-related, who is or was a POW, or is officially MIA; state police officer whose death was service-related; or state employee of the Department of Transportation routinely employed in job-related activities on the state highway system whose death was job-related. Visit Website for deadline.

Amount of award:	Full tuition
Number of applicants:	2

Contact:
Delaware Higher Education Commission
820 North French Street
Wilmington, DE 19801
Phone: 302-577-5240
Fax: 302-577-6765
Web: www.doe.k12.de.us/high-ed

Herman M. Holloway, Sr. Memorial Scholarship

Type of award: Scholarship, renewable.
Intended use: For full-time freshman study at 4-year institution. Designated institutions: Delaware State University.
Eligibility: Applicant must be high school senior. Applicant must be U.S. citizen or permanent resident residing in Delaware.
Basis for selection: Applicant must demonstrate high academic achievement.
Application requirements: Essay, transcript. FAFSA.
Additional information: Applicants must rank in upper half of class and have combined score of at least 1350 on SAT. Awards full tuition, fees, room, board, and books. Visit Website for deadline information.

Amount of award:	Full tuition
Number of awards:	1
Number of applicants:	60

Contact:
Delaware Higher Education Commission
820 North French Street
Wilmington, DE 19801
Phone: 302-577-5240
Fax: 302-577-6765
Web: www.doe.k12.de.us/programs/dhec/how_to_apply/
financial_aid

Robert C. Byrd Honors Scholarship

Type of award: Scholarship, renewable.
Intended use: For full-time undergraduate study at accredited postsecondary institution in United States. Designated institutions: Nonprofit, regionally accredited schools.
Eligibility: Applicant must be high school senior. Applicant must be U.S. citizen or permanent resident residing in Delaware.
Basis for selection: Applicant must demonstrate high academic achievement.
Application requirements: Essay, transcript. SAT scores.
Additional information: Applicant must be in top 25 percent of graduating class or GED recipient with score of at least 300. Minimum combined score of 1800 on SAT. Program dependent on federal funding. Renewable up to three years. Visit Website for deadline information.

Amount of award:	$1,500
Number of awards:	20
Number of applicants:	176

Contact:
Delaware Higher Education Commission
820 North French Street
Wilmington, DE 19801
Phone: 302-577-5240
Fax: 302-577-6765
Web: www.doe.k12.de.us/programs/dhec/how_to_apply/
financial_aid

Discover Financial Services

Discover Scholarship Program

Type of award: Scholarship.
Intended use: For undergraduate study at accredited postsecondary institution.
Eligibility: Applicant must be high school junior. Applicant must be U.S. citizen or permanent resident.
Basis for selection: Applicant must demonstrate leadership and service orientation.
Application requirements: Recommendations, essay, transcript. Community service verification.
Additional information: Applicant must have minimum cumulative 2.75 GPA for ninth and tenth grades and must have faced significant roadblock or challenge. Submit application online at International Scholarship and Tuition Services Website. More information at www.discoverfinancial.com/community.

Amount of award:	$40,000
Number of awards:	10
Number of applicants:	16,707
Application deadline:	January 31
Notification begins:	April 1
Total amount awarded:	$300,000

Contact:
Phone: 866-756-7932
Web: www.discoverfinancial.com/community

District of Columbia Higher Education Financial Services

DC Adoption Scholarship

Type of award: Scholarship, renewable.
Intended use: For undergraduate study at 2-year or 4-year institution. Designated institutions: Title IV-approved institutions.
Eligibility: Applicant must be no older than 24. Applicant must be U.S. citizen or permanent resident residing in District of Columbia.
Application requirements: Transcript, proof of eligibility. Current utility bill, FAFSA, SAR, adoption decree or parent/guardian's death certificate.
Additional information: Award for District of Columbia children adopted on or after October 1, 2001, from the D.C. Child and Family Services Agency or children who lost one or both parents as a result of the events of September 11, 2001. Applicant must have graduated high school or received GED. Applicant must be DC resident for 12 months prior to enrollment and throughout college. Award may not be used at proprietary institutions. Visit Website to apply.

Amount of award:	$10,000
Application deadline:	June 30

Contact:
Higher Education Financial Services
Van Ness Elementary School
1150 5th St, SE
Washington, DC 20003
Phone: 202-727-2824
Web: www.seo.dc.gov

DC Tuition Assistance Grant Program (DCTAG)

Type of award: Scholarship, renewable.
Intended use: For undergraduate study at 2-year or 4-year institution in United States. Designated institutions: DCTAG-eligible institutions that can participate in Title IV programs.
Eligibility: Applicant must be no older than 24. Applicant must be U.S. citizen or permanent resident residing in District of Columbia.
Application requirements: Transcript, proof of eligibility. Student Aid Report, FAFSA, current utility bill.
Additional information: Applicant must be DC resident for 12 months prior to enrollment and throughout college. Award may not be used at proprietary institutions. Awards vary, visit Website for details.

Amount of award:	$2,500-$10,000
Application deadline:	June 30

Contact:
Higher Education Financial Services
Van Ness Elementary School
1150 5th St, SE
Washington, DC 20003
Phone: 202-727-2824
Web: www.seo.dc.gov

District of Columbia Leveraging Educational Assistance Partnership Program

Type of award: Scholarship, renewable.
Intended use: For undergraduate study at 2-year or 4-year institution in or outside United States. Designated institutions: Postsecondary institutions certified to participate in Title IV Student Aid Programs.
Eligibility: Applicant must be no older than 23. Applicant must be U.S. citizen or permanent resident residing in District of Columbia.
Basis for selection: Applicant must demonstrate financial need.
Application requirements: Transcript, proof of eligibility. Student Aid Report, FAFSA, current utility bill.
Additional information: Must be D.C. resident for 12 months prior to application and throughout college. Must be eligible for Pell Grant. Award may not be used at proprietary institutions. Apply online.

Amount of award:	$1,500-$5,000
Application deadline:	June 30

Contact:
Higher Education Financial Services
Van Ness Elementary School
1150 5th St, SE
Washington, DC 20003
Phone: 202-727-2824
Web: www.seo.dc.gov

Dolphin Scholarship Foundation

Dolphin Scholarship

Type of award: Scholarship, renewable.
Intended use: For full-time undergraduate study at accredited 4-year institution.
Eligibility: Applicant must be single, no older than 23. Applicant must be U.S. citizen. Must be child/stepchild of member or former member of U.S. Navy who served in, or in support of, Submarine Force.
Basis for selection: Applicant must demonstrate financial need, high academic achievement and service orientation.
Application requirements: Recommendations, essay, transcript, proof of eligibility. SAT/ACT scores.
Additional information: Applicant must be high school senior or college student. Applicant must demonstrate commitment to extracurricular activities and community service.

Amount of award:	$3,400
Number of awards:	137
Number of applicants:	231
Application deadline:	March 15
Notification begins:	May 1
Total amount awarded:	$445,250

Contact:
Dolphin Scholarship Foundation
4966 Euclid Road
Suite 109
Virginia Beach, VA 23462
Phone: 757-671-3200 ext. 111
Fax: 757-671-3330
Web: www.dolphinscholarship.org

Eastern Orthodox Committee on Scouting

Boy and Girl Scouts Scholarship

Type of award: Scholarship.
Intended use: For full-time freshman study at accredited 4-year institution in United States.
Eligibility: Applicant must be high school senior. Applicant must be Eastern Orthodox. Applicant must be U.S. citizen.
Basis for selection: Applicant must demonstrate depth of character and service orientation.
Application requirements: Four letters of recommendation with application, one from each of following groups: religious institution, school, community leader, and head of Scouting unit.
Additional information: Eligible applicant must be registered member of Boy or Girl Scouts unit; Eagle Scout or Gold Award recipient; active member of Eastern Orthodox Church; have received Alpha Omega Religious Scout Award; have demonstrated practical citizenship in his or her church, school, Scouting unit, and community. Offers one $1,000 scholarship and one $500 scholarship upon acceptance to four-year accredited college or university.

Amount of award:	$500-$1,000
Number of awards:	2
Number of applicants:	250
Application deadline:	May 1
Total amount awarded:	$1,500

Contact:
EOCS Scholarship Committee
862 Guy Lombardo Avenue
Freeport, NY 11520
Phone: 516-868-4050
Web: www.eocs.org

Edmund F. Maxwell Foundation

Edmund F. Maxwell Foundation Scholarship

Type of award: Scholarship, renewable.
Intended use: For full-time freshman study. Designated institutions: Private colleges and universities.
Eligibility: Applicant must be U.S. citizen or permanent resident residing in Washington.
Basis for selection: Applicant must demonstrate financial need, high academic achievement, depth of character, leadership, seriousness of purpose and service orientation.
Application requirements: Essay, transcript. Financial aid worksheet.
Additional information: Must be resident of western Washington. Combined reading and math SAT scores must be greater than 1200. Applicants encouraged to apply early in year. Visit Website for application and more information.

Amount of award:	$5,000
Application deadline:	April 30
Notification begins:	June 1

Contact:
The Edmund F. Maxwell Foundation
P.O. Box 22537
Seattle, WA 98122-0537
Web: www.maxwell.org

Elie Wiesel Foundation for Humanity

Elie Wiesel Prize in Ethics

Type of award: Scholarship.
Intended use: For full-time junior or senior study at accredited 4-year institution in United States.
Basis for selection: Competition/talent/interest in writing/journalism. Major/career interest in ethnic/cultural studies; social/behavioral sciences or governmental public relations.
Application requirements: Proof of eligibility. Letter from college/university verifying full-time junior or senior status. Sponsorship by faculty member. Submit three copies of essay concerning an ethical dilemma, issue, or question related to the contest's annual topic. In 3,000 to 4,000 words, students are encouraged to raise questions, single out issues, and identify dilemmas.
Additional information: First prize is $5,000; second prize is $2,500; third prize is $1,500; two honorable mentions are $500 each. See Website for more information.

Amount of award:	$500-$5,000
Number of awards:	5
Number of applicants:	304
Application deadline:	January 4
Notification begins:	May 31
Total amount awarded:	$10,000

Contact:
Elie Wiesel Prize in Ethics
The Elie Wiesel Foundation for Humanity
555 Madison Avenue, 20th Floor
New York, NY 10022
Phone: 212-490-7788
Fax: 212-490-6006
Web: www.eliewieselfoundation.org

Elizabeth Greenshields Foundation

The Elizabeth Greenshields Grant

Type of award: Scholarship, renewable.
Intended use: For undergraduate, graduate or non-degree study at postsecondary institution.
Basis for selection: Major/career interest in arts, general.
Application requirements: Jpeg on CD.
Additional information: For artists (fine arts) in early stages of careers creating representational or figurative works through painting, drawing, printmaking, or sculpture. Must make a commitment to making art a lifetime career. Applications are welcome throughout the year. All award amounts are in Canadian dollars. Funds may be used for any art-related purpose.

Amount of award: $12,500
Number of awards: 50
Number of applicants: 1,000
Contact:
Elizabeth Greenshields Foundation
1814 Sherbrooke Street West, Suite 1
Montreal
Quebec, Canada, H3H 1E4
Phone: 514-937-9225

Elks National Foundation

Elks Most Valuable Student Scholarship

Type of award: Scholarship.
Intended use: For full-time undergraduate study at accredited postsecondary institution in United States.
Eligibility: Applicant must be high school senior. Applicant must be U.S. citizen.
Basis for selection: Applicant must demonstrate financial need, high academic achievement and leadership.
Application requirements: Transcript. Counselor report, SAT/ACT scores, income range.
Additional information: Applications available starting September 1 from local Benevolent and Protective Order of Elks Lodge; also available on Website or by sending SASE to foundation. Application deadline is in November. Award is distributed over four years. Membership in Elks not required, but application must be endorsed by and submitted to local Elks Lodge for entry into competition. Judging occurs at lodge, district, and state level before reaching national competition.
Amount of award: $4,000-$60,000
Number of awards: 500
Number of applicants: 20,000
Application deadline: November 1
Notification begins: April 1
Total amount awarded: $2,296,000
Contact:
Elks National Foundation
2750 North Lakeview Avenue
Chicago, IL 60614-1889
Phone: 773-755-4732
Fax: 773-755-4733
Web: www.elks.org/enf/scholars

Elks National Foundation Legacy Awards

Type of award: Scholarship.
Intended use: For full-time undergraduate study at accredited postsecondary institution in United States.
Eligibility: Applicant must be high school senior. Applicant must be U.S. citizen.
Basis for selection: Applicant must demonstrate high academic achievement and leadership.
Application requirements: Essay, transcript. SAT/ACT scores.
Additional information: Application deadline in mid-January. Applicant must be child or grandchild of Elks member who has been paid-up and in good standing for two consecutive years. Application available September 1 from Website. Eligible applicants from Guam, Panama, Puerto Rico, and the

Philippines may attend schools in those countries. Visit Website for additional information.
Amount of award: $4,000
Number of awards: 250
Application deadline: January 1
Notification begins: April 15
Total amount awarded: $1,000,000
Contact:
Elks National Foundation
2750 North Lakeview Avenue
Chicago, IL 60614-1889
Phone: 773-755-4732
Fax: 773-755-4733
Web: www.elks.org/enf/scholars

Engineers Foundation of Ohio

Engineers Foundation of Ohio Scholarships

Type of award: Scholarship.
Intended use: For freshman study at accredited 4-year institution in United States. Designated institutions: ABET-accredited schools in Ohio and University of Notre Dame.
Eligibility: Applicant must be high school senior. Applicant must be U.S. citizen residing in Ohio.
Basis for selection: Major/career interest in engineering. Applicant must demonstrate high academic achievement.
Application requirements: Essay, transcript.
Additional information: Minimum 3.0 GPA. Must have minimum 600 SAT (Math) and 500 SAT (Reading or Composition) or 29 ACT Math and 25 ACT English. EFO offers up to 10 scholarships per year with various requirements; see Website for specifics. Some awards renewable.
Amount of award: $500-$2,500
Number of awards: 25
Application deadline: December 15
Total amount awarded: $25,000
Contact:
Engineers Foundation of Ohio
400 South Fifth Street
Suite 300
Columbus, OH 43215-5430
Phone: 614-223-1177
Fax: 614-223-1131
Web: www.ohioengineer.com

The Entomological Foundation

The Entomological Foundation BioQuip Undergraduate Scholarship

Type of award: Scholarship.
Intended use: For full-time junior or senior study at 4-year institution. Designated institutions: Institutions in United States, Canada, or Mexico.

Basis for selection: Competition/talent/interest in study abroad. Major/career interest in entomology; zoology; biology or science, general. Applicant must demonstrate financial need.
Application requirements: Recommendations, essay, transcript.
Additional information: Applicant must have been enrolled as undergraduate student in entomology in the fall prior to application deadline. If student's college or university does not offer a degree in entomology, student must be preparing to become an entomologist through his/her studies. By September 1 following application deadline, student must accumulate at least 90 credit hours and either complete two junior-level entomology courses or a research project in entomology. See Website for more information.

Amount of award:	$2,000
Number of awards:	1
Number of applicants:	72
Application deadline:	July 1
Notification begins:	September 30
Total amount awarded:	$2,000

Contact:
The Entomological Foundation
Undergraduate Scholarship
9332 Annapolis Road, Suite 210
Lanham, MD 20706-3115
Phone: 301-459-9082
Fax: 301-459-9084
Web: www.entfdn.org

Stan Beck Fellowship

Type of award: Scholarship, renewable.
Intended use: For undergraduate or graduate study at 4-year or graduate institution. Designated institutions: Colleges or universities in the United States, Mexico, or Canada.
Basis for selection: Major/career interest in entomology; biology or zoology. Applicant must demonstrate financial need.
Application requirements: Recommendations, essay, transcript, proof of eligibility.
Additional information: Award amount varies. Need is based on physical limitations or economic, minority, or environmental conditions. Applications must be submitted electronically. See Website for additional information.

Number of awards:	1
Application deadline:	July 1
Total amount awarded:	$1,000

Contact:
The Entomological Foundation
Stan Beck Fellowship
9332 Annapolis Road, Suite 210
Lanham, MD 20706-3115
Phone: 301-459-9082
Fax: 301-459-9084
Web: www.entfdn.org

The Environmental Institute for Golf

GCSAA Legacy Awards

Type of award: Scholarship.
Intended use: For full-time undergraduate or graduate study at accredited postsecondary institution.

Basis for selection: Applicant must demonstrate high academic achievement, leadership and service orientation.
Application requirements: Essay, transcript, proof of eligibility. Letter of acceptance from college or university (high school seniors).
Additional information: Applicant's parent or grandparent must have been a Golf Course Superintendents Association of America (GCSAA) member for five or more consecutive years and must be current active member in one of the following classifications: A, Superintendent Member, C, Retired-A, Retired-B, or AA Life. Children or grandchildren of deceased members also eligible if member was active at time of death. Award limited to one student per family. Children of Syngenta Professional Products employees, The Environmental Institute for Golf's Board of Trustees, and GCSAA staff not eligible.

Amount of award:	$1,500
Application deadline:	April 15
Notification begins:	June 15

Contact:
Golf Course Superintendents Association of America
Scholarship Program
1421 Research Park Drive
Lawrence, KS 66049-3859
Phone: 785-832-4445 or 800-472-7878 ext. 4445
Web: www.gcsaa.org

GCSAA Scholars Competition

Type of award: Scholarship.
Intended use: For sophomore, junior or senior study at accredited 2-year or 4-year institution.
Basis for selection: Major/career interest in turf management. Applicant must demonstrate high academic achievement and leadership.
Application requirements: Recommendations, essay, transcript, proof of eligibility.
Additional information: Must be member of Golf Course Superintendents Association of America. Must be planning career in golf course management or closely related profession. First and second place winners receive all-expense paid trip to GCSAA-sponsored Golf Industry Show. Children of GCSAA Environmental Institute for Golf's Board of Trustees, GCSAA Board of Directors, and GCSAA staff not eligible. Visit Website for details and application.

Amount of award:	$500-$6,000
Number of awards:	28
Application deadline:	June 1
Notification begins:	August 1

Contact:
Golf Course Superintendents Association of America
Scholarship Program
1421 Research Park Drive
Lawrence, KS 66049-3859
Phone: 785-832-4445 or 800-472-7878 ext. 4445
Web: www.gcsaa.org

GCSAA Student Essay Contest

Type of award: Scholarship.
Intended use: For undergraduate or graduate study at postsecondary institution.
Basis for selection: Competition/talent/interest in writing/journalism, based on essay focusing on golf course management. Major/career interest in turf management.
Application requirements: Essay, proof of eligibility.
Additional information: Must be member of Golf Course Superintendents Association of America. Must be pursuing degree in turfgrass science, agronomy, or any other field related

to golf course management. First prize is $2000; second prize, $1500; third prize, $1000. Visit Website for details.

Amount of award:	$1,000-$2,000
Number of awards:	3
Application deadline:	March 31

Contact:
Golf Course Superintendents Association of America
Student Essay Contest
1421 Research Park Drive
Lawrence, KS 66049-3859
Phone: 800-472-7878 ext. 4445
Web: www.gcsaa.org

Epilepsy Foundation

Behavioral Sciences Student Fellowship

Type of award: Research grant.
Intended use: For undergraduate or graduate study in United States.
Basis for selection: Major/career interest in social/behavioral sciences; sociology; social work; psychology; anthropology; nursing; economics; rehabilitation/therapeutic services or political science/government.
Application requirements: Recommendations, research proposal. Research proposal.
Additional information: Three-month fellowship for epilepsy study project. Professor or advisor must supervise student's project. Other appropriate fields include vocational rehabilitation, counseling, and subjects relevant to epilepsy research or practice. Women and minorities are especially encouraged to apply. Visit Website for application instructions and for more information.

Amount of award:	$3,000
Application deadline:	March 1
Notification begins:	May 31
Total amount awarded:	$3,000

Contact:
Epilepsy Foundation
8301 Professional Place
Landover, MD 20785-2267
Phone: 301-459-3700
Fax: 301-577-2684
Web: www.epilepsyfoundation.org/grants

Epilepsy Foundation of San Diego County

Epilepsy Foundation of San Diego County Scholarship

Type of award: Scholarship.
Intended use: For undergraduate study at vocational, 2-year or 4-year institution.
Eligibility: Applicant must be residing in California.
Basis for selection: Applicant must demonstrate financial need and high academic achievement.
Additional information: Two categories of eligibility: 1) Student being treated for epilepsy who is or will be enrolled in

a college, university, or trade school in the Fall. 2) Full-time college or university student involved in an epilepsy research project in health or social science with minimum 3.0 GPA. All applicants must be residents of San Diego or Imperial counties, but may be attending school outside the area.

Amount of award:	$250-$2,000
Number of awards:	6
Number of applicants:	8
Application deadline:	June 1
Total amount awarded:	$4,000

Contact:
Epilepsy Foundation of San Diego County
2055 El Cajon Boulevard
San Diego, CA 92104
Phone: 619-296-0161
Web: www.epilepsysandiego.org

EqualityMaine Foundation

The Joel Abromson Memorial Scholarship

Type of award: Scholarship.
Intended use: For freshman study at postsecondary institution.
Eligibility: Applicant must be high school senior. Applicant must be U.S. citizen or permanent resident residing in Maine.
Basis for selection: Competition/talent/interest in gay/lesbian, based on involvement and leadership in promoting equality for lesbian, gay, bisexual, and transgender people in schools and community. Applicant must demonstrate depth of character and service orientation.
Application requirements: Recommendations, essay. Cover letter. Acceptance letter from chosen higher education institution.
Additional information: Visit Website for essay question and additional information.

Amount of award:	$1,000
Number of awards:	2
Application deadline:	April 15

Contact:
EqualityMaine
P.O. Box 1951
Portland, ME 04104
Phone: 207-761-3732
Fax: 207-761-3752
Web: www.equalitymaine.org

ESA Foundation

ESA Foundation Scholarship Program

Type of award: Scholarship, renewable.
Intended use: For undergraduate or graduate study at vocational, 2-year, 4-year or graduate institution.
Basis for selection: Applicant must demonstrate financial need, high academic achievement, depth of character, leadership and service orientation.
Application requirements: $5 application fee. Recommendations, essay, transcript.

Additional information: Individual scholarships have specific requirements; visit Website for details and application form.

Amount of award:	$330-$5,000
Number of awards:	160
Number of applicants:	6,106
Application deadline:	February 1
Notification begins:	June 1
Total amount awarded:	$160,906

Contact:
ESA Foundation
P.O. Box 270517
Fort Collins, CO 80527
Phone: 970-223-2824
Fax: 970-223-4456
Web: www.esaintl.com/esaf/

Executive Women International

Executive Women International Scholarship

Type of award: Scholarship, renewable.
Intended use: For full-time undergraduate study at accredited 4-year institution in United States.
Eligibility: Applicant must be high school junior.
Basis for selection: Applicant must demonstrate high academic achievement, depth of character, leadership, seriousness of purpose and service orientation.
Application requirements: Interview, recommendations, essay.
Additional information: Applicant must reside within boundaries of participating Executive Women International chapter. Scholarship awarded each academic year, for up to five consecutive years, until student completes degree. Applicants must have sponsoring teacher at their school. Must have a major/career interest in a professional field.

Amount of award:	$1,000-$10,000
Application deadline:	April 30
Notification begins:	June 1

Contact:
Executive Women International
515 South 700 East
Suite 2A
Salt Lake City, UT 84102
Phone: 801-355-2800
Fax: 801-355-2852
Web: www.ewiconnect.com

Experimental Aircraft Association

David Alan Quick Scholarship

Type of award: Scholarship.
Intended use: For junior or senior study at accredited 4-year institution.
Basis for selection: Major/career interest in aerospace or engineering.

Additional information: Must be Experimental Aircraft Association member or recommended by EAA member. Awarded to student pursuing degree in aerospace or aeronautical engineering. Apply online.

Amount of award:	$500
Number of awards:	1
Application deadline:	February 28
Notification begins:	April 30

Contact:
EAA Scholarship Department
P.O. 3086
Oshkosh, WI 54903-3086
Phone: 920-426-6823
Web: www.youngeagles.org/programs/scholarships

Hansen Scholarship

Type of award: Scholarship, renewable.
Intended use: For undergraduate study at accredited vocational, 2-year or 4-year institution.
Basis for selection: Major/career interest in aerospace; aviation or engineering. Applicant must demonstrate financial need, high academic achievement, depth of character, leadership and service orientation.
Additional information: Must be Experimental Aircraft Association member or recommended by an EAA member to apply. Student should be pursuing degree in aerospace engineering or aeronautical engineering. Visit Website for details and application.

Amount of award:	$1,000
Number of awards:	1
Application deadline:	February 28
Notification begins:	April 30
Total amount awarded:	$1,000

Contact:
EAA Scholarship Department
P.O. 3086
Oshkosh, WI 54903-3086
Phone: 920-426-6823
Web: www.youngeagles.org/programs/scholarships

H.P. "Bud" Milligan Aviation Scholarship

Type of award: Scholarship, renewable.
Intended use: For undergraduate study at accredited vocational, 2-year or 4-year institution.
Basis for selection: Major/career interest in aviation. Applicant must demonstrate depth of character, leadership and service orientation.
Application requirements: Essay.
Additional information: Must be Experimental Aircraft Association member or recommended by EAA member. Complete application online.

Amount of award:	$500
Number of awards:	1
Application deadline:	February 28
Notification begins:	April 30

Contact:
EAA Scholarship Department
P.O. 3086
Oshkosh, WI 54903-3086
Phone: 920-426-6823
Web: www.youngeagles.org/programs/scholarships

Hudner Medal of Honor Scholarship

Type of award: Scholarship.
Intended use: For undergraduate study at postsecondary institution.
Eligibility: Applicant must be residing in Wisconsin.
Basis for selection: Major/career interest in aviation; military science or public administration/service. Applicant must demonstrate financial need, leadership and service orientation.
Additional information: Must have strong record of involvement with Experimental Aircraft Association and express intent to serve the country through military or public service. Winner must attend award presentation dinner. Apply online.

Amount of award:	$500
Number of awards:	1
Application deadline:	February 28
Notification begins:	April 30

Contact:
EAA Scholarship Department
P.O. 3086
Oshkosh, WI 54903-3086
Phone: 920-426-6823
Web: www.youngeagles.org/programs/scholarships

Payzer Scholarship

Type of award: Scholarship.
Intended use: For undergraduate study at accredited postsecondary institution.
Basis for selection: Major/career interest in engineering; mathematics; physical sciences; biology or aviation. Applicant must demonstrate financial need, depth of character, leadership and service orientation.
Additional information: Must be current Experimental Aircraft Association member or recommended by EAA member. Complete application online.

Amount of award:	$5,000
Number of awards:	1
Application deadline:	February 28
Notification begins:	April 30
Total amount awarded:	$5,000

Contact:
EAA Scholarship Department
P.O. 3086
Oshkosh, WI 54903-3086
Phone: 920-426-6823
Web: www.youngeagles.org/programs/scholarships

Richard Lee Vernon Aviation Scholarship

Type of award: Scholarship.
Intended use: For undergraduate study at postsecondary institution.
Basis for selection: Major/career interest in aviation. Applicant must demonstrate financial need.
Additional information: Must be Experimental Aircraft Association member or recommended by EAA member. Awarded to a student pursuing training leading to professional aviation occupation. Apply online.

Amount of award:	$500
Number of awards:	1
Application deadline:	February 28
Notification begins:	April 30

Contact:
EAA Scholarship Department
P.O. 3086
Oshkosh, WI 54903-3086
Phone: 920-426-6823
Web: www.youngeagles.org/programs/scholarships

Explorers Club

Explorers Club Youth Activity Fund

Type of award: Research grant.
Intended use: For undergraduate study at postsecondary institution.
Basis for selection: Competition/talent/interest in research paper, based on proposal's scientific and practical merit, investigator's competence, and budget's appropriateness. Major/career interest in natural sciences. Applicant must demonstrate seriousness of purpose.
Application requirements: Research proposal. Physical release. Recommendation from supervising instructor.
Additional information: For field research in the natural sciences under supervision of qualified scientist or institution. For full-time high school students or undergraduates only. Recipients of grants must provide one- to two-page report on their exploration or research within year of receiving the grant. Photographs are encouraged. Request application form from club. See Website for more details.

Amount of award:	$500-$1,500
Number of applicants:	52
Application deadline:	December 15

Contact:
The Explorers Club c/o Annie Lee
46 East 70th Street
New York, NY 10021
Phone: 212-628-8383
Fax: 212-288-4449
Web: www.explorers.org

Federal Employee Education and Assistance Fund

Federal Employee Education and Assistance Fund Scholarship

Type of award: Scholarship.
Intended use: For undergraduate, master's or doctoral study at accredited 2-year, 4-year or graduate institution.
Eligibility: Applicant or parent must be employed by Federal/U.S. Government.
Basis for selection: Applicant must demonstrate high academic achievement.
Application requirements: Recommendations, essay, transcript. List of community service/extracurricular activities.
Additional information: Current civilian federal and postal employees with minimum three years' service by the end of August of the application year and their dependents are eligible. Applicant must have completed community service activities. Minimum 3.0 GPA. Employee applicants eligible for part-time

study; dependents must enroll full-time. Visit Website for application materials beginning in January.

Amount of award:	$500-$2,000
Number of applicants:	3,411
Application deadline:	March 26
Notification begins:	September 30
Total amount awarded:	$533,000

Contact:
Federal Employee Education and Assistance Fund
3333 S. Wadsworth Blvd.
Suite 300
Lakewood, CO 80227
Phone: 800-323-4140
Web: www.feea.org

Finance Authority of Maine

Maine Robert C. Byrd Honors Scholarship

Type of award: Scholarship, renewable.
Intended use: For full-time undergraduate study at 2-year or 4-year institution.
Eligibility: Applicant must be high school senior. Applicant must be U.S. citizen residing in Maine.
Basis for selection: Applicant must demonstrate high academic achievement.
Application requirements: Essay, transcript. High school profile from guidance office with SAT scores, list of scholastic achievements, awards and honors. FAFSA.
Additional information: Information available through Maine high school guidance offices and Finance Authority of Maine. See Website for details.

Amount of award:	$1,500
Number of awards:	36
Number of applicants:	470
Application deadline:	May 1
Notification begins:	June 1
Total amount awarded:	$54,000

Contact:
Finance Authority of Maine
5 Community Drive
P.O. Box 949
Augusta, ME 04332-0949
Phone: 800-228-3734
Fax: 207-623-0095
Web: www.famemaine.com

Financial Service Centers of New York

Rewarding Young Leaders in Our Community Scholarship

Type of award: Scholarship.
Intended use: For freshman study at postsecondary institution.
Eligibility: Applicant must be U.S. citizen or permanent resident.
Basis for selection: Applicant must demonstrate high academic achievement, leadership and service orientation.

Application requirements: Essay, transcript. Written verification of community involvement.
Additional information: Applicant must have contributed at least 50 hours of volunteer service per year in high school.

Amount of award:	$500-$7,500
Number of awards:	16
Total amount awarded:	$40,000

Contact:
Financial Service Centers of New York
Mr. Sanford Herman, Chairman
286 Madison Avenue, Suite 907
New York, NY 10017
Phone: 212-268-1911
Web: www.fscny.org/scholar.htm

First Catholic Slovak Ladies Association

First Catholic Slovak Ladies Association Scholarship Program

Type of award: Scholarship.
Intended use: For full-time undergraduate or graduate study at accredited postsecondary institution in United States or Canada.
Basis for selection: Applicant must demonstrate high academic achievement, leadership and service orientation.
Application requirements: Recommendations, essay, transcript, proof of eligibility. SAT/ACT scores. Photograph of candidate encouraged.
Additional information: Applicant must be member of First Catholic Slovak Ladies Association for at least three years prior to date of application, and on a $1,000 legal reserve certificate, a $5,000 term certificate, or have an annuity certificate. Minimum 2.5 GPA. Visit Website for more information.

Amount of award:	$1,250-$1,750
Number of awards:	135
Number of applicants:	384
Application deadline:	March 1
Notification begins:	May 15
Total amount awarded:	$177,750

Contact:
First Catholic Slovak Ladies Association
Director of Fraternal Scholarship Aid
24950 Chagrin Boulevard
Beachwood, OH 44122
Phone: 800-464-4642
Fax: 216-464-9260
Web: www.fcsla.org

First Marine Division Association

First Marine Division Association Scholarship

Type of award: Scholarship, renewable.
Intended use: For full-time undergraduate study at accredited vocational, 2-year or 4-year institution in United States.

Eligibility: Applicant must be no older than 22. Applicant must be U.S. citizen. Applicant must be dependent of disabled veteran or deceased veteran who served in the Marines. Must have served specifically in any unit part of, attached to, or in support of First Marine Division.

Basis for selection: Applicant must demonstrate depth of character and seriousness of purpose.

Application requirements: Essay, proof of eligibility. Veteran sponsor's DD214 if available (if not, applicant must complete Standard Form 180). Death certificate or affidavit proving veteran's 100 percent and permanent disability. Copy of applicant's birth certificate. Photograph. See Website for other required information.

Additional information: Number of awards varies. Visit Website for application deadline and details.

    Amount of award: $1,750

Contact:
First Marine Division Association
403 North Freeman St.
Oceanside, CA 92054
Phone: 760-967-8561
Fax: 760-967-8567
Web: www.1stmarinedivisionassociation.org/scholarships.php

Fisher Communications, Inc.

Fisher Broadcasting Company Scholarship for Minorities

Type of award: Scholarship.

Intended use: For full-time sophomore, junior or senior study at accredited vocational, 2-year or 4-year institution in United States.

Eligibility: Applicant must be Alaskan native, Asian American, African American, Mexican American, Hispanic American, Puerto Rican, American Indian or Native Hawaiian/Pacific Islander. Applicant must be U.S. citizen.

Basis for selection: Major/career interest in radio/television/film; journalism or marketing. Applicant must demonstrate financial need and high academic achievement.

Application requirements: Recommendations, essay, transcript, proof of eligibility. Estimated expense/income worksheet.

Additional information: Must have career interest in broadcast communications. Amount of award varies each year. Minimum 2.5 GPA. For use at schools in Washington, California, Oregon, Idaho, and Montana, or for students with permanent addresses in those states who attend school out of state.

    Number of applicants: 25
    Application deadline: April 30
    Notification begins: July 30
    Total amount awarded: $12,950

Contact:
Fisher Communications Inc. Minority Scholarship
Attn: Human Resources
140 4th Ave. N.
Seattle, WA 98109
Web: www.fsci.com/scholarship.html

Florida Department of Education

Access to Better Learning and Education (ABLE) Grant Program

Type of award: Scholarship, renewable.

Intended use: For full-time undergraduate study at accredited postsecondary institution in United States. Designated institutions: Eligible private Florida colleges and universities.

Eligibility: Applicant must be U.S. citizen or permanent resident residing in Florida.

Basis for selection: Applicant must demonstrate financial need.

Additional information: Each participating institution determines application procedures, deadlines, and student eligibility. The amount of ABLE award plus all other scholarships and grants specifically designated for payment of tuition and fees cannot exceed the total amount of tuition and fees charged by the institution. May not be enrolled in program of study leading to degree in theology or divinity.

    Amount of award: $986

Contact:
Office of Student Financial Assistance
325 West Gaines Street
Tallahassee, FL 32399-0400
Phone: 888-827-2004
Web: www.floridastudentfinancialaid.org

Florida Academic Scholars Award

Type of award: Scholarship, renewable.

Intended use: For undergraduate study at postsecondary institution in United States. Designated institutions: Eligible Florida post-secondary institutions.

Eligibility: Applicant must be high school senior. Applicant must be U.S. citizen or permanent resident residing in Florida.

Basis for selection: Applicant must demonstrate high academic achievement and service orientation.

Additional information: Applicant must have minimum 3.5 GPA, taken 15 credits of college preparatory academic courses, completed 75 hours of community service, and scored at least 1270 on SAT or 28 on ACT (excluding writing sections). Applicant with highest academic ranking in each county will receive Academic Top Scholars award of $1,500. Application available online, and must be completed before high school graduation. Check Website for additional information and requirements.

    Amount of award: Full tuition

Contact:
Office of Student Financial Assistance
325 West Gaines Street
Tallahassee, FL 32399-0400
Phone: 888-827-2004
Web: www.floridastudentfinancialaid.org

Florida Gold Seal Vocational Scholars Award

Type of award: Scholarship, renewable.

Intended use: For undergraduate study at vocational, 2-year or 4-year institution. Designated institutions: Eligible Florida post-secondary institutions.

Eligibility: Applicant must be high school senior. Applicant must be U.S. citizen or permanent resident residing in Florida.
Basis for selection: Applicant must demonstrate high academic achievement.
Additional information: Minimum 3.0 GPA in core credits, 3.5 GPA in minimum of three vocational credits. Specific CPT, SAT, or ACT test scores required. Check Website for additional information and requirements. Applications available online and must be completed before high school graduation.
Contact:
Office of Student Financial Assistance
325 West Gaines Street
Tallahassee, FL 32399-0400
Phone: 888-827-2004
Web: www.floridastudentfinancialaid.org

Florida Medallion Scholars Award

Type of award: Scholarship, renewable.
Intended use: For undergraduate study at 2-year or 4-year institution. Designated institutions: Eligible Florida post-secondary institutions.
Eligibility: Applicant must be high school senior. Applicant must be U.S. citizen or permanent resident residing in Florida.
Basis for selection: Applicant must demonstrate high academic achievement.
Additional information: Minimum 3.0 GPA. Minimum composite score of 970/SAT or 20/ACT (excluding writing sections). Must have taken 15 credits of college preparatory academic courses. Applications available online, and must be completed before high school graduation. Check Website for additional information and requirements.
Contact:
Office of Student Financial Assistance
325 West Gaines Street
Tallahassee, FL 32399-0400
Phone: 888-827-2004
Web: www.floridastudentfinancialaid.org

Florida Student Assistance Grant Program

Type of award: Scholarship, renewable.
Intended use: For full-time undergraduate study at 2-year or 4-year institution. Designated institutions: Eligible Florida postsecondary institutions.
Eligibility: Applicant must be U.S. citizen or permanent resident residing in Florida.
Basis for selection: Applicant must demonstrate financial need.
Application requirements: Proof of eligibility. FAFSA.
Additional information: Each participating institution determines application deadlines, student eligibility, and award amounts. Applications available from participating schools' financial aid offices. Visit Website for more information.
Amount of award: $200-$2,069
Contact:
Office of Student Financial Assistance
325 West Gaines Street
Tallahassee, FL 32399-0400
Phone: 888-827-2004
Web: www.floridastudentfinancialaid.org

Jose Marti Scholarship Challenge Grant Fund

Type of award: Scholarship, renewable.

Intended use: For full-time freshman or graduate study at 2-year, 4-year or graduate institution in United States. Designated institutions: Florida public or eligible private institutions.
Eligibility: Applicant must be Mexican American, Hispanic American or Puerto Rican. Applicant must be U.S. citizen or permanent resident residing in Florida.
Basis for selection: Applicant must demonstrate financial need and high academic achievement.
Application requirements: FAFSA.
Additional information: Minimum 3.0 GPA. Must be of Spanish culture, born in Mexico or Hispanic country of the Caribbean, Central America, or South America, or child of same. Award number is limited to the amount of available funds. First priority given to renewal applicants, second priority to graduating high school seniors, third priority to graduate students. Applications available from high school guidance office or college financial aid office. Visit Website for more information.
Amount of award: $2,000
Application deadline: April 1
Contact:
Office of Student Financial Assistance
325 West Gaines Street
Tallahassee, FL 32399-0400
Phone: 888-827-2004
Web: www.floridastudentfinancialaid.org

Mary McLeod Bethune Scholarship

Type of award: Scholarship, renewable.
Intended use: For full-time undergraduate study at 4-year institution in United States. Designated institutions: Bethune-Cookman University, Edward Waters College, Florida A&M University, and Florida Memorial University.
Eligibility: Applicant must be U.S. citizen or permanent resident residing in Florida.
Basis for selection: Applicant must demonstrate financial need and high academic achievement.
Additional information: Minimum 3.0 high school GPA. Deadlines established by participating institutions. Award funds contingent upon matching contributions raised by the eligible institutions. Applications can be obtained from any of four designated institutions' financial aid offices. Visit Website for more information.
Amount of award: $3,000
Contact:
Office of Student Financial Assistance
325 West Gaines Street
Tallahassee, FL 32399-0400
Phone: 888-827-2004
Web: www.floridastudentfinancialaid.org

Robert C. Byrd Honors Scholarship Program

Type of award: Scholarship, renewable.
Intended use: For full-time undergraduate study at 2-year or 4-year institution in United States.
Eligibility: Applicant must be high school senior. Applicant must be U.S. citizen or permanent resident residing in Florida.
Basis for selection: Applicant must demonstrate high academic achievement.
Application requirements: Proof of eligibility, nomination by high school principal, adult education director, or school district superintendent.

Additional information: Nomination based on cumulative unweighted GPA multiplied by ACT score. Applicants are ranked with members of designated geographic region. Number and award amount determined annually.

Amount of award:	$1,500
Application deadline:	April 15

Contact:
Office of Student Financial Assistance
325 West Gaines Street
Tallahassee, FL 32399-0400
Phone: 888-827-2004
Web: www.floridastudentfinancialaid.org

Rosewood Family Scholarship Program

Type of award: Scholarship, renewable.
Intended use: For full-time undergraduate study at vocational, 2-year or 4-year institution in United States. Designated institutions: Public post-secondary institutions.
Eligibility: Applicant must be Alaskan native, Asian American, African American, Mexican American, Hispanic American, Puerto Rican, American Indian or Native Hawaiian/Pacific Islander. Applicant must be U.S. citizen or permanent resident.
Basis for selection: Applicant must demonstrate financial need.
Application requirements: Transcript. FAFSA. If not Florida resident, copy of Student Aid Report (SAR) must be postmarked to OSFA by May 15th.
Additional information: Applicant must be descendent of African-American Rosewood families affected by the incidents of January 1923; renewal applicants given priority. Award covers annual cost of tuition and fees up to $4,000 per semester for up to eight semesters. Visit Website for more information.

Amount of award:	$4,000
Number of awards:	25
Application deadline:	April 1

Contact:
Office of Student Financial Assistance
325 West Gaines Street
Tallahassee, FL 32399-0400
Phone: 888-827-2004
Web: www.floridastudentfinancialaid.org

Scholarships for Children and Spouses of Deceased or Disabled Veterans and Servicemembers

Type of award: Scholarship, renewable.
Intended use: For undergraduate study at postsecondary institution. Designated institutions: Eligible Florida postsecondary institutions.
Eligibility: Applicant must be at least 16, no older than 22. Applicant must be U.S. citizen or permanent resident residing in Florida. Applicant must be dependent of disabled veteran, deceased veteran or POW/MIA; or spouse of disabled veteran or deceased veteran.
Application requirements: Proof of eligibility.
Additional information: Child applicant must be between ages of 16 and 22. Spouse of deceased service member must not be remarried. Service members must be certified by Florida Department of Veterans Affairs. Award for students of eligible private schools based on average cost of Florida public tuition/fees. Award amount varies. Visit Website for additional information.

Application deadline:	April 1

Contact:
Office of Student Financial Assistance
325 West Gaines Street
Tallahassee, FL 32399-0400
Phone: 888-827-2004
Web: www.floridastudentfinancialaid.org

William L. Boyd, IV, Florida Resident Access Grant Program

Type of award: Scholarship, renewable.
Intended use: For full-time undergraduate study at accredited 4-year institution. Designated institutions: Eligible private, nonprofit Florida colleges and universities.
Eligibility: Applicant must be U.S. citizen or permanent resident residing in Florida.
Application requirements: Proof of eligibility.
Additional information: Applicant must not have previously received bachelor's degree and may not use award for study of divinity or theology. Amount of award plus all other scholarships and grants may not exceed total amount of tuition. Contact financial aid office of eligible institutions for application and more information.

Amount of award:	$2,529

Contact:
Office of Student Financial Assistance
325 West Gaines Street
Tallahassee, FL 32399-0400
Phone: 888-827-2004
Web: www.floridastudentfinancialaid.org

Foundation for Surgical Technology

Foundation Student Scholarship

Type of award: Scholarship.
Intended use: For undergraduate study in United States.
Basis for selection: Major/career interest in surgical technology. Applicant must demonstrate financial need and high academic achievement.
Application requirements: Recommendations, transcript, proof of eligibility.
Additional information: Applicant must be enrolled in surgical technology program accredited by CAAHEP or ABHES and be eligible to sit for the NBSTSA national surgical technologist certifying examination. Award amount varies. Visit Website for application.

Number of awards:	23
Number of applicants:	200
Application deadline:	March 1
Notification begins:	June 15
Total amount awarded:	$23,500

Contact:
The Foundation for Surgical Technology Attn: Scholarship Department
6 West Dry Creek Circle
Suite 200
Littleton, CO 80120
Phone: 303-694-9130
Fax: 303-694-9169
Web: www.ast.org/educators/scholarships.aspx

Foundation of the National Student Nurses Association, Inc.

National Student Nurses Association Scholarship

Type of award: Scholarship.
Intended use: For full-time undergraduate study at accredited 2-year or 4-year institution. Designated institutions: State-approved schools of nursing or pre-nursing.
Eligibility: Applicant must be U.S. citizen or permanent resident.
Basis for selection: Major/career interest in nursing or nurse practitioner. Applicant must demonstrate financial need, high academic achievement and service orientation.
Application requirements: $10 application fee. Essay, transcript, proof of eligibility. National Student Nurses Association members must submit proof of membership.
Additional information: All applicants considered for following scholarships: General Scholarships, Career Mobility Scholarships, Breakthrough to Nursing Scholarships, Specialty Scholarships, and Promise of Nursing Scholarships. Applicants must be enrolled in nursing or pre-nursing program. Awards granted for use in summer, fall of the same year and only spring of following academic year. Number of awards varies. Application deadline in January. Applications available from May through January. See Website for deadline and application.

Amount of award:	$1,000-$5,000
Number of applicants:	212
Total amount awarded:	$120,000

Contact:
Foundation of the National Student Nurses Association, Inc.
45 Main Street
Suite 606
Brooklyn, NY 11201
Phone: 718-210-0705
Fax: 718-210-0710
Web: www.nsna.org

Francis Ouimet Scholarship Fund

The Ouimet Scholarship

Type of award: Scholarship, renewable.
Intended use: For full-time undergraduate study at postsecondary institution.
Basis for selection: Competition/talent/interest in athletics/sports. Applicant must demonstrate financial need and high academic achievement.
Application requirements: Interview, recommendations, essay, transcript. FAFSA and CSS Profile, SAT scores. Photo.
Additional information: Applicants must have worked on golf course in Massachusetts for at least two years. Contact the Ouimet Fund office in June to be put on application mailing list for awards for following school year, or sign up for application online.

Amount of award:	$1,500-$7,500
Number of awards:	350
Number of applicants:	364
Application deadline:	December 1
Notification begins:	August 31
Total amount awarded:	$1,325,000

Contact:
Francis Ouimet Scholarship Fund
William F. Connell Golf House & Museum
300 Arnold Palmer Blvd.
Norton, MA 02766
Phone: 774-430-9090
Fax: 774-430-9091
Web: www.ouimet.org

Fred G. Zahn Foundation

Fred G. Zahn Foundation Scholarship

Type of award: Scholarship, renewable.
Intended use: For undergraduate study at accredited 2-year or 4-year institution in United States. Designated institutions: Institutions in Washington state.
Eligibility: Applicant must be residing in Washington.
Basis for selection: Applicant must demonstrate financial need, high academic achievement and depth of character.
Application requirements: Essay, transcript. Student Aid Report.
Additional information: Must have graduated from Washington state high school. Preference to juniors and seniors with minimum 3.75 GPA. May obtain application and more information at eligible Washington state institutions. Do not contact foundation.

Amount of award:	$1,500
Number of awards:	25
Application deadline:	April 15
Notification begins:	June 15

Contact:
Fred G. Zahn Foundation Scholarship c/o Bank of America Trust Service
715 Peachtree Street, 8th Floor
Atlanta, GA 30308
Phone: 800-832-9071
Fax: 800-552-3182

Freedom From Religion Foundation

FFRF Student/Youth Activist Award

Type of award: Scholarship.
Intended use: For undergraduate study at postsecondary institution.
Application requirements: Nomination by FFRF member.
Additional information: Given to students who have done something specific to separate church and state (e.g., stopped religious programs in public schools, been a plaintiff in a church-state lawsuit, etc.) or to promote nontheism. Nomination

period varies but preference is to give award in person at foundation's fall national convention. Private nomination only.

Amount of award: $1,000
Number of awards: 2
Number of applicants: 2
Total amount awarded: $2,000
Contact:
Freedom From Religion Foundation
FFRF Student/Youth Activist Award
P.O. Box 750
Madison, WI 53701
Phone: 608-256-8900
Web: www.ffrf.org

Henry Buschong Scholarship

Type of award: Scholarship.
Intended use: For freshman study at postsecondary institution.
Eligibility: Applicant must be high school senior.
Basis for selection: Competition/talent/interest in writing/journalism, based on best-written essays.
Application requirements: Essay, proof of eligibility. Essay should be three to four pages, double-spaced with standard margins. Include autobiographical paragraph giving permanent address, phone numbers, and e-mail. Identify high school and college/university to be attended. Include intended major and other interests.
Additional information: Applicant must be college-bound high school senior. Essay topics and requirements change annually and are announced in February. Students are requested not to inquire before then. Send SASE or visit Website for more information. First place receives $2,000; second place, $1,000; third place, $500; honorable mention(s), $200.

Amount of award: $200-$2,000
Number of applicants: 200
Application deadline: June 1
Notification begins: August 1
Total amount awarded: $4,500
Contact:
Freedom From Religion Foundation
High School Essay Competition
P.O. Box 750
Madison, WI 53701
Phone: 608-256-8900
Web: www.ffrf.org

Michael Hakeem Memorial Award

Type of award: Scholarship.
Intended use: For full-time undergraduate or graduate study at postsecondary institution.
Eligibility: Applicant must be U.S. citizen.
Basis for selection: Competition/talent/interest in writing/journalism, based on best-written essays.
Application requirements: Essay. Essay should be four to five pages, typed and double-spaced with standard margins. Include autobiographical paragraph giving both campus and permanent addresses, phone numbers, and e-mail. Identify college/university, major, and interests. Essay on free thought concerning religion; essay most suitable for atheistic and agnostic student.
Additional information: Applicant must be currently enrolled college student. Essay topics and requirements change annually and are announced in February. Check Website for current topic. Students are requested not to inquire before then. Send SASE or visit Website for more information. First place receives $2,000; second place, $1,000; third place, $500; honorable mention(s), $200.

Amount of award: $200-$2,000
Number of applicants: 200
Application deadline: July 1
Notification begins: September 1
Total amount awarded: $6,300
Contact:
Freedom From Religion Foundation
College Essay Competition
P.O. Box 750
Madison, WI 53701
Phone: 608-256-8900
Web: www.ffrf.org

Garden Club of America

Award in Desert Studies

Type of award: Scholarship.
Intended use: For junior, senior or graduate study at accredited postsecondary institution in United States.
Basis for selection: Major/career interest in horticulture; botany; environmental science or landscape architecture.
Application requirements: Recommendations, essay. Resume, itemized budget, research/project proposal.
Additional information: Projects must pertain to arid environment, preference given to projects that generate scientifically sound water and plant management. Visit www.dbg.org for application information.

Amount of award: $4,000
Application deadline: January 15
Notification begins: March 31
Contact:
Desert Botanical Garden
Attn: Cathy Babcock, Director of Horticulture
1201 N. Galvin Parkway
Phoenix, AZ 85008
Phone: 480-481-8162
Web: www.gcamerica.org or www.desertbotanical.org

Caroline Thorn Kissel Summer Environmental Studies Scholarship

Type of award: Scholarship.
Intended use: For undergraduate or graduate study at postsecondary institution.
Eligibility: Applicant must be U.S. citizen residing in New Jersey.
Basis for selection: Major/career interest in environmental science.
Application requirements: Recommendations, essay.
Additional information: Must be either New Jersey resident or non-resident studying in New Jersey. All application elements must be mailed together in one envelope.

Amount of award: $2,000
Number of awards: 1
Application deadline: February 10
Contact:
Garden Club of America
Ms. Judy Smith
14 East 60th Street
New York, NY 10022-1002
Phone: 212-753-8287
Fax: 212-753-0134
Web: www.gcamerica.org

Field Botany Scholarships

Type of award: Scholarship.
Intended use: For sophomore, junior, senior or master's study at postsecondary institution in United States.
Basis for selection: Major/career interest in botany or horticulture.
Application requirements: Recommendations, essay, transcript.
Additional information: One application for two awards: GCA Scholarship in Field Botany and Joan K. and Rachel M. Hunt Summer Scholarship in Field Botany. Study may be used in North, Central, or South America, or in the U.S. Preference given to study in U.S. Mail all information in one envelope. Visit Website for application.

Amount of award:	$2,000
Application deadline:	February 1

Contact:
Garden Club of America
Ms. Judy Smith
14 East 60th Street
New York, NY 10022-1002
Phone: 212-753-8287
Fax: 212-753-0134
Web: www.gcamerica.org

Francis M. Peacock Native Bird Habitat Scholarship

Type of award: Scholarship.
Intended use: For senior or graduate study at postsecondary institution.
Basis for selection: Major/career interest in ornithology.
Application requirements: Project proposal of no more than five pages.
Additional information: Grant for advanced study of U.S. winter/summer habitat of threatened or endangered native birds. Awarded in cooperation with the Cornell Lab of Ornithology. Second semester juniors may apply for senior year. No phone calls. To apply, contact: www.birds.cornell.edu/about/jobs.html.

Amount of award:	$4,000
Number of awards:	1
Application deadline:	January 15
Total amount awarded:	$4,000

Contact:
Cornell Lab of Ornithology
Scott Sutcliffe
159 Sapsucker Woods Road
Ithaca, NY 14850
Fax: 607-254-2415
Web: www.gcamerica.org

Garden Club of America Summer Environmental Awards

Type of award: Scholarship.
Intended use: For freshman, sophomore or junior study at 4-year institution.
Basis for selection: Major/career interest in environmental science or ecology.
Application requirements: Recommendations, essay, transcript.
Additional information: Three awards for summer study in field of ecology and environmental studies: The Mary T. Carothers Scholarship, The Clara Carter Higgins/GCA Scholarship, and The Elizabeth Gardner Norweb Scholarship.

Amount of award:	$2,000
Number of awards:	3
Application deadline:	February 10

Contact:
Garden Club of America Awards for Summer Environmental Studies
Ms. Judy Smith
14 East 60th Street
New York, NY 10022-1002
Phone: 212-753-8287
Fax: 212-753-0134
Web: www.gcamerica.org

Katharine M. Grosscup Scholarship

Type of award: Scholarship.
Intended use: For sophomore, junior, senior or graduate study at accredited 4-year or graduate institution in United States. Designated institutions: Kentucky, Indiana, Michigan, Ohio, Pennsylvania, West Virginia institutions.
Basis for selection: Major/career interest in horticulture. Applicant must demonstrate financial need and high academic achievement.
Application requirements: Interview, recommendations, essay, transcript.
Additional information: Minimum 3.5 GPA. Several scholarships available. Preference given to college juniors and seniors who are residents of Pennsylvania, Ohio, West Virginia, Michigan, Indiana and, Kentucky. Major can be in related field. Please do not contact by phone. Application available on Website.

Amount of award:	$3,000
Application deadline:	January 15

Contact:
Katharine M. Grosscup Scholarship Committee/Cleveland Botanical Garden
11030 East Boulevard
Cleveland, OH 44106
Fax: 216-721-2056
Web: www.gcamerica.org

The Loy McCandless Marks Scholarship

Type of award: Scholarship.
Intended use: For sophomore, junior, senior or graduate study at accredited 4-year or graduate institution in United States.
Eligibility: Applicant must be U.S. citizen.
Basis for selection: Major/career interest in botany; horticulture or landscape architecture.
Application requirements: Recommendations, essay, transcript. Budget.
Additional information: For study and research at appropriate foreign institution specializing in study of tropical plants. Visit Website for application.

Amount of award:	$2,000
Number of awards:	1
Application deadline:	January 15

Contact:
Garden Club of America
Ms. Judy Smith
14 East 60th Street
New York, NY 10022-1002
Phone: 212-753-8287
Fax: 212-753-0134
Web: www.gcamerica.org

Zeller Summer Scholarship in Medicinal Botany

Type of award: Scholarship.
Intended use: For undergraduate or graduate study at accredited postsecondary institution in United States.
Basis for selection: Major/career interest in botany.
Application requirements: Recommendations, essay, transcript.
Additional information: Mail all application materials together in one envelope.

Amount of award:	$2,000
Number of awards:	1
Application deadline:	February 1

Contact:
Garden Club of America
Ms. Judy Smith
14 East 60th Street
New York, NY 10022-1002
Phone: 212-753-8287
Fax: 212-753-0134
Web: www.gcamerica.org

Georgia Student Finance Commission

Accel Program Grant

Type of award: Scholarship.
Intended use: For undergraduate study at accredited vocational, 2-year or 4-year institution.
Eligibility: Applicant must be high school junior or senior. Applicant must be U.S. citizen or permanent resident residing in Georgia.
Application requirements: Must submit completed application to high school for each participating term.
Additional information: Assistance for high school students to take college level coursework for credit in both high school and college. Must be approved by both high school and college as a dual credit enrollment student. Public college award includes tuition, approved mandatory fees, and book allowance. For students enrolled at private colleges, award is up to $1,750 per semester. Awards are pro-rated for students taking less than 12 hours per semester. Amount awarded varies. Students must apply on or before the last day of school term or student's withdrawal date, whichever is first. Unlimited number of awards available. Visit Website for application.

Number of applicants:	3,739
Total amount awarded:	$5,764,625

Contact:
Georgia Student Finance Commission
2082 East Exchange Place
Suite 100
Tucker, GA 30084
Phone: 800-505-4732
Fax: 770-724-9004
Web: www.gacollege411.org

Georgia Hope Grant - GED Recipient

Type of award: Scholarship.

Intended use: For undergraduate study at accredited vocational, 2-year or 4-year institution. Designated institutions: HOPE-eligible colleges and universities in Georgia.
Eligibility: Applicant must be U.S. citizen or permanent resident residing in Georgia.
Application requirements: Proof of eligibility.
Additional information: Must have received GED from Georgia Department of Technical and Adult Education after June 30, 1993. Submit HOPE voucher upon enrollment. Students receiving GED from DTAE receive voucher automatically. Unlimited number of awards available.

Amount of award:	$500
Number of applicants:	4,947
Total amount awarded:	$2,467,836

Contact:
Georgia Student Finance Commission
2082 East Exchange Place
Suite 100
Tucker, GA 30084
Phone: 800-505-4732
Fax: 770-724-9004
Web: www.gacollege411.org

Georgia Hope Grant - Public Technical Institution

Type of award: Scholarship, renewable.
Intended use: For undergraduate study at accredited vocational, 2-year or 4-year institution. Designated institutions: Branches and affiliates of the Georgia Department of Technical and Adult Education and branches of the University System of Georgia.
Eligibility: Applicant must be U.S. citizen or permanent resident residing in Georgia. Applicant may also be dependent child of military personnel stationed in Georgia.
Additional information: Scholarship covers tuition, mandatory fees, plus book allowance up to $150 per semester. Award covers full tuition. Unlimited number of awards available. Must be enrolled, matriculated technical certificate or diploma student.

Amount of award:	Full tuition
Number of applicants:	114,288
Total amount awarded:	$128,700,000

Contact:
Georgia Student Finance Commission
2082 East Exchange Place
Suite 100
Tucker, GA 30084
Phone: 800-505-4732
Fax: 770-724-9004
Web: www.gacollege411.org

Georgia Hope Scholarship - Private Institution

Type of award: Scholarship, renewable.
Intended use: For undergraduate study at accredited 2-year or 4-year institution. Designated institutions: Eligible Georgia private colleges and universities.
Eligibility: Applicant must be U.S. citizen or permanent resident residing in Georgia.
Basis for selection: Applicant must demonstrate high academic achievement.
Additional information: Award is up to $3,500 per semester for full-time students and up to $1,750 per semester for half-time students.

Amount of award:	$3,500
Number of awards:	13,980
Number of applicants:	13,980
Total amount awarded:	$43,300,000

Contact:
Georgia Student Finance Commission
2082 East Exchange Place
Suite 100
Tucker, GA 30084
Phone: 800-505-4732
Fax: 770-724-9004
Web: www.gacollege411.org

Georgia Hope Scholarship - Public College or University

Type of award: Scholarship, renewable.
Intended use: For undergraduate study at accredited 2-year or 4-year institution. Designated institutions: Eligible Georgia public colleges and universities.
Eligibility: Applicant must be U.S. citizen or permanent resident residing in Georgia.
Basis for selection: Applicant must demonstrate high academic achievement.
Application requirements: Proof of eligibility.
Additional information: Minimum 3.0 GPA. Must be designated HOPE scholar. HOPE assistance includes tuition, HOPE-approved mandatory fees, and book allowance up to $150 per semester.

Amount of award:	Full tuition
Number of awards:	89,751
Number of applicants:	89,751
Total amount awarded:	$348,100,000

Contact:
Georgia Student Finance Commission
2082 East Exchange Place
Suite 100
Tucker, GA 30084
Phone: 800-505-4732
Fax: 770-724-9004
Web: www.gacollege411.org

Georgia Law Enforcement Personnel Dependents Grant

Type of award: Scholarship, renewable.
Intended use: For full-time undergraduate study at accredited vocational, 2-year or 4-year institution. Designated institutions: Georgia colleges and public technical institutions.
Eligibility: Applicant must be U.S. citizen or permanent resident residing in Georgia. Applicant's parent must have been killed or disabled in work-related accident as firefighter, police officer or public safety officer.
Application requirements: Proof of eligibility.
Additional information: Must complete preliminary document that verifies claim with parent's former employer and doctors. Parent must have been permanently disabled or killed in the line of duty as Georgia police officer, firefighter, emergency medical technician, or corrections officer.

Amount of award:	$2,000
Total amount awarded:	$64,270

Contact:
Georgia Student Finance Commission
2082 East Exchange Place
Suite 100
Tucker, GA 30084
Phone: 800-505-4732
Fax: 770-724-9004
Web: www.gacollege411.org

Georgia LEAP Grant

Type of award: Scholarship, renewable.
Intended use: For undergraduate study at vocational, 2-year or 4-year institution.
Eligibility: Applicant must be U.S. citizen or permanent resident residing in Georgia.
Basis for selection: Applicant must demonstrate financial need.
Application requirements: FAFSA.
Additional information: Must submit application on or before the last day of school term. Must apply for and be eligible to receive Federal Pell Grant. Unlimited number of awards available.

Amount of award:	$150-$2,000
Total amount awarded:	$1,475,500

Contact:
Georgia Student Finance Commission
2082 East Exchange Place
Suite 100
Tucker, GA 30084
Phone: 800-505-4732
Fax: 770-724-9004
Web: www.gacollege411.org

Georgia Robert C. Byrd Scholarship

Type of award: Scholarship, renewable.
Intended use: For full-time undergraduate study at accredited 2-year or 4-year institution in United States.
Eligibility: Applicant must be high school senior. Applicant must be U.S. citizen or permanent resident residing in Georgia.
Basis for selection: Applicant must demonstrate high academic achievement.
Application requirements: Essay, transcript, proof of eligibility. SAT/ACT scores.
Additional information: Obtain application from high school guidance office and submit to Georgia Department of Education.

Amount of award:	$1,500
Number of awards:	200
Application deadline:	February 1
Total amount awarded:	$1,023,545

Contact:
Georgia Student Finance Commission
2082 East Exchange Place
Suite 100
Tucker, GA 30084
Phone: 800-505-4732
Fax: 770-724-9004
Web: www.gacollege411.org

Georgia Tuition Equalization Grant

Type of award: Scholarship, renewable.
Intended use: For full-time undergraduate study at accredited 2-year or 4-year institution. Designated institutions: GSFC approved institutions.

Eligibility: Applicant must be U.S. citizen or permanent resident residing in Georgia.
Application requirements: Proof of eligibility. Mileage affidavit (for out-of-state schools only).
Additional information: Must be enrolled at eligible private college or university in Georgia, or be a junior or senior with no Georgia public college within 50 miles of home and enrolled at eligible public college outside Georgia. Amount of award determined by Georgia General Assembly appropriations. Application deadlines set by schools. Award amount varies. Visit Website for list of approved institutions.

Total amount awarded:	$31,242,792

Contact:
Georgia Student Finance Commission
2082 East Exchange Place
Suite 100
Tucker, GA 30084
Phone: 800-505-4732
Fax: 770-724-9004
Web: www.gacollege411.org

Glamour Magazine

Top 10 College Women Competition

Type of award: Scholarship.
Intended use: For full-time junior study at accredited 4-year institution in United States or Canada.
Eligibility: Applicant must be female.
Basis for selection: Applicant must demonstrate high academic achievement, leadership and service orientation.
Application requirements: Recommendations, essay, transcript. List of activities, black-and-white or color photograph.
Additional information: See Website for deadline, application, and details.

Number of awards:	10

Contact:
Glamour's Top 10 College Women Competition
4 Times Square
16th Floor
New York, NY 10036-6593
Fax: 212-286-6922
Web: www.glamour.com/about/top-10-college-women

The Global Challenge Award

Global Challenge Awards

Type of award: Scholarship.
Intended use: For freshman study at postsecondary institution.
Eligibility: Applicant must be enrolled in high school.
Basis for selection: Competition/talent/interest in science project, based on specific criteria outlined on Website. Applicant's talent/interest in science, math, engineering, business, global collaboration, and/or environmental topics must be shown in final project.
Application requirements: Research proposal. Register online.

Additional information: Students, aged 14-17, work in international teams to learn, research, and address various issues of climate change and energy use. The four team-based projects are the Global Business Plan, the Technical Innovation Plan, GCA-350, and Explorations. Rolling deadline. Visit Website for more details.

Amount of award:	$150-$1,000
Number of awards:	16
Number of applicants:	200
Notification begins:	June 1, December 1
Total amount awarded:	$30,850

Contact:
The Global Challenge Award Inc.
100 Notchbrook Road
Stowe, VT 05672
Phone: 802-472-3200
Web: www.globalchallengeaward.org

Golden Apple

Golden Apple Scholars of Illinois Program

Type of award: Scholarship.
Intended use: For undergraduate study at 4-year institution in United States. Designated institutions: Participating Illinois universities.
Eligibility: Applicant must be high school senior. Applicant must be U.S. citizen residing in Illinois.
Basis for selection: Major/career interest in education; education, early childhood; education, special or education, teacher. Applicant must demonstrate high academic achievement.
Application requirements: Transcript. SAT/ACT scores.
Additional information: Must obtain teacher's certification and teach for five years in Illinois school of need. Must participate in Summer Institutes. Must be high school senior or college sophomore. Scholars receive $2,000 stipend for attending Summer Institute program. Visit Website for application and nomination forms.

Amount of award:	$5,000-$10,000
Number of awards:	100
Number of applicants:	100
Application deadline:	November 15
Notification begins:	March 1
Total amount awarded:	$492,500

Contact:
Golden Apple
8 South Michigan Avenue
Suite 700
Chicago, IL 60603
Phone: 312-407-0006
Fax: 312-407-0344
Web: www.goldenapple.org

Golden Key International Honour Society

Business Achievement Awards

Type of award: Scholarship.
Intended use: For undergraduate or graduate study at accredited postsecondary institution.
Basis for selection: Major/career interest in business. Applicant must demonstrate high academic achievement.
Application requirements: Recommendations, transcript. Business-related paper/report (must not exceed ten typed pages).
Additional information: Open to Golden Key members only. First-place winner receives $2,000; second place, $1,500; third place, $1,000. Visit Website for application.

Amount of award:	$1,000-$2,000
Number of awards:	3
Application deadline:	March 1

Contact:
Scholarship Program Administrators Attn: Golden Key Awards
P.O. Box 23737
Nashville, TN 37202-3737
Phone: 800-377-2401
Fax: 615-627-9685
Web: www.goldenkey.org

Community Service Award

Type of award: Scholarship.
Intended use: For undergraduate or graduate study at accredited postsecondary institution.
Basis for selection: Applicant must demonstrate service orientation.
Application requirements: Recommendations, essay. List of extracurricular activities.
Additional information: Only Golden Key members who were enrolled as students during previous academic year eligible to apply. Winner and charity of winner's choice will each receive $500. Visit Website for application.

Amount of award:	$500
Number of awards:	1
Application deadline:	March 1

Contact:
Scholarship Program Administrators Attn: Golden Key Awards
P.O. Box 23737
Nashville, TN 37202-3737
Phone: 800-377-2401
Fax: 615-627-9685
Web: www.goldenkey.org

Education Achievement Awards

Type of award: Scholarship.
Intended use: For undergraduate or graduate study at accredited postsecondary institution.
Basis for selection: Major/career interest in education. Applicant must demonstrate high academic achievement.
Application requirements: Recommendations, essay, transcript. An education-related paper (no more than ten pages).
Additional information: Open to Golden Key members only. Visit Website for application.

Amount of award:	$1,000-$2,000
Number of awards:	3
Application deadline:	March 1

Contact:
Scholarship Program Administrators Attn: Golden Key Awards
P.O. Box 23737
Nashville, TN 37202-3737
Phone: 800-377-2401
Fax: 615-627-9685
Web: www.goldenkey.org

Engineering/Technology Achievement Awards

Type of award: Scholarship.
Intended use: For undergraduate or graduate study at accredited postsecondary institution.
Basis for selection: Major/career interest in engineering or technology. Applicant must demonstrate high academic achievement.
Application requirements: Recommendations, essay, transcript. An engineering-related paper (no more than ten pages of text).
Additional information: Open to Golden Key members only. First-place winner receives $2,000; second place, $1,500; third place, $1,000. Visit Website for application.

Amount of award:	$1,000-$2,000
Number of awards:	3
Application deadline:	March 1

Contact:
Scholarship Program Administrators Attn: Golden Key Awards
P.O. Box 23737
Nashville, TN 37202-3737
Phone: 800-377-2401
Fax: 615-627-9685
Web: www.goldenkey.org

GEICO Life Scholarship

Type of award: Scholarship.
Intended use: For undergraduate study at accredited 4-year institution.
Eligibility: Applicant must be returning adult student.
Basis for selection: Applicant must demonstrate high academic achievement.
Application requirements: Recommendations, essay, transcript. Essay should be no more than 500 words and describe educational goals, other commitments, and obstacles overcome to achieve academic excellence.
Additional information: Only Golden Key members eligible to apply. Applicants must have completed at least 12 credit hours since returning to school. Visit Website for details and application.

Amount of award:	$1,000
Number of awards:	10
Application deadline:	April 1

Contact:
Scholarship Program Administrators Attn: Golden Key Awards
P.O. Box 23737
Nashville, TN 37202-3737
Phone: 800-377-2401
Fax: 615-627-9685
Web: www.goldenkey.org

Literary Achievement Awards

Type of award: Scholarship.
Intended use: For undergraduate or graduate study at accredited postsecondary institution.
Basis for selection: Competition/talent/interest in writing/journalism.

Application requirements: Original composition, not to exceed 1,500 words.

Additional information: Open to Golden Key members only. Previously published works not accepted. Four contest categories: fiction, non-fiction, poetry, and news writing. Only one entry per category per member. Visit Website for details and application.

Amount of award:	$1,000
Number of awards:	4
Application deadline:	March 1
Total amount awarded:	$4,000

Contact:
Scholarship Program Administrators Attn: Golden Key Awards
P.O. Box 23737
Nashville, TN 30202-3737
Phone: 800-377-2401
Fax: 615-627-9685
Web: www.goldenkey.org

Regional Student Leader of the Year Award

Type of award: Scholarship.
Intended use: For undergraduate or graduate study at accredited postsecondary institution in United States.
Basis for selection: Applicant must demonstrate high academic achievement and leadership.
Application requirements: Recommendations, essay, transcript. List of personal Golden Key involvement and other extracurricular activities.
Additional information: Open to Golden Key members only. Applicant must be active member in good standing. Winners at regional level will be considered for International Student Leader Award. Visit Website for details and application. E-mail submission preferred.

Amount of award:	$500
Number of awards:	13
Application deadline:	April 1

Contact:
Golden Key International Honour Society Attn: Student Leader Awards
621 North Avenue NE
Suite C-100
Atlanta, GA 30308
Phone: 800-377-2401 ext. 6723
Web: www.goldenkey.org

Study Abroad Scholarships

Type of award: Scholarship.
Intended use: For undergraduate or graduate study at postsecondary institution.
Basis for selection: Competition/talent/interest in study abroad, based on relevance of study abroad program to major field of study. Applicant must demonstrate high academic achievement.
Application requirements: Transcript, proof of eligibility. Description of planned academic program at host university. One-page statement of relevance of program to degree signed by professor/academic advisor.
Additional information: Only Golden Key members eligible to apply. Three awards presented for the October 1 deadline and seven for the April 1 deadline. Visit Website for details and application.

Amount of award:	$1,000
Number of awards:	10
Application deadline:	April 1, October 1

Contact:
Scholarship Program Administrators Attn: Golden Key Awards
P.O. Box 23737
Nashville, TN 37202-3737
Phone: 800-377-2401
Fax: 615-627-9685
Web: www.goldenkey.org

Undergraduate Research Grants

Type of award: Research grant.
Intended use: For undergraduate or graduate study.
Basis for selection: Applicant must demonstrate high academic achievement.
Application requirements: Transcript. Budget summary and description of proposed research.
Additional information: Only Golden Key members eligible to apply. Grant for members to travel to professional conferences and student research symposia, or to conduct thesis research. Four awards will be presented for the October 1 deadline, six for the April 1 deadline. Visit Website for details and application.

Amount of award:	$1,000
Number of awards:	10
Application deadline:	April 1, October 1

Contact:
Scholarship Program Administrators Attn: Golden Key Awards
P.O. Box 23737
Nashville, TN 37202-3737
Phone: 800-377-2401
Fax: 615-627-9685
Web: www.goldenkey.org

Visual and Performing Arts Achievement Awards

Type of award: Scholarship.
Intended use: For undergraduate or graduate study at accredited postsecondary institution.
Basis for selection: Competition/talent/interest in visual arts, based on quality of work submitted.
Application requirements: Slides, photographs, or CD of visual work; VHS tape, CD, or DVD of performance (ten minute maximum).
Additional information: Open to Golden Key members only. One award in each of nine categories: painting, drawing, mixed media, sculpture, photography, computer-generated art/illustration/graphic design, instrumental performance, vocal performance, and dance. One entry per member per category. Visit Website for details and application.

Amount of award:	$1,000
Number of awards:	9
Application deadline:	March 1

Contact:
Scholarship Program Administrators Attn: Golden Key Awards
P.O. Box 23737
Nashville, TN 37202-3737
Phone: 800-377-2401
Fax: 615-627-9685
Web: www.goldenkey.org

Grange Insurance Association

Grange Insurance Scholarship

Type of award: Scholarship.
Intended use: For full-time undergraduate or graduate study at accredited vocational, 2-year, 4-year or graduate institution.
Eligibility: Applicant must be U.S. citizen or permanent resident residing in Wyoming, California, Oregon, Idaho, Washington or Colorado.
Basis for selection: Applicant must demonstrate financial need, high academic achievement, depth of character, leadership, patriotism, seriousness of purpose and service orientation.
Application requirements: Essay, transcript. Cover letter.
Additional information: Applicant must be one of the following: current GIA policyholder (or child/grandchild of GIA policyholder), Grange member (or child/grandchild of Grange member), or child/grandchild of current GIA company employee. Previous recipients also eligible to apply. Application must be postmarked by deadline.

Amount of award:	$1,000-$1,500
Number of awards:	26
Number of applicants:	81
Application deadline:	April 15
Notification begins:	May 15
Total amount awarded:	$26,000

Contact:
Grange Insurance Association
Scholarship Committee
P.O. Box 21089
Seattle, WA 98111-3089
Phone: 800-247-2643 ext. 2200
Web: www.grange.com

Great Minds in Stem

Great Minds in Stem Scholars Program

Type of award: Scholarship, renewable.
Intended use: For full-time undergraduate or graduate study at 2-year, 4-year or graduate institution.
Basis for selection: Major/career interest in engineering; mathematics; science, general or technology. Applicant must demonstrate high academic achievement and leadership.
Application requirements: Recommendations, essay. Resume.
Additional information: Minimum 3.0 GPA. All sciences except medicine eligible. Include SASE with application request, or download application from Website. Amount of award varies.

Amount of award:	$500-$5,000
Number of awards:	80
Application deadline:	April 30
Notification begins:	July 15
Total amount awarded:	$250,000

Contact:
Great Minds in Stem
Student Scholarship Committee
3900 Whiteside Street
Los Angeles, CA 90063
Phone: 323-262-0997
Web: www.greatmindsinstem.org

Greater Kanawha Valley Foundation

Greater Kanawha Valley Scholarship Program

Type of award: Scholarship, renewable.
Intended use: For full-time undergraduate or graduate study at 4-year or graduate institution.
Eligibility: Applicant must be residing in West Virginia.
Basis for selection: Applicant must demonstrate high academic achievement and depth of character.
Application requirements: Recommendations, transcript. First page of parents' federal income tax return.
Additional information: Minimum 20 ACT score. Foundation offers more than 80 scholarships, each with specific eligibility criteria. Visit Website for complete listing, and to apply.

Amount of award:	$1,000
Number of awards:	565
Number of applicants:	750
Application deadline:	January 15
Notification begins:	May 15
Total amount awarded:	$865,000

Contact:
The Greater Kanawha Valley Foundation
P.O. Box 3041
Charleston, WV 25331
Phone: 304-346-3620
Web: www.tgkvf.org

Greenhouse Partners

Greenhouse Scholars

Type of award: Scholarship, renewable.
Intended use: For full-time undergraduate study at 4-year institution.
Eligibility: Applicant must be high school senior. Applicant must be U.S. citizen or permanent resident residing in Colorado.
Basis for selection: Based on commitment to community, ability to persevere through difficult circumstances, strong sense of accountability. Applicant must demonstrate financial need, high academic achievement and leadership.
Application requirements: Transcript. Three letters of recommendation, ACT scores.
Additional information: The Greenhouse Scholars Program is a scholarship and mentorship program for under-resourced, high-achieving students. The program uses a 'Whole Person' approach to address the intellectual, academic, professional, and financial needs of students. Minimum 3.5 GPA. Renewable for four years. Visit Website for application and more information.

Amount of award:	$1,000-$5,000
Number of awards:	15
Number of applicants:	150
Application deadline:	January 20
Notification begins:	February 22
Total amount awarded:	$90,000

Contact:
Greenhouse Scholars
1011 Walnut Street, Third Floor
Boulder, CO 80302
Phone: 303-464-7811
Fax: 303-464-7796
Web: www.greenhousescholars.org

Harness Tracks of America

Harness Tracks of America Scholarship Fund

Type of award: Scholarship.
Intended use: For full-time undergraduate or graduate study at accredited postsecondary institution.
Eligibility: Applicant or parent must be member/participant of Harness Racing Industry.
Basis for selection: Applicant must demonstrate financial need and high academic achievement.
Application requirements: Essay, transcript, proof of eligibility. FAFSA and U.S. or Canadian tax return.
Additional information: Must be child of licensed driver, trainer, breeder, owner or caretaker of harness horses or be personally active in harness racing industry. Children of deceased industry members also eligible. Recommendations not required but considered if included with application. Awards based on financial need, academic excellence, and active harness racing involvement. Visit Website for more information.

Amount of award:	$5,000
Number of awards:	5
Number of applicants:	31
Application deadline:	June 15
Notification begins:	September 15
Total amount awarded:	$25,000

Contact:
Harness Tracks of America
4640 East Sunrise Drive
Suite 200
Tucson, AZ 85718
Phone: 520-529-2525
Fax: 520-529-3235
Web: www.harnesstracks.com

Havana National Bank

McFarland Charitable Foundation Scholarship

Type of award: Scholarship, renewable.
Intended use: For full-time undergraduate study at accredited vocational, 2-year or 4-year institution in United States.
Eligibility: Applicant must be residing in Illinois.
Basis for selection: Major/career interest in nursing. Applicant must demonstrate seriousness of purpose.

Application requirements: Interview, recommendations, transcript, proof of eligibility. Letter of acceptance to RN program.
Additional information: Award recipients must contractually obligate themselves to return to Havana, Illinois, and work as registered nurses for two years for each year of funding. Reverts to loan if work obligation is not met. Two Cosigners are required. To fund RN programs only. Number of awards and amounts varies.

Amount of award:	$1,000-$20,000
Number of applicants:	6
Application deadline:	May 15
Notification begins:	June 15
Total amount awarded:	$75,000

Contact:
Havana National Bank
112 South Orange
P.O. Box 200
Havana, IL 62644-0200
Phone: 309-543-3361
Web: www.havanabank.com

Hawaii Community Foundation

100th Infantry Battalion Memorial Scholarship Fund

Type of award: Scholarship.
Intended use: For full-time undergraduate or graduate study at 2-year or 4-year institution in United States.
Eligibility: Applicant must be U.S. citizen or permanent resident. Must be direct descendant of a 100th Infantry Battalion World War II Veteran.
Basis for selection: Applicant must demonstrate financial need, high academic achievement, depth of character and service orientation.
Application requirements: Recommendations, essay, transcript, proof of eligibility. SAR, Personal Statement. Essay on topic: "What is the legacy of the 100th Infantry Battalion of WWII and how will you contribute to forwarding this legacy?" Name World War II 100th Battalion and your relationship to individual.
Additional information: Minimum 3.5 GPA. Applicant does not have to reside in Hawaii.

Application deadline:	March 1

Contact:
Hawaii Community Foundation Scholarships
1164 Bishop Street
Suite 800
Honolulu, HI 96813
Phone: 888-731-3863
Fax: 808-521-6286
Web: www.hawaiicommunityfoundation.org

ABC Stores Jumpstart Scholarship

Type of award: Scholarship.
Intended use: For undergraduate or graduate study at accredited 2-year, 4-year or graduate institution in United States.
Eligibility: Applicant must be residing in Hawaii or Nevada.
Basis for selection: Applicant must demonstrate financial need, high academic achievement and depth of character.

Application requirements: Recommendations, essay, transcript. SAR, FAFSA, Personal Statement. Name of ABC Stores Employee and relationship (i.e., mother).
Additional information: Must be resident of Hawaii, Nevada, Guam or Saipan. Minimum 2.7 GPA. Applicants must have permanent address in Hawaii. Amount of award may change yearly. Applicants must be employee or dependent of ABC Stores or Company Island Gourmet Markets employee.

    Application deadline: March 1
Contact:
Hawaii Community Foundation Scholarships
1164 Bishop Street
Suite 800
Honolulu, HI 96813
Phone: 888-731-3863
Fax: 808-521-6286
Web: www.hawaiicommunityfoundation.org

Aiea General Hospital Association Scholarship

Type of award: Scholarship, renewable.
Intended use: For full-time undergraduate or graduate study at accredited 2-year, 4-year or graduate institution in United States.
Eligibility: Applicant must be U.S. citizen or permanent resident residing in Hawaii.
Basis for selection: Major/career interest in health-related professions. Applicant must demonstrate financial need, high academic achievement and depth of character.
Application requirements: Recommendations, essay, transcript. FAFSA and SAR.
Additional information: Minimum 2.7 GPA. Applicant must be resident of Leeward Oahu ZIP Codes: 96701, 96706, 96707, 96782, 96792, or 98797. Amount and number of awards vary.

    Number of awards: 26
    Application deadline: March 1
Contact:
Hawaii Community Foundation Scholarships
1164 Bishop Street
Suite 800
Honolulu, HI 96813
Phone: 888-731-3863
Fax: 808-521-6286
Web: www.hawaiicommunityfoundation.org

Allan Eldin & Agnes Sutorik Geiger Scholarship Fund

Type of award: Scholarship.
Intended use: For full-time undergraduate or graduate study at accredited 2-year or 4-year institution in United States.
Eligibility: Applicant must be U.S. citizen residing in Hawaii.
Basis for selection: Major/career interest in veterinary medicine. Applicant must demonstrate financial need, high academic achievement and depth of character.
Application requirements: Recommendations, essay, transcript. SAR, FAFSA, Personal Statement.
Additional information: Minimum 3.0 GPA. Applicants must have permanent address in Hawaii. Applicants taking up mainland residency must have relatives living in Hawaii. Amount of award may change yearly.

    Application deadline: March 1

Contact:
Hawaii Community Foundation Scholarships
1164 Bishop Street
Suite 800
Honolulu, HI 96813
Phone: 888-731-3863
Fax: 808-521-6286
Web: www.hawaiicommunityfoundation.org

Alma White-Delta Kappa Gamma Scholarship

Type of award: Scholarship.
Intended use: For full-time junior, senior or graduate study at accredited postsecondary institution in United States.
Eligibility: Applicant must be U.S. citizen or permanent resident residing in Hawaii.
Basis for selection: Major/career interest in education. Applicant must demonstrate financial need, high academic achievement and depth of character.
Application requirements: Recommendations, essay, transcript. FAFSA and SAR. Official letter confirming enrollment in education program.
Additional information: Applicants must have permanent address in Hawaii. Applicants taking up mainland residency must have relatives living in Hawaii. Amount and number of awards vary and may change yearly.

    Number of awards: 10
    Application deadline: March 1
Contact:
Hawaii Community Foundation Scholarships
1164 Bishop Street
Suite 800
Honolulu, HI 96813
Phone: 888-731-3863
Fax: 808-521-6286
Web: www.hawaiicommunityfoundation.org

Bal Dasa Scholarship Fund

Type of award: Scholarship.
Intended use: For full-time undergraduate study at accredited 2-year or 4-year institution in United States.
Eligibility: Applicant must be U.S. citizen or permanent resident residing in Hawaii.
Basis for selection: Applicant must demonstrate financial need, high academic achievement and depth of character.
Application requirements: Essay, transcript. FAFSA and SAR.
Additional information: Must be graduate of Waipahu High School. Award amount varies yearly. Applicants taking up mainland residency must have relatives living in Hawaii.

    Number of awards: 1
    Application deadline: March 1
Contact:
Hawaii Community Foundation Scholarships
1164 Bishop Street
Suite 800
Honolulu, HI 96813
Phone: 888-731-3863
Fax: 808-521-6286
Web: www.hawaiicommunityfoundation.org

Blossom Kalama Evans Memorial Scholarship

Type of award: Scholarship, renewable.

Intended use: For full-time junior, senior or graduate study at accredited 4-year or graduate institution in United States.
Eligibility: Applicant must be Native Hawaiian/Pacific Islander. Applicant must be U.S. citizen or permanent resident residing in Hawaii.
Basis for selection: Major/career interest in Hawaiian studies. Applicant must demonstrate financial need, high academic achievement and depth of character.
Application requirements: Transcript. FAFSA and SAR. Personal essay stating how applicant's knowledge will be used to serve the needs of the Native Hawaiian community.
Additional information: Minimum 2.7 GPA. Students must be of Hawaiian ancestry. Applicants must have permanent address in Hawaii. Applicants who take up mainland residency must have relatives living in Hawaii. Amount and number of awards vary.

> **Number of awards:** 9
> **Application deadline:** March 1

Contact:
Hawaii Community Foundation Scholarships
1164 Bishop Street
Suite 800
Honolulu, HI 96813
Phone: 888-731-3863
Fax: 808-521-6286
Web: www.hawaiicommunityfoundation.org

Camille C. Chidiac Fund

Type of award: Scholarship.
Intended use: For full-time undergraduate study at accredited 2-year or 4-year institution in United States.
Eligibility: Applicant must be high school senior. Applicant must be U.S. citizen or permanent resident residing in Hawaii.
Basis for selection: Applicant must demonstrate financial need, high academic achievement and depth of character.
Application requirements: Essay, transcript. FAFSA and SAR. Essay must state why it is important for Hawaii students to be internationally aware.
Additional information: Applicant must be student at Ka'u High School. Amount of scholarship varies yearly. Applicants taking up mainland residency must have relatives living in Hawaii.

> **Number of awards:** 1
> **Application deadline:** March 1

Contact:
Hawaii Community Foundation Scholarships
1164 Bishop Street
Suite 800
Honolulu, HI 96813
Phone: 888-731-3863
Fax: 808-521-6286
Web: www.hawaiicommunityfoundation.org

Candon, Todd, & Seabolt Scholarship Fund

Type of award: Scholarship.
Intended use: For junior or senior study at 4-year institution in United States.
Eligibility: Applicant must be U.S. citizen residing in Hawaii.
Basis for selection: Major/career interest in accounting or finance/banking.
Application requirements: Recommendations, essay, transcript. SAR.
Additional information: Minimum 3.2 GPA.

> **Number of awards:** 1
> **Application deadline:** March 1

Contact:
Hawaii Community Foundation Scholarships
1164 Bishop St
Suite 800
Honolulu, HI 96813
Phone: 888-731-3863
Fax: 808-521-6286
Web: www.hawaiicommunityfoundation.org

Castle & Cooke Mililani Technology Park Scholarship Fund

Type of award: Scholarship.
Intended use: For full-time freshman study at accredited 2-year or 4-year institution in United States.
Eligibility: Applicant must be high school senior. Applicant must be U.S. citizen or permanent resident residing in Hawaii.
Basis for selection: Major/career interest in science, general; engineering or computer/information sciences. Applicant must demonstrate financial need and high academic achievement.
Application requirements: Essay, transcript. FAFSA and SAR.
Additional information: Applicants must be graduating senior from Leilehua, Mililani, or Waialua high schools. Preference given to majors in technology fields. Applicants must have permanent address in Hawaii. Applicants taking up mainland residency must have relatives living in Hawaii. Amount and number of awards vary and may change yearly.

> **Number of awards:** 10
> **Application deadline:** March 1

Contact:
Hawaii Community Foundation Scholarships
1164 Bishop Street
Suite 800
Honolulu, HI 96813
Phone: 888-731-3863
Fax: 808-521-6286
Web: www.hawaiicommunityfoundation.org

Castle & Cooke W. Y. Yim Scholarship Fund

Type of award: Scholarship.
Intended use: For full-time undergraduate or graduate study at accredited 2-year or 4-year institution in United States.
Eligibility: Applicant must be U.S. citizen residing in Hawaii.
Basis for selection: Applicant must demonstrate financial need, high academic achievement and depth of character.
Application requirements: Recommendations, essay, transcript. SAR, FAFSA, Personal Statement. Castle & Cooke employee name, position, and relationship to applicant.
Additional information: Minimum 3.0 GPA. Must be a dependent of current employee with at least one year of service with Castle & Cooke Hawaii affiliated company. Applicants must have permanent address in Hawaii. Applicants taking up mainland residency must have relatives living in Hawaii. Amount of award may change yearly.

> **Application deadline:** March 1

Contact:
Hawaii Community Foundation Scholarships
1164 Bishop Street
Suite 800
Honolulu, HI 96813
Phone: 888-731-3863
Fax: 808-521-6286
Web: www.hawaiicommunityfoundation.org

Cayetano Foundation Scholarship

Type of award: Scholarship.
Intended use: For full-time undergraduate study at accredited 2-year or 4-year institution.
Eligibility: Applicant must be high school senior. Applicant must be residing in Hawaii.
Basis for selection: Applicant must demonstrate financial need, high academic achievement and depth of character.
Application requirements: Recommendations, essay, transcript. FAFSA and SAR. SAT scores. Personal statement should describe community service. In personal essay imagine yourself in your late 50s: Reflect on your adult life, list the major accomplishments in your life, and explain why you consider them to be significant. Also include, on a separate piece of paper, your name, the occupations of your parents and your yearly income.
Additional information: Minimum 3.5 GPA. Preference given to students with greatest financial need. Applicants must have permanent Hawaii address. Applicants taking up mainland residency must have relatives living in Hawaii.

    Number of awards: 14
    Application deadline: March 1
Contact:
Hawaii Community Foundation Scholarships
1164 Bishop Street
Suite 800
Honolulu, HI 96813
Phone: 888-731-3863
Fax: 808-521-6286
Web: www.hawaiicommunityfoundation.org

Community Scholarship Fund

Type of award: Scholarship, renewable.
Intended use: For full-time undergraduate or graduate study at accredited 2-year or 4-year institution in United States.
Eligibility: Applicant must be U.S. citizen or permanent resident residing in Hawaii.
Basis for selection: Major/career interest in arts, general; architecture; education; humanities/liberal arts or social/behavioral sciences. Applicant must demonstrate financial need, high academic achievement, depth of character and service orientation.
Application requirements: Essay, transcript. FAFSA and SAR.
Additional information: Minimum 3.0 GPA. Must show potential for fulfilling a community need; demonstrate accomplishment, motivation, initiative, vision, and intention of returning to or staying in Hawaii to work. Must have permanent address in Hawaii. Applicants taking up mainland residency must have relatives living in Hawaii. Amount and number of awards vary and may change yearly.

    Application deadline: March 1

Contact:
Hawaii Community Foundation Scholarships
1164 Bishop Street
Suite 800
Honolulu, HI 96813
Phone: 888-731-3863
Fax: 808-521-6286
Web: www.hawaiicommunityfoundation.org

Cora Aguda Manayan Fund

Type of award: Scholarship, renewable.
Intended use: For full-time undergraduate or graduate study in United States.
Eligibility: Applicant must be of Filipino ancestry. Applicant must be U.S. citizen or permanent resident residing in Hawaii.
Basis for selection: Major/career interest in health-related professions. Applicant must demonstrate financial need, high academic achievement and depth of character.
Application requirements: Essay, transcript. FAFSA and SAR.
Additional information: Preference given to students studying in Hawaii. Applicants must have permanent address in Hawaii. Applicants who take up mainland residency must have relatives living in Hawaii. Amount and number of awards vary.

    Number of awards: 10
    Application deadline: March 1
Contact:
Hawaii Community Foundation Scholarships
1164 Bishop Street
Suite 800
Honolulu, HI 96813
Phone: 888-731-3863
Fax: 808-521-6286
Web: www.hawaiicommunityfoundation.org

David L. Irons Memorial Scholarship Fund

Type of award: Scholarship.
Intended use: For full-time undergraduate study at accredited 2-year or 4-year institution in United States.
Eligibility: Applicant must be high school senior. Applicant must be U.S. citizen or permanent resident residing in Hawaii.
Basis for selection: Applicant must demonstrate financial need, high academic achievement and depth of character.
Application requirements: Essay, transcript. FAFSA and SAR. Essay must respond to following questions: 1) How would you spend a free day? 2) Who is a hero of yours, and what is an overriding quality that makes this person your hero?
Additional information: Applicant must be student at Punahou School. Applicants taking up mainland residency must have relatives living in Hawaii. Amount of award may change yearly.

    Number of awards: 1
    Application deadline: March 1
Contact:
Hawaii Community Foundation Scholarships
1164 Bishop Street
Suite 800
Honolulu, HI 96813
Phone: 888-731-3863
Fax: 808-521-6286
Web: www.hawaiicommunityfoundation.org

Dolly Ching Scholarship Fund

Type of award: Scholarship.

Intended use: For full-time undergraduate study at accredited postsecondary institution in United States. Designated institutions: Institutions in University of Hawaii system.
Eligibility: Applicant must be high school senior. Applicant must be U.S. citizen or permanent resident residing in Hawaii.
Basis for selection: Applicant must demonstrate financial need, high academic achievement, depth of character and service orientation.
Application requirements: Recommendations, essay, transcript. FAFSA and SAR.
Additional information: Minimum 2.7 GPA. Must be resident of Kauai. Amount and number of awards vary.

    Number of awards: 1
    Application deadline: March 1
Contact:
Hawaii Community Foundation Scholarships
1164 Bishop Street
Suite 800
Honolulu, HI 96813
Phone: 888-731-3863
Fax: 808-521-6286
Web: www.hawaiicommunityfoundation.org

Doris & Clarence Glick Classical Music Scholarship

Type of award: Scholarship.
Intended use: For full-time undergraduate study at accredited 2-year or 4-year institution in United States.
Eligibility: Applicant must be residing in Hawaii.
Basis for selection: Major/career interest in music. Applicant must demonstrate financial need, high academic achievement and depth of character.
Application requirements: Essay, transcript. FAFSA and SAR. Describe in personal statement how program of study relates to classical music.
Additional information: Must major in music, with emphasis on classical music. Applicants must have permanent address in Hawaii. Applicants taking up mainland residency must have relatives living in Hawaii. Amount and number of awards vary and may change yearly.

    Number of awards: 4
    Application deadline: March 1
Contact:
Hawaii Community Foundation Scholarships
1164 Bishop Street
Suite 800
Honolulu, HI 96813
Phone: 888-731-3863
Fax: 808-521-6286
Web: www.hawaiicommunityfoundation.org

Dr. Alvin and Monica Saake Scholarship

Type of award: Scholarship.
Intended use: For full-time junior, senior or graduate study at accredited 2-year, 4-year or graduate institution.
Eligibility: Applicant must be residing in Hawaii.
Basis for selection: Major/career interest in physical education; athletic training; sports/sports administration; physical therapy or occupational therapy. Applicant must demonstrate financial need, high academic achievement and depth of character.
Application requirements: Essay, transcript. FAFSA and SAR.

Additional information: Must be majoring in kinesiology, leisure science, physical education, athletic training, exercise science, sports medicine, physical therapy, or occupational therapy. Applicant must have permanent Hawaii address. Applicants taking up mainland residency must have relatives living in Hawaii.

    Number of awards: 12
    Application deadline: March 1
Contact:
Hawaii Community Foundation Scholarships
1164 Bishop Street
Suite 800
Honolulu, HI 96813
Phone: 888-731-3863
Fax: 808-521-6286
Web: www.hawaiicommunityfoundation.org

Dr. and Mrs. Moon Park Scholarship

Type of award: Scholarship.
Intended use: For full-time undergraduate or graduate study at accredited 2-year or 4-year institution in United States.
Eligibility: Applicant must be U.S. citizen residing in Hawaii.
Basis for selection: Applicant must demonstrate financial need and high academic achievement.
Application requirements: Recommendations, essay, transcript. SAR, FAFSA, Personal Statement. Clinical Laboratories of Hawaii, LLC employee name and relationship to applicant.
Additional information: Minimum 3.0 GPA. Must be an employee or child dependent with minimum one year of service of Clinical Laboratories of Hawaii, LLP and/or Pan Pacific Pathologies, LLC. Applicants must have permanent address in Hawaii. Applicants taking up mainland residency must have relatives living in Hawaii. Amount of award may change yearly.

    Application deadline: March 1
Contact:
Hawaii Community Foundation Scholarships
1164 Bishop Street
Suite 800
Honolulu, HI 96813
Phone: 888-731-3863
Fax: 808-521-6286
Web: www.hawaiicommunityfoundation.org

Dr. Hans & Clara Zimmerman Foundation Education Scholarship

Type of award: Scholarship.
Intended use: For full-time undergraduate or graduate study at accredited 2-year or 4-year institution in United States.
Eligibility: Applicant must be U.S. citizen or permanent resident residing in Hawaii.
Basis for selection: Major/career interest in education or education, teacher. Applicant must demonstrate financial need, high academic achievement, depth of character and leadership.
Application requirements: Recommendations, essay, transcript. FAFSA and SAR. Personal statement describing applicant's community service projects or activities. Essay must also answer question "What is your teaching philosophy and how is it applied in classroom today?" (with one example). Applicants disqualified if they fail to address essay topic in personal statement.
Additional information: Minimum 2.8 GPA. Preference given to nontraditional students with at least two years of teaching experience. Preference given to students of Hawaiian

ethnicity. Applicants must have permanent address in Hawaii. Amount and number of awards vary and may change yearly.

Number of awards: 28
Application deadline: March 1
Contact:
Hawaii Community Foundation Scholarships
1164 Bishop Street
Suite 800
Honolulu, HI 96813
Phone: 888-731-3863
Fax: 808-521-6286
Web: www.hawaiicommunityfoundation.org

Dr. Hans and Clara Zimmerman Foundation Health Scholarship

Type of award: Scholarship, renewable.
Intended use: For full-time junior, senior or graduate study at accredited postsecondary institution in United States.
Eligibility: Applicant must be U.S. citizen or permanent resident residing in Hawaii.
Basis for selection: Major/career interest in health sciences; health-related professions or medicine. Applicant must demonstrate financial need, high academic achievement and depth of character.
Application requirements: Transcript. FAFSA and SAR. Personal statement including description of applicant's community service projects or activities.
Additional information: Minimum 3.0 GPA. Applicants must have permanent address in Hawaii. Applicants who take up mainland residency must have relatives living in Hawaii. Sports medicine and some psychology majors ineligible. Amount and number of awards vary.

Number of awards: 190
Application deadline: March 1
Contact:
Hawaii Community Foundation Scholarships
1164 Bishop Street
Suite 800
Honolulu, HI 96813
Phone: 888-731-3863
Fax: 808-521-6286
Web: www.hawaiicommunityfoundation.org

Eastside & Northshore Kauai Scholarship Fund

Type of award: Scholarship.
Intended use: For full-time undergraduate or graduate study at accredited 2-year or 4-year institution in United States.
Eligibility: Applicant must be U.S. citizen residing in Hawaii.
Basis for selection: Applicant must demonstrate financial need, high academic achievement and depth of character.
Application requirements: Recommendations, essay, transcript. SAR, FAFSA, Personal Statement.
Additional information: Minimum 2.5 GPA. Must be resident of one of the following East and Northshore Kaua[00e2][0080][0098]i areas: Anahola (96703), Kapa[00e2][0080][0098]a (96746), Kilauea (96754), Hanalei (96714), Princeville (96722), Kealia (96751), Wailua (96746).

Application deadline: March 1

Contact:
Hawaii Community Foundation Scholarships
1164 Bishop Street
Suite 800
Honolulu, HI 96813
Phone: 888-731-3863
Fax: 808-521-6286
Web: www.hawaiicommunityfoundation.org

Edward Payson and Bernice Pi'ilani Irwin Scholarship Trust Fund

Type of award: Scholarship.
Intended use: For full-time junior, senior or graduate study at accredited 4-year institution in United States.
Eligibility: Applicant must be U.S. citizen or permanent resident residing in Hawaii.
Basis for selection: Major/career interest in journalism or communications. Applicant must demonstrate financial need, high academic achievement and depth of character.
Application requirements: Essay, transcript. FAFSA and SAR.
Additional information: Must have permanent address in Hawaii. Applicants who take up mainland residency must have relatives living in Hawaii. Amount and number of awards vary and may change yearly.

Application deadline: March 1
Contact:
Hawaii Community Foundation Scholarships
1164 Bishop Street
Suite 800
Honolulu, HI 96813
Phone: 888-731-3863
Fax: 808-521-6286
Web: www.hawaiicommunityfoundation.org

E.E. Black Scholarship

Type of award: Scholarship, renewable.
Intended use: For full-time undergraduate study at accredited postsecondary institution in United States.
Eligibility: Applicant must be U.S. citizen or permanent resident residing in Hawaii.
Basis for selection: Applicant must demonstrate financial need, high academic achievement and depth of character.
Application requirements: Essay, transcript. FAFSA and SAR. Name of Tesoro employee and relationship.
Additional information: Minimum 3.0 GPA. Must be dependent of an employee of Tesoro Hawaii or its subsidiaries. Applicants must have permanent address in Hawaii. Applicants who take up mainland residency must have relatives living in Hawaii. Amount and number of awards vary.

Number of awards: 11
Application deadline: March 1
Contact:
Hawaii Community Foundation Scholarships
1164 Bishop Street
Suite 800
Honolulu, HI 96813
Phone: 888-731-3863
Fax: 808-521-6286
Web: www.hawaiicommunityfoundation.org

Eizo & Toyo Sakumoto Trust Scholarship

Type of award: Scholarship.

Intended use: For full-time senior or graduate study at accredited 2-year or 4-year institution in United States. Designated institutions: Hawaii institutions.
Eligibility: Applicant must be Japanese. Applicant must be U.S. citizen residing in Hawaii.
Basis for selection: Applicant must demonstrate financial need, high academic achievement and depth of character.
Application requirements: Recommendations, essay, transcript. SAR, FAFSA, Personal Statement.
Additional information: Minimum 3.5 GPA. Must be of Japanese ancestry. Must have been born in Hawaii. Applicants must have permanent address in Hawaii. Applicants taking up mainland residency must have relatives living in Hawaii. Amount of award may change yearly.
   Application deadline: March 1
Contact:
Hawaii Community Foundation Scholarships
1164 Bishop Street
Suite 800
Honolulu, HI 96813
Phone: 888-731-3863
Fax: 808-521-6286
Web: www.hawaiicommunityfoundation.org

Elena Albano "Maka'alohilohi" Scholarship Fund

Type of award: Scholarship.
Intended use: For full-time undergraduate or graduate study at 2-year or 4-year institution in United States.
Eligibility: Applicant must be U.S. citizen residing in Hawaii.
Basis for selection: Applicant must demonstrate financial need, high academic achievement and depth of character.
Application requirements: Recommendations, essay, transcript. SAR, FAFSA, Personal Statement. Two letters of recommendation from mentors, teachers, counselors, or other mental health professionals.
Additional information: Minimum 2.7 GPA. Must be in recovery from mental health/behavioral/psychological disability. Must be resident of Maui county. Preference given to students of Hawaiian ancestry and renewal applicants. Applicants must have permanent address in Hawaii. Applicants taking up mainland residency must have relatives living in Hawaii. Amount of award may change yearly.
   Application deadline: March 1
Contact:
Hawaii Community Foundation Scholarships
1164 Bishop Street
Suite 800
Honolulu, HI 96813
Phone: 888-731-3863
Fax: 808-521-6286
Web: www.hawaiicommunityfoundation.org

Ellison Onizuka Memorial Scholarship

Type of award: Scholarship.
Intended use: For full-time undergraduate study at accredited 2-year or 4-year institution in United States.
Eligibility: Applicant must be high school senior. Applicant must be U.S. citizen or permanent resident residing in Hawaii.
Basis for selection: Major/career interest in aerospace. Applicant must demonstrate financial need and depth of character.
Application requirements: Recommendations, transcript. SAT scores, FAFSA, SAR and personal statement describing

extracurricular activities, club affiliations, and community service projects.
Additional information: Applicants must have permanent address in Hawaii. Applicants who take up mainland residency must have relatives living in Hawaii. Amount and number of awards vary.
   Number of awards: 5
   Application deadline: March 1
Contact:
Hawaii Community Foundation Scholarships
1164 Bishop Street
Suite 800
Honolulu, HI 96813
Phone: 888-731-3863
Fax: 808-521-6286
Web: www.hawaiicommunityfoundation.org

Esther Kanagawa Memorial Art Scholarship

Type of award: Scholarship.
Intended use: For full-time undergraduate or graduate study at accredited 2-year or 4-year institution in United States.
Eligibility: Applicant must be U.S. citizen or permanent resident residing in Hawaii.
Basis for selection: Major/career interest in arts, general. Applicant must demonstrate financial need, high academic achievement and depth of character.
Application requirements: Essay, transcript. FAFSA and SAR.
Additional information: Must major in fine art, drawing, painting, sculpture, ceramics, or photography. Applicants must have permanent address in Hawaii. Applicants taking up mainland residency must have relatives living in Hawaii. Amount of award varies yearly.
   Number of awards: 2
   Application deadline: March 1
Contact:
Hawaii Community Foundation Scholarships
1164 Bishop Street
Suite 800
Honolulu, HI 96813
Phone: 888-731-3863
Fax: 808-521-6286
Web: www.hawaiicommunityfoundation.org

F. Koehnen Ltd. Scholarship Fund

Type of award: Scholarship.
Intended use: For full-time undergraduate or graduate study at accredited 4-year institution in United States.
Eligibility: Applicant must be U.S. citizen residing in Hawaii.
Basis for selection: Applicant must demonstrate financial need, high academic achievement and depth of character.
Application requirements: Recommendations, essay, transcript. SAR, FAFSA, Personal Statement. Name of employee, retail establishment and phone number of human resources department of retail establishment.
Additional information: Minimum 2.5 GPA. Must be graduate of high school on island of Hawaii. Must be son, daughter or grandchild of employee of retail establishment on island of Hawaii.
   Application deadline: March 1

Contact:
Hawaii Community Foundation Scholarships
1164 Bishop Street
Suite 800
Honolulu, HI 96813
Phone: 888-731-3863
Fax: 808-521-6286
Web: www.hawaiicommunityfoundation.org

The Filipino Nurses' Organization of Hawaii Scholarship

Type of award: Scholarship.
Intended use: For full-time undergraduate study at accredited 2-year or 4-year institution in United States.
Eligibility: Applicant must be of Filipino ancestry. Applicant must be U.S. citizen or permanent resident residing in Hawaii.
Basis for selection: Major/career interest in nursing. Applicant must demonstrate financial need, high academic achievement, depth of character and service orientation.
Application requirements: Essay, transcript. FAFSA and SAR.
Additional information: Must have permanent address in Hawaii. Applicants taking up mainland residency must have relatives living in Hawaii. Amount of award may vary yearly.

  Number of awards: 2
  Application deadline: March 1
Contact:
Hawaii Community Foundation Scholarships
1164 Bishop Street
Suite 800
Honolulu, HI 96813
Phone: 888-731-3863
Fax: 808-521-6286
Web: www.hawaiicommunityfoundation.org

Financial Women International Scholarship

Type of award: Scholarship.
Intended use: For full-time junior, senior or graduate study at accredited 2-year or 4-year institution in United States.
Eligibility: Applicant must be female. Applicant must be U.S. citizen or permanent resident residing in Hawaii.
Basis for selection: Major/career interest in business. Applicant must demonstrate financial need, high academic achievement and depth of character.
Application requirements: Essay, transcript. FAFSA and SAR.
Additional information: Minimum 3.5 GPA. Applicant must have permanent address in Hawaii. Applicants taking up mainland residency must have relatives living in Hawaii. Amount of award may change yearly.

  Number of awards: 1
  Application deadline: March 1
Contact:
Hawaii Community Foundation Scholarships
1164 Bishop Street
Suite 800
Honolulu, HI 96813
Phone: 888-731-3863
Fax: 808-521-6286
Web: www.hawaiicommunityfoundation.org

Fletcher & Fritzi Hoffmann Education Fund

Type of award: Scholarship.
Intended use: For full-time undergraduate study at accredited vocational, 2-year or 4-year institution. Designated institutions: College or vocational school on island of Hawaii.
Eligibility: Applicant must be U.S. citizen or permanent resident residing in Hawaii.
Basis for selection: Applicant must demonstrate financial need, high academic achievement and depth of character.
Application requirements: Essay, transcript. FAFSA and SAR. Personal statement must include information on family's history and roots in the Hamakua area.
Additional information: Minimum 2.7 GPA. Preference given to applicants whose families worked in sugar plantation industry and Honoka'a high school graduates. Must be longtime resident of Hamakua Coast in Hawaii. Amount of award may change yearly.

  Number of awards: 1
  Application deadline: March 1
Contact:
Hawaii Community Foundation Scholarships
1164 Bishop Street
Suite 800
Honolulu, HI 96813
Phone: 888-731-3863
Fax: 808-521-6286
Web: www.hawaiicommunityfoundation.org

Friends of Hawaii Public Housing Scholarship

Type of award: Scholarship.
Intended use: For full-time undergraduate or graduate study at accredited 2-year or 4-year institution in United States.
Eligibility: Applicant must be U.S. citizen or permanent resident residing in Hawaii.
Basis for selection: Applicant must demonstrate financial need, high academic achievement and depth of character.
Application requirements: Essay, transcript, proof of eligibility. FAFSA and SAR. Must include name of public housing complex in personal statement.
Additional information: Applicant must be resident of public housing unit in Hawaii. Amount and number of awards may change yearly.

  Number of awards: 6
  Application deadline: March 1
Contact:
Hawaii Community Foundation Scholarships
1164 Bishop Street
Suite 800
Honolulu, HI 96813
Phone: 888-731-3863
Fax: 808-521-6286
Web: www.hawaiicommunityfoundation.org

George Mason Business Scholarship Fund

Type of award: Scholarship.
Intended use: For full-time senior study at accredited 4-year institution.
Eligibility: Applicant must be residing in Hawaii.
Basis for selection: Major/career interest in business or business/management/administration. Applicant must

demonstrate financial need, high academic achievement and depth of character.

Application requirements: Essay, transcript. FAFSA and SAR. Essay must state why you have chosen business as an intended career and how you expect to make a difference in the business world.

Additional information: Minimum 3.0 GPA. Applicant must have permanent Hawaii address.

> **Number of awards:** 1
> **Application deadline:** March 1

Contact:
Hawaii Community Foundation Scholarships
1164 Bishop Street
Suite 800
Honolulu, HA 96813
Phone: 888-731-3863
Fax: 808-521-6286
Web: www.hawaiicommunityfoundation.org

Gerrit R. Ludwig Scholarship

Type of award: Scholarship.
Intended use: For full-time undergraduate or graduate study at accredited 2-year, 4-year or graduate institution.
Eligibility: Applicant must be residing in Hawaii.
Basis for selection: Major/career interest in classics or arts, general. Applicant must demonstrate financial need, high academic achievement and depth of character.
Application requirements: Essay, transcript. FAFSA and SAR.
Additional information: Minimum 2.5 GPA. Preference given to applicants pursuing a degree in fine arts or classics. Must be graduate from East Hawaii public school: Hilo, Honoka'a, Kea'au, Laupahoehoe, Pahoa, and Waiakea. Applicants taking up mainland residency must have relatives living in Hawaii.

> **Number of awards:** 3
> **Application deadline:** March 1

Contact:
Hawaii Community Foundation Scholarships
1164 Bishop Street
Suite 800
Honolulu, HI 96813
Phone: 888-731-3863
Fax: 808-521-6286
Web: www.hawaiicommunityfoundation.org

Good Eats Scholarship Fund

Type of award: Scholarship.
Intended use: For full-time undergraduate or graduate study at accredited vocational, 2-year or 4-year institution in United States.
Eligibility: Applicant must be U.S. citizen residing in Hawaii.
Basis for selection: Major/career interest in culinary arts; agriculture or food production/management/services. Applicant must demonstrate depth of character.
Application requirements: Recommendations, essay, transcript. SAR, FAFSA, Personal Statement.
Additional information: Minimum 2.7 GPA. Must pursue post high school studies in culinary arts or agriculture. Must demonstrate interest in food production and preparation.

Contact:
Hawaii Community Foundation Scholarships
1164 Bishop Street
Suite 800
Honolulu, HI 96813
Phone: 888-731-3863
Fax: 808-521-6286
Web: www.hawaiicommunityfoundation.org

Grace Pacific Outstanding Scholars Fund

Type of award: Scholarship.
Intended use: For full-time undergraduate or graduate study at accredited 2-year or 4-year institution in United States.
Eligibility: Applicant must be high school senior. Applicant must be U.S. citizen residing in Hawaii.
Basis for selection: Applicant must demonstrate financial need, high academic achievement and depth of character.
Application requirements: Recommendations, essay, transcript. SAR, FAFSA, Personal Statement.
Additional information: Minimum 2.7 GPA. Must be former participant of Grace Pacific Outstanding Keiki Scholars Program. Applicants must have permanent address in Hawaii. Applicants taking up mainland residency must have relatives living in Hawaii. Amount of award may change yearly.

> **Application deadline:** March 1

Contact:
Hawaii Community Foundation Scholarships
1164 Bishop Street
Suite 800
Honolulu, HI 96813
Phone: 888-731-3863
Fax: 808-521-6286
Web: www.hawaiicommunityfoundation.org

Guy Marshall Scholarship Fund

Type of award: Scholarship.
Intended use: For full-time freshman study at accredited 2-year or 4-year institution in United States.
Eligibility: Applicant must be U.S. citizen residing in Hawaii.
Basis for selection: Applicant must demonstrate financial need, high academic achievement and depth of character.
Application requirements: Recommendations, essay, transcript. SAR, FAFSA, Personal Statement.
Additional information: Minimum 2.7 GPA. Must plan to attend college in continental United States. Must be graduate of Hawaii high school.

> **Application deadline:** March 1

Contact:
Hawaii Community Foundation Scholarships
1164 Bishop Street
Suite 800
Honolulu, HI 96813
Phone: 888-731-3863
Fax: 808-521-6286
Web: www.hawaiicommunityfoundation.org

Hawaii Pacific Gerontological Society Nursing Scholarship Fund

Type of award: Scholarship.
Intended use: For full-time undergraduate or graduate study at accredited 2-year or 4-year institution in United States.
Eligibility: Applicant must be U.S. citizen residing in Hawaii.

Basis for selection: Major/career interest in nursing. Applicant must demonstrate financial need, high academic achievement and depth of character.
Application requirements: Recommendations, essay, transcript. SAR, FAFSA, Personal Statement.
Additional information: Minimum 2.7 GPA.
  Application deadline: March 1
Contact:
Hawaii Community Foundation Scholarships
1164 Bishop Street
Suite 800
Honolulu, HI 96813
Phone: 888-731-3863
Fax: 808-521-6286
Web: www.hawaiicommunityfoundation.org

Hawaii Pizza Hut Scholarship Fund

Type of award: Scholarship.
Intended use: For full-time undergraduate study at accredited 2-year or 4-year institution in United States.
Eligibility: Applicant must be U.S. citizen residing in Hawaii.
Basis for selection: Applicant must demonstrate financial need, high academic achievement and depth of character.
Application requirements: Recommendations, essay, transcript. SAR, FAFSA, Personal Statement.
Additional information: GPA must be between 2.5 and 3.5.
  Application deadline: March 1
Contact:
Hawaii Community Foundation Scholarships
1164 Bishop Street
Suite 800
Honolulu, HI 96813
Phone: 888-731-3863
Fax: 808-521-6286
Web: www.hawaiicommunityfoundation.org

Hawaii Society of Certified Public Accountants Scholarship Fund

Type of award: Scholarship.
Intended use: For full-time junior, senior or graduate study at 4-year institution in United States. Designated institutions: Four-year colleges and universities in Hawaii.
Eligibility: Applicant must be U.S. citizen residing in Hawaii.
Basis for selection: Major/career interest in accounting. Applicant must demonstrate financial need, high academic achievement and depth of character.
Application requirements: Recommendations, essay, transcript. SAR, FAFSA, Personal Statement.
Additional information: Minimum 3.0 GPA. Must have already completed two or more 300-level accounting courses.
  Application deadline: March 1
Contact:
Hawaii Community Foundation Scholarships
1164 Bishop Street
Suite 800
Honolulu, HI 96813
Phone: 888-731-3863
Fax: 808-521-6286
Web: www.hawaiicommunityfoundation.org

Hawaiian Homes Commission Scholarship

Type of award: Scholarship.

Intended use: For full-time undergraduate or graduate study at accredited 2-year or 4-year institution in United States.
Eligibility: Applicant must be U.S. citizen.
Basis for selection: Applicant must demonstrate financial need, high academic achievement and depth of character.
Application requirements: Recommendations, essay, transcript. SAR, FAFSA, Personal Statement.
Additional information: Minimum 2.0 GPA undergraduates, 3.0 graduates. Must either be native Hawaiian or lessee of Department of Hawaiian Home Lands (DHHL). Applicant not required to be Hawaii resident.
  Application deadline: March 1
Contact:
Hawaii Community Foundation Scholarships
1164 Bishop Street
Suite 800
Honolulu, HI 96813
Phone: 888-731-3863
Fax: 808-521-6286
Web: www.hawaiicommunityfoundation.org

Henry A. Zuberano Scholarship

Type of award: Scholarship.
Intended use: For full-time undergraduate study at accredited 2-year or 4-year institution.
Eligibility: Applicant must be residing in Hawaii.
Basis for selection: Major/career interest in political science/ government; international relations; business, international or public administration/service. Applicant must demonstrate financial need, high academic achievement and depth of character.
Application requirements: Essay, transcript. FAFSA and SAR.
Additional information: Applicant must have permanent Hawaii address. Applicants taking up mainland residency must have relatives living in Hawaii.
  Number of awards: 9
  Application deadline: March 1
Contact:
Hawaii Community Foundation Scholarships
1164 Bishop Street
Suite 800
Honolulu, HI 96813
Phone: 888-731-3863
Fax: 808-521-6286
Web: www.hawaiicommunityfoundation.org

Herbert & Ollie Brook Fund

Type of award: Scholarship.
Intended use: For full-time undergraduate or graduate study at accredited 2-year or 4-year institution in United States.
Eligibility: Applicant must be U.S. citizen residing in Hawaii.
Basis for selection: Applicant must demonstrate financial need, high academic achievement and depth of character.
Application requirements: Recommendations, essay, transcript. SAR, FAFSA, Personal Statement.
Additional information: Minimum 2.7 GPA. Must be high school senior in Maui County. Preference given to those who plan to return to Maui County after completing education to contribute to community.
  Application deadline: March 1

Contact:
Hawaii Community Foundation Scholarships
1164 Bishop Street
Suite 800
Honolulu, HI 96813
Phone: 888-731-3863
Fax: 808-521-6286
Web: www.hawaiicommunityfoundation.org

Hideko & Zenzo Matsuyama Scholarship Fund

Type of award: Scholarship.
Intended use: For full-time undergraduate or graduate study at 2-year or 4-year institution in United States.
Eligibility: Applicant must be U.S. citizen residing in Hawaii.
Basis for selection: Applicant must demonstrate financial need, high academic achievement and depth of character.
Application requirements: Recommendations, essay, transcript. SAR, FAFSA, Personal Statement.
Additional information: Minimum 3.0 GPA. Must be graduate of high school in Hawaii or have received GED in Hawaii. Preference given to students of Japanese ancestry born in Hawaii.
   Application deadline: March 1
Contact:
Hawaii Community Foundation Scholarships
1164 Bishop Street
Suite 800
Honolulu, HI 96813
Phone: 888-731-3863
Fax: 808-521-6286
Web: www.hawaiicommunityfoundation.org

Hilo Chinese School Scholarship

Type of award: Scholarship.
Intended use: For full-time undergraduate or graduate study at accredited 2-year or 4-year institution in United States.
Eligibility: Applicant must be U.S. citizen residing in Hawaii.
Basis for selection: Applicant must demonstrate financial need, high academic achievement and depth of character.
Application requirements: Recommendations, essay, transcript. SAR, FAFSA, Personal Statement.
Additional information: Minimum 2.7 GPA. Must be resident of Hawaii island. Preference given to descendants of Hilo Chinese School alumni and students of Chinese ancestry.
   Application deadline: March 1
Contact:
Hawaii Community Foundation Scholarships
1164 Bishop Street
Suite 800
Honolulu, HI 96813
Phone: 888-731-3863
Fax: 808-521-6286
Web: www.hawaiicommunityfoundation.org

Hokuli'a Foundation Scholarship Fund

Type of award: Scholarship.
Intended use: For full-time undergraduate or graduate study at accredited 2-year or 4-year institution in United States.
Eligibility: Applicant must be U.S. citizen residing in Hawaii.
Basis for selection: Major/career interest in health-related professions; education or social work. Applicant must demonstrate financial need, high academic achievement, depth of character and service orientation.
Application requirements: Recommendations, essay, transcript. SAR, FAFSA, Personal Statement should include record of community service and how future career will benefit Hawaii residents.
Additional information: Minimum 2.7 GPA. Must be resident of South Kona. Preference given to students demonstrating emphasis in advancing native Hawaiian culture.
   Application deadline: March 1
Contact:
Hawaii Community Foundation Scholarships
1164 Bishop Street
Suite 800
Honolulu, HI 96813
Phone: 888-731-3863
Fax: 808-521-6286
Web: www.hawaiicommunityfoundation.org

Hon Chew Hee Scholarship Fund

Type of award: Scholarship.
Intended use: For full-time undergraduate or graduate study at accredited 2-year or 4-year institution in United States.
Eligibility: Applicant must be U.S. citizen residing in Hawaii.
Basis for selection: Major/career interest in art/art history. Applicant must demonstrate financial need, high academic achievement and depth of character.
Application requirements: Recommendations, essay, transcript. SAR, FAFSA, Personal Statement. Two letters of recommendation required. One from an art instructor, one from a non-related person.
Additional information: Minimum 2.7 GPA. Major in fine arts with preference given to stduents focusing on painting, drawing, sculpting, ceramics, printmaking, and textiles.
   Application deadline: March 1
Contact:
Hawaii Community Foundation
1164 Bishop Street
Suite 800
Honolulu, HI 96813
Phone: 888-731-3863
Fax: 808-521-6286
Web: www.hawaiicommunityfoundation.org

Ho'omaka Hou Scholarship

Type of award: Scholarship.
Intended use: For full-time undergraduate or graduate study at accredited 2-year or 4-year institution in United States.
Eligibility: Applicant must be U.S. citizen residing in Hawaii.
Basis for selection: Applicant must demonstrate financial need, high academic achievement and depth of character.
Application requirements: Recommendations, essay, transcript. SAR, FAFSA, Personal Statement should describe problems and how they were overcome.
Additional information: Minimum 2.7 GPA. Applicant must have overcome substance abuse.
   Application deadline: March 1
Contact:
Hawaii Community Foundation Scholarships
1164 Bishop Street
Suite 800
Honolulu, HI 96813
Phone: 888-731-3863
Fax: 808-521-6286
Web: www.hawaiicommunityfoundation.org

Ian Doane Smith Scholarship Fund

Type of award: Scholarship.
Intended use: For full-time undergraduate or graduate study at accredited 2-year or 4-year institution in United States.
Eligibility: Applicant must be high school senior. Applicant must be U.S. citizen residing in Hawaii.
Basis for selection: Applicant must demonstrate financial need, high academic achievement, depth of character and service orientation.
Application requirements: Recommendations, essay, transcript. SAR, FAFSA, Personal Statement must detail community service and experiences with surfing or soccer.
Additional information: Minimum 2.7 GPA. Must resident of island of Maui. Must be active in soccer and/or surfing.
   Application deadline: March 1
Contact:
Hawaii Community Foundation Scholarships
1164 Bishop Street
Suite 800
Honolulu, HI 96813
Phone: 888-731-3863
Fax: 808-521-6286
Web: www.hawaiicommunityfoundation.org

Ida M. Pope Memorial Scholarship

Type of award: Scholarship.
Intended use: For full-time undergraduate or graduate study at accredited 2-year or 4-year institution in United States.
Eligibility: Applicant must be Native Hawaiian/Pacific Islander. Applicant must be female. Applicant must be U.S. citizen residing in Hawaii.
Basis for selection: Applicant must demonstrate depth of character.
Application requirements: Recommendations, essay, transcript. SAR, FAFSA, Personal Statement. Birth certificate.
Additional information: Minimum 3.0 GPA.
   Application deadline: March 1
Contact:
Hawaii Community Foundation Scholarships
1164 Bishop Street
Suite 800
Honolulu, HI 96813
Phone: 888-731-3863
Fax: 808-521-6286
Web: www.hawaiicommunityfoundation.org

Isemoto Contracting Co., Ltd. Scholarship Fund

Type of award: Scholarship.
Intended use: For full-time sophomore, junior, senior or graduate study at accredited 2-year or 4-year institution in United States.
Eligibility: Applicant must be U.S. citizen residing in Hawaii.
Basis for selection: Major/career interest in engineering; nursing or education. Applicant must demonstrate financial need, high academic achievement and depth of character.
Application requirements: Recommendations, essay, transcript. SAR, FAFSA, Personal Statement.
Additional information: Minimum 2.7 GPA. Must be graduate of high school on island of Hawaii.
   Application deadline: March 1

Contact:
Hawaii Community Foundation Scholarships
1164 Bishop Street
Suite 800
Honolulu, HI 96813
Phone: 888-731-3863
Fax: 808-521-6286
Web: www.hawaiicommunityfoundation.org

Jean Fitzgerald Scholarship Fund

Type of award: Scholarship, renewable.
Intended use: For full-time freshman study at accredited 2-year or 4-year institution in United States.
Eligibility: Applicant must be female, high school senior. Applicant must be U.S. citizen or permanent resident residing in Hawaii.
Basis for selection: Applicant must demonstrate financial need, high academic achievement and depth of character.
Application requirements: Essay, transcript. FAFSA and SAR.
Additional information: Applicant must be active tennis player; preference may be given to USTA/Hawaii Pacific Section members. Applicants must have permanent address in Hawaii. Applicants who take up mainland residency must have relatives living in Hawaii. Amount and number of awards vary.
   Number of awards: 2
   Application deadline: March 1
   Total amount awarded: $7,000
Contact:
Hawaii Community Foundation Scholarships
1164 Bishop Street
Suite 800
Honolulu, HI 96813
Phone: 888-731-3863
Fax: 808-521-6286
Web: www.hawaiicommunityfoundation.org

John Dawe Dental Education Fund

Type of award: Scholarship, renewable.
Intended use: For full-time undergraduate or graduate study at accredited postsecondary institution in United States.
Eligibility: Applicant must be U.S. citizen or permanent resident residing in Hawaii.
Basis for selection: Major/career interest in dentistry; dental hygiene or dental assistant. Applicant must demonstrate financial need, high academic achievement and depth of character.
Application requirements: Recommendations, essay, transcript, proof of eligibility. FAFSA and SAR. Must submit Dawe Supplemental Financial Form (download from Website). Letter from their school confirming enrollment in the dental hygiene or dentistry program.
Additional information: Applicants must have permanent address in Hawaii. Applicants taking up mainland residency must have relatives living in Hawaii. Amount and number of awards vary.
   Number of awards: 6
   Application deadline: March 1
Contact:
Hawaii Community Foundation Scholarships
1164 Bishop Street
Suite 800
Honolulu, HI 96813
Phone: 888-731-3863
Fax: 808-521-6286
Web: www.hawaiicommunityfoundation.org

Joseph & Alice Duarte Memorial Fund

Type of award: Scholarship.
Intended use: For full-time undergraduate or graduate study at accredited 2-year or 4-year institution in United States.
Eligibility: Applicant must be U.S. citizen residing in Hawaii.
Basis for selection: Applicant must demonstrate financial need, high academic achievement and depth of character.
Application requirements: Recommendations, essay, transcript. SAR, FAFSA, Personal Statement.
Additional information: Minimum 2.7 GPA. Must be from North or South Kona districts of Hawaii. Preference given to graduates of Holualoa Elementary School.

Application deadline: March 1
Contact:
Hawaii Community Foundation Scholarships
1164 Bishop Street
Suite 800
Honolulu, HI 96813
Phone: 888-731-3863
Fax: 808-521-6286
Web: www.hawaiicommunityfoundation.org

Ka'iulani Home for Girls Trust Scholarship

Type of award: Scholarship, renewable.
Intended use: For full-time freshman or sophomore study at accredited postsecondary institution in United States.
Eligibility: Applicant must be Native Hawaiian/Pacific Islander. Applicant must be female. Applicant must be U.S. citizen or permanent resident residing in Hawaii.
Basis for selection: Applicant must demonstrate financial need, high academic achievement and depth of character.
Application requirements: Essay, transcript, proof of eligibility. FAFSA and SAR, birth certificate.
Additional information: Minimum 3.0 GPA. Must be of Hawaiian ancestry. First time applicants must be freshmen or sophomores. Juniors and seniors who are past recipients also eligible. Must have permanent address in Hawaii. Applicants taking up mainland residency must have relatives living in Hawaii. Amount and number of awards vary and may change yearly.

Number of awards: 222
Application deadline: March 1
Contact:
Hawaii Community Foundation Scholarships
1164 Bishop Street
Suite 800
Honolulu, HI 96813
Phone: 888-731-3863
Fax: 808-521-6286
Web: www.hawaiicommunityfoundation.org

Ka'a'awa Community Fund

Type of award: Scholarship.
Intended use: For full-time undergraduate or graduate study at accredited 2-year or 4-year institution in United States.
Eligibility: Applicant must be U.S. citizen or permanent resident residing in Hawaii.
Basis for selection: Applicant must demonstrate financial need, high academic achievement and depth of character.
Application requirements: Essay, transcript. FAFSA and SAR.

Additional information: Must be resident of the Ka'a'awa area on Windward O'ahu. Preference given to long-time residents. Amount and number of awards vary and may change yearly.

Application deadline: March 1
Contact:
Hawaii Community Foundation Scholarships
1164 Bishop Street
Suite 800
Honolulu, HI 96813
Phone: 888-731-3863
Fax: 808-521-6286
Web: www.hawaiicommunityfoundation.org

Kahala Nui Residents Scholarship Fund

Type of award: Scholarship.
Intended use: For full-time undergraduate or graduate study at accredited 2-year or 4-year institution.
Eligibility: Applicant must be U.S. citizen residing in Hawaii.
Basis for selection: Applicant must demonstrate financial need, high academic achievement and depth of character.
Application requirements: Recommendations, essay, transcript. SAR, FAFSA, personal statement.
Additional information: Minimum 2.7 GPA. Applicant must be an employee or a dependent of an employee of Kahala Senior Living Community, Inc. for at least 6 months prior to application deadline. Amount of award varies.

Application deadline: March 1
Contact:
Hawaii Community Foundation Scholarships
1164 Bishop Street
Suite 800
Honolulu, HI 96813
Phone: 888-731-3863
Fax: 808-521-6286
Web: www.hawaiicommunityfoundation.org

Kahiau Scholarship Fund

Type of award: Scholarship.
Intended use: For full-time undergraduate or graduate study at accredited 2-year or 4-year institution in United States.
Eligibility: Applicant must be U.S. citizen residing in Hawaii.
Basis for selection: Applicant must demonstrate financial need, high academic achievement and depth of character.
Application requirements: Recommendations, essay, transcript. SAR, FAFSA, personal statement.
Additional information: Minimum 2.7 GPA. Amount of award varies. Applicant must be a graduate from Kohala High School. Applicant's family must have lived in the North Kohala community for at least two generations. Applicant must be attending an out-of-state college or university, or a four year university on O'ahu.

Application deadline: March 1
Contact:
Hawaii Community Foundation Scholarships
1164 Bishop Street
Suite 800
Honolulu, HI 96813
Phone: 888-731-3863
Fax: 808-521-6286
Web: www.hawaiicommunityfoundation.org

Scholarships

Kapolei Community & Business Scholarship

Type of award: Scholarship.
Intended use: For full-time undergraduate study at accredited 2-year or 4-year institution in United States.
Eligibility: Applicant must be high school senior. Applicant must be U.S. citizen or permanent resident residing in Hawaii.
Basis for selection: Applicant must demonstrate financial need, high academic achievement and depth of character.
Application requirements: Essay, transcript. FAFSA and SAR.
Additional information: Applicant must be a senior from Campbell, Nanakuli, or Waianae high schools. Applicants taking up mainland residency must have relatives living in Hawaii. Amount of award may vary yearly.
  Number of awards: 4
  Application deadline: March 1
Contact:
Hawaii Community Foundation Scholarships
1164 Bishop Street
Suite 800
Honolulu, HI 96813
Phone: 888-731-3863
Fax: 808-521-6286
Web: www.hawaiicommunityfoundation.org

Kawasaki-McGaha Scholarship Fund

Type of award: Scholarship.
Intended use: For full-time undergraduate study at postsecondary institution. Designated institutions: Hawaii Pacific University.
Eligibility: Applicant must be permanent resident residing in Hawaii.
Basis for selection: Major/career interest in computer/information sciences or international studies. Applicant must demonstrate financial need, high academic achievement and depth of character.
Application requirements: Essay, transcript. FAFSA and SAR.
Additional information: Applicants must have permanent address in Hawaii. Applicants taking up mainland residency must have relatives living in Hawaii. Amount and number of awards vary and may change yearly.
  Number of awards: 2
  Application deadline: March 1
Contact:
Hawaii Community Foundation Scholarships
1164 Bishop Street
Suite 800
Honolulu, HI 96813
Phone: 888-731-3863
Fax: 808-521-6286
Web: www.hawaiicommunityfoundation.org

Kazuma and Ichiko Hisanaga Scholarship Fund

Type of award: Scholarship.
Intended use: For full-time undergraduate study at accredited 2-year or 4-year institution in United States. Designated institutions: NAIA or Division III school in the contiguous United States.

Eligibility: Applicant must be high school senior. Applicant must be U.S. citizen residing in Hawaii.
Basis for selection: Applicant must demonstrate financial need, high academic achievement, depth of character, leadership and service orientation.
Application requirements: Recommendations, essay, transcript. SAR, FAFSA, Personal Statement.
Additional information: Minimum 3.0 GPA. Amount of award varies. Applicant must be a graduating senior at Hilo High School; if Hilo has no eligible applicants from Hilo High School, seniors from other Hawai'i Island high schools will be considered in the following order: Waiakea High School, St. Joseph High School, other Hawai'i Island high schools. Applicant must be an athlete that participated in more than one varsity high school sport. Must have served as the captain of a varsity sports team, a student government leader or an officer of an extracurricular program.
  Application deadline: March 1
Contact:
Hawaii Community Foundation Scholarships
1164 Bishop Street
Suite 800
Honolulu, HI 96813
Phone: 888-731-3863
Fax: 808-521-6286
Web: www.hawaiicommunityfoundation.org

King Kekaulike High School Scholarship

Type of award: Scholarship.
Intended use: For full-time undergraduate study at accredited 2-year or 4-year institution in United States.
Eligibility: Applicant must be high school senior. Applicant must be U.S. citizen or permanent resident residing in Hawaii.
Basis for selection: Applicant must demonstrate financial need, high academic achievement, depth of character and service orientation.
Application requirements: Essay, transcript. FAFSA and SAR. Additional 500-word essay on how well Na Ali'i 3 R's (Respect, Relevance, and Rigor) relate to your future goals.
Additional information: Minimum 2.8 GPA and three or more hours of community service required. Applicant must be student at King Kekaulike High School. Children of KKHS staff members not eligible. Amount of award may change yearly. Applicants taking up mainland residency must have relatives living in Hawaii.
  Number of awards: 1
  Application deadline: March 1
Contact:
Hawaii Community Foundation Scholarships
1164 Bishop Street
Suite 800
Honolulu, HI 96813
Phone: 888-731-3863
Fax: 808-521-6286
Web: www.hawaiicommunityfoundation.org

K.M. Hatano Scholarship

Type of award: Scholarship, renewable.
Intended use: For full-time undergraduate study at accredited 4-year institution in United States. Designated institutions: Institutions in Hawaii.
Eligibility: Applicant must be high school senior. Applicant must be U.S. citizen or permanent resident residing in Hawaii.

Basis for selection: Applicant must demonstrate financial need, high academic achievement and depth of character.
Application requirements: Essay, transcript. FAFSA and SAR.
Additional information: Applicant must be high school graduate of Maui, including Lanai or Molokai counties. Must attend college in Hawaii. Applicant must have permanent address in Hawaii. Applicants taking up mainland residency must have relatives living in Hawaii. Amount and number of awards vary and may change yearly.

  Number of awards: 8
  Application deadline: March 1
Contact:
Hawaii Community Foundation Scholarships
1164 Bishop Street
Suite 800
Honolulu, HI 96813
Phone: 888-731-3863
Fax: 808-521-6286
Web: www.hawaiicommunityfoundation.org

Kohala Ditch Education Fund

Type of award: Scholarship.
Intended use: For full-time undergraduate study at accredited 2-year or 4-year institution in United States.
Eligibility: Applicant must be high school senior. Applicant must be U.S. citizen or permanent resident residing in Hawaii.
Basis for selection: Applicant must demonstrate financial need, high academic achievement and depth of character.
Application requirements: Essay, transcript. FAFSA and SAR.
Additional information: Applicant must be student at Kohala High School. Amount of award may change yearly. Applicants taking up mainland residency must have relatives living in Hawaii.

  Number of awards: 3
  Application deadline: March 1
Contact:
Hawaii Community Foundation Scholarships
1164 Bishop Street
Suite 800
Honolulu, HI 96813
Phone: 888-731-3863
Fax: 808-521-6286
Web: www.hawaiicommunityfoundation.org

Koloa Scholarship

Type of award: Scholarship, renewable.
Intended use: For full-time undergraduate or graduate study at accredited vocational, 2-year or 4-year institution in United States.
Eligibility: Applicant must be U.S. citizen or permanent resident residing in Hawaii.
Basis for selection: Applicant must demonstrate financial need, high academic achievement and depth of character.
Application requirements: Recommendations, transcript. FAFSA and SAR. Personal essay explaining personal understanding of meaning of "aloha," how it has played a part in personal development and how applicant hopes to use chosen field to further this meaning among family and community. Must include how long applicant has lived in Koloa area, list of books or other publications read on Hawaii's history, and list of relatives born in Koloa District, including relationship to applicant, and place and approximate year of birth.
Additional information: Minimum 2.0 GPA. Applicant must be resident of one of the following Kauai areas in Hawaii:

Koloa, including Omao and Poipu (96756), Lawai (96765), or Kalaheo (96741). Applicants taking up mainland residency must have relatives living in Hawaii. Amount of award varies and may change yearly.

  Number of awards: 4
  Application deadline: March 1
Contact:
Hawaii Community Foundation Scholarships
1164 Bishop Street
Suite 800
Honolulu, HI 96813
Phone: 888-731-3863
Fax: 808-521-6286
Web: www.hawaiicommunityfoundation.org

Korean University Club Scholarship Fund

Type of award: Scholarship.
Intended use: For full-time undergraduate or graduate study at accredited 2-year or 4-year institution in United States.
Eligibility: Applicant must be U.S. citizen residing in Hawaii.
Basis for selection: Applicant must demonstrate financial need, high academic achievement and depth of character.
Application requirements: Recommendations, essay, transcript. SAR, FAFSA, Personal Statement.
Additional information: Minimum 2.7 GPA. Must be of Korean ancestry.

  Application deadline: March 1
Contact:
Hawaii Community Foundation Scholarships
1164 Bishop Street
Suite 800
Honolulu, HI 96813
Phone: 888-731-3863
Fax: 808-521-6286
Web: www.hawaiicommunityfoundation.org

Kurt W. Schneider Memorial Scholarship Fund

Type of award: Scholarship.
Intended use: For full-time undergraduate study at accredited 2-year or 4-year institution in United States.
Eligibility: Applicant must be high school senior. Applicant must be U.S. citizen or permanent resident residing in Hawaii.
Basis for selection: Major/career interest in tourism/travel. Applicant must demonstrate financial need, high academic achievement and depth of character.
Application requirements: Essay, transcript. FAFSA and SAR.
Additional information: Applicant must be student at Lana'i High School. Preference given to travel industry management majors. Applicants taking up mainland residency must have relatives living in Hawaii. Amount of award may change yearly.

  Number of awards: 1
  Application deadline: March 1
Contact:
Hawaii Community Foundation Scholarships
1164 Bishop Street
Suite 800
Honolulu, HI 96813
Phone: 888-731-3863
Fax: 808-521-6286
Web: www.hawaiicommunityfoundation.org

Laheenae Rebecca Hart Gay Scholarship

Type of award: Scholarship.
Intended use: For full-time undergraduate or graduate study at accredited 2-year or 4-year institution in United States.
Eligibility: Applicant must be U.S. citizen residing in Hawaii.
Basis for selection: Major/career interest in arts, general. Applicant must demonstrate financial need, high academic achievement and depth of character.
Application requirements: Recommendations, essay, transcript. SAR, FAFSA, Personal Statement.
Additional information: Minimum 2.7 GPA. Amount of award varies. Scholarship does not apply to study of video, film, performing arts or the culinary arts.
  Application deadline:　　　March 1
Contact:
Hawaii Community Foundation Scholarships
1164 Bishop Street
Suite 800
Honolulu, HI 96813
Phone: 888-731-3863
Fax: 808-521-6286
Web: www.hawaiicommunityfoundation.org

Laura N. Dowsett Fund

Type of award: Scholarship, renewable.
Intended use: For full-time junior, senior or graduate study at accredited 2-year, 4-year or graduate institution in United States.
Eligibility: Applicant must be U.S. citizen or permanent resident residing in Hawaii.
Basis for selection: Major/career interest in occupational therapy. Applicant must demonstrate financial need, high academic achievement and depth of character.
Application requirements: Essay, transcript. FAFSA and SAR.
Additional information: Minimum 2.7 GPA. Applicants must have permanent address in Hawaii. Applicants who take up mainland residency must have relatives living in Hawaii. Amount and number of awards vary.
  Number of awards:　　　2
  Application deadline:　　　March 1
Contact:
Hawaii Community Foundation Scholarships
1164 Bishop Street
Suite 800
Honolulu, HI 96813
Phone: 888-731-3863
Fax: 808-521-6286
Web: www.hawaiicommunityfoundation.org

Laura Rowe Burdick Scholarship Fund

Type of award: Scholarship.
Intended use: For full-time undergraduate study at accredited 2-year or 4-year institution in United States.
Eligibility: Applicant must be high school senior. Applicant must be U.S. citizen residing in Hawaii.
Basis for selection: Applicant must demonstrate financial need, high academic achievement, depth of character and service orientation.
Application requirements: Recommendations, essay, transcript. SAR, FAFSA, Personal Statement.

Additional information: Minimum 2.7 GPA. Amount of award varies. Applicant must be a high school senior in Maui County. Preference given to applicants who want to return to Maui County after completing their education or training in order to contribute to the community that formed them.
  Application deadline:　　　March 1
Contact:
Hawaii Community Foundation Scholarships
1164 Bishop Street
Suite 800
Honolulu, HI 96813
Phone: 888-731-3863
Fax: 808-521-6286
Web: www.hawaiicommunityfoundation.org

Margaret Jones Memorial Nursing Scholarship

Type of award: Scholarship, renewable.
Intended use: For full-time junior, senior or graduate study at accredited 4-year or graduate institution in United States. Designated institutions: University of Hawaii, Manoa; University of Hawaii, Hilo; Hawaii Pacific University; or PhD programs in Hawaii or mainland U.S.
Eligibility: Applicant must be U.S. citizen or permanent resident residing in Hawaii.
Basis for selection: Major/career interest in nursing. Applicant must demonstrate financial need, high academic achievement and depth of character.
Application requirements: Essay, transcript. FAFSA and SAR.
Additional information: Minimum 3.0 GPA. Applicants must be enrolled in BSN, MSN, or doctoral nursing program. Preference may be given to members of Hawaii Nurses Association. Applicants must have permanent address in Hawaii. Applicant taking up mainland residency must have relatives living in Hawaii. Amount and number of awards vary and change yearly.
  Number of awards:　　　13
  Application deadline:　　　March 1
Contact:
Hawaii Community Foundation Scholarships
1164 Bishop Street
Suite 800
Honolulu, HI 96813
Phone: 888-731-3863
Fax: 808-521-6286
Web: www.hawaiicommunityfoundation.org

Marion Maccarrell Scott Scholarship

Type of award: Scholarship, renewable.
Intended use: For full-time undergraduate or graduate study at accredited postsecondary institution in United States. Designated institutions: Institutions on U.S. mainland.
Eligibility: Applicant must be U.S. citizen or permanent resident residing in Hawaii.
Basis for selection: Applicant must demonstrate financial need, high academic achievement and depth of character.
Application requirements: Essay, transcript. FAFSA and SAR. Essay (2-3 typed pages, double-spaced) must demonstrate commitment to international understanding and world peace.
Additional information: Minimum 2.8 GPA. Must be graduate of Hawaii public high school and attend accredited mainland U.S. college or university. Applicant must have permanent address in Hawaii. Applicants taking up mainland

residency must have relatives living in Hawaii. Amount and number of awards vary and may change yearly.

Number of awards: 331
Application deadline: March 1
Contact:
Hawaii Community Foundation Scholarships
1164 Bishop Street
Suite 800
Honolulu, HI 96813
Phone: 888-731-3863
Fax: 808-521-6286
Web: www.hawaiicommunityfoundation.org

Mary Josephine Bloder Scholarship

Type of award: Scholarship.
Intended use: For full-time undergraduate study at accredited 2-year or 4-year institution in United States.
Eligibility: Applicant must be high school senior. Applicant must be U.S. citizen or permanent resident residing in Hawaii.
Basis for selection: Applicant must demonstrate financial need, high academic achievement and depth of character.
Application requirements: Recommendations, essay, transcript. FAFSA and SAR. One of the two letters of recommendation must be from Lahainaluna High School science teacher.
Additional information: Must be student at Lahainaluna High School. Preference given to boarding students. Must have high GPA in sciences. Applicants taking up mainland residency must have relatives living in Hawaii. Amount and number of awards vary and may change yearly.

Application deadline: March 1
Contact:
Hawaii Community Foundation Scholarships
1164 Bishop Street
Suite 800
Honolulu, HI 96813
Phone: 888-731-3863
Fax: 808-521-6286
Web: www.hawaiicommunityfoundation.org

Mildred Towle Scholarship - Study Abroad

Type of award: Scholarship, renewable.
Intended use: For full-time junior, senior or graduate study at accredited postsecondary institution outside United States.
Eligibility: Applicant must be residing in Hawaii.
Basis for selection: Applicant must demonstrate financial need, high academic achievement and depth of character.
Application requirements: Essay, transcript. FAFSA and SAR. Essay must include intended country and semester of study.
Additional information: Minimum 3.0 GPA. Award for Hawaii residents studying abroad. Amount and number of awards vary and may change yearly.

Number of awards: 6
Application deadline: March 1
Contact:
Hawaii Community Foundation Scholarships
1164 Bishop Street
Suite 800
Honolulu, HI 96813
Phone: 888-731-3863
Fax: 808-521-6286
Web: www.hawaiicommunityfoundation.org

Mildred Towle Scholarship for African-Americans

Type of award: Scholarship.
Intended use: For undergraduate study at postsecondary institution.
Eligibility: Applicant must be African American. Applicant must be U.S. citizen residing in Hawaii.
Application requirements: Recommendations, essay, transcript. SAR.
Additional information: Minimum 3.0 GPA. Must attend school in Hawaii. Hawaii residency not required.
Number of awards: 11
Total amount awarded: $11,000
Contact:
Hawaii Community Foundation Scholarships
1164 Bishop Street
Suite 800
Honolulu, HI 96813
Phone: 888-731-3863
Fax: 808-521-6286
Web: www.hawaiicommunityfoundation.org

Nick Van Pernis Scholarship

Type of award: Scholarship.
Intended use: For full-time undergraduate study at accredited 2-year or 4-year institution in United States.
Eligibility: Applicant must be U.S. citizen or permanent resident residing in Hawaii.
Basis for selection: Major/career interest in oceanography/marine studies; bioengineering; health sciences or education, early childhood. Applicant must demonstrate financial need, high academic achievement, depth of character and service orientation.
Application requirements: Essay, transcript. FAFSA and SAR. Essay must include record of community service and description of how student's education and career will benefit Hawaii residents.
Additional information: Must be graduate of public or private school in the North Kona, South Kona, North Kohala, South Kohala, or Ka'u districts. Applicants taking up mainland residency must have relatives living in Hawaii. Amount and number of awards may vary yearly.

Application deadline: March 1
Contact:
Hawaii Community Foundation Scholarships
1164 Bishop Street
Suite 800
Honolulu, HI 96813
Phone: 888-731-3863
Fax: 808-521-6286
Web: www.hawaiicommunityfoundation.org

Office of Hawaiian Affairs Scholarship Fund

Type of award: Scholarship.
Intended use: For undergraduate or graduate study at accredited 2-year or 4-year institution in United States.
Eligibility: Applicant must be Native Hawaiian/Pacific Islander. Applicant must be U.S. citizen.
Basis for selection: Applicant must demonstrate financial need, high academic achievement and depth of character.
Application requirements: Recommendations, essay, transcript, proof of eligibility. SAR, FAFSA, Personal Statement.

Additional information: Minimum 2.0 GPA for undergraduate students, 3.0 GPA for graduate students. Applicant must be of Hawaiian ancestry; ancestry must be verified through OHA's Hawaiian Registry Program. Amount of award varies.

Application deadline: March 1
Contact:
Hawaii Community Foundation Scholarships
1164 Bishop Street
Suite 800
Honolulu, HI 96813
Phone: 888-731-3863
Fax: 808-521-6286
Web: www.hawaiicommunityfoundation.org

Oscar and Rosetta Fish Fund

Type of award: Scholarship.
Intended use: For full-time undergraduate or graduate study at 2-year or 4-year institution. Designated institutions: Any University of Hawaii campus, excluding Manoa.
Eligibility: Applicant must be U.S. citizen or permanent resident residing in Hawaii.
Basis for selection: Major/career interest in business. Applicant must demonstrate financial need, high academic achievement and depth of character.
Application requirements: Essay, transcript. FAFSA and SAR.
Additional information: Must have permanent address in Hawaii. Amount and number of awards vary and may change yearly.

Application deadline: March 1
Contact:
Hawaii Community Foundation Scholarships
1164 Bishop Street
Suite 800
Honolulu, HI 96813
Phone: 888-731-3863
Fax: 808-521-6286
Web: www.hawaiicommunityfoundation.org

Paulina L. Sorg Scholarship

Type of award: Scholarship.
Intended use: For full-time senior or graduate study at accredited 2-year or 4-year institution in United States.
Eligibility: Applicant must be U.S. citizen residing in Hawaii.
Basis for selection: Major/career interest in physical therapy. Applicant must demonstrate financial need and depth of character.
Application requirements: Recommendations, essay, transcript. SAR, FAFSA, Personal Statement.
Additional information: Minimum 2.7 GPA. Amount of award varies.

Application deadline: March 1
Contact:
Hawaii Community Foundation Scholarships
1164 Bishop Street
Suite 800
Honolulu, HI 96813
Phone: 888-731-3863
Fax: 808-521-6286
Web: www.hawaiicommunityfoundation.org

Perry & Sally Sorenson Scholarship for Dependents of Hospitality Workers

Type of award: Scholarship.
Intended use: For full-time undergraduate or graduate study at accredited 2-year or 4-year institution in United States.
Eligibility: Applicant must be U.S. citizen residing in Hawaii.
Basis for selection: Applicant must demonstrate financial need, high academic achievement and depth of character.
Application requirements: Recommendations, essay, transcript, proof of eligibility. SAR, FAFSA, personal statement, name of Outrigger employee/position at company.
Additional information: Minimum 2.7 GPA. Amount of award varies. Applicant must be a dependent of an employee currently employed by Outrigger Enterprises in Hawaii working in a hospitality industry position.

Application deadline: March 1
Contact:
Hawaii Community Foundation Scholarships
1164 Bishop Street
Suite 800
Honolulu, HI 96813
Phone: 888-731-3863
Fax: 808-521-6286
Web: www.hawaiicommunityfoundation.org

Perry & Sally Sorenson Scholarship for Foster Youth

Type of award: Scholarship.
Intended use: For full-time undergraduate or graduate study at accredited 4-year or graduate institution in United States.
Eligibility: Applicant must be at least 18, no older than 25. Applicant must be U.S. citizen residing in Hawaii.
Basis for selection: Applicant must demonstrate financial need, high academic achievement and depth of character.
Application requirements: Recommendations, essay, transcript. SAR, FAFSA, Personal Statement.
Additional information: Minimum 2.0 GPA. Amount of award varies. Applicant must be permanently or temporarily separated from birth parent(s) and aged out of the foster care system in the state of Hawaii.

Application deadline: March 1
Contact:
Hawaii Community Foundation Scholarships
1164 Bishop Street
Suite 800
Honolulu, HI 96813
Phone: 888-731-3863
Fax: 808-521-6286
Web: www.hawaiicommunityfoundation.org

Peter Papworth Scholarship

Type of award: Scholarship.
Intended use: For full-time sophomore, junior, senior or graduate study at accredited 2-year or 4-year institution in United States.
Eligibility: Applicant must be U.S. citizen residing in Hawaii.
Basis for selection: Applicant must demonstrate financial need, high academic achievement and depth of character.
Application requirements: Recommendations, essay, transcript. SAR, FAFSA, Personal Statement.

Additional information: Applicant must be a graduate of Campbell High School. Minimum 2.7 GPA. Amount of award varies.

   Application deadline: March 1
Contact:
Hawaii Community Foundation Scholarships
1164 Bishop Street
Suite 800
Honolulu, HI 96813
Phone: 888-731-3863
Fax: 808-521-6286
Web: www.hawaiicommunityfoundation.org

PRSA-Hawaii/Roy Leffingwell Public Relations Scholarship

Type of award: Scholarship.
Intended use: For full-time junior, senior or graduate study at accredited 2-year or 4-year institution in United States.
Eligibility: Applicant must be U.S. citizen or permanent resident residing in Hawaii.
Basis for selection: Major/career interest in public relations; communications or journalism. Applicant must demonstrate financial need, high academic achievement and depth of character.
Application requirements: Essay, transcript. FAFSA and SAR.
Additional information: Must intend to pursue career in public relations. Award amount varies.

   Number of awards: 1
   Application deadline: March 1
Contact:
Hawaii Community Foundation Scholarships
1164 Bishop Street
Suite 800
Honolulu, HI 96813
Phone: 888-731-3863
Fax: 808-521-6286
Web: www.hawaiicommunityfoundation.org

Ray Yoshida Kauai Fine Arts Scholarship

Type of award: Scholarship.
Intended use: For full-time undergraduate study at accredited 2-year or 4-year institution in United States.
Eligibility: Applicant must be high school senior. Applicant must be U.S. citizen residing in Hawaii.
Basis for selection: Major/career interest in arts, general. Applicant must demonstrate financial need, high academic achievement and depth of character.
Application requirements: Recommendations, essay, transcript. SAR, FAFSA, Personal Statement.
Additional information: Minimum 2.7 GPA. Amount of award varies. Applicant must be a high school senior from a school on the island of Kauai, and must pursue studies in Fine Arts.

   Application deadline: March 1
Contact:
Hawaii Community Foundation Scholarships
1164 Bishop Street
Suite 800
Honolulu, HI 96813
Phone: 888-731-3863
Fax: 808-521-6286
Web: www.hawaiicommunityfoundation.org

Raymond F. Cain Scholarship Fund

Type of award: Scholarship.
Intended use: For full-time undergraduate or graduate study at accredited 2-year or 4-year institution in United States.
Eligibility: Applicant must be U.S. citizen residing in Hawaii.
Basis for selection: Major/career interest in landscape architecture. Applicant must demonstrate financial need, high academic achievement and depth of character.
Application requirements: Recommendations, essay, transcript. SAR, FAFSA, Personal Statement.
Additional information: Minimum 2.7 GPA. Amount of award varies.

   Application deadline: March 1
Contact:
Hawaii Community Foundation Scholarships
1164 Bishop Street
Suite 800
Honolulu, HI 96813
Phone: 888-731-3863
Fax: 808-521-6286
Web: www.hawaiicommunityfoundation.org

Rich Meiers Health Administration Fund

Type of award: Scholarship.
Intended use: For full-time senior or graduate study at accredited 2-year or 4-year institution in United States.
Designated institutions: Hawaii institutions.
Eligibility: Applicant must be U.S. citizen residing in Hawaii.
Basis for selection: Major/career interest in health services administration. Applicant must demonstrate financial need, high academic achievement and depth of character.
Application requirements: Recommendations, essay, transcript. SAR, FAFSA, Personal Statement.
Additional information: Minimum 2.7 GPA. Amount of award varies. Majors may also include hospital administration, health care administration and long-term care administration.

   Application deadline: March 1
Contact:
Hawaii Community Foundation Scholarships
1164 Bishop Street
Suite 800
Honolulu, HI 96813
Phone: 888-731-3863
Fax: 808-521-6286
Web: www.hawaiicommunityfoundation.org

Richie Gregory Fund

Type of award: Scholarship.
Intended use: For full-time undergraduate or graduate study at accredited 2-year or 4-year institution in United States.
Eligibility: Applicant must be U.S. citizen residing in Hawaii.
Basis for selection: Major/career interest in arts, general. Applicant must demonstrate financial need, high academic achievement and depth of character.
Application requirements: Recommendations, essay, transcript. SAR, FAFSA, Personal Statement.
Additional information: Minimum 2.7 GPA. Amount of award varies. Applicant must major in Art.

   Application deadline: March 1

Contact:
Hawaii Community Foundation Scholarships
1164 Bishop Street
Suite 800
Honolulu, HI 96813
Phone: 888-731-3863
Fax: 808-521-6286
Web: www.hawaiicommunityfoundation.org

Robanna Fund

Type of award: Scholarship.
Intended use: For full-time undergraduate study at accredited 2-year or 4-year institution in United States.
Eligibility: Applicant must be U.S. citizen residing in Hawaii.
Basis for selection: Major/career interest in health-related professions. Applicant must demonstrate financial need, high academic achievement and depth of character.
Application requirements: Recommendations, essay, transcript. SAR, FAFSA, Personal Statement.
Additional information: Minimum 2.7 GPA. Amount of award varies.

    Application deadline: March 1
Contact:
Hawaii Community Foundation Scholarships
1164 Bishop Street
Suite 800
Honolulu, HI 96813
Phone: 888-731-3863
Fax: 808-521-6286
Web: www.hawaiicommunityfoundation.org

Ron Bright Scholarship

Type of award: Scholarship.
Intended use: For full-time undergraduate study at accredited 2-year or 4-year institution in United States.
Eligibility: Applicant must be high school senior. Applicant must be U.S. citizen or permanent resident residing in Hawaii.
Basis for selection: Major/career interest in education. Applicant must demonstrate financial need, high academic achievement and depth of character.
Application requirements: Essay, transcript. FAFSA and SAR. Grades from first semester of 12th grade.
Additional information: Must attend one of the following Windward Oahu high schools: Castle, Kahuku, Kailua, Kalaheo, or Olomana. Preference given to students with extracurricular activities in the performing arts. Must have permanent address in Hawaii. Applicants taking up mainland residency must have relatives living in Hawaii. Amount and number of awards vary and may change yearly.

    Application deadline: March 1
Contact:
Hawaii Community Foundation Scholarships
1164 Bishop Street
Suite 800
Honolulu, HI 96813
Phone: 888-731-3863
Fax: 808-521-6286
Web: www.hawaiicommunityfoundation.org

Rosemary & Nellie Ebrie Fund

Type of award: Scholarship.
Intended use: For full-time undergraduate or graduate study at accredited 2-year or 4-year institution in United States.

Eligibility: Applicant must be Native Hawaiian/Pacific Islander. Applicant must be U.S. citizen or permanent resident residing in Hawaii.
Basis for selection: Applicant must demonstrate financial need, high academic achievement and depth of character.
Application requirements: Essay, transcript. FAFSA and SAR.
Additional information: Must be of Hawaiian ancestry. Must be long-term resident born and currently living on the island of Hawaii. Applicants taking up mainland residency must have relatives living in Hawaii. Amount of award may change yearly.
    Number of awards: 15
    Application deadline: March 1
Contact:
Hawaii Community Foundation Scholarships
1164 Bishop Street
Suite 800
Honolulu, HI 96813
Phone: 888-731-3863
Fax: 808-521-6286
Web: www.hawaiicommunityfoundation.org

Safeway Foundation Hawaii Scholarship Fund

Type of award: Scholarship.
Intended use: For full-time undergraduate or graduate study at accredited 2-year or 4-year institution in United States. Designated institutions: Hawaii institutions.
Eligibility: Applicant must be U.S. citizen residing in Hawaii.
Basis for selection: Applicant must demonstrate financial need, high academic achievement and depth of character.
Application requirements: Recommendations, essay, transcript. SAR, FAFSA, Personal Statement.
Additional information: Minimum 3.0 GPA. Amount of award varies. Preference for current and past employees of Safeway Hawaii & their dependents.
    Application deadline: March 1
Contact:
Hawaii Community Foundation Scholarships
1164 Bishop Street
Suite 800
Honolulu, HI 96813
Phone: 888-731-3863
Fax: 808-521-6286
Web: www.hawaiicommunityfoundation.org

Senator Richard M. & Dr. Ruth Matsuura Scholarship Fund

Type of award: Scholarship.
Intended use: For full-time undergraduate or graduate study at accredited 2-year or 4-year institution in United States.
Eligibility: Applicant must be U.S. citizen residing in Hawaii.
Basis for selection: Applicant must demonstrate financial need, high academic achievement and depth of character.
Application requirements: Recommendations, essay, transcript. SAR, FAFSA, Personal Statement.
Additional information: Applicant must be a graduate of Hilo High School or Waiakea High School and a resident of the island of Hawaii. Minimum 2.7 GPA. Amount of award varies.
    Application deadline: March 1

Contact:
Hawaii Community Foundation Scholarships
1164 Bishop Street
Suite 800
Honolulu, HI 96813
Phone: 888-731-3863
Fax: 808-521-6286
Web: www.hawaiicommunityfoundation.org

Shirley McKown Scholarship Fund

Type of award: Scholarship.
Intended use: For full-time junior, senior or graduate study at accredited 4-year institution in United States.
Eligibility: Applicant must be U.S. citizen or permanent resident residing in Hawaii.
Basis for selection: Major/career interest in advertising; journalism or public relations. Applicant must demonstrate depth of character.
Application requirements: Essay, transcript. FAFSA and SAR.
Additional information: Minimum 3.0 GPA. Applicants must have permanent address in Hawaii. Applicants taking up mainland residency must have relatives living in Hawaii.
  Number of awards: 1
  Application deadline: March 1
Contact:
Hawaii Community Foundation Scholarships
1164 Bishop Street
Suite 800
Honolulu, HI 96813
Phone: 888-731-3863
Fax: 808-521-6286
Web: www.hawaiicommunityfoundation.org

Shuichi, Katsu and Itsuyo Suga Scholarship

Type of award: Scholarship.
Intended use: For full-time undergraduate or graduate study at accredited 2-year or 4-year institution in United States.
Eligibility: Applicant must be U.S. citizen or permanent resident residing in Hawaii.
Basis for selection: Major/career interest in mathematics; physics; science, general; computer/information sciences or technology. Applicant must demonstrate financial need, high academic achievement and depth of character.
Application requirements: Essay, transcript. FAFSA and SAR.
Additional information: Minimum 3.0 GPA. Applicants must have permanent address in Hawaii. Applicants taking up mainland residency must have relatives living in Hawaii. Amount of award may change yearly.
  Number of awards: 9
  Application deadline: March 1
Contact:
Hawaii Community Foundation Scholarships
1164 Bishop Street
Suite 800
Honolulu, HI 96813
Phone: 888-731-3863
Fax: 808-521-6286
Web: www.hawaiicommunityfoundation.org

Takehiko Hasegawa Academic Scholarship

Type of award: Scholarship.
Intended use: For full-time undergraduate or graduate study at accredited 2-year or 4-year institution in United States.
Eligibility: Applicant must be U.S. citizen residing in Hawaii.
Basis for selection: Applicant must demonstrate financial need, high academic achievement and depth of character.
Application requirements: Recommendations, essay, transcript. SAR, FAFSA, Personal statement.
Additional information: Minimum GPA of 3.5. Must be a resident of the Island of Kaua'i. Amount of award varies.
  Application deadline: March 1
Contact:
Hawaii Community Foundation Scholarships
1164 Bishop Street
Suite 800
Honolulu, HI 96813
Phone: 888-731-3863
Fax: 808-521-6286
Web: www.hawaiicommunityfoundation.org

Thz Fo Farm Fund

Type of award: Scholarship.
Intended use: For full-time undergraduate or graduate study at accredited postsecondary institution in United States.
Eligibility: Applicant must be Chinese. Applicant must be U.S. citizen or permanent resident residing in Hawaii.
Basis for selection: Major/career interest in gerontology. Applicant must demonstrate financial need, high academic achievement and depth of character.
Application requirements: FAFSA and SAR.
Additional information: Minimum 2.7 GPA. Applicants must have permanent address in Hawaii. Applicants who take up mainland residency must have relatives living in Hawaii. Amount of award varies.
  Number of awards: 6
Contact:
Hawaii Community Foundation Scholarships
1164 Bishop Street
Suite 800
Honolulu, HI 96813
Phone: 888-731-3863
Fax: 808-521-6286
Web: www.hawaiicommunityfoundation.org

Tommy Lee Memorial Scholarship Fund

Type of award: Scholarship.
Intended use: For full-time undergraduate study at accredited 2-year or 4-year institution in United States.
Eligibility: Applicant must be high school senior. Applicant must be U.S. citizen or permanent resident residing in Hawaii.
Basis for selection: Applicant must demonstrate financial need, high academic achievement and depth of character.
Application requirements: Recommendations, essay, transcript. FAFSA and SAR.
Additional information: Must be high school senior residing in the Waialua or Haleiwa area. Applicants taking up mainland residency must have relatives living in Hawaii. Amount of award may change yearly.
  Number of awards: 4
  Application deadline: March 1

Contact:
Hawaii Community Foundation Scholarships
1164 Bishop Street
Suite 800
Honolulu, HI 96813
Phone: 888-731-3863
Fax: 808-521-6286
Web: www.hawaiicommunityfoundation.org

The Tongan Cultural Society Scholarship

Type of award: Scholarship.
Intended use: For full-time undergraduate or graduate study at accredited 2-year or 4-year institution in United States. Designated institutions: Hawaii institutions.
Eligibility: Applicant must be U.S. citizen residing in Hawaii.
Basis for selection: Applicant must demonstrate financial need, high academic achievement and depth of character.
Application requirements: Recommendations, essay, transcript. SAR, FAFSA, Personal Statement.
Additional information: Must be of primarily Tongan ancestry. Must attend school in Hawaii. Minimum 2.7 GPA. Amount of awards varies.

  Application deadline: March 1
Contact:
Hawaii Community Foundation Scholarships
1164 Bishop Street
Suite 800
Honolulu, HI 96813
Phone: 888-731-3863
Fax: 808-521-6286
Web: www.hawaiicommunityfoundation.org

Toraji & Toki Yoshinaga Scholarship

Type of award: Scholarship.
Intended use: For full-time sophomore study at accredited 2-year or 4-year institution. Designated institutions: Brigham Young University-Hawaii, Chaminade University, Hawaii Pacific University, Heald College.
Eligibility: Applicant must be U.S. citizen or permanent resident residing in Hawaii.
Basis for selection: Applicant must demonstrate financial need, high academic achievement and depth of character.
Application requirements: Essay, transcript. FAFSA and SAR.
Additional information: Minimum 2.7 GPA. Applicants must have permanent address in Hawaii. Applicants taking up mainland residency must have relatives living in Hawaii. Amount of award may change yearly.

  Number of awards: 2
  Application deadline: March 1
Contact:
Hawaii Community Foundation Scholarships
1164 Bishop Street
Suite 800
Honolulu, HI 96813
Phone: 888-731-3863
Fax: 808-521-6286
Web: www.hawaiicommunityfoundation.org

Vicki Willder Scholarship Fund

Type of award: Scholarship.

Intended use: For full-time undergraduate study at accredited 2-year or 4-year institution in United States.
Eligibility: Applicant must be U.S. citizen or permanent resident residing in Hawaii.
Basis for selection: Major/career interest in culinary arts or tourism/travel. Applicant must demonstrate financial need, high academic achievement and depth of character.
Application requirements: Essay, transcript. FAFSA and SAR.
Additional information: Applicant must be employee or dependent of employee of Kamehameha Schools food services department or a graduate of Kamehameha Schools. Preference given to students majoring in culinary arts or travel industry management. Applicants taking up mainland residency must have relatives living in Hawaii. Amount and number of awards vary and may change yearly.

  Number of awards: 13
  Application deadline: March 1
Contact:
Hawaii Community Foundation Scholarships
1164 Bishop Street
Suite 800
Honolulu, HI 96813
Phone: 888-731-3863
Fax: 808-521-6286
Web: www.hawaiicommunityfoundation.org

Walter H. Kupau Memorial Fund

Type of award: Scholarship.
Intended use: For full-time undergraduate study at accredited 2-year or 4-year institution in United States.
Eligibility: Applicant must be U.S. citizen or permanent resident residing in Hawaii.
Basis for selection: Applicant must demonstrate financial need, high academic achievement and depth of character.
Application requirements: Essay, transcript. FAFSA and SAR. Name and social security number of Local 745 member, along with relationship to applicant.
Additional information: Applicant must be descendant of Hawaii Carpenter's Union Local 745 member in good standing; preference given to descendants of retired members. Applicant must have permanent address in Hawaii. Applicants taking up mainland residency must have relatives living in Hawaii. Amount and number of awards vary.

  Number of awards: 5
  Application deadline: March 1
Contact:
Hawaii Community Foundation Scholarships
1164 Bishop Street
Suite 800
Honolulu, HI 96813
Phone: 888-731-3863
Fax: 808-521-6286
Web: www.hawaiicommunityfoundation.org

Will J. Henderson Scholarship Fund in Hawaii

Type of award: Scholarship.
Intended use: For full-time undergraduate or graduate study at accredited vocational, 2-year or 4-year institution in United States. Designated institutions: Institutions approved by the Hawaii Community Foundation.
Eligibility: Applicant must be U.S. citizen residing in Hawaii.
Basis for selection: Applicant must demonstrate financial need, high academic achievement and depth of character.

Application requirements: Recommendations, essay, transcript. SAR, FAFSA, Personal Statement, name/job title of parent employed by Queen's Medical Center.
Additional information: Minimum 2.0 GPA. Amount of award varies. Applicant must be a child dependent of a current employee at Queen's Medical Center, and must attend or plan to attend an institution approved by the Hawaii Community Foundation.

Application deadline:	March 1

Contact:
Hawaii Community Foundation Scholarships
1164 Bishop Street
Suite 800
Honolulu, HI 96813
Phone: 888-731-3863
Fax: 808-521-6286
Web: www.hawaiicommunityfoundation.org

William James & Dorothy Bading Lanquist Fund

Type of award: Scholarship.
Intended use: For full-time undergraduate or graduate study at accredited 2-year or 4-year institution in United States.
Eligibility: Applicant must be U.S. citizen or permanent resident residing in Hawaii.
Basis for selection: Major/career interest in physical sciences. Applicant must demonstrate financial need, high academic achievement and depth of character.
Application requirements: Essay, transcript. FAFSA and SAR.
Additional information: Must major in the physical sciences or related fields, excluding biological and social sciences. Must have permanent address in Hawaii. Applicants taking up mainland residency must have relatives living in Hawaii. Amount and number of awards vary and may change yearly.

Application deadline:	March 1

Contact:
Hawaii Community Foundation Scholarships
1164 Bishop Street
Suite 800
Honolulu, HI 96813
Phone: 888-731-3863
Fax: 808-521-6286
Web: www.hawaiicommunityfoundation.org

Helicopter Association International

Aviation Maintenance Technician Scholarship Award

Type of award: Scholarship.
Intended use: For undergraduate or non-degree study at vocational institution. Designated institutions: U.S. helicopter airframe and engine manufacturers; aviation maintenance schools.
Basis for selection: Major/career interest in aviation repair.
Application requirements: Recommendations.
Additional information: For students who wish to study helicopter maintenance. Award includes full tuition to aviation maintenance program and stipend of $650-1600. Applicant must be about to graduate from FAA-approved Aviation Maintenance

Technician School, or a recent recipient of Airframe and Powerplant (A&P) certificate or international equivalent. Applications available on Website.

Amount of award:	Full tuition
Number of awards:	8
Number of applicants:	45
Application deadline:	January 15

Contact:
Aviation Maintenance Technician Scholarship
Helicopter Association International
1635 Prince Street
Alexandria, VA 22314-2818
Phone: 703-683-4646
Fax: 703-683-4745
Web: www.rotor.com

Herschel C. Price Educational Foundation

Herschel C. Price Educational Scholarship

Type of award: Scholarship, renewable.
Intended use: For undergraduate or graduate study at accredited 2-year, 4-year or graduate institution in United States.
Eligibility: Applicant must be U.S. citizen.
Basis for selection: Applicant must demonstrate financial need and high academic achievement.
Application requirements: Interview, transcript.
Additional information: Applicant must reside in West Virginia or attend West Virginia college or university. Achievement in community activities also considered. Preference given to undergraduates. Limited number of applications available by written request in January for fall term or August for spring term. Limited number of applications available.

Amount of award:	$250-$5,000
Number of awards:	175
Number of applicants:	350
Application deadline:	April 1, October 1
Notification begins:	May 15, November 15
Total amount awarded:	$242,000

Contact:
Herschel C. Price Educational Foundation
P.O. Box 412
Huntington, WV 25708-0412
Phone: 304-529-3852

Higher Education Services Corporation (HESC)

NYC World Trade Center Memorial Scholarship

Type of award: Scholarship, renewable.
Intended use: For full-time undergraduate study at postsecondary institution. Designated institutions: Approved New York State institutions.

Basis for selection: Applicant must demonstrate financial need.

Application requirements: Proof of eligibility. FAFSA, TAP.

Additional information: Applicants must be children, spouses and financial dependents of deceased or severely and permanently disabled victims of the Sept. 11, 2001 terrorist attacks on the United States or the subsequent rescue and recovery operations; this includes victims at the World Trade Center site, at the Pentagon, or on flights 11, 77, 93, or 175. Applicants may also be survivors of the terrorist attacks who are severely and permanently disabled as a result of injuries sustained in the attacks or the subsequent rescue and recovery operations. Applicant must have graduated from high school in the United States, earned a GED, or passed a federally approved "Ability to Benefit" test as defined by the Commissioner of the State Education Department. Applicant must have "C" minimum grade average, and must not be in default on a student loan guaranteed by HESC or on any repayment of state awards. Award covers up to four years of full-time undergraduate study (or five years in an approved five-year bachelor's degree program).

Amount of award:	Full tuition
Application deadline:	May 1

Contact:
New York State Higher Education Services Corporation
99 Washington Avenue
Albany, NY 12255
Phone: 518-473-1574
Web: www.hesc.com/content.nsf/SFC/0/
NYS_World_Trade_Center_Memorial_Scholarship

Hispanic College Fund

Google Hispanic College Fund Scholarship Program

Type of award: Scholarship.

Intended use: For junior, senior, master's or doctoral study at postsecondary institution in or outside United States. Designated institutions: Institutions in the United States or Puerto Rico.

Eligibility: Applicant must be Hispanic American. Applicant must be U.S. citizen or permanent resident.

Basis for selection: Major/career interest in computer/information sciences or engineering, computer. Applicant must demonstrate financial need.

Application requirements: Recommendations, essay, transcript. Proof of family income, proof of citizenship status, resume.

Additional information: Minimum 3.5 GPA. Visit Website for application and more information.

Amount of award:	$10,000
Number of awards:	20
Number of applicants:	18
Total amount awarded:	$180,000

Contact:
Hispanic College Fund
Scholarship Processing
1301 K St. NW, Ste. 450-A West
Washington, DC 20005
Phone: 800-644-4223
Fax: 202-296-3774
Web: www.hispanicfund.org

HCF Scholarship Program

Type of award: Scholarship.

Intended use: For full-time undergraduate or graduate study at accredited postsecondary institution. Designated institutions: Institutions in the United States and Puerto Rico.

Eligibility: Applicant must be Hispanic American. Applicant must be U.S. citizen or permanent resident.

Basis for selection: Applicant must demonstrate financial need.

Application requirements: Recommendations, essay, transcript, proof of eligibility. Resume, proof of family income, proof of citizenship status.

Additional information: Minimum 3.0 GPA. Deadline in February. Check Website for details.

Amount of award:	$500-$5,000
Number of applicants:	1,151
Total amount awarded:	$1,000,000

Contact:
Hispanic College Fund
Scholarship Processing
1301 K Street NW, Suite 450-A West
Washington, DC 20005
Phone: 800-644-4223
Fax: 202-296-3774
Web: www.hispanicfund.org

Marriott Scholars Program

Type of award: Scholarship.

Intended use: For full-time freshman or sophomore study at accredited postsecondary institution in United States. Designated institutions: Colleges in U.S. and Puerto Rico.

Eligibility: Applicant must be Mexican American, Hispanic American or Puerto Rican. Applicant must be U.S. citizen or permanent resident.

Basis for selection: Major/career interest in culinary arts; food production/management/services; hospitality administration/management or hotel/restaurant management. Applicant must demonstrate financial need.

Application requirements: Recommendations, essay, transcript. Resume, proof of family income, proof of citizenship status, financial aid verification.

Additional information: Must plan to pursue a degree in hospitality management or related field. Minimum 3.5 GPA. Visit Website for deadline.

Amount of award:	$9,000

Contact:
Hispanic College Fund
1301 K Street NW, Suite 450-A West
Washington, DC 20005
Phone: 800-644-4223
Fax: 202-296-3774
Web: www.hispanicfund.org

Scholarships for Students of Puerto Rican Descent

Type of award: Scholarship.

Intended use: For full-time undergraduate study at 4-year institution. Designated institutions: Colleges and universities in the United States and Puerto Rico.

Eligibility: Applicant must be Puerto Rican. Applicant must be U.S. citizen.

Application requirements: Recommendations, essay, transcript. Resume, proof of family income, proof of citizenship, birth certificate.

Additional information: Minimum 3.0 GPA. Must be Puerto Rican or of Puerto Rican descent. Preference given to students who live in Puerto Rico.

    Amount of award: $500-$1,500

Contact:
Hispanic College Fund
1301 K Street, NW
Suite 450-A West
Washington, DC 20005
Phone: 800-644-4223
Fax: 202-296-3774
Web: www.hispanicfund.org

Hispanic Heritage Foundation

Hispanic Heritage Youth Awards Program

Type of award: Scholarship.
Intended use: For full-time undergraduate study at postsecondary institution.
Eligibility: Applicant must be Hispanic American. Applicant must be high school junior. Applicant must be U.S. citizen or permanent resident.
Basis for selection: Applicant must demonstrate high academic achievement, depth of character, leadership and service orientation.
Application requirements: Recommendations, essay, transcript, proof of eligibility.
Additional information: Applicant must have at least one parent of Hispanic/Latino ancestry. Foundation offers regional and national awards in a number of categories; amount of award and application deadlines vary by year. Awards may also be used for education related expenses, or to establish a community service effort in the student's community. Applications due in June or July. Visit Website for application and updates regarding Youth Awards Program.

    Amount of award: $1,000
    Number of awards: 140
    Number of applicants: 13,000
    Total amount awarded: $600,000

Contact:
Hispanic Heritage Foundation
Hispanic Heritage Youth Awards
1775 Wiehle Ave, Suite 400
Reston, VA 20190
Phone: 703-871-4841
Fax: 703-773-5000
Web: www.hispanicheritage.org

Hispanic Scholarship Fund

Atrisco Heritage Foundation Scholarship

Type of award: Scholarship.
Intended use: For full-time undergraduate or graduate study at accredited 2-year, 4-year or graduate institution in United States.

Eligibility: Applicant must be Mexican American, Hispanic American or Puerto Rican. Applicant must be U.S. citizen or permanent resident.
Application requirements: Proof of eligibility. Heir registration number. FAFSA.
Additional information: Available to Hispanic students who are verified heirs of Atrisco Land Grant of New Mexico. To access application, contact Anita Lucero at (505) 836-0306 at Atrisco Companies to obtain Heir Registration Number. Minimum 2.0 GPA.

    Amount of award: $2,000
    Application deadline: February 28

Contact:
Hispanic Scholarship Fund
55 Second Street
Suite 1500
San Francisco, CA 94105
Phone: 877-473-4636
Fax: 415-808-2302
Web: www.hsf.net

BB&T Charitable Scholarship Program

Type of award: Scholarship.
Intended use: For full-time undergraduate study at accredited 4-year institution in United States.
Eligibility: Applicant must be African American. Applicant must be U.S. citizen or permanent resident.
Basis for selection: Major/career interest in accounting; economics; finance/banking; business; law or arts, general. Applicant must demonstrate financial need and high academic achievement.
Application requirements: FAFSA.
Additional information: Minimum 3.0 GPA. Must attend school in or be a resident of one of the following states: Alabama, Florida, Georgia, Indiana, Maryland, North Carolina, Kentucky, Puerto Rico, South Carolina, Tennessee, Virginia, Washington, D.C., West Virginia. Recipients may have potential internship opportunity with BB&T. Visit Website for deadline.

Contact:
Hispanic Scholarship Fund
55 Second Street
Suite 1500
San Francisco, CA 94105
Phone: 877-473-4636
Fax: 415-808-2302
Web: www.hsf.net

General College Scholarship

Type of award: Scholarship.
Intended use: For full-time undergraduate or graduate study at 2-year, 4-year or graduate institution in or outside United States. Designated institutions: Colleges in United States, Puerto Rico, U.S. Virgin Islands, and Guam.
Eligibility: Applicant must be Mexican American, Hispanic American or Puerto Rican. Applicant must be U.S. citizen or permanent resident.
Basis for selection: Applicant must demonstrate financial need, high academic achievement, seriousness of purpose and service orientation.
Application requirements: Recommendations, essay, transcript, proof of eligibility. FAFSA and SAR. Copy of permanent resident card or passport stamped I-551 (if applicable).

Additional information: Minimum 3.0 GPA. Must be pursuing first undergraduate or graduate degree. Visit Website or contact via e-mail for application deadlines and tips on how to apply.

  Amount of award: $1,000-$5,000
  Application deadline: April 1
Contact:
General Selection Committee Hispanic Scholarship Fund
55 Second Street
Suite 1500
San Francisco, CA 94105
Phone: 877-473-4636
Fax: 415-808-2302
Web: www.hsf.net

HSBC-North America Scholarship Program

Type of award: Scholarship.
Intended use: For full-time junior, senior or graduate study at accredited 2-year, 4-year or graduate institution in United States.
Eligibility: Applicant must be Mexican American, Hispanic American or Puerto Rican. Applicant must be U.S. citizen or permanent resident residing in New York, Texas, Nevada, Florida, California, District of Columbia, Virginia or Illinois.
Basis for selection: Major/career interest in accounting; business; business/management/administration; economics; finance/banking; advertising; engineering, computer; marketing or public relations. Applicant must demonstrate financial need and high academic achievement.
Application requirements: FAFSA.
Additional information: Minimum 3.0 GPA. Must be pursuing first undergraduate or graduate degree. Must reside in one of the following areas: Los Angeles, CA; Monterey/Salinas, CA; Chicago, IL, New York, NY; Las Vegas, NV. Visit Website for deadline.

  Application deadline: December 15
Contact:
Hispanic Scholarship Fund
55 Second Street
Suite 1500
San Francisco, CA 94105
Phone: 877-473-4636
Fax: 415-808-2302
Web: www.hsf.net

Macy's College Scholarship Program

Type of award: Scholarship.
Intended use: For full-time junior or senior study at accredited 4-year institution in United States. Designated institutions: Baruch College, Columbia University, New York University, Pennsylvania State University, Texas A&M University, The Ohio State University, University of Arizona, University of California - Berkeley, University of Florida, University of Georgia, University of Maryland - College Park, University of Southern California, University of Texas - Austin, University of Washington.
Eligibility: Applicant must be Mexican American, Hispanic American or Puerto Rican. Applicant must be U.S. citizen or permanent resident.
Basis for selection: Applicant must demonstrate financial need and high academic achievement.
Application requirements: FAFSA.
Additional information: Minimum 3.0 GPA.

  Amount of award: $5,000
Contact:
Hispanic Scholarship Fund
55 Second Street
Suite 1500
San Francisco, CA 94105
Phone: 877-473-4636
Fax: 415-808-2302
Web: www.hsf.net

Marathon Oil Corporation College Scholarship

Type of award: Scholarship, renewable.
Intended use: For junior or master's study at 4-year institution.
Eligibility: Applicant must be Alaskan native, African American, Hispanic American, American Indian or Native Hawaiian/Pacific Islander. Applicant must be U.S. citizen or permanent resident.
Basis for selection: Major/career interest in engineering, chemical; engineering, civil; engineering, electrical/electronic; engineering, mechanical; engineering, petroleum; geology/earth sciences; geophysics; accounting or marketing. Applicant must demonstrate leadership and seriousness of purpose.
Application requirements: Recommendations, essay, transcript. Resume and FAFSA.
Additional information: Other acceptable fields of study are global procurement or supply chain management, environmental health and safety, energy management, petroleum land management, transportation and logistics, and geotechnical engineering. Must agree to participate in a possible paid summer internship. Minimum 3.0 GPA. See Website for application and further requirements.

  Amount of award: $15,000
  Number of awards: 20
  Application deadline: August 15
Contact:
HSF/ Marathon Oil Corporation Scholarship Committee
55 Second Street
Suite 1500
San Francisco, CA 94105
Phone: 877-473-4636
Fax: 415-808-2302
Web: www.hsf.net

MassMutual Multicultural College Scholarship

Type of award: Scholarship.
Intended use: For full-time sophomore, junior or senior study at accredited postsecondary institution in United States.
Eligibility: Applicant must be Asian American, African American, Mexican American, Hispanic American, Puerto Rican or Native Hawaiian/Pacific Islander. Applicant must be U.S. citizen or permanent resident.
Basis for selection: Major/career interest in accounting; business; economics; engineering; finance/banking; marketing; mathematics or statistics. Applicant must demonstrate financial need and high academic achievement.
Application requirements: FAFSA.
Additional information: Minimum 3.0 GPA. Must have a permanent address in one of the following cities: Atlanta, Houston, Los Angeles, or San Francisco. Visit Website for deadline.

  Amount of award: $5,000

Contact:
Hispanic Scholarship Fund
55 Second Street
Suite 1500
San Francisco, CA 94105
Phone: 877-473-4636
Fax: 415-808-2302
Web: www.hsf.net

McNamara Family Creative Arts Project Grant

Type of award: Scholarship.
Intended use: For full-time undergraduate or graduate study at accredited 4-year or graduate institution in United States.
Eligibility: Applicant must be Mexican American, Hispanic American or Puerto Rican. Applicant must be U.S. citizen or permanent resident.
Basis for selection: Major/career interest in arts, general; communications; film/video or performing arts. Applicant must demonstrate financial need and high academic achievement.
Application requirements: FAFSA.
Additional information: Minimum 3.0 GPA. Grant intended to assist students in completing an art project. Must be majoring in Arts, including but not limited to media, film, performing arts, communications, or writing. Visit Website for deadline.

  Amount of award: $15,000
  Application deadline: December 15
Contact:
Hispanic Scholarship Fund
55 Second Street
Suite 1500
San Francisco, CA 94105
Phone: 877-473-4636
Fax: 415-808-2302
Web: www.hsf.net

Nissan Community College Transfer Scholarship

Type of award: Scholarship.
Intended use: For full-time undergraduate study at accredited postsecondary institution in United States. Designated institutions: Accredited four-year postsecondary institutions in United States, Puerto Rico, U.S. Virgin Islands, and Guam.
Eligibility: Applicant must be Mexican American, Hispanic American or Puerto Rican. Applicant must be U.S. citizen or permanent resident.
Basis for selection: Major/career interest in business; engineering; communications or radio/television/film. Applicant must demonstrate financial need and high academic achievement.
Application requirements: Recommendations, essay, transcript, proof of eligibility. FAFSA and copy of permanent resident card or passport stamped I-551 (if applicable).
Additional information: Must reside in or transfer to school in one of the following locations: Atlanta, Georgia; Chicago, Illinois; Dallas/Fort Worth, Texas; Denver Colorado; Los Angeles, California; Miami/Ft. Lauderdale, Florida; Nashville, Tennessee; New York City/New Jersey metropolitan area; San Antonio, Texas; Washington, D.C. Must be enrolled part-time or full-time at community college and plan to transfer to four-year institution in fall or spring of next academic year. Minimum 3.0 GPA. Visit Website or contact via e-mail for more information.

  Amount of award: $2,500

Contact:
Community College Transfer Program Hispanic Scholarship Fund
55 Second Street
Suite 1500
San Francisco, CA 94105
Phone: 877-473-4636
Fax: 415-808-2302
Web: www.hsf.net

Procter & Gamble Scholarship

Type of award: Scholarship.
Intended use: For full-time undergraduate study at accredited postsecondary institution in United States.
Eligibility: Applicant must be Mexican American, Hispanic American or Puerto Rican. Applicant must be U.S. citizen or permanent resident.
Basis for selection: Major/career interest in engineering; mathematics; science, general or technology.
Application requirements: FAFSA.
Additional information: Minimum 3.0 GPA. Must reside in one of the following states: Georgia, Indiana, Kentucky, New York, North Carolina, Ohio, Texas or one of the following cities: Chicago, Miami, or Los Angeles.

  Amount of award: $2,500
  Application deadline: February 28
Contact:
Hispanic Scholarship Fund
55 Second Street
Suite 1500
San Francisco, CA 94105
Phone: 877-473-4636
Fax: 415-808-2302
Web: www.hsf.net

Toyota Motor Sales U.S.A., Inc. Scholarship

Type of award: Scholarship.
Intended use: For full-time undergraduate study at accredited 4-year institution in United States. Designated institutions: Schools in Greater Los Angeles, Houston, or San Antonio.
Eligibility: Applicant must be Mexican American, Hispanic American or Puerto Rican. Applicant must be U.S. citizen or international student residing in California or Texas.
Basis for selection: Applicant must demonstrate financial need and high academic achievement.
Application requirements: FAFSA.
Additional information: Minimum 3.0 GPA. Must reside and attend school in Greater Los Angeles, Houston, or San Antonio.
  Application deadline: May 15
Contact:
Hispanic Scholarship Fund
55 Second Street
Suite 1500
San Francisco, CA 94105
Phone: 877-473-4636
Fax: 415-808-2302
Web: www.hsf.net

Wal-Mart Stores, Inc. High School Scholarship

Type of award: Scholarship.
Intended use: For full-time freshman study at accredited 4-year institution in United States.

Eligibility: Applicant must be Mexican American, Hispanic American or Puerto Rican. Applicant must be high school senior. Applicant must be U.S. citizen or permanent resident.
Basis for selection: Applicant must demonstrate financial need and high academic achievement.
Application requirements: FAFSA.
Additional information: Minimum 3.0 GPA. Must reside in one of the following areas: Baltimore, Boston, Chicago, Detroit, Los Angeles, Miami, Minneapolis/Twin Cities, New York, Philadelphia, Portland, Sacramento, San Diego, San Francisco, Seattle, or Washington, D.C.

Amount of award:	$2,500
Application deadline:	January 31

Contact:
Hispanic Scholarship Fund
55 Second Street
Suite 1500
San Francisco, CA 94105
Phone: 877-473-4636
Fax: 415-808-2302
Web: www.hsf.net

Wells Fargo Scholarship

Type of award: Scholarship.
Intended use: For full-time junior study at 4-year institution.
Eligibility: Applicant must be Mexican American, Hispanic American or Puerto Rican. Applicant must be U.S. citizen or permanent resident.
Basis for selection: Major/career interest in accounting; business; computer/information sciences; economics; engineering, computer or finance/banking. Applicant must demonstrate financial need and high academic achievement.
Application requirements: FAFSA.
Additional information: Minimum 3.0 GPA. Must be junior during award year. First priority given to students attending following schools: Arizona State University, California State University - Fullerton, California State University - Fresno, California State University - San Francisco, Columbia University, Iowa State University, San Jose State University, Santa Clara University, Stanford University, Texas A&M University, University of Arizona, University of California - Berkeley, University of California - Davis, University of California - Los Angeles, University of California - San Diego, University of Minnesota, University of Southern California, University of Texas at Austin, University of Washington. Second priority given to residents of the following states: Alaska, Arkansas, Arizona, California, Colorado, Iowa, Idaho, Illinois, Indiana, Michigan, Minnesota, Montana, Nebraska, Nevada, New Mexico, North Dakota, Ohio, Oregon, South Dakota, Texas, Utah, Washington, Wisconsin, Wyoming. Visit Website for deadline.

Amount of award:	$2,000
Application deadline:	December 15

Contact:
Hispanic Scholarship Fund
55 Second Street
Suite 1500
San Francisco, CA 94105
Phone: 877-473-4636
Fax: 415-808-2302
Web: www.hsf.net

Hopi Tribe Grants and Scholarship Program

Hopi BIA Higher Education Grant

Type of award: Scholarship, renewable.
Intended use: For undergraduate or graduate study at accredited 2-year, 4-year or graduate institution.
Eligibility: Applicant must be American Indian. Must be enrolled member of the Hopi Tribe.
Basis for selection: Applicant must demonstrate financial need.
Additional information: Entering freshmen must have minimum 2.0 GPA for high school coursework or minimum composite score of 45% on GED Exam. Continuing students must have minimum 2.0 GPA for all graduate coursework. Four deadlines per year: November 1st (for winter quarter), December 1st (for spring), May 1st (for summer), and July 1st (for fall). Must reapply each academic year or semester.

Amount of award:	$3,000
Number of applicants:	150
Application deadline:	December 1, July 1

Contact:
Hopi Tribe Grants and Scholarship Program
P.O. Box 123
Kykotsmovi, AZ 86039
Phone: 800-762-9630
Fax: 928-734-9575

Hopi Education Award

Type of award: Scholarship, renewable.
Intended use: For undergraduate or graduate study at accredited 2-year, 4-year or graduate institution.
Eligibility: Applicant must be American Indian. Must be enrolled member of the Hopi Tribe.
Basis for selection: Applicant must demonstrate financial need.
Additional information: Entering freshmen must have minimum 2.5 GPA for high school coursework or minimum composite score of 45 percent on the GED Exam. Continuing students must have minimum 2.5 GPA for all college work. $3,000 may be awarded each semester. Four deadlines per year: November 1st (for winter quarter), December 1st (for spring), May 1st (for summer), and July 1st (for fall). Must reapply each academic year or semester.

Amount of award:	$1,000-$6,000
Number of applicants:	140
Application deadline:	December 1, July 1

Contact:
Hopi Tribe Grants and Scholarship Program
P.O. Box 123
Kykotsmovi, AZ 86039
Phone: 800-762-9630
Fax: 928-734-9575

Hopi Tribal Priority Award

Type of award: Scholarship, renewable.
Intended use: For full-time junior, senior or graduate study at accredited 4-year or graduate institution.
Eligibility: Applicant must be American Indian. Must be enrolled member of the Hopi Tribe.

Basis for selection: Applicant must demonstrate high academic achievement, depth of character, leadership and seriousness of purpose.
Application requirements: Recommendations, transcript, proof of eligibility.
Additional information: Award is based on amount of college cost. Preference given to those majoring in fields considered to be of tribal priority. Applicant must have college submit financial needs analysis to determine amount of award.

Amount of award:	Full tuition
Number of awards:	5
Number of applicants:	2
Application deadline:	July 1

Contact:
Hopi Tribe Grants and Scholarship Program
P.O. Box 123
Kykotsmovi, AZ 86039
Phone: 800-762-9630
Fax: 928-734-9575

Horatio Alger Association

Horatio Alger Ak-Sar-Ben Scholarship Program

Type of award: Scholarship.
Intended use: For full-time undergraduate study at accredited 2-year or 4-year institution in United States.
Eligibility: Applicant must be high school senior. Applicant must be U.S. citizen residing in Iowa or Nebraska.
Basis for selection: Applicant must demonstrate financial need, high academic achievement, seriousness of purpose and service orientation.
Application requirements: Essay, transcript. Letter of support, income statement.
Additional information: Minimum 2.0 GPA. Program assists high school seniors who have faced and overcome great obstacles and have participated in co-curricular and community activities. Must plan to pursue bachelor's degree. See Website for application and list of eligible Iowa counties.

Amount of award:	$5,000
Number of awards:	50
Application deadline:	October 30

Contact:
Horatio Alger Association
99 Canal Center Plaza, Suite 320
Alexandria, VA 22314
Phone: 703-684-9444
Fax: 703-684-9445
Web: www.horatioalger.org/scholarships

Horatio Alger Arizona Scholarship

Type of award: Scholarship.
Intended use: For full-time freshman study at 2-year or 4-year institution in United States.
Eligibility: Applicant must be high school senior. Applicant must be U.S. citizen residing in Arizona.
Basis for selection: Applicant must demonstrate financial need, high academic achievement, seriousness of purpose and service orientation.
Application requirements: Essay, transcript. Letter of support, income statement.

Additional information: Minimum 2.0 GPA. Program assists high school seniors who have faced and overcome great obstacles and have participated in co-curricular and community activities. Must plan to pursue bachelor's degree.

Amount of award:	$5,000
Number of awards:	50
Application deadline:	October 30

Contact:
Horatio Alger Association
99 Canal Center Plaza, Suite 320
Alexandria, VA 22314
Phone: 703-684-9444
Fax: 703-684-9445
Web: www.horatioalger.org/scholarships

Horatio Alger California Scholarship Program

Type of award: Scholarship.
Intended use: For full-time undergraduate study at accredited 2-year or 4-year institution in United States.
Eligibility: Applicant must be high school senior. Applicant must be U.S. citizen residing in California.
Basis for selection: Applicant must demonstrate financial need, high academic achievement, seriousness of purpose and service orientation.
Application requirements: Essay, transcript. Letter of support, income statement.
Additional information: Minimum 2.0 GPA. Program assists high school seniors who have faced and overcome great obstacles and have participated in co-curricular and community activities. Applicant should have strong commitment to use college degree in service to others. Must plan to pursue bachelor's degree. See Website for application.

Amount of award:	$4,000
Number of awards:	37
Application deadline:	October 30

Contact:
Horatio Alger Association
99 Canal Center Plaza, Suite 320
Alexandria, VA 22314
Phone: 703-684-9444
Fax: 703-684-9445
Web: www.horatioalger.org/scholarships

Horatio Alger Delaware Scholarship Program

Type of award: Scholarship.
Intended use: For full-time undergraduate study at accredited 2-year or 4-year institution in United States.
Eligibility: Applicant must be high school senior. Applicant must be U.S. citizen residing in Delaware.
Basis for selection: Applicant must demonstrate financial need, high academic achievement and service orientation.
Application requirements: Essay, transcript. Letter of support, income statement.
Additional information: Minimum 2.0 GPA. Program assists high school seniors who have faced and overcome great obstacles and have participated in co-curricular and community activities. Must plan to pursue bachelor's degree. See Website for application.

Amount of award:	$5,000
Number of awards:	5
Application deadline:	October 30

Contact:
Horatio Alger Association
99 Canal Center Drive, Suite 320
Alexandria, VA 22314
Phone: 703-684-9444
Fax: 703-684-9445
Web: www.horatioalger.org/scholarships

Horatio Alger District of Columbia, Maryland and Virginia Scholarship Program

Type of award: Scholarship.
Intended use: For full-time undergraduate study at accredited 2-year or 4-year institution in United States.
Eligibility: Applicant must be high school senior. Applicant must be U.S. citizen residing in District of Columbia.
Basis for selection: Applicant must demonstrate financial need, high academic achievement, seriousness of purpose and service orientation.
Application requirements: Essay, transcript. Letter of support, income statement.
Additional information: Minimum 2.0 GPA. Applicant must reside in D.C. metro area. Program assists high school seniors who have faced and overcome great obstacles and have participated in co-curricular and community activities. See Website for list of eligible counties. Must plan to pursue bachelor's degree. See Website for application.

Amount of award:	$2,500
Number of awards:	25
Application deadline:	October 30

Contact:
Horatio Alger Association
99 Canal Center Plaza, Suite 320
Alexandria, VA 22314
Phone: 703-684-9444
Fax: 703-684-9445
Web: www.horatioalger.com/scholarships/

Horatio Alger Franklin Scholarship

Type of award: Scholarship.
Intended use: For full-time undergraduate study at accredited 2-year or 4-year institution in United States.
Eligibility: Applicant must be high school senior. Applicant must be U.S. citizen residing in Pennsylvania.
Basis for selection: Applicant must demonstrate financial need, high academic achievement, seriousness of purpose and service orientation.
Application requirements: Essay, transcript. Letter of support, income statement.
Additional information: Minimum 2.0 GPA. Program assists high school seniors who have faced and overcome great obstacles and have participated in co-curricular and community activities. Must plan to pursue bachelor's degree. Visit Website for application.

Amount of award:	$10,000
Number of awards:	25
Application deadline:	October 30

Contact:
Horatio Alger Association
99 Canal Center Plaza, Suite 320
Alexandria, VA 22314
Phone: 703-684-9444
Fax: 703-684-9445
Web: www.horatioalger.org/scholarships

Horatio Alger Georgia Scholarship Program

Type of award: Scholarship.
Intended use: For full-time undergraduate study at accredited 2-year or 4-year institution in United States.
Eligibility: Applicant must be high school senior. Applicant must be U.S. citizen residing in Georgia.
Basis for selection: Applicant must demonstrate financial need, high academic achievement, seriousness of purpose and service orientation.
Application requirements: Essay, transcript. Letter of support, income statement.
Additional information: Minimum 2.0 GPA. Program assists high school seniors who have faced and overcome great obstacles and have participated in co-curricular and community activities. Preference given to students who reside in Walker and Catoosa counties. Must plan to pursue bachelor's degree. Visit Website for application.

Amount of award:	$5,000
Number of awards:	50
Application deadline:	October 30

Contact:
Horatio Alger Assocation
99 Canal Center Plaza, Suite 320
Alexandria, VA 22314
Phone: 703-684-9444
Fax: 703-684-9445
Web: www.horatioalger.org/scholarships

Horatio Alger Idaho Scholarship Program

Type of award: Scholarship.
Intended use: For full-time undergraduate study in United States. Designated institutions: University of Idaho, North Idaho College, and Lewis-Clark State College (Coeur d'Alene or Lewiston).
Eligibility: Applicant must be high school senior. Applicant must be U.S. citizen residing in Idaho.
Basis for selection: Applicant must demonstrate financial need, high academic achievement, depth of character and service orientation.
Application requirements: Essay, transcript. Letter of support, income statement.
Additional information: Program assists high school seniors who have faced and overcome great obstacles and have participated in co-curricular and community activities. Must attend high school in Benewah, Boundary, Bonner, Kootenai, or Latah, or Shoshone counties. Must plan to pursue bachelor's degree. See Website for application, county eligibility, and additional information.

Amount of award:	$5,000
Number of awards:	25
Application deadline:	October 30

Contact:
Horatio Alger Association
99 Canal Center Plaza, Suite 320
Alexandria, VA 22314
Phone: 703-684-9444
Fax: 703-684-9445
Web: www.horatioalger.org/scholarships

Horatio Alger Illinois Scholarship Program

Type of award: Scholarship.
Intended use: For full-time undergraduate study at accredited 2-year or 4-year institution in United States.
Eligibility: Applicant must be high school senior. Applicant must be U.S. citizen residing in Illinois.
Basis for selection: Applicant must demonstrate financial need, high academic achievement and service orientation.
Application requirements: Essay, transcript. Letter of support, income statement.
Additional information: Minimum 2.0 GPA. Program assists high school seniors who have faced and overcome great obstacles and have participated in co-curricular and community activities. Must plan to pursue bachelor's degree. Visit Website for application.

Amount of award:	$5,000
Number of awards:	25
Application deadline:	October 30

Contact:
Horatio Alger Association
99 Canal Center Plaza, Suite 320
Alexandria, VA 22314
Phone: 703-684-9444
Fax: 703-684-9445
Web: www.horatioalger.org/scholarships

Horatio Alger Louisiana Scholarship Program

Type of award: Scholarship.
Intended use: For full-time undergraduate study at accredited 2-year or 4-year institution in United States. Designated institutions: Louisiana colleges and universities.
Eligibility: Applicant must be high school senior. Applicant must be U.S. citizen residing in Louisiana.
Basis for selection: Applicant must demonstrate financial need, high academic achievement, seriousness of purpose and service orientation.
Application requirements: Essay, transcript. Letter of support, income statement.
Additional information: Minimum 2.0 GPA. Program assists high school seniors who have faced and overcome great obstacles and have participated in co-curricular and community activities. Must plan to pursue bachelor's degree. See Website for application.

Amount of award:	$10,500
Number of awards:	25
Application deadline:	October 30

Contact:
Horatio Alger Association
99 Canal Center Plaza, Suite 320
Alexandria, VA 22314
Phone: 703-684-9444
Fax: 703-684-9445
Web: www.horatioalger.org/scholarships

Horatio Alger Minnesota Scholarship Program

Type of award: Scholarship.
Intended use: For full-time undergraduate study at accredited 2-year or 4-year institution in United States.
Eligibility: Applicant must be high school senior. Applicant must be U.S. citizen residing in Minnesota.

Basis for selection: Applicant must demonstrate financial need, high academic achievement and service orientation.
Application requirements: Essay, transcript. Letter of support, income statement.
Additional information: Minimum 2.0 GPA. Program assists high school seniors who have faced and overcome great obstacles and have participated in co-curricular and community activities. Must plan to pursue bachelor's degree. Applicant must be resident of Anoka, Carver, Dakota, Hennepin, Ramsey, Scott, or Washington counties. See Website for application.

Amount of award:	$4,000
Number of awards:	42
Application deadline:	October 30

Contact:
Horatio Alger Association
99 Canal Center Plaza, Suite 320
Alexandria, VA 22314
Phone: 703-684-9444
Fax: 703-684-9445
Web: www.horatioalger.org/scholarships

Horatio Alger Missouri Scholarship Program

Type of award: Scholarship.
Intended use: For full-time undergraduate study at accredited 2-year or 4-year institution in United States.
Eligibility: Applicant must be high school senior. Applicant must be U.S. citizen residing in Missouri.
Basis for selection: Applicant must demonstrate financial need, high academic achievement, seriousness of purpose and service orientation.
Application requirements: Essay, transcript. Letter of support, income statement.
Additional information: Minimum 2.0 GPA. Program assists high school seniors who have faced and overcome great obstacles and have participated in co-curricular and community activities. Must plan to pursue bachelor's degree. See Website for application.

Amount of award:	$5,000
Number of awards:	50
Application deadline:	October 30

Contact:
Horatio Alger Association
99 Canal Center Plaza, Suite 320
Alexandria, VA 22314
Phone: 703-684-9444
Fax: 703-684-9445
Web: www.horatioalger.org/scholarships

Horatio Alger Montana Scholarship Program

Type of award: Scholarship.
Intended use: For full-time undergraduate study in United States. Designated institutions: University of Montana institutions.
Eligibility: Applicant must be high school senior. Applicant must be U.S. citizen residing in Montana.
Basis for selection: Applicant must demonstrate financial need, high academic achievement and service orientation.
Application requirements: Essay, transcript. Letter of support, income statement.
Additional information: Minimum 2.0 GPA. Program assists high school seniors who have faced and overcome great obstacles and have participated in co-curricular and community

activities. Must plan to pursue bachelor's degree. See Website for application.

Amount of award:	$5,000
Number of awards:	50
Application deadline:	October 30

Contact:
Horatio Alger Association
99 Canal Center Plaza, Suite 320
Alexandria, VA 22314
Phone: 703-684-9444
Fax: 703-684-9445
Web: www.horatioalger.org/scholarships

Horatio Alger National Scholarship

Type of award: Scholarship.
Intended use: For full-time undergraduate study at accredited 2-year or 4-year institution in United States.
Eligibility: Applicant must be high school senior. Applicant must be U.S. citizen.
Basis for selection: Based on co-curricular and community activities. Applicant must demonstrate financial need, high academic achievement, seriousness of purpose and service orientation.
Application requirements: Essay, transcript. Letter of support, income statement.
Additional information: Minimum 2.0 GPA. Program assists high school seniors who have faced and overcome great obstacles and have participated in co-curricular and community activities. Must plan to pursue bachelor's degree. Visit Website for application.

Amount of award:	$20,000
Number of awards:	104
Application deadline:	October 30

Contact:
Horatio Alger Association
99 Canal Center Plaza, Suite 320
Alexandria, VA 22314
Phone: 703-684-9444
Fax: 703-684-9445
Web: www.horatioalger.org/scholarships

Horatio Alger North Dakota Scholarship Program

Type of award: Scholarship.
Intended use: For full-time undergraduate study at accredited 2-year or 4-year institution in United States.
Eligibility: Applicant must be high school senior. Applicant must be U.S. citizen residing in North Dakota.
Basis for selection: Applicant must demonstrate financial need, high academic achievement, seriousness of purpose and service orientation.
Application requirements: Essay, transcript. Letter of support, income statement.
Additional information: Minimum 2.0 GPA. Program assists high school seniors who have faced and overcome great obstacles and have participated in co-curricular and community activities. Must plan to pursue bachelor's degree. Visit Website for application.

Amount of award:	$5,000
Number of awards:	25
Application deadline:	October 30

Contact:
Horatio Alger Association
99 Canal Center Plaza, Suite 320
Alexandria, VA 22314
Phone: 703-684-9444
Fax: 703-684-9445
Web: www.horatioalger.org/scholarships

Horatio Alger Pennsylvania Scholarship Program

Type of award: Scholarship.
Intended use: For full-time undergraduate study at accredited 2-year or 4-year institution in United States.
Eligibility: Applicant must be high school senior. Applicant must be U.S. citizen residing in Pennsylvania.
Basis for selection: Applicant must demonstrate financial need, high academic achievement and service orientation.
Application requirements: Essay, transcript. Letter of support, income statement.
Additional information: Minimum 2.0 GPA. Program assists high school seniors who have faced and overcome great obstacles and have participated in co-curricular and community activities. Must plan to pursue bachelor's degree. See Website for application.

Amount of award:	$5,000
Number of awards:	50
Application deadline:	October 30

Contact:
Horatio Alger Association
99 Canal Center Drive, Suite 320
Alexandria, VA 22314
Phone: 703-684-9444
Fax: 703-684-9445
Web: www.horatioalger.org/scholarships

Horatio Alger South Dakota Scholarship Program

Type of award: Scholarship.
Intended use: For full-time undergraduate study at accredited 2-year or 4-year institution in United States.
Eligibility: Applicant must be high school senior. Applicant must be U.S. citizen residing in South Dakota.
Basis for selection: Applicant must demonstrate financial need, high academic achievement, seriousness of purpose and service orientation.
Application requirements: Essay, transcript. Letter of support, income statement.
Additional information: Minimum 2.0 GPA. Program assists high school seniors who have faced and overcome great obstacles and have participated in co-curricular and community activities. Must plan to pursue bachelor's degree. See Website for application and more information.

Amount of award:	$5,000
Number of awards:	25
Application deadline:	October 30

Contact:
The Horatio Alger Association
99 Canal Center Plaza, Suite 320
Alexandria, VA 22314
Phone: 703-684-9444
Fax: 703-684-9445
Web: www.horatioalger.org/scholarships

Scholarships

Horatio Alger Texas Ft. Worth Scholarship Program

Type of award: Scholarship.
Intended use: For full-time undergraduate study at accredited 2-year or 4-year institution in United States.
Eligibility: Applicant must be high school senior. Applicant must be U.S. citizen residing in Texas.
Basis for selection: Applicant must demonstrate financial need, high academic achievement, seriousness of purpose and service orientation.
Application requirements: Essay, transcript. Letter of support, income statement.
Additional information: Minimum 2.0 GPA. Applicant must reside in Forth Worth, Texas. Program assists high school seniors who have faced and overcome great obstacles and have participated in co-curricular and community activities. Must plan to pursue bachelor's degree. Visit Website for application.

Amount of award:	$5,000
Number of awards:	12
Application deadline:	October 30

Contact:
Horatio Alger Assocation
99 Canal Center Plaza, Suite 320
Alexandria, VA 22314
Phone: 703-684-9444
Fax: 703-684-9445
Web: www.horatioalger.org/scholarships

Horatio Alger Texas Scholarship Program

Type of award: Scholarship.
Intended use: For full-time undergraduate study at accredited 2-year or 4-year institution in United States.
Eligibility: Applicant must be high school senior. Applicant must be U.S. citizen residing in Texas.
Basis for selection: Applicant must demonstrate financial need, high academic achievement, depth of character and service orientation.
Application requirements: Essay, transcript. Letter of support, income statement.
Additional information: Program assists high school seniors who have faced and overcome great obstacles and have participated in co-curricular and community activities. Must plan to pursue bachelor's degree. See Website for application.

Amount of award:	$5,000
Number of awards:	7
Application deadline:	October 30

Contact:
Horatio Alger Association
99 Canal Center Plaza, Suite 320
Alexandria, VA 22314
Phone: 703-684-9444
Fax: 703-684-9445
Web: www.horatioalger.org/scholarships

Horatio Alger Utah Scholarship Program

Type of award: Scholarship.
Intended use: For full-time undergraduate study at accredited 2-year or 4-year institution in United States.
Eligibility: Applicant must be high school senior. Applicant must be U.S. citizen residing in Utah.

Basis for selection: Applicant must demonstrate financial need, high academic achievement, seriousness of purpose and service orientation.
Application requirements: Essay, transcript. Letter of support, income statement.
Additional information: Minimum 2.0 GPA. Program assists high school seniors who have faced and overcome great obstacles and have participated in co-curricular and community activities. Must plan to pursue bachelor's degree. Visit Website for application.

Amount of award:	$5,000
Number of awards:	25
Application deadline:	October 30

Contact:
Horatio Alger Association
99 Canal Center Plaza, Suite 320
Alexandria, VA 22314
Phone: 703-684-9444
Fax: 703-684-9445
Web: www.horatioalger.org/scholarships

Horatio Alger Wyoming Scholarship Program

Type of award: Scholarship.
Intended use: For full-time undergraduate study at accredited 2-year or 4-year institution in United States.
Eligibility: Applicant must be high school senior. Applicant must be U.S. citizen residing in Wyoming.
Basis for selection: Applicant must demonstrate financial need, high academic achievement, seriousness of purpose and service orientation.
Application requirements: Essay, transcript. Letter of support, income statement.
Additional information: Minimum 2.0 GPA. Program assists high school seniors who have faced and overcome great obstacles and have participated in co-curricular and community activities. Must plan to pursue bachelor's degree. Visit Website for application.

Amount of award:	$5,000
Number of awards:	25
Application deadline:	October 30

Contact:
Horatio Alger Association
99 Canal Center Plaza, Suite 320
Alexandria, VA 22314
Phone: 703-684-9444
Fax: 703-684-9445
Web: www.horatioalger.org/scholarships

Horticultural Research Institute

Carville M. Akehurst Memorial Scholarship

Type of award: Scholarship.
Intended use: For full-time junior or senior study at accredited 2-year, 4-year or graduate institution.
Eligibility: Applicant must be residing in Virginia, West Virginia or Maryland.

Basis for selection: Major/career interest in horticulture or landscape architecture. Applicant must demonstrate high academic achievement.

Application requirements: Recommendations, essay, transcript. Resume.

Additional information: Minimum 2.7 overall GPA and minimum 3.0 in major. Must have junior standing in four-year curriculum or senior standing in two-year curriculum. Preference given to applicants who plan to work within industry following graduation. Previous winners eligible for additional funding. Visit Website for application and more information.

Amount of award:	$2,000
Number of awards:	1
Number of applicants:	10
Application deadline:	May 31
Total amount awarded:	$4,000

Contact:
Horticultural Research Institute
1000 Vermont Avenue NW
Suite 300
Washington, DC 20005-4914
Phone: 202-789-2900
Fax: 202-478-7288
Web: www.hriresearch.org

Horticultural Research Institute Spring Meadow Scholarship

Type of award: Scholarship.

Intended use: For full-time undergraduate study at accredited vocational, 2-year, 4-year or graduate institution.

Basis for selection: Major/career interest in horticulture or landscape architecture.

Application requirements: Recommendations, essay, transcript. Resume.

Additional information: Must have minimum 2.25 overall GPA, and minimum 2.7 in major. Must be enrolled in accredited landscape, horticulture or related program. Must be interested in woody plant production, propogation, and breeding or horticulture sales and marketing. Preference given to those who plan to work in industry following graduation. Visit Website for application and more information.

Amount of award:	$1,500
Number of awards:	1
Number of applicants:	69
Application deadline:	May 31
Total amount awarded:	$2,500

Contact:
Horticultural Research Institute
1000 Vermont Avenue NW
Suite 300
Washington, DC 20005-4914
Phone: 202-789-2900
Fax: 202-478-7288
Web: www.hriresearch.org

Muggets Scholarship

Type of award: Scholarship, renewable.

Intended use: For full-time undergraduate or graduate study at vocational, 2-year, 4-year or graduate institution in United States. Designated institutions: California state colleges and universities.

Eligibility: Applicant must be residing in California.

Basis for selection: Major/career interest in landscape architecture or horticulture.

Application requirements: Recommendations, essay, transcript. Cover letter and resume.

Additional information: Students enrolled in vocational agricultural programs also eligible. Preference given to applicants who plan to work within the industry after graduation. Minimum 2.5 GPA overall; minimum 2.7 GPA in major. Visit Website for application.

Amount of award:	$1,000
Number of awards:	1
Application deadline:	May 31

Contact:
Endowment Program Administrator, Horticultural Research Institute
1000 Vermont Ave. NW
Suite 300
Washington, DC 20005-4914
Phone: 202-789-5980 ext. 3014
Fax: 202-478-7288
Web: www.hriresearch.org

Timothy S. and Palmer W. Bigelow Scholarship

Type of award: Scholarship.

Intended use: For full-time undergraduate or graduate study at accredited 2-year, 4-year or graduate institution.

Eligibility: Applicant must be residing in Vermont, New Hampshire, Connecticut, Maine, Massachusetts or Rhode Island.

Basis for selection: Major/career interest in landscape architecture or horticulture. Applicant must demonstrate financial need, high academic achievement, depth of character and seriousness of purpose.

Application requirements: Recommendations, essay, transcript. Resume and cover letter.

Additional information: Minimum 2.25 GPA for undergraduates and 3.0 GPA for graduate students. Must be enrolled in accredited landscape or horticulture program. Applicant must have senior standing in two-year program, junior standing in four-year program, or graduate standing. Applicant must be resident of one of the six New England states, but need not attend institution there. Preference given to applicants who plan to work with industry after graduation. Preference also given to applicants who demonstrate financial need. Visit Website for application.

Amount of award:	$1,000-$3,500
Number of awards:	1
Number of applicants:	8
Application deadline:	May 31
Notification begins:	July 1
Total amount awarded:	$1,750

Contact:
Horticultural Research Institute
1000 Vermont Ave. NW
Suite 300
Washington, DC 20005-4914
Phone: 202-789-2900 ext. 3014
Fax: 202-478-7288
Web: www.hriresearch.org

Houston Livestock Show and Rodeo

Area Go Texan Scholarships

Type of award: Scholarship.
Intended use: For undergraduate study at postsecondary institution. Designated institutions: Texas colleges and universities.
Eligibility: Applicant must be high school senior. Applicant must be U.S. citizen residing in Texas.
Basis for selection: Applicant must demonstrate financial need, high academic achievement, depth of character, leadership and service orientation.
Application requirements: Recommendations, essay, transcript, proof of eligibility. Class standing and photograph. SAT/ACT scores.
Additional information: Scholarships awarded to one eligible public high school student from each of 60 Area Go Texan counties. Minimum 1350 SAT combined score, or minimum 19 ACT score. Applicant must attend public high school and be in top third of graduating class. Applicant cannot receive more than $40,000 from financial aid or other scholarships. Contact sponsor or visit Website for eligible counties, deadline, and application.

Amount of award:	$15,000
Number of awards:	70

Contact:
Houston Livestock Show and Rodeo
Office of Education Programs
P.O. Box 20070
Houston, TX 77225-0070
Phone: 832-667-1000
Web: http://www99.rodeohouston.com/about/scholarship/s-go-texan.aspx

Metropolitan Scholarships

Type of award: Scholarship, renewable.
Intended use: For undergraduate study at accredited 4-year institution in United States. Designated institutions: Colleges and universities in Texas.
Eligibility: Applicant must be high school senior. Applicant must be U.S. citizen residing in Texas.
Basis for selection: Applicant must demonstrate financial need, high academic achievement, depth of character and leadership.
Application requirements: Recommendations, essay, transcript. SAT/ACT Scores.
Additional information: Must be graduating from Houston-area public school districts in Brazoria, Chambers, Fort Bend, Galveston, Harris, Liberty, Montgomery, and Waller Counties. Must be in top quarter of graduating class and have minimum 1350 SAT or 19 ACT score.

Amount of award:	$3,750
Number of awards:	221

Contact:
Houston Livestock Show and Rodeo
Office of Education Programs
P.O. Box 20070
Houston, TX 77225-0070
Phone: 832-667-1000
Web: www99.rodeohouston.com/about/scholarship/s-metropolitan.aspx

Opportunity Scholarship

Type of award: Scholarship, renewable.
Intended use: For full-time undergraduate study at 4-year institution. Designated institutions: Texas colleges and universities.
Eligibility: Applicant must be high school senior. Applicant must be U.S. citizen residing in Texas.
Basis for selection: Applicant must demonstrate financial need, high academic achievement, depth of character, leadership and service orientation.
Application requirements: Recommendations, transcript, proof of eligibility. Up to three references. Two-page essay must describe importance of college and career goals. Class standing and photograph. SAT/ACT scores.
Additional information: Must have minimum 1210 SAT or 17 ACT. Must be graduating in top half of class from specified Texas school districts in Brazoria, Chambers, Fort Bend, Galveston, Harris, Liberty, Montgomery, or Waller counties. Visit Website for list of eligible districts, application, and more information. For applications, contact guidance counselor or Office of Education Programs.

Amount of award:	$15,000
Number of awards:	106
Total amount awarded:	$1,500,000

Contact:
Houston Livestock Show and Rodeo
Office of Education Programs
P.O. Box 20070
Houston, TX 77225-0070
Phone: 832-667-1000
Web: www99.rodeohouston.com/about/scholarship/s-opportunity.aspx

School Art Scholarships

Type of award: Scholarship, renewable.
Intended use: For undergraduate study at accredited 4-year institution in United States. Designated institutions: Colleges and universities in Texas.
Eligibility: Applicant must be high school senior. Applicant must be U.S. citizen or international student residing in Texas.
Basis for selection: Applicant must demonstrate financial need, high academic achievement, depth of character and leadership.
Application requirements: Recommendations, essay, transcript. SAT/ACT scores.
Additional information: Must attend accredited public high school that participates in School Art Program of the Houston Livestock Show and Rodeo. Must be in top quarter of class and have minimum 1350 SAT or 19 ACT score. Visit Website for deadline.

Amount of award:	$3,750
Number of awards:	15

Contact:
Houston Livestock Show and Rodeo
Office of Education Programs
P.O. Box 20070
Houston, TX 77225-0070
Phone: 832-667-1000
Web: www99.rodeohouston.com/about/scholarship/s-school-art.aspx

ICMA Retirement Corporation

Vantagepoint Public Employee Memorial Scholarship Fund

Type of award: Scholarship.
Intended use: For full-time undergraduate or graduate study at accredited postsecondary institution.
Basis for selection: Applicant must demonstrate financial need, high academic achievement, leadership and service orientation.
Application requirements: Recommendations, essay, transcript, proof of eligibility. Statement of goals and aspirations, official letter from deceased employee's place of work certifying employee died in line of duty.
Additional information: High school seniors and graduates, as well as current undergraduate or graduate students eligible. Must be child or spouse of deceased local or state government employee who has died in the line of duty. Work experience, goals and aspirations, and unusual personal or family circumstances also factored into selection. Award amount varies; maximum is $10,000 (tuition and fees only). Visit Website for complete information and application.

Amount of award:	$10,000
Number of awards:	7
Number of applicants:	40
Application deadline:	March 15
Notification begins:	June 1
Total amount awarded:	$90,000

Contact:
Vantagepoint Public Employee Memorial Scholarship Program
c/o Scholarship America
One Scholarship Way, PO Box 297
St. Peter, MN 56082
Phone: 507-931-1682
Web: www.vantagescholar.org

Idaho State Board of Education

Grow Your Own Teacher Scholarship Program

Type of award: Scholarship.
Intended use: For undergraduate study at 2-year or 4-year institution. Designated institutions: Boise State University, Idaho State University, Lewis-Clark State College, College of Southern Idaho.
Eligibility: Applicant must be residing in Idaho.
Basis for selection: Major/career interest in education.
Application requirements: FAFSA.
Additional information: Program established to aid students becoming bilingual education, ESL and Native American teachers. Minimum 3.0 GPA. Award for part-time students based on credit hours. Contact college of education at intended institution of matriculation for more information.

Amount of award:	$3,000
Application deadline:	February 15

Contact:
Idaho State Board of Education
650 West State Street
P.O. Box 83720
Boise, ID 83720-0037
Phone: 208-332-1574
Web: www.boardofed.idaho.gov/scholarships

Idaho Governor's Cup Scholarship

Type of award: Scholarship, renewable.
Intended use: For full-time undergraduate study at postsecondary institution. Designated institutions: Idaho colleges and universities.
Eligibility: Applicant must be high school senior. Applicant must be residing in Idaho.
Basis for selection: Applicant must demonstrate high academic achievement, leadership and service orientation.
Application requirements: Recommendations, essay, transcript. SAT/ACT scores. Documentation of volunteer work, leadership, and public service.
Additional information: Minimum 2.8 GPA. Must have demonstrated commitment to public service. For more information, contact high school guidance counselor or Idaho State Board of Education.

Amount of award:	$3,000
Number of awards:	12
Application deadline:	January 15

Contact:
Idaho State Board of Education
650 West State Street
P.O. Box 83720
Boise, ID 83720-0037
Phone: 208-332-1574
Web: www.boardofed.idaho.gov/scholarships

Idaho Minority/"At-Risk" Scholarship

Type of award: Scholarship, renewable.
Intended use: For full-time undergraduate study at postsecondary institution. Designated institutions: Boise State University, Brigham Young University-Idaho, Idaho State University, North Idaho College, Eastern Idaho Technical College, Lewis-Clark State College, Northwest Nazarene University, University of Idaho, College of Southern Idaho, College of Western Idaho, The College of Idaho.
Eligibility: Applicant must be U.S. citizen residing in Idaho.
Basis for selection: Applicant must demonstrate financial need.
Additional information: Must be talented student at risk of failing to realize ambitions due to cultural, economic, or physical circumstances. Must be graduate of Idaho high school. Must meet three of the following criteria: be first-generation college student; be disabled; be migrant worker or dependent of one; have substantial financial need; be member of ethnic minority historically underrepresented in higher education in Idaho (of Native American, African American, or Hispanic American descent). Maximum award is $3,000. Contact high school counselor or financial aid office of participating postsecondary institutions for specific requirements and application.

Amount of award:	$3,000
Number of awards:	45
Total amount awarded:	$120,000

Contact:
Financial aid office at designated institution, or Dana Kelly.
Phone: 208-332-1574
Web: www.boardofed.idaho.gov/scholarships

Idaho Robert C. Byrd Scholarship

Type of award: Scholarship, renewable.
Intended use: For full-time freshman study at 2-year or 4-year institution.
Eligibility: Applicant must be high school senior. Applicant must be U.S. citizen or permanent resident residing in Idaho.
Basis for selection: Applicant must demonstrate high academic achievement.
Application requirements: Transcript, proof of eligibility. Statement of Selective Service registration status.
Additional information: Maximum award is $1,500 per year, renewable for up to four years. Visit Website or contact high school counselor for application, deadlines and more information.
  Amount of award: $1,500
  Application deadline: January 15
Contact:
Idaho State Board of Education
650 West State Street
P.O. Box 83720
Boise, ID 83720-0037
Phone: 208-332-1574
Web: www.boardofed.idaho.gov/scholarships

Leveraging Educational Assistance State Partnership Program (LEAP)

Type of award: Scholarship, renewable.
Intended use: For undergraduate or graduate study at vocational, 2-year, 4-year or graduate institution. Designated institutions: Eligible Idaho public and private colleges and universities.
Eligibility: Applicant must be U.S. citizen or permanent resident.
Basis for selection: Applicant must demonstrate financial need.
Application requirements: FAFSA.
Additional information: Formerly the Idaho State Student Incentive Grant. Institution makes recommendations to Idaho State Board of Education. Visit Website for list of eligible institutions. Contact financial aid office of institution for materials or additional information.
  Amount of award: $400-$5,000
Contact:
Financial aid offices at Idaho colleges
Phone: 208-332-1574
Web: www.boardofed.idaho.gov

Robert R. Lee Promise Category A Scholarship

Type of award: Scholarship, renewable.
Intended use: For full-time freshman study at postsecondary institution. Designated institutions: Idaho state-funded colleges and universities.
Eligibility: Applicant must be high school senior. Applicant must be residing in Idaho.
Additional information: Academic applicants must have minimum 28 ACT and 3.5 GPA, and be in top ten percent of graduating class. Applicants for professional-technical programs must have minimum 2.8 GPA and take COMPASS exam. Apply

online or contact Idaho State Board of Education for application.
  Amount of award: $3,000
  Number of awards: 25
  Number of applicants: 3,000
  Application deadline: January 15
  Total amount awarded: $75,000
Contact:
Dana Kelly, Idaho State Board of Education
650 West State Street
P.O. Box 83720
Boise, ID 83720-0037
Phone: 208-332-1574
Web: www.boardofed.idaho.gov/scholarships

Robert R. Lee Promise Category B Scholarship

Type of award: Scholarship, renewable.
Intended use: For full-time freshman study at postsecondary institution. Designated institutions: Boise State University, College of Southern Idaho, Eastern Idaho Technical College, Idaho State University, Lewis-Clark State College, North Idaho College, University of Idaho, Northwest Nazarene University, BYU-Idaho, The College of Idaho, College of Western Idaho.
Eligibility: Applicant must be no older than 21. Applicant must be residing in Idaho.
Additional information: Minimum 3.0 GPA or ACT score of 20. Must be younger than 22 on July 1 of academic term of award. Must have completed high school, or equivalent, in Idaho. For more information, contact college or university.
  Amount of award: $300
Contact:
Dana Kelly, Idaho State Board of Education
650 West State Street
P.O. Box 83720
Boise, ID 83720-0037
Phone: 208-332-1574
Web: www.boardofed.idaho.gov/scholarships

Illinois Department of Veterans' Affairs

MIA/POW Scholarship

Type of award: Scholarship, renewable.
Intended use: For full-time undergraduate study at accredited postsecondary institution in United States. Designated institutions: Illinois state-supported schools.
Eligibility: Applicant must be U.S. citizen. Applicant must be dependent of disabled veteran, deceased veteran or POW/MIA; or spouse of disabled veteran, deceased veteran or POW/MIA.
Application requirements: Proof of eligibility.
Additional information: Available to dependents of veterans who have been declared prisoners of war, missing in action, become permanently disabled, or have died due to service related disability. Veteran must have been Illinois resident within six months of entering service.
  Amount of award: Full tuition

Contact:
Illinois Department of Veterans' Affairs
833 South Spring Street
P.O. Box 19432
Springfield, IL 62794-9432
Phone: 217-782-6641
Web: www.veterans.illinois.gov/benefits

Illinois State Board of Education

Illinois General Assembly Legislative Scholarships

Type of award: Scholarship, renewable.
Intended use: For undergraduate study at accredited postsecondary institution in United States. Designated institutions: Illinois state-supported universities.
Eligibility: Applicant must be U.S. citizen residing in Illinois.
Application requirements: Nomination by member of Illinois General Assembly.
Additional information: Each member of General Assembly annually awards two scholarships from his or her district. Contact your County Clerk's Election office to determine the name and phone number of your legislators. Student must be resident of legislative district of the awarding legislator.

    Amount of award: Full tuition
Contact:
Contact your state senator and state representative for application.
Web: www.isbe.state.il.us

Illinois Student Assistance Commission

Bonus Incentive Grant (BIG)

Type of award: Scholarship.
Intended use: For undergraduate study at 2-year or 4-year institution in United States. Designated institutions: Approved Illinois public and private colleges, universities, and hospital schools.
Eligibility: Applicant must be U.S. citizen or permanent resident residing in Illinois.
Additional information: Bonus Incentive Grants are non-need based grants available to beneficiaries of Illinois College Savings Bonds, if at least 70 percent of bond proceeds are used for costs at eligible institution. Must have owned bond for at least 12 consecutive months. Grant amounts range from $40 to $440 per bond. Grants can be used for educational purposes only. Not for use at religious institutions, for divinity programs, or for studies in preparation for the priesthood, regardless of denomination or faith. Contact sponsor for more information, or visit Website.

    Amount of award: $40-$440
    Number of awards: 427
    Total amount awarded: $322,220

Contact:
Illinois Student Assistance Commission
ISAC College Zone Counselor
1755 Lake Cook Road
Deerfield, IL 60015
Phone: 800-899-ISAC
Web: www.collegezone.com

Grant Program for Dependents of Correctional Officers

Type of award: Scholarship, renewable.
Intended use: For freshman study at 2-year or 4-year institution in United States. Designated institutions: ISAC-approved institutions in Illinois.
Eligibility: Applicant must be U.S. citizen or permanent resident. Applicant's parent must have been killed or disabled in work-related accident as public safety officer.
Application requirements: Proof of eligibility.
Additional information: Must be child or spouse of Illinois corrections officer killed or at least 90 percent disabled in line of duty. Award is equal to full tuition and mandatory fees at public Illinois institutions; at private schools a corresponding amount is awarded. Applicant need not be Illinois resident at time of enrollment. Beneficiaries may receive the equivalent of eight semesters or 12 quarters of assistance. Contact ISAC or visit Website for additional information.

    Amount of award: Full tuition
    Number of awards: 74
    Total amount awarded: $469,426

Contact:
Illinois Student Assistance Commission
ISAC College Zone Counselor
1755 Lake Cook Road
Deerfield, IL 60015
Phone: 800-899-ISAC
Web: www.collegezone.com

Grant Program for Dependents of Police or Fire Officers

Type of award: Scholarship, renewable.
Intended use: For undergraduate or graduate study at 2-year, 4-year or graduate institution. Designated institutions: ISAC-approved institutions in Illinois.
Eligibility: Applicant must be U.S. citizen or permanent resident. Applicant's parent must have been killed or disabled in work-related accident as firefighter or police officer.
Application requirements: Proof of eligibility.
Additional information: Grant for tuition and fees for spouses and children of Illinois policemen or firemen killed or at least 90 percent disabled in line of duty. Award amount adjusted annually. Applicant need not be Illinois resident at time of enrollment. Beneficiaries may receive the equivalent of eight semesters or 12 quarters of assistance. Contact ISAC or visit Website for additional information.

    Amount of award: Full tuition
    Number of awards: 69
    Application deadline: October 1
    Total amount awarded: $349,997

Contact:
Illinois Student Assistance Commission
ISAC College Zone Counselor
1755 Lake Cook Road
Deerfield, IL 60015
Phone: 800-899-ISAC
Web: www.collegezone.com

Higher Education License Plate (HELP) Program

Type of award: Scholarship.
Intended use: For undergraduate study at accredited postsecondary institution in United States. Designated institutions: Participating Illinois universities.
Eligibility: Applicant must be U.S. citizen.
Application requirements: FAFSA.
Additional information: Provides grants to students who attend Illinois colleges for which collegiate license plates are available. Contact your college to determine if it participates in the HELP program. Number and amount of awards contingent on number of license plates sold.
Contact:
Illinois Student Assistance Commission
1755 Lake Cook Road
Deerfield, IL 60015
Phone: 800-899-ISAC
Web: www.collegezone.com

Illinois Future Teacher Corps

Type of award: Scholarship, renewable.
Intended use: For junior, senior or graduate study at accredited 2-year or 4-year institution. Designated institutions: Approved Illinois public and private four-year colleges and universities offering teacher program, and certain other degree-granting institutions.
Eligibility: Applicant must be U.S. citizen or permanent resident residing in Illinois.
Basis for selection: Major/career interest in education; education, teacher or education, early childhood. Applicant must demonstrate financial need and high academic achievement.
Application requirements: FAFSA and Teacher Education Program Application.
Additional information: Scholarships for students planning to pursue careers as preschool, elementary school, and secondary school teachers in Illinois. Priority given to students with financial need, minority students, and students planning to teach in teacher shortage discipline and/or hard-to-staff school. Must fulfill teaching commitment or scholarship becomes loan. Minimum 2.5 GPA. See Website for application.
Amount of award:	$5,000-$10,000
Number of awards:	549
Application deadline:	March 1
Total amount awarded:	$3,823,541
Contact:
Illinois Student Assistance Commission
ISAC College Zone Counselor
1755 Lake Cook Road
Deerfield, IL 60015
Phone: 800-899-ISAC
Web: www.collegezone.com

Illinois National Guard Grant

Type of award: Scholarship, renewable.
Intended use: For undergraduate or graduate study at 2-year or 4-year institution. Designated institutions: Approved Illinois institutions.
Eligibility: Applicant must be residing in Illinois. Applicant must be in military service in the Reserves/National Guard. Must have served at least one year of active duty in Illinois National Guard or Naval Militia.
Application requirements: Proof of eligibility.

Additional information: Available to enlisted and company grade officers up to rank of captain who have either served one year active duty; are currently on active duty status; or have been active for at least five consecutive years and have been called to federal active duty for at least six months and be within 12 months after discharge date. Applied toward tuition and certain fees. Recipients may use award for eight semesters or 12 quarters (or the equivalent). Award amount varies. Deadlines: 10/1 for full year, 3/1 for second/third term, and 6/15 for summer term. Applications available from ISAC or National Guard units. Contact ISAC or National Guard units or visit Website for additional information.
Number of awards:	1,897
Application deadline:	October 1
Total amount awarded:	$4,470,595
Contact:
Illinois Student Assistance Commission
ISAC College Zone Counselor
1755 Lake Cook Road
Deerfield, IL 60015
Phone: 800-899-ISAC
Web: www.collegezone.com

Illinois Veteran Grant (IVG) Program

Type of award: Scholarship, renewable.
Intended use: For undergraduate or graduate study at postsecondary institution.
Eligibility: Applicant must be U.S. citizen or permanent resident residing in Illinois. Applicant must be veteran. Must have been Illinois resident or Illinois college student six months prior to entering service and must have returned to Illinois to reside within six months of leaving service. Must have served one year of federal active duty or have served in a foreign country in a time of hostilities in that country.
Application requirements: Proof of eligibility.
Additional information: Provides payment of tuition and mandatory fees to qualified Illinois veterans or military service members. Grant is available for equivalent of four academic years of full-time enrollment for undergraduate and graduate study. Recipient not required to enroll for minimum number of credit hours each term. One-time application only. See Website for additional information and application.
Amount of award:	Full tuition
Number of awards:	11,462
Total amount awarded:	$19,223,139
Contact:
Illinois Student Assistance Commission
ISAC College Zone Counselor
1755 Lake Cook Road
Deerfield, IL 60015
Phone: 800-899-ISAC
Web: www.collegezone.com

Minority Teachers of Illinois Scholarship

Type of award: Scholarship, renewable.
Intended use: For undergraduate or graduate study at postsecondary institution. Designated institutions: ISAC-approved institutions in Illinois.
Eligibility: Applicant must be Alaskan native, Asian American, African American, Mexican American, Hispanic American, Puerto Rican or American Indian. Applicant must be U.S. citizen or permanent resident residing in Illinois.

Basis for selection: Major/career interest in education, teacher or education.

Application requirements: Teacher Education Program application.

Additional information: Minimum 2.5 GPA. Applicant should be in course of study leading to teacher certification. Recipient must sign commitment to teach one year in Illinois for each year assistance is received. Must teach at nonprofit Illinois preschool, elementary school, or secondary school with at least 30 percent minority enrollment. If teaching commitment is not fulfilled, scholarship converts to loan, and entire amount, plus interest, must be paid. Contact ISAC or visit Website for additional information.

Amount of award:	$5,000
Number of awards:	583
Application deadline:	March 1
Total amount awarded:	$2,715,787

Contact:
Illinois Student Assistance Commission
ISAC College Zone Counselor
1755 Lake Cook Road
Deerfield, IL 60015
Phone: 800-899-ISAC
Web: www.collegezone.com

Monetary Award Program (MAP)

Type of award: Scholarship, renewable.

Intended use: For undergraduate study at 2-year or 4-year institution. Designated institutions: ISAC/MAP-approved institutions in Illinois.

Eligibility: Applicant must be U.S. citizen or permanent resident residing in Illinois.

Basis for selection: Applicant must demonstrate financial need.

Application requirements: FAFSA.

Additional information: Must reapply every year for renewal. Contact ISAC or visit Website for application, deadlines, and additional information. Amount of award dependent on legislative action and available funding in any given year.

Amount of award:	$4,968
Number of awards:	145,543
Number of applicants:	597,441
Application deadline:	September 30
Total amount awarded:	$383,817,064

Contact:
Illinois Student Assistance Commission
ISAC College Zone Counselor
1755 Lake Cook Road
Deerfield, IL 60015
Phone: 800-899-ISAC
Web: www.collegezone.com

Robert C. Byrd Honors Scholarship Program

Type of award: Scholarship, renewable.

Intended use: For full-time undergraduate study at accredited postsecondary institution in United States.

Eligibility: Applicant must be high school senior. Applicant must be U.S. citizen or permanent resident residing in Illinois.

Basis for selection: Applicant must demonstrate high academic achievement.

Additional information: Names of qualifying students submitted by high school guidance counselors. Student must be high school senior and enrolled, or accepted for enrollment, as full-time undergraduate. May not be used for military service academies. Eligibility based on standardized test scores, high school rank, and GPA.

Amount of award:	$1,500
Number of awards:	1,067
Total amount awarded:	$1,571,593

Contact:
Illinois Student Assistance Commission
ISAC College Zone Counselor
1755 Lake Cook Road
Deerfield, IL 60015
Phone: 800-899-ISAC
Web: www.collegezone.com

Silas Purnell Illinois Incentive for Access

Type of award: Scholarship.

Intended use: For freshman study at postsecondary institution. Designated institutions: ISAC-approved institutions.

Eligibility: Applicant must be U.S. citizen or permanent resident residing in Illinois.

Basis for selection: Applicant must demonstrate financial need.

Application requirements: FAFSA.

Additional information: Applicant must have been determined by federal needs calculation to have an expected family contribution (EFC) of $0. Must meet Monetary Award Program eligibility requirements. Contact ISAC or visit Website for additional information.

Amount of award:	$500
Number of awards:	21,335
Number of applicants:	45,000
Application deadline:	September 30
Total amount awarded:	$8,363,500

Contact:
Illinois Student Assistance Commission
ISAC College Zone Counselor
1755 Lake Cook Road
Deerfield, IL 60015
Phone: 800-899-ISAC
Web: www.collegezone.com

Special Education Teacher Tuition Waiver

Type of award: Scholarship, renewable.

Intended use: For undergraduate or graduate study at postsecondary institution in United States. Designated institutions: Eligible four-year institutions in Illinois: Chicago State University, Eastern Illinois University, Governors State University, Illinois State University, Northeastern Illinois University, Northern Illinois University, Southern Illinois University (Carbondale and Edwardsville), University of Illinois (Chicago, Springfield, Urbana), and Western Illinois University.

Eligibility: Applicant must be U.S. citizen or permanent resident residing in Illinois.

Basis for selection: Major/career interest in education, special.

Additional information: Must be Illinois high school graduate and rank in upper half of graduating class. Must not already hold valid teaching certificate in special education. Recipients must teach in Illinois for two years, or scholarship becomes loan. See Website for application and more details.

Amount of award:	Full tuition
Number of awards:	245
Application deadline:	March 1
Notification begins:	July 1

Contact:
Illinois Student Assistance Commission
1755 Lake Cook Road
Deerfield, IL 60015
Phone: 800-899-ISAC
Web: www.collegezone.com

Student-to-Student (STS) Program

Type of award: Scholarship, renewable.
Intended use: For undergraduate study at postsecondary institution. Designated institutions: Participating institutions in Illinois.
Eligibility: Applicant must be U.S. citizen or permanent resident residing in Illinois.
Basis for selection: Applicant must demonstrate financial need.
Additional information: Voluntary student contributions are matched, dollar for dollar, by ISAC, and paid to participating institutions. Need-based grants are then made available to students through procedures established by campus financial aid administrator and local student government. Deadline for application set by individual schools. Recipient must attend school on at least half-time basis. Must reapply for renewal. Contact college or university financial aid office, or visit ISAC Website for additional information.

Number of awards:	3,023
Total amount awarded:	$949,994

Contact:
Illinois Student Assistance Commission
ISAC College Zone Counselor
1755 Lake Cook Road
Deerfield, IL 60015
Phone: 800-899-ISAC
Web: www.collegezone.com

Institute for Humane Studies

Humane Studies Fellowship

Type of award: Scholarship.
Intended use: For full-time junior, senior or graduate study at postsecondary institution.
Basis for selection: Applicant must demonstrate high academic achievement.
Application requirements: $25 application fee. Recommendations, essay, transcript. Test scores (GRE, LSAT, GMAT, SAT, ACT, etc.), resume and writing sample. Sample is typically draft dissertation or academic paper; 30 page maximum.
Additional information: Applicants should have demonstrated interest in the principles, practices, and institutions necessary to a free society. Amounts awarded take into account the cost of tuition at the recipient's institution and any other funds received. Number of fellowships awarded each year varies. IHS begins accepting applications online in September.

Amount of award:	$2,000-$12,000
Number of awards:	165
Number of applicants:	760
Application deadline:	December 31
Notification begins:	April 20
Total amount awarded:	$450,000

Contact:
Institute for Humane Studies at George Mason University
3301 N. Fairfax Drive
Suite 440
Arlington, VA 22201
Phone: 800-697-8799
Fax: 703-993-4890
Web: www.theihs.org

Institute of Food Technologists

Institute of Food Technologists Freshman Scholarship

Type of award: Scholarship, renewable.
Intended use: For full-time freshman study at 4-year institution in United States or Canada. Designated institutions: Educational institutions with approved programs in food science/technology.
Eligibility: Applicant must be high school senior.
Basis for selection: Major/career interest in food science/technology. Applicant must demonstrate high academic achievement.
Application requirements: Recommendations, essay, transcript. SAT/ACT report. Essay should be one page statement regarding applicant's desire to become food scientist/technologist.
Additional information: IFT Scholarship recipients must join IFT student association. Applicant must be high school senior or high school graduate entering college for first time. Minimum 3.0 GPA required. Must have a well-rounded personality. Must enroll in IFT-approved program. Program descriptions and application available on Website. All inquiries and completed applications should be directed to department head of approved school.

Amount of award:	$1,000
Number of awards:	16
Application deadline:	March 15
Notification begins:	April 15
Total amount awarded:	$16,000

Contact:
Scholarship Department Institute of Food Technologists
525 W. Van Buren, Suite 1000
Chicago, IL 60607
Phone: 317-782-8424
Fax: 312-782-8348
Web: www.ift.org

Institute of Food Technologists Junior/Senior Scholarship

Type of award: Scholarship, renewable.
Intended use: For full-time junior or senior study at 4-year institution in United States or Canada. Designated institutions: Educational institutions with approved programs in food science/technology.
Basis for selection: Major/career interest in food science/technology. Applicant must demonstrate high academic achievement.
Application requirements: Recommendations, transcript.
Additional information: Applicant must have minimum 3.0 GPA and must be enrolled in IFT-approved program. Program

description and application available through Website or via fax. All other inquiries and completed applications should be directed to department head of approved school. Previous scholarship recipients must be IFT members to reapply.

Amount of award:	$1,000-$10,535
Number of awards:	44
Notification begins:	April 15
Total amount awarded:	$50,000

Contact:
Scholarship Department
Institute of Food Technologists
525 W. Van Buren, Suite 1000
Chicago, IL 60601
Phone: 312-782-8424
Fax: 312-782-8348
Web: www.ift.org

Institute of Food Technologists Sophomore Scholarship

Type of award: Scholarship, renewable.
Intended use: For full-time sophomore study at 4-year institution in United States or Canada. Designated institutions: Educational institutions with approved programs in food science/technology.
Basis for selection: Major/career interest in food science/technology. Applicant must demonstrate high academic achievement.
Application requirements: Recommendations, essay, transcript, proof of eligibility. SAT/ACT report. Essay must be one-page statement regarding desire to continue studies in food science/technology. Non-food majors must submit one page explaining desire to become food scientist/technologist.
Additional information: Applicant must be college freshman. Scholarship recipients must be member of IFT student association. Must have minimum 3.0 GPA. Must be enrolled in or plan to enroll in IFT-approved program. Program descriptions and application available through Website or via fax. All inquiries and completed applications should be directed to the department head of approved school. Previous scholarship recipients must be IFT members to reapply.

Amount of award:	$1,000
Number of awards:	15
Application deadline:	March 1
Notification begins:	April 15
Total amount awarded:	$16,000

Contact:
Institute of Food Technologists
Scholarship Department
525 West Van Buren, Suite 1000
Chicago, IL 60607
Phone: 312-782-8424
Fax: 312-782-8348
Web: www.ift.org

Institute of Real Estate Management Foundation

George M. Brooker Collegiate Scholarship for Minorities

Type of award: Scholarship.

Intended use: For full-time junior, senior, master's or doctoral study at 4-year or graduate institution.
Eligibility: Applicant must be Alaskan native, Asian American, African American, Mexican American, Hispanic American, Puerto Rican or American Indian. Applicant must be U.S. citizen.
Basis for selection: Major/career interest in real estate; business or business/management/administration. Applicant must demonstrate high academic achievement, depth of character, leadership and seriousness of purpose.
Application requirements: Interview, recommendations, essay, transcript.
Additional information: Must have 3.0 GPA in major. Must intend to enter the field of real estate management. Award notification is made on an ongoing basis.

Amount of award:	$2,500-$5,000
Number of awards:	3
Number of applicants:	5
Application deadline:	June 30, December 31
Total amount awarded:	$4,500

Contact:
Institute of Real Estate Management Foundation
Scholarship and Grant Program
430 North Michigan Avenue
Chicago, IL 60611-4090
Phone: 312-329-6008
Fax: 312-410-7908
Web: www.irem.org

Insurance Scholarship Foundation of America

ISFA Education Foundation College Scholarship

Type of award: Scholarship.
Intended use: For junior, senior or graduate study at accredited 4-year or graduate institution.
Basis for selection: Major/career interest in insurance/actuarial science.
Application requirements: Recommendations, essay, transcript.
Additional information: Applicant must have major or minor in insurance, risk management, or actuarial science with a minimum 3.0 GPA. Must have completed or be currently enrolled in two insurance, actuarial science, or risk-management-related courses, a minimum of three credit hours each. Postmark dates have no bearing on application deadline. Visit Website for application.

Amount of award:	$500-$5,000
Number of awards:	168
Number of applicants:	428
Application deadline:	January 15
Total amount awarded:	$211,595

Contact:
NAIW Education Foundation
Insurance Scholarship Foundation of America
P.O. Box 866
Hendersonville, NC 28793-0866
Phone: 828-890-3328
Fax: 828-891-2667
Web: www.inssfa.org

Scholarships

International Association of Fire Fighters

W.H. McClennan Scholarship

Type of award: Scholarship, renewable.
Intended use: For full-time undergraduate study at accredited vocational, 2-year or 4-year institution.
Eligibility: Applicant's parent must have been killed or disabled in work-related accident as firefighter.
Basis for selection: Applicant must demonstrate financial need, high academic achievement, depth of character, seriousness of purpose and service orientation.
Application requirements: Recommendations, essay, transcript, proof of eligibility. IA77 McClennan application.
Additional information: Open to children of firefighters who were killed in the line of duty and were members in good standing of IAFF at the time of deaths. Minimum 2.0 GPA.

Amount of award:	$2,500
Number of applicants:	51
Application deadline:	February 1
Notification begins:	August 1
Total amount awarded:	$127,500

Contact:
W. H. McClennan Scholarship/International Association of Fire Fighters
1750 New York Ave., NW
3rd Floor, Dept. of Education
Washington, DC 20006
Phone: 202-737-8484
Fax: 202-737-8418
Web: www.iaff.org

International Buckskin Horse Association, Inc.

Buckskin Horse Association Scholarship

Type of award: Scholarship, renewable.
Intended use: For full-time undergraduate study at accredited postsecondary institution in United States.
Eligibility: Applicant must be high school senior. Applicant must be U.S. citizen.
Basis for selection: Applicant must demonstrate financial need, high academic achievement, depth of character, leadership and seriousness of purpose.
Application requirements: Portfolio, recommendations, proof of eligibility.
Additional information: Available to children of association members. Parent must have been member for at least 2 years.

Amount of award:	$500-$1,000
Number of awards:	12
Number of applicants:	8
Application deadline:	February 1
Notification begins:	September 15
Total amount awarded:	$7,500

Contact:
International Buckskin Horse Association, Inc.
P.O. Box 268
Shelby, IN 46377
Phone: 219-552-1013
Fax: 219-552-1013
Web: www.ibha.net

International Executive Housekeepers Association

IEHA Educational Foundation Scholarship

Type of award: Scholarship.
Intended use: For undergraduate or non-degree study at accredited postsecondary institution.
Basis for selection: Major/career interest in hospitality administration/management.
Application requirements: Essay, transcript. Letter from school official verifying enrollment. Class schedule and coursework curriculum. Original and three copies of prepared manuscript on housekeeping (maximum 2,000 words, double-spaced). Photographs must be black-and-white glossy prints.
Additional information: Applicant must be member of International Executive Housekeepers Association. Scholarship will be awarded to student submitting best original manuscript on housekeeping within any industry segment (e.g., hospitality, healthcare, education, rehabilitation centers, government buildings). Other major/career interest: facilities management. Can be used for IEHA certification program. No set limit on number of awards granted.

Amount of award:	$800
Number of awards:	15
Application deadline:	January 10
Notification begins:	June 1
Total amount awarded:	$8,000

Contact:
International Executive Housekeepers Association
Educational Foundation Scholarships
1001 Eastwind Drive, Suite 301
Westerville, OH 43081-3361
Phone: 800-200-6342
Fax: 614-895-1248
Web: www.ieha.org

International Foodservice Editorial Council

Foodservice Communicators Scholarship

Type of award: Scholarship.
Intended use: For full-time undergraduate or master's study at accredited postsecondary institution in United States.
Basis for selection: Major/career interest in food science/technology; food production/management/services; culinary arts; communications; public relations or journalism. Applicant must demonstrate financial need, high academic achievement, depth

of character, leadership, seriousness of purpose and service orientation.

Application requirements: Recommendations, transcript, proof of eligibility.

Additional information: Applicant must pursue academic study in editorial or public relations within the food service industry. Writing ability considered. Applications may be requested by e-mail or downloaded from Website. Four to six awards granted each year for total of $8,000 to $15,000.

Amount of award:	$1,000-$3,750
Number of awards:	4
Number of applicants:	85
Application deadline:	March 15
Notification begins:	July 1
Total amount awarded:	$15,000

Contact:
International Foodservice Editorial Council (IFEC)
P.O. Box 491
Hyde Park, NY 12538
Phone: 845-229-6973
Fax: 845-229-6993
Web: www.ifeconline.com

International Furnishings and Design Association Educational Foundation

International Furnishings and Design Association Educational Foundation Leaders Commemorative Scholarship

Type of award: Scholarship.
Intended use: For undergraduate study at postsecondary institution.
Eligibility: Applicant must be U.S. citizen or permanent resident.
Basis for selection: Major/career interest in design or interior design. Applicant must demonstrate depth of character, leadership and service orientation.
Application requirements: Portfolio, recommendations, essay, transcript. Copies of two examples of original design work, recommendation from professor on official school stationery.
Additional information: Must be member of IFDA. Must have completed four courses in interior design (or related field) at post-secondary level. Student must be involved with volunteer or community service and held leadership positions during past five years. See Website for further requirements and application.

Amount of award:	$1,500
Number of awards:	1
Number of applicants:	16
Application deadline:	March 31
Total amount awarded:	$1,000

Contact:
International Furnishings and Design Association
Attn: Merry Mabbett Dean
10765 SW Canterbury Lane, #101
Tigard, OR 97244
Web: www.ifdaef.org

International Furnishings and Design Association Student Member Scholarships

Type of award: Scholarship.
Intended use: For full-time undergraduate or graduate study at accredited postsecondary institution in United States.
Basis for selection: Major/career interest in architecture or interior design. Applicant must demonstrate high academic achievement, depth of character, seriousness of purpose and service orientation.
Application requirements: Recommendations, essay, transcript. Two to three examples of student work, four copies of each element of application. One recommendation must be from IFPA member.
Additional information: Must be member of IFDA. Must have completed four courses in interior design (or related field) at post-secondary level. Must have completed at least one semester of postsecondary school. Furniture design majors also eligible. See Website for further requirements and application.

Amount of award:	$2,000
Number of awards:	1
Number of applicants:	2
Application deadline:	March 31
Notification begins:	July 31
Total amount awarded:	$2,000

Contact:
IFDA Educational Foundation
Attn: Merry Mabbett Dean
10765 SW Canterbury Lane, #101
Tigard, OR 97244
Web: www.ifdaef.org

Marketing Internship Scholarship

Type of award: Scholarship.
Intended use: For at postsecondary institution.
Eligibility: Applicant must be U.S. citizen or permanent resident.
Basis for selection: Major/career interest in marketing or public relations.
Application requirements: Recommendations, essay. Letter from internship supervisor at university or institution, letter from employer on company letterhead confirming responsibilities, outline of how one would promote product through marketing, list of four completed courses in marketing or related subjects, list of awards, extracurricular and volunteer work.
Additional information: Must be member of IFDA. Available to full-time college students or someone entering job market. IFDA does not provide internships or internship information. Internship must directly involve marketing, promoting or advertising design industry. Internship must last two to six months. Must have completed four courses in marketing or related subjects. See Website for further requirements and application.

Amount of award:	$1,500
Number of awards:	1
Number of applicants:	12
Total amount awarded:	$1,500

Contact:
International Furnishings and Design Association
Attn: Merry Mabbett Dean
10765 SW Canterbury Lane, #101
Tigard, OR 97244
Web: www.ifdaef.org

Part-Time Student Scholarship

Type of award: Scholarship.
Intended use: For half-time undergraduate study at postsecondary institution.
Basis for selection: Major/career interest in interior design.
Application requirements: Portfolio, recommendations, essay, transcript. Two examples of the student's original work. Resume. Four copies of all application materials.
Additional information: Applicants must have completed four courses in interior design or related field. Must be currently enrolled in at least two interior design-related courses. Visit Website for application and additional information.

Amount of award:	$1,000
Number of awards:	1
Number of applicants:	13
Application deadline:	March 31
Notification begins:	July 31
Total amount awarded:	$1,500

Contact:
IFDA Educational Foundation
Attn: Merry Mabbett Dean
10765 SW Canterbury Lane, #101
Tigard, OR 97224
Web: www.ifdaef.org

Ruth Clark Furniture Design Scholarship

Type of award: Scholarship.
Intended use: For full-time undergraduate or graduate study at postsecondary institution.
Eligibility: Applicant must be U.S. citizen or permanent resident.
Basis for selection: Major/career interest in design.
Application requirements: Portfolio, recommendations, essay, transcript. Letter from instructor on official school stationery. Five examples of original furniture designs.
Additional information: Must be member of IFDA. Must have completed four courses in interior design (or related field) at post-secondary level. Must be major in design with focus on residential upholstered and/or wood furniture design. See Website for further requirements and application.

Amount of award:	$3,000
Number of awards:	1
Number of applicants:	12
Application deadline:	March 31
Total amount awarded:	$2,500

Contact:
International Furnishings and Design Association
Attn: Merry Mabbett Dean
10765 SW Canterbury Lane, #101
Tigard, OR 97244
Web: www.ifdaef.org

International Order of the King's Daughters and Sons

Health Career Scholarship

Type of award: Scholarship, renewable.
Intended use: For full-time junior, senior, master's or first professional study at accredited 4-year or graduate institution in United States or Canada.
Eligibility: Applicant must be U.S. citizen or Canadian citizen.
Basis for selection: Major/career interest in medicine; dentistry; pharmacy/pharmaceutics/pharmacology; nursing; health sciences; health-related professions; physical therapy or occupational therapy. Applicant must demonstrate financial need, high academic achievement, depth of character, leadership, seriousness of purpose and service orientation.
Application requirements: Recommendations, essay, transcript, proof of eligibility.
Additional information: To request application, student must write to director stating field and present level of study and include business-size SASE. Pre-med students not eligible. R.N., M.D. and D.D.S. students must have completed first year. Number of scholarships varies year to year.

Amount of award:	$1,000
Application deadline:	April 1

Contact:
International Order of the King's Daughters and Sons
Director, Health Careers Department
P.O. Box 1040
Chautauqua, NY 14722-1040
Phone: 716-357-4951
Fax: 716-357-3762
Web: www.iokds.org

North American Indian Scholarship

Type of award: Scholarship, renewable.
Intended use: For full-time undergraduate study at accredited 2-year or 4-year institution in United States.
Eligibility: Applicant must be American Indian. Applicant must be U.S. citizen.
Basis for selection: Applicant must demonstrate financial need, depth of character, leadership, seriousness of purpose and service orientation.
Application requirements: Recommendations, essay, transcript, proof of eligibility. Written documentation of tribal registration and other requirements.
Additional information: Offers scholarships with no restrictions as to tribal affiliations or Indian blood quantum. For more information, send SASE to director of North American Indian Department.

Amount of award:	$650
Number of awards:	30
Application deadline:	April 1
Notification begins:	July 1
Total amount awarded:	$19,500

Contact:
International Order of the King's Daughters and Sons
Director, North American Indian Dept.
P.O. Box 1040
Chautauqua, NY 14722-1040
Phone: 716-357-4951
Fax: 716-357-3762
Web: www.iokds.org

Intertribal Timber Council

Truman D. Picard Scholarship

Type of award: Scholarship, renewable.

Intended use: For full-time undergraduate or graduate study at accredited 2-year, 4-year or graduate institution in United States.

Eligibility: Applicant must be Alaskan native or American Indian. Must be enrolled member of a federally recognized tribe. Applicant must be U.S. citizen.

Basis for selection: Major/career interest in natural resources/conservation; forestry; wildlife/fisheries or agriculture. Applicant must demonstrate financial need, high academic achievement, depth of character, leadership, seriousness of purpose and service orientation.

Application requirements: Recommendations, transcript. Resume, and two-page (maximum) letter of application.

Additional information: Check Website for application deadline dates.

Amount of award:	$1,500-$2,000
Number of awards:	33
Number of applicants:	50
Notification begins:	November 1
Total amount awarded:	$64,500

Contact:
Intertribal Timber Council
Education Committee
1112 NE 21st Avenue, Ste. 4
Portland, OR 97232-2114
Phone: 503-282-4296
Fax: 503-282-1274
Web: www.itcnet.org

Iowa College Student Aid Commission

All Iowa Opportunity Scholarship

Type of award: Scholarship.

Intended use: For undergraduate study at accredited 2-year or 4-year institution in United States. Designated institutions: Eligible Iowa colleges and universities.

Eligibility: Applicant must be U.S. citizen residing in Iowa.

Application requirements: FAFSA.

Additional information: Minimum 2.5 GPA. Awards of up to average tuition and fee rate of Regents University for current academic year. Priority given to students who participated in federal TRIO programs, students who graduated from alternative high schools, and homeless youth.

Application deadline:	March 15

Contact:
Iowa College Student Aid Commission
200 10th Street, Fourth Floor
Des Moines, IA 50309-3609
Phone: 877-272-4456
Fax: 515-725-3401
Web: www.iowacollegeaid.gov

Governor Terry E. Branstad Iowa State Fair Scholarship

Type of award: Scholarship.

Intended use: For undergraduate study at postsecondary institution in United States. Designated institutions: Iowa colleges and universities.

Eligibility: Applicant must be high school senior. Applicant must be U.S. citizen residing in Iowa.

Application requirements: Recommendations, essay. Proof of involvement in Iowa State Fair.

Additional information: Must be graduating senior from Iowa state high school who has been actively involved with the Iowa State Fair. Visit Website for application.

Amount of award:	$500-$1,000
Number of awards:	4
Application deadline:	May 1

Contact:
Iowa College Student Aid Commission
200 10th Street, Fourth Floor
Des Moines, IA 50309-3609
Phone: 877-272-4456
Fax: 515-725-3401
Web: www.iowacollegeaid.gov

Iowa Farm Bureau Federation Scholarship

Type of award: Scholarship.

Intended use: For undergraduate study at accredited 2-year or 4-year institution in United States. Designated institutions: Iowa colleges and universities.

Eligibility: Applicant must be U.S. citizen residing in Iowa.

Basis for selection: Major/career interest in agriculture; agricultural economics; horticulture; economics; education; forestry or veterinary medicine. Applicant must demonstrate financial need and high academic achievement.

Application requirements: Recommendations, essay, transcript.

Additional information: Must be child of Iowa Farm Bureau member. Must be working toward degree in agriculture-related field. Visit Website for application.

Application deadline:	March 1

Contact:
Iowa College Student Aid Commission
200 10th Street, Fourth Floor
Des Moines, IA 50309-3609
Phone: 877-272-4456
Fax: 515-725-3401
Web: www.iowacollegeaid.gov

Iowa Grant

Type of award: Scholarship, renewable.

Intended use: For undergraduate study at vocational, 2-year or 4-year institution.

Eligibility: Applicant must be U.S. citizen or permanent resident residing in Iowa.

Basis for selection: Applicant must demonstrate financial need.

Application requirements: FAFSA.

Additional information: Award amount adjusted for part-time study. Eligible colleges and universities receive Iowa grant allocations and award grants to students with greatest financial need.

Amount of award:	$100-$1,000
Notification begins:	March 20
Total amount awarded:	$1,029,784

Contact:
Iowa College Student Aid Commission
200 Tenth Street, Fourth Floor
Des Moines, IA 50309-3609
Phone: 877-272-4456
Fax: 515-725-3401
Web: www.iowacollegeaid.org

Iowa National Guard Educational Assistance Program

Type of award: Scholarship, renewable.
Intended use: For undergraduate study at accredited postsecondary institution.
Eligibility: Applicant must be U.S. citizen residing in Iowa. Applicant must be in military service in the Reserves/National Guard.
Application requirements: National Guard application.
Additional information: Applicant must be in military service in the Iowa Reserves/National Guard. Selection is based on National Guard designation. Award varies yearly and ranges from 50 to 100 percent of tuition for students at public institutions; for students at private institutions, award is equal to average tuition rate at Iowa Regents Universities. Must apply through National Guard unit.

Amount of award:	Full tuition
Number of awards:	1,217
Number of applicants:	1,326
Application deadline:	August 31
Total amount awarded:	$4,111,816

Contact:
Iowa National Guard Headquarters
Military Personnel Office
77000 NW Beaver Drive
Johnston, IA 50131-1902
Web: www.iowacollegeaid.org

Iowa Robert C. Byrd Honor Scholarship

Type of award: Scholarship.
Intended use: For full-time undergraduate or graduate study at accredited 2-year or 4-year institution in United States.
Eligibility: Applicant must be high school senior. Applicant must be U.S. citizen or permanent resident residing in Iowa.
Basis for selection: Applicant must demonstrate high academic achievement, leadership and service orientation.
Application requirements: Recommendations, essay, transcript, proof of eligibility. AP scores.
Additional information: Eligible applicants must have completed three years of social studies, math (beyond general math and pre-Algebra) and science (beyond general science), two years of the same foreign language, and four years of English. Must have minimum 28 ACT or 1860 SAT, and 3.5 GPA. Must rank in top ten percent of class. Award amount varies; maximum is $1,500.

Amount of award:	$1,500
Number of awards:	249
Number of applicants:	297
Application deadline:	May 1
Notification begins:	July 15
Total amount awarded:	$366,000

Contact:
Todd Brown, Byrd Scholarship Competition
Iowa College Student Aid Commission
200 Tenth Street, Fourth Floor
Des Moines, IA 50309-3609
Phone: 877-272-4456
Fax: 515-725-3401
Web: www.iowacollegeaid.org

Iowa Tuition Grant

Type of award: Scholarship, renewable.

Intended use: For undergraduate study at accredited 2-year or 4-year institution. Designated institutions: Private colleges in Iowa.
Eligibility: Applicant must be U.S. citizen or permanent resident residing in Iowa.
Basis for selection: Applicant must demonstrate financial need.
Application requirements: Proof of eligibility. FAFSA.

Amount of award:	$3,565
Number of awards:	17,531
Number of applicants:	33,889
Application deadline:	July 1
Total amount awarded:	$53,637,612

Contact:
Iowa College Student Aid Commission
200 Tenth Street, Fourth Floor
Des Moines, IA 50309-3609
Phone: 877-272-4456
Fax: 515-725-3401
Web: www.iowacollegeaid.org

Iowa Vocational-Technical Tuition Grant

Type of award: Scholarship, renewable.
Intended use: For undergraduate study at vocational or 2-year institution.
Eligibility: Applicant must be U.S. citizen or permanent resident residing in Iowa.
Basis for selection: Applicant must demonstrate financial need.
Application requirements: Proof of eligibility. FAFSA.
Additional information: Only vocational-technical career majors considered.

Amount of award:	$1,200
Number of awards:	3,397
Number of applicants:	19,611
Application deadline:	January 1
Total amount awarded:	$2,776,222

Contact:
Iowa College Student Aid Commission
200 Tenth Street, Fourth Floor
Des Moines, IA 50309-3609
Phone: 877-272-4456
Fax: 515-725-3401
Web: www.iowacollegeaid.org

Robert D. Blue Scholarship

Type of award: Scholarship.
Intended use: For undergraduate study at postsecondary institution in United States. Designated institutions: Iowa colleges and universities.
Eligibility: Applicant must be U.S. citizen residing in Iowa.
Basis for selection: Applicant must demonstrate financial need, high academic achievement, depth of character, leadership and seriousness of purpose.
Application requirements: Recommendations, essay, transcript.
Additional information: Visit Website for application.

Amount of award:	$500-$1,000
Application deadline:	May 10

Contact:
Iowa College Student Aid Commission
200 10th Street, Fourth Floor
Des Moines, IA 50309-3609
Phone: 877-272-4456
Fax: 515-725-3401
Web: www.iowacollegeaid.gov

Italian Catholic Federation

Italian Catholic Federation Scholarship

Type of award: Scholarship, renewable.
Intended use: For full-time freshman study at accredited 2-year or 4-year institution.
Eligibility: Applicant must be high school senior. Applicant must be Italian. Applicant must be Roman Catholic. Applicant must be U.S. citizen residing in California, Illinois, Arizona or Nevada.
Basis for selection: Applicant must demonstrate financial need and high academic achievement.
Application requirements: Recommendations, essay, transcript.
Additional information: Minimum 3.2 GPA. Also open to non-Italian students whose parents or grandparents are members of Federation. First year's scholarship award is $400. Larger amounts available for advanced scholarships.

Amount of award:	$400
Number of awards:	200
Number of applicants:	460
Application deadline:	March 15
Notification begins:	May 1
Total amount awarded:	$79,600

Contact:
Italian Catholic Federation
8393 Capwell Drive
Suite 110
Oakland, CA 94621
Phone: 510-633-9058
Fax: 510-633-9758
Web: www.icf.org

IUE-CWA

Bruce van Ess Scholarship

Type of award: Scholarship.
Intended use: For full-time undergraduate study at accredited vocational, 2-year or 4-year institution.
Eligibility: Applicant or parent must be member/participant of International Union of EESMF Workers, AFL-CIO.
Basis for selection: Applicant must demonstrate depth of character, leadership, seriousness of purpose and service orientation.
Application requirements: Proof of GPA, short statement on civic contributions. 500-word essay on importance of labor movement.
Additional information: Available to all IUE-CWA members and employees (including retired or deceased members and employees) and their children and grandchildren. Apply online.

Amount of award:	$2,500
Number of awards:	1
Application deadline:	March 31
Total amount awarded:	$2,500

Contact:
Trudy Humphrey IUE Department of Education
Int'l Union of EESMF Workers, ALF-CIO
1275 K Street, NW
Washington, DC 20005-4064
Web: www.iue-cwa.org/advantage/scholarships

David J. Fitzmaurice Scholarship

Type of award: Scholarship.
Intended use: For full-time undergraduate study at accredited vocational, 2-year or 4-year institution.
Eligibility: Applicant or parent must be member/participant of International Union of EESMF Workers, AFL-CIO.
Basis for selection: Major/career interest in engineering. Applicant must demonstrate depth of character, leadership, seriousness of purpose and service orientation.
Application requirements: Proof of GPA, 150-word essay on civic contributions, 500-word essay on importance of labor movement.
Additional information: Available to children and grandchildren of all IUE-CWA members and employees (including retired or deceased members and employees). Applicant must be in engineering program. Apply online.

Amount of award:	$2,000
Number of awards:	1
Application deadline:	March 31
Total amount awarded:	$2,000

Contact:
Trudy Humphrey IUE Department of Education
Int'l Union of EESMF Workers, AFL-CIO
1275 K Street, NW
Washington, DC 20005-4064
Web: www.iue-cwa.org/advantage/scholarships

James B. Carey Scholarship

Type of award: Scholarship.
Intended use: For full-time undergraduate study at accredited postsecondary institution in United States.
Eligibility: Applicant or parent must be member/participant of International Union of EESMF Workers, AFL-CIO.
Basis for selection: Applicant must demonstrate depth of character, leadership, seriousness of purpose and service orientation.
Application requirements: Recommendations, transcript, proof of eligibility. 150-word essay on civic contributions, 500-word essay on importance of labor movement.
Additional information: Available to children and grandchildren of all IUE-CWA members and employees (including retired or deceased members and employees) and their children and grandchildren. Must be accepted or enrolled in college, university, nursing school, or technical school. Apply online.

Amount of award:	$1,000
Number of awards:	9
Application deadline:	March 31
Total amount awarded:	$9,000

Contact:
Trudy Humphrey, IUE Department of Education
Int'l Union of EESMF Workers, AFL-CIO
1275 K Street, N.W.
Washington, DC 20005-4064
Web: www.iue-cwa.org/advantage/scholarships

Paul Jennings Scholarship

Type of award: Scholarship.
Intended use: For full-time undergraduate study in United States.
Eligibility: Applicant must be high school senior.
Basis for selection: Applicant must demonstrate depth of character, leadership and service orientation.
Application requirements: Transcript, proof of eligibility. 150-word essay on civic contributions, 500-word essay on importance of labor movement.
Additional information: Award available to children and grandchildren of IUE-CWA members who are now or have been local union elected officials. Families of full-time union officers or employees not eligible. Must be accepted or enrolled in college, university, nursing school, or technical school. Apply online.

Amount of award:	$3,000
Number of awards:	1
Application deadline:	March 31
Total amount awarded:	$3,000

Contact:
Trudy Humphrey, IUE Department of Education
Int'l Union of EESMF Workers, AFL-CIO
1275 K Street, N.W.
Washington, DC 20005-4064
Web: www.iue-cwa.org/advantage/scholarships

Robert L. Livingston Scholarship

Type of award: Scholarship.
Intended use: For full-time undergraduate study at accredited vocational, 2-year or 4-year institution.
Basis for selection: Applicant must demonstrate depth of character, leadership, seriousness of purpose and service orientation.
Application requirements: Proof of GPA, short statement which includes applicant's civic contributions, career objectives, and extracurricular activities.
Additional information: Open to dependents of IUE-CWA Automotive Conference Board members (active, retired or deceased). Dependents of IUE-CWA Division employees ineligible. Apply online.

Amount of award:	$1,500
Number of awards:	2
Application deadline:	March 31
Total amount awarded:	$3,000

Contact:
Trudy Humphrey IUE Department of Education
Int'l Union of EESMF Workers, ALF-CIO
1275 K Street, NW
Washington, DC 20005-4064
Web: www.iue-cwa.org/advantage/scholarships

Sal Ingrassia Scholarship

Type of award: Scholarship.
Intended use: For full-time undergraduate study at accredited vocational, 2-year or 4-year institution.
Eligibility: Applicant or parent must be member/participant of International Union of EESMF Workers, AFL-CIO.
Basis for selection: Applicant must demonstrate depth of character, leadership, seriousness of purpose and service orientation.
Application requirements: Proof of GPA, 150-word essay on civic contributions, 500-word essay on relationship to labor movement.

Additional information: Available to all IUE-CWA members and employees (including retired or deceased members and employees) and their children and grandchildren. Apply online.

Amount of award:	$2,500
Number of awards:	1
Application deadline:	March 31
Total amount awarded:	$2,500

Contact:
Trudy Humphrey IUE Department of Education
Int'l Union of EESMF Workers, ALF-CIO
1275 K Street, NW
Washington, DC 20005-4064
Web: www.iue-cwa.org/advantage/scholarships

Willie Rudd Scholarship

Type of award: Scholarship.
Intended use: For full-time undergraduate study at accredited vocational, 2-year or 4-year institution.
Eligibility: Applicant or parent must be member/participant of International Union of EESMF Workers, AFL-CIO.
Basis for selection: Applicant must demonstrate depth of character, leadership, seriousness of purpose and service orientation.
Application requirements: Proof of GPA, 150-word essay on civic contributions, 500-word essay on importance of labor movement.
Additional information: Available to all IUE-CWA members and employees and their children and grandchildren (including retired or deceased members and employees). Apply online.

Amount of award:	$1,000
Number of awards:	1
Application deadline:	March 31
Total amount awarded:	$1,000

Contact:
Trudy Humphrey IUE Department of Education
Int'l Union of EESMF Workers, AFL-CIO
1275 K Street, NW
Washington, DC 20005-4064
Web: www.iue-cwa.org/advantage/scholarships

Jackie Robinson Foundation

Education and Leadership Development Program

Type of award: Scholarship, renewable.
Intended use: For full-time undergraduate study at accredited 4-year institution in United States.
Eligibility: Applicant must be Alaskan native, Asian American, African American, Mexican American, Hispanic American, Puerto Rican or American Indian. Applicant must be high school senior. Applicant must be U.S. citizen.
Basis for selection: Applicant must demonstrate financial need, high academic achievement, leadership and service orientation.
Application requirements: Interview, recommendations, essay, transcript.
Additional information: Applicants must have minimum SAT score of 1000 or ACT score of 23. Award amount varies up to $6,000. Applications available online and must be submitted via website.

Amount of award:	$6,000
Number of awards:	50
Number of applicants:	3,000
Application deadline:	March 15
Notification begins:	June 1
Total amount awarded:	$1,800,000

Contact:
Jackie Robinson Foundation
Attn: Scholarship Programs
One Hudson Sq., 75 Varick Street, 2nd floor
New York, NY 10013-1917
Phone: 212-290-8600
Fax: 212-290-8081
Web: www.jackierobinson.org

James Beard Foundation

American Restaurant Scholarship

Type of award: Scholarship.
Intended use: For undergraduate study at accredited postsecondary institution. Designated institutions: Licensed or accredited culinary schools.
Application requirements: Proof of eligibility.

Amount of award:	$4,000
Number of awards:	1
Application deadline:	May 15

Contact:
Scholarship America
1 Scholarship Way
P.O. Box 297
St. Peter, MN 56082
Phone: 507-931-1682
Web: www.jamesbeard.org

Bern Laxer Memorial Scholarship

Type of award: Scholarship.
Intended use: For undergraduate study at accredited postsecondary institution. Designated institutions: Licensed or accredited culinary schools.
Eligibility: Applicant must be residing in Florida.
Basis for selection: Major/career interest in culinary arts; hospitality administration/management or food science/technology. Applicant must demonstrate financial need.
Application requirements: Recommendations, essay, transcript, proof of eligibility. Proof of residency, financial statement, resume.
Additional information: Must have at least one year of culinary experience and have high school diploma or equivalent. Up to three scholarships granted annually, one in each of the following categories: culinary studies, hospitality management, and viticulture/oenology. Recipients who reapply will be given priority consideration over new applicants. May be received for a maximum of four years, but applicant must maintain a B- GPA.

Amount of award:	$2,500
Number of awards:	3
Application deadline:	May 15
Total amount awarded:	$7,500

Contact:
Scholarship America
1 Scholarship Way
P.O. Box 297
St. Peter, MN 56082
Phone: 507-931-1682
Web: www.jamesbeard.org

Bob Zappatelli Memorial Scholarship

Type of award: Scholarship.
Intended use: For undergraduate study at accredited postsecondary institution.
Basis for selection: Major/career interest in culinary arts; food production/management/services; food science/technology; hospitality administration/management or hotel/restaurant management.
Application requirements: Recommendations, essay, transcript.
Additional information: Must plan to enroll in culinary school. Preference given to Benchmark employees or relatives of employees. Must have experience in food and beverage industry.

Amount of award:	$3,000
Number of awards:	1
Application deadline:	May 15
Total amount awarded:	$5,000

Contact:
Scholarship America
1 Scholarship Way
P.O. Box 297
St. Peter, MN 56082
Phone: 504-931-1682
Web: www.jamesbeard.org

Chefs of Louisiana Cookery Scholarship

Type of award: Scholarship.
Intended use: For undergraduate study at postsecondary institution. Designated institutions: Culinary schools in Louisiana.
Eligibility: Applicant must be U.S. citizen residing in Louisiana.
Basis for selection: Major/career interest in culinary arts; food production/management/services; food science/technology; hospitality administration/management or hotel/restaurant management. Applicant must demonstrate financial need.
Application requirements: Recommendations, essay, transcript.
Additional information: Must plan to enroll in Louisiana culinary school.

Amount of award:	$2,000
Number of awards:	2
Application deadline:	May 15

Contact:
Scholarship America
1 Scholarship Way
P.O. Box 297
St. Peter, MN 56082
Phone: 504-931-1682
Web: www.jamesbeard.org

Christian Wolffer Scholarship

Type of award: Scholarship.

Intended use: For undergraduate study at accredited postsecondary institution. Designated institutions: Licensed or accredited culinary schools.
Eligibility: Applicant must be residing in New York.
Basis for selection: Major/career interest in culinary arts; food production/management/services or food science/technology. Applicant must demonstrate high academic achievement.
Application requirements: Recommendations, essay, transcript, proof of eligibility. Proof of residency, financial statement, resume.
Additional information: Minimum 3.0 GPA. Must be enrolled or planning to enroll in accredited culinary or wine studies program.

Amount of award:	$2,000
Number of awards:	1
Application deadline:	May 15
Total amount awarded:	$5,000

Contact:
Scholarship America
1 Scholarship Way
P.O. Box 297
St. Peter, MN 56082
Phone: 507-931-1682
Web: www.jamesbeard.org

Clat Triplette Scholarship

Type of award: Scholarship.
Intended use: For undergraduate study at accredited postsecondary institution.
Basis for selection: Major/career interest in culinary arts; food production/management/services or food science/technology. Applicant must demonstrate financial need.
Application requirements: Recommendations, transcript, proof of eligibility. Proof of residency, financial statement, resume, 250 word essay on James Beard.
Additional information: Applicants must be enrolled or planning to enroll in accredited baking or pastry studies program at licensed or accredited culinary school.

Amount of award:	$4,000
Number of awards:	3
Application deadline:	May 15
Total amount awarded:	$12,000

Contact:
Scholarship America
1 Scholarship Way
P.O. Box 297
St. Peter, MN 56082
Phone: 507-931-1682
Web: www.jamesbeard.org

Deseo at the Westin Scholarship

Type of award: Scholarship.
Intended use: For undergraduate study at postsecondary institution.
Eligibility: Applicant must be residing in Arizona.
Basis for selection: Major/career interest in culinary arts; food production/management/services or food science/technology. Applicant must demonstrate financial need.
Application requirements: Recommendations, essay, transcript, proof of eligibility. Proof of residency, financial statement, resume.
Additional information: Applicants must have participated in Arizona Careers Through Culinary Arts program and be recommended by Arizona C-CAP.

Amount of award:	$2,500
Number of awards:	2
Application deadline:	May 15
Total amount awarded:	$6,250

Contact:
Scholarship America
1 Scholarship Way
P.O. Box 297
St. Peter, MN 56082
Phone: 507-931-1682
Web: www.jamesbeard.org

Fifth Floor Restaurant Scholarship

Type of award: Scholarship.
Intended use: For undergraduate study in United States. Designated institutions: Licensed or accredited culinary schools.
Basis for selection: Major/career interest in journalism; culinary arts; food production/management/services or food science/technology. Applicant must demonstrate financial need.
Application requirements: Recommendations, transcript. Financial statement, resume.
Additional information: Must plan to enroll in licensed or accredited culinary school.

Amount of award:	$2,500
Number of awards:	1
Application deadline:	May 15

Contact:
Scholarship America
1 Scholarship Way
P.O. Box 297
St. Peter, MN 56082
Phone: 507-931-1682
Web: www.jamesbeard.org

Inn at Blackberry Farm Scholarship

Type of award: Scholarship.
Intended use: For undergraduate study at accredited postsecondary institution. Designated institutions: Licensed or accredited culinary institutions.
Basis for selection: Major/career interest in culinary arts; food production/management/services; food science/technology; hospitality administration/management or hotel/restaurant management. Applicant must demonstrate financial need, high academic achievement, leadership, seriousness of purpose and service orientation.
Application requirements: Recommendations, essay, transcript. Resume, financial statement.
Additional information: Must plan to enroll in licensed or accredited culinary school.

Amount of award:	$4,125
Number of awards:	2
Application deadline:	May 15
Total amount awarded:	$7,700

Contact:
Scholarship America
1 Scholarship Way
P.O. Box 297
St. Peter, MN 56082
Phone: 507-931-1682
Web: www.jamesbeard.org

La Toque Scholarship in Wine Studies

Type of award: Scholarship.

Intended use: For undergraduate study at postsecondary institution. Designated institutions: Licensed or accredited culinary schools.
Basis for selection: Major/career interest in culinary arts or food production/management/services. Applicant must demonstrate financial need.
Application requirements: Recommendations, essay, transcript, proof of eligibility. Proof of residency, financial statement, resume.
Additional information: Applicants must be enrolled in or be planning to enroll in an accredited wine studies program.

Amount of award:	$3,000
Number of awards:	1
Application deadline:	May 15
Total amount awarded:	$6,000

Contact:
Scholarship America
1 Scholarship Way
P.O. Box 297
St. Peter, MN 56082
Phone: 507-931-1682
Web: www.jamesbeard.org

The Peter Cameron/Housewares Charity Foundation Scholarship

Type of award: Scholarship.
Intended use: For undergraduate study at accredited postsecondary institution. Designated institutions: Licensed or accredited culinary schools.
Eligibility: Applicant must be high school senior.
Basis for selection: Major/career interest in culinary arts; food production/management/services or food science/technology. Applicant must demonstrate financial need and high academic achievement.
Application requirements: Recommendations, essay, transcript, proof of eligibility. Financial statement, resume.
Additional information: Minimum 3.0 GPA.

Amount of award:	$4,000
Number of awards:	1
Application deadline:	May 15
Total amount awarded:	$4,000

Contact:
Scholarship America
1 Scholarship Way
P.O. Box 297
St. Peter, MN 56082
Phone: 507-931-1682
Web: www.jamesbeard.org

Peter Kump Memorial Scholarship

Type of award: Scholarship.
Intended use: For undergraduate study at accredited postsecondary institution. Designated institutions: Licensed or accredited culinary schools.
Eligibility: Applicant must be high school senior.
Basis for selection: Major/career interest in culinary arts; food production/management/services or food science/technology. Applicant must demonstrate financial need and high academic achievement.
Application requirements: Recommendations, essay, transcript, proof of eligibility. Proof of residency, financial statement, resume.
Additional information: Minimum 3.0 GPA. Minimum one year substantiated culinary experience.

Amount of award:	$4,000
Number of awards:	3
Application deadline:	May 15
Total amount awarded:	$12,000

Contact:
Scholarship America
1 Scholarship Way
P.O. Box 297
St. Peter, MN 56082
Phone: 507-931-1682
Web: www.jamesbeard.org

Poggio Scholarship

Type of award: Scholarship.
Intended use: For undergraduate study at accredited postsecondary institution. Designated institutions: Licensed or accredited culinary schools.
Basis for selection: Major/career interest in culinary arts. Applicant must demonstrate financial need.
Application requirements: Recommendations, essay, transcript. Financial statement, resume.
Additional information: Must plan to attend licensed or accredited culinary school.

Amount of award:	$5,000
Number of awards:	1
Application deadline:	May 15

Contact:
Scholarship America
1 Scholarship Way
P.O. Box 297
St. Peter, MN 56082
Phone: 507-931-1682
Web: www.jamesbeard.org

The Publican Scholarship

Type of award: Scholarship.
Intended use: For undergraduate study at accredited postsecondary institution.
Basis for selection: Major/career interest in culinary arts; food production/management/services or food science/technology. Applicant must demonstrate financial need.
Application requirements: Recommendations, essay, transcript, proof of eligibility. Financial statement, resume.
Additional information: Must plan to attend culinary school.

Amount of award:	$4,500
Number of awards:	1
Application deadline:	May 15

Contact:
Scholarship America
1 Scholarship Way
P.O. Box 297
St. Peter, MN 56082
Phone: 507-931-1682
Web: www.jamesbeard.org

Puckemin Inn Scholarship

Type of award: Scholarship.
Intended use: For undergraduate study at accredited postsecondary institution. Designated institutions: Licensed or accredited culinary schools.
Basis for selection: Major/career interest in culinary arts. Applicant must demonstrate financial need.
Application requirements: Recommendations, transcript. Financial statement, resume.

Additional information: Must plan to enroll in licensed or accredited culinary school.

Amount of award:	$3,500
Number of awards:	1
Application deadline:	May 15

Contact:
Scholarship America
1 Scholarship Way
P.O. Box 297
St. Peter, MN 56082
Phone: 507-931-1682
Web: www.jamesbeard.org

Spencer's Scholarship

Type of award: Scholarship.
Intended use: For undergraduate, graduate or non-degree study at postsecondary institution in or outside United States or Canada.
Basis for selection: Major/career interest in culinary arts.
Application requirements: Recommendations, essay, transcript. Resume, financial statement.
Additional information: Must plan to enroll in licensed or accredited culinary school. Visit Website for application and additional information.

Amount of award:	$5,000
Number of awards:	1
Application deadline:	May 15

Contact:
Scholarship America
1 Scholarship Way
P.O. Box 297
St. Peter, MN 56082
Phone: 507-931-1682
Web: www.jamesbeard.org

Studio at the Montage Resort & Spa Scholarship

Type of award: Scholarship.
Intended use: For undergraduate study at accredited postsecondary institution. Designated institutions: Licensed or accredited culinary schools.
Basis for selection: Major/career interest in culinary arts. Applicant must demonstrate financial need.
Application requirements: Recommendations, essay, transcript. Financial statement, resume.
Additional information: Must plan to attend licensed or accredited culinary school.

Amount of award:	$2,500
Number of awards:	2
Application deadline:	May 15
Total amount awarded:	$10,000

Contact:
Scholarship America
1 Scholarship Way
P.O. Box 297
St. Peter, MN 56082
Phone: 507-931-1682
Web: www.jamesbeard.org

Zov's Bistro Scholarship

Type of award: Scholarship.
Intended use: For undergraduate study at accredited postsecondary institution. Designated institutions: Licensed or accredited culinary schools.

Basis for selection: Major/career interest in culinary arts. Applicant must demonstrate financial need.
Application requirements: Recommendations, essay, transcript. Financial statement, resume.
Additional information: Must plan to enroll in licensed or accredited culinary school.

Amount of award:	$3,000
Number of awards:	1
Application deadline:	May 15

Contact:
Scholarship America
1 Scholarship Way
P.O. Box 297
St. Peter, MN 56082
Phone: 507-931-1682
Web: www.jamesbeard.org

James F. Byrnes Foundation

James F. Byrnes Scholarship

Type of award: Scholarship, renewable.
Intended use: For full-time freshman study at accredited 4-year institution.
Eligibility: Applicant must be U.S. citizen residing in South Carolina.
Basis for selection: Applicant must demonstrate financial need, high academic achievement, depth of character, leadership, patriotism, seriousness of purpose and service orientation.
Application requirements: Interview, essay, transcript. SAT/ACT scores, photograph, autobiography (three typed pages maximum) describing home situation, death of parent/s, desire for college education, college ambitions, reasons financial assistance is needed, how college will be financed, etc. Two non-relative references (one from current guidance counselor or teacher).
Additional information: Applicant must be high school senior or college freshman. Applicant must have minimum 2.5 GPA. One or both parents of applicant must be deceased. Visit Website for additional information.

Amount of award:	$3,250
Number of awards:	6
Number of applicants:	126
Application deadline:	February 15
Notification begins:	April 20

Contact:
James F. Byrnes Foundation
P.O. Box 6781
Columbia, SC 29260-6781
Phone: 803-254-9325
Fax: 803-254-9354
Web: www.byrnesscholars.org

Japanese American Association of New York

Japanese American General Scholarship

Type of award: Scholarship.
Intended use: For full-time freshman study at accredited 2-year or 4-year institution in United States.
Eligibility: Applicant must be high school senior. Applicant must be Japanese. Applicant must be U.S. citizen or permanent resident residing in Connecticut, New York or New Jersey.
Basis for selection: Applicant must demonstrate financial need, high academic achievement and service orientation.
Application requirements: Essay, transcript. SAT scores, photograph. Letter of recommendation from a JAA member if no one in family is a member.
Additional information: Open to Japanese students who hold green cards and Asian-Americans of Japanese descent. Two awards given are need-based. Awards given every other year. Contact sponsor or visit Website for future competitions and deadlines.

Amount of award:	$1,000-$6,000
Number of awards:	10
Number of applicants:	30
Application deadline:	May 1
Notification begins:	May 20
Total amount awarded:	$38,000

Contact:
Japanese American Association of New York
15 West 44 Street
New York, NY 10036
Phone: 212-840-6942
Fax: 212-840-0616
Web: www.jaany.org

Japanese American Music Scholarship Competition

Type of award: Scholarship.
Intended use: For undergraduate or graduate study at postsecondary institution.
Eligibility: Applicant must be Japanese. Applicant must be U.S. citizen or permanent resident.
Basis for selection: Competition/talent/interest in music performance/composition, based on piano performance. Major/career interest in music.
Application requirements: Photograph.
Additional information: Open to Japanese students who hold green cards and Asian-Americans of Japanese descent. Awards given every other year. Contact sponsor or visit Website for future competitions and deadlines.

Amount of award:	$1,500
Number of awards:	3
Total amount awarded:	$4,500

Contact:
Japanese American Association of New York
15 West 44 Street
New York, NY 10036
Phone: 212-840-6942
Fax: 212-840-0616
Web: www.jaany.org

Jaycee War Memorial Fund

Charles R. Ford Scholarship

Type of award: Scholarship.
Intended use: For undergraduate study at postsecondary institution.
Eligibility: Applicant must be returning adult student. Applicant must be U.S. citizen.
Basis for selection: Applicant must demonstrate financial need, high academic achievement and leadership.
Application requirements: $10 application fee.
Additional information: Must be active member of Jaycees who wishes to return to college or university to complete education. To receive application, send business-size SASE with application fee between July 1 and February 1. Make check or money order payable to the Jaycee War Memorial Fund. Visit Website for more information.

Amount of award:	$2,500
Number of awards:	1
Application deadline:	February 1
Notification begins:	May 15

Contact:
Jaycee War Memorial Fund
Ford Scholarship
7447 S. Lewis Ave.
Tulsa, OK 74136
Phone: 918-584-2481
Fax: 918-584-4422
Web: www.usjaycees.org

Jaycee War Memorial Scholarship

Type of award: Scholarship.
Intended use: For full-time undergraduate study at accredited vocational, 2-year or 4-year institution.
Eligibility: Applicant must be U.S. citizen.
Basis for selection: Applicant must demonstrate financial need, high academic achievement and leadership.
Application requirements: $10 application fee.
Additional information: To receive application, send business-size SASE with application fee between July 1 and February 1. Make check or money order payable to the Jaycee War Memorial Fund. Visit Website for additional information.

Amount of award:	$1,000
Number of awards:	10
Application deadline:	February 1
Notification begins:	May 15
Total amount awarded:	$25,000

Contact:
Jaycee War Memorial Scholarship
Jycee War Memorial Scholarship
7447 S. Lewis Ave.
Tulsa, OK 74136
Phone: 918-584-2481
Fax: 918-584-4422
Web: www.usjaycees.org

Thomas Wood Baldridge Scholarship

Type of award: Scholarship.
Intended use: For full-time undergraduate study at accredited 2-year or 4-year institution.
Eligibility: Applicant or parent must be member/participant of Jaycees. Applicant must be U.S. citizen.

Basis for selection: Applicant must demonstrate financial need, high academic achievement and leadership.
Application requirements: $10 application fee.
Additional information: Applicant must be member or have immediate family who is Jaycee member. To receive application, send business-size SASE along with application fee between July 1 and February 1. Make check or money order payable to the Jaycee War Memorial Fund. Visit Website for additional information.

Amount of award:	$3,000
Number of awards:	1
Application deadline:	February 1
Total amount awarded:	$3,000

Contact:
Jaycee War Memorial Fund
Baldridge Scholarship
7447 S. Lewis Ave.
Tulsa, OK 74136
Phone: 918-584-2481
Fax: 918-584-4422
Web: www.usjaycees.org

Jeannette Rankin Foundation

Jeanette Rankin Foundation Scholarship

Type of award: Scholarship.
Intended use: For undergraduate study at accredited vocational, 2-year or 4-year institution in United States.
Eligibility: Applicant must be female, at least 35. Applicant must be U.S. citizen.
Basis for selection: Applicant must demonstrate financial need, depth of character and seriousness of purpose.
Application requirements: Recommendations, essay.
Additional information: Applicant must be 35+ as of March 1 and meet low-income guidelines. Must display courage and attainable goals. Download application from Website from November through mid-February, or send SASE with application request.

Amount of award:	$2,000
Number of awards:	80
Number of applicants:	800
Application deadline:	March 1
Notification begins:	June 30
Total amount awarded:	$80,000

Contact:
Jeannette Rankin Foundation
1 Huntington Road, # 701
Athens, GA 30606
Phone: 706-208-1211
Web: www.rankinfoundation.org

Jewish Vocational Service

Jewish Vocational Service Scholarship Fund

Type of award: Scholarship, renewable.

Intended use: For full-time undergraduate or graduate study at accredited postsecondary institution in United States.
Eligibility: Applicant must be Jewish. Applicant must be U.S. citizen or permanent resident residing in California.
Basis for selection: Applicant must demonstrate financial need.
Application requirements: Recommendations, essay, transcript. FAFSA and tax returns.
Additional information: Minimum 2.7 GPA. Must be Jewish and legal, permanent resident of Los Angeles County with verifiable financial need. Number of awards varies. Visit Website for electronic application.

Amount of award:	$1,000-$5,000
Number of applicants:	400
Application deadline:	March 12
Notification begins:	June 15
Total amount awarded:	$369,900

Contact:
JVS Scholarship Fund
c/o Cathy Kersh
6505 Wilshire Blvd., Suite 200
Los Angeles, CA 90048
Phone: 323-761-8888 ext. 8868
Fax: 323-761-8580
Web: www.jvsla.org

Jewish War Veterans of the United States of America

Jewish War Veterans of the United States of America Bernard Rotberg Memorial Scholarship

Type of award: Scholarship.
Intended use: For freshman study at accredited 4-year institution.
Eligibility: Applicant must be high school senior. Applicant must be Jewish.
Basis for selection: Applicant must demonstrate financial need and high academic achievement.
Additional information: Applicant must be direct descendant of Jewish War Veterans member. Must be in upper 25 percent of high school class; must have participated in extracurricular activities in school as well as in Jewish community. SAT scores and recommendations encouraged. Visit Website for application and more information.

Amount of award:	$1,000
Number of awards:	1

Contact:
Jewish War Veterans of the United States of America
National Scholarship Committee
1811 R Street NW
Washington, DC 20009
Phone: 202-265-6280
Fax: 202-234-5662
Web: www.jwv.org

Jewish War Veterans of the United States of America JWV Grant

Type of award: Research grant.
Intended use: For freshman study at accredited vocational or 4-year institution.

Eligibility: Applicant must be high school senior. Applicant must be Jewish.
Basis for selection: Applicant must demonstrate financial need and high academic achievement.
Additional information: Applicant must be direct descendant of JWV member. Must be in upper 25 percent of high school class; must have participated in extracurricular activities in school as well as in Jewish community. SAT and recommendations encouraged. Visit Website for application and more information.

Amount of award:	$500
Number of awards:	1

Contact:
Jewish War Veterans of the United States of America
National Scholarship Committee
1811 R Street NW
Washington, DC 20009
Phone: 202-265-6280
Fax: 202-234-5662
Web: www.jwv.org

Jewish War Veterans of the United States of America XX Olympiad Memorial Award

Type of award: Scholarship.
Intended use: For undergraduate study at accredited 4-year institution.
Eligibility: Applicant must be high school senior.
Basis for selection: Applicant must demonstrate high academic achievement, leadership and service orientation.
Application requirements: SAT scores.
Additional information: Selection based on merit with focus on athletic achievement. Application deadline March - May. Visit Website for application and more information.

Amount of award:	$200-$1,000
Number of awards:	1

Contact:
Jewish War Veterans of the United States of America
National Scholarship Committee
1811 R Street NW
Washington, DC 20009
Phone: 202-265-6280
Fax: 202-234-5662
Web: www.jwv.org

Louis S. Silvey Grant

Type of award: Research grant.
Intended use: For freshman study at accredited 4-year institution.
Eligibility: Applicant must be high school senior. Applicant must be Jewish.
Basis for selection: Applicant must demonstrate financial need and high academic achievement.
Additional information: Applicant must be direct descendant of JWV member. Must be in upper 25 percent of high school class; must have participated in extracurricular activities in school as well as in Jewish community. SAT and recommendations encouraged. Visit Website for application and more information.

Amount of award:	$750
Number of awards:	1

Contact:
Jewish War Veterans of the United States of America
National Scholarship Committee
1811 R Street NW
Washington, DC 20009
Phone: 202-265-6280
Fax: 202-234-5662
Web: www.jwv.org

Kansas Board of Regents

Kansas Comprehensive Grant

Type of award: Scholarship, renewable.
Intended use: For full-time undergraduate study at accredited 4-year institution. Designated institutions: Kansas post-secondary institutions.
Eligibility: Applicant must be U.S. citizen or permanent resident residing in Kansas.
Basis for selection: Applicant must demonstrate financial need.
Application requirements: Proof of eligibility. FAFSA.
Additional information: Up to $1,100 for those attending public institutions; up to $3,000 for those attending private institutions.

Number of awards:	10,074
Number of applicants:	22,229
Application deadline:	April 1
Notification begins:	May 1
Total amount awarded:	$16,451,614

Contact:
Kansas Board of Regents
1000 SW Jackson Street
Suite 520
Topeka, KS 66612-1368
Phone: 785-296-3517
Fax: 785-296-0983
Web: www.kansasregents.org

Kansas Ethnic Minority Scholarship

Type of award: Scholarship, renewable.
Intended use: For full-time undergraduate study at postsecondary institution. Designated institutions: Kansas post-secondary institutions.
Eligibility: Applicant must be Alaskan native, Asian American, African American, Mexican American, Hispanic American, Puerto Rican or American Indian. Applicant must be U.S. citizen or permanent resident residing in Kansas.
Basis for selection: Applicant must demonstrate financial need and high academic achievement.
Application requirements: $12 application fee. Proof of eligibility. State of Kansas Student Aid Application. FAFSA.
Additional information: Minimum 3.0 GPA.

Amount of award:	$1,850
Number of awards:	222
Number of applicants:	777
Application deadline:	May 1
Total amount awarded:	$387,224

Contact:
Kansas Board of Regents
1000 SW Jackson Street
Suite 520
Topeka, KS 66612-1368
Phone: 785-296-3517
Fax: 785-296-0983
Web: www.kansasregents.org

Kansas Nursing Service Scholarship

Type of award: Scholarship, renewable.
Intended use: For full-time undergraduate study at postsecondary institution. Designated institutions: Kansas postsecondary schools with approved nursing programs.
Eligibility: Applicant must be U.S. citizen or permanent resident residing in Kansas.
Basis for selection: Major/career interest in nursing. Applicant must demonstrate financial need.
Application requirements: $12 application fee. State of Kansas Student Aid Application. FAFSA.
Additional information: Must obtain sponsorship from adult-care home licensed under the Adult Care Home Licensure Act; state agency that employs LPNs or RNs; or state-licensed medical care facility, psychiatric hospital, home health agency or local health department. Must agree to work in Kansas one year for each year that scholarship is received. If recipient does not meet obligation, award becomes loan.

Amount of award:	$2,500-$3,500
Number of awards:	201
Number of applicants:	346
Application deadline:	May 1
Total amount awarded:	$589,250

Contact:
Kansas Board of Regents
1000 SW Jackson Street
Suite 520
Topeka, KS 66612-1368
Phone: 785-296-3518
Fax: 785-296-0983
Web: www.kansasregents.org

Kansas ROTC Service Scholarship

Type of award: Scholarship.
Intended use: For full-time undergraduate study at postsecondary institution.
Eligibility: Applicant or parent must be member/participant of Reserve Officers Training Corps (ROTC). Applicant must be residing in Kansas.
Additional information: Applicant must be Kansas resident enrolled in Kansas ROTC program. Must be full-time undergraduate with at least 12 credit hours. Scholarship limited to eight semesters. Award amount may be up to tuition and costs of average four-year regents institution; average award is $1,650.

Number of awards:	24
Number of applicants:	24
Application deadline:	August 1
Total amount awarded:	$147,621

Contact:
Kansas Board of Regents Director of Student Financial Assistance
1000 SW Jackson Street
Suite 520
Topeka, KS 66612-1368
Phone: 785-296-3518
Fax: 785-296-0983
Web: www.kansasregents.org

Kansas State Scholarship

Type of award: Scholarship, renewable.
Intended use: For full-time undergraduate study at postsecondary institution.
Eligibility: Applicant must be residing in Kansas.
Basis for selection: Applicant must demonstrate financial need and high academic achievement.
Application requirements: $12 application fee. Proof of eligibility. FAFSA.
Additional information: Applicant must be Kansas resident, high school senior or undergraduate, and must be designated State Scholar in senior year of high school. Must be enrolled in Kansas school. Must have high GPA (average: 3.9) and ACT scores (average: 29).

Amount of award:	$1,000
Number of awards:	1,241
Number of applicants:	3,074
Application deadline:	May 1
Total amount awarded:	$1,178,768

Contact:
Kansas Board of Regents
1000 SW Jackson Street
Suite 520
Topeka, KS 66612-1368
Phone: 785-296-3517
Fax: 785-296-0983
Web: www.kansasregents.org

Kansas Teacher Service Scholarship

Type of award: Scholarship, renewable.
Intended use: For full-time undergraduate or post-bachelor's certificate study at 4-year or graduate institution.
Eligibility: Applicant must be residing in Kansas.
Basis for selection: Major/career interest in education, teacher or education, special. Applicant must demonstrate high academic achievement.
Application requirements: $12 application fee. Recommendations, transcript, proof of eligibility. FAFSA. Personal statement.
Additional information: Applicant must be Kansas resident enrolled in Kansas school that offers education degree. Must identify a "hard-to fill" or "underserved" area. Scholarships are competitive; selection based on ACT score, GPA, high school rank, transcript and recommendation. Preference given to juniors and seniors, or currently licensed teachers pursuing licensure or endorsement in hard-to-fill disciplines.

Amount of award:	$5,000
Number of awards:	419
Number of applicants:	1,008
Application deadline:	May 1
Total amount awarded:	$1,507,482

Contact:
Kansas Board of Regents
1000 SW Jackson Street
Suite 520
Topeka, KS 66612-1368
Phone: 785-296-3517
Fax: 785-296-0983
Web: www.kansasregents.org

Kansas Vocational Education Scholarship

Type of award: Scholarship, renewable.
Intended use: For full-time undergraduate study at vocational or 2-year institution. Designated institutions: Kansas institutions.
Eligibility: Applicant must be U.S. citizen or permanent resident residing in Kansas.
Application requirements: $12 application fee. Essay, proof of eligibility.
Additional information: Applicant must be Kansas resident and graduate of Kansas high school. Must take vocational test given on first Saturday of November or March and complete Vocational Education application. Renewals awarded first; remaining scholarships offered to those with highest exam scores.

Amount of award:	$500
Number of awards:	320
Number of applicants:	377
Application deadline:	May 1, February 1
Notification begins:	May 15
Total amount awarded:	$160,000

Contact:
Kansas Board of Regents
1000 SW Jackson Street
Suite 520
Topeka, KS 66612-0983
Phone: 785-296-3518
Fax: 785-296-0983
Web: www.kansasregents.org

National Guard Educational Assistance Program

Type of award: Scholarship, renewable.
Intended use: For undergraduate study at postsecondary institution. Designated institutions: Kansas institutions.
Eligibility: Applicant must be U.S. citizen residing in Kansas.
Additional information: Award amount varies. Requires service obligation.

Number of awards:	283
Number of applicants:	304
Application deadline:	August 1
Total amount awarded:	$942,631

Contact:
Kansas Board of Regents Attn: Diane Lindeman
1000 SW Jackson Street
Suite 520
Topeka, KS 66612-1368
Phone: 785-296-3518
Fax: 785-296-0983
Web: www.kansasregents.org

Kappa Kappa Gamma Foundation

Kappa Kappa Gamma Scholarship

Type of award: Scholarship, renewable.
Intended use: For full-time undergraduate or graduate study at 4-year or graduate institution in United States.
Basis for selection: Applicant must demonstrate financial need and high academic achievement.
Application requirements: Recommendations, transcript.
Additional information: Applicant must be active member in good standing of Kappa Kappa Gamma fraternity, with minimum 3.0 GPA. Recipients must reapply each year. Must be U.S. citizen or permanent resident from Canada.

Amount of award:	$500-$3,000
Number of awards:	141
Number of applicants:	427
Application deadline:	February 1
Total amount awarded:	$448,529

Contact:
Kappa Kappa Gamma Foundation
P.O. Box 38
Columbus, OH 43216-0038
Phone: 614-228-6515
Fax: 614-228-6303
Web: www.kappa.org

KarMel Scholarship Committee

KarMel Scholarship

Type of award: Scholarship.
Intended use: For undergraduate or graduate study at postsecondary institution in United States.
Eligibility: Applicant must be U.S. citizen.
Basis for selection: Competition/talent/interest in gay/lesbian, based on artistic or written ability on Gay/Lesbian subject. Applicant must demonstrate depth of character, leadership and seriousness of purpose.
Application requirements: Artistic work or writing samples.
Additional information: Open to high school seniors, undergraduates, and graduate students. Applicant need not be gay/lesbian/bi to apply for scholarship, but must submit works that include gay/lesbian/bi content. Scholarship is divided into two categories: Best "Written" Gay/Lesbian/Bi Themed Work and Best "Artistic" Gay/Lesbian/Bi Themed Work. Applicant may submit up to three works in both categories. Written work of any length will be accepted. All applicants may submit work via e-mail or postal mail. Visit Website for more information.

Amount of award:	$50-$400
Number of awards:	35
Number of applicants:	1,300
Application deadline:	March 31
Notification begins:	July 31
Total amount awarded:	$3,000

Contact:
KarMel Scholarship Committee
P.O. Box 70382
Sunnyvale, CA 94086
Web: www.karenandmelody.com

Kentucky Higher Education Assistance Authority (KHEAA)

Early Childhood Development Scholarship

Type of award: Scholarship.
Intended use: For half-time undergraduate study at 2-year or 4-year institution. Designated institutions: Approved Kentucky institutions.
Eligibility: Applicant must be U.S. citizen or permanent resident residing in Kentucky.
Basis for selection: Major/career interest in education, early childhood. Applicant must demonstrate financial need.
Application requirements: FAFSA.
Additional information: Part-time students working at least twenty hours in childcare facility eligible. Must agree to service commitment. To apply register through Zip Access on Website. Must reapply for each term. Deadlines: July 15 for fall, November 15 for spring, April 15 for summer.

Amount of award:	$1,800
Number of awards:	1,180
Number of applicants:	1,700
Application deadline:	July 15, November 15
Total amount awarded:	$1,282,000

Contact:
Kentucky Higher Education Assistance Authority
P.O. Box 798
Frankfort, KY 40602-0798
Phone: 800-928-8926
Fax: 502-696-7373
Web: www.kheaa.com

Go Higher Grant

Type of award: Scholarship.
Intended use: For at postsecondary institution in United States. Designated institutions: Kentucky colleges and universities.
Eligibility: Applicant must be at least 24. Applicant must be U.S. citizen or permanent resident residing in Kentucky.
Basis for selection: Applicant must demonstrate financial need.
Application requirements: FAFSA.
Additional information: For less than half-time adult students who are at least 24 years old.

Amount of award:	$1,000
Number of awards:	250
Number of applicants:	530
Total amount awarded:	$237,000

Contact:
Kentucky Higher Education Assistance Authority (KHEAA)
P.O. Box 798
Frankfort, KY 40602-0798
Phone: 800-928-8926
Web: www.kheaa.com

Kentucky College Access Program Grant (CAP)

Type of award: Scholarship, renewable.
Intended use: For undergraduate study at postsecondary institution.
Eligibility: Applicant must be U.S. citizen or permanent resident residing in Kentucky.
Basis for selection: Applicant must demonstrate financial need.
Application requirements: Proof of eligibility. FAFSA.
Additional information: Applicant ineligible if family contribution exceeds $4,617. May be used at eligible schools. Visit Website for additional information.

Amount of award:	$50-$1,900
Number of awards:	40,000
Number of applicants:	212,000
Application deadline:	March 15
Total amount awarded:	$61,197,000

Contact:
Kentucky Higher Education Assistance Authority (KHEAA)
Grant Programs
P.O. Box 798
Frankfort, KY 40602-0798
Phone: 800-928-8926
Fax: 502-696-7373
Web: www.kheaa.com

Kentucky Educational Excellence Scholarship (KEES)

Type of award: Scholarship, renewable.
Intended use: For undergraduate study at accredited vocational, 2-year or 4-year institution in United States. Designated institutions: Participating public and private postsecondary institutions in Kentucky and selected out-of-state institutions if program of study not offered in Kentucky.
Eligibility: Applicant must be enrolled in high school. Applicant must be U.S. citizen or permanent resident residing in Kentucky.
Basis for selection: Applicant must demonstrate high academic achievement.
Additional information: Scholarship is earned each year of high school. Minimum annual high school GPA of 2.5. Supplemental award is given for highest ACT score (or SAT equivalent) achieved by high school graduation, based on minimum ACT score of 15. Recipient must be enrolled in postsecondary program at least half-time. Visit Website or contact via e-mail for additional information.

Amount of award:	$125-$2,500
Number of awards:	65,400
Number of applicants:	65,400
Total amount awarded:	$90,789,000

Contact:
Kentucky Higher Education Assistance Authority (KHEAA)
P.O. Box 798
Frankfort, KY 40602-0798
Phone: 800-928-8926
Fax: 502-696-7373
Web: www.kheaa.com

Kentucky Teacher Scholarship

Type of award: Scholarship, renewable.
Intended use: For full-time undergraduate or graduate study at accredited 2-year, 4-year or graduate institution. Designated institutions: Participating Kentucky institutions.

Eligibility: Applicant must be U.S. citizen residing in Kentucky.
Basis for selection: Major/career interest in education, teacher; education, early childhood or education, special. Applicant must demonstrate financial need.
Application requirements: Proof of eligibility. FAFSA.
Additional information: Must enroll in course of study leading to initial Kentucky teacher certification. Loan forgiveness for teaching in Kentucky schools: one semester for each semester of financial assistance, two semesters if service is in teacher shortage area. Scholarship becomes loan if recipient does not complete education program or fulfill teaching obligation. Visit Website for application (see ZipAccess) and additional information.

Amount of award:	$300-$5,000
Number of awards:	600
Number of applicants:	1,450
Application deadline:	May 1
Notification begins:	May 30
Total amount awarded:	$2,135,000

Contact:
Kentucky Higher Education Assistance Authority (KHEAA)
Teacher Scholarship Program
P.O. Box 798
Frankfort, KY 40602-0798
Phone: 800-928-8926
Fax: 502-696-7373
Web: www.kheaa.com

Kentucky Tuition Grant

Type of award: Scholarship, renewable.
Intended use: For full-time undergraduate study at 2-year or 4-year institution. Designated institutions: Eligible private institutions in Kentucky.
Eligibility: Applicant must be U.S. citizen residing in Kentucky.
Basis for selection: Applicant must demonstrate financial need.
Application requirements: Proof of eligibility. FAFSA.
Additional information: Visit Website for additional information.

Amount of award:	$200-$3,000
Number of awards:	12,600
Number of applicants:	36,600
Application deadline:	March 15
Notification begins:	April 15
Total amount awarded:	$32,002,000

Contact:
Kentucky Higher Education Assistance Authority
Grant Programs
P.O. Box 798
Frankfort, KY 40602-0798
Phone: 800-928-8926
Fax: 502-696-7373
Web: www.kheaa.com

Mary Jo Young Scholarship

Type of award: Scholarship.
Intended use: For freshman or non-degree study at postsecondary institution.
Eligibility: Applicant must be enrolled in high school. Applicant must be residing in Kentucky.
Basis for selection: Applicant must demonstrate financial need.
Additional information: Provides college tuition assistance to disadvantaged high school students taking dual credit college

courses or AP courses through the Kentucky Virtual High School. Eligibility for free or reduced lunch through high school required. Award amounts are: $375 per semester if taking one course; $750 per semester if taking two courses.

Number of awards:	500
Number of applicants:	960
Application deadline:	May 1
Total amount awarded:	$259,000

Contact:
Kentucky Higher Education Assistance Authority (KHEAA)
P.O. Box 798
Frankfort, KY 40602-0798
Phone: 800-928-8926
Fax: 502-696-7373
Web: www.kheaa.com

Robert C. Byrd Honors Scholarship

Type of award: Scholarship, renewable.
Intended use: For undergraduate study at 2-year or 4-year institution in United States.
Eligibility: Applicant must be high school senior. Applicant must be U.S. citizen residing in Kentucky.
Basis for selection: Applicant must demonstrate high academic achievement.
Application requirements: Recommendation from school official or GED coordinator, who must certify eligibility on KHEAA Website.
Additional information: Minimum 3.5 GPA, and minimum 23 ACT score or minimum 1060 SAT score; or 2700 GED score. Maximum award is $1,500 per year, renewable for four years. See Website or school guidance counselor for more information. Apply through ZipAccess on Website.

Amount of award:	$1,500
Number of awards:	380
Number of applicants:	1,700
Application deadline:	February 1
Notification begins:	May 30
Total amount awarded:	$543,000

Contact:
Kentucky Higher Education Assistance Authority
P.O. Box 798
Frankfort, KY 40602-0798
Phone: 800-928-8926
Fax: 502-696-7373
Web: www.kheaa.com

The Kim and Harold Louie Family Foundation

The Louie Foundation Scholarship

Type of award: Scholarship.
Intended use: For full-time undergraduate study at vocational, 2-year or 4-year institution.
Eligibility: Applicant must be U.S. citizen or permanent resident.
Basis for selection: Applicant must demonstrate financial need and high academic achievement.
Application requirements: Recommendations, transcript, proof of eligibility. Proof of acceptance to college, personal essays, SAR, proof of citizenship or legal residency.
Additional information: Minimum 3.5 GPA; SAT score of 1800. Special consideration will be noted for applicants whose

parents did not attend college, whose parents are United States veterans, who have overcome significant adversity, or who are first-generation immigrants to the United States.

Number of awards:	20
Number of applicants:	400
Application deadline:	March 1
Total amount awarded:	$100,000

Contact:
The Kim and Harold Louie Family Foundation - Scholarship
102 Fey Drive
Burlingame, CA 94010
Phone: 650-491-3434
Fax: 650-490-3153
Web: www.louiefamilyfoundation.org

Knights of Columbus

Matthews/Swift Educational Trust - Military Dependants

Type of award: Scholarship, renewable.
Intended use: For full-time undergraduate study at 4-year institution in United States. Designated institutions: Catholic colleges and universities.
Eligibility: Applicant or parent must be member/participant of Knights of Columbus. Applicant must be Roman Catholic. Applicant must be veteran; or dependent of disabled veteran or deceased veteran who served in the Army, Air Force, Marines, Navy, Coast Guard or Reserves/National Guard during Korean War, Persian Gulf War, WW II or Vietnam. Veterans of Iraq, Afghanistan and Pakistan conflicts and their dependents are also eligible. Parent must have been active Knights of Columbus member who died or became totally disabled while serving in the military during hostile action.
Application requirements: Proof of eligibility.
Additional information: Application must be filed within two years of death or determination of disability. Award pays tuition up to $25,000 for bachelor's degree at Catholic college. No application deadline.

Amount of award:	$25,000

Contact:
Knights of Columbus
Department of Scholarships
P.O. Box 1670
New Haven, CT 06507-0901
Phone: 203-752-4332
Fax: 203-752-4103

Matthews/Swift Educational Trust - Police/Firefighters

Type of award: Scholarship, renewable.
Intended use: For full-time undergraduate study at 4-year institution in United States. Designated institutions: Catholic colleges and universities.
Eligibility: Applicant or parent must be member/participant of Knights of Columbus. Applicant must be Roman Catholic. Applicant's parent must have been killed or disabled in work-related accident as firefighter or police officer.
Application requirements: Proof of eligibility.
Additional information: Parent must have been active Knights of Columbus member who died as the result of criminal violence while performing duties as full-time firefighter or law enforcement officer. Application must be filed within two

years of death or determination of disability. Award pays tuition up to $25,000 for bachelor's degree at Catholic college. No application deadline.

Amount of award:	Full tuition
Total amount awarded:	$25,000

Contact:
Knights of Columbus
Department of Scholarships
P.O. Box 1670
New Haven, CT 06507-0901
Phone: 203-752-4332
Fax: 203-752-4103

Pro Deo/Pro Patria Scholarship

Type of award: Scholarship, renewable.
Intended use: For full-time freshman study at 4-year institution in United States. Designated institutions: Catholic colleges and universities.
Eligibility: Applicant or parent must be member/participant of Knights of Columbus. Applicant must be high school senior. Applicant must be Roman Catholic. Applicant must be U.S. citizen.
Basis for selection: Applicant must demonstrate high academic achievement.
Application requirements: Recommendations, essay, transcript, proof of eligibility.
Additional information: Must be Knights of Columbus member in good standing; child of such a member or deceased member; or member in good standing of Columbian Squires. There are 12 scholarships designated for students at the Catholic University of America in Washington, DC; 50 scholarships available to students entering other Catholic colleges in the United States. Scholarships are renewable for up to four years, pending satisfactory academic performance. Obtain application from Department of Scholarships, Knights of Columbus, in New Haven, CT.

Amount of award:	$1,500
Number of awards:	62
Number of applicants:	600
Application deadline:	March 1
Notification begins:	May 1
Total amount awarded:	$305,250

Contact:
Knights of Columbus
Department of Scholarships
P.O. Box 1670
New Haven, CT 06507-0901
Phone: 203-752-4332
Fax: 203-752-4103

Kosciuszko Foundation

Kosciuszko Foundation Year Abroad Program

Type of award: Scholarship, renewable.
Intended use: For sophomore, junior, senior or graduate study at 4-year or graduate institution in Poland. Designated institutions: Jagiellonian University, Institute of Polish Diaspora and Ethnic Studies (formerly the Polonia Institute, Krakow).
Eligibility: Applicant must be U.S. citizen or permanent resident.

Basis for selection: Competition/talent/interest in study abroad. Major/career interest in Polish language/studies. Applicant must demonstrate high academic achievement.

Application requirements: $50 application fee. Recommendations, essay, transcript. Certificate of proficiency in Polish, two passport-sized photos with full name on reverse side of each. Graduates must submit copies of degree diplomas, Polish Ministry of Education application completed in English.

Additional information: Must have interest in Polish subjects and/or involvement in Polish-American community. Scholarship covers tuition and stipend for housing and living expenses for one academic year or semester. Airfare not included. Minimum 3.0 GPA. Visit Website for more information and application. Applications available from October 1 to December 30.

Amount of award:	Full tuition
Number of applicants:	12
Total amount awarded:	$11,475

Contact:
Kosciuszko Foundation
Year Abroad Program
15 East 65th Street
New York, NY 10065
Phone: 212-734-2130 ext.210
Fax: 212-628-4552
Web: www.kosciuszkofoundation.org

Massachusetts Federation of Polish Women's Clubs Scholarships

Type of award: Scholarship.

Intended use: For full-time sophomore, junior or senior study at postsecondary institution in United States.

Eligibility: Applicant must be Polish. Applicant must be U.S. citizen or permanent resident.

Basis for selection: Applicant must demonstrate financial need and high academic achievement.

Application requirements: $35 application fee. Recommendations, essay, transcript, proof of eligibility. Proof of Polish ancestry. Two passport-sized photos with full name printed on reverse side of each. SASE.

Additional information: Applicant must be member of Massachusetts Federation of Polish Women's Clubs. Children and grandchildren of federation members also eligible. Minimum 3.0 GPA. Selection based on academic excellence, motivation, and interest in Polish subjects and involvement in Polish-American community. Only one member per immediate family may receive Massachusetts Federation of Polish Women's Scholarship during any given academic year. Visit Website for more information and application.

Amount of award:	$1,250
Number of applicants:	3
Application deadline:	January 5
Notification begins:	May 1
Total amount awarded:	$7,000

Contact:
Kosciuszko Foundation
15 East 65th Street
New York, NY 10065
Phone: 212-734-2130 ext.210
Fax: 212-628-4552
Web: www.kosciuszkofoundation.org

The Polish American Club of North Jersey Scholarships

Type of award: Scholarship, renewable.

Intended use: For full-time undergraduate or graduate study at accredited postsecondary institution in United States.

Eligibility: Applicant must be Polish. Applicant must be U.S. citizen or permanent resident.

Basis for selection: Applicant must demonstrate financial need and high academic achievement.

Application requirements: $35 application fee. Recommendations, essay, transcript, proof of eligibility. Proof of Polish ancestry. Two passport-sized photos with full name printed on reverse side of each. SASE.

Additional information: Applicant must be an active member of Polish American Club of North Jersey. Children and grandchildren of Polish American Club of North Jersey members also eligible. Minimum 3.0 GPA. Only one member per immediate family may receive a Polish American Club of North Jersey Scholarship during any given academic year. Selection based on academic excellence, motivation, and interest in Polish subjects and involvement in the Polish-American community. Number of awards varies. Applications available October 1 through December 30. Visit Website for application and more information.

Amount of award:	$500-$2,000
Number of applicants:	7
Application deadline:	January 5
Notification begins:	May 1
Total amount awarded:	$7,200

Contact:
Kosciuszko Foundation
15 East 65th Street
New York, NY 10065
Phone: 212-734-2130 ext.210
Fax: 212-628-4552
Web: www.kosciuszkofoundation.org

The Polish National Alliance of Brooklyn, USA, Inc. Scholarships

Type of award: Scholarship, renewable.

Intended use: For full-time undergraduate study at accredited postsecondary institution in United States.

Eligibility: Applicant or parent must be member/participant of Polish National Alliance of Brooklyn. Applicant must be Polish. Applicant must be U.S. citizen or permanent resident.

Basis for selection: Applicant must demonstrate financial need and high academic achievement.

Application requirements: $35 application fee. Recommendations, essay, transcript, proof of eligibility. Proof of Polish ancestry. Two passport-sized photos with full name printed on reverse side of each. SASE.

Additional information: Applicant must be member in good standing of Polish National Alliance of Brooklyn, USA, Inc. Minimum 3.0 GPA. Only one member per immediate family may receive scholarship during any given academic year. Selection based on academic excellence, motivation, and interest in Polish subjects and involvement in the Polish-American community. Applications available October 1 through December 30. Visit Website for application and more information.

Amount of award:	$2,000
Number of awards:	3
Number of applicants:	7
Application deadline:	January 5
Notification begins:	May 15
Total amount awarded:	$6,000

Contact:
Kosciuszko Foundation
15 East 65th Street
New York, NY 10065
Phone: 212-734-2130 ext.210
Fax: 212-628-4552
Web: www.kosciuszkofoundation.org

The Lagrant Foundation

Lagrant Scholarships

Type of award: Scholarship.
Intended use: For full-time sophomore, junior, senior or graduate study at accredited 4-year or graduate institution.
Eligibility: Applicant must be Alaskan native, African American, Mexican American, Hispanic American, Puerto Rican, American Indian or Native Hawaiian/Pacific Islander. Applicant must be U.S. citizen or permanent resident.
Basis for selection: Major/career interest in advertising; marketing or public relations.
Application requirements: Recommendations, essay, transcript. Resume.
Additional information: Minimum 2.75 GPA for undergraduates; 3.2 GPA for graduate students. Chosen applicant must attend The Lagrant Foundation's career development workshop and awards reception to receive scholarship. In addition, recipient must make one-year commitment to maintain contact with TLF to receive professional guidance and academic support. Visit Website for application and deadline.

Amount of award:	$5,000-$10,000
Number of awards:	20
Number of applicants:	150
Application deadline:	February 25
Total amount awarded:	$125,000

Contact:
The Lagrant Foundation
600 Wilshire Boulevard, Suite 1520
Los Angeles, CA 90017-3247
Phone: 323-469-8680
Web: www.lagrantfoundation.org

Lambda Alpha National Collegiate Honors Society for Anthropology

Senior Scholarship

Type of award: Scholarship.
Intended use: For senior study in United States.
Eligibility: Applicant or parent must be member/participant of Lambda Alpha. Applicant must be U.S. citizen or permanent resident.
Basis for selection: Major/career interest in anthropology. Applicant must demonstrate high academic achievement and seriousness of purpose.
Application requirements: Recommendations, transcript, nomination by faculty sponsor from department of anthropology. Curriculum vitae, writing sample.

Additional information: Institution must have a chartered Lambda Alpha chapter. Apply in senior year.

Amount of award:	$5,000
Number of awards:	1
Number of applicants:	16
Application deadline:	March 1
Notification begins:	May 1
Total amount awarded:	$5,000

Contact:
Lambda Alpha National Collegiate Honors Society for Anthropology
Department of Anthropology, Attn: B.K. Swartz
Ball State University
Muncie, IN 47306-0435
Phone: 765-285-1575
Web: www.lambdaalpha.com

Landscape Architecture Foundation

ASLA Council of Fellows Scholarship

Type of award: Scholarship.
Intended use: For junior or senior study at accredited 4-year institution in United States.
Eligibility: Applicant must be U.S. citizen or permanent resident.
Basis for selection: Applicant must demonstrate financial need.
Application requirements: Recommendations, essay. Photo in jpg format; two letters of recommendation, at least one from a faculty member, 500-word essay about how applicant will contribute to the profession of landscape architecture; 250-word statement describing financial need; SAR.
Additional information: Two scholarships awarded; one specifically available to students of under-represented populations. Applicants seeking consideration for diversity scholarship should indicate specific cultural or ethnic group. Each winner will receive a one-year student ASLA membership and airfare to attend ASLA meeting where award is presented.

Amount of award:	$4,000
Number of awards:	2
Application deadline:	February 16
Total amount awarded:	$8,000

Contact:
Landscape Architecture Foundation
818 18th Street
Suite 810
Washington, DC 20006
Phone: 202-331-7070
Fax: 202-898-1185
Web: www.lafoundation.org

Courtland Paul Scholarship

Type of award: Scholarship.
Intended use: For junior or senior study at accredited postsecondary institution. Designated institutions: Schools accredited by the Landscape Architecture Accreditation Board.
Eligibility: Applicant must be U.S. citizen.
Basis for selection: Major/career interest in landscape architecture. Applicant must demonstrate financial need and seriousness of purpose.

Application requirements: Recommendations, essay. Cover sheet, personal profile.

Additional information: All application materials must be sent together in one email, except for the recommendation letters which must be sent by email from the author. Minimum 'C' GPA. Award must be used for tuition and/or books within the school year of the award.

Amount of award:	$5,000
Number of applicants:	37
Application deadline:	February 16

Contact:
Landscape Architecture Foundation
818 18th Street
Suite 810
Washington, DC 20006
Phone: 202-331-7070
Fax: 202-898-1185
Web: www.lafoundation.org

David T. Woolsey Scholarship

Type of award: Scholarship.

Intended use: For full-time junior, senior or graduate study at accredited 4-year or graduate institution.

Eligibility: Applicant must be permanent resident residing in Hawaii.

Basis for selection: Major/career interest in landscape architecture. Applicant must demonstrate service orientation.

Application requirements: Recommendations, essay. Photo. Cover Letter. Three 8 1/2x11 work samples as jpg or pdf. Personal profile, proof of Hawaii residency.

Additional information: Applicant must be enrolled in landscape architecture program at accredited college or university. Visit Website for more information.

Amount of award:	$2,000
Number of awards:	1
Application deadline:	February 16

Contact:
Landscape Architecture Foundation
818 18th Street
Suite 810
Washington, DC 20006
Phone: 202-331-7070
Fax: 202-898-1185
Web: www.lafoundation.org

The EDSA Minority Scholarship

Type of award: Scholarship.

Intended use: For junior or senior study at postsecondary institution.

Eligibility: Applicant must be Alaskan native, Asian American, African American, Mexican American, Hispanic American, Puerto Rican, American Indian or Native Hawaiian/Pacific Islander.

Basis for selection: Major/career interest in landscape architecture. Applicant must demonstrate financial need and seriousness of purpose.

Application requirements: Recommendations, transcript. Cover letter, personal profile, 500-word essay describing design effort you plan to pursue and its contribution to the advancement of the profession and your ethnic heritage, three work samples (jpg or pdf).

Additional information: Visit Website for more information.

Amount of award:	$5,000
Number of awards:	1
Number of applicants:	7
Application deadline:	February 16

Contact:
Landscape Architecture Foundation
818 18th Street
Suite 810
Washington, DC 20006
Phone: 202-331-7070
Fax: 202-898-1185
Web: www.lafoundation.org

Landscape Forms Design for People Scholarship

Type of award: Scholarship.

Intended use: For full-time senior study at postsecondary institution. Designated institutions: Schools with LAAB-accredited program.

Basis for selection: Major/career interest in landscape architecture. Applicant must demonstrate financial need and seriousness of purpose.

Application requirements: Portfolio, recommendations, transcript. Cover sheet, personal profile, 300-word essay describing qualities essential to great and successful public spaces, three work samples (jpg or pdf).

Additional information: Must show proven contribution to design of public spaces that promote social interaction.

Amount of award:	$3,000
Number of awards:	1
Number of applicants:	17
Application deadline:	February 16

Contact:
Landscape Architecture Foundation
818 18th Street
Suite 810
Washington, DC 20006
Phone: 202-331-7070
Fax: 202-898-1185
Web: www.lafoundation.org

Peridian International Inc./Rae L. Price FASLA Scholarship

Type of award: Scholarship.

Intended use: For junior or senior study at postsecondary institution. Designated institutions: UCLA.

Eligibility: Applicant must be U.S. citizen.

Basis for selection: Major/career interest in landscape architecture. Applicant must demonstrate financial need and high academic achievement.

Application requirements: Recommendations, essay. Photo in jpg format.

Additional information: Award restricted to tuition, books, and program required supplies. Minimum 'B' GPA.

Amount of award:	$5,000
Application deadline:	February 16

Contact:
Landscape Architecture Foundation
818 18th Street
Suite 810
Washington, DC 20006
Phone: 202-331-7070
Fax: 202-898-1185
Web: www.lafoundation.org

Rain Bird Intelligent Use of Water Company Scholarship

Type of award: Scholarship.

Intended use: For full-time junior or senior study at accredited 4-year institution.
Basis for selection: Major/career interest in landscape architecture; horticulture; hydrology or urban planning. Applicant must demonstrate high academic achievement.
Application requirements: Essay. Photo, personal profile. Cover letter explaining enclosures and interests. 300-word essay stating career goals and how applicant will continue advancement of landscape architecture.
Additional information: Visit Website for more information.

Amount of award:	$2,500
Number of awards:	1
Number of applicants:	30
Application deadline:	February 16

Contact:
Landscape Architecture Foundation
818 18th Street
Suite 810
Washington, DC 20006
Phone: 202-331-7070
Fax: 202-898-1185
Web: www.lafoundation.org

Steven G. King Play Environments Scholarship

Type of award: Scholarship.
Intended use: For full-time junior, senior or graduate study. Designated institutions: LAAB-accredited schools.
Basis for selection: Major/career interest in landscape architecture. Applicant must demonstrate financial need and seriousness of purpose.
Application requirements: Recommendations, transcript. Cover sheet, personal profile, 500-word essay explaining value of play and of integrating playgrounds into recreation environments, plan or details of play environment of applicant's design (jpg or pdf).
Additional information: Must have demonstrated interest in park and playground planning.

Amount of award:	$5,000
Number of awards:	1
Number of applicants:	9
Application deadline:	February 16

Contact:
Landscape Architecture Foundation
818 18th Street
Suite 810
Washington, DC 20006
Phone: 202-331-7070
Fax: 202-898-1185
Web: www.lafoundation.org

Latin American Educational Foundation

Latin American Educational Scholarship

Type of award: Scholarship, renewable.
Intended use: For full-time undergraduate or non-degree study at accredited postsecondary institution in United States.

Eligibility: Applicant must be Mexican American, Hispanic American or Puerto Rican. Applicant must be residing in Colorado.
Basis for selection: Applicant must demonstrate financial need, high academic achievement, leadership and service orientation.
Application requirements: Recommendations, essay, transcript. Previous year's tax return.
Additional information: Minimum 3.0 GPA. SAT/ACT scores required for high school seniors. Must be Hispanic American or actively involved in Hispanic American community. Recipients must fulfill ten hours of community service during the award year. Applicants must reapply each year.

Amount of award:	$750-$2,000
Number of awards:	100
Number of applicants:	350
Application deadline:	March 15
Notification begins:	June 15
Total amount awarded:	$135,000

Contact:
Latin American Education Foundation
561 Santa Fe Drive
Denver, CO 80214
Phone: 303-446-0541 ext. 12
Fax: 303-446-0526
Web: www.laef.org

League of United Latin American Citizens

GE Business/Engineering Scholarship for Minority Students

Type of award: Scholarship, renewable.
Intended use: For full-time sophomore study at accredited 2-year or 4-year institution in United States.
Eligibility: Applicant must be Alaskan native, Asian American, African American, Mexican American, Hispanic American, Puerto Rican, American Indian or Native Hawaiian/Pacific Islander. Applicant must be U.S. citizen or permanent resident.
Basis for selection: Major/career interest in business or engineering. Applicant must demonstrate high academic achievement, seriousness of purpose and service orientation.
Application requirements: Recommendations, essay, transcript, proof of eligibility.
Additional information: Must be minority student with minimum 3.25 GPA who is entering sophomore year in the fall. Recipients may be offered temporary summer or internship positions with GE businesses; however, the students are under no obligation to accept GE employment. Application available on Website.

Amount of award:	$5,000
Number of awards:	11
Application deadline:	July 15
Notification begins:	August 15
Total amount awarded:	$55,000

Contact:
League of United Latin American Citizens
Attn: GE Scholarship
2000 L Street NW, Suite 610
Washington, DC 20036
Phone: 202-835-9646
Web: www.lnesc.org

LULAC National Scholarship Fund Honors Awards

Type of award: Scholarship.
Intended use: For full-time undergraduate or graduate study at accredited vocational, 2-year, 4-year or graduate institution in United States.
Eligibility: Applicant must be Mexican American, Hispanic American or Puerto Rican. Applicant must be U.S. citizen or permanent resident.
Basis for selection: Applicant must demonstrate high academic achievement.
Application requirements: Essay, transcript, proof of eligibility. Verification of admittance to institution.
Additional information: Students are ineligible for scholarship if related to scholarship committee member, council president, or individual contributor to the local funds of the council. Minimum 3.25 GPA. Entering freshmen must have scored at least 23 on ACT or 1100 on SAT. Submit application to local participating LULAC council. See Website for application and list of participating LULAC councils. Local LULAC council may require additional information and personal interview.

Amount of award:	$500-$2,000
Application deadline:	March 31
Notification begins:	May 15

Contact:
Phone: 202-835-9646
Web: www.lnesc.org

LULAC National Scholarship Fund National Scholastic Achievement Awards

Type of award: Scholarship.
Intended use: For full-time undergraduate or graduate study at accredited 2-year, 4-year or graduate institution in United States.
Eligibility: Applicant must be Hispanic American. Applicant must be U.S. citizen or permanent resident.
Basis for selection: Applicant must demonstrate high academic achievement.
Application requirements: Essay, transcript, proof of eligibility. Verification of admittance to institution.
Additional information: Students are ineligible for scholarship if related to scholarship committee member, council president, or individual contributor to the local funds of the council. Entering freshmen must have scored at least 29 on ACT or 1350 on SAT. Minimum 3.5 GPA. Minimum amount of award is $1,000. See Website for list of participating LULAC councils. Local LULAC council may require additional information and personal interview.

Amount of award:	$2,000
Application deadline:	March 31
Notification begins:	May 15

Contact:
Contact local LULAC council for more information.
Phone: 202-833-6130
Web: www.lnesc.org

LULAC National Scholarshp Fund General Awards

Type of award: Scholarship.
Intended use: For undergraduate or graduate study at accredited vocational, 2-year, 4-year or graduate institution in United States.
Eligibility: Applicant must be Mexican American, Hispanic American or Puerto Rican. Applicant must be U.S. citizen or permanent resident.
Basis for selection: Applicant must demonstrate financial need, high academic achievement, depth of character, leadership and service orientation.
Application requirements: Interview, essay, transcript, proof of eligibility. Verification of admittance to institution.
Additional information: Academic performance considered, however motivation, sincerity, and integrity will also be considered in selection process. Students are ineligible for scholarship if related to scholarship committee member, council president, or individual contributor to the local funds of the council. Submit application to local participating LULAC council. See Website for application and list of participating councils. Local council may require additional information and personal interview.

Amount of award:	$250-$1,000
Application deadline:	March 31
Notification begins:	May 15
Total amount awarded:	$750,000

Contact:
Phone: 202-835-9646
Web: www.lnesc.org

Learning for Life

Captain James J. Regan Memorial Scholarship

Type of award: Scholarship.
Intended use: For full-time undergraduate study at accredited postsecondary institution.
Eligibility: Applicant or parent must be member/participant of Learning for Life. Applicant must be U.S. citizen or permanent resident.
Basis for selection: Major/career interest in criminal justice/law enforcement. Applicant must demonstrate high academic achievement, leadership and seriousness of purpose.
Application requirements: Essay, transcript, proof of eligibility. Certification from post advisor, head of participating organization, Learning for Life representative. Three letters of recommendation (two from outside of law enforcement). Additional essay (minimum of 250 words) on "How Will Technology Affect Law Enforcement in the 21st Century?" Black-and-white photo (preferably in uniform). Must submit original and four copies of all materials.
Additional information: Program open to Learning for Life's Law Enforcement Explorers. Visit Website for application and more information.

Amount of award:	$500
Number of awards:	2
Application deadline:	March 31
Total amount awarded:	$1,000

Contact:
National Law Enforcement Scholarships and Awards
1325 West Walnut Hill Lane
P.O. Box 152079
Irving, TX 75015
Phone: 972-580-2433
Fax: 972-580-2502
Web: www.learning-for-life.org/exploring

Sheryl A. Horak Law Enforcement Explorer Scholarship

Type of award: Scholarship.
Intended use: For full-time undergraduate study at accredited 2-year or 4-year institution.
Eligibility: Applicant or parent must be member/participant of Learning for Life. Applicant must be high school senior. Applicant must be U.S. citizen or permanent resident.
Basis for selection: Major/career interest in criminal justice/ law enforcement. Applicant must demonstrate high academic achievement, leadership and service orientation.
Application requirements: Transcript. Certification from post advisor, head of participating organization, Learning for Life representative. Three letters of recommendation (two from outside of law enforcement). Essay (500 words minimum) on "Why I Want to Pursue a Career in Law Enforcement." Black-and-white photo (preferably in uniform). Must submit original and two copies of all materials.
Additional information: Program open to Learning for Life's Law Enforcement Explorers. Number of awards granted varies. Visit Website for application and more information.

Amount of award:	$1,000
Application deadline:	March 31

Contact:
National Law Enforcement Scholarships and Awards
1325 West Walnut Hill Lane
P.O. Box 152079
Irving, TX 75015
Phone: 972-580-2433
Fax: 972-580-2502
Web: www.learning-for-life.org/exploring

Life and Health Insurance Foundation for Education

LIFE Lessons Essay Contest

Type of award: Scholarship.
Intended use: For undergraduate study at postsecondary institution in United States.
Eligibility: Applicant must be at least 17, no older than 24. Applicant must be U.S. citizen or permanent resident.
Basis for selection: Competition/talent/interest in writing/ journalism, based on 500-word essay or 3-minute video describing how applicant has experienced personal and financial challenges caused by death of parent or legal guardian.
Application requirements: Proof of eligibility. Essay of 500 words or 3-minute video describing personal and financial challenges caused by death of a parent.

Additional information: Applicant must have experienced the death of a parent or legal guardian. Apply online, or e-mail or call to receive paper application. Employees of Life and Health Insurance Foundation for Education ("LIFE" or "Sponsor"), Weber Shandwick, and their respective parents, affiliates, subsidiaries, and advertising, and promotion agencies, and any such employee's immediate family members and those living in their same households, whether or not related, are not eligible.

Amount of award:	$1,000-$10,000
Number of awards:	51
Application deadline:	April 15
Total amount awarded:	$65,000

Contact:
Life and Health Insurance Foundation for Education
Attn: Life Lessons Scholarship Essay Contest
1655 North Fort Meyer Drive, Suite 610
Arlington, VA 22209
Phone: 202-464-5000 ext. 4446
Fax: 202-464-5011
Web: www.lifehappens.org/life-lessons

Liggett-Stashower, Inc.

David L. Stashower Scholarship

Type of award: Scholarship.
Intended use: For senior study at 4-year institution. Designated institutions: Ohio colleges and universities.
Eligibility: Applicant must be residing in Ohio.
Basis for selection: Major/career interest in advertising; graphic arts/design; public relations or communications. Applicant must demonstrate high academic achievement.
Application requirements: Recommendations, essay, transcript. Optional: Portfolio of work, writing samples, or other form of appropriate communication.
Additional information: Award includes trip to Cleveland in August for awards ceremony at Liggett-Stashower.

Amount of award:	$2,000
Number of awards:	2
Number of applicants:	23
Total amount awarded:	$4,000

Contact:
Scholarship Award Committee Liggett-Stashower, Inc
LS Brand Building
1240 Huron Road
Cleveland, OH 44115
Phone: 216-348-8500
Web: www.liggett.com

Lighthouse International

Christine H. Eidie Memorial Scholarship

Type of award: Scholarship.
Intended use: For full-time undergraduate or graduate study at accredited 4-year or graduate institution.
Eligibility: Applicant must be visually impaired.
Application requirements: Essay, proof of eligibility. Proof of legal blindness.

Amount of award:	$500
Number of awards:	1
Number of applicants:	2
Application deadline:	January 15, September 2
Total amount awarded:	$1,000

Contact:
Lighthouse International
Attn: Dr. Cynthia Stuen
111 East 59th Street
New York, NY 10022-1202
Phone: 212-821-9428
Fax: 212-821-9703
Web: www.lighthouse.org

Lighthouse College-Bound Award

Type of award: Scholarship.
Intended use: For full-time freshman study at accredited 2-year or 4-year institution in United States.
Eligibility: Applicant must be visually impaired. Applicant must be high school senior. Applicant must be U.S. citizen residing in Virginia, Vermont, West Virginia, or South Carolina.
Basis for selection: Applicant must demonstrate high academic achievement.
Application requirements: Recommendations, essay, transcript, proof of eligibility. Official documentation of legal blindness. Recommendations required from two people other than family members. Personal essay should be at least 500 words. Letter of acceptance to college.
Additional information: Applicant must be legally blind. College-bound high school seniors or recent high school graduates now planning to begin college may apply. Previous SCA recipients and Lighthouse employees and members are ineligible.

Amount of award:	$5,000
Number of awards:	1
Number of applicants:	65
Application deadline:	February 27
Total amount awarded:	$5,000

Contact:
Lighthouse International
Scholarship Awards Program
111 East 59 Street
New York, NY 10022-1202
Phone: 212-821-9200
Fax: 212-821-9707
Web: www.lighthouse.org/sca

Lighthouse Undergraduate Award

Type of award: Scholarship.
Intended use: For full-time undergraduate study at postsecondary institution.
Eligibility: Applicant must be visually impaired. Applicant must be U.S. citizen.
Basis for selection: Applicant must demonstrate high academic achievement.
Application requirements: Recommendations, essay, transcript, proof of eligibility. Official documentation of legal blindness. Recommendations required from two people other than family members. Personal essay should be at least 500 words.
Additional information: Applicant must be legally blind. Previous SCA recipients and Lighthouse members and employees are ineligible.

Amount of award:	$5,000
Number of awards:	1
Number of applicants:	65
Application deadline:	February 27
Total amount awarded:	$5,000

Contact:
Lighthouse International
Scholarship Awards Program
111 East 59 Street
New York, NY 10022-1202
Phone: 212-821-9200
Fax: 212-821-9707
Web: www.lighthouse.org

Los Padres Foundation

Los Padres Foundation College Tuition Assistance Program

Type of award: Scholarship, renewable.
Intended use: For full-time undergraduate or graduate study at 4-year or graduate institution in United States.
Eligibility: Applicant must be Mexican American, Hispanic American or Puerto Rican. Applicant must be high school senior. Applicant must be U.S. citizen or permanent resident residing in New York or New Jersey.
Basis for selection: Applicant must demonstrate seriousness of purpose and service orientation.
Additional information: Applicant must have minimum 3.0 GPA and proof of low income. Applicant must be first generation in family to attend college. Award is renewable up to four years. Must complete 100 hours of community service by June 1st of first college year. Application available at financial aid office, high school counselor's office, and online.

Amount of award:	$2,000
Number of applicants:	30
Application deadline:	January 23

Contact:
Los Padres Foundation
CTA Program
P.O. Box 8421
McLean, VA 22106
Phone: 877-843-7555
Fax: 866-810-1361
Web: www.lospadresfoundation.org

Second Chance Program

Type of award: Scholarship.
Intended use: For undergraduate study at accredited vocational, 2-year or 4-year institution.
Eligibility: Applicant must be Mexican American, Hispanic American or Puerto Rican. Applicant must be U.S. citizen or permanent resident residing in New York, Puerto Rico or New Jersey.
Basis for selection: Applicant must demonstrate financial need.
Application requirements: Transcript, proof of eligibility. Proof of low income.
Additional information: Applicant must have high school diploma or GED and be out of high school for more than a year prior to submitting and never attended a postsecondary institution. Awardees must complete 100 hours of non-faith-based community service by June 1 of the first year in program.

Amount of award: $2,000
Application deadline: October 29
Contact:
Los Padres Foundation
Second Chance Program
P.O. Box 8421
McLean, VA 22106
Phone: 877-843-7555
Fax: 866-810-1361
Web: www.lospadresfoundation.org

Louisiana Department of Veterans Affairs

Louisiana Veterans Affairs Educational Assistance for Dependent Children

Type of award: Scholarship, renewable.
Intended use: For full-time undergraduate, graduate or non-degree study at vocational, 2-year, 4-year or graduate institution. Designated institutions: Louisiana public institutions.
Eligibility: Applicant must be at least 16, no older than 25. Applicant must be residing in Louisiana. Applicant must be dependent of disabled veteran or deceased veteran. Deceased veteran must have died of wartime injuries.
Application requirements: Proof of eligibility. Certification of eligibility.
Additional information: Award is a tuition waiver at all Louisiana state-supported schools. Veteran must have been Louisiana resident for at least two years prior to entering service. Disability must be at least 90 percent as rated by U.S. Department of Veterans Affairs to qualify. Applicant also eligible if disability rating is 60 percent or more but employability rating is 100 percent unemployable. Waiver available for five year period before applicant turns 25. Award amounts vary.
Amount of award: Full tuition
Contact:
Louisiana Department of Veterans Affairs
P.O. Box 94095, Capitol Station
Baton Rouge, LA 70804-9095
Phone: 225-922-0500 ext. 203
Fax: 225-922-0511
Web: www.vetaffairs.la.gov

Louisiana Veterans Affairs Educational Assistance for Surviving Spouse

Type of award: Scholarship, renewable.
Intended use: For full-time undergraduate, graduate or non-degree study at postsecondary institution. Designated institutions: Louisiana public institutions.
Eligibility: Applicant must be single. Applicant must be residing in Louisiana. Applicant must be spouse of deceased veteran. Veteran must have been a Louisiana resident at least 12 months prior to entering service.
Application requirements: Proof of eligibility. Certification of eligibility.
Amount of award: Full tuition

Contact:
Louisiana Department of Veterans Affairs
P.O. Box 94095, Capitol Station
Baton Rouge, LA 70804-9095
Phone: 225-922-0500 ext. 203
Fax: 225-922-0511
Web: www.vetaffairs.la.gov

Louisiana Office of Student Financial Assistance

Louisiana Go Grants

Type of award: Scholarship, renewable.
Intended use: For undergraduate study at postsecondary institution.
Eligibility: Applicant must be residing in Louisiana.
Basis for selection: Applicant must demonstrate financial need.
Application requirements: FAFSA.
Additional information: Financial aid for nontraditional and low to moderate income students. Must receive Pell grant to qualify.
Amount of award: $200-$2,000
Number of awards: 11,000
Number of applicants: 15,973
Total amount awarded: $26,026,000
Contact:
Louisiana Office of Student Financial Assistance
P.O. Box 91202
Baton Rouge, LA 70821-9202
Phone: 800-259-5626 ext 1012
Fax: 225-922-0790
Web: www.osfa.la.gov

Louisiana Rockefeller Wildlife Scholarship

Type of award: Scholarship, renewable.
Intended use: For full-time undergraduate or graduate study at 4-year or graduate institution.
Eligibility: Applicant must be U.S. citizen residing in Louisiana.
Basis for selection: Major/career interest in wildlife/fisheries; forestry or oceanography/marine studies. Applicant must demonstrate high academic achievement.
Application requirements: FAFSA, Rockefeller State Wildlife Application/Promissory Note.
Additional information: Minimum 2.5 GPA for undergraduate students or 3.0 for graduate students.
Amount of award: $1,000
Number of awards: 60
Number of applicants: 50
Application deadline: July 1
Total amount awarded: $60,000
Contact:
Louisiana Office of Student Financial Assistance
P.O. Box 91202
Baton Rouge, LA 70821-9202
Phone: 800-259-5626 ext. 1012
Fax: 225-922-0790
Web: www.osfa.la.gov

Scholarships

Louisiana Taylor Opportunity Program for Students (TOPS) Award

Type of award: Scholarship, renewable.
Intended use: For full-time undergraduate study at postsecondary institution. Designated institutions: Eligible Louisiana postsecondary institutions.
Eligibility: Applicant must be U.S. citizen or permanent resident residing in Louisiana.
Basis for selection: Applicant must demonstrate high academic achievement.
Application requirements: FAFSA. SAT or ACT scores.
Additional information: Open to Louisiana residents who will be first-time, full-time freshmen at Louisiana public or LAICU private postsecondary institutions no later than fall following first anniversary of high school graduation. Must have no criminal convictions. Must have completed 17.5 units college-prep TOPS core curriculum. Individual requirements for awards below; please send one inquiry, only, for all award levels: TOPS OPPORTUNITY AWARD: Equal to tuition at public institution (or weighted average tuition at LAICU member institution). Must have minimum 2.5 GPA, minimum ACT score based on state's prior year average (never below 20) or minimum SAT of 940. TOPS PERFORMANCE AWARDS: Equal to tuition at public institution (or weighted average tuition at LAICU member institution) plus $400/yr stipend. Minimum 3.0 GPA, minimum ACT score of 23 or SAT score of 1050. TOPS HONORS AWARDS: Equal to tuition at public institution (or weighted average tuition at LAICU member institution) plus $800/yr stipend. Minimum 3.0 GPA, ACT score of 27 or SAT score of 1210. Contact Public Information Rep for more details.

Amount of award:	Full tuition
Number of applicants:	31,022
Application deadline:	July 1
Notification begins:	June 1
Total amount awarded:	$117,300,000

Contact:
Louisiana Office of Student Financial Assistance
P.O. Box 91202
Baton Rouge, LA 70821-9202
Phone: 800-259-5626 ext. 1012
Fax: 225-922-0790
Web: www.osfa.la.gov

Louisiana State Department of Education

Robert C. Byrd Honors Scholarship

Type of award: Scholarship, renewable.
Intended use: For full-time undergraduate study at vocational, 2-year or 4-year institution.
Eligibility: Applicant must be U.S. citizen or permanent resident residing in Louisiana.
Basis for selection: Applicant must demonstrate high academic achievement.
Application requirements: Proof of eligibility. FAFSA.
Additional information: Minimum 3.5 GPA and 23 ACT or 970 SAT score or 620 GED score. Must have received high school diploma or GED in Louisiana. Award amount varies; maximum is $1,500 per year, renewable for up to four years.

Must be registered with the Selective Service, if required. Students at military academies not eligible. Award may be used for tuition for schools outside Louisiana.

Amount of award:	$1,500

Contact:
Louisiana State Department of Education
P.O. Box 94064
Baton Rouge, LA 70804
Phone: 225-342-2098 or 877-453-2721
Fax: 225-342-3432
Web: www.doe.state.la.us/lde/students.html

Maine Division of Veterans Services

Maine Veterans Services Dependents Educational Benefits

Type of award: Scholarship.
Intended use: For undergraduate or master's study at vocational, 2-year or 4-year institution.
Eligibility: Applicant must be at least 16, no older than 26. Applicant must be residing in Maine. Applicant must be dependent of disabled veteran; or spouse of disabled veteran. Must apply for program prior to 22nd birthday, or before 26th birthday if applicant was enrolled in the U.S. Armed Forces. Age limits apply to child applicants only, not spouses.
Application requirements: Proof of eligibility. Proof of veteran's disability, birth certificate. Stepchildren must provide parent's marriage certificate. Adopted children must provide adoption certificate or proof of paternity to natural parent. Spouse must provide marriage certificate.
Additional information: Applicant must have graduated from high school and must be dependent of permanently and totally disabled veteran. Parent or spouse must have been resident of Maine prior to enlistment or resident of Maine for five years preceding application for aid. Provides tuition at all branches of University of Maine system, all State of Maine vocational-technical colleges, and Maine Maritime Academy for eight semesters to be used within six years. Must maintain "C" average to continue receiving benefits.

Amount of award:	Full tuition

Contact:
Maine Division of Veterans Services
117 State House Station
Augusta, ME 04333-0117
Phone: 207-626-4464
Fax: 207-626-4471
Web: www.mainebvs.org

Maine Innkeepers Association

Maine Innkeepers Association Scholarship

Type of award: Scholarship.
Intended use: For full-time undergraduate or graduate study at accredited vocational, 4-year or graduate institution in United

States. Designated institutions: Institutions with fully accredited programs in hotel administration or culinary arts.
Eligibility: Applicant must be U.S. citizen or permanent resident residing in Maine.
Basis for selection: Major/career interest in culinary arts; hotel/restaurant management or hospitality administration/management. Applicant must demonstrate financial need and high academic achievement.
Application requirements: Recommendations, essay, transcript.
Additional information: Applicant must be Maine resident who is high school senior or college undergraduate.

Amount of award:	$500-$2,000
Number of awards:	10
Number of applicants:	30
Application deadline:	April 9
Notification begins:	January 1
Total amount awarded:	$8,000

Contact:
Maine Innkeepers Association
Scholarship Chairperson
304 US Route 1
Freeport, ME 04032
Phone: 207-865-6100
Fax: 207-865-6120
Web: www.maineinns.com

Maine Metal Products Association Education Fund

Maine Metal Products Association Scholarship

Type of award: Scholarship.
Intended use: For undergraduate study at postsecondary institution.
Eligibility: Applicant must be permanent resident residing in Maine.
Basis for selection: Major/career interest in engineering or welding. Applicant must demonstrate financial need, high academic achievement, depth of character, leadership, seriousness of purpose and service orientation.
Application requirements: Recommendations, essay, transcript, proof of eligibility.
Additional information: Applicant must have career interest in Maine precision machining technology or manufacturing technology industry or related majors. Amount of award varies based on need and fund account. Visit Website for more information.

Number of awards:	12
Number of applicants:	31
Application deadline:	May 1
Total amount awarded:	$2,400

Contact:
Dorota Olaru, Director of Finance and Administration
Maine Metal Products Association
386 Bridgton Road
Westbrook, ME 04092
Phone: 207-854-2153
Fax: 207-854-3865
Web: www.mainemfg.com

Maine Restaurant Association

Russ Casey Scholarship

Type of award: Scholarship.
Intended use: For undergraduate or graduate study at accredited 2-year, 4-year or graduate institution. Designated institutions: New England colleges and universities.
Eligibility: Applicant must be U.S. citizen residing in Maine.
Basis for selection: Major/career interest in culinary arts.
Application requirements: Transcript. Two recommendations from high school or college teachers, one from restaurant owner/manager or allied member of Maine Restaurant Association. Cover letter detailing applicant's interest in and connection to food service industry in 300 words or less.
Additional information: Open to Maine students pursuing career in food service industry.

Amount of award:	$1,000-$1,500
Number of awards:	8
Application deadline:	April 1
Total amount awarded:	$10,000

Contact:
Chairman, Scholarship Committee Maine Restaurant Association
P.O. Box 5060
5 Wade Street
Augusta, ME 04332
Phone: 207-623-2178
Fax: 207-623-8377
Web: www.mainerestaurant.com

Maine Society of Professional Engineers

Maine Society of Professional Engineers Scholarship Program

Type of award: Scholarship.
Intended use: For freshman study at 2-year or 4-year institution in United States. Designated institutions: ABET-accredited schools.
Eligibility: Applicant must be high school senior. Applicant must be permanent resident residing in Maine.
Basis for selection: Major/career interest in engineering or engineering, civil.
Application requirements: Recommendations, essay, transcript. SAT/ACT scores.
Additional information: Applicant must intend to earn a degree in engineering and to enter the practice of engineering after graduation. Must go to ABET-accredited school. Money awarded only after successful completion of first semester. Must be resident of Maine but awardees do not have to attend school in Maine.

Amount of award:	$1,500-$2,500
Number of awards:	2
Number of applicants:	50
Application deadline:	March 1
Notification begins:	May 30
Total amount awarded:	$5,000

Contact:
Colon Hewett
Maine Society of Professional Engineers
P.O. Box 318
Winthrop, ME 04364
Phone: 207-449-0339
Web: www.mespe.org

Maine State Society of Washington, DC

Maine State Society of Washington, DC, Foundation Scholarship Program

Type of award: Scholarship.
Intended use: For full-time sophomore, junior or senior study at accredited 4-year institution. Designated institutions: Maine institutions.
Eligibility: Applicant must be no older than 25. Applicant must be U.S. citizen.
Basis for selection: Applicant must demonstrate high academic achievement and seriousness of purpose.
Application requirements: Portfolio, essay, transcript, proof of eligibility.
Additional information: Applicant must have been born in Maine or have been legal resident of Maine for at least four years or have at least one parent who was born in Maine or who has been legal resident of Maine for at least four years. Applicant must currently attend college in Maine, with a minimum GPA of 3.0 for latest academic year. Requests for applications must include SASE. Visit Website for application.

Amount of award:	$1,000-$1,500
Number of awards:	12
Number of applicants:	73
Application deadline:	April 1
Notification begins:	May 15
Total amount awarded:	$7,000

Contact:
Maine State Society of Washington DC Foundation Scholarship Program
4718 Columbia Road
Annandale, VA 22003
Phone: 703-256-4524
Web: www.mainestatesociety.org/MSSFoundation.htm

Manomet Center for Conservation Sciences

Kathleen S. Anderson Award

Type of award: Research grant.
Intended use: For junior, senior or graduate study in or outside United States. Designated institutions: Institutions in Western Hemisphere.
Basis for selection: Major/career interest in ornithology. Applicant must demonstrate leadership and seriousness of purpose.

Application requirements: Recommendations, research proposal.
Additional information: Research grant: Either one $1,000 award or two $500 awards. Kathleen Anderson is asked to choose winner from five finalists submitted by Manomet staff. Apply via email only.

Amount of award:	$500-$1,000
Number of awards:	2
Number of applicants:	20
Application deadline:	December 1
Notification begins:	March 1
Total amount awarded:	$1,000

Contact:
Manomet Center for Conservation Sciences
c/o Jennie Robbins
P.O. Box 1770
Manomet, MA 02345
Phone: 508-224-6521
Fax: 508-224-9220
Web: www.manomet.org

Marin Community Foundation

Goldman Family Fund: New Leader Scholarship

Type of award: Scholarship, renewable.
Intended use: For full-time junior, senior or graduate study at postsecondary institution. Designated institutions: University of California, Berkeley; California State University East Bay; San Francisco State University; San Jose State University; Sonoma State University.
Eligibility: Applicant must be U.S. citizen or permanent resident residing in California.
Basis for selection: Major/career interest in economics; health sciences; law; medicine; psychology; social work or sociology. Applicant must demonstrate financial need, high academic achievement, leadership and service orientation.
Application requirements: Interview, recommendations, essay, transcript. Financial statement.
Additional information: Preference given to recent immigrants and students of color. Applicants do not need to be Marin County residents to apply. Applicants should demonstrate commitment to giving back to their communities and plan to pursue career in public, legal, psychological, health, or social services. Graduate students may be considered if they have received scholarship as undergraduate and are attending California public universities. See Website (www.goldmanfamilyfund.com) for more information. Minimum 3.5 GPA.

Amount of award:	$3,000-$7,000
Number of awards:	11
Number of applicants:	40
Application deadline:	March 15
Total amount awarded:	$50,000

Contact:
Marin Education Fund
New Leader Scholarship of Goldman Family Fund
781 Lincoln Avenue, Suite 140
San Rafael, CA 94901
Phone: 415-459-4240
Fax: 415-459-0527
Web: www.goldmanfamilyfund.org,
www.marineducationfund.org

Marin Education Fund

Marin Education Undergraduate Scholarships

Type of award: Scholarship, renewable.
Intended use: For undergraduate study at accredited 2-year or 4-year institution in United States.
Eligibility: Applicant must be residing in California.
Basis for selection: Applicant must demonstrate financial need.
Additional information: Must be resident of Marin County. Must be enrolled for minimum of nine units per term. Applicants automatically considered for six other scholarships ranging from $1,500-5,000. Visit Website for more information.
  Amount of award: $1,000-$5,000
Contact:
Marin Education Fund
781 Lincoln Avenue
San Rafael, CA 94901
Phone: 415-459-4240
Fax: 415-459-0527
Web: www.marineducationfund.org

Marine Corps Scholarship Foundation

Marine Corps Scholarship

Type of award: Scholarship, renewable.
Intended use: For undergraduate study at accredited vocational, 2-year or 4-year institution in United States.
Eligibility: Applicant must be U.S. citizen. Applicant must be dependent of active service person or veteran in the Marines. Must be child of active Marine, Marine reservist, or Marine who has received honorable discharge.
Basis for selection: Applicant must demonstrate financial need.
Application requirements: Essay, transcript, proof of eligibility. FAFSA, Tax return.
Additional information: Gross family income must not exceed $82,000. Open to high school seniors and undergraduates attending post-high school vocational/technical institutions.
  Amount of award: $500-$10,000
  Number of awards: 1,000
  Number of applicants: 1,400
  Application deadline: April 1
  Total amount awarded: $3,500,000

Contact:
Marine Corps Scholarship Foundation
P.O. Box 3008
Princeton, NJ 08543-3008
Phone: 800-292-7777
Fax: 609-452-2259
Web: www.mcsf.org

Maryland Higher Education Commission Office of Student Financial Assistance

Charles W. Riley Fire and Emergency Medical Services Tuition Reimbursement Program

Type of award: Scholarship, renewable.
Intended use: For undergraduate study at postsecondary institution.
Eligibility: Applicant must be U.S. citizen or permanent resident residing in Maryland.
Basis for selection: Major/career interest in fire science/technology or medical emergency.
Application requirements: Transcript, proof of eligibility.
Additional information: Applicant must be active career/volunteer firefighter or ambulance/rescue squad member serving the Maryland community while taking courses, and must agree to continue to serve for one year after completing courses. Must maintain satisfactory academic progress and remain enrolled in eligible program to renew award.
  Amount of award: Full tuition
  Number of awards: 108
  Number of applicants: 207
  Application deadline: July 1
  Total amount awarded: $340,979
Contact:
Maryland Higher Ed. Commission Office of Student Financial Assistance
Reimbursement of Firefighters
839 Bestgate Road, Suite 400
Annapolis, MD 21401-3013
Phone: 800-974-1024
Fax: 410-260-3200
Web: www.mhec.state.md.us/financialaid/descriptions

Howard P. Rawlings Guaranteed Access Grant

Type of award: Scholarship, renewable.
Intended use: For full-time undergraduate study at accredited postsecondary institution.
Eligibility: Applicant must be high school senior. Applicant must be U.S. citizen or permanent resident residing in Maryland.
Basis for selection: Applicant must demonstrate financial need.
Application requirements: Proof of eligibility. FAFSA.
Additional information: Applicant must be high school senior who has completed college preparatory program or has graduated prior to the academic year and provides written

documentation explaining why he or she was unable to attend college within one year of graduation from high school. Minimum 2.5 GPA. Must meet Guaranteed Access Family Grant income requirements; award equals 100% of student's financial need.

Amount of award:	$400-$13,700
Number of awards:	1,156
Number of applicants:	2,808
Application deadline:	March 1
Total amount awarded:	$10,862,060

Contact:
Maryland Higher Ed. Commission Office of Student Financial Assistance
Guaranteed Access Grant
839 Bestgate Road, Suite 400
Annapolis, MD 21401-3103
Phone: 800-974-1024
Fax: 410-260-3200
Web: www.mhec.state.md.us/financialaid/descriptions

Maryland Delegate Scholarship

Type of award: Scholarship, renewable.
Intended use: For undergraduate or graduate study at vocational, 2-year, 4-year or graduate institution.
Eligibility: Applicant must be high school senior. Applicant must be U.S. citizen or permanent resident residing in Maryland.
Application requirements: Proof of eligibility, nomination by local state delegate. FAFSA.
Additional information: Applicant's parents (if applicant is dependent) must be Maryland residents. Rolling application deadline. Certain vocational programs eligible. Out-of-state institutions eligible only if major not offered in Maryland. Each state delegate makes awards to students. If OSFA makes awards for delegates, applicant must demonstrate financial need. Non-U.S. citizens living in Maryland may be eligible. Applicants must reapply yearly for renewal and maintain satisfactory academic progress.

Amount of award:	$200-$19,000
Number of awards:	5,510
Notification begins:	July 1
Total amount awarded:	$4,736,357

Contact:
Maryland Higher Ed. Commission Office of Student Financial Assistance
Delegate Scholarship
839 Bestgate Road, Suite 400
Annapolis, MD 21401-3013
Phone: 800-974-1024
Fax: 410-260-3200
Web: www.mhec.state.md.us/financialaid/descriptions

Maryland Distinguished Scholar: Achievement

Type of award: Scholarship, renewable.
Intended use: For full-time undergraduate study at 2-year or 4-year institution. Designated institutions: Eligible Maryland institutions.
Eligibility: Applicant must be high school junior. Applicant must be U.S. citizen or permanent resident residing in Maryland.
Basis for selection: Applicant must demonstrate high academic achievement.
Application requirements: Transcript, nomination by high school. SAT scores from tests taken in January of junior year or

earlier. PSAT or ACT scores may be submitted if student has not taken SAT 1.
Additional information: Applicant's parents (if applicant is dependent) must be Maryland residents. Applications must be submitted to high school guidance office in February of junior year. Guidance counselor submits talent nominations in March. Applicant must have minimum 3.7 GPA. Students not funded initially will be placed on waiting list; funds may not be available to award all eligible students. Award automatically renewed up to three additional years if annual minimum 3.0 GPA and other eligibility requirements maintained.

Amount of award:	$3,000
Number of awards:	1,245
Number of applicants:	5,227
Notification begins:	June 30
Total amount awarded:	$3,638,250

Contact:
Maryland Higher Ed. Commission Office of Student Financial Assistance
Distinguished Scholar Program
839 Bestgate Road, Suite 400
Annapolis, MD 21401-3013
Phone: 800-974-1024
Fax: 410-260-3200
Web: www.mhec.state.md.us/financialaid/descriptions

Maryland Distinguished Scholar: National Merit and National Achievement Finalists

Type of award: Scholarship, renewable.
Intended use: For full-time undergraduate study at 2-year or 4-year institution in United States. Designated institutions: Eligible Maryland institutions.
Eligibility: Applicant must be high school junior. Applicant must be U.S. citizen or permanent resident residing in Maryland.
Basis for selection: Applicant must demonstrate high academic achievement.
Additional information: Applicant's parents (if applicant is dependent) must be Maryland residents. Applicant must be National Merit Finalist or National Achievement Finalist. Award automatically offered to students in these scholarship programs when they have been selected as finalists and indicate they will attend a Maryland institution. Award automatically renewed up to three additional years if annual minimum 3.0 GPA and other eligibility requirements maintained.

Amount of award:	$3,000
Number of awards:	1,245
Number of applicants:	5,227
Total amount awarded:	$3,638,250

Contact:
Maryland Higher Ed. Commission Office of Student Financial Assistance
Distinguished Scholar Program
839 Bestgate Road, Suite 400
Annapolis, MD 21401-3013
Phone: 800-974-1024
Fax: 410-260-3200
Web: www.mhec.state.md.us/financialaid/descriptions

Maryland Distinguished Scholar: Talent in the Arts

Type of award: Scholarship, renewable.

Scholarships

325

Scholarships

Contact:
Maryland Higher Ed. Commission Office of Student Financial
Assistance
Jack F. Tolbert Memorial Grant
839 Bestgate Road, Suite 400
Annapolis, MD 21401-3013
Phone: 800-974-0203
Fax: 410-260-3200
Web: www.mhec.state.md.us/financialaid/descriptions

Maryland Part-Time Grant Program

Type of award: Scholarship, renewable.
Intended use: For half-time undergraduate study at accredited
postsecondary institution. Designated institutions: Accredited
institutions in Maryland.
Eligibility: Applicant must be enrolled in high school.
Applicant must be residing in Maryland.
Basis for selection: Applicant must demonstrate financial
need.
Additional information: Applicant's parents (if applicant is
dependent) must be Maryland residents. Must be taking 6 to 11
semester credit hours. Apply through financial aid office of
Maryland institution. Applicants simultaneously enrolled in
secondary school and an institution of higher education are also
eligible. To renew award, student must maintain satisfactory
academic progress and submit FAFSA by March 1 each year;
may receive award up to eight years.

Amount of award:	$200-$2,000
Number of awards:	8,667
Application deadline:	March 1
Total amount awarded:	$5,964,385

Contact:
Maryland Higher Ed. Commission Office of Student Financial
Assistance
Part-Time Grant Program
839 Bestgate Road, Suite 400
Annapolis, MD 21401-3013
Phone: 800-974-1024
Fax: 410-260-3200
Web: www.mhec.state.md.us/financialaid/descriptions

Maryland Senatorial Scholarship

Type of award: Scholarship, renewable.
Intended use: For undergraduate or graduate study at
postsecondary institution.
Eligibility: Applicant must be residing in Maryland.
Basis for selection: Applicant must demonstrate financial
need.
Application requirements: Nomination by local state senator.
FAFSA.
Additional information: Applicant and parents (if applicant
is dependent) must be Maryland residents. SAT or ACT
required for freshmen at four-year institutions unless applicant
graduated from high school five years prior to aid application or
has earned 24 college credit hours. Out-of-state institutions
eligible only if major not offered in Maryland. Contact state
senator's office for more information. Award automatically
renewed if satisfactory academic progress is maintained. Full-
time students may be awarded four years total, part-time
students eight years total.

Amount of award:	$400-$9,000
Number of awards:	6,874
Application deadline:	March 1
Total amount awarded:	$5,769,725

Contact:
Maryland Higher Ed. Commission Office of Student Financial
Assistance
Senatorial Scholarship Program
839 Bestgate Road, Suite 400
Annapolis, MD 21401-3013
Phone: 800-974-1024
Fax: 410-260-3200
Web: www.mhec.state.md.us/financialaid/descriptions

Maryland Tuition Reduction for Non-Resident Nursing Students

Type of award: Scholarship, renewable.
Intended use: For undergraduate study at postsecondary
institution.
Eligibility: Applicant must be U.S. citizen.
Basis for selection: Major/career interest in nursing.
Additional information: Must be resident of state other than
Maryland and accepted into Maryland degree-granting nursing
program at two- or four-year public institution. Awardees fulfill
service obligation in Maryland following graduation; two years
for two-year program, four years for four-year program. Service
must begin within six months of graduation. Award amount
varies; college may reduce tuition so that non-residents pay
tuition charged to Maryland resident.

Number of applicants:	51

Contact:
Maryland Higher Ed. Commission Office of Student Financial
Assistance
Out-of-State Nursing Program
839 Bestgate Road, Suite 400
Annapolis, MD 21401-3013
Phone: 800-974-1024
Fax: 410-260-3200
Web: www.mhec.state.md.us/financialaid/descriptions

Tuition Waiver for Foster Care Recipients

Type of award: Scholarship, renewable.
Intended use: For undergraduate study at 2-year or 4-year
institution. Designated institutions: Eligible Maryland public
institutions.
Eligibility: Applicant must be no older than 20. Applicant
must be residing in Maryland.
Application requirements: FAFSA.
Additional information: Applicant must have resided in
Maryland foster care home at time of high school graduation or
completion of GED. Also open to applicants who resided in
Maryland foster care home on 14th birthday and were
subsequently adopted. The Department of Human Resources
must confirm applicant's eligibility. Applicant must be enrolled
as a degree-seeking student before age of 21. Award renewal
possible if satisfactory academic progress and enrollment in
eligible program maintained.

Amount of award:	Full tuition
Application deadline:	March 1

Contact:
Maryland Higher Ed. Commission Office of Student Financial
Assistance
839 Bestgate Road, Suite 400
Annapolis, MD 21401-3013
Phone: 800-974-1024
Fax: 410-260-3200
Web: www.mhec.state.md.us/financialaid/descriptions

Massachusetts Board of Higher Education

Massachusetts Christian A. Herter Memorial Scholarship Program

Type of award: Scholarship, renewable.
Intended use: For full-time undergraduate study at accredited vocational, 2-year or 4-year institution. Designated institutions: Massachusetts institutions.
Eligibility: Applicant must be high school sophomore or junior. Applicant must be U.S. citizen or permanent resident residing in Massachusetts.
Basis for selection: Applicant must demonstrate financial need, depth of character and seriousness of purpose.
Application requirements: Interview, recommendations, essay, transcript, nomination by high school principal, counselor, teacher, or social service agency.
Additional information: Program provides grant assistance for students from low income or disadvantaged backgrounds who have had to overcome adverse circumstances. Selection made during sophomore and junior years in high school. Award amount is up to half of student's demonstrated financial need. Minimum 2.5 GPA.

Amount of award:	$15,000
Number of awards:	25
Number of applicants:	200
Application deadline:	April 1
Total amount awarded:	$900,000

Contact:
Office of Student Financial Assistance
Massachusetts Board of Higher Education
454 Broadway, Suite 200
Revere, MA 02151
Phone: 617-727-9420
Fax: 617-727-0667
Web: www.osfa.mass.edu

Massachusetts Gilbert Matching Student Grant

Type of award: Scholarship, renewable.
Intended use: For full-time undergraduate study at accredited 2-year or 4-year institution. Designated institutions: Independent colleges or hospital schools of nursing in Massachusetts.
Eligibility: Applicant must be U.S. citizen or permanent resident residing in Massachusetts.
Basis for selection: Major/career interest in nursing. Applicant must demonstrate financial need.
Additional information: Deadline depends on institution. Applicant must be dependent of parent who has been a Massachusetts resident for at least 12 months prior to start of academic year. Must not have received prior bachelor's degree.

Amount of award:	$200-$2,500
Total amount awarded:	$18,600,000

Contact:
Apply to college financial aid office.
Phone: 617-727-9420
Fax: 617-727-0667
Web: www.osfa.mass.edu

Massachusetts MASSgrant Program

Type of award: Scholarship, renewable.

Intended use: For full-time undergraduate study at accredited vocational, 2-year or 4-year institution. Designated institutions: Schools in Massachusetts, Connecticut, Maine, New Hampshire, Vermont, Rhode Island, Pennsylvania or Washington, DC.
Eligibility: Applicant must be U.S. citizen or permanent resident residing in Vermont, Maine, Pennsylvania, Massachusetts, District of Columbia, Connecticut, New Hampshire or Rhode Island.
Basis for selection: Applicant must demonstrate financial need.
Application requirements: FAFSA.
Additional information: Applicant must have expected family contribution of $4,617 or less and be eligible for Title IV financial aid. Applicant must maintain satisfactory academic progress. Must not have received prior bachelor's degree. Award amount varies.

Number of awards:	28,553
Number of applicants:	250,000
Application deadline:	May 1
Notification begins:	June 15
Total amount awarded:	$24,000,000

Contact:
Office of Student Financial Assistance
Massachusetts Board of Higher Education
454 Broadway, Suite 200
Revere, MA 02151
Phone: 617-727-9420
Fax: 617-727-0667
Web: www.osfa.mass.edu

Massachusetts Public Service Grant Program

Type of award: Scholarship, renewable.
Intended use: For full-time undergraduate study at accredited 2-year or 4-year institution. Designated institutions: Massachusetts colleges and universities.
Eligibility: Applicant must be U.S. citizen or permanent resident residing in Massachusetts.
Application requirements: Proof of eligibility.
Additional information: Awards available for children or widowed spouse of deceased firefighters, police officers, or corrections officers who died from injuries received performing his or her duties. Children of veterans killed in action or Vietnam POWs also eligible. Award in form of entitlement grant. Applicant must be resident of Massachusetts at least one year prior to start of school. For recipients attending Massachusetts public college or university, award shall equal cost of tuition. Recipients attending Massachusetts independent college or university, award will be equivalent to highest tuition amount paid to public institution.

Amount of award:	Full tuition
Application deadline:	May 1
Notification begins:	June 1
Total amount awarded:	$22,665

Contact:
Office of Student Financial Assistance
Massachusetts Board of Higher Education
454 Broadway, Suite 200
Revere, MA 02151
Phone: 617-727-9420
Fax: 617-727-0667
Web: www.osfa.mass.edu

Paul Tsongas Scholarship Program

Type of award: Scholarship.

Intended use: For undergraduate study at postsecondary institution. Designated institutions: Massachusetts state colleges.
Eligibility: Applicant must be U.S. citizen or permanent resident residing in Massachusetts.
Basis for selection: Applicant must demonstrate financial need.
Additional information: Minimum 3.75 GPA and SAT score of 1200. Tuition waiver for full tuition and related fees. For renewal, must maintain 3.3 GPA.

Amount of award:	Full tuition
Number of awards:	45

Contact:
Contact State College financial aid office.
Phone: 617-727-9420
Fax: 617-727-0667
Web: www.osfa.mass.edu

Massachusetts Democratic Party

John F. Kennedy Scholars Award

Type of award: Scholarship.
Intended use: For junior or senior study at 4-year institution.
Eligibility: Applicant must be U.S. citizen or permanent resident residing in Massachusetts.
Basis for selection: Major/career interest in political science/ government or public administration/service. Applicant must demonstrate financial need, high academic achievement, leadership, seriousness of purpose and service orientation.
Additional information: Awarded to one male and one female at Massachusetts Democratic State Convention. Preference given to registered Democrats and students with 3.0 GPA or higher. Visit Website or contact local chairperson for more information and important dates.

Amount of award:	$1,500
Number of awards:	2
Number of applicants:	10
Application deadline:	April 16
Total amount awarded:	$3,000

Contact:
Massachusetts Democratic Party
MDP Office, Attn: Gloribell Mota
56 Roland Street, Suite 203
Boston, MA 02129
Phone: 617-776-2676
Fax: 617-776-2579
Web: www.massdems.org

Massachusetts Department of Education

Massachusetts Robert C. Byrd Honors Scholarship

Type of award: Scholarship, renewable.
Intended use: For full-time undergraduate study at accredited postsecondary institution.

Eligibility: Applicant must be high school senior. Applicant must be U.S. citizen or permanent resident residing in Massachusetts.
Basis for selection: Applicant must demonstrate high academic achievement, leadership and service orientation.
Application requirements: Nomination by high school.
Additional information: Minimum 3.5 GPA or class rank in top five percent required. Must have paid employment. Military academy students are ineligible. Students are nominated by high school. See guidance officer for additional information and application procedure. Number of awards varies.

Amount of award:	$1,500
Number of applicants:	235
Application deadline:	June 1

Contact:
Massachusetts Department of Education
Sally Teixeira
75 Pleasant Street
Malden, MA 02148-4906
Phone: 781-338-6304
Web: www.doe.mass.edu

McKee Scholars

John McKee Scholarship

Type of award: Scholarship, renewable.
Intended use; For undergraduate study at vocational or 4-year institution.
Eligibility: Applicant must be male, no older than 19, enrolled in high school. Applicant must be U.S. citizen residing in Pennsylvania.
Basis for selection: Applicant must demonstrate financial need and high academic achievement.
Application requirements: Interview, transcript. SAT/ACT scores.
Additional information: For male applicants whose fathers are dead, missing, permanently absent, or dysfunctional. Applicant must be a resident of Philadelphia, Bucks, Chester, Montgomery or Delaware counties. Award allotment after initial award year is based on upheld academic standards. Application available on Website.

Amount of award:	$1,000-$5,500
Number of awards:	70
Number of applicants:	70
Application deadline:	February 1
Total amount awarded:	$320,000

Contact:
John McKee Scholarship Committee
c/o George S. Forde, Jr., Executive Secretary
2005 Market Street, 26th Floor
Philadelphia, PA 19103-7098
Fax: 215-242-1475
Web: www.mckeescholars.org

Scholarships

Menominee Indian Tribe of Wisconsin

Menominee Adult Vocational Training Grant

Type of award: Scholarship, renewable.
Intended use: For undergraduate or non-degree study at accredited vocational or 2-year institution in United States.
Eligibility: Applicant must be American Indian. Applicant must be enrolled member of Menominee Indian tribe of Wisconsin.
Basis for selection: Applicant must demonstrate financial need.
Application requirements: FAFSA and Menominee Tribal Grant Application.
Additional information: Award also applicable toward associate's degree. Must apply through college financial aid office.

Amount of award:	$550-$2,200
Number of applicants:	100
Application deadline:	October 30, March 1

Contact:
Menominee Indian Tribe of Wisconsin
P.O. Box 910
Keshena, WI 54135
Phone: 715-799-5118 or 715-799-5110
Fax: 715-799-5102
Web: www.menominee-nsn.gov/education/educationhome.asp

Menominee Higher Education Grant

Type of award: Scholarship, renewable.
Intended use: For undergraduate study at accredited 2-year or 4-year institution in United States.
Eligibility: Applicant must be American Indian. Applicant must be enrolled member of Menominee Indian tribe.
Basis for selection: Applicant must demonstrate financial need.
Application requirements: FAFSA and Menominee Tribal Grant Application.
Additional information: Applications and deadline dates available through Tribal Education office.

Amount of award:	$550-$2,200
Number of awards:	97
Number of applicants:	200
Application deadline:	October 30, March 1

Contact:
Menominee Indian Tribe of Wisconsin
P.O. Box 910
Keshena, WI 54135
Phone: 715-799-5118 or 715-799-5110
Fax: 715-799-5102
Web: www.menominee-nsn.gov/education/educationhome.asp

The Merchants Exchange

The Merchants Exhange Scholarship Fund

Type of award: Scholarship, renewable.

Intended use: For sophomore, junior or senior study at postsecondary institution.
Eligibility: Applicant must be residing in Wyoming, California, Montana, Alaska, Oregon, Idaho or Washington.
Basis for selection: Major/career interest in international relations. Applicant must demonstrate high academic achievement and depth of character.
Application requirements: Transcript. Signed letter of intent to enroll in a program related to maritime affairs/international trade.
Additional information: Scholarship is for students from the Pacific Northwest studying maritime affairs/international trade. Minimum 2.5 GPA. Financial need may be considered if all other factors are equal. Application deadline in mid-June. Visit Website for exact deadline and application.

Amount of award:	$1,500
Number of awards:	7
Number of applicants:	5

Contact:
The Merchants Exchange
200 SW Market, Suite 190
Portland, OR 97201
Phone: 503-220-2092
Web: www.pdxmex.com

Michigan Higher Education Assistance Authority

Children of Veterans Tuition Grant

Type of award: Scholarship, renewable.
Intended use: For undergraduate study at postsecondary institution. Designated institutions: Michigan institutions.
Eligibility: Applicant must be at least 16, no older than 25. Applicant must be U.S. citizen or permanent resident residing in Michigan. Applicant must be dependent of disabled veteran or deceased veteran.
Additional information: Veteran must have been killed in action, been listed as MIA, or been permanently disabled due to service-related injuries. Veteran must have been a Michigan resident before entering military service or must have established residency in Michigan after entering military service.

Amount of award:	$1,400-$2,800
Number of awards:	399
Total amount awarded:	$859,930

Contact:
Michigan Higher Education Assistance Authority
Office of Scholarships and Grants
P.O. Box 30462
Lansing, MI 48909-7962
Phone: 888-447-2687
Web: www.michigan.gov/osg

Michigan Competitive Scholarship

Type of award: Scholarship, renewable.
Intended use: For undergraduate study at postsecondary institution. Designated institutions: Michigan institutions.
Eligibility: Applicant must be U.S. citizen or permanent resident residing in Michigan.
Basis for selection: Applicant must demonstrate financial need.

Application requirements: FAFSA and qualifying ACT score.

Amount of award:	$100-$1,610
Number of awards:	27,885
Application deadline:	March 1
Total amount awarded:	$37,071,451

Contact:
Michigan Higher Education Assistance Authority
Office of Scholarships and Grants
P.O. Box 30462
Lansing, MI 48909-7962
Phone: 888-447-2687
Web: www.michigan.gov/osg

Michigan Robert C. Byrd Honors Scholarship

Type of award: Scholarship, renewable.
Intended use: For full-time undergraduate study at accredited postsecondary institution in United States.
Eligibility: Applicant must be high school senior. Applicant must be U.S. citizen or permanent resident residing in Michigan.
Basis for selection: Applicant must demonstrate high academic achievement.
Application requirements: Nomination by high school principal.

Amount of award:	$1,500
Number of awards:	230
Total amount awarded:	$1,399,500

Contact:
Michigan Higher Education Assistance Authority
Office of Scholarships and Grants
P.O. Box 30462
Lansing, MI 48909-7962
Phone: 888-447-2687
Web: www.michigan.gov/osg

Michigan Tuition Grant

Type of award: Scholarship, renewable.
Intended use: For undergraduate, master's or doctoral study at 2-year, 4-year or graduate institution. Designated institutions: Michigan institutions.
Eligibility: Applicant must be U.S. citizen or permanent resident residing in Michigan.
Basis for selection: Applicant must demonstrate financial need.
Application requirements: FAFSA.
Additional information: Theology or religious education students ineligible.

Amount of award:	$100-$1,610
Number of awards:	35,518
Application deadline:	July 1
Total amount awarded:	$53,088,352

Contact:
Michigan Higher Education Assistance Authority
Office of Scholarships and Grants
P.O. Box 30462
Lansing, MI 48909-7962
Phone: 888-447-2687
Web: www.michigan.gov/osg

Tuition Incentive Program

Type of award: Scholarship, renewable.
Intended use: For undergraduate study at postsecondary institution. Designated institutions: Michigan institutions.

Eligibility: Applicant must be U.S. citizen or permanent resident residing in Michigan.
Basis for selection: Applicant must demonstrate financial need.
Application requirements: Proof of eligibility.
Additional information: Eligibility determined by Medicaid status. Provides tuition assistance for up to 24 semesters or 36 term credits for first two years. Up to $2,000 total assistance for third and fourth years.

Number of awards:	12,041
Total amount awarded:	$21,798,128

Contact:
Michigan Higher Education Assistance Authority
Office of Scholarships and Grants
P.O. Box 30462
Lansing, MI 48909-7962
Phone: 888-447-2687
Web: www.michigan.gov/osg

Michigan Society of Professional Engineers

Michigan Society of Professional Engineers Scholarships for High School Seniors

Type of award: Scholarship.
Intended use: For undergraduate study at accredited 4-year institution. Designated institutions: ABET-accredited schools in Michigan.
Eligibility: Applicant must be high school senior. Applicant must be U.S. citizen residing in Michigan.
Basis for selection: Major/career interest in engineering. Applicant must demonstrate high academic achievement, depth of character, leadership and service orientation.
Application requirements: Recommendations, essay, transcript. ACT scores.
Additional information: Minimum 3.0 GPA and 26 ACT score. Contact guidance counselor or local MSPE chapter for application and specific eligibility requirements. Applications must be submitted to local MSPE chapter.

Amount of award:	$1,000-$3,000
Number of awards:	29
Number of applicants:	295
Application deadline:	February 15, April 1
Notification begins:	April 1
Total amount awarded:	$46,000

Contact:
Scholarship Coordinator Local MSPE Chapter
215 North Walnut Street
Lansing, MI 48933
Phone: 517-487-9388
Fax: 517-487-0635
Web: www.michiganspe.org

Microscopy Society of America

Microscopy Society of America Undergraduate Research Scholarship

Type of award: Research grant.
Intended use: For full-time junior or senior study at postsecondary institution.
Basis for selection: Major/career interest in science, general; biology; physics; chemistry; natural sciences or engineering, materials. Applicant must demonstrate seriousness of purpose.
Application requirements: Recommendations. Resume, budget, research proposal, letter from laboratory supervisor, letter from MSA member (may be same as supervisor or professor). Four hard copies of all application materials if not submitting electronically.
Additional information: Award for students interested in pursuing microscopy as career or major research tool. Applicant should be sponsored by MSA member. Must supply abstract of research project. Funds must be spent within year of award date, but in special cases may be extended to cover additional research during summer semester following graduation. Visit Website for more information and application.

Amount of award:	$3,000
Number of awards:	6
Number of applicants:	20
Application deadline:	December 31
Notification begins:	April 1
Total amount awarded:	$9,000

Contact:
Microscopy Society of America
Undergraduate Research Scholarship
12100 Sunset Hills Road, Suite 130
Reston, VA 20190
Phone: 800-538-3672
Fax: 703-435-4390
Web: www.microscopy.org

Microsoft Corporation

Microsoft General Scholarship

Type of award: Scholarship.
Intended use: For full-time undergraduate study at 4-year institution. Designated institutions: Colleges and universities in the United States, Canada, and Mexico.
Basis for selection: Major/career interest in computer/ information sciences; engineering, computer; mathematics or physics. Applicant must demonstrate financial need and high academic achievement.
Application requirements: Recommendations, essay, transcript. Resume.
Additional information: Minimum 3.0 GPA. Scholarship will cover up to 100 percent of tuition for one academic year. All recipients required to complete salaried summer internship of 12 weeks or more at Microsoft in Redmond, Washington. Applicant must be enrolled in degree-granting program in computer science, computer engineering, or related technical

discipline, with demonstrated interest in computer science. See Website for important dates, more information and application.

Amount of award:	Full tuition
Application deadline:	February 1
Notification begins:	March 20
Total amount awarded:	$500,000

Contact:
Microsoft Scholarship Program
Microsoft Corporation
One Microsoft Way
Redmond, WA 98052-8303
Web: www.microsoft.com/college/en/us/collegescholarship.aspx

Midwestern Higher Education Compact

Midwest Student Exchange Program

Type of award: Scholarship, renewable.
Intended use: For full-time undergraduate, master's, doctoral or first professional study at accredited 2-year, 4-year or graduate institution in United States. Designated institutions: Participating institutions in Indiana, Kansas, Michigan, Minnesota, Missouri, Nebraska, North Dakota, and Wisconsin.
Eligibility: Applicant must be residing in Wisconsin, Michigan, Minnesota, Kansas, Indiana, Nebraska, Illinois, Missouri or North Dakota.
Application requirements: Proof of eligibility.
Additional information: Reduced tuition rate for Indiana, Kansas, Michigan, Minnesota, Missouri, Nebraska, North Dakota, and Wisconsin residents attending participating out-of-state institutions in one of six other states in designated institutions or programs of study. For information, contact high school counselor or college admissions officer. For list of participating institutions and programs, and for individual state contact information, visit Website.

Amount of award:	$4,430
Number of applicants:	3,290
Total amount awarded:	$14,580,276

Contact:
Midwestern Higher Education Compact
Attn: Jennifer Dahlquist
1300 S. Second St., Suite 130
Minneapolis, MN 55454-1079
Phone: 612-626-1602
Fax: 612-626-8290
Web: msep.mhec.org

Military Officers Association of America

General John Paul Ratay Educational Fund Grants

Type of award: Scholarship.
Intended use: For undergraduate study at postsecondary institution.
Eligibility: Applicant must be U.S. citizen. Applicant must be dependent of veteran.

Additional information: Grants available to children of surviving spouse of retired officers. Must be seeking first undergraduate degree. Students cannot receive both an MOAA loan and Ratay grant.

Amount of award:	$4,000
Application deadline:	March 1

Contact:
Military Officers Association of America
201 N. Washington Street
Alexandria, VA 22314
Phone: 703-549-2311
Web: www.moaa.org/education

MOAA American Patriot Scholarship Program

Type of award: Scholarship, renewable.
Intended use: For undergraduate study at postsecondary institution.
Eligibility: Applicant must be no older than 24. Applicant must be dependent of disabled veteran or deceased veteran.
Basis for selection: Applicant must demonstrate financial need.
Additional information: Must be dependent of an active duty uniformed service member (including Drilling Reserve and National Guard). Minimum 3.0 GPA. Military academy cadets are ineligible. Must be seeking first undergraduate degree. Amount and number of awards given vary.

Amount of award:	$2,500
Number of awards:	50
Number of applicants:	60
Application deadline:	March 1
Total amount awarded:	$300,000

Contact:
MOAA Scholarship Fun
American Patriot Scholarships Department 889
201 North Washington Street
Alexandria, VA 22314-2529
Phone: 800-234-6622 ext. 169
Web: www.moaa.org/education

Military Order of the Purple Heart

Military Order of the Purple Heart Scholarship

Type of award: Scholarship, renewable.
Intended use: For full-time undergraduate or graduate study at postsecondary institution.
Eligibility: Applicant must be U.S. citizen. Applicant must be descendant of veteran or disabled while on active duty; or dependent of disabled veteran or deceased veteran; or spouse of disabled veteran or deceased veteran. Applicant must be either a recipient of the Purple Heart or a descendent, spouse or widow of a recipient of the Purple Heart, a veteran killed in action, or a veteran who died of wounds incurred during service.
Basis for selection: Applicant must demonstrate high academic achievement.
Application requirements: $15 application fee. Recommendations, essay, transcript, proof of eligibility.
Additional information: Applicant must either be a recipient of the Purple Heart or descendant of recipient of the Purple

Heart, or descendant or spouse of veteran killed in action or who died of wounds. Must have minimum 2.75 GPA. Deadline in mid-late February. Contact the Military Order of the Purple Heart for applications, deadline information, award amounts, and other details.

Amount of award:	$3,000
Number of awards:	83
Number of applicants:	400
Total amount awarded:	$250,000

Contact:
Military Order of the Purple Heart
Scholarship Coordinator
5413-B Backlick Road
Springfield, VA 22151
Phone: 703-642-5360
Fax: 703-642-2054
Web: www.PurpleHeart.org

Milk Processor's Education Program

Scholar Athlete Milk Mustache of the Year Awards

Type of award: Scholarship.
Intended use: For undergraduate study at postsecondary institution.
Eligibility: Applicant must be high school senior. Applicant must be U.S. citizen.
Basis for selection: Competition/talent/interest in athletics/sports. Applicant must demonstrate high academic achievement, leadership and service orientation.
Application requirements: Essay. A description, in 75 words or less, of how drinking milk is part of applicant's life and training regimen.
Additional information: Minimum 3.2 GPA. Must be participant in high school sport or club sport. In addition to scholarship, winners receive spot in SAMMY Hall of Fame located in Milk House at Disney's Wide World of Sports and trip to Disney World to be honored in special ceremony. SAMMY award winners will be selected based on four criteria: academic performance, athletic excellence, leadership skills, and community service. Visit Website for application and more information.

Amount of award:	$7,500
Number of awards:	25

Contact:
Visit Website for more information.
Web: www.bodybymilk.com/sammy_scholarship.php

Minnesota Department of Veterans Affairs

Minnesota Educational Assistance for Surviving Spouse or Dependent

Type of award: Scholarship, renewable.

Intended use: For full-time undergraduate study at accredited vocational, 2-year or 4-year institution. Designated institutions: Approved Minnesota public institutions.
Eligibility: Applicant must be residing in Minnesota. Applicant must be dependent of deceased veteran; or spouse of deceased veteran. Parent or spouse must have been in Minnesota at time of entry on active duty (and for six months prior). Veteran's death must have been on active duty or service connected condition.
Application requirements: Proof of eligibility.
Additional information: All recipients also receive $750 stipend. Applicant must be resident of Minnesota for two years prior to application. Adopted children eligible. Step-children and foster children not eligible. Available until recipient obtains bachelor's degree or equivalent. Information also available from institution or county veterans service office.

   Amount of award: Full tuition
Contact:
Minnesota Department of Veterans Affairs
Veterans Service Building, 2nd Floor
20 West 12 Street
St. Paul, MN 55155-2079
Phone: 651-296-2562
Fax: 651-296-3954
Web: www.mdva.state.mn.us/education

Minnesota Educational Assistance for Veterans

Type of award: Scholarship.
Intended use: For undergraduate or graduate study at postsecondary institution. Designated institutions: Approved Minnesota institutions.
Eligibility: Applicant must be U.S. citizen residing in Minnesota. Applicant must be veteran. Applicant must have been Minnesota resident at time of entry into active duty and for six months immediately preceding entry. Must have served 181 consecutive days of active duty.
Application requirements: Proof of eligibility. Military Service DD Form 214.
Additional information: Applicant must have exhausted eligible federal educational benefits prior to the delimiting date or within the eligibility period in which benefits were available. Grant is one-time award. Contact county veterans service officer or institution for more information.

   Amount of award: $750
Contact:
Minnesota Department of Veterans Affairs
Veterans Service Building, 2nd Floor
20 West 12 Street
St. Paul, MN 55155-2079
Phone: 651-296-2562
Fax: 651-296-3954
Web: www.mdva.state.mn.us/education

Minnesota Office of Higher Education

Minnesota Achieve Scholarship

Type of award: Scholarship.
Intended use: For undergraduate study at postsecondary institution.
Eligibility: Applicant must be residing in Minnesota.

Application requirements: Transcript. FAFSA. Must qualify for Pell or stage grant.
Additional information: Applicant must have graduated from Minnesota high school after January 1, 2008. Must have completed one of four eligible rigorous high school course programs and graduated with unweighted GPA of 2.5 or higher.
   Amount of award: $1,200-$4,022
   Number of applicants: 3,853
   Total amount awarded: $2,073,240
Contact:
Minnesota Office of Higher Education
1450 Energy Park Drive, Suite 350
Saint Paul, MN 55108-5227
Phone: 800-657-3866
Fax: 651-642-0675
Web: www.getreadyforcollege.org/achieve

Minnesota GI Bill

Type of award: Scholarship, renewable.
Intended use: For undergraduate or graduate study at postsecondary institution. Designated institutions: Eligible Minnesota institutions.
Eligibility: Applicant must be residing in Minnesota. Applicant must be in military service or veteran; or dependent of disabled veteran or deceased veteran; or spouse of disabled veteran or deceased veteran who serves or served in the Army, Air Force, Marines, Navy, Coast Guard or Reserves/National Guard.
Additional information: Applicant must be a veteran, or spouse or child of military personnel who died or became permanently disabled on or since September 11, 2001. Applicant may also be non-veteran who has served a total of five years in the United States military with any part of service occurring after September 11, 2001.
   Amount of award: $100-$3,000
   Number of applicants: 1,466
   Total amount awarded: $1,263,514
Contact:
Minnesota Office of Higher Education
1450 Energy Park Drive, Suite 350
St. Paul, MN 55108-5227
Phone: 800-657-3866
Web: www.getreadyforcollege.org/military

Minnesota Indian Scholarship Program

Type of award: Scholarship.
Intended use: For undergraduate or graduate study in United States. Designated institutions: Eligible Minnesota institutions.
Eligibility: Applicant must be American Indian. Applicant must be residing in Minnesota.
Application requirements: Proof of one-fourth or more Indian ancestry. FAFSA.
Additional information: Applicant must be at least one-quarter American Indian. Undergraduates must be enrolled at least three-quarters time and graduate students must be enrolled at least half-time. Must be eligible for Pell grant or Minnesota state grant. Awards made on first-come, first-served basis.
   Amount of award: $4,000-$6,000
   Number of applicants: 2,052
   Application deadline: July 1
   Total amount awarded: $1,875,000

Contact:
Minnesota Office of Higher Education
1450 Energy Park Drive, Suite 350
St. Paul, MN 55108-5227
Phone: 800-657-3866
Web: www.getreadyforcollege.org/indianscholarship

Minnesota Post-Secondary Child Care Grant

Type of award: Scholarship, renewable.
Intended use: For undergraduate study at accredited postsecondary institution. Designated institutions: Eligible Minnesota schools.
Eligibility: Applicant must be no older than 22. Applicant must be U.S. citizen or permanent resident residing in Minnesota.
Basis for selection: Applicant must demonstrate financial need.
Additional information: Apply at college's financial aid office. Award amount prorated upon enrollment. Award based on family income and size. Eligibility limited to applicants with children 12 years or younger; maximum of $2600 per eligible child per academic year. Applicant cannot be receiving Aid to Families With Dependent Children, Minnesota Family Investment Program, or tuition reciprocity, or be in default of loan. Those with bachelor's degree or eight semesters or 12 quarters of credit, or equivalent, are not eligible. Applicant must be enrolled at least half-time in nonsectarian program and must be in good academic standing. Deadlines established by individual institution.

Amount of award:	$2,600
Number of applicants:	2,873
Total amount awarded:	$5,937,721

Contact:
Minnesota Office of Higher Education
1450 Energy Park Drive, Suite 350
St. Paul, MN 55108-5227
Phone: 800-657-3866
Web: www.getreadyforcollege.org

Minnesota Public Safety Officers Survivors Program

Type of award: Scholarship.
Intended use: For undergraduate study at accredited 2-year or 4-year institution. Designated institutions: Eligible Minnesota schools.
Eligibility: Applicant must be residing in Minnesota. Applicant's parent must have been killed or disabled in work-related accident as firefighter, police officer or public safety officer.
Application requirements: Proof of eligibility. Eligibility certificate.
Additional information: Must be enrolled in degree or certificate program at institution participating in State Grant Program. Applicant must be the surviving spouse or dependent child of a public safety officer killed in the line of duty. Also eligible if parent or spouse, not officially employed in public safety, was killed while assisting public safety officer or offering emergency medical assistance. Maximum age is 22 unless called for active military service, in which case maximum age is 29. Obtain eligibility certificate from Nancy Reissner, Department of Public Safety, 211 Transportation Building, St. Paul, MN 55155. Apply through financial aid office. Award covers tuition and fees up to $9,838 at four-year college and $5,808 at two-year college.

Number of awards:	16
Number of applicants:	12
Total amount awarded:	$56,594

Contact:
Minnesota Office of Higher Education
1450 Energy Park Drive, Suite 350
St. Paul, MN 55108-5227
Phone: 800-657-3866
Web: www.getreadyforcollege.org

Minnesota State Grant Program

Type of award: Scholarship, renewable.
Intended use: For undergraduate study at accredited vocational, 2-year or 4-year institution.
Eligibility: Applicant must be U.S. citizen or permanent resident residing in Minnesota.
Basis for selection: Applicant must demonstrate financial need.
Application requirements: Proof of eligibility. FAFSA.
Additional information: Applicant must not have completed four years of college. If not Minnesota high school graduate and parents not residents of Minnesota, applicant must be resident of Minnesota for at least one year without being enrolled half-time or more. Cannot be in default on loans or delinquent on child-support payments. FAFSA used as application for Minnesota State Grant. Application deadline is 30 days from term start date.

Amount of award:	$100-$8,661
Number of awards:	84,518
Number of applicants:	150,000
Total amount awarded:	$143,520,000

Contact:
Minnesota Office of Higher Education
1450 Energy Park Drive, Suite 350
St. Paul, MN 55108-5227
Phone: 800-657-3866
Web: www.getreadyforcollege.org

Miss America Organization

Allman Medical Scholarships

Type of award: Scholarship, renewable.
Intended use: For undergraduate or graduate study at postsecondary institution.
Eligibility: Applicant must be female.
Basis for selection: Major/career interest in medicine. Applicant must demonstrate financial need and high academic achievement.
Application requirements: Recommendations, essay, transcript, proof of eligibility. MCAT scores.
Additional information: Must be pursuing a degree in medicine. Must have competed in Miss America system at local, state, or national level after 1998. Notification begins in August.

Application deadline:	June 30

Contact:
Miss America Organization Attn: Scholarship Department
222 New Road, Suite 700
Attn: Scholarships
Linwood, NJ 08221
Phone: 609-653-8700
Web: www.missamerica.org/scholarships

Eugenia Vellner Fischer Award for the Performing Arts

Type of award: Scholarship.
Intended use: For undergraduate or graduate study at postsecondary institution.
Eligibility: Applicant must be female.
Basis for selection: Major/career interest in performing arts. Applicant must demonstrate financial need and high academic achievement.
Application requirements: Recommendations, essay, transcript, proof of eligibility.
Additional information: Must be pursuing degree in the performing arts, such as dance or music. Must have competed in Miss America system in local, state, or national level after 1998. Visit Website for more information.

  Application deadline: June 30
  Notification begins: September 1
Contact:
Miss America Organization
Attn: Scholarships
222 New Road, Suite 700
Linwood, NJ 08221
Phone: 609-653-8700
Web: www.missamerica.org

Miss America Competition Awards

Type of award: Scholarship.
Intended use: For undergraduate, graduate or non-degree study at accredited postsecondary institution.
Eligibility: Applicant must be single, female, at least 17, no older than 24. Applicant must be U.S. citizen.
Basis for selection: Competition/talent/interest in poise/talent/fitness. Applicant must demonstrate depth of character, leadership, patriotism, seriousness of purpose and service orientation.
Application requirements: Proof of eligibility.
Additional information: Local winners go on to compete at state level, and state winners compete for Miss America. Contestants will apply their talent, intelligence, and speaking ability, and demonstrate their commitment to community service. Cash and tuition-based scholarships available at every level of competition. Deadlines for local competitions vary. Contact the Miss America Organization for more information or visit Website.

  Amount of award: $1,000-$50,000
  Total amount awarded: $40,000,000
Contact:
Miss America Organization
Attn: Scholarships
222 New Road, Suite 700
Linwood, NJ 08221
Phone: 609-653-8700
Web: www.missamerica.org/scholarships

Mississippi Office of Student Financial Aid

Leveraging Educational Assistance Partnership Program (LEAP)

Type of award: Scholarship, renewable.

Intended use: For full-time undergraduate study at accredited 2-year or 4-year institution. Designated institutions: Mississippi institutions.
Eligibility: Applicant must be enrolled in high school. Applicant must be U.S. citizen or permanent resident residing in Mississippi.
Basis for selection: Applicant must demonstrate financial need and high academic achievement.
Application requirements: Recommendations, proof of eligibility. FAFSA.
Additional information: Must meet general requirements for participation in federal student aid program. Award amount varies. Apply to college financial aid office.

  Number of awards: 1,381
Contact:
Mississippi Student Financial Aid
3825 Ridgewood Road
Jackson, MS 39211-6453
Phone: 800-327-2980
Web: www.mississippi.edu/riseupms/financialaid-state.php

Mississippi Eminent Scholars Grant

Type of award: Scholarship, renewable.
Intended use: For full-time undergraduate study at accredited vocational, 2-year or 4-year institution. Designated institutions: Eligible Mississippi institutions.
Eligibility: Applicant must be residing in Mississippi.
Basis for selection: Applicant must demonstrate high academic achievement.
Application requirements: Transcript. State of Mississippi tax return.
Additional information: Applicant may be high school senior. Must be Mississippi resident for at least one year. Minimum 3.5 GPA. Must have minimum ACT of 29 or SAT of 1280, or be in top 25 percent of class.

  Amount of award: $2,500
  Number of awards: 1,829
  Application deadline: September 15
  Total amount awarded: $4,337,024
Contact:
Mississippi Office of Student Financial Aid
3825 Ridgewood Road
Jackson, MS 39211-6453
Phone: 800-327-2980
Web: www.mississippi.edu/riseupms

Mississippi Higher Education Legislative Plan

Type of award: Scholarship, renewable.
Intended use: For full-time sophomore or junior study at accredited 2-year or 4-year institution. Designated institutions: Eligible Mississippi institutions.
Eligibility: Applicant must be U.S. citizen residing in Mississippi.
Basis for selection: Applicant must demonstrate financial need.
Application requirements: FAFSA. Household verification form.
Additional information: Minimum 2.5 GPA or must rank in top 50 percent of class. Must be legal resident of Mississippi for at least two years. Must have graduated from high school within two years of application. Preference given to early applicants. Covers tuition and fees up to ten semesters. Visit Website for application and more details.

Amount of award: Full tuition
Application deadline: March 31
Total amount awarded: $1,753,252
Contact:
Mississippi Office of Student Financial Aid
3825 Ridgewood Road
Jackson, MS 39211-6453
Phone: 800-327-2980
Web: www.mississippi.edu/riseupms

Mississippi Tuition Assistance Grant

Type of award: Scholarship, renewable.
Intended use: For full-time undergraduate study at accredited vocational, 2-year or 4-year institution. Designated institutions: Eligible Mississippi institutions.
Eligibility: Applicant must be U.S. citizen residing in Mississippi.
Application requirements: FAFSA and Student Aid Report.
Additional information: Applicant must be resident of Mississippi for at least one year. Must be receiving less than full Federal Pell Grant. High school seniors must have minimum 2.5 GPA. Other first-time applicants must have minimum 2.5 GPA. Award is up to $500 per year for freshmen and sophomores; up to $1,000 per year for juniors and seniors. Recipients must maintain minimum 2.5 GPA to reapply. Applicants must not be in default on an educational loan. Apply online.

Amount of award: $500-$1,000
Number of awards: 26,295
Application deadline: September 15
Total amount awarded: $15,286,070
Contact:
Mississippi Office of Student Financial Aid
3825 Ridgewood Road
Jackson, MS 39211-6453
Phone: 800-327-2980
Web: www.mississippi.edu/riseupms

Nissan Scholarship

Type of award: Scholarship, renewable.
Intended use: For full-time undergraduate study at 2-year or 4-year institution. Designated institutions: Mississippi public institutions.
Eligibility: Applicant must be high school senior. Applicant must be residing in Mississippi.
Basis for selection: Applicant must demonstrate financial need, high academic achievement, leadership, seriousness of purpose and service orientation.
Application requirements: Recommendations, transcript. FAFSA, 200-word essay. Resume. SAT/ACT scores.
Additional information: Minimum 2.5 GPA and 20 ACT or 940 SAT. Minimum 2.5 GPA or must rank in top 50 percent of class. Visit Website for more information and application. Number and amount of awards vary.

Amount of award: Full tuition
Application deadline: March 1
Contact:
Mississippi Office of Student Financial Aid
3825 Ridgewood Road
Jackson, MS 39211-6453
Phone: 800-327-2980
Web: www.mississippi.edu/riseupms

Missouri Department of Elementary and Secondary Education

Missouri Robert C. Byrd Honors Scholarship

Type of award: Scholarship, renewable.
Intended use: For undergraduate study at accredited 4-year institution in United States. Designated institutions: Eligible Missouri institutions.
Eligibility: Applicant must be high school senior. Applicant must be U.S. citizen or permanent resident residing in Missouri.
Basis for selection: Applicant must demonstrate high academic achievement.
Application requirements: Seventh semester transcripts.
Additional information: Applicant must be completing high school or GED in year of application. Must score in 90th percentile on ACT. Final selection at each congressional district level based on SAT/ACT scores and GPA. Award amount varies; contact sponsor for more information. Applicant's high school guidance counselor must sign and verify application form. Applications may be renewed for total of four years.

Amount of award: $1,500
Number of applicants: 700
Application deadline: April 15
Notification begins: October 1
Total amount awarded: $750,000
Contact:
Missouri Department of Elementary and Secondary Education
Robert C. Byrd Honors Scholarship
P.O. Box 480
Jefferson City, MO 65102
Phone: 573-751-1668
Fax: 573-526-3580
Web: www.dese.mo.gov

Missouri Department of Higher Education

Access Missouri Financial Assistance Program

Type of award: Scholarship, renewable.
Intended use: For full-time undergraduate study at vocational, 2-year or 4-year institution. Designated institutions: Approved Missouri institutions.
Eligibility: Applicant must be U.S. citizen or permanent resident residing in Missouri.
Basis for selection: Applicant must demonstrate financial need.
Application requirements: FAFSA.
Additional information: Must be used only toward first baccalaureate degree and may not be used towards theology or divinity studies. Eligibility based on Expected Family Contribution (EFC), with individuals with EFC of $12,000 or less eligible. Award amounts vary. No paper application. Students must apply for renewal each year.

Amount of award: $300-$4,600
Number of awards: 43,039
Number of applicants: 81,965
Application deadline: April 1
Total amount awarded: $92,582,925
Contact:
Missouri Department of Higher Education
3515 Amazonas Drive
Jefferson City, MO 65109
Phone: 800-473-6757, option 4
Fax: 573-751-6635
Web: www.dhe.mo.gov

Marguerite Ross Barnett Memorial Scholarship

Type of award: Scholarship, renewable.
Intended use: For half-time undergraduate study at accredited vocational, 2-year or 4-year institution in United States.
Designated institutions: Participating Missouri schools.
Eligibility: Applicant must be at least 18. Applicant must be U.S. citizen or permanent resident residing in Missouri.
Basis for selection: Applicant must demonstrate financial need.
Application requirements: Proof of eligibility. FAFSA.
Additional information: For students employed at least 20 hours per week while attending school part-time. Scholarship awarded on first-come, first-served basis. Maximum award is the lesser of the following: tuition charged at school of part-time enrollment or amount of tuition charged to Missouri undergraduate resident enrolled part-time in same class level at University of Missouri-Columbia. Employer must verify applicant's employment. Recipient may not be pursuing degree in theology or divinity.

Amount of award: Full tuition
Number of awards: 190
Number of applicants: 246
Application deadline: August 1
Total amount awarded: $439,358
Contact:
Missouri Department of Higher Education
3515 Amazonas Drive
Jefferson City, MO 65109
Phone: 800-473-6757, option 4
Fax: 573-751-6635
Web: www.dhe.mo.gov

Missouri Department of Higher Education Vietnam Veteran's Survivor Grant Program

Type of award: Scholarship, renewable.
Intended use: For full-time undergraduate study at accredited vocational, 2-year or 4-year institution in United States.
Designated institutions: Approved Missouri public and private schools.
Eligibility: Applicant must be U.S. citizen or permanent resident residing in Missouri. Applicant must be dependent of deceased veteran; or spouse of deceased veteran during Vietnam.
Additional information: For children and spouses of Vietnam veterans whose death was attributed to or caused by exposure to toxic chemicals during Vietnam conflict. Applicant cannot pursue degree in theology or divinity. Applications accepted in January; end date based on fund availability. Amount of award varies. Maximum amount is the lesser of actual tuition charged

for twelve credit hours at school where applicant is enrolled, or the average amount of tuition charged for twelve credit hours to undergraduate Missouri resident enrolled full-time in same class level and academic major at regional four-year public Missouri institutions.

Number of awards: 9
Number of applicants: 9
Total amount awarded: $31,008
Contact:
Missouri Department of Higher Education
3515 Amazonas Drive
Jefferson City, MO 65109
Phone: 800-473-6757, option 4
Fax: 573-751-6635
Web: www.dhe.mo.gov

Missouri Higher Education "Bright Flight" Academic Scholarship

Type of award: Scholarship, renewable.
Intended use: For full-time undergraduate study at accredited vocational, 2-year or 4-year institution in United States.
Designated institutions: Approved Missouri public and private schools.
Eligibility: Applicant must be U.S. citizen or permanent resident residing in Missouri.
Basis for selection: Applicant must demonstrate high academic achievement.
Application requirements: Proof of eligibility. SAT/ACT scores.
Additional information: May only be used for first baccalaureate degree. May not be used for theology or divinity studies. SAT/ACT composite scores must be in top five percent of state students. Must achieve qualifying scores by June assessment date of senior year. GED and home-schooled students may also qualify. Application deadline is June assessment date of senior year. No paper application needed. Check with high school counselor or financial aid administrator for additional information. Also see Website.

Amount of award: $1,000-$3,000
Number of awards: 8,192
Number of applicants: 10,338
Application deadline: June 11
Total amount awarded: $15,596,202
Contact:
Missouri Department of Higher Education
3515 Amazonas Drive
Jefferson City, MO 65109
Phone: 800-473-6757, option 4
Fax: 573-751-6635
Web: www.dhe.mo.gov

Missouri Minority Teaching Scholarship

Type of award: Scholarship, renewable.
Intended use: For full-time undergraduate or master's study at accredited 2-year or 4-year institution in United States.
Designated institutions: Missouri institutions with approved teacher education programs.
Eligibility: Applicant must be Alaskan native, Asian American, African American, Mexican American, Hispanic American, Puerto Rican or American Indian. Applicant must be U.S. citizen residing in Missouri.
Basis for selection: Major/career interest in education. Applicant must demonstrate high academic achievement.

Application requirements: Recommendations, essay, transcript, proof of eligibility.

Additional information: Must rank in top 25 percent of class or score in top 25 percent on ACT or SAT. If in college, may have 3.0 GPA at 30 hours to qualify. If college graduate, may receive award if returning to a master's level math or science education program. Upon graduation, recipient must teach for five years in Missouri public schools or scholarship becomes loan. Applicant may be renewed for up to 4 years.

Amount of award:	$3,000
Number of awards:	100
Number of applicants:	75
Application deadline:	February 15
Notification begins:	April 15
Total amount awarded:	$150,000

Contact:
Missouri Department of Higher Education
3515 Amazonas Drive
Jefferson City, MO 65109
Phone: 800-473-6757, option 4
Fax: 573-731-6635
Web: www.dhe.mo.gov

Missouri Public Safety Officer or Employee's Child Survivor Grant

Type of award: Scholarship, renewable.

Intended use: For full-time undergraduate study at accredited vocational, 2-year or 4-year institution in United States. Designated institutions: Approved Missouri public and private schools.

Eligibility: Applicant must be U.S. citizen or permanent resident residing in Missouri. Applicant's parent must have been killed or disabled in work-related accident as firefighter, police officer or public safety officer.

Application requirements: Proof of eligibility.

Additional information: For public safety officers who were permanently disabled in the line of duty or for children and spouses of Missouri public service officers killed or permanently disabled in the line of duty. Children or spouses of Missouri Department of Highway and Transportation employees also eligible if parent died or was permanently disabled during performance of job. May not be used for theology or divinity studies. Award amounts vary; contact sponsor for information. Estimated amount is based on 12 credit hours at chosen institution or no more than 12 hours at University of Missouri. Applications accepted in January; end date based on fund availability.

Number of awards:	20
Number of applicants:	20
Total amount awarded:	$88,014

Contact:
Missouri Department of Higher Education
3515 Amazonas Drive
Jefferson City, MO 65109
Phone: 800-473-6757, option 4
Fax: 573-751-6635
Web: www.dhe.mo.gov

Missouri League for Nursing

Margo Ballard and Vivian Meinecke Memorial Scholarship

Type of award: Scholarship.

Intended use: For sophomore, junior, senior or graduate study at postsecondary institution.

Eligibility: Applicant must be U.S. citizen residing in Missouri.

Basis for selection: Major/career interest in nursing. Applicant must demonstrate financial need.

Application requirements: Recommendations, proof of eligibility. Names and addresses of three persons who will know the student's address for next five years.

Additional information: Minimum 3.0 GPA. Applications must be submitted by dean at current school. Applications submitted by students not considered.

Contact:
Contact deans at accredited nursing schools in Missourri.
Web: www.mlnmonursing.org

Missouri League for Nursing Scholarship

Type of award: Scholarship, renewable.

Intended use: For full-time sophomore, junior, senior or master's study at accredited postsecondary institution. Designated institutions: Eligible institutions in Missouri.

Eligibility: Applicant must be U.S. citizen residing in Missouri.

Basis for selection: Major/career interest in nursing. Applicant must demonstrate financial need and high academic achievement.

Application requirements: Recommendations.

Additional information: Minimum 3.0 GPA. Scholarship must be used for study in Missouri. Amount of award varies. Applications can be obtained from dean of nationally recognized accredited schools of nursing in Missouri.

Amount of award:	$2,000
Number of awards:	2
Number of applicants:	30
Application deadline:	November 15

Contact:
Contact deans of school of nursing programs in Missouri.
Phone: 573-635-5355
Fax: 573-635-7908
Web: www.mlnmonursing.org

Montana Board of Regents

Governor's High School Merit Scholarship

Type of award: Scholarship, renewable.

Intended use: For full-time undergraduate study at 2-year or 4-year institution. Designated institutions: Montana University system or tribal colleges.

Eligibility: Applicant must be residing in Montana.

Basis for selection: Applicant must demonstrate high academic achievement.
Additional information: Applications available on Website. Must have minimum 3.0 GPA or 20 ACTscore or 1440 SAT score.

Amount of award:	$2,000
Number of awards:	480
Number of applicants;	1,500
Application deadline:	February 15
Total amount awarded:	$500,000

Contact:
Governor's High School Merit Scholarship
c/o MGSLP
P.O. Box 203101
Helena, MT 59604-3101
Phone: 406-444-1869
Fax: 406-444-0638
Web: www.mgslp.org

Governor's Merit-at-Large Scholarship

Type of award: Scholarship.
Intended use: For full-time undergraduate study at 2-year or 4-year institution in United States. Designated institutions: Montana University System school or tribal college in Montana.
Eligibility: Applicant must be residing in Montana.
Basis for selection: Applicant must demonstrate high academic achievement.
Additional information: Applications available on Website. Must have minimum 3.0 GPA or 20 ACT score or 1440 SAT score.

Amount of award:	$2,000
Number of awards:	480
Number of applicants:	1,500
Application deadline:	March 1
Total amount awarded:	$500,000

Contact:
Montana Board of Regents
c/o MGSLP
P.O. Box 203101
Helena, MT 59604-3101
Phone: 406-444-1869
Fax: 406-444-0638
Web: www.mgslp.org

Governor's Need Based Scholarship

Type of award: Scholarship.
Intended use: For undergraduate study at 2-year or 4-year institution in United States. Designated institutions: Montana University System schools or Montana tribal colleges.
Eligibility: Applicant must be residing in Montana.
Basis for selection: Applicant must demonstrate financial need.
Application requirements: FAFSA.
Additional information: Applications available through college financial aid office.

Amount of award:	$1,000
Number of awards:	480
Number of applicants:	1,500
Total amount awarded:	$500,000

Contact:
Montana Board of Regents
c/o MGSLP
P.O. Box 203101
Helena, MT 59604-3101
Phone: 406-444-1869
Fax: 406-444-0638
Web: www.mgslp.org

Montana Higher Education Grant

Type of award: Scholarship.
Intended use: For undergraduate study at postsecondary institution. Designated institutions: Eligible Montana institutions.
Eligibility: Applicant must be residing in Montana.
Basis for selection: Applicant must demonstrate financial need.
Application requirements: FAFSA.

Number of awards:	1,000
Total amount awarded:	$600,000

Contact:
Contact college financial aid office for application information.
Web: www.mgslp.org

Montana Tuition Fee Waiver for Veterans

Type of award: Scholarship.
Intended use: For undergraduate or graduate study at postsecondary institution. Designated institutions: Montana University system institutions.
Eligibility: Applicant must be permanent resident residing in Montana. Applicant must be veteran. Must have been honorably discharged person who served with the United States forces during wartime.
Application requirements: Proof of eligibility.
Additional information: Veterans who have served in the armed forces subsequent to the conflict in Vietnam are eligible for a fee waiver if the following conditions are met: 1) The veteran has been awarded an Armed Forces Expeditionary Medal for service in Lebanon, Grenada, or Panama or the veteran served in a combat theater in the Persian Gulf between August 2, 1990, and April 11, 1991, and received the Southwest Asia Service Medal; 2) The veteran is pursuing his or her initial undergraduate degree. Must have used up all federal veterans educational assistance benefits. Contact college financial aid office.

Amount of award:	Full tuition

Contact:
Montana University System
P.O. Box 203101
Helena, MT 59620-3101
Phone: 800-537-7508
Fax: 406-444-1869
Web: www.mgslp.org

Montana University System Community College Honor Scholarship

Type of award: Scholarship.
Intended use: For junior study at 4-year institution. Designated institutions: Montana University system institutions.
Eligibility: Applicant must be residing in Montana.
Basis for selection: Applicant must demonstrate high academic achievement.

Application requirements: Proof of eligibility.
Recommendation from president/faculty of accredited Montana
community college.
Additional information: Holder of scholarship must enter
Montana University System within nine months after receiving
associate degree. Award provides for tuition/fee waiver in any
unit of Montana University System. The waiver will be valid
through the completion of the first academic year (two
semesters) of enrollment, exclusive of any credits earned prior
to high school or community college graduation.

Amount of award:	Full tuition

Contact:
Financial aid office of community college.
Web: www.mgslp.org

Montana University System Honor Scholarship

Type of award: Scholarship, renewable.
Intended use: For freshman study at 4-year institution.
Designated institutions: Campuses in Montana University
system, as well as Dawson, Flathead Valley, and Miles
community colleges.
Eligibility: Applicant must be high school senior. Applicant
must be U.S. citizen residing in Montana.
Basis for selection: Applicant must demonstrate high
academic achievement.
Application requirements: Recommendations, transcript,
proof of eligibility. College acceptance letter, SAT/ACT scores.
Additional information: Must be high school senior enrolled
at accredited Montana high school for at least three years.
Recipients ranked based on GPA and ACT or SAT score.
Minimum 3.4 GPA. Must have met college preparatory
requirements. Must submit completed application to high school
guidance counselor. See Website for more details.

Amount of award:	Full tuition
Number of awards:	200
Number of applicants:	1,006
Application deadline:	February 15

Contact:
Montana Board of Regents of Higher Education
P.O. Box 203101
Helena, MT 59620-3101
Web: www.mgslp.org

Montana Trappers Association

MTA Doug Slifka Memorial Scholarship

Type of award: Scholarship.
Intended use: For undergraduate study at postsecondary
institution.
Eligibility: Applicant must be at least 15, no older than 25.
Basis for selection: Major/career interest in environmental
science; life sciences; natural resources/conservation or wildlife/
fisheries. Applicant must demonstrate depth of character and
seriousness of purpose.
Application requirements: Interview, transcript. Essay or
story on trapping or conservation. Recommendations by MTA
members, teachers, or other pertinent individuals. Endorsement
of MTA District Director (or sub-director) where applicant

resides. Student involvement in activities that include MTA
programs, trapping, school programs, and community service.
Additional information: Applicant must be member of MTA
for at least one year or minor dependent of MTA member.
Member must have been member of Association for one year
prior to application. MTA members out of state and their
families also eligible to apply. For application, complete request
form on Website or contact local director, officer or committee
member.

Amount of award:	$500
Number of awards:	2
Application deadline:	June 1
Total amount awarded:	$1,000

Contact:
Montana Trappers Association MTA Scholarship Committee
C/O Gary VanHaele
P.O. Box 264
Hysham, MT 59038
Phone: 406-342-5552
Web: www.montanatrappers.org/programs/scholarship.htm

The Moody's Foundation

Moody's Mega Math "M3" Challenge

Type of award: Scholarship.
Intended use: For freshman, sophomore or junior study at
2-year or 4-year institution.
Eligibility: Applicant must be high school junior or senior.
Applicant must be residing in New York, Delaware,
Massachusetts, Virginia, Connecticut, Vermont, Maine,
Maryland, Pennsylvania, Florida, Georgia, South Carolina,
District of Columbia, New Hampshire, West Virginia, New
Jersey, North Carolina or Rhode Island.
Basis for selection: Competition/talent/interest in academics,
based on responses to the assigned modeling problem.
Additional information: Each school may enter up to two
teams of three to five students. Team prizes range from $1,000
to $20,000. Visit Website for details and to register.

Amount of award:	$1,000-$20,000
Number of awards:	46
Number of applicants:	2,086
Total amount awarded:	$80,000

Contact:
Society for Industrial and Applied Mathematics
3600 Market Street, 6th Floor
Philadelphia, PA 19104
Phone: 267-350-6388
Fax: 215-525-2756
Web: m3challenge.siam.org

NAACP

Agnes Jones Jackson Scholarship

Type of award: Scholarship, renewable.
Intended use: For full-time undergraduate or graduate study at
accredited 4-year or graduate institution.
Eligibility: Applicant must be no older than 24. Applicant
must be U.S. citizen.

Basis for selection: Applicant must demonstrate financial need.

Application requirements: Recommendations, essay, transcript, proof of eligibility. Financial aid forms or copies of parents' latest income tax forms. Send one personal reference, one academic reference, and one NAACP reference (from an officer). Proof of enrollment.

Additional information: Must be current regular member of NAACP. Minimum 2.5 GPA for undergraduates, 3.0 GPA for graduate students. Award amounts: $1,500 undergraduate, $2,500 graduate. Graduate students may be full-time or part-time. Applications may be requested after January 1; include business-sized SASE. Scholarship application administered by United Negro College Fund. Visit Website for application, deadline, and more information.

    Amount of award: $1,500-$2,500

Contact:
United Negro College Fund: Scholarships and Grants
Administration
Attn: Kimberly Hall
8260 Willow Oaks Corporate Drive
Fairfax, VA 22301
Phone: 800-331-2244
Web: www.naacp.org/youth/scholarships

Earl G. Graves Scholarship

Type of award: Scholarship.

Intended use: For full-time junior, senior or graduate study at accredited 4-year or graduate institution in United States.

Basis for selection: Major/career interest in business. Applicant must demonstrate high academic achievement.

Application requirements: Essay, transcript, proof of eligibility. One personal and two academic recommendations.

Additional information: Applicants must be in top 20 percent of their class. May apply during sophomore year. Scholarship application administered by United Negro College Fund. Visit Website for application, deadline, and more information.

    Amount of award: $5,000

Contact:
United Negro College Fund: Scholarships and Grants
Administration
Attn: Kimberly Hall
8260 Willow Oaks Corporate Drive
Fairfax, VA 22031
Phone: 800-331-2244
Web: www.naacp.org/youth/scholarships

Hubertus W.V. Wellems Scholarship for Male Students

Type of award: Scholarship, renewable.

Intended use: For full-time undergraduate or graduate study at accredited 2-year, 4-year or graduate institution in United States.

Eligibility: Applicant must be male. Applicant must be U.S. citizen.

Basis for selection: Major/career interest in engineering; chemistry; physics or mathematics. Applicant must demonstrate financial need.

Application requirements: Essay, transcript, proof of eligibility. Two recommendations from teachers or professors in field of study. Financial aid forms. Proof of enrollment, application for admissions.

Additional information: Applications may be requested after January 1. Send 9x12 SASE. Minimum 2.5 GPA for

undergraduates and 3.0 GPA for graduate students. Active membership in NAACP highly desirable. Award is $2,000 for undergraduates, $3,000 for graduate students. Graduate students may be enrolled part-time. Scholarship application administered by the United Negro College Fund. Visit Website for application, deadline, and more information.

    Amount of award: $2,000-$3,000

Contact:
United Negro College Fund: Scholarships and Grants
Administration
Attn: Kimberly Hall
8260 Willow Oaks Corporate Drive
Fairfax, VA 22031
Phone: 800-331-2244
Web: www.naacp.org/youth/scholarships

Lillian and Samuel Sutton Education Scholarship

Type of award: Scholarship, renewable.

Intended use: For full-time undergraduate or graduate study at accredited 2-year, 4-year or graduate institution in United States. Designated institutions: Historically Black Colleges and Universities.

Eligibility: Applicant must be U.S. citizen.

Basis for selection: Major/career interest in education; education, early childhood; education, special or education, teacher. Applicant must demonstrate leadership.

Application requirements: Essay, transcript, proof of eligibility. Two recommendations from teachers or professors in major field of study. Proof of enrollment, acceptance letter from college or university. Financial aid forms.

Additional information: Undergraduates must have minimum 2.5 GPA, graduate students must have minimum 3.0 GPA. Applications available in January. Include business-sized SASE. Graduate students may be enrolled part-time. NAACP membership and participation highly desirable. Award $1,000 for undergraduates; $2,000 for graduates. Scholarship application administered by United Negro College Fund. Visit Website for deadline, application, and more information.

    Amount of award: $1,000-$2,000

Contact:
United Negro College Fund: Scholarships and Grants
Administration
Attn: Kimberly Hall
8260 Willow Oaks Corporate Drive
Fairfax, VA 22031
Phone: 800-331-2244
Web: www.naacp.org/youth/scholarships

Roy Wilkins Scholarship

Type of award: Scholarship.

Intended use: For full-time freshman study at accredited 4-year institution in United States.

Eligibility: Applicant must be U.S. citizen.

Application requirements: Recommendations, essay, transcript, proof of eligibility. Send financial aid forms along with copy of letter of acceptance from college or university. Business-sized SASE.

Additional information: Must be entering college freshman. Minimum 2.5 GPA. Highly desirable that applicant be active member of NAACP. Applications may be requested after January 1. United Negro College Fund administers application process. Visit Website for deadline, application, and more information.

    Amount of award: $1,000

Contact:
United Negro College Fund: Scholarships and Grants
Administration
Attn: Kimberly Hall
8260 Willow Oaks Corporate Drive
Fairfax, VA 22031
Phone: 800-331-2244
Web: www.naacp.org/youth/scholarships

NAACP Legal Defense and Education Fund, Inc.

Herbert Lehman Educational Fund

Type of award: Scholarship, renewable.
Intended use: For full-time freshman or sophomore study at accredited 4-year institution in United States.
Eligibility: Applicant must be African American. Applicant must be high school senior. Applicant must be U.S. citizen.
Basis for selection: Applicant must demonstrate financial need, high academic achievement, depth of character, leadership, seriousness of purpose and service orientation.
Application requirements: Recommendations, essay, transcript. Standardized test scores.
Additional information: Application request should be made in writing between November 1 and February 15 with statement of career and educational goals, reason why assistance is needed, and name of college to be attended. See Website for additional information.

Amount of award:	$2,000
Application deadline:	April 30
Notification begins:	August 1

Contact:
The Herbert Lehman Fund
NAACP Legal Defense and Educational Fund, Inc
99 Hudson Street Suite 1600
New York, NY 10013
Phone: 212-965-2200 or 212-965-2225
Fax: 212-219-1595
Web: www.naacpldf.org

NASA Alabama Space Grant Consortium

NASA Space Grant Undergraduate Scholarship

Type of award: Scholarship, renewable.
Intended use: For full-time junior or senior study at accredited 4-year institution. Designated institutions: Alabama Space Grant member universities: University of Alabama Huntsville, Alabama A&M, University of Alabama, University of Alabama Birmingham, University of South Alabama, Auburn University, Tuskegee University.
Eligibility: Applicant must be U.S. citizen residing in Alabama.
Basis for selection: Major/career interest in aerospace; engineering or science, general. Applicant must demonstrate high academic achievement.

Application requirements: Recommendations, essay, transcript, nomination by faculty advisor at Alabama Space Grant Consortium member institution. Resume.
Additional information: Applicants must have minimum 3.0 GPA and attend Alabama University. Must be in final term of sophomore year or later when applying. The Consortium actively encourages women, minority, and physically challenged students to apply, but others not excluded.

Amount of award:	$1,000
Number of awards:	40
Number of applicants:	36
Application deadline:	March 1
Notification begins:	April 15
Total amount awarded:	$36,000

Contact:
NASA Alabama Space Grant Consortium
University of Alabama in Huntsville
301 Sparkman Dr. Materials Science Bldg, 205
Huntsville, AL 35899
Phone: 256-824-6800
Fax: 256-824-6061
Web: www.uah.edu/ASGC/applications.php

NASA Connecticut Space Grant Consortium

NASA Connecticut Space Grant Undergraduate Fellowship

Type of award: Research grant, renewable.
Intended use: For full-time undergraduate study at accredited 4-year institution in United States. Designated institutions: Connecticut Space Grant Consortium member institutions.
Eligibility: Applicant must be U.S. citizen.
Basis for selection: Major/career interest in aerospace; engineering or science, general.
Application requirements: Recommendations, transcript, proof of eligibility, research proposal. Resume.
Additional information: Minimum 3.0 GPA. Consortium actively encourages women, minority, and disabled students to apply. Award amount varies; maximum is $4,500.

Amount of award:	$4,500
Number of awards:	13
Number of applicants:	20
Application deadline:	October 31
Total amount awarded:	$58,500

Contact:
NASA Connecticut Space Grant Consortium
University of Hartford
200 Bloomfield Ave.
West Hartford, CT 06117
Phone: 860-768-4813
Fax: 860-768-5073
Web: uhaweb.hartford.edu/ctspgrant

Scholarships

343

NASA Delaware Space Grant Consortium

Delaware Space Grant Undergraduate Tuition Scholarship

Type of award: Scholarship, renewable.
Intended use: For full-time sophomore, junior or senior study at postsecondary institution. Designated institutions: University of Delaware, Delaware Technical and Community College, Swarthmore College, Delaware State University at Dover, Villanova University, Wesley College, Wilmington University.
Eligibility: Applicant must be U.S. citizen.
Basis for selection: Major/career interest in aerospace; astronomy; communications; engineering; geography; geology/earth sciences; geophysics; physics or oceanography/marine studies.
Application requirements: Recommendations, transcript, nomination by department chair, DESGC Consortium Representative, or advisor. Applicant statement; letter from Department Chairperson.
Additional information: Must have proven interest in space-related studies. Recipient must currently attend Delaware Space Grant Consortium member institution. Award amounts vary and are available pending funding. Contact Consortium office for deadlines and additional information.

Amount of award:	$2,000
Number of awards:	10
Number of applicants:	17
Application deadline:	April 24
Total amount awarded:	$49,000

Contact:
Delaware Space Grant Consortium Program Office
University of Delaware
106 Sharp Lab
Newark, DE 19716
Phone: 302-831-1094
Fax: 302-831-1843
Web: www.delspace.org

NASA District of Columbia Space Grant Consortium

NASA District of Columbia Undergraduate Scholarship

Type of award: Scholarship, renewable.
Intended use: For full-time undergraduate or graduate study at postsecondary institution. Designated institutions: The American University, Catholic University, Gallaudet University, George Washington University, Georgetown University, Howard University, Trinity University, University of District of Columbia.
Eligibility: Applicant must be U.S. citizen.
Basis for selection: Major/career interest in science, general; mathematics; engineering; aerospace; physical education; political science/government or engineering. Applicant must demonstrate high academic achievement.
Application requirements: Recommendations, transcript, proof of eligibility.

Additional information: Number of grants, amount of funding, deadlines, and application requirements vary by year and by institution. See Website for more information.
Contact:
DC Space Grant Consortium American University - Dept. of Physics
4400 Massachusetts Ave, NW
McKinley Building Suite 102
Washington, DC 20016-8058
Phone: 202-885-2755
Fax: 202-885-2723
Web: www.dcspacegrant.org

NASA Georgia Space Grant Consortium

NASA Space Grant Georgia Fellowship Program

Type of award: Scholarship, renewable.
Intended use: For full-time junior, senior, master's or doctoral study at accredited postsecondary institution in United States. Designated institutions: Albany State University, Clark Atlanta University, Columbus State University, Fort Valley State University, Georgia Institute of Technology, Georgia State University, Kennesaw State University, Mercer University, Morehouse College, Spelman College, State University of West Georgia, University of Georgia.
Eligibility: Applicant must be U.S. citizen residing in Georgia.
Basis for selection: Major/career interest in engineering; science, general; aerospace; physics; atmospheric sciences/meteorology; computer/information sciences; education or chemistry. Applicant must demonstrate seriousness of purpose and service orientation.
Application requirements: Interview, portfolio, recommendations, essay, transcript.
Additional information: Funding available for students in all areas of engineering and science, and many areas of social science.

Amount of award:	$300

Contact:
Georgia Space Grant Consortium
Georgia Tech-Aerospace and Engineering
Space Science and Technology Bldg., Room 210
Atlanta, GA 30332-0150
Phone: 404-894-0521
Fax: 404-894-9313
Web: www.ae.gatech.edu/research/gsgc

NASA Hawaii Space Grant Consortium

NASA Space Grant Hawaii Undergraduate Fellowship

Type of award: Scholarship.
Intended use: For full-time undergraduate study at accredited postsecondary institution in United States. Designated

institutions: Consortium member schools: University of Hawaii at Manoa and Hilo.

Eligibility: Applicant must be U.S. citizen residing in Hawaii.

Basis for selection: Major/career interest in astronomy; geology/earth sciences; oceanography/marine studies; physics; zoology; engineering or geography.

Application requirements: Recommendations, transcript. Abstract, research proposal, budget, resume. Three copies of all application materials.

Additional information: Must be resident of Hawaii or attend school at one of the designated institutions. Must be sponsored by a faculty member willing to act as the student's mentor during the award period. Field of study must be relevant to NASA's goals, e.g. areas of math, science, engineering, computer science (concerned with utilizing or exploring space), and air transportation. Full-time undergraduates at Manoa, Hilo with major declared can apply for two-semester fellowships. Stipend of $3,000 per semester. Also up to $500 for supplies or travel. Recipients expected to work 10-15 hours per week on space-related projects. Women, under-represented minorities (specifically Native Hawaiians, Filipinos, other Pacific Islanders, Native Americans, Blacks, Hispanics), and physically challenged students who have interest in space-related fields are encouraged to apply. Visit Website for more information and application.

Amount of award:	$3,000
Number of applicants:	20
Application deadline:	June 15, December 1
Total amount awarded:	$135,000

Contact:
Phone: 808-956-3138
Fax: 808-956-6322
Web: www.spacegrant.hawaii.edu

NASA Idaho Space Grant Consortium

NASA Idaho Space Grant Undergraduate Scholarship

Type of award: Scholarship, renewable.

Intended use: For full-time undergraduate study at accredited 4-year institution. Designated institutions: College of Idaho, Boise State University, College of Southern Idaho, Idaho State University, Lewis Clark State College, North Idaho College, Northwest Nazarene University, BYU-Idaho, and the University of Idaho.

Eligibility: Applicant must be U.S. citizen.

Basis for selection: Major/career interest in engineering; mathematics or science, general.

Application requirements: Recommendations, essay. High school and college transcripts, SAT or ACT scores.

Additional information: Applicants must attend Idaho Space Grant Consortium member institution in Idaho and maintain a 3.0 GPA. Women, minority students, and disabled students encouraged to apply. Application essay should not exceed 500 words. Applications available on Website.

Amount of award:	$1,000-$2,000
Number of awards:	25
Number of applicants:	75
Application deadline:	March 1
Notification begins:	June 1
Total amount awarded:	$40,000

Contact:
NASA Space Grant Idaho Space Grant Consortium
University of Idaho
P.O. Box 441011
Moscow, ID 83844-1011
Phone: 208-885-6438
Fax: 208-885-1399
Web: www.id.spacegrant.org

NASA Illinois Space Grant Consortium

NASA Space Grant Illinois Undergraduate Scholarship

Type of award: Scholarship, renewable.

Intended use: For full-time undergraduate study at postsecondary institution. Designated institutions: Illinois Space Grant Consortium member institutions.

Eligibility: Applicant must be U.S. citizen.

Basis for selection: Major/career interest in engineering or aerospace. Applicant must demonstrate high academic achievement.

Application requirements: Recommendations, essay, transcript.

Additional information: Minimum 2.5 GPA. Contact sponsor for deadline information.

Amount of award:	$3,000
Number of awards:	15
Number of applicants:	62
Total amount awarded:	$50,000

Contact:
Associate Director/ Illinois Space Grant Consortium
U of Illinois-Urbana, 306 Talbot Lab
104 S. Wright Street
Urbana, IL 61801-2935
Phone: 217-244-8048
Fax: 217-244-0720
Web: www.ae.illinois.edu/ISGC

NASA Kentucky Space Grant Consortium

NASA Space Grant Kentucky Undergraduate Scholarship

Type of award: Scholarship, renewable.

Intended use: For full-time undergraduate study at accredited 4-year institution in United States. Designated institutions: Consortium member institutions: Bellarmine University, Centre College, Eastern Kentucky University, Kentucky Center for Space Enterprise, Kentucky State University, Morehead State University, Murray State University, Northern Kentucky University, Thomas More College, Transylvania University, Tribo Flow Separations, University of Kentucky, University of Louisville, Western Kentucky University.

Eligibility: Applicant must be U.S. citizen.

Basis for selection: Major/career interest in aerospace; astronomy; education; engineering or physics. Applicant must demonstrate high academic achievement.

Application requirements: Interview, recommendations, essay, transcript, nomination by professor/mentor at participating institution. Research proposal, written with mentor.

Additional information: Preference given to schools that waive tuition for recipient. Consortium actively encourages women, minority students, and physically challenged students to apply. Applicants doing work related to space exploration may qualify for funding, whatever their field of study may be.

Amount of award:	$5,000
Number of applicants:	10

Contact:
NASA/Kentucky Space Grant Consortium
University of Kentucky
151 Ralph G. Anderson Building
Lexington, KY 40506-0503
Phone: 859-257-6336 ext. 80663
Web: www.uky.edu/KSGC

NASA Maine Space Grant Consortium

NASA Space Grant Maine Consortium Annual Scholarship and Fellowship Program

Type of award: Research grant, renewable.

Intended use: For full-time undergraduate or graduate study at accredited 4-year or graduate institution. Designated institutions: University of Maine (Orono), University of Maine (Presque Isle), University of Southern Maine, University of New England, Maine Maritime Academy, College of the Atlantic, Bowdoin College, Colby College, Bates College.

Eligibility: Applicant must be U.S. citizen.

Basis for selection: Major/career interest in astronomy; geology/earth sciences; geophysics; engineering; aerospace; biology or medicine.

Additional information: Applicants from out of state who attend one of the designated institutions are eligible. Research project must be in an aerospace-related field. Applications from academic institutions in Maine other than those designated will be reviewed for consideration. Visit Website for additional details.

Amount of award:	$3,000-$6,000
Total amount awarded:	$135,000

Contact:
Maine Space Grant Consortium
87 Winthrop Street
Suite 200
Augusta, ME 04330
Phone: 877-397-7223
Fax: 207-622-4548
Web: www.msgc.org

NASA Michigan Space Grant Consortium

MSGC Undergraduate Underrepresented Minority Fellowship Program

Type of award: Research grant.

Intended use: For full-time undergraduate study at 4-year institution in United States. Designated institutions: Michigan Space Grant Consortium member institutions.

Eligibility: Applicant must be African American, Hispanic American, American Indian or Native Hawaiian/Pacific Islander. Applicant must be U.S. citizen residing in Michigan.

Basis for selection: Major/career interest in aerospace; engineering; science, general or mathematics. Applicant must demonstrate high academic achievement.

Application requirements: Recommendations, essay, transcript, research proposal. Description of project expectations and specifications; 150 word abstract.

Additional information: Offers support in form of undergraduate research and public service fellowships to students in aerospace, space science, Earth system science and other related science, engineering, or math fields. Students working on educational research topics in math, science, or technology also eligible to apply. Preference given to projects directly related to aerospace, space science, earth system science, and directly related educational efforts. Students required to identify a mentor with whom they intend to work. Underrepresented minority students who have a GPA below 3.0, but have strong mentorship, do qualify for an award. Visit Website for more information.

Amount of award:	$2,500
Application deadline:	November 20
Notification begins:	February 28
Total amount awarded:	$14,000

Contact:
NASA Michigan Space Grant Consortium
University of Michigan
1320 Beal Ave., 1216-C FXB
Ann Arbor, MI 48109-2140
Phone: 734-764-9508
Fax: 734-763-6904
Web: www.umich.edu/~msgc

NASA Space Grant Michigan Undergraduate Fellowship

Type of award: Research grant, renewable.

Intended use: For undergraduate study at accredited 4-year institution. Designated institutions: Michigan Space Grant Consortium member institutions.

Eligibility: Applicant must be U.S. citizen.

Basis for selection: Major/career interest in aerospace; engineering; science, general or mathematics. Applicant must demonstrate high academic achievement.

Application requirements: Essay, transcript. Two letters of recommendation; description of project expectations and specifications; 150 word abstract.

Additional information: Offers support in form of undergraduate research and public service fellowships to students in aerospace, space science, Earth system science and other related science, engineering, or math fields. Students working on educational research topics in math, science, or technology also eligible to apply. Preference given to projects directly related to aerospace, space science, Earth system science, and directly related educational efforts. Announcements for next funding interval can be found on Website.

Amount of award:	$2,500-$5,000
Application deadline:	November 20
Notification begins:	February 28
Total amount awarded:	$100,000

Contact:
NASA Space Grant Michigan Space Grant Consortium
University of Michigan
1320 Beal Ave., 1216-C FXB
Ann Arbor, MI 48109-2140
Phone: 734-764-9508
Fax: 734-763-6904
Web: www.umich.edu/~msgc

NASA Minnesota Space Grant Consortium

NASA Minnesota Space Grant Consortium Wide Scholarship

Type of award: Scholarship, renewable.
Intended use: For full-time undergraduate study at accredited 4-year institution in United States. Designated institutions: Augsburg College, Bethel University, Bemidji State University, Carleton College, Concordia College, Fond du Lac Tribal and Community College, Leech Lake Tribal College, Macalester College, Southwest Minnesota State University, St. Catherine University, University of Minnesota - Duluth, University of Minnesota - Twin Cities, University of St. Thomas.
Eligibility: Applicant must be U.S. citizen.
Basis for selection: Major/career interest in aerospace; astronomy; atmospheric sciences/meteorology; mathematics; engineering, mechanical; chemistry; engineering, electrical/electronic; engineering, chemical; engineering, civil or engineering, computer.
Application requirements: Recommendations, transcript. Letter of intent.
Additional information: Minimum 3.2 GPA. Women, minority, and physically challenged students encouraged to apply. Applicant must be attending a Minnesota Space Grant Consortium school but does not have to be a resident of the state. Must major in aerospace, astronomy, physics, geology, chemistry, or engineering. Visit Website for application.

Amount of award:	$500-$2,500
Number of awards:	15
Number of applicants:	40
Application deadline:	May 15

Contact:
NASA Minnesota Space Grant Consortium
U of M: Dept of Aerospace Engineering
110 Union St. SE
Minneapolis, MN 55455
Phone: 612-626-9295
Web: www.aem.umn.edu/mnsgc

NASA Missouri Space Grant Consortium

NASA Missouri State Space Grant Undergraduate Scholarship

Type of award: Scholarship, renewable.
Intended use: For full-time undergraduate study at accredited 4-year institution in United States. Designated institutions: Missouri State University, University of Missouri - Columbia, University of Missouri - Kansas City, Missouri University of Science and Technology, University of Missouri - St. Louis, and Washington University in St. Louis.
Eligibility: Applicant must be U.S. citizen residing in Missouri.
Basis for selection: Major/career interest in aerospace; astronomy; engineering; geology/earth sciences; physics; mathematics or engineering, mechanical.
Application requirements: Recommendations, essay, transcript.
Additional information: Program encourages applications from eligible space science students. Awardees must attend Missouri Space Grant Consortium affiliate institution. Women, minority students, and physically challenged students are actively encouraged to apply. Deadline varies but is usually the first week in April. Check sponsor for exact date. Awards normally granted sometime in May.

Amount of award:	$1,500-$3,500
Number of awards:	45
Number of applicants:	43
Total amount awarded:	$140,000

Contact:
NASA Missouri Space Grant Consortium
Missouri University of Science and Technology
137 Toomey Hall
Rolla, MO 65409-0050
Phone: 573-341-4887
Fax: 573-341-4607
Web: www.mst.edu/~spaceg

NASA Montana Space Grant Consortium

NASA Space Grant Montana Undergraduate Scholarship Program

Type of award: Scholarship, renewable.
Intended use: For full-time undergraduate study at accredited 2-year or 4-year institution in United States. Designated institutions: Montana Space Grant Consortium member institutions.
Eligibility: Applicant must be U.S. citizen.
Basis for selection: Major/career interest in aerospace; biology; chemistry; geology/earth sciences; physics; astronomy; computer/information sciences; engineering, chemical; engineering, civil or engineering, electrical/electronic. Applicant must demonstrate depth of character and leadership.
Application requirements: Recommendations, essay, transcript.

Additional information: Awards for one year, renewable on a competitive basis. Recipients must agree to provide MSGC with information about studies and employment beyond period of award. Visit Website for more information.

Amount of award:	$1,500
Number of awards:	24
Number of applicants:	45
Application deadline:	April 1
Total amount awarded:	$24,000

Contact:
NASA Space Grant Montana Space Grant Consortium
Montana State University
416 Cobleigh Hall, P.O. Box 173835
Bozeman, MT 59717-3835
Phone: 406-994-4223
Fax: 406-994-4452
Web: www.spacegrant.montana.edu

NASA Nevada Space Grant Consortium

NASA Space Grant Nevada Undergraduate Scholarship

Type of award: Scholarship.
Intended use: For full-time undergraduate or graduate study at accredited postsecondary institution in United States. Designated institutions: Nevada System of Higher Education institutions.
Eligibility: Applicant must be U.S. citizen.
Basis for selection: Major/career interest in aerospace; astronomy; biology; chemistry; computer/information sciences; geology/earth sciences; engineering; mathematics; science, general or physics.
Application requirements: Transcript. Resume. Career goal statement, including applicant's motivation toward aerospace career.
Additional information: Applicant must attend school in Nevada. Math, science, engineering, or majors in relevant fields eligible to apply. Application available on Website. Contact institution of interest for more information. Application deadline usually in mid-April.

Amount of award:	$5,000-$13,333
Number of awards:	13
Number of applicants:	45
Total amount awarded:	$150,000

Contact:
Nevada Space Grant Consortium Program Coordinator
Desert Research Institute
2215 Raggio Parkway
Reno, NV 89512
Phone: 775-673-7674
Fax: 775-673-7485
Web: www.nvspacegrant.org

NASA New Mexico Space Grant Consortium

NASA Space Grant New Mexico Undergraduate Scholarship

Type of award: Research grant, renewable.
Intended use: For full-time sophomore, junior, senior or graduate study at accredited 4-year institution in United States. Designated institutions: New Mexico Space Grant Consortium institutions.
Eligibility: Applicant must be U.S. citizen.
Basis for selection: Major/career interest in astronomy; biology; chemistry; computer/information sciences; engineering, chemical; engineering, civil; engineering, electrical/electronic; engineering, mechanical; physics or mathematics.
Application requirements: Transcript, research proposal, nomination by faculty mentor.
Additional information: Minimum 3.0 GPA. Geology, earth science, environmental science, agriculture, range science, and fishery and wildlife science majors also eligible. Preference given to applicants who can show nonfederal matching funds. Women, minority students, and physically challenged students encouraged to apply. Visit Website for application and more information.

Amount of award:	$5,000
Number of applicants:	20
Application deadline:	March 15
Notification begins:	March 30
Total amount awarded:	$100,000

Contact:
NASA New Mexico Space Grant Consortium
Program Office, New Mexico State University
3050 Knox St, Sugarman Space Grant Building
Las Cruces, NM 88003-0001
Phone: 505-646-6414
Fax: 505-646-7791
Web: spacegrant.nmsu.edu

NASA North Carolina Space Grant Consortium

Undergraduate Research Scholarship

Type of award: Scholarship.
Intended use: For full-time junior or senior study at postsecondary institution. Designated institutions: North Carolina Space Grant Consortium member institution, including Appalachian State University, Elizabeth City State University, North Carolina State University, North Carolina Central University, Duke University, North Carolina A&T State University, Winston-Salem State University, University of North Carolina at Asheville, University of North Carolina at Charlotte, University of North Carolina at Chapel Hill, and University of North Carolina at Pembroke.
Eligibility: Applicant must be returning adult student. Applicant must be U.S. citizen.

Basis for selection: Major/career interest in science, general; engineering; aerospace; mathematics or technology. Applicant must demonstrate high academic achievement and leadership.
Application requirements: Recommendations, transcript, research proposal.
Additional information: Minimum 3.0 GPA. Visit Website for more information and application.

Amount of award:	$3,000-$7,000
Number of awards:	25
Number of applicants:	40
Application deadline:	February 15
Notification begins:	April 15
Total amount awarded:	$100,000

Contact:
NASA North Carolina Space Grant
NCSU Box 7515
Raleigh, NC 27695-7515
Phone: 919-515-4240
Fax: 919-515-5934
Web: www.ncspacegrant.org/fs/

Undergraduate Scholarship Program

Type of award: Scholarship, renewable.
Intended use: For full-time freshman or sophomore study at 4-year institution. Designated institutions: North Carolina Space Grant Consortium Member Institutions.
Eligibility: Applicant must be U.S. citizen.
Basis for selection: Major/career interest in science, general; engineering or aerospace. Applicant must demonstrate high academic achievement and leadership.
Application requirements: Recommendations, essay, transcript.
Additional information: Minimum 3.0 GPA. May be new or returning adult student. Visit Website for application and more information.

Amount of award:	$1,000-$2,000
Number of awards:	10
Number of applicants:	15
Application deadline:	February 15
Notification begins:	April 15
Total amount awarded:	$10,000

Contact:
NASA North Carolina Space Grant
NCSU Box 7515
Raleigh, NC 27695-7515
Phone: 919-515-4240
Fax: 919-515-5934
Web: www.ncspacegrant.org/fs/

NASA North Dakota Space Grant Consortium

NASA Space Grant North Dakota Consortium Lillian Goettler Scholarship

Type of award: Scholarship.
Intended use: For full-time undergraduate study at accredited postsecondary institution in United States. Designated institutions: North Dakota State University.
Eligibility: Applicant must be female. Applicant must be U.S. citizen.

Basis for selection: Major/career interest in engineering; mathematics or science, general.
Additional information: Must have minimum 3.5 GPA and ideally be involved in research project of interest to NASA. Contact coordinator for deadline information.

Amount of award:	$2,500

Contact:
North Dakota Space Grant Consortium
U of North Dakota, Space Studies Dept.
P.O. Box 9008
Grand Forks, ND 58202-9008
Phone: 701-777-4856
Web: www.nd.spacegrant.org

NASA Space Grant North Dakota Undergraduate Scholarship

Type of award: Scholarship, renewable.
Intended use: For full-time undergraduate study at 2-year or 4-year institution. Designated institutions: Tribal or public NDSGC member institutions.
Eligibility: Applicant must be U.S. citizen.
Basis for selection: Major/career interest in biology; chemistry; engineering; geology/earth sciences; computer/information sciences or mathematics.
Application requirements: Recommendations, transcript, nomination by participating North Dakota Space Grant Consortium member institution.
Additional information: Minimum 3.0 GPA. Consortium actively encourages women, minority students, and physically challenged students to apply. Deadlines vary. Contact financial aid office at institutions directly.

Amount of award:	$500-$750

Contact:
Financial Aid office at eligible institutions.
Web: www.nd.spacegrant.org

Pearl I. Young Scholarship

Type of award: Scholarship.
Intended use: For full-time undergraduate study at accredited postsecondary institution in United States. Designated institutions: University of North Dakota.
Eligibility: Applicant must be female. Applicant must be U.S. citizen or permanent resident.
Basis for selection: Major/career interest in biology; chemistry; engineering; geology/earth sciences; computer/information sciences or mathematics.
Additional information: Applicants must have minimum 3.5 GPA and ideally be involved in research project of interest to NASA. Contact coordinator for deadline information.

Amount of award:	$2,500
Number of awards:	1

Contact:
NASA Space Grant North Dakota Space Grant Consortium
U of North Dakota, Space Studies Dept.
P.O. Box 9008
Grand Forks, ND 58202-9008
Phone: 701-777-4856
Web: www.nd.spacegrant.org

Scholarships

NASA Ohio Space Grant Consortium

NASA Ohio Space Grant Junior/Senior Scholarship Program

Type of award: Scholarship, renewable.
Intended use: For full-time junior or senior study at accredited 4-year institution. Designated institutions: Ohio Space Grant Consortium members: Case Western Reserve University, Cedarville College, Central State University, Cleveland State University, Marietta College, Miami University, Ohio Northern University, Ohio University, Ohio State University, University of Akron, University of Cincinnati, University of Dayton, University of Toledo, Wilberforce University, Wright State University, and Youngstown State University.
Eligibility: Applicant must be U.S. citizen.
Basis for selection: Major/career interest in science, general; engineering; aerospace or mathematics.
Application requirements: Recommendations, essay, transcript. Proposal of research project.
Additional information: Applications available at OSGC office at Consortium member institutions. Awardees required to participate in research projects and present results at annual OSGC Research Symposium.

Amount of award:	$3,000-$4,000
Number of awards:	50
Number of applicants:	75
Application deadline:	March 1
Notification begins:	April 30
Total amount awarded:	$130,000

Contact:
OSGC campus representative.
Phone: 800-828-6742
Web: www.osgc.org/scholarship.html

NASA Oregon Space Grant Consortium

NASA Space Grant Oregon Undergraduate Scholarship

Type of award: Scholarship.
Intended use: For undergraduate study at accredited 2-year or 4-year institution in United States. Designated institutions: Oregon State University, University of Oregon, Portland State University, Eastern Oregon University, Southern Oregon University, Oregon Institute of Technology, Western Oregon University, George Fox University, Portland Community Colleges (Sylvania, Rock Creek and Cascades Campuses), Lane Community College, and Pacific University.
Eligibility: Applicant must be U.S. citizen residing in Oregon.
Basis for selection: Major/career interest in science, general; engineering; aerospace; mathematics or physical sciences. Applicant must demonstrate high academic achievement.
Application requirements: Recommendations, essay, transcript.
Additional information: Contact Space Grant Consortium representative on campus or see Website for application deadlines and more information.

Amount of award:	$2,000-$6,000
Number of awards:	40
Number of applicants:	85
Application deadline:	January 15
Total amount awarded:	$30,000

Contact:
Oregon NASA Space Grant Consortium
Oregon State University
92 Kerr Administration Bldg.
Corvallis, OR 97331-2103
Phone: 541-737-2414
Fax: 541-737-9946
Web: spacegrant.oregonstate.edu

NASA Pennsylvania Space Grant Consortium

NASA Pennsylvania Space Grant Sylvia Stein Memorial Scholarship

Type of award: Scholarship.
Intended use: For full-time junior or senior study at accredited 4-year institution in United States. Designated institutions: Pennsylvania State University.
Eligibility: Applicant must be U.S. citizen.
Basis for selection: Major/career interest in science, general; mathematics; engineering; education; aerospace or astronomy. Applicant must demonstrate high academic achievement.
Application requirements: Recommendations, essay, transcript. Resume, SAT scores, description of research project and plan of study.
Additional information: Contact campus Space Grant Consortium representative for details. Consortium actively encourages women, minority, and physically challenged students to apply.

Amount of award:	$4,000
Number of awards:	2
Number of applicants:	12
Application deadline:	April 1
Total amount awarded:	$8,000

Contact:
NASA Pennsylvania Space Grant Consortium
Penn State, University Park
2217 Earth-Engineering Sciences Building
University Park, PA 16802
Phone: 814-865-2535
Fax: 814-863-9563
Web: www.pa.spacegrant.org

NASA Rhode Island Space Grant Consortium

NASA Space Grant Rhode Island Undergraduate Research Scholarship

Type of award: Scholarship.
Intended use: For sophomore, junior or senior study at postsecondary institution. Designated institutions: Rhode Island

Space Grant Consortium member institutions: Brown University, Bryant College, Community College of Rhode Island, Providence College, Roger Williams University, Rhode Island College, Rhode Island School of Design, Salve Regina University, University of Rhode Island, Wheaton College.
Eligibility: Applicant must be U.S. citizen.
Basis for selection: Major/career interest in aerospace; biology; engineering; geology/earth sciences or physics. Applicant must demonstrate high academic achievement.
Application requirements: Interview, recommendations, essay, transcript. Research proposal, resume.
Additional information: Awardees expected to work full-time with 75 percent of time devoted to research and the other 25 percent to science education outreach. Applications due in late February; call sponsor for exact dates. Number of awards may vary. Topics of study in space sciences also funded. Students should contact campus representative or the Rhode Island Space Grant office.

Amount of award:	$4,500
Number of awards:	4
Number of applicants:	15

Contact:
NASA Rhode Island Space Grant Consortium
Brown University
Box 1846
Providence, RI 02912
Phone: 401-863-1151
Fax: 401-863-3978
Web: www.spacegrant.brown.edu/RI_Space_Grant/

Summer Undergraduate Scholarship

Type of award: Scholarship, renewable.
Intended use: For sophomore, junior or senior study at postsecondary institution. Designated institutions: Rhode Island Space Grant Consortium member institutions: Brown University, Bryant College, Community College of Rhode Island, Providence College, Roger Williams University, Rhode Island College, Rhode Island School of Design, Salve Regina University, University of Rhode Island, Wheaton College.
Eligibility: Applicant must be U.S. citizen.
Basis for selection: Major/career interest in aerospace; biology; engineering; geology/earth sciences or physics. Applicant must demonstrate high academic achievement.
Application requirements: Interview, recommendations, essay, transcript. Research proposal, resume.
Additional information: Awardees expected to devote four hours per week to science education outreach. Application deadline in late February; call sponsor for exact dates. Number of awards may vary. Topics of study in space sciences also funded. Students should contact their campus representative or the Rhode Island Space Grant office.

Amount of award:	$3,000
Number of awards:	3
Number of applicants:	5

Contact:
NASA Rhode Island Space Grant Consortium
Brown University
Box 1846
Providence, RI 02912
Phone: 401-863-1151
Fax: 401-863-3978
Web: www.spacegrant.brown.edu/RI_Space_Grant/

NASA Rocky Mountain Space Grant Consortium

NASA Rocky Mountain Space Grant Consortium Undergraduate Scholarship

Type of award: Scholarship, renewable.
Intended use: For full-time undergraduate or graduate study at accredited postsecondary institution in United States. Designated institutions: Brigham Young University, Dixie State College, Salt Lake Community College, Snow College, Southern Utah University, Utah College of Applied Technology, Utah Science Center, Utah State University, Utah Valley University, University of Utah, Weaver State University, Weber State University, and Westminster College.
Eligibility: Applicant must be U.S. citizen.
Basis for selection: Major/career interest in science, general; mathematics; engineering or technology. Applicant must demonstrate high academic achievement.
Application requirements: Recommendations, transcript, research proposal. Resume.
Additional information: Award varies from year to year. Contact sponsor for deadline information. Must be used at Rocky Mountain Space Grant Consortium member institution. Award amounts are per month during academic year.

Amount of award:	$500-$1,500
Number of awards:	20
Number of applicants:	60
Total amount awarded:	$22,000

Contact:
Rocky Mountain NASA Space Grant Consortium
Utah State University
4140 Old Main Hill
Logan, UT 84322-4140
Phone: 435-797-3666
Fax: 435-797-3382
Web: utahspacegrant.com

NASA South Carolina Space Grant Consortium

Kathryn D. Sullivan Science and Engineering Fellowship

Type of award: Scholarship, renewable.
Intended use: For full-time senior study at 4-year institution. Designated institutions: SCSGC member institutions.
Eligibility: Applicant must be high school senior. Applicant must be U.S. citizen.
Basis for selection: Major/career interest in science, general; engineering; mathematics or aerospace. Applicant must demonstrate high academic achievement.
Application requirements: Recommendations, essay, transcript. Faculty sponsorship. Resume.
Additional information: Applicants must attend South Carolina member institution. Applicants must have sponsorship from faculty advisor. The Consortium actively encourages women, minority, and disabled students to apply. Application deadline usually in January.

Amount of award: $7,000
Number of awards: 1
Contact:
NASA South Carolina Space Grant Consortium Tara B. Scozzaro, MPA
College of Charleston
66 George Street
Charleston, SC 29424
Phone: 843-953-5463
Fax: 843-953-5446
Web: www.cofc.edu/~scsgrant/scholar/overview.html

NASA Space Grant South Carolina Undergraduate Student Research Fellowship

Type of award: Research grant, renewable.
Intended use: For full-time sophomore, junior or senior study at accredited 4-year institution in United States. Designated institutions: SCSGC member institutions.
Eligibility: Applicant must be U.S. citizen.
Basis for selection: Major/career interest in aerospace; astronomy; atmospheric sciences/meteorology; engineering; environmental science; geophysics; mathematics or science, general. Applicant must demonstrate high academic achievement.
Application requirements: Recommendations, essay, transcript, research proposal. Faculty sponsorship. Resume.
Additional information: Applicants must attend South Carolina Space Grant Consortium member institution. Applicants must have sponsorship from a faculty advisor. Applicants may have a field of study or interest related to any NASA enterprise. Presentation and written report on project findings due within one year of completion. Consortium actively encourages women, minority, and disabled students to apply. See Website for application and more information.
Amount of award: $5,000
Contact:
NASA South Carolina Space Grant Consortium Tara B. Scozzaro MPA
College of Charleston
66 George Street
Charleston, SC 29424
Phone: 843-953-5463
Fax: 843-953-5446
Web: www.cofc.edu/~scsgrant/scholar/overview.html

NASA Texas Space Grant Consortium

NASA Space Grant Texas Columbia Crew Memorial Undergraduate Scholarships

Type of award: Scholarship.
Intended use: For junior or senior study at accredited 2-year or 4-year institution in United States. Designated institutions: Texas Space Grant member institutions.
Eligibility: Applicant must be U.S. citizen.
Basis for selection: Major/career interest in engineering; mathematics; science, general or technology. Applicant must demonstrate high academic achievement and leadership.

Application requirements: Recommendations, essay, transcript, proof of eligibility.
Additional information: First or second year medical school students also eligible. Must attend Texas Space Grant Consortium member institution. Online application.
Amount of award: $1,000
Number of awards: 15
Number of applicants: 40
Application deadline: March 20
Total amount awarded: $15,000
Contact:
Texas Space Grant Consortium
3925 W. Braker Lane
Suite 200
Austin, TX 78759-5321
Phone: 800-248-8742
Web: www.tsgc.utexas.edu

STEM Scholarship

Type of award: Scholarship.
Intended use: For sophomore, junior or senior study at 2-year or 4-year institution in United States. Designated institutions: Texas Space Grant Consortium member institutions.
Eligibility: Applicant must be U.S. citizen.
Basis for selection: Major/career interest in science, general; technology; engineering or mathematics. Applicant must demonstrate high academic achievement.
Application requirements: Recommendations, transcript.
Additional information: First and second year medical students also eligible.
Number of applicants: 100
Contact:
NASA Texas Space Grant Consortium
University of Texas at Austin
3925 West Braker Lane
Austin, TX 78759-5321
Phone: 800-248-8742
Web: www.tsgc.utexas.edu

NASA Vermont Space Grant Consortium

NASA Space Grant Vermont Consortium Undergraduate Scholarships

Type of award: Scholarship, renewable.
Intended use: For full-time undergraduate study at accredited postsecondary institution in United States. Designated institutions: Vermont institutions.
Eligibility: Applicant must be high school senior. Applicant must be U.S. citizen residing in Vermont.
Basis for selection: Major/career interest in science, general; engineering; mathematics; aerospace or physics.
Application requirements: Recommendations, essay, transcript.
Additional information: Open to high school seniors in Vermont who intend to be enrolled full-time in the following year. Applicant must be enrolled in program relevant to NASA's goals at a Vermont institution. Minimum 3.0 GPA. Out-of-state recipients qualify for in-state tuition. Three awards designated for Native American applicants; three scholarships

designated for Burlington Technical Center Aviation & Technical Center, Aerospace Work Force Development, and Aviation Technical School. Can be used at any accredited Vermont institution of higher education.

Amount of award:	$2,500
Number of awards:	10
Number of applicants:	15
Application deadline:	April 13
Total amount awarded:	$18,000

Contact:
Vermont Space Grant Consortium
Votey Hall, College of Engineering and Math
University of Vermont
Burlington, VT 05405-0156
Phone: 802-656-1429
Web: www.cems.uvm.edu/VSGC

NASA Virginia Space Grant Consortium

Aerospace Undergraduate Research Scholarship Program

Type of award: Scholarship.
Intended use: For full-time undergraduate study at accredited 4-year institution in United States. Designated institutions: Space Grant Consortium schools.
Eligibility: Applicant must be U.S. citizen.
Basis for selection: Major/career interest in aerospace; astronomy; chemistry; computer/information sciences; engineering; geology/earth sciences; mathematics or physics. Applicant must demonstrate high academic achievement.
Application requirements: Recommendations, essay, transcript, research proposal. Resume. Budget proposal.
Additional information: Any undergraduate major that includes coursework related to an understanding of aerospace is eligible. Minimum 3.0 GPA. Awards can include $3,000 stipend plus $1,000 travel/research during the academic year, and $3,500 stipend plus $1,000 travel/research during the summer (ten weeks). Awardees must attend a Virginia Space Grant Consortium member institution and participate in USGC's Annual Student Research Conference. The consortium actively encourages women, minorities, and students with disabilities to apply.

Amount of award:	$3,000-$4,500
Notification begins:	April 15

Contact:
Virginia Space Grant Consortium
600 Butler Farm Road, Suite 2253
Hampton, VA 23666
Phone: 757-766-5210
Fax: 757-766-5205
Web: www.vsgc.odu.edu

NASA Space Grant Teacher Education Scholarship

Type of award: Scholarship.
Intended use: For full-time undergraduate or graduate study at 2-year, 4-year or graduate institution in United States. Designated institutions: VSGC member institutions.
Eligibility: Applicant must be U.S. citizen.

Basis for selection: Major/career interest in computer/information sciences; education; engineering; environmental science; geology/earth sciences; mathematics; science, general or technology.
Application requirements: Recommendations, essay, transcript. Resume.
Additional information: Applicants must be enrolled in course of study leading to precollege teacher certification. Priority given to technology education, mathematics, and earth/space/environmental science majors. Minimum 3.0 GPA. High school seniors eligible. See Website for application and additional information.

Amount of award:	$1,000
Notification begins:	April 1
Total amount awarded:	$10,000

Contact:
Virginia Space Grant Consortium
600 Butler Farm Road, Suite 2253
Hampton, VA 23666
Phone: 757-766-5210
Fax: 757-766-5205
Web: www.vsgc.odu.edu

NASA Space Grant Virginia Community College Scholarship

Type of award: Scholarship.
Intended use: For sophomore study at accredited 2-year institution in United States. Designated institutions: Virginia community colleges.
Eligibility: Applicant must be U.S. citizen.
Basis for selection: Major/career interest in aerospace; computer/information sciences; electronics; engineering; mathematics; science, general or technology.
Application requirements: Recommendations, essay, transcript. Resume, photograph and biographical information.
Additional information: Awards are generally to full-time students (12 semester hours), but part-time students (six to nine hours) demonstrating academic achievements are also eligible. Minimum 3.0 GPA. Scholarship is open to students at all community colleges in Virginia. Application deadline may vary. Women, minorities, and students with disabilities are encouraged to apply. Visit Website for application.

Amount of award:	$1,500
Notification begins:	April 1

Contact:
Virginia Space Grant Consortium
600 Butler Farm Road, Suite 2253
Hampton, VA 23666
Phone: 757-766-5210
Fax: 757-766-5205
Web: www.vsgc.odu.edu

NASA West Virginia Space Grant Consortium

NASA West Virginia Space Grant Undergraduate Research Fellowship

Type of award: Scholarship.
Intended use: For full-time undergraduate study at accredited 4-year institution in United States. Designated institutions: West Virginia University, Bethany College, Bluefield State College,

Fairmont State College, Marshall University, Shepherd University, West Virginia State University, Wheeling-Jesuit University, West Liberty State College, and West Virginia Wesleyan College.

Eligibility: Applicant must be U.S. citizen.

Basis for selection: Major/career interest in aerospace; science, general; engineering or mathematics. Applicant must demonstrate high academic achievement and seriousness of purpose.

Application requirements: Recommendations, essay, research proposal. Resume. One recommendation must be from research advisor. Proposal must include statement of purpose, methodology, expected results, and timeline.

Additional information: Visit Website for more information and application. Female and minority students encouraged to apply.

Amount of award:	$4,500-$5,000
Notification begins:	April 1

Contact:
NASA West Virginia Space Grant Consortium, West Virginia University
G-68 Engineering Sciences Building
P.O. Box 6070
Morgantown, WV 26506-6070
Phone: 304-293-4099 ext. 3738
Fax: 304-293-4970
Web: www.nasa.wvu.edu

NASA Wisconsin Space Grant Consortium

NASA Space Grant Wisconsin Consortium Undergraduate Research Program

Type of award: Research grant.

Intended use: For full-time undergraduate study at 2-year or 4-year institution. Designated institutions: WSGC colleges and universities.

Eligibility: Applicant must be U.S. citizen.

Basis for selection: Major/career interest in aerospace; astronomy; engineering; science, general; architecture; law; business or medicine. Applicant must demonstrate high academic achievement and seriousness of purpose.

Application requirements: Recommendations, transcript, research proposal. Project proposal with budget.

Additional information: Funding for qualified students to create and implement a research project related to aerospace, space science, or other interdisciplinary space-related studies. For academic year or summer term use. Minimum 3.0 GPA and above-average SAT/ACT scores required. Consortium encourages applications from women, minorities, and students with disabilities. For more information, see Website.

Amount of award:	$3,500-$4,000
Number of awards:	8
Application deadline:	February 1
Notification begins:	March 30
Total amount awarded:	$28,000

Contact:
Wisconsin Space Grant Consortium
University of Wisconsin, Green Bay
2420 Nicolet Drive
Green Bay, WI 54311-7001
Phone: 608-263-4206
Fax: 608-263-4203
Web: www.uwgb.edu/wsgc

NASA Space Grant Wisconsin Consortium Undergraduate Scholarship

Type of award: Scholarship, renewable.

Intended use: For full-time undergraduate study at accredited 4-year institution in United States. Designated institutions: WSGC colleges and universities.

Eligibility: Applicant must be U.S. citizen.

Basis for selection: Major/career interest in aerospace; astronomy; engineering; physics or science, general. Applicant must demonstrate high academic achievement.

Application requirements: Recommendations, essay, transcript.

Additional information: Applicant must attend Wisconsin Space Grant Consortium member institution and reside in Wisconsin during school year. Minimum 3.0 GPA and above-average SAT/ACT scores required. Qualified students may also apply for summer session's Undergraduate Research Award. Consortium actively encourages women, minorities, and students with disabilities to apply. See Website for application and details.

Amount of award:	$1,500
Application deadline:	February 1
Notification begins:	March 30

Contact:
Wisconsin Space Grant Consortium
University of Wisconsin, Green Bay
2420 Nicolet Drive
Green Bay, WI 54311-7001
Phone: 920-465-2108
Web: www.uwgb.edu/wsgc

National Academy for Nuclear Training

Scholarship Educational Assistance Program

Type of award: Scholarship, renewable.

Intended use: For full-time junior or senior study at accredited 4-year institution in United States.

Eligibility: Applicant must be U.S. citizen.

Basis for selection: Major/career interest in engineering, chemical; engineering, mechanical; engineering, electrical/electronic or engineering, nuclear. Applicant must demonstrate high academic achievement, depth of character, leadership, seriousness of purpose and service orientation.

Application requirements: Recommendations, transcript, proof of eligibility, nomination by INPO member utility.

Additional information: Minimum 3.0 GPA. Renewal for eligible students. Additional field of study: power generation health physics. Study of chemical engineering must include nuclear or power option. Applicant should be considering career

Scholarships

in nuclear utility industry. For additional information and application deadline, contact by e-mail or visit Website.

Amount of award:	$1,250-$2,500
Number of awards:	120
Number of applicants:	95
Notification begins:	August 1
Total amount awarded:	$300,000

Contact:
National Academy for Nuclear Training Scholarship Program
301 ACT Drive
P.O. Box 4030
Iowa City, IA 52243-4030
Phone: 800-294-7492
Fax: 319-337-1204
Web: www.nei.org/nantscholarships

National Amateur Baseball Federation, Inc.

National Amateur Baseball Federation Scholarship

Type of award: Scholarship, renewable.
Intended use: For undergraduate study at accredited postsecondary institution in United States or Canada.
Basis for selection: Competition/talent/interest in athletics/sports. Major/career interest in athletic training. Applicant must demonstrate financial need and high academic achievement.
Application requirements: Recommendations, transcript, proof of eligibility, nomination by National Amateur Baseball Federation member association. Written statement. Documentation of previous awards received from sponsoring association, nomination by president or director of franchised member team.
Additional information: Amount of award determined annually. Applicant must have participated in National Amateur Baseball Federation event in the current season and be sponsored by National Amateur Baseball Federation member association. Send SASE for application packet.

Amount of award:	$500-$1,000
Number of awards:	5
Number of applicants:	5
Application deadline:	October 1
Notification begins:	January 1
Total amount awarded:	$5,000

Contact:
National Amateur Baseball Federation
Attn: Chairman Awards Committee
P.O. Box 705
Bowie, MD 20718
Phone: 410-721-4727
Fax: 410-721-4940
Web: www.nabf.com

National Art Materials Trade Association

NAMTA Educational Scholarship

Type of award: Scholarship.

Intended use: For undergraduate or graduate study at accredited vocational, 2-year, 4-year or graduate institution.
Eligibility: Applicant or parent must be member/participant of National Art Materials Trade Association.
Basis for selection: Applicant must demonstrate financial need and high academic achievement.
Application requirements: Essay, transcript. Proof of acceptance.
Additional information: Applicant must be employee or family member of employee of NAMTA member firm. Applicants must have graduated high school by July 1 of the year scholarship is awarded. All application materials must be mailed together.

Amount of award:	$2,500
Number of awards:	1
Number of applicants:	18
Application deadline:	March 1
Notification begins:	April 15
Total amount awarded:	$2,500

Contact:
National Art Materials Trade Association
15806 Brookway Drive
Suite 300
Huntersville, NC 28078
Phone: 704-892-6244
Fax: 704-892-6247
Web: www.namta.org

NAMTA Foundation Visual Arts Major Scholarship

Type of award: Scholarship.
Intended use: For undergraduate study at accredited vocational, 2-year or 4-year institution.
Eligibility: Applicant or parent must be member/participant of National Art Materials Trade Association.
Basis for selection: Major/career interest in arts, general; arts management or art/art history. Applicant must demonstrate financial need and high academic achievement.
Application requirements: Essay, transcript. Proof of acceptance, two to three examples of work via electronic means only (CD or email).
Additional information: Applicant must major in visual arts or visual arts education. Applicants judged primarily on artistic talent/potential, however financial need and GPA may also be considered.

Amount of award:	$2,500
Number of awards:	8
Number of applicants:	57
Application deadline:	March 1
Notification begins:	April 15
Total amount awarded:	$10,000

Contact:
Karen Brown, National Art Materials Trade Association
15806 Brookway Drive
Suite 300
Huntersville, NC 28078
Phone: 704-892-6244
Fax: 704-892-6247
Web: www.namtafoundation.org

National Association of Black Accountants Inc.

NABA National Scholarship Program

Type of award: Scholarship.
Intended use: For full-time undergraduate or master's study at 4-year or graduate institution.
Eligibility: Applicant must be Alaskan native, Asian American, African American, Mexican American, Hispanic American, Puerto Rican or American Indian.
Basis for selection: Major/career interest in accounting; business or finance/banking. Applicant must demonstrate depth of character, leadership and service orientation.
Application requirements: Recommendations, essay, transcript, proof of eligibility. Resume.
Additional information: Must be active National Association of Black Accountants member. Applicants must have minimum 2.5 GPA for some awards, 3.3 GPA for others. Applicants must join association by December 31.

Amount of award:	$1,000-$10,000
Application deadline:	January 31
Notification begins:	September 1

Contact:
National Association of Black Accountants Inc.
National Scholarship Program
7474 Greenway Center Drive, #1120
Greenbelt, MD 20770
Phone: 301-474-6222
Fax: 301-474-3114
Web: www.nabainc.org

National Association of Black Journalists

Allison E. Fisher Scholarship

Type of award: Scholarship.
Intended use: For undergraduate or graduate study at postsecondary institution.
Eligibility: Applicant must be U.S. citizen, permanent resident or international student.
Basis for selection: Major/career interest in journalism. Applicant must demonstrate service orientation.
Application requirements: Essay, transcript. Resume. Applicants must submit minimum of five samples of published work in print, radio, television, photography, slideshows, website, or flash animation. Must send four copies of all application materials.
Additional information: Minimum 3.0 GPA. Must be a print or broadcast journalism major and a member of NABJ.

Number of awards:	1
Total amount awarded:	$2,500

Contact:
National Association of Black Journalists
100 Knight Hall, Suite 3100
College Park, MD 20742
Phone: 301-405-0248
Fax: 301-314-1714
Web: www.nabj.org

Carole Simpson Scholarship

Type of award: Scholarship.
Intended use: For undergraduate or graduate study at accredited 4-year or graduate institution.
Eligibility: Applicant must be U.S. citizen, permanent resident or international student.
Basis for selection: Major/career interest in journalism or radio/television/film.
Application requirements: Essay, transcript. Resume, cover letter. Applicants must submit minimum of five samples of published work in print, radio, television, photography, slideshows, website, or flash animation.
Additional information: Minimum 2.5 GPA. Must be member of National Association of Black Journalists and major in broadcast journalism.

Amount of award:	$2,500
Number of awards:	1
Total amount awarded:	$2,500

Contact:
National Association of Black Journalists
1100 Knight Hall, Suite 3100
College Park, MD 20742
Phone: 301-405-0248
Fax: 301-314-1714
Web: www.nabj.org

Larry Whiteside Scholarship

Type of award: Scholarship.
Intended use: For junior or senior study at accredited 4-year institution.
Eligibility: Applicant must be African American.
Basis for selection: Major/career interest in journalism.
Application requirements: Portfolio, recommendations, essay, transcript. Resume, cover letter. Must submit three samples of work.
Additional information: Minimum 2.5 GPA in major and 2.0 major overall. Must be member of National Association of Black Journalists and be pursuing career in sports journalism.

Amount of award:	$2,500
Number of awards:	1
Total amount awarded:	$2,500

Contact:
National Association of Black Journalists
1100 Knight Hall, Suite 3100
College Park, MD 20742
Phone: 301-405-0248
Fax: 301-314-1714
Web: www.nabj.org

Sports Illustrated Scholarship

Type of award: Scholarship.
Intended use: For junior study at accredited 4-year institution.
Eligibility: Applicant must be African American. Applicant must be female.
Basis for selection: Major/career interest in journalism.
Application requirements: Portfolio, recommendations, essay, transcript. Resume, cover letter. Applicants must submit minimum of five samples of published work in print, radio, television, photography, slideshows, website, or flash animation.
Additional information: Minimum 2.5 GPA. Must be female member of National Association of Black Journalists. Must major in journalism or be pursuing a career in sports journalism.

Amount of award:	$5,000
Number of awards:	1
Total amount awarded:	$5,000

Contact:
National Association of Black Journalists
1100 Knight Hall, Suite 3100
College Park, MD 20742
Phone: 301-405-0248
Fax: 301-314-1714
Web: www.nabj.org

Visual Task Force (VTF) Scholarship

Type of award: Scholarship.
Intended use: For sophomore, junior, senior or graduate study at 4-year or graduate institution.
Eligibility: Applicant must be African American.
Basis for selection: Major/career interest in journalism.
Application requirements: Portfolio, recommendations, essay, transcript. Resume, cover letter. Applicants must submit minimum of five samples of published work in print, radio, television, photography, slideshows, Website, or flash animation.
Additional information: Minimum 2.75 GPA. Must be member of National Association of Black Journalists and have declared a concentration in visual journalism. Must have experience working on campus newspaper or TV studio and have had one internship.

Amount of award:	$1,250
Number of awards:	2
Total amount awarded:	$2,500

Contact:
National Association of Black Journalists
1100 Knight Hall, Suite 3100
College Park, MD 20742
Phone: 301-405-0248
Fax: 301-314-1714
Web: www.nabj.org

National Association of Letter Carriers

Costas G. Lemonopoulos Scholarship

Type of award: Scholarship, renewable.
Intended use: For full-time undergraduate study at accredited 4-year institution. Designated institutions: St. Petersburg Junior College or four-year public Florida university.
Eligibility: Applicant must be high school senior.
Basis for selection: Applicant must demonstrate high academic achievement.
Application requirements: Transcript. SAT/ACT scores and NALC form.
Additional information: Applicant must be child of National Association of Letter Carriers member in good standing (active, retired, or deceased). Preliminary application available on Website; required for further details and primary application form. Notification published in March issue of Postal Record magazine.

Number of awards:	20
Number of applicants:	150
Application deadline:	June 1

Contact:
National Association of Letter Carriers
Costas G. Lemonopoulos Scholarship Trust
100 Indiana Avenue NW
Washington, DC 20001-2144
Phone: 202-393-4695
Fax: 202-737-1540
Web: www.nalc.org/nalc/members/scholarships.html

William C. Doherty - John T. Donelon Scholarships

Type of award: Scholarship, renewable.
Intended use: For full-time undergraduate study at accredited 4-year institution.
Eligibility: Applicant must be high school senior.
Basis for selection: Applicant must demonstrate financial need and high academic achievement.
Application requirements: Recommendations, essay, transcript, proof of eligibility. SAT/ACT scores.
Additional information: Applicant must be child of National Association of Letter Carriers member in good standing (active, retired, or deceased) for at least one year. Preliminary application on Website due December 31; supporting materials due March 31. Notification published in July issue of Postal Record magazine.

Amount of award:	$1,000-$4,000
Number of awards:	5
Number of applicants:	5
Application deadline:	December 31
Total amount awarded:	$21,000

Contact:
National Association of Letter Carriers
Scholarship Committee
100 Indiana Avenue NW
Washington, DC 20001-2144
Phone: 202-393-4695
Fax: 202-737-1540
Web: www.nalc.org/nalc/members/scholarships.html

National Association of Water Companies (NJ Chapter)

Water Companies (NJ Chapter) Scholarship

Type of award: Scholarship.
Intended use: For freshman, sophomore, junior, senior or graduate study at accredited 2-year, 4-year or graduate institution in United States. Designated institutions: New Jersey colleges and universities.
Eligibility: Applicant must be U.S. citizen residing in New Jersey.
Basis for selection: Major/career interest in hydrology; natural resources/conservation; science, general; engineering, environmental; finance/banking; communications; accounting; business; computer/information sciences or law. Applicant must demonstrate financial need, high academic achievement, depth of character, leadership, seriousness of purpose and service orientation.

Application requirements: Recommendations, essay, transcript. Essay must illustrate interest in water utility industry or related field.

Additional information: Applicant must have interest in fields of study related to water industry. Acceptable fields of study also include consumer affairs and human resources. At least five years residence in New Jersey required. Minimum 3.0 GPA.

Amount of award:	$2,500
Number of awards:	2
Number of applicants:	80
Application deadline:	April 1
Notification begins:	June 1
Total amount awarded:	$2,500

Contact:
Nat'l Assn. of Water Companies (NJ Chapter)
Gail P. Brady
49 Howell Drive
Verona, NJ 07044
Phone: 973-669-5807

National Association of Women in Construction

Construction Trades Scholarship

Type of award: Scholarship.
Intended use: For undergraduate study at postsecondary institution.
Basis for selection: Major/career interest in construction or construction management.
Application requirements: Resume, list of extracurricular activities.
Additional information: Must be currently enrolled in construction-related training program approved by the Bureau of Apprenticeship Training or home state's Postsecondary Education Commission. Visit Website for application.

Amount of award:	$1,000-$2,000
Application deadline:	March 15
Total amount awarded:	$25,000

Contact:
National Association of Women in Construction
327 South Adams
Fort Worth, TX 76104
Web: www.nawic.org

National Association of Women in Construction Founders' Scholarship

Type of award: Scholarship.
Intended use: For full-time undergraduate study at accredited 2-year or 4-year institution in United States or Canada.
Eligibility: Applicant must be U.S. citizen.
Basis for selection: Major/career interest in construction; construction management; engineering, construction or architecture. Applicant must demonstrate financial need and high academic achievement.
Application requirements: Interview, recommendations, essay, transcript. Resume.
Additional information: Number and amount of awards vary. Interest in construction, extracurricular activities, and employment experience also taken into consideration. Applicants must have completed one term of study in construction-related field. Minimum 3.0 GPA. Only semifinalists

will be interviewed. Visit Website for additional information and application.

Amount of award:	$1,000-$2,000
Application deadline:	March 15
Notification begins:	April 1
Total amount awarded:	$25,000

Contact:
National Association of Women in Construction
327 South Adams Street
Fort Worth, TX 76104
Web: www.nawic.org

National Athletic Trainers' Association Research & Education Foundation

Athletic Trainers' Entry Level Scholarship

Type of award: Scholarship.
Intended use: For full-time junior, senior, master's or doctoral study at 4-year or graduate institution.
Basis for selection: Major/career interest in athletic training. Applicant must demonstrate high academic achievement.
Application requirements: Recommendations, essay, transcript, proof of eligibility, nomination by BOC certified trainer.
Additional information: Must be National Athletic Trainers' Association member. Minimum 3.2 GPA. Intention to pursue the profession of athletic training as career required. Must be sponsored by a certified athletic trainer. Must be enrolled in Commission on Accreditation of Athletic Training Education (CAATE)-accredited undergraduate or master's program. See complete guidelines on Website.

Amount of award:	$2,300
Number of applicants:	203
Notification begins:	April 15
Total amount awarded:	$150,000

Contact:
National Athletic Trainers' Association
Research & Education Foundation
2952 Stemmons Freeway
Dallas, TX 75247
Phone: 800-879-6282 ext. 121
Fax: 214-637-2206
Web: www.natafoundation.org

National Black Nurses Association

Black Nurses Scholarship

Type of award: Scholarship.
Intended use: For undergraduate or graduate study at postsecondary institution.
Eligibility: Applicant must be African American.
Basis for selection: Major/career interest in nursing or nurse practitioner. Applicant must demonstrate leadership, seriousness of purpose and service orientation.

Application requirements: Recommendations, essay, transcript. Evidence of participation in both student nursing activities and the African-American community.

Additional information: Must be member of National Black Nurses Association and member of local chapter if one exists. Must be currently enrolled in a nursing program and have at least one full year of school left. Must be in good academic standing. Call association for current information on program.

Amount of award:	$500-$2,000
Application deadline:	April 15
Notification begins:	July 1

Contact:
National Black Nurses Association
8630 Fenton Street
Silver Spring, MD 20910
Phone: 301-589-3200
Fax: 301-589-3223
Web: www.nbna.org

National Black Police Association

Alphonso Deal Scholarship

Type of award: Scholarship.

Intended use: For freshman study at 2-year or 4-year institution in United States.

Eligibility: Applicant must be enrolled in high school. Applicant must be U.S. citizen.

Basis for selection: Major/career interest in law or criminal justice/law enforcement. Applicant must demonstrate high academic achievement, depth of character, seriousness of purpose and service orientation.

Application requirements: Recommendations, essay, transcript. Photo of applicant required.

Additional information: Award provides higher education training for the betterment of the criminal justice system. Applicant must be accepted by a college or university prior to date of award.

Amount of award:	$500
Number of awards:	5
Number of applicants:	5
Application deadline:	June 1
Total amount awarded:	$2,500

Contact:
National Black Police Association Scholarship Award
30 Kennedy St.
Suite 101
Washington, DC 20011-2103
Phone: 202-986-2070
Fax: 202-986-0410
Web: www.blackpolice.org

National Center For Learning Disabilities

Anne Ford and Allegra Ford Scholarship

Type of award: Scholarship, renewable.

Intended use: For undergraduate study at 4-year institution.

Eligibility: Applicant must be learning disabled. Applicant must be high school senior. Applicant must be U.S. citizen.

Basis for selection: Applicant must demonstrate financial need, depth of character, leadership, seriousness of purpose and service orientation.

Application requirements: Recommendations, essay, transcript, proof of eligibility. Personal statement may be written or recorded (audio or video). Financial statements, SAT/ACT scores.

Additional information: Applicants must have identifiable learning disability. Minimum 3.0 GPA. Recipients receive $10,000 over 4 years ($2,500 per year). Minorities encouraged to apply. Must be willing to mentor future scholars.

Amount of award:	$10,000
Number of awards:	2
Number of applicants:	400
Application deadline:	December 31
Notification begins:	April 1

Contact:
Anne Ford and Allegra Ford Scholarship
National Center for Learning Disabilities
381 Park Avenue South, Suite 1401
New York, NY 10016-8806
Phone: 212-545-7510
Fax: 212-545-9665
Web: www.ncld.org

National Commission for Cooperative Education

National Co-op Scholarship

Type of award: Scholarship, renewable.

Intended use: For undergraduate study at postsecondary institution. Designated institutions: Drexel University, Johnson & Wales University, Kettering University, Pace University, Rochester Institute of Technology, University of Cincinnati, University of Toledo, Wentworth Institute of Technology.

Eligibility: Applicant must be high school senior. Applicant must be residing in Washington or U.S. Territories.

Application requirements: One-page essay on decision to pursue a college cooperative education program.

Additional information: Applicants must be accepted to and attend one of the ten participating institutions. Minimum 3.5 GPA. Visit Website for more information and application.

Amount of award:	$6,000
Number of awards:	170
Number of applicants:	2,251
Application deadline:	February 15
Total amount awarded:	$4,500,000

Contact:
National Commission for Cooperative Education
360 Huntington Avenue, 384 CP
Boston, MA 02115-5096
Phone: 617-373-3770
Fax: 617-373-3463
Web: www.co-op.edu

National Dairy Shrine

Core Scholarship

Type of award: Scholarship, renewable.
Intended use: For full-time freshman study at accredited 4-year institution.
Eligibility: Applicant must be U.S. citizen.
Basis for selection: Major/career interest in agriculture; animal sciences or dairy. Applicant must demonstrate high academic achievement, leadership and seriousness of purpose.
Application requirements: Recommendations, essay, transcript.
Additional information: Minimum 2.5 GPA. Student must have commitment to career in dairy.

Amount of award:	$1,000
Number of awards:	1
Number of applicants:	12
Application deadline:	May 1
Notification begins:	August 1
Total amount awarded:	$1,000

Contact:
National Dairy Shrine
P.O. Box 1
Maribel, WI 54227
Phone: 920-863-6333
Fax: 920-863-8328
Web: www.dairyshrine.org

Dairy Student Recognition Program

Type of award: Scholarship.
Intended use: For senior study at postsecondary institution.
Basis for selection: Major/career interest in agriculture; business; dairy; environmental science; food production/management/services; food science/technology; law; manufacturing; marketing or veterinary medicine. Applicant must demonstrate leadership.
Application requirements: Recommendations, essay, transcript, nomination by college or university dairy-science department.
Additional information: Cash awards for graduating seniors planning career in dairy cattle. Two candidates eligible per institution. First-place winner receives $1,500; second, $1,000; third through seventh, $500. National Dairy Shrine chooses final winners. Students who placed in top five in previous years not eligible for further competition.

Amount of award:	$500-$1,500
Number of awards:	9
Number of applicants:	23
Application deadline:	May 1
Notification begins:	August 1
Total amount awarded:	$6,000

Contact:
National Dairy Shrine
P.O. Box 1
Maribel, WI 54227
Phone: 920-863-6333
Fax: 920-863-8328
Web: www.dairyshrine.org

DMI Milk Marketing Scholarships

Type of award: Scholarship.
Intended use: For sophomore or junior study at postsecondary institution.
Basis for selection: Major/career interest in agriculture; animal sciences; dairy; dietetics/nutrition or education.
Application requirements: Recommendations, essay, transcript.
Additional information: For students interested in careers marketing milk or dairy products. Minimum 2.5 GPA. Visit Website for more details.

Amount of award:	$1,000-$1,500
Number of awards:	8
Number of applicants:	22
Application deadline:	May 1
Notification begins:	August 1
Total amount awarded:	$8,500

Contact:
National Dairy Shrine
Attn: Maurice E. Core
P.O. Box 1
Maribel, WI 54227
Phone: 920-863-6333
Fax: 920-863-8328
Web: www.dairyshrine.org

Iager Dairy Scholarship

Type of award: Scholarship.
Intended use: For undergraduate study at 2-year institution.
Basis for selection: Major/career interest in food production/management/services; food science/technology or dairy. Applicant must demonstrate high academic achievement and leadership.
Application requirements: Recommendations, essay, transcript.
Additional information: Must be second-year college student in two-year agricultural college. Minimum 2.5 GPA. May request application from Website or National Dairy Shrine.

Amount of award:	$1,000
Number of awards:	1
Number of applicants:	4
Application deadline:	May 1
Notification begins:	August 1
Total amount awarded:	$1,000

Contact:
National Dairy Shrine
P.O. Box 1
Maribel, WI 54227
Phone: 920-863-6333
Fax: 920-863-8328
Web: www.dairyshrine.org

Klussendorf Scholarship

Type of award: Scholarship.
Intended use: For sophomore, junior or senior study at 2-year or 4-year institution.

Basis for selection: Major/career interest in animal sciences; dairy; food production/management/services or food science/technology.
Application requirements: Recommendations, essay, transcript.
Additional information: For dairy or animal science majors in second, third, or fourth year of college. Must plan to become dairy cattle breeder, owner, herdsperson, or fitter. May request application from Website or National Dairy Shrine.

Amount of award:	$1,500
Number of awards:	5
Number of applicants:	20
Application deadline:	May 1
Notification begins:	August 1
Total amount awarded:	$7,500

Contact:
National Dairy Shrine
P.O. Box 1
Maribel, WI 54227
Phone: 920-863-6333
Fax: 920-863-8328
Web: www.dairyshrine.org

Marshall E. McCullough Undergraduate Scholarship

Type of award: Scholarship.
Intended use: For full-time senior study at accredited 4-year institution in United States.
Eligibility: Applicant must be high school senior. Applicant must be U.S. citizen.
Basis for selection: Major/career interest in animal sciences; dairy; communications or journalism.
Application requirements: Recommendations, essay, transcript.
Additional information: Five finalists will be asked to submit video responding to specific questions about the dairy industry. Two awards: one for $2,500; one for $1,000. Must major in dairy/animal science with communications emphasis or agricultural journalism with dairy/animal science emphasis.

Amount of award:	$1,000-$2,500
Number of awards:	2
Number of applicants:	10
Application deadline:	May 1
Notification begins:	August 1
Total amount awarded:	$3,500

Contact:
National Dairy Shrine
P.O. Box 1
Maribel, WI 54227
Phone: 920-863-6333
Fax: 920-863-8328
Web: www.dairyshrine.org

National Dairy Shrine Kildee Scholarship

Type of award: Scholarship.
Intended use: For junior, senior or graduate study at postsecondary institution.
Basis for selection: Major/career interest in animal sciences; dairy; food production/management/services or food science/technology. Applicant must demonstrate high academic achievement and leadership.
Application requirements: Recommendations, essay, transcript.

Additional information: Applicant must have placed in top 25 in National 4-H, FFA or National Intercollegiate Judging Contests. Platinum winners from National Dairy Challenge are eligible to compete for graduate study scholarships. Up to two $3,000 scholarships for graduate study and one $2,000 scholarship for undergraduate study awarded. May request application from Website or National Dairy Shrine.

Amount of award:	$2,000-$3,000
Number of awards:	3
Number of applicants:	8
Application deadline:	May 1
Notification begins:	August 1
Total amount awarded:	$5,000

Contact:
National Dairy Shrine
P.O. Box 1
Maribel, WI 54227
Phone: 920-863-6333
Fax: 920-863-8328
Web: www.dairyshrine.org

National Eagle Scout Association

Hall/McElwain Merit Scholarship

Type of award: Scholarship.
Intended use: For undergraduate study at postsecondary institution.
Eligibility: Applicant must be male.
Basis for selection: Applicant must demonstrate leadership.
Application requirements: Recommendations, proof of eligibility.
Additional information: Applicant must be Eagle Scout. Must have strong record of participation in activities outside of scouting. Visit Website for more information and application.

Amount of award:	$1,000
Number of awards:	70
Number of applicants:	2,500
Application deadline:	January 31
Notification begins:	July 1
Total amount awarded:	$56,000

Contact:
NESA, Sum 222
1325 W. Walnut Hill Lane
P.O. Box 152079
Irving, TX 75015-2079
Phone: 972-580-2032
Web: www.nesa.org

NESA Academic Scholarships

Type of award: Scholarship.
Intended use: For freshman study at accredited 4-year institution.
Eligibility: Applicant must be male, high school senior.
Basis for selection: Applicant must demonstrate financial need, high academic achievement and leadership.
Application requirements: Recommendations, transcript.
Additional information: Applicant must be Eagle Scout. Award may not be used at military institution. Minimum 1200 SAT or 28 ACT score.

Amount of award:	$2,500-$48,000
Number of applicants:	2,500
Application deadline:	January 31
Notification begins:	July 1
Total amount awarded:	$300,000

Contact:
NESA, Sum 222
1325 West Walnut Hill Lane
P.O. Box 152079
Irving, TX 75015-2079
Phone: 972-580-2032
Web: www.nesa.org

National Environmental Health Association/ American Academy of Sanitarians

NEHA/AAS Scholarship

Type of award: Scholarship.
Intended use: For full-time junior, senior or graduate study at accredited 4-year or graduate institution.
Basis for selection: Major/career interest in environmental science or public health. Applicant must demonstrate financial need, high academic achievement and seriousness of purpose.
Application requirements: Transcript, proof of eligibility. Three letters of recommendation (one from active NEHA member, two from faculty members at applicant's school).
Additional information: Undergraduates must be enrolled in an Environmental Health Accreditation Council accredited school or National Environmental Health Association Institutional/Educational or sustaining member school (list available at sponsor Website). Graduates must be enrolled in environmental health science and/or public health program. Visit Website for further information and updates.

Amount of award:	$1,000-$1,500
Number of awards:	3
Number of applicants:	100
Application deadline:	February 1
Total amount awarded:	$3,500

Contact:
National Environmental Health Association
NEHA/AAS Scholarship
720 South Colorado Boulevard., 1000-N
Denver, CO 80246-1925
Phone: 303-756-9090
Fax: 303-691-9490
Web: www.neha.org

National Federation of the Blind

Charles and Melva T. Owen Memorial Scholarship

Type of award: Scholarship, renewable.

Intended use: For full-time undergraduate or graduate study at postsecondary institution.
Eligibility: Applicant must be visually impaired.
Basis for selection: Applicant must demonstrate financial need, high academic achievement and service orientation.
Application requirements: Recommendations, essay, transcript. Interview with NFB affiliate president, SAT/ACT scores (high school seniors only), proof of legal blindness.
Additional information: Applicant must be legally blind in both eyes. Field of study should be directed toward attaining financial independence. Excludes study of religion and those seeking only to further general or cultural education. Recipients of Federation scholarships need not be members of National Federation of the Blind. Visit Website for application.

Amount of award:	$3,000-$10,000
Number of awards:	2
Application deadline:	March 31
Notification begins:	June 1
Total amount awarded:	$10,000

Contact:
National Federation of the Blind Scholarship Committee
NFB at Jernigan Place
200 East Wells Street
Baltimore, MD 21230
Phone: 410-659-9134 ext. 2415
Fax: 410-685-5653
Web: www.nfb.org/scholarships

Computer Science Scholarship

Type of award: Scholarship, renewable.
Intended use: For full-time undergraduate or graduate study at postsecondary institution.
Eligibility: Applicant must be visually impaired.
Basis for selection: Major/career interest in computer/information sciences; engineering, computer or computer graphics. Applicant must demonstrate financial need, high academic achievement and service orientation.
Application requirements: Recommendations, essay, transcript. Proof of legal blindness, interview with NFB affiliate president, SAT/ACT scores (high school seniors only).
Additional information: Applicant must be legally blind in both eyes. Recipients of Federation scholarships need not be members of National Federation of the Blind. Visit Website for application.

Amount of award:	$3,000
Number of awards:	1
Application deadline:	March 31
Notification begins:	June 1
Total amount awarded:	$3,000

Contact:
National Federation of the Blind Scholarship Committee
NFB at Jernigan Place
200 East Wells Street
Baltimore, MD 21230
Phone: 410-659-9134 ext. 2415
Fax: 410-685-5653
Web: www.nfb.org/scholarships

E.U. Parker Memorial Scholarship

Type of award: Scholarship, renewable.
Intended use: For full-time undergraduate or graduate study at postsecondary institution.
Eligibility: Applicant must be visually impaired.
Basis for selection: Applicant must demonstrate financial need, high academic achievement and service orientation.

Application requirements: Recommendations, essay, transcript. Proof of legal blindness, interview with NFB affiliate president, SAT/ACT scores (high school seniors only).
Additional information: Applicant must be legally blind in both eyes. Recipients of Federation scholarships need not be members of National Federation of the Blind. Visit Website for application.

Amount of award:	$3,000
Number of awards:	1
Application deadline:	March 31
Notification begins:	June 1
Total amount awarded:	$3,000

Contact:
National Federation of the Blind Scholarship Committee
NFB at Jernigan Place
200 East Wells Street
Baltimore, MD 21230
Phone: 410-659-9134 ext. 2415
Fax: 410-685-5653
Web: www.nfb.org/scholarships

Hank LeBonne Scholarship

Type of award: Scholarship.
Intended use: For full-time undergraduate or graduate study at postsecondary institution in United States.
Eligibility: Applicant must be visually impaired.
Basis for selection: Applicant must demonstrate financial need, high academic achievement and service orientation.
Application requirements: Recommendations, essay, transcript. Interview with NFB affiliate president, ACT/SAT scores (high school seniors only), proof of legal blindness.
Additional information: Applicant must be legally blind in both eyes. Recipients of scholarships need not be members of Federation. Visit Website for application.

Amount of award:	$5,000
Number of awards:	1
Application deadline:	March 31

Contact:
National Federation for the Blind Scholarship Committee
NFB at Jernigan Place
200 East Wells Street
Baltimore, MD 21230
Phone: 410-659-9134 ext. 2415
Fax: 410-685-5653
Web: www.nfb.org/scholarships

Hermione Grant Calhoun Scholarship

Type of award: Scholarship, renewable.
Intended use: For full-time undergraduate or graduate study at postsecondary institution.
Eligibility: Applicant must be visually impaired. Applicant must be female.
Basis for selection: Applicant must demonstrate financial need, high academic achievement and service orientation.
Application requirements: Recommendations, essay, transcript. Interview with NFB affiliate president, SAT/ACT scores (high school seniors only), proof of legal blindness.
Additional information: Applicant must be female who is legally blind in both eyes. Recipients of Federation scholarships need not be members of National Federation of the Blind. Visit Website for application.

Amount of award:	$3,000
Number of awards:	1
Application deadline:	March 31
Notification begins:	June 1
Total amount awarded:	$3,000

Contact:
National Federation of the Blind Scholarship Committee
NFB at Jernigan Place
200 East Wells Street
Baltimore, MD 21230
Phone: 410-659-9134 ext. 2415
Fax: 410-685-5653
Web: www.nfb.org/scholarship

Howard Brown Rickard Scholarship

Type of award: Scholarship, renewable.
Intended use: For full-time undergraduate or graduate study at postsecondary institution.
Eligibility: Applicant must be visually impaired.
Basis for selection: Major/career interest in law; medicine; engineering; architecture or natural sciences. Applicant must demonstrate financial need, high academic achievement and service orientation.
Application requirements: Recommendations, essay, transcript. Interview with NFB affiliate president, ACT/SAT scores (high school seniors only), proof of legal blindness.
Additional information: Applicant must be legally blind in both eyes. Recipients of Federation scholarships need not be members of National Federation of the Blind. Visit Website for application.

Amount of award:	$3,000
Number of awards:	1
Application deadline:	March 31
Notification begins:	June 1
Total amount awarded:	$3,000

Contact:
National Federation of the Blind Scholarship Committee
NFB at Jernigan Place
200 East Wells Street
Baltimore, MD 21230
Phone: 410-659-9134 ext. 2415
Fax: 410-685-5653
Web: www.nfb.org/scholarships

Jeannette C. Eyerly Memorial Scholarship

Type of award: Scholarship.
Intended use: For full-time undergraduate study at postsecondary institution in United States.
Eligibility: Applicant must be visually impaired. Applicant must be U.S. citizen or permanent resident.
Basis for selection: Applicant must demonstrate high academic achievement.
Application requirements: Recommendations, transcript. SAT/ACT scores, NFB affiliate president's letter, proof of legal blindness.
Additional information: Must be legally blind in both eyes. Awardees must attend NFB National Convention and all scholarship program activities.

Amount of award:	$3,000
Number of awards:	1
Application deadline:	March 31

Contact:
National Federation of the Blind Scholarship Committee
NFB at Jernigan Place
200 East Wells Street
Baltimore, MD 21230
Phone: 410-659-9314, ext. 2415
Fax: 410-685-5653
Web: www.nfb.org/scholarships

Kenneth Jernigan Memorial Scholarship

Type of award: Scholarship, renewable.
Intended use: For full-time undergraduate or graduate study at postsecondary institution.
Eligibility: Applicant must be visually impaired.
Basis for selection: Applicant must demonstrate financial need, high academic achievement and service orientation.
Application requirements: Recommendations, essay, transcript. Proof of blindness, interview with NFB affiliate president, SAT/ACT scores (high school seniors only).
Additional information: Applicant must be legally blind in both eyes. Recipients of Federation scholarships need not be members of Federation. Must participate in NFB Annual Convention and all scheduled scholarship activities. Visit Website for application.

Amount of award:	$12,000
Number of awards:	1
Application deadline:	March 31
Notification begins:	June 1
Total amount awarded:	$12,000

Contact:
National Federation of the Blind Scholarship Committee
NFB at Jernigan Place
200 East Wells Street
Baltimore, MD 21230
Phone: 410-659-9134 ext. 2415
Fax: 410-685-5653
Web: www.nfb.org/scholarships

Kuchler-Killian Memorial Scholarship

Type of award: Scholarship, renewable.
Intended use: For full-time undergraduate or graduate study at postsecondary institution.
Eligibility: Applicant must be visually impaired.
Basis for selection: Applicant must demonstrate financial need, high academic achievement and service orientation.
Application requirements: Recommendations, essay, transcript. Interview with NFB affiliate president, SAT/ACT scores (high school seniors only), proof of legal blindness.
Additional information: Applicant must be legally blind in both eyes. Recipients of Federation scholarships need not be members of National Federation of the Blind. Visit Website for application.

Amount of award:	$3,000
Number of awards:	1
Application deadline:	March 31
Notification begins:	June 1
Total amount awarded:	$3,000

Contact:
National Federation of the Blind Scholarship Committee
NFB at Jernigan Place
200 East Wells Street
Baltimore, MD 21230
Phone: 410-659-9134 ext. 2415
Fax: 410-685-5653
Web: www.nfb.org/scholarships

National Federation of the Blind Educator of Tomorrow Award

Type of award: Scholarship, renewable.
Intended use: For full-time undergraduate or graduate study at postsecondary institution.
Eligibility: Applicant must be visually impaired.
Basis for selection: Major/career interest in education, teacher or education. Applicant must demonstrate financial need, high academic achievement and service orientation.
Application requirements: Recommendations, essay, transcript. Interview with NFB affiliate president, SAT/ACT scores (high school seniors only), proof of legal blindness.
Additional information: Applicant must be legally blind in both eyes. Must be planning career in elementary, secondary, or postsecondary teaching. Recipients of Federation scholarships need not be members of National Federation of the Blind. Visit Website for application.

Amount of award:	$3,000
Number of awards:	1
Application deadline:	March 31
Notification begins:	June 1
Total amount awarded:	$3,000

Contact:
National Federation of the Blind Scholarship Committee
NFB at Jernigan Place
200 East Wells Street
Baltimore, MD 21230
Phone: 410-659-9134 ext. 2415
Fax: 410-685-5653
Web: www.nfb.org/scholarships

National Federation of the Blind Scholarships

Type of award: Scholarship, renewable.
Intended use: For full-time undergraduate or graduate study at postsecondary institution.
Eligibility: Applicant must be visually impaired.
Basis for selection: Major/career interest in humanities/liberal arts. Applicant must demonstrate financial need, high academic achievement and service orientation.
Application requirements: Recommendations, essay, transcript. Interview with NFB affiliate president, SAT/ACT scores (high school seniors only), proof of legal blindness.
Additional information: Applicant must be legally blind in both eyes. Recipients of Federation scholarships need not be members of National Federation of the Blind. Visit Website for application.

Amount of award:	$3,000-$7,000
Number of awards:	19
Application deadline:	March 31
Notification begins:	June 1

Contact:
National Federation of the Blind Scholarship Committee
NFB at Jernigan Place
200 East Wells Street
Baltimore, MD 21230
Phone: 410-659-9134 ext. 2415
Fax: 410-685-5653
Web: www.nfb.org/scholarships

National FFA

National FFA Collegiate Scholarship Program

Type of award: Scholarship.
Intended use: For undergraduate study at postsecondary institution.
Additional information: Open to FFA members as well as a small number of qualifying non-members. Visit Website for more information and application.

Amount of award:	$1,000-$10,000
Application deadline:	February 15
Notification begins:	June 1
Total amount awarded:	$2,000,000

Contact:
National FFA
Attn. Scholarship Office
P.O. Box 68960
Indianapolis, IN 46268-0960
Web: www.ffa.org

National Ground Water Research and Education Foundation

NGWREF Len Assante Scholarship Fund

Type of award: Scholarship.
Intended use: For full-time undergraduate study at accredited 2-year or 4-year institution.
Basis for selection: Applicant must demonstrate financial need, high academic achievement, depth of character, leadership, patriotism, seriousness of purpose and service orientation.
Application requirements: Essay, transcript, proof of eligibility. Essay should be one-page biography.
Additional information: Applicant must be studying in a ground water-related field. Students in two-year well drilling associate degree program also eligible. Minimum 2.5 GPA. Amount and number of awards vary annually. Application available on Website.

Number of awards:	6
Number of applicants:	14
Application deadline:	April 1

Contact:
NGWREF Len Assante Scholarship Fund
601 Dempsey Road
Westerville, OH 43081
Phone: 800-551-7379
Fax: 614-898-7786
Web: www.ngwa.org

National Inventors Hall of Fame

Collegiate Inventors Competition

Type of award: Scholarship.
Intended use: For full-time undergraduate or graduate study at postsecondary institution in United States or Canada.
Basis for selection: Competition/talent/interest in science project, based on invention's potential for society and scope of use.
Application requirements: Advisor letter; four copies of application and any supplementary material; personal essay describing invention, including a title page and one-paragraph overview of invention.
Additional information: Amount of awards varies. Entry must include summary of current literature and patent search, test data and invention's benefit. Entry must be original idea that has not been made available to public as a commercial product/process. Must not have been patented or published more than one year prior to date of submission. Competition accepts individual and team entries. Students must be (or have been) enrolled full-time at least part of 12-month period prior to date entry submitted. For teams, at least one member must meet full-time eligibility criteria. Other team members must have been enrolled on part-time basis (at minimum) sometime during 24-month period prior to date entry submitted. See Website for more information.

Amount of award:	$15,000-$25,000
Number of awards:	3
Application deadline:	May 16

Contact:
The Collegiate Inventors Competition
The National Inventors Hall of Fame
520 South Main Street, Suite 2423
Akron, OH 44311
Phone: 800-968-4332 ext. 5
Web: www.invent.org/collegiate

National Italian American Foundation

Emanuele and Emilia Inglese Memorial Scholarship

Type of award: Scholarship.
Intended use: For undergraduate study at accredited postsecondary institution.
Eligibility: Applicant must be Italian. Applicant must be U.S. citizen or permanent resident.
Basis for selection: Applicant must demonstrate financial need and high academic achievement.

Application requirements: Essay, transcript. Teacher Evaluation Form, Student Aid Report from FAFSA.

Additional information: Applicant must be first generation of family to attend college. Must be able to trace lineage to Lombardy region in Italy. Minimum 3.0 GPA. Applications must be submitted online. See Website for details and application.

Amount of award:	$2,500
Number of awards:	1
Number of applicants:	3
Application deadline:	March 4
Total amount awarded:	$2,500

Contact:
The Inglese Memorial Scholarship c/o NIAF
1860 19th Street NW
Washington, DC 20009
Phone: 202-387-0600
Web: www.niaf.org/scholarships/index.asp

National Italian American Foundation Scholarship Program

Type of award: Scholarship.

Intended use: For full-time undergraduate or graduate study at accredited 4-year or graduate institution in United States.

Eligibility: Applicant must be U.S. citizen or permanent resident.

Basis for selection: Applicant must demonstrate high academic achievement, depth of character, leadership, seriousness of purpose and service orientation.

Application requirements: Recommendations, transcript. FAFSA (optional).

Additional information: Completed application and teacher evaluation submitted online. Awards in two categories. General Category I Awards: Open to Italian-American students who demonstrate outstanding potential and high academic achievement. General Category II Awards: Open to those students majoring or minoring in Italian Language, Italian studies, Italian American Studies, or related fields. Awards not applicable for summer study. Minimum 3.5 GPA.

Amount of award:	$2,000-$12,000
Number of awards:	150
Number of applicants:	4,000
Application deadline:	March 4

Contact:
The National Italian American Foundation
1860 19th Street NW
Washington, DC 20009
Phone: 202-387-0600
Web: www.niaf.org/scholarships/index.asp

National Jewish Committee on Scouting

Rick Arkans Eagle Scout Scholarship

Type of award: Scholarship.

Intended use: For undergraduate study at postsecondary institution.

Eligibility: Applicant must be high school senior.

Basis for selection: Applicant must demonstrate financial need.

Application requirements: Recommendation from a volunteer or professional scout leader. FAFSA.

Additional information: Applicant must be registered, active member of a Boy Scout troop, Varsity Scout team, or Venturing crew. Must have received Eagle Scout Award. Must be active member of synagogue and have received Ner Tamid or Etz Chaim emblem. Contact National Jewish Committee on Scouting to request application form. Visit Website for more information.

Amount of award:	$1,000
Number of awards:	1
Number of applicants:	15
Application deadline:	February 28
Notification begins:	May 1
Total amount awarded:	$1,000

Contact:
National Jewish Committee on Scouting
1325 W. Walnut Hill Lane
P.O. Box 152079
Irving, TX 75015-2079
Phone: 972-580-2119
Fax: 972-580-2535
Web: www.jewishscouting.org

National Jewish Committee on Scouting, Boy Scouts of America

Chester M. Vernon Memorial Eagle Scout Scholarship

Type of award: Scholarship, renewable.

Intended use: For full-time undergraduate study at accredited 2-year or 4-year institution.

Eligibility: Applicant must be male, high school senior. Applicant must be Jewish. Applicant must be U.S. citizen or permanent resident.

Basis for selection: Applicant must demonstrate financial need, depth of character, leadership and service orientation.

Application requirements: Recommendation from a volunteer or professional scout leader. FAFSA.

Additional information: Applicant must be registered, active member of a Boy Scout troop, Varsity Scout team, or Venturing crew. Must have received Eagle Scout Award. Must be active member of synagogue and have received Ner Tamid or Etz Chaim emblem. Award renewable for four years. Contact National Jewish Committee on Scouting to request application form. Visit Website for more information.

Amount of award:	$1,000
Number of awards:	1
Number of applicants:	15
Application deadline:	February 28
Notification begins:	May 1
Total amount awarded:	$1,000

Contact:
National Jewish Committee on Scouting, BSA
1325 W. Walnut Hill Lane
P.O. Box 152079
Irving, TX 75015-2079
Phone: 972-580-2119
Fax: 972-580-2535
Web: www.jewishscouting.org

Frank L. Weil Memorial Eagle Scout Scholarship

Type of award: Scholarship.
Intended use: For full-time undergraduate study at accredited 2-year or 4-year institution.
Eligibility: Applicant must be male, high school senior. Applicant must be Jewish. Applicant must be U.S. citizen or permanent resident.
Basis for selection: Applicant must demonstrate depth of character, leadership and service orientation.
Application requirements: Recommendation from volunteer or professional scout leader. FAFSA.
Additional information: Recipient of scholarship receives $1,000. Two $500 second-place scholarship awards also given. Applicant must be registered, active member of a Boy Scout troop, Varsity Scout team, or Venturing crew. Must have received Eagle Scout Award. Must be active member of synagogue and have received Ner Tamid or Etz Chaim emblem. Contact National Jewish Committee on Scouting to request application form. Visit Website for more information.

Amount of award:	$500-$1,000
Number of awards:	3
Number of applicants:	15
Application deadline:	February 28
Notification begins:	May 1
Total amount awarded:	$2,000

Contact:
National Jewish Committee on Scouting, BSA
1325 West Walnut Hill Lane
P.O. Box 152079
Irving, TX 75015-2079
Phone: 972-580-2119
Fax: 972-580-2535
Web: www.jewishscouting.org

National Junior Classical League

Latin Honor Society Scholarship

Type of award: Scholarship.
Intended use: For full-time freshman study at 2-year or 4-year institution.
Eligibility: Applicant must be high school senior.
Basis for selection: Major/career interest in classics or education. Applicant must demonstrate high academic achievement.
Application requirements: Recommendations, essay, transcript.
Additional information: Must have been member in good standing of NJCL for at least three years and must be member of NJCL Latin Honor Society for current academic year and at least one preceding year. Must be planning to major in and teach Latin, Greek, or classics. Application available online.

Amount of award:	$1,500
Number of awards:	1
Number of applicants:	7
Application deadline:	May 1
Total amount awarded:	$1,500

Contact:
National Junior Classical League Attn: Scholarships
Miami University
422 Wells Mill Drive
Oxford, OH 45056
Phone: 513-529-7741
Fax: 513-529-7742
Web: www.aclclassics.org

National Junior Classical League Scholarship

Type of award: Scholarship.
Intended use: For full-time freshman study at 2-year or 4-year institution.
Eligibility: Applicant must be high school senior.
Basis for selection: Major/career interest in classics; education or humanities/liberal arts. Applicant must demonstrate financial need, high academic achievement, leadership, seriousness of purpose and service orientation.
Application requirements: Recommendations, essay, transcript. List of awards and activities.
Additional information: Must be NJCL member. Preference given to applicants who intend to teach Latin, Greek, or classical humanities.

Amount of award:	$1,000-$2,000
Number of awards:	9
Number of applicants:	12
Application deadline:	May 1

Contact:
National Junior Classical League Attn: Scholarships
Miami University
422 Wells Mill Drive
Oxford, OH 45056
Phone: 513-529-7741
Fax: 513-529-7742
Web: www.aclclassics.org

National Merit Scholarship Corporation

National Achievement Scholarships

Type of award: Scholarship.
Intended use: For full-time undergraduate study at accredited postsecondary institution in United States.
Eligibility: Applicant must be African American. Applicant must be enrolled in high school. Applicant must be U.S. citizen or permanent resident.
Basis for selection: Applicant must demonstrate high academic achievement and leadership.
Application requirements: Recommendations, essay.
Additional information: A privately financed academic competition for Black American high school students. To enter, students must meet published participation requirements and request consideration in program when they take PSAT/NMSQT and enter National Merit Program. Entry requirements published each year in PSAT/NMSQT Official Student Guide, sent to schools for distribution to students before October test administration, and on NMSC's Website. Some 1,600 of highest scoring participants named Semifinalists on regional representation basis. Semifinalists must meet additional requirements and advance to Finalist standing to compete for about 800 National Achievement Scholarships offered annually.

There are 700 National Achievement $2,500 Scholarships for which all Finalists compete and about 100 corporate-sponsored scholarships for Finalists who meet specified criteria of sponsoring organization.

Number of awards:	800
Number of applicants:	160,000
Notification begins:	February 15
Total amount awarded:	$2,500,000

Contact:
National Achievement Scholarship Program
1560 Sherman Avenue
Suite 200
Evanston, IL 60201-4897
Phone: 847-866-5100
Web: www.nationalmerit.org

National Merit Scholarships

Type of award: Scholarship.
Intended use: For full-time undergraduate study at accredited postsecondary institution in United States.
Eligibility: Applicant must be enrolled in high school. Applicant must be U.S. citizen or permanent resident.
Basis for selection: Applicant must demonstrate high academic achievement and leadership.
Application requirements: Recommendations, essay.
Additional information: Open to U.S. high school students who take PSAT/NMSQT in specified year in high school and meet other entry requirements. Entry requirements published each year in PSAT/NMSQT Official Student Guide, sent to schools for distribution to students before October test administration, and on NMSC's Website. Some 16,000 high-scoring participants designated Semifinalists on state representational basis. Applications sent to students through their schools. Semifinalists must meet additional requirements and advance to Finalist standing to be considered for National Merit Scholarships. About 8,200 awards of three types offered annually: 2,500 National Merit $2,500 Scholarships for which all Finalists compete; about 1,100 corporate-sponsored Merit Scholarship awards for Finalists who meet criteria of sponsoring corporate organization; and over 4,600 college-sponsored Merit Scholarship awards for Finalists who will attend sponsor college/university. Corporate organizations also provide about 1,500 Special Scholarships for other high performers in competition who are not Finalists. Permanent residents eligible if in process of becoming U.S. citizen.

Number of awards:	9,700
Number of applicants:	1,500,000
Notification begins:	March 1
Total amount awarded:	$49,000,000

Contact:
National Merit Scholarship Program
1560 Sherman Avenue
Suite 200
Evanston, IL 60201-4897
Phone: 847-866-5100
Web: www.nationalmerit.org

National Poultry & Food Distributors Association

NPFDA Scholarship

Type of award: Scholarship, renewable.

Intended use: For full-time junior or senior study at 4-year institution in United States.
Basis for selection: Major/career interest in dietetics/nutrition; agriculture; agricultural economics; agribusiness or food science/technology. Applicant must demonstrate high academic achievement.
Application requirements: Essay, transcript, proof of eligibility. Recommendation by dean.
Additional information: Poultry science, animal science, or related agricultural business majors also eligible.

Amount of award:	$1,500-$2,000
Number of awards:	4
Number of applicants:	80
Application deadline:	May 31
Notification begins:	January 1
Total amount awarded:	$6,500

Contact:
National Poultry & Food Distributors Association
2014 Osborne Road
St. Mary's, GA 31558
Phone: 770-535-9901
Fax: 770-535-7385
Web: www.npfda.org

National Press Photographers Foundation

Bob Baxter Scholarship

Type of award: Scholarship.
Intended use: For full-time undergraduate or graduate study at postsecondary institution in United States or Canada.
Basis for selection: Major/career interest in journalism. Applicant must demonstrate financial need.
Application requirements: Recommendations, essay. Portfolio of six slides (digital formats also accepted), statement of financial need.
Additional information: Applicants must be studying photojournalism. Visit Website for more information and application.

Amount of award:	$2,000
Number of awards:	1
Application deadline:	March 1

Contact:
Danielle Richards
Phone: 201-646-4130
Web: www.nppf.org

Bob East Scholarship Fund

Type of award: Scholarship.
Intended use: For undergraduate or graduate study at postsecondary institution in United States or Canada.
Eligibility: Applicant must be U.S. citizen or permanent resident residing in Florida.
Basis for selection: Major/career interest in journalism. Applicant must demonstrate financial need.
Application requirements: Portfolio, recommendations, essay. Portfolio must include at least five single images in addition to picture story. Digital portfolios accepted; see Website for instructions.
Additional information: Open to students studying photojournalism for newspapers. Must be undergraduate in first three and one half years of college, or be planning to pursue

postgraduate work and offer indication of acceptance in such program.

Amount of award:	$2,000
Number of awards:	1
Application deadline:	March 1
Total amount awarded:	$2,000

Contact:
The Miami Herald
Attn: Chuck Fadely
One Herald Plaza
Miami, FL 33132
Phone: 305-376-2015
Web: www.nppf.org

College Photographer of the Year Competition

Type of award: Scholarship.
Intended use: For undergraduate study at 4-year institution in United States or Canada.
Basis for selection: Major/career interest in journalism. Applicant must demonstrate financial need and high academic achievement.
Application requirements: Portfolio, recommendations, proof of eligibility. Portfolio must include five single images in addition to picture story. Digital portfolios accepted; see Website for instructions.
Additional information: Contest recognizes outstanding work of student photojournalists. NPPF Booster club provides $1,000 Col. William Lookadoo Award and $500 Milton Frier Award.

Amount of award:	$500-$1,000
Number of awards:	2
Application deadline:	October 1
Total amount awarded:	$1,500

Contact:
University of Missouri School of Journalism
Rita Reed, CPOY Dir., University of Missouri
106 Lee Hills Hall
Columbia, MO 65211
Phone: 573-882-4442
Web: www.nppf.org

Jimi Lott Scholarship

Type of award: Scholarship.
Intended use: For undergraduate study in United States or Canada.
Eligibility: Applicant must be U.S. citizen or permanent resident.
Basis for selection: Major/career interest in journalism.
Application requirements: Portfolio, recommendations, essay, transcript. Portfolio must include at least five single images in addition to picture story. Digital portfolios accepted; see Website for instructions.
Additional information: Applicants must be studying photojournalism. Visit Website for more information and application.

Amount of award:	$2,000
Number of awards:	1
Application deadline:	March 1
Total amount awarded:	$2,000

Contact:
National Press Photographers Foundation
Web: www.nppf.org

National Press Photographers Foundation Still and Multimedia Scholarship

Type of award: Scholarship.
Intended use: For sophomore, junior or senior study at 4-year institution in United States or Canada.
Basis for selection: Major/career interest in journalism. Applicant must demonstrate financial need and high academic achievement.
Application requirements: Portfolio, proof of eligibility. Portfolio must include five single images in addition to picture story. Digital portfolios accepted; see Website for instructions.
Additional information: Awards aimed at those with journalism potential, but with little opportunity and great need. Must have completed one year at recognized four-year college or university with courses in photojournalism. Must be continuing in program leading to bachelor's degree.

Amount of award:	$2,000
Number of awards:	1
Application deadline:	March 1
Total amount awarded:	$2,000

Contact:
Bill Sanders
Ashville Citizen-Times
P.O. Box 2090
Ashville, NC 28802
Web: www.nppf.org

National Press Photographers Foundation Television News Scholarship

Type of award: Scholarship.
Intended use: For undergraduate study at 4-year institution in United States or Canada.
Basis for selection: Major/career interest in radio/television/ film or journalism. Applicant must demonstrate financial need and high academic achievement.
Application requirements: Portfolio, recommendations, essay. Videotape containing no more than three complete stories no longer than six minutes total with voice narration and natural sound. One-page biographical sketch including personal statement addressing professional goals.
Additional information: Must be enrolled in recognized four-year college or university with courses in TV news photojournalism. Must be continuing program leading to bachelor's degree.

Amount of award:	$2,000
Number of awards:	1
Application deadline:	March 1
Total amount awarded:	$2,000

Contact:
Ed Dooks
5 Mohawk Drive
Lexington, MA 02421-6217
Phone: 781-861-6062
Web: www.nppf.org

Reid Blackburn Scholarship

Type of award: Scholarship.
Intended use: For sophomore, junior or senior study at 4-year institution in United States or Canada.

Basis for selection: Major/career interest in journalism. Applicant must demonstrate financial need, high academic achievement and seriousness of purpose.
Application requirements: Portfolio, essay, proof of eligibility. Statement of philosophy and goals. Portfolio must include at least five single images in addition to picture story. Digital portfolios accepted; see Website for instructions.
Additional information: Must have completed at least one year at recognized four-year college or university with courses in photojournalism and must have at least half-year of undergraduate schooling remaining at time of award. Program must be leading to bachelor's degree.

Amount of award:	$2,000
Number of awards:	1
Application deadline:	March 1
Total amount awarded:	$2,000

Contact:
The Columbian
Attn: Fay Blackburn
P.O. Box 180
Vancouver, WA 98666
Phone: 360-759-8027
Web: www.nppf.org

National Restaurant Association Educational Foundation

Academic Scholarship for High School Seniors and GED Graduates

Type of award: Scholarship.
Intended use: For undergraduate study at vocational, 2-year or 4-year institution.
Eligibility: Applicant must be U.S. citizen or permanent resident.
Basis for selection: Major/career interest in food science/technology; hotel/restaurant management; food science/technology; culinary arts or marketing.
Application requirements: Transcript. One to three letters of recommendation verifying work hours, on business or school letterhead, from current or previous employer in the restaurant or food service industry, paystubs, two essays: one stating food service background and career goals, the other discussing what person or experience influenced you to select food industry and how this will help you reach your career goals.
Additional information: Must be first-time freshman accepted into accredited culinary school, or in college or university majoring in food service related major. Must plan to enroll in minimum of two terms for following school year. Must have minimum 250 hours of food-service-related work experience. Deadline in August. Visit Website for application.

Amount of award:	$2,500

Contact:
National Restaurant Association Educational Foundation
Scholarships and Mentoring Initiative
175 West Jackson Boulevard, Suite 1500
Chicago, IL 60604-2702
Phone: 800-765-2122 ext. 6738
Fax: 312-566-9733
Web: www.nraef.org/scholarships

Academic Scholarship for Undergraduate Students

Type of award: Scholarship.
Intended use: For undergraduate study at accredited vocational, 2-year or 4-year institution in United States.
Eligibility: Applicant must be U.S. citizen or permanent resident.
Basis for selection: Major/career interest in food production/management/services; culinary arts; hotel/restaurant management; hospitality administration/management or food science/technology. Applicant must demonstrate high academic achievement.
Application requirements: Recommendations, transcript. Copy of college curriculum. Letter from current or previous employer in the restaurant or food service industry, with paychecks or paystubs verifying restaurant employment. Two essays: One discussing food service background and career goals, the other discussing how either sustainability, food safety, or nutrition affect the industry and what you would do to address this issue.
Additional information: Applicant must have completed at least one term of two- or four-year degree program. Must be enrolled in food service related program for minimum of nine credit hours per semester. Must have performed minimum 750 hours foodservice-related work. Visit Website for application and more information, .

Amount of award:	$2,500
Application deadline:	March 31, July 31

Contact:
National Restaurant Association Educational Foundation
Attn: Scholarships Program
175 West Jackson Boulevard, Suite 1500
Chicago, IL 60604-2702
Phone: 800-765-2122 ext. 6738
Fax: 312-566-9733
Web: www.nraef.org/scholarships

ManageFirst Program Scholarship

Type of award: Scholarship.
Intended use: For undergraduate study at accredited vocational, 2-year or 4-year institution in United States.
Eligibility: Applicant must be U.S. citizen or permanent resident.
Basis for selection: Major/career interest in culinary arts or food production/management/services.
Application requirements: Recommendations, essay, transcript. Topical essay. Copy of college curriculum.
Additional information: Must be enrolled in food service-related program at an accredited culinary school, college, or university. Must have earned at least one ManageFirst certificate, not including ServSafe Food Safety and ServSafe Alcohol. Deadlines are March 31, July 31, and October 1. Visit Website for application.

Amount of award:	$2,500
Application deadline:	March 31, July 31

Contact:
National Restaurant Association
Attn: Scholarships Program
175 West Jackson Boulevard, Suite 1500
Chicago, IL 60604-2702
Phone: 800-765-2122 ext. 6738
Web: www.nraef.org/scholarships

ProStart National Certificate of Achievement Scholarship

Type of award: Scholarship.
Intended use: For undergraduate study at accredited 2-year or 4-year institution in United States.
Eligibility: Applicant must be high school senior. Applicant must be U.S. citizen or permanent resident.
Basis for selection: Major/career interest in food production/ management/services; food science/technology; culinary arts or hotel/restaurant management.
Application requirements: Essay, transcript. 250-300 word case study. Letter of intent or acceptance. Copy of ProStart Certification. Copy of college curriculum.
Additional information: Applicant must earn ProStart National Certificate of Achievement by application deadline. Must have applied and gained acceptance to a college with an accredited restaurant- and/or food service-related post-secondary program. Must plan to attend college for minimum nine credit hours per semester. Visit Website for application and more information.

Amount of award:	$2,500
Application deadline:	May 15, August 15

Contact:
National Restaurant Association Educational Foundation
Attn: Scholarships Program
175 West Jackson Boulevard, Suite 1500
Chicago, IL 60604-2702
Phone: 800-765-2122 ext. 6738
Fax: 312-566-9726
Web: www.nraef.org/scholarships

National Rifle Association

Jeanne E. Bray Law Enforcement Dependents Scholarship

Type of award: Scholarship.
Intended use: For full-time undergraduate or graduate study at accredited 2-year, 4-year or graduate institution in United States.
Eligibility: Applicant must be U.S. citizen. Applicant's parent must have been killed or disabled in work-related accident as police officer.
Basis for selection: Applicant must demonstrate high academic achievement and service orientation.
Application requirements: Recommendations, transcript, proof of eligibility. Letter from employing law enforcement agency; 500-700 word essay on the Second Amendment.
Additional information: Number of awards varies. Parent must be member of National Rifle Association. Parent must be active, disabled, deceased, discharged, or retired peace officer. Minimum 2.5 GPA, SAT score of 950 or ACT score of 25. Award given for up to four years or until applicable monetary cap is reached, as long as student maintains eligibility. Applications accepted on continuous basis.

Amount of award:	$500-$2,000
Number of applicants:	35
Application deadline:	November 15
Notification begins:	February 15

Contact:
National Rifle Association, Attn: Sandy S. Elkin
Jeanne E. Bray Memorial Scholarship
11250 Waples Mill Road
Fairfax, VA 22030
Phone: 703-267-1131
Fax: 703-267-1083
Web: www.nrahq.org/law/lebenefits.asp

National Science Teachers Association

Toshiba/NSTA ExploraVision Award

Type of award: Scholarship.
Intended use: For undergraduate or non-degree study at postsecondary institution in United States or Canada.
Eligibility: Applicant must be no older than 21, enrolled in high school.
Basis for selection: Competition/talent/interest in science project, based on scientific accuracy, creativity, communication and feasibility of vision. Major/career interest in science, general.
Application requirements: Essay. Written description of research and design project, five graphics simulating Web pages.
Additional information: Applicant must attend public, private, or home school. Must be full-time student, no older than 21. Technology study project. Open to grades K-12. Each student member of first-place team receives $10,000 savings bond, each student member of second-place team receives $5,000 savings bond, and regional winners receive Toshiba products. Contact sponsor for entry kit, and visit Website to download application.

Amount of award:	$5,000-$10,000
Number of applicants:	4,500
Application deadline:	February 1
Notification begins:	March 1
Total amount awarded:	$240,000

Contact:
Toshiba/NSTA ExploraVision Awards
1840 Wilson Boulevard
Arlington, VA 22201-3000
Phone: 800-EXPLOR9
Web: www.exploravision.org

National Sculpture Society

Sculpture Society Scholarship

Type of award: Scholarship.
Intended use: For undergraduate, master's or doctoral study at postsecondary institution in United States.
Eligibility: Applicant must be U.S. citizen or permanent resident.
Basis for selection: Competition/talent/interest in visual arts, based on images of figurative or representational sculpture created by applicant. Major/career interest in arts, general. Applicant must demonstrate financial need.
Application requirements: Recommendations, essay, proof of eligibility. Brief letter of application including biography and

background in sculpture; six to fifteen images of at least three works submitted on CD; list of works shown on CD; proof of financial need; SASE.

Additional information: Must be studying figurative or representational sculpture. Work inspired by nature, or figurative or realistic sculpture, preferred.

Amount of award:	$2,000
Number of awards:	4
Number of applicants:	35
Total amount awarded:	$8,000

Contact:
National Sculpture Society
c/o ANS
75 Varick Street, 11th Floor
New York, NY 10013
Phone: 212-764-5645
Fax: 212-764-5651
Web: www.nationalsculpture.org

National Security Agency

National Security Agency Stokes Educational Scholarship Program

Type of award: Scholarship, renewable.
Intended use: For full-time undergraduate study in United States.
Eligibility: Applicant must be U.S. citizen.
Basis for selection: Major/career interest in computer/information sciences; engineering, computer or engineering, electrical/electronic. Applicant must demonstrate high academic achievement, depth of character, leadership, patriotism, seriousness of purpose and service orientation.
Application requirements: Interview, recommendations, essay, transcript, proof of eligibility. Resume.
Additional information: Current applications available September 1-30 of each year. Preference given to those with minimum 3.0 GPA, 1600 SAT score and/or 25 ACT score. Must undergo polygraph and security screening. Freshmen must major in computer science or electrical or computer engineering. College sophomores should check Website for eligible majors. Awardees must work at NSA in area related to major for 12 weeks in summer and after graduation for at least one and a half times length of study. If work debt not repaid, scholarship reverts to debt. Scholarship covers tuition, fees, and includes a book allowance of $1500. See Website for current program information.

Amount of award:	Full tuition
Number of applicants:	700
Application deadline:	November 30
Notification begins:	April 1

Contact:
National Security Agency Stokes Scholars Program
9800 Savage Road
Suite 6779
Fort Meade, MD 20755-6779
Phone: 410-854-4725 or 866-NSA-HIRE
Fax: 410-854-3002
Web: www.nsa.gov

National Society of Accountants

Louis and Fannie Sager Memorial Scholarship

Type of award: Scholarship.
Intended use: For sophomore, junior or senior study at accredited 2-year or 4-year institution in United States. Designated institutions: Virginia colleges and universities.
Eligibility: Applicant must be U.S. citizen or permanent resident.
Basis for selection: Major/career interest in accounting. Applicant must demonstrate financial need, high academic achievement and leadership.
Application requirements: Transcript. Appraisal form.
Additional information: Must be graduate of Virginia public school. Must have minimum "B" average.

Amount of award:	$500-$1,000

Contact:
National Society of Accountants
1010 North Fairfax Street
Fairfax, VA 22314-1574
Phone: 800-966-6679 ext. 1307
Web: www.nsacct.org

Stanley H. Stearman Award

Type of award: Scholarship.
Intended use: For sophomore, junior or senior study at accredited 2-year or 4-year institution in United States.
Eligibility: Applicant must be U.S. citizen or permanent resident.
Basis for selection: Major/career interest in accounting. Applicant must demonstrate financial need, high academic achievement and leadership.
Application requirements: Transcript. Appraisal form.
Additional information: Must be relative of active or retired NSA member. Minimum "B" average.

Amount of award:	$2,000
Number of awards:	1
Total amount awarded:	$2,000

Contact:
National Society of Accountants
1010 North Fairfax Street
Alexandria, VA 22314-1574
Phone: 800-966-6679 ext. 1307
Web: www.nsacct.org

National Society of Accountants Scholarship Foundation

National Society of Accountants Scholarship

Type of award: Scholarship.
Intended use: For sophomore, junior or senior study at accredited vocational, 2-year or 4-year institution in United States.

Eligibility: Applicant must be U.S. citizen or Canadian citizen.
Basis for selection: Major/career interest in accounting. Applicant must demonstrate financial need, high academic achievement and leadership.
Application requirements: Transcript. Appraisal form.
Additional information: Minimum 3.0 GPA. Student must be enrolled in undergraduate accounting program at time of application. Competition's most outstanding student receives additional stipend. Visit Website for more information and application.

Amount of award:	$500-$2,000
Number of awards:	32
Number of applicants:	1,200
Application deadline:	March 10
Total amount awarded:	$40,000

Contact:
National Society of Accountants Scholarship Program
Scholarship America
One Scholarship Way, P.O. Box 297
St. Peter, MN 56082
Phone: 507-931-1682
Web: www.nsacct.org

National Society of Black Engineers

Batttelle Collegiate Scholarship

Type of award: Scholarship.
Intended use: For junior or senior study at postsecondary institution.
Eligibility: Applicant or parent must be member/participant of National Society of Black Engineers. Applicant must be African American.
Basis for selection: Major/career interest in engineering; mathematics; chemistry; computer/information sciences or physics.
Application requirements: Transcript. Resume.
Additional information: Eligible applicants must apply online through their membership account.

Amount of award:	$5,000
Number of awards:	6
Total amount awarded:	$70,000

Contact:
National Society of Black Engineers
205 Daingerfield Road
Alexandria, VA 22314
Phone: 703-549-2207
Fax: 703-683-5312
Web: national.nsbe.org

Bechtel Group Foundation Scholarship

Type of award: Scholarship.
Intended use: For sophomore, junior or senior study at 4-year institution.
Eligibility: Applicant or parent must be member/participant of National Society of Black Engineers. Applicant must be African American.
Basis for selection: Major/career interest in engineering; engineering, civil; engineering, electrical/electronic; engineering, environmental; engineering, mechanical or architecture.

Application requirements: Transcript. Resume.
Additional information: Minimum 3.0 GPA required. Eligible applicants must apply online through their membership account.

Amount of award:	$5,500
Number of awards:	2
Total amount awarded:	$11,000

Contact:
National Society of Black Engineers
205 Daingerfield Road
Alexandria, VA 22314
Phone: 703-549-2207
Fax: 703-683-5312
Web: national.nsbe.org

BP Corporate Scholarship

Type of award: Scholarship.
Intended use: For full-time sophomore, junior, senior or graduate study at 4-year institution.
Eligibility: Applicant or parent must be member/participant of National Society of Black Engineers. Applicant must be African American.
Basis for selection: Major/career interest in engineering.
Application requirements: Transcript. Resume.
Additional information: Minimum 3.0 GPA required. Must demonstrate interest in energy industry career. Consideration given to availability to employment opportunity at BP. NSBE membership required. All eligible applicants must apply online through their membership account.

Amount of award:	$2,500
Number of awards:	4
Total amount awarded:	$10,000

Contact:
National Society of Black Engineers
205 Daingerfield Road
Alexandria, VA 22314
Phone: 703-549-2207
Fax: 703-683-5312
Web: national.nsbe.org

Caterpillar Corporate Scholarship

Type of award: Scholarship.
Intended use: For sophomore, junior or senior study at 4-year institution.
Eligibility: Applicant or parent must be member/participant of National Society of Black Engineers. Applicant must be African American.
Basis for selection: Major/career interest in engineering.
Application requirements: Transcript. Resume.
Additional information: Minimum 2.8 GPA required. Financial NSBE membership required. All eligible applicants must apply online through their membership account.

Amount of award:	$2,000
Number of awards:	5
Total amount awarded:	$10,000

Contact:
National Society of Black Engineers
205 Daingerfield Road
Alexandria, VA 22314
Phone: 703-549-2207
Fax: 703-683-5312
Web: national.nsbe.org

Cummins Inc. Corporate Scholarship

Type of award: Scholarship, renewable.

Intended use: For sophomore or junior study at 4-year institution.
Eligibility: Applicant or parent must be member/participant of National Society of Black Engineers. Applicant must be African American.
Basis for selection: Major/career interest in engineering.
Application requirements: Essay, transcript. Resume.
Additional information: Minimum 3.0 GPA required. Must demonstrate interest in employment with Cummins, Inc. and must be available to accept internship if offered. NSBE membership required. All eligible applicants must apply online through their membership account.

Amount of award:	$5,000
Number of awards:	4
Total amount awarded:	$20,000

Contact:
National Society of Black Engineers
205 Daingerfield Road
Alexandria, VA 22314
Phone: 703-549-2207
Fax: 703-683-5312
Web: national.nsbe.org

ExxonMobil Corporate Scholarship

Type of award: Scholarship.
Intended use: For freshman, sophomore or junior study at postsecondary institution.
Eligibility: Applicant or parent must be member/participant of National Society of Black Engineers. Applicant must be African American.
Basis for selection: Major/career interest in engineering, chemical; engineering, civil; engineering, electrical/electronic or engineering, mechanical.
Application requirements: Essay, transcript. Resume.
Additional information: Minimum 3.3 GPA required. All eligible applicants must apply online through their membership account.

Amount of award:	$1,500-$2,000
Number of awards:	13
Number of applicants:	836
Total amount awarded:	$20,000

Contact:
National Society of Black Engineers
205 Daingerfield Road
Alexandria, VA 22314
Phone: 703-549-2207
Fax: 703-683-5312
Web: national.nsbe.org

Fulfilling the Legacy Scholarship

Type of award: Scholarship.
Intended use: For full-time undergraduate or graduate study at accredited postsecondary institution.
Eligibility: Applicant or parent must be member/participant of National Society of Black Engineers.
Basis for selection: Major/career interest in engineering. Applicant must demonstrate high academic achievement, depth of character, leadership, seriousness of purpose and service orientation.
Application requirements: Essay, transcript, proof of eligibility. Resume.
Additional information: National Society of Black Engineers membership required. Number of awards and amount depend on total contributions made by members and others. All eligible applicants must apply online through their membership accounts.

Amount of award:	$1,000
Number of awards:	15
Number of applicants:	6,990
Notification begins:	February 1
Total amount awarded:	$15,000

Contact:
National Society of Black Engineers
205 Daingerfield Road
Alexandria, VA 22314
Phone: 703-549-2207
Fax: 703-683-5312
Web: national.nsbe.org

International Studies Scholarship

Type of award: Scholarship.
Intended use: For full-time undergraduate or graduate study in or outside United States or Canada.
Eligibility: Applicant or parent must be member/participant of National Society of Black Engineers. Applicant must be African American.
Basis for selection: Major/career interest in engineering.
Application requirements: Essay, transcript.
Additional information: Minimum 3.2 GPA or "B" average required. Must be full-time student in country other than his or her country of citizenship. Summer study-abroad programs are acceptable. Must hold NSBE International student membership status in NSBE Online. All eligible applicants must apply online through their membership account.

Amount of award:	$500
Number of awards:	2
Total amount awarded:	$1,000

Contact:
National Society of Black Engineers
205 Daingerfield Road
Alexandria, VA 22314
Phone: 703-549-2207
Fax: 703-683-5312
Web: national.nsbe.org

Lockheed Martin Corporate Scholarship

Type of award: Scholarship.
Intended use: For junior or senior study at postsecondary institution.
Eligibility: Applicant or parent must be member/participant of National Society of Black Engineers. Applicant must be African American.
Basis for selection: Major/career interest in engineering; engineering, computer; engineering, electrical/electronic; aerospace; mathematics or engineering, mechanical.
Application requirements: Essay, transcript. Resume.
Additional information: Minimum 3.0 GPA required. Must demonstrate interest in employment with Lockheed Martin. NSBE membership required. All eligible applicants must apply online through their membership account.

Amount of award:	$2,000
Number of awards:	5
Total amount awarded:	$10,000

Contact:
National Society of Black Engineers
205 Daingerfield Road
Alexandria, VA 22314
Phone: 703-549-2207
Fax: 703-683-5312
Web: national.nsbe.org

National Society of Black Engineers Golden Torch Awards

Type of award: Scholarship, renewable.
Intended use: For full-time undergraduate study at accredited 4-year institution.
Eligibility: Applicant or parent must be member/participant of National Society of Black Engineers. Applicant must be high school senior.
Basis for selection: Major/career interest in engineering; computer/information sciences or mathematics. Applicant must demonstrate depth of character, leadership and service orientation.
Application requirements: Recommendations, essay, transcript.
Additional information: National Society of Black Engineers Junior membership required. Minimum 3.0 GPA. All eligible applicants must apply online through their membership accounts. Renewable over four years; must maintain minimum 2.75 GPA in engineering/technology program. Award amount may vary.

Amount of award:	$1,000
Number of awards:	7
Number of applicants:	495
Application deadline:	March 1
Notification begins:	February 1
Total amount awarded:	$7,000

Contact:
GTA Scholarship PCI
National Society of Black Engineers
205 Daingerfield Road
Alexandria, VA 22314
Phone: 703-549-2207
Fax: 703-683-5312
Web: national.nsbe.org

National Society of Black Engineers Leroy Callendar PCI Award Program

Type of award: Scholarship.
Intended use: For undergraduate study at 4-year institution.
Eligibility: Applicant or parent must be member/participant of National Society of Black Engineers. Applicant must be African American. Applicant must be high school senior.
Basis for selection: Applicant must demonstrate high academic achievement and service orientation.
Application requirements: Recommendations, transcript.
Additional information: Applicants must reside in Host Region Six of National Society of Black Engineers National Convention. NSBE Junior membership required. All eligible applicants must apply online through their membership accounts.

Amount of award:	$500
Number of awards:	2
Number of applicants:	357
Total amount awarded:	$1,000

Contact:
Leroy Callendar Award PCI Programs
National Society of Black Engineers
205 Daingerfield Road
Alexandria, VA 22314
Phone: 703-549-2207
Fax: 703-683-5312
Web: national.nsbe.org

Northrop Grumman Corporate Scholarship

Type of award: Scholarship.
Intended use: For sophomore, junior or senior study at postsecondary institution.
Eligibility: Applicant or parent must be member/participant of National Society of Black Engineers. Applicant must be African American. Applicant must be U.S. citizen.
Basis for selection: Major/career interest in engineering, computer; engineering, electrical/electronic; architecture or computer/information sciences. Applicant must demonstrate leadership.
Application requirements: Transcript. Resume.
Additional information: Minimum 3.0 GPA required. Must demonstrate interest in employment with Northrop Grumman. NSBE membership required. All eligible applicants must apply online through their membership account.

Amount of award:	$5,000
Number of awards:	5
Number of applicants:	857
Total amount awarded:	$25,000

Contact:
National Society of Black Engineers
205 Daingerfield Road
Alexandria, VA 22314
Phone: 703-549-2207
Fax: 703-683-5312
Web: national.nsbe.org

NSBE Fellows Scholarship

Type of award: Scholarship.
Intended use: For full-time undergraduate or graduate study at accredited 4-year or graduate institution in or outside United States or Canada.
Eligibility: Applicant or parent must be member/participant of National Society of Black Engineers.
Basis for selection: Major/career interest in engineering. Applicant must demonstrate high academic achievement, depth of character, leadership, seriousness of purpose and service orientation.
Application requirements: Essay, transcript, proof of eligibility. Resume.
Additional information: Must be member of National Society of Black Engineers. Minimum 2.7 GPA. Must be dedicated to Society's cause and other community organizations, and show promise in studies and professional pursuits. Recipients receive $500 stipend for travel to annual NSBE convention in Las Vegas, NV. All eligible applicants must apply online through their membership accounts.

Amount of award:	$1,000-$3,000
Number of awards:	100
Number of applicants:	5,858
Notification begins:	February 1

Contact:
National Society of Black Engineers
205 Daingerfield Road
Alexandria, VA 22314
Phone: 703-549-2207
Fax: 703-683-5312
Web: national.nsbe.org

PBS&J Corporate Scholarship

Type of award: Scholarship.

Intended use: For junior or senior study at postsecondary institution.
Eligibility: Applicant or parent must be member/participant of National Society of Black Engineers. Applicant must be African American.
Basis for selection: Major/career interest in architecture; engineering, civil or engineering, structural.
Application requirements: Essay, transcript. Resume.
Additional information: Minimum 3.0 GPA required. Must demonstrate interest in employment with PBS&J. NSBE membership required. All eligible applicants must apply online through their membership account.

Amount of award:	$1,000-$2,500
Number of awards:	3
Number of applicants:	397
Total amount awarded:	$5,000

Contact:
National Society of Black Engineers
205 Daingerfield Road
Alexandria, VA 22314
Phone: 703-549-2207
Fax: 703-683-5312
Web: national.nsbe.org

Toyota Corporate Scholarship

Type of award: Scholarship.
Intended use: For sophomore, junior or senior study at postsecondary institution.
Eligibility: Applicant or parent must be member/participant of National Society of Black Engineers. Applicant must be African American.
Basis for selection: Major/career interest in engineering; engineering, chemical; engineering, electrical/electronic; engineering, industrial; engineering, materials or engineering, mechanical.
Application requirements: Transcript. Resume.
Additional information: Minimum 3.0 GPA required. NSBE membership required. Must be interested in employment with Toyota. All eligible applicants must apply online through their membership account.

Amount of award:	$2,500
Number of awards:	4
Number of applicants:	1,829
Total amount awarded:	$10,000

Contact:
National Society of Black Engineers
205 Daingerfield Road
Alexandria, VA 22314
Phone: 703-549-2207
Fax: 703-683-5312
Web: national.nsbe.org

U.S. Steel NSBE Academic Scholarship

Type of award: Scholarship.
Intended use: For full-time junior study at 4-year institution. Designated institutions: Alabama A&M University, Auburn University, California University of Pennsylvania, Cleveland State University, Colorado School of Mines, Georgia Institute of Technology, Howard University, Michigan State University, North Carolina A&T State University, North Dakota State University, Penn State University, Purdue University, Southern University, Southern Illinois University, Tennessee State University, Tuskegee University, University of Alabama, University of Illinois, University of Michigan, University of

Minnesota, University of Missouri, University of North Dakota, University of Pittsburgh, University of Texas, Wayne State University, West Virginia University.
Eligibility: Applicant or parent must be member/participant of National Society of Black Engineers. Applicant must be African American. Applicant must be U.S. citizen or permanent resident.
Basis for selection: Major/career interest in engineering; computer/information sciences; chemistry; materials science; mathematics or physics.
Application requirements: Transcript. Resume.
Additional information: Minimum 2.75 GPA required. Financial NSBE membership required. All eligible applicants must apply online through their membership account.

Amount of award:	$5,000
Number of awards:	1
Number of applicants:	306
Total amount awarded:	$5,000

Contact:
National Society of Black Engineers
205 Daingerfield Road
Alexandria, VA 22314
Phone: 703-549-2207
Fax: 703-683-5312
Web: national.nsbe.org

Verizon Corporate Scholarship

Type of award: Scholarship.
Intended use: For undergraduate or graduate study at postsecondary institution.
Eligibility: Applicant or parent must be member/participant of National Society of Black Engineers. Applicant must be African American.
Basis for selection: Major/career interest in engineering; engineering, computer; engineering, electrical/electronic; technology or business.
Application requirements: Transcript. Resume.
Additional information: Minimum 3.0 GPA required. NSBE membership required. Applicant must demonstrate interest in employment with Verizon and its affiliated companies. All eligible applicants must apply online through their membership account.

Amount of award:	$5,000-$6,500
Number of awards:	3
Number of applicants:	2,236
Total amount awarded:	$16,500

Contact:
National Society of Black Engineers
205 Daingerfield Road
Alexandria, VA 22314
Phone: 703-549-2207
Fax: 703-683-5312
Web: national.nsbe.org

Wal-Mart Stores Inc. Corporate Scholarship

Type of award: Scholarship.
Intended use: For junior or senior study at 4-year institution.
Eligibility: Applicant or parent must be member/participant of National Society of Black Engineers. Applicant must be African American.
Basis for selection: Major/career interest in engineering; engineering, civil; engineering, electrical/electronic; engineering, industrial; technology or computer/information sciences.

Application requirements: Essay, transcript. Resume.
Additional information: Minimum 3.0 GPA required.
Financial NSBE membership required. All eligible applicants
must apply online through their membership account. Must
demonstrate interest in employment with Wal-Mart Stores, Inc.
Recipient eligible for paid summer internship.

Amount of award:	$3,000
Number of awards:	3
Number of applicants:	1,411
Total amount awarded:	$9,000

Contact:
National Society of Black Engineers
205 Daingerfield Road
Alexandria, VA 22314
Phone: 703-549-2207
Fax: 703-683-5312
Web: national.nsbe.org

National Society of the Sons of the American Revolution

Arthur M. and Berdena King Eagle Scout Scholarship

Type of award: Scholarship.
Intended use: For undergraduate study at postsecondary
institution.
Eligibility: Applicant must be male, no older than 18.
Basis for selection: Applicant must demonstrate depth of
character, leadership and patriotism.
Application requirements: Essay, proof of eligibility. Essay
should be 500 words on Revolutionary War, subject of
applicant's choice. Four generation ancestor chart.
Additional information: Open to all Eagle Scouts currently
registered in active unit who will not reach 19th birthday during
year of application. Competition conducted in three phases:
Chapter (local), Society (state), and National. Applicants need
only apply at Chapter level. Winners at local level entered into
state competition; state winners used in National contest.
Number of awards varies. Awards may also be available at
chapter and state level. See Website for more information and
application.

Amount of award:	$2,000-$8,000
Number of awards:	3
Application deadline:	December 31
Total amount awarded:	$14,000

Contact:
National Society of the Sons of the American Revolution
1000 South Fourth Street
Louisville, KY 40203
Phone: 502-589-1776
Web: www.sar.org/youth/eagle.html

National Speakers Association

National Speakers Association Scholarship

Type of award: Scholarship.
Intended use: For full-time junior, senior or graduate study at
4-year or graduate institution.
Basis for selection: Major/career interest in communications.
Applicant must demonstrate financial need, high academic
achievement, leadership and seriousness of purpose.
Application requirements: Recommendations, essay,
transcript.
Additional information: Applicant must have above-average
academic record, major or minor in speech or communication-
related studies, and desire to be professional speaker.
Application available on Website.

Amount of award:	$5,000
Number of awards:	4
Number of applicants:	100
Application deadline:	June 1
Notification begins:	September 1
Total amount awarded:	$20,000

Contact:
National Speakers Association
1500 South Priest Drive
Tempe, AZ 85281
Phone: 480-968-2552
Fax: 480-968-0911
Web: www.nsafoundation.org

National Stone, Sand & Gravel Association

Barry K. Wendt Commitment Award and Scholarship

Type of award: Scholarship.
Intended use: For full-time undergraduate study in United
States. Designated institutions: Engineering schools.
Eligibility: Applicant must be U.S. citizen or permanent
resident.
Basis for selection: Major/career interest in engineering.
Applicant must demonstrate high academic achievement.
Application requirements: Recommendations, essay.
Additional information: Must be planning career in
aggregate industry. Visit Website for details and application.

Number of awards:	1

Contact:
Wendt Memorial Scholarship Committee
c/o NSSGA
1605 King Street
Alexandria, VA 22314
Phone: 703-525-8788
Fax: 703-525-7782
Web: www.nssga.org/careerscholarships/scholarships.cfm

Jennifer Curtis Byler Scholarship Fund for the Study of Public Affairs

Type of award: Scholarship.
Intended use: For full-time undergraduate study in United States.
Basis for selection: Major/career interest in public administration/service. Applicant must demonstrate high academic achievement, seriousness of purpose and service orientation.
Application requirements: Recommendations, essay.
Additional information: Applicant must be graduating high school senior or student already enrolled in public affairs program in college. Must be child of aggregate company employee. Must demonstrate commitment to career in public affairs. Visit Website for details and application.

Number of awards:	1
Application deadline:	August 31
Notification begins:	September 30

Contact:
Jennifer Curtis Byler Scholarship
c/o NSSGA
1605 King Street
Alexandria, VA 22314
Phone: 703-526-1063
Fax: 703-525-7782
Web: www.nssga.org/careerscholarships/scholarships.cfm

Native Daughters of the Golden West

Native Daughters of the Golden West Scholarship

Type of award: Scholarship, renewable.
Intended use: For full-time undergraduate or graduate study at accredited postsecondary institution in United States. Designated institutions: Schools in California.
Eligibility: Applicant or parent must be member/participant of Native Daughters of the Golden West. Applicant must be U.S. citizen residing in California.
Basis for selection: Applicant must demonstrate financial need, high academic achievement, depth of character, leadership, patriotism, seriousness of purpose and service orientation.
Application requirements: Recommendations, essay, transcript, nomination by local club or parlor.
Additional information: Applicant must have been born in California. Requirements vary for different awards; contact Grand Parlor Office for more information.
Contact:
Native Daughters of the Golden West
543 Baker Street
San Francisco, CA 94117-1405
Phone: 415-563-9091
Fax: 415-563-5230
Web: www.ndgw.org

Navy Supply Corps Foundation

Navy Supply Corps Foundation Scholarship

Type of award: Scholarship, renewable.
Intended use: For full-time undergraduate study at accredited 2-year or 4-year institution.
Eligibility: Applicant must be U.S. citizen. Applicant must be dependent of veteran who served in the Navy. Applicant must be family member of Supply Corps Officer/Warrant Officer.
Basis for selection: Applicant must demonstrate financial need, high academic achievement, depth of character, leadership and service orientation.
Application requirements: Transcript, proof of eligibility.
Additional information: Minimum 2.5 GPA. Any family member of Foundation member or enlisted member (active duty, reservist, or retired) is eligible for consideration. Number of awards varies. Visit Website for application and more information.

Amount of award:	$1,000-$10,000
Number of applicants:	200
Application deadline:	March 26
Notification begins:	May 10
Total amount awarded:	$254,500

Contact:
Navy Supply Corps Foundation
Navy Supply Corps School
Phone: 706-354-4111
Web: www.usnscf.com

Navy-Marine Corps Relief Society

Gold Star Scholarship Program

Type of award: Scholarship, renewable.
Intended use: For undergraduate study at postsecondary institution.
Eligibility: Applicant must be dependent of deceased veteran; or spouse of disabled veteran who served in the Marines or Navy. Service member must have died on active duty, in combat situation, or after retirement.
Basis for selection: Applicant must demonstrate financial need.
Application requirements: Current military dependent ID card; DD214 and death certificate or DD1300.
Additional information: Minimum 2.0 GPA. Visit Website for more information and application. Must be child or spouse of Navy or Marine Corps. service member who died on active duty, in combat situation, or after retirement.

Amount of award:	$500-$2,500
Number of applicants:	50
Application deadline:	March 1
Total amount awarded:	$132,000

Contact:
Navy-Marine Corps Relief Society
875 North Randolph Street, Suite 225
Arlington, VA 22203-1977
Phone: 703-696-4960
Web: www.nmcrs.org/education

NCAA

NCAA Division I Degree-Completion Award Program

Type of award: Scholarship.
Intended use: For senior study at 4-year institution.
Designated institutions: Colleges in Division I of the NCAA.
Basis for selection: Competition/talent/interest in athletics/sports. Applicant must demonstrate financial need, depth of character, leadership and service orientation.
Application requirements: Recommendations, essay, transcript. Endorsement and signature from dean of college or head of department and director of athletics; statement and signature from financial aid office, official tax forms, list of extracurricular activities.
Additional information: Program established to assist student athletes who have exhausted their eligibility for institutional financial aid (in five years). Applicants must have received athletics-related grant-in-aid at NCAA Division I institution and must be within 30 semester hours or 45 quarter hours of their degree requirements. Award will not exceed full athletics-related grant-in-aid as defined by institution and is renewable for second term, given completion of 12 hours with 2.0 GPA or better. Award covers tuition and fees plus book allowance.

Amount of award:	Full tuition
Number of applicants:	135
Total amount awarded:	$950,000

Contact:
NCAA Division I Degree-Completion Program
Karen Cooper
P.O. Box 6222
Indianapolis, IN 46206-6222
Phone: 317-917-6307
Fax: 317-917-6364
Web: www.ncaa.org

Nebraska Coordinating Commission for Postsecondary Education

Nebraska State Grant

Type of award: Scholarship.
Intended use: For undergraduate study at postsecondary institution.
Eligibility: Applicant must be residing in Nebraska.
Basis for selection: Applicant must demonstrate financial need.
Application requirements: FAFSA.
Additional information: Applicant must be eligible for Pell Grant. Award amount, application deadline, and requirements determined by individual institutions. Awards made on rolling basis. Notification begins in January preceding award year.

Number of applicants:	28,071
Total amount awarded:	$12,611,384

Contact:
Contact financial aid office at eligible institution
Phone: 402-471-2847
Fax: 402-471-2886
Web: www.ccpe.state.ne.us

Nebraska State Department of Education

Nebraska Robert C. Byrd Honors Scholarship

Type of award: Scholarship, renewable.
Intended use: For full-time freshman study at accredited postsecondary institution in United States.
Eligibility: Applicant must be high school senior. Applicant must be U.S. citizen or permanent resident residing in Nebraska.
Basis for selection: Applicant must demonstrate high academic achievement.
Application requirements: Transcript. ACT scores.
Additional information: Renewable up to four years with good academic standing. Minimum ACT score of 30. Applications mailed to counselors at all Nebraska high schools in January. Award not available to students of U.S. military academies.

Amount of award:	$1,500
Number of awards:	40
Number of applicants:	350
Application deadline:	March 15
Total amount awarded:	$234,000

Contact:
Nebraska State Department of Education Robert C. Byrd Scholarship
301 Centennial Mall South
P.O. Box 94987
Lincoln, NE 68509-4987
Phone: 402-471-3962
Web: www.nde.state.ne.us/byrd

Nevada Department of Education

Nevada Robert C. Byrd Honors Scholarship

Type of award: Scholarship, renewable.
Intended use: For undergraduate study at postsecondary institution.
Eligibility: Applicant must be high school senior. Applicant must be U.S. citizen or permanent resident residing in Nevada.
Basis for selection: Applicant must demonstrate high academic achievement, depth of character and seriousness of purpose.

Additional information: Applicant must be Nevada High School Scholar. Minimum 3.5 GPA and 1100 SAT or 25 ACT score required. Renewable up to four years.

Amount of award:	$1,500
Number of awards:	40
Number of applicants:	300
Notification begins:	May 1
Total amount awarded:	$324,000

Contact:
Nevada Department of Education
700 East Fifth Street
Carson City, NV 89710
Phone: 775-687-9150
Fax: 775-687-9113
Web: www.doe.nv.gov

Nevada Student Incentive Grant

Type of award: Scholarship.
Intended use: For undergraduate or graduate study at vocational, 2-year, 4-year or graduate institution.
Eligibility: Applicant must be U.S. citizen or permanent resident residing in Nevada.
Basis for selection: Applicant must demonstrate financial need.
Application requirements: FAFSA.
Additional information: Must apply through post-secondary financial aid office. Deadlines vary by institution. Maximum award is $5,000.

Amount of award:	$5,000
Notification begins:	July 1

Contact:
Nevada Department of Education
700 East Fifth Street
Carson City, NV 87910
Phone: 775-687-9150
Fax: 775-687-9113
Web: www.doe.nv.gov

New England Board of Higher Education

NEBHE's Tuition Break Regional Student Program

Type of award: Scholarship.
Intended use: For undergraduate or graduate study in United States. Designated institutions: New England public colleges and universities.
Eligibility: Applicant must be permanent resident residing in Vermont, New Hampshire, Connecticut, Maine, Massachusetts or Rhode Island.
Additional information: Regional Student Program provides tuition discount to New England residents who study majors not offered at public institutions in their own state at out-of-state public colleges in New England. Must be enrolling in approved major listed in annual catalog.

Contact:
New England Board of Higher Education
45 Temple Place
Boston, MA 02111
Phone: 617-357-9620
Web: www.nebhe.org/tuitionbreak

New England Employee Benefits Council

NEEBC Scholarship

Type of award: Scholarship, renewable.
Intended use: For undergraduate or graduate study at accredited postsecondary institution.
Basis for selection: Major/career interest in business/management/administration; human resources; insurance/actuarial science or health services administration. Applicant must demonstrate high academic achievement, depth of character, leadership, seriousness of purpose and service orientation.
Application requirements: Recommendations, transcript. 500-word essay; minimum of two references from college professors, NEEBC members or other benefits professionals.
Additional information: Applicants must aspire to career in employee benefits. Applicants must reside or attend college in New England.

Amount of award:	$2,500-$5,000
Number of applicants:	2
Application deadline:	April 1
Notification begins:	May 1
Total amount awarded:	$5,000

Contact:
New England Benefits Council
240 Bear Hill Road
Suite 102
Waltham, MA 02451
Phone: 781-684-8700
Web: www.neebc.org

New Hampshire Postsecondary Education Commission

New Hampshire Incentive Program

Type of award: Scholarship, renewable.
Intended use: For undergraduate study at accredited vocational, 2-year or 4-year institution. Designated institutions: Eligible institutions in New England (Connecticut, Maine, Massachusetts, New Hampshire, Rhode Island, Vermont).
Eligibility: Applicant must be U.S. citizen or permanent resident residing in New Hampshire.
Basis for selection: Applicant must demonstrate financial need.
Application requirements: Proof of eligibility. FAFSA.
Additional information: Application online at www.fafsa.org.

Amount of award:	$125-$1,000
Number of awards:	4,000
Application deadline:	May 1
Total amount awarded:	$3,182,132

Contact:
New Hampshire Postsecondary Education Commission
Cynthia Capodestria
3 Barrell Court, Suite 300
Concord, NH 03301-8543
Phone: 603-271-2555 ext. 360
Fax: 603-271-2696
Web: www.nh.gov/postsecondary/financial

New Hampshire Scholarship for Orphans of Veterans

Type of award: Scholarship, renewable.
Intended use: For undergraduate or graduate study at vocational, 2-year or 4-year institution.
Eligibility: Applicant must be at least 16, no older than 25. Applicant must be U.S. citizen residing in New Hampshire. Applicant must be dependent of deceased veteran during Korean War, WW I, WW II or Vietnam. Dependents of deceased veterans of Gulf War or deceased veterans awarded an armed forces expeditionary medal.
Application requirements: Proof of eligibility.
Additional information: Parent must have been legal resident of New Hampshire at time of service-related death.

Amount of award:	$2,500
Number of applicants:	1
Total amount awarded:	$3,750

Contact:
New Hampshire Postsecondary Education Commission
Judith Knapp
3 Barrell Court, Suite 300
Concord, NH 03301-8543
Phone: 603-271-2555 ext. 352
Fax: 603-271-2696
Web: www.nh.gov/postsecondary

New Jersey Commission on Higher Education

New Jersey Educational Opportunity Fund Grant

Type of award: Scholarship, renewable.
Intended use: For full-time undergraduate or graduate study at accredited 2-year or 4-year institution. Designated institutions: Participating New Jersey community colleges, four-year colleges and universities.
Eligibility: Applicant must be U.S. citizen or permanent resident residing in New Jersey.
Basis for selection: Applicant must demonstrate financial need.
Application requirements: FAFSA.
Additional information: For students from educationally disadvantaged backgrounds with demonstrated financial need. Must be New Jersey resident for at least 12 consecutive months prior to enrollment. Students are admitted into EOF program by college. Program includes summer sessions, tutoring, counseling, and student leadership development. Award amounts vary; undergraduate $200-$2,500, graduate $200-$4,350. Contact EOF director at institution for specific application requirements.

Number of awards:	18,259
Application deadline:	October 1
Notification begins:	April 1
Total amount awarded:	$26,643,935

Contact:
New Jersey Commission on Higher Education
P.O. Box 542
Trenton, NJ 08625-0542
Phone: 609-984-2709
Fax: 609-984-2709
Web: www.nj.gov/highereducation/EOF

New Jersey Department of Military and Veterans Affairs

New Jersey POW/MIA Tuition Benefit Program

Type of award: Scholarship, renewable.
Intended use: For full-time undergraduate study at accredited 4-year institution in United States. Designated institutions: New Jersey colleges and universities.
Eligibility: Applicant must be residing in New Jersey. Applicant must be dependent of active service person or POW/MIA. Parent must have been officially declared Prisoner of War or Missing in Action after January 1, 1960 and must have been resident of New Jersey.
Application requirements: Proof of eligibility. Copy of DD 1300.
Additional information: Award does not include room, board, or expenses.

Amount of award:	Full tuition

Contact:
New Jersey Department of Military and Veterans Affairs
DVS-VBB-Patty Richter
P.O. Box 340
Trenton, NJ 08625-7005
Phone: 609-530-6854
Fax: 609-530-6970
Web: www.state.nj.us/military

New Jersey War Orphans Tuition Assistance Program

Type of award: Scholarship, renewable.
Intended use: For undergraduate or graduate study at postsecondary institution in United States.
Eligibility: Applicant must be at least 16, no older than 21. Applicant must be residing in New Jersey. Applicant must be veteran who served in the Army, Air Force, Marines, Navy, Coast Guard or Reserves/National Guard during Vietnam. Child of service personnel who died due to service-connected disabilities or who is officially listed as Missing In Action. Veteran must have been New Jersey resident.
Application requirements: Proof of eligibility.
Additional information: Must have been New Jersey resident for one year prior to application.

Amount of award:	$500
Number of applicants:	1

Contact:
New Jersey Department of Military and Veterans Affairs
DVS-VBB-Patty Richter
P.O. Box 340
Trenton, NJ 08625-7005
Phone: 609-530-6854
Fax: 609-530-6970
Web: www.state.nj.us/military

New Jersey Higher Education Student Assistance Authority

Dana Christmas Scholarship for Heroism

Type of award: Scholarship.
Intended use: For undergraduate or graduate study at postsecondary institution.
Eligibility: Applicant must be U.S. citizen or permanent resident residing in New Jersey.
Additional information: Honors young New Jersey residents for acts of heroism. Students must be age 21 or younger at time of act of heroism. Applicant must be resident of New Jersey upon application and at time act of heroism was performed. Application can be obtained by calling HESAA or by visiting Website.

  Application deadline: October 15
  Notification begins: December 1
Contact:
New Jersey Higher Education Student Assistance Authority
P.O. Box 540
Trenton, NJ 08625-0540
Phone: 800-792-8670
Web: www.hesaa.org

Law Enforcement Officer Memorial Scholarship

Type of award: Scholarship.
Intended use: For full-time undergraduate study at postsecondary institution. Designated institutions: New Jersey institutions.
Eligibility: Applicant must be residing in New Jersey. Applicant's parent must have been killed or disabled in work-related accident as police officer.
Application requirements: Proof of eligibility.
Additional information: Must be dependent of law enforcement officer killed in the line of duty. Award may cover up to the cost of attendance at any approved institution of higher education in New Jersey. Awards are renewable for up to four years.

  Amount of award: Full tuition
  Application deadline: October 1, March 1
Contact:
New Jersey Higher Education Student Assistance Authority
P.O. Box 540
Trenton, NJ 08625-0540
Phone: 800-792-8670
Web: www.hesaa.org

New Jeresy Student Tuition Assistance Reward Scholarship (NJSTARS)

Type of award: Scholarship, renewable.
Intended use: For full-time undergraduate study at 2-year institution. Designated institutions: New Jersey county colleges.
Eligibility: Applicant must be U.S. citizen or permanent resident residing in New Jersey.
Basis for selection: Applicant must demonstrate high academic achievement.
Application requirements: FAFSA.
Additional information: Must be resident of New Jersey for 12 months prior to high school graduation. Provides tuition and approved fees for up to 18 credits per semester for up to five semesters at a county college for students graduating in top 15 percent of high school class. To be eligible for renewal, students must have minimum 3.0 GPA.

  Application deadline: June 1, October 1
Contact:
New Jersey Higher Education Student Assistance Authority
P.O. Box 540
Trenton, NJ 08625-0540
Phone: 800-792-8670
Web: www.hesaa.org

New Jersey Edward J. Bloustein Distinguished Scholars

Type of award: Scholarship, renewable.
Intended use: For full-time undergraduate study at accredited 2-year or 4-year institution. Designated institutions: Approved New Jersey colleges, universities, and degree-granting proprietary institutions.
Eligibility: Applicant must be high school senior. Applicant must be U.S. citizen or permanent resident residing in New Jersey.
Basis for selection: Applicant must demonstrate high academic achievement.
Application requirements: Nomination by high school. SAT scores, junior year class rank.
Additional information: Students may not apply directly to this program. Candidates will be selected for consideration by their secondary schools based upon academic criteria. Must be a New Jersey resident for at least 12 consecutive months prior to receiving the award. Candidates are notified in fall of senior year. See guidance counselor for more information.

  Amount of award: $1,000
Contact:
New Jersey Higher Education Student Assistance Authority
4 Quakerbridge Plaza
P.O. Box 540
Trenton, NJ 08625-0540
Phone: 800-792-8670
Web: www.hesaa.org

New Jersey STARS II

Type of award: Scholarship, renewable.
Intended use: For full-time undergraduate study at accredited 4-year institution in United States. Designated institutions: New Jersey public institutions.
Eligibility: Applicant must be U.S. citizen or permanent resident or New Jersey.
Basis for selection: Applicant must demonstrate financial need and high academic achievement.

Application requirements: FAFSA.
Additional information: Must be successful NJ STARS scholar receiving associate's degree with a minimum 3.25 GPA. Provides for tuition and approved fees for up to 18 credits per semester for four semesters at a New Jersey public four-year institution.

Amount of award:	$6,000-$7,000
Application deadline:	June 1, October 1

Contact:
New Jersey Higher Education Student Assistance Authority
P.O. Box 540
Trenton, NJ 08625-0540
Phone: 800-792-8670
Web: www.hesaa.org

New Jersey Survivor Tuition Benefits Program

Type of award: Scholarship, renewable.
Intended use: For undergraduate study. Designated institutions: Approved New Jersey colleges, universities, and degree-granting institutions.
Eligibility: Applicant's parent must have been killed or disabled in work-related accident as firefighter, police officer or public safety officer.
Application requirements: Proof of eligibility.
Additional information: Parent or spouse must have been New Jersey firefighter, law enforcement officer, or emergency service personnel killed in line of duty. Applications available on agency's website or by calling toll-free hotline. Grants pay cost of tuition up to highest amount charged at a New Jersey public postsecondary school.

Amount of award:	Full tuition
Application deadline:	October 1, March 1

Contact:
New Jersey Higher Education Student Assistance Authority
4 Quakerbridge Plaza
P.O. Box 540
Trenton, NJ 08625-0540
Phone: 800-792-8670
Web: www.hesaa.org

New Jersey Tuition Aid Grants (TAG)

Type of award: Scholarship, renewable.
Intended use: For full-time undergraduate study in United States. Designated institutions: Approved New Jersey colleges, universities, and degree-granting proprietary institutions.
Eligibility: Applicant must be U.S. citizen or permanent resident residing in New Jersey.
Basis for selection: Applicant must demonstrate financial need.
Application requirements: FAFSA.
Additional information: Students must maintain satisfactory academic progress. Deadline is June 1 for renewal students; October 1 for new applicants. Notification begins in March.

Number of applicants:	500,000
Application deadline:	June 1, October 1

Contact:
New Jersey Higher Education Student Assistance Authority
4 Quakerbridge Plaza
P.O. Box 540
Trenton, NJ 08625-0540
Phone: 800-792-8670
Fax: 609-558-2228
Web: www.hesaa.org

New Jersey Urban Scholars

Type of award: Scholarship, renewable.
Intended use: For full-time undergraduate study at accredited 2-year institution in United States. Designated institutions: Approved New Jersey colleges and degree-granting institutions.
Eligibility: Applicant must be U.S. citizen or permanent resident residing in New Jersey.
Basis for selection: Applicant must demonstrate high academic achievement.
Application requirements: Nomination by high school. Junior year class rank and GPA.
Additional information: Students may not apply directly for award. Open to students in top 10 percent of their high school class, with minimum 3.0 GPA or equivalent, attending high schools in New Jersey's urban and economically distressed areas. Candidates nominated for consideration will receive notification by fall of senior year. See guidance counselor for more information.

Amount of award:	$1,000

Contact:
New Jersey Higher Education Student Assistance Authority
4 Quakerbridge Plaza
P.O. Box 540
Trenton, NJ 08625-0540
Phone: 800-792-8670
Web: www.hesaa.org

New Jersey World Trade Center Scholarship

Type of award: Scholarship, renewable.
Intended use: For full-time undergraduate study at postsecondary institution.
Eligibility: Applicant must be residing in New Jersey.
Additional information: Must be spouse or dependent of New Jersey resident who was killed or is presumed dead as a result of the terrorist attacks of September 11, 2001. This includes first responders and rescue workers who died as a result of illness caused by attack sites.

Application deadline:	October 1, March 1

Contact:
New Jersey Higher Education Student Assistance Authority
P.O. Box 540
Trenton, NJ 08625-0540
Phone: 800-792-8670
Web: www.hesaa.org

Part-Time Tuition Aid Grant for County Colleges

Type of award: Scholarship, renewable.
Intended use: For half-time undergraduate study at postsecondary institution. Designated institutions: Participating New Jersey county colleges.
Eligibility: Applicant must be U.S. citizen or permanent resident residing in New Jersey.
Basis for selection: Applicant must demonstrate financial need.
Application requirements: FAFSA.
Additional information: Must be enrolled part-time (6-11 credits). Must be legal New Jersey resident for at least 12 months prior to enrollment. Must maintain satisfactory academic progress. Renewals due June 1; new applications due October 1. Visit Website for application and additional information.

Application deadline:	June 1, October 1

Contact:
New Jersey Higher Education Student Assistance Authority
P.O. Box 540
Trenton, NJ 08625-0540
Phone: 800-792-8670
Web: www.hesaa.org

New Jersey State Golf Association

Caddie Scholarship

Type of award: Scholarship, renewable.
Intended use: For full-time undergraduate study at accredited 2-year or 4-year institution in United States. Designated institutions: Members of Association of American Colleges and Universities.
Basis for selection: Applicant must demonstrate financial need and high academic achievement.
Application requirements: Proof of eligibility. Recommendation from golf club.
Additional information: Applicants must have been a caddie for at least two seasons at a member club of New Jersey State Golf Association. Must be in top half of class and have minimum 900 SAT and 2.5 GPA. Awards renewable for up to four years. Foundation also offers one full scholarship award at Rutgers University.

Amount of award:	$2,500-$5,000
Number of awards:	50
Number of applicants:	102
Application deadline:	May 1
Notification begins:	June 15
Total amount awarded:	$630,000

Contact:
New Jersey State Golf Association
Caddie Scholarship Foundation
P.O. Box 6947
Freehold, NJ 07728
Phone: 908-241-4653
Fax: 908-245-4696
Web: www.njsga.org

New Mexico Commission on Higher Education

New Mexico Competitive Scholarships

Type of award: Scholarship.
Intended use: For full-time undergraduate study at 4-year institution in United States. Designated institutions: Public New Mexico institutions.
Basis for selection: Applicant must demonstrate high academic achievement.
Additional information: Awards to encourage out-of-state students who have demonstrated high academic achievement in high school to enroll in public institutions in New Mexico. Recipients of at least $100 in competitive scholarships per semester eligible for resident tuition and fees. Applicants must meet GPA/ACT score requirements, which vary by institution.

Contact financial aid office of any New Mexico public postsecondary institution or see Website.
Contact:
New Mexico Commission on Higher Education
Financial Aid and Student Services
1068 Cerrillos Road
Santa Fe, NM 87505
Phone: 800-279-9777
Web: www.hed.state.nm.us

New Mexico Legislative Endowment Program

Type of award: Scholarship, renewable.
Intended use: For undergraduate study at accredited postsecondary institution. Designated institutions: Public institutions in New Mexico.
Eligibility: Applicant must be U.S. citizen or permanent resident residing in New Mexico.
Basis for selection: Applicant must demonstrate financial need.
Application requirements: FAFSA.
Additional information: Contact financial aid office of any public postsecondary institution in New Mexico. Four-year public institutions may award up to $2,500 per student per academic year. Two-year public institutions may award up to $1,000 per student per year. Part-time students eligible for prorated awards. Deadlines set by institutions.

Amount of award:	$1,000-$2,500

Contact:
New Mexico Commission on Higher Education
Financial Aid and Student Services
2048 Galisteo Street
Santa Fe, NM 87505
Phone: 505-476-8400
Web: www.hed.state.nm.us

New Mexico Legislative Lottery Scholarship

Type of award: Scholarship.
Intended use: For full-time undergraduate study at postsecondary institution. Designated institutions: Eligible New Mexico public colleges and universities.
Eligibility: Applicant must be high school senior. Applicant must be residing in New Mexico.
Additional information: Must complete 12 graded credit hours with 2.5 GPA in the first regular semester immediately following graduation from New Mexico high school. Deadlines vary according to institution; see Website or apply through financial aid office.

Amount of award:	Full tuition

Contact:
New Mexico Commission on Higher Education
Financial Aid and Student Services
2048 Galisteo Street
Santa Fe, NM 87505
Phone: 505-476-8400
Web: www.hed.state.nm.us

New Mexico Scholars Program

Type of award: Scholarship, renewable.
Intended use: For full-time undergraduate study at accredited 2-year or 4-year institution. Designated institutions: Public institutions in New Mexico or the following private institutions:

College of Santa Fe, St. John's College, College of the Southwest.
Eligibility: Applicant must be no older than 21. Applicant must be U.S. citizen or permanent resident residing in New Mexico.
Basis for selection: Applicant must demonstrate financial need and high academic achievement.
Application requirements: FAFSA.
Additional information: Award includes books and required fees. Number of awards based on availability of funds. Must be graduate of New Mexico high school. Must have 25 ACT score or be in top five percent of class. Must attend eligible university by end of 21st birthday. Combined family income may not exceed $30,000 per year. Contact financial aid office of New Mexico postsecondary institution of choice for information and application. Application deadline set by institution.

Amount of award:	Full tuition

Contact:
New Mexico Commission on Higher Education
Financial Aid and Student Services
2048 Galisteo Street
Santa Fe, NM 87505
Phone: 505-476-8400
Web: www.hed.state.nm.us

New Mexico Student Choice Grant

Type of award: Scholarship, renewable.
Intended use: For undergraduate study at postsecondary institution. Designated institutions: St. John's College, College of the Southwest, College of Santa Fe.
Eligibility: Applicant must be U.S. citizen or permanent resident residing in New Mexico.
Basis for selection: Applicant must demonstrate financial need.
Application requirements: FAFSA.
Additional information: Amount of award and application deadline determined by institution. Apply to financial aid office at one of designated colleges. Part-time students eligible for pro-rated awards.
Contact:
New Mexico Commission on Higher Education
Financial Aid and Student Services
2048 Galisteo Street
Santa Fe, NM 87505
Phone: 505-476-8400
Web: www.hed.state.nm.us

New Mexico Student Incentive Grant

Type of award: Scholarship, renewable.
Intended use: For undergraduate study at accredited postsecondary institution. Designated institutions: College of Santa Fe, St. John's College, College of the Southwest, Institute of American Indian Art, Crownpoint Institute of Technology, Dine College, Southwest Indian Polytechnic Institute.
Eligibility: Applicant must be U.S. citizen or permanent resident residing in New Mexico.
Basis for selection: Applicant must demonstrate financial need.
Application requirements: FAFSA.
Additional information: Must demonstrate exceptional financial need. Contact financial aid office of designated institutions for information, application, and deadline. Part-time students eligible for pro-rated awards.

Amount of award:	$200-$2,500

Contact:
New Mexico Commission on Higher Education
Financial Aid and Student Services
2048 Galisteo Street
Santa Fe, NM 87505
Phone: 505-476-8400
Web: www.hed.state.nm.us

New Mexico Vietnam Veteran's Scholarship

Type of award: Scholarship, renewable.
Intended use: For undergraduate or graduate study at postsecondary institution. Designated institutions: College of Santa Fe, St. John's College, College of the Southwest.
Eligibility: Applicant must be U.S. citizen residing in New Mexico. Applicant must be veteran during Vietnam. Must have been awarded Vietnam campaign medal during period of August 5, 1964 to termination of Vietnam conflict.
Application requirements: Proof of eligibility.
Additional information: Maximum award provides tuition, fees, and book allowance on first come, first served basis. Eligibility and coursework must be certified by New Mexico Veterans Service Commission. Contact financial aid office of any New Mexico public postsecondary institution for information, deadline, and application. Must have been honorably discharged from U.S. armed forces. Must have been resident of New Mexico at original time of entry into armed forces or have lived in New Mexico for ten years or more.

Amount of award:	Full tuition

Contact:
New Mexico Veteran's Service Commission
P.O. Box 2324
Santa Fe, NM 87505
Phone: 505-827-6300
Web: www.hed.state.nm.us

New York State Education Department

New York State Arthur O. Eve Higher Education Opportunity Program (HEOP)

Type of award: Scholarship.
Intended use: For undergraduate study at 2-year or 4-year institution. Designated institutions: Independent New York State colleges and universities.
Eligibility: Applicant must be residing in New York.
Basis for selection: Applicant must demonstrate financial need.
Additional information: Applicant must be resident of New York State for one year preceding entry into HEOP and be academically and economically disadvantaged. Contact college or university of interest for application and additional information, and apply at time of admission. Support services include presession summer program and tutoring, counseling, and special coursework during academic year. Award amounts vary; contact sponsor for information. For general information, contact New York State Education Department.

Number of applicants:	5,368

Contact:
Contact Financial Aid Office
Phone: 518-474-5313
Fax: 518-486-5221
Web: www.highered.nysed.gov

New York State Robert C. Byrd Federal Honors Scholarship

Type of award: Scholarship, renewable.
Intended use: For full-time undergraduate study at accredited 2-year or 4-year institution in United States.
Eligibility: Applicant must be high school senior. Applicant must be U.S. citizen or permanent resident residing in New York.
Basis for selection: Applicant must demonstrate high academic achievement.
Application requirements: Nomination by high school.
Additional information: Must have 1875 SAT score, minimum 95 average, or 410 GED score. Applicants will be ranked within county of legal residence based on final ranking score composed of 75 percent GPA or GED and 25 percent SAT score. Applications available in early fall at student's high school.

Amount of award:	$1,500
Number of awards:	400
Number of applicants:	6,000
Application deadline:	March 1
Total amount awarded:	$700,000

Contact:
New York State Education Department
Scholarships Dept.
Room 967 EBA
Albany, NY 12234
Phone: 518-486-1319
Fax: 518-474-0060
Web: www.highered.nysed.gov

New York State Scholarships for Academic Excellence

Type of award: Scholarship.
Intended use: For undergraduate study at 2-year or 4-year institution in United States. Designated institutions: New York state postsecondary institutions.
Eligibility: Applicant must be high school senior. Applicant must be U.S. citizen or permanent resident residing in New York.
Application requirements: Regents test scores.
Additional information: Scholarship winners are selected by their high school based on academic excellence as measured by scores on Regents examinations taken prior to the senior year. Bulletins and applications available at high school. See Website for more information.

Amount of award:	$500-$1,500
Number of awards:	8,000
Number of applicants:	8,000
Application deadline:	December 18
Total amount awarded:	$6,000,000

Contact:
New York State Higher Education Services Corporation
Scholarships Dept.
Room 967 EBA
Albany, NY 12234
Phone: 888-697-4372
Fax: 518-474-0060
Web: www.highered.nysed.gov

New York State Grange

Caroline Kark Scholarship

Type of award: Scholarship.
Intended use: For undergraduate study at postsecondary institution.
Eligibility: Applicant must be residing in New York.
Basis for selection: Major/career interest in deafness studies.
Additional information: Award available to Grange members preparing for a career working with the deaf or hearing impaired and to non-members who are deaf and want to further their education beyond high school. Hearing applicants must have been a Grange member for one year prior to applying. Deaf applicants must show sufficient hearing loss to receive full-time amplification.

Application deadline:	April 15

Contact:
New York State Grange
100 Grange Place
Cortland, NY 13045
Phone: 607-756-7553
Fax: 607-756-7757
Web: www.nysgrange.org

Grange Denise Scholarship

Type of award: Scholarship, renewable.
Intended use: For full-time undergraduate study at 2-year or 4-year institution.
Eligibility: Applicant must be residing in New York.
Basis for selection: Major/career interest in agriculture; agribusiness; agricultural education; agricultural economics or natural resources/conservation. Applicant must demonstrate financial need.
Application requirements: Recommendations, transcript.
Additional information: Send SASE for application.

Amount of award:	$1,000
Number of awards:	6
Number of applicants:	20
Application deadline:	April 15
Notification begins:	June 15
Total amount awarded:	$6,000

Contact:
New York State Grange
100 Grange Place
Cortland, NY 13045
Phone: 607-756-7553
Fax: 607-756-7757
Web: www.nysgrange.org

Grange Susan W. Freestone Education Award

Type of award: Scholarship, renewable.
Intended use: For full-time undergraduate or graduate study at 2-year or 4-year institution in United States. Designated institutions: Approved institutions in New York state.
Eligibility: Applicant must be residing in New York.
Basis for selection: Applicant must demonstrate financial need, depth of character and service orientation.
Application requirements: Transcript.
Additional information: Applicant must be current New York State Grange member. Must have been Junior Grange member to qualify for maximum award. Send SASE for application. Activity in Grange work considered.

Scholarships

Amount of award: $1,000
Number of awards: 2
Number of applicants: 5
Application deadline: April 15
Notification begins: June 15
Total amount awarded: $2,000

Contact:
New York State Grange
100 Grange Place
Cortland, NY 13045
Phone: 607-756-7553
Fax: 607-756-7757
Web: www.nysgrange.org

June Gill Nursing Scholarship

Type of award: Scholarship, renewable.
Intended use: For undergraduate study at postsecondary institution.
Eligibility: Applicant or parent must be member/participant of New York State Grange. Applicant must be residing in New York.
Basis for selection: Major/career interest in nursing. Applicant must demonstrate financial need and high academic achievement.
Application requirements: Transcript, proof of eligibility. Career statement.
Additional information: Grandchild of member of the New York State Grange also eligible. Award amounts vary.

Amount of award: $1,000
Number of awards: 2
Application deadline: April 15
Notification begins: June 1

Contact:
New York State Grange
100 Grange Place
Cortland, NY 13045
Phone: 607-756-7553
Fax: 607-756-7757
Web: www.nysgrange.org

New York State Higher Education Services Corporation

City University SEEK/College Discovery Program

Type of award: Scholarship.
Intended use: For undergraduate study at 2-year or 4-year institution. Designated institutions: City University of New York campuses.
Eligibility: Applicant must be U.S. citizen or permanent resident residing in New York.
Basis for selection: Applicant must demonstrate financial need.
Application requirements: Proof of eligibility. FAFSA, TAP.
Additional information: Applicant must be both academically and economically disadvantaged. Available at CUNY and community college campuses. Apply to CUNY financial aid office. For SEEK, student must have resided in New York State for at least one year; for College Discovery,

student must have resided in New York City for at least one year.
Contact:
City University of New York
Office of Admission Services
1114 Avenue of the Americas
New York, NY 10036
Phone: 212-997-CUNY
Web: www.cuny.edu

Flight 587 Memorial Scholarships

Type of award: Scholarship, renewable.
Intended use: For full-time undergraduate study at postsecondary institution. Designated institutions: Approved New York state institutions.
Eligibility: Applicant must be residing in New York.
Application requirements: FAFSA. TAP. Scholarship supplement. Proof of applicant's relationship to the deceased (birth certificate, marriage license, etc.)
Additional information: Provides financial aid to children, spouses, and financial dependents of individuals killed as a direct result of American Airlines Flight 587's crash in the Belle Harbor neighborhood of Queens, New York, on the morning of November 12, 2001. Award is full tuition for students attending public colleges and universities in New York State, and the monetary equivalent for students attending private New York schools.

Amount of award: Full tuition
Application deadline: May 1

Contact:
New York State Higher Education Services Corporation
HESC Scholarship Unit
99 Washington Avenue, Room 1430A
Albany, NY 12255
Phone: 888-NYS-HESC
Web: www.hesc.com

Military Service Recognition Scholarship (MSRS)

Type of award: Scholarship, renewable.
Intended use: For full-time undergraduate study at 2-year or 4-year institution. Designated institutions: Approved New York State institutions.
Eligibility: Applicant must be residing in New York. Applicant must be disabled while on active duty; or dependent of disabled veteran, deceased veteran or POW/MIA; or spouse of disabled veteran, deceased veteran or POW/MIA. Must be child, spouse, or financial dependent of member of the U.S. armed forces or state-organized militia who, at any time after August 2, 1990, while New York State resident, (1) died or became permanently disabled as a result of injury or illness in a combat theater or combat zone or during military training operations in preparation for duty in a combat theater or (2) is classified as MIA in a combat theater or combat zone of operations.
Application requirements: FAFSA, TAP application.
Additional information: At public colleges and universities (CUNY or SUNY), award covers actual tuition and mandatory educational fees; actual room and board for living on campus (or an allowance for commuters); and allowances for books, supplies, and transportation. At private institutions, award amount equals SUNY four-year college tuition and fees and allowances for room and board, books, supplies, and transportation. New York State resident family members who were enrolled in undergraduate programs at U.S. colleges or

universities outside of New York State on September 11, 2001, are also eligible. See Website for more details.

Amount of award: Full tuition
Application deadline: May 1
Contact:
New York State Higher Education Services Corporation
Scholarships and Grants
99 Washington Avenue
Albany, NY 12255
Phone: 888-NYS-HESC
Web: www.hesc.com

New York State Aid for Part-time Study Program

Type of award: Scholarship, renewable.
Intended use: For half-time undergraduate study at postsecondary institution. Designated institutions: Participating New York state institutions.
Eligibility: Applicant must be U.S. citizen or permanent resident residing in New York.
Basis for selection: Applicant must demonstrate financial need.
Application requirements: Proof of eligibility.
Additional information: Must fall within income limits. Campus-based program; recipients selected and award amount determined by school. Maximum award is $2,000. Must not have used up TAP eligibility or be in default on Federal Family Education Loan. Student must maintain minimum 2.0 GPA. Applications available from individual colleges.

Amount of award: $2,000
Contact:
New York State Higher Education Services Corporation
Scholarships and Grants
99 Washington Avenue
Albany, NY 12255
Phone: 888-NYS-HESC
Web: www.hesc.com

New York State Memorial Scholarship for Families of Deceased Police/Volunteer Firefighters/Peace Officers and Emergency Medical Service Workers

Type of award: Scholarship, renewable.
Intended use: For full-time undergraduate study at 2-year or 4-year institution. Designated institutions: Approved New York institutions.
Eligibility: Applicant must be U.S. citizen residing in New York. Applicant's parent must have been killed or disabled in work-related accident as firefighter, police officer or public safety officer.
Application requirements: Proof of eligibility. Memorial Scholarship Supplement, FAFSA, and Express TAP Application.
Additional information: Spouse and/or children of police officer/firefighter/peace officer/EMS worker who died as result of injuries sustained in line of duty in service to New York State are eligible. Award will equal applicant's actual tuition cost or SUNY undergraduate tuition cost, whichever is less. Also provides funds to meet non-tuition costs, such as room and board, books, supplies, and transportation. Visit Website for additional information.

Amount of award: Full tuition
Application deadline: May 1

Contact:
New York State Higher Education Services Corporation
Scholarships and Grants
99 Washington Avenue
Albany, NY 12255
Phone: 888-NYS-HESC
Web: www.hesc.com

New York State Regents Awards for Children of Deceased and Disabled Veterans

Type of award: Scholarship.
Intended use: For full-time undergraduate or non-degree study at 2-year or 4-year institution.
Eligibility: Applicant must be residing in New York. Applicant must be dependent of veteran, disabled veteran or deceased veteran during Korean War, Persian Gulf War, WW I, WW II or Vietnam. Student's parent must have been disabled or deceased veteran or POW, or classified as MIA. Student whose parent has received Armed Forces, Navy, or Marine Corps expeditionary medal for participation in operations in Lebanon, Grenada, and Panama also eligible, as are students born with spina bifida whose parent(s) served in Vietnam between 12/22/61 and 5/7/75.
Application requirements: Proof of eligibility. FAFSA and Express TAP Application.
Additional information: Student must initially establish eligibility by submitting a Child of Veteran Award Supplement before applying. Veteran must be a resident of New York state. Visit Website for additional information.

Amount of award: $450
Application deadline: May 1
Contact:
New York State Higher Education Services Corporation
Scholarships and Grants
99 Washington Avenue
Albany, NY 12255
Phone: 888-NYS-HESC
Web: www.hesc.com

New York State Tuition Assistance Program

Type of award: Scholarship, renewable.
Intended use: For undergraduate or graduate study at accredited postsecondary institution in United States. Designated institutions: TAP-eligible schools in New York.
Eligibility: Applicant must be U.S. citizen or permanent resident residing in New York.
Basis for selection: Applicant must demonstrate financial need.
Application requirements: Proof of eligibility. FAFSA.
Additional information: Must fall within income limits. Submit FAFSA to receive prefilled Express TAP Application (ETA) to review, sign, and return. Award subject to budget appropriations. Must maintain at least C average. Must not be in default on a HESC-guaranteed loan. Part-time, first-time freshmen attending CUNY, SUNY, or not-for-profit independent degree-granting colleges also eligible. Visit Website for additional information.

Application deadline: May 1

Contact:
New York State Higher Education Services Corporation
Grants and Scholarships
99 Washington Avenue
Albany, NY 12255
Phone: 888-NYS-HESC
Web: www.hesc.com

New York State Veterans Tuition Award

Type of award: Scholarship, renewable.
Intended use: For undergraduate or graduate study at accredited vocational, 2-year, 4-year or graduate institution in United States. Designated institutions: Approved postsecondary schools in New York.
Eligibility: Applicant must be returning adult student. Applicant must be U.S. citizen or permanent resident residing in New York. Applicant must be veteran during Persian Gulf War or Vietnam. Must have served in armed forces in hostilities in Indochina between December 1961 and May 1975, or in Persian Gulf on or after August 2, 1990. Veterans of the conflict in Afghanistan also eligible. Must not have been dishonorably discharged.
Application requirements: Proof of eligibility. FAFSA. Express Tap Application (ETA). Documentation of Indochina, Persian Gulf, or Afghanistan service.
Additional information: Students must have also applied for TAP and Federal Pell Grant awards. Visit Website for additional information.

  Amount of award: $4,895
  Application deadline: May 1

Contact:
New York State Higher Education Services Corporation
Scholarships and Grants
99 Washington Avenue
Albany, NY 12255
Phone: 888-NYS-HESC
Web: www.hesc.com

New York State World Trade Center Memorial Scholarship

Type of award: Scholarship, renewable.
Intended use: For full-time undergraduate study at 2-year or 4-year institution. Designated institutions: Approved New York colleges and universities.
Application requirements: Proof of eligibility. FAFSA, Express TAP Application.
Additional information: Must be child, spouse, or financial dependent of person who died or became severely and permanently disabled due to the September 11th attacks or rescue and recovery operation. At public colleges and universities (CUNY or SUNY), award covers actual tuition and mandatory educational fees; actual room and board for living on campus (or an allowance for commuters); and allowances for books, supplies, and transportation. At private institutions, award amount equals SUNY four-year college tuition and fees, and allowances for room and board, books, supplies, and transportation. New York State resident family members who were enrolled in undergraduate programs at U.S. colleges or universities outside of New York State on September 11, 2001, are also eligible. See Website for details.

  Amount of award: Full tuition
  Application deadline: May 1

Contact:
New York State Higher Education Services Corporation
Grants and Scholarships
99 Washington Avenue
Albany, NY 12255
Phone: 888-NYS-HESC
Web: www.hesc.com

New York State Native American Education Unit

New York State Native American Student Aid Program

Type of award: Scholarship, renewable.
Intended use: For undergraduate study at accredited vocational, 2-year or 4-year institution.
Eligibility: Applicant must be American Indian. Must be on official tribal roll of New York State tribe or be a child of enrolled member. Applicant must be residing in New York.
Application requirements: Transcript, proof of eligibility. Tribal certification form, documentation of high school graduation, college acceptance letter.
Additional information: Must reapply to renew award each semester. Minimum 2.0 semester GPA required. Students taking 12 or more credits receive $500; under 12 credits, $42 per credit hour.

  Amount of award: $1,000
  Application deadline: July 15, December 31

Contact:
New York State Native American Education Unit
New York State Education Department
Room 478, Education Building Annex
Albany, NY 12234
Phone: 518-474-0537
Fax: 518-474-3666
Web: www.emsc.nysed.gov/rss/natamer

New York Women in Communications Foundation

New York Women in Communications Foundation Scholarship

Type of award: Scholarship, renewable.
Intended use: For undergraduate or graduate study at accredited postsecondary institution.
Eligibility: Applicant must be U.S. citizen.
Basis for selection: Major/career interest in communications. Applicant must demonstrate financial need, high academic achievement, leadership and service orientation.
Application requirements: Interview, recommendations, essay, transcript, proof of eligibility. Resume.
Additional information: Minimum 3.2 GPA. Applicant must be majoring in a communications-related field or a high school senior intending to declare a major in a communications-related

field. Must be attending school in New York City or be a resident of New York, New Jersey, Connecticut, or Pennsylvania. Finalists will be required to attend an in-person interview in New York City in February. Visit Website for application and additional requirements.

Amount of award:	$2,500-$10,000
Number of awards:	18
Number of applicants:	500
Application deadline:	January 30
Notification begins:	April 1
Total amount awarded:	$100,000

Contact:
New York Women in Communications Foundation Scholarship Program
355 Lexington Avenue, 15th Floor
New York, NY 10017-6603
Web: www.nywici.org

Nisei Student Relocation Commemorative Fund

Nisei Student Relocation Commemorative Fund

Type of award: Scholarship.
Intended use: For freshman study at vocational, 2-year or 4-year institution in United States.
Eligibility: Applicant must be Southeast Asian (Vietnamese, Cambodian, Hmong, Laotian, Amerasian) refugee or immigrant. Applicant must be high school senior.
Basis for selection: Applicant must demonstrate financial need and high academic achievement.
Application requirements: Recommendations, essay, transcript.
Additional information: Applicant must be high school senior living in city/area/region of the U.S. where scholarships are awarded, as determined annually by organization's board of directors. Location changes yearly; contact group for information. Number of awards varies.

Amount of award:	$1,000-$2,000
Number of awards:	30
Number of applicants:	80
Total amount awarded:	$37,500

Contact:
Nisei Student Relocation Commemorative Fund
c/o Y. Kobayashi or J. Hibino
19 Scenic Drive
Portland, CT 06480
Phone: 860-342-1731
Web: www.nsrcfund.org

NMIA Ohio

NMIA Ohio Scholarship Program

Type of award: Scholarship, renewable.
Intended use: For full-time junior, senior or graduate study at accredited 4-year or graduate institution in United States.
Eligibility: Applicant must be U.S. citizen residing in Ohio.

Basis for selection: Applicant must demonstrate high academic achievement.
Additional information: Applicant must be interested in a career in Intelligence. Funds awarded may be used for tuition, room, board, and/or laboratory fees and will be payable to the student's institution. Size and number of awards depends on funding; one to six awards will be given each year. Scholarships for full-time students will be greater than scholarships for part-time students. Applicant must not be relative of NMIA or scholarship committee members. Preference is given to students attending Ohio colleges and universities. The decision of the Scholarship Committee is final and not subject to external review.

Amount of award:	$500-$2,000
Number of awards:	6
Number of applicants:	7
Application deadline:	March 1
Notification begins:	April 1
Total amount awarded:	$3,000

Contact:
NMIA Ohio
c/o Deanne Otto
P.O. Box 341508
Beavercreek, OH 45434
Phone: 937-429-7601
Fax: 937-429-7602
Web: www.nmiaohio.org

Non Commissioned Officers Association

Non Commissioned Officers Association Scholarship for Children of Members

Type of award: Scholarship, renewable.
Intended use: For full-time undergraduate study in United States.
Application requirements: Transcript. Autobiography, ACT/SAT scores, and minimum 200-word essay on Americanism. Include two recommendation letters from school and one personal recommendation letter from adult who is not a relative.
Additional information: Applicant's parent must be member of Non Commissioned Officers Association.

Amount of award:	$900-$1,000
Number of awards:	11
Number of applicants:	200
Application deadline:	March 31
Notification begins:	June 1
Total amount awarded:	$21,000

Contact:
Non Commissioned Officers Association
P.O. Box 33790
San Antonio, TX 78265
Phone: 210-653-6161
Fax: 210-637-3337
Web: www.ncoausa.org

Non Commissioned Officers Association Scholarship for Spouses

Type of award: Scholarship, renewable.

Intended use: For full-time undergraduate study in United States.

Application requirements: Transcript. Copy of high school diploma or GED, brief biographical background, and certificates for any training courses completed. Letter of intent describing degree course of study, plans for completion of program, and a closing paragraph on "What a College Degree Means to Me."

Additional information: Must be spouse of member of Non Commissioned Officers Association. Recipient must apply for auxiliary membership in Non Commissioned Officers Association.

Amount of award:	$900
Number of awards:	4
Number of applicants:	30
Application deadline:	March 31
Notification begins:	June 1
Total amount awarded:	$7,200

Contact:
Non Commissioned Officers Association
P.O. Box 33790
San Antonio, TX 78265
Phone: 210-653-6161
Fax: 210-637-3337
Web: www.ncoausa.org

North American Limousin Foundation

Limi Boosters National Educational Grant

Type of award: Scholarship.

Intended use: For undergraduate study at vocational, 2-year or 4-year institution.

Basis for selection: Major/career interest in agriculture. Applicant must demonstrate financial need, high academic achievement, depth of character, leadership, patriotism, seriousness of purpose and service orientation.

Application requirements: Recommendations, proof of eligibility. Recent photo. One of the three recommendations must be from active NALF member other than relative or guardian, two must be from the following: school superintendent, school principal, minister, 4-H leader, FFA instructor, county agent, or teacher.

Additional information: Experience with Limousin cattle preferred. Proven excellence in Limousin activities as well as leadership skills demonstrated in NALJA, 4-H, and FFA. Must be NALF Junior member.

Amount of award:	$500-$750
Application deadline:	May 15

Contact:
North American Limousin Junior Association
Attn: Donna Etherton
8961 Oak Crest Road
Dawson, IL 62520-3301
Phone: 303-220-1693
Fax: 303-220-1884
Web: www.nalf.org

Limi Boosters Scholarship

Type of award: Scholarship.

Intended use: For undergraduate or graduate study at 2-year or 4-year institution.

Basis for selection: Applicant must demonstrate financial need, high academic achievement, depth of character, leadership, patriotism, seriousness of purpose and service orientation.

Application requirements: Transcript, proof of eligibility. Three recommendations, one of which must be from active NALF member other than relative or guardian.

Additional information: Must be NALF member and be active in 4H and FFA work. Must rank in top third of class.

Amount of award:	$500-$750
Number of awards:	2
Application deadline:	May 15
Total amount awarded:	$3,000

Contact:
North American Limousin Foundation
Attn: Donna Etherton
8961 Oak Crest Road
Dawson, IL 62520-3301
Phone: 303-220-1693
Fax: 303-220-1884
Web: www.nalf.org

North Carolina Community Colleges Foundation

North Carolina Community Colleges Wachovia Technical Scholarship

Type of award: Scholarship.

Intended use: For full-time sophomore study at vocational or 2-year institution.

Eligibility: Applicant must be residing in North Carolina.

Basis for selection: Applicant must demonstrate financial need and high academic achievement.

Additional information: Scholarships distributed through the 58 community colleges in the system; apply through financial aid office of institution where enrolled.

Amount of award:	$500

Contact:
North Carolina Community Colleges Foundation
200 West Jones Street
Raleigh, NC 27603
Phone: 919-807-7106
Fax: 919-807-7173
Web: www.ncccs.cc.nc.us

Rodney E. Powell Memorial Scholarship

Type of award: Scholarship.

Intended use: For full-time undergraduate study at 2-year institution. Designated institutions: Community colleges in Progress Energy's service area.

Eligibility: Applicant must be residing in North Carolina.

Basis for selection: Major/career interest in engineering, electrical/electronic; electronics or technology. Applicant must demonstrate financial need and high academic achievement.

Application requirements: Essay.

Additional information: Minimum 3.0 GPA. Scholarship for students of electronic technology. Applicant must be enrolled full-time or must intend to enroll as new student at designated institution. Number of awards varies.

Amount of award: $1,000
Number of awards: 1
Contact:
North Carolina Department of Community Colleges
Attn: Lee McCollum
410 S. Wilmington Street PEB 7
Raleigh, NC 27601
Phone: 919-546-7585
Fax: 919-546-7652
Web: www.ncccs.cc.nc.us

North Carolina Division of Veterans Affairs

North Carolina Scholarships for Children of War Veterans

Type of award: Scholarship, renewable.
Intended use: For undergraduate or graduate study at accredited postsecondary institution.
Eligibility: Applicant must be no older than 24. Applicant must be residing in North Carolina. Applicant must be dependent of disabled veteran, deceased veteran or POW/MIA who served in the Army, Air Force, Marines, Navy or Coast Guard. Parent must have served during a period of war.
Basis for selection: Applicant must demonstrate financial need.
Application requirements: Interview, transcript, proof of eligibility. Birth certificate.
Additional information: For state schools, award is tuition waiver plus maximum of $2,200 room and board allowance for up to four years. For private schools, award is up to $4,500 per year. Parent must have been North Carolina resident at time of enlistment or child must have been born in and reside permanently in North Carolina. See Website for deadline information.
Amount of award: Full tuition
Number of applicants: 555
Contact:
North Carolina Division of Veterans Affairs
1315 Mail Service Center
Albemarle Building, Suite 1065
Raleigh, NC 27699-1315
Web: www.doa.state.nc.us/vets/benefits-scholarships.htm

North Carolina Division of Vocational Rehabilitation Services

North Carolina Vocational Rehabilitation Award

Type of award: Scholarship, renewable.
Intended use: For full-time undergraduate study at accredited vocational, 2-year or 4-year institution.
Eligibility: Applicant must be physically challenged or learning disabled. Applicant must be residing in North Carolina.

Basis for selection: Applicant must demonstrate financial need.
Application requirements: Interview, proof of eligibility. Proof of mental, physical, or learning disability that is an impediment to employment.
Additional information: This program provides educational assistance for individuals who meet eligibility requirements and require training to reach their vocational goals.
Amount of award: $2,670
Contact:
North Carolina Division of Vocational Rehabilitation Services
2801 Mail Service Center
Raleigh, NC 27699-2801
Phone: 919-855-3500
Fax: 919-715-0616
Web: dvr.dhhs.state.nc.us

North Carolina State Board of Refrigeration Examiners

North Carolina State Board of Refrigeration Examiners Scholarship

Type of award: Scholarship.
Intended use: For undergraduate study at 2-year institution.
Eligibility: Applicant must be residing in North Carolina.
Basis for selection: Major/career interest in air conditioning/heating/refrigeration technology. Applicant must demonstrate financial need and high academic achievement.
Application requirements: Essay.
Additional information: Number of awards varies. Must enroll in Associate of Applied Science degree of study in commercial refrigeration or HVAC/R technology.
Number of awards: 2
Application deadline: February 1
Contact:
North Carolina State Board of Refrigeration Examiners
Suite 208
893 Highway 70 W
Garner, NC 27529
Phone: 919-779-4711
Web: www.refrigerationboard.org/wp/

North Carolina State Education Assistance Authority

GlaxoSmithKline Opportunity Scholarship

Type of award: Scholarship.
Intended use: For undergraduate study at vocational, 2-year or 4-year institution in United States.
Eligibility: Applicant must be U.S. citizen residing in North Carolina.
Basis for selection: Applicant must demonstrate depth of character and seriousness of purpose.

Additional information: Applicant must have been a permanent resident of Durham, Orange, or Wake county for one year prior to application. GlaxoSmithKline and Triangle Community Foundation employees or their families not eligible. Visit Website for application.

Amount of award:	$5,000
Number of awards:	5
Application deadline:	March 15

Contact:
Triangle Community Foundation Scholarship Program
Attn: Libby Long
324 Blackwell Street, Suite 1220
Durham, NC 27701
Phone: 919-474-8370
Fax: 919-941-9208
Web: www.trianglecf.org

Golden LEAF Scholars Program - Two-Year Colleges

Type of award: Scholarship.
Intended use: For undergraduate study at 2-year institution. Designated institutions: Member institutions of North Carolina Community College system.
Eligibility: Applicant must be residing in North Carolina.
Basis for selection: Applicant must demonstrate financial need, high academic achievement, depth of character, leadership and service orientation.
Application requirements: Disclosure of other financial aid awards.
Additional information: Applicant must demonstrate need under federal TRIO formula. Award is up to $750 per semester (including summer) for curriculum students; up to $250 per semester for occupational education students. Finalist will undergo merit competition and be judged on academics, leadership, community service, and the effect of the tobacco industry's and economy's decline on his/her family. Must be permanent resident of one of 73 eligible counties. Visit Website for more information. Contact financial aid office for application.

Amount of award:	$500-$1,500

Contact:
Contact financial aid office at local community college.
Phone: 800-700-1775 ext. 650
Fax: 919-549-8481
Web: www.cfnc.org

Golden LEAF Scholarship - Four-Year University Program

Type of award: Scholarship, renewable.
Intended use: For undergraduate study at 4-year institution. Designated institutions: Public universities.
Eligibility: Applicant must be high school senior. Applicant must be residing in North Carolina.
Basis for selection: Applicant must demonstrate financial need.
Application requirements: FAFSA.
Additional information: Must be incoming freshman, transfer student from a North Carolina community college, or previous recipient applying for renewal. New applicants must be permanent resident of economically distressed and/or tobacco-dependent rural county. Recipients of other aid amounting to 75 percent or more of total education costs will be given low priority. Visit Website for application and more information.

Amount of award:	$3,000
Number of awards:	580
Application deadline:	March 15

Contact:
North Carolina State Education Assistance Authority
P.O. Box 14103
Research Triangle Park, NC 27709
Phone: 800-700-1775 ext. 650
Web: www.ncseaa.edu

Jagannathan Scholarship

Type of award: Scholarship, renewable.
Intended use: For full-time freshman study at 4-year institution in United States. Designated institutions: Constituent institutions of the University of North Carolina.
Eligibility: Applicant must be high school senior. Applicant must be U.S. citizen or permanent resident residing in North Carolina.
Basis for selection: Applicant must demonstrate financial need, high academic achievement and leadership.
Application requirements: Proof of eligibility, nomination by high school guidance counselor, financial office of UNC institution, or Tolaram Polymers, Cookson Fibers, or related company. SAT scores, College Scholarship Service's PROFILE (register and file by February 8), and documented proof of financial need.
Additional information: Special consideration given to students whose parents are employees of Tolaram Polymers, Cookson Fibers, or related companies. Applications available at all North Carolina public high schools. Check Website for specific details.

Amount of award:	$3,500
Number of awards:	4
Number of applicants:	4
Notification begins:	May 1
Total amount awarded:	$14,000

Contact:
North Carolina State Education Assistance Authority
P.O. Box 14103
Research Triangle Park, NC 27709-3663
Phone: 800-700-1775
Web: www.cfnc.org/jag

Latino Diamante Scholarship Fund

Type of award: Scholarship.
Intended use: For freshman or sophomore study at postsecondary institution. Designated institutions: North Carolina institutions.
Eligibility: Applicant must be Hispanic American. Applicant must be residing in North Carolina.
Application requirements: Recommendations, essay, transcript.
Additional information: Minimum 2.5 GPA. Visit Website for application and more information.

Amount of award:	$750
Number of awards:	2
Application deadline:	August 15
Notification begins:	September 15

Contact:
Diamante, Inc.
315 North Academy Street
Cary, NC 27513
Phone: 919-852-0075
Web: www.cfnc.org

NC Sheriff's Association Criminal Justice Scholarship

Type of award: Scholarship.
Intended use: For full-time undergraduate study in United States. Designated institutions: Appalachian State University, East Carolina University, Elizabeth City State University, Fayetteville State University, North Carolina Central University, North Carolina State University, the University of North Carolina at Charlotte, the University of North Carolina at Pembroke, the University of North Carolina at Wilmington, Western Carolina University.
Eligibility: Applicant must be residing in North Carolina.
Basis for selection: Major/career interest in criminal justice/law enforcement.
Application requirements: Recommendations, essay, transcript.
Additional information: Application available at financial aid offices of eligible institutions. Application and supplemental material should be submitted to sheriff of county where applicant resides. First priority given to child of sheriff/law enforcement officer killed in the line of duty; second priority given to child of retired or deceased sheriff/law enforcement officer; third priority given to criminal justice students.

Amount of award:	$2,000
Number of awards:	10
Number of applicants:	50
Total amount awarded:	$20,000

Contact:
North Carolina State Education Assistance Authority
P.O. Box 14103
Research Triangle Park, NC 27709-3663
Phone: 800-700-1775 ext. 650
Web: www.ncseaa.edu

North Carolina Aubrey Lee Brooks Scholarship

Type of award: Scholarship, renewable.
Intended use: For full-time undergraduate study at 4-year institution in United States. Designated institutions: North Carolina State University, University of North Carolina at Chapel Hill, University of North Carolina at Greensboro.
Eligibility: Applicant must be high school senior. Applicant must be U.S. citizen residing in North Carolina.
Basis for selection: Applicant must demonstrate financial need, depth of character, leadership and seriousness of purpose.
Application requirements: Proof of eligibility.
Additional information: Award amount varies; maximum $8,600 per year, plus one-time computer award up to $3,000. Scholarship pays additional amounts for approved summer study or internships. Applications available through high school. Applicants must reside and attend high school in one of the following counties: Alamance, Bertie, Caswell, Durham, Forsyth, Granville, Guilford, Orange, Person, Rockingham, Stokes, Surry, Swain, or Warren. One additional scholarship awarded to student from cities of Greensboro and High Point and to eligible senior at North Carolina School of Science and Mathematics.

Amount of award:	$8,600
Number of awards:	17
Application deadline:	February 1

Contact:
North Carolina State Education Assistance Authority
P.O. Box 14103
Research Triangle Park, NC 27709-3663
Phone: 800-700-1775 ext. 650
Web: www.cfnc.org

North Carolina Legislative Tuition Grant

Type of award: Scholarship, renewable.
Intended use: For undergraduate study at accredited 2-year or 4-year institution. Designated institutions: Eligible North Carolina private institutions.
Eligibility: Applicant must be U.S. citizen or permanent resident residing in North Carolina.
Additional information: Award not applicable for theology, divinity, or religious education programs. Award amount determined by North Carolina General Assembly. Applications available from eligible institutions' financial aid offices.

Amount of award:	$1,950
Number of awards:	24,078
Total amount awarded:	$43,911,790

Contact:
North Carolina State Education Assistance Authority
P.O. Box 14103
Research Triangle Park, NC 27709-3663
Phone: 800-700-1775 ext. 650
Web: www.cfnc.org

North Carolina Student Incentive Grant

Type of award: Scholarship, renewable.
Intended use: For full-time undergraduate study at postsecondary institution. Designated institutions: Approved institutions in North Carolina.
Eligibility: Applicant must be U.S. citizen residing in North Carolina.
Basis for selection: Applicant must demonstrate financial need.

Amount of award:	$700
Number of awards:	8,110
Number of applicants:	395,913
Application deadline:	March 15
Total amount awarded:	$5,101,881

Contact:
North Carolina State Education Assistance Authority
P.O. Box 14103
Research Triangle Park, NC 27709-3663
Phone: 800-700-1775
Web: www.cfnc.org

State Contractual Scholarship Fund

Type of award: Scholarship, renewable.
Intended use: For undergraduate study at accredited 2-year or 4-year institution. Designated institutions: Private institutions in North Carolina.
Eligibility: Applicant must be U.S. citizen or permanent resident residing in North Carolina.
Basis for selection: Applicant must demonstrate financial need.
Application requirements: Proof of eligibility.
Additional information: Theology and divinity students not eligible. Contact school's financial aid office or NCSEAA for more information. Must be enrolled in degree-seeking program.

394

Award amount varies; check with private institution's financial aid office for current award amount.

Contact:
North Carolina State Education Assistance Authority
P.O. Box 14103
Research Triangle Park, NC 27709-3663
Phone: 800-700-1775 ext. 650
Web: www.cfnc.org

Teacher Assistant Scholarship Fund

Type of award: Scholarship, renewable.
Intended use: For undergraduate study at 2-year or 4-year institution in United States. Designated institutions: North Carolina institutions offering teacher licensure programs (visit Website for list).
Eligibility: Applicant must be residing in North Carolina.
Basis for selection: Major/career interest in education; education, early childhood; education, special or education, teacher. Applicant must demonstrate financial need.
Application requirements: FAFSA.
Additional information: Applicant must be full-time teacher assistant for at least one year at public or federal school in North Carolina. Must be enrolled in program leading toward initial teacher licensure. Minimum 3.0 GPA. Must maintain minimum 2.8 GPA to renew. Students at two-year schools receive up to $1,800 per year; those at four-year schools receive up to $3,600 per year. Students cannot receive more than $25,200 in total aid. Must not be in default on a student loan.

Amount of award:	$600-$3,600
Application deadline:	April 15

Contact:
North Carolina State Education Assistance Authority
P.O. Box 14103
Research Triangle Park, NC 27709-3663
Phone: 800-700-1775 ext. 650
Web: www.cfnc.org

North Dakota University System

North Dakota Indian Scholarship Program

Type of award: Scholarship, renewable.
Intended use: For full-time undergraduate or graduate study at vocational, 2-year or 4-year institution.
Eligibility: Applicant must be American Indian. Must be enrolled member of Indian tribe. Applicant must be U.S. citizen residing in North Dakota.
Basis for selection: Applicant must demonstrate financial need.
Application requirements: Transcript, proof of eligibility. Budget completed by financial aid officer at institution student is attending/will attend.
Additional information: Minimum 2.0 GPA. Priority given to undergraduates with cumulative 3.5 GPA or higher.

Amount of award:	$800-$2,000
Number of awards:	175
Number of applicants:	400
Application deadline:	July 15
Total amount awarded:	$102,000

Contact:
North Dakota University System, Indian Scholarship Program
BSC Horizon Building
1815 Schaefer Street, Suite 202
Bismarck, ND 58501
Phone: 701-224-2497
Web: www.ndus.nodak.edu

North Dakota Scholars Program

Type of award: Scholarship, renewable.
Intended use: For full-time undergraduate study at postsecondary institution.
Eligibility: Applicant must be high school senior. Applicant must be residing in North Dakota.
Basis for selection: Applicant must demonstrate high academic achievement.
Application requirements: Proof of eligibility.
Additional information: Applicant must take ACT between October and June of junior year and score in upper five percentile of all North Dakota ACT test-takers. Numeric sum of English, math, reading, and science reasoning scores may be considered. Award is full-tuition scholarship for students attending ND's public and tribal colleges; equal to NDSU/UND tuition for students attending private institutions. Recipients must maintain 3.5 GPA for renewal. Contact sponsor for more information and deadline.

Number of awards:	50
Number of applicants:	400

Contact:
North Dakota University System Student Financial Assistance Program
600 East Boulevard
Dept. 215
Bismarck, ND 58505-0230
Phone: 701-328-4114
Web: www.ndus.edu

North Dakota State Student Incentive Grant

Type of award: Scholarship, renewable.
Intended use: For full-time undergraduate study at vocational, 2-year or 4-year institution. Designated institutions: North Dakota colleges.
Eligibility: Applicant must be U.S. citizen or permanent resident residing in North Dakota.
Basis for selection: Applicant must demonstrate financial need.
Application requirements: Proof of eligibility. FAFSA.
Additional information: Application automatic with FAFSA. Applicant must be first-time undergraduate student. Must not be in default on any federal loans or owe refund on any Title IV grants or loans.

Amount of award:	$600-$1,000
Number of awards:	7,900
Number of applicants:	28,000
Application deadline:	March 15
Total amount awarded:	$2,220,000

Contact:
North Dakota University System Student Financial Assistance Program
600 East Boulevard
Dept. 215
Bismarck, ND 58505-0230
Phone: 701-328-4114
Web: www.ndus.edu

Northern Cheyenne Tribal Education Department

Northern Cheyenne Higher Education Program

Type of award: Scholarship, renewable.
Intended use: For undergraduate study at postsecondary institution.
Eligibility: Applicant must be American Indian. Must be enrolled with Northern Cheyenne Tribe. Applicant must be U.S. citizen.
Basis for selection: Applicant must demonstrate financial need.
Application requirements: Recommendations, essay, transcript, proof of eligibility. FAFSA.
Additional information: Award amount varies, depends on unmet need. Deadlines: October 1 for spring, April 1 for summer, and March 1 for fall.

Amount of award:	$175-$6,000
Number of awards:	84
Number of applicants:	62
Application deadline:	March 1, April 1
Total amount awarded:	$282,000

Contact:
Northern Cheyenne Tribal Education Department
Attn: Norma Bixby
Box 307
Lame Deer, MT 59043
Phone: 406-477-6602
Fax: 406-477-8150
Web: www.cheyennenation.com

Northwest Danish Association

The Kaj Christensen Scholarship for Vocational Training

Type of award: Scholarship, renewable.
Intended use: For undergraduate or graduate study at postsecondary institution in or outside United States.
Eligibility: Applicant must be no older than 17. Applicant must be U.S. citizen or permanent resident.
Basis for selection: Applicant must demonstrate depth of character and service orientation.
Application requirements: Recommendations, transcript. Personal essay on educational goals, two references.
Additional information: Must be member of Northwest Danish Foundation. Must demonstrate some connection to Denmark via life experience, travel, heritage, etc. Must be resident of Oregon or Washington, or be enrolled in accredited school in those states. Must have interest in vocational training.

Amount of award:	$500
Number of awards:	5
Number of applicants:	40
Application deadline:	March 31
Notification begins:	May 1

Contact:
Northwest Danish Association
1833 North 105th Street
Suite 203
Seattle, WA 98133-8973
Phone: 800-564-7736
Fax: 206-729-6997
Web: www.northwestdanishfoundation.org

Northwest Danish Association Scholarship

Type of award: Scholarship.
Intended use: For undergraduate or graduate study at postsecondary institution in United States.
Additional information: Must be of Danish descent or married to someone of Danish descent, who actively participates in Danish community. Consideration given to those of non-Danish descent who show exceptional involvment with Danish community. Must either reside or attend university in Oregon or Washington. Those training for artistic careers also considered.

Application deadline:	March 31

Contact:
Northwest Danish Association
1833 North 105th Street
Suite 203
Seattle, WA 98133
Phone: 206-523-3263
Fax: 206-729-6997
Web: www.northwestdanishfoundation.org

Scan/Design Foundation by Inger and Jens Bruun Scholarship for Study in Denmark

Type of award: Scholarship.
Intended use: For undergraduate study at postsecondary institution.
Eligibility: Applicant must be at least 18.
Application requirements: Essay on why you wish to study in Denmark, written statement on what has prepared you to take full advantage of your study experience, two references.
Additional information: Open to current residents of Washington or Oregon, or students currently registered in a school, university, or institution of learning in those states, who wish to study in Denmark.

Amount of award:	$5,000
Number of awards:	1
Application deadline:	March 31

Contact:
Northwest Danish Association
1833 North 105 Street
Suite 203
Seattle, WA 98133-8973
Phone: 800-564-7736
Fax: 206-729-6997
Web: www.northwestdanishfoundation.org

OCA

OCA-AXA Achievement Scholarships

Type of award: Scholarship.
Intended use: For freshman study at postsecondary institution.
Eligibility: Applicant must be Asian American or Native Hawaiian/Pacific Islander. Applicant must be U.S. citizen or permanent resident.
Basis for selection: Applicant must demonstrate high academic achievement, leadership and service orientation.
Application requirements: Recommendations, essay. Resume.
Additional information: Minimum 3.0 GPA. Number of awards varies. Visit Website for more information and deadline.

Amount of award:	$2,000
Total amount awarded:	$20,000

Contact:
OCA
1322 18th Street, NW
Washington, DC 20036
Phone: 202-223-5500
Fax: 202-296-0540
Web: www.ocanational.org

OCA/UPS Foundation Gold Mountain College Scholarship

Type of award: Scholarship.
Intended use: For full-time freshman study in United States.
Eligibility: Applicant must be Asian American or Native Hawaiian/Pacific Islander. Applicant must be U.S. citizen or permanent resident.
Basis for selection: Applicant must demonstrate financial need.
Application requirements: Recommendations, essay. Resume, FAFSA.
Additional information: Minimum 3.0 GPA. Applicant must be Asian Pacific American and first person in family to go to college in the United States. Visit Website for deadline.

Amount of award:	$2,000
Number of awards:	12
Number of applicants:	250
Total amount awarded:	$24,000

Contact:
OCA
1322 18th Street, NW
Washington, DC 20036
Phone: 202-223-5500
Fax: 202-296-0540
Web: www.ocanational.org

OCA/Verizon Foundation College Scholarship

Type of award: Scholarship.
Intended use: For full-time sophomore, junior or senior study at 4-year institution.
Eligibility: Applicant must be Asian American. Applicant must be U.S. citizen or permanent resident.
Basis for selection: Major/career interest in accounting; business/management/administration; electronics; engineering; education; engineering, electrical/electronic; finance/banking; human resources; marketing or engineering, mechanical. Applicant must demonstrate financial need.
Application requirements: Recommendations, essay. FAFSA.
Additional information: Minimum 3.0 GPA. Visit Website for full list of eligible majors and deadline.

Amount of award:	$2,000
Number of awards:	10
Number of applicants:	10
Total amount awarded:	$20,000

Contact:
OCA
1322 18th Street, NW
Washington, DC 20036
Phone: 202-223-5500
Fax: 202-296-0540
Web: www.ocanational.org

Office of Vocational and Educational Services for Individuals with Disabilities

New York State Readers Aid Program

Type of award: Scholarship, renewable.
Intended use: For undergraduate, master's or doctoral study at 2-year, 4-year or graduate institution.
Eligibility: Applicant must be visually impaired or hearing impaired. Applicant must be residing in New York.
Application requirements: Interview, proof of eligibility.
Additional information: Applicant must be legally blind or deaf. Number of awards varies. Applications available at degree-granting institutions. Award provides funds for note-takers, readers, or interpreters. Applicant may be attending out-of-state institution.

Amount of award:	$800
Number of applicants:	411
Application deadline:	March 15, June 30
Total amount awarded:	$300,000

Contact:
Vocational and Educational Services for People with Disabilities
Readers Aid Program Att: Bryan Baszczuk
One Commerce Plaza, Room 1605
Albany, NY 12234
Phone: 518-474-2925
Fax: 518-473-6073
Web: www.vesid.nysed.gov

Ohio Board of Regents

Ohio College Opportunity Grant

Type of award: Scholarship, renewable.
Intended use: For freshman study at accredited 2-year or 4-year institution. Designated institutions: Ohio and select Pennsylvania schools.
Eligibility: Applicant must be residing in Ohio.

Basis for selection: Applicant must demonstrate financial need.

Application requirements: FAFSA.

Additional information: Must be pursuing associates degree, bachelors degree, or nursing diploma. Amount of award varies. Visit Website for more information.

Number of awards:	77,481
Application deadline:	October 1
Total amount awarded:	$157,446,201

Contact:
Ohio Board of Regents
30 E. Broad Street
36th Floor
Columbus, OH 43215-3414
Phone: 888-833-1133
Fax: 614-752-5903
Web: www.regents.ohio.gov/sgs/ocog/

Ohio Safety Officers College Memorial Fund

Type of award: Scholarship, renewable.

Intended use: For undergraduate study at accredited 2-year or 4-year institution. Designated institutions: Ohio institutions.

Eligibility: Applicant must be U.S. citizen or permanent resident residing in Ohio. Applicant's parent must have been killed or disabled in work-related accident as firefighter, police officer or public safety officer.

Application requirements: Proof of eligibility.

Additional information: Applicant whose spouse was killed in the line of duty as a firefighter, police officer, or public safety officer also eligible. Visit Website for more information.

Number of applicants:	55
Total amount awarded:	$319,947

Contact:
Ohio Board of Regents
30 E. Broad Street
36th Floor
Columbus, OH 43215-3414
Phone: 888-833-1133
Fax: 614-752-5903
Web: www.regents.ohio.gov/sgs/oso/

Ohio War Orphans Scholarship

Type of award: Scholarship, renewable.

Intended use: For full-time undergraduate study at accredited 2-year or 4-year institution. Designated institutions: Ohio institutions.

Eligibility: Applicant must be at least 16. Applicant must be U.S. citizen or permanent resident residing in Ohio. Applicant must be dependent of veteran, disabled veteran, deceased veteran or POW/MIA. Child of disabled veteran who has combined disability rating of 60% or more.

Application requirements: Proof of eligibility.

Additional information: Visit Website for more information.

Number of awards:	812
Application deadline:	July 1
Notification begins:	August 1
Total amount awarded:	$4,210,157

Contact:
Ohio Board of Regents
30 E. Broad Street
6th Floor
Columbus, OH 43215-3414
Phone: 888-833-1133
Fax: 614-752-5903
Web: www.regents.ohio.gov/sgs/war_orphans

Ohio National Guard

Ohio National Guard Scholarship Program

Type of award: Scholarship, renewable.

Intended use: For undergraduate study at accredited postsecondary institution. Designated institutions: Degree-granting institutions in Ohio approved by Ohio Board of Regents.

Eligibility: Applicant must be residing in Ohio. Applicant must be in military service in the Reserves/National Guard. Must enlist, re-enlist, or extend current enlistment to equal six years with Ohio National Guard. Must remain in good standing.

Application requirements: Proof of eligibility.

Additional information: Minimum six credit hours per semester or quarter. Award covers 100 percent of instructional and general fees for state-assisted institutions; average of state-assisted university fees for proprietary institutions. Application deadlines: July 1 (fall), November 1 (winter quarter/spring semester), February 1 (spring quarter), April 1 (summer). Must not already possess bachelor's degree. Lifetime maximum of 12 full-time quarters or eight full-time semesters. Number of awards varies.

Amount of award:	Full tuition
Number of awards:	6,645
Number of applicants:	5,000

Contact:
Adjutant General's Department
Ohio National Guard Scholarship Program
2825 West Dublin Granville Road
Columbus, OH 43235
Phone: 888-400-6484 or 614-336-7032
Fax: 614-336-7318
Web: www.ongsp.org

Ohio Newspapers Foundation

Harold K. Douthit Scholarship

Type of award: Scholarship.

Intended use: For sophomore, junior or senior study at postsecondary institution. Designated institutions: Ohio institutions.

Eligibility: Applicant must be U.S. citizen residing in Ohio.

Basis for selection: Major/career interest in communications or journalism. Applicant must demonstrate financial need and high academic achievement.

Application requirements: Essay, transcript. Two letters of recommendation from faculty members.

Additional information: Applicant must be resident of one of the following Ohio counties: Cuyahoga, Lorain, Huron, Erie, Wood, Geauga, Sandusky, Ottawa, or Lucas. Minimum 3.0 GPA. Student may provide up to two published writing samples.

Amount of award:	$1,500
Number of awards:	1
Number of applicants:	14
Application deadline:	March 31
Notification begins:	May 15
Total amount awarded:	$1,500

Contact:
Ohio Newspapers Foundation Douthit Scholarship
1335 Dublin Road
Suite 216-B
Columbus, OH 43215
Phone: 614-486-6677
Web: www.ohionews.org

Ohio Newspapers Minority Scholarship

Type of award: Scholarship.
Intended use: For full-time freshman study at postsecondary institution. Designated institutions: Ohio institutions.
Eligibility: Applicant must be Asian American, African American, Hispanic American or American Indian. Applicant must be high school senior. Applicant must be residing in Ohio.
Basis for selection: Major/career interest in journalism. Applicant must demonstrate high academic achievement.
Application requirements: Recommendations, essay, transcript, proof of eligibility. Up to two writing samples or published articles.
Additional information: Minimum 2.5 GPA.

Amount of award:	$1,500
Number of awards:	1
Number of applicants:	8
Application deadline:	March 31
Notification begins:	May 15
Total amount awarded:	$4,500

Contact:
Ohio Newspapers Foundation Minority Scholarship
1335 Dublin Road
Suite 216-B
Columbus, OH 43215
Phone: 614-486-6677
Web: www.ohionews.org

Ohio Newspapers Women's Scholarship

Type of award: Scholarship.
Intended use: For junior or senior study at postsecondary institution. Designated institutions: Ohio institutions.
Eligibility: Applicant must be residing in Ohio.
Basis for selection: Major/career interest in communications or journalism.
Application requirements: Recommendations, transcript. Three or four newspaper clippings demonstrating applicant's writing skills. Answers to questions: Who or what was your inspiration to get involved in the field of journalism and why did you select print journalism as your area of interest? Why do you need a scholarship? What do you think qualifies you for a scholarship? What do you hope to accomplish during your career as a professional journalist?
Additional information: Applicants may be male or female.

Amount of award:	$1,500
Number of awards:	1
Application deadline:	March 31

Contact:
Ohio Newspapers Foundation Women's Scholarship
1335 Dublin Road
Suite 216-B
Columbus, OH 43215
Phone: 614-486-6677
Web: www.ohionews.org

University Journalism Scholarship

Type of award: Scholarship.
Intended use: For sophomore, junior or senior study at 2-year or 4-year institution. Designated institutions: Ohio institutions.
Eligibility: Applicant must be residing in Ohio.
Basis for selection: Major/career interest in communications or journalism.
Application requirements: Essay, transcript. Two letters of recommendation from faculty members and published writing samples.
Additional information: Minimum 2.5 GPA. Preference given to applicants demonstrating career commitment to newspaper journalism.

Amount of award:	$1,500
Number of awards:	3
Number of applicants:	6
Application deadline:	March 31
Notification begins:	May 15

Contact:
Ohio Newspaper Foundation University Journalism Scholarship
1335 Dublin Road
Suite 216-B
Columbus, OH 43215
Phone: 614-486-6677
Web: www.ohionews.org

Oklahoma Engineering Foundation

Oklahoma Engineering Foundation Scholarship

Type of award: Scholarship, renewable.
Intended use: For undergraduate study at accredited 4-year institution in United States. Designated institutions: Oklahoma Christian University of Science & Arts, Oklahoma State University, University of Oklahoma, University of Central Oklahoma, Oral Roberts University, University of Tulsa.
Eligibility: Applicant must be high school senior. Applicant must be U.S. citizen residing in Oklahoma.
Basis for selection: Major/career interest in engineering. Applicant must demonstrate depth of character, leadership and service orientation.
Application requirements: Interview, essay, transcript.
Additional information: Minimum 3.0 GPA, ACT composite score of 24-29, and ACT Math component score of 28 or above. Applicants eligible for National Merit or Oklahoma Regents Scholarships not eligible for this award. Visit Website for pre-qualification form and application deadline.

Amount of award:	$1,000
Number of awards:	12
Number of applicants:	52
Total amount awarded:	$12,000

Contact:
Oklahoma Engineering Foundation Executive Director
201 Northeast 27th Street
Room 125
Oklahoma City, OK 73105
Phone: 405-528-1435
Web: www.ospe.org

Oklahoma State Department of Education Professional Services Division

Robert C. Byrd Honors Scholarship Program

Type of award: Scholarship, renewable.
Intended use: For full-time undergraduate study at postsecondary institution.
Eligibility: Applicant must be high school senior. Applicant must be U.S. citizen or permanent resident residing in Oklahoma.
Basis for selection: Applicant must demonstrate high academic achievement.
Application requirements: Recommendations, essay, transcript.
Additional information: Students receive award for first year of study at eligible postsecondary institutions. Scholarships renewable up to three additional years of study provided students continue to meet eligibility requirements as defined by the institution they are attending. Award amount varies based on funding. Deadlines vary; check Website for details. Must have minimum ACT composite score of 32 and/or minimum SAT combined score of 2130 or GED score of 700.

Application deadline: April 11
Contact:
Oklahoma State Department of Education
Oliver Hodge Building
2500 N. Lincoln Boulevard, Room 212
Oklahoma City, OK 73105-4599
Phone: 405-521-2062
Web: www.sde.state.ok.us

Oklahoma State Regents for Higher Education

Academic Scholars Program

Type of award: Scholarship, renewable.
Intended use: For full-time undergraduate study at postsecondary institution. Designated institutions: Oklahoma institutions.
Eligibility: Applicant must be residing in Oklahoma.

Basis for selection: Applicant must demonstrate high academic achievement.
Application requirements: Transcript, proof of eligibility.
Additional information: Applicant must be National Merit Scholar or Finalist; Presidential Scholar; have SAT/ACT in 99.5 percentile for Oklahoma residents. Application deadline varies.

Amount of award: $1,800-$5,500
Contact:
Oklahoma State Regents for Higher Education
P.O. Box 108850
Oklahoma City, OK 73101-8850
Phone: 800-858-1840
Fax: 405-225-9230
Web: www.okhighered.org

Future Teachers Scholarship

Type of award: Scholarship, renewable.
Intended use: For undergraduate or graduate study at accredited 2-year or 4-year institution.
Eligibility: Applicant must be U.S. citizen or permanent resident residing in Oklahoma.
Basis for selection: Major/career interest in education, early childhood or education. Applicant must demonstrate high academic achievement.
Application requirements: Essay, transcript, proof of eligibility, nomination by college. SAT/ACT scores.
Additional information: Application deadline varies; visit Website for more information. Priority given to full-time students. Minimum 2.5 GPA. Recipient must agree to teach in shortage area (Math, Science, English, Foreign Language, Early Childhood Education, Counseling, Library Media, Speech Language Pathologist) in Oklahoma public schools for at least three years after graduation and licensure. Must apply for renewal.

Amount of award: $500-$1,500
Number of awards: 85
Contact:
Oklahoma State Regents for Higher Education
P.O. Box 108850
Oklahoma City, OK 73101-8850
Phone: 800-858-1840
Fax: 405-225-9230
Web: www.okhighered.org

Heartland Scholarship Fund

Type of award: Scholarship.
Intended use: For full-time undergraduate study at accredited 2-year or 4-year institution.
Eligibility: Applicant must be residing in Oklahoma.
Application requirements: Proof of eligibility.
Additional information: Applicant must be dependent child of individual killed as a result of the April 19, 1995 bombing of Alfred P. Murrah Federal Building in Oklahoma City. Award applicable to cost of tuition, fees, books, and room and board. For details, contact Oklahoma State Regents for Higher Education.

Amount of award: $3,500-$5,500
Contact:
Oklahoma State Regents for Higher Education
P.O. Box 108850
Oklahoma City, OK 73101-8850
Phone: 800-858-1840
Fax: 405-225-9230
Web: www.okhighered.org

Independent Living Act (Department of Human Services Tuition Waiver)

Type of award: Scholarship.
Intended use: For undergraduate study at vocational, 2-year or 4-year institution.
Eligibility: Applicant must be no older than 21. Applicant must be residing in Oklahoma.
Application requirements: Proof of eligibility.
Additional information: Awards tuition waivers to eligible individuals who have been or are in the Oklahoma Department of Human Services foster care program. Applicant must have been in DHS custody for at least nine months between the ages of 16 and 18. Within last three years, applicant must have graduated from State Board of Education-accredited high school, the Oklahoma School of Science and Mathematics, or approved school in a bordering state, or have attained GED.
Amount of award: Full tuition
Contact:
Oklahoma State Regents for Higher Education
P.O. Box 108850
Oklahoma City, OK 73101-8850
Phone: 800-858-1840
Fax: 405-225-9230
Web: www.okhighered.org

National Guard Tuition Waiver

Type of award: Scholarship.
Intended use: For undergraduate study at 2-year or 4-year institution.
Eligibility: Applicant must be residing in Oklahoma. Applicant must be bona fide member in good standing of Oklahoma National Guard.
Application requirements: Proof of eligibility. Statement of Understanding and Certificate of Basic Eligibility.
Additional information: Applicant must be enrolled in degree-granting program. Applicant cannot currently have a bachelor's or graduate degree. Waivers not awarded for certificate-granting courses, continuing education courses, or career technology courses.
Amount of award: Full tuition
Contact:
Oklahoma National Guard
P.O. Box 108850
Oklahoma City, OK 73101-8850
Phone: 800-858-1840 or 800-464-8273
Fax: 405-225-9230
Web: www.okhighered.org or www.ok.ngb.army.mil

Oklahoma Tuition Aid Grant

Type of award: Scholarship, renewable.
Intended use: For undergraduate study at vocational, 2-year or 4-year institution. Designated institutions: Approved Oklahoma institutions.
Eligibility: Applicant must be residing in Oklahoma.
Basis for selection: Applicant must demonstrate financial need.
Application requirements: Proof of eligibility. FAFSA.
Additional information: Award is $1,000 for public schools and $1,300 for private non-profit institutions. For best consideration, apply as soon as possible after January 1.

Amount of award: $1,000-$1,300
Number of awards: 26,000
Number of applicants: 50,000
Total amount awarded: $19,750,576
Contact:
Oklahoma Tuition Aid Grant Program
P.O. Box 108850
Oklahoma City, OK 73101-8850
Phone: 877-662-6231
Fax: 405-225-9230
Web: www.okhighered.org

Oklahoma's Promise - Oklahoma Higher Learning Access Program

Type of award: Scholarship.
Intended use: For undergraduate study at 2-year or 4-year institution.
Eligibility: Applicant must be residing in Oklahoma.
Basis for selection: Applicant must demonstrate financial need, high academic achievement and seriousness of purpose.
Additional information: Scholarship for students in families earning less than $50,000 per year. Student must enroll in the program in eighth, ninth, or tenth grade and demonstrate commitment to academic success in high school; homeschooled students must be age 13, 14, or 15. Deadline for homeschooled students must occur before student's 16th birthday. Minimum 2.5 GPA. Award amount varies; full tuition at public institutions or portion of tuition at private institutions in OK. See counselor or visit Website for details.
Number of awards: 19,000
Number of applicants: 9,334
Application deadline: June 30
Total amount awarded: $43,000,000
Contact:
Oklahoma State Regents for Higher Education
P.O. Box 108850
Oklahoma City, OK 73101-8850
Phone: 800-858-1840
Fax: 405-225-9230
Web: www.okpromise.org

Regional University Baccalaureate Scholarship

Type of award: Scholarship.
Intended use: For full-time undergraduate study at postsecondary institution. Designated institutions: Oklahoma regional universities.
Eligibility: Applicant must be residing in Oklahoma.
Basis for selection: Applicant must demonstrate high academic achievement.
Additional information: Must have ACT score of at least 30 or be National Merit Semifinalist or Commended Student. Award is $3,000 plus resident tuition waiver. Application deadlines vary by institution.
Amount of award: $3,000
Contact:
Oklahoma State Regents for Higher Education
P.O. Box 108850
Oklahoma City, OK 73101-8850
Phone: 800-858-1840
Fax: 405-225-9230
Web: www.okhighered.org

OMNE/Nursing Leaders of Maine

OMNE/Nursing Leaders of Maine Scholarship

Type of award: Scholarship.
Intended use: For undergraduate or graduate study at accredited 4-year or graduate institution. Designated institutions: Maine institutions.
Eligibility: Applicant must be U.S. citizen residing in Maine.
Basis for selection: Major/career interest in nursing. Applicant must demonstrate high academic achievement, seriousness of purpose and service orientation.
Application requirements: Recommendations, transcript, proof of eligibility. Brief note explaining how scholarship would help applicant.
Additional information: Applicant must be enrolled in baccalaureate or graduate nursing program. Minimum 2.0 GPA.

Amount of award:	$500
Number of awards:	2
Number of applicants:	14
Application deadline:	May 1
Notification begins:	June 30
Total amount awarded:	$500

Contact:
Diane York, RN, MS Chair, OMNE Scholarship Subcommittee
Rumford Hospital
420 Franklin Street
Rumford, ME 04276
Web: www.omne.org/omne_scholarship.html

ONS Foundation

Bachelor's Scholarships

Type of award: Scholarship.
Intended use: For undergraduate study at accredited 4-year institution in United States. Designated institutions: Schools accredited by National League for Nursing or Commission on Collegiate Nursing Education.
Basis for selection: Major/career interest in nursing or oncology. Applicant must demonstrate high academic achievement, depth of character, leadership and service orientation.
Application requirements: $5 application fee. Essay, transcript, proof of eligibility.
Additional information: Must be currently enrolled in bachelor's nursing degree program. At the end of each year of scholarship participation, recipient shall submit a summary of education activities in which he/she participated.

Amount of award:	$2,000
Application deadline:	February 1
Notification begins:	March 15

Contact:
ONS Foundation
125 Enterprise Drive
Pittsburgh, PA 15275-1214
Phone: 412-859-6100
Fax: 412-859-6163
Web: www.nursingawards.org

OP Loftbed

OP Loftbed $500 Scholarship Award

Type of award: Scholarship.
Intended use: For undergraduate or graduate study at accredited postsecondary institution in United States.
Eligibility: Applicant must be U.S. citizen.
Additional information: Must submit application online. Applications first accepted in February. Recipients selected based on creativity of answers to a given set of questions. Guidelines and additional information available on Website.

Amount of award:	$500
Number of awards:	1
Number of applicants:	1
Application deadline:	January 31, July 31
Notification begins:	February 21, August 15

Contact:
OP Loftbed
P.O. Box 573
Thomasville, NC 27361-0573
Phone: 866-567-5638
Web: www.oploftbed.com

Oregon Collectors Association

Bob Hasson Memorial Scholarship Fund Essay

Type of award: Scholarship.
Intended use: For full-time freshman study at vocational, 2-year or 4-year institution. Designated institutions: Oregon institutions.
Eligibility: Applicant must be high school senior. Applicant must be U.S. citizen or permanent resident residing in Oregon.
Application requirements: Transcript. FAFSA. Three- to four-page essay: "Credit in the 21st Century." Applicant's name/address/social security number, parent name/telephone number, high school name/telephone number, and name of intended college must appear on first page of essay.
Additional information: Must enroll in Oregon college within 12 months of high school graduation. Children and grandchildren of owners and officers of collection agencies in Oregon not eligible. Finalists must read their essays at Association's annual spring meeting. Essays may be printed/published at discretion of Association. Apply by mailing essays or submitting online. Visit Website for details and application.

Amount of award:	$1,000-$3,000
Application deadline:	March 1

Contact:
ORCA Scholarship Fund
c/o Doug Jones
1541 SW 201st Avenue
Beaverton, OR 97006
Phone: 888-622-3588
Fax: 503-430-8670
Web: www.orcascholarshipfund.com

Oregon Student Assistance Commission

Ahmad-Sehar Saleha Ahmad and Abrahim Ekramullah Zafar Foundation

Type of award: Scholarship, renewable.
Intended use: For undergraduate study at accredited 4-year institution in United States. Designated institutions: Oregon institutions.
Eligibility: Applicant must be female, high school senior. Applicant must be U.S. citizen or permanent resident residing in Oregon.
Basis for selection: Major/career interest in English. Applicant must demonstrate high academic achievement.
Application requirements: Essay, transcript. FAFSA.
Additional information: Must be graduating from Oregon high school. Minimum 3.8 GPA. Female students given preference. Visit Website for details and application.
   Application deadline: March 1
Contact:
Oregon Student Assistance Commission
Grants and Scholarship Division
1500 Valley River Drive, Suite 100
Eugene, OR 97401
Phone: 800-452-8807
Web: www.osac.state.or.us

Albina Fuel Company Scholarship

Type of award: Scholarship.
Intended use: For undergraduate study in United States.
Eligibility: Applicant must be residing in Oregon or Washington.
Application requirements: Transcript.
Additional information: Applicant must be dependent child of current Albina Fuel Company employee who has been employed by Albina for at least one year by October 1 prior to application deadline. Early bird deadline Feb. 15. Visit Website for more details.
   Application deadline: March 1
Contact:
Oregon Student Assistance Commission
Grants and Scholarship Division
1500 Valley River Drive, Suite 100
Eugene, OR 97401
Phone: 800-452-8807
Web: www.osac.state.or.us

Allcott/Hunt Share It Now II Scholarship

Type of award: Scholarship.
Intended use: For undergraduate study in United States.
Eligibility: Applicant must be residing in Oregon.
Basis for selection: Applicant must demonstrate financial need.
Application requirements: Transcript. Names, addresses, and phone numbers of two community or school references. FAFSA strongly recommended. Essay (250-350 words): Describe why you might be the best candidate for the Share It Now II Scholarship and your experience living or working in diverse environments.

Additional information: Preference given to first- or second-generation immigrants to the U.S. Early bird deadline Feb. 15. Visit Website for details.
   Application deadline: March 1
Contact:
Oregon Student Assistance Commission
Grants and Scholarship Division
1500 Valley River Drive, Suite 100
Eugene, OR 97401
Phone: 800-452-8807
Web: www.osac.state.or.us

Alpha Delta Kappa/Harriet Simmons Scholarship

Type of award: Scholarship, renewable.
Intended use: For full-time senior or graduate study at accredited postsecondary institution in United States. Designated institutions: Oregon institutions.
Eligibility: Applicant must be U.S. citizen or permanent resident residing in Oregon.
Basis for selection: Major/career interest in education. Applicant must demonstrate financial need and high academic achievement.
Application requirements: Transcript. FAFSA. Two essays.
Additional information: Applicants must be elementary or secondary education majors. Visit Website for details and application.
   Amount of award: $500
   Application deadline: March 1
Contact:
Oregon Student Assistance Commission
Grants and Scholarship Division
1500 Valley River Drive, Suite l00
Eugene, OR 97401
Phone: 800-452-8807
Web: www.osac.state.or.us

American Council of Engineering Companies of Oregon Scholarship

Type of award: Scholarship, renewable.
Intended use: For freshman study at 4-year institution. Designated institutions: Oregon colleges offering ABET-accredited programs.
Eligibility: Applicant must be U.S. citizen or permanent resident residing in Oregon.
Basis for selection: Major/career interest in engineering, chemical; engineering, civil; engineering, electrical/electronic or engineering, mechanical.
Application requirements: Transcript. FAFSA. Essay (500-700 words): Describe why you are interested in a career in consulting engineering and how you expect your career to contribute to society.
Additional information: Applicant must be graduating high school senior or have had no previous college education. Preference given to applicants interested in the consulting engineering profession. Visit Website for details and application.
   Application deadline: March 1
Contact:
Oregon Student Assistance Commission
Grants and Scholarship Division
1500 Valley River Drive, Suite 100
Eugene, OR 97401
Phone: 800-452-8807
Web: www.osac.state.or.us

American Ex-Prisoner of War, Peter Connacher Memorial Scholarship

Type of award: Scholarship, renewable.
Intended use: For full-time undergraduate or graduate study at postsecondary institution in United States.
Eligibility: Applicant must be U.S. citizen or permanent resident. Must be former American prisoner of war or descendant.
Basis for selection: Applicant must demonstrate financial need and high academic achievement.
Application requirements: Transcript, proof of eligibility. FAFSA, two essays, copy of POW's military discharge papers and proof of POW status. State relationship to POW on supporting documents.
Additional information: Preference given to Oregon residents and their dependents. Visit Website for details and application.
  Amount of award: $500
  Application deadline: March 1
Contact:
Oregon Student Assistance Commission
Grants and Scholarship Division
1500 Valley River Drive, Suite 100
Eugene, OR 97401
Phone: 800-452-8807
Web: www.osac.state.or.us

American Federation of State, County, and Municipal Employees (AFSCME) Oregon Council #75

Type of award: Scholarship, renewable.
Intended use: For undergraduate or graduate study at 4-year or graduate institution in United States.
Eligibility: Applicant must be U.S. citizen or permanent resident.
Application requirements: Transcript. FAFSA. Essay: What is the importance of organizing political action and contract bargaining for workers?
Additional information: Applicant, spouse (including life partner), parent, or grandparent must be member (active, laid-off, retired, or disabled) of Oregon AFSCME Council. Must have been member for at least one year prior to scholarship deadline or for one year prior to death, layoff, disability, or retirement. Part-time enrollment (minimum six credit hours) considered for active members and spouses or laid-off members. Visit Website for application and details.
  Application deadline: March 1
Contact:
Oregon Student Assistance Commission
Grants and Scholarship Division
1500 Valley River Drive, Suite 100
Eugene, OR 97401
Phone: 800-452-8807
Web: www.osac.state.or.us

Bandon Submarine Cable Council Scholarship

Type of award: Scholarship, renewable.
Intended use: For freshman study at postsecondary institution in United States.
Eligibility: Applicant must be high school senior. Applicant must be residing in Oregon.
Basis for selection: Applicant must demonstrate financial need.

Application requirements: Essay, transcript.
Additional information: First preference given to members of the Bandon Submarine Cable Council or their dependent children. Second preference given to commercial fishermen or their family members residing in Coos County. Third preference given to any commercial fishermen or family member. Fourth preference given to postsecondary students residing in Clatsop, Coos, Curry, Lane, Lincoln, or Tillamook counties. Fifth preference to any postsecondary student in Oregon. Early bird deadline February 15. Visit Website for essay topic.
  Application deadline: March 1
Contact:
Oregon Student Assistance Commission
Grants and Scholarship Division
1500 Valley River Drive, Suite 100
Eugene, OR 97401
Phone: 800-452-8807
Web: www.osac.state.or.us

Bank of the Cascades Scholarship

Type of award: Scholarship.
Intended use: For undergraduate or graduate study at postsecondary institution. Designated institutions: Non-profit colleges or universities in Oregon or Idaho.
Eligibility: Applicant must be at least 17, no older than 25. Applicant must be residing in Oregon or Idaho.
Additional information: Applicant must be Bank of the Cascades employee or child/stepchild of employee. Age requirements apply only to children. Employee must have been continuously employed for at least one year at 20 hours or more per week at the deadline. Children of members of the Cascades Board of Directors ineligible. Minimum 3.0 GPA. Early bird deadline February 15. Visit Website for more details.
  Application deadline: March 1
  Total amount awarded: $500
Contact:
Oregon Student Assistance Commission
Grants and Scholarship Division
1500 Valley River Drive, Suite 100
Eugene, OR 97401
Phone: 800-452-8807
Web: www.osac.state.or.us

Ben Selling Scholarship

Type of award: Scholarship, renewable.
Intended use: For sophomore, junior or senior study at postsecondary institution in United States.
Eligibility: Applicant must be U.S. citizen or permanent resident residing in Oregon.
Basis for selection: Applicant must demonstrate financial need and high academic achievement.
Application requirements: Essay, transcript. FAFSA.
Additional information: Minimum 3.5 GPA. Visit Website for details and application.
  Amount of award: $500
  Application deadline: March 1
Contact:
Oregon Student Assistance Commission
Grants and Scholarship Division
1500 Valley River Drive, Suite 100
Eugene, OR 97401
Phone: 800-452-8807
Web: www.osac.state.or.us

Benjamin Franklin/Edith Green Scholarship

Type of award: Scholarship.
Intended use: For full-time undergraduate study at accredited 4-year institution. Designated institutions: Oregon public colleges.
Eligibility: Applicant must be high school senior. Applicant must be U.S. citizen or permanent resident residing in Oregon.
Basis for selection: Applicant must demonstrate financial need and high academic achievement.
Application requirements: Essay, transcript. FAFSA.
Additional information: Minimum 3.45 GPA. Must show improvements in grades from freshman year. Visit Website for details and application.

    Amount of award: $500
    Application deadline: March 1
Contact:
Oregon Student Assistance Commission
Grants and Scholarship Division
1500 Valley River Drive, Suite l00
Eugene, OR 97401
Phone: 800-452-8807
Web: www.osac.state.or.us

Bertha P. Singer Scholarship

Type of award: Scholarship, renewable.
Intended use: For full-time undergraduate or graduate study at accredited postsecondary institution. Designated institutions: Oregon institutions.
Eligibility: Applicant must be U.S. citizen or permanent resident residing in Oregon.
Basis for selection: Major/career interest in nursing.
Application requirements: Essay, transcript, proof of eligibility. FAFSA.
Additional information: Employees of U.S. Bank, their children, or near relatives not eligible. Minimum 3.0 GPA. Visit Website for details and application.

    Amount of award: $500
    Application deadline: March 1
Contact:
Oregon Student Assistance Commission
Grants and Scholarship Division
1500 Valley River Drive, Suite 100
Eugene, OR 97401
Phone: 800-452-8807
Web: www.osac.state.or.us

Chafee Education and Training Scholarship

Type of award: Scholarship, renewable.
Intended use: For undergraduate or graduate study in United States.
Eligibility: Applicant must be at least 14, no older than 20. Applicant must be residing in Oregon.
Basis for selection: Applicant must demonstrate financial need and service orientation.
Application requirements: Transcript. Two essays, FAFSA.
Additional information: Applicant must currently be in or previously been in foster care placement with the Oregon Department of Human Services or federally recognized Oregon Tribes; be a former foster youth with 180 days of substitute care after age 14 with Oregon DHS or an Oregon Tribe; and exited substitute care at age 16 or older. Deadline for fall, August 1; spring, February 1; summer, May 1; winter,

November 1. Students may continue receiving award until age 23, but first-time recipients must be no older than 20. May apply for fall after deadline, but all funds may already be allocated. Visit Website for details and supplemental information form.

    Amount of award: $4,000
    Application deadline: August 1, February 1
Contact:
Oregon Student Assistance Commission
Chafee Program
1500 Valley River Drive, Suite 100
Eugene, OR 97401
Phone: 800-452-8807 ext. 7443
Fax: 541-687-7414
Web: www.osac.state.or.us/chafeetv.html

Clark-Phelps Scholarship

Type of award: Scholarship.
Intended use: For undergraduate or graduate study at 4-year or graduate institution. Designated institutions: Oregon public institutions.
Eligibility: Applicant must be U.S. citizen or permanent resident residing in Oregon or Alaska.
Basis for selection: Major/career interest in dentistry; medicine or nursing. Applicant must demonstrate financial need.
Application requirements: Transcript. FAFSA.
Additional information: Preference given to Oregon Health and Science University students and graduates of Oregon and Alaskan high schools. Award amount varies. Early bird application deadline is February 15. Visit Website for details and application.

    Application deadline: March 1
Contact:
Oregon Student Assistance Commission
Grants and Scholarship Division
1500 Valley River Drive, Suite 100
Eugene, OR 97401
Phone: 800-452-8807
Web: www.osac.state.or.us

Darfur Humanitarian Essay

Type of award: Scholarship.
Intended use: For undergraduate study in United States.
Eligibility: Applicant must be no older than 21. Applicant must be residing in Oregon.
Basis for selection: Competition/talent/interest in writing/journalism, based on 350-500 word essay exploring the meaning and global significance of the humanitarian crisis in Darfur.
Application requirements: Transcript.
Additional information: Early bird deadline February 15. Visit Website for more details.

    Application deadline: March 1
Contact:
Oregon Student Assistance Commission
Grants and Scholarship Division
1500 Valley River Drive, Suite 100
Eugene, OR 97401
Phone: 800-452-8807
Web: www.osac.state.or.us

Darlene Hooley for Oregon Veterans Scholarship

Type of award: Scholarship.

Intended use: For undergraduate or graduate study at postsecondary institution in United States. Designated institutions: Oregon institutions.

Eligibility: Applicant must be U.S. citizen or permanent resident residing in Oregon. Applicant must be veteran who served in the Army, Air Force, Marines, Navy, Coast Guard or Reserves/National Guard. Must have served in armed services during Global War on Terror.

Basis for selection: Applicant must demonstrate financial need.

Application requirements: Transcript, proof of eligibility. FAFSA.

Additional information: Award amount varies. Early bird application deadline is February 15. Visit Website for details and application.

    Application deadline: March 1

Contact:
Oregon Student Assistance Commission
Grants and Scholarship Division
1500 Valley River Drive, Suite 100
Eugene, OR 97401
Phone: 800-452-8807
Web: www.osac.state.or.us

David Family Scholarship

Type of award: Scholarship, renewable.

Intended use: For sophomore, junior, senior or graduate study at postsecondary institution in United States.

Eligibility: Applicant must be U.S. citizen or permanent resident residing in Oregon.

Basis for selection: Major/career interest in health-related professions; health education; health sciences; education or health services administration. Applicant must demonstrate financial need and high academic achievement.

Application requirements: Essay, transcript. FAFSA.

Additional information: Minimum 2.5 GPA. Intended for residents of Benton, Clackamas, Lane, Multnomah, and Washington counties. Preference given to applicants enrolling at least half-time in upper-division or graduate health- or education-related programs at four-year colleges. Visit Website for details and application.

    Amount of award: $500
    Application deadline: March 1

Contact:
Oregon Student Assistance Commission
Grants and Scholarship Division
1500 Valley River Drive, Suite 100
Eugene, OR 97401
Phone: 800-452-8807
Web: www.osac.state.or.us

Dorothy Campbell Memorial Scholarship

Type of award: Scholarship, renewable.

Intended use: For full-time undergraduate study at accredited 4-year institution. Designated institutions: Oregon institutions.

Eligibility: Applicant must be female, high school senior. Applicant must be U.S. citizen or permanent resident residing in Oregon.

Basis for selection: Applicant must demonstrate financial need and high academic achievement.

Application requirements: Transcript. FAFSA. Essay (one page): Describe strong continuing interest in golf and contribution the sport has made to applicant's development.

Additional information: Must have strong interest in golf. Minimum 2.75 GPA. Visit Website for details and application.

    Application deadline: March 1

Contact:
Oregon Student Assistance Commission
Grants and Scholarship Division
1500 Valley River Drive, Suite 100
Eugene, OR 97401
Phone: 800-452-8807
Web: www.osac.state.or.us

Eugene Bennet Visual Arts Scholarship

Type of award: Scholarship.

Intended use: For undergraduate or graduate study in United States.

Eligibility: Applicant must be residing in Oregon.

Basis for selection: Major/career interest in arts, general. Applicant must demonstrate financial need.

Application requirements: Interview, transcript.

Additional information: Applicants must be graduates of a Jackson County high school, or GED recipients or home-schooled graduates from Jackson County. Minimum 2.75 GPA. Career interest should be in fine/visual arts, not performing arts. Early bird deadline February 15. Visit Website for details.

    Application deadline: March 1

Contact:
Oregon Student Assistance Commission
Grants and Scholarship Division
1500 Valley River Drive, Suite 100
Eugene, OR 97401
Phone: 800-452-8807
Web: www.osac.state.or.us

Fashion Group International of Portland Scholarship

Type of award: Scholarship.

Intended use: For sophomore, junior or senior study at postsecondary institution in United States. Designated institutions: California, Idaho, Oregon, or Washington institutions.

Eligibility: Applicant must be U.S. citizen or permanent resident residing in California, Oregon, Idaho or Washington.

Basis for selection: Major/career interest in fashion/fashion design/modeling.

Application requirements: Interview, essay, transcript. FAFSA.

Additional information: Minimum 3.0 GPA. See Website for details and application.

    Application deadline: March 1

Contact:
Oregon Student Assistance Commission
Grants and Scholarship Division
1500 Valley River Drive, Suite 100
Eugene, OR 97401
Phone: 800-452-8807
Web: www.osac.state.or.us

Ford Opportunity Program

Type of award: Scholarship, renewable.

Intended use: For full-time undergraduate study at accredited 2-year or 4-year institution. Designated institutions: Oregon institutions.

Eligibility: Applicant must be single. Applicant must be U.S. citizen or permanent resident residing in Oregon.
Basis for selection: Applicant must demonstrate financial need and high academic achievement.
Application requirements: Essay, transcript. FAFSA.
Additional information: Minimum 3.0 GPA or 2650 GED score, unless application is accompanied by special recommendation form from counselor or OSAC. Must be single head of household with custody of dependent child/children. Interviews required of all semifinalists. Visit Website for details and application.

Number of awards:	30
Application deadline:	March 1

Contact:
Oregon Student Assistance Commission
Grants and Scholarship Division
1500 Valley River Drive, Suite 100
Eugene, OR 97401
Phone: 800-452-8807
Web: www.osac.state.or.us

Ford Scholars Program

Type of award: Scholarship, renewable.
Intended use: For full-time undergraduate study at accredited 2-year or 4-year institution. Designated institutions: Oregon institutions.
Eligibility: Applicant must be U.S. citizen or permanent resident residing in Oregon.
Basis for selection: Applicant must demonstrate financial need and high academic achievement.
Application requirements: Interview, essay, transcript. FAFSA.
Additional information: Minimum 3.0 GPA or 2650 GED score, unless application accompanied by special recommendation form from counselor or OSAC. Intended for high school graduates who have not yet been full-time undergraduates, or for individuals who have completed two years at Oregon community college and are entering junior year at Oregon four-year college. Visit Website for details and application.

Amount of award:	$500
Application deadline:	March 1

Contact:
Oregon Student Assistance Commission
Grants and Scholarship Division
1500 Valley River Drive, Suite 100
Eugene, OR 97401
Phone: 800-452-8807
Web: www.osac.state.or.us

Frank Stenzel M.D. and Kathryn Stenzel II Scholarship

Type of award: Scholarship, renewable.
Intended use: For undergraduate or graduate study at postsecondary institution in United States.
Eligibility: Applicant must be U.S. citizen or permanent resident residing in Oregon.
Basis for selection: Applicant must demonstrate financial need.
Application requirements: Transcript. FAFSA.
Additional information: Not open to graduating high school seniors. Not open to medicine, nursing, or physician assistant majors. Preference given to nontraditional students, first-generation college students, and students approaching final year of program. Minimum 2.5 GPA. Award amount varies. Early

bird application deadline is February 15. Visit Website for details and application.

Application deadline:	March 1

Contact:
Oregon Student Assistance Commission
Grants and Scholarship Division
1500 Valley River Drive, Suite 100
Eugene, OR 97401
Phone: 800-452-8807
Web: www.osac.state.or.us

Glenn Jackson Scholars

Type of award: Scholarship, renewable.
Intended use: For full-time undergraduate study at postsecondary institution in United States.
Eligibility: Applicant must be high school senior. Applicant must be U.S. citizen or permanent resident residing in Oregon.
Basis for selection: Applicant must demonstrate financial need.
Application requirements: Essay, transcript. FAFSA.
Additional information: For dependents of employees/retirees of Oregon Department of Transportation or Parks and Recreation Department. Parent must have been employed by their department at least three years. Financial need not required, but considered. Visit Website for details and application.

Amount of award:	$500
Application deadline:	March 1

Contact:
Oregon Student Assistance Commission
Grants and Scholarship Division
1500 Valley River Drive, Suite 100
Eugene, OR 97401
Phone: 800-452-8807
Web: www.osac.state.or.us

Healthy Waters Institute of the Freshwater Trust

Type of award: Scholarship.
Intended use: For freshman study in United States.
Eligibility: Applicant must be high school senior. Applicant must be U.S. citizen or permanent resident residing in Oregon.
Basis for selection: Major/career interest in biology; environmental science or wildlife/fisheries. Applicant must demonstrate financial need.
Application requirements: Essay, transcript. FAFSA.
Additional information: Must either participate in stewardship project (high school junior or senior year) addressing the health of local waters and satisfying real community need, or be planning a career in conservation-related field. Must graduate from Oregon high school. Award amount varies. Early bird application deadline is February 15. Visit Website for details and application.

Application deadline:	March 1

Contact:
Oregon Student Assistance Commission
Grants and Scholarship Division
1500 Valley River Drive, Suite 100
Eugene, OR 97401
Phone: 800-452-8807
Web: www.osac.state.or.us

Homestead Capital Housing Scholarship

Type of award: Scholarship.
Intended use: For junior or senior study at 4-year institution. Designated institutions: Oregon institutions.
Eligibility: Applicant must be U.S. citizen or permanent resident or Oregon.
Basis for selection: Major/career interest in accounting; architecture; business/management/administration; construction management; engineering, civil; engineering, structural; finance/banking; landscape architecture; public administration/service or urban planning. Applicant must demonstrate financial need.
Application requirements: Essay, transcript. FAFSA.
Additional information: Applicant must be graduate of Oregon high school. Minimum 2.75 GPA. Visit Website for essay topic and application.

  Application deadline: March 1
  Total amount awarded: $500
Contact:
Oregon Student Assistance Commission
Grants and Scholarship Division
1500 Valley River Drive, Suite 100
Eugene, OR 97401
Phone: 800-452-8807
Web: www.osac.state.or.us

Ida M. Crawford Scholarship

Type of award: Scholarship, renewable.
Intended use: For full-time undergraduate study at accredited postsecondary institution in United States.
Eligibility: Applicant must be U.S. citizen or permanent resident residing in Oregon.
Basis for selection: Applicant must demonstrate financial need and high academic achievement.
Application requirements: Essay, transcript, proof of eligibility. FAFSA.
Additional information: Minimum 3.5 GPA. Must be graduate of accredited Oregon high school. Not available to students majoring in law, medicine, music, theology, or education. U.S. Bank employees, their children, and near relatives not eligible. Visit Website for details and application.

  Amount of award: $500
  Application deadline: March 1
Contact:
Oregon Student Assistance Commission
Grants and Scholarship Division
1500 Valley River Drive, Suite l00
Eugene, OR 97401
Phone: 800-452-8807
Web: www.osac.state.or.us

Jackson Foundation Journalism Scholarship

Type of award: Scholarship, renewable.
Intended use: For full-time undergraduate study at postsecondary institution. Designated institutions: Oregon institutions.
Eligibility: Applicant must be U.S. citizen or permanent resident residing in Oregon.
Basis for selection: Major/career interest in journalism. Applicant must demonstrate financial need and high academic achievement.
Application requirements: Essay, transcript. FAFSA.

Additional information: Must be graduate of an Oregon high school. Preference given to applicants who have strong SAT writing scores. Visit Website for details and application.
  Amount of award: $500
  Application deadline: March 1
Contact:
Oregon Student Assistance Commission
Grants and Scholarship Division
1500 Valley River Drive, Suite 100
Eugene, OR 97401
Phone: 800-452-8807
Web: www.osac.state.or.us

James Carlson Memorial Scholarship

Type of award: Scholarship.
Intended use: For full-time senior or graduate study at accredited 4-year institution in United States.
Eligibility: Applicant must be U.S. citizen or permanent resident residing in Oregon.
Basis for selection: Major/career interest in education; education, teacher; education, special or education, early childhood. Applicant must demonstrate financial need and high academic achievement.
Application requirements: Essay, transcript. FAFSA.
Additional information: Available to elementary or secondary education majors entering senior year or fifth year of study, or to graduate students in fifth year for elementary or secondary certificate. Preference given to students with experience living or working in diverse environments (250-350 word essay describing this experience required for applicants qualifying under this preference); dependents of Oregon Education Association members; and students committed to teaching autistic children. Visit Website for details and application.

  Amount of award: $500
  Application deadline: March 1
Contact:
Oregon Student Assistance Commission
Grants and Scholarship Division
1500 Valley River Drive, Suite 100
Eugene, OR 97401
Phone: 800-452-8807
Web: www.osac.state.or.us

Jeffrey Alan Scoggins Memorial Scholarship

Type of award: Scholarship.
Intended use: For junior or senior study at 4-year institution. Designated institutions: Oregon public institutions.
Eligibility: Applicant must be U.S. citizen or permanent resident residing in Oregon.
Basis for selection: Major/career interest in engineering. Applicant must demonstrate financial need.
Application requirements: Essay, transcript. FAFSA.
Additional information: Minimum 3.0 GPA. Preference given to applicants attending Oregon State University and to members of Sigma Chi fraternity. Award amount varies. Early bird application deadline is February 15. Visit Website for details and application.
  Application deadline: March 1

Contact:
Oregon Student Assistance Commission
Grants and Scholarship Division
1500 Valley River Drive, Suite 100
Eugene, OR 97401
Phone: 800-452-8807
Web: www.osac.state.or.us

Jerome B. Steinbach Scholarship

Type of award: Scholarship.
Intended use: For full-time sophomore, junior or senior study at accredited postsecondary institution in United States.
Eligibility: Applicant must be U.S. citizen residing in Oregon.
Basis for selection: Applicant must demonstrate financial need and high academic achievement.
Application requirements: Essay, transcript, proof of eligibility. FAFSA.
Additional information: Minimum 3.5 GPA. U.S. Bank employees, their children, and near relatives not eligible. Visit Website for details and application.
    Amount of award: $500
    Application deadline: March 1
Contact:
Oregon Student Assistance Commission
Grants and Scholarship Division
1500 Valley River Drive, Suite 100
Eugene, OR 97401
Phone: 800-452-8807
Web: www.osac.state.or.us

Jose D. Garcia Migrant Education Scholarship

Type of award: Scholarship.
Intended use: For freshman study at postsecondary institution in United States.
Eligibility: Applicant must be U.S. citizen or permanent resident residing in Oregon.
Basis for selection: Applicant must demonstrate financial need.
Application requirements: Essay, transcript. FAFSA.
Additional information: Applicant must be high school graduate or GED recipient participating in Oregon Migrant Education Program. Visit Website for details and application.
    Amount of award: $500
    Application deadline: March 1
Contact:
Oregon Student Assistance Commission
Grants and Scholarship Division
1500 Valley River Drive, Suite 100
Eugene, OR 97401
Phone: 800-452-8807
Web: www.osac.state.or.us

Laurence R. Foster Memorial Scholarship

Type of award: Scholarship, renewable.
Intended use: For undergraduate or graduate study at accredited 4-year institution in United States.
Eligibility: Applicant must be U.S. citizen or permanent resident residing in Oregon.
Basis for selection: Major/career interest in nursing; medical specialties/research; physician assistant; public health; medical assistant; health-related professions or nurse practitioner.

Applicant must demonstrate financial need and service orientation.
Application requirements: Essay, transcript. FAFSA. Two additional essays.
Additional information: Applicant must be seeking career in public health, not private practice. General preference given to applicants of diverse cultures. Preference also given to persons working in (or graduate students majoring in) public health and to undergraduates entering junior/senior-year health programs. Visit Website for essay topic and application.
    Amount of award: $500
    Application deadline: March 1
Contact:
Oregon Student Assistance Commission
Grants and Scholarship Division
1500 Valley River Drive, Suite 100
Eugene, OR 97401
Phone: 800-452-8807
Web: www.osac.state.or.us

Maria C. Jackson-General George A. White Scholarship

Type of award: Scholarship, renewable.
Intended use: For full-time undergraduate or graduate study at postsecondary institution. Designated institutions: Oregon institutions.
Eligibility: Applicant must be U.S. citizen or permanent resident residing in Oregon. Applicant must be veteran; or dependent of active service person or veteran in the Army, Air Force, Marines, Navy or Coast Guard. Must have been Oregon resident at time of enlistment.
Basis for selection: Applicant must demonstrate financial need and high academic achievement.
Application requirements: Essay, transcript, proof of eligibility. FAFSA.
Additional information: Minimum 3.75 GPA for undergraduates; no GPA requirement for graduate students or students at technical schools. U.S. Bank employees, children, and near relatives not eligible. Visit Website for details and application.
    Application deadline: March 1
Contact:
Oregon Student Assistance Commission
Grants and Scholarship Division
1500 Valley River Drive, Suite 100
Eugene, OR 97401
Phone: 800-452-8807
Web: www.osac.state.or.us

Neil Hamilton Memorial Scholarship

Type of award: Scholarship.
Intended use: For undergraduate study at 2-year institution. Designated institutions: Oregon community colleges.
Eligibility: Applicant must be U.S. citizen or permanent resident residing in Oregon.
Basis for selection: Major/career interest in fire science/technology.
Application requirements: Transcript. FAFSA.
Additional information: Minimum 2.5 GPA or 2500 GED. Award amount varies. Early bird application deadline is February 15. Visit Website for details and application.
    Application deadline: March 1

Scholarships

Contact:
Oregon Student Assistance Commission
Grants and Scholarship Division
1500 Valley River Drive, Suite 100
Eugene, OR 97401
Phone: 800-452-8807
Web: www.osac.state.or.us

Oregon Dungeness Crab Commission

Type of award: Scholarship.
Intended use: For full-time undergraduate study at postsecondary institution in United States.
Eligibility: Applicant must be no older than 23. Applicant must be U.S. citizen or permanent resident residing in Oregon.
Basis for selection: Major/career interest in wildlife/fisheries' or environmental science. Applicant must demonstrate financial need and high academic achievement.
Application requirements: Essay, transcript. FAFSA. Identify name of vessel in place of "worksite" on item 16 of application.
Additional information: Major/career interest restrictions do not apply to high school seniors. For dependents of licensed Oregon Dungeness Crab fishermen or crew. Visit Website for details and application.
  Application deadline: March 1
Contact:
Oregon Student Assistance Commission
Grants and Scholarship Division
1500 Valley River Drive, Suite 100
Eugene, OR 97401
Phone: 800-452-8807
Web: www.osac.state.or.us

Oregon Foundation for Blacktail Deer Outdoor & Wildlife Scholarship

Type of award: Scholarship.
Intended use: For undergraduate study at postsecondary institution. Designated institutions: Oregon institutions.
Eligibility: Applicant must be residing in Oregon.
Basis for selection: Major/career interest in forestry; biology; wildlife/fisheries or zoology. Applicant must demonstrate financial need and seriousness of purpose.
Application requirements: Transcript. FAFSA. Essay (250 words) discussing the challenges of wildlife management in the coming ten years. Copy of previous year's hunting license.
Additional information: Must have serious commitment to career in wildlife management. Early bird deadline February 15. Visit Website for details.
  Application deadline: March 1
Contact:
Oregon Student Assistance Commission
Grants and Scholarship Division
1500 Valley River Drive, Suite 100
Eugene, OR 97401
Phone: 800-452-8807
Web: www.osac.state.or.us

Oregon Occupational Safety and Health Division Workers Memorial Scholarship

Type of award: Scholarship, renewable.
Intended use: For full-time undergraduate or graduate study at postsecondary institution in United States.
Eligibility: Applicant must be U.S. citizen or permanent resident residing in Oregon.
Basis for selection: Applicant must demonstrate financial need and high academic achievement.
Application requirements: Essay, transcript. FAFSA. Additional 500-word essay: "How has the injury or death of your parent or spouse affected or influenced your decision to further your education?" Must provide name, last four digits of social security number, or workers compensation claim number of worker permanently disabled or fatally injured; date of death or injury; location of incident; and exact relationship to applicant.
Additional information: Applicant must be dependent or spouse of Oregon worker permanently disabled on the job or be the recipient of fatality benefits as dependent or spouse of worker fatally injured in Oregon. Visit Website for details and application.
  Application deadline: March 1
Contact:
Oregon Student Assistance Commission
Grants and Scholarship Division
1500 Valley River Drive, Suite 100
Eugene, OR 97401
Phone: 800-452-8807
Web: www.osac.state.or.us

Oregon Robert C. Byrd Honors Scholarship

Type of award: Scholarship, renewable.
Intended use: For full-time freshman study at accredited postsecondary institution in United States.
Eligibility: Applicant must be U.S. citizen or permanent resident residing in Oregon.
Basis for selection: Applicant must demonstrate high academic achievement.
Application requirements: Essay, transcript.
Additional information: Minimum 3.85 GPA or Oregon GED of 3300. Minimum 1300 on SAT (Math and Reading) or 29 on ACT. Must be graduating senior of Oregon high school, homeschooled senior, or GED recipient. Visit Website for details and application.
  Application deadline: March 1
Contact:
Oregon Student Assistance Commission
Grants and Scholarship Division
1500 Valley River Drive, Suite 100
Eugene, OR 97401
Phone: 800-452-8807
Web: www.osac.state.or.us

Oregon Scholarship Fund Community College Student Award Programs

Type of award: Scholarship, renewable.
Intended use: For undergraduate study at accredited 2-year institution. Designated institutions: Oregon community colleges.
Eligibility: Applicant must be high school senior. Applicant must be U.S. citizen or permanent resident residing in Oregon.
Basis for selection: Applicant must demonstrate financial need and high academic achievement.
Application requirements: Transcript. FAFSA and two essays.

Additional information: Visit Website for details and application.

Application deadline: March 1

Contact:
Oregon Student Assistance Commission
Grants and Scholarship Division
1500 Valley River Drive, Suite 100
Eugene, OR 97401
Phone: 800-452-8807 ext. 7395
Web: www.osac.state.or.us

Professional Land Surveyors of Oregon Scholarship

Type of award: Scholarship, renewable.
Intended use: For full-time undergraduate study at 2-year or 4-year institution. Designated institutions: Oregon institutions.
Eligibility: Applicant must be U.S. citizen or permanent resident residing in Oregon.
Basis for selection: Major/career interest in surveying/mapping. Applicant must demonstrate financial need.
Application requirements: Essay, transcript. FAFSA. Names, addresses, and phone numbers of two references (do not submit letters).
Additional information: Students must be enrolled in curricula leading to land-surveying career. Community college applicants must intend to transfer to eligible four-year schools. Four-year applicants must intend to take Fundamentals of Land Surveying (FLS) exam. Maximum award based on year in school. Visit Website for details and application.

Application deadline: March 1

Contact:
Oregon Student Assistance Commission
Grants and Scholarship Division
1500 Valley River Drive, Suite 100
Eugene, OR 97401
Phone: 800-452-8807
Web: www.osac.state.or.us

Richard F. Brentano Memorial Scholarship

Type of award: Scholarship, renewable.
Intended use: For full-time undergraduate study at postsecondary institution in United States.
Eligibility: Applicant must be no older than 24. Applicant must be U.S. citizen or permanent resident.
Basis for selection: Applicant must demonstrate high academic achievement.
Application requirements: Essay, transcript.
Additional information: Intended for children or IRS-legal dependents of employees of Waste Control Systems, Inc., and subsidiaries. Maximum age extended to 26 for applicants who entered U.S. Armed Forces directly from high school. Parent must have been employed by Waste Control Systems one year as of deadline. Visit Website for details and application.

Application deadline: March 1

Contact:
Oregon Student Assistance Commission
Grants and Scholarship Division
1500 Valley Drive, Suite 100
Eugene, OR 97401
Phone: 800-452-8807
Web: www.osac.state.or.us

Roger W. Emmons Memorial Scholarship

Type of award: Scholarship, renewable.
Intended use: For full-time undergraduate study at accredited postsecondary institution in United States.
Eligibility: Applicant must be high school senior. Applicant must be U.S. citizen or permanent resident.
Basis for selection: Applicant must demonstrate high academic achievement.
Application requirements: Essay, transcript, proof of eligibility.
Additional information: Parent(s) or grandparent(s) must have been solid waste company owner(s) or employee(s) for at least three years and member of Oregon Refuse & Recycling Association. Visit Website for details and application.

Application deadline: March 1

Contact:
Oregon Student Assistance Commission
Grants and Scholarship Division
1500 Valley River Drive, Suite 100
Eugene, OR 97401
Phone: 800-452-8807
Web: www.osac.state.or.us

Teamsters Clyde C. Crosby/Joseph M. Edgar Memorial Scholarship

Type of award: Scholarship, renewable.
Intended use: For full-time undergraduate study at postsecondary institution in United States.
Eligibility: Applicant must be high school senior. Applicant must be U.S. citizen or permanent resident residing in Oregon.
Basis for selection: Applicant must demonstrate financial need and high academic achievement.
Application requirements: Essay, transcript. FAFSA.
Additional information: Minimum 3.0 cumulative GPA. Must be child or dependent stepchild of active, retired, disabled, or deceased member of local unions affiliated with Joint Council of Teamsters #37. Qualifying members must have been active at least one year. Visit Website for details and application.

Application deadline: March 1

Contact:
Oregon Student Assistance Commission
Grants and Scholarship Division
1500 Valley River Drive, Suite 100
Eugene, OR 97401
Phone: 800-452-8807
Web: www.osac.state.or.us

Teamsters Council #37 Federal Credit Union Scholarship

Type of award: Scholarship.
Intended use: For undergraduate or graduate study at postsecondary institution in United States.
Eligibility: Applicant must be U.S. citizen or permanent resident residing in Oregon.
Basis for selection: Applicant must demonstrate financial need and high academic achievement.
Application requirements: Essay, transcript. FAFSA.
Additional information: For members (or dependents) of Council #37 credit union. Members must have been active in local affiliated with the Joint Council of Teamsters #37 at least

one year. Applicant must have cumulative GPA between 2.0 and 3.0. Visit Website for details and application.

Application deadline: March 1
Contact:
Oregon Student Assistance Commission
Grants and Scholarship Division
1500 Valley River Drive, Suite 100
Eugene, OR 97401
Phone: 800-452-8807
Web: www.osac.state.or.us

Teamsters Local 305 Scholarship

Type of award: Scholarship, renewable.
Intended use: For full-time undergraduate study at postsecondary institution in United States.
Eligibility: Applicant must be high school senior. Applicant must be U.S. citizen or permanent resident residing in Oregon.
Basis for selection: Applicant must demonstrate high academic achievement.
Application requirements: Essay, transcript.
Additional information: Must be child or dependent stepchild of active, retired, disabled, or deceased member of Local 305 of the Joint Council of Teamsters #37. Member must have been active at least one year. Visit Website for details and application.

Application deadline: March 1
Contact:
Oregon Student Assistance Commission
Grants and Scholarship Division
1500 Valley River Drive, Suite 100
Eugene, OR 97401
Phone: 800-452-8807
Web: www.osac.state.or.us

Walter and Marie Schmidt Scholarship

Type of award: Scholarship, renewable.
Intended use: For undergraduate study at postsecondary institution in United States.
Eligibility: Applicant must be U.S. citizen or permanent resident residing in Oregon.
Basis for selection: Major/career interest in nursing or gerontology. Applicant must demonstrate financial need and high academic achievement.
Application requirements: Essay, transcript. FAFSA. Additional essay describing desire to pursue nursing career in geriatric healthcare.
Additional information: Available to students enrolling in programs to become registered nurses and intending to pursue careers in geriatric healthcare. Priority given to students: 1) attending Lane Community College; 2) enrolled in another two-year nursing program. U.S. Bank employees, children, and near relatives not eligible. Visit Website for details and application.

Application deadline: March 1
Contact:
Oregon Student Assistance Commission
Grants and Scholarship Division
1500 Valley River Drive, Suite 100
Eugene, OR 97401
Phone: 800-452-8807
Web: www.osac.state.or.us

Wild Bill Fogle Memorial Scholarship

Type of award: Scholarship.
Intended use: For undergraduate or graduate study at 2-year, 4-year or graduate institution. Designated institutions: Non-profit institutions in Oregon, Idaho, Montana, and Washington.
Eligibility: Applicant must be U.S. citizen or permanent resident.
Basis for selection: Major/career interest in veterinary medicine.
Application requirements: Transcript. FAFSA.
Additional information: Preference for applicants attending Oregon State University and Linn-Benton Community College. Minimum 3.2 GPA. Pre-veterinary medicine majors also eligible. Award amount varies. Early bird application deadline is February 15. Visit Website for details and application.

Application deadline: March 1
Contact:
Oregon Student Assistance Commission
1500 Valley River Drive, Suite 100
Eugene, OR 97401
Phone: 800-452-8807
Web: www.osac.state.or.us

The Orthotic and Prosthetic Education and Development Fund

Chester Haddan Scholarship Program

Type of award: Scholarship.
Intended use: For undergraduate or post-bachelor's certificate study at accredited 2-year or 4-year institution in United States.
Eligibility: Applicant must be U.S. citizen.
Basis for selection: Major/career interest in orthotics/prosthetics or medical specialties/research. Applicant must demonstrate financial need, depth of character, leadership, seriousness of purpose and service orientation.
Application requirements: Recommendations, transcript. A 200-word essay on why student wants to work in orthotics or prosthetics. Recent W-2 or letter from current employer.
Additional information: Students may apply directly or professors may nominate them. Applicants must be willing to financially contribute to their education.

Amount of award: $1,000
Number of awards: 1
Application deadline: January 29
Contact:
The Orthotic and Prosthetic Education and Development Fund
c/o The Academy
1331 H Street, NW, Suite 501
Washington, DC 20005
Phone: 202-380-3663 ext. 206
Web: www.oandp.org/education

Dan McKeever Scholarship Program

Type of award: Scholarship.

Intended use: For senior study at accredited 4-year institution in United States. Designated institutions: American Academy of Orthotists and Prosthetists-accredited institutions.

Eligibility: Applicant must be U.S. citizen.

Basis for selection: Major/career interest in orthotics/prosthetics or medical specialties/research. Applicant must demonstrate financial need, leadership, seriousness of purpose and service orientation.

Application requirements: Recommendations, transcript. A 200-word essay on why student wants to work in orthotics or prosthetics. Recent W-2 or letter from current employer.

Additional information: Students may apply directly or professors may nominate them. Must maintain minimum 3.0 GPA. Applicants must be willing to financially contribute to their education.

Amount of award:	$1,000
Number of awards:	3
Application deadline:	May 29

Contact:
Orthotic and Prosthetic Education and Development Fund
The Academy
1331 H Street, NW, Suite 501
Washington, DC 20005
Phone: 202-380-3663 ext. 206
Web: www.oandp.org/education

Ken Chagnon Scholarship

Type of award: Scholarship.

Intended use: For undergraduate study at accredited 2-year or 4-year institution in United States.

Eligibility: Applicant must be U.S. citizen.

Basis for selection: Major/career interest in orthotics/prosthetics or medical specialties/research. Applicant must demonstrate financial need, leadership and seriousness of purpose.

Application requirements: Recommendations, transcript. A 200-word essay on why student wants to work in orthotics or prosthetics. Recent W-2 or letter from current employer.

Additional information: Students may apply directly or professors may nominate them. Applicants must be willing to financially contribute to their education. Applicants must be enrolled in technician program and show exceptional technical aptitude.

Amount of award:	$500
Number of awards:	1
Application deadline:	January 29

Contact:
Orthotic and Prosthetic Education and Development Fund
The Academy
1331 H Street, NW, Suite 501
Washington, DC 20005
Phone: 202-380-3663 ext. 206
Web: www.oandp.org/education

Osage Tribal Education Committee

Osage Tribal Education Scholarship

Type of award: Scholarship, renewable.

Intended use: For undergraduate or graduate study at accredited postsecondary institution in United States.

Eligibility: Applicant must be American Indian. Must be a member of the Osage Nation. Applicant must be U.S. citizen.

Application requirements: Proof of Osage Indian blood.

Additional information: Must maintain 2.0 GPA. Award amount varies.

Application deadline:	July 1, December 31

Contact:
Osage Tribal Education Committee
Oklahoma Area Education Office
200 Northwest 4th, Suite 4049
Oklahoma City, OK 73102
Phone: 405-605-6051 ext. 304
Fax: 405-605-6057

Papercheck.com

Papercheck.com Charles Shafae' Scholarship Fund

Type of award: Scholarship.

Intended use: For undergraduate study at accredited 4-year institution in United States.

Eligibility: Applicant must be U.S. citizen or permanent resident.

Basis for selection: Competition/talent/interest in writing/journalism. Applicant must demonstrate high academic achievement.

Application requirements: Transcript. Minimum 1,000-word essay in MLA format. Include "works cited" page with at least two sources.

Additional information: Minimum 3.2 GPA. Applicant must be in good standing at institution. Visit Website for essay questions, guidelines, and deadline. Complete entry form online. Contact via e-mail.

Amount of award:	$500
Number of awards:	2

Contact:
Papercheck.com
Charles Shafae' Scholarship
P.O. Box 642
Half Moon Bay, CA 94019
Phone: 866-693-EDIT
Web: www.papercheck.com

Par Aide

Par Aide's Joseph S. Garske Collegiate Grant Program

Type of award: Scholarship, renewable.

Intended use: For undergraduate study at vocational, 2-year or 4-year institution.

Eligibility: Applicant must be high school senior.

Basis for selection: Applicant must demonstrate high academic achievement, leadership and service orientation.

Application requirements: Transcript. A 500-word essay evaluating a significant experience, achievement, or risk and its effect on the student.

Additional information: Minimum 2.0 GPA. Applicant's parent or stepparent must be Golf Course Superintendents Association of America member for five or more consecutive years in one of the following classifications: A, Superintendent Member, C, Retired-A, Retired-B, or AA life. Children or stepchildren of deceased members eligible if member was active for five years at time of death. Children of Par Aide employees, the Environmental Institute for Golf's Board of Trustees, the GCSAA Board of Directors, and GCSAA staff not eligible. First place award is $2,500; second place, $1,500; third place, $1,000. First-place awardees eligible for one-year renewal.

Amount of award:	$1,000-$2,500
Number of awards:	3
Application deadline:	March 15
Notification begins:	May 15
Total amount awarded:	$5,000

Contact:
Golf Course Superintendents Association of America
Garske Grant Program
1421 Research Park Drive
Lawrence, KS 66049-3859
Phone: 785-832-4445
Web: www.gcsaa.org

Patient Advocate Foundation

Scholarships for Survivors

Type of award: Scholarship.
Intended use: For full-time undergraduate or graduate study at accredited 2-year, 4-year or graduate institution.
Eligibility: Applicant must be no older than 25.
Basis for selection: Applicant must demonstrate financial need, depth of character, leadership and service orientation.
Application requirements: Recommendations, essay, transcript, proof of eligibility. Previous year's tax returns. Written documentation from physician stating medical history.
Additional information: Must be survivor of life-threatening, chronic, or debilitating disease. Must maintain 3.0 overall GPA. Must complete 20 hours of community service in year scholarship will be dispensed. Check Website for application deadline.

Amount of award:	$3,000
Number of awards:	10
Number of applicants:	150
Total amount awarded:	$30,000

Contact:
Patient Advocate Foundation
700 Thimble Shoals Blvd., Suite 200
Newport News, VA 23606
Web: www.patientadvocate.org

Peacock Productions, Inc.

Audria M. Edwards Scholarship Fund

Type of award: Scholarship, renewable.
Intended use: For full-time undergraduate study at accredited vocational, 2-year or 4-year institution in United States.

Eligibility: Applicant must be U.S. citizen residing in Oregon or Washington.
Basis for selection: Major/career interest in arts, general. Applicant must demonstrate financial need, depth of character and leadership.
Application requirements: Recommendations, essay, transcript, proof of eligibility.
Additional information: Applicant must be gay, lesbian, bisexual, or transgendered; or the child of gay, lesbian, bisexual, or transgendered parents. Applicant must be pursuing degree in academic field, trade, vocation, or the arts. Applicants living in Washington must reside in Clark, Cowlitz, Lewis, Pacific, Skamania, or Wahkiakum counties. Visit Website for application information.

Application deadline:	May 1
Total amount awarded:	$6,250

Contact:
Peacock Productions, Inc.
Audria M. Edwards Scholarship Fund
P.O. Box 8854
Portland, OR 97207-8854
Web: www.peacockinthepark.com

Penguin Putnam, Inc.

Signet Classic Student Scholarship Essay Contest

Type of award: Scholarship.
Intended use: For undergraduate study at postsecondary institution.
Eligibility: Applicant must be high school junior or senior. Applicant must be U.S. citizen or permanent resident.
Basis for selection: Competition/talent/interest in writing/journalism, based on style, content, grammar, and originality; judges look for clear, concise writing that is articulate, logically organized, and well-supported. Major/career interest in English or literature.
Application requirements: Proof of eligibility, nomination by high school English teacher. Entrant must read designated book and answer one of several book-related questions in two- to three-page essay. Cover letter on school letterhead from teacher. Only one junior and one senior essay may be submitted per teacher. Parent or legal guardian must submit essay for home-schooled students.
Additional information: Home-schooled entrants must be between ages 16 and 18. Immediate relatives of employees of Penguin Group (USA) Inc. and its affiliates ineligible. Visit Website for details and application. Winner also receives Signet Classic library for school (or for public library in the case of home-schooled winner).

Amount of award:	$1,000
Number of awards:	5
Application deadline:	April 15
Notification begins:	June 15
Total amount awarded:	$5,000

Contact:
Penguin Group Signet Classic Student Scholarship Essay Contest
Academic Marketing Department
375 Hudson Street
New York, NY 10014
Web: us.penguingroup.com/static/pages/services-academic/essayhome.html

Pennsylvania Higher Education Assistance Agency

Chafee Education and Training Grant (ETG) Program

Type of award: Scholarship, renewable.
Intended use: For undergraduate study at accredited vocational, 2-year or 4-year institution. Designated institutions: Institutions approved by U.S. Department of Education for Title IV student assistance programs.
Eligibility: Applicant must be residing in Pennsylvania.
Basis for selection: Applicant must demonstrate financial need.
Application requirements: FAFSA.
Additional information: Must be eligible for services under the Commonwealth's Chafee Foster Care Independence Program. Must be in foster care or adopted from foster care after age 16. Must participate in ETG program on 21st birthday until age 23. Must maintain satisfactory academic progress. Visit Website for details and application.
   Amount of award: $5,000
Contact:
PHEAA State Grant and Special Programs
1200 North Seventh Street
Harrisburg, PA 17102-1444
Phone: 800-692-7392
Web: www.pheaa.org

Gaining Early Awareness and Readiness for Undergraduate Programs (GEAR UP) Scholarship

Type of award: Scholarship.
Intended use: For freshman study at postsecondary institution in United States.
Eligibility: Applicant must be no older than 22. Applicant must be U.S. citizen residing in Pennsylvania.
Application requirements: FAFSA.
Additional information: Must have graduated within 2008 through 2013 from one of the following high schools in the Philadelphia or Harrisburg school districts: Young Women's Leadership School at E.W. Rhodes High School, John Bartram Main High School, Martin Luther King High School, Strawberry Mansion High School, or Harrisburg High School (including SciTech High School, William Penn High School, ACTS, and CTA). Must be deemed scholarship-eligible through participation in college readiness activities. Must be eligible for a Federal Pell Grant each year. Must meet all federal student aid requirements. The annual maximum GEAR UP scholarship is equal to the maximum Federal Pell Grant for the same academic year. The GEAR UP scholarship may be reduced based on enrollment status, Expected Family Contribution (EFC), fund availability, or unmet cost as determined by the school's financial aid office. Awards are contingent upon federal funding and are not guaranteed.
Contact:
PHEAA State Grant and Special Programs
P.O. Box 8157
Harrisburg, PA 17105-8157
Phone: 800-692-7392
Web: www.pheaa.org

Partnership for Access to Higher Education (PATH)

Type of award: Scholarship, renewable.
Intended use: For undergraduate study at postsecondary institution in United States. Designated institutions: Pennsylvania State Grant-approved postsecondary institution in Pennsylvania.
Eligibility: Applicant must be U.S. citizen residing in Pennsylvania.
Basis for selection: Applicant must demonstrate financial need and high academic achievement.
Application requirements: Nomination by participating PATH organization (visit PHEAA Website for list). FAFSA.
Additional information: Must receive a scholarship from participating PHEAA PATH organization for the academic year that PATH aid is requested. Must be Pennsylvania State Grant recipient for academic year or period for which PHEAA PATH aid is requested. Amount of award varies, and is up to $3,500 per academic year.
Contact:
Contact local participating PHEAA PATH organization or foundation.
Phone: 800-692-7392
Web: www.pheaa.org

Pennsylvania Robert C. Byrd Honors Scholarship

Type of award: Scholarship, renewable.
Intended use: For full-time freshman study at accredited postsecondary institution in United States.
Eligibility: Applicant must be high school senior. Applicant must be U.S. citizen or permanent resident residing in Pennsylvania.
Basis for selection: Applicant must demonstrate high academic achievement.
Application requirements: Transcript. SAT/ACT or GED scores.
Additional information: Applicant must rank in top five percent of class, have minimum 3.5 GPA, 1150 SAT (Math and Reading) or 25 ACT, or 3550 GED. Must graduate from high school same year scholarship is awarded. Information available from high school guidance office.
   Application deadline: April 1
Contact:
Pennsylvania Higher Education Assistance Agency
Robert C. Byrd Scholarship
P.O. Box 8114
Harrisburg, PA 17105-8114
Phone: 800-692-7392
Web: www.pheaa.org

Pennsylvania State Grant Program

Type of award: Scholarship, renewable.
Intended use: For undergraduate study at accredited vocational, 2-year or 4-year institution in United States.
Eligibility: Applicant must be residing in Pennsylvania.
Basis for selection: Applicant must demonstrate financial need.
Application requirements: Proof of eligibility. FAFSA.
Additional information: Applicant must be high school graduate or GED recipient enrolled in PHEAA-approved program. Applicant must not already have four-year undergraduate degree. Grants are portable to approved institutions in other states. Number and amount of awards vary.

Scholarships

Deadlines: August 1 for first-time applicants in business, trade, technical, or nursing schools or terminal two-year programs; May 1 for other applicants.

Amount of award:	$4,120
Application deadline:	May 1, August 1

Contact:
PHEAA State Grant and Special Programs Division
1200 North Seventh Street
Harrisburg, PA 17102-1444
Phone: 800-692-7392
Web: www.pheaa.org

Pennsylvania Work-Study Program

Type of award: Scholarship, renewable.
Intended use: For undergraduate, master's, doctoral or first professional study at accredited postsecondary institution. Designated institutions: PHEAA-approved institutions.
Eligibility: Applicant must be U.S. citizen or permanent resident residing in Pennsylvania.
Basis for selection: Applicant must demonstrate financial need.
Application requirements: Interview, proof of eligibility. Proof of state grant or subsidized Stafford loan.
Additional information: Student must demonstrate ability to benefit from career-related high-tech or community service work experience. Funds earned must be used to pay school costs. Applicant must be state grant or subsidized federal loan recipient and not owe state grant refund or be in default on student loan. Recipient must secure a job with PHEAA-approved on or off-campus SWSP employer. Amount and number of awards vary. Deadlines: Fall term only and academic year, October 1; spring term only, January 31; summer, May 31.

Application deadline:	October 1, January 31

Contact:
PHEAA State Grant and Special Programs Division
1200 North Seventh Street
Harrisburg, PA 17102
Phone: 800-692-7392
Web: www.pheaa.org

Postsecondary Educational Gratuity Program

Type of award: Scholarship, renewable.
Intended use: For full-time undergraduate study at 2-year or 4-year institution. Designated institutions: Pennsylvania public institutions.
Eligibility: Applicant must be no older than 25. Applicant must be residing in Pennsylvania. Applicant must be dependent of deceased veteran. Applicant's parent must have been killed or disabled in work-related accident as firefighter, police officer or public safety officer.
Application requirements: Record of application for other financial aid. Certified copy of birth certificate.
Additional information: Applicant must be: child by birth or adoption of deceased police officer, firefighter, rescue or ambulance squad member, corrections facility employee, or active National Guard member who died after January 1, 1976 as direct result of performing official duties; or child by birth or adoption of deceased sheriff, deputy sheriff, National Guard member, or certain other individual on federal or state active military duty who died since September 11, 2001 as direct result of performing official duties. Award may include waiver of tuition, fees, and room and board costs. Must apply for other

available financial aid prior to application to this program. Visit Website for application.

Amount of award:	Full tuition

Contact:
PHEAA State Grant and Special Programs
1200 North Seventh Street
Harrisburg, PA 17102-1444
Phone: 800-692-7392
Web: www.pheaa.org

SciTech Scholarship

Type of award: Scholarship, renewable.
Intended use: For full-time sophomore, junior or senior study at 4-year institution in United States. Designated institutions: Approved Pennsylvania institutions.
Eligibility: Applicant must be residing in Pennsylvania.
Basis for selection: Major/career interest in science, general; technology or health-related professions.
Additional information: Must apply for Federal Pell and Pennsylvania State Grants. Minimum 3.0 GPA at time of application; must maintain to be eligible for renewal. Must complete approved internship or relevant work experience with Pennsylvania company prior to graduation. Must begin employment in state within one year of graduation and work one year for each year scholarship was awarded. Must provide employment verification every six months. Students pursuing full-time graduate study within one year of receiving bachelor's may request deferment of work obligation. Award is renewable for maximum of three years (some exceptions made for approved five-year programs). Scholarship converts to loan if student fails to satisfy work obligation.

Amount of award:	$3,000

Contact:
PHEAA State Grant and Special Programs
1200 North Seventh Street
Harrisburg, PA 17102-1444
Phone: 800-692-7392
Web: www.pheaa.org

Technology Scholarship

Type of award: Scholarship, renewable.
Intended use: For undergraduate study at vocational, 2-year or 4-year institution. Designated institutions: PHEAA-approved institutions.
Eligibility: Applicant must be residing in Pennsylvania.
Additional information: Applicant must apply for Federal Pell Grant and Pennsylvania State Grant. Minimum 3.0 GPA. Applicant must begin employment in Pennsylvania within one year of graduation and work one year for each year scholarship was awarded. Employment verification must be provided every six months. Deferment of work obligation possible if student begins full-time graduate study within one year of receiving bachelor's. Scholarship converts to loan if student fails to satisfy work obligation.

Amount of award:	$1,000

Contact:
PHEAA State Grant and Special Programs
1200 North Seventh Street
Harrisburg, PA 17102-1444
Phone: 800-692-7392
Web: www.pheaa.org

Pennsylvania State System of Higher Education Foundation, Inc.

Dr. & Mrs. Arthur William Phillips Scholarship

Type of award: Scholarship.
Intended use: For full-time freshman study at 4-year institution in United States. Designated institutions: Pennsylvania State System of Higher Education universities.
Eligibility: Applicant must be residing in Pennsylvania.
Basis for selection: Applicant must demonstrate financial need and high academic achievement.
Additional information: Must be resident of Butler, Clarion, Forest, Jefferson, Lawrence, Mercer, or Venango counties. Visit Website for deadline and other information.

Amount of award:	$500-$1,000
Notification begins:	May 31
Total amount awarded:	$1,000

Contact:
Pennsylvania State System of Higher Education Foundation, Inc.
2896 N. 2nd Street
Harrisburg, PA 17110
Phone: 717-720-4065
Fax: 717-720-7082
Web: www.thepafoundation.org

Fitz Dixon Memorial Scholarship

Type of award: Scholarship.
Intended use: For undergraduate or graduate study at 4-year or graduate institution in United States. Designated institutions: Pennsylvania State System of Higher Education (PASSHE) universities.
Basis for selection: Applicant must demonstrate financial need, high academic achievement and service orientation.
Application requirements: Recommendations, essay. Community/University service form.
Additional information: Undergraduate applicants must have passed 45 credits at a PASSHE university with a minimum GPA of 3.0. Graduate students must have passed nine credits at a PASSHE university with a minimum GPA of 3.5.

Amount of award:	$500
Number of awards:	1
Application deadline:	March 31

Contact:
Pennsylvania State System of Higher Education Foundation, Inc.
2896 N. 2nd St.
Harrisburg, PA 17110
Phone: 717-720-4065
Fax: 717-720-7082
Web: www.thepafoundation.org

Harry & Lorraine Ausprich Endowed Scholarship for the Arts

Type of award: Scholarship.
Intended use: For full-time undergraduate study at 4-year institution in United States. Designated institutions: Pennsylvania State System of Higher Education universities.
Basis for selection: Major/career interest in music; theater arts; arts, general or dance.
Application requirements: Recommendations, essay.
Additional information: Pre-architecture students also eligible. Minimum 3.0 GPA. One to two scholarships are awarded yearly dependent on available funds. Amount of award varies. Visit Website for deadline.

Total amount awarded:	$500

Contact:
Pennsylvania State System of Higher Education Foundation, Inc.
2896 N. 2nd St.
Harrisburg, PA 17110
Phone: 717-720-4065
Fax: 717-720-7082
Web: www.thepafoundation.org

Highmark Scholarship

Type of award: Scholarship.
Intended use: For full-time freshman study at postsecondary institution in United States. Designated institutions: Pennsylvania State System of Higher Education universities.
Basis for selection: Major/career interest in biology; health education; health sciences; health services administration; health-related professions; nursing or physical therapy.
Additional information: Other healthcare majors including pre-physician assistant, pre-medicine, medical imagery, and exercise science also eligible. Visit Website for list of PASSHE universities. Contact university for requirements.

Amount of award:	$1,000
Number of awards:	140
Total amount awarded:	$140,000

Contact:
Pennsylvania State System of Higher Education Foundation, Inc.
2896 N. 2nd Street
Harrisburg, PA 17110
Phone: 717-720-4065
Fax: 717-720-7082
Web: www.thepafoundation.org

James Hughes Memorial Scholarship Fund

Type of award: Scholarship, renewable.
Intended use: For full-time undergraduate study at postsecondary institution in United States. Designated institutions: Pennsylvania State System of Higher Education universities.
Eligibility: Applicant must be residing in Pennsylvania.
Basis for selection: Applicant must demonstrate financial need and high academic achievement.
Application requirements: Recommendations, essay, transcript.
Additional information: Applicants must have graduated from public or charter school in the School District of Philadelphia. Minimum 2.0 GPA required for renewals. Application available on Website.

Amount of award:	$750-$1,500
Application deadline:	March 31
Notification begins:	May 1
Total amount awarded:	$81,000

Contact:
Pennsylvania State System of Higher Education Foundation, Inc.
2986 N. 2nd Street
Harrisburg, PA 17110
Phone: 717-720-4065
Fax: 717-720-7082
Web: www.thepafoundation.org

Robert Noyce Scholarship Program

Type of award: Scholarship, renewable.
Intended use: For full-time junior, senior, post-bachelor's certificate or postgraduate study at 4-year or graduate institution in United States. Designated institutions: Pennsylvania State System of Higher Education universities.
Eligibility: Applicant must be residing in Pennsylvania.
Basis for selection: Major/career interest in education; mathematics; engineering; technology or science, general. Applicant must demonstrate high academic achievement.
Application requirements: Recommendations, essay, transcript.
Additional information: For science, technology, engineering, and math (STEM) majors and STEM professionals with a commitment to becoming mathematics or science teachers. Each semester awarded requires one year of teaching in Pennsylvania high-needs school. Minimum 3.0 GPA. Transfer students or post-baccalaureates must complete semester or more of coursework at a state system university to establish qualifying GPA. Awardees who default on their obligations must repay award. Visit Website for list of eligible schools, terms, and responsibilities.

Amount of award:	$7,500-$10,000
Application deadline:	April 20
Total amount awarded:	$36,156

Contact:
Pennsylvania State System of Higher Education Foundation, Inc.
2986 N. 2nd Street
Harrisburg, PA 17110
Phone: 717-720-4065
Web: www.iup.edu/natsciandmath/default.aspx

Wayne G. Failor Scholarship

Type of award: Scholarship.
Intended use: For full-time freshman study at postsecondary institution in United States. Designated institutions: Pennsylvania State System of Higher Education universities.
Eligibility: Applicant must be high school senior. Applicant must be residing in Pennsylvania.
Basis for selection: Major/career interest in business. Applicant must demonstrate financial need and high academic achievement.
Additional information: Number of awards varies yearly. Applicants must be graduating from a West Shore School District high school. Must have "B" average or better by the end of junior year. Visit Website for deadline and other information.

Amount of award:	$500
Application deadline:	May 1
Total amount awarded:	$500

Contact:
Pennsylvania State System of Higher Education Foundation, Inc.
2986 N. 2nd Street
Harrisburg, PA 17110
Phone: 717-720-4065
Fax: 717-720-7082
Web: www.thepafoundation.org

The Persian Scholarship Foundation

The Persian Scholarship Recognition Award

Type of award: Scholarship.
Intended use: For undergraduate or graduate study in United States.
Application requirements: Transcript. Cover letter, digital copy of valid student ID, scanned copy of published article, MS Word copy of article, scanned copy of official transcript.
Additional information: Applicant must be of Iranian descent. Must have published an essay or article in a school, local, or national newspaper discussing the positive achievements of Iranian people and society. One winner each will be selected from high school, undergraduate, and graduate levels. Visit Website for deadline and more information.

Amount of award:	$500-$1,000
Number of awards:	3
Total amount awarded:	$2,500

Contact:
The Persian Scholarship Foundation
1434 Westwood Boulevard, #5
Los Angeles, CA 90024
Web: www.persianscholarship.org

PFLAG National Office

PFLAG National Scholarship Program

Type of award: Scholarship.
Intended use: For full-time freshman study at 2-year or 4-year institution.
Eligibility: Applicant must be high school senior.
Additional information: Applicants who graduated within last year also eligible. Must self-identify as gay, lesbian, bisexual, transgender, or ally/supporter of LGBT people who has worked on behalf of the LGBT community or overcome odds because of identity. Applications and full details available online in December.

Amount of award:	$1,000-$5,000
Number of awards:	16
Number of applicants:	300
Application deadline:	March 11
Total amount awarded:	$35,000

Contact:
PFLAG National Office
1726 M Street, NW, Suite 400
Washington, DC 20036
Phone: 202-467-8180, ext. 219
Web: www.pflag.org

The Phillips Foundation

Ronald Reagan College Leaders Scholarship Program

Type of award: Scholarship, renewable.
Intended use: For full-time junior or senior study at accredited 4-year institution in United States.
Eligibility: Applicant must be U.S. citizen.
Basis for selection: Applicant must demonstrate high academic achievement, depth of character, leadership, patriotism, seriousness of purpose and service orientation.
Application requirements: Recommendations, essay. Proof of full-time enrollment in good standing; proof of leadership activities.
Additional information: Number of awards varies based on merit. Recipients will be notified in late March/early April. Visit Website for application and more information.

Amount of award:	$1,000-$10,000
Number of awards:	93
Number of applicants:	430
Application deadline:	January 15
Total amount awarded:	$217,000

Contact:
The Phillips Foundation
Attn: Jeff Hollingsworth
1 Massachusetts Avenue NW, Suite 620
Washington, DC 20001
Phone: 202-250-3887, ext. 628
Web: www.thephillipsfoundation.org

Plumbing-Heating-Cooling Contractors - National Assoc. Educational Foundation

A.O. Smith Water Heaters Scholarship

Type of award: Scholarship.
Intended use: For full-time undergraduate study at accredited vocational, 2-year or 4-year institution in United States.
Eligibility: Applicant must be U.S. citizen or Canadian citizen.
Basis for selection: Major/career interest in air conditioning/heating/refrigeration technology; business/management/administration; construction management or engineering, mechanical.
Application requirements: Recommendations, essay, transcript. SAT/ACT scores. List of extracurricular activities.
Additional information: Students enrolled or planning to enroll in PHCC-approved apprenticeship program also eligible.

Other eligible majors include mechanical CAD design, plumbing or HVACR installation, and others directly related to the plumbing-heating-cooling profession. Must be sponsored by active member of PHCC National Association. Minimum 2.0 GPA. Visit Website for details and application.

Amount of award:	$2,500
Number of awards:	2
Application deadline:	May 1

Contact:
A.O. Smith Scholarship Program Foundation Scholarship Coordinator
P.O. Box 6808
Falls Church, VA 22040
Phone: 800-533-7694
Fax: 703-237-7442
Web: www.foundation.phccweb.org/Scholarships

Bradford White Scholarship

Type of award: Scholarship.
Intended use: For full-time undergraduate study at accredited vocational or 2-year institution in United States.
Eligibility: Applicant must be U.S. citizen or Canadian citizen.
Basis for selection: Major/career interest in air conditioning/heating/refrigeration technology; business/management/administration; construction management or engineering, mechanical.
Application requirements: Recommendations, essay, transcript. SAT/ACT scores. List of extracurricular activities.
Additional information: Students enrolled or planning to enroll in PHCC-approved apprenticeship program also eligible. Other eligible majors include mechanical CAD design, plumbing or HVACR installation, and others directly related to the plumbing-heating-cooling profession. Must be sponsored by active member of PHCC National Association. Minimum 2.0 GPA. Visit Website for details and application.

Amount of award:	$2,500
Number of awards:	3
Application deadline:	May 1

Contact:
Bradford White Scholarship Program
P.O. Box 6808
Falls Church, VA 22040
Phone: 800-533-7694
Fax: 703-237-7442
Web: www.foundation.phccweb.org/scholarships

Delta Faucet Company Scholarship

Type of award: Scholarship.
Intended use: For full-time undergraduate study at accredited vocational, 2-year or 4-year institution in United States.
Eligibility: Applicant must be U.S. citizen or Canadian citizen.
Basis for selection: Major/career interest in air conditioning/heating/refrigeration technology; business/management/administration; construction management or engineering, mechanical.
Application requirements: Recommendations, essay, transcript. SAT/ACT scores, list of extracurricular activities.
Additional information: Applicants must pursue studies in major related to plumbing-heating-cooling industry or apprentice in a PHCC-approved program. Must be sponsored by active member of PHCC National Association. Minimum 2.0 GPA. Visit Website for application.

Amount of award:	$2,500
Number of awards:	6
Number of applicants:	45
Application deadline:	May 1
Total amount awarded:	$15,000

Contact:
Delta Faucet Scholarship Program
P.O. Box 6808
Falls Church, VA 22040
Phone: 800-533-7694
Fax: 703-237-7442
Web: www.foundation.phccweb.org/scholarships

PHCC Auxiliary of Massachusetts Scholarship

Type of award: Scholarship.
Intended use: For full-time undergraduate study at accredited 4-year institution in United States.
Eligibility: Applicant must be high school senior. Applicant must be U.S. citizen residing in Massachusetts.
Application requirements: Recommendations, essay, transcript. SAT/ACT scores. List of extracurricular activities.
Additional information: Must be sponsored by active member of PHCC National Auxiliary residing in MA. Minimum 2.0 GPA. Visit Website for details and application.

Amount of award:	$1,500
Number of awards:	1
Application deadline:	May 1

Contact:
Education Foundation Scholarship Coordinator
P.O. Box 6808
Falls Church, VA 22040
Phone: 800-533-7694
Fax: 703-237-7442
Web: www.foundation.phccweb.org/scholarships

PHCC Educational Foundation Need-Based Scholarship

Type of award: Scholarship.
Intended use: For full-time undergraduate study at accredited vocational, 2-year or 4-year institution in United States.
Eligibility: Applicant must be U.S. citizen or Canadian citizen.
Basis for selection: Major/career interest in air conditioning/ heating/refrigeration technology; business/management/ administration; construction management or engineering, mechanical. Applicant must demonstrate financial need.
Application requirements: Recommendations, essay, transcript. SAT/ACT scores. List of extracurricular activities.
Additional information: Students enrolled or planning to enroll in PHCC-approved apprenticeship program also eligible. Other eligible majors include mechanical CAD design, plumbing or HVACR installation, and others directly related to the plumbing-heating-cooling profession. Must be sponsored by active member of PHCC National Association. Minimum 2.0 GPA. Visit Website for details and application.

Amount of award:	$2,500
Number of awards:	1
Application deadline:	May 1

Contact:
PHCC Educational Foundation Need-Based Scholarship
Program
P.O. Box 6808
Falls Church, VA 22040
Phone: 800-533-7694
Fax: 703-237-7442
Web: www.foundation.phccweb.org/scholarships

Plumbing-Heating-Cooling Contractors - National Association Educational Foundation Scholarship

Type of award: Scholarship, renewable.
Intended use: For full-time undergraduate study at accredited vocational, 2-year or 4-year institution in United States.
Eligibility: Applicant must be U.S. citizen or Canadian citizen.
Basis for selection: Major/career interest in air conditioning/ heating/refrigeration technology; architecture; business; engineering, construction or construction management. Applicant must demonstrate high academic achievement.
Application requirements: Recommendations, transcript. SAT/ACT scores, list of extracurricular activities.
Additional information: Applicants must pursue studies in major related to plumbing-heating-cooling industry or apprentice in a PHCC-approved program. Must be sponsored by active member of PHCC National Association. Must maintain minimum 2.0 GPA.

Amount of award:	$2,500
Number of awards:	2
Application deadline:	May 1
Notification begins:	August 1
Total amount awarded:	$5,000

Contact:
PHCC Educational Foundation Scholarship Program
P.O. Box 6808
Falls Church, VA 22040
Phone: 800-533-7694
Fax: 703-237-7442
Web: www.foundation.phccweb.org/scholarships

Point Foundation

Point Scholarship

Type of award: Scholarship.
Intended use: For undergraduate or graduate study at accredited 4-year institution in United States.
Basis for selection: Competition/talent/interest in gay/lesbian. Applicant must demonstrate financial need, high academic achievement, depth of character, leadership, seriousness of purpose and service orientation.
Application requirements: Transcript. Two or three letters of recommendation, two of them from a teacher or professor. Applicants who have been out of school five years or more may substitute a reference from a supervisor for one letter.
Additional information: Applicants should have a history of leadership in the lesbian, gay, bisexual, and transgendered community and plan to be a LGBT leader in the future. Award amount varies based on available funds; average award $13,600. Scholars must be willing to speak publicly at Foundation events, provide the Foundation with transcripts, remain in contact with Foundation, and do an individual community service project with the LGBT community. Must

maintain 3.3. GPA. Deadline occurs in February; visit Website for exact date and application.

Number of awards:	11
Number of applicants:	2,463
Total amount awarded:	$1,819,375

Contact:
Point Foundation
5757 Wilshire Blvd., Suite #370
Los Angeles, CA 90036
Phone: 323-933-1234
Web: www.pointfoundation.org

Presbyterian Church (USA)

National Presbyterian Scholarship

Type of award: Scholarship, renewable.
Intended use: For full-time undergraduate study in United States. Designated institutions: Presbyterian-affiliated colleges.
Eligibility: Applicant must be high school senior. Applicant must be Presbyterian. Applicant must be U.S. citizen or permanent resident.
Basis for selection: Applicant must demonstrate financial need and high academic achievement.
Application requirements: Transcript. Recommendation from church pastor, biographical questionnaire, and record from high school guidance counselor.
Additional information: SAT/ACT must be taken no later than December 15 of senior year of high school.

Amount of award:	$500-$1,400
Number of awards:	440
Number of applicants:	206
Application deadline:	January 31
Notification begins:	April 1

Contact:
Presbyterian Church (USA)
Financial Aid for Studies
100 Witherspoon Street
Louisville, KY 40202-1396
Phone: 888-728-7228 ext. 5776
Fax: 502-569-8766
Web: www.pcusa.org/financialaid

Native American Education Grant

Type of award: Scholarship.
Intended use: For full-time undergraduate study at accredited postsecondary institution in United States.
Eligibility: Applicant must be Alaskan native or American Indian.
Basis for selection: Applicant must demonstrate financial need.
Additional information: Minimum 2.5 GPA. Must demonstrate Cost of Attendance with preference given to students demonstrating financial need. Preference is given to members of Presbyterian Church (USA). Native American students from all faith traditions are encouraged to apply. Award is renewable up to first degree; after first degree dependent upon availability of funds. Visit Website to request application.

Amount of award:	$500-$1,500
Application deadline:	June 15

Contact:
Presbyterian Church (USA)
100 Witherspoon Street
Louisville, KY 40202-1396
Phone: 888-728-7228 ext. 5776
Fax: 502-569-8766
Web: www.pcusa.org/financialaid

Presbyterian Student Opportunity Scholarship

Type of award: Scholarship, renewable.
Intended use: For full-time junior or senior study at accredited 4-year institution in United States.
Eligibility: Applicant must be Presbyterian. Applicant must be U.S. citizen or permanent resident.
Basis for selection: Major/career interest in religion/theology; education; health sciences or social/behavioral sciences. Applicant must demonstrate financial need.
Application requirements: Recommendations, transcript, proof of eligibility.
Additional information: Applicants studying Sacred Music also eligible. Preference given to students of African American, Asian American, Hispanic American, Alaskan Native, and Native American descent. Minimum 2.5 GPA. Must reapply annually for renewal.

Amount of award:	$200-$3,000
Number of awards:	156
Number of applicants:	156
Application deadline:	June 15
Notification begins:	August 1
Total amount awarded:	$175,000

Contact:
Presbyterian Church (USA)
Financial Aid for Studies
100 Witherspoon Street
Louisville, KY 40202-1396
Phone: 888-728-7228 ext. 5776
Fax: 502-569-8766
Web: www.pcusa.org/financialaid

Samuel Robinson Award

Type of award: Scholarship.
Intended use: For full-time junior or senior study at 4-year institution. Designated institutions: One of 69 colleges affiliated with Presbyterian Church (USA).
Eligibility: Applicant must be Presbyterian. Applicant must be U.S. citizen or permanent resident.
Application requirements: A 2,000-word essay on assigned topic related to the Catechism.
Additional information: Applicant must successfully recite answers of the Westminster Shorter Catechism. Amount of award based on annual funds.

Amount of award:	$200-$5,000
Number of awards:	12
Application deadline:	April 1
Notification begins:	May 15
Total amount awarded:	$60,000

Contact:
Presbyterian Church (USA)
Financial Aid for Studies
100 Witherspoon Street
Louisville, KY 40202-1396
Phone: 888-728-7228 ext. 5776
Fax: 502-569-8766
Web: www.pcusa.org/financialaid

Press Club of Houston Educational Foundation

Press Club of Houston Scholarship

Type of award: Scholarship.
Intended use: For full-time junior or senior study at accredited 4-year institution in United States.
Eligibility: Applicant must be U.S. citizen.
Basis for selection: Major/career interest in journalism; radio/television/film or communications. Applicant must demonstrate financial need and high academic achievement.
Application requirements: Interview, recommendations, transcript. Writing samples, statement from college financial aid office about current financial aid package, personal statement outlining career goal and reasons behind that goal.
Additional information: Applicant must be student at college in greater Houston area (Harris, Brazoria, Chambers, Fort Bend, Galveston, Liberty, Montgomery, and Waller counties) or resident of greater Houston area attending college anywhere. Applications available after January 1. Total amount available for awards depends on proceeds from annual Gridiron Show. Deadline varies; visit Website for details and application.

Amount of award:	$500-$3,000
Application deadline:	July 1
Total amount awarded:	$10,000

Contact:
Press Club of Houston Educational Foundation
Scholarship Chairman
P.O. Box 541038
Houston, TX 77254-1038
Phone: 713-743-1822
Web: www.houstonpressclub.com

Pride of the Greater Lehigh Valley

Rainbow Scholarship

Type of award: Scholarship.
Intended use: For undergraduate study at postsecondary institution.
Eligibility: Applicant must be residing in Pennsylvania.
Application requirements: Recommendations, transcript.
Additional information: Three awards available to students who identify as gay, lesbian, bisexual, transgender, intersex, or ally. Queer Student of the Year, awarded to a queer teen who is a positive force in the GBLTI community through involvement and participation in community activities; Rainbow Award, awarded to a queer teen for academic excellence; Diversity Essay Contest, open to all college-bound youth, regardless of sexual orientation or gender identity. Must live in Berks, Bucks, Carbon, Lehigh, Monroe, Montgomery, Northampton, Schuylkill, or Warren counties. Visit Website for more information and application.

Amount of award:	$200-$500
Number of awards:	3
Number of applicants:	2
Application deadline:	June 1

Contact:
The Rainbow Scholarship
c/o Pride-GLV
1101 West Hamilton Street
Allentown, PA 18101-1043
Phone: 610-770-6200
Web: www.prideglv.org

The Princess Grace Foundation USA

Princess Grace Award for Dance

Type of award: Scholarship.
Intended use: For sophomore, junior or senior study in United States. Designated institutions: Non-profit institutions.
Eligibility: Applicant must be U.S. citizen or permanent resident.
Basis for selection: Major/career interest in dance.
Application requirements: Nomination by dean or department head.
Additional information: Award amount varies.

Number of awards:	6
Application deadline:	April 30

Contact:
Princess Grace Foundation USA
150 E. 58th Street
25th Floor
New York, NY 10155
Phone: 212-317-1470
Fax: 212-317-1473
Web: www.pgfusa.org

Princess Grace Award For Film

Type of award: Scholarship.
Intended use: For senior or graduate study at accredited 4-year or graduate institution. Designated institutions: Eligible film schools.
Eligibility: Applicant must be U.S. citizen or permanent resident.
Basis for selection: Major/career interest in film/video.
Application requirements: Nomination by dean or department head.
Additional information: Award amount varies. Scholarships to help produce thesis projects. Only students of invited film schools are eligible to apply.

Number of awards:	6
Application deadline:	June 2

Contact:
The Princess Grace Foundation USA
150 E. 58th Street
25th Floor
New York, NY 10155
Phone: 212-317-1470
Fax: 212-317-1473
Web: www.pgfusa.org

Princess Grace Award For Playwriting

Type of award: Scholarship.
Intended use: For undergraduate study in United States.

Eligibility: Applicant must be U.S. citizen or permanent resident.
Basis for selection: Major/career interest in playwriting/ screenwriting.
Application requirements: One unproduced play.
Additional information: Award given directly to individual through residency at New Dramatists, Inc. in New York. Applicant must not have had any professional productions. Readings, workshops, and Equity showcases are admissible. See Website for application.

Amount of award:	$7,500
Number of awards:	1
Application deadline:	March 31

Contact:
The Princess Grace Foundation USA
150 E. 58th Street
25th Floor
New York, NY 10155
Phone: 212-317-1470
Fax: 212-317-1473
Web: www.pgfusa.org

Princess Grace Award For Theater

Type of award: Scholarship.
Intended use: For senior or master's study at accredited 4-year or graduate institution.
Eligibility: Applicant must be U.S. citizen or permanent resident.
Basis for selection: Major/career interest in theater arts or theater/production/technical.
Application requirements: Nomination by dean or department head.
Additional information: Scholarships awarded to students for their last year (undergraduate or graduate) of professional training in acting; directing; or scenic, lighting, sound, or costume design. Award amount varies.

Number of awards:	6
Application deadline:	March 31

Contact:
The Princess Grace Foundation USA
150 E. 58th Street
25th Floor
New York, NY 10155
Phone: 212-317-1470
Fax: 212-317-1473
Web: www.pgfusa.org

Print and Graphics Scholarship Foundation

PGSF Annual Scholarship Competition

Type of award: Scholarship, renewable.
Intended use: For full-time undergraduate study at 2-year or 4-year institution.
Eligibility: Applicant must be U.S. citizen.
Basis for selection: Major/career interest in graphic arts/ design; printing or publishing. Applicant must demonstrate high academic achievement.
Application requirements: Recommendations, transcript. Biographical information including extracurricular activities and academic honors. Photocopy of intended course of study. High school students must submit SAT, PSAT/NMSQT, or ACT scores.
Additional information: To renew, recipients must maintain 3.0 GPA and continue as graphic arts/printing technology major. Application deadline March 1 for high school seniors and high school graduates not currently attending college and April 1 for current undergraduates. Recipients granted membership in the Graphic Arts Technical Foundation. Application requirements and criteria may vary by trust fund member institution. Visit Website for application.

Amount of award:	$1,000-$5,000
Number of awards:	300
Number of applicants:	1,200
Application deadline:	March 1, April 1
Notification begins:	June 30
Total amount awarded:	$440,000

Contact:
Print and Graphics Scholarship Foundation
200 Deer Run Road
Sewickley, PA 15143-2600
Phone: 800-910-4283 or 412-259-1740
Fax: 412-741-2311
Web: www.pgsf.org

Professional Association of Georgia Educators Foundation, Inc.

PAGE Foundation Scholarships

Type of award: Scholarship.
Intended use: For junior, senior or post-bachelor's certificate study at accredited 4-year or graduate institution in United States.
Eligibility: Applicant must be U.S. citizen or permanent resident residing in Georgia.
Basis for selection: Major/career interest in education. Applicant must demonstrate high academic achievement and service orientation.
Application requirements: Recommendations, essay, transcript.
Additional information: Minimum 3.0 GPA. Must be PAGE or SPAGE member. Intended for future teachers and certified teachers seeking advanced degrees. Must agree to teach in Georgia for three years. Applications available from September to April. Visit Website for additional information, deadline, and application procedures.

Amount of award:	$1,000
Number of awards:	15
Number of applicants:	125
Application deadline:	April 30
Notification begins:	July 1
Total amount awarded:	$15,000

Contact:
PAGE Foundation
P.O. Box 942270
Atlanta, GA 31141-2270
Phone: 800-334-6861
Fax: 770-216-9672
Web: www.pagefoundation.org

Quill and Scroll Foundation

Edward J. Nell Memorial Scholarship

Type of award: Scholarship.
Intended use: For full-time freshman study at accredited 2-year or 4-year institution in United States.
Eligibility: Applicant must be high school senior. Applicant must be U.S. citizen.
Basis for selection: Major/career interest in journalism. Applicant must demonstrate seriousness of purpose.
Application requirements: Recommendations, essay, transcript. Statement of intent to major in journalism. Three selections of student's journalistic work. One color photo of applicant.
Additional information: Open only to winners of Quill and Scroll's Annual National Yearbook Excellence or International Writing/Photo Contests at any time during high school career.

Amount of award:	$500-$1,500
Number of awards:	10
Number of applicants:	30
Application deadline:	May 10
Notification begins:	June 1
Total amount awarded:	$6,000

Contact:
Quill and Scroll Foundation
School of Journalism and Mass Communication
University of Iowa
Iowa City, IA 52242-1401
Phone: 319-335-3457
Fax: 319-335-3989
Web: www.uiowa.edu/~quill-sc

Radio-Television News Director Foundation (RTNDF)

Carole Simpson Scholarship

Type of award: Scholarship.
Intended use: For full-time sophomore, junior or senior study at 4-year institution.
Basis for selection: Major/career interest in communications; film/video; journalism or radio/television/film. Applicant must demonstrate depth of character and seriousness of purpose.
Application requirements: Recommendations, essay, proof of eligibility. Resume. One to three samples (audio or video cassettes or CD, maximum 15 minutes) showing journalistic skills, accompanied by script.
Additional information: Must be preparing for career in electronic journalism. Preference given to students of color. Visit Website for deadline and application.

Amount of award:	$2,000
Number of awards:	1
Number of applicants:	20
Total amount awarded:	$2,000

Contact:
RTNDF Scholarships
4121 Plank Road, #512
Fredericksburg, VA 22407
Phone: 202-467-5214
Fax: 202-223-4007
Web: www.rtndf.org

Ed Bradley Scholarship

Type of award: Scholarship.
Intended use: For full-time sophomore, junior, senior or graduate study at 4-year institution.
Basis for selection: Major/career interest in communications; film/video; journalism or radio/television/film. Applicant must demonstrate seriousness of purpose.
Application requirements: Recommendations, essay, proof of eligibility. Resume. One to three samples (audio or video cassettes or CD, maximum 15 minutes) showing journalistic skills, accompanied by script.
Additional information: Must have at least one full year of school remaining. Must be preparing for career in electronic journalism. Preference given to undergraduate students of color. Visit Website for deadline and application.

Amount of award:	$10,000
Number of awards:	1
Number of applicants:	47
Total amount awarded:	$10,000

Contact:
RTNDF Scholarships
4121 Plank Road, #512
Fredericksburg, VA 22407
Phone: 202-467-5214
Fax: 202-223-4007
Web: www.rtndf.org

The George Foreman Tribute to Lyndon B. Johnson Scholarship

Type of award: Scholarship.
Intended use: For full-time sophomore, junior, senior or graduate study at 4-year institution in United States. Designated institutions: University of Texas at Austin.
Eligibility: Applicant must be U.S. citizen or permanent resident residing in Texas.
Basis for selection: Major/career interest in communications; film/video; journalism or radio/television/film.
Application requirements: Recommendations, essay, proof of eligibility. Resume. One to three samples (audio or video cassettes or CD, maximum 15 minutes) showing journalistic skills, accompanied by script.
Additional information: Must be preparing for career in electronic journalism. Visit Website for deadline and application.

Amount of award:	$6,000
Number of awards:	1
Number of applicants:	9
Total amount awarded:	$6,000

Contact:
RTNDF Scholarships
4121 Plank Road, #512
Fredericksburg, VA 22407
Phone: 202-467-5214
Fax: 202-223-4007
Web: www.rtndf.org

RTNDF Scholarships
4121 Plank Road, #512
Fredericksburg, VA 22407
Phone: 202-467-5214
Fax: 202-223-4007
Web: www.rtndf.org

Ken Kashiwahara Scholarship

Type of award: Scholarship.
Intended use: For full-time sophomore, junior, senior or graduate study at postsecondary institution in United States.
Eligibility: Applicant must be U.S. citizen or permanent resident.
Basis for selection: Major/career interest in communications; film/video; journalism or radio/television/film.
Application requirements: Recommendations, essay, proof of eligibility. Resume. One to three samples (audio or video cassettes or CD, maximum 15 minutes) showing journalistic skills, accompanied by script.
Additional information: Applicant must be in good standing and preparing for a career in electronic journalism. Preference given to undergraduate students of color. Visit Website for deadline and application.

Amount of award:	$2,500
Number of awards:	1
Number of applicants:	27
Total amount awarded:	$2,500

Contact:
RTNDF Scholarships
4121 Plank Road, #512
Fredericksburg, VA 22407
Phone: 202-467-5214
Fax: 202-223-4007
Web: www.rtndf.org

Lou and Carole Prato Sports Reporting Scholarship

Type of award: Scholarship.
Intended use: For full-time sophomore, junior or senior study at postsecondary institution.
Basis for selection: Major/career interest in communications; film/video; journalism; radio/television/film or sports/sports administration.
Application requirements: Recommendations, essay, proof of eligibility. Resume. One to three samples (audio or video cassettes or CD, maximum 15 minutes) showing journalistic skills, accompanied by script.
Additional information: Must be planning career as sports reporter in television or radio. Visit Website for deadline and application.

Amount of award:	$1,000
Number of awards:	1
Number of applicants:	15
Total amount awarded:	$1,000

Contact:
RTNDF Scholarships
4121 Plank Road, #512
Fredericksburg, VA 22407
Phone: 202-467-5214
Fax: 202-223-4007
Web: www.rtndf.org

Pete Wilson Journalism Scholarship

Type of award: Scholarship.
Intended use: For full-time undergraduate or graduate study at accredited 4-year or graduate institution. Designated institutions: San Francisco Bay area institutions.
Eligibility: Applicant must be residing in California.
Basis for selection: Major/career interest in communications; film/video; journalism or radio/television/film.

Application requirements: Recommendations, essay, proof of eligibility. Resume. One to three samples (audio or video cassettes or CD, maximum 15 minutes) showing journalistic skills, accompanied by script.
Additional information: Must be preparing for career in electronic journalism. Must have one full year of school left to be eligible. Visit Website for deadline and application.

Amount of award:	$4,000

Contact:
RTNDF Scholarships
4121 Plank Road, #512
Fredericksburg, VA 22407
Phone: 202-467-5214
Fax: 202-223-4007
Web: www.rtndf.org

Presidents' $2,500 Scholarships

Type of award: Scholarship.
Intended use: For full-time sophomore, junior or senior study at 2-year or 4-year institution.
Basis for selection: Major/career interest in communications; film/video; journalism or radio/television/film. Applicant must demonstrate high academic achievement and seriousness of purpose.
Application requirements: Recommendations, essay, proof of eligibility. Resume. One to three samples (audio or video cassettes or CD, maximum 15 minutes) showing journalistic skills, accompanied by script.
Additional information: Must be preparing for career in electronic journalism. Visit Website for deadline and application.

Amount of award:	$2,500
Number of awards:	2
Number of applicants:	79
Total amount awarded:	$2,500

Contact:
RTNDF Scholarships
4121 Plank Road, #512
Fredericksburg, VA 22407
Phone: 202-467-5214
Fax: 202-223-4007
Web: www.rtndf.org

Recording for the Blind and Dyslexic

Marion Huber Learning Through Listening Award

Type of award: Scholarship.
Intended use: For undergraduate study at vocational, 2-year or 4-year institution.
Eligibility: Applicant must be learning disabled. Applicant must be high school senior.
Basis for selection: Applicant must demonstrate high academic achievement, leadership and service orientation.
Application requirements: Recommendations, essay, transcript. List of honors, achievements, and activities.
Additional information: Applicant must be registered member of Recording for the Blind and Dyslexic for at least one year prior to application deadline. Must have 3.0 GPA or better in grades 10-12.

Amount of award: $2,000-$6,000
Number of awards: 6
Application deadline: April 1
Total amount awarded: $24,000
Contact:
Recording for the Blind and Dyslexic LTL Awards
c/o Melissa Greenwald
20 Roszel Road
Princeton, NJ 08540
Phone: 609-243-7087 or 866-732-3585
Web: www.rfbd.org

Mary P. Oenslager Scholastic Achievement Award

Type of award: Scholarship.
Intended use: For senior, master's or doctoral study at accredited 4-year or graduate institution in United States.
Eligibility: Applicant must be visually impaired.
Basis for selection: Applicant must demonstrate high academic achievement, leadership and service orientation.
Application requirements: Recommendations, essay, transcript. List of honors, achievements, and community activities.
Additional information: Must receive degree during the current year. Minimum 3.0 GPA on 4.0 scale or equivalent. Must be registered member of Recording for the Blind and Dyslexic for at least one year prior to application deadline. Continuing education beyond bachelor's degree not required.

Amount of award: $1,000-$6,000
Number of awards: 9
Application deadline: March 1
Total amount awarded: $30,000
Contact:
Recording for the Blind and Dyslexic SAA Awards
c/o Melissa Greenwald
20 Roszel Road
Princeton, NJ 08540
Phone: 609-243-7087 or 866-732-3585
Web: www.rfbd.org

Red River Valley Fighter Pilots Association

Red River Valley Fighter Pilots Association (RRVA) Scholarship Program

Type of award: Scholarship, renewable.
Intended use: For undergraduate or graduate study at accredited vocational, 2-year, 4-year or graduate institution in United States.
Eligibility: Applicant must be U.S. citizen.
Basis for selection: Applicant must demonstrate financial need, high academic achievement and service orientation.
Application requirements: Transcript, proof of eligibility. SAT/ACT scores.
Additional information: Applicants are eligible if they are one of the following: 1) Dependent (legal son, daughter, or spouse) of deceased veteran, dependent of POW/MIA, dependent of member of any branch of the U.S. Armed Forces listed as KIA or MIA since August 1964, dependent of military aircrew members killed in combat or non-combat military

missions, or dependent of current or deceased RRVA member in good standing; 2) pursuing a career in field related to aviation/space. See Website for application and more information.

Amount of award: $500-$3,500
Number of awards: 32
Number of applicants: 42
Application deadline: May 15
Total amount awarded: $67,000
Contact:
Red River Valley Fighter Pilots Association
P.O. Box 1553
Front Royal, VA 22630
Phone: 540-636-9798
Fax: 540-636-9776
Web: www.river-rats.org

Reserve Officers Association

Henry J. Reilly Memorial College Scholarship

Type of award: Scholarship, renewable.
Intended use: For full-time undergraduate or graduate study at accredited 4-year or graduate institution in United States.
Eligibility: Applicant must be U.S. citizen.
Basis for selection: Applicant must demonstrate high academic achievement, depth of character, leadership and seriousness of purpose.
Application requirements: Essay, transcript, proof of eligibility. SAT or ACT scores.
Additional information: For undergraduate applicants: Parent or grandparent must be member of either Reserve Officers Association or Reserve Officers Association League (ROAL). For graduate applicants: Must be a member of either Reserve Officers Association or ROAL. Minimum SAT score of 1875 for applicants who took the SAT on or after March 2005; miniumum SAT score of 1250 for applicants who took the SAT prior to March 2005. Minimum 3.0 GPA for applicants already attending college; minimum 3.3 GPA for applicants still attending high school. Must have registered for the draft if eligible. Number of awards and award amounts vary. Visit Website for more information.

Number of applicants: 125
Application deadline: April 10
Notification begins: June 30
Total amount awarded: $45,000
Contact:
Reserve Officers Association
Ms. Betsy Allen
One Constitution Avenue, NE
Washington, DC 20002-5655
Phone: 800-809-9448
Web: www.roa.org/scholarships

Restaurant Association of Maryland Education Foundation

Letitia B. Carter Scholarship

Type of award: Scholarship.
Intended use: For undergraduate study in United States.
Eligibility: Applicant must be enrolled in high school. Applicant must be U.S. citizen residing in Maryland.
Basis for selection: Major/career interest in hospitality administration/management. Applicant must demonstrate high academic achievement.
Application requirements: Recommendations, essay. Paystub from most recent employer in industry related work. Two typed and double-spaced essays: 1) Describe any personal skills and characteristics that will help you meet the future challenges of the food service/hospitality industry; 2) Which person was most influential in helping you choose a career in the food service/ hospitality industry?
Additional information: Applicant must have applied to an RAMEF-recognized professional development program in hospitality or enrolled in a RAMEF-recognized food service/ hospitality program. Any high school or college student applying for scholarship must have a minimum 3.0 cumulative GPA and a minimum of 400 hours documented industry experience. Any teachers or instructors applying must have a minimum of 1,500 hours documented industry experience. Visit Website for more information.

Amount of award:	$500-$2,000
Number of applicants:	10
Application deadline:	April 1
Notification begins:	May 11
Total amount awarded:	$5,000

Contact:
Restaurant Association of Maryland Education Foundation
6301 Hillside Court
Columbia, MD 21046
Phone: 410-290-6800
Fax: 410-290-6882
Web: www.ramef.org

Marcia S. Harris Legacy Fund Scholarship

Type of award: Scholarship.
Intended use: For undergraduate study at postsecondary institution.
Eligibility: Applicant must be residing in Maryland.
Basis for selection: Major/career interest in culinary arts; food production/management/services; food science/technology; hospitality administration/management or hotel/restaurant management. Applicant must demonstrate financial need and high academic achievement.
Application requirements: Interview. Proof of employment in culinary or hospitality industry. Three essays.
Additional information: Selection based on grades in food service coursework, essays, and work experience.

Number of awards:	2
Number of applicants:	11
Application deadline:	April 1
Total amount awarded:	$2,000

Contact:
Restaurant Association of Maryland Education Foundation
6301 Hillside Court
Columbia, MD 21046
Phone: 410-290-6800 ext. 1015
Fax: 410-290-6882
Web: www.ramef.org

Rhode Island Higher Education Assistance Authority

College Bound Fund Academic Promise Scholarship

Type of award: Scholarship, renewable.
Intended use: For full-time undergraduate study at vocational, 2-year or 4-year institution. Designated institutions: Institutions participating in at least one Title IV financial aid program.
Eligibility: Applicant must be U.S. citizen or permanent resident residing in Rhode Island.
Basis for selection: Applicant must demonstrate financial need and high academic achievement.
Application requirements: FAFSA. SAT or ACT scores.
Additional information: Initial eligibility based on SAT/ACT scores and expected family contribution; renewal subject to maintenance of specified GPA. Dependent applicant's parent must reside in Rhode Island. Award notification begins in late spring.

Amount of award:	$2,500
Number of awards:	100
Number of applicants:	1,450
Application deadline:	March 1
Total amount awarded:	$1,000,000

Contact:
Rhode Island Higher Education Assistance Authority
560 Jefferson Boulevard
Warwick, RI 02886
Phone: 401-736-1170
Fax: 401-732-3541
Web: www.riheaa.org

Rhode Island State Grant

Type of award: Scholarship, renewable.
Intended use: For undergraduate study at vocational, 2-year or 4-year institution in or outside United States or Canada. Designated institutions: U.S., Canadian, or Mexican institutions that participate in at least one federal financial aid program.
Eligibility: Applicant must be U.S. citizen or permanent resident residing in Rhode Island.
Basis for selection: Applicant must demonstrate financial need.
Application requirements: FAFSA.
Additional information: Must meet all Title IV eligibility requirements. Dependent applicant's parent must reside in Rhode Island. Award notification begins in late spring.

Amount of award:	$250-$900
Number of awards:	15,000
Number of applicants:	54,298
Application deadline:	March 1
Total amount awarded:	$12,577,151

Contact:
Rhode Island Higher Education Assistance Authority
560 Jefferson Boulevard
Warwick, RI 02886
Phone: 401-736-1170
Fax: 401-736-1178
Web: www.riheaa.org

Rocky Mountain Coal Mining Institute

RCMI Technical/Trade School Scholarship

Type of award: Scholarship.
Intended use: For sophomore study at vocational or 2-year institution.
Eligibility: Applicant must be U.S. citizen residing in Wyoming, Utah, Texas, Montana, New Mexico, Colorado, North Dakota or Arizona.
Basis for selection: Major/career interest in engineering, mining or geology/earth sciences.
Additional information: Applicant must be first-year student at a two-year technical school in good standing. Must be studying an applicable trade and be interested in coal as a career path.

Amount of award:	$1,000
Number of awards:	8
Number of applicants:	4
Application deadline:	February 1
Notification begins:	March 1
Total amount awarded:	$3,000

Contact:
Rocky Mountain Coal Mining Institute
8057 South Yukon Way
Littleton, CO 80128-5510
Phone: 303-948-3300
Fax: 303-948-1132
Web: www.rmcmi.org

Rocky Mountain Coal Mining Institute Scholarship

Type of award: Scholarship, renewable.
Intended use: For full-time junior or senior study in United States. Designated institutions: Mining schools approved by Rocky Mountain Coal Mining Institute.
Eligibility: Applicant must be U.S. citizen residing in Wyoming, Utah, Texas, Montana, New Mexico, Colorado, Arizona or North Dakota.
Basis for selection: Major/career interest in engineering; engineering, mining or geology/earth sciences. Applicant must demonstrate high academic achievement.
Application requirements: Interview, recommendations.
Additional information: Must have career interest in western coal mining. Recommended 3.0 GPA or higher. One new award per Rocky Mountain Coal Mining Institute member state per year. Can be renewed as senior or post-graduate.

Amount of award:	$2,500
Number of awards:	8
Number of applicants:	25
Application deadline:	February 1
Notification begins:	March 1
Total amount awarded:	$32,000

Contact:
Rocky Mountain Coal Mining Institute
8057 South Yukon Way
Littleton, CO 80128-5510
Phone: 303-948-3300
Fax: 303-948-1132
Web: www.rmcmi.org

Ronald McDonald House Charities

RMHC Scholarship Programs

Type of award: Scholarship.
Intended use: For full-time undergraduate study at accredited vocational, 2-year or 4-year institution.
Eligibility: Applicant must be high school senior. Applicant must be U.S. citizen or permanent resident.
Basis for selection: Applicant must demonstrate financial need, high academic achievement, leadership and service orientation.
Application requirements: Recommendations, essay, transcript, proof of eligibility. IRS Form 1040.
Additional information: Intended for those who live within geographic boundaries of a RMHC chapter that offers scholarships. Geographic areas listed on Website. Some requirements include: RMHC/ASIA: Applicant must have at least one parent of Asian heritage; RMHC/Future African American Achievers: Applicant must have at least one parent of African American or Black/Caribbean heritage; RMHC/HACER: Applicant must have at least one parent of Hispanic heritage; RMHC/Scholars: No race restrictions. Number of awards varies. Minimum award $1000. Award notification begins in May. See Website for contact information and application.

Application deadline:	February 15
Notification begins:	May 1
Total amount awarded:	$2,800,000

Contact:
Ronald McDonald House Charities Scholarship Program Administrators
One Kroc Drive
Oak Brook, IL 60523
Phone: 630-623-7048
Fax: 630-623-7488
Web: www.rmhc.org

The Rotary Foundation

Academic-Year Ambassadorial Scholarship

Type of award: Scholarship.

Intended use: For full-time undergraduate, graduate, postgraduate or non-degree study at postsecondary institution in in another country where there are Rotary Clubs.
Eligibility: Applicant must be citizen of country that has Rotary Clubs.
Basis for selection: Competition/talent/interest in study abroad. Applicant must demonstrate high academic achievement, leadership, seriousness of purpose and service orientation.
Application requirements: Interview, recommendations, essay, transcript, proof of eligibility. Proof of language ability.
Additional information: Deadlines set by the local Rotary Clubs and fall between March and August of year prior to when studies begin. Must have interest in international understanding and peace. Scholarship provides funding for one academic year of study in another country and is intended to defray costs associated with tuition, room and board, round-trip transportation, and one month of language training (if necessary). Need not be current student but must have completed two years of postsecondary work or have equivalent professional experience and be proficient in the language of the proposed host country. Number of awards varies from year to year. Spouses or descendants of Rotarians ineligible. Visit Website or check with local Rotary Club for more information and scholarship availability.

Amount of award: $26,000
Contact:
The Rotary Foundation
One Rotary Center
1560 Sherman Avenue
Evanston, IL 60201-3698
Phone: 866-9ROTARY
Web: www.rotary.org

ROTC/Air Force

ROTC/Air Force Four-Year Scholarship (Types 1, 2, and 7)

Type of award: Scholarship.
Intended use: For freshman study at accredited 4-year institution in United States.
Eligibility: Applicant must be at least 17, no older than 25, high school senior. Applicant must be U.S. citizen.
Basis for selection: Applicant must demonstrate high academic achievement.
Application requirements: Interview, recommendations, transcript. SAT/ACT scores, physical fitness assessment, resume.
Additional information: Recipients agree to serve four years' active duty. Minimum 3.0 GPA. At least 24 ACT or 1100 SAT. Opportunities available in any major. Applicants must not be enrolled in college full-time prior to application. Type 1 provides full tuition, most fees, $900 for textbooks, and $300-500 monthly stipend during academic year. Type 2 provides tuition, most fees up to $18,000 per year, $900 for textbooks, and $300-500 monthly stipend. Type 7 provides tuition and fees up to the equivalent of the in-state rate, $900 for books, and $300-500 monthly stipend. Scholarship board decides which type is offered. For all scholarships, amount of stipend is based on student's academic year. To contact a local ROTC recruiter, visit www.afrotc.com/admissions/locateRep.php.

Amount of award: Full tuition
Application deadline: December 1

Contact:
Contact local ROTC recruiter.
Phone: 866-423-7682
Fax: 334-953-6167
Web: www.afrotc.com

ROTC/United States Army

Four-Year Nursing Scholarship

Type of award: Scholarship.
Intended use: For freshman study at accredited 4-year institution in United States.
Eligibility: Applicant must be at least 17, no older than 26. Applicant must be U.S. citizen.
Basis for selection: Major/career interest in military science or nursing. Applicant must demonstrate high academic achievement and depth of character.
Application requirements: Interview, transcript.
Additional information: Must enlist to serve in the Army on Active Duty or in a Reserve Component for eight years. Minimum 920 SAT (Math and Reading) or 19 ACT. Must maintain minimum 2.5 GPA in college. Scholarships offered at different levels, providing college tuition and educational fees. All applicants considered for each level. Includes living allowance (increasing each year) for each year of scholarship, plus allowance for books and other educational items. Travel expenses not included. Limited number of three- and two-year scholarships available once student is on campus; check with school's professor of military science or contact local Army ROTC recruiter.

Amount of award: Full tuition
Application deadline: January 1

Contact:
Army ROTC Scholarship
U.S. Army Cadet Command
Fort Monroe, VA 23651-1052
Phone: 800-USA-ROTC
Web: www.goarmy.com/rotc/nurse_program.jsp

Four-Year Scholarship

Type of award: Scholarship, renewable.
Intended use: For freshman study at accredited 4-year institution in United States.
Eligibility: Applicant must be at least 17, no older than 26. Applicant must be U.S. citizen. Must enlist in Army on active duty, or in Army Reserve or Army National Guard for minimum eight years.
Basis for selection: Major/career interest in military science. Applicant must demonstrate high academic achievement and depth of character.
Application requirements: Interview, recommendations, transcript. SAT/ACT scores. Proof of high school class rank.
Additional information: Recipient receives living allowance (increasing each year) for each year of scholarship, plus allowance for books and other educational items. Minimum 920 SAT (Math and Reading) or 19 ACT. Minimum 2.5 GPA. Limited number of three- and two-year scholarships available once student is on campus; check with professor of military science once enrolled. Contact local Army ROTC recruiter or visit Website for application.

Amount of award: Full tuition
Application deadline: January 10

Contact:
Army ROTC Scholarship
U.S. Army Cadet Command
Fort Monroe, VA 23651-1052
Phone: 800-USA-ROTC
Web: www.goarmy.com/rotc or www.rotc.monroe.army.mil

Sachs Foundation

Sachs Foundation Undergraduate Grant

Type of award: Scholarship, renewable.
Intended use: For full-time undergraduate study at accredited 2-year or 4-year institution.
Eligibility: Applicant must be African American. Applicant must be high school senior. Applicant must be U.S. citizen or permanent resident residing in Colorado.
Basis for selection: Applicant must demonstrate financial need, depth of character and leadership.
Application requirements: Interview, recommendations, transcript, proof of eligibility. Financial statement and parents' tax returns. Small recent photo. A copy of Colorado School Enrollment form.
Additional information: Must have been resident of Colorado for at least five years. Minimum 3.4 GPA. Must maintain at least 2.5 GPA throughout college for renewal consideration.

Amount of award:	$4,000
Number of awards:	200
Number of applicants:	200
Application deadline:	March 1
Total amount awarded:	$1,000,000

Contact:
Sachs Foundation
90 South Cascade Avenue
Suite 1410
Colorado Springs, CO 80903
Phone: 719-633-2353
Web: www.sachsfoundation.org

SAE International

BMW/SAE Engineering Scholarships

Type of award: Scholarship, renewable.
Intended use: For full-time freshman study at accredited 4-year institution in United States. Designated institutions: ABET-accredited engineering schools.
Eligibility: Applicant must be high school senior. Applicant must be U.S. citizen.
Basis for selection: Major/career interest in engineering or computer/information sciences. Applicant must demonstrate high academic achievement, depth of character and leadership.
Application requirements: Essay, transcript. SAT or ACT scores, list of extracurricular activities.
Additional information: Must have 3.75 GPA and rank in 90th percentile on ACT composite or SAT I (Math and Reading). Must maintain 3.0 GPA to renew scholarship.

Renewable for four years. Visit Website for more information. For list of ABET-accredited schools, visit www.abet.org.

Amount of award:	$1,500
Number of awards:	1
Application deadline:	January 15
Notification begins:	June 30

Contact:
SAE International
SAE Engineering Scholarships
400 Commonwealth Drive
Warrendale, PA 15096-0001
Phone: 724-776-4841
Web: www.sae.org/scholarships

Edward D. Hendrickson/SAE Engineering Scholarship

Type of award: Scholarship, renewable.
Intended use: For undergraduate study at accredited postsecondary institution. Designated institutions: ABET-accredited institutions.
Eligibility: Applicant must be high school senior. Applicant must be U.S. citizen.
Basis for selection: Major/career interest in engineering. Applicant must demonstrate high academic achievement.
Application requirements: Essay, transcript. SAT or ACT scores, list of extracurricular activities.
Additional information: Minimum 3.75 GPA. Must rank in 90th percentile on SAT (Math and Reading) or composite ACT. Award renewable for three years if student maintains 3.0 GPA. Visit Website for application. For list of ABET-accredited schools, visit www.abet.org.

Amount of award:	$1,000
Number of awards:	1
Application deadline:	January 15
Notification begins:	June 30

Contact:
SAE International
SAE Engineering Scholarships
400 Commonwealth Drive
Warrendale, PA 15096-0001
Phone: 724-776-4841
Web: www.sae.org/scholarships

Fred M. Young, Sr./SAE Engineering Scholarship

Type of award: Scholarship, renewable.
Intended use: For undergraduate study at accredited postsecondary institution. Designated institutions: ABET-accredited institutions.
Eligibility: Applicant must be high school senior. Applicant must be U.S. citizen.
Basis for selection: Major/career interest in engineering. Applicant must demonstrate high academic achievement.
Application requirements: Essay, transcript. SAT or ACT scores, list of extracurricular activities.
Additional information: Minimum 3.75 GPA. Applicants must rank in the 90th percentile on SAT (Math and Reading) or ACT. Award renewable for three years if student maintains 3.0 GPA. Visit Website for application. For list of ABET-accredited schools, visit www.abet.org.

Amount of award:	$1,000
Number of awards:	1
Application deadline:	January 15
Notification begins:	June 30

Contact:
SAE International
SAE Engineering Scholarships
400 Commonwealth Drive
Warrendale, PA 15096-0001
Phone: 724-776-4841
Web: www.sae.org/scholarships

Ralph K. Hillquist Honorary SAE Scholarship

Type of award: Scholarship.
Intended use: For full-time junior study at accredited 4-year institution in United States. Designated institutions: ABET-accredited engineering schools.
Eligibility: Applicant must be U.S. citizen.
Basis for selection: Major/career interest in engineering, mechanical. Applicant must demonstrate high academic achievement.
Additional information: Minimum 3.0 GPA. Any automotive-related engineering majors are eligible. Preference given to those with areas of expertise related to noise and vibration (statics, dynamic, physics, vibration). Award is given every other year at the SAE Noise & Vibration Conference. For list of ABET-accredited schools, visit www.abet.org.

Amount of award:	$1,000
Number of awards:	1
Application deadline:	January 15
Notification begins:	June 30

Contact:
SAE Engineering Scholarships
400 Commonwealth Drive
Warrendale, PA 15096-0001
Phone: 724-776-4841
Web: www.sae.org/scholarships

SAE Detroit Section Technical Scholarship

Type of award: Scholarship, renewable.
Intended use: For freshman study at accredited 2-year or 4-year institution. Designated institutions: ABET-accredited schools.
Eligibility: Applicant must be high school senior. Applicant must be U.S. citizen.
Basis for selection: Major/career interest in engineering or computer/information sciences. Applicant must demonstrate financial need.
Application requirements: Essay, transcript. FAFSA, SAT or ACT scores, list of extracurricular activities.
Additional information: Applicant must be child or grandchild of current SAE Detroit Section member. Minimum 3.0 GPA and 1200 SAT (exclusive of Writing) or 28 ACT. Must maintain 2.5 GPA to renew scholarship. Renewable and transferable up to three consecutive years. Visit Website for application. For list of ABET-accredited schools, visit www.abet.org.

Amount of award:	$5,000
Number of awards:	2
Application deadline:	January 15
Notification begins:	June 30

Contact:
SAE International
SAE Engineering Scholarships
400 Commonwealth Drive
Warrendale, PA 15096-0001
Phone: 724-776-4841
Web: www.sae.org/scholarships

SAE Long-Term Member Sponsored Scholarship

Type of award: Scholarship.
Intended use: For full-time senior study at 4-year institution.
Basis for selection: Major/career interest in engineering. Applicant must demonstrate leadership.
Application requirements: Recommendations, proof of eligibility.
Additional information: Applicant must be active SAE student member. Must demonstrate support for SAE activities and programs. Must be junior in college at time of application. Number of awards varies. Apply online.

Amount of award:	$1,000
Application deadline:	February 15
Notification begins:	June 30

Contact:
SAE International
SAE Engineering Scholarships
400 Commonwealth Drive
Warrendale, PA 15096-0001
Phone: 724-776-4841
Web: www.sae.org/scholarships

SAE Women Engineers Committee Scholarship

Type of award: Scholarship.
Intended use: For freshman study. Designated institutions: ABET-accredited engineering schools.
Eligibility: Applicant must be female, high school senior. Applicant must be U.S. citizen.
Basis for selection: Major/career interest in engineering.
Application requirements: Essay, transcript. SAT or ACT scores, list of extracurricular activities.
Additional information: Minimum 3.0 GPA. Visit Website for application. For list of ABET-accredited schools, visit www.abet.org.

Amount of award:	$2,000
Number of awards:	1
Application deadline:	January 15
Notification begins:	June 30

Contact:
SAE International
SAE Engineering Scholarships
400 Commonwealth Drive
Warrendale, PA 15096-0001
Phone: 724-776-4841
Web: www.sae.org/scholarships

SAE/David Hermance Hybird Technologies Scholarship

Type of award: Scholarship.
Intended use: For junior study at accredited 2-year or 4-year institution in United States. Designated institutions: ABET-accredited engineering schools.
Eligibility: Applicant must be U.S. citizen.
Basis for selection: Major/career interest in engineering.

Additional information: Minimum 3.5 GPA. For list of ABET-accredited schools, visit www.abet.org.

Amount of award:	$2,500
Number of awards:	1
Application deadline:	February 15
Notification begins:	June 30

Contact:
SAE Engineering Scholarships
400 Commonwealth Drive
Warrendale, PA 15096-0001
Phone: 724-776-4841
Web: www.sae.org/scholarships

SAE/Ford Partnership for Advanced Studies Scholarship

Type of award: Scholarship.
Intended use: For full-time freshman study at accredited 4-year institution in United States. Designated institutions: ABET-accredited engineering schools.
Eligibility: Applicant must be high school senior. Applicant must be U.S. citizen.
Additional information: Minimum 3.0 GPA. Must rank in the 90th percentile in both math and critical reading on SAT I or the composite ACT scores. Must be a past or present student of a Ford PAS program at their high school or in a Ford PAS afterschool/weekend/summer/college program. For list of ABET-accredited schools, visit www.abet.org.

Amount of award:	$5,000
Number of awards:	1
Application deadline:	January 15
Notification begins:	June 30

Contact:
SAE International
SAE Engineering Scholarships
400 Commonwealth Drive
Warrendale, PA 15096-0001
Phone: 724-776-4841
Web: www.sae.org/scholarships

Siegel Service Technology Scholarships

Type of award: Scholarship.
Intended use: For sophomore study at 4-year institution in United States. Designated institutions: University of Montana-Helena, University of Montana-Missoula, Montana State University-Billings, Montana State University-Great Falls, Montana State University-Northern Havre, Montana Tech-Butte.
Eligibility: Applicant must be U.S. citizen residing in Montana.
Basis for selection: Major/career interest in automotive technology or agriculture. Applicant must demonstrate high academic achievement.
Additional information: Minimum 3.0 GPA. Other eligible service technology fields are aircraft, heavy truck, auto body repair and refinishing, off-highway equipment, and related mobility technology.

Amount of award:	$1,000
Number of awards:	6
Application deadline:	May 15
Total amount awarded:	$6,000

Contact:
SAE International
SAE Engineering Scholarships
400 Commonwealth Drive
Warrendale, PA 15096-0001
Phone: 724-776-4841
Web: www.sae.org/scholarships

Tau Beta Pi/SAE Engineering Scholarship

Type of award: Scholarship.
Intended use: For freshman study at accredited postsecondary institution. Designated institutions: ABET-accredited engineering schools.
Eligibility: Applicant must be high school senior. Applicant must be U.S. citizen.
Basis for selection: Major/career interest in engineering. Applicant must demonstrate high academic achievement.
Application requirements: Essay, transcript. SAT or ACT scores, list of extracurricular activities.
Additional information: Minimum 3.75 GPA. Applicant must rank in 90th percentile on SAT (Math and Reading) or composite ACT. Visit Website for application. For list of ABET-accredited schools, visit www.abet.org.

Amount of award:	$1,000
Number of awards:	6
Application deadline:	January 15
Notification begins:	June 30

Contact:
SAE International
SAE Engineering Scholarships
400 Commonwealth Drive
Warrendale, PA 15096-0001
Phone: 724-776-4841
Web: www.sae.org/scholarships

TMC/SAE Donald D. Dawson Technical Scholarship

Type of award: Scholarship, renewable.
Intended use: For undergraduate study. Designated institutions: ABET-accredited engineering schools.
Eligibility: Applicant must be U.S. citizen.
Basis for selection: Major/career interest in engineering.
Application requirements: Transcript. Essay showing evidence of hands-on automotive experience or activity, SAT or ACT scores, list of extracurricular activities.
Additional information: Graduating high school seniors must have minimum 3.25 GPA, 600 SAT (Math) and 550 SAT (Reading), 27 ACT. Transfer students from four-year schools with 3.0 GPA, and students/graduates of technical/vocational schools with 3.5 GPA also eligible. Award renewable for four years as long as a 3.0 GPA maintained. Visit Website for application. For list of ABET-accredited schools, visit www.abet.org.

Amount of award:	$1,500
Number of awards:	1
Application deadline:	January 15
Notification begins:	June 30

Contact:
SAE International
SAE Engineering Scholarships
400 Commonwealth Drive
Warrendale, PA 15096-0001
Phone: 724-776-4841
Web: www.sae.org/scholarships

Yanmar/SAE Scholarship

Type of award: Scholarship, renewable.
Intended use: For full-time senior or graduate study at accredited 4-year institution. Designated institutions: ABET-accredited engineering schools.
Eligibility: Applicant must be U.S. citizen or Canadian or Mexican citizen.
Basis for selection: Major/career interest in engineering. Applicant must demonstrate high academic achievement and leadership.
Application requirements: Essay, transcript, proof of eligibility. List of extracurricular activities.
Additional information: Must pursue course of study or research related to conservation of energy in transportation, agriculture and construction, or power generation. Emphasis placed on research or study related to internal combustion engine. Must be junior in college at time of application. Scholarship renewable for one additional year. Visit Website for application. For list of ABET-accredited schools, visit www.abet.org.

Amount of award:	$1,000
Number of awards:	1
Application deadline:	February 15
Notification begins:	June 30

Contact:
SAE International
SAE Scholarship & Award Program
400 Commonwealth Drive
Warrendale, PA 15096-0001
Phone: 724-776-4841
Web: www.sae.org/scholarships

Sallie Mae Fund

911 Education Fund Scholarship Program

Type of award: Scholarship, renewable.
Intended use: For full-time undergraduate study at accredited 2-year or 4-year institution.
Eligibility: Applicant's parent must have been killed or disabled in work-related accident as firefighter, police officer or public safety officer.
Basis for selection: Applicant must demonstrate financial need.
Application requirements: Proof of eligibility. Insurance determination letter or referral letter from family member verifying death of parent.
Additional information: Applicant must be child of police officer, fire safety officer, or medical personnel victim of September 11, 2001 attacks. Visit Website for application. Students must submit application to their school's financial aid administrator.

Amount of award:	$2,500
Application deadline:	May 15
Notification begins:	September 1

Contact:
The Sallie Mae 911 Education Fund Scholarship Program
CFNCR
1201 15th Street, NW, Suite 420
Washington, DC 20005
Phone: 800-441-4043
Web: www.salliemae.com

Unmet Need Scholarship Program

Type of award: Scholarship.
Intended use: For full-time undergraduate study at accredited postsecondary institution in or outside United States. Designated institutions: Title IV eligible institutions in United States and Puerto Rico.
Eligibility: Applicant must be U.S. citizen or permanent resident.
Basis for selection: Applicant must demonstrate financial need.
Application requirements: Transcript. SAR, FAFSA, financial aid award letter from institution.
Additional information: Family's adjusted gross income must be $30,000 or less. Minimum 2.5 GPA or GED score of 42. Visit Website for more information and application.

Amount of award:	$1,000-$3,000
Application deadline:	May 31

Contact:
The Sallie Mae Fund Unmet Need Scholarship Program
Scholarship America
One Scholarship Way, P.O. Box 297
Saint Peter, MN 56082
Phone: 507-931-1682
Web: www.salliemae.com

Salute to Education, Inc.

Salute to Education Scholarship

Type of award: Scholarship.
Intended use: For undergraduate study at postsecondary institution.
Eligibility: Applicant must be high school senior. Applicant must be U.S. citizen residing in Florida.
Basis for selection: Applicant must demonstrate financial need, high academic achievement, depth of character, leadership, seriousness of purpose and service orientation.
Additional information: Minimum 3.0 GPA. Number of awards varies from 140 to 200 per year. Applicant must be a resident of and attend an accredited public or private high school in Miami-Dade or Broward County. Scholarships in following categories: athletics, language arts and foreign languages, leadership/service, mathematics/computer science, natural science, performing arts, and visual arts. Visit Website for application and deadline.

Amount of award:	$1,000
Number of awards:	140
Number of applicants:	1,400
Notification begins:	April 15
Total amount awarded:	$140,000

Contact:
Salute to Education, Inc.
P.O. Box 833425
Miami, FL 33283
Phone: 305-799-6726
Fax: 786-515-9864
Web: www.stescholarships.org

Scarlett Family Foundation Scholarship Program

Scarlett Family Foundation Scholarship

Type of award: Scholarship, renewable.
Intended use: For full-time undergraduate study at postsecondary institution. Designated institutions: Not-for-profit institutions.
Eligibility: Applicant must be residing in Tennessee.
Basis for selection: Major/career interest in accounting; business; business, international; business/management/ administration or finance/banking. Applicant must demonstrate financial need.
Application requirements: Essay, transcript. FAFSA.
Additional information: Minimum award is $2500. Amount of award varies based on need. Applicant's minimum high school or college GPA must be 2.5. Applicant must be from one of 39 counties in Tennessee. Visit Website for details.

Number of awards:	21
Application deadline:	December 15
Notification begins:	September 15
Total amount awarded:	$370,000

Contact:
Scarlett Family Foundation Scholarship Program
c/o ISTS, Inc.
P.O. Box 23737
Nashville, TN 37202-3737
Phone: 615-320-3149
Fax: 615-627-9685
Web: www.scarlettfoundation.org

Screen Actors Guild Foundation

John L. Dales Standard Scholarship

Type of award: Scholarship, renewable.
Intended use: For full-time undergraduate or graduate study at accredited 2-year, 4-year or graduate institution in United States.
Eligibility: Applicant or parent must be member/participant of Screen Actor's Guild.
Basis for selection: Applicant must demonstrate financial need.
Application requirements: Recommendations, essay, transcript, proof of eligibility. Most recent federal income tax return and additional financial information. SAT/ACT scores.
Additional information: Member under the age of 22 must have been a member for five years and have lifetime earnings of $30,000. Parent of applicant must have ten vested years of pension credits or lifetime earnings of $150,000. Consult office or Website for more information. Number and amount of awards vary.

Number of awards:	93
Number of applicants:	124
Application deadline:	March 16
Notification begins:	July 7
Total amount awarded:	$372,000

Contact:
Screen Actors Guild Foundation
John L. Dales Scholarship Fund
5757 Wilshire Boulevard, Suite 124
Los Angeles, CA 90036
Phone: 323-549-6649
Fax: 323-549-6710
Web: www.sagfoundation.org

John L. Dales Transitional Scholarship

Type of award: Scholarship, renewable.
Intended use: For full-time undergraduate or graduate study at accredited postsecondary institution in United States.
Basis for selection: Applicant must demonstrate financial need.
Application requirements: Recommendations, essay, transcript, proof of eligibility. Most recent federal income tax return and additional financial information. SAT/ACT scores.
Additional information: Must be member of Screen Actors Guild. Applicant must have ten vested years of pension credits with SAG or lifetime earnings of $150,000. Consult office or visit Website for more information. Number and amount of awards vary.

Number of awards:	9
Number of applicants:	16
Application deadline:	March 16
Notification begins:	July 7
Total amount awarded:	$36,000

Contact:
Screen Actors Guild Foundation
John L. Dales Scholarship Fund
5757 Wilshire Boulevard, Suite 124
Los Angeles, CA 90036
Phone: 323-549-6649
Fax: 323-549-6710
Web: www.sagfoundation.org

Seabee Memorial Scholarship Association, Inc.

Seabee Memorial Scholarship

Type of award: Scholarship, renewable.
Intended use: For full-time undergraduate study at accredited 4-year institution in United States.
Eligibility: Applicant must be U.S. citizen. Applicant must be descendant of veteran who served in the Navy. Applicant must be child or grandchild of a currently enlisted, honorably discharged, or deceased member of Naval Construction FORCE (Seabees) or Navy CEC (Civil Engineer Corps).
Basis for selection: Applicant must demonstrate financial need, high academic achievement, depth of character, leadership, patriotism, seriousness of purpose and service orientation.
Application requirements: Essay, transcript, proof of eligibility. IRS Form 1040. Official document (DD214, reenlistment certificate, transfer orders, etc.) that verifies rate/ rank of sponsor.
Additional information: Award is renewable for up to four years. Download application from Website.

Contact:
Screen Actors Guild Foundation
John L. Dales Scholarship Fund
5757 Wilshire Boulevard, Suite 124
Los Angeles, CA 90036
Phone: 323-549-6649
Fax: 323-549-6710
Web: www.sagfoundation.org

Amount of award:	$1,800-$5,000
Number of applicants:	350
Application deadline:	April 15
Notification begins:	June 15

Contact:
Scholarship Committee
P.O. Box 6574
Silver Spring, MD 20916
Phone: 301-570-2850
Fax: 301-570-2873
Web: www.seabee.org

Seattle Jaycees

Seattle Jaycees Scholarship

Type of award: Scholarship, renewable.
Intended use: For undergraduate or graduate study at accredited vocational, 2-year, 4-year or graduate institution.
Designated institutions: Institutions in Washington state.
Eligibility: Applicant must be residing in Washington.
Basis for selection: Applicant must demonstrate depth of character, leadership and service orientation.
Application requirements: $5 application fee. Recommendations, essay, transcript. List of community service, civic, and other extra-curricular activities.
Additional information: Scholarships granted for exemplary civic involvement, volunteerism, and community service. Renewable one time. Visit Website for application and more information.

Amount of award:	$1,000
Number of awards:	20
Number of applicants:	480
Application deadline:	April 1
Notification begins:	June 1

Contact:
Seattle Jaycees
Scholarship Committee
P.O. Box 9640
Seattle, WA 98109
Phone: 206-286-2014
Web: www.seattlejaycees.org

Second Marine Division Association

Second Marine Division Association Scholarship Fund

Type of award: Scholarship, renewable.
Intended use: For full-time undergraduate study at accredited vocational, 2-year or 4-year institution.
Eligibility: Must be dependent child or grandchild of person who serves or served in Second Marine Division, U.S. Marine Corps, or unit attached to the division.
Basis for selection: Applicant must demonstrate financial need.
Application requirements: Recommendations, essay, transcript, proof of eligibility.

Additional information: Family's adjusted gross income should not exceed $65,000 for the taxable year prior to application. Exceptions may be made for larger families. Minimum 2.75 GPA. Must reapply for renewal. Include SASE when requesting application. Parent or grandparent who served in the Second Marine Division must join SMDA, if not already a member, once scholarship is awarded.

Amount of award:	$1,200
Number of awards:	38
Number of applicants:	44
Application deadline:	April 1, July 1
Notification begins:	September 15
Total amount awarded:	$32,000

Contact:
Second Marine Division Association Memorial Scholarship Fund
P.O. Box 8180
Camp Lejeune, NC 28547
Phone: 910-451-3167
Web: www.2Dmardiv.com

Senator George J. Mitchell Scholarship Research Institute

Senator George J. Mitchell Scholarship

Type of award: Scholarship, renewable.
Intended use: For freshman study at accredited 2-year or 4-year institution in United States.
Eligibility: Applicant must be high school senior. Applicant must be U.S. citizen residing in Maine.
Basis for selection: Applicant must demonstrate financial need, high academic achievement and service orientation.
Application requirements: Essay, transcript, proof of eligibility. Letter from guidance counselor, SAR, copy of financial aid award from college student plans to attend.
Additional information: One award made to graduating senior from every public high school in Maine. Renewable for up to four years. Award total is $5,000 -- $1,250 per year for four years. Scholarship to be applied to spring semester bill. Application due April 1, supporting materials due May 1.

Amount of award:	$1,250-$5,000
Number of awards:	130
Number of applicants:	1,000
Application deadline:	April 1
Notification begins:	June 1

Contact:
Senator George J. Mitchell Scholarship Research Institute
22 Monument Square
Suite 200
Portland, ME 04101
Phone: 207-773-7700
Fax: 207-773-1133
Web: www.mitchellinstitute.org

Seneca Nation and BIA

Seneca Nation Higher Education Program

Type of award: Scholarship, renewable.
Intended use: For undergraduate or graduate study at accredited 2-year, 4-year or graduate institution.
Eligibility: Applicant must be American Indian. Must be an enrolled member of Seneca Nation of Indians. Applicant must be U.S. citizen.
Basis for selection: Applicant must demonstrate financial need.
Application requirements: Essay, transcript, proof of eligibility. Proof of tribal enrollment, letter of reference from non-relative.
Additional information: Amount and number of awards vary. Residency requirements: Level 1- New York State residents living on reservation; Level 2- New York State residents living in New York; Level 3- Enrolled members living outside New York. Application deadlines: fall, July 1; spring, December 1; summer, May 1. Contact sponsor or see Website for more information.

Application deadline:	July 1, December 1

Contact:
Seneca Nation of Indians
Higher Education Program
P.O. Box 231
Salamanca, NY 14779
Phone: 716-945-1790 ext. 3103
Web: www.sni.org

Sertoma

Sertoma Scholarships for Students Who are Hard of Hearing or Deaf

Type of award: Scholarship, renewable.
Intended use: For full-time undergraduate study at 4-year institution in United States.
Eligibility: Applicant must be hearing impaired. Applicant must be U.S. citizen or permanent resident.
Basis for selection: Applicant must demonstrate high academic achievement, depth of character and seriousness of purpose.
Application requirements: Transcript. Statement of purpose, two letters of recommendation, documentation of hearing impairment in form of recent audiogram or signed statement by hearing-health professional.
Additional information: Applicant must have minimum of 40 dB bilateral hearing loss. Must have minimum 3.2 GPA. Visit Website for application and more information.

Amount of award:	$1,000
Number of awards:	40
Number of applicants:	160
Application deadline:	May 1
Notification begins:	June 1
Total amount awarded:	$40,000

Contact:
Sertoma
Attn: Scholarships
1912 East Meyer Boulevard
Kansas City, MO 64132-1174
Web: www.sertoma.org

Service Employees International Union

Charles Hardy Memorial Scholarship

Type of award: Scholarship, renewable.
Intended use: For full-time freshman study at accredited 2-year or 4-year institution in United States.
Eligibility: Applicant or parent must be member/participant of Service Employees International Union. Applicant must be high school senior. Applicant must be residing in California.
Application requirements: Recommendations, essay, transcript.
Additional information: Contact local union office for application.

Amount of award:	$1,000
Number of awards:	4
Application deadline:	March 15
Total amount awarded:	$4,000

Contact:
Service Employees International Union
California State Council
1007 7th Street, 4th Floor
Sacramento, CA 95814-3407
Phone: 916-442-3838
Fax: 916-442-0976
Web: www.seiucal.org

Shoshone Tribe

Shoshone Tribal Scholarship

Type of award: Scholarship, renewable.
Intended use: For undergraduate or graduate study at accredited vocational, 2-year or 4-year institution in United States.
Eligibility: Applicant must be American Indian. Must be enrolled member of Eastern Shoshone Tribe.
Basis for selection: Applicant must demonstrate financial need.
Application requirements: Transcript, proof of eligibility.
Additional information: Must first apply for Pell Grant and appropriate campus-based aid. Minimum 2.5 GPA. Award renewable for maximum ten semesters. Application deadlines: academic year, June 1; spring, November 15; summer, April 15. Number of awards varies.

Amount of award:	$50-$15,000
Number of awards:	60
Number of applicants:	100
Application deadline:	June 1, November 15
Total amount awarded:	$300,000

Contact:
Eastern Shoshone Tribe
PL102-447 Program
104 Washakie Street, P.O. Box 1210
Fort Washakie, WY 82514
Phone: 307-332-8052
Fax: 307-332-8055

Sid Richardson Memorial Fund

Sid Richardson Scholarship

Type of award: Scholarship, renewable.
Intended use: For full-time undergraduate or graduate study at accredited postsecondary institution.
Basis for selection: Major/career interest in humanities/liberal arts. Applicant must demonstrate financial need and high academic achievement.
Application requirements: Essay, transcript, proof of eligibility. SAT or ACT scores.
Additional information: Must be direct descendant (child or grandchild) of persons who qualified for early retirement, normal retirement, disability retirement, or death benefits from The Retirement Plan for Employees of Bass Enterprises Production Co.; or direct descendant of persons presently employed with a minimum of three years' full-time service with any of the following employers: Sid Richardson Carbon and Energy Co. (Sid Richardson Carbon and Gasoline Company or Sid Richardson Carbon Company) and SRCE, L.P.; Bass Enterprises Production Co.; BEPCO, L.P.; Bass Brothers Enterprises, Inc.; Richardson Oils, Inc.; Perry R. Bass, Inc. (Sid W. Richardson, Inc.); Chisholm Trail Ventures, L.P.; Sid W. Richardson Foundation; San Jose Cattle Company (Fairview Farms); City Center Development Co.; Richardson Aviation; Sid Richardson Carbon, Ltd.; SRCG Aviation, Inc.; Leapartners, L.P.; Barbnet Investments Co.; City Club of Fort Worth (City Center Development Co.); City Center Development Co., L.P. (DBA City Center Development Co. and City Center Executive Suite); Sundance Square; Sundance Square Partners, L.P. (DBA Sundance Square, the Cassidy, and Sundance Square Development); Sundance Square Management, L.P. (DBA Sundance Square Management Co. and Sundance Square Management); BOPCO, L.P., Sid Richardson Energy Services, Ltd. (Sid Richardson Energy Services Co., Sid Richardson Gasoline, Ltd., or Sid Richardson Gasoline Co.) and Richardson Energy Marketing, Ltd. (Richardson Products II, Ltd.). Apply by mail, email, or fax. Must include student name, address, qualifying employee name, Social Security number of employee, qualifying company name, and dates of employment.

Amount of award:	$500-$7,000
Number of applicants:	82
Application deadline:	March 31
Notification begins:	May 15
Total amount awarded:	$230,750

Contact:
Sid Richardson Memorial Fund
309 Main Street
Fort Worth, TX 76102
Phone: 817-336-0494
Fax: 817-332-2176

Siemens Foundation

Siemens Awards for Advanced Placement

Type of award: Scholarship.
Intended use: For full-time freshman study at accredited 4-year institution.
Eligibility: Applicant must be enrolled in high school. Applicant must be U.S. citizen or permanent resident.
Basis for selection: Competition/talent/interest in academics, based on the most scores of "5" on AP tests in eight subjects: Calculus BC, Computer Science A, Statistics, Chemistry, Biology, Environmental Science, Physics C: Mechanics, and Physics C: Electricity.
Additional information: A $2,000 college scholarship awarded each spring to up to one male and one female student from each of the 50 states. No application for award. Two additional national winners (one male, one female) will be awarded $5,000 college scholarship. Students must still be in high school in the spring when the award is announced. Must attain a score of 5 on at least two of the aforementioned exams. Composite exams used as tiebreaker if multiple students attain same number of 5's. All U.S. high school students who have taken an AP exam in year prior to applying are eligible, as well as homeschooled students. Students may be awarded state or national award only once, but state winners may be considered for national award in subsequent years. See Website for more details.

Amount of award:	$2,000-$5,000
Number of awards:	102
Notification begins:	February 1
Total amount awarded:	$210,000

Contact:
The College Board
Attn: Siemens Awards for AP
11955 Democracy Drive
Reston, VA 20190
Phone: 800-626-9795
Fax: 703-935-7795
Web: www.collegeboard.com/siemens or www.siemens-foundation.org

Siemens Competition in Math, Science and Technology

Type of award: Scholarship.
Intended use: For full-time undergraduate or graduate study at accredited 4-year or graduate institution.
Eligibility: Applicant must be enrolled in high school. Applicant must be U.S. citizen or permanent resident.
Basis for selection: Competition/talent/interest in science project, based on originality, scientific importance, validity, creativity, academic rigor, clarity of expression, comprehensiveness, experimental work, field knowledge. Major/career interest in biology; chemistry; engineering; environmental science; materials science; mathematics; physics; computer/information sciences or medicine.
Application requirements: Proof of eligibility, research proposal. An 18-page (maximum) research report followed by poster and oral presentations for Regional Finalists. Confirmation page signed by school administrator. Completed supplemental form and project advisor or mentor comments form.

Additional information: Competition to encourage students to do research in math, science, or technology, giving young scientists the opportunity to present their research to leading scientists in their field. Regional Finalists awarded trip to compete at one of six regional competitions. At regional event, after presenting a poster, giving an oral presentation, and participating in Q&A session, the student or team of students will qualify for $1,000 or $3,000 scholarship. National Finalists qualify for $10,000 to $100,000 scholarship. Solo applicants must be seniors; team applicants may be freshmen, sophomores, juniors, or seniors. Register at Website.

Amount of award:	$1,000-$100,000
Number of awards:	60
Number of applicants:	1,786
Application deadline:	October 3
Notification begins:	October 21
Total amount awarded:	$450,000

Contact:
Siemens Competition Program Manager
c/o The College Board
11955 Democracy Drive, 10th floor
Reston, VA 20190
Phone: 800-626-9795 ext. 5849
Fax: 703-935-7795
Web: www.collegeboard.com/siemens

Siemens Merit Scholarship

Type of award: Scholarship.
Intended use: For full-time junior study at 4-year institution in United States.
Eligibility: Applicant must be high school junior. Applicant must be U.S. citizen or permanent resident.
Basis for selection: Applicant must demonstrate financial need and high academic achievement.
Application requirements: Proof of eligibility. PSAT/NMSQT scores.
Additional information: Award is $6,000 distributed at $1,500 each year for up to four years of undergraduate study or until baccalaureate degree requirements are completed, whichever comes first. High school students who are sons and daughters of employees of Siemens or its designated operating companies are eligible. Students must also meet all requirements for participation in the National Merit Scholarship Program that are published in the Official Student Guide to the PSAT/NMSQT which is updated annually and distributed to students through their high schools. Number of awards varies. Visit Website for deadline and more details.

Amount of award:	$6,000

Contact:
Siemens Foundation c/o Kiesha Boykins
170 Wood Avenue South
Iselin, NJ 08830
Phone: 732-321-3150
Web: www.siemens-foundation.org

Slovak Gymnastic Union Sokol, USA

Milan Getting Scholarship

Type of award: Scholarship, renewable.
Intended use: For full-time undergraduate study at accredited 4-year institution.

Eligibility: Applicant must be high school junior or senior. Applicant must be U.S. citizen.
Basis for selection: Applicant must demonstrate high academic achievement, depth of character, leadership, patriotism and seriousness of purpose.
Application requirements: Recommendations, transcript.
Additional information: Applicant must be member in good standing of Slovak Gymnastic Union Sokol, USA, for at least three years. Minimum scholastic average of C+ or equivalent required. Award renewable for four years. Number of awards varies. Deadline in March. Contact sponsor for application form and more information.

Amount of award:	$500
Number of awards:	2
Number of applicants:	6
Total amount awarded:	$7,500

Contact:
Slovak Gymnastic Union Sokol, USA
P.O. Box 189
East Orange, NJ 07019
Phone: 973-676-0280

Slovenian Women's Union of America

Slovenian Women's Union Scholarship For Returning Adults

Type of award: Scholarship.
Intended use: For undergraduate certificate or non-degree study at vocational, 2-year or 4-year institution in United States.
Eligibility: Applicant must be returning adult student.
Basis for selection: Applicant must demonstrate financial need, depth of character, leadership and service orientation.
Application requirements: Resume and/or personal statement or autobiography.
Additional information: Applicant must be member of Slovenian Women's Union or active participant of organization's activities for three years. Open to men and women with interest in promoting Slovene culture. Contact Mary Turvey at SWUA for more information.

Amount of award:	$500
Number of awards:	2
Application deadline:	March 1
Total amount awarded:	$1,000

Contact:
Slovenian Women's Union of America
Scholarship Director
4 Lawrence Drive
Marquette, MI 49855
Phone: 906-249-4288
Web: www.swua.org

Slovenian Women's Union Scholarship Foundation

Type of award: Scholarship.
Intended use: For full-time undergraduate study at accredited 2-year or 4-year institution in United States.
Basis for selection: Applicant must demonstrate financial need, depth of character, leadership and service orientation.
Application requirements: Recommendations, essay, transcript. FAFSA, resume, and photograph.

Additional information: Applicant must be member of
Slovenian Women's Union or active participant of
organization's activities for three years. Open to women and
men with interest in promoting Slovene culture.
Recommendation must be from SWUA branch officer and
instructor. Number of awards varies. Contact Mary Turvey at
SWUA for more information.

Amount of award:	$1,000-$3,000
Number of awards:	5
Number of applicants:	15
Application deadline:	March 1
Notification begins:	April 1
Total amount awarded:	$7,000

Contact:
Slovenian Women's Union of America
Scholarship Director
4 Lawrence Drive
Marquette, MI 49855
Phone: 906-249-4288
Web: www.swua.org

SNM

Nuclear Medicine Student Fellowship Award

Type of award: Research grant.
Intended use: For undergraduate, master's, doctoral or first
professional study at postsecondary institution.
Basis for selection: Major/career interest in nuclear medicine;
medicine or pharmacy/pharmaceutics/pharmacology.
Application requirements: Recommendations, research
proposal. Resume.
Additional information: Major/career interest may also
include molecular imaging. Maximum three-month research
internship assisting in clinical and basic research activities in
nuclear medicine. Competence in physical and/or biological
aspects of radioactivity essential. Recipients must give
foundation summary of activities before receiving final monthly
allocation. Visit Website for application and deadline.

Amount of award:	$3,000
Number of awards:	4
Number of applicants:	25
Total amount awarded:	$12,000

Contact:
Attn: SNM Awards Committee
SNM Development Office
1850 Samuel Morse Drive
Reston, VA 20190-5316
Phone: 703-652-6795
Web: www.snm.org/grants

SNM Technologist Section

Paul Cole Scholarship

Type of award: Scholarship.
Intended use: For undergraduate study at accredited 2-year or
4-year institution. Designated institutions: Schools accredited by
the Joint Review Committee on Educational Programs in
Nuclear Medicine Technology (JRCNMT).

Basis for selection: Major/career interest in nuclear medicine.
Applicant must demonstrate financial need and high academic
achievement.
Application requirements: Recommendations, essay,
transcript, proof of eligibility.
Additional information: Minimum 2.5 GPA. Applicant must
be in a program to receive Associates or Bachelors degree in
nuclear medicine technology. Special consideration will be
given to applicants who are not only academically capable but
who might be financially unable to attend training program
without the scholarship. Deadline in January; notification begins
in October. Visit Website for more information.

Amount of award:	$1,000
Number of awards:	15
Number of applicants:	85
Total amount awarded:	$15,000

Contact:
SNM Development Office
Attn: SNMTS Awards Committee
1850 Samuel Morse Drive
Reston, VA 20190-5316
Phone: 703-708-9000
Web: www.snm.org/grants

Sociedad Honoraria Hispanica

Joseph S. Adams Scholarship

Type of award: Scholarship.
Intended use: For full-time freshman study in United States.
Eligibility: Applicant must be high school senior.
Basis for selection: Major/career interest in Latin American
studies or foreign languages. Applicant must demonstrate high
academic achievement, depth of character, leadership,
patriotism, seriousness of purpose and service orientation.
Application requirements: Recommendations, essay,
transcript, proof of eligibility, nomination by local high school
chapter sponsor.
Additional information: Applicant must be active senior
member of Sociedad Honoraria Hispanica. Applicant must be
presently enrolled in high school Spanish or Portuguese class.
SHH members should contact their sponsor, not the national
director, regarding application before December 31. All majors
eligible; strong interest in Latin American Studies, Spanish,
Portuguese preferred. Only one member per chapter may apply.

Amount of award:	$1,000-$2,000
Number of awards:	52
Number of applicants:	200
Application deadline:	February 15
Notification begins:	April 15
Total amount awarded:	$64,000

Contact:
Upakar c/o Mukunda
10237 Nolan Drive
Rockville, MD 20850
Phone: 847-550-0455
Fax: 847-550-0460
Web: www.sociedadhonorariahispanica.org

Society for Range Management

Masonic Range Science Scholarship

Type of award: Scholarship, renewable.
Intended use: For full-time freshman or sophomore study at postsecondary institution. Designated institutions: Colleges or universities with range science programs.
Basis for selection: Major/career interest in range science. Applicant must demonstrate high academic achievement and leadership.
Application requirements: Recommendations, essay, transcript, nomination by member of Society for Range Management, National Association of Conservation Districts, or Soil and Water Conservation Society. SAT/ACT scores.
Additional information: Award amount varies. Renewable for maximum of eight semesters. Student must maintain 2.5 GPA first two semesters, 3.0 GPA any subsequent semesters. Visit Website for more information and application.

Number of awards:	1
Number of applicants:	18
Application deadline:	January 15
Notification begins:	March 1
Total amount awarded:	$6,200

Contact:
Society for Range Management
Paul Loeffler, Texas General Land Office
500 West Avenue H, Suite 101, Box 2
Alpine, TX 79830-6008
Phone: 303-986-3309
Fax: 303-986-3892
Web: www.rangelands.org

Society for Science & the Public

Intel International Science and Engineering Fair

Type of award: Scholarship.
Intended use: For undergraduate study at postsecondary institution.
Eligibility: Applicant must be enrolled in high school.
Basis for selection: Competition/talent/interest in science project, based on merit at Intel ISEF-affiliated regional or state fair. Major/career interest in science, general or engineering.
Additional information: World's largest precollege science competition. Students compete at Intel ISEF-affiliated regional or state fair; winners advance to Intel ISEF. All paperwork must be received by SSP within 12 days after regional or state fair is held. Visit Website for more information.

Amount of award:	$100-$50,000
Number of awards:	800
Number of applicants:	1,554
Total amount awarded:	$4,000,000

Contact:
Intel ISEF
Society for Science and the Public
1719 N Street NW
Washington, DC 20036
Phone: 202-785-2255
Fax: 202-785-1243
Web: www.societyforscience.org

Intel Science Talent Search

Type of award: Scholarship.
Intended use: For undergraduate study at postsecondary institution.
Eligibility: Applicant must be high school senior.
Basis for selection: Competition/talent/interest in science project, based on creative thinking and scientific originality of individual research reports in science, math, or engineering. Major/career interest in biology; science, general; physics or mathematics.
Application requirements: Recommendations, transcript, proof of eligibility. Twenty-page research paper on independent research in science, math, or engineering; standardized test scores.
Additional information: Any students in their last year of secondary school who have completed the courses necessary for college enrollment are eligible. Award may be used for tuition, books, lodging, or meals. Highly competitive program for college-bound students. Visit Website for more information.

Amount of award:	$1,000-$100,000
Number of awards:	300
Number of applicants:	1,736
Application deadline:	November 16
Total amount awarded:	$1,250,000

Contact:
Intel Science Talent Search
Society for Science and the Public
1719 N Street NW
Washington, DC 20036
Phone: 202-785-2255
Fax: 202-785-1243
Web: www.societyforscience.org

Society of Daughters of the United States Army

Society of Daughters of United States Army Scholarship Program

Type of award: Scholarship, renewable.
Intended use: For full-time undergraduate study at accredited postsecondary institution.
Eligibility: Applicant must be female. Applicant must be daughter or granddaughter (including step or adopted) of a career warrant (WO 1-5) or commissioned officer (2nd & 1st LT, CPT, MAJ, LTC, COL, or General) of U.S. Army who (1) is currently on active duty; (2) retired from active duty after at least 20 years of service; (3) was medically retired before 20 years of active service; (4) died while on active duty; or (5) died after retiring from active duty with 20 or more years of service.
Basis for selection: Applicant must demonstrate high academic achievement, depth of character, leadership, patriotism and seriousness of purpose.

Additional information: Minimum 3.0 GPA. Scholarships cover academic expenses only. Request for application must include parent or grandparent's name, rank, component (Active, Regular, Reserve), inclusive dates of active service, and relationship to applicant. Number of awards varies annually. Send business-size SASE and one letter of request only. Do not send birth certificate or original documents. Do not use registered/certified mail. All application submissions become property of DUSA.

Amount of award:	$1,000
Number of applicants:	150
Application deadline:	March 1
Notification begins:	June 1
Total amount awarded:	$12,000

Contact:
Society of Daughters of the United States Army
Mary P. Maroney, Scholarship Chairman
11804 Grey Birch Place
Reston, VA 20191-4223

Society of Exploration Geophysicists

SEG Foundation Scholarship

Type of award: Scholarship, renewable.
Intended use: For undergraduate or graduate study in or outside United States.
Basis for selection: Major/career interest in physics; mathematics; geology/earth sciences or geophysics. Applicant must demonstrate high academic achievement and seriousness of purpose.
Application requirements: Recommendations, essay, transcript, proof of eligibility.
Additional information: Applicant must pursue college course directed toward career in geophysics or a closely related field and must possess an interest in and aptitude for physics, mathematics, and geology. Amount and number of awards vary. Visit Website for more information and application.

Amount of award:	$500-$14,000
Number of awards:	172
Number of applicants:	600
Application deadline:	March 1
Notification begins:	September 1
Total amount awarded:	$415,020

Contact:
SEG Foundation
P.O. Box 702740
Tulsa, OK 74170-2740
Phone: 918-497-5500
Fax: 918-497-5560
Web: www.seg.org

Society of Exploration Geophysicists Scholarship

Type of award: Scholarship, renewable.
Intended use: For full-time undergraduate or graduate study at accredited 4-year or graduate institution.
Basis for selection: Major/career interest in geophysics; geology/earth sciences; physics or environmental science. Applicant must demonstrate high academic achievement.
Application requirements: Recommendations, essay, transcript, proof of eligibility. List of extracurricular activities;

SAT or ACT scores for high school and undergraduate students, GRE or TOEFL scores for graduate students.
Additional information: Number of scholarships available yearly depends on the number of sponsors and the amount they contribute. Applicants must intend to pursue career in exploration geophysics (graduate students in operations, teaching, or research). Visit Website for more information.

Amount of award:	$500-$14,000
Application deadline:	March 1
Notification begins:	September 1
Total amount awarded:	$415,020

Contact:
SEG Foundation
Scholarship Committee
P.O. Box 702740
Tulsa, OK 74170-2740
Phone: 918-497-5500
Web: www.seg.org

Society of Manufacturing Engineers Education Foundation

Albert E. Wischmeyer Memorial Scholarship Award

Type of award: Scholarship, renewable.
Intended use: For full-time undergraduate study at accredited 4-year institution. Designated institutions: Institutions located in the state of New York.
Eligibility: Applicant must be U.S. citizen or permanent resident residing in New York.
Basis for selection: Major/career interest in manufacturing; engineering or technology. Applicant must demonstrate high academic achievement.
Application requirements: Recommendations, essay, transcript. Resume, SAT or ACT scores for current high school students.
Additional information: Applicants must reside in New York State west of Interstate 81. Minimum 2.5 GPA. Must reapply for renewal. Application available on Website.

Amount of award:	$1,000-$2,500
Number of awards:	2
Application deadline:	February 1
Total amount awarded:	$4,000

Contact:
Society of Manufacturing Engineers
Scholarship Review Committee
One SME Drive, P.O. Box 930
Dearborn, MI 48121-0930
Phone: 313-425-3300
Web: www.smeef.org

Arthur and Gladys Cervenka Scholarship

Type of award: Scholarship, renewable.
Intended use: For full-time sophomore, junior or senior study at accredited 4-year institution in United States or Canada.
Eligibility: Applicant must be U.S. citizen, permanent resident or Canadian resident.

Basis for selection: Major/career interest in manufacturing; engineering or technology. Applicant must demonstrate high academic achievement.
Application requirements: Recommendations, essay, transcript. Resume.
Additional information: Applicant must have completed minimum of 30 college credit hours. Minimum 3.0 GPA. Preference given to students attending institutions in Florida.

Amount of award:	$1,000-$2,500
Number of awards:	1
Application deadline:	February 1

Contact:
Society of Manufacturing Engineers
Scholarship Review Committee
One SME Drive, P.O. Box 930
Dearborn, MI 48121-0930
Phone: 313-425-3300
Web: www.smeef.org

Caterpillar Scholars Award

Type of award: Scholarship, renewable.
Intended use: For full-time undergraduate study at 4-year institution in United States or Canada.
Eligibility: Applicant must be U.S. citizen, permanent resident or Canadian resident.
Basis for selection: Major/career interest in manufacturing or engineering. Applicant must demonstrate high academic achievement.
Application requirements: Recommendations, essay, transcript. Resume.
Additional information: Freshmen must supply SAT or ACT scores. Applicants must be enrolled in manufacturing engineering degree program and have completed minimum 30 college credit hours. Minority applicants may apply as incoming freshmen. Minimum 3.0 GPA. Applicants must reapply for renewal. Application available on Website.

Amount of award:	$1,000-$2,500
Number of awards:	5
Application deadline:	February 1
Total amount awarded:	$10,000

Contact:
Society of Manufacturing Engineers
Scholarship Review Committee
One SME Drive, P.O. Box 930
Dearborn, MI 48121-0930
Phone: 313-425-3300
Web: www.smeef.org

Chapter 17 St. Louis Scholarship

Type of award: Scholarship, renewable.
Intended use: For freshman, sophomore or junior study at accredited 2-year or 4-year institution.
Basis for selection: Major/career interest in manufacturing; engineering; engineering, mechanical or technology. Applicant must demonstrate high academic achievement, depth of character and seriousness of purpose.
Application requirements: Recommendations, essay, transcript. Resume, SAT or ACT scores for current high school students.
Additional information: Applicants must be enrolled in manufacturing engineering, industrial technology, or related degree program. Preference given to applicants residing in boundaries of St. Louis Chapter 17. Second preference given to applicants living in Missouri. Minimum 2.5 GPA. Must reapply for renewal. Application available on Website.

Amount of award:	$1,000-$2,500
Number of awards:	2
Application deadline:	February 1
Total amount awarded:	$3,000

Contact:
Society of Manufacturing Engineers
Scholarship Review Committee
One SME Drive, P.O. Box 930
Dearborn, MI 48121-0930
Phone: 313-425-3300
Web: www.smeef.org

Chapter 198 - Downriver Detroit Scholarship

Type of award: Scholarship.
Intended use: For full-time undergraduate or graduate study at accredited 2-year, 4-year or graduate institution. Designated institutions: Michigan institutions.
Eligibility: Applicant must be U.S. citizen, permanent resident or Canadian resident.
Basis for selection: Major/career interest in manufacturing; engineering, mechanical or engineering.
Application requirements: Recommendations, essay, transcript. Resume, SAT or ACT scores for current high school students.
Additional information: First preference given to children or grandchildren of current SME Downriver Chapter 198 members. Second preference given to members of student SME chapters sponsored by Chapter 198. Third preference given to residents of Michigan. Fourth preference given to applicants planning to attend college/university in Michigan. Minimum 2.5 GPA.

Amount of award:	$1,000-$2,500
Number of awards:	1
Application deadline:	February 1

Contact:
Society of Manufacturing Engineers Education Foundation
Scholarship Review Committee
One SME Drive, P.O. Box 930
Dearborn, MI 48121-0930
Phone: 313-425-3300
Web: www.smeef.org

Chapter 4 - Lawrence A. Wacker Memorial Scholarship

Type of award: Scholarship, renewable.
Intended use: For undergraduate study at accredited 4-year institution in United States. Designated institutions: Wisconsin institutions.
Eligibility: Applicant must be U.S. citizen or permanent resident residing in Wisconsin.
Basis for selection: Major/career interest in manufacturing; engineering, industrial or engineering, mechanical. Applicant must demonstrate high academic achievement.
Application requirements: Recommendations, essay, transcript. Resume, SAT or ACT scores for current high school students.
Additional information: Applicants must be seeking bachelor's degree in manufacturing, mechanical, or industrial engineering. Minimum 3.0 GPA. One scholarship granted to graduating high school senior, one to current undergraduate. First preference given to SME Chapter 4 members or spouses, children, or grandchildren of members. Second preference given to residents of Milwaukee, Ozaukee, Washington, and Waukesha counties. Third preference given to Wisconsin

residents. Applicants must reapply for renewal. Application available on Website.

Amount of award:	$1,000-$2,500
Number of awards:	2
Application deadline:	February 1
Total amount awarded:	$3,000

Contact:
Society of Manufacturing Engineers
Scholarship Review Committee
One SME Drive, P.O. Box 930
Dearborn, MI 48121-0930
Phone: 313-425-3300
Web: www.smeef.org

Chapter 52 - Wichita Scholarship

Type of award: Scholarship.
Intended use: For undergraduate or graduate study at accredited 2-year, 4-year or graduate institution in United States. Designated institutions: Kansas, Oklahoma, or Missouri institutions.
Eligibility: Applicant must be U.S. citizen, permanent resident or Canadian resident. Applicant must be residing in Oklahoma, Kansas or Missouri.
Basis for selection: Major/career interest in engineering or engineering, mechanical.
Application requirements: Recommendations, essay, transcript. Resume, SAT or ACT scores for current high school students.
Additional information: First preference given to children, grandchildren, or other relatives of current SME Wichita Chapter 52 members. Second preference given to residents of Kansas, Oklahoma, and Missouri. Third preference given to applicants attending colleges or universities in Kansas. Minimum 2.5 GPA.

Amount of award:	$1,000-$2,500
Number of awards:	1
Application deadline:	February 1

Contact:
Society of Manufacturing Engineers Education Foundation
Scholarship Review Committee
One SME Drive, P.O. Box 930
Dearborn, MI 48121-0930
Phone: 313-425-3300
Web: www.smeef.org

Chapter 56 - Fort Wayne Scholarship

Type of award: Scholarship.
Intended use: For undergraduate or graduate study at 2-year, 4-year or graduate institution. Designated institutions: Indiana institutions.
Eligibility: Applicant must be U.S. citizen, permanent resident or Canadian resident. Applicant must be residing in Indiana.
Basis for selection: Major/career interest in engineering or engineering, mechanical.
Application requirements: Recommendations, essay, transcript. Resume, SAT or ACT scores for high school students.
Additional information: First preference given to children or grandchildren of current members of SME Fort Wayne Chapter 56. Second preference given to members of SME student chapters sponsored by Chapter 56. Third preference given to residents of Indiana. Fourth preference given to applicants attending or planning to attend Indiana institutions. Minimum 2.5 GPA.

Amount of award:	$1,000-$2,500
Number of awards:	3
Application deadline:	February 1

Contact:
Society of Manufacturing Engineers Education Foundation
Scholarship Review Committee
One SME Drive, P.O. Box 930
Dearborn, MI 48121-0930
Phone: 313-425-3300
Web: www.smeef.org

Chapter 6 - Fairfield County Scholarship

Type of award: Scholarship.
Intended use: For full-time undergraduate study in United States or Canada.
Eligibility: Applicant must be U.S. citizen, permanent resident or Canadian resident.
Basis for selection: Major/career interest in engineering; manufacturing or technology.
Application requirements: Recommendations, essay, transcript. Resume, SAT or ACT scores for current high school students.
Additional information: Minimum 3.0 GPA. Preference given to residents of the eastern United States.

Amount of award:	$1,000-$2,500
Number of awards:	1
Application deadline:	February 1

Contact:
Society of Manufacturing Engineers Education Foundation
Scholarship Review Committee
One SME Drive, P.O. Box 930
Dearborn, MI 48121-0930
Phone: 313-425-3300
Web: www.smeef.org

Chapter 67 - Phoenix Scholarship

Type of award: Scholarship, renewable.
Intended use: For full-time undergraduate study. Designated institutions: Arizona institutions.
Eligibility: Applicant must be U.S. citizen, permanent resident or Canadian resident. Applicant must be residing in Arizona.
Basis for selection: Major/career interest in engineering or manufacturing.
Application requirements: Recommendations, essay, transcript. Resume, SAT or ACT scores for current high school students.
Additional information: Minimum 2.5 overall GPA; maintain 3.0 in manufacturing courses to continue eligibility in future years.

Amount of award:	$1,000-$2,500
Number of awards:	2
Application deadline:	February 1

Contact:
Society of Manufacturing Engineers Education Foundation
Scholarship Review Committee
One SME Drive, P.O. Box 930
Dearborn, MI 48121-0930
Phone: 313-425-3300
Web: www.smeef.org

The Clarence & Josephine Myers Scholarship

Type of award: Scholarship.

Intended use: For undergraduate or graduate study at 2-year, 4-year or graduate institution.
Eligibility: Applicant must be residing in Indiana.
Basis for selection: Major/career interest in engineering, mechanical; engineering or manufacturing.
Application requirements: Recommendations, essay, transcript. Resume, SAT or ACT scores for current high school students.
Additional information: Preference given to students planning to attend or currently attending college or university in Indiana, students who attend Arsenal Technological High School in Indianapolis, members of SME student chapters sponsored by SME Chapter 37, and children or grandchildren of current SME Chapter 37 members. Minimum 3.0 GPA.

Amount of award:	$1,000-$2,500
Number of awards:	1
Application deadline:	February 1
Total amount awarded:	$1,200

Contact:
Society of Manufacturing Engineers Education Foundation
Scholarship Review Committee
One SME Drive, P.O. Box 930
Dearborn, MI 48121-0930
Phone: 313-425-3300
Web: www.smeef.org

Clinton J. Helton Manufacturing Scholarship Award

Type of award: Scholarship.
Intended use: For full-time sophomore, junior or senior study at accredited 4-year institution. Designated institutions: Colorado State University and all University of Colorado campuses.
Eligibility: Applicant must be residing in Colorado.
Basis for selection: Major/career interest in manufacturing; engineering or technology. Applicant must demonstrate high academic achievement and depth of character.
Application requirements: Recommendations, essay, transcript. Resume.
Additional information: Applicants must be enrolled in manufacturing engineering or technology degree program and must have completed at least 30 credit hours. Minimum 3.0 GPA. Applicants must reapply for renewal. Application available on Website.

Amount of award:	$1,000-$2,500
Application deadline:	February 1

Contact:
Society of Manufacturing Engineers Education Foundation
Scholarship Review Committee
One SME Drive, P.O. Box 930
Dearborn, MI 48121-0930
Phone: 313-425-3300
Web: www.smeef.org

Connie and Robert T. Gunter Scholarship

Type of award: Scholarship.
Intended use: For full-time sophomore, junior or senior study at accredited 4-year institution.
Eligibility: Applicant must be U.S. citizen, permanent resident or resident of Canada.
Basis for selection: Major/career interest in manufacturing; engineering or technology. Applicant must demonstrate high academic achievement, depth of character and seriousness of purpose.

Application requirements: Recommendations, essay, transcript. Resume.
Additional information: Applicants must be enrolled in manufacturing engineering degree program and must have completed at least 30 credit hours. Minimum 3.5 GPA. Applicants must reapply for renewal. Application available on Website.

Amount of award:	$1,000-$2,500
Number of awards:	1
Application deadline:	February 1
Total amount awarded:	$6,000

Contact:
Society of Manufacturing Engineers Education Foundation
Scholarship Review Committee
One SME Drive, P.O. Box 930
Dearborn, MI 48121-0930
Phone: 313-425-3300
Web: www.smeef.org

Detroit Chapter One - Founding Chapter Scholarship Award

Type of award: Scholarship, renewable.
Intended use: For undergraduate or graduate study at accredited 2-year, 4-year or graduate institution. Designated institutions: Wayne State University, Lawrence Technological University, University of Detroit Mercy, Focus: HOPE Center for Advanced Technologies, Henry Ford Community College, Macomb Community College, University of Michigan.
Basis for selection: Major/career interest in manufacturing or engineering. Applicant must demonstrate high academic achievement, depth of character and leadership.
Application requirements: Recommendations, essay, transcript. Resume.
Additional information: Awarded to one student each at associate, baccalaureate, and graduate levels. Applicants must be enrolled in manufacturing engineering, manufacturing engineering technology, or closely related degree or certificate program. Student must be member of SME student chapter sponsored by Detroit Chapter 1. Minimum 3.0 GPA. Applicants must reapply for renewal. Financial need considered only between two otherwise equal applicants. Application available on Website.

Amount of award:	$1,000-$2,500
Number of awards:	3
Application deadline:	February 1
Total amount awarded:	$7,000

Contact:
Society of Manufacturing Engineers Education Foundation
Scholarship Review Committee
One SME Drive, P.O. Box 930
Dearborn, MI 48121-0930
Phone: 313-425-3300
Web: www.smeef.org

Directors Scholarship

Type of award: Scholarship, renewable.
Intended use: For full-time sophomore, junior or senior study at accredited 4-year institution in United States or Canada.
Eligibility: Applicant must be U.S. citizen, permanent resident or Canadian resident.
Basis for selection: Major/career interest in manufacturing. Applicant must demonstrate high academic achievement and leadership.
Application requirements: Recommendations, essay, transcript. Resume.

Additional information: Applicants must have completed minimum 30 college credit hours. Minimum 3.5 GPA. Applicants must reapply for renewal. Preference given to applicants who demonstrate leadership skills in a community, academic, or professional environment. Application available on Website.

Amount of award:	$1,000-$2,500
Number of awards:	2
Application deadline:	February 1
Total amount awarded:	$10,000

Contact:
Society of Manufacturing Engineers
Scholarship Review Committee
One SME Drive, P.O. Box 930
Dearborn, MI 48121-0930
Phone: 313-425-3300
Web: www.smeef.org

E. Wayne Kay Co-op Scholarship

Type of award: Scholarship, renewable.
Intended use: For full-time sophomore, junior or senior study at accredited postsecondary institution in United States or Canada.
Eligibility: Applicant must be U.S. citizen, permanent resident or Canadian resident.
Basis for selection: Major/career interest in manufacturing; engineering or technology. Applicant must demonstrate high academic achievement.
Application requirements: Essay, transcript, proof of eligibility. Letter of recommendation from employer and letter of support from faculty member at college or university.
Additional information: Applicants must be enrolled in manufacturing engineering or technology degree program and working through co-op program in a manufacturing-related environment. Applicants must have completed minimum 30 college credit hours. Must provide evidence of demonstrated excellence related to manufacturing engineering or technology which may include project completed for employer. Minimum 3.0 GPA. Applicants must reapply for renewal. Application available on Website.

Amount of award:	$1,000-$2,500
Number of awards:	2
Application deadline:	February 1
Total amount awarded:	$5,000

Contact:
Society of Manufacturing Engineers
Scholarship Review Committee
One SME Drive, P.O. Box 930
Dearborn, MI 48121-0930
Phone: 313-425-3300
Web: www.smeef.org

E. Wayne Kay Community College Scholarship

Type of award: Scholarship, renewable.
Intended use: For full-time freshman study at accredited vocational or 2-year institution in United States or Canada.
Eligibility: Applicant must be high school senior. Applicant must be U.S. citizen, permanent resident or Canadian resident.
Basis for selection: Major/career interest in manufacturing or technology. Applicant must demonstrate high academic achievement.
Application requirements: Recommendations, essay, transcript. Resume, SAT or ACT scores.

Additional information: Applicants must be enrolled in manufacturing engineering or closely related degree program. Entering freshman or sophomore students with 60 or fewer college credits are also eligible. Minimum 3.0 GPA. Must reapply for renewal. Application available on Website.

Amount of award:	$1,000
Number of awards:	3
Application deadline:	February 1
Total amount awarded:	$3,000

Contact:
Society of Manufacturing Engineers
Scholarship Review Committee
One SME Drive, P.O. Box 930
Dearborn, MI 48121-0930
Phone: 313-425-3300
Web: www.smeef.org

E. Wayne Kay High School Scholarship

Type of award: Scholarship, renewable.
Intended use: For full-time freshman study at accredited 4-year institution in United States or Canada.
Eligibility: Applicant must be high school senior. Applicant must be U.S. citizen, permanent resident or Canadian resident.
Basis for selection: Major/career interest in manufacturing or engineering. Applicant must demonstrate high academic achievement.
Application requirements: Recommendations, essay, transcript. Resume, SAT or ACT scores.
Additional information: Applicant must commit to enrolling in manufacturing engineering or technology degree program. Minimum 3.0 GPA. Application available on Website.

Amount of award:	$1,000-$2,500
Number of awards:	2
Application deadline:	February 1
Total amount awarded:	$5,000

Contact:
Society of Manufacturing Engineers
Scholarship Review Committee
One SME Drive, P.O. Box 930
Dearborn, MI 48121-0930
Phone: 313-425-3300
Web: www.smeef.org

E. Wayne Kay Scholarship

Type of award: Scholarship, renewable.
Intended use: For full-time undergraduate study at accredited 4-year institution in United States or Canada.
Eligibility: Applicant must be U.S. citizen, permanent resident or Canadian resident.
Basis for selection: Major/career interest in manufacturing or engineering. Applicant must demonstrate high academic achievement.
Application requirements: Recommendations, essay, transcript. Resume.
Additional information: Applicants must be enrolled in manufacturing engineering or technology degree program or closely related field. Minimum 3.0 GPA. Must reapply for renewal. Application available on Website.

Amount of award:	$1,000-$2,500
Number of awards:	2
Application deadline:	February 1

Contact:
Society of Manufacturing Engineers
Scholarship Review Committee
One SME Drive, P.O. Box 930
Dearborn, MI 48121-0930
Phone: 313-425-3300
Web: www.smeef.org

Edward S. Roth Manufacturing Engineering

Type of award: Scholarship, renewable.
Intended use: For full-time undergraduate or graduate study at accredited 4-year institution in United States. Designated institutions: California State Polytechnic University; University of Miami, FL; Bradley University, IL; Central State University, OH; Miami University, OH; Boston University; Worcester Polytechnic Institute, MA; University of Massachusetts; St. Cloud State University, MN; University of Texas-Pan American; Brigham Young University, UT; Utah State University.
Eligibility: Applicant must be U.S. citizen.
Basis for selection: Major/career interest in manufacturing or engineering. Applicant must demonstrate high academic achievement, depth of character and seriousness of purpose.
Application requirements: Recommendations, essay, transcript. Resume.
Additional information: Applicants must be enrolled in manufacturing engineering degree program. Minimum 3.0 GPA. Preference given to students demonstrating financial need, minority students, and students participating in co-op program. Must reapply for renewal. Application available on Website.

Amount of award:	$1,000-$2,500
Number of awards:	1
Application deadline:	February 1
Total amount awarded:	$2,500

Contact:
Society of Manufacturing Engineers Education Foundation
Scholarship Review Committee
One SME Drive, P.O. Box 930
Dearborn, MI 48121-0930
Phone: 313-425-3300
Web: www.smeef.org

Future Leaders of Manufacturing Scholarships

Type of award: Scholarship.
Intended use: For full-time undergraduate or graduate study at postsecondary institution.
Eligibility: Applicant must be U.S. citizen, permanent resident or Canadian resident.
Basis for selection: Major/career interest in manufacturing; engineering or technology.
Application requirements: Recommendations, transcript, nomination by SME student chapter faculty advisor. Resume.
Additional information: Applicant must be current SME student member. Faculty advisors may only nominate one student from the chapter. Visit Website for nomination form and application.

Amount of award:	$1,000-$2,500
Number of awards:	10
Application deadline:	February 1

Contact:
Society of Manufacturing Engineers Education Foundation
Future Leaders of Manufacturing
One SME Drive, P.O. Box 930
Dearborn, MI 48121-0930
Phone: 313-425-3300
Web: www.smeef.org

Giuliano Mazzetti Scholarship

Type of award: Scholarship, renewable.
Intended use: For full-time sophomore, junior or senior study at accredited 4-year institution in United States or Canada.
Eligibility: Applicant must be U.S. citizen, permanent resident or Canadian resident.
Basis for selection: Major/career interest in manufacturing; engineering or technology. Applicant must demonstrate high academic achievement.
Application requirements: Recommendations, essay, transcript. Resume.
Additional information: Applicants must be enrolled in manufacturing engineering, technology, or closely related degree program and must have completed minimum 30 college credit hours. Minimum 3.0 GPA. Must reapply for renewal. Financial need considered only between two otherwise equal applicants. Application available on Website.

Amount of award:	$1,000-$2,500
Number of awards:	3
Application deadline:	February 1
Total amount awarded:	$6,000

Contact:
Society of Manufacturing Engineers
Scholarship Review Committee
One SME Drive, P.O. Box 930
Dearborn, MI 48121-0930
Phone: 313-425-3300
Web: www.smeef.org

Lucile B. Kaufman Women's Scholarship

Type of award: Scholarship, renewable.
Intended use: For full-time sophomore, junior or senior study at 4-year institution in United States or Canada.
Eligibility: Applicant must be female. Applicant must be U.S. citizen, permanent resident or Canadian resident.
Basis for selection: Major/career interest in manufacturing or engineering. Applicant must demonstrate high academic achievement.
Application requirements: Recommendations, essay, transcript. Resume.
Additional information: Applicants must be enrolled in manufacturing engineering or manufacturing engineering technology degree program and must have completed minimum 30 credits. Minimum 3.0 GPA. Must reapply for renewal. Application available on Website.

Amount of award:	$1,000-$2,500
Number of awards:	2
Application deadline:	February 1
Total amount awarded:	$3,000

Contact:
Society of Manufacturing Engineers
Scholarship Review Committee
One SME Drive, P.O. Box 930
Dearborn, MI 48121-0930
Phone: 313-425-3300
Web: www.smeef.org

Scholarships

Myrtle and Earl Walker Scholarship

Type of award: Scholarship, renewable.
Intended use: For full-time undergraduate study at accredited 4-year institution in United States or Canada.
Eligibility: Applicant must be U.S. citizen, permanent resident or Canadian resident.
Basis for selection: Major/career interest in manufacturing or engineering. Applicant must demonstrate high academic achievement.
Application requirements: Recommendations, essay, transcript. Resume.
Additional information: Applicants must be enrolled in manufacturing engineering degree or technology program and must have completed minimum 15 credits. Minimum 3.0 GPA. Must reapply for renewal. Application available on Website.

Amount of award:	$1,000-$2,500
Number of awards:	20
Application deadline:	February 1
Total amount awarded:	$40,000

Contact:
Society of Manufacturing Engineers
Scholarship Review Committee
One SME Drive, P.O. Box 930
Dearborn, MI 48121-0930
Phone: 313-425-3300
Web: www.smeef.org

North Central Region Scholarship

Type of award: Scholarship.
Intended use: For full-time undergraduate study at 2-year or 4-year institution. Designated institutions: Institutions in Iowa, Minnesota, Nebraska, North Dakota, South Dakota, Wisconsin, or the upper peninsula of Michigan.
Eligibility: Applicant must be U.S. citizen, permanent resident or Canadian resident. Applicant must be residing in Michigan, Wisconsin, Iowa, South Dakota, Minnesota, Nebraska or North Dakota.
Basis for selection: Major/career interest in manufacturing; engineering or engineering, mechanical.
Application requirements: Recommendations, essay, transcript. Resume, SAT or ACT scores for current high school students.
Additional information: First preference given to applicants from the North Central Region who are SME members, spouses of members, or children or grandchildren of members. Second preference given to residents of Iowa, Minnesota, Nebraska, North Dakota, South Dakota, Wisconsin, and the upper peninsula of Michigan. Minimum 3.0 GPA.

Amount of award:	$1,000-$2,500
Number of awards:	1
Application deadline:	February 1

Contact:
Society of Manufacturing Engineers Education Foundation
Scholarship Review Committee
One SME Drive, P.O. Box 930
Dearborn, MI 48121-0930
Phone: 313-425-3300
Web: www.smeef.org

SME Education Foundation Family Scholarship

Type of award: Scholarship.
Intended use: For full-time freshman or sophomore study in United States or Canada.
Eligibility: Applicant must be U.S. citizen, permanent resident or Canadian resident.
Basis for selection: Major/career interest in engineering or manufacturing. Applicant must demonstrate high academic achievement, leadership and seriousness of purpose.
Application requirements: Recommendations, essay, transcript, proof of eligibility. Resume, SAT/ACT scores, list of extracurricular activities.
Additional information: Applicant must have parent or grandparent who has been SME member in good standing for at least two years. Graduating high school seniors and current undergraduates with fewer than 30 credit hours are eligible. Minimum 3.0 GPA. Minimum 1000 SAT or 21 ACT.

Amount of award:	$1,000-$2,500
Number of awards:	3
Application deadline:	February 1

Contact:
Society of Manufacturing Engineers Education Foundation
Scholarship Review Committee
One SME Drive, P.O. Box 930
Dearborn, MI 48121-0930
Phone: 313-425-3300
Web: www.smeef.org

Walt Bartram Memorial Education Award (Region 12 and Chapter 119)

Type of award: Scholarship, renewable.
Intended use: For full-time undergraduate study at accredited 2-year or 4-year institution. Designated institutions: Schools with manufacturing engineering programs within Desert Pacific Region 12 (Arizona, New Mexico, Southern California).
Eligibility: Applicant must be high school senior. Applicant must be residing in California, New Mexico or Arizona.
Basis for selection: Major/career interest in manufacturing or engineering. Applicant must demonstrate high academic achievement, depth of character and seriousness of purpose.
Application requirements: Recommendations, essay, transcript. Resume, SAT or ACT scores for current high school students.
Additional information: Applicant must reside within Desert Pacific Region 12 and, unless high school senior, must be member of SME. Applicant must be enrolled in manufacturing engineering or closely related degree program. Minimum 3.5 GPA. Application available on Website.

Amount of award:	$1,000-$2,500
Number of awards:	1
Application deadline:	February 1
Total amount awarded:	$1,500

Contact:
Society of Manufacturing Engineers
Scholarship Review Committee
One SME Drive, P.O. Box 930
Dearborn, MI 48121-0930
Phone: 313-425-3300
Web: www.smeef.org

William E. Weisel Scholarship

Type of award: Scholarship, renewable.
Intended use: For full-time sophomore, junior or senior study at 4-year institution in United States or Canada.
Eligibility: Applicant must be U.S. citizen or Canadian citizen.
Basis for selection: Major/career interest in manufacturing; engineering or robotics. Applicant must demonstrate high academic achievement.

Application requirements: Recommendations, essay, transcript. Resume.

Additional information: Applicant must be enrolled in manufacturing engineering degree program and must have completed minimum 30 credits. Preference given to applicants seeking career in robotics or automated systems used in manufacturing. Consideration given to students who intend to apply knowledge to career in medical robotics. Minimum 3.0 GPA. Applicants must reapply for renewal. Financial need considered only between two otherwise equal applicants. Application available on Website.

Amount of award:	$1,000-$2,500
Number of awards:	1
Application deadline:	February 1
Total amount awarded:	$2,000

Contact:
Society of Manufacturing Engineers
Scholarship Review Committee
One SME Drive, P.O. Box 930
Dearborn, MI 48121-0930
Phone: 313-425-3300
Web: www.smeef.org

Society of Physics Students

Society of Physics Students Leadership Scholarship

Type of award: Scholarship.

Intended use: For full-time junior or senior study at 2-year or 4-year institution.

Basis for selection: Major/career interest in physics. Applicant must demonstrate high academic achievement and seriousness of purpose.

Application requirements: Transcript. Letters of recommendation from at least two full-time faculty members.

Additional information: Awards payable in equal installments at the beginning of each semester or quarter of full-time study in final year of baccalaureate degree. Applicants in two-year schools should apply after completing one semester of physics. Must be active participant in Society of Physics Students. Must show intention for continued scholastic development in physics. Number of awards varies. Obtain application from Website or SPS Chapter Adviser.

Amount of award:	$2,000-$5,000
Number of awards:	18
Application deadline:	February 15
Notification begins:	April 1
Total amount awarded:	$36,000

Contact:
SPS Scholarships Committee
One Physics Ellipse
College Park, MD 20740
Phone: 301-209-3007
Fax: 301-209-0839
Web: www.spsnational.org

Society of Plastics Engineers

Extrusion Division/Lew Erwin Memorial Scholarship

Type of award: Scholarship.

Intended use: For full-time senior or master's study at 4-year or graduate institution.

Basis for selection: Major/career interest in chemistry; engineering; engineering, chemical; engineering, materials; engineering, mechanical or physics. Applicant must demonstrate financial need.

Application requirements: Research proposal. One- to two-page typed statement explaining reasons for application, qualifications, and educational/career goals in the plastics industry. Recommendation letter from faculty adviser associated with project.

Additional information: All applicants must be in good academic standing and have a demonstrated interest in the plastics industry. Applicants must be working on senior or MS research project in polymer extrusion that the scholarship will help support. The project must be described in writing, including background, objective, and proposed experiments. Recipient will be expected to furnish final research summary report. Visit Website for more information.

Amount of award:	$2,500
Number of awards:	1
Application deadline:	March 1
Total amount awarded:	$2,500

Contact:
Society of Plastics Engineers
13 Church Hill Road
Newtown, CT 06470
Phone: 203-740-5447
Fax: 203-775-8490
Web: www.4spe.org

Fleming/Blaszcak Scholarship

Type of award: Scholarship.

Intended use: For full-time undergraduate or graduate study at 4-year or graduate institution.

Eligibility: Applicant must be Mexican American. Applicant must be U.S. citizen or permanent resident.

Basis for selection: Major/career interest in chemistry; engineering; engineering, chemical; engineering, materials; engineering, mechanical or physics. Applicant must demonstrate financial need.

Application requirements: Transcript. One- to two-page typed statement explaining reasons for application, qualifications, and educational/career goals in the plastics industry. Three recommendation letters: two from teachers or school officials and one from an employer or non-relative.

Additional information: All applicants must be in good standing and have a demonstrated interest in the plastics industry. Visit Website for more information.

Amount of award:	$2,000
Number of awards:	1
Application deadline:	January 15
Total amount awarded:	$2,000

Contact:
Society of Plastics Engineers
13 Church Hill Road
Newtown, CT 06470
Phone: 203-740-5447
Fax: 203-775-8490
Web: www.4spe.org

Gulf Coast Hurricane Scholarships

Type of award: Scholarship.
Intended use: For full-time undergraduate or graduate study at 2-year, 4-year or graduate institution in United States.
Eligibility: Applicant must be residing in Texas, Mississippi, Alabama, Louisiana or Florida.
Basis for selection: Major/career interest in chemistry; engineering; engineering, chemical; engineering, materials; engineering, materials or physics. Applicant must demonstrate financial need and high academic achievement.
Application requirements: Recommendations, essay, transcript. A listing of employment history, including description of work with plastics/polymers. A list of current and past school activities and community activities and honors.
Additional information: Applicants must have a demonstrated or expressed interest in the plastics industry. Applicants must be majoring in or taking courses that are beneficial to a career in the plastics/polymer industry. One four-year university scholarship of $6,000 (funds distributed on a yearly basis) and two two-year junior or technical institute scholarships of $2,000 (funds distributed on a yearly basis) are available. Applicants must be a resident of, and attending college in, a Gulf Coast State (Florida, Alabama, Mississippi, Louisiana, and Texas).

Amount of award:	$2,000-$6,000
Number of awards:	3
Application deadline:	January 15
Total amount awarded:	$10,000

Contact:
Society of Plastics Engineers
13 Church Hill Road
Newtown, CT 06470
Phone: 203-740-5447
Fax: 203-740-8490
Web: www.4spe.org/spe-foundation

K. K. Wang Scholarship

Type of award: Scholarship.
Intended use: For full-time undergraduate or graduate study at 2-year, 4-year or graduate institution.
Basis for selection: Major/career interest in chemistry; engineering; engineering, chemical; engineering, materials; engineering, mechanical or physics. Applicant must demonstrate financial need and high academic achievement.
Application requirements: Recommendations, essay, transcript. A listing of employment history, including description of work in the plastics/polymers industry. A list of current and past school activities, community activities, and honors.
Additional information: Applicants must have a demonstrated or expressed interest in the plastics industry, and must be majoring or taking courses that are beneficial to a career in the plastics/polymer industry. Applicants must have experience in injection molding and computer-aided engineering (CAE), such as courses taken, research conducted, or jobs held.

Amount of award:	$2,000
Number of awards:	1
Application deadline:	January 15

Contact:
Society of Plastics Engineers
13 Church Hill Road
Newtown, CT 06470
Phone: 203-740-5447
Fax: 203-775-8490
Web: www.4spe.org/spe-foundation

Pittsburgh Scholarship

Type of award: Scholarship, renewable.
Intended use: For full-time undergraduate or graduate study at 2-year, 4-year or graduate institution.
Eligibility: Applicant must be residing in Pennsylvania.
Basis for selection: Major/career interest in chemistry; engineering, chemical; engineering, mechanical; physics or engineering, industrial. Applicant must demonstrate financial need.
Application requirements: Recommendations, essay, transcript, proof of eligibility. List of current and past school and community activities and honors. List of employment history with detailed description of any involvement in plastics/polymers.
Additional information: All applicants must be in good standing with their colleges and must have a demonstrated or expressed interest in the plastics industry. Plastics engineering and polymer science majors also eligible. Must be resident of one of the following Pennsylvania counties: Alleghany, Armstrong, Beaver, Bedford, Blair, Brooke, Butler, Cambria, Clarion, Clearfield, Fayette, Greene, Hancock, Indiana, Jefferson, Lawrence, Mercer, Somerset, Venango, Washington, or Westmoreland. Visit Website for more information.

Number of awards:	2
Application deadline:	January 15
Total amount awarded:	$4,000

Contact:
Society of Plastics Engineers
13 Church Hill Road
Newtown, CT 06470
Phone: 203-740-5447
Fax: 203-775-8490
Web: www.4spe.org/spe-foundation

Plastics Pioneers Scholarships

Type of award: Scholarship, renewable.
Intended use: For full-time undergraduate study at 2-year or 4-year institution.
Basis for selection: Major/career interest in chemistry; engineering, chemical; engineering, mechanical; physics or engineering, industrial. Applicant must demonstrate financial need.
Application requirements: Recommendations, essay, transcript. List of current and past school activities and community activities and honors. List of employment history with detailed description of any involvement in plastics/polymers.
Additional information: All applicants must be in good standing with their colleges and must have a demonstrated or expressed interest in the plastics industry. Must be committed to becoming "hands on" worker in the plastics industry as plastics technician or engineer. Plastics engineering and polymer science majors also eligible. Visit Website for more information.

Amount of award:	$3,000
Number of awards:	10
Application deadline:	January 15
Total amount awarded:	$30,000

Contact:
Society of Plastics Engineers
13 Church Hill Road
Newtown, CT 06470
Phone: 203-740-5447
Fax: 203-775-8490
Web: www.4spe.org/spe-foundation

Society of Plastics Engineers General Scholarships

Type of award: Scholarship, renewable.
Intended use: For full-time undergraduate or graduate study at vocational, 2-year, 4-year or graduate institution.
Basis for selection: Major/career interest in chemistry; engineering; engineering, chemical; engineering, mechanical; engineering, materials or physics. Applicant must demonstrate financial need and seriousness of purpose.
Application requirements: Transcript. One- to two-page typed statement explaining reasons for application, qualifications, and educational/career goals in the plastics industry. Three recommendation letters: two from teachers or school officials and one from an employer or non-relative.
Additional information: All applicants must be in good standing with their colleges and must have a demonstrated interest in the plastics industry. Recipients must re-apply for renewal, for up to three additional years. Visit Website for more information.

Amount of award:	$1,000-$4,000
Application deadline:	January 15
Total amount awarded:	$65,000

Contact:
Society of Plastics Engineers
13 Church Hill Road
Newtown, CT 06470
Phone: 203-740-5447
Fax: 203-775-8490
Web: www.4spe.org

The SPE Foundation Blow Molding Division Memorial Scholarships

Type of award: Scholarship.
Intended use: For junior study at 4-year institution.
Basis for selection: Major/career interest in engineering. Applicant must demonstrate financial need.
Application requirements: Recommendations, transcript. Essay on the importance of blow molding to the technical parts and packing industries.
Additional information: Applicants must be members of a Society of Plastics Engineers Student Chapter and be in second year of four-year undergraduate plastics engineering program. Award is $8,000, payable over two years.

Amount of award:	$8,000
Number of awards:	2
Application deadline:	January 15
Total amount awarded:	$16,000

Contact:
Society of Plastics Engineers
13 Church Hill Road
Newtown, CT 06470
Phone: 203-740-5447
Fax: 203-775-8490
Web: www.4spe.org

Thermoforming Division Memorial Scholarships

Type of award: Scholarship.
Intended use: For full-time undergraduate or graduate study at vocational, 2-year, 4-year or graduate institution.
Basis for selection: Major/career interest in chemistry; engineering; engineering, chemical; engineering, materials; engineering, mechanical or physics. Applicant must demonstrate financial need.
Application requirements: Transcript. One- to two-page typed statement explaining reasons for application, qualifications, and educational/career goals. Statement detailing exposure to the thermostat industry, including courses, research conducted, or jobs held. Three recommendation letters: two from teachers or school officials, and one from an employer or other non-relative.
Additional information: All applicants must be in good standing and have a demonstrated interest in the plastics industry. Visit Website for more information.

Amount of award:	$5,000
Number of awards:	2
Application deadline:	January 15
Total amount awarded:	$10,000

Contact:
Society of Plastics Engineers
13 Church Hill Road
Newtown, CT 06470
Phone: 203-740-5447
Fax: 203-775-8490
Web: www.4spe.org

Thermoset Division/James I. MacKenzie Memorial Scholarship

Type of award: Scholarship.
Intended use: For full-time undergraduate or graduate study at vocational, 2-year or 4-year institution.
Basis for selection: Major/career interest in chemistry; engineering; engineering, chemical; engineering, materials; engineering, mechanical or physics. Applicant must demonstrate financial need.
Application requirements: Transcript. One- to two-page typed statement explaining reasons for application, qualifications, and educational/ career goals. Statement detailing exposure to the thermoset industry. Three recommendation letters: two from teachers or school officials and one from an employer or non-relative.
Additional information: All applicants must be in good academic standing and have a demonstrated interest in the plastics industry. Must have experience in the thermoset industry, such as courses taken, research conducted, or jobs held. Visit Website for more information.

Amount of award:	$2,500
Number of awards:	2
Application deadline:	January 15
Total amount awarded:	$5,000

Contact:
Society of Plastics Engineers
13 Church Hill Road
Newtown, CT 06470
Phone: 203-740-5447
Fax: 203-775-8490
Web: www.4spe.org

Western Plastics Pioneers Scholarship

Type of award: Scholarship, renewable.
Intended use: For full-time undergraduate study at 2-year or 4-year institution. Designated institutions: Institutions in Arizona, California, Oregon, or Washington state.
Basis for selection: Major/career interest in chemistry; engineering, chemical; engineering, mechanical; physics or engineering, industrial. Applicant must demonstrate financial need.
Application requirements: Recommendations, essay, transcript. List of current and past school activities and community activities and honors. List of employment history with detailed description of any involvement in plastics/polymers.
Additional information: All applicants must be in good standing with their colleges and must have a demonstrated or expressed interest in the plastics industry. Plastics engineering and polymer science majors also eligible. Visit Website for more information.

Amount of award:	$2,000
Number of awards:	1
Application deadline:	January 15
Total amount awarded:	$2,000

Contact:
Society of Plastics Engineers
13 Church Hill Road
Newtown, CT 06470
Phone: 203-740-5447
Fax: 203-775-8490
Web: www.4spe.org/spe-foundation

The Society of the Descendants of the Signers of the Declaration of Independence

Annual Scholarship

Type of award: Scholarship, renewable.
Intended use: For full-time undergraduate or graduate study at accredited vocational, 2-year, 4-year or graduate institution in or outside United States.
Basis for selection: Applicant must demonstrate high academic achievement, depth of character, leadership, patriotism, seriousness of purpose and service orientation.
Application requirements: Recommendations, essay, transcript, proof of eligibility. Resume.
Additional information: Applicant must be member of the Society of the Descendants of the Signers of the Declaration of Independence. Applicant must reapply for renewal. Number and amount of awards vary. See Website for application deadline and more information.

Number of applicants:	75
Total amount awarded:	$200,000

Contact:
Descendants of the Signers of the Declaration of Independence
Scholarship Committee
P.O. Box 8223
Savannah, GA 31412
Web: www.dsdi1776.com

Society of Women Engineers

Ada I. Pressman Memorial Scholarship

Type of award: Scholarship.
Intended use: For full-time sophomore, junior, senior or graduate study at accredited 4-year institution.
Eligibility: Applicant must be female. Applicant must be U.S. citizen.
Basis for selection: Major/career interest in engineering. Applicant must demonstrate high academic achievement.
Application requirements: Recommendations, essay, transcript, proof of eligibility.
Additional information: Applicants must be enrolled or plan to be enrolled in ABET- or CSAB-accredited program. Minimum 3.0 GPA. Application forms available through deans of engineering at eligible schools, through SWE sections, SWE student sections, SWE Headquarters, or on Website. Visit www.abet.org for list of ABET-accredited schools.

Amount of award:	$5,000
Number of awards:	6
Application deadline:	February 15
Notification begins:	June 15
Total amount awarded:	$30,000

Contact:
Society of Women Engineers
230 E. Ohio Street
Suite 400
Chicago, IL 60611-3265
Phone: 312-596-5223
Fax: 312-596-5252
Web: www.societyofwomenengineers.swe.org

Admiral Grace Murray Hopper Scholarship

Type of award: Scholarship.
Intended use: For full-time freshman study at accredited 4-year institution in United States.
Eligibility: Applicant must be female, high school senior. Applicant must be U.S. citizen or permanent resident.
Basis for selection: Major/career interest in engineering or engineering, computer. Applicant must demonstrate high academic achievement.
Application requirements: Recommendations, essay, transcript, proof of eligibility.
Additional information: Applicants must plan to enroll in ABET- or CSAB-accredited program or SWE-approved school. Preference given to computer-related engineering majors. Application forms available through deans of engineering at eligible schools, through SWE sections, SWE student sections, SWE Headquarters, or on Website. Visit www.abet.org for list of ABET-accredited schools.

Amount of award:	$1,500
Number of awards:	5
Application deadline:	May 15
Notification begins:	September 15
Total amount awarded:	$7,500

Contact:
Society of Women Engineers
230 E. Ohio Street
Suite 400
Chicago, IL 60611-3265
Phone: 312-596-5223
Fax: 312-596-5252
Web: www.societyofwomenengineers.swe.org

Anne Maureen Whitney Barrow Memorial

Type of award: Scholarship.
Intended use: For full-time undergraduate study at accredited 4-year institution in United States.
Eligibility: Applicant must be female. Applicant must be U.S. citizen or permanent resident.
Basis for selection: Major/career interest in engineering.
Application requirements: Recommendations, essay, transcript, proof of eligibility.
Additional information: Minimum 3.0 GPA. Applicants must plan to enroll in an ABET- or CSAB-accredited program. Application forms available through deans of engineering at eligible schools, through SWE sections, SWE student sections, SWE Headquarters, or on Website. Visit www.abet.org for list of ABET-accredited schools.

Amount of award:	$7,000
Number of awards:	1
Application deadline:	February 15, May 15
Notification begins:	June 15, September 15

Contact:
Society of Women Engineers
230 E. Ohio Street
Suite 400
Chicago, IL 60611-3265
Phone: 312-596-5223
Fax: 312-596-5252
Web: www.societyofwomenengineers.swe.org

B. K. Krenzer Re-entry Scholarship

Type of award: Scholarship.
Intended use: For undergraduate or graduate study at accredited 4-year or graduate institution in United States.
Eligibility: Applicant must be female, returning adult student. Applicant must be U.S. citizen or permanent resident.
Basis for selection: Major/career interest in engineering. Applicant must demonstrate high academic achievement.
Application requirements: Recommendations, essay, transcript, proof of eligibility.
Additional information: Eligibility restricted to women who have been out of school and the engineering or technology workforce for at least two years prior to re-entry. Applicants must be enrolled or plan to be enrolled in an ABET- or CSAB-accredited program. Application forms available through deans of engineering at eligible schools, through SWE sections, SWE student sections, SWE Headquarters, or on Website. Visit www.abet.org for list of ABET-accredited schools.

Amount of award:	$2,000
Number of awards:	1
Application deadline:	February 15, May 15
Notification begins:	June 15, September 15
Total amount awarded:	$2,000

Contact:
Society of Women Engineers
230 E. Ohio Street
Suite 400
Chicago, IL 60611-3265
Phone: 312-596-5223
Fax: 312-596-5252
Web: www.societyofwomenengineers.swe.org

Baker Hughes Scholarship

Type of award: Scholarship.
Intended use: For full-time sophomore, junior or senior study at accredited 4-year institution in United States.
Eligibility: Applicant must be female. Applicant must be U.S. citizen or permanent resident.
Basis for selection: Major/career interest in engineering, chemical; engineering, electrical/electronic; engineering, mechanical or engineering, petroleum. Applicant must demonstrate high academic achievement.
Application requirements: Recommendations, essay, transcript, proof of eligibility.
Additional information: Underrepresented groups preferred. Applicants must be enrolled or plan to enroll in ABET- or CSAB-accredited program. Minimum 3.0 GPA. Application forms available through deans of engineering at eligible schools, through SWE sections, SWE student sections, SWE headquarters, or on Website. Visit www.abet.org for list of ABET-accredited schools.

Amount of award:	$5,000
Number of awards:	3
Application deadline:	February 15
Notification begins:	June 15
Total amount awarded:	$15,000

Contact:
Society of Women Engineers
230 E. Ohio Street
Suite 400
Chicago, IL 60611
Phone: 312-596-5223
Fax: 312-596-5252
Web: www.societyofwomenengineers.swe.org

Bechtel Foundation Scholarship

Type of award: Scholarship.
Intended use: For full-time sophomore, junior or senior study at accredited 4-year institution in United States.
Eligibility: Applicant must be female. Applicant must be U.S. citizen or permanent resident.
Basis for selection: Major/career interest in engineering, civil; engineering, electrical/electronic; engineering, environmental; engineering, mechanical; engineering or architecture. Applicant must demonstrate high academic achievement.
Application requirements: Recommendations, essay, transcript, proof of eligibility.
Additional information: Applicant must be member of SWE. Architectural engineering technology majors also eligible. Applicants must be enrolled or plan to be enrolled in an ABET- or CSAB-accredited program. Minimum 3.0 GPA. Application forms available through deans of engineering at eligible schools, through SWE sections, SWE student sections, SWE Headquarters, or on Website. Visit www.abet.org for list of ABET-accredited schools.

Amount of award:	$1,400
Number of awards:	2
Application deadline:	February 15
Notification begins:	June 15
Total amount awarded:	$2,800

Contact:
Society of Women Engineers
230 E. Ohio Street
Suite 400
Chicago, IL 60611-3265
Phone: 312-596-5223
Fax: 312-596-5252
Web: www.societyofwomenengineers.swe.org

Bertha Lamme Memorial Scholarship

Type of award: Scholarship.
Intended use: For full-time freshman study at 4-year institution in United States.
Eligibility: Applicant must be female. Applicant must be U.S. citizen.
Basis for selection: Major/career interest in engineering, electrical/electronic.
Application requirements: Recommendations, transcript, proof of eligibility.
Additional information: Applicants must plan to enroll in an ABET- or CSAB-accredited program. Application forms available through deans of engineering at eligible schools, through SWE sections, SWE student sections, SWE Headquarters, or on Website. Visit www.abet.org for list of ABET-accredited schools.

Amount of award:	$1,200
Number of awards:	1
Application deadline:	May 15
Notification begins:	September 15

Contact:
Society of Women Engineers
230 E. Ohio Street
Suite 400
Chicago, IL 60611-3265
Phone: 312-596-5223
Fax: 312-596-5252
Web: www.societyofwomenengineers.swe.org

B.J. Harrod Scholarships

Type of award: Scholarship.
Intended use: For full-time freshman study at accredited 4-year institution in United States.
Eligibility: Applicant must be female, high school senior. Applicant must be U.S. citizen or permanent resident.
Basis for selection: Major/career interest in engineering. Applicant must demonstrate high academic achievement.
Application requirements: Essay, transcript, proof of eligibility. Two letters of reference: one from a high school teacher, one from a person who knows the applicant but is not a family member.
Additional information: Applicants must plan to enroll in an ABET- or CSAB-accredited program. Application forms available through deans of engineering at eligible schools, through SWE sections, SWE student sections, SWE headquarters, or on Website. Visit www.abet.org for list of ABET-accredited schools.

Amount of award:	$2,000
Number of awards:	2
Application deadline:	May 15
Notification begins:	September 15
Total amount awarded:	$2,000

Contact:
Society of Women Engineers
230 E. Ohio Street
Suite 400
Chicago, IL 60611-3265
Phone: 312-596-5223
Fax: 312-596-5252
Web: www.societyofwomenengineers.swe.org

Boston Scientific Scholarship

Type of award: Scholarship.
Intended use: For full-time senior study at 4-year institution in United States. Designated institutions: SWE-approved schools (contact sponsor for list).
Eligibility: Applicant must be female. Applicant must be U.S. citizen or permanent resident.
Basis for selection: Major/career interest in computer/information sciences; engineering, chemical; engineering, computer; engineering, electrical/electronic; engineering, materials; engineering, mechanical or engineering, industrial. Applicant must demonstrate high academic achievement.
Application requirements: Recommendations, essay, transcript, proof of eligibility.
Additional information: Manufacturing engineering majors also eligible. Minimum 3.5 GPA. Applicants must be enrolled in an ABET- or CSAB-accredited program. Application forms available through deans of engineering at eligible schools, through SWE sections, SWE student sections, SWE Headquarters, or on Website. Visit www.abet.org for list of ABET-accredited schools.

Amount of award:	$5,000
Number of awards:	2
Application deadline:	February 15
Notification begins:	June 15

Contact:
Society of Women Engineers
230 E. Ohio Street
Suite 400
Chicago, IL 60611-3265
Phone: 312-596-5223
Fax: 312-596-5252
Web: www.societyofwomenengineers.swe.org

Brill Family Scholarship

Type of award: Scholarship.
Intended use: For full-time sophomore, junior or senior study at accredited 4-year institution in United States.
Eligibility: Applicant must be female. Applicant must be U.S. citizen or permanent resident.
Basis for selection: Major/career interest in biomedical; aerospace or engineering. Applicant must demonstrate high academic achievement.
Application requirements: Recommendations, essay, transcript, proof of eligibility.
Additional information: Must be aerospace engineering or biomedical engineering major. Applicants must be enrolled or plan to enroll in ABET- or CSAB-accredited program. Minimum 3.0 GPA. Application forms available through deans of engineering at eligible schools, through SWE sections, SWE student sections, SWE headquarters, or on Website. Visit www.abet.org for list of ABET-accredited schools.

Amount of award: $1,000
Number of awards: 1
Application deadline: February 15
Notification begins: June 15
Contact:
Society of Women Engineers
230 E. Ohio Street
Suite 400
Chicago, IL 60611
Phone: 312-596-5223
Fax: 312-596-5252
Web: www.societyofwomenengineers.swe.org

Caterpillar Inc. Scholarship

Type of award: Scholarship.
Intended use: For full-time sophomore, junior, senior or graduate study at 4-year or graduate institution in United States.
Eligibility: Applicant must be female.
Basis for selection: Major/career interest in engineering, agricultural; engineering, chemical; engineering, electrical/electronic; engineering, materials; engineering, mechanical; engineering or engineering, industrial.
Application requirements: Recommendations, essay, transcript, proof of eligibility.
Additional information: Manufacturing engineering majors also eligible. Minimum 3.0 GPA. Applicants must be enrolled in or plan to enroll in ABET- or CSAB-accredited program. Non-U.S. citizens must be eligible to work in U.S. Application forms available through deans of engineering at eligible schools, through SWE sections, SWE student sections, SWE headquarters, or on Website. Visit www.abet.org for list of ABET-accredited schools.

Amount of award: $2,400
Number of awards: 3
Application deadline: February 15
Notification begins: June 15
Contact:
Society of Women Engineers
230 E. Ohio Street
Suite 400
Chicago, IL 60611-3265
Phone: 312-596-5223
Fax: 312-596-5252
Web: www.societyofwomenengineers.swe.org

Central New Mexico Scholarship

Type of award: Scholarship, renewable.
Intended use: For sophomore, junior, senior or graduate study at 4-year institution. Designated institutions: New Mexico engineering or technology institutions.
Eligibility: Applicant must be female. Applicant must be U.S. citizen or permanent resident residing in New Mexico.
Basis for selection: Major/career interest in engineering.
Application requirements: Recommendations, transcript, proof of eligibility.
Additional information: Applicants must be enrolled or plan to enroll in ABET- or CSAB-accredited program. Application forms available through deans of engineering at eligible schools, through SWE sections, SWE student sections, SWE headquarters, or on Website. Minimum 3.0 GPA. Visit www.abet.org for list of ABET-accredited schools.

Amount of award: $1,250
Number of awards: 1
Application deadline: February 15
Notification begins: June 15

Contact:
Society of Women Engineers
230 E. Ohio Street
Suite 400
Chicago, IL 60611-3265
Phone: 312-596-5228
Fax: 312-596-5252
Web: www.societyofwomenengineers.swe.org

Chevron Corporation Scholarships

Type of award: Scholarship.
Intended use: For full-time sophomore or junior study at accredited 4-year institution in United States. Designated institutions: Approved institutions (contact sponsor for list).
Eligibility: Applicant must be female. Applicant must be U.S. citizen or permanent resident.
Basis for selection: Major/career interest in engineering, civil; engineering, chemical; engineering, petroleum; engineering, mechanical; engineering, electrical/electronic or computer/information sciences. Applicant must demonstrate high academic achievement.
Application requirements: Recommendations, essay, transcript, proof of eligibility.
Additional information: Applicant must be active SWE student member. Applicants must be enrolled or plan to be enrolled in ABET- or CSAB-accredited program. Minimum 3.0 GPA. Application forms available through deans of engineering at eligible schools, through SWE sections, SWE student sections, SWE Headquarters, or on Website. Visit www.abet.org for list of ABET-accredited schools.

Amount of award: $2,000
Number of awards: 8
Application deadline: February 15
Notification begins: June 15
Total amount awarded: $16,000
Contact:
Society of Women Engineers
230 E. Ohio Street
Suite 400
Chicago, IL 60611-3265
Phone: 312-596-5223
Fax: 312-596-5252
Web: www.societyofwomenengineers.swe.org

Chrysler Foundation Scholarship

Type of award: Scholarship.
Intended use: For full-time sophomore, junior or senior study at accredited 4-year institution in United States.
Eligibility: Applicant must be female. Applicant must be U.S. citizen or permanent resident.
Basis for selection: Major/career interest in computer/information sciences; engineering, electrical/electronic or engineering, mechanical. Applicant must demonstrate high academic achievement.
Application requirements: Recommendations, essay, transcript, proof of eligibility.
Additional information: Applicants must be enrolled or plan to enroll in ABET- or CSAB-accredited program. Minimum 3.0 GPA. Application forms available through deans of engineering at eligible schools, through SWE sections, SWE student sections, SWE headquarters, or on Website. Visit www.abet.org for list of ABET-accredited schools.

Scholarships

Amount of award: $3,000
Number of awards: 5
Application deadline: February 15
Notification begins: June 15
Total amount awarded: $15,000

Contact:
Society of Women Engineers
230 E. Ohio Street
Suite 400
Chicago, IL 60611
Phone: 312-596-5223
Fax: 312-596-5252
Web: www.societyofwomenengineers.swe.org

Cummins Scholarship

Type of award: Scholarship.
Intended use: For full-time sophomore, junior, senior or graduate study at accredited 4-year or graduate institution in United States.
Eligibility: Applicant must be female. Applicant must be U.S. citizen or permanent resident.
Basis for selection: Major/career interest in engineering; engineering, chemical; engineering, computer; engineering, electrical/electronic; engineering, industrial or engineering, mechanical. Applicant must demonstrate high academic achievement.
Application requirements: Recommendations, essay, transcript, proof of eligibility.
Additional information: Underrepresented groups preferred. Automotive engineering, manufacturing engineering, and materials science/engineering majors are also eligible. Applicants must be enrolled or plan to enroll in ABET- or CSAB-accredited program. Minimum 3.5 GPA. Application forms available through deans of engineering at eligible schools, through SWE sections, SWE student sections, SWE headquarters, or on Website. Visit www.abet.org for list of ABET-accredited schools.

Amount of award: $1,000
Number of awards: 2
Application deadline: February 15
Notification begins: June 15
Total amount awarded: $2,000

Contact:
Society of Women Engineers
230 E. Ohio Street
Suite 400
Chicago, IL 60611
Phone: 312-596-5223
Fax: 312-596-5252
Web: www.societyofwomenengineers.swe.org

Dell Inc. Scholarship

Type of award: Scholarship.
Intended use: For full-time junior or senior study at 4-year institution in United States.
Eligibility: Applicant must be female. Applicant must be U.S. citizen or permanent resident.
Basis for selection: Major/career interest in engineering, electrical/electronic; engineering, computer; engineering, mechanical or computer/information sciences. Applicant must demonstrate financial need.
Application requirements: Recommendations, essay, transcript, proof of eligibility.
Additional information: Minimum 3.0 GPA. Applicants must be enrolled in an ABET- or CSAB-accredited program. Application forms available through deans of engineering at

eligible schools, through SWE sections, SWE student sections, SWE Headquarters, or on Website. Visit www.abet.org for list of ABET-accredited schools.

Amount of award: $2,250
Number of awards: 2
Application deadline: February 15
Notification begins: June 15

Contact:
Society of Women Engineers
230 E. Ohio Street
Suite 400
Chicago, IL 60611-3265
Phone: 312-596-5223
Fax: 312-596-5252
Web: www.societyofwomenengineers.swe.org

Dorothy Lemke Howarth Scholarships

Type of award: Scholarship.
Intended use: For full-time sophomore study at accredited 4-year institution.
Eligibility: Applicant must be female. Applicant must be U.S. citizen.
Basis for selection: Major/career interest in engineering. Applicant must demonstrate high academic achievement.
Application requirements: Recommendations, essay, transcript, proof of eligibility.
Additional information: Applicants must be enrolled or plan to enroll in ABET- or CSAB-accredited program. Minimum 3.0 GPA. Application forms available through deans of engineering at eligible schools, through SWE sections, SWE student sections, SWE headquarters, or on Website. Visit www.abet.org for list of ABET-accredited schools.

Amount of award: $2,500
Number of awards: 6
Application deadline: February 15
Notification begins: June 15
Total amount awarded: $15,000

Contact:
Society of Women Engineers
230 E. Ohio Street
Suite 400
Chicago, IL 60611-3265
Phone: 312-596-5223
Fax: 312-596-5252
Web: www.societyofwomenengineers.swe.org

Dorothy M. & Earl S. Hoffman Scholarships

Type of award: Scholarship, renewable.
Intended use: For full-time freshman study at accredited 4-year institution in United States. Designated institutions: Bucknell University and Rensselaer Polytechnic University.
Eligibility: Applicant must be female, high school senior. Applicant must be U.S. citizen or permanent resident.
Basis for selection: Major/career interest in engineering. Applicant must demonstrate high academic achievement.
Application requirements: Recommendations, essay, transcript, proof of eligibility.
Additional information: Applicants must plan to enroll in ABET- or CSAB-accredited program. Application forms available through deans of engineering at eligible schools, through SWE sections, SWE student sections, SWE headquarters, or on Website. Visit www.abet.org for list of ABET-accredited schools.

Amount of award:	$3,000
Number of awards:	5
Application deadline:	May 15
Notification begins:	September 15

Contact:
Society of Women Engineers
230 E. Ohio Street
Suite 400
Chicago, IL 60611-3265
Phone: 312-596-5223
Fax: 312-596-5252
Web: www.societyofwomenengineers.swe.org

Dorothy P. Morris Scholarship

Type of award: Scholarship.
Intended use: For full-time sophomore, junior or senior study at 4-year institution in United States.
Eligibility: Applicant must be female. Applicant must be U.S. citizen.
Basis for selection: Major/career interest in engineering.
Application requirements: Recommendations, essay, transcript, proof of eligibility.
Additional information: Minimum 3.0 GPA. Applicants must be enrolled or plan to enroll in an ABET- or CSAB-accredited program. Application forms available through deans of engineering at eligible schools, through SWE sections, SWE student sections, SWE headquarters, or on Website. Visit www.abet.org for list of ABET-accredited schools.

Amount of award:	$1,000
Number of awards:	1
Application deadline:	February 15
Notification begins:	June 15

Contact:
Society of Women Engineers
230 E. Ohio Street
Suite 400
Chicago, IL 60611-3265
Phone: 312-596-5223
Fax: 312-596-5252
Web: www.societyofwomenengineers.swe.org

DuPont Company Scholarship

Type of award: Scholarship.
Intended use: For full-time sophomore, junior or senior study at 4-year institution in United States. Designated institutions: Eastern U.S. institutions.
Eligibility: Applicant must be female. Applicant must be U.S. citizen or permanent resident.
Basis for selection: Major/career interest in engineering, chemical or engineering, mechanical.
Application requirements: Recommendations, transcript, proof of eligibility.
Additional information: Minimum 3.0 GPA. Applicants must be enrolled or plan to enroll in ABET- or CSAB-accredited program. Application forms available through deans of engineering at eligible schools, through SWE sections, SWE student sections, SWE headquarters, or on Website. Visit www.abet.org for list of ABET-accredited schools.

Amount of award:	$1,000
Number of awards:	2
Application deadline:	February 15
Notification begins:	June 15

Contact:
Society of Women Engineers
230 E. Ohio Street
Suite 400
Chicago, IL 60611-3265
Phone: 312-596-5223
Fax: 312-596-5252
Web: www.societyofwomenengineers.swe.org

Electronics for Imaging Scholarship

Type of award: Scholarship.
Intended use: For sophomore, junior, senior or graduate study at 4-year or graduate institution in United States. Designated institutions: Approved institutions (contact sponsor for list).
Eligibility: Applicant must be female. Applicant must be U.S. citizen or permanent resident.
Basis for selection: Major/career interest in engineering.
Application requirements: Recommendations, transcript, proof of eligibility.
Additional information: Minimum 3.0 GPA. Application forms available through deans of engineering at eligible schools, through SWE sections, SWE student sections, SWE headquarters, or on Website.

Amount of award:	$4,000
Number of awards:	4
Application deadline:	February 15

Contact:
Society of Women Engineers
230 E. Ohio Street
Suite 400
Chicago, IL 60611
Phone: 312-596-5223
Fax: 312-596-5252
Web: www.societyofwomenengineers.swe.org

Elizabeth McLean Memorial Scholarship

Type of award: Scholarship.
Intended use: For full-time sophomore, junior or senior study at accredited 4-year institution in United States.
Eligibility: Applicant must be female. Applicant must be U.S. citizen or permanent resident.
Basis for selection: Major/career interest in engineering, civil.
Application requirements: Recommendations, transcript, proof of eligibility.
Additional information: Minimum 3.0 GPA. Applicant must be enrolled in an ABET- or CSAB-accredited degree program. Application forms available through deans of engineering at eligible schools, through SWE sections, SWE student sections, SWE headquarters, or on Website. Visit www.abet.org for list of ABET-accredited schools.

Amount of award:	$1,000
Number of awards:	1
Application deadline:	February 15
Notification begins:	June 15

Contact:
Society of Women Engineers
230 E. Ohio Street
Suite 400
Chicago, IL 60611
Phone: 312-596-5223
Fax: 312-596-5252
Web: www.societyofwomenengineers.swe.org

Exelon Scholarship

Type of award: Scholarship.
Intended use: For full-time freshman study at 4-year institution in United States.
Eligibility: Applicant must be female, high school senior. Applicant must be U.S. citizen or permanent resident.
Basis for selection: Major/career interest in engineering.
Application requirements: Recommendations, transcript, proof of eligibility.
Additional information: Applicants must plan to enroll in an ABET- or CSAB-accredited program. Application forms available through deans of engineering at eligible schools, through SWE sections, SWE student sections, SWE headquarters, or on Website. Visit www.abet.org for list of ABET-accredited schools.

Amount of award:	$1,000
Number of awards:	5
Application deadline:	May 15
Notification begins:	September 15

Contact:
Society of Women Engineers
230 E. Ohio Street
Suite 400
Chicago, IL 60611-3265
Phone: 312-596-5223
Fax: 312-596-5252
Web: www.societyofwomenengineers.swe.org

Ford Motor Company Scholarship

Type of award: Scholarship.
Intended use: For full-time sophomore or junior study at accredited 4-year institution.
Eligibility: Applicant must be female. Applicant must be U.S. citizen or permanent resident.
Basis for selection: Major/career interest in engineering, electrical/electronic; engineering, mechanical; automotive technology; manufacturing or engineering, industrial. Applicant must demonstrate high academic achievement and leadership.
Application requirements: Recommendations, transcript, proof of eligibility.
Additional information: Manufaturing engineering majors also eligible. Minimum 3.5 GPA. Applicants must be enrolled or plan to enroll in ABET- or CSAB-accredited program. Application forms available through deans of engineering at eligible schools, through SWE sections, SWE student sections, SWE headquarters, or on Website. Visit www.abet.org for list of ABET-accredited schools.

Amount of award:	$1,500
Number of awards:	3
Application deadline:	February 15
Notification begins:	June 15

Contact:
Society of Women Engineers
230 E. Ohio Street
Suite 400
Chicago, IL 60611
Phone: 312-596-5223
Fax: 312-596-5252
Web: www.societyofwomenengineers.swe.org

General Electric Foundation Scholarship

Type of award: Scholarship.

Intended use: For full-time freshman study at 4-year institution in United States.
Eligibility: Applicant must be female, high school senior. Applicant must be U.S. citizen.
Basis for selection: Major/career interest in engineering.
Application requirements: Recommendations, transcript, proof of eligibility.
Additional information: Applicants must plan to enroll in an ABET- or CSAB-accredited program. Scholarship includes travel grant for SWE National Conference. Application forms available through deans of engineering at eligible schools, through SWE sections, SWE student sections, SWE headquarters, or on Website. Visit www.abet.org for list of ABET-accredited schools.

Amount of award:	$1,500
Number of awards:	3
Application deadline:	May 15
Notification begins:	September 15

Contact:
Society of Women Engineers
230 E. Ohio Street
Suite 400
Chicago, IL 60611-3265
Phone: 312-596-5223
Fax: 312-596-5252
Web: www.societyofwomenengineers.swe.org

General Electric Women's Network Scholarship

Type of award: Scholarship.
Intended use: For full-time sophomore, junior or senior study at accredited 4-year institution in United States. Designated institutions: Preferred schools (contact sponsor for list).
Eligibility: Applicant must be female. Applicant must be U.S. citizen.
Basis for selection: Major/career interest in engineering.
Additional information: Minimum 3.0 GPA. Application forms available through deans of engineering at eligible schools, through SWE sections, SWE student sections, SWE headquarters, or on Website.

Amount of award:	$2,500
Number of awards:	15
Application deadline:	February 15
Notification begins:	June 15
Total amount awarded:	$37,500

Contact:
Society of Women Engineers
230 E. Ohio Street
Suite 400
Chicago, IL 60611
Phone: 312-596-5223
Fax: 312-596-5252
Web: www.societyofwomenengineers.swe.org

General Motors Foundation Scholarships

Type of award: Scholarship, renewable.
Intended use: For full-time sophomore or junior study at accredited 4-year institution in United States. Designated institutions: Approved institutions (contact sponsor for list).
Eligibility: Applicant must be female. Applicant must be U.S. citizen or permanent resident.
Basis for selection: Major/career interest in engineering; automotive technology; engineering, electrical/electronic; engineering, mechanical; manufacturing or engineering,

industrial. Applicant must demonstrate financial need, high academic achievement and leadership.

Application requirements: Recommendations, essay, transcript, proof of eligibility.

Additional information: Manufacturing engineering majors also eligible. Applicants must be enrolled or plan to enroll in ABET- or CSAB-accredited program. Applicants should have career interest in automotive industry or manufacturing. Minimum 3.5 GPA. Application forms available through deans of engineering at eligible schools, through SWE sections, SWE student sections, SWE headquarters, or on Website. Visit www.abet.org for list of ABET-accredited schools.

Amount of award:	$3,000
Number of awards:	3
Application deadline:	February 15
Notification begins:	June 15
Total amount awarded:	$9,000

Contact:
Society of Women Engineers
230 E. Ohio Street
Suite 400
Chicago, IL 60611-3265
Phone: 312-596-5223
Fax: 312-596-5252
Web: www.societyofwomenengineers.swe.org

Goldman, Sachs and Co. Scholarship

Type of award: Scholarship.
Intended use: For full-time junior or senior study at accredited 4-year institution in United States.
Eligibility: Applicant or parent must be member/participant of Society of Women Engineers. Applicant must be female. Applicant must be U.S. citizen or permanent resident.
Basis for selection: Major/career interest in engineering, computer; engineering, electrical/electronic or computer/information sciences.
Application requirements: Recommendations, transcript, proof of eligibility.
Additional information: Minimum 3.2 GPA. Applicants must be enrolled in ABET- or CSAB-accredited program. Application forms available through deans of engineering at eligible schools, through SWE sections, SWE student sections, SWE headquarters, or on Website. Visit www.abet.org for list of ABET-accredited schools.

Amount of award:	$2,000
Number of awards:	4
Application deadline:	February 15
Notification begins:	June 15
Total amount awarded:	$8,000

Contact:
Society of Women Engineers
230 E. Ohio Street
Suite 400
Chicago, IL 60611
Phone: 312-596-5223
Fax: 312-596-5252
Web: www.societyofwomenengineers.swe.org

Honeywell International Inc. Scholarship

Type of award: Scholarship.
Intended use: For full-time undergraduate study at accredited 4-year institution in United States.

Eligibility: Applicant must be female. Applicant must be U.S. citizen.
Basis for selection: Major/career interest in engineering, chemical; engineering, computer; engineering, electrical/electronic; engineering, mechanical; engineering, materials; computer/information sciences; aerospace; architecture; manufacturing or engineering, industrial. Applicant must demonstrate financial need and high academic achievement.
Application requirements: Recommendations, transcript, proof of eligibility.
Additional information: Minimum 3.5 GPA. Architectural and manufacturing engineering majors also eligible. Applicants must be enrolled or plan to enroll in ABET- or CSAB-accredited program. Application forms available through deans of engineering at eligible schools, through SWE sections, SWE student sections, SWE headquarters, or on Website. Visit www.abet.org for list of ABET-accredited schools.

Amount of award:	$5,000
Number of awards:	3
Application deadline:	February 15, May 15
Notification begins:	June 15, September 15
Total amount awarded:	$15,000

Contact:
Society of Women Engineers
230 E. Ohio Street
Suite 400
Chicago, IL 60611
Phone: 312-596-5223
Fax: 312-596-5252
Web: www.societyofwomenengineers.swe.org

IBM Corporation Scholarship

Type of award: Scholarship.
Intended use: For full-time sophomore or junior study at accredited 4-year institution in United States.
Eligibility: Applicant must be female. Applicant must be U.S. citizen or permanent resident.
Basis for selection: Major/career interest in engineering, electrical/electronic; engineering, computer or computer/information sciences.
Application requirements: Recommendations, transcript, proof of eligibility.
Additional information: Underrepresented groups preferred. Applicants must be enrolled or plan to enroll in ABET- or CSAB-accredited program. Minimum 3.4 GPA. Application forms available through deans of engineering at eligible schools, through SWE sections, SWE student sections, SWE headquarters, or on Website. Visit www.abet.org for list of ABET-accredited schools.

Amount of award:	$1,000
Number of awards:	4
Application deadline:	February 15
Notification begins:	June 15

Contact:
Society of Women Engineers
230 E. Ohio Street
Suite 400
Chicago, IL 60611
Phone: 312-596-5223
Fax: 312-596-5252
Web: www.societyofwomenengineers.swe.org

ITT Scholarship

Type of award: Scholarship.
Intended use: For full-time junior, senior or graduate study at accredited 4-year or graduate institution in United States.

Designated institutions: Contact sponsor for list of preferred institutions.

Eligibility: Applicant must be female. Applicant must be U.S. citizen or permanent resident.

Basis for selection: Major/career interest in engineering, chemical; engineering, civil; computer/information sciences; engineering, environmental; engineering, industrial; engineering, mechanical or engineering, electrical/electronic. Applicant must demonstrate high academic achievement.

Application requirements: Recommendations, essay, transcript, proof of eligibility.

Additional information: Manufacturing engineering, aerospace engineering, and electronic engineering technology majors also eligible. Applicants must be enrolled or plan to enroll in ABET- or CSAB-accredited program. Minimum 3.0 GPA. Application forms available through deans of engineering at eligible schools, through SWE sections, SWE student sections, SWE headquarters, or on Website. Visit www.abet.org for list of ABET-accredited schools.

Amount of award:	$2,500-$5,000
Number of awards:	4
Application deadline:	February 15
Notification begins:	June 15
Total amount awarded:	$15,000

Contact:
Society of Women Engineers
230 E. Ohio Street
Suite 400
Chicago, IL 60611
Phone: 312-596-5223
Fax: 312-596-5252
Web: www.societyofwomenengineers.swe.org

Ivy Parker Memorial Scholarship

Type of award: Scholarship.

Intended use: For full-time junior or senior study at accredited 4-year institution in United States.

Eligibility: Applicant must be female. Applicant must be U.S. citizen or permanent resident.

Basis for selection: Major/career interest in engineering. Applicant must demonstrate financial need and high academic achievement.

Application requirements: Recommendations, essay, transcript, proof of eligibility.

Additional information: Applicants must be enrolled in ABET- or CSAB-accredited program. Minimum 3.0 GPA. Application forms available through deans of engineering at eligible schools, through SWE sections, SWE student sections, SWE headquarters, or on Website. Visit www.abet.org for list of ABET-accredited schools.

Amount of award:	$2,500
Number of awards:	1
Application deadline:	February 15
Notification begins:	June 15
Total amount awarded:	$2,500

Contact:
Society of Women Engineers
230 E. Ohio Street
Suite 400
Chicago, IL 60611-3265
Phone: 312-596-5223
Fax: 312-596-5252
Web: www.societyofwomenengineers.swe.org

Jill S. Tietjen P.E. Scholarship

Type of award: Scholarship.

Intended use: For full-time sophomore, junior or senior study at accredited 4-year institution in United States.

Eligibility: Applicant must be female. Applicant must be U.S. citizen.

Basis for selection: Major/career interest in engineering.

Application requirements: Recommendations, transcript, proof of eligibility.

Additional information: Applicants must be enrolled or plan to enroll in ABET- or CSAB-accredited program. Minimum 3.0 GPA. Application forms available through deans of engineering at eligible schools, through SWE sections, SWE student sections, SWE headquarters, or on Website. Visit www.abet.org for list of ABET-accredited schools.

Amount of award:	$1,500
Number of awards:	1
Application deadline:	February 15
Notification begins:	June 15

Contact:
Society of Women Engineers
230 E. Ohio Street
Suite 400
Chicago, IL 60611
Phone: 312-596-5223
Fax: 312-596-5252
Web: www.societyofwomenengineers.swe.org

Judith Resnik Memorial Scholarship

Type of award: Scholarship.

Intended use: For full-time sophomore, junior or senior study at accredited 4-year institution.

Eligibility: Applicant must be female. Applicant must be U.S. citizen or permanent resident.

Basis for selection: Major/career interest in engineering or aerospace. Applicant must demonstrate high academic achievement.

Application requirements: Recommendations, essay, transcript, proof of eligibility.

Additional information: Must be aeronautical/aerospace engineering or astronautical engineering major. Applicants must be enrolled or plan to enroll in ABET- or CSAB-accredited program. Applicant must be SWE student member. Minimum 3.0 GPA. Application forms available through deans of engineering at eligible schools, through SWE sections, SWE student sections, SWE headquarters, or on Website. Visit www.abet.org for list of ABET-accredited schools.

Amount of award:	$3,000
Number of awards:	1
Application deadline:	February 15
Notification begins:	June 15
Total amount awarded:	$3,000

Contact:
Society of Women Engineers
230 E. Ohio Street
Suite 400
Chicago, IL 60611-3265
Phone: 312-596-5223
Fax: 312-596-5252
Web: www.societyofwomenengineers.swe.org

Lehman Scholarship

Type of award: Scholarship.

Intended use: For full-time sophomore study at accredited 4-year institution in United States.

Eligibility: Applicant must be female. Applicant must be U.S. citizen or permanent resident.
Basis for selection: Major/career interest in engineering, computer; computer/information sciences or engineering, electrical/electronic. Applicant must demonstrate high academic achievement.
Application requirements: Recommendations, essay, transcript, proof of eligibility.
Additional information: Contact sponsor for full list of eligible majors. Applicants must be enrolled or plan to enroll in ABET- or CSAB-accredited program. Minimum 3.5 GPA. Application forms available through deans of engineering at eligible schools, through SWE sections, SWE student sections, SWE headquarters, or on Website. Visit www.abet.org for list of ABET-accredited schools.

Amount of award:	$2,500
Number of awards:	3
Application deadline:	February 15
Notification begins:	June 15
Total amount awarded:	$7,500

Contact:
Society of Women Engineers
230 E. Ohio Street
Suite 400
Chicago, IL 60611
Phone: 312-596-5223
Fax: 312-596-5252
Web: www.societyofwomenengineers.swe.org

Lillian Moller Gilbreth Scholarship

Type of award: Scholarship.
Intended use: For full-time junior or senior study at accredited 4-year institution in United States.
Eligibility: Applicant must be female. Applicant must be U.S. citizen or permanent resident.
Basis for selection: Major/career interest in engineering. Applicant must demonstrate high academic achievement.
Application requirements: Recommendations, essay, transcript, proof of eligibility.
Additional information: Renewable for continuing undergraduate study only. Applicants must be enrolled in ABET- or CSAB-accredited program. Minimum 3.0 GPA. Application forms available through deans of engineering at eligible schools, through SWE sections, SWE student sections, SWE headquarters, or on Website. Visit www.abet.org for list of ABET-accredited schools.

Amount of award:	$10,000
Number of awards:	1
Application deadline:	February 15
Notification begins:	June 15
Total amount awarded:	$10,000

Contact:
Society of Women Engineers
230 E. Ohio Street
Suite 400
Chicago, IL 60611-3265
Phone: 312-596-5223
Fax: 312-596-5252
Web: www.societyofwomenengineers.swe.org

Lockheed Martin Aeronautics Company Scholarships

Type of award: Scholarship.
Intended use: For full-time junior study at accredited 4-year institution in United States.

Eligibility: Applicant must be female. Applicant must be U.S. citizen or permanent resident.
Basis for selection: Major/career interest in engineering, electrical/electronic or engineering, mechanical. Applicant must demonstrate high academic achievement.
Application requirements: Recommendations, essay, transcript, proof of eligibility.
Additional information: Awards given to one student in each of above majors. Applicants must be enrolled in an ABET- or CSAB-accredited program. Minimum 3.5 GPA. Application forms available through deans of engineering at eligible schools, through SWE sections, SWE student sections, SWE headquarters, or on Website. Visit www.abet.org for list of ABET-accredited schools.

Amount of award:	$1,000
Number of awards:	2
Application deadline:	February 15
Notification begins:	June 15
Total amount awarded:	$2,000

Contact:
Society of Women Engineers
230 E. Ohio Street
Suite 400
Chicago, IL 60611-3265
Phone: 312-596-5223
Fax: 312-596-5252
Web: www.societyofwomenengineers.swe.org

Lockheed Martin Foundation Scholarships

Type of award: Scholarship.
Intended use: For full-time freshman study at accredited 4-year institution in United States.
Eligibility: Applicant must be female, high school senior. Applicant must be U.S. citizen or permanent resident.
Basis for selection: Major/career interest in engineering. Applicant must demonstrate high academic achievement.
Application requirements: Recommendations, essay, transcript, proof of eligibility.
Additional information: Includes travel grant for SWE National Conference. Applicants must plan to enroll in an ABET- or CSAB-accredited program. Application forms available through deans of engineering at eligible schools, through SWE sections, SWE student sections, SWE headquarters, or on Website. Visit www.abet.org for list of ABET-accredited schools.

Amount of award:	$3,000
Number of awards:	2
Application deadline:	May 15
Notification begins:	September 15
Total amount awarded:	$6,000

Contact:
Society of Women Engineers
230 E. Ohio Street
Suite 400
Chicago, IL 60611-3265
Phone: 312-596-5223
Fax: 312-596-5252
Web: www.societyofwomenengineers.swe.org

Lydia I. Pickup Memorial Scholarship

Type of award: Scholarship.

Intended use: For full-time sophomore, junior, senior or graduate study at accredited 4-year or graduate institution in United States.
Eligibility: Applicant must be female. Applicant must be U.S. citizen or permanent resident.
Basis for selection: Major/career interest in engineering. Applicant must demonstrate high academic achievement.
Application requirements: Recommendations, essay, transcript, proof of eligibility.
Additional information: Graduate students are preferred, but undergraduate sophomores, juniors, and seniors are encouraged to apply. Applicants must be enrolled or plan to enroll in ABET- or CSAB-accredited program. Minimum 3.0 GPA. Application forms available through deans of engineering at eligible schools, through SWE sections, SWE student sections, SWE headquarters, or on Website. Visit www.abet.org for list of ABET-accredited schools.

Amount of award:	$4,000
Number of awards:	1
Application deadline:	February 15
Notification begins:	June 15

Contact:
Society of Women Engineers
230 E. Ohio Street
Suite 400
Chicago, IL 60611
Phone: 312-596-5223
Fax: 312-596-5252
Web: www.societyofwomenengineers.swe.org

Mary V. Munger Scholarship

Type of award: Scholarship.
Intended use: For full-time sophomore, junior or senior study at accredited 4-year institution in United States.
Eligibility: Applicant must be female. Applicant must be U.S. citizen or permanent resident.
Basis for selection: Major/career interest in engineering. Applicant must demonstrate high academic achievement.
Application requirements: Recommendations, essay, transcript, proof of eligibility.
Additional information: Applicants must be enrolled or plan to enroll in ABET- or CSAB-accredited program. Minimum 3.0 GPA. Application forms available through deans of engineering at eligible schools, through SWE sections, SWE student sections, SWE headquarters, or on Website. Visit www.abet.org for list of ABET-accredited schools.

Amount of award:	$4,000
Number of awards:	1
Application deadline:	February 15
Notification begins:	June 15

Contact:
Society of Women Engineers
230 E. Ohio Street
Suite 400
Chicago, IL 60611
Phone: 312-596-5223
Fax: 312-596-5252
Web: www.societyofwomenengineers.swe.org

MASWE Scholarships

Type of award: Scholarship.
Intended use: For full-time sophomore, junior or senior study at accredited 4-year institution in United States.
Eligibility: Applicant must be female. Applicant must be U.S. citizen or permanent resident.

Basis for selection: Major/career interest in engineering. Applicant must demonstrate financial need and high academic achievement.
Application requirements: Recommendations, essay, transcript, proof of eligibility.
Additional information: Applicants must be enrolled or plan to enroll in ABET- or CSAB-accredited program. Minimum 3.0 GPA. Application forms available through deans of engineering at eligible schools, through SWE sections, SWE student sections, SWE headquarters, or on Website. Visit www.abet.org for list of ABET-accredited schools.

Amount of award:	$2,000
Number of awards:	4
Application deadline:	February 15
Notification begins:	June 15
Total amount awarded:	$8,000

Contact:
Society of Women Engineers
230 E. Ohio Street
Suite 400
Chicago, IL 60611-3265
Phone: 312-596-5223
Fax: 312-596-5252
Web: www.societyofwomenengineers.swe.org

Meridith Thoms Memorial Scholarships

Type of award: Scholarship.
Intended use: For full-time sophomore, junior or senior study at accredited 4-year institution in United States.
Eligibility: Applicant must be female. Applicant must be U.S. citizen or permanent resident.
Basis for selection: Major/career interest in engineering. Applicant must demonstrate high academic achievement.
Application requirements: Recommendations, essay, transcript, proof of eligibility.
Additional information: Minimum 3.0 GPA. Applicants must be enrolled or plan to enroll in an ABET- or CSAB-accredited program. Application forms available through deans of engineering at eligible schools, through SWE sections, SWE student sections, SWE headquarters, or on Website. Visit www.abet.org for list of ABET-accredited schools.

Amount of award:	$2,000
Number of awards:	6
Application deadline:	February 15
Notification begins:	June 15
Total amount awarded:	$12,000

Contact:
Society of Women Engineers
230 E. Ohio Street
Suite 400
Chicago, IL 60611-3265
Phone: 312-596-5223
Fax: 312-596-5252
Web: www.societyofwomenengineers.swe.org

Microsoft Corporation Scholarships

Type of award: Scholarship.
Intended use: For full-time sophomore, junior, senior or graduate study at accredited 4-year or graduate institution in United States.
Eligibility: Applicant must be female. Applicant must be U.S. citizen or permanent resident.

Basis for selection: Major/career interest in engineering, computer or computer/information sciences. Applicant must demonstrate high academic achievement.
Application requirements: Recommendations, essay, transcript, proof of eligibility.
Additional information: Master's students eligible only in first year. Applicants must be enrolled or plan to enroll in an ABET- or CSAB-accredited program. Minimum 3.5 GPA. Application forms available through deans of engineering at eligible schools, through SWE sections, SWE student sections, SWE headquarters, or on Website. Visit www.abet.org for list of ABET-accredited schools.

Amount of award:	$2,500
Number of awards:	2
Application deadline:	February 15
Notification begins:	June 15
Total amount awarded:	$5,000

Contact:
Society of Women Engineers
230 E. Ohio Street
Suite 400
Chicago, IL 60611-3265
Phone: 312-596-5223
Fax: 312-596-5252
Web: www.societyofwomenengineers.swe.org

New Jersey Scholarship

Type of award: Scholarship.
Intended use: For full-time freshman study at accredited 4-year institution in United States.
Eligibility: Applicant must be female, high school senior. Applicant must be U.S. citizen or permanent resident residing in New Jersey.
Basis for selection: Major/career interest in engineering. Applicant must demonstrate high academic achievement.
Application requirements: Recommendations, essay, transcript, proof of eligibility.
Additional information: Applicants must plan to enroll in an ABET- or CSAB-accredited program. Application forms available through deans of engineering at eligible schools, through SWE sections, SWE student sections, SWE headquarters, or on Website. Visit www.abet.org for list of ABET-accredited schools.

Amount of award:	$5,000
Number of awards:	1
Application deadline:	May 15
Notification begins:	September 15
Total amount awarded:	$5,000

Contact:
Society of Women Engineers
230 E. Ohio Street
Suite 400
Chicago, IL 60611-3265
Phone: 312-596-5223
Fax: 312-596-5252
Web: www.societyofwomenengineers.swe.org

Northrop Grumman Corporation Scholarship

Type of award: Scholarship.
Intended use: For full-time freshman study at accredited 4-year institution in United States.
Eligibility: Applicant must be female. Applicant must be U.S. citizen or permanent resident.

Basis for selection: Major/career interest in engineering, materials; engineering, civil; engineering, computer; computer/information sciences; engineering, electrical/electronic or engineering, industrial. Applicant must demonstrate high academic achievement.
Application requirements: Recommendations, essay, transcript, proof of eligibility.
Additional information: Systems engineering and aerospace engineering majors also eligible. Minimum 3.0 GPA. Applicants must plan to enroll in ABET- or CSAB-accredited program. Application forms available through deans of engineering at eligible schools, through SWE sections, SWE student sections, SWE headquarters, or on Website. Visit www.abet.org for list of ABET-accredited schools.

Amount of award:	$5,000
Number of awards:	1
Application deadline:	May 15
Notification begins:	September 15

Contact:
Society of Women Engineers
230 E. Ohio Street
Suite 400
Chicago, IL 60611-3265
Phone: 312-596-5223
Fax: 312-596-5252
Web: www.societyofwomenengineers.swe.org

Olive Lynn Salembier Re-entry Scholarship

Type of award: Scholarship.
Intended use: For undergraduate or graduate study at accredited 4-year or graduate institution in United States.
Eligibility: Applicant must be female, returning adult student. Applicant must be U.S. citizen or permanent resident.
Basis for selection: Major/career interest in engineering.
Application requirements: Recommendations, essay, transcript, proof of eligibility.
Additional information: Must have been out of school or engineering workforce at least two years prior to re-entry. Applicants must be enrolled or plan to enroll in ABET- or CSAB-accredited program. Application forms available through deans of engineering at eligible schools, through SWE sections, SWE student sections, SWE headquarters, or on Website. Visit www.abet.org for list of ABET-accredited schools.

Amount of award:	$2,000
Number of awards:	1
Application deadline:	February 15, May 15
Notification begins:	June 15, September 15
Total amount awarded:	$2,000

Contact:
Society of Women Engineers
230 E. Ohio Street
Suite 400
Chicago, IL 60611-3265
Phone: 312-596-5223
Fax: 312-596-5252
Web: www.societyofwomenengineers.swe.org

Past Presidents Scholarships

Type of award: Scholarship.
Intended use: For full-time undergraduate or graduate study at accredited 4-year or graduate institution in United States.
Eligibility: Applicant must be female. Applicant must be U.S. citizen.

Basis for selection: Major/career interest in engineering. Applicant must demonstrate high academic achievement.
Application requirements: Recommendations, essay, transcript, proof of eligibility.
Additional information: Minimum 3.0 GPA. Applicants must be enrolled or plan to enroll in an ABET- or CSAB-accredited program. Application forms available through deans of engineering at eligible schools, through SWE sections, SWE student sections, SWE headquarters, or on Website. Visit www.abet.org for list of ABET-accredited schools.

Amount of award:	$2,000
Number of awards:	2
Application deadline:	February 15, May 15
Notification begins:	June 15, September 15
Total amount awarded:	$4,000

Contact:
Society of Women Engineers
230 E. Ohio Street
Suite 400
Chicago, IL 60611-3265
Phone: 312-596-5223
Fax: 312-596-5252
Web: www.societyofwomenengineers.swe.org

Phoenix Section Scholarship

Type of award: Scholarship.
Intended use: For full-time freshman study at accredited 4-year institution in United States.
Eligibility: Applicant must be high school senior. Applicant must be U.S. citizen or permanent resident residing in Arizona.
Basis for selection: Major/career interest in engineering. Applicant must demonstrate high academic achievement.
Application requirements: Recommendations, essay, transcript, proof of eligibility.
Additional information: Non-residents attending school in Arizona also eligible. Applicants must plan to enroll in an ABET- or CSAB-accredited program. Application forms available through deans of engineering at eligible schools, through SWE sections, SWE student sections, SWE headquarters, or on Website. Visit www.abet.org for list of ABET-accredited schools.

Amount of award:	$1,000
Number of awards:	2
Application deadline:	May 15
Notification begins:	September 15

Contact:
Society of Women Engineers
230 E. Ohio Street
Suite 400
Chicago, IL 60611-3265
Phone: 312-596-5223
Fax: 312-596-5252
Web: www.societyofwomenengineers.swe.org

Rockwell Automation Scholarships

Type of award: Scholarship.
Intended use: For full-time junior or senior study at accredited 4-year institution in United States.
Eligibility: Applicant must be female. Applicant must be U.S. citizen or permanent resident.
Basis for selection: Major/career interest in engineering; engineering, computer; engineering, electrical/electronic; engineering, mechanical; computer/information sciences; manufacturing or engineering, industrial. Applicant must demonstrate leadership.

Application requirements: Recommendations, essay, transcript, proof of eligibility.
Additional information: Software engineering and manufacturing engineering majors also eligible. Applicants must be enrolled in ABET- or CSAB-accredited program. Minimum 3.0 GPA. Application forms available through deans of engineering at eligible schools, through SWE sections, SWE student sections, SWE headquarters, or on Website. Visit www.abet.org for list of ABET-accredited schools.

Amount of award:	$2,500
Number of awards:	2
Application deadline:	February 15
Notification begins:	June 15
Total amount awarded:	$5,000

Contact:
Society of Women Engineers
230 E. Ohio Street
Suite 400
Chicago, IL 60611-3265
Phone: 312-596-5223
Fax: 312-596-5252
Web: www.societyofwomenengineers.swe.org

Susan Miszkowitz Memorial Scholarship

Type of award: Scholarship.
Intended use: For full-time sophomore, junior, senior or graduate study at accredited 4-year institution in United States.
Eligibility: Applicant must be female. Applicant must be U.S. citizen or permanent resident.
Basis for selection: Major/career interest in engineering. Applicant must demonstrate high academic achievement.
Application requirements: Recommendations, transcript, proof of eligibility.
Additional information: Minimum 3.0 GPA. Applicants must be enrolled or plan to enroll in an ABET- or CSAB-accredited program. Application forms available through deans of engineering at eligible schools, through SWE sections, SWE student sections, SWE headquarters, or on Website. Visit www.abet.org for list of ABET-accredited schools.

Amount of award:	$1,500
Number of awards:	1
Application deadline:	February 15
Notification begins:	June 15

Contact:
Society of Women Engineers
230 E. Ohio Street
Suite 400
Chicago, IL 60611-3265
Phone: 312-596-5223
Fax: 312-596-5252
Web: www.societyofwomenengineers.swe.org

Soil and Water Conservation Society

Donald A. Williams Soil Conservation Scholarship

Type of award: Scholarship.
Intended use: For undergraduate study at postsecondary institution.

Basis for selection: Major/career interest in natural resources/conservation. Applicant must demonstrate financial need, depth of character and seriousness of purpose.

Application requirements: Recommendations, essay.

Additional information: Applicant must have been member of Soil and Water Conservation Society for at least one year at time of application. Must demonstrate competence in line of work. Must have completed at least one year of full-time employment and be currently employed in a natural resource conservation endeavor. Number of awards varies. Visit Website for application and deadline.

Amount of award:	$1,000
Number of awards:	1
Number of applicants:	3

Contact:
Soil and Water Conservation Society
945 SW Ankeny Road
Ankeny, IA 50023
Phone: 515-289-2331
Fax: 515-289-1227
Web: www.swcs.org

Sons of Italy Foundation

Charles Evans Scholarship

Type of award: Scholarship.

Intended use: For undergraduate or graduate study at accredited 4-year or graduate institution in United States.

Eligibility: Applicant must be Italian. Applicant must be U.S. citizen.

Application requirements: $30 application fee. Recommendations, essay, transcript. Standardized test scores, resume.

Additional information: Must have at least one Italian or Italian American grandparent. $30 processing fee includes a one-year national at-large membership to the Order Sons of Italy in America and a subscription to Italian America magazine.

Application deadline:	February 25

Contact:
Sons of Italy Foundation
219 E Street, NE
Washington, DC 20002
Phone: 202-547-2900
Web: www.osia.org

General Scholarship

Type of award: Scholarship.

Intended use: For undergraduate or graduate study at accredited 4-year institution.

Eligibility: Applicant must be Italian. Applicant must be U.S. citizen.

Application requirements: $30 application fee. Recommendations, essay, transcript. Resume, cover letter. SAT/ACT scores.

Additional information: Must have at least one Italian or Italian-American grandparent. Visit Website for application.

Application deadline:	February 25

Contact:
Sons of Italy Foundation
219 E Street NE
Washington, DC 20002
Phone: 202-547-2900
Web: www.osia.org

Henry Salvatori Scholarship

Type of award: Scholarship.

Intended use: For full-time undergraduate study.

Eligibility: Applicant must be high school senior. Applicant must be Italian. Applicant must be U.S. citizen.

Basis for selection: Applicant must demonstrate high academic achievement, depth of character, leadership, patriotism, seriousness of purpose and service orientation.

Application requirements: $30 application fee. Transcript, proof of eligibility. SAT/ACT scores. Cover letter, resume. Two letters of recommendation from public figures who have demonstrated the ideals of liberty, freedom, and equality in their work; and 750-1,000 word essay discussing the relevance of the Declaration of Independence, the Constitution, and the Bill of Rights to the principles of liberty, freedom, and equality in the U.S. today.

Additional information: Must have at least one Italian or Italian-American grandparent. Visit Website for application.

Amount of award:	$5,000
Number of awards:	1
Number of applicants:	200
Application deadline:	February 25
Notification begins:	April 15
Total amount awarded:	$5,000

Contact:
Sons of Italy Foundation
219 E Street NE
Washington, DC 20002
Phone: 202-547-2900
Web: www.osia.org

Italian Language Scholarship

Type of award: Scholarship.

Intended use: For junior or senior study.

Eligibility: Applicant must be Italian. Applicant must be U.S. citizen.

Basis for selection: Major/career interest in Italian.

Application requirements: $30 application fee. Recommendations, essay, transcript. Resume, cover letter. SAT/ACT scores. Essay must be in Italian.

Additional information: Must have at least one Italian or Italian-American grandparent. Visit Website for application.

Application deadline:	February 25

Contact:
Sons of Italy Foundation
219 E Street NE
Washington, DC 20002
Phone: 202-547-2900
Web: www.osia.org

Jospeh L. Bracone Memorial Scholarship

Type of award: Scholarship.

Intended use: For undergraduate study at accredited 4-year institution.

Eligibility: Applicant must be Italian. Applicant must be U.S. citizen.

Application requirements: $30 application fee.
Recommendations, essay, transcript. SAT/ACT scores, cover
letter, resume.
Additional information: Must have at least one Italian or
Italian-American grandparent. Preference given to those
studying business, finance, or pre-law. Visit Website for
application.

    Application deadline: February 25
Contact:
Sons of Italy Foundation
219 E Street NE
Washington, DC 20002
Phone: 202-547-2900
Web: www.osia.org

National Leadership Grant

Type of award: Scholarship.
Intended use: For full-time undergraduate, master's, doctoral
or first professional study at accredited 4-year or graduate
institution in United States.
Eligibility: Applicant must be Italian. Applicant must be U.S.
citizen.
Basis for selection: Applicant must demonstrate high
academic achievement, depth of character, leadership,
seriousness of purpose and service orientation.
Application requirements: $30 application fee.
Recommendations, essay, transcript, proof of eligibility. SAT/
ACT scores, resume.
Additional information: Must have at least one Italian or
Italian-American grandparent. Amount and number of awards
vary. Visit Website for application.

    Amount of award: $5,000-$25,000
    Number of awards: 8
    Number of applicants: 600
    Application deadline: February 25
    Notification begins: April 15
Contact:
Sons of Italy Foundation
219 E Street NE
Washington, DC 20002
Phone: 202-547-2900
Web: www.osia.org

Sorrento Lingue Scholarship

Type of award: Scholarship.
Intended use: For junior, senior or graduate study at
postsecondary institution outside United States.
Eligibility: Applicant must be Italian. Applicant must be U.S.
citizen.
Basis for selection: Major/career interest in Italian.
Application requirements: $30 application fee.
Recommendations, essay, transcript. Essay must be submitted in
Italian. SAT/ACT scores. Resume, cover letter.
Additional information: Scholarship for study abroad in
Sorrento, Italy from January to June. Must have at least one
Italian or Italian-American grandparent. Basic knowledge of
Italian language preferred. Visit Website for application and
more information.

    Application deadline: February 25
Contact:
Sons of Italy Foundation
219 E Street NE
Washington, DC 20002
Phone: 202-547-2900
Web: www.osia.org

Sons of Norway Foundation

Astrid G. Cates Scholarship Fund and Myrtle Beinhauer Scholarship

Type of award: Scholarship.
Intended use: For undergraduate study at postsecondary
institution.
Eligibility: Applicant or parent must be member/participant of
Sons of Norway. Applicant must be U.S. citizen.
Basis for selection: Applicant must demonstrate financial
need, high academic achievement, depth of character and
service orientation.
Application requirements: Recommendations, transcript,
proof of eligibility. Recent photo.
Additional information: Applicant, parent, or grandparent
must be current member of Sons of Norway District 1-6.
Student must include the following information with
application: GPA, what type of study is intended, where and
when. Related fees must be specified, as well as long-term
career goals, Sons of Norway involvement, extracurricular
activities and financial need. The Cates Scholarship is $1,000;
Beinhauer Scholarship awards $3,000 to the most qualified of
all candidates. Student can be awarded maximum two
scholarships within five-year period. Visit Website for
application.

    Amount of award: $1,000-$3,000
    Number of awards: 8
    Number of applicants: 99
    Application deadline: March 1
    Notification begins: May 1
Contact:
Sons of Norway Foundation
Attn: Cates/Beinhauer Scholarship
1455 West Lake Street
Minneapolis, MN 55408-2666
Web: www.sonsofnorway.com/foundation

King Olav V Norwegian-American Heritage Fund

Type of award: Scholarship.
Intended use: For full-time undergraduate or graduate study at
accredited postsecondary institution in United States.
Eligibility: Applicant must be at least 18.
Basis for selection: Major/career interest in Scandinavian
studies/research. Applicant must demonstrate financial need,
high academic achievement, depth of character, leadership and
service orientation.
Application requirements: Recommendations, transcript,
proof of eligibility. SAT or ACT scores. Recent photo. Essay of
maximum 500 words about reasons for application; course of
study to be pursued; length of the course; name, tuition, and
other costs of institution; amount of financial assistance desired;
and how the applicant's course of study will benefit his or her
community and accord with the goals and objectives of the
Sons of Norway Foundation.
Additional information: Open to Americans who have
demonstrated keen and sincere interest in Norwegian heritage or
Norwegians who have demonstrated interest in American
heritage and have desire to further study heritage (arts, crafts,
literature, history, music, folklore, etc.) at recognized
educational institution. Number and amount of awards varies.
Visit Website for application.

Amount of award:	$1,000-$1,500
Number of awards:	7
Number of applicants:	100
Application deadline:	March 1
Notification begins:	May 1

Contact:
Sons of Norway Foundation
Attn: King Olav Fund
1455 West Lake Street
Minneapolis, MN 55408-2666
Web: www.sonsofnorway.com/foundation

Nancy Lorraine Jensen Memorial Scholarship

Type of award: Scholarship, renewable.
Intended use: For full-time undergraduate study.
Eligibility: Applicant or parent must be member/participant of Sons of Norway. Applicant must be female, at least 17, no older than 35. Applicant must be U.S. citizen.
Basis for selection: Major/career interest in chemistry; physics; engineering, electrical/electronic; engineering, mechanical or engineering, chemical. Applicant must demonstrate high academic achievement, depth of character and seriousness of purpose.
Application requirements: Recommendations, essay, transcript, proof of eligibility. SAT/ACT scores. Recent photo.
Additional information: Applicant or applicant's parent or grandparent must have been a member of Sons of Norway for at least three years. Must have completed at least one semester of undergraduate study in current program. Award is no less than 50 percent of one semester's tuition and no more than full tuition for one year. Minimum 1800 SAT (or at least 600 Math) or 26 ACT. Must apply each year. Visit Website for application.

Number of awards:	6
Application deadline:	April 1

Contact:
Sons of Norway Foundation
Attn: Nancy L. Jensen Memorial Scholarship
1455 West Lake Street
Minneapolis, MN 55408-2666
Web: www.sonsofnorway.com/foundation

South Carolina Commission on Higher Education

Dayco Scholarship Program

Type of award: Scholarship, renewable.
Intended use: For full-time freshman study at 4-year institution in United States. Designated institutions: South Carolina institutions.
Eligibility: Applicant must be high school senior. Applicant must be U.S. citizen or permanent resident residing in South Carolina.
Basis for selection: Applicant must demonstrate financial need and high academic achievement.
Application requirements: Transcript, proof of eligibility. Need analysis, affidavit documenting that student has never been convicted of felonies or alcohol- or drug-related misdemeanor offenses.
Additional information: Must be either an employee or dependent of an employee of a branch of Dayco Products, Inc. in South Carolina. Employee must be employed by Dayco for

at least four calendar years. In the event that there are no eligible dependents meeting above critera, the award will be given to a resident of one of the counties of Walterboro, Williston, or Easley. Minimum 3.25 GPA. Must rank in top 20% of graduating high school class. Must have completed 12 credit hours at time of scholarship disbursement. Must not owe refund or repayment to a grant program or be under default on a loan. Must not have criminal record. Must reapply and meet eligibility requirements annually. Amount of award varies.
Contact:
South Carolina Commission on Higher Education
1333 Main Street, Suite 200
Columbia, SC 29201
Phone: 803-737-2260
Fax: 803-737-2297
Web: www.che.sc.gov

LIFE Scholarship Program

Type of award: Scholarship, renewable.
Intended use: For full-time freshman study at vocational, 2-year or 4-year institution. Designated institutions: Eligible institutions in South Carolina.
Eligibility: Applicant must be U.S. citizen or permanent resident residing in South Carolina.
Basis for selection: Applicant must demonstrate high academic achievement.
Application requirements: Transcript. SAT/ACT scores.
Additional information: First-time entering freshmen at four-year institutions must meet two of three criteria: 3.0 high school GPA on Uniform Grading Policy (UGP); minimum 1100 SAT or 24 ACT; rank in top 30 percent of graduating class. First-time entering freshmen at two-year institution must have 3.0 high school GPA on UGP. Applicant must graduate from high school as South Carolina resident. No application required; college/university will determine eligibility based on transcript and will notify student directly. Maximum award $5,000 for four-year schools, average in-state tuition for two-year schools, and up to full in-state tuition at technical schools, not to exceed $5,000. Students in approved math and science programs could earn an additional $2,500.

Amount of award:	$5,000
Number of awards:	31,004
Total amount awarded:	$150,595,333

Contact:
South Carolina Commission on Higher Education
1333 Main Street, Suite 200
Columbia, SC 29201
Phone: 803-737-2260
Fax: 803-737-2297
Web: www.che.sc.gov

Lottery Tuition Assistance Program

Type of award: Scholarship, renewable.
Intended use: For undergraduate study at vocational or 2-year institution. Designated institutions: Eligible South Carolina institutions.
Eligibility: Applicant must be U.S. citizen or permanent resident residing in South Carolina.
Application requirements: FAFSA or FAFSA waiver.
Additional information: Award may not exceed cost of tuition. Award based on lottery revenue and number of applicants. Amount varies by semester. All federal grants and need-based grants must be awarded first before determining amount for which student is eligible. Student must be degree-seeking and enrolled in minimum six credit hours. Visit Website for more information.

Number of awards: 45,628
Number of applicants: 59,486
Total amount awarded: $47,641,997
Contact:
South Carolina Commission on Higher Education
1333 Main Street, Suite 200
Columbia, SC 29201
Phone: 803-737-2262
Fax: 803-737-2297
Web: www.che.sc.gov

Palmetto Fellows Scholarship Program

Type of award: Scholarship, renewable.
Intended use: For full-time undergraduate study at 4-year institution. Designated institutions: Eligible South Carolina institutions.
Eligibility: Applicant must be high school senior. Applicant must be U.S. citizen or permanent resident residing in South Carolina.
Basis for selection: Applicant must demonstrate high academic achievement.
Application requirements: Transcript. ACT/SAT scores. Must apply through guidance counselor.
Additional information: Minimum 1200 SAT (Math and Reading) or 27 ACT, 3.5 GPA on the SC Uniform Grading Policy, and rank in top six percent of class. Class ranking requirement waived for students with 1400 SAT (Math and Reading) or 32 ACT and 4.0 GPA. High school graduates or students who have completed home-school program as prescribed by law may be eligible. For more information, contact guidance counselor or S.C. Commission.
  Amount of award: $6,700-$7,500
  Application deadline: December 15, June 15
  Notification begins: February 15, August 15
  Total amount awarded: $44,035,892
Contact:
South Carolina Commission on Higher Education
1333 Main Street, Suite 200
Columbia, SC 29201
Phone: 877-349-7183 or 803-787-2286
Fax: 803-737-2297
Web: www.che.sc.gov

South Carolina HOPE Scholarships

Type of award: Scholarship.
Intended use: For freshman study at 4-year institution. Designated institutions: Eligible South Carolina institutions.
Eligibility: Applicant must be U.S. citizen or permanent resident residing in South Carolina.
Basis for selection: Applicant must demonstrate high academic achievement.
Application requirements: Transcript, proof of eligibility.
Additional information: No application necessary. College or university will determine eligibility based on official high school transcript and will notify students directly. Minimum 3.0 cumulative GPA upon high school graduation. Student must certify that he/she has not been convicted of any felonies or any second drug/alcohol misdemeanors within past academic year. Contact institution's financial aid office for more information.
  Amount of award: $2,800
  Number of awards: 2,724
  Total amount awarded: $7,037,260

Contact:
South Carolina Commission on Higher Education
1333 Main Street, Suite 200
Columbia, SC 29201
Phone: 803-737-2260
Fax: 803-737-2297
Web: www.che.sc.gov

South Carolina Need-Based Grants Program

Type of award: Scholarship.
Intended use: For undergraduate study at vocational, 2-year or 4-year institution. Designated institutions: Eligible South Carolina public institutions.
Eligibility: Applicant must be U.S. citizen or permanent resident residing in South Carolina.
Basis for selection: Applicant must demonstrate financial need.
Application requirements: FAFSA.
Additional information: May receive award for maximum eight full-time equivalent terms or until degree is earned, whichever is less. Must enroll in at least 12 credit hours per semester if full-time or six if part-time. Visit Website for more information.
  Amount of award: $1,250-$2,500
  Number of awards: 28,051
  Number of applicants: 28,507
  Total amount awarded: $26,989,583
Contact:
South Carolina Commission on Higher Education
1333 Main Street, Suite 200
Columbia, SC 29201
Phone: 803-737-2262
Fax: 803-737-2297
Web: www.che.sc.gov

South Carolina Higher Education Tuition Grants Commission

South Carolina Tuition Grants

Type of award: Scholarship, renewable.
Intended use: For full-time undergraduate study at accredited 2-year or 4-year institution in United States. Designated institutions: SACS-accredited South Carolina private, nonprofit institutions (visit Website for list).
Eligibility: Applicant must be U.S. citizen residing in South Carolina.
Basis for selection: Applicant must demonstrate financial need.
Application requirements: FAFSA.
Additional information: Award amount varies. Recipient may reapply for up to four years. Incoming freshmen must score 900 SAT (Math and Reading) or 19 ACT, graduate in top three-fourths of high school class, or graduate from South Carolina high school with 2.0 GPA. Upperclassmen must complete 24 semester hours and meet college's satisfactory progress requirements. Application is automatic with FAFSA; submit to federal processor and list eligible college in college choice section. All eligible applicants funded if deadline is met. Contact campus financial aid office for details.

Amount of award:	$2,460-$2,800
Number of awards:	14,200
Number of applicants:	27,206
Application deadline:	June 30
Total amount awarded:	$37,948,782

Contact:
South Carolina Higher Education Tuition Grants Commission
800 Dutch Square Blvd., Suite 260A
Columbia, SC 29210-7317
Phone: 803-896-1120
Fax: 803-896-1126
Web: www.sctuitiongrants.com

South Dakota Board of Regents

South Dakota Annis I. Fowler/ Kaden Scholarship

Type of award: Scholarship.
Intended use: For freshman study at postsecondary institution. Designated institutions: University of South Dakota, Black Hills State University, Dakota State University, and Northern State University.
Eligibility: Applicant must be high school senior. Applicant must be U.S. citizen residing in South Dakota.
Basis for selection: Major/career interest in education. Applicant must demonstrate high academic achievement, depth of character, leadership, seriousness of purpose and service orientation.
Application requirements: Recommendations, essay, transcript, proof of eligibility. ACT scores.
Additional information: Open to high school seniors who have a cumulative GPA of 3.0 after three years. Applicants must select elementary education as major field. Special consideration given to applicants with demonstrated motivation or disability, or who are self-supporting. Transcript must include class rank, cumulative GPA, and list of courses to be taken during senior year.

Amount of award:	$1,000
Number of awards:	2
Number of applicants:	30
Notification begins:	April 15

Contact:
South Dakota Board of Regents
Scholarship Committee
306 E. Capitol Avenue, Suite 200
Pierre, SD 57501-3159
Phone: 605-773-3455
Web: www.sdbor.edu

South Dakota Ardell Bjugstad Scholarship

Type of award: Scholarship.
Intended use: For freshman study at postsecondary institution in United States.
Eligibility: Applicant must be American Indian. Must be member of federally recognized Indian tribe whose reservation is in North Dakota or South Dakota. Applicant must be high school senior. Applicant must be U.S. citizen residing in South Dakota or North Dakota.

Basis for selection: Major/career interest in agribusiness; agriculture; natural resources/conservation or environmental science. Applicant must demonstrate high academic achievement, depth of character, leadership and seriousness of purpose.
Application requirements: Recommendations, transcript. Verification of tribal enrollment.
Additional information: Transcript must include class rank and cumulative GPA.

Amount of award:	$500
Number of awards:	1
Number of applicants:	3
Notification begins:	April 15

Contact:
South Dakota Board of Regents
Scholarship Committee
306 E. Capitol Avenue, Suite 200
Pierre, SD 57501-3159
Phone: 605-773-3455
Web: www.sdbor.edu

South Dakota Haines Memorial Scholarship

Type of award: Scholarship.
Intended use: For full-time sophomore, junior or senior study at accredited 4-year institution in United States. Designated institutions: University of South Dakota, Black Hills State University, Dakota State University, Northern State University, South Dakota State University.
Eligibility: Applicant must be residing in South Dakota.
Basis for selection: Major/career interest in education; education, early childhood; education, special or education, teacher. Applicant must demonstrate depth of character, leadership, seriousness of purpose and service orientation.
Application requirements: Proof of eligibility. Resume. Two two-page essays: one describing personal philosophy and another describing philosophy of education.
Additional information: Minimum 2.5 GPA.

Amount of award:	$2,150
Number of awards:	1
Number of applicants:	20
Notification begins:	April 15

Contact:
South Dakota Board of Regents Scholarship Committee
306 E. Capitol, Suite 200
Pierre, SD 57501-3159
Phone: 605-773-3455
Web: www.sdbor.edu

South Dakota Marlin R. Scarborough Memorial Scholarship

Type of award: Scholarship.
Intended use: For full-time junior study at accredited 4-year institution in United States. Designated institutions: Public institutions in South Dakota.
Eligibility: Applicant must be residing in South Dakota.
Basis for selection: Applicant must demonstrate high academic achievement, depth of character, leadership, seriousness of purpose and service orientation.
Application requirements: Nomination by participating South Dakota public university. Essay explaining leadership and academic qualities, career plans, and educational interests.
Additional information: Must be sophomore at time of application. Submit application to school financial aid office. Minimum 3.5 GPA. Must have completed three full semesters

at same university. Each South Dakota public university may nominate one student. Application deadlines vary by university; visit Website for dates and application.

Amount of award:	$1,000
Number of awards:	1
Notification begins:	April 15

Contact:
South Dakota Board of Regents Scholarship Committee
306 East Capitol, Suite 200
Pierre, SD 57501-3159
Phone: 605-773-3455
Web: www.sdbor.edu

South Dakota Opportunity Scholarship Program

Type of award: Scholarship.
Intended use: For undergraduate study at accredited vocational, 2-year or 4-year institution in United States. Designated institutions: Augustana College, Colorado Technical University, Dakota Wesleyan University, Lake Area Technical Institute, Mitchell Technical Institute, Northern State University, South Dakota School of Mines & Technology, Southeast Technical Institute, University of Sioux Falls, Black Hills State University, Dakota State University, Kilian Community College, Mount Mary College, National American University, Presentation College, South Dakota State University, University of South Dakota, Western Dakota Technical Institute.
Eligibility: Applicant must be U.S. citizen or permanent resident residing in South Dakota.
Basis for selection: Applicant must demonstrate high academic achievement.
Application requirements: Transcript. SAT/ACT scores.
Additional information: Award is distributed bi-annually over four academic years. Minimum 1090 SAT (Verbal and Math) and 24 ACT. Minimum 3.0 GPA. Must complete Regents Scholar Curriculum with a minimum 2.0. Completed applications must be submitted directly to the institution to which applicant is applying. Visit Website for detailed credit hour requirements.

Amount of award:	$5,000
Application deadline:	September 1, January 15

Contact:
South Dakota Board of Regents c/o Dr. Paul D. Turman
306 E. Capitol Ave., Suite 200
Pierre, SD 57501-2545
Phone: 605-773-3455
Web: www.sdbor.edu

South Dakota Department of Education

South Dakota Robert C. Byrd Honors Scholarship

Type of award: Scholarship, renewable.
Intended use: For full-time undergraduate study in United States.
Eligibility: Applicant must be high school senior. Applicant must be U.S. citizen or permanent resident residing in South Dakota.
Basis for selection: Applicant must demonstrate high academic achievement.

Application requirements: Transcript.
Additional information: Minimum 3.5 GPA. Must have at least 30 ACT score.

Amount of award:	$1,500
Number of awards:	71
Number of applicants:	137
Application deadline:	March 20
Notification begins:	February 6
Total amount awarded:	$107,250

Contact:
South Dakota Department of Education
700 Governors Drive
Pierre, SD 57501-2291
Phone: 605-773-3248
Fax: 605-773-6139
Web: www.doe.sd.gov/scholarships/byrd

Southern Nursery Organization

Southern Nursery Organization Sidney B. Meadows Scholarship

Type of award: Scholarship.
Intended use: For full-time junior, senior, master's or doctoral study at accredited 4-year or graduate institution.
Eligibility: Applicant must be U.S. citizen residing in Tennessee, Louisiana, Virginia, Mississippi, Alabama, Kentucky, Missouri, Texas, Arkansas, Maryland, Florida, Georgia, South Carolina, Oklahoma, West Virginia or North Carolina.
Basis for selection: Major/career interest in horticulture.
Additional information: Must be enrolled in ornamental horticulture or related discipline in good standing. Minimum 2.75 GPA for undergraduates, 3.0 for graduates. Must be resident of one of 16 states in Southern Nursery Organization, but matriculation in these states is not mandatory. Preference given to applicants who plan to work in the horticulture industry after graduation, and for those who demonstrate financial need. Visit Website for application and additional information.

Amount of award:	$2,500
Number of awards:	7
Application deadline:	May 15
Notification begins:	July 1
Total amount awarded:	$17,500

Contact:
Sidney B. Meadows Scholarship Endowment Fund c/o Dr. Mark Windham
205 Ellington Plant Sciences Bldg.
University of Tennessee
Knoxville, TN 37996-4560
Phone: 865-974-0206
Fax: 865-974-4744
Web: www.sna.org/education.cfm

Southern Scholarship Foundation

Southern Scholarship Foundation Scholarships

Type of award: Scholarship, renewable.
Intended use: For undergraduate or graduate study in United States. Designated institutions: Florida State University, Florida A&M, University of Florida, Florida Gulf Coast University.
Basis for selection: Applicant must demonstrate financial need, high academic achievement, depth of character and service orientation.
Application requirements: Interview, recommendations, essay, transcript, proof of eligibility. Resume, FAFSA, SAR, recent photograph.
Additional information: Number of awards varies. Minimum 3.0 GPA. Applicants encouraged to submit early in spring semester. Graduating high school students and students currently attending community college are eligible to apply. Awards given in the form of housing at one of 25 Florida-based scholarship houses. Awardees do not pay rent, but are responsible for basic household expenses. Each student contributes approximately $950/semester. Florida Gulf Coast University awards are for females only.

Number of awards:	80
Number of applicants:	300

Contact:
Southern Scholarship Foundation
Attn: Sydney Smith
322 Stadium Drive
Tallahassee, FL 32304
Phone: 850-222-3833
Fax: 850-222-6750
Web: www.southernscholarship.org

SPIE - The International Society for Optical Engineering

SPIE Educational Scholarship in Optical Science and Engineering

Type of award: Scholarship, renewable.
Intended use: For undergraduate, graduate or non-degree study in or outside United States.
Basis for selection: Major/career interest in engineering or physics. Applicant must demonstrate seriousness of purpose.
Application requirements: Recommendations, essay.
Additional information: Open only to SPIE student members; nonmembers may submit SPIE student membership application and dues with scholarship application. High school and pre-university students may receive one-year complimentary membership. Applicant must be enrolled in optics, photonics, imaging, optoelectronics, or related program at accredited institution for year in which award will be used (unless high school student). Award amount varies. Students must reapply for renewal. Visit Website for application and deadline.

Amount of award:	$1,000-$11,000

Contact:
SPIE Scholarship Committee
P.O. Box 10
Bellingham, WA 98227-0010
Phone: 360-685-5452
Fax: 360-647-1445
Web: www.spie.org/scholarships

Spina Bifida Association

Spina Bifida Association One-Year Scholarship

Type of award: Scholarship.
Intended use: For undergraduate study at postsecondary institution in United States.
Basis for selection: Applicant must demonstrate financial need, high academic achievement, leadership, seriousness of purpose and service orientation.
Application requirements: Recommendations, essay, transcript, proof of eligibility. SAT, ACT, or GRE scores. Statement verifying disability from physician. Verification of high school diploma or GED; verification of acceptance at school/college. FAFSA or financial aid forms.
Additional information: Open to all persons with spina bifida. Applicant must be enrolled in/accepted by college, junior college, graduate program, or approved trade or vocational program. Number of awards varies. Immediate family members of SBA Board, scholarship committee, or staff are not eligible. Visit Website for deadline and more information.

Amount of award:	$2,000

Contact:
Scholarship Committee
4590 MacArthur Boulevard, NW
Suite 250
Washington, DC 20007-4226
Phone: 202-944-3285 or 800-621-3141
Fax: 202-944-3295
Web: www.spinabifidaassociation.org

Staples

Staples Associates Annual Scholarships Plan

Type of award: Scholarship, renewable.
Intended use: For undergraduate, graduate or non-degree study at vocational, 2-year, 4-year or graduate institution.
Application requirements: Proof of eligibility.
Additional information: Applicants must have worked at Staples for 90 days, averaging at least 18 hours per week. Contact Human Resources for complete details and application. Number of awards granted depends on funding.

Amount of award:	$750-$2,000
Number of applicants:	2,600
Application deadline:	September 30
Notification begins:	November 15
Total amount awarded:	$2,000,000

Contact:
Staples
500 Staples Drive
Framingham, MA 01702

State Council of Higher Education for Virginia

Virginia Academic Common Market

Type of award: Scholarship.
Intended use: For full-time undergraduate or graduate study at 4-year or graduate institution. Designated institutions: Eligible public institutions in 15 southern states.
Eligibility: Applicant must be U.S. citizen or permanent resident residing in Virginia.
Additional information: Awards Virginia residents in-state tuition at participating out-of-state institutions in the South. Institution must offer program unavailable at Virginia public institutions. Applicant must be domiciled in Virginia. Deadlines vary by institution.

Number of awards: 100
Contact:
Academic Common Market/SCHEV
James Monroe Building
101 North Fourteenth Street
Richmond, VA 23219
Phone: 877-516-0138
Fax: 804-225-2604
Web: www.schev.edu

Virginia Tuition Assistance Grant

Type of award: Scholarship, renewable.
Intended use: For full-time undergraduate, master's, doctoral or first professional study at accredited postsecondary institution. Designated institutions: Private, nonprofit institutions in Virginia.
Eligibility: Applicant must be residing in Virginia.
Application requirements: Proof of eligibility.
Additional information: Must be in eligible degree program in participating Virginia private college. Graduate students must be enrolled in health-related major. Applicant must be domiciled in Virginia. Theology and divinity majors not eligible. Award is $3200 for undergraduates; $1900 for graduate students. If funding is insufficient, priority given first to renewals, then to new applicants who apply prior to deadline. Interested students should contact financial aid office of qualifying postsecondary institution.

Amount of award: $1,900-$3,200
Number of awards: 20,000
Application deadline: July 31
Total amount awarded: $60,000,000
Contact:
Web: www.schev.edu

State of Alabama

Alabama Scholarship for Dependents of Blind Parents

Type of award: Scholarship, renewable.
Intended use: For undergraduate study at vocational, 2-year or 4-year institution. Designated institutions: Alabama public institutions.
Eligibility: Parent must be visually impaired. Applicant must be U.S. citizen or permanent resident residing in Alabama.
Basis for selection: Applicant must demonstrate financial need.
Application requirements: Proof of eligibility.
Additional information: Award waives instructional fees and tuition costs and pays for portion of books. Parent must be head of household and legally blind, and family income must be at or below 1.3 times the federal poverty guidelines. Applicant must have been Alabama resident for five years prior to application. Must reapply for renewal. Award available for all eligible applicants.

Amount of award: Full tuition
Application deadline: June 30, September 30
Contact:
Alabama Department of Rehabilitation Services
Attn: Debra Culver
7 Bemiston Avenue
Talladega, AL 35160
Phone: 256-362-0638
Fax: 256-362-6941

State Student Assistance Commission of Indiana

Frank O'Bannon Grant

Type of award: Scholarship, renewable.
Intended use: For full-time undergraduate study at 2-year or 4-year institution. Designated institutions: Eligible Indiana schools.
Eligibility: Applicant must be U.S. citizen or permanent resident residing in Indiana.
Basis for selection: Applicant must demonstrate financial need.
Application requirements: FAFSA.
Additional information: Submitting FAFSA automatically fulfills application requirement. All eligible students offered an award. Amount of award varies. Visit Website for list of eligible schools.

Number of awards: 50,000
Number of applicants: 54,554
Application deadline: March 10
Notification begins: July 1
Total amount awarded: $196,838,902
Contact:
State Student Assistance Commission of Indiana
W462 Indiana Government Center
402 West Washington Street
Indianapolis, IN 46204
Phone: 317-232-2350
Web: www.in.gov/ssaci

Scholarships

471

Indiana Minority Teacher & Special Education Services Scholarship

Type of award: Scholarship, renewable.
Intended use: For full-time undergraduate or graduate study at accredited 4-year or graduate institution.
Eligibility: Applicant must be African American, Mexican American, Hispanic American or Puerto Rican. Applicant must be U.S. citizen or permanent resident residing in Indiana.
Basis for selection: Major/career interest in education; education, special; occupational therapy or physical therapy. Applicant must demonstrate high academic achievement.
Application requirements: Proof of eligibility. FAFSA.
Additional information: Minimum 2.0 GPA. Applicant must be black or Latino, unless applicant is entering field of special education, or occupational/physical therapy. All qualified applicants receive an award. Contact college financial aid office for more information.

Amount of award:	$1,000-$4,000
Number of awards:	267
Number of applicants:	267
Total amount awarded:	$448,616

Contact:
Phone: 317-232-2350
Fax: 317-232-3260
Web: www.in.gov/ssaci

Indiana National Guard Supplemental Grant

Type of award: Scholarship, renewable.
Intended use: For undergraduate study at 2-year or 4-year institution. Designated institutions: Indiana state-funded colleges and universities.
Eligibility: Applicant must be residing in Indiana. Applicant must be member of Indiana Air and Army National Guard. Applicant must be in active drilling status and be certified by Indiana National Guard (ING).
Application requirements: FAFSA.
Additional information: Room, board, and textbooks not covered. Contact unit commander with eligibility and certification questions.

Amount of award:	Full tuition
Number of applicants:	726
Application deadline:	March 10
Notification begins:	September 1
Total amount awarded:	$2,509,489

Contact:
State Student Assistance Commission of Indiana
W462 Indiana Government Center
402 West Washington St.
Indianapolis, IN 46204
Phone: 317-232-2350
Web: www.in.gov/ssaci

Indiana Nursing Scholarship

Type of award: Scholarship, renewable.
Intended use: For undergraduate study at accredited vocational, 2-year or 4-year institution. Designated institutions: Eligible Indiana schools.
Eligibility: Applicant must be U.S. citizen residing in Indiana.
Basis for selection: Major/career interest in nursing. Applicant must demonstrate financial need and high academic achievement.
Application requirements: Proof of eligibility. FAFSA.

Additional information: Minimum 2.0 GPA. Must be admitted to eligible Indiana school. Must commit to work two years as nurse in specific Indiana health care settings. All qualified applicants receive an award. Contact financial aid office of institution for application or e-mail State Student Assistance Commission of Indiana. Deadline varies by institution.

Amount of award:	$50-$5,000
Number of awards:	549
Number of applicants:	549
Total amount awarded:	$451,533

Contact:
Web: www.in.gov/ssaci

Indiana Robert C. Byrd Honors Scholarship

Type of award: Scholarship, renewable.
Intended use: For full-time undergraduate study at accredited 2-year or 4-year institution in United States.
Eligibility: Applicant must be high school senior. Applicant must be U.S. citizen residing in Indiana.
Basis for selection: Applicant must demonstrate high academic achievement.
Application requirements: Transcript, proof of eligibility.
Additional information: Minimum 1300 SAT, 29 ACT, or 65 GED. Minimum 3.0 GPA. Cannot be in debt to federal government or have been sentenced for drug offense. All qualified applicants receive an award. Award cannot exceed $6,000 over four years. Visit Website for application.

Amount of award:	$1,500
Number of awards:	492
Number of applicants:	492
Application deadline:	April 26
Notification begins:	June 1
Total amount awarded:	$731,813

Contact:
Contact high school guidance counselor for information.
Web: www.in.gov/ssaci

Indiana Twenty-First Century Scholars Program

Type of award: Scholarship.
Intended use: For full-time undergraduate study at accredited 2-year or 4-year institution. Designated institutions: Participating Indiana schools.
Eligibility: Applicant must be high school senior. Applicant must be U.S. citizen or permanent resident residing in Indiana.
Basis for selection: Applicant must demonstrate financial need.
Application requirements: FAFSA.
Additional information: Minimum 2.0 high school GPA. Must enroll in 6th, 7th, or 8th grade by taking pledge to remain drug, alcohol, and crime free. Must file affirmation that pledge was fulfilled in high school senior year. Full tuition waiver after other financial aid applied. Number and amount of awards varies. Visit Website for details.

Number of awards:	9,875
Number of applicants:	9,875
Application deadline:	March 10
Notification begins:	July 1
Total amount awarded:	$22,787,104

Contact:
State Student Assistance Commission of Indiana
150 West Market Street, Suite 500
Indianapolis, IN 46204
Phone: 317-233-2100
Fax: 317-232-3260

Stephen T. Marchello Scholarship Foundation

Legacy of Hope

Type of award: Scholarship.
Intended use: For undergraduate study at accredited vocational, 2-year or 4-year institution in United States.
Eligibility: Applicant must be high school senior. Applicant must be U.S. citizen , Montana or Colorado.
Application requirements: Interview, recommendations, essay, transcript, proof of eligibility. SAT/ACT scores (when available).
Additional information: Some awards renewable depending on fund availability; all others are one-time grants. Applicant must be survivor of childhood cancer. Visit Website for more information. Submit application online or send SASE to address below. Number and amount of awards vary.

Number of applicants:	25
Application deadline:	March 15
Total amount awarded:	$7,500

Contact:
Stephen T. Marchello Scholarship Foundation
1170 East Long Place
Centennial, CO 80122
Phone: 303-886-5018
Web: www.stmfoundation.org

Studio Art Centers International

Anna K. Meredith Fund Scholarship

Type of award: Scholarship.
Intended use: For undergraduate study in Florence, Italy. Designated institutions: Studio Art Centers International (SACI).
Basis for selection: Competition/talent/interest in study abroad. Major/career interest in arts, general or art/art history. Applicant must demonstrate financial need and high academic achievement.
Application requirements: Portfolio of 20 labeled slides of own work (CD format accepted) or at least two art history writing samples for non-studio study. SAR/FAFSA.
Additional information: Must demonstrate artistic talent. Must be accepted to study with Studio Art Centers International. Number of awards varies depending on budget.

Amount of award:	$500-$2,000
Application deadline:	March 15, October 1
Notification begins:	April 15, November 1

Contact:
Studio Art Centers International
50 Broad Street
Suite 1617
New York, NY 10004-2372
Phone: 212-248-7225 or 877-257-7225
Fax: 212-248-7222
Web: www.saci-florence.org

Clare Brett Smith Scholarship

Type of award: Scholarship.
Intended use: For undergraduate or graduate study in Florence, Italy. Designated institutions: Studio Art Centers International (SACI).
Basis for selection: Competition/talent/interest in study abroad. Major/career interest in arts, general. Applicant must demonstrate financial need.
Application requirements: Portfolio of 20 labeled slides of own work (CD format accepted). SAR/FAFSA.
Additional information: Must be accepted to study with Studio Art Centers International. Applicant must be studying photography. Number of awards varies depending on budget.

Amount of award:	$1,000
Application deadline:	March 15, October 1
Notification begins:	April 15, November 1

Contact:
Studio Art Centers International
50 Broad Street
Suite 1617
New York, NY 10004-2372
Phone: 212-248-7225 or 877-257-7225
Fax: 212-248-7222
Web: www.saci-florence.org

Elizabeth A. Sackler Museum Educational Trust

Type of award: Scholarship.
Intended use: For undergraduate study in Florence, Italy. Designated institutions: Studio Art Centers International (SACI).
Eligibility: Applicant must be female.
Basis for selection: Major/career interest in arts, general or art/art history. Applicant must demonstrate financial need and high academic achievement.
Application requirements: FAFSA/SAR, statement of intent, six passport-sized photos, one letter of recommendation, portfolio on CD or set of 20 labeled slides (name, medium, size, date) presented in slide portfolio sleeve.
Additional information: Must be accepted to study with Studio Art Centers International. Must attend SACI for one full academic year. Must exhibit exceptional artistic talent in painting, drawing, printmaking, sculpture, ceramics, photography, art history, or art conservation. Visit Website for application and more information.

Number of awards:	1
Application deadline:	March 15
Notification begins:	May 1
Total amount awarded:	$15,000

Contact:
Studio Art Centers International
50 Broad Street
Suite 1617
New York, NY 10004-2372
Phone: 212-248-7225 or 877-257-7225
Fax: 212-248-7222
Web: www.saci-florence.org/admissions/sackler.htm

International Incentive Awards

Type of award: Scholarship.
Intended use: For sophomore, junior or senior study in Florence, Italy. Designated institutions: Studio Art Centers International (SACI).
Basis for selection: Competition/talent/interest in study abroad. Major/career interest in arts, general or art/art history. Applicant must demonstrate financial need and high academic achievement.
Application requirements: Portfolio of 20 labeled slides of own work (CD format accepted). SAR/FAFSA.
Additional information: Must be accepted to study with Studio Art Centers International. Minimum 3.0 GPA. Special efforts made to encourage applications from minorities and underrepresented groups. Number of awards varies depending on budget.

Amount of award:	$1,500
Application deadline:	March 15, October 1
Notification begins:	April 15, November 1

Contact:
Studio Art Centers International
50 Broad Street
Suite 1617
New York, NY 10004-2372
Phone: 212-248-7225 or 877-257-7225
Fax: 212-248-7222
Web: www.saci-florence.org

Jules Maidoff Scholarship

Type of award: Scholarship.
Intended use: For undergraduate or graduate study in Florence, Italy. Designated institutions: Studio Art Centers International (SACI).
Basis for selection: Competition/talent/interest in study abroad. Major/career interest in arts, general or art/art history. Applicant must demonstrate financial need.
Application requirements: Portfolio. FAFSA/SAR.
Additional information: Must be accepted to study with Studio Art Centers International. Awarded to students exhibiting both exceptional artistic talent and financial need. Number of awards varies depending on budget.

Amount of award:	$2,500
Application deadline:	March 15, October 1
Notification begins:	April 15, November 1

Contact:
Studio Art Centers International
50 Broad Street
Suite 1617
New York, NY 10004-2372
Phone: 212-248-7225 or 877-257-7225
Fax: 212-248-7222
Web: www.saci-florence.org

Lele Cassin Scholarship

Type of award: Scholarship.

Intended use: For undergraduate or graduate study in Florence, Italy. Designated institutions: Studio Art Centers International (SACI).
Basis for selection: Competition/talent/interest in study abroad. Major/career interest in film/video. Applicant must demonstrate financial need.
Application requirements: Video (no longer than 15 minutes) of own work. SAR/FAFSA.
Additional information: Must be accepted to study with Studio Art Centers International. Number of awards offered varies yearly according to budget.

Amount of award:	$1,000
Application deadline:	March 15, October 1
Notification begins:	April 15, November 1

Contact:
Studio Art Centers International
50 Broad Street
Suite 1617
New York, NY 10004-2372
Phone: 212-248-7225 or 877-257-7225
Fax: 212-248-7222
Web: www.saci-florence.org

SACI Consortium Scholarship

Type of award: Scholarship.
Intended use: For undergraduate or graduate study in Florence, Italy. Designated institutions: Studio Art Centers International (SACI) consortium institutions.
Basis for selection: Competition/talent/interest in study abroad. Major/career interest in arts, general or art/art history. Applicant must demonstrate financial need.
Application requirements: Portfolio, nomination by SACI consortium school. FAFSA/SAR.
Additional information: Must be accepted to study with Studio Art Centers International. Each consortium school may submit one nominee. Award for one semester; one award available per semester. See Website for list of eligible institutions.

Amount of award:	Full tuition
Number of awards:	2
Application deadline:	March 15, October 1
Notification begins:	April 15, November 1

Contact:
Studio Art Centers International
50 Broad Street
Suite 1617
New York, NY 10004-2372
Phone: 212-248-7225 or 877-257-7225
Fax: 212-248-7222
Web: www.saci-florence.org

Scholarships for Children of SACI Alumni

Type of award: Scholarship.
Intended use: For undergraduate or graduate study at postsecondary institution in Florence, Italy. Designated institutions: Studio Art Centers International (SACI).
Basis for selection: Major/career interest in arts, general or art/art history. Applicant must demonstrate financial need and high academic achievement.
Application requirements: CD or set of 20 labeled slides in portfolio sleeve. Two art history writing samples, for students seeking scholarships in non-studio study. FAFSA/SAR. Statement indicating the name of parent who attended SACI and dates of attendance.

Additional information: Must be accepted to study with Studio Art Centers International and have a parent who attended SACI. Applicants for late spring or summer terms must submit materials by the admissions deadline of the term they wish to enroll. Number of awards varies depending on budget.

Amount of award:	$500-$2,500
Application deadline:	March 15, October 1
Notification begins:	April 15, November 1

Contact:
Studio Art Centers International
50 Broad Street
Suite 1617
New York, NY 10004-2372
Phone: 212-248-7225 or 877-257-7225
Fax: 212-248-7222
Web: www.saci-florence.com

Sunkist Growers

A.W. Bodine Sunkist Memorial Scholarship

Type of award: Scholarship, renewable.
Intended use: For full-time undergraduate study at accredited 2-year or 4-year institution.
Basis for selection: Applicant must demonstrate financial need, high academic achievement, depth of character, leadership, seriousness of purpose and service orientation.
Application requirements: Recommendations, essay, transcript, proof of eligibility. SAT or ACT scores, tax return (or parents' tax return for applicants younger than 21).
Additional information: Applicant or someone in immediate family must have derived majority of income from California- or Arizona-based agriculture. All majors eligible. Award renewable up to four years based on annual review. Must maintain 2.7 GPA and carry 12 credits per semester to qualify for renewal. Number of awards varies. Visit Website for application.

Amount of award:	$2,000
Number of applicants:	300
Application deadline:	April 30

Contact:
A.W. Bodine Sunkist Memorial Scholarship
Sunkist Growers
P.O. Box 7888
Van Nuys, CA 91409-7888
Phone: 818-986-4800
Web: www.sunkist.com/about/bodine_scholarship.aspx

Supreme Guardian Council, International Order of Job's Daughters

The Grotto Scholarships

Type of award: Scholarship.
Intended use: For full-time undergraduate study at 2-year or 4-year institution.
Eligibility: Applicant must be single, female, no older than 30.

Basis for selection: Major/career interest in dentistry. Applicant must demonstrate financial need, high academic achievement, depth of character, leadership and seriousness of purpose.
Application requirements: Recommendations, transcript, proof of eligibility. Personal letter.
Additional information: Applicant must be member of Job's Daughters. Job's Daughters activities, financial self-help, and achievements outside of Job's Daughters are also factors in awarding scholarships. Training in the handicapped field is preferred. Minimum 2.5 GPA. Visit Website for more information.

Amount of award:	$1,500
Application deadline:	April 30

Contact:
International Order of Job's Daughters
Phone: 402-592-7987
Fax: 402-592-2177
Web: www.iojd.org

Supreme Guardian Council, International Order of Job's Daughters Scholarship

Type of award: Scholarship.
Intended use: For full-time undergraduate study at vocational, 2-year or 4-year institution.
Eligibility: Applicant must be single, female, no older than 30.
Basis for selection: Applicant must demonstrate financial need, high academic achievement, depth of character, leadership, seriousness of purpose and service orientation.
Application requirements: Recommendations, transcript, proof of eligibility. Personal letter.
Additional information: Applicant must be member of Job's Daughters. Job's Daughters activities, applicant's financial self-help, and achievements outside of Job's Daughters are also factors in awarding scholarships. Number of awards varies. Visit Website for more information.

Amount of award:	$750
Number of applicants:	100
Application deadline:	April 30

Contact:
Supreme Guardian Council
Phone: 402-592-7987
Fax: 402-592-2177
Web: www.iojd.org

Susie Holmes Memorial Scholarship

Type of award: Scholarship.
Intended use: For full-time undergraduate study at vocational, 2-year or 4-year institution.
Eligibility: Applicant must be single, female, no older than 30.
Basis for selection: Applicant must demonstrate financial need, depth of character and seriousness of purpose.
Application requirements: Recommendations, transcript, proof of eligibility. Personal letter.
Additional information: Applicant must be member of Job's Daughters. Must be high school graduate with 2.5 GPA; show dedicated, continuous, joyful service to Job's Daughters; and regularly attend Grand and/or Supreme Session and participate in competitions. Job's Daughter's activities, applicant's financial self-help, and achievements outside of Job's Daughters are also factors in awarding scholarships. Visit Website for more details.

Amount of award:	$1,000
Application deadline:	April 30

Contact:
Supreme Guardian Council, International Order of Job's
Daughters
Phone: 402-592-7987
Fax: 402-592-2177
Web: www.iojd.org

Swiss Benevolent Society of New York

Sonia Streuli Maguire Outstanding Scholastic Achievement Award

Type of award: Scholarship.
Intended use: For full-time senior, post-bachelor's certificate, master's, doctoral or first professional study at accredited 4-year or graduate institution in United States.
Eligibility: Applicant must be Swiss. Applicant must be permanent resident residing in New York, Connecticut, Delaware, New Jersey or Pennsylvania.
Basis for selection: Applicant must demonstrate high academic achievement.
Application requirements: Recommendations, transcript, proof of eligibility. SAT/GRE results.
Additional information: Applicant or parent must be Swiss national. Must have minimum 3.8 GPA. Visit Website for application.

Amount of award:	$2,500-$5,000
Number of awards:	2
Application deadline:	March 31
Notification begins:	June 1
Total amount awarded:	$5,000

Contact:
Swiss Benevolent Society Scholarship Committee
500 Fifth Avenue
Room 1800
New York, NY 10110
Phone: 212-246-0655
Fax: 212-246-1366
Web: www.sbsny.org/sbs_scholarships.html

Swiss Benevolent Society Medicus Student Exchange

Type of award: Scholarship.
Intended use: For full-time junior, senior, post-bachelor's certificate, master's, doctoral or first professional study in universities and polytechnic institutes in Switzerland.
Eligibility: Applicant must be Swiss. Applicant must be U.S. citizen or permanent resident.
Basis for selection: Competition/talent/interest in study abroad. Applicant must demonstrate financial need and high academic achievement.
Application requirements: Recommendations, transcript, proof of eligibility. SAT or GRE scores. Letter of acceptance from Swiss institution. Statement of funding. Proof of fluency in language of instruction.
Additional information: Provides partial financial support for U.S. students accepted to Swiss post-secondary institutions. Applicant or parent must be Swiss national. Visit Website for application.

Application deadline:	March 31
Notification begins:	June 1

Contact:
Swiss Benevolent Society Scholarship Committee
500 Fifth Avenue
Room 1800
New York, NY 10110
Phone: 212-246-0655
Fax: 212-246-1366
Web: www.sbsny.org/sbs_scholarships.html

Swiss Benevolent Society Pellegrini Scholarship

Type of award: Scholarship, renewable.
Intended use: For undergraduate, graduate or non-degree study at accredited postsecondary institution in United States.
Eligibility: Applicant must be Swiss. Applicant must be permanent resident residing in New York, Connecticut, Delaware, New Jersey or Pennsylvania.
Basis for selection: Applicant must demonstrate financial need and high academic achievement.
Application requirements: Recommendations, transcript, proof of eligibility. SAT or GRE scores. Proof of Swiss parentage and tax return. Copy of bursar's bill. Incoming freshmen should provide figures of anticipated cost.
Additional information: Applicant or parent must be Swiss national. Minimum 3.0 GPA. Visit Website for application.

Amount of award:	$500-$4,000
Number of awards:	55
Number of applicants:	61
Application deadline:	March 31
Notification begins:	June 1
Total amount awarded:	$95,550

Contact:
Swiss Benevolent Society Scholarship Committee
500 Fifth Avenue
Room 1800
New York, NY 10110
Phone: 212-246-0655
Fax: 212-246-1366
Web: www.sbsny.org/sbs_scholarships.html

TAG Education Collaborative

Web Challenge Contest

Type of award: Scholarship.
Intended use: For full-time undergraduate study.
Eligibility: Applicant must be enrolled in high school. Applicant must be U.S. citizen or permanent resident residing in Georgia.
Basis for selection: Competition/talent/interest in web-site design, based on use of technology to create a theme-based project. Major/career interest in computer/information sciences or computer graphics. Applicant must demonstrate seriousness of purpose.
Application requirements: Proof of eligibility.
Additional information: Applicants work in teams of up to four members to create projects using free and/or open source technologies. Team must be sponsored by faculty adviser. Total amount awarded varies. Visit Website for registration information, deadline, and contest information and theme.

Number of awards: 25
Number of applicants: 100
Total amount awarded: $21,100
Contact:
TAG Education Collaborative
75 Fifth Street, NW
Suite 625
Atlanta, GA 30308
Phone: 404-920-2038
Web: www.tagforstem.org

Taglit-Birthright Israel

Taglit-Birthright Israel Gift

Type of award: Scholarship.
Intended use: For undergraduate or graduate study at postsecondary institution.
Eligibility: Applicant must be at least 18, no older than 26. Applicant must be Jewish.
Application requirements: Proof of eligibility. Passport.
Additional information: Applicant must be out of high school. All eligible applicants receive free trip to Israel under the auspices of Aish HaTorah, Hillel, and other organizations. Round-trip airfare and ten days of program activity (including hotel, transportation, and most meals) are funded. Must not have visited Israel previously on an educational peer-group trip or study program. Must not have lived in Israel past age 12. Visit Website or contact sponsor for current offerings.
Number of awards: 20,000
Contact:
Phone: 888-99-ISRAEL
Web: www.birthrightisrael.com

Tennessee Student Assistance Corporation

Dual Enrollment Grant

Type of award: Scholarship, renewable.
Intended use: For undergraduate study at postsecondary institution.
Eligibility: Applicant must be high school junior or senior. Applicant must be residing in Tennessee.
Additional information: Student must meet dual enrollment requirements for high school and postsecondary institution. Must be a Tennessee resident for at least one year prior to enrollment. Visit Website for designated institutions. Application deadline is 9/15 for fall; 2/1 for spring; 5/1 for summer.
Amount of award: $600
Number of awards: 13,384
Number of applicants: 10,931
Application deadline: September 15, February 1
Total amount awarded: $5,776,905

Contact:
Tennessee Student Assistance Corporation
Parkway Towers, Suite 1510
404 James Robertson Parkway
Nashville, TN 37243-0820
Phone: 800-342-1663
Fax: 615-741-6101
Web: www.tn.gov/collegepays

Helping Heroes Grant

Type of award: Scholarship, renewable.
Intended use: For undergraduate study at 2-year or 4-year institution.
Eligibility: Applicant must be residing in Tennessee. Applicant must be veteran who served in the Army, Air Force, Marines, Navy or Reserves/National Guard. Must be a veteran who was honorably discharged and was awarded the Iraq Campaign Medal, Afghanistan Campaign Medal, or Global War on Terrorism Expeditionary Medal.
Additional information: Award amount is up to $2,000. Fall application deadline is 9/1; spring deadline is 2/1; summer deadline is 5/1. Scholarships are given on a first-come, first-served basis, with up to $750,000 awarded per academic year.
Amount of award: $2,000
Number of awards: 259
Application deadline: September 1, February 1
Total amount awarded: $365,614

Contact:
Tennessee Student Assistance Corporation
Parkway Towers, Suite 1510
404 James Robertson Parkway
Nashville, TN 37243-0820
Phone: 800-342-1633
Fax: 615-741-6101
Web: www.tn.gov/collegepays

Hope Foster Child Tuition Grant

Type of award: Scholarship, renewable.
Intended use: For undergraduate study at 2-year or 4-year institution.
Eligibility: Applicant must be residing in Tennessee.
Application requirements: Proof of eligibility.
Additional information: Must meet the academic requirements for the HOPE Scholarship or HOPE Access Grant. Must have been in custody of Tennessee Department of Children's Services for at least one year after age 14.
Amount of award: Full tuition
Number of awards: 24
Application deadline: September 1
Notification begins: January 1
Total amount awarded: $83,058

Contact:
Tennessee Student Assistance Corporation
Parkway Towers, Suite 1510
404 James Robertson Parkway
Nashville, TN 37243-0820
Phone: 800-342-1663
Fax: 615-741-6101
Web: www.tn.gov/collegepays

HOPE-Aspire Award

Type of award: Scholarship.
Intended use: For freshman or sophomore study at postsecondary institution. Designated institutions: Eligible Tennessee institutions.

Eligibility: Applicant must be residing in Tennessee.
Basis for selection: Applicant must demonstrate financial need.
Application requirements: FAFSA.
Additional information: Applicant must be eligible for HOPE. Entering freshman must have a minimum 21 ACT or 980 SAT or 3.0 GPA. Parent's or student's income must be $36,000 or less. Applicant must be a Tennessee resident for one year prior to enrollment.

Amount of award:	$1,500
Number of awards:	14,450
Application deadline:	September 1
Notification begins:	January 1
Total amount awarded:	$67,801,866

Contact:
Tennessee Student Assistance Corporation
Parkway Towers, Suite 1510
404 James Robertson Parkway
Nashville, TN 37243-0820
Phone: 800-342-1663
Fax: 615-741-6101
Web: www.tn.gov/collegepays

Hope-General Assembly Merit Scholarship

Type of award: Scholarship, renewable.
Intended use: For undergraduate study at postsecondary institution. Designated institutions: Eligible Tennessee institutions.
Eligibility: Applicant must be residing in Tennessee.
Basis for selection: Applicant must demonstrate high academic achievement.
Application requirements: FAFSA.
Additional information: Supplement to HOPE Scholarship. Entering freshman must have minimum 3.75 weighted GPA and 29 ACT or 1280 SAT. Applicant must be a resident of Tennessee for one year prior to enrollment.

Amount of award:	$1,000
Number of awards:	5,232
Application deadline:	September 1
Notification begins:	January 1
Total amount awarded:	$25,377,778

Contact:
Tennessee Student Assistance Corporation
Parkway Towers, Suite 1510
404 James Robertson Parkway
Nashville, TN 37243-0820
Phone: 800-342-1663
Fax: 614-741-6101
Web: www.tn.gov/collegepays

Tennessee Dependent Children Scholarship Program

Type of award: Scholarship, renewable.
Intended use: For full-time undergraduate study at accredited postsecondary institution.
Eligibility: Applicant must be U.S. citizen residing in Tennessee. Applicant's parent must have been killed or disabled in work-related accident as firefighter or police officer.
Basis for selection: Applicant must demonstrate financial need.
Application requirements: Proof of eligibility. FAFSA.
Additional information: Applicant must be enrolled in a degree-granting program. Applicant's parent may also be

emergency medical technician killed or disabled in work-related accident. Award based on student's financial aid package.

Amount of award:	Full tuition
Number of awards:	32
Number of applicants:	85
Application deadline:	July 15
Total amount awarded:	$183,223

Contact:
Tennessee Student Assistance Corporation
Parkway Towers, Suite 1510
404 James Robertson Parkway
Nashville, TN 37243-0820
Phone: 800-342-1663
Fax: 615-741-6101
Web: www.tn.gov/collegepays

Tennessee HOPE Access Grant

Type of award: Scholarship.
Intended use: For freshman study at 2-year or 4-year institution. Designated institutions: Eligible Tennessee institutions.
Eligibility: Applicant must be residing in Tennessee.
Basis for selection: Applicant must demonstrate financial need.
Application requirements: FAFSA.
Additional information: Award amount is $2,750 for four-year institutions or $1,750 for two-year institutions. Minimum 2.75 GPA. Minimum 18 ACT, 860 SAT. Parents' or independent student and spouse's adjusted gross income must be $36,000 or less on IRS tax form. Applicant must be a Tennessee resident for one year prior to enrollment.

Amount of award:	$1,750-$2,750
Number of awards:	411
Application deadline:	September 1
Notification begins:	January 1
Total amount awarded:	$877,014

Contact:
Tennessee Student Assistance Corporation
Parkway Towers, Suite 1510
404 James Robertson Parkway
Nashville, TN 37243-0820
Phone: 800-342-1663
Fax: 615-741-6101
Web: www.tn.gov/collegepays

Tennessee HOPE Scholarship

Type of award: Scholarship.
Intended use: For undergraduate study at postsecondary institution. Designated institutions: Eligible Tennessee institutions.
Eligibility: Applicant must be residing in Tennessee.
Application requirements: FAFSA.
Additional information: Applicant must be a Tennessee resident for one year prior to enrollment. Award amount is $4,000 for four-year institutions, $2,000 for two-year institutions. Minimum 3.0 GPA or 21 ACT/980 SAT.

Amount of award:	$2,000-$4,000
Number of awards:	41,516
Application deadline:	September 1
Notification begins:	January 1
Total amount awarded:	$142,721,455

Contact:
Tennessee Student Assistance Corporation
Parkway Towers, Suite 1510
404 James Robertson Parkway
Nashville, TN 37243-0820
Phone: 800-342-1663
Fax: 615-741-6101
Web: www.tn.gov/collegepays

Tennessee Ned McWherter Scholars Program

Type of award: Scholarship, renewable.
Intended use: For full-time freshman study at accredited 2-year or 4-year institution.
Eligibility: Applicant must be high school senior. Applicant must be U.S. citizen residing in Tennessee.
Basis for selection: Applicant must demonstrate high academic achievement and leadership.
Application requirements: Transcript, proof of eligibility. List of leadership activities.
Additional information: Applicant must score at 95th percentile on ACT/SAT. Minimum 3.5 cumulative GPA. Difficulty of high school courses considered.

Amount of award:	$6,000
Number of awards:	177
Number of applicants:	1,299
Application deadline:	February 15
Total amount awarded:	$514,500

Contact:
Tennessee Student Assistance Corporation
Parkway Towers, Suite 1510
404 James Robertson Parkway
Nashville, TN 37243-0820
Phone: 800-342-1663
Fax: 615-741-6101
Web: www.tn.gov/collegepays

Tennessee Robert C. Byrd Honors Scholarship Program

Type of award: Scholarship, renewable.
Intended use: For full-time freshman study at accredited vocational, 2-year or 4-year institution in United States.
Eligibility: Applicant must be high school senior. Applicant must be U.S. citizen or permanent resident residing in Tennessee.
Basis for selection: Applicant must demonstrate high academic achievement.
Application requirements: Transcript, proof of eligibility.
Additional information: Minimum 3.5 GPA. May also qualify with 3.0 GPA and 24 ACT or 1090 SAT. At least 570 GED also accepted.

Amount of award:	$1,500
Number of awards:	532
Number of applicants:	5,218
Application deadline:	March 1
Total amount awarded:	$762,625

Contact:
Tennessee Student Assistance Corporation
Parkway Towers, Suite 1510
404 James Robertson Parkway
Nashville, TN 37243-0820
Phone: 800-342-1663
Fax: 615-741-6101
Web: www.tn.gov/collegepays

Tennessee Student Assistance Award Program

Type of award: Scholarship, renewable.
Intended use: For undergraduate study at postsecondary institution.
Eligibility: Applicant must be U.S. citizen residing in Tennessee.
Basis for selection: Applicant must demonstrate financial need.
Application requirements: FAFSA.
Additional information: Applicant's expected family contribution must be $2,100 or less. Award is up to $4,000 for private institutions; up to $2,000 for public, based on funding.

Number of awards:	26,851
Number of applicants:	351,711
Application deadline:	February 15
Total amount awarded:	$55,635,206

Contact:
Tennessee Student Assistance Corporation
Parkway Towers, Suite 1510
404 James Robertson Parkway
Nashville, TN 37243-0820
Phone: 800-342-1663
Fax: 615-741-6101
Web: www.tn.gov/collegepays

Wilder-Naifeh Technical Skills Grant

Type of award: Scholarship.
Intended use: For freshman or sophomore study at vocational institution. Designated institutions: Tennessee Technology Centers.
Eligibility: Applicant must be residing in Tennessee.
Application requirements: FAFSA.
Additional information: Applicant must be Tennessee resident for one year prior to enrollment. Application deadline varies. See Website for details.

Amount of award:	$2,000
Number of awards:	11,604
Number of applicants:	10,429
Notification begins:	January 1
Total amount awarded:	$13,314,583

Contact:
Tennessee Student Assistance Corporation
Parkway Towers, Suite 1510
404 James Robertson Parkway
Nashville, TN 37243-0820
Phone: 800-342-1663
Fax: 615-741-6101
Web: www.tn.gov/collegepays

Texas 4-H Club

Texas 4-H Opportunity Scholarships

Type of award: Scholarship, renewable.
Intended use: For undergraduate study at accredited 4-year institution in United States. Designated institutions: Colleges and universities in Texas.
Eligibility: Applicant must be high school senior. Applicant must be U.S. citizen residing in Texas.

Basis for selection: Applicant must demonstrate financial need and high academic achievement.

Application requirements: Recommendations, essay, transcript. SAT/ACT scores.

Additional information: Must be current Texas 4-H member in good standing. Must graduate from Texas public high school in top fourth of class. Must have minimum 1350 SAT or 19 ACT score. Cannot have applied for scholarship though FFA or FCCLA.

Amount of award:	$500-$16,000
Number of awards:	245
Number of applicants:	350
Application deadline:	January 1
Notification begins:	June 1

Contact:
Texas 4-H Club
P.O. Box 11020
College Station, TX 77840
Phone: 979-845-1212
Fax: 979-845-6495
Web: texas4-h.tamu.edu

Texas Association, Family Career and Community Leaders of America

Blue Bell Scholarship

Type of award: Scholarship.

Intended use: For full-time undergraduate study at accredited postsecondary institution in United States. Designated institutions: Colleges and universities in Texas.

Eligibility: Applicant must be high school senior. Applicant must be U.S. citizen residing in Texas.

Basis for selection: Applicant must demonstrate financial need, high academic achievement, depth of character and leadership.

Application requirements: Recommendations, essay, transcript. SAT/ACT scores.

Additional information: Must be active member of Family Career and Community Leaders of America in good standing. Must have passed TAKS Mastery/Exit Level exam and be in top fourth of graduating class.

Amount of award:	$1,000
Number of awards:	5
Application deadline:	March 1
Total amount awarded:	$5,000

Contact:
Texas Association, Family Career and Community Leaders of America
6513 Circle S Road
TX 78745
Phone: 512-306-0099
Fax: 512-442-7100
Web: www.texasfccla.org

C. J. Davidson Scholarship

Type of award: Scholarship, renewable.

Intended use: For undergraduate study at accredited postsecondary institution in United States. Designated institutions: Texas colleges with family and consumer sciences departments.

Eligibility: Applicant must be high school senior. Applicant must be U.S. citizen residing in Texas.

Basis for selection: Major/career interest in education. Applicant must demonstrate financial need and high academic achievement.

Application requirements: Recommendations, essay, transcript. SAT/ACT scores.

Additional information: Must graduate from a Texas high school with 85 average. Must be active member of Family Career and Community Leaders of America for at least one year. Must major in and receive a teaching certificate for family/consumer sciences.

Amount of award:	$4,000
Number of awards:	10
Application deadline:	March 1

Contact:
Texas Association, Family Career and Community Leaders of America
6513 Circle S Road
Austin, TX 78745
Phone: 512-306-0099
Fax: 512-442-7100
Web: www.texasfccla.org

Houston Livestock Show and Rodeo Scholarships

Type of award: Scholarship, renewable.

Intended use: For full-time undergraduate study at accredited 4-year institution in United States. Designated institutions: Colleges and universities in Texas.

Eligibility: Applicant must be high school senior. Applicant must be U.S. citizen residing in Texas.

Basis for selection: Applicant must demonstrate financial need, high academic achievement, depth of character and leadership.

Application requirements: Recommendations, essay, transcript. SAT/ACT scores.

Additional information: Must be current member of Family Career and Community Leaders of America in good standing. Must graduate from Texas public high school in top fourth of class and have minimum 1350 SAT or 19 ACT score. Cannot have applied for scholarship through Texas 4-H or FFA.

Amount of award:	$3,750
Number of awards:	10
Number of applicants:	77
Application deadline:	March 1

Contact:
Texas Association, Family Career and Community Leaders of America
6513 Circle S Road
Austin, TX 78745
Phone: 512-306-0099
Fax: 512-442-7100
Web: www.texasfccla.org

Texas Farm Bureau Scholarship

Type of award: Scholarship.

Intended use: For full-time undergraduate study at accredited postsecondary institution in United States. Designated institutions: Texas colleges and universities with family and consumer sciences departments.

Eligibility: Applicant must be high school senior. Applicant must be U.S. citizen residing in Texas.

Basis for selection: Applicant must demonstrate financial need, high academic achievement, depth of character and leadership.
Application requirements: Recommendations, essay, transcript. SAT/ACT scores, two copies of autobiography.
Additional information: Must be active Family Career and Community Leaders of America member in good standing for at least one year. Must be FFCLA regional or state officer. Must be a graduate of Texas high school with minimum 85 average. Must major in family/consumer sciences.

Amount of award:	$1,000
Number of awards:	1
Application deadline:	March 1
Total amount awarded:	$1,000

Contact:
Texas Association, Family Career and Community Leaders of America
6513 Circle S Road
Austin, TX 78745
Phone: 512-306-0099
Fax: 512-442-7100
Web: www.texasfccla.org

Texas Future Farmers of America

FFA Scholarships

Type of award: Scholarship, renewable.
Intended use: For undergraduate study at accredited 4-year institution in United States. Designated institutions: Colleges and universities in Texas.
Eligibility: Applicant must be high school senior. Applicant must be U.S. citizen residing in Texas.
Basis for selection: Applicant must demonstrate financial need and high academic achievement.
Application requirements: Interview, recommendations, essay, transcript. SAT/ACT scores.
Additional information: Must be current member of Texas FFA in good standing. Must have graduated from Texas public high school in top half of class. Must have minimum 1350 SAT or 19 ACT score. Cannot have applied for scholarship through Texas 4-H or FCCLA. Preliminary deadlines vary based on area; visit Website for more information.

Amount of award:	$2,000-$15,000
Number of awards:	170

Contact:
Texas Future Farmers of America
614 East 12th Street
Austin, TX 78701
Phone: 512-480-8045
Fax: 512-476-2894
Web: www.texasffa.org

Texas Higher Coordinating Board

Engineering Scholarship Program

Type of award: Scholarship, renewable.

Intended use: For sophomore study at 4-year institution in United States. Designated institutions: Texas public or private universities.
Eligibility: Applicant must be residing in Texas.
Basis for selection: Major/career interest in engineering.
Additional information: Minimum 3.5 high school GPA in mathematics and science. Must have graduated in top 20 percent of graduating high school class. Minimum 3.0 college GPA. Exemptions apply for those enrolled in Selective Service. Depending on funding, recipients may receive up to $5,000 per year.
Contact:
Contact engineering department in which student is enrolled.
Phone: 800-242-3062
Web: www.collegeforalltexans.com

Texas Higher Education Coordinating Board

Concurrent Enrollment Waiver (Enrollment in Two Texas Community Colleges)

Type of award: Scholarship.
Intended use: For undergraduate study at 2-year or 4-year institution in United States. Designated institutions: Texas public colleges or universities.
Eligibility: Applicant must be residing in Texas.
Application requirements: Proof of eligibility. Proof of concurrent enrollment.
Additional information: Waiver provides a break in tuition charges to students enrolled at two public Texas community colleges at the same time. Award is reduced tuition at second institution of enrollment (student pays minimum tuition rate at second institution). No funds may be used to pay tuition for continuing education classes for which the college receives no state tax support.
Contact:
Contact registrar at second college in which you are enrolled.
Phone: 800-242-3062
Web: www.collegeforalltexans.com

Educational Aide Exemption

Type of award: Scholarship.
Intended use: For undergraduate or graduate study at postsecondary institution in United States. Designated institutions: Texas public colleges and universities.
Eligibility: Applicant must be U.S. citizen or permanent resident residing in Texas.
Basis for selection: Major/career interest in education; education, early childhood; education, special or education, teacher. Applicant must demonstrate financial need.
Application requirements: Proof of certification by Texas Board of Teacher Certification as a Certified Aide. FAFSA.
Additional information: Assists educational aides by exempting them from payment of tuition and fees (other than lab or class fees). Applicant must have applied for financial aid through college of attendance, including filing FAFSA or qualifying based on income. Applicant must have worked as educational aide (includes library, computer lab, and P.E. aides) for at least one out of last five years or as substitute teacher for 180 days of the past five school years. Applicant must also be

working in some capacity in Texas public school during semester for which exemption is applied and must be enrolled in classes toward teacher certification. Must maintain good academic standing. The timelines for applying are: fall, June 1 through February 1; spring, November 1 through July 1. Visit Website or call for application.

Amount of award:	Full tuition
Number of awards:	4,000
Application deadline:	February 1, July 1

Contact:
Texas Higher Education Coordinating Board
Student Services Division
P.O. Box 12788
Austin, TX 78711-2788
Phone: 800-242-3062 ext. 6387 or 512-427-6387
Fax: 512-427-6420
Web: www.collegeforalltexans.com

Exemption for Peace Officers Disabled in the Line of Duty

Type of award: Scholarship.
Intended use: For undergraduate study at postsecondary institution in United States. Designated institutions: Texas public colleges and universities.
Eligibility: Applicant must be residing in Texas.
Application requirements: Proof of eligibility. Satisfactory evidence of status as a disabled peace officer as required by institution.
Additional information: Award for persons injured in the line of duty while serving as peace officers in Texas. Must enroll in classes for which college receives tax support. Maximum award is exemption from payment of tuition and fees for not more than 12 semesters or sessions. Contact college for additional information.

Amount of award:	Full tuition

Contact:
Texas Higher Education Coordinating Board
Student Services Division
P.O. Box 12788
Austin, TX 78711-2788
Phone: 800-242-3062
Fax: 512-427-6420
Web: www.collegeforalltexans.com

Exemption for the Surviving Spouse and Dependent Children of Certain Deceased Public Servants (Employees)

Type of award: Scholarship.
Intended use: For full-time undergraduate study at postsecondary institution in United States. Designated institutions: Texas public colleges and universities.
Eligibility: Applicant must be residing in Texas.
Application requirements: Proof of eligibility.
Additional information: Exemption for surviving spouse and/or dependent children of certain public employees (defined by Texas Government Code 615.003) killed in the line of duty. Public employee must have died on or after September 1, 2000. Program covers cost of tuition and fees, textbooks, and possibly room and board. Visit Website for link to list of eligible public servants. Contact registrar's office at college/university for information on claiming this exemption.

Amount of award:	Full tuition

Contact:
Texas Higher Education Coordinating Board
Student Services Division
P.O. Box 12788
Austin, TX 78711-2788
Phone: 800-242-3062
Fax: 512-427-6420
Web: www.collegeforalltexans.com

Reduction in Tuition Charges for Students Taking 15 or More Semester Credit Hours Per Term

Type of award: Scholarship.
Intended use: For full-time undergraduate study at postsecondary institution. Designated institutions: Texas public colleges and universities.
Eligibility: Applicant must be residing in Texas.
Application requirements: Proof of eligibility.
Additional information: Applicant must be enrolled in at least 15 credit hours at institution during semester/term for which reduction is offered. Must be making satisfactory progress toward completion of a degree program. Contact registrar's office at college/university to inquire whether they offer reduction.

Contact:
Texas Higher Education Coordinating Board
Student Services Division
P.O. Box 12788
Austin, TX 78711-2788
Phone: 800-242-3062
Fax: 512-427-6420
Web: www.collegeforalltexans.com

Robert C. Byrd Honors Scholarship

Type of award: Scholarship, renewable.
Intended use: For undergraduate study at vocational, 2-year or 4-year institution.
Eligibility: Applicant must be high school senior. Applicant must be U.S. citizen or permanent resident residing in Texas.
Basis for selection: Applicant must demonstrate high academic achievement.
Application requirements: Transcript, nomination by high school guidance counselor or GED-center director.
Additional information: Those completing GED eligible to receive initial award only. Must be in top ten percent of class. Students attending a U.S. Military Academy not eligible. Visit Website for deadline.

Amount of award:	$1,500
Number of awards:	3,839

Contact:
High school guidance office or GED center director.
Phone: 800-242-3062 or 512-427-6340
Fax: 512-427-6420
Web: www.collegeforalltexans.com

Senior Citizen, 65 or Older, Free Tuition for Up to 6 Credit Hours

Type of award: Scholarship.
Intended use: For half-time undergraduate or graduate study at 2-year or 4-year institution in United States. Designated institutions: Participating Texas public colleges and universities.
Eligibility: Applicant must be at least 65, returning adult student.
Application requirements: Proof of eligibility.

Additional information: Program allows senior citizens to take up to 6 credit hours per semester, tuition-free. Texas institutions not required to offer program; applicants should check with registrar. Classes must not already be filled with students paying at full price and must use tax support for some of their cost. Contact college for additional information.

Contact:
Texas Higher Education Coordinating Board
Student Services Division
P.O. Box 12788
Austin, TX 78711-2788
Phone: 800-242-3062
Fax: 512-427-6420
Web: www.collegeforalltexans.com

TANF (Temporary Assistance to Needy Families) Exemption

Type of award: Scholarship.
Intended use: For undergraduate certificate or freshman study at accredited 2-year or 4-year institution in United States. Designated institutions: Texas public colleges and universities.
Eligibility: Applicant must be no older than 22. Applicant must be U.S. citizen or permanent resident residing in Texas.
Application requirements: Proof of eligibility. Proof that a parent received TANF (Temporary Assistance to Needy Families) for at least six months of student's senior year of high school.
Additional information: Award includes tuition and fees for student's first academic year. Must enroll within two years of graduation from Texas public high school. Must enroll in classes for which college receives state tax support. Contact financial aid office at college or university for more information.
   Amount of award: Full tuition
Contact:
Phone: 800-242-3062
Fax: 512-427-6420
Web: www.collegeforalltexans.com

Texas Early High School Graduation Scholarship

Type of award: Scholarship, renewable.
Intended use: For undergraduate study at accredited postsecondary institution in United States.
Eligibility: Applicant must be U.S. citizen or permanent resident residing in Texas.
Application requirements: Proof of eligibility.
Additional information: Applicant must have completed recommended high school curriculum at Texas public high school in less than 45 months. Must register for selective service unless exempt. If award is to be used at private institution, college must provide matching scholarship. Visit Website for application.
   Amount of award: $500-$3,000
Contact:
Phone: 800-242-3062
Fax: 512-427-6420
Web: www.collegeforalltexans.com

Texas Fifth-Year Accounting Student Scholarship Program

Type of award: Scholarship.

Intended use: For senior, post-bachelor's certificate or master's study at accredited postsecondary institution in United States. Designated institutions: Texas institutions.
Eligibility: Applicant must be residing in Texas.
Basis for selection: Major/career interest in accounting. Applicant must demonstrate financial need.
Application requirements: Proof of eligibility. Signed statement of intent to take CPA exam in Texas. FAFSA.
Additional information: Must be enrolled as fifth-year accounting student who has completed at least 120 credit hours, including 15 hours of accounting. Contact college financial aid office for application.
   Amount of award: $5,000
Contact:
Phone: 800-242-3062
Web: www.collegeforalltexans.com

Texas Foster Care Students Exemption

Type of award: Scholarship, renewable.
Intended use: For undergraduate or graduate study at accredited vocational, 2-year or 4-year institution in United States. Designated institutions: Texas public colleges and universities.
Eligibility: Applicant must be no older than 21. Applicant must be U.S. citizen or permanent resident residing in Texas.
Application requirements: Proof of eligibility from the Department of Family and Protective Services.
Additional information: Applicants must have been either in the care or conservatorship of Texas Department of Family and Protective Services on the day before their 18th birthday, the day of their graduation from high school, or the day of receipt of GED; or in the care or conservatorship of the TDFS on 14th birthday and then adopted. Must enroll in college before third anniversary of discharge from foster care. Program awards tuition and fees; once student determined eligible for the benefit, it continues indefinitely. Contact college's financial aid office for application.
   Amount of award: Full tuition
Contact:
Contact college/university financial aid office to apply.
Phone: 800-242-3062
Fax: 512-427-6420
Web: www.collegeforalltexans.com

Texas Good Neighbor Scholarship

Type of award: Scholarship.
Intended use: For undergraduate or graduate study at accredited 2-year, 4-year or graduate institution in United States. Designated institutions: Texas public colleges and universities.
Eligibility: Applicant must be native-born citizen of any Western Hemisphere country other than Cuba. Applicant must be residing in Texas.
Application requirements: Proof of eligibility.
Additional information: Must plan to return to native country. Contact institution's financial aid office or the international student affairs office for application. Award covers one year of tuition.
   Amount of award: Full tuition
   Application deadline: March 15
Contact:
Phone: 800-242-3062
Fax: 512-427-6420
Web: www.collegeforalltexans.com

TEXAS Grant (Toward Excellence, Access, and Success)

Type of award: Scholarship, renewable.
Intended use: For undergraduate study at vocational, 2-year or 4-year institution. Designated institutions: Texas public colleges or universities.
Eligibility: Applicant must be U.S. citizen or permanent resident residing in Texas.
Basis for selection: Applicant must demonstrate financial need and high academic achievement.
Application requirements: Selective Service registration or exemption from requirement. FAFSA.
Additional information: Applicant must have completed Recommended High School Program or Distinguished Achievement Program, enroll in college at least 3/4-time (unless granted hardship waiver) within 16 months of high school graduation, and must receive first award prior to completing 30 hours on campus. Also eligible are students with associate degrees from public technical or community colleges in Texas, who enroll in public Texas universities within 12 months of receiving associate's. Expected Family Contribution (EFC) to education must be less than $4,000. Minimum 2.5 GPA required to renew award. Applicant must not have been convicted of felony or crime involving controlled substance. Award not to exceed student's need or public institution tuition and fees. Contact financial aid office at specific college/university for application deadline and procedures.

Amount of award:	Full tuition

Contact:
Phone: 800-242-3062
Fax: 512-427-6420
Web: www.collegeforalltexans.com

Texas Hazlewood Act Tuition Exemption: Veterans

Type of award: Scholarship, renewable.
Intended use: For undergraduate or graduate study at accredited 2-year, 4-year or graduate institution. Designated institutions: Texas public colleges and universities.
Eligibility: Applicant must be U.S. citizen residing in Texas. Applicant must be veteran; or dependent of disabled veteran or deceased veteran. Must have served at least 181 days of active military duty, excluding basic training. Must have received honorable discharge or general discharge under honorable conditions. If dependent of disabled veteran, parent must be totally disabled for purposes of employability as result of service-related injury or illness.
Application requirements: Proof of eligibility.
Additional information: Must have tuition and fee charges that exceed all federal education benefits. Veteran must have been resident of Texas prior to enlistment. Award amount includes all dues, fees, and charges, excluding property deposit, student services, and lodging/board/clothing fees. Must be enrolled in courses receiving state tax support. Applicants should contact specific school's financial aid office for more information.

Amount of award:	Full tuition

Contact:
Phone: 800-242-3062
Fax: 512-427-6420
Web: www.collegeforalltexans.com

Texas Highest Ranking High School Graduate Tuition Exemption

Type of award: Scholarship.
Intended use: For freshman study at accredited postsecondary institution. Designated institutions: Texas public colleges and universities.
Eligibility: Applicant must be residing in Texas.
Basis for selection: Applicant must demonstrate high academic achievement.
Application requirements: Proof of eligibility. Valedictorian certificate issued by Texas Education Agency.
Additional information: Must be highest-ranking graduate of accredited public or private Texas high school. Award covers tuition during both semesters of first regular session immediately following the student's high school graduation; fees not included. Deadline varies.

Amount of award:	Full tuition
Number of awards:	1,000

Contact:
Contact college/university financial aid office to apply.
Phone: 800-242-3062 or 512-463-3070
Web: www.collegeforalltexans.com

Texas National Guard Tuition Assistance Program

Type of award: Scholarship.
Intended use: For undergraduate or graduate study at postsecondary institution in United States. Designated institutions: Texas institutions.
Eligibility: Applicant must be residing in Texas.
Application requirements: Proof of eligibility.
Additional information: Program provides tuition exemption to active, drilling members of Texas National Guard, Texas Air Guard, or State Guard. Must be registered for Selective Service or exempt from this requirement. Awards at public colleges/universities are for student's tuition charges up to 12 credit hours per semester. Awards for private, non-profit institutions are based on public university amount. For more information, visit Texas National Guard Website at www.agd.state.tx.us. Applicants may also contact the commander of their National Guard, Air Guard, or State Guard unit, or the education officer via information below.

Amount of award:	Full tuition

Contact:
State Adjutant General's Office
P.O. Box 5218/AGTX-PAE
Austin, TX 78763-5218
Phone: 512-782-5515
Web: www.collegeforalltexans.com

Texas Public Educational Grant

Type of award: Scholarship.
Intended use: For undergraduate or graduate study at accredited vocational, 2-year or 4-year institution. Designated institutions: Texas public colleges and universities.
Eligibility: Applicant must be residing in Texas.
Basis for selection: Applicant must demonstrate financial need.
Application requirements: FAFSA.
Additional information: Award amount varies; may not exceed student's financial need. Deadline varies. Applicant must register for Selective Service, unless exempt. Contact financial aid office at college/university for more information.

Contact:
Phone: 800-242-3062
Web: www.collegeforalltexans.com

Texas Scholarships for Nursing Students

Type of award: Scholarship.
Intended use: For undergraduate or graduate study at accredited vocational, 2-year, 4-year or graduate institution. Designated institutions: Texas public colleges and universities.
Eligibility: Applicant must be U.S. citizen or permanent resident residing in Texas.
Basis for selection: Major/career interest in nursing or health-related professions. Applicant must demonstrate financial need and high academic achievement.
Application requirements: Proof of eligibility.
Additional information: A variety of scholarships for vocational or professional nursing students. Award amount varies; maximum is $2,500. Must register for the Selective Service (unless exempt). Contact institutional financial aid office to apply.
Amount of award: $2,500
Contact:
Phone: 800-242-3062
Fax: 512-427-6420
Web: www.collegeforalltexans.com

Texas Tuition Exemption for Blind or Deaf Students

Type of award: Scholarship, renewable.
Intended use: For undergraduate or graduate study at accredited 2-year or 4-year institution in United States. Designated institutions: Texas public colleges and universities.
Eligibility: Applicant must be visually impaired or hearing impaired. Applicant must be U.S. citizen or permanent resident residing in Texas.
Basis for selection: Applicant must demonstrate depth of character.
Application requirements: Recommendations, transcript, proof of eligibility. Certification of disability. FAFSA. Written statement indicating which certificate, degree program, or professional enhancement applicant intends to pursue.
Additional information: Must be certified by Texas Department of Assistive and Rehabilitative Services and have high school diploma or equivalent. Applicant must enroll in classes for which the college receives tax support. Award does not include fees or charges for lodging, board, or clothing. Application deadline varies. Contact financial aid office at college/university for more information.
Amount of award: Full tuition
Contact:
Phone: 800-242-3062
Fax: 512-427-6420
Web: www.collegeforalltexans.com

Tuition Equalization Grant (TEG)

Type of award: Scholarship.
Intended use: For full-time undergraduate or graduate study at accredited 2-year or 4-year institution in United States. Designated institutions: Private, non-profit Texas colleges and universities.
Eligibility: Applicant must be U.S. citizen or permanent resident residing in Texas.

Basis for selection: Applicant must demonstrate financial need.
Application requirements: Proof of eligibility. Selective Service registration or exemption from requirement. FAFSA.
Additional information: Non-resident National Merit Finalists also eligible. Not open to athletic scholarship recipients. Award cannot exceed difference between applicant's tuition at private institution and what applicant would pay at public institution. Award amount varies; maximum is $3,808, but students with exceptional need may receive up to $5,712. Applicants should contact the financial aid office at the Texas private college/university they plan to attend for more information.
Number of awards: 28,000
Contact:
Phone: 800-242-3062
Web: www.collegeforalltexans.com

Tuition Exemption for Children of Disabled or Deceased Firefighters, Peace Officers, Game Wardens, and Employees of Correctional Institutions

Type of award: Scholarship, renewable.
Intended use: For undergraduate or graduate study at 2-year or 4-year institution in United States. Designated institutions: Texas public colleges and universities.
Eligibility: Applicant must be no older than 21. Applicant must be residing in Texas. Applicant's parent must have been killed or disabled in work-related accident as firefighter, police officer or public safety officer.
Application requirements: Proof of eligibility.
Additional information: Applicant must be child of paid or volunteer firefighter; paid municipal, county or state peace officer; custodial employee of Department of Corrections; or game warden disabled or killed in Texas in the line of duty. Persons eligible to participate in a school district's special education program under section 29.003 at age 22 may also apply. Applicant must enroll in courses that use tax support to cover some of their cost. Applicant must obtain certification form from Texas Higher Education Coordinating Board, have parent's former employer complete it, and submit to Texas Higher Education Coordinating Board. The Board will notify applicant's institution of eligibility. Students may be exempted from tuition and fees for the first 120 semester credits or until age 26, whichever comes first.
Amount of award: Full tuition
Contact:
Texas Higher Education Coordinating Board
Student Services Division
P.O. Box 12788
Austin, TX 78711-2788
Phone: 800-242-3062
Web: www.collegeforalltexans.com

Tuition Exemption for Children of U.S. Military POW/MIAs from Texas

Type of award: Scholarship, renewable.
Intended use: For undergraduate study at accredited 2-year or 4-year institution. Designated institutions: Texas public colleges or universities.

Eligibility: Applicant must be no older than 25. Applicant must be U.S. citizen or permanent resident residing in Texas. Applicant must be dependent of POW/MIA.
Application requirements: Proof of eligibility. Documentation from Department of Defense that a parent, classified as Texas resident, is MIA or a POW. FAFSA.
Additional information: Applicants 22 to 25 years of age must receive most of their support from a parent. Applicant must enroll in courses that use tax support to cover some of their cost. Award does not include room, board, clothing, or property deposits. Applicants should contact the registrar at the college/university they plan to attend for more information.

> **Amount of award:**   Full tuition

Contact:
Phone: 800-242-3062
Web: www.collegeforalltexans.com

Tuition Rebate for Certain Undergraduates

Type of award: Scholarship.
Intended use: For full-time undergraduate study at postsecondary institution in United States. Designated institutions: Texas public colleges and universities.
Eligibility: Applicant must be residing in Texas.
Additional information: Program provides tuition rebates for students who efficiently acquire their bachelor's degrees. Students must graduate in a timely manner to receive rebate: within four years for four-year degree, five years for five-year degree. Student must have taken all coursework at Texas public institutions, and must have been entitled to pay in-state tuition at all times while pursuing degree. Student must complete bachelor's degree with no more than 3 hours in excess of degree plan, excluding up to 9 hours of credit by examination. Students must apply for tuition rebate prior to receiving bachelor's degree. Contact business office at college/university for more information.

> **Amount of award:** $1,000

Contact:
Texas Higher Education Coordinating Board
Student Services Division
P.O. Box 12788
Austin, TX 78711-2788
Phone: 800-242-3062
Fax: 512-427-6420
Web: www.collegeforalltexans.com

Third Marine Division Association

Memorial Scholarship Fund

Type of award: Scholarship, renewable.
Intended use: For undergraduate study at accredited 2-year or 4-year institution in United States or Canada.
Eligibility: Applicant must be U.S. citizen. Applicant must be dependent of active service person or deceased veteran who serves or served in the Marines or Navy during Vietnam. Must be dependent child of qualified member or deceased member (Marine or Navy Corpsman) of the Third Marine Division Association, or dependent child of any military personnel who served in any Third Marine Division (Reinf) unit and who died as result of combat actions while serving in Vietnam between March 8, 1965 and November 27, 1969, or in operations Desert Shield, Desert Storm, or any other qualified Persian Gulf operations after August 2, 1990. Dependent children of deceased Third Marine Division personnel who served in above operations whose post-service deaths have been certified by the Department of Veterans Affairs to have been the result of combat-related wounds or other disabilities incurred during the period of eligible combat service, and were not the result of any misconduct by the veteran, are also eligible.
Basis for selection: Applicant must demonstrate financial need.
Application requirements: Proof of eligibility. Financial aid form.
Additional information: Minimum 2.0 GPA. Number of awards varies. Eligible dependent children participating automatically receive renewal application forms.

> **Amount of award:** $500-$1,500
> **Number of applicants:**   12
> **Application deadline:**   April 15
> **Notification begins:**   June 15
> **Total amount awarded:** $11,500

Contact:
MGySgt James G. Kyser USMC (Ret)
Secretary, Memorial Scholarship Fund
15727 Vista Drive
Dumfries, VA 22025-1810
Web: www.caltrap.com

Thurgood Marshall College Fund

Thurgood Marshall Scholarship Award

Type of award: Scholarship, renewable.
Intended use: For full-time undergraduate or graduate study at 4-year or graduate institution in United States. Designated institutions: One of 47 designated historically black public universities.
Eligibility: Applicant must be U.S. citizen.
Basis for selection: Applicant must demonstrate financial need, high academic achievement and service orientation.
Application requirements: Recommendations, essay, transcript. Resume, headshot or personal photograph.
Additional information: Must have high school or current GPA of 3.0 or higher, and must maintain throughout duration of scholarship. Must have minimum 1650 SAT or 25 ACT score. Contact university's Thurgood Marshall College Fund campus coordinator directly for more information, or visit Website.

> **Amount of award:** $4,400
> **Number of awards:**   500
> **Number of applicants:**   500
> **Application deadline:**   July 15
> **Total amount awarded:** $2,000,000

Contact:
Thurgood Marshall College Fund
80 Maiden Lane
Suite 2204
New York, NY 10038
Phone: 212-573-8888
Web: www.thurgoodmarshallfund.org

Tourism Cares

A.J. Spielman Scholarship

Type of award: Scholarship, renewable.
Intended use: For undergraduate certificate or non-degree study at vocational institution in United States or Canada.
Eligibility: Applicant must be returning adult student. Applicant must be U.S. citizen, permanent resident or Canadian resident.
Basis for selection: Major/career interest in tourism/travel.
Application requirements: Recommendations, essay, transcript. Copy of driver's license, resume.
Additional information: Minimum 3.0 GPA. Visit Website for application and deadline date. Submit all supporting items in electronic form except transcript, which should be mailed directly from school. Amount of award varies.
   Number of awards: 1
Contact:
Tourism Cares
275 Turnpike Street
Suite 307
Canton, MA 02021
Fax: 781-821-8949
Web: www.tourismcares.org/scholarships

Alaska Airlines Scholarship

Type of award: Scholarship.
Intended use: For junior or senior study at accredited 4-year institution in United States or Canada.
Eligibility: Applicant must be U.S. citizen, permanent resident or Canadian resident.
Basis for selection: Major/career interest in tourism/travel.
Application requirements: Recommendations, essay, transcript. Copy of driver's license, resume.
Additional information: Minimum 3.0 GPA. Submit all supporting items in electronic form except transcript, which should be mailed directly from school. Check Website for deadline. Amount of award varies.
   Number of awards: 1
Contact:
Tourism Cares
275 Turnpike Street
Suite 307
Canton, MA 02021
Fax: 781-821-8949
Web: www.tourismcares.org/scholarships

Alexander Harris Scholarship

Type of award: Scholarship.
Intended use: For junior or senior study at accredited 4-year institution in United States.
Eligibility: Applicant must be U.S. citizen or permanent resident residing in New York or New Jersey.
Basis for selection: Major/career interest in hospitality administration/management or tourism/travel. Applicant must demonstrate high academic achievement.
Application requirements: Transcript. Resume. Copy of driver's license or passport. Two letters of recommendation (one from tourism-related faculty member, one from tourism professional). Two-page essay describing what segment of the industry you are focusing on, and how your academic and extracurricular activities tie in to future goals.

Additional information: Minimum 3.0 GPA. All application materials must be scanned to PDF and submitted electronically (except transcript). Visit Website for application and deadline.
   Amount of award: $1,000
   Number of awards: 1
Contact:
Tourism Cares
275 Turnpike Street
Suite 307
Canton, MA 02021
Web: www.tourismcares.org/scholarships

American Express Travel Scholarship

Type of award: Scholarship, renewable.
Intended use: For freshman study at accredited 2-year or 4-year institution in United States or Canada.
Eligibility: Applicant must be high school senior. Applicant must be U.S. citizen or permanent resident.
Basis for selection: Major/career interest in hospitality administration/management or tourism/travel.
Application requirements: Recommendations, essay, transcript. Copy of driver's license or passport, resume, proof of enrollment. Two-page essay describing what segment of the industry you are focusing on, and how your academic and extracurricular activities tie in to future goals.
Additional information: Minimum 3.0 GPA. Hospitality students must have focus on travel and tourism. Visit Website for deadline and to apply. Submit all supporting items in electronic form except transcript, which should be mailed directly from school.
   Amount of award: $1,000
   Number of awards: 1
Contact:
Tourism Cares
275 Turnpike Street
Suite 307
Canton, MA 02021
Web: www.tourismcares.org/scholarships

Arizona Chapter Dependent Scholarship

Type of award: Scholarship, renewable.
Intended use: For sophomore, junior or senior study at accredited 2-year or 4-year institution in United States.
Eligibility: Applicant or parent must be member/participant of ASTA Arizona Chapter. Applicant must be U.S. citizen or permanent resident residing in Arizona.
Application requirements: Recommendations, essay, transcript. Copy of driver's license, letter from Arizona Chapter Member travel agency, resume.
Additional information: Minimum 3.0 GPA. Open to applicants in all fields of study; major in travel and tourism not required. Applicant must be enrolled in final year at two-year college or in junior or senior year at four-year university. Visit Website for application and deadline date. Submit all supporting items in electronic form except transcript, which should be mailed directly from school. Amount of award varies.
   Number of awards: 1

Contact:
Tourism Cares
275 Turnpike Street
Suite 307
Canton, MA 02021
Fax: 781-821-8949
Web: www.tourismcares.org/scholarships

Arizona Scholarship

Type of award: Scholarship, renewable.
Intended use: For sophomore, junior or senior study at accredited 2-year or 4-year institution in United States. Designated institutions: Colleges and universities in Arizona.
Eligibility: Applicant must be U.S. citizen, permanent resident or Canadian citizen/resident. Applicant must be residing in Arizona.
Basis for selection: Major/career interest in tourism/travel.
Application requirements: Recommendations, transcript. Resume, copy of driver's license or passport. Two-page essay describing what segment of the industry you are focusing on, and how your academic and extracurricular activities tie in to future goals.
Additional information: Minimum 3.0 GPA. Applicants attending two-year schools must be entering second year of program; students attending four-year schools must be entering junior or senior years. Visit Website for application and deadline date. Submit all supporting items in electronic form except transcript, which should be mailed directly from school.

Amount of award:	$2,000
Number of awards:	1

Contact:
Tourism Cares
275 Turnpike Street
Suite 307
Canton, MA 02021
Web: www.tourismcares.org/scholarships

Canada Scholarship

Type of award: Scholarship.
Intended use: For senior or graduate study at accredited 2-year or 4-year institution in United States or Canada.
Eligibility: Applicant must be permanent resident of Canada.
Basis for selection: Major/career interest in tourism/travel or hospitality administration/management.
Application requirements: Transcript. Resume. Copy of Canadian driver's license or passport. One recommendation from tourism-related faculty, one from a professional in the tourism industry. Two-page essay addressing one of the following topics: future of international inbound tourism, impact of technology on distribution channels, challenges to group travel of changing demographics and lifestyles, impact of mass tourism on visited communities, sustainable tourism, niche marketing, culture and heritage tourism, or learning and enrichment travel.
Additional information: Student may also attend three-year school in Quebec. Minimum 3.0 GPA. Must demonstrate focus and commitment to tourism. All application materials must be scanned to PDF and submitted electronically (except transcript). Visit Website for application and deadline.

Amount of award:	$1,000
Number of awards:	1

Contact:
Tourism Cares
275 Turnpike Street
Suite 307
Canton, MA 02021
Web: www.tourismcares.org/scholarships

Connecticut Scholarship

Type of award: Scholarship.
Intended use: For full-time junior or senior study at accredited 4-year institution in United States. Designated institutions: Connecticut institutions.
Eligibility: Applicant must be U.S. citizen or permanent resident residing in Connecticut.
Basis for selection: Major/career interest in hospitality administration/management or tourism/travel. Applicant must demonstrate high academic achievement.
Application requirements: Transcript. Resume. Copy of driver's license or passport. Two letters of recommendation (one from tourism-related faculty member, one from tourism professional). Two-page essay describing what segment of the industry you are focusing on, and how your academic and extracurricular activities tie in to future goals.
Additional information: Minimum 3.0 GPA. All application materials must be scanned to PDF and submitted electronically (except transcript). Visit Website for application and deadline.

Amount of award:	$1,000
Number of awards:	1

Contact:
Tourism Cares
275 Turnpike Street
Suite 307
Canton, MA 02021
Web: www.tourismcares.org/scholarships

Contiki Vacations Scholarship

Type of award: Scholarship.
Intended use: For sophomore, junior or senior study at accredited 2-year or 4-year institution in United States.
Eligibility: Applicant must be U.S. citizen or permanent resident.
Basis for selection: Major/career interest in tourism/travel or hospitality administration/management.
Application requirements: Recommendations, transcript. Copy of driver's license or passport, resume. Two-page essay describing what segment of the industry you are focusing on, and how your academic and extracurricular activities tie in to future goals.
Additional information: Minimum 3.0 GPA. Applicant must either be entering the second year of a two-year school, or junior or senior year of a four- or five-year school. Employees of Contiki Vacations or family members of employees of Contiki Vacations are not eligible for consideration. Submit all items in electronic form except transcript, which should be sent directly from school. Visit Website for deadline.

Amount of award:	$1,500
Number of awards:	1

Contact:
Tourism Cares
275 Turnpike Street
Suite 307
Canton, MA 02021
Web: www.tourismcares.org/scholarships

Dave Herren Memorial Scholarship

Type of award: Scholarship.

Intended use: For junior, senior or graduate study at accredited 4-year institution in United States.

Eligibility: Applicant must be U.S. citizen or permanent resident.

Basis for selection: Major/career interest in hospitality administration/management or tourism/travel. Applicant must demonstrate high academic achievement.

Application requirements: Transcript. Resume. Copy of driver's license or passport. Two letters of recommendation (one from tourism-related faculty member, one from tourism professional). Two-page essay describing what segment of the industry you are focusing on, and how your academic and extracurricular activities tie in to your future goals.

Additional information: Minimum 3.0 GPA. All application materials must be scanned to PDF and submitted electronically (except transcript). Visit Website for application and deadline.

   Amount of award: $1,000

   Number of awards: 1

Contact:
Tourism Cares
275 Turnpike Street
Suite 307
Canton, MA 02021
Web: www.tourismcares.org/scholarships

Florida Scholarship

Type of award: Scholarship.

Intended use: For junior or senior study at accredited 2-year or 4-year institution in United States. Designated institutions: Florida institutions.

Eligibility: Applicant must be U.S. citizen or permanent resident residing in Florida.

Basis for selection: Major/career interest in hospitality administration/management or tourism/travel. Applicant must demonstrate high academic achievement.

Application requirements: Transcript. Resume. Copy of driver's license or passport. Two letters of recommendation (one from tourism-related faculty member, one from tourism professional). Two-page essay describing what segment of the industry you are focusing on, and how your academic and extracurricular activities tie in to future goals.

Additional information: Minimum 3.0 GPA. All application materials must be scanned to PDF and submitted electronically (except transcript). Visit Website for application and deadline.

   Amount of award: $1,500

   Number of awards: 1

Contact:
Tourism Cares
275 Turnpike Street
Suite 307
Canton, MA 02021
Web: www.tourismcares.org/scholarships

George Reinke Scholarship

Type of award: Scholarship.

Intended use: For undergraduate study at vocational institution in United States.

Eligibility: Applicant must be returning adult student. Applicant must be U.S. citizen or permanent resident.

Basis for selection: Major/career interest in tourism/travel.

Application requirements: Recommendations, essay, transcript. Copy of driver's license, resume.

Additional information: Must be re-entering the job market in travel and tourism industry. Minimum 3.0 GPA. See Website for application and deadline date. Submit all supporting items in electronic form except transcript, which should be mailed directly from school. Amount of awards vary.

   Number of awards: 2

Contact:
Tourism Cares
275 Turnpike Street
Suite 307
Canton, MA 02021
Fax: 781-821-8949
Web: www.tourismcares.org/scholarships

Hawaii Chuck Yim Gee Scholarship

Type of award: Scholarship.

Intended use: For junior or senior study at accredited 4-year institution in United States. Designated institutions: Hawaii institutions.

Eligibility: Applicant must be U.S. citizen or permanent resident residing in Hawaii.

Basis for selection: Major/career interest in hospitality administration/management or tourism/travel. Applicant must demonstrate high academic achievement.

Application requirements: Transcript. Resume. Copy of driver's license or passport. Two letters of recommendation (one from tourism-related faculty member, one from tourism professional). Two-page essay describing what segment of the industry you are focusing on, and how your academic and extracurricular activities tie in to future goals.

Additional information: Minimum 3.0 GPA. All application materials must be scanned to PDF and submitted electronically (except transcript). Visit Website for application and deadline.

   Amount of award: $1,500

   Number of awards: 1

Contact:
Tourism Cares
275 Turnpike Street
Suite 307
Canton, MA 02021
Web: www.tourismcares.org/scholarships

Kathy LeTarte Scholarship

Type of award: Scholarship.

Intended use: For junior or senior study at accredited 4-year institution in United States or Canada.

Eligibility: Applicant must be residing in Michigan.

Basis for selection: Major/career interest in tourism/travel or hospitality administration/management.

Application requirements: Transcript. Resume. Copy of Michigan driver's license or passport. One recommendation from tourism-related faculty and one from a professional in tourism industry. Two-page essay on niche markets with an emphasis on student markets.

Additional information: Minimum 3.0 GPA. All application materials must be scanned to PDF and submitted electronically (except transcript). Visit Website for application and deadline.

   Amount of award: $1,000

   Number of awards: 1

Contact:
Tourism Cares
275 Turnpike Street
Suite 307
Canton, MA 02021
Web: www.tourismcares.org/scholarships

LaMacchia Family Scholarship

Type of award: Scholarship.
Intended use: For full-time junior or senior study at 4-year institution. Designated institutions: Wisconsin institutions.
Basis for selection: Major/career interest in tourism/travel or hospitality administration/management.
Application requirements: Transcript. Resume. Photocopy of Wisconsin Driver's license or passport. Two letters of recommendation (one from tourism-related faculty member, one from tourism professional). Two-page essay describing what segment of the industry you are focusing on, and how your academic and extracurricular activities tie in to future goals.
Additional information: Must have minimum 3.0 GPA. Students enrolled in hospitality programs must have focus on travel/tourism. All application materials must be scanned to PDF and submitted electronically (except transcript). Vist Website for application and deadline.

| Amount of award: | $1,000 |
| Number of awards: | 1 |

Contact:
Tourism Cares
275 Turnpike Street
Suite 307
Canton, MA 02021
Web: www.tourismcares.org/scholarships

Massachusetts Scholarship

Type of award: Scholarship.
Intended use: For sophomore, junior or senior study at accredited 2-year or 4-year institution in United States. Designated institutions: Massachusetts institutions.
Eligibility: Applicant must be U.S. citizen or permanent resident residing in Massachusetts.
Basis for selection: Major/career interest in hospitality administration/management or tourism/travel. Applicant must demonstrate high academic achievement.
Application requirements: Transcript. Resume. Copy of driver's license or passport. Two letters of recommendation (one from tourism-related faculty member, one from tourism professional). Two-page essay describing what segment of the industry you are focusing on, and how your academic and extracurricular activities tie in to future goals.
Additional information: Minimum 3.0 GPA. Applicants attending two-year schools must be entering second year of program; students attending four-year schools must be entering junior or senior years. All application materials must be scanned to PDF and submitted electronically (except transcript). Visit Website for application and deadline.

| Amount of award: | $1,000 |
| Number of awards: | 1 |

Contact:
Tourism Cares
275 Turnpike Street
Suite 307
Canton, MA 02021
Web: www.tourismcares.org/scholarships

Michigan Scholarship

Type of award: Scholarship.
Intended use: For sophomore, junior or senior study at accredited 2-year or 4-year institution in United States.
Eligibility: Applicant must be U.S. citizen or permanent resident residing in Michigan.

Basis for selection: Major/career interest in hospitality administration/management or tourism/travel. Applicant must demonstrate high academic achievement.
Application requirements: Transcript. Resume. Copy of driver's license or passport. Two letters of recommendation (one from tourism-related faculty member, one from tourism professional). Two-page essay describing what segment of the industry you are focusing on, and how your academic and extracurricular activities tie in to future goals.
Additional information: Minimum 3.0 GPA. Applicant must be entering second year of a two-year school, or junior or senior year of a four-year school. All application materials must be scanned to PDF and submitted electronically (except transcript). Visit Website for application and deadline.

| Amount of award: | $1,000 |
| Number of awards: | 1 |

Contact:
Tourism Cares
275 Turnpike Street
Suite 307
Canton, MA 02021
Web: www.tourismcares.org/scholarships

National Tour Association State Scholarship

Type of award: Scholarship.
Intended use: For junior, senior or graduate study at accredited 4-year or graduate institution in United States or Canada.
Eligibility: Applicant must be U.S. citizen, permanent resident or Canadian citizen/permanent resident.
Basis for selection: Major/career interest in hospitality administration/management or tourism/travel. Applicant must demonstrate high academic achievement.
Application requirements: Transcript. Resume. Copy of driver's license or passport. Two letters of recommendation (one from tourism-related faculty member, one from tourism professional). Two-page essay describing what segment of the industry you are focusing on, and how your academic and extracurricular activities tie in to future goals.
Additional information: Minimum 3.0 GPA. All application materials must be scanned to PDF and submitted electronically (except transcript). Students enrolled in hospitality program must have focus on travel and tourism. Visit Website for application and deadline.

| Amount of award: | $1,000 |
| Number of awards: | 13 |

Contact:
Tourism Cares
275 Turnpike Street
Suite 307
Canton, MA 02021
Web: www.tourismcares.org/scholarships

New Horizons Rene Campbell Memorial Scholarship

Type of award: Scholarship.
Intended use: For junior or senior study at accredited 4-year institution in United States or Canada.
Eligibility: Applicant must be residing in North Carolina.
Basis for selection: Major/career interest in tourism/travel or hospitality administration/management.
Application requirements: Transcript. Resume. Two letters of recommendation (one from tourism-related faculty member, one from tourism professional). Copy of North Carolina

driver's license or passport. Two-page essay describing what segment of the industry you are focusing on, and how your academic and extracurricular activities tie in to future goals.
Additional information: Minimum 3.0 GPA. Hospitality students must have focus on travel/tourism. All application materials must be scanned to PDF and submitted electronically (except transcript). Visit Website for application and deadline.

Amount of award:	$1,000
Number of awards:	1

Contact:
Tourism Cares
275 Turnpike Street
Suite 307
Canton, MA 02021
Web: www.tourismcares.org/scholarships

New Jersey Scholarship

Type of award: Scholarship.
Intended use: For sophomore, junior or senior study at accredited 2-year or 4-year institution in United States. Designated institutions: New Jersey institutions.
Eligibility: Applicant must be U.S. citizen or permanent resident residing in New Jersey.
Basis for selection: Major/career interest in hospitality administration/management or tourism/travel. Applicant must demonstrate high academic achievement.
Application requirements: Transcript. Resume. Copy of driver's license or passport. Two letters of recommendation (one from tourism-related faculty member, one from tourism professional). Two-page essay describing what segment of the industry you are focusing on, and how your academic and extracurricular activities tie in to future goals.
Additional information: Minimum 3.0 GPA. Applicant must be entering the second year of a two-year school, or junior or senior year of a four-year school. All application materials must be scanned to PDF and submitted electronically (except transcript). Visit Website for application and deadline.

Amount of award:	$1,000
Number of awards:	1

Contact:
Tourism Cares
275 Turnpike Street
Suite 307
Canton, MA 02021
Web: www.tourismcares.org/scholarships

New York Scholarship

Type of award: Scholarship.
Intended use: For full-time sophomore, junior or senior study at accredited 2-year or 4-year institution in United States. Designated institutions: New York institutions.
Eligibility: Applicant must be U.S. citizen or permanent resident residing in New York.
Basis for selection: Major/career interest in hospitality administration/management or tourism/travel. Applicant must demonstrate high academic achievement.
Application requirements: Transcript. Resume. Copy of driver's license or passport. Two letters of recommendation (one from tourism-related faculty member, one from tourism professional). Two-page essay describing what segment of the industry you are focusing on, and how your academic and extracurricular activities tie in to future goals.
Additional information: Minimum 3.0 GPA. Applicants attending two-year schools must be entering second year of program; students at four-year schools must be entering junior or senior years. All application materials must be scanned to

PDF and submitted electronically (except transcript). Visit Website for application and deadline.

Amount of award:	$1,000
Number of awards:	1

Contact:
Tourism Cares
275 Turnpike Street
Suite 307
Canton, MA 02021
Web: www.tourismcares.org/scholarships

Northern California Chapter - Richard Epping Scholarship

Type of award: Scholarship, renewable.
Intended use: For sophomore, junior or senior study at accredited 2-year or 4-year institution in United States. Designated institutions: Colleges and universities in northern California.
Eligibility: Applicant must be U.S. citizen, permanent resident or Canadian resident. Applicant must be residing in California.
Basis for selection: Major/career interest in hospitality administration/management or tourism/travel.
Application requirements: Recommendations, transcript. Copy of driver's license or passport, resume. Two-page essay describing what segment of the industry you are focusing on, and how your academic and extracurricular activities tie in to future goals.
Additional information: Minimum 3.0 GPA. Must be entering second year at two-year school, or junior or senior year at four-year school. Hospitality students must have focus on travel/tourism. Visit Website for application and deadline date. Submit all items in electronic form except transcript, which should be sent directly from school.

Amount of award:	$2,000
Number of awards:	1

Contact:
Tourism Cares
275 Turnpike Street
Suite 307
Canton, MA 02021
Web: www.tourismcares.org/scholarships

Ohio Scholarship

Type of award: Scholarship.
Intended use: For sophomore, junior or senior study at accredited 2-year or 4-year institution in United States. Designated institutions: Ohio institutions.
Eligibility: Applicant must be U.S. citizen or permanent resident residing in Ohio.
Basis for selection: Major/career interest in hospitality administration/management or tourism/travel. Applicant must demonstrate high academic achievement.
Application requirements: Transcript. Resume. Copy of driver's license or passport. Two letters of recommendation (one from tourism-related faculty member, one from tourism professional). Two-page essay describing what segment of the industry you are focusing on, and how your academic and extracurricular activities tie in to future goals.
Additional information: Minimum 3.0 GPA. Applicants attending two-year schools must be entering second year of program; students at four-year schools must be entering junior or senior years. All application materials must be scanned to PDF and submitted electronically (except transcript). Visit Website for application and deadline.

Amount of award: $1,000
Number of awards: 1
Contact:
Tourism Cares
275 Turnpike Street
Suite 307
Canton, MA 02021
Web: www.tourismcares.org/scholarships

Pacific Northwest Chapter/William Hunt Scholarship

Type of award: Scholarship.
Intended use: For sophomore, junior or senior study at accredited 2-year or 4-year institution in United States or Canada.
Eligibility: Applicant must be U.S. citizen or permanent resident residing in Oregon, Montana, Alaska, Idaho or Washington.
Basis for selection: Major/career interest in tourism/travel or hospitality administration/management.
Application requirements: Recommendations, transcript. Copy of U.S. driver's license as proof of state residency, resume. Two-page essay describing what segment of the industry you are focusing on, and how your academic and extracurricular activities tie in to future goals.
Additional information: Minimum 3.0 GPA. Must be entering the second year of a two-year school, or junior or senior year of a four-year school. Submit all items in electronic form except transcript, which should be sent directly from school. Visit Website for deadline.

Amount of award: $1,500
Number of awards: 2
Total amount awarded: $3,000
Contact:
Tourism Cares
275 Turnpike Street
Suite 307
Canton, MA 02021
Web: www.tourismcares.org/scholarships

Pat & Jim Host Scholarship

Type of award: Scholarship.
Intended use: For full-time undergraduate or graduate study at accredited 4-year institution. Designated institutions: Kentucky institutions.
Eligibility: Applicant must be residing in Kentucky.
Basis for selection: Major/career interest in tourism/travel; hotel/restaurant management or hospitality administration/management. Applicant must demonstrate high academic achievement.
Application requirements: Recommendations, transcript. Resume. Copy of Kentucky driver's license or passport. For returning students only: two letters of recommendation (one from tourism-related faculty member; other from tourism industry professional). Two-page essay describing what segment of the industry you are focusing on, and how your academic and extracurricular activities tie in to future goals.
Additional information: Minimum 3.0 GPA. Must demonstrate a clear focus on and commitment to tourism. All application materials must be scanned to PDF and submitted electronically (except transcript). Visit Website for application and deadline.

Number of awards: 1
Total amount awarded: $1,000

Contact:
Tourism Cares
275 Turnpike Street
Suite 307
Canton, MA 02021
Web: www.tourismcares.org/scholarships

Princess Cruises Scholarship

Type of award: Scholarship, renewable.
Intended use: For sophomore, junior or senior study at accredited 2-year or 4-year institution in United States or Canada.
Eligibility: Applicant must be U.S. citizen, permanent resident or Canadian citizen/resident.
Basis for selection: Major/career interest in hospitality administration/management or tourism/travel.
Application requirements: Recommendations, essay, transcript. Copy of driver's license, resume.
Additional information: Minimum 3.0 GPA. Must be entering second year at two-year school, or junior or senior year at four-year school. Hospitality students must have focus on travel/tourism. Visit Website for application and deadline date. Submit all supporting items in electronic form except transcript, which should be mailed directly from school. Amount of award varies.

Number of awards: 1
Contact:
Tourism Cares
275 Turnpike Street
Suite 307
Canton, MA 02021
Fax: 781-821-8949
Web: www.tourismcares.org/scholarships

Quebec Scholarship

Type of award: Scholarship.
Intended use: For senior or graduate study at accredited 4-year institution in United States or Canada.
Eligibility: Applicant must be permanent resident of Quebec.
Basis for selection: Major/career interest in tourism/travel or hospitality administration/management.
Application requirements: Transcript. Resume. Copy of Quebec driver's license or passport. One recommendation from tourism-related faculty, one from a professional in the tourism industry. Two-page essay addressing one of the following topics; future of international inbound tourism, impact of technology on distribution channels, challenges to group travel of changing demographics and lifestyles, impact of mass tourism on visited communities, sustainable tourism, niche marketing, culture and heritage tourism, or learning and enrichment travel.
Additional information: Students may also attend three-year schools in Quebec. Minimum 3.0 GPA. All application materials must be scanned to PDF and submitted electronically (except transcript). Transcript should be sent directly from school. Visit Website for application and deadline.

Amount of award: $1,500
Number of awards: 1
Contact:
Tourism Cares
275 Turnpike Street
Suite 307
Canton, MA 02021
Web: www.tourismcares.org/scholarships

Southern California Chapter - Pleasant Holidays Scholarship

Type of award: Scholarship, renewable.
Intended use: For sophomore, junior or senior study at accredited 2-year or 4-year institution in United States or Canada.
Eligibility: Applicant must be U.S. citizen or permanent resident.
Basis for selection: Major/career interest in tourism/travel.
Application requirements: Recommendations, essay, transcript. Copy of driver's license, resume.
Additional information: Minimum 3.0 GPA. Must be entering second year at two-year school, or junior or senior year at four-year school. Visit Website for application and deadline date. Submit all supporting items in electronic form except transcript, which should be mailed directly from school. Amount of award varies.

    Number of awards: 1
Contact:
Tourism Cares
275 Turnpike Street
Suite 307
Canton, MA 02021
Fax: 781-821-8949
Web: www.tourismcares.org/scholarships

Stan and Leone Pollard Scholarship

Type of award: Scholarship, renewable.
Intended use: For sophomore study at accredited 2-year institution in United States or Canada.
Eligibility: Applicant must be returning adult student. Applicant must be U.S. citizen, permanent resident or Canadian citizen/resident.
Basis for selection: Major/career interest in hospitality administration/management or tourism/travel.
Application requirements: Recommendations, essay, transcript. Copy of driver's license, resume.
Additional information: Minimum 3.0 GPA. Check Website for deadline and application. Submit all supporting items in electronic form except transcript, which should be mailed directly from school. Amount of award varies.

    Number of awards: 1
Contact:
Tourism Cares
275 Turnpike Street
Suite 307
Canton, MA 02021
Fax: 781-821-8949
Web: www.tourismcares.org/scholarships

Utah Keith Griffall Scholarship

Type of award: Scholarship.
Intended use: For full-time junior or senior study at accredited 4-year institution in United States. Designated institutions: Utah institutions.
Eligibility: Applicant must be U.S. citizen or permanent resident residing in Utah.
Basis for selection: Major/career interest in hospitality administration/management or tourism/travel. Applicant must demonstrate high academic achievement.
Application requirements: Transcript. Resume. Copy of driver's license or passport. Two letters of recommendation (one from tourism-related faculty member, one from tourism professional). Two-page essay describing what segment of the industry you are focusing on, and how your academic and extracurricular activities tie in to future goals.
Additional information: Minimum 3.0 GPA. All application materials must be scanned to PDF and submitted electronically (except transcript). Visit Website for application and deadline.

    Amount of award: $1,000
    Number of awards: 1
Contact:
Tourism Cares
275 Turnpike Street
Suite 307
Canton, MA 02021
Web: www.tourismcares.org/scholarships

Yellow Ribbon Scholarship

Type of award: Scholarship.
Intended use: For undergraduate or graduate study at accredited postsecondary institution in United States or Canada.
Eligibility: Applicant must be visually impaired, hearing impaired or physically challenged. Applicant must be U.S. citizen, permanent resident or Canadian citizen or resident.
Basis for selection: Major/career interest in tourism/travel; hospitality administration/management or hotel/restaurant management. Applicant must demonstrate high academic achievement.
Application requirements: Transcript, proof of eligibility. Two recommendation letters (one from tourism-related faculty member, one from tourism industry professional). Copy of U.S./Canadian driver's license or passport. Letter from an accredited physician attesting to applicant's disability. Resume. Two-page essay. Undergraduates: Describe what segment of the industry you are focusing on, and how your academic and extracurricular activities tie in to future goals. Graduates: Discuss the changes you've observed in the industry, and your future potential in the industry.
Additional information: Minimum 2.5 GPA. All application materials must be scanned to PDF and submitted electronically (except transcript). Visit Website for application and deadline.

    Number of awards: 1
    Total amount awarded: $5,000
Contact:
Tourism Cares
275 Turnpike Street
Suite 307
Canton, MA 02021
Phone: 781-821-5990
Fax: 781-821-8949
Web: www.tourismcares.org/scholarships

Transportation Clubs International

Alice Glaisyer Warfield Memorial Scholarship

Type of award: Scholarship.
Intended use: For undergraduate or graduate study at accredited postsecondary institution.
Basis for selection: Major/career interest in transportation. Applicant must demonstrate financial need, high academic achievement and depth of character.
Application requirements: Recommendations, essay, transcript. Small current photograph (for publication).

Scholarships

Amount of award: $1,500
Number of awards: 1
Application deadline: May 31
Total amount awarded: $1,500
Contact:
Transportation Clubs International Scholarships
Attn: Bill Blair
15710 JFK Boulevard
Houston, TX 77032
Web: www.transportationclubsinternational.com

Charlotte Woods Memorial Scholarship

Type of award: Scholarship.
Intended use: For undergraduate or graduate study.
Eligibility: Applicant or parent must be member/participant of Transportation Clubs International.
Basis for selection: Major/career interest in transportation. Applicant must demonstrate financial need, high academic achievement and depth of character.
Application requirements: Recommendations, essay, transcript. Small current photograph (for publication).
Amount of award: $1,500
Number of awards: 1
Application deadline: May 31
Total amount awarded: $1,500
Contact:
Transportation Clubs International Scholarships
Attn: Bill Blair
15710 JFK Boulevard
Houston, TX 77032
Web: www.transportationclubsinternational.com

Denny Lydic Scholarship

Type of award: Scholarship.
Intended use: For undergraduate or graduate study at accredited vocational, 4-year or graduate institution.
Basis for selection: Major/career interest in transportation. Applicant must demonstrate financial need, high academic achievement and depth of character.
Application requirements: Recommendations, essay, transcript. Small current photograph (for publication).
Additional information: Minimum 3.0 GPA. Award amount varies; up to $1,000.
Amount of award: $1,000
Number of awards: 1
Application deadline: May 15
Total amount awarded: $1,000
Contact:
Transportation Clubs International Scholarships
Attn: Bill Blair
15710 JFK Boulevard
Houston, TX 77032
Web: www.transportationclubsinternational.com

Ginger and Fred Deines Canada Scholarship

Type of award: Scholarship.
Intended use: For undergraduate or graduate study in United States or Canada.
Eligibility: Applicant must be Canadian citizen.
Basis for selection: Major/career interest in transportation. Applicant must demonstrate financial need, high academic achievement and depth of character.

Application requirements: Recommendations, essay, transcript. Small current photograph (for publication).
Amount of award: $2,000
Number of awards: 1
Application deadline: May 31
Total amount awarded: $2,000
Contact:
Transportation Clubs International Scholarships
Attn: Bill Blair
15710 JFK Boulevard
Houston, TX 77032
Web: www.transportationclubsinternational.com

Ginger and Fred Deines Mexico Scholarship

Type of award: Scholarship.
Intended use: For undergraduate or graduate study. Designated institutions: Institutions in U.S. or Mexico.
Eligibility: Applicant must be Mexican citizen.
Basis for selection: Major/career interest in transportation. Applicant must demonstrate financial need, high academic achievement and depth of character.
Application requirements: Recommendations, essay, transcript. Small current photograph (for publication).
Amount of award: $2,000
Number of awards: 1
Application deadline: May 31
Total amount awarded: $2,000
Contact:
Transportation Clubs International Scholarships
Attn: Bill Blair
15710 JFK Boulevard
Houston, TX 77032
Web: www.transportationclubsinternational.com

Hooper Memorial Scholarship

Type of award: Scholarship.
Intended use: For undergraduate or graduate study.
Basis for selection: Major/career interest in transportation. Applicant must demonstrate financial need, high academic achievement and depth of character.
Application requirements: Recommendations, essay, transcript. Small current photograph (for publication).
Amount of award: $2,000
Number of awards: 1
Application deadline: May 31
Total amount awarded: $2,000
Contact:
Transportation Clubs International Scholarships
Attn: Bill Blair
15710 JFK Boulevard
Houston, TX 77032
Web: www.transportationclubsinternational.com

Texas Transportation Scholarship

Type of award: Scholarship.
Intended use: For undergraduate or graduate study.
Basis for selection: Major/career interest in transportation. Applicant must demonstrate financial need, high academic achievement and depth of character.
Application requirements: Recommendations, essay, transcript. Small current photograph (for publication).
Additional information: Applicant must have been enrolled in a Texas school for some phase of elementary through high school education.

Amount of award: $1,500
Number of awards: 1
Application deadline: May 31
Total amount awarded: $1,500
Contact:
Transportation Clubs International Scholarships
Attn: Bill Blair
15710 JFK Boulevard
Houston, TX 77032
Web: www.transportationclubsinternational.com

Treacy Company

Treacy Company Scholarship

Type of award: Scholarship, renewable.
Intended use: For full-time freshman or sophomore study at postsecondary institution.
Eligibility: Applicant must be residing in Montana, Idaho or North Dakota.
Basis for selection: Applicant must demonstrate financial need, leadership, seriousness of purpose and service orientation.
Application requirements: Transcript. Letter stating reason for applying, including personal information.
Additional information: Student may attend school outside of ND, ID, and MT. Must write for application; applications available from January to end of May.

Amount of award: $1,000
Number of awards: 25
Number of applicants: 55
Application deadline: June 15
Notification begins: July 31
Total amount awarded: $28,000
Contact:
Treacy Company
P.O. Box 1479
Helena, MT 59624

Trinity Episcopal Church

Shannon Scholarship

Type of award: Scholarship, renewable.
Intended use: For undergraduate study at postsecondary institution.
Eligibility: Applicant must be female. Applicant must be Episcopal. Applicant must be residing in Pennsylvania.
Basis for selection: Applicant must demonstrate financial need.
Application requirements: Proof of eligibility.
Additional information: Only open to daughters of Episcopal clergy in state of Pennsylvania. Must apply for state and federal financial assistance first. Previous recipients may reapply. Number of awards varies. For more information, contact church office.

Amount of award: $500-$7,500
Number of applicants: 8
Application deadline: April 30
Total amount awarded: $26,000

Contact:
Trinity Episcopal Church
200 South Second Street
Pottsville, PA 17901
Phone: 570-622-8720

Two Ten Footwear Foundation

Two Ten Footwear Design Scholarship

Type of award: Scholarship, renewable.
Intended use: For undergraduate or graduate study in or outside United States.
Eligibility: Applicant must be U.S. citizen or permanent resident.
Basis for selection: Based on design talent. Major/career interest in design. Applicant must demonstrate financial need.
Application requirements: Portfolio, recommendations, essay, transcript.
Additional information: Rolling deadline. Must be committed to career in footwear design.

Amount of award: $1,000-$5,000
Contact:
Two Ten Footwear Foundation
Scholarship Department
1466 Main Street
Waltham, MA 02451
Phone: 800-346-3210 ext. 1510
Fax: 781-736-1555
Web: www.twoten.org

Two Ten Footwear Foundation Scholarship

Type of award: Scholarship, renewable.
Intended use: For undergraduate study at accredited vocational, 2-year or 4-year institution.
Eligibility: Applicant or parent must be employed by Footwear/Leather Industry. Applicant must be U.S. citizen.
Basis for selection: Applicant must demonstrate financial need and high academic achievement.
Application requirements: Recommendations, essay, transcript, proof of eligibility.
Additional information: Applicant must have worked 500 hours in footwear or leather industries or have parent currently employed in this field for at least two years. Top-ranking applicant is candidate for $15,000 super-scholarship, renewable up to four years. Must show personal promise. Additional information and application available on Website.

Amount of award: $300-$15,000
Application deadline: February 16
Notification begins: June 15
Total amount awarded: $700,000
Contact:
Two Ten Footwear Foundation
Attn: Scholarship Department
1466 Main Street
Waltham, MA 02451-1623
Phone: 800-346-3210 ext. 1512
Fax: 781-736-1555
Web: www.twoten.org

UCB Pharma Inc.

Keppra Family Epilepsy Scholarship Program

Type of award: Scholarship.
Intended use: For undergraduate or graduate study at vocational, 2-year, 4-year or graduate institution in United States.
Eligibility: Applicant must be U.S. citizen or permanent resident.
Basis for selection: Applicant must demonstrate high academic achievement, leadership and service orientation.
Application requirements: Transcript. Essay or artistic presentation explaining why applicant should be selected for scholarship (awards received, community involvement, etc.) and how epilepsy has impacted his or her life. Photograph. Three letters of recommendation: one from a school official, one from a community member, and one from applicant's epilepsy healthcare team.
Additional information: Scholarships are awarded to people with epilepsy, and to caregivers and family members of epilepsy patients. Visit Website for deadline and application.

Amount of award:	$5,000
Number of awards:	40
Total amount awarded:	$200,000

Contact:
UCB Pharma Inc.
1950 Lake Park Drive
Smyrna, GA 30080
Phone: 866-825-1920
Web: www.keppra.com

Unico Foundation, Inc.

Alphonse A. Miele Scholarship

Type of award: Scholarship.
Intended use: For undergraduate study at postsecondary institution.
Eligibility: Applicant must be high school senior. Applicant must be Italian.
Basis for selection: Applicant must demonstrate financial need, high academic achievement, depth of character and leadership.
Application requirements: Recommendations, essay, transcript, proof of eligibility. SAT/ACT scores.
Additional information: Applications must be acquired from and submitted through a participating local UNICO chapter. Must be of Italian heritage. Award is $1,500 per year for four years.

Amount of award:	$6,000
Number of awards:	1
Application deadline:	April 15

Contact:
Unico Foundation, Inc.
271 US Highway, 46 #A108
Fairfield, NJ 07004
Phone: 973-808-0035
Web: www.unico.org

Major Don S. Gentile Scholarship

Type of award: Scholarship.
Intended use: For undergraduate study at postsecondary institution.
Eligibility: Applicant must be high school senior. Applicant must be Italian.
Basis for selection: Applicant must demonstrate financial need, high academic achievement, depth of character and leadership.
Application requirements: Recommendations, essay, transcript, proof of eligibility. SAT/ACT scores.
Additional information: Applications must be acquired from and submitted through a participating local UNICO chapter. Must be of Italian heritage. Award is $1,500 per year for four years.

Amount of award:	$6,000
Number of awards:	1
Application deadline:	April 15

Contact:
Unico Foundation, Inc.
271 US Highway 46 #A108
Fairfield, NJ 07004-2458
Phone: 973-808-0035
Web: www.unico.org

Theodore Mazza Scholarship

Type of award: Scholarship.
Intended use: For undergraduate study at postsecondary institution.
Eligibility: Applicant must be high school senior. Applicant must be Italian.
Basis for selection: Applicant must demonstrate financial need, high academic achievement, depth of character and leadership.
Application requirements: Recommendations, essay, transcript, proof of eligibility. SAT/ACT scores.
Additional information: Applications must be acquired from and submitted through a participating local UNICO chapter. Must be of Italian heritage. Award is $1,500 per year for four years.

Amount of award:	$6,000
Number of awards:	1
Application deadline:	April 15

Contact:
Unico Foundation, Inc.
271 US Highway 46 #A108
Fairfield, NJ 07004-2458
Web: www.unico.org

William C. Davini Scholarship

Type of award: Scholarship.
Intended use: For undergraduate study at postsecondary institution.
Eligibility: Applicant must be high school senior. Applicant must be Italian.
Basis for selection: Applicant must demonstrate financial need, high academic achievement, depth of character and leadership.
Application requirements: Recommendations, essay, transcript, proof of eligibility. SAT/ACT scores.
Additional information: Applications must be acquired from and submitted through a participating local UNICO chapter. Must be of Italian heritage. Award is $1,500 per year for four years.

Amount of award:	$6,000
Number of awards:	1
Application deadline:	April 15

Contact:
Unico Foundation, Inc.
271 US Highway 46 #A108
Fairfield, NJ 07004-2458
Web: www.unico.org

Union Plus

Union Plus Scholarship

Type of award: Scholarship.
Intended use: For undergraduate or graduate study at accredited vocational, 2-year, 4-year or graduate institution.
Basis for selection: Applicant must demonstrate financial need, high academic achievement, depth of character and leadership.
Application requirements: Recommendations, essay, proof of eligibility.
Additional information: Open to current or retired members, and dependents and spouses of current or retired members, of unions that participate in Union Plus programs. Check Website for deadline.

Amount of award:	$500-$4,000
Number of awards:	108
Number of applicants:	4,237
Notification begins:	May 31
Total amount awarded:	$150,000

Contact:
Union Plus Education Foundation c/o Union Privilege
1125 15th St., NW
Suite 300
Washington, DC 20005
Fax: 202-293-5311
Web: www.unionplus.org

Unitarian Universalist Association

Stanfield and D'Orlando Art Scholarship

Type of award: Scholarship.
Intended use: For full-time undergraduate or graduate study in United States.
Eligibility: Applicant must be Unitarian Universalist.
Basis for selection: Major/career interest in arts, general. Applicant must demonstrate financial need, depth of character and service orientation.
Application requirements: Portfolio, recommendations, essay, transcript, proof of eligibility.
Additional information: Number of awards varies; on average, five are given. Applicant must be preparing for fine arts career in fields such as painting, drawing, sculpture, or photography. Art therapy and performing arts majors not eligible. Returning adult students also eligible. See Website for application and more information.

Amount of award:	$1,000-$4,500
Number of awards:	5
Number of applicants:	15
Application deadline:	March 1
Notification begins:	March 31
Total amount awarded:	$22,500

Contact:
Unitarian Universalist Funding Program
P.O. Box 301149
Jamaica Plain, MA 02130
Phone: 617-971-9600
Fax: 617-971-0029
Web: www.uua.org/giving/awardsscholarships/

United Food and Commercial Workers International Union

United Food and Commercial Workers International Union Scholarship Program

Type of award: Scholarship.
Intended use: For undergraduate or graduate study at accredited postsecondary institution.
Eligibility: Applicant or parent must be member/participant of United Food and Commerical Workers.
Basis for selection: Applicant must demonstrate high academic achievement and service orientation.
Application requirements: Essay, transcript. Complete biographical questionnaire.
Additional information: Award is $2,000 per year for up to four years; 14-20 awards are available yearly. Open to current and prospective high school graduates and GED recipients. Applicant or applicant's parent must be member of United Food and Commercial Workers International Union for one year prior to application. Dependents of members must be under age 20.

Amount of award:	$8,000
Number of awards:	14
Number of applicants:	3,500
Application deadline:	April 15
Notification begins:	July 1
Total amount awarded:	$112,000

Contact:
United Food and Commercial Workers International Union
1775 K Street, N.W.
Washington, DC 20006
Phone: 202-223-3111
Web: www.ufcw.org/scholarship

United Methodist Church General Board of Higher Education and Ministry

United Methodist Scholarships

Type of award: Scholarship, renewable.

Intended use: For full-time undergraduate or graduate study at accredited 2-year, 4-year or graduate institution in United States.
Eligibility: Applicant must be United Methodist.
Basis for selection: Applicant must demonstrate seriousness of purpose.
Application requirements: Recommendations, essay, transcript. Online application.
Additional information: Sponsor administers more than 60 scholarship programs. All recipients must be full active members of United Methodist Church for minimum of one year prior to application and maintain minimum 2.5 GPA. Deadlines vary. Some scholarships are renewable. Visit Website for more information.

Notification begins:	January 5

Contact:
United Methodist Church General Board of Higher Education and Ministry
Office of Loans and Scholarships
P.O. Box 340007
Nashville, TN 37203-0007
Phone: 614-340-7344
Web: www.gbhem.org

United Methodist Communications

Leonard M. Perryman Communications Scholarship for Ethnic Minority Students

Type of award: Scholarship.
Intended use: For full-time junior or senior study at accredited 4-year institution in United States.
Eligibility: Applicant must be Alaskan native, Asian American, African American, Mexican American, Hispanic American, Puerto Rican, American Indian or Native Hawaiian/Pacific Islander. Applicant must be United Methodist.
Basis for selection: Major/career interest in journalism; communications; radio/television/film or religion/theology. Applicant must demonstrate seriousness of purpose.
Application requirements: Recommendations, essay, transcript. Three examples of journalistic work in any medium; photograph (appropriate for publicity purposes).
Additional information: Must plan to pursue career in religious journalism or religious communication. Application forms may be downloaded from Website.

Amount of award:	$2,500
Number of awards:	1
Number of applicants:	6
Application deadline:	March 15
Total amount awarded:	$2,500

Contact:
United Methodist Communications
Communications Ministry Team
P.O. Box 320, 810 12th Avenue South
Nashville, TN 37202-0320
Phone: 888-278-4862
Web: www.umcom.org

United Negro College Fund

Cargill Scholarship Program

Type of award: Scholarship.
Intended use: For full-time freshman, sophomore or junior study at accredited 2-year or 4-year institution. Designated institutions: UNCF member institutions and Kansas State University, University of Illinois, University of Minnesota, Iowa State University, North Carolina A&T State University, and University of Wisconsin-Madison.
Eligibility: Applicant must be U.S. citizen or permanent resident.
Basis for selection: Major/career interest in accounting; agriculture; animal sciences; biochemistry; chemistry; computer/information sciences; engineering, chemical; engineering, mechanical; finance/banking or microbiology. Applicant must demonstrate financial need and high academic achievement.
Application requirements: Recommendations, transcript. FAFSA; resume; 250-word essay about yourself, selected major, and career goals and how they might be fulfilled at Cargill.
Additional information: Minimum 3.0 GPA. Internship opportunities may become available for recipients. Visit Website for deadline and list of UNCF eligible schools.

Amount of award:	$5,000

Contact:
United Negro College Fund
8260 Willow Oaks Corporate Drive
P.O. Box 10444
Fairfax, VA 22031-8044
Phone: 800-331-2244
Web: www.uncf.org

Earl & Patricia Armstrong Scholarship

Type of award: Scholarship.
Intended use: For full-time undergraduate or graduate study at accredited 4-year institution in United States. Designated institutions: UNCF member institutions.
Eligibility: Applicant must be U.S. citizen or permanent resident.
Basis for selection: Major/career interest in medicine; biology or health sciences. Applicant must demonstrate financial need and high academic achievement.
Application requirements: Recommendations, essay, transcript, proof of eligibility. FAFSA and SAR.
Additional information: Minimum 3.0 GPA. Visit Website for application.

Amount of award:	$3,000

Contact:
United Negro College Fund
8260 Willow Oaks Corporate Drive
P.O. Box 10444
Fairfax, VA 22031-8044
Phone: 800-331-2244
Web: www.uncf.org

Gates Millennium Scholars Program

Type of award: Scholarship, renewable.
Intended use: For full-time freshman or graduate study at accredited 4-year or graduate institution in United States.
Eligibility: Applicant must be Alaskan native, Asian American, African American, Mexican American, Hispanic American,

Puerto Rican, American Indian or Native Hawaiian/Pacific Islander. Applicant must be U.S. citizen or permanent resident.
Basis for selection: Major/career interest in education; engineering; library science; mathematics or public health. Applicant must demonstrate financial need, high academic achievement, leadership and service orientation.
Application requirements: Recommendations, transcript, nomination by high school principal, teacher, counselor, college president, professor, or dean. Nominee Personal Information Form, FAFSA, GMS information sheet, admission letter.
Additional information: Must be eligible for Pell Grant. Must participate in community service, volunteer work, or extracurricular activities. Minimum 3.3 GPA. Scholarship provides tuition, room, materials, and board not covered by existing financial aid. Eliminates loans, work-study, and outside jobs for scholarship recipients. Funded by Bill and Melinda Gates Foundation. Visit Website for application and deadline.

Number of awards:	1,000
Number of applicants:	13,350
Total amount awarded:	$61,415,141

Contact:
Gates Millenium Scholars
P.O. Box 1434
Alexandria, VA 22313
Phone: 877-690-4677
Fax: 703-205-2079
Web: www.uncf.org or www.gmsp.org

Janet Jackson Rhythm Nation Scholarships

Type of award: Scholarship, renewable.
Intended use: For full-time undergraduate study at accredited 4-year institution in United States. Designated institutions: UNCF member institutions.
Basis for selection: Major/career interest in communications; performing arts; English or music.
Application requirements: Recommendations, essay, proof of eligibility. FAFSA, resume, photograph, and SAR must be sent to school's financial aid office.
Additional information: Minimum 3.0 GPA. Fine arts majors also eligible. Awards are made annually and may be used for tuition costs, room and board, or to repay federal student loans. Visit Website for list of eligible schools, application, and deadline.

Amount of award:	$2,000

Contact:
United Negro College Fund
8260 Willow Oaks Corporate Drive
P.O. Box 10444
Fairfax, VA 22031-8044
Phone: 800-331-2244
Web: www.uncf.org

John W. Anderson Foundation Scholarship

Type of award: Scholarship, renewable.
Intended use: For full-time undergraduate study at accredited 4-year institution in United States. Designated institutions: UNCF member institutions.
Eligibility: Applicant must be U.S. citizen or permanent resident residing in Indiana.
Basis for selection: Applicant must demonstrate financial need and high academic achievement.
Application requirements: FAFSA and SAR.

Additional information: Minimum 2.5 GPA. See Website for more information.

Amount of award:	$3,000

Contact:
United Negro College Fund
8260 Willow Oaks Corporate Drive
P.O. Box 10444
Fairfax, VA 22031-8044
Phone: 800-331-2244
Web: www.uncf.org

Malcolm X Scholarship for Exceptional Courage

Type of award: Scholarship, renewable.
Intended use: For full-time junior study at accredited 4-year institution in United States. Designated institutions: UNCF member institutions.
Basis for selection: Applicant must demonstrate financial need, high academic achievement, leadership and seriousness of purpose.
Application requirements: Recommendations, essay, transcript, proof of eligibility. FAFSA and SAR sent to school's financial aid office.
Additional information: Minimum 2.5 GPA. Application and list of eligible colleges available online. Renewable each year until graduation. Scholarship is awarded to students who have overcome tremendous hardships and special circumstances. Deadline varies, visit Website for details. FAFSA and SAR must be sent to school's financial aid office.

Amount of award:	$4,000

Contact:
United Negro College Fund
8260 Willow Oaks Corporate Drive
P.O. Box 10444
Fairfax, VA 22031-8044
Phone: 800-331-2244
Web: www.uncf.org

Maya Angelou/Vivian Baxter Scholarship

Type of award: Scholarship, renewable.
Intended use: For full-time undergraduate study at accredited 4-year institution in United States. Designated institutions: UNCF member institutions.
Eligibility: Applicant must be residing in North Carolina.
Basis for selection: Applicant must demonstrate financial need, high academic achievement, leadership and service orientation.
Application requirements: FAFSA and SAR.
Additional information: Minimum 2.5 GPA. Visit Website for details.

Amount of award:	$2,500

Contact:
United Negro College Fund
8260 Willow Oaks Corporate Drive
P.O. Box 10444
Fairfax, VA 22031-8044
Phone: 800-331-2244
Web: www.uncf.org

UBS/PaineWebber Scholarships

Type of award: Scholarship, renewable.

Intended use: For full-time sophomore or junior study at accredited 4-year institution. Designated institutions: UNCF member institutions.
Basis for selection: Major/career interest in accounting; business; business/management/administration; economics; finance/banking or marketing.
Application requirements: Recommendations, essay, transcript, proof of eligibility. FAFSA and photograph.
Additional information: Minimum 3.0 GPA. Visit Website for list of eligible schools, application, and deadline.

Amount of award:	$8,000

Contact:
United Negro College Fund
8260 Willow Oaks Corporate Drive
P.O. Box 10444
Fairfax, VA 22031-8044
Phone: 800-331-2244
Web: www.uncf.org

United States Association of Blind Athletes

Arthur and Helen Copeland Scholarship for Females

Type of award: Scholarship.
Intended use: For full-time undergraduate study at 2-year or 4-year institution.
Eligibility: Applicant must be visually impaired. Applicant must be U.S. citizen.
Basis for selection: Applicant must demonstrate high academic achievement and service orientation.
Application requirements: Transcript, proof of eligibility. Autobiographical sketch outlining USABA involvement, academic goals, and objective for which scholarship funds will be used.
Additional information: Applicants must be legally blind. Priority given to USABA members. $500 award may be split into two $250 scholarships if there are two qualified applicants.

Amount of award:	$250-$500
Number of awards:	2
Application deadline:	August 15
Notification begins:	November 1
Total amount awarded:	$500

Contact:
U.S. Association of Blind Athletes
33 North Institute Street
Colorado Springs, CO 80903
Phone: 719-630-0422
Fax: 719-630-0616
Web: www.usaba.org

Arthur E. Copeland Scholarship

Type of award: Scholarship.
Intended use: For full-time undergraduate study at 2-year or 4-year institution.
Eligibility: Applicant must be visually impaired. Applicant must be U.S. citizen.
Basis for selection: Applicant must demonstrate high academic achievement and service orientation.
Application requirements: Transcript, proof of eligibility. Autobiographical sketch outlining community service and academic goals. References.

Additional information: Applicant must be legally blind. Must be high school senior or in college. Must be current United States Association of Blind Athletes member. Must have participated in USABA sports programs or plan on participating in future programs; preference given to athletes.

Amount of award:	$500
Number of awards:	1
Application deadline:	August 15
Notification begins:	November 1

Contact:
Mark Lucas
33 North Institute Street
Colorado Springs, CO 80903
Phone: 719-630-0422
Fax: 719-630-0616
Web: www.usaba.org

United States Institute of Peace

National Peace Essay Contest

Type of award: Scholarship.
Intended use: For undergraduate study at postsecondary institution.
Eligibility: Applicant must be enrolled in high school. Applicant must be U.S. citizen or permanent resident.
Basis for selection: Competition/talent/interest in writing/journalism. Major/career interest in international relations.
Application requirements: Three-part maximum 1500-word essay on topic chosen by the Institute. Student form and coordinator form.
Additional information: Home-schooled students, foreign exchange students, or those enrolled in correspondence programs also eligible. Non-International Relations majors are also eligible and encouraged to submit essay. Applicant must submit essay to contest coordinator before deadline; the coordinator will submit essay to the Institute. State-level winners receive $1,000 and will compete for national awards of $10,000, $5,000, and $2,500 (national amount includes state award). Also invited to attend awards program in Washington, DC. Visit Website for more information.

Amount of award:	$1,000-$10,000
Number of awards:	53
Number of applicants:	1,200
Application deadline:	February 1
Notification begins:	May 1
Total amount awarded:	$67,500

Contact:
United States Institute of Peace
1200 17th Street NW
Suite 200
Washington, DC 20036-3011
Phone: 202-429-4710
Fax: 202-429-6063
Web: www.usip.org/npec

United Transportation Union Insurance Association

United Transportation Union Insurance Association Scholarship

Type of award: Scholarship, renewable.
Intended use: For full-time undergraduate study at accredited vocational, 2-year or 4-year institution in or outside United States.
Eligibility: Applicant or parent must be member/participant of United Transportation Union. Applicant must be no older than 25. Applicant must be permanent resident.
Application requirements: Proof of eligibility.
Additional information: Scholarships awarded by lottery. Applicant must be accepted to or enrolled in an eligible institution. Members and direct descendants of living or deceased members eligible. Notification takes place prior to fall enrollment.

Amount of award:	$500
Number of awards:	50
Number of applicants:	900
Application deadline:	March 31

Contact:
United Transportation Union Insurance Association
14600 Detroit Ave.
Cleveland, OH 44107-4250
Phone: 216-228-9400
Web: www.utu.org

University Film and Video Association

Carole Fielding Video Grant

Type of award: Research grant.
Intended use: For undergraduate or graduate study at accredited 2-year or 4-year institution.
Basis for selection: Major/career interest in film/video.
Application requirements: Resume, budget, research/production proposal.
Additional information: Project categories include narrative, documentary, experimental, multimedia/installation, animation, and research. Applicant must be sponsored by faculty member who is active member of University Film and Video Association. Number of awards varies. Visit Website for application.

Amount of award:	$500-$4,000
Application deadline:	December 15
Notification begins:	March 31

Contact:
Prof. Adrianne Carageorge, UFVA Carole Fielding Student Grants Chair
Rochester Inst. Of Tech., Bldg. 7B, Rm. 2270
Rochester, NY 14623-5604
Web: www.ufva.org

Upakar

Indian American Scholarship

Type of award: Scholarship, renewable.
Intended use: For freshman study.
Eligibility: Applicant must be Asian American. Applicant must be U.S. citizen or permanent resident.
Basis for selection: Applicant must demonstrate financial need and high academic achievement.
Application requirements: Recommendations, essay.
Additional information: Applicant must have either been born or have one grandparent/parent who was born in the Republic of India. Applicant must have cumulative, unadjusted GPA over 3.6. Applicant's family must have Adjusted Gross Income of less than $75,000.

Amount of award:	$3,000
Number of awards:	20
Number of applicants:	250
Application deadline:	April 28
Notification begins:	June 1
Total amount awarded:	$60,000

Contact:
Upakar c/o M. Mukunda
10237 Nolan Drive
Rockville, MD 20850
Web: www.upakar.org

U.S. Army Recruiting Command

Montgomery GI Bill (MGIB)

Type of award: Scholarship.
Intended use: For undergraduate or graduate study at accredited postsecondary institution in United States.
Eligibility: Applicant must be at least 17, no older than 41. Applicant must be U.S. citizen. Applicant must be in military service in the Army.
Basis for selection: Applicant must demonstrate depth of character, leadership, patriotism, seriousness of purpose and service orientation.
Application requirements: Interview. Armed Services Vocational Aptitude Battery.
Additional information: Award amount varies depending on type of service. Visit Website for award amounts and service requirements.
Contact:
Phone: 888-550-ARMY
Web: www.goarmy.com

Selected Reserve Montgomery GI Bill

Type of award: Scholarship.
Intended use: For undergraduate or graduate study at accredited postsecondary institution.
Eligibility: Applicant must be at least 17, no older than 41. Applicant must be U.S. citizen. Applicant must be veteran who served in the Army or Reserves/National Guard.

Basis for selection: Applicant must demonstrate depth of character, leadership, patriotism, seriousness of purpose and service orientation.

Application requirements: Interview. Armed Services Vocational Aptitude Battery.

Additional information: Award amount varies. Visit Website for award amounts and service requirements.

Contact:
Phone: 888-550-ARMY
Web: www.goarmy.com

U.S. Department of Agriculture

USDA/1890 National Scholars Program

Type of award: Scholarship, renewable.

Intended use: For full-time freshman study at 4-year institution in United States. Designated institutions: One of the 1890 Historically Black Land-Grant Institutions: Alabama A&M University, Alcorn State University (MS), Delaware State University, Florida A&M University, Fort Valley State University (GA), Kentucky State University, Lincoln University (MO), Langston University (OK), North Carolina A&T University, Prairie View A&M University (TX), South Carolina State University, Southern University (LA), Tennessee State University, Tuskegee University (AL), University of Arkansas at Pine Bluff, University of Maryland at Eastern Shore, Virginia State University, and West Virginia State University.

Eligibility: Applicant must be high school senior. Applicant must be U.S. citizen.

Basis for selection: Major/career interest in agriculture; agribusiness; agricultural education; agricultural economics; animal sciences; botany; food science/technology; wildlife/fisheries; forestry or horticulture. Applicant must demonstrate high academic achievement, leadership and service orientation.

Application requirements: Transcript. One recommendation from school counselor and one recommendation from high school teacher. SAT/ACT scores.

Additional information: Must be seeking bachelor's degree in agriculture, food, natural resource sciences, or related disciplines. Scholarship covers full tuition and fees, plus room and board, for four years, up to $120,000. Upon completion of academic degree program, recipient has obligation of one year of service to USDA for each year of financial support. Number of awards varies depending on funding. Minimum 1000 SAT (Math and Reading; 1500 Math/Reading/Writing) or minimum 21 ACT and 3.0 GPA. Program includes summer employment. Upon successful completion of summer program, students are eligible for non-competitive transition as permanent employees. Contact designated institutions for more information and application.

Amount of award:	Full tuition
Number of applicants:	421
Application deadline:	February 1
Notification begins:	May 1
Total amount awarded:	$2,280,000

Contact:
Contact 1890 program at one or more of the designated universities.
Web: www.ascr.usda.gov/1890programs.html

U.S. Department of Education

Federal Pell Grant Program

Type of award: Scholarship, renewable.

Intended use: For undergraduate study at 2-year or 4-year institution.

Eligibility: Applicant must be U.S. citizen or permanent resident.

Basis for selection: Applicant must demonstrate financial need.

Application requirements: Proof of eligibility. FAFSA.

Additional information: Grant based on financial need, costs to attend school, and enrollment status. Must not have previously earned baccalaureate or professional degree. Amount of award varies; the maximum amount is $5,550. Visit Website for more information.

Application deadline:	June 30

Contact:
Federal Student Aid Information Center
P.O. Box 84
Washington, DC 20044-0084
Phone: 800-4-FED-AID or 800-730-8913
Web: www.studentaid.ed.gov

Federal Supplemental Educational Opportunity Grant Program

Type of award: Scholarship, renewable.

Intended use: For undergraduate study at accredited vocational, 2-year or 4-year institution in United States.

Eligibility: Applicant must be U.S. citizen or permanent resident.

Basis for selection: Applicant must demonstrate financial need.

Application requirements: Proof of eligibility. FAFSA.

Additional information: Priority given to Federal Pell Grant recipients with exceptional financial need. Must not have defaulted on federal grant or educational loan. Awards not generally made to students enrolled less than half-time. Check with institution's financial aid office for deadline.

Amount of award:	$100-$4,000

Contact:
Federal Student Aid Information Center
P.O. Box 84
Washington, DC 20044-0084
Phone: 800-4-FED-AID
Web: www.studentaid.ed.gov

Federal Work-Study Program

Type of award: Scholarship.

Intended use: For undergraduate or graduate study at accredited postsecondary institution in United States.

Eligibility: Applicant must be U.S. citizen or permanent resident.

Basis for selection: Applicant must demonstrate financial need.

Application requirements: Proof of eligibility. FAFSA.

Additional information: Part-time on-campus and off-campus jobs based on class schedule and academic progress. Students earn at least federal minimum wage. Visit Website for more information.

Application deadline:	June 30

Contact:
Federal Student Aid Information Center
P.O. Box 84
Washington, DC 20044-0084
Phone: 800-4-FED-AID
Web: www.studentaid.ed.gov

Robert C. Byrd Honors Scholarship Program

Type of award: Scholarship, renewable.
Intended use: For full-time undergraduate study at postsecondary institution in United States.
Eligibility: Applicant must be high school senior. Applicant must be U.S. citizen or permanent resident.
Basis for selection: Applicant must demonstrate high academic achievement.
Application requirements: Proof of eligibility.
Additional information: Merit-based. Renewable up to three years. Selections by state education agencies (SEAs) supervising public elementary/secondary schools. Awards made in all 50 states, District of Columbia, Puerto Rico, and insular areas. Deadlines vary by state; contact high school guidance counselor or SEA for details.

Amount of award:	$1,500

Contact:
Federal Student Aid Information Center
P.O. Box 84
Washington, DC 20044
Phone: 800-4-FED-AID
Web: www.studentaid.ed.gov

U.S. Department of Education Rehabilitation Services Administration

Vocational Rehabilitation Assistance

Type of award: Scholarship, renewable.
Intended use: For undergraduate or graduate study at postsecondary institution in United States.
Additional information: Number of awards varies; amount varies depending on institution. Award applicable to many fields/majors, but must be consistent with applicant's abilities, interest, and informed choice. Must contact state vocational rehabilitation agency to become eligible. See Website for more information.

Contact:
Rehabilitation Services Administration
400 Maryland Ave SW
PCP Room 5014
Washington, DC 20202-2800
Web: www.ed.gov/about/offices/list/osers/rsa/index.html

U.S. Department of Health and Human Services

National Health Service Corps Scholarship

Type of award: Scholarship.
Intended use: For full-time undergraduate or graduate study at accredited 4-year or graduate institution in United States.
Eligibility: Applicant must be U.S. citizen.
Basis for selection: Major/career interest in dentistry; nursing; nurse practitioner; physician assistant or midwifery. Applicant must demonstrate depth of character, seriousness of purpose and service orientation.
Application requirements: Interview, recommendations, essay, transcript, proof of eligibility. Resume, tuition bill, W-4.
Additional information: Students pursuing degree in allopathic or osteopathic medicine also eligible. Doctorate nurse training and "pre-professional" students ineligible. Awardees commit to providing health-care services in a National Health Service Corps approved site. One year of service owed for every year of scholarship support. Minimum service commitment two years; maximum four years. Award includes monthly stipend. Must be in training program. Visit Website for deadline and application.

Amount of award:	Full tuition
Number of awards:	100
Number of applicants:	1,400

Contact:
United States Department of Health and Human Services
c/o Discovery Logic
1375 Piccard Drive, Suite 360
Rockville, MD 20850
Phone: 800-638-0824
Web: www.nhsc.hrsa.gov

U.S. Environmental Protection Agency

EPA National Network for Environmental Management Studies Fellowship

Type of award: Research grant.
Intended use: For undergraduate or graduate study.
Eligibility: Applicant must be U.S. citizen or permanent resident.
Basis for selection: Major/career interest in environmental science; public relations; communications; computer/information sciences or law. Applicant must demonstrate leadership and seriousness of purpose.
Application requirements: Transcript. Resume. One-page work-plan proposal. Letter of reference from faculty member or department head familiar with student's work and qualifications; letter must discuss student's aptitude and/or experience for project.
Additional information: Program provides students with research opportunities and experience at EPA locations nationwide. NNEMS develops and distributes annual catalog listing available research opportunities for coming year.

Scholarships

Selected students receive stipend for performing research project. Projects also available in environmental management/ administration and environmental policy, regulation, and law. Undergraduate applicants must: 1) be enrolled in program directly related to pollution control or environmental protection; 2) have 3.0 GPA; 3) have already completed four courses related to environmental field. Seniors who graduate prior to completion of advertised NNEMS fellowship period ineligible unless admitted to graduate school with submittable verification. Visit Website for award information and deadline. Catalog of available research opportunities available at www.epa.gov/ education/students.html.

Number of awards:	25
Number of applicants:	345
Total amount awarded:	$316,087

Contact:
Ginger Potter, NNEMS Program, Division 1704A
Office of Environmental Education
1200 Pennsylvania Ave., NW
Washington, DC 20460
Phone: 202-564-0443
Web: www.epa.gov/enviroed/students.html

Greater Research Opportunities Undergraduate Student Fellowships

Type of award: Scholarship.
Intended use: For full-time junior or senior study at accredited 4-year institution in United States.
Eligibility: Applicant must be U.S. citizen or permanent resident.
Basis for selection: Major/career interest in life sciences; environmental science; engineering; social/behavioral sciences; physical sciences; mathematics; computer/information sciences or economics. Applicant must demonstrate financial need, high academic achievement and seriousness of purpose.
Application requirements: Recommendations, essay, transcript, proof of eligibility. Pre-application form. Resident Aliens must include green card number. EPA may verify number with the Immigration and Naturalization Service.
Additional information: Award provides funding for last two years of four-year education. Students must apply before beginning of junior year. Applicant must attend a four-year institution or be in the second year at a two-year school at the time of applying, with the intent of transferring to a four-year institution. Minimum 3.0 GPA. Fellowship provides up to $19,250 per year for two years to cover tuition and fees as well as $8,000 of internship support for a three month period. Stipends and expense allowance also provided. Recipient must complete summer internship at EPA facility between funded junior and senior years. Preference given to applicants attending academic institutions that are not highly funded for development of environmental research. See Website for link to list. Applicants must submit preapplication form first; following a merit review, top-ranked applicants will be asked to submit formal application. See Website for application and deadline.

Amount of award:	$46,500
Number of awards:	30
Total amount awarded:	$1,395,000

Contact:
U.S. Environmental Protection Agency
Peer Review Division (8703R), Ariel Rios Bldg
1200 Pennsylvania Avenue, NW
Washington, DC 20460
Phone: 800-490-9194
Web: www.epa.gov/ncer/fellow

U.S. Navy/Marine NROTC College Scholarship Program

ROTC/Navy Nurse Corps Scholarship Program

Type of award: Scholarship.
Intended use: For full-time freshman study at accredited 4-year institution in United States. Designated institutions: NROTC-approved nursing schools.
Eligibility: Applicant must be at least 17, no older than 23. Applicant must be U.S. citizen.
Basis for selection: Major/career interest in nursing. Applicant must demonstrate high academic achievement and leadership.
Application requirements: Interview, recommendations, transcript, proof of eligibility.
Additional information: Scholarships are highly competitive and based on individual merit. Scholarships pay for college tuition, fees, books, uniforms, and offer $250 monthly allowance, which increases yearly. Electronic application is first step in application process. Number of awards varies. Applicant must be medically qualified for the NROTC Scholarship Program. Minimum 530 SAT (Reading), 520 (Math); minimum 22 ACT (English), 21 (Math). Participation in extracurricular activities and work experience required. Applicants must have fewer than 30 hours college credit. Obligation of eight years commissioned service, four of which must be active duty. Contact local recruiter for more details.

Amount of award:	Full tuition
Number of applicants:	300
Application deadline:	January 31

Contact:
Contact local recruitment officer.
Phone: 800-NAV-ROTC
Web: https://www.nrotc.navy.mil

ROTC/Navy/Marine Four-Year Scholarship

Type of award: Scholarship.
Intended use: For full-time freshman study at accredited 4-year institution in United States. Designated institutions: Colleges and universities hosting NROTC program.
Eligibility: Applicant must be at least 17, no older than 23. Applicant must be U.S. citizen.
Basis for selection: Applicant must demonstrate high academic achievement and leadership.
Application requirements: Interview, recommendations, transcript, proof of eligibility.
Additional information: Scholarships are highly competitive and based on individual merit. Provide full tuition, fees, book allowance, and $250 monthly allowance, which increases annually. Number of awards varies. Applicant must be medically qualified for NROTC Scholarship. Minimum 530 SAT (Reading), 520 (Math); minimum 22 ACT (English), 21 (Math). Participation in extracurricular activities and work experience required. Applicant must have fewer than 30 hours college credit. Obligation of eight years commissioned service, five of which must be active duty. Contact nearest NROTC unit for more information. Visit Website to fill out electronic application.

Amount of award:	Full tuition
Number of applicants:	5,300
Application deadline:	January 31

Contact:
Contact your local recruitment officer.
Phone: 800-NAV-ROTC
Web: https://www.nrotc.navy.mil

ROTC/Navy/Marine Two-Year Scholarship

Type of award: Scholarship.
Intended use: For full-time junior or senior study at 4-year institution in United States. Designated institutions: Colleges and universities hosting NROTC programs.
Eligibility: Applicant must be at least 17, no older than 23. Applicant must be U.S. citizen.
Basis for selection: Applicant must demonstrate high academic achievement and leadership.
Application requirements: Interview, recommendations, transcript, proof of eligibility.
Additional information: Scholarships are highly competitive and based on individual merit. Scholarships open to students who have completed sophomore year, or third year in a five-year curriculum. NROTC scholarships pay for college tuition, fees, book allowance, uniforms, and $250 monthly allowance, which increases annually. Minimum 530 SAT (Reading), 520 (Math); minimum 22 ACT (English), 21 ACT (Math). Participation in extracurricular activities and work experience required. Total military service obligation is eight years, five of which must be active duty. Contact local NROTC unit of university you wish to attend for more information.

Amount of award:	Full tuition
Number of applicants:	100
Application deadline:	March 15

Contact:
Contact local recruitment officer.
Phone: 800-NAV-ROTC
Web: https://www.nrotc.navy.mil

USTA Tennis and Education Foundation

USTA Scholarships

Type of award: Scholarship, renewable.
Intended use: For full-time undergraduate study at accredited 2-year or 4-year institution.
Eligibility: Applicant must be high school senior.
Basis for selection: Applicant must demonstrate financial need, high academic achievement, leadership and seriousness of purpose.
Application requirements: Interview, recommendations, essay, transcript. Photograph, FAFSA or SAR, ACT/SAT reports.
Additional information: Applicant must have participated in USTA or other organized youth tennis program. The USTA offers six scholarship programs. Amount and number of awards vary. Applications available online and must be mailed to local USTA Section office. Visit Website for application, deadline, and individual scholarship requirements.

Amount of award:	$1,000-$15,000
Number of awards:	76
Total amount awarded:	$379,000

Contact:
United States Tennis Association
70 West Red Oak Lane
White Plains, NY 10604
Phone: 914-696-7000
Web: www.usta.com

Utah Higher Education Assistance Authority (UHEAA)

Leveraging Educational Assistance Partnership (LEAP)

Type of award: Scholarship, renewable.
Intended use: For undergraduate study in United States. Designated institutions: Participating Utah public institutions.
Eligibility: Applicant must be residing in Utah.
Basis for selection: Applicant must demonstrate financial need.
Application requirements: FAFSA.
Additional information: Allocations made to participating Utah institutions. Contact participating institution's financial aid office.

Amount of award:	$300-$2,500
Number of awards:	3,343
Number of applicants:	3,343
Total amount awarded:	$1,743,173

Contact:
Contact institution's financial aid office.

UHEAA Grant

Type of award: Scholarship, renewable.
Intended use: For undergraduate or graduate study at 4-year or graduate institution in United States. Designated institutions: Participating Utah institutions.
Eligibility: Applicant must be residing in Utah.
Basis for selection: Applicant must demonstrate financial need.
Application requirements: Nomination by participating institution's financial aid director.
Additional information: Awards range from $300 to $2,800 for undergraduates; $300 to $4,500 for graduates. Awards are made by individual institutions from allotments from UHEAA as part of campus-based financial aid. Contact institution for deadlines.

Amount of award:	$300-$4,500
Number of awards:	871
Number of applicants:	519
Total amount awarded:	$415,228

Contact:
Contact participating institution's financial aid office.

Utah Centennial Opportunity Program for Education (UCOPE)

Type of award: Scholarship, renewable.
Intended use: For undergraduate study at postsecondary institution.
Eligibility: Applicant must be residing in Utah.

Basis for selection: Applicant must demonstrate financial need.

Application requirements: FAFSA.

Additional information: Allocations are made to participating Utah institutions. Contact participating institution's financial aid office.

Amount of award:	$300-$5,000
Number of awards:	7,375
Number of applicants:	6,288
Total amount awarded:	$5,257,309

Contact:
Contact institution's financial aid office.

Utah State Office of Education

Utah Robert C. Byrd Honors Scholarship

Type of award: Scholarship, renewable.

Intended use: For full-time undergraduate study in United States.

Eligibility: Applicant must be high school senior. Applicant must be U.S. citizen residing in Utah.

Basis for selection: Applicant must demonstrate high academic achievement.

Application requirements: Transcript. SAT or ACT scores. Proof of U.S. citizenship. College or university acceptance letter.

Additional information: Minimum 3.7 GPA. Minimum 25 ACT score or 1940 SAT score. Home-schooled students also eligible. Contact high school counselor or financial aid adviser after January for application, or see Website. Deadline in late March.

Amount of award:	$1,500
Number of awards:	62
Number of applicants:	500
Notification begins:	June 30
Total amount awarded:	$384,000

Contact:
The Robert C. Byrd Scholarship
Utah State Office of Education
250 East 500 South, P.O. Box 144200
Salt Lake City, UT 84114-4200
Web: www.schools.utah.gov/curr/Early_College/Byrd.htm

The Vegetarian Resource Group

The Vegetarian Resource Group College Scholarships

Type of award: Scholarship.

Intended use: For freshman study at postsecondary institution in United States.

Eligibility: Applicant must be high school senior. Applicant must be U.S. citizen.

Application requirements: Essay.

Additional information: Award for graduating high school students who have promoted vegetarianism or veganism in their schools or communities. Students will be judged on having shown compassion, courage and a strong commitment to promoting a peaceful world through a vegetarian or vegan diet/lifestyle. Visit Website for application information.

Amount of award:	$5,000
Number of awards:	2
Number of applicants:	200
Application deadline:	February 20
Total amount awarded:	$10,000

Contact:
The Vegetarian Resource Group
P.O. Box 1463
Baltimore, MD 21203
Phone: 410-366-8343
Web: www.vrg.org

Ventura County Japanese-American Citizens League

Ventura County Japanese-American Citizens League Scholarships

Type of award: Scholarship.

Intended use: For freshman study at vocational, 2-year, 4-year or graduate institution in United States.

Eligibility: Applicant must be high school senior. Applicant must be Japanese. Applicant must be U.S. citizen residing in California.

Application requirements: Recommendations, essay, transcript, proof of eligibility. SAT scores.

Additional information: Applicant must be a Ventura County high school senior and a member of the Japanese American Citizens League. Amount and number of awards depend on available funding. Visit Website for application.

Application deadline:	April 1
Total amount awarded:	$10,000

Contact:
Ventura County JACL Scholarship Committee
P.O. Box 1092
Camarillo, CA 93011
Phone: 805-498-0764
Web: www.vcjacl.org

Vermont Golf Association Scholarship Fund, Inc.

Vermont Golf Association Scholarship

Type of award: Scholarship, renewable.

Intended use: For full-time undergraduate study at 2-year or 4-year institution.

Eligibility: Applicant must be high school senior. Applicant must be permanent resident residing in Vermont.

Application requirements: Interview, recommendations, transcript. FAFSA.

Additional information: Must be graduate of Vermont high school and in top 40 percent of class or have GPA of 3.0 and 1500 SAT. Students of Hanover High School, NH, Riverdell Interstate School District, NH, and Grandville High School, NY, are also eligible. Applicant must have valid connection to golf.

Amount of award:	$1,000
Number of awards:	10
Number of applicants:	38
Application deadline:	April 20
Total amount awarded:	$10,000

Contact:
Vermont Golf Association Scholarship Fund
P.O. Box 1612
Station A
Rutland, VT 05701
Phone: 802-775-7837
Fax: 802-773-7182
Web: www.vtga.org

Vermont Student Assistance Corporation

AIWF Culinary Scholarship

Type of award: Scholarship.
Intended use: For undergraduate study at accredited postsecondary institution. Designated institutions: Institutions approved for federal Title IV funding.
Eligibility: Applicant must be U.S. citizen or permanent resident residing in Vermont.
Basis for selection: Major/career interest in culinary arts. Applicant must demonstrate financial need.
Application requirements: Recommendations, essay. Personal interview (if necessary).
Additional information: Must attend school at least three-quarters time. Deadline in early March.

Amount of award:	$2,500
Number of awards:	1
Number of applicants:	18

Contact:
VSAC Scholarships Program
10 East Allen Street
P.O. Box 2000
Winooski, VT 05404
Phone: 888-253-4819
Web: www.vsac.org/scholarships

Alfred T. Granger Student Art Fund

Type of award: Scholarship.
Intended use: For undergraduate or graduate study at accredited postsecondary institution. Designated institutions: Institutions approved for federal Title IV funding.
Eligibility: Applicant must be U.S. citizen or permanent resident residing in Vermont.
Basis for selection: Major/career interest in architecture; interior design; arts, general or design. Applicant must demonstrate financial need and high academic achievement.
Application requirements: Portfolio, recommendations.
Additional information: Architectural engineering, lighting design, and mechanical drawing (CAD) majors also eligible. Four awards of $2,500 each for undergraduates and two $5,000 awards for graduate students. Deadline in early March.

Amount of award:	$2,500-$5,000
Number of awards:	6
Number of applicants:	57

Contact:
VSAC Scholarships Program
10 East Allen Road
P.O. Box 2000
Winooski, VT 05404
Phone: 888-253-4819
Web: www.vsac.org/scholarships

Calvin Coolidge Memorial Foundation Scholarship

Type of award: Scholarship.
Intended use: For undergraduate study at accredited postsecondary institution. Designated institutions: Institutions approved for federal Title IV funding.
Eligibility: Applicant must be U.S. citizen or permanent resident residing in Vermont.
Basis for selection: Major/career interest in archaeology; anthropology; criminal justice/law enforcement; economics; geography; history; international relations; philosophy; political science/government or psychology. Applicant must demonstrate high academic achievement and service orientation.
Application requirements: Recommendations, essay.
Additional information: Must be enrolled at least three-quarters time. Social work, sociology, urban studies, and other social science majors also eligible. Deadline in early March.

Amount of award:	$1,000
Number of awards:	1
Number of applicants:	195

Contact:
VSAC Scholarships Program
10 East Allen Street
P.O. Box 2000
Winooski, VT 05404
Phone: 888-253-4819
Web: www.vsac.org/scholarships

Champlain Valley Kennel Club Scholarship

Type of award: Scholarship.
Intended use: For full-time undergraduate or graduate study at accredited postsecondary institution. Designated institutions: Institutions approved for federal Title IV funding.
Eligibility: Applicant must be residing in Vermont.
Basis for selection: Major/career interest in veterinary medicine. Applicant must demonstrate financial need and high academic achievement.
Application requirements: Recommendations, essay, transcript. FAFSA.
Additional information: Graduating high school seniors also eligible. Applicant must have been Vermont resident for at least five years at time of application.

Amount of award:	$250
Number of awards:	1
Number of applicants:	20
Application deadline:	May 10

Contact:
Pamela Parshall CVKC Scholarship Chair
77 Range Road
Underhill, VT 05489-9410
Phone: 802-899-2994
Web: www.vsac.org

Charles E. Leonard Memorial Scholarship

Type of award: Scholarship.
Intended use: For undergraduate or graduate study at accredited postsecondary institution. Designated institutions: Institutions approved for federal Title IV funding.
Eligibility: Applicant of parent must be visually impaired. Applicant must be U.S. citizen or permanent resident residing in Vermont.
Basis for selection: Applicant must demonstrate financial need and high academic achievement.
Application requirements: Essay.
Additional information: Applicants pursuing career in education/rehabilitation of blind or visually impaired people also eligible. Deadline in early March.

Amount of award:	$500
Number of awards:	4
Number of applicants:	8

Contact:
VSAC Scholarships Program
10 East Allen Street
P.O. Box 2000
Winooski, VT 05404
Phone: 888-253-4819
Web: www.vsac.org

Chittenden Bank Scholarship

Type of award: Scholarship, renewable.
Intended use: For full-time freshman study at accredited 2-year or 4-year institution in United States. Designated institutions: Vermont postsecondary schools approved for federal Title IV funding.
Eligibility: Applicant must be high school senior. Applicant must be residing in Vermont.
Basis for selection: Applicant must demonstrate financial need, high academic achievement and service orientation.
Application requirements: Recommendations, essay.
Additional information: Minimum 3.0 GPA. Deadline in early March.

Amount of award:	$2,500
Number of awards:	2
Number of applicants:	305

Contact:
VSAC Scholarships Program
10 East Allen Street
P.O. Box 2000
Winooski, VT 05404
Phone: 888-253-4819
Web: www.vsac.org/scholarships

Emily Lester Vermont Opportunity Scholarship

Type of award: Scholarship, renewable.
Intended use: For undergraduate study at accredited postsecondary institution. Designated institutions: Vermont schools approved for federal Title IV funding.
Eligibility: Applicant must be residing in Vermont.
Basis for selection: Applicant must demonstrate financial need.
Application requirements: Proof of eligibility.
Additional information: Applicant must be under the custody of the Vermont commissioner of social and rehabilitation services or be between the ages of 18 and 24 and have been under the custody of the commissioner for at least six months between ages 16 and 18. Graduating high school seniors also eligible. Deadline in early March.

Amount of award:	$1,000-$3,000
Total amount awarded:	$22,500

Contact:
VSAC Scholarship Program
10 East Allen Street
P.O. Box 2000
Winooski, VT 05404
Phone: 888-253-4819
Web: www.vsac.org/scholarships

Jedidiah Zabrosky Scholarship

Type of award: Scholarship.
Intended use: For full-time undergraduate study at 2-year or 4-year institution in United States. Designated institutions: Castleton State College, Lyndon State College, Johnson State College, Community College of Vermont, Vermont Technical College, University of Vermont.
Eligibility: Applicant must be residing in Vermont.
Basis for selection: Major/career interest in business or education. Applicant must demonstrate financial need, high academic achievement and service orientation.
Application requirements: Recommendations, essay.
Additional information: Minimum 2.5 GPA. Applicant must be employed at time of application working minimum ten hours per week. Deadline in early March.

Amount of award:	$2,000
Number of awards:	1
Number of applicants:	40

Contact:
VSAC Scholarships Progam
10 East Allen Street
P.O. Box 2000
Winooski, VT 05404
Phone: 888-253-4819
Web: www.vsac.org/scholarships

Kittredge Coddington Memorial Scholarship

Type of award: Scholarship.
Intended use: For undergraduate study at accredited postsecondary institution. Designated institutions: Vermont institutions approved for federal Title IV funding.
Eligibility: Applicant must be enrolled in high school. Applicant must be U.S. citizen or permanent resident residing in Vermont.
Basis for selection: Major/career interest in business; business, international or business/management/administration.
Application requirements: Recommendations, essay.
Additional information: Must be planning career in business or industry. One award to female, one to male. Deadline in early March.

Amount of award:	$500
Number of awards:	1
Number of applicants:	55

Contact:
VSAC Scholarships Program
10 East Allen Street
P.O. Box 2000
Winooski, VT 05404
Phone: 888-253-4819
Web: www.vsac.org/scholarships

Lee A. Lyman Memorial Music Scholarship

Type of award: Scholarship.
Intended use: For undergraduate or graduate study at accredited postsecondary institution. Designated institutions: Institutions approved for federal Title IV funding.
Eligibility: Applicant must be U.S. citizen or permanent resident residing in Vermont.
Basis for selection: Major/career interest in music. Applicant must demonstrate financial need and high academic achievement.
Application requirements: Recommendations, essay.
Additional information: Must demonstrate participation in music-related activities, performances, or groups. Deadline in early March.

Amount of award:	$1,000
Number of awards:	4
Number of applicants:	34
Total amount awarded:	$4,000

Contact:
VSAC Scholarships Program
10 East Allen Street
P.O. Box 2000
Winooski, VT 05404
Phone: 888-253-4819
Web: www.vsac.org/scholarships

Operation Enduring Freedom and Operation Iraqi Freedom Scholarship

Type of award: Scholarship, renewable.
Intended use: For full-time undergraduate study at accredited 4-year institution. Designated institutions: Schools approved for federal Title IV funding.
Eligibility: Applicant must be U.S. citizen or permanent resident residing in Vermont. Applicant must be dependent of active service person, veteran, disabled veteran or deceased veteran who serves or served in the Army, Air Force, Marines, Navy, Coast Guard or Reserves/National Guard. For dependents of those who served in Operation Iraqi Freedom or Operation Enduring Freedom. Preference given to those whose parent was killed, wounded, or permanently disabled as result of service.
Basis for selection: Applicant must demonstrate financial need.
Application requirements: Recommendations, essay.
Additional information: Deadline in early March.

Amount of award:	$3,500-$7,000
Number of awards:	14
Number of applicants:	25

Contact:
VSAC Scholarships Program
10 East Allen Street
P.O. Box 2000
Winooski, VT 05404
Phone: 888-253-4819
Web: www.vsac.org/scholarships

Patrick and Judith McHugh Scholarship

Type of award: Scholarship.
Intended use: For undergraduate or graduate study at accredited postsecondary institution. Designated institutions: Institutions approved for federal Title IV funding.

Eligibility: Applicant must be U.S. citizen or permanent resident residing in Vermont.
Basis for selection: Major/career interest in health-related professions; dentistry; medicine; mental health/therapy; nursing; pharmacy/pharmaceutics/pharmacology or psychology. Applicant must demonstrate financial need.
Application requirements: Recommendations, essay.
Additional information: Must be enrolled at least three-quarters time. Deadline in early March.

Amount of award:	$1,000
Number of awards:	1
Number of applicants:	260

Contact:
VSAC Scholarships Program
10 East Allen Street
P.O. Box 2000
Winooski, VT 05404
Phone: 888-253-4819
Web: www.vsac.org/scholarships

Philip and Alice Angell Eastern Star Scholarship

Type of award: Scholarship.
Intended use: For undergraduate study at accredited 2-year or 4-year institution. Designated institutions: Postsecondary institutions approved for federal Title IV funding.
Eligibility: Applicant must be residing in Vermont.
Basis for selection: Major/career interest in business or education. Applicant must demonstrate financial need and high academic achievement.
Application requirements: Recommendations, essay.
Additional information: Minimum 3.5 GPA. Graduating high school seniors eligible. Deadline in early March.

Amount of award:	$500
Number of awards:	1
Number of applicants:	118

Contact:
VSAC Scholarships Program
10 East Allen Street
P.O. Box 2000
Winooski, VT 05404
Phone: 888-253-4819
Web: www.vsac.org/scholarships

RehabGYM Scholarship

Type of award: Scholarship.
Intended use: For undergraduate study at accredited postsecondary institution. Designated institutions: Institutions approved for federal Title IV funding.
Eligibility: Applicant must be physically challenged. Applicant must be U.S. citizen or permanent resident residing in Vermont.
Basis for selection: Applicant must demonstrate financial need.
Application requirements: Essay.
Additional information: Must be enrolled at least three-quarters time. Must have overcome significant physical challenge or illness. Deadline in early March.

Amount of award:	$1,000
Number of awards:	1
Number of applicants:	47

Contact:
VSAC Scholarships Program
10 East Allen Street
P.O. Box 2000
Winooski, VT 05404
Phone: 888-253-4819
Web: www.vsac.org/scholarships

Samara Foundation of Vermont Scholarship

Type of award: Scholarship.
Intended use: For undergraduate study at vocational, 2-year or 4-year institution.
Eligibility: Applicant must be high school senior. Applicant must be residing in Vermont.
Basis for selection: Competition/talent/interest in gay/lesbian.
Application requirements: Recommendations, essay.
Additional information: Applicant must demonstrate, through personal experience and/or public commitment, dedication to the interests of the gay, lesbian, bisexual, transgendered, and questioning community. Up to $5,000 is awarded annually. Deadline in early March.

Number of awards:	3
Number of applicants:	15

Contact:
VSAC Scholarships Programs
10 East Allen Street
P.O. Box 2000
Winooski, VT 05404
Phone: 888-253-4819
Web: www.vsac.org/scholarships

Students With Disabilities Endowed Scholarship Honoring Elizabeth Daley Jeffords

Type of award: Scholarship.
Intended use: For undergraduate study at accredited postsecondary institution. Designated institutions: Institutions approved for federal Title IV funding.
Eligibility: Applicant must be visually impaired, hearing impaired, physically challenged or learning disabled. Applicant must be U.S. citizen or permanent resident residing in Vermont.
Basis for selection: Applicant must demonstrate financial need and seriousness of purpose.
Application requirements: Recommendations, essay, proof of eligibility. Personal interview (if necessary).
Additional information: Number of awards varies. Deadline in early March.

Amount of award:	$1,500
Number of awards:	1
Number of applicants:	58

Contact:
VSAC Scholarships Program
10 East Allen Street
P.O. Box 2000
Winooski, VT 05404
Phone: 888-253-4819
Web: www.vsac.org/scholarships

Vermont Alliance for Arts Education (VAEE) Scholarship

Type of award: Scholarship.

Intended use: For undergraduate study at accredited postsecondary institution. Designated institutions: Institutions approved for federal Title IV funding.
Eligibility: Applicant must be high school senior. Applicant must be U.S. citizen or permanent resident residing in Vermont.
Basis for selection: Major/career interest in arts, general; dance; music or theater arts. Applicant must demonstrate financial need and high academic achievement.
Application requirements: Portfolio, recommendations, essay.
Additional information: Recipients may be invited to perform and/or exhibit at VAAE functions. Deadline in early March.

Amount of award:	$500
Number of awards:	4
Number of applicants:	35

Contact:
VSAC Scholarships Program
10 East Allen Street
P.O. Box 2000
Winooski, VT 05404
Phone: 888-253-4819
Web: www.vsac.org/scholarships

Vermont Incentive Grant

Type of award: Scholarship.
Intended use: For full-time undergraduate study in United States.
Eligibility: Applicant must be U.S. citizen or permanent resident residing in Vermont.
Basis for selection: Applicant must demonstrate financial need.
Application requirements: Proof of eligibility. FAFSA.
Additional information: Must not yet have bachelor's degree. Vermont residents who attend Vermont College of Medicine or who are enrolled in Doctor of Veterinary Science program also eligible. Application may be completed online.

Amount of award:	$500-$10,800
Number of applicants:	15,825
Total amount awarded:	$16,521,900

Contact:
Grant Department
VSAC
P.O. Box 2000
Winooski, VT 05404
Phone: 800-882-4166 or 802-654-3750
Web: www.vsac.org

Vermont John H. Chafee Education and Training Scholarship

Type of award: Scholarship.
Intended use: For undergraduate study at accredited vocational, 2-year or 4-year institution. Designated institutions: Institutions approved for federal Title IV funding.
Eligibility: Applicant must be no older than 21. Applicant must be U.S. citizen or permanent resident residing in Vermont.
Basis for selection: Applicant must demonstrate financial need.
Additional information: Must be under custody of Vermont Commissioner of the Department for Children and Families (DCF) through eighteenth birthday or be adopted after age 16. Deadline in early March.

Amount of award:	$1,000-$5,000

Contact:
VSAC Scholarships Program
10 East Allen Street
P.O. Box 2000
Winooski, VT 05404
Phone: 888-253-4819
Web: www.vsac.org/scholarships

Vermont Non-Degree Program

Type of award: Scholarship.
Intended use: For non-degree study at postsecondary institution in United States.
Eligibility: Applicant must be permanent resident residing in Vermont.
Basis for selection: Applicant must demonstrate financial need.
Application requirements: Proof of eligibility.
Additional information: Award amount varies. Applicants must be enrolled in non-degree course that will improve employability or encourage further study. Applications available at Vermont Department of Employment and Training offices, schools and vocation centers, and VSAC.

Number of applicants:	1,290
Total amount awarded:	$645,732

Contact:
Grant Department
VSAC
P.O. Box 2000
Winooski, VT 05404
Phone: 800-882-4166 or 802-654-3750
Web: www.vsac.org

Vermont Part-Time Grant

Type of award: Scholarship.
Intended use: For half-time undergraduate study at vocational, 2-year or 4-year institution in United States.
Eligibility: Applicant must be permanent resident residing in Vermont.
Basis for selection: Applicant must demonstrate financial need.
Application requirements: Proof of eligibility. FAFSA.
Additional information: Must be taking fewer than 12 credits and not yet received bachelor's degree. Award amounts vary according to number of credits.

Number of applicants:	3,743
Total amount awarded:	$1,016,909

Contact:
Grant Department
VSAC
P.O. Box 2000
Winooski, VT 05404
Phone: 800-882-4166 or 802-654-3750
Web: www.vsac.org

Veterans of Foreign Wars

Voice of Democracy Scholarship

Type of award: Scholarship.
Intended use: For undergraduate or graduate study at postsecondary institution in United States.
Eligibility: Applicant must be enrolled in high school.

Application requirements: Audiotape or CD of essay. Participants are judged by tape or CD, not written essay script.
Additional information: Student must be 19 or younger to apply. Must apply through high school or local Veterans of Foreign Wars post. Not all VFW posts participate in program. Any entry submitted to VFW National Headquarters will be returned to sender. Selection based on interpretation of assigned patriotic theme, content, and presentation of recorded 3-5 minute audio-essay. Visit Website for additional information and application form. Award is non-renewable.

Amount of award:	$1,000-$30,000
Number of awards:	60
Number of applicants:	80,000
Application deadline:	November 1
Total amount awarded:	$146,000

Contact:
Veterans of Foreign Wars National Headquarters
Voice of Democracy Program
406 West 34 Street
Kansas City, MO 64111
Phone: 816-968-1117
Fax: 816-968-1149
Web: www.vfw.org

Virgin Islands Board of Education

Virgin Islands Leveraging Educational Assistance Partnership Program

Type of award: Scholarship, renewable.
Intended use: For full-time undergraduate or graduate study at postsecondary institution.
Eligibility: Applicant must be U.S. citizen or permanent resident residing in Virgin Islands.
Basis for selection: Applicant must demonstrate financial need.
Application requirements: Transcript. Acceptance letter from institution for first-time applicants or transfer students.
Additional information: Minimum 2.0 GPA. Number of awards varies.

Amount of award:	$500-$5,000
Number of applicants:	50
Application deadline:	May 1

Contact:
Virgin Islands Board of Education Financial Aid Office
P.O. Box 11900
St. Thomas, VI 00801
Phone: 340-774-4546

Virgin Islands Music Scholarship

Type of award: Scholarship, renewable.
Intended use: For full-time undergraduate study at accredited 2-year or 4-year institution in United States.
Eligibility: Applicant must be high school senior. Applicant must be U.S. citizen or permanent resident residing in Virgin Islands.
Basis for selection: Major/career interest in music. Applicant must demonstrate financial need.
Application requirements: Transcript. Acceptance letter from college or university if first-time applicant.

Additional information: Minimum 2.0 GPA.

Amount of award:	$2,000
Number of awards:	8
Number of applicants:	20
Application deadline:	May 1
Total amount awarded:	$16,000

Contact:
Virgin Islands Board of Education Financial Aid Office
P.O. Box 11900
St. Thomas, VI 00801
Phone: 340-774-4546

Virginia Department of Education

Virginia Lee-Jackson Scholarship

Type of award: Scholarship.

Intended use: For full-time freshman study at accredited 2-year or 4-year institution in United States.

Eligibility: Applicant must be high school junior or senior. Applicant must be residing in Virginia.

Basis for selection: Competition/talent/interest in writing/ journalism.

Application requirements: Essay demonstrating appreciation for virtues exemplified by General Robert E. Lee or General "Stonewall" Jackson.

Additional information: Award amount varies depending on essay. Additional awards for exceptional essays. Students must submit essay and application form to high school principal or guidance counselor. Application deadline is generally in mid-December. Community college awardees must plan to enroll in their college's transfer program. See Website for more information.

Amount of award:	$1,000-$10,000
Number of awards:	27
Total amount awarded:	$44,000

Contact:
The Lee-Jackson Foundation
P.O. Box 8121
Charlottesville, VA 22906
Phone: 434-977-1861
Web: www.lee-jackson.org

Virginia Robert C. Byrd Honors Scholarship

Type of award: Scholarship, renewable.

Intended use: For full-time undergraduate study at accredited postsecondary institution in United States.

Eligibility: Applicant must be high school senior. Applicant must be U.S. citizen or permanent resident residing in Virginia.

Basis for selection: Applicant must demonstrate high academic achievement and service orientation.

Application requirements: Recommendations, transcript, nomination by high school. SAT/ACT scores. Must file a Statement of Selective Service Registration Status.

Additional information: Students with a GED are also eligible. Application and information sent to principals of public and private high schools in February. Number of awards varies; 180-210 expected in 2010. Award renewable for three years during first four years of higher education. Visit Website for application. Deadline in early April.

Amount of award:	$1,500
Number of applicants:	320
Total amount awarded:	$1,027,750

Contact:
Robert C. Byrd Scholarships
CTE Resource Center Robert C. Byrd Scholarsh
2002 Bremo Road, Lower Level
Richmond, VA 23226
Phone: 804-786-9377
Fax: 804-786-5466
Web: www.doe.virginia.gov

Virginia Department of Health

Mary Marshall Nursing LPN Scholarship

Type of award: Scholarship.

Intended use: For full-time undergraduate study. Designated institutions: Virginia nursing schools.

Eligibility: Applicant must be U.S. citizen or permanent resident residing in Virginia.

Basis for selection: Major/career interest in nursing. Applicant must demonstrate financial need.

Application requirements: Recommendations, transcript. FAFSA.

Additional information: Award amount varies. Provides awards to students who agree to work in nursing profession in Virginia at rate of one month for every $100 of aid received. Must reside in Virginia at least one year prior to application. Recipient may reapply for up to four succeeding years. Applications and guidelines available from dean or financial aid office at applicant's nursing school, or from address listed.

Amount of award:	$200-$500
Number of awards:	91
Application deadline:	June 30

Contact:
Virginia Department of Health Minority Health & Public Health Policy
109 Governor Street
Suite 1016-E
Richmond, VA 23219
Phone: 804-864-7435
Web: www.vdh.virginia.gov

Nurse Pracitioner Nurse Midwife Scholarship

Type of award: Scholarship.

Intended use: For full-time undergraduate study at postsecondary institution. Designated institutions: Institutions in Virginia.

Eligibility: Applicant must be residing in Virginia.

Basis for selection: Major/career interest in nurse practitioner. Applicant must demonstrate high academic achievement and depth of character.

Application requirements: Recommendations, transcript.

Additional information: Applicant must commit to post-graduate employment in a medically underserved area of Virginia, in a setting that provides services to persons unable to pay and participates in all government-sponsored insurance programs. Employment must last for number of years equal to the number of annual scholarships received. If work commitment is not fulfilled or student does not complete studies, the award amount converts to loan. Minimum 3.0 GPA. Award amount and number of awards varies.

Amount of award:	$5,000
Number of awards:	5
Application deadline:	July 31
Notification begins:	September 15
Total amount awarded:	$25,000

Contact:
Virginia Department of Health Minority Health & Public Policy Office
109 Governor Street
Suite 1016-E
Richmond, VA 23219
Phone: 804-864-7435
Web: www.vdh.virginia.gov

Virginia Department of Rehabilitative Services

Virginia Rehabilitative Services College Program

Type of award: Scholarship.
Intended use: For undergraduate study at postsecondary institution.
Eligibility: Applicant must be visually impaired, hearing impaired, physically challenged or learning disabled. Applicant must be residing in Virginia.
Basis for selection: Applicant must demonstrate financial need.
Application requirements: Proof of eligibility. Proof must be furnished at least 60 days before start of school or educational program.
Additional information: Applicant must have a disability and an employment goal. This program is not a true scholarship, but rather a source of funding for eligible individuals if need remains after other federal, state, and private sources are used. Program provides vocational rehabilitation and related services to Virginians with disabilities in order to foster the skills necessary to achieve greater self-sufficiency, independence, and employment. Contact nearest Department of Rehabilitative Services office or visit Website for numbers.
Contact:
Virginia Department of Rehabilitative Services
8004 Franklin Farms Drive
Richmond, VA 23229
Phone: 804-662-7000
Web: www.vadrs.org

Virginia Museum of Fine Arts

Virginia Museum of Fine Arts Fellowship

Type of award: Scholarship, renewable.

Intended use: For full-time undergraduate or graduate study at accredited 4-year or graduate institution.
Eligibility: Applicant must be U.S. citizen or permanent resident residing in Virginia.
Basis for selection: Major/career interest in arts, general; film/video or art/art history. Applicant must demonstrate financial need.
Application requirements: Portfolio, transcript. Eight images on CD representing recent work or three of the following: 16mm or video format films, videos, DVD, research papers, or published articles. References.
Additional information: May apply in one of the following categories on the undergraduate or graduate level: crafts, drawing, sculpture, filmmaking, painting, photography, printmaking, video. Candidates in art history may apply on the graduate level only. Visit Website for guidelines and application.

Amount of award:	$2,000-$8,000
Number of awards:	35
Number of applicants:	587
Application deadline:	November 12
Notification begins:	February 1
Total amount awarded:	$202,000

Contact:
Virginia Museum of Fine Arts Fellowships
Statewide Partnerships
200 N. Boulevard
Richmond, VA 23220-4007
Phone: 804-204-2670
Fax: 804-204-2675
Web: www.vmfa.museum

Wal-Mart Foundation

Higher REACH Scholarship

Type of award: Scholarship.
Intended use: For undergraduate study at accredited 2-year or 4-year institution in United States.
Eligibility: Applicant must be U.S. citizen or permanent resident.
Basis for selection: Applicant must demonstrate financial need and leadership.
Additional information: Awarded to nontraditional students who have been employed by Wal-Mart Stores, Inc. for at least six months. Award amount varies depending on part-time or full-time enrollment. Students enrolled in a two-year program receive up to $2,000; students enrolled in a four-year program receive up to $3,000. Applicants must be out of high school for one year. Must maintain 2.0 GPA to renew. Visit Website for application and deadline.

Amount of award:	$500-$3,000
Application deadline:	January 29

Contact:
Higher Reach Scholarship, Wal-Mart Scholarship Program
301 ACT Drive
P.O. Box 4030
Iowa City, IA 52243-4030
Phone: 877-333-0284
Fax: 319-337-1204
Web: www.walmartstores.com/communitygiving

Sam Walton Community Scholarship

Type of award: Scholarship.
Intended use: For full-time freshman study at accredited 2-year or 4-year institution in United States.
Eligibility: Applicant must be high school senior. Applicant must be U.S. citizen or permanent resident.
Basis for selection: Applicant must demonstrate financial need, high academic achievement and leadership.
Application requirements: Transcript, proof of eligibility. ACT/SAT scores, list of school/community/extracurricular involvement and work experience.
Additional information: Applicant must not be an employee of Wal-Mart Stores, Inc., or child/dependent of an employee. Applications available first week of November on Website. Minimum 2.5 GPA. Student must have his/her local Sam's Club or Wal-Mart store's 4-digit location number to apply. Deadline varies, visit Website for details.

Amount of award:	$3,000
Number of awards:	2,500
Number of applicants:	42,564
Application deadline:	January 29

Contact:
Sam Walton Community Scholarship, Wal-Mart Scholarship Program
301 ACT Drive
P.O. Box 4030
Iowa City, IA 52243-4030
Phone: 887-333-0284
Fax: 319-337-1204
Web: www.walmartstores.com/communitygiving

Wal-Mart Associate Scholarship

Type of award: Scholarship.
Intended use: For full-time undergraduate study at accredited 2-year or 4-year institution in United States.
Eligibility: Applicant or parent must be employed by Wal-Mart Stores, Inc. Applicant must be high school senior. Applicant must be U.S. citizen or permanent resident.
Basis for selection: Applicant must demonstrate financial need and high academic achievement.
Application requirements: Transcript, proof of eligibility. SAT/ACT scores and financial data.
Additional information: Award for Wal-Mart employees and their dependents who are not eligible for the Walton Foundation Scholarship. Employee must have been working at Wal-Mart for at least six consecutive months. Minimum 2.5 GPA. Minimum 18 ACT or 800 SAT. Visit Website for application and deadline information.

Amount of award:	$3,000
Number of awards:	26
Number of applicants:	2,600
Application deadline:	January 29

Contact:
Wal-Mart Associate Scholarship, Wal-Mart Scholarship Program
301 ACT Drive
P.O. Box 4030
Iowa City, IA 52243-4030
Phone: 877-333-0284
Fax: 319-337-1204
Web: www.walmartstores.com/communitygiving

Walton Family Foundation Scholarship

Type of award: Scholarship.
Intended use: For full-time undergraduate study at accredited 2-year or 4-year institution.
Eligibility: Applicant must be high school senior. Applicant must be U.S. citizen or permanent resident.
Basis for selection: Applicant must demonstrate financial need and high academic achievement.
Application requirements: Transcript, proof of eligibility. SAT/ACT scores and financial data.
Additional information: Award is $13,000 payable over four years. Applicant's parent or guardian must have been employed with Wal-Mart full-time (32 hours/week) for at least one year. Minimum 22 ACT or 1030 SAT. Maintenance of 3.0 GPA required for renewal. Recipients attending two-year institutions must agree to transfer to four-year institution by beginning of third academic year. Visit Website for application and deadline.

Amount of award:	$13,000
Number of awards:	150
Number of applicants:	800
Application deadline:	January 29
Total amount awarded:	$960,000

Contact:
Walton Family Foundation Scholarship, Wal-Mart Scholarship Program
301 ACT Drive
P.O. Box 4030
Iowa City, IA 52243-4030
Phone: 877-333-0284
Fax: 319-337-1204
Web: www.walmartstores.com/communitygiving

Washington Crossing Foundation

Washington Crossing Foundation Scholarship

Type of award: Scholarship.
Intended use: For full-time undergraduate study at accredited 4-year institution.
Eligibility: Applicant must be high school senior. Applicant must be U.S. citizen residing in Pennsylvania.
Basis for selection: Major/career interest in political science/government or public administration/service. Applicant must demonstrate high academic achievement, depth of character, leadership, patriotism, seriousness of purpose and service orientation.
Application requirements: Recommendations, transcript. Essay on why student is planning a career in government service, including any inspiration derived from Washington's famous crossing of the Delaware. SAT/ACT scores.
Additional information: Number of awards varies.

Amount of award:	$1,000-$5,000
Application deadline:	January 15
Notification begins:	June 30
Total amount awarded:	$42,000

Contact:
Washington Crossing Foundation
Attn: Vice Chairman
P.O. Box 503
Levittown, PA 19058
Phone: 215-949-8841
Web: www.gwcf.org

Washington State Higher Education Coordinating Board

Washington State American Indian Endowed Scholarship

Type of award: Scholarship.
Intended use: For full-time undergraduate or graduate study at accredited vocational, 2-year, 4-year or graduate institution.
Eligibility: Applicant must be U.S. citizen residing in Washington.
Basis for selection: Applicant must demonstrate financial need, high academic achievement and service orientation.
Application requirements: Recommendations, essay, transcript, proof of eligibility. FAFSA.
Additional information: Must have close social and cultural ties to American Indian community within Washington State and strong commitment to return service to state's American Indian community. Applicants pursuing degree in theology not eligible.

Amount of award:	$500-$2,000
Number of awards:	15
Application deadline:	February 1
Notification begins:	March 1

Contact:
Washington State Higher Education Coordinating Board
917 Lakeridge Way
P.O. Box 43430
Olympia, WA 98504-3430
Phone: 360-753-7843
Web: www.hecb.wa.gov

Washington State Need Grant

Type of award: Scholarship, renewable.
Intended use: For undergraduate study at accredited vocational, 2-year or 4-year institution. Designated institutions: Eligible postsecondary institutions in Washington.
Eligibility: Applicant must be U.S. citizen or permanent resident residing in Washington.
Basis for selection: Applicant must demonstrate financial need.
Application requirements: Proof of eligibility. FAFSA.
Additional information: Grants are given only to students from low-income families. Must meet qualifications every year for renewal, up to five years. Contact institution's financial aid office for additional requirements and deadlines. Must not be pursuing a degree in theology. Number of awards varies. Visit Website for family income requirements and more information.

Amount of award:	$845-$6,876
Total amount awarded:	$182,735,778

Contact:
Washington State Higher Education Coordinating Board
917 Lakeridge Way
P.O. Box 43430
Olympia, WA 98504-3430
Phone: 360-753-7850
Web: www.hecb.wa.gov

Washington State Scholars Program

Type of award: Scholarship.
Intended use: For undergraduate study at accredited vocational, 2-year or 4-year institution. Designated institutions: Eligible colleges and universities in Washington state.
Eligibility: Applicant must be high school senior. Applicant must be U.S. citizen or permanent resident residing in Washington.
Basis for selection: Applicant must demonstrate high academic achievement, depth of character, leadership, seriousness of purpose and service orientation.
Application requirements: Nomination by high school principal or guidance counselor. SAT/ACT scores.
Additional information: Four-year award based on tuition, which may be prorated. Must rank in top one percent of class. May not defer enrollment. Eligible high school seniors should contact their high school counselors for more information. Must not pursue a degree in theology.

Amount of award:	$2,633-$6,840
Number of awards:	147
Application deadline:	January 19
Notification begins:	March 15
Total amount awarded:	$2,300,000

Contact:
Washington State Higher Education Coordinating Board
917 Lakeridge Way
P.O. Box 43430
Olympia, WA 98504-3430
Phone: 360-753-7843
Fax: 360-704-6243
Web: www.hecb.wa.gov

Washington State PTA

Washington State Scholarship Program

Type of award: Scholarship.
Intended use: For full-time freshman study at accredited vocational, 2-year or 4-year institution.
Eligibility: Applicant must be residing in Washington.
Basis for selection: Applicant must demonstrate financial need, high academic achievement, depth of character, leadership, seriousness of purpose and service orientation.
Application requirements: Recommendations, essay, transcript, proof of eligibility.
Additional information: Must be graduate of a Washington State public high school. Grant administered according to college's determination. Not transferable to another institution if already enrolled in classes. Visit Website for additional information, application, and deadline.

Amount of award:	$1,000-$2,000
Number of awards:	60
Number of applicants:	2,000
Total amount awarded:	$65,000

Contact:
Washington State Scholarship Program
2003 65 Avenue West
Tacoma, WA 98466-6215
Phone: 253-565-2153
Fax: 253-565-7753
Web: www.wastatepta.org

Wells Fargo

CollegeSTEPS Program

Type of award: Scholarship.
Intended use: For undergraduate study at postsecondary institution.
Eligibility: Applicant must be high school freshman, sophomore, junior or senior. Applicant must be U.S. citizen.
Additional information: Awardees selected via random drawing. Visit Website to apply. Employees of Wells Fargo and immediate family members not eligible for tuition prize.

Amount of award:	$1,000
Number of awards:	20
Total amount awarded:	$20,000

Contact:
Education Financial Services
Wells Fargo
P.O. Box 5185
Sioux Falls, SD 57117-5185
Phone: 888-511-7302
Web: www.wellsfargo.com/collegesteps

Welsh Society of Philadelphia

Undergraduate Scholarship

Type of award: Scholarship.
Intended use: For full-time undergraduate study at accredited 2-year or 4-year institution in United States.
Eligibility: Applicant must be Welsh. Applicant must be residing in Delaware, New Jersey, Maryland or Pennsylvania.
Basis for selection: Applicant must demonstrate high academic achievement, leadership, seriousness of purpose and service orientation.
Application requirements: Recommendations, essay, transcript, proof of eligibility.
Additional information: Applicant must be of Welsh descent. Must live or attend school within 125 miles of Philadelphia. Must rank in top third of class.

Amount of award:	$500-$1,000
Number of awards:	7
Number of applicants:	40
Application deadline:	May 1
Total amount awarded:	$5,000

Contact:
Welsh Society of Philadelphia Scholarship Committee
c/o Dr. Donald Marcus
P.O. Box 7287
Saint Davids, PA 19087-7287
Web: www.welsh-society-phila.org

Welsh Heritage Scholarship

Type of award: Scholarship, renewable.
Intended use: For full-time undergraduate study at accredited 2-year or 4-year institution.
Eligibility: Applicant must be Welsh.
Basis for selection: Applicant must demonstrate high academic achievement and seriousness of purpose.
Application requirements: Recommendations, essay, transcript. Statement of purpose.
Additional information: Applicant must be of Welsh descent. Applicant must live or attend college within 100 miles of Philadelphia. Participation in Welsh/Welsh-American organizations or events preferred.

Amount of award:	$500-$1,000
Number of awards:	5
Number of applicants:	50
Application deadline:	May 1
Total amount awarded:	$5,000

Contact:
Welsh Society of Philadelphia
Scholarship Committee Chairman
P.O. Box 7287
St. David's, PA 19087-7287

West Pharmaceutical Services, Inc.

Herman O. West Foundation Scholarship Program

Type of award: Scholarship, renewable.
Intended use: For full-time undergraduate study at accredited 2-year or 4-year institution.
Eligibility: Applicant or parent must be employed by West Pharmaceutical Services, Inc. Applicant must be high school senior. Applicant must be U.S. citizen.
Basis for selection: Applicant must demonstrate high academic achievement.
Application requirements: Recommendations, essay, transcript, proof of eligibility. List of extracurricular activities.
Additional information: Parent must be employee of West Pharmaceutical Services, Inc. Award is renewable annually for maximum of four years.

Amount of award:	$2,500
Number of awards:	7
Number of applicants:	26
Application deadline:	February 28
Notification begins:	May 1
Total amount awarded:	$50,000

Contact:
H.O. West Foundation
101 Gordon Drive
Lionville, PA 19341
Phone: 610-594-2945

West Virginia Division of Veterans Affairs

West Virginia War Orphans Educational Assistance

Type of award: Scholarship, renewable.
Intended use: For undergraduate, graduate or non-degree study in United States.
Eligibility: Applicant must be at least 16, no older than 25. Applicant must be U.S. citizen residing in West Virginia. Applicant must be dependent of deceased veteran who served in the Army, Air Force, Marines, Navy, Coast Guard or Reserves/National Guard. Applicant's parent must be veteran who was killed while on active duty during wartime or who died of injury or illness resulting from wartime service.
Application requirements: Proof of eligibility.
Additional information: Award is waiver of tuition and registration fees for West Virginia residents attending a West Virginia school. If attending a private school in West Virginia or out of state college, may only receive a maximum of $2,000 for academic year. Non-West Virginia residents exempt.

Amount of award:	Full tuition
Number of awards:	23
Number of applicants:	14
Application deadline:	July 1, December 1
Notification begins:	July 15, December 15
Total amount awarded:	$24,000

Contact:
West Virginia Division of Veterans Affairs
1321 Plaza East, Suite 109
Charleston, WV 25301-1400
Phone: 888-838-2332
Fax: 304-558-3662
Web: www.wvs.state.wv.us/va

West Virginia Higher Education Policy Commission

PROMISE Scholarship

Type of award: Scholarship, renewable.
Intended use: For undergraduate study at 2-year or 4-year institution.
Eligibility: Applicant must be U.S. citizen or permanent resident residing in West Virginia.
Basis for selection: Applicant must demonstrate high academic achievement.
Application requirements: FAFSA.
Additional information: Merit-based scholarship; all eligible applicants will receive award up to $4,750. Minimum 22 composite ACT, with scores of at least 20 in math, science, English, and reading, or 1020 SAT (Math and Reading) with minimum 480 Math and 490 Reading. Minimum 3.0 GPA. Tuition waiver only for public institutions. Students attending private institutions will receive tuition assistance based on average cost of public college tuition and fees. See Website for more information.

Amount of award:	$4,750
Number of awards:	10,000
Number of applicants:	8,000
Application deadline:	March 1
Notification begins:	April 1
Total amount awarded:	$30,000,000

Contact:
West Virginia Higher Education Policy Commission
1018 Kanawha Boulevard East
Suite 700
Charleston, WV 25301
Phone: 877-987-7664 or 304-558-4417
Fax: 304-558-4622
Web: www.cswv.com

West Virginia Engineering, Science, and Technology Scholarship

Type of award: Scholarship, renewable.
Intended use: For full-time undergraduate study at 2-year or 4-year institution in United States. Designated institutions: Eligible West Virginia institutions.
Eligibility: Applicant must be U.S. citizen or permanent resident residing in West Virginia.
Basis for selection: Major/career interest in science, general; engineering; engineering, civil; engineering, computer; engineering, electrical/electronic; engineering, mechanical; computer/information sciences; life sciences; physical sciences or natural sciences. Applicant must demonstrate high academic achievement and seriousness of purpose.
Application requirements: Essay, transcript.
Additional information: Recipients should obtain degree/certificate in engineering, science, or technology and pursue career in West Virginia. Recipient must, within one year after ceasing to be a full-time student, work full-time in engineering, science, or technology field in West Virginia, or begin a program of community service relating to these fields in West Virginia for a duration of one year for each year scholarship was received. If work requirement fails to be met, recipient must repay scholarship plus interest and any required collection fees. Interested high school students should apply through high school counselor; currently enrolled college/university students should apply through their institution. Minimum 3.0 GPA. Application available on Website.

Amount of award:	$3,000
Number of awards:	100
Number of applicants:	400
Application deadline:	March 1
Total amount awarded:	$395,802

Contact:
West Virginia Higher Education Policy Commission
Engineering, Science, and Technology Program
1018 Kanawha Boulevard East, Suite 700
Charleston, WV 25301-2800
Phone: 304-558-4614
Web: www.cswv.com

West Virginia Higher Education Adult Part-time Student (HEAPS) Grant Program

Type of award: Scholarship, renewable.
Intended use: For half-time undergraduate certificate, freshman, sophomore, junior or senior study at postsecondary institution.

Eligibility: Applicant must be returning adult student. Applicant must be U.S. citizen or permanent resident residing in West Virginia.
Basis for selection: Applicant must demonstrate financial need.
Application requirements: FAFSA and any supplemental materials required by individual institutions.
Additional information: Applicant must be out of high school for at least two years and plan to continue education on part-time basis. Must either be enrolled in college with cumulative 2.0 GPA (for renewal applicants), or be accepted for enrollment by intended institution (for first-time applicants); must have complied with Military Selective Service Act; must qualify as independent student according to federal financial aid criteria; must not be in default on higher education loan; and must not be incarcerated in correctional facility. At public colleges/universities, award is actual amount of tuition and fees. At independent colleges/universities and vocational/technical schools, award is based upon average per credit/term hours tuition and fee charges assessed by all public undergraduate institutions. Contact school's financial aid office, or visit Website for additional information.
Contact:
West Virginia Higher Education Policy Commission
Melissa Samples
1018 Kanawha Boulevard East, Fifth Floor
Charleston, WV 25301
Phone: 304-558-4618
Web: www.cswv.com

West Virginia Higher Education Grant

Type of award: Scholarship, renewable.
Intended use: For full-time undergraduate study at accredited 2-year or 4-year institution. Designated institutions: West Virginia or Pennsylvania institutions.
Eligibility: Applicant must be U.S. citizen residing in West Virginia or Pennsylvania.
Basis for selection: Applicant must demonstrate financial need and high academic achievement.
Application requirements: Transcript. FAFSA. ACT/SAT scores.
Additional information: Applicants must fill out common application for state-level financial aid programs. Visit Website for application.

Amount of award:	$350-$2,756
Number of awards:	9,800
Number of applicants:	34,000
Application deadline:	March 1
Notification begins:	April 1
Total amount awarded:	$34,600,000

Contact:
West Virginia Higher Education Grant Program
Office of Financial Aid and Outreach Services
1018 Kanawha Boulevard East, Suite 700
Charleston, WV 25301-2800
Phone: 888-825-5707 or 304-558-4618
Fax: 304-558-4622
Web: www.cswv.com

West Virginia Robert C. Byrd Honors Scholarship

Type of award: Scholarship, renewable.
Intended use: For full-time freshman study at vocational, 2-year or 4-year institution in United States.

Eligibility: Applicant must be high school senior. Applicant must be U.S. citizen or permanent resident residing in West Virginia.
Basis for selection: Applicant must demonstrate high academic achievement.
Application requirements: Transcript, proof of eligibility, nomination by high school. SAT or ACT scores.
Additional information: Because of limited funding, high schools with senior class enrollment of 1-199 may submit one application for consideration and high schools with senior class of 200+ may submit two applications for consideration. Students should apply through their high school counselor.

Amount of award:	$1,500
Number of awards:	36
Number of applicants:	400
Application deadline:	March 1
Notification begins:	April 1
Total amount awarded:	$211,500

Contact:
West Virginia Higher Education Policy Commission
Robert C. Byrd Honors Scholarship Program
1018 Kanawha Boulevard East, Suite 700
Charleston, WV 25301-2800
Phone: 304-558-4614
Web: www.cswv.com

West Virginia Underwood-Smith Teacher Scholarship

Type of award: Scholarship, renewable.
Intended use: For full-time junior, senior or graduate study at 4-year or graduate institution.
Eligibility: Applicant must be U.S. citizen or permanent resident residing in West Virginia.
Basis for selection: Major/career interest in education; education, early childhood; education, special or education, teacher. Applicant must demonstrate high academic achievement.
Application requirements: Essay, proof of eligibility.
Additional information: Undergraduate applicants must have cumulative 3.25 GPA; graduate students must rank in top 10 percent of class or have 3.5 GPA. Number of applicants varies. Recipients must agree to teach at the public school level in West Virginia for two years for each year the scholarship is received or be willing to repay the scholarship on a pro rata basis. Visit Website for details and application.

Amount of award:	$5,000
Number of awards:	54
Number of applicants:	100
Application deadline:	March 1
Notification begins:	July 1
Total amount awarded:	$235,000

Contact:
West Virginia Higher Education Policy Commission
Underwood-Smith Teacher Scholarship Program
1018 Kanawha Boulevard East, Suite 700
Charleston, WV 25301-2800
Phone: 304-558-4614
Web: www.cswv.com

Western European Architecture Foundation

Gabriel Prize

Type of award: Research grant.
Intended use: For non-degree study at postsecondary institution.
Eligibility: Applicant must be U.S. citizen.
Basis for selection: Major/career interest in architecture. Applicant must demonstrate seriousness of purpose.
Application requirements: Portfolio, recommendations, research proposal. Resume.
Additional information: Award to encourage personal investigative and critical studies of French architectural compositions completed between 1630 and 1930. Work is expected to be executed in France under supervision of foundation's European representative. Winner is required to begin studies in France by May 1, keep a traveling sketchbook, and prepare three large colored drawings within three months. Must use stipend for travel and study. Send SASE for return of materials. Visit Website for application and deadline.

Amount of award:	$20,000
Number of awards:	1
Number of applicants:	24
Total amount awarded:	$20,000

Contact:
Western European Architecture Foundation
306 West Sunset, Suite 115
San Antonio, TX 78209
Phone: 210-829-4040
Fax: 210-829-4049
Web: www.gabrielprize.org

Western Golf Association/ Evans Scholars Foundation

Chick Evans Caddie Scholarship

Type of award: Scholarship, renewable.
Intended use: For full-time undergraduate study at accredited 4-year institution in United States.
Eligibility: Applicant must be high school senior.
Basis for selection: Competition/talent/interest in athletics/ sports, based on consistent caddie record at Western Golf Association-affiliated club. Applicant must demonstrate financial need, high academic achievement, depth of character and leadership.
Application requirements: Recommendations, transcript, proof of eligibility. Tax returns, financial aid profile.
Additional information: Scholarship for full tuition, plus housing where applicable. Must have caddied minimum two years at Western Golf Association-affiliated club and maintain at least B average in college prep classes. Must have strong caddie record and work at sponsoring club during summer of application. Most recipients attend one of 14 universities where Evans Scholars Foundation owns and operates chapter house. Approximately 200 new Evans Scholarships awarded each year. Renewable up to four years. See Website for designated institutions.

Amount of award:	Full tuition
Number of awards:	200
Number of applicants:	585
Application deadline:	September 30
Total amount awarded:	$8,000,000

Contact:
Scholarship Committee
Western Golf Assoc./Evans Scholars Foundation
1 Briar Road
Golf, IL 60029
Phone: 847-724-4600
Fax: 847-724-7133
Web: www.evansscholarsfoundation.com

William Randolph Hearst Foundation

Hearst Journalism Award

Type of award: Scholarship.
Intended use: For undergraduate study at accredited 4-year institution. Designated institutions: Institutions accredited by Accrediting Council on Education in Journalism and Mass Communication.
Basis for selection: Competition/talent/interest in writing/ journalism, based on newsworthiness, research, excellence of journalistic writing, photojournalism, or broadcast news. Major/ career interest in journalism; radio/television/film or communications.
Additional information: Field of study may also include photojournalism or broadcast news. Applicants must be actively involved in campus media and submit work that has been published or aired. Competition consists of monthly contests and one championship. Scholarships awarded to student winners with matching grants awarded to their departments of journalism. Entries must be submitted by journalism department. For additional information and deadlines, applicants should contact journalism department chair or visit Website. Only two applicants per competition per school.

Amount of award:	$500-$2,000
Number of awards:	14
Total amount awarded:	$500,000

Contact:
Hearst Journalism Awards Program
90 New Montgomery Street
Suite 1212
San Francisco, CA 94105-4504
Phone: 415-908-4560 or 800-841-7048 ext. 4560
Web: www.hearstfdn.org

United States Senate Youth Program

Type of award: Scholarship.
Intended use: For undergraduate study at accredited 2-year or 4-year institution in United States.
Eligibility: Applicant must be high school junior or senior. Applicant must be U.S. citizen or permanent resident.
Basis for selection: Applicant must demonstrate leadership and service orientation.
Application requirements: Nomination by high school principal or teacher.
Additional information: Applicant must be permanent resident of and currently enrolled in public or private secondary school located in the state (including District of Columbia) in

519

which parent or guardian legally resides. Must be currently serving in elected capacity as student body officer; class officer; student council representative; or student representative to district, regional, or state-level civic or educational organization. Selection process managed by state-level department of education. Scholarship includes all-expenses-paid week in Washington, D.C., in March. Application deadline is in early fall for most states; application available from high school principal or teacher. Visit Website for more information.

Amount of award:	$5,000
Number of awards:	104
Notification begins:	December 1
Total amount awarded:	$520,000

Contact:
Rayne Guilford, Program Director William Randolph Hearst Foundation
90 New Montgomery Street
Suite 1212
San Francisco, CA 94105-4504
Phone: 800-841-7048 ext. 4540
Fax: 415-243-0760
Web: www.ussenateyouth.org

Wilson Ornithological Society

George A. Hall/Harold F. Mayfield Award

Type of award: Research grant.
Intended use: For non-degree study at postsecondary institution.
Basis for selection: Major/career interest in ornithology.
Application requirements: Recommendations, research proposal. Budget. Research proposal must be no longer than three pages.
Additional information: Research proposal must not exceed three pages. Award restricted to amateur researchers, including high school students, without access to funds and facilities of academic institutions or governmental agencies. Willingness to report research results as oral or poster paper is condition of award. Applicants whose first language is not English may also submit proposal in their first language. Award should be used for equipment, supplies, travel, or living expenses. Visit Website for contact information and application.

Amount of award:	$1,000
Number of awards:	1
Number of applicants:	4
Application deadline:	February 1
Total amount awarded:	$1,000

Contact:
Phone: 202-633-0787
Web: www.wilsonsociety.org/awards

Paul A. Stewart Award

Type of award: Research grant.
Intended use: For undergraduate, master's, doctoral, postgraduate or non-degree study at postsecondary institution.
Basis for selection: Major/career interest in ornithology.
Application requirements: Recommendations, research proposal. Research budget.
Additional information: Research proposal should not exceed three pages. Preference given to proposals studying bird

movements based on banding, analysis of recoveries, and returns of banded birds, with an emphasis on economic ornithology. Willingness to report research results as oral or poster paper is condition of award. Applicants whose first language is not English may also submit proposal in their first language. Visit Website for contact information and application.

Amount of award:	$500
Number of awards:	8
Number of applicants:	18
Application deadline:	February 1
Total amount awarded:	$4,000

Contact:
Phone: 202-633-0787
Web: www.wilsonsociety.org/awards

Wisconsin Department of Veterans Affairs

Wisconsin Veterans Affairs Retraining Grant

Type of award: Scholarship.
Intended use: For undergraduate study at accredited vocational institution. Designated institutions: Wisconsin technical colleges; occupational/technical schools approved by the Wisconsin Educational Approval Board; Wisconsin on-the-job training programs.
Eligibility: Applicant must be residing in Wisconsin. Applicant must be veteran. Must have served two years of continuous active duty during peacetime or 90 days of active duty during designated wartime period.
Basis for selection: Applicant must demonstrate financial need.
Additional information: Applicant must be recently unemployed or underemployed and registered for or enrolled in education program that will lead to re-employment and be completed within two years. Must have been involuntarily laid off within a period beginning one year before WDVA receives application. Must have been employed for six consecutive months with same employer or in the same or similar occupation. Must have been a resident of Wisconsin on entry into military service or a continuous resident of Wisconsin for at least five years after separation from military service. Apply year-round at local county Veterans Service Office to establish eligibility.

Amount of award:	$3,000

Contact:
Wisconsin Department of Veterans Affairs
P.O. Box 7843
30 West Mifflin Street
Madison, WI 53707-7843
Phone: 800-947-8387
Web: www.dva.state.wi.us

Wisconsin Veterans Education GI Bill Tuition Remission Program

Type of award: Scholarship, renewable.
Intended use: For undergraduate study at vocational, 2-year or 4-year institution. Designated institutions: University of Wisconsin system schools, Wisconsin Technical College system schools.

Eligibility: Applicant must be residing in Wisconsin. Applicant must be veteran; or dependent of veteran, disabled veteran or deceased veteran; or spouse of veteran, disabled veteran or deceased veteran.

Basis for selection: Applicant must demonstrate financial need.

Application requirements: Proof of eligibility. Federal tax return or proof of annual income.

Additional information: Veteran must have been Wisconsin resident at time of entry into active duty; children of veterans must be between ages 17-25; widowed spouse of veteran must not be remarried. Veterans and spouses of veterans rated by the federal VA with a combined service-connected disability rating of 30% or greater are also eligible. Family income limit of $50,000; limit increases by $1,000 for each independent child. Veterans may receive up to 100 percent reimbursement of cost of tuition and fees. May receive reimbursement for up to eight semesters of full-time study. Visit Website for list of eligible schools, further requirements, and deadlines.

Contact:
Wisconsin Department of Veterans Affairs
P.O. Box 7843
30 West Mifflin Street
Madison, WI 53707-7843
Phone: 800-947-8387
Web: www.dva.state.wi.us

Wisconsin Higher Educational Aids Board

Wisconsin Academic Excellence Scholarship

Type of award: Scholarship, renewable.
Intended use: For full-time undergraduate study at vocational, 2-year or 4-year institution. Designated institutions: Wisconsin non-profit colleges or universities.
Eligibility: Applicant must be high school senior. Applicant must be residing in Wisconsin.
Basis for selection: Applicant must demonstrate high academic achievement.
Application requirements: Nomination by high school guidance counselor.
Additional information: Awarded to Wisconsin high school seniors who have the highest grade point average in each public and private high school throughout Wisconsin. 3.0 GPA must be maintained for renewal.

Amount of award:	$2,250
Number of awards:	2,670
Application deadline:	February 15
Total amount awarded:	$2,894,469

Contact:
Higher Educational Aids Board
Attn: Nancy Wilkison
131 West Wilson, Suite 902
Madison, WI 53707-7885
Phone: 608-267-2213
Web: www.heab.state.wi.us/programs.html

Wisconsin Hearing & Visually Handicapped Student Grant

Type of award: Scholarship, renewable.

Intended use: For undergraduate study at postsecondary institution. Designated institutions: Non-profit Wisconsin institutions; some out-of-state schools.
Eligibility: Applicant must be visually impaired or hearing impaired. Applicant must be residing in Wisconsin.
Basis for selection: Applicant must demonstrate financial need.
Application requirements: Proof of eligibility. FAFSA.

Amount of award:	$250-$1,800
Number of awards:	54
Total amount awarded:	$85,910

Contact:
Higher Educational Aids Board
Attn: Sandy Thomas
P.O. Box 7885
Madison, WI 53707-7885
Phone: 608-266-0888
Web: www.heab.state.wi.us

Wisconsin Higher Education Grant

Type of award: Scholarship, renewable.
Intended use: For undergraduate study at vocational or 4-year institution. Designated institutions: University of Wisconsin, Wisconsin Technical College, Tribal institutions. Some exceptions for hard of hearing or visually handicapped students.
Eligibility: Applicant must be residing in Wisconsin.
Basis for selection: Applicant must demonstrate financial need.
Application requirements: Proof of eligibility.
Additional information: Apply with FAFSA through high school guidance counselor or financial aid office of institution. Rolling deadline.

Amount of award:	$250-$3,000
Number of awards:	37,172
Total amount awarded:	$35,060,586

Contact:
Higher Educational Aids Board
Attn: Sandy Thomas
P.O. Box 7885
Madison, WI 53707-7885
Phone: 608-266-0888
Web: www.heab.state.wi.us

Wisconsin Indian Student Assistance Grant

Type of award: Scholarship, renewable.
Intended use: For undergraduate or graduate study at postsecondary institution. Designated institutions: Wisconsin institutions.
Eligibility: Applicant must be American Indian. Must be at least one-quarter Native American. Applicant must be residing in Wisconsin.
Basis for selection: Major/career interest in humanities/liberal arts. Applicant must demonstrate financial need.
Application requirements: Proof of eligibility. FAFSA.

Amount of award:	$250-$1,100
Number of awards:	837
Total amount awarded:	$784,857

Contact:
Higher Educational Aids Board
Attn: Sandy Thomas
P.O. Box 7885
Madison, WI 53707-7885
Phone: 608-266-0888
Web: www.heab.state.wi.us

Wisconsin Minority Undergraduate Retention Grant

Type of award: Scholarship, renewable.
Intended use: For sophomore, junior or senior study at vocational, 2-year or 4-year institution. Designated institutions: Wisconsin technical colleges, independent colleges and universities, or tribal colleges.
Eligibility: Applicant must be Asian American, African American, Mexican American, Hispanic American, Puerto Rican or American Indian. Asian American applicants must be former citizens or children of former citizens of Laos, Vietnam, or Cambodia admitted to United States after 12/31/75. Applicant must be U.S. citizen or permanent resident residing in Wisconsin.
Basis for selection: Applicant must demonstrate financial need.
Application requirements: FAFSA and nomination by Financial Aid Office.

Amount of award:	$250-$2,500
Number of awards:	913
Number of applicants:	915
Total amount awarded:	$687,596

Contact:
Higher Educational Aids Board
Attn: May Lou Kuzdas
P.O. Box 7885
Wisconsin, WI 53707-7885
Phone: 608-267-2212
Web: www.heab.state.wi.us

Wisconsin Talent Incentive Program Grant

Type of award: Scholarship, renewable.
Intended use: For freshman study at postsecondary institution. Designated institutions: Non-profit Wisconsin institutions.
Eligibility: Applicant must be residing in Wisconsin.
Basis for selection: Applicant must demonstrate financial need.
Application requirements: Nomination by financial aid department or Wisconsin Educational Opportunity Programs. FAFSA.
Additional information: Applicant must meet at least one of non-traditional/economically disadvantaged criteria. Visit Website for list. Eligibility cannot exceed ten semesters.

Amount of award:	$250-$1,800
Number of awards:	4,146
Total amount awarded:	$5,489,498

Contact:
Higher Educational Aids Board
Attn: John Whitt
P.O. Box 7885
Madison, WI 53707-7885
Phone: 608-266-1665
Web: www.heab.state.wi.us

Wisconsin Tuition Grant

Type of award: Scholarship, renewable.
Intended use: For undergraduate study at postsecondary institution. Designated institutions: Independent, nonprofit institutions in Wisconsin.
Eligibility: Applicant must be residing in Wisconsin.
Basis for selection: Applicant must demonstrate financial need.
Application requirements: FAFSA.

Additional information: Minimum award $250; maximum award amount set annually by HEAB.

Number of awards:	12,343
Total amount awarded:	$23,247,820

Contact:
Higher Educational Aids Board
Attn: Mary Lou Kuzdas
P.O. Box 7885
Madison, WI 53707-7885
Phone: 608-267-2212
Web: www.heab.state.wi.us

Women Grocers of America

Mary Macey Scholarship

Type of award: Scholarship, renewable.
Intended use: For sophomore, junior, senior or graduate study at accredited 2-year, 4-year or graduate institution in United States.
Basis for selection: Major/career interest in food production/management/services.
Application requirements: Recommendations, essay, transcript.
Additional information: Must plan on a career in the independent sector of the grocery industry. Majors in public health and hotel management are not eligible. Minimum 2.0 GPA. Minimum of two $1000 awards each year.

Number of applicants:	15
Application deadline:	June 28
Notification begins:	July 31
Total amount awarded:	$5,000

Contact:
Women Grocers of America
1005 North Glebe Road
Suite 250
Arlington, VA 22201-5758
Phone: 703-516-0700
Fax: 703-812-1821
Web: www.nationalgrocers.org

Women in Defense, A National Security Organization

Horizons Scholarship

Type of award: Scholarship.
Intended use: For junior, senior or graduate study at accredited 4-year institution in United States.
Eligibility: Applicant must be female. Applicant must be U.S. citizen.
Basis for selection: Major/career interest in science, general; engineering; mathematics; computer/information sciences; physics; business; law; international relations or political science/government. Applicant must demonstrate financial need and high academic achievement.
Application requirements: Recommendations, essay, transcript.

Additional information: Scholarship intended to provide financial assistance to women either employed or planning careers in defense or national security areas. Minimum 3.25 GPA. Studies must be aimed at national defense/national security. Visit Website for details and application (no phone calls).

Amount of award:	$500-$2,000
Number of awards:	5
Number of applicants:	40
Application deadline:	July 1
Total amount awarded:	$10,000

Contact:
Women in Defense
2111 Wilson Blvd., Suite 400
Arlington, VA 22201-3061
Phone: 703-247-2552
Fax: 703-522-1885
Web: wid.ndia.org

Women's Western Golf Foundation

Women's Western Golf Foundation Scholarship

Type of award: Scholarship, renewable.
Intended use: For full-time freshman study at accredited 4-year institution in United States.
Eligibility: Applicant must be female, high school senior. Applicant must be U.S. citizen.
Basis for selection: Competition/talent/interest in athletics/sports. Applicant must demonstrate financial need, high academic achievement, depth of character, leadership and seriousness of purpose.
Application requirements: Essay, transcript, proof of eligibility. SAT/ACT scores, FAFSA. Personal recommendation required from high school teacher or counselor. List of high school activities.
Additional information: Must be in top 15 percent of class. 3.5 GPA is recommended. Must demonstrate involvement in golf, but skill not criterion. Deadline to request application is March 1; SASE required. Awards renew for each of four years, assuming scholarship terms are fulfilled (financial need, GPA above 3.0). About 20 new awards each year, plus 50 renewals.

Amount of award:	$2,000
Number of awards:	22
Number of applicants:	500
Application deadline:	April 5
Notification begins:	May 20
Total amount awarded:	$150,000

Contact:
Director of Scholarship
Women's Western Golf Foundation
393 Ramsay Road
Deerfield, IL 60015

Woodrow Wilson National Fellowship Foundation

Thomas R. Pickering Foreign Affairs Fellowship

Type of award: Scholarship.
Intended use: For full-time senior or graduate study at accredited 4-year or graduate institution in United States. Designated institutions: Institutions affiliated with Association of Professional Schools of International Affairs (graduate portion of fellowship).
Eligibility: Applicant must be U.S. citizen.
Basis for selection: Major/career interest in international relations; communications; history; economics; political science/government; foreign languages or business/management/administration. Applicant must demonstrate financial need, high academic achievement, depth of character, leadership, seriousness of purpose and service orientation.
Application requirements: Recommendations, essay, transcript, proof of eligibility. Resume, SAT or ACT scores, SAR, if applicable.
Additional information: Award is up to $50,000 toward tuition, mandatory fees, books, travel, and living stipend. Undergraduates must apply as juniors; applicants for graduate fellowship must be seeking admission to graduate school for the following academic year. Must have interest in career as Foreign Service officer. Number of fellowships determined by available funding. Finalists will attend interview session in Washington, D.C.; transportation to interview site paid. Orientation in Washington, D.C. Medical and security clearances required for program participation. Applicants must have minimum 3.2 GPA at time of application and maintain GPA throughout fellowship. Women and members of minority groups historically underrepresented in the Foreign Service encouraged to apply. Successful applicants obligated to a minimum of three years as a Foreign Service officer. Must register and apply online. Deadline varies; visit Website for details.
Contact:
Dr. Richard O. Hope, Pickering Foreign Affairs Fellowship Program
Woodrow Wilson National Fellowship Foundation
P.O. Box 2437
Princeton, NJ 08543-2437
Phone: 609-452-7007
Web: www.woodrow.org

Worldstudio Foundation

Worldstudio AIGA Scholarship

Type of award: Scholarship.
Intended use: For full-time undergraduate or graduate study at accredited 2-year or 4-year institution in United States.
Eligibility: Applicant must be U.S. citizen or permanent resident.
Basis for selection: Major/career interest in graphic arts/design or arts, general. Applicant must demonstrate financial need, seriousness of purpose and service orientation.
Application requirements: Portfolio, recommendations, transcript. Statement of purpose and self-portrait.

Additional information: Illustration, art direction for advertising, interactive design/motion graphics, and photography majors also eligible. The foundation's primary aim is to increase diversity in the creative professions and to foster social and environmental responsibility in the artists, designers, and studios of tomorrow. Applicants must be enrolled in courses related to or planning a career in design arts professions, and must demonstrate a social agenda in their work. Students with minority status given preference. Minimum 2.0 GPA. Visit Website for guidelines and application. Deadline in early April. Awards not offered for performing arts.

Amount of award:	$500-$5,000
Number of awards:	20
Number of applicants:	400
Total amount awarded:	$65,000

Contact:
Worldstudio Foundation AIGA Scholarships
164 Fifth Avenue
New York, NY 10010
Phone: 212-807-1990
Fax: 212-807-1799
Web: www.scholarships.worldstudioinc.com

Xerox

Technical Minority Scholarship

Type of award: Scholarship.
Intended use: For full-time undergraduate or graduate study in United States.
Eligibility: Applicant must be Alaskan native, Asian American, African American, Mexican American, Hispanic American, Puerto Rican, American Indian or Native Hawaiian/Pacific Islander. Applicant must be U.S. citizen or permanent resident.
Basis for selection: Major/career interest in chemistry; engineering; science, general; information systems; physics or computer/information sciences. Applicant must demonstrate high academic achievement, leadership, patriotism and seriousness of purpose.
Application requirements: Resume and cover letter.
Additional information: Minimum 3.0 GPA. Spouses and children of Xerox employees not eligible. Visit Website for application and more information.

Amount of award:	$1,000-$10,000
Number of awards:	99
Number of applicants:	1,524
Application deadline:	September 30
Notification begins:	December 31
Total amount awarded:	$160,000

Contact:
Xerox
Technical Minority Scholarship Program
150 State Street, 4th Floor
Rochester, NY 14614
Web: www.xerox.com/careers

Yakama Nation Higher Education Program

Yakama Nation Tribal Scholarship

Type of award: Scholarship.
Intended use: For undergraduate, master's or doctoral study at accredited 2-year, 4-year or graduate institution.
Eligibility: Must be enrolled member of Yakama Nation.
Application requirements: Transcript. High school or GED score sheet. Tribal ID card copy. Enrollment verification, FAFSA, college acceptance letter.
Additional information: Maximum $3,000 awarded to undergraduate students; maximum $6,000 awarded to graduate students. Recipients notified two weeks prior to the start of semester to which aid will be applied.

Amount of award:	$3,000-$6,000
Number of awards:	300
Number of applicants:	299
Application deadline:	July 1
Notification begins:	July 10
Total amount awarded:	$200,000

Contact:
Yakama Nation Higher Education Program
P.O. Box 151
Toppenish, WA 98948
Phone: 509-865-5121
Fax: 509-865-6994

Internships

Academy of Television Arts & Sciences Foundation

Student Internship Program

Type of award: Internship.
Intended use: For full-time undergraduate or graduate study in United States.
Eligibility: Applicant must be U.S. citizen or permanent resident.
Basis for selection: Major/career interest in film/video or radio/television/film.
Application requirements: Recommendations, essay, transcript. Resume.
Additional information: Designed to expose students to professional TV production, techniques, and practices. Opportunities available in many fields; see Website for categories and special requirements. Internships are full-time for eight weeks. Interns responsible for housing, transportation, and living expenses. Interns must have car for transportation in Los Angeles. Apply online.

Amount of award:	$4,000
Number of awards:	41
Number of applicants:	1,100
Application deadline:	March 15
Notification begins:	May 1

Contact:
Nancy Robinson Academy of Television Arts & Sciences Foundation
Student Internship Program
5220 Lankershim Boulevard
North Hollywood, CA 91601-3109
Phone: 818-754-2800
Web: www.emmysfoundation.org

Accuracy in Media/ American Journalism Center

Accuracy in Media Internships

Type of award: Internship.
Intended use: For undergraduate or graduate study.
Basis for selection: Major/career interest in journalism; marketing or public relations.
Application requirements: Cover letter and resume. Writing sample.
Additional information: Accuracy in Media is a nonprofit media watchdog group that reports on media bias. Internships open to applicants from all majors, though some positions require experience in a particular field. Internships pay $50 per day. High school students may apply, as well as recent college graduates. Applications are processed on rolling basis; send early for best chance and to allow time to find housing. Deadlines: April 15 for summer, August 15 for fall,

December 15 for spring. See Website for application and more information.

Amount of award:	$3,000
Number of awards:	24
Application deadline:	April 15, August 15

Contact:
Accuracy in Media/American Journalism Center
Internship Coordinator
4455 Connecticut Avenue, NW, Suite 330
Washington, DC 20008
Phone: 202-364-4401 ext. 110
Fax: 202-364-4098
Web: www.aimajc.org

Allstate

Allstate Internships

Type of award: Internship, renewable.
Intended use: For full-time undergraduate study at accredited 4-year institution.
Basis for selection: Major/career interest in insurance/actuarial science; accounting; marketing; business; business/management/ administration; computer/information sciences; finance/banking; mathematics or statistics. Applicant must demonstrate high academic achievement.
Application requirements: Resume and cover letter.
Additional information: In addition to salary, eligible interns receive subsidized transportation to and from Allstate Home Office in Northbrook, IL, at beginning and end of internship; daily transportation; and subsidized housing. Please respond directly to position posted on Website.
Contact:
Allstate Insurance Company
2775 Sanders Road
Northbrook, IL 60062
Web: www.allstate.jobs

American Association of Advertising Agencies

Multicultural Advertising Intern Program

Type of award: Internship, renewable.
Intended use: For full-time senior or graduate study at accredited 4-year or graduate institution.
Eligibility: Applicant must be Asian American, African American, Mexican American, Hispanic American, Puerto Rican, American Indian or Native Hawaiian/Pacific Islander. Applicant must be U.S. citizen or permanent resident.
Basis for selection: Major/career interest in advertising. Applicant must demonstrate seriousness of purpose.

Application requirements: Recommendations, transcript. Resume, work samples (if applying for creative internship).
Additional information: Applicants must have completed at least junior year of college and have strong interest in advertising. Minimum 3.0 GPA. Applicants with lower GPA (2.7-2.9) must complete additional essay question on application. Students are placed in member agency offices for ten weeks during the summer. Salary minimum $350 per week. AAAA covers 70 percent of housing and travel costs (if applicable). Can apply for following departments: account management, digital/interactive technologies, media planning/buying, broadcast/print production, traffic, art direction, copywriting, public relations, or strategic/account planning. Agency professionals interview semifinalists before selection. Number of awards varies. See Website for more information.

Number of applicants:	360
Application deadline:	December 4
Notification begins:	January 25

Contact:
American Association of Advertising Agencies
405 Lexington Avenue, 18th Floor
New York, NY 10174-1801
Phone: 800-676-9333
Fax: 212-682-2028
Web: www.adunity.aaaa.org

American Bar Foundation

Summer Research Diversity Fellowships in Law and Social Sciences for Undergraduate Students

Type of award: Internship.
Intended use: For sophomore or junior study at 4-year institution.
Eligibility: Applicant must be U.S. citizen or permanent resident.
Basis for selection: Major/career interest in law; social/behavioral sciences; criminal justice/law enforcement; public administration/service or humanities/liberal arts. Applicant must demonstrate high academic achievement.
Application requirements: Recommendations, essay, transcript.
Additional information: Interns work eight 35-hour weeks as research assistants at American Bar Foundation in Chicago. Fellowships are intended for, but not limited to, persons who are African American, Hispanic/Latino, Native American, or Puerto Rican. Applicants must have minimum 3.0 GPA and intend to pursue academic major in social sciences or humanities. See Website for application deadline.

Amount of award:	$3,600
Number of awards:	4
Notification begins:	April 1

Contact:
American Bar Foundation - Summer Diversity Fellowships
750 North Lake Shore Drive, Fourth Floor
Chicago, IL 60611
Phone: 312-988-6560
Fax: 312-988-6579
Web: www.americanbarfoundation.org

American Conservatory Theater

American Conservatory Theater Production Internships

Type of award: Internship.
Intended use: For undergraduate, graduate or non-degree study.
Eligibility: Applicant must be U.S. citizen or permanent resident.
Basis for selection: Major/career interest in performing arts; theater arts or theater/production/technical.
Application requirements: Recommendations, essay. Resume. Writing sample, if required by specific internship.
Additional information: Provides intern with practical experience in many areas of theater production. Departments include costume rentals, costume shop, properties, sound design, stage management, wig construction/makeup, and production management. Internships are full-time for duration of entire season (September to June). A small weekly stipend is available. Visit Website for more information.

Number of awards:	9
Number of applicants:	200
Application deadline:	April 9
Notification begins:	June 4

Contact:
American Conservatory Theater
Internship Coordinator
30 Grant Avenue, 6th Floor
San Francisco, CA 94108-5834
Phone: 415-834-3200
Web: www.act-sf.org

Artistic and Administrative Internships

Type of award: Internship.
Intended use: For undergraduate, graduate or non-degree study.
Eligibility: Applicant must be U.S. citizen or permanent resident.
Basis for selection: Major/career interest in theater arts; theater/production/technical; arts management; performing arts; public relations; marketing; English or literature.
Application requirements: Recommendations, essay. Resume. Writing sample if required by specific internship.
Additional information: Provides intern with opportunity to work in dramaturgy, publications, arts management, development, literary or marketing/public relations departments. Internship is full-time for duration of entire season (September to June). A weekly stipend is available. Visit Website for more information.

Number of awards:	6
Number of applicants:	200
Application deadline:	April 9
Notification begins:	June 4

Contact:
American Conservatory Theater
Internship Coordinator
30 Grant Avenue, 6th Floor
San Francisco, CA 94108-5834
Phone: 415-834-3200
Web: www.act-sf.org

American Federation of State, County and Municipal Employees

AFSCMA/UNCF Union Scholars Program

Type of award: Internship.
Intended use: For junior or senior study at 4-year institution.
Eligibility: Applicant must be Alaskan native, Asian American, African American, Mexican American, Hispanic American, Puerto Rican, American Indian or Native Hawaiian/Pacific Islander.
Basis for selection: Major/career interest in ethnic/cultural studies; women's studies; sociology; anthropology; history; political science/government; psychology; social work; economics or public administration/service.
Application requirements: Recommendations.
Additional information: Labor studies and American studies majors also eligible. Minimum 2.5 GPA. Must demonstrate interest in working for social and economic justice through the labor movement. Must have a driver's license. Award is a ten-week summer field placement to participate in union organizing campaign in one of several U.S. locations. Includes on-site housing and week-long orientation and training. Scholars receive up to $4,000 stipend and up to $5,000 academic scholarship for upcoming school year.

Amount of award:	$4,000-$9,000
Number of awards:	10
Application deadline:	February 28

Contact:
AFSCME
Attn: Education Department
1625 L Street, NW
Washington, DC 20036
Phone: 866-671-7237
Web: www.afscme.org

American Museum of Natural History

Anthropology Internship Program

Type of award: Internship.
Intended use: For undergraduate or graduate study.
Basis for selection: Major/career interest in anthropology; archaeology or museum studies.
Application requirements: Essay, transcript. Resume, contact information of academic advisor.
Additional information: Must specify whether applying for paid, academic credit, or unpaid internship. Deadlines: April 1 for summer; August 27 for fall; December 1 for spring. Internships may range from three to six months. Number of awards varies.

Application deadline:	April 1, December 1

Contact:
American Museum of Natural History
Attn: Anita Caltabiano
Central Park West at 79th Street
New York, NY 10024-5192
Phone: 212-769-5375
Web: www.research.amnh.org/anthropology/about/internship

Research Experiences for Undergraduates in Systematics and Evolutionary Biology

Type of award: Internship.
Intended use: For undergraduate study at accredited postsecondary institution in United States.
Eligibility: Applicant must be U.S. citizen or permanent resident.
Basis for selection: Major/career interest in science, general; biology or microbiology. Applicant must demonstrate high academic achievement and seriousness of purpose.
Application requirements: Essay. List of courses. List of references. Ranking of first two choices among summer projects listed on Website and explanation of why applicant chose them.
Additional information: Applicant must have strong scientific background. Amount of stipend varies. Internship lasts from beginning of June to mid-August. College seniors may not apply. See Website for detailed descriptions of summer projects and application, which must be submitted electronically. Deadline in February; see Website for exact date.

Number of awards:	8
Number of applicants:	110

Contact:
Mark E. Siddall Office of Grants and Fellowships
REU, American Museum of Natural History
Central Park West at 79th Street
New York, NY 10024-5192
Phone: 212-769-5055
Web: www.rggs.amnh.org

Research Experiences for Undergraduates in the Physical Sciences

Type of award: Internship.
Intended use: For undergraduate study at accredited postsecondary institution in United States.
Eligibility: Applicant must be U.S. citizen or permanent resident.
Basis for selection: Major/career interest in physical sciences; astronomy or geophysics. Applicant must demonstrate high academic achievement and seriousness of purpose.
Application requirements: Essay, transcript. List of courses. List of references. Ranking of first two choices among summer projects listed on Website and explanation of why applicant chose them.
Additional information: Nearby university dormitory housing provided, as well as travel to and from New York City, as per need. Visit Website for updated list of projects offered and application. Application must be submitted electronically. Contact Dr. James Webster (jdw@amnh.org) for more information on the Earth and Planetary Science program or Dr. Charles Liu (cliu@amnh.org) for the Astrophysics program. Amount of award varies. Deadline in February; check Website for exact date.

Number of awards:	8
Number of applicants:	165

Contact:
Richard Gilder Graduate School, REU Program in Physical Sciences
American Museum of Natural History
Central Park West at 79th Street
New York, NY 10024-5192
Phone: 212-769-5055
Web: www.rggs.amnh.org

American Society of International Law

American Society of International Law Internships

Type of award: Internship.
Intended use: For undergraduate or graduate study at accredited postsecondary institution.
Basis for selection: Major/career interest in accounting; communications; international relations; law; library science; public administration/service or public relations.
Application requirements: Cover letter, resume.
Additional information: Positions require a minimum commitment of 15 hours per week during fall and spring semesters, and 20 hours per week during summer semester. All internships unpaid; students may arrange academic credit. Address application to one of the following departments: communications and development, finance office, legal research, or library and information services. See Website for more information. Applications accepted on rolling basis.
Contact:
American Society of International Law
Internship Coordinator
2223 Massachusetts Avenue, NW
Washington, DC 20008
Fax: 202-797-7133
Web: www.asil.org/asil-internships.cfm

Americans for the Arts

Arts & Business Council of New York Internship

Type of award: Internship.
Intended use: For undergraduate or graduate study.
Basis for selection: Major/career interest in nonprofit administration; arts, general or arts management.
Application requirements: Cover letter, resume.
Additional information: Ten-week internship available on part-time basis for winter/spring and fall terms. Interns receive a stipend. Recent college graduates also eligible. Application deadlines are 7/28 for fall, and 12/4 for winter/spring. Visit Website for details. Internship takes place in New York City. Candidates should have a passion for the arts, knowledge of Microsoft Office, and be able to multi-task and work with minimal supervision.
Number of awards: 1

Contact:
Americans for the Arts
Attn: Human Resources
1000 Vermont Avenue, NW, 6th Floor
Washington, DC 20005
Phone: 202-371-2830
Fax: 202-371-0424
Web: www.americansforthearts.org

Arts Action Fund Internship

Type of award: Internship.
Intended use: For undergraduate or graduate study at postsecondary institution.
Basis for selection: Major/career interest in arts management; nonprofit administration or political science/government.
Application requirements: Cover letter, resume.
Additional information: Applicant may also be recent college graduate. Ten-week positions available part-time for winter/spring and fall and full-time for summer. Application deadlines are 3/15 for summer, 7/28 for fall, and 12/4 for winter/spring. Internship not always available for all seasons. Check Website for more details. All interns receive stipend. Must have excellent written and organizational skills, some experience in campaigns or political activities, strong computer skills (including proficiency in Adobe Creative Suite), and interest in basic Website management. Download application from Website or apply online.
Number of awards: 1
Contact:
Americans for the Arts
Attn: Human Resources
1000 Vermont Avenue NW, 6th Floor
Washington, DC 20005
Phone: 202-371-2830
Fax: 202-371-0424
Web: www.americansforthearts.org

Arts Policy Internship

Type of award: Internship.
Intended use: For undergraduate or graduate study.
Basis for selection: Major/career interest in arts management; arts, general or nonprofit administration.
Application requirements: Cover letter, resume.
Additional information: Internship takes place in New York City office. Recent college graduates may apply. Positions available part-time for winter/spring and fall and full-time for summer. Application deadlines are 3/15 for summer, 7/28 for fall, and 12/4 for winter/spring. Internship not always available for all seasons. Check Website for details. All interns receive stipend. Must know MS office (especially Excel), be able to work independently, have good communication skills, and an interest in arts and culture policy.
Number of awards: 1
Contact:
Americans for the Arts
Attn: Human Resources
1000 Vermont Avenue NW, 6th Floor
Washington, DC 20005
Phone: 202-371-2830
Fax: 202-371-0424
Web: www.americansforthearts.org

Government and Public Affairs Internship

Type of award: Internship.

Intended use: For undergraduate or graduate study at postsecondary institution.
Basis for selection: Major/career interest in arts management; arts, general; education; governmental public relations; public administration/service or nonprofit administration.
Application requirements: Cover letter, resume.
Additional information: Recent college graduates may apply. Ten-week positions available part-time for winter/spring and fall and full-time for summer. Application deadlines are 3/15 for summer, 7/28 for fall, and 12/4 for winter/spring. Internship not always available for all seasons. Check Website for details. All interns receive stipend. Must know MS Office and have good communication skills. Download application from Website or apply online.

   Number of awards: 1
Contact:
Americans for the Arts
Attn: Human Resources
1000 Vermont Avenue NW, 6th Floor
Washington, DC 20005
Phone: 202-371-2830
Fax: 202-371-0424
Web: www.americansforthearts.org

Local Arts Agency Services Intern

Type of award: Internship.
Intended use: For undergraduate or graduate study at postsecondary institution.
Basis for selection: Major/career interest in arts management; arts, general; communications or nonprofit administration.
Application requirements: Cover letter, resume.
Additional information: Recent college graduates may apply. Ten-week position available part-time for winter/spring and fall and full-time for summer. Application deadlines are 4/15 for summer, 7/31 for fall, and 12/12 for winter/spring. Internship not always available for all seasons. All interns receive stipend. Must know Microsoft Office and Outlook, and have exceptional written and verbal communication skills. Check Website for details and application.

   Amount of award: $500-$1,000
   Number of awards: 1
Contact:
Americans for the Arts
Attn: Human Resources
1000 Vermont Avenue NW, 6th Floor
Washington, DC 20005
Phone: 202-371-2830
Fax: 202-371-0424
Web: www.americansforthearts.org

Marketing and Communications Internship

Type of award: Internship.
Intended use: For undergraduate or graduate study at postsecondary institution.
Basis for selection: Major/career interest in public relations; marketing; communications or nonprofit administration.
Application requirements: Cover letter, resume.
Additional information: Recent college graduates may apply. Ten-week positions available part-time for winter/spring and fall and full-time for summer. Application deadlines are 3/15 for summer, 7/28 for fall, and 12/4 for winter/spring. Internship not always available for all seasons. Check Website for details. All interns receive stipend. Must know MS Office and have good phone manner. Experience with database software, HTML, and proofreading/editing a plus. Download application from Website or apply online.

   Number of awards: 1
Contact:
Americans for the Arts
Attn: Human Resources
1000 Vermont Avenue NW, 6th Floor
Washington, DC 20005
Phone: 202-371-2830
Fax: 202-371-0424
Web: www.americansforthearts.org

Meetings and Events/Executive Office Internship

Type of award: Internship.
Intended use: For undergraduate study.
Basis for selection: Major/career interest in hospitality administration/management; hotel/restaurant management; communications; public relations or nonprofit administration.
Application requirements: Cover letter, resume.
Additional information: Recent college graduatates also eligible. Ten-week internship available on part-time basis for winter/spring and fall terms and full-time for summer. Interns receive a stipend. Application deadlines are 3/15 for summer, 7/28 for fall, and 12/4 for winter/spring. Internship not always available for all seasons. Must have strong knowledge of Microsoft Office. Candidate should have interest in event planning and/or nonprofit sector. Visit Website for details.

   Number of awards: 1
Contact:
Americans for the Arts
Attn: Human Resources
1000 Vermont Avenue, NW, 6th Floor
Washington, DC 20005
Phone: 202-371-2830
Fax: 202-371-0424
Web: www.americansforthearts.org

Membership Internship

Type of award: Internship.
Intended use: For undergraduate or graduate study.
Basis for selection: Major/career interest in nonprofit administration; arts management; arts, general or marketing.
Application requirements: Cover letter, resume.
Additional information: Recent college graduates also eligible. Ten-week internship available full-time for winter/spring and fall and part-time for summer. Application deadlines are 3/15 for summer, 7/28 for fall, and 12/4 for winter/spring. Internship not always available for all seasons. Check Website for details. Must have knowledge of Microsoft Office; experience using database software a plus. Ideal candidate has interest and experience in marketing, membership, or arts administration.

   Number of awards: 1
Contact:
Americans for the Arts
Attn: Human Resources
1000 Vermont Avenue, NW, 6th Floor
Washington, DC 20005
Phone: 202-371-2830
Fax: 202-371-0424
Web: www.americansforthearts.org

Private-Sector Initiatives Internship

Type of award: Internship.

Intended use: For undergraduate or graduate study at postsecondary institution.
Basis for selection: Major/career interest in business; arts, general; arts management or nonprofit administration.
Application requirements: Cover letter, resume.
Additional information: Recent college graduates may apply. Position is based in New York, NY. Major/career interest in program management, research, and development. Ten-week internship available part-time for winter/spring and fall and full-time for summer. Application deadlines are 3/15 for summer, 7/28 for fall, and 12/4 for winter/spring. Internship not always available for all seasons. Check Website for details. All interns receive stipend. Must have excellent writing and research skills, know MS Office (especially) Excel, and have interest in the business value of the arts. Download application from Website or apply online.

Number of awards:	1

Contact:
Americans for the Arts
Attn: Human Resources
1000 Vermont Avenue NW, 6th Floor
Washington, DC 20005
Phone: 202-371-2830
Fax: 202-371-0424
Web: www.americansforthearts.org

Research Services Internship

Type of award: Internship.
Intended use: For undergraduate or graduate study.
Basis for selection: Major/career interest in nonprofit administration; arts management or arts, general.
Application requirements: Cover letter, resume.
Additional information: Recent college graduates also eligible. Ten-week positions available part-time for winter/spring and fall and full-time for summer. Application deadlines are 3/15 for summer, 7/28 for fall, and 12/4 for winter/spring. Interns receive stipend. Must have knowledge of Microsoft Office and be able to work independently. Commitment to serve the nonprofit arts field required. Internship may not be available every year, check Website for details.

Number of awards:	1

Contact:
Americans for the Arts
Attn: Human Resources
1000 Vermont Avenue, NW, 6th Floor
Washington, DC 20005
Phone: 202-371-2830
Fax: 202-371-0424
Web: www.americansforthearts.org

Applied Arts

Applied Arts Internships

Type of award: Internship.
Intended use: For undergraduate study at postsecondary institution.
Basis for selection: Major/career interest in arts, general; public administration/service; marketing; education or arts management.
Application requirements: Resume, cover letter.
Additional information: Internships are for college credit and are open to all high school/college/international students or graduates. Available in the following fields: education TA in fine arts (painting, drawing, sculpture, digital media, and photography); arts management; events management; office assistant; public service; youth program assistant; marketing/ promotion. Rolling application deadline and open duration. E-mail applications preferred.

Number of awards:	10
Number of applicants:	100

Contact:
Applied Arts
Attn: Internship Coordinator
P.O. Box 1336
Amagansett, NY 11930
Phone: 631-267-2787
Fax: 631-267-3428
Web: www.appliedartsschool.com/internships.html

Elizabeth Dow Ltd. Internships

Type of award: Internship.
Intended use: For undergraduate or graduate study.
Basis for selection: Major/career interest in arts, general; interior design; marketing; design or arts management.
Application requirements: Recommendations. Resume, cover letter.
Additional information: High school students and recent college graduates also eligible to apply. Internship is unpaid, but college credit available. Program has rolling admission; duration of internship is flexible.

Number of awards:	30
Number of applicants:	100

Contact:
Elizabeth Dow Ltd.
Attn: Internship Coordinator
P.O. Box 2310
Amagansett, NY 11930
Phone: 631-267-3401
Fax: 631-267-3428
Web: www.appliedartsschool.com/internships.html

Applied Materials, Global College Programs

Internship and Co-op Program

Type of award: Internship.
Intended use: For undergraduate or graduate study at accredited postsecondary institution.
Basis for selection: Major/career interest in accounting; business; business/management/administration; computer/ information sciences; engineering, chemical; engineering, electrical/electronic; engineering, mechanical; finance/banking; materials science or physics. Applicant must demonstrate high academic achievement.
Application requirements: Resume.
Additional information: Applicant should have interest in semi-conductor industry. Paid, summer, and year-round internships and co-op positions based in Texas and California. Visit Website to submit resume and to find out when internship interviews will be held at college campuses. Minimum 3.0 GPA.

Number of awards:	100

Contact:
Applied Materials, Global College Programs
2881 Scott Blvd.
MS 2005
Santa Clara, CA 95050
Web: www.appliedmaterials.com/careers

Arts and Business Council of New York

Multicultural Arts Management Internship Program

Type of award: Internship.
Intended use: For sophomore, junior or senior study at 2-year or 4-year institution.
Eligibility: Applicant must be U.S. citizen.
Basis for selection: Major/career interest in arts management.
Application requirements: Interview, essay. Resume, cover letter.
Additional information: Interns spend ten weeks (June to August) working full-time at a New York City arts organization. Preference given to African-American, Asian-American, Latino/a, and Native American students. Must have taken arts, business, or marketing courses, or been involved in similar extracurricular activities. Students who will graduate right before start of internship are eligible but must explain how internship relates to career goals. Application available online.

Amount of award:	$2,500
Number of awards:	11
Number of applicants:	80
Application deadline:	February 19
Notification begins:	April 10

Contact:
Arts and Business Council of New York
Attn: Internship Program
One East 53rd Street, 3rd Floor
New York, NY 10022
Phone: 212-279-5910
Fax: 212-279-5915
Web: www.artsandbusiness-ny.org/leadership_development/
arts_management/default.asp

Bernstein-Rein Advertising

Advertising Internship

Type of award: Internship.
Intended use: For junior study.
Basis for selection: Major/career interest in advertising; communications or marketing.
Application requirements: Interview. Resume, cover letter, three reference names, one-page writing sample.
Additional information: Internship runs for nine weeks in summer. Applicant must have one or two semesters left before graduation. Pay is $10 per hour. Two positions each in account management, media, and creative. Application available online.

Number of awards:	6
Number of applicants:	122
Application deadline:	February 1
Notification begins:	March 1

Contact:
Bernstein-Rein
Human Resources
4600 Madison, Suite 1500
Kansas City, MO 64112
Phone: 816-756-0640
Fax: 816-399-6000
Web: www.bernstein-rein.com

Black & Veatch Corporation

Summer Internship Program

Type of award: Internship.
Intended use: For full-time junior or senior study in United States.
Eligibility: Applicant must be U.S. citizen or permanent resident.
Basis for selection: Major/career interest in architecture; economics; engineering, civil; engineering, electrical/electronic; engineering or finance/banking. Applicant must demonstrate high academic achievement.
Application requirements: Resume.
Additional information: Internship compensation varies by discipline. Minimum 2.75 GPA. Positions offered across the U.S. Students should apply for internships as soon as the fall career fairs, and positions will be posted online until filled.
Contact:
Web: www.bv.com/careers

BMI Foundation, Inc.

Pete Carpenter Fellowship

Type of award: Internship.
Intended use: For non-degree study.
Eligibility: Applicant must be no older than 34.
Basis for selection: Competition/talent/interest in music performance/composition, based on original one- to three-minute composition or selection from score appropriate for theatrical or TV film or series theme music. Major/career interest in music or radio/television/film.
Application requirements: One- to three-minute composition in CD format.
Additional information: Winner will work for four to five weeks with composer Mike Post at his studio in Los Angeles. Visit Website for application. Completed application must be notarized. Application deadline in last week of January; see Website for exact date.

Amount of award:	$3,000
Number of awards:	1
Number of applicants:	130
Notification begins:	June 1
Total amount awarded:	$3,000

Contact:
Linda Livingston
BMI Foundation/Pete Carpenter Fellowship
8730 Sunset Boulevard, 3rd Floor West
Los Angeles, CA 90069
Web: www.bmifoundation.org

Board of Governors of the Federal Reserve System

Economic Research Division Project Internships

Type of award: Internship, renewable.
Intended use: For undergraduate or graduate study at postsecondary institution.
Basis for selection: Major/career interest in economics; statistics; computer/information sciences; mathematics or finance/banking. Applicant must demonstrate high academic achievement.
Application requirements: Recommendations, transcript. Resume, cover letter.
Additional information: Paid internship lasts from June to September. Submit application by e-mail.

Application deadline:	April 1

Contact:
Board of Governors of the Federal Reserve System
20th Street and Constitution Avenue NW
Washington, DC 20551
Phone: 202-452-3880
Web: www.federalreserve.gov/careers/intern_research.htm

Boeing Company

Boeing Internships

Type of award: Internship.
Intended use: For undergraduate or graduate study in United States.
Eligibility: Applicant must be U.S. citizen or permanent resident.
Basis for selection: Major/career interest in aerospace; computer/information sciences; finance/banking; human resources; manufacturing; marketing; public relations; engineering; mathematics or business.
Application requirements: Resume.
Additional information: Internships available at Boeing sites in Seattle, WA; Arizona; Florida; Southern California; St. Louis, MO; Texas; Philadelphia, PA; Huntsville, AL; Washington, D.C.; Chicago, IL; and Wichita, KS. Deadlines, eligibility requirements, and compensation vary depending on position. See Website for detailed information on available positions and to submit resume.

Number of awards:	800

Contact:
Web: www.boeing.com/collegecareers

Boston Globe

Boston Globe Summer Internship

Type of award: Internship.
Intended use: For junior, senior or graduate study at 4-year or graduate institution.
Basis for selection: Major/career interest in journalism.
Application requirements: Interview, recommendations. Writing samples/clips.
Additional information: Full-time, 12-week summer internship at approximately $700 per week. Current undergraduate students in any major may apply, as well as journalism graduate students without professional experience as newspaper reporter. Applicants must have had at least one previous internship at daily newspaper. Must have driver's license and be able to type 30 words per minute. Application available online in September.

Number of awards:	10
Number of applicants:	500
Application deadline:	November 1
Notification begins:	December 31

Contact:
The Boston Globe
Attn: Mary Rourke
P.O. Box 55819
Boston, MA 02205-5819
Phone: 617-929-2000
Web: www.bostonglobe.com/newsintern

Chevron Corporation

Chevron Internship Program

Type of award: Internship.
Intended use: For full-time junior, senior, master's or doctoral study at postsecondary institution.
Basis for selection: Major/career interest in business; business/management/administration; computer/information sciences; engineering; finance/banking; geology/earth sciences; human resources; information systems; marketing or political science/government.
Application requirements: Transcript. Resume and cover letter.
Additional information: Paid, full-time internships, terms vary. International students must be qualified to work in U.S. Apply through campus visits or special recruiting events, or for those attending non-recruited schools, apply for internships posted online. Visit Website for more details. Application deadline is rolling.

Number of awards:	300

Contact:
Web: careers.chevron.com/students/

Citizens for Global Solutions

Citizens for Global Solutions Internship

Type of award: Internship, renewable.
Intended use: For undergraduate or graduate study at postsecondary institution.
Basis for selection: Major/career interest in international relations; international studies; information systems; journalism; nonprofit administration; political science/government or web design.
Application requirements: Resume, cover letter, three- to five- page writing sample.
Additional information: Recent graduates also eligible. Internship includes $10 per day stipend. Application deadlines are April 1 for summer, August 1 for fall, and December 1 for spring. Visit Website for more information.

   Application deadline: April 1, August 1
Contact:
Citizens for Global Solutions
418 7th Street SE
Washington, DC 20003-2796
Phone: 202-546-3950 ext. 100
Fax: 202-546-3749
Web: www.globalsolutions.org/about/internships

Congressional Hispanic Caucus Institute

CHCI Congressional Internship

Type of award: Internship.
Intended use: For full-time sophomore, junior or senior study at accredited 2-year or 4-year institution.
Eligibility: Applicant must be U.S. citizen or permanent resident.
Basis for selection: Applicant must demonstrate high academic achievement, leadership and service orientation.
Application requirements: Recommendations, transcript. Three personal essays, resume.
Additional information: Spring (12 week), fall (12 week) and summer (eight week) internship in Washington, D.C. congressional offices. Transportation, housing, and stipend provided; $2,500 for eight week program, and $3,750 for 12 week program. Must have excellent writing and analytical skills and active participation in community service activities. Work experience is complemented by leadership development sessions. Minimum 3.0 GPA preferred. Visit Website for deadline information and application.

   Number of awards: 30
   Number of applicants: 134
Contact:
CHCI Internship Program
911 Second Street, NE
Washington, DC 20002
Phone: 202-543-1771
Fax: 202-546-2143
Web: www.chci.org/internships

Congressional Institute, Inc.

Congressional Institute Internships

Type of award: Internship.
Intended use: For undergraduate study at accredited 2-year or 4-year institution in United States.
Eligibility: Applicant must be U.S. citizen.
Basis for selection: Major/career interest in political science/government; public administration/service; law or communications. Applicant must demonstrate high academic achievement.
Application requirements: Recommendations. Resume and writing samples.
Additional information: Paid internships available throughout the year on flexible terms. Must have interest in public policy or legislative policy issues. Visit Website for application and additional information.
Contact:
Congressional Institute, Inc.
1001 N. Fairfax Street
#410
Alexandria, VA 22314
Phone: 703-837-8812
Fax: 703-837-8817
Web: www.conginst.org

Creede Repertory Theatre

CRT Internship Program

Type of award: Internship.
Intended use: For undergraduate study at postsecondary institution.
Eligibility: Applicant must be at least 18.
Basis for selection: Major/career interest in business; design; humanities/liberal arts; performing arts; theater arts; theater/production/technical; education or marketing.
Application requirements: Recommendations. Statement of intent. Resume.
Additional information: Potential internship positions available depending on seasons' needs/limitations: wardrobe, prop assistant, stage management, actors, box office/front of house, or business/marketing. Interns receive $125 weekly stipend and free housing. Application deadline on rolling basis. See Website for more information or e-mail with questions.
Contact:
CRT Internship Program Attn: Renee Stynchula
Creede Repertory Theatre
P.O. Box 269
Creede, CO 81130
Phone: 719-658-2540 ext. 27
Web: www.creederep.org

Cushman School

Cushman School Internship

Type of award: Internship, renewable.
Intended use: For undergraduate or graduate study.

Basis for selection: Major/career interest in education.
Application requirements: Resume, cover letter.
Additional information: Internship is 17 weeks on Cushman School campus for fall and spring semesters. Interns assist staff in grading papers, supervising students, and performing administrative work. Internships are full-time, 8 a.m. to 3:30 p.m., Monday to Friday. Stipend of $2,000 for U.S. students and $3,000 for international students awarded each semester. International students must have J1 visa. Rolling application deadline.

> Amount of award: $2,000-$3,000
> Number of awards: 2

Contact:
Cushman School
592 Northeast 60th Street
Miami, FL 33137
Phone: 305-757-1966
Fax: 305-757-1632
Web: www.cushmanschool.org

Denver Rescue Mission

Denver Rescue Mission Center for Mission Studies Internships

Type of award: Internship.
Intended use: For junior, senior or graduate study at postsecondary institution in United States.
Basis for selection: Major/career interest in social work; religion/theology; ministry; nonprofit administration; health services administration; public relations; marketing or information systems. Applicant must demonstrate service orientation.
Additional information: Denver Rescue Mission is a nondenominational Christian charity offering internships in the following areas: child development, family studies, human services, management information systems, medical office administration, public relations/marketing, social work, volunteer relations, counseling, family therapy, shelter management, and nonprofit administration. Internships vary in length, and some may have gender, age, level-of-study, or other requirements. Full-time interns earn $400 per month, and are held to a minimum work commitment of four months. See Website for details and to apply.

> Number of awards: 100
> Number of applicants: 200

Contact:
Denver Rescue Mission
P.O. Box 5206
Denver, CO 80217
Phone: 303-953-3955
Web: www.denverrescuemission.org/internships.html

Dow Jones News Fund

Business Reporting Intern Program

Type of award: Internship.
Intended use: For full-time junior, senior or graduate study at 2-year or 4-year institution.

Eligibility: Applicant must be U.S. citizen, permanent resident or international student.
Basis for selection: Major/career interest in journalism or business. Applicant must demonstrate high academic achievement and seriousness of purpose.
Application requirements: Interview, essay, transcript, proof of eligibility. Resume, three to five recently published clips, reporting test.
Additional information: May have any major, but must plan to pursue journalism career. Special interest in business a plus. Applications available online August to October 30. All applicants notified by January 31. Applicants must take reporting test administered by designated professor on applicant's campus. Telephone interview required for finalists. Paid summer internships as business reporters at daily newspapers last at least 10 to 12 weeks. Interns returning to school receive scholarship at end of summer to apply toward following year. All interns attend pre-internship training that lasts one week. International students must have work visa.

> Amount of award: $1,000
> Number of awards: 12
> Application deadline: November 1
> Notification begins: January 15
> Total amount awarded: $12,000

Contact:
Dow Jones News Fund
Business Reporting Intern Program
P.O. Box 300
Princeton, NJ 08543-0300
Phone: 609-452-2820
Web: www.newsfund.org

Multimedia Intern Program

Type of award: Internship.
Intended use: For full-time junior, senior or graduate study at 4-year or graduate institution in United States.
Eligibility: Applicant must be U.S. citizen, permanent resident or international student.
Basis for selection: Major/career interest in journalism. Applicant must demonstrate high academic achievement and seriousness of purpose.
Application requirements: Essay, transcript. Resume, exam.
Additional information: May have any major but must intend to pursue journalism career. Applications available online August through October 30. Must take editing test administered by designated professor on applicant's campus. Finalists undergo telephone interview. Paid 10 to 12-week summer internships as editors at daily newspapers, online newspapers, or news services. Must attend one-week pre-internship training. Interns returning to school receive scholarship. International students must have work visa.

> Amount of award: $1,000
> Number of awards: 12
> Number of applicants: 600
> Application deadline: November 1
> Notification begins: December 15
> Total amount awarded: $12,000

Contact:
Dow Jones News Fund
Multimedia Editing Intern Program
P.O. Box 300
Princeton, NJ 08543-0300
Phone: 609-452-2820
Web: www.newsfund.org

News Copy Editing Intern Program

Type of award: Internship.
Intended use: For full-time junior, senior or graduate study at 4-year or graduate institution in United States.
Eligibility: Applicant must be U.S. citizen, permanent resident or international student.
Basis for selection: Major/career interest in journalism. Applicant must demonstrate high academic achievement and seriousness of purpose.
Application requirements: Essay, transcript. Resume, editing test.
Additional information: May have any major but must plan to pursue journalism career. Applications available online August to October 30. All applicants notified by December 31. Applicants may apply for sports, multimedia, and/or news copy editing programs using common application. Editing test administered by designated professor on applicant's campus. Telephone interview required for finalists. Paid summer internships, as editors at daily newspapers, online newspapers, or real-time financial news services, last 10 to 12 weeks. Interns returning to school receive scholarship at end of summer to apply toward following year. All interns attend pre-internship training that lasts one to two weeks. International students must have work visa.

Amount of award:	$1,000
Number of awards:	100
Number of applicants:	600
Application deadline:	November 1
Notification begins:	December 15
Total amount awarded:	$70,000

Contact:
Dow Jones News Fund
News Copy Editing Intern Program
P.O. Box 300
Princeton, NJ 08543-0300
Phone: 609-452-2820
Web: www.newsfund.org

Sports Copy Editing Intern Program

Type of award: Internship.
Intended use: For full-time junior, senior or graduate study.
Eligibility: Applicant must be U.S. citizen, permanent resident or international student.
Basis for selection: Major/career interest in journalism.
Application requirements: Essay, transcript. Editing exam, resume.
Additional information: Applicants may have any major but must plan to pursue career in journalism. Interns will work on sports copy desks at daily newspapers and attend training at the University of Nebraska at Lincoln, taught by Dr. Charlyne Berens. The seminars last two weeks. Applicants may apply for sports, online, and/or news copy editing programs using common application form. International students must have work visa.

Amount of award:	$1,000
Number of awards:	12
Application deadline:	November 1
Notification begins:	December 15
Total amount awarded:	$12,000

Contact:
Dow Jones News Fund
Sports Copy Editing Intern Program
P.O. Box 300
Princeton, NJ 08543-0300
Phone: 609-452-2820
Web: www.newsfund.org

DuPont Company

DuPont Co-ops

Type of award: Internship.
Intended use: For full-time sophomore, junior or senior study at accredited 4-year institution in United States.
Eligibility: Applicant must be U.S. citizen or permanent resident.
Basis for selection: Major/career interest in accounting; engineering, chemical; engineering, electrical/electronic; engineering, mechanical; finance/banking; marketing or science, general.
Application requirements: Resume and cover letter.
Additional information: Co-ops available at DuPont company sites throughout U.S. Participants alternate work assignments and academic terms. Applicants can start no earlier than after completion of freshman year and work a minimum of three industrial work periods. Preference given to juniors and seniors. Must be registered with school's co-op office. Competitive compensation. Minimum 3.0 GPA. Must apply through Website.
Contact:
Web: www.dupont.com/careers

DuPont Internships

Type of award: Internship.
Intended use: For full-time sophomore, junior, senior or master's study at accredited 4-year institution in United States.
Eligibility: Applicant must be U.S. citizen or permanent resident.
Basis for selection: Major/career interest in accounting; engineering, chemical; engineering, electrical/electronic; engineering, mechanical; finance/banking; marketing or science, general.
Application requirements: Resume and cover letter.
Additional information: Interns normally work in summer between junior and senior years at DuPont company sites throughout U.S. May apply for extended internship. Minimum 3.0 GPA. Number and amount of awards vary. Must apply through Website.
Contact:
Web: www.dupont.com/careers

Eastman Kodak Company

Cooperative Internship Programs

Type of award: Internship.
Intended use: For full-time sophomore, junior, senior or graduate study.
Basis for selection: Major/career interest in accounting; business; chemistry; computer/information sciences; engineering; finance/banking; manufacturing; marketing or physics.
Application requirements: Resume and cover letter.
Additional information: Internship must be minimum ten consecutive weeks any time during year (most occur in summer). Positions offered in Rochester, NY, Windsor, CO, and Dayton, OH. Internship includes competitive salary based upon discipline and education level, and travel expenses. Applicant

must be drug-screened as condition of employment. Minimum 3.0 GPA highly desired. Apply online.

Number of awards: 60

Contact:
Eastman Kodak Company
Talent Acquisition
343 State Street
Rochester, NY 14650-1139
Web: www.kodak.com/go/careers

Entergy

Entergy Jumpstart Co-ops and Internships

Type of award: Internship, renewable.
Intended use: For full-time undergraduate or graduate study at accredited 4-year or graduate institution in United States.
Eligibility: Applicant must be U.S. citizen or permanent resident.
Basis for selection: Major/career interest in engineering, civil; business; accounting; computer/information sciences; human resources; engineering, electrical/electronic; engineering, mechanical; engineering, nuclear; information systems or finance/banking. Applicant must demonstrate high academic achievement and depth of character.
Additional information: Paid co-ops and internships available. Minimum 3.0 GPA. Apply online. Visit Website for application deadline, list of targeted campuses in the South, recruiting schedule, and current openings. Must have work experience and give graduation date.

Contact:
Phone: 504-576-4000
Web: www.entergy.com/careers

Entertainment Weekly

Entertainment Weekly Internship Program

Type of award: Internship.
Intended use: For junior, senior or postgraduate study at postsecondary institution.
Basis for selection: Major/career interest in journalism or publishing.
Application requirements: Resume, cover letter, and five clips/writing samples.
Additional information: Internships in editorial department last 12-18 weeks and pay $10 per hour. Summer internships open to rising seniors and recent graduates. Fall and spring internships for recent college graduates only. Application deadlines are Feb. 15 for summer, Jun. 15 for fall, and Oct. 15 for winter.

Number of awards:	2
Number of applicants:	200
Application deadline:	February 15, June 15
Notification begins:	March 1, July 1

Contact:
Tanner Stransky Entertainment Weekly Internship Coordinator
135 W. 50th Street, 3rd Floor
New York, NY 10020
Phone: 212-522-5600
Fax: 212-522-6104
Web: www.ew.com

The Environmental Institute for Golf

The Scotts Company Scholars Program

Type of award: Internship.
Intended use: For undergraduate study at accredited 2-year or 4-year institution.
Basis for selection: Major/career interest in turf management. Applicant must demonstrate high academic achievement and leadership.
Application requirements: Recommendations, transcript. Letter of acceptance from college or university (high school seniors).
Additional information: Must be pursuing career in golf course management industry. Summer internship includes opportunity to learn more about golf course industry and compete for two $2500 scholarships. Scholarship awardees receive all-expense paid trip to GCSAA-sponsored Golf Industry Show. Interns receive $500 to supplement internship income. Women, minorities, and individuals with disabilities encouraged to apply. Children of The Scotts Company employees, GCSAA Environmental Institute for Golf's Board of Trustees, GCSAA Board of Directors, and GCSAA staff not eligible. Visit Website for application and more information.

Amount of award:	$500-$2,500
Number of awards:	5
Application deadline:	March 1
Notification begins:	May 1

Contact:
Golf Course Superintendents Association of America
Scholarship Program
1421 Research Park Drive
Lawrence, KS 66049-3859
Phone: 785-832-4445 or 800-472-7878 ext. 4445
Web: www.gcsaa.org

ESPN Inc.

ESPN Internship

Type of award: Internship.
Intended use: For full-time junior, senior or graduate study.
Eligibility: Applicant must be U.S. citizen or permanent resident.
Basis for selection: Major/career interest in sports/sports administration; communications; computer/information sciences; statistics; graphic arts/design; journalism; marketing or radio/television/film. Applicant must demonstrate high academic achievement.
Application requirements: Resume and cover letter.

Additional information: Applicants should be within 12 months of graduation. Internships last ten weeks at 40 hours per week. Most positions based in Bristol, CT or New York, NY, with limited opportunities at other locations. CT and NY interns may qualify for subsidized housing. Previous internship experience a plus. Competitive pay. Course credit offered based on college requirements. Internships offered in spring, summer and fall. Applications processed on rolling basis; apply online.

Number of applicants:	10,000
Application deadline:	March 1, July 1

Contact:
ESPN Inc.
Phone: 860-766-2000
Web: www.espncareers.com/campus

Essence Magazine

Essence Summer Internship

Type of award: Internship, renewable.
Intended use: For undergraduate or graduate study at accredited 4-year institution in United States.
Basis for selection: Major/career interest in advertising; business; fashion/fashion design/modeling; graphic arts/design; journalism; marketing; public relations or publishing.
Application requirements: Resume and writing sample or digital portfolio.
Additional information: Must be authorized to work in U.S. Nine-week summer internships available in several departments: sales and marketing, Essence.com, fashion and beauty, art/photo, public relations, business office, and editorial. Interns responsible for finding their own housing. Receive bi-weekly paycheck. Must have appreciation for magazine industry; be self-motivated and detail-oriented. Visit Website for application and more information.

Number of awards:	10
Number of applicants:	300
Application deadline:	January 15
Notification begins:	April 15

Contact:
Essence Magazine
Internship Coordinator
135 West 50th Street, 4th Floor
New York, NY 10020
Phone: 212-522-1212
Fax: 212-467-2357
Web: www.essence.com/internships

Federal Reserve Bank of New York

Undergraduate Summer Internship

Type of award: Internship.
Intended use: For full-time senior study at postsecondary institution.
Basis for selection: Major/career interest in finance/banking; economics; business; computer/information sciences; accounting or public administration/service. Applicant must demonstrate high academic achievement.
Application requirements: Interview. Resume.

Additional information: Paid internships begin in late May/early June. Applicants must have completed junior year of college before beginning internship. Opportunities generally available in bank supervision and regulation, domestic and international research, and information technology and markets. Applicants must be available for in-person interviews in March/April. Housing not provided. International students must be legally authorized to work in U.S. on a multi-year basis for other than practical training purposes. Submit resume online.

Application deadline:	January 31

Contact:
Federal Reserve Bank of New York
Summer Internship Coordinator
33 Liberty Street
New York, NY 10045
Phone: 212-720-5000
Web: www.ny.frb.org/careers/summerintern.html

Feminist Majority Foundation

Feminism & Leadership Internship

Type of award: Internship.
Intended use: For undergraduate study at accredited 4-year institution.
Basis for selection: Major/career interest in women's studies or political science/government. Applicant must demonstrate high academic achievement and leadership.
Application requirements: Resume, cover letter, writing sample.
Additional information: Full-time or part-time internships for a minimum of two months available year-round in the Washington, DC, area and Los Angeles. Interns have various responsibilities, such as monitoring press conferences and coalition meetings, researching, attending rallies, and organizing events. Internships unpaid, but students may be able to earn small stipend in exchange for administrative work. Applicants with experience working on women's issues preferred. People of color, people with disabilities, and math/science majors encouraged to apply. Application deadlines for DC office are March 31 for summer, June 30 for fall, and September 30 for spring. Applications processed on rolling basis for LA office. See Website for more information.

Number of awards:	50
Number of applicants:	200
Application deadline:	March 31, June 30

Contact:
Feminist Majority Foundation
Attn: Internship Coordinator
1600 Wilson Boulevard, Suite 801
Arlington, VA 22209
Phone: 703-522-2214
Fax: 703-522-2219
Web: www.feminist.org/intern

Internships

Filoli Center

Filoli Center Garden Internships and Apprenticeships

Type of award: Internship.
Intended use: For undergraduate, graduate or non-degree study at postsecondary institution. Designated institutions: Filoli Center.
Basis for selection: Major/career interest in horticulture; landscape architecture or botany. Applicant must demonstrate high academic achievement, depth of character, leadership and seriousness of purpose.
Application requirements: Interview, recommendations, transcript. Resume and cover letter outlining interests.
Additional information: Also for students pursuing careers in public garden management and landscape maintenance. Students paid $8 per hour and may earn college credit for ten-week internship program or six-month apprenticeship program. Applicants must have at least 15 units of horticulture classes and 3.0 GPA. Ability to work well with public and work teams essential. Maximum five students per internship. Visit Website for deadlines and application.

Amount of award:	$3,200-$8,320
Number of awards:	12
Total amount awarded:	$32,000

Contact:
Filoli Center
Filoli Garden Internships
86 Cañada Road
Woodside, CA 94062
Phone: 650-364-8300 ext. 214
Fax: 650-366-7836
Web: www.filoli.org/education/garden-internships.html

Florida Department of Education

Florida Work Experience Program

Type of award: Internship, renewable.
Intended use: For undergraduate study at vocational, 2-year or 4-year institution. Designated institutions: Eligible Florida postsecondary institutions.
Eligibility: Applicant must be U.S. citizen or permanent resident residing in Florida.
Basis for selection: Applicant must demonstrate financial need.
Application requirements: Proof of eligibility. FAFSA.
Additional information: Minimum 2.0 GPA. Provides students with opportunity to be employed off-campus in jobs related to their academic major or area of career interest. Applications available from participating schools' financial aid offices. Amount of award determined by institution and may not exceed student's financial need.
Contact:
Office of Student Financial Assistance
325 West Gaines Street
Tallahassee, FL 32399-0400
Phone: 888-827-2004
Web: www.floridastudentfinancialaid.org

Florida Power & Light Company

Florida Power & Light Internship Program

Type of award: Internship, renewable.
Intended use: For full-time undergraduate study at accredited vocational or 4-year institution in United States.
Eligibility: Applicant must be U.S. citizen or permanent resident.
Basis for selection: Major/career interest in engineering; engineering, nuclear; engineering, mechanical; engineering, electrical/electronic; engineering, civil; engineering, industrial; finance/banking; accounting or computer/information sciences. Applicant must demonstrate high academic achievement.
Application requirements: Resume.
Additional information: Positions are paid. Minimum 3.0 GPA. Apply online or check Website for campus recruiting calendar.
Contact:
Florida Power & Light Company
Ms. Toni Scholze
P.O. Box 14000, HRR/JB
Juno Beach, FL 33408-0420
Phone: 561-694-4664
Web: www.fplcareers.com/recruiting/contents/college_recruiting.shtml

Fox Group

Fox Internship

Type of award: Internship.
Intended use: For sophomore, junior, senior or graduate study at accredited 4-year or graduate institution.
Eligibility: Applicant must be International students eligible to work in United States.
Basis for selection: Major/career interest in advertising; accounting; business; communications; film/video; finance/banking; journalism; marketing; public relations or theater/production/technical.
Application requirements: Resume and cover letter that includes areas of interest.
Additional information: Internships are available in all departments within Film, Television and Digital Media. Applicants must be eligible to receive college credit. Apply via Website.
Contact:
Web: www.foxcareers.com

Franklin D. Roosevelt Library

Roosevelt Archival Internships

Type of award: Internship.

Intended use: For undergraduate or graduate study at postsecondary institution.

Basis for selection: Major/career interest in education; computer/information sciences; museum studies; history; political science/government or library science.

Application requirements: Transcript.

Additional information: Interns work at FDR library with other interns and staff organizing and automating archival materials, making indices, finding aids and databases, digitizing documents and photographs, and assisting with other projects. Internship can last up to eight weeks and must take place during summer break (mid-May through end of August). Housing not provided. Work Monday through Friday, 9 a.m. to 5 p.m. Stipend of $300 per week. Number of awards depends on funding. Familiarity with FDR presidency helpful. Visit Website for application.

Number of awards:	3
Number of applicants:	75
Application deadline:	April 15
Notification begins:	April 24

Contact:
Franklin D. Roosevelt Library
Roosevelt Archival Internship Program
4079 Albany Post Road
Hyde Park, NY 12538
Phone: 845-486-7745
Fax: 845-486-1147
Web: www.fdrlibrary.marist.edu/intern.html

Garden Club of America

GCA Internship in Garden History and Design

Type of award: Internship.

Intended use: For undergraduate or graduate study.

Basis for selection: Major/career interest in botany; horticulture; landscape architecture or museum studies.

Application requirements: Recommendations, essay, transcript. Two letters of recommendation (one from professor in major, one from advisor).

Additional information: May apply to Archives of American Gardens in Washington, DC or at other eligible institutions (contact sponsor to verify). Interns at Archives of American Gardens, Smithsonian Institutes work for 10 to 16 weeks and receive stipends of $360/week for undergraduates, $420 for graduate students; GCA funds act as supplement.

Amount of award:	$2,000
Number of awards:	1
Application deadline:	February 15

Contact:
Garden Club of America
Ms. Judy Smith
14 East 60th Street
New York, NY 10022-1002
Phone: 212-753-8287
Fax: 212-753-0134
Web: www.gcamerica.org

Genentech, Inc.

Genentech, Inc. Internship Program

Type of award: Internship, renewable.

Intended use: For full-time undergraduate or graduate study at accredited 4-year institution.

Basis for selection: Major/career interest in biology; business; chemistry; computer/information sciences; engineering; engineering, biomedical; engineering, chemical; law; life sciences or medicine. Applicant must demonstrate high academic achievement.

Application requirements: Resume and cover letter.

Additional information: Paid summer internships last 10-12 weeks and are available in various research and business areas. International students must have work authorization. Apply online or check Website for campus recruiting schedule.

Number of awards:	250

Contact:
Genentech, Inc.
1 DNA Way
South San Francisco, CA 94080-4990
Phone: 650-225-1000
Fax: 650-225-6000
Web: www.gene.com/gene/careers/university

Georgia-Pacific, LLC

Georgia-Pacific Internship and Co-op Programs

Type of award: Internship.

Intended use: For undergraduate or master's study in United States.

Eligibility: Applicant must be U.S. citizen or permanent resident.

Basis for selection: Major/career interest in engineering, chemical; engineering, electrical/electronic; engineering, mechanical or finance/banking. Applicant must demonstrate high academic achievement.

Application requirements: Transcript, proof of eligibility.

Additional information: Internships and co-ops are paid, and number awarded varies. Basic qualifications vary by department. Submit profile and resume through Website form. Supply chain/logistics majors also eligible.

Number of awards:	50
Number of applicants:	50

Contact:
Georgia-Pacific, LLC Attn: College Relations Program Manager
133 Peachtree Street, NE
Floor 39
Atlanta, GA 30303
Phone: 404-652-4000
Web: www.gp.com/careers

Hannaford Bros Co.

Hannaford Internships

Type of award: Internship.

Intended use: For undergraduate or master's study at postsecondary institution.

Eligibility: Applicant must be U.S. citizen, permanent resident or international student.

Basis for selection: Major/career interest in pharmacy/pharmaceutics/pharmacology.

Application requirements: Cover letter and resume.

Additional information: Twelve week summer internship, beginning early June. Interns at Hannaford are exposed to a multicultural organization with support systems and training opportunities. Internships available at Hannaford's corporate office, distribution centers, and retail locations. Pharmacy internships also available. Inquire at campus placement office to schedule recruiting interview or e-mail for additional information. Minimum 3.0 GPA. Must be legally authorized to work in United States. Amount of payment or course credit awarded varies. International students must have work authorization. Visit Website for more information. Applications accepted online only.

Application deadline: February 15

Contact:
Hannaford Brothers Company Employment Department
Phone: 800-442-6049
Fax: 207-885-2859
Web: www.hannaford.com

Hispanic Association of Colleges and Universities

HACU National Internship Program

Type of award: Internship.

Intended use: For sophomore, junior, senior or graduate study at 2-year, 4-year or graduate institution. Designated institutions: Institutions with significant number of Hispanic students.

Eligibility: Applicant must be U.S. citizen or permanent resident.

Basis for selection: Applicant must demonstrate high academic achievement and service orientation.

Application requirements: Essay, transcript. Resume.

Additional information: Paid internships provide opportunities for students from institutions with significant numbers of Hispanic students to explore potential careers with federal agencies and private corporations. Interns work in Washington, DC, area and field sites throughout country. Some internships require U.S. citizenship to participate. Applicants must have 3.0 GPA and have completed freshman year of college before internship begins. Weekly pay varies according to class level: $450 for sophomores and juniors, $480 for seniors and $550 for graduates. Must be active in college and community service. Fall and spring internships last 15 weeks; summer internships last ten weeks. Deadlines: November for spring, February for summer, June for fall. Visit Website for more information.

Contact:
Hispanic Association of Colleges and Universities
One Dupont Circle, NW
Suite 430
Washington, DC 20036
Phone: 202-467-0893
Fax: 202-496-9177
Web: www.hnip.net

Hoffman-La Roche Inc.

Hoffman-La Roche Inc. Student Internship

Type of award: Internship.

Intended use: For full-time freshman, sophomore, junior or graduate study at postsecondary institution.

Basis for selection: Major/career interest in pharmacy/pharmaceutics/pharmacology; engineering; computer/information sciences; science, general; business; business/management/administration; biology; chemistry or biochemistry.

Application requirements: Interview. Cover letter, resume.

Additional information: Applicant must be authorized to work in the United States. Internship fields, topics, and amount of compensation vary. Send materials to address provided. If deadline is missed, application will be considered after those students who have met deadline. Visit Website for more information and internship descriptions.

Contact:
University Relations Department Hoffman-La Roche, Inc.
340 Kingsland Street
Nutley, NJ 07110-1199
Phone: 973-235-4035 or 973-235-5000
Web: www.rocheusa.com

IBM

IBM Co-op and Intern Program

Type of award: Internship.

Intended use: For full-time sophomore, junior, senior or graduate study at accredited 4-year or graduate institution in United States.

Basis for selection: Major/career interest in computer/information sciences; engineering, computer; engineering, electrical/electronic; information systems; accounting or finance/banking. Applicant must demonstrate high academic achievement and leadership.

Application requirements: Interview.

Additional information: Applicants chosen on competitive basis, based on relevant work or research experience, communication, team skills, and high evaluation during interview process. Most awardees are undergraduate juniors or first year masters students. Competitive salary based on number of credits completed towards degree. Applicants hired on semester basis. Must submit resume via IBM Website.

Contact:
IBM Co-op and Intern Program
27409
Web: www.ibm.com/employment/us/

The Indianapolis Star

Pulliam Journalism Fellowship

Type of award: Internship.

Intended use: For undergraduate or postgraduate study at postsecondary institution.

Basis for selection: Competition/talent/interest in writing/ journalism. Major/career interest in humanities/liberal arts or journalism. Applicant must demonstrate high academic achievement, depth of character, leadership and seriousness of purpose.

Application requirements: Recommendations, transcript, proof of eligibility. Writing samples. Recent photograph.

Additional information: Paid fellowship lasts ten weeks during summer. Ten recipients work for The Indianapolis Star, ten for The Arizona Republic in Phoenix. Applicants must be college students. Early deadline in November; final postmark deadline in March. Visit Website for application and more information.

Amount of award:	$6,500
Number of awards:	20
Number of applicants:	200
Application deadline:	November 1

Contact:
Russell B. Pulliam, Director
The Pulliam Fellowship
P.O. Box 145
Indianapolis, IN 46206-0145
Phone: 317-444-6001
Web: www.indystar.com/pjf

INROADS, Inc.

INROADS Internship

Type of award: Internship, renewable.

Intended use: For full-time freshman or sophomore study.

Eligibility: Applicant must be Alaskan native, Asian American, African American, Mexican American, Hispanic American, Puerto Rican or American Indian. Applicant must be high school senior. Applicant must be U.S. citizen or permanent resident.

Basis for selection: Major/career interest in engineering; business; computer/information sciences; communications; retailing/merchandising or health-related professions. Applicant must demonstrate high academic achievement, leadership and service orientation.

Application requirements: Interview, transcript. Resume. National College Component Application.

Additional information: Applicant must have minimum high school 3.0 GPA or college 2.8 GPA; minimum 1000 SAT or 20 ACT. Internship duration and compensation varies, and deadlines vary according to local affiliate office. Visit Website for additional information.

Number of awards:	4,000
Number of applicants:	20,000
Application deadline:	March 31

Contact:
INROADS, Inc.
10 S. Broadway
Suite 300
St. Louis, MO 63102
Phone: 314-241-7488
Fax: 314-241-9325
Web: www.inroads.org

International Radio and Television Society Foundation

International Radio and Television Society Foundation Summer Fellowship Program

Type of award: Internship.

Intended use: For junior, senior or graduate study at postsecondary institution.

Basis for selection: Major/career interest in communications.

Additional information: Nine week internship. Applicants must have prior internship experience and demonstrated interest in the field of communications. Fellows are awarded travel and housing expenses and small stipend. Visit Website for deadlines, information, and application.

Number of awards:	25
Application deadline:	December 1

Contact:
International Radio and Television Society Foundation
420 Lexington Avenue, Suite 1601
New York, NY 10170
Phone: 212-867-6650 ext. 303
Fax: 212-867-6653
Web: www.irts.org

J. Paul Getty Trust

Multicultural Undergraduate Summer Internships at the Getty Center

Type of award: Internship.

Intended use: For full-time undergraduate study at 4-year institution.

Eligibility: Applicant must be Asian American, African American, Mexican American, Hispanic American, Puerto Rican, American Indian or Native Hawaiian/Pacific Islander.

Basis for selection: Major/career interest in arts management; communications; humanities/liberal arts; architecture; museum studies/administration or art/art history.

Application requirements: Interview, recommendations. Supplemental application (plus three copies), all official transcripts (plus three copies), and SASE.

Additional information: Ten-week internship in specific departments of Getty Museum and other programs located at the Getty Center in Los Angeles. Interns receive $3500 stipend. Limited to students attending school in or residing in Los Angeles County. Intended for outstanding students who are members of groups currently underrepresented in museum professions and fields related to visual arts and humanities. Applicants must have completed at least one semester of college by June and not be graduating before December. Housing and transportation not included. Applications accepted in December, and applicants notified of acceptance in early May.

Internships

Amount of award: $3,500
Number of applicants: 124
Application deadline: March 1
Contact:
Multicultural Undergraduate Internships at the Getty Center
The Getty Foundation
1200 Getty Center Dr., Suite 800
Los Angeles, CA 90049-1685
Phone: 310-440-7320
Fax: 310-440-7703
Web: www.getty.edu/grants/education

John Deere

John Deere Student Training Programs

Type of award: Internship.
Intended use: For full-time sophomore, junior, senior or graduate study at accredited 2-year, 4-year or graduate institution.
Eligibility: Applicant must be U.S. citizen or permanent resident.
Basis for selection: Major/career interest in accounting; finance/banking; human resources; health services administration; engineering; information systems or marketing. Applicant must demonstrate high academic achievement.
Application requirements: Recommendations.
Additional information: Deere and Company offers paid internships, course credit, and academic scholarships through Student Training Program. Applicants may also be interested/majoring in supply management and credit. Open to undergraduates; graduate students may also be eligible. Minimum 3.0 GPA. Apply through Career Section on Website. Co-op applicants must be enrolled undergraduates and meet academic requirement. Number and amount of awards vary. For co-ops, students must apply through and be recommended by Cooperative Education Office at college or university.
Contact:
Recruitment Coordinator
Deere and Company
One John Deere Place
Moline, IL 61265
Phone: 309-765-8000
Web: www.deere.com

The John F. Kennedy Center for the Performing Arts

Kennedy Center Arts Management Internship

Type of award: Internship.
Intended use: For junior, senior or post-bachelor's certificate study at accredited 4-year or graduate institution.
Basis for selection: Major/career interest in arts management.
Application requirements: Interview, transcript. Cover letter stating career goals. Two letters of recommendation. Resume and writing sample.

Additional information: Arts education majors also eligible. Three- to four-month full-time internship in areas such as advertising, development, education, National Symphony Orchestra, press relations, production, programming, technology, volunteer management, and finance. Interns receive $225 stipend per week to defray housing and transportation costs. College credit may be available. Interns attend weekly sessions led by executives of Kennedy Center and other major arts institutions in Washington, D.C. Interns may attend performances, workshops, classes, and courses presented by center, free of charge (space available), during their internship. Application deadline for fall, June 15 and for winter/spring, October 25. Visit Website for application and more information.
Number of awards: 60
Number of applicants: 800
Application deadline: June 15, October 25
Contact:
Vilar Institute for Arts Management/Internships
2700 F Street N.W
Washington, DC 20566
Phone: 202-416-8800
Web: www.kennedy-center.org/education/artsmanagement/internships

John F. Kennedy Library Foundation

Kennedy Library Archival Internship

Type of award: Internship.
Intended use: For undergraduate or graduate study at postsecondary institution. Designated institutions: John F. Kennedy Presidential Library.
Eligibility: Applicant must be U.S. citizen or permanent resident.
Basis for selection: Major/career interest in history; political science/government; library science; English; journalism; communications or museum studies. Applicant must demonstrate high academic achievement.
Application requirements: Interview, recommendations, transcript.
Additional information: Minimum 12 hours per week, $12.50 per hour. Provides intern with opportunity to work on projects such as digitizing papers of Kennedy and his administration. Interns given career-relevant archival experience. Internships open up as vacancies occur. Library considers proposals for unpaid internships, independent study, work-study, and internships undertaken for academic credit. See Website for application and more information.
Notification begins: April 1
Contact:
Archival Internships c/o Intern Coordinator
John F. Kennedy Presidential Library & Museum
Columbia Point
Boston, MA 02125-3313
Fax: 617-514-1629
Web: www.jfklibrary.org

John Wiley and Sons, Inc.

John Wiley and Sons, Inc. Internship Program

Type of award: Internship.
Intended use: For full-time junior or senior study at 4-year institution.
Basis for selection: Major/career interest in marketing; publishing; information systems or public relations.
Application requirements: Resume. Letter addressing why applicant would like to be selected for the program and listing areas of interest.
Additional information: Summer internship programs available for students who have completed junior year; program runs from mid-June through mid-August. Internships available in marketing, editorial, production, information technology, new media, and publicity; based at corporate offices in Hoboken and Somerset in NJ, Indianapolis, San Francisco, and Malden, MA. Interns receive weekly stipend. Those interested in interning in Hoboken, NJ, Somerset, NJ, San Francisco, CA, Indianapolis, IN, and Malden, MA should visit www.wiley.com for more information. Application address varies by city. See Website for details.

Application deadline:	April 1

Contact:
John Wiley and Sons, Inc. Attn: Internship Program
Human Resources Department
111 River Street
Hoboken, NJ 07030-5774
Fax: 201-748-6049
Web: www.wiley.com

Johnson Controls

Johnson Controls Co-op and Internship Programs

Type of award: Internship, renewable.
Intended use: For full-time undergraduate or graduate study at accredited 4-year institution in United States.
Basis for selection: Major/career interest in engineering; law; business/management/administration; manufacturing or automotive technology. Applicant must demonstrate high academic achievement.
Application requirements: Proof of eligibility. Resume, cover letter.
Additional information: Johnson Controls offers several co-op and internship programs in locations throughout the U.S. and abroad. The Engineering Co-op Program develops and trains students in all aspects of the Automotive Systems Group at Johnson Controls. Over a period of two to five years, mechanical and design engineering students alternate between work terms at Johnson Controls and school terms at college or university. Paid summer internships and positions in most other company divisions also available. Visit Website for complete program descriptions and application.

Contact:
Johnson Controls
Human Resources
5757 N. Green Bay Ave.
Glendale, WI 53209
Phone: 414-524-1200
Web: www.johnsoncontrols.com

J.W. Saxe Memorial Fund

J.W. Saxe Memorial Prize for Public Service

Type of award: Internship.
Intended use: For undergraduate, graduate or non-degree study.
Basis for selection: Major/career interest in public administration/service. Applicant must demonstrate financial need, depth of character, leadership, seriousness of purpose and service orientation.
Application requirements: Resume, letter of support from faculty member, three recommendations, and an essay on short- and long-term goals.
Additional information: Award enables public-service-minded college or university students to gain practical experience working no-pay or low-pay public service job or internship during summer or other term. Preference given to applicants who have already found public service-oriented position, but require additional funds. Interns receive $2000 stipend. Number of awards varies.

Amount of award:	$2,000
Number of applicants:	200
Application deadline:	March 15
Notification begins:	May 1
Total amount awarded:	$24,000

Contact:
J.W. Saxe Memorial Fund
1524 31 St. N.W.
Washington, DC 20007-3074
Web: www.jwsaxefund.org

Kentucky Higher Education Assistance Authority (KHEAA)

Kentucky Work-Study Program

Type of award: Internship, renewable.
Intended use: For undergraduate, master's, doctoral, first professional or postgraduate study at vocational, 2-year, 4-year or graduate institution. Designated institutions: Approved Kentucky institutions.
Eligibility: Applicant must be U.S. citizen residing in Kentucky.
Application requirements: Interview, proof of eligibility.
Additional information: Job must be related to major course of study. Work-study wage is at least federal minimum wage. May also be enrolled in technical schools. Visit Website for additional information.

543

Number of awards: 830
Number of applicants: 830
Total amount awarded: $678,000
Contact:
Kentucky Higher Education Assistance Authority (KHEAA)
KHEAA Work-Study Program
P.O. Box 798
Frankfort, KY 40602-0798
Phone: 800-928-8926
Fax: 502-696-7373
Web: www.kheaa.com

KIMT

KIMT Weather/News Internships

Type of award: Internship.
Intended use: For undergraduate study.
Eligibility: Applicant must be at least 18.
Basis for selection: Major/career interest in atmospheric sciences/meteorology; journalism; radio/television/film or sports/ sports administration.
Application requirements: Interview. Resume.
Additional information: Applicant must be majoring in field directly related to the department of internship. All internships for college credit only. Student must arrange to receive college credit. Internships available year-round. Hours are flexible.
Contact:
KIMT
Attn: Human Resources Coordinator
112 North Pennsylvania
Mason City, IA 50401
Phone: 641-423-2540

Library of Congress

Hispanic Division Huntington Fellowship

Type of award: Internship.
Intended use: For senior study at accredited 4-year or graduate institution. Designated institutions: Library of Congress.
Eligibility: Applicant must be U.S. citizen or permanent resident.
Basis for selection: Major/career interest in library science or Latin American studies. Applicant must demonstrate seriousness of purpose.
Application requirements: Interview, recommendations, transcript. Resume and cover letter including contact information and interview availability.
Additional information: Fellowships last approximately eight weeks during the summer, where fellows will be required to work full-time (40 hours per week) in the Hispanic Division of the Library of Congress. Fellows receive stipend of $1200 per month. Women, minorities, and people with disabilities encouraged to apply. Applicant must be fluent in Spanish. Visit Website for application. Fax completed applications to 202-707-2005.

Amount of award: $1,200
Number of awards: 2
Number of applicants: 35
Application deadline: May 1
Total amount awarded: $2,400
Contact:
Library of Congress
Chief of Hispanic Division
Washington, DC 20540-4850
Phone: 202-707-5400
Fax: 202-707-2005
Web: www.loc.gov

Louis Carr Internship Foundation (LCIF)

Louis Carr Summer Internship

Type of award: Internship.
Intended use: For full-time freshman, sophomore or junior study in United States.
Eligibility: Applicant must be African American. Applicant must be U.S. citizen.
Basis for selection: Major/career interest in advertising; marketing or communications. Applicant must demonstrate high academic achievement, depth of character, leadership and seriousness of purpose.
Application requirements: Recommendations, essay, transcript. Resume.
Additional information: Paid, ten-week summer internship in New York, Chicago, Detroit, or Washington D.C.
Amount of award: $4,000
Number of awards: 10
Number of applicants: 16
Application deadline: March 1
Notification begins: April 15
Total amount awarded: $84,000
Contact:
Louis Carr Internship Foundation
P.O. Box 81859
Chicago, IL 60681-0589
Phone: 312-819-8617
Fax: 312-540-1109
Web: www.louiscarrfoundation.org

Macy's, Inc.

Internships at Macy's and Bloomingdale's

Type of award: Internship, renewable.
Intended use: For full-time undergraduate study.
Basis for selection: Applicant must demonstrate high academic achievement.
Application requirements: Resume.
Additional information: Eight- to ten-week paid internships offered in buying, planning, store management, product development, design, and macys.com. Apply online or visit Website for campus recruiting schedule.
Number of awards: 350

Contact:
Macy's, Inc.
Web: www.macysjobs.com/college/internships

Makovsky & Company Inc.

Public Relations Internship

Type of award: Internship.
Intended use: For senior study at 4-year institution in United States or Canada.
Basis for selection: Major/career interest in public relations; communications; English or political science/government. Applicant must demonstrate high academic achievement.
Application requirements: Interview. Resume, cover letter, writing sample.
Additional information: Two to four full- or part-time (20 hours minimum) paid positions offered in summer. Compensation $10/hr. Must major in public relations or related subject. Applicant must be responsible, diligent, and energetic. Provides opportunity to receive hands-on experience in all facets of public relations under direction of forums staff.

Number of awards:	4
Number of applicants:	200
Application deadline:	March 15

Contact:
Makovsky & Company, Inc. Internship Coordinator
16 East 34th Street
New York, NY 10016
Phone: 212-508-9639
Fax: 212-751-9710
Web: www.makovsky.com

Massachusetts Democratic Party

John Joseph Moakely Democratic Internship

Type of award: Internship.
Intended use: For junior or senior study at accredited 4-year institution.
Eligibility: Applicant must be at least 18, no older than 23. Applicant must be U.S. citizen or permanent resident residing in Massachusetts.
Basis for selection: Major/career interest in political science/government or public administration/service. Applicant must demonstrate financial need, high academic achievement, leadership, seriousness of purpose and service orientation.
Additional information: Preference given to registered Democrats. Eleven-week summer internship at Massachusetts Democratic State Convention Headquarters. Interns receive $3,500 stipend. Visit Website for more program information and important dates.

Amount of award:	$3,500
Number of awards:	1
Number of applicants:	10
Application deadline:	April 16

Contact:
Massachusetts Democratic Party
MDP Office, Attn: Gloribell Mota
56 Roland St., Suite 203
Boston, MA 02129
Phone: 617-776-2676
Fax: 617-776-2579
Web: www.massdems.org

MCC Theater

MCC Theater Internships

Type of award: Internship.
Intended use: For undergraduate study at vocational institution.
Eligibility: Applicant must be residing in New York.
Basis for selection: Major/career interest in theater arts; theater/production/technical; performing arts; design; business/management/administration or arts management.
Application requirements: Resume.
Additional information: Rolling application deadlines, negotiable schedule. Internships available in general management/theater administration, development, marketing, production, and literary and arts education. College credit available. E-mail resume to apply.
Contact:
MCC Theater
311 West 43rd Street, Suite 302
New York, NY 10036
Phone: 212-727-7722
Fax: 212-727-7780
Web: www.mcctheater.org/jobs

Metropolitan Museum of Art

The Cloisters Summer Internship Program

Type of award: Internship.
Intended use: For undergraduate study at postsecondary institution.
Basis for selection: Major/career interest in art/art history; history; museum studies or museum studies/administration.
Application requirements: $35 application fee. Recommendations, essay, transcript. Resume and list of art history courses taken.
Additional information: Must be currently enrolled college student at time of internship. First- and second-year students especially encouraged to apply. Interns receive $2,750 stipend. Interest in medieval history appreciated. Nine-week full-time internship from mid-June to mid-August. Five-day, 35-hour work week.

Amount of award:	$2,750
Number of awards:	8
Notification begins:	April 10

Internships

Contact:
The Cloisters
College Internship Program
Fort Tryon Park
New York, NY 10040
Phone: 212-650-2280
Web: www.metmuseum.org/education

Mentoring Program for College Juniors

Type of award: Internship.
Intended use: For sophomore or junior study at postsecondary institution.
Application requirements: $35 application fee. Recommendations, transcript.
Additional information: Interns work full-time for 6 weeks over the summer. Designed to encourage college juniors from diverse backgrounds to pursue museum careers. Participants work in one of the Museum's departments (curatorial, administrative, or educational). Includes a two-week orientation of the Museum, meetings with Museum professionals, a Museum mentor, and field trips to other institutions. Visit Website for deadline and application details.

> **Amount of award:** $3,250

Contact:
Metropolitan Museum of Art
1000 Fifth Avenue
New York, NY 10028
Phone: 212-570-3710
Web: www.metmuseum.org/education

Six-Month Internship

Type of award: Internship.
Intended use: For senior, graduate or non-degree study at 4-year or graduate institution.
Eligibility: Applicant must be U.S. citizen or international student.
Basis for selection: Major/career interest in art/art history; museum studies or history.
Application requirements: $35 application fee. Recommendations, transcript, proof of eligibility. Resume. List of art history and other relevant courses taken and foreign languages spoken. 500-word essay describing career goals, interest in museum work, specific areas of interest within the museum, and reasons for applying to the program.
Additional information: Interns work full-time from early June to early December and participate in summer orientation program. Interns receive $11,000 stipend. International students must have permission to earn stipend in U.S. Visit Website for more information.

> **Amount of award:** $11,000

Contact:
Metropolitan Museum of Art
1000 Fifth Avenue
New York, NY 10028-0198
Phone: 212-570-3710
Web: www.metmuseum.org/education

Summer Internship Program

Type of award: Internship.
Intended use: For junior, senior, graduate or non-degree study at postsecondary institution.
Eligibility: Applicant must be U.S. citizen or international student.
Basis for selection: Major/career interest in art/art history; arts management or museum studies/administration. Applicant must demonstrate seriousness of purpose.
Application requirements: $35 application fee. Typed paper indicating desired internship and include name, home and school addresses and phone numbers. Resume. Two academic recommendations. Transcripts. Separate list with art history or relevant courses taken and knowledge of foreign languages. 500-word (maximum) essay describing career goals, interest in museum work, specific areas of interest within the museum, and reason for applying.
Additional information: Ten-week program for college students, recent college graduates who have not yet entered graduate school, and graduate students who have completed at least one year of graduate work in art history or related field. Interns work full-time. International students must have permission to work in U.S. Applicants should have broad background in art history. Program begins in June with two-week orientation, ends in August, and includes $3,250 honorarium for college interns and recent graduates and $3,500 for graduate interns. Visit Website for more information.

> **Amount of award:** $3,250-$3,500

Contact:
Attn: Internship Programs
Metropolitan Museum of Art
1000 Fifth Avenue
New York, NY 10028-0198
Phone: 212-570-3710
Web: www.metmuseum.org/education

Minnesota Office of Higher Education

Minnesota Work-Study Program

Type of award: Internship.
Intended use: For undergraduate or graduate study.
Eligibility: Applicant must be U.S. citizen or permanent resident residing in Minnesota.
Basis for selection: Applicant must demonstrate financial need.
Application requirements: Interview.
Additional information: This is a work-study program, but it may be applied to internships. Work placement must be approved by school or nonprofit agency. Must be used at Minnesota college or for internship with nonprofit or private sector employer located in Minnesota. Must be enrolled for at least six credit hours. Priority given to those enrolled for 12 or more credit hours. Apply to financial aid office of school. Award maximum set at cost of attendance minus EFC and other financial aid.

> **Number of awards:** 11,000
> **Number of applicants:** 10,515
> **Total amount awarded:** $12,207,557

Contact:
Minnesota Office of Higher Education
1450 Energy Park Drive, Suite 350
St. Paul, MN 55108-5227
Phone: 800-657-3866
Web: www.getreadyforcollege.org

Morris Arboretum of the University of Pennsylvania

Arboriculture Internship

Type of award: Internship.
Intended use: For undergraduate or graduate study at postsecondary institution.
Basis for selection: Major/career interest in horticulture; forestry or landscape architecture.
Application requirements: Recommendations, transcript. Letter of intent, resume.
Additional information: Applicant should have interest in arboriculture. Internships train students in most up-to-date tree care techniques. Interns work 40 hours per week at hourly rate of $9.18 for full year. Intern works with Chief Arborist in all aspects of tree care, including tree assessment, pruning, cabling, and removal. Safety-conscious techniques are emphasized, and recent innovations in climbing and rigging are demonstrated and put into practice. Other opportunities include assisting with outreach activities including workshops and off-site consulting. Benefits include health insurance and dental plan. Must have solid academic background in arboriculture and horticulture. Tree climbing ability helpful. Driver's license required. Academic credit given.
    Application deadline: February 15
Contact:
Morris Arboretum of the University of Pennsylvania
Jan McFarlan, Education Coordinator
100 Northwestern Avenue
Philadelphia, PA 19118
Phone: 215-247-5777 ext. 156
Web: www.upenn.edu/arboretum

Morris Arboretum Education Internship

Type of award: Internship.
Intended use: For undergraduate or graduate study at postsecondary institution.
Basis for selection: Major/career interest in education; botany; horticulture; ecology or education, teacher.
Application requirements: Recommendations, transcript. Letter of intent, resume.
Additional information: Interns work 40 hours/week at hourly wage of $9.18 for full year. Interns develop workshops for experienced guides, training sessions for new guides, occasionally lead tours. Other responsibilities include supervising the school tour program, running special programs for the public, helping to prepare the adult education course brochure, and writing promotional copy including a newsletter for volunteer guides. Benefits include insurance, dental plan, and tuition benefits. Academic background or experience in education or educational programming preferred. Knowledge of plant-related subjects helpful. Strong writing and interpersonal skills essential. Academic credit given.
    Application deadline: February 15
Contact:
Morris Arboretum of the University of Pennsylvania
Jan McFarlan, Education Coordinator
100 Northwestern Avenue
Philadelphia, PA 19118
Phone: 215-247-5777 ext. 156
Web: www.upenn.edu/arboretum

Morris Arboretum Horticulture Internship

Type of award: Internship.
Intended use: For undergraduate or graduate study at postsecondary institution.
Basis for selection: Major/career interest in horticulture.
Application requirements: Recommendations, transcript. Letter of intent, resume.
Additional information: Intern assists in all phases of garden development and care of collections. Specific emphasis on refining practical horticultural skills. Supervisory skills are developed by directing activities of volunteers and part-time staff. Other activities include developing Integrated Pest Management skills, arboricultural techniques, and the operation and maintenance of garden machinery. Special projects will be assigned to develop individual skills in garden planning and management. Must have strong academic background in horticulture or closely related field. Interns work 40 hours per week at hourly wage of $9.18 for full year. Benefits include health insurance, dental plan, and tuition benefits. Some internships require travel. Driver's license required. Academic credit given.
    Application deadline: February 15
Contact:
Morris Arboretum of the University of Pennsylvania
Jan McFarlan, Education Coordinator
100 Northwestern Avenue
Philadelphia, PA 19118
Phone: 215-247-5777 ext. 156
Web: www.upenn.edu/arboretum

Plant Propagation Internship

Type of award: Internship.
Intended use: For undergraduate or graduate study at postsecondary institution.
Basis for selection: Major/career interest in botany or horticulture.
Application requirements: Recommendations, transcript. Letter of intent, resume.
Additional information: Strong background in woody landscape plants, plant propagation, nursery management, and plant physiology required. Interns work 40 hours/week at hourly rate of $9.18 for full year. Benefits include health insurance, dental plan, and tuition benefits. Academic credit given. Intern assists propagator in the development of plant propagation and production schemes for arboretum. Emphasis is placed on the refinement of skills in traditional methods of plant propagation, nursery production, and greenhouse management. Other duties include management of the field nursery and data collection for ongoing research projects.
    Application deadline: February 15
Contact:
Morris Arboretum of the University of Pennsylvania
Jan McFarlan, Education Coordinator
100 Northwestern Avenue
Philadelphia, PA 19118
Phone: 215-247-5777 ext. 156
Web: www.upenn.edu/arboretum

Plant Protection Internship

Type of award: Internship.
Intended use: For undergraduate or graduate study at postsecondary institution.

Basis for selection: Major/career interest in horticulture; entomology or botany.
Application requirements: Recommendations, transcript. Letter of intent, resume.
Additional information: Interns work 40 hours per week at hourly wage of $9.18 for full year. Course work in entomology or plant pathology required. Intern assists arboretum's plant pathologist with the Integrated Pest Management program, which includes regular monitoring of the living collection and communicating information on pests and diseases to staff members. Related projects include establishing threshold levels for specific plant pests and evaluating the effectiveness of control measures. Modern laboratory facilities are available for identifying plant pests and pathogens. Intern also participates in Plant Clinic's daily operations, providing diagnostic services to the public about horticultural problems. Benefits include health insurance, dental plan, and tuition benefits. Strong writing skills essential. Academic credit given.
  Application deadline: February 15
Contact:
Morris Arboretum of the University of Pennsylvania
Jan McFarlan, Education Coordinator
100 Northwestern Avenue
Philadelphia, PA 19118
Phone: 215-247-5777 ext. 156
Web: www.upenn.edu/arboretum

Rose and Flower Garden Internship

Type of award: Internship.
Intended use: For undergraduate or graduate study at postsecondary institution.
Basis for selection: Major/career interest in horticulture. Applicant must demonstrate seriousness of purpose.
Application requirements: Recommendations, transcript. Letter of intent, resume.
Additional information: Intern assists Rosarian in garden development, management, and care of collections. Emphasis on mastering skills used in the culture of modern and antique roses, developing pest management skills, and refining horticulture skills including formal garden maintenance. Other duties include plant record keeping, support for volunteer gardeners, operation of garden machinery, and supervision of part-time staff. Interns work 40-hour week at hourly rate of $9.18 for full year. Benefits include health insurance, dental plan, and tuition benefits. Applicant should have strong academic background in horticulture with course work in herbaceous and woody landscape plants. Driver's license required. Academic credit given.
  Application deadline: February 15
Contact:
Morris Arboretum of the University of Pennsylvania
Jan McFarlan, Education Coordinator
100 Northwestern Avenue
Philadelphia, PA 19118
Phone: 215-247-5777 ext. 156
Web: www.upenn.edu/arboretum

Urban Forestry Internship

Type of award: Internship.
Intended use: For undergraduate study at postsecondary institution.
Basis for selection: Major/career interest in forestry; horticulture; landscape architecture or ecology.
Application requirements: Recommendations, transcript. Letter of intent, resume.

Additional information: Intern will engage in urban forestry and natural resources programs and strategies for public gardens, government agencies, and educational and community organizations; learn and teach stewardship concepts and practical applications through riparian and woodland restoration projects; develop community partnership, urban vegetation analysis, and management planning skills. Interns work 40 hours per week at hourly wage of $9.18 for full year. Benefits include health insurance, dental plan, and tuition benefits. Academic background in urban forestry, horticulture, landscape design, or related field. Communication skills essential. Car required; mileage reimbursed. Academic credit given.
  Application deadline: February 15
Contact:
Morris Arboretum of the University of Pennsylvania
Jan McFarlan, Education Coordinator
100 Northwestern Avenue
Philadelphia, PA 19118
Phone: 215-247-5777 ext. 156
Web: www.upenn.edu/arboretum

Mother Jones

Mother Jones Ben Bagdikian Fellowship Program

Type of award: Internship.
Intended use: For junior, senior, graduate or non-degree study at postsecondary institution.
Basis for selection: Major/career interest in political science/government; communications; journalism or publishing. Applicant must demonstrate high academic achievement.
Application requirements: Interview, recommendations. Resume with cover letter; contact information for two references; writing samples.
Additional information: Deadlines are rolling. Internships are full-time and run six months with stipend of $1,000/month with seven-day vacation allowance. After six months, interns may apply for fellowship program which also runs six months with $1,400/month stipend. Hours vary according to magazine production schedule. No course credit offered. Reporting, writing, and research skills preferred. See Website for more information. Application deadlines occur twice a year: April 1st and October 1st.
  Number of awards: 10
  Application deadline: April 1, October 1
Contact:
Mother Jones
Attn: Ben Bagdikian Fellowship Program
222 Sutter Street, Suite 600
San Francisco, CA 94108
Web: www.motherjones.com

Museum of Modern Art

Museum of Modern Art Internship

Type of award: Internship.
Intended use: For junior, senior or graduate study at postsecondary institution.

Eligibility: Applicant must be U.S. citizen, permanent resident or international student.
Basis for selection: Major/career interest in arts management; museum studies/administration; arts, general or art/art history.
Application requirements: Interview, essay, transcript. Resume and one recommendation.
Additional information: Course credit available. Fall, spring, summer, and 12-month internships. Twelve-month internships are paid, full-time programs for recent college graduates. Fall, spring, and summer internships are part-time and unpaid. Fields of study encompass broad spectrum of topics. Visit Website for complete list of departments, applications, and deadline information.

Number of awards:	100
Number of applicants:	1,600

Contact:
The Museum of Modern Art
Internship Coordinator, Dept. of Education
11 W. 53rd Street
New York, NY 10019
Web: www.moma.org

NASA Arizona Space Grant Consortium

NASA Space Grant Arizona Undergraduate Research Internship

Type of award: Internship, renewable.
Intended use: For full-time sophomore, junior or senior study at accredited 2-year or 4-year institution in United States. Designated institutions: Arizona Space Grant Consortium (AZSGC) Colleges and Universities.
Eligibility: Applicant must be U.S. citizen residing in Arizona.
Basis for selection: Major/career interest in aerospace; astronomy; engineering; physics; geology/earth sciences; science, general; journalism or education.
Additional information: Approximately 100 students will be employed for 10-20 hours per week for the academic year in research programs, working alongside upper-level graduate students and practicing scientists. Hourly wage offered. Awardees must attend Arizona Space Grant Consortium member institution. Availability of internships varies. Some internships are renewable. Current announcements/application posted on Website.

Number of applicants:	350
Application deadline:	June 30

Contact:
NASA Space Grant Arizona Space Grant Consortium
Lunar and Planetary Laboratory, Room 349
U of Arizona, 1629 E. University Blvd.
Tucson, AZ 85721-0092
Phone: 520-621-8556
Web: spacegrant.arizona.edu

NASA Delaware Space Grant Consortium

Delaware Space Grant Undergraduate Research Internship

Type of award: Internship, renewable.
Intended use: For full-time sophomore, junior or senior study at postsecondary institution. Designated institutions: University of Delaware, Delaware Technical and Community College, Swarthmore College, Delaware State University at Dover, Villanova University, Wesley College, Wilmington University.
Eligibility: Applicant must be U.S. citizen.
Basis for selection: Major/career interest in geography; mathematics; science, general or technology.
Application requirements: Recommendations, transcript. Description of proposed research project.
Additional information: Must have proven interest in space science-related studies. Recipient must attend a Delaware Space Grant Consortium member institution. Stipend offered. Contact Consortium office for deadlines and additional information.

Amount of award:	$3,500
Number of awards:	10
Number of applicants:	17
Application deadline:	April 24
Total amount awarded:	$50,000

Contact:
Delaware Space Grant Consortium Program Office
University of Delaware
106 Sharp Lab
Newark, DE 19716
Phone: 302-831-1094
Fax: 302-831-1843
Web: www.delspace.org

NASA Hawaii Space Grant Consortium

NASA Hawaii Undergraduate Student Research Program

Type of award: Internship.
Intended use: For full-time junior or senior study in United States. Designated institutions: Consortium member schools: University of Hawaii at Manoa and Hilo.
Eligibility: Applicant must be U.S. citizen residing in Hawaii.
Basis for selection: Major/career interest in science, general; mathematics or engineering.
Application requirements: Recommendations, transcript. Two-page research proposal, budget, resume.
Additional information: Minimum 3.0 GPA. Must major in STEM discipline. Student must have faculty mentor. Contact sponsor for application details. Women, minority, and physically challenged students who have interest in space-related fields encouraged to apply. Visit Website for more information and application.

Number of applicants:	10

Contact:
Phone: 808-956-3138
Fax: 808-956-6322
Web: www.spacegrant.hawaii.edu

NASA New Jersey Space Grant Consortium

Undergraduate Summer Fellowships in Engineering and Science

Type of award: Internship, renewable.
Intended use: For junior or senior study at accredited 4-year institution in United States. Designated institutions: Georgian Court University, New Jersey Institute of Technology, Princeton University, Raritan Valley Community College, Rutgers University, Stevens Institute of Technology, University of Medicine and Dentistry of NJ, New Jersey City University, Rowan University, Seton Hall, College of New Jersey.
Eligibility: Applicant must be U.S. citizen.
Basis for selection: Major/career interest in aerospace; biology; computer/information sciences; engineering, computer; engineering, chemical; engineering, electrical/electronic; engineering, mechanical; materials science; natural sciences or physical sciences.
Application requirements: Recommendations, essay. Biographical sketch, statement that describes career goals and what applicant hopes to accomplish as Space Grant Fellow, plan for immediate future and reference letter from faculty advisor.
Additional information: Applicants must have completed at least two but preferably three years of college. Consortium actively encourages women, minority students, and physically challenged students to apply. Awardees must attend NJSGC member institution. Academic year ($2,000 stipend) and summer fellowships ($5,500 stipend) offered. Summer fellowship deadline in April. Academic year fellowship has ongoing deadline. Visit Website for important dates and additional information.

Amount of award:	$2,000-$5,500
Number of awards:	20
Number of applicants:	25
Application deadline:	April 1

Contact:
Program Director New Jersey Space Grant Consortium
Rutgers University, College of Engineering
Room B213, 98 Brett Road
Piscataway, NJ 08854
Phone: 732-445-2440
Web: www.njsgc.org

NASA Pennsylvania Space Grant Consortium

NASA Academy Internship

Type of award: Internship.
Intended use: For full-time junior, senior or graduate study at accredited 4-year or graduate institution in United States. Designated institutions: Pennsylvania colleges and universities.

Eligibility: Applicant must be U.S. citizen or permanent resident residing in Pennsylvania.
Basis for selection: Major/career interest in engineering; science, general; mathematics; aerospace or astronomy. Applicant must demonstrate high academic achievement and leadership.
Application requirements: Recommendations, essay, transcript.
Additional information: Awards are for ten-week internships at participating NASA centers. Minimum B average required. Stipend, plus room and board and travel expenses. Earth science students also eligible. Awardees must attend Pennsylvania institution or be a full-time resident. Interns receive $4,000 stipend. Consortium actively encourages women, minority, and physically challenged students to apply. Visit the NASA Academy Website for application information.

Amount of award:	$5,000
Number of awards:	3
Number of applicants:	24
Application deadline:	January 15
Total amount awarded:	$15,000

Contact:
NASA Pennsylvania Space Grant Consortium
Penn State, University Park
2217 Earth-Engineering Sciences Building
University Park, PA 16802
Phone: 814-865-2535
Fax: 814-863-9563
Web: www.pa.spacegrant.org

National Association of Black Journalists

NABJ Internships

Type of award: Internship.
Intended use: For full-time undergraduate study at postsecondary institution.
Eligibility: Applicant must be African American.
Basis for selection: Major/career interest in journalism or radio/television/film.
Application requirements: Portfolio, recommendations, essay. Resume, cover letter. Applicants must submit minimum of five samples of published work in print, radio, television, photography, slideshows, website, or flash animation.
Additional information: Ten-week paid internship in print, broadcast, online, sports, or photojournalism. Must have prior experience in collegiate or professional media. Must be member of National Association of Black Journalists. Weekly stipend varies between $400 and $600. Some internships are unpaid. Visit Website for more information.

Contact:
National Association of Black Journalists
1100 Knight Hall, Suite 3100
College Park, MD 20742
Phone: 301-405-0248
Fax: 301-314-1714
Web: www.nabj.org

Newhouse Foundation Scholarship

Type of award: Internship, renewable.
Intended use: For undergraduate study at accredited 4-year institution.

Internships

Eligibility: Applicant must be U.S. citizen, permanent resident or international student.
Basis for selection: Major/career interest in journalism. Applicant must demonstrate financial need.
Application requirements: Essay, transcript. Resume, five published works that demonstrate reporting, editing, or producing skills. Must provide four copies of all application materials.
Additional information: Minimum 3.0 GPA. Must be member of National Association of Black Journalists and work for campus newspaper. Must major in print journalism.

    Amount of award: $5,000
Contact:
National Association of Black Journalists
University of Maryland
1100 Knight Hall, Suite 3100
College Park, MD 20742
Phone: 301-405-0248
Fax: 301-314-1714
Web: www.nabj.org

National Basketball Association

NBA Internship Program

Type of award: Internship.
Intended use: For sophomore or junior study at postsecondary institution.
Basis for selection: Major/career interest in sports/sports administration; marketing; theater/production/technical; public relations; finance/banking or computer/information sciences.
Application requirements: Resume and cover letter.
Additional information: Ten-week internship program. Interns participate in series of events and activities exposing them to many facets of NBA's business.
Contact:
National Basketball Association
Internship Coordinator
645 Fifth Avenue
New York, NY 10022
Phone: 212-407-8800
Web: www.nba.com/careers

National Geographic Society

Geography Students Internship

Type of award: Internship.
Intended use: For junior, senior or master's study at 4-year or graduate institution in United States.
Basis for selection: Major/career interest in geography or cartography.
Application requirements: Recommendations, essay, transcript. Resume.
Additional information: Spring, summer, and fall internships for 14 to 16 weeks in Washington, D.C., at $400 per week. Application deadline for all internships in the fall. Emphasis on editorial and cartographic research. Students should contact

their school's geography department chair or call internship hotline for more information.
    Number of awards: 30
    Number of applicants: 100
Contact:
National Geographic Society
Robert E. Dulli
1145 17 Street, NW
Washington, DC 20036-4688
Phone: 202-857-7134
Web: www.nationalgeographic.com

National Museum of the American Indian

National Museum of the American Indian Internship

Type of award: Internship.
Intended use: For undergraduate, graduate or non-degree study at postsecondary institution.
Basis for selection: Major/career interest in museum studies.
Application requirements: Recommendations, essay, transcript. Resume.
Additional information: Provides educational work/research experience for students in museum practice and related programming using resources of museum and other Smithsonian offices. Internships available at NMAI in Suitland, MD; Washington, DC; and New York City. Applicants must have minimum 3.0 GPA. Four 10-week internships, deadlines as follows: February 6 for summer; July 12 for fall; October 10 for winter; and November 20 for spring. Selection based on professional and educational goals of student; needs of museum. Students receiving stipends must work full-time; other interns must work at least 20 hours per week. Museum will grant academic credit if student makes arrangements with school. Visit Website or contact via e-mail for more information.
    Number of awards: 20
    Number of applicants: 40
    Application deadline: November 20, February 6
Contact:
Internship Program, National Museum of the American Indian
Cultural Resources Center- Community Services
4220 Silver Hill Road
Suitland, MD 20746-2863
Phone: 301-238-1541
Fax: 301-238-3200
Web: www.nmai.si.edu

National Museum of Women in the Arts

Museum Coca-Cola Internship

Type of award: Internship.
Intended use: For junior, senior, graduate or non-degree study in United States.
Basis for selection: Major/career interest in public relations; advertising; library science; journalism; museum studies; art/art

Internships

history; museum studies/administration; accounting; education or retailing/merchandising. Applicant must demonstrate high academic achievement and seriousness of purpose.

Application requirements: Recommendations, transcript. Resume, cover letter, and one- to two-page writing sample.

Additional information: Internship available to students interested in pursuing careers in museum environments. Minimum 3.25 GPA. Interns receive $1500 stipend. Full-time internship lasts 12 weeks; application deadline for spring is October 15; summer is March 15; fall is June 15.

Amount of award:	$1,500
Number of awards:	3
Number of applicants:	50
Application deadline:	October 15, March 15
Total amount awarded:	$1,500

Contact:
National Museum of Women in the Arts
Manager of Public Programs Education Dept.
1250 New York Avenue, NW
Washington, DC 20005-3970
Phone: 202-783-7996
Fax: 202-393-3234
Web: www.nmwa.org

Southern California Council Endowed Internship

Type of award: Internship, renewable.

Intended use: For junior, senior or graduate study at postsecondary institution. Designated institutions: Art and design institutions in Los Angeles County area.

Eligibility: Applicant must be residing in California.

Basis for selection: Major/career interest in art/art history; arts management; arts, general; museum studies or museum studies/administration.

Application requirements: Recommendations, essay, transcript. Cover letter, brief writing sample, resume.

Additional information: Full-time, twelve-week internship. $2,000 stipend. Applicant must be resident of Los Angeles County. Minimum 3.25 GPA. Application deadline for spring is October 15; summer is March 15; fall is June 15.

Amount of award:	$2,000
Number of awards:	1
Number of applicants:	1
Application deadline:	March 15, June 15

Contact:
National Museum of Women in the Arts
Manager of Public Programs Education Dept.
1250 New York Avenue, NW
Washington, DC 20005-3970
Phone: 202-783-7996
Fax: 202-393-3234
Web: www.nmwa.org

National Science Foundation

Research Experiences for Undergraduates - Maria Mitchell Observatory

Type of award: Internship.

Intended use: For undergraduate study at 4-year institution. Designated institutions: Maria Mitchell Observatory, Nantucket, MA.

Eligibility: Applicant must be U.S. citizen or permanent resident.

Basis for selection: Major/career interest in astronomy. Applicant must demonstrate high academic achievement.

Application requirements: Recommendations, essay, transcript.

Additional information: Positions provide chance for students to conduct independent research and to participate in common project. Students expected to develop their ability to communicate with the public. Furnished housing is available at no cost. Partial travel funds available. Internship runs from June through August, with $1,700 monthly stipend. Applicant must demonstrate motivation in research. Minimum of one year undergraduate physics required.

Number of awards:	6
Number of applicants:	100
Application deadline:	February 15
Notification begins:	March 1

Contact:
Maria Mitchell Observatory
4 Vestal Street
Nantucket, MA 02554
Phone: 508-228-9273
Fax: 508-228-1031
Web: www.mmo.org

NCR Corporation

NCR Summer Internships

Type of award: Internship.

Intended use: For full-time undergraduate study at accredited 4-year institution.

Basis for selection: Major/career interest in accounting; computer/information sciences; engineering, computer; finance/banking; human resources; information systems or marketing.

Application requirements: Interview, proof of eligibility. Resume.

Additional information: Minimum 3.0 GPA. Must have at least one semester or two quarters remaining before graduation. Interns paid hourly wage. Applicants must complete personal profile, including resume, on Website before applying for positions. Applicants encouraged to visit Website frequently during spring to review newly added offerings and important information.

Contact:
Visit Website for more information.
Web: www.ncr.com/careers

New Dramatists

Bernard B. Jacobs Internship Program

Type of award: Internship.

Intended use: For undergraduate or graduate study at postsecondary institution.

Basis for selection: Major/career interest in theater arts; performing arts or arts management.
Application requirements: Interview, recommendations, essay. Resume.
Additional information: Must have passion for new plays and playwrights. Twelve- to twenty-week internships, three to five days per week. Internships run September to December, January to May, and June to August. Stipend is $25 per week for three days, $50 per week for five days. College credit may be available. Computer and writing skills essential. Applications must be filled out online.

Application deadline:	December 1, March 31

Contact:
New Dramatists
Internship Coordinator
424 West 44th Street
New York, NY 10036
Web: www.newdramatists.org

New Mexico Commission on Higher Education

New Mexico Work-Study Program

Type of award: Internship, renewable.
Intended use: For undergraduate study at postsecondary institution. Designated institutions: College of Santa Fe, St. John's College, College of the Southwest, Institute of American Indian Art, Crownpoint Institute of Technology, Diné College, Southwest Indian Polytechnic Institute.
Eligibility: Applicant must be U.S. citizen or permanent resident residing in New Mexico.
Basis for selection: Applicant must demonstrate financial need.
Application requirements: FAFSA.
Additional information: Awards vary. Limit of 20 hours per week, on-campus or off-campus in federal, state, or local public agency. New Mexico residents receive state portion of funding. Contact financial aid office of New Mexico public postsecondary institutions for information, deadlines, and application.
Contact:
New Mexico Commission on Higher Education
Financial Aid and Student Services
2048 Galisteo Street
Santa Fe, NM 87505
Phone: 505-476-8400
Web: www.hed.state.nm.us

The New Republic

The New Republic Internship

Type of award: Internship.
Intended use: For senior, graduate or non-degree study at postsecondary institution.
Eligibility: Applicant must be U.S. citizen.
Basis for selection: Major/career interest in journalism. Applicant must demonstrate depth of character and seriousness of purpose.

Application requirements: Cover letter, resume, two writing samples (one showing reporting ability, other showing opinion writing ability), plus one 750-word critique of politics section of recent New Republic issue.
Additional information: Year-long full-time internship beginning in summer for college graduates and soon-to-be college graduates with journalism experience. Must be fluent with LexisNexis and other research tools. Payment is $300 (excluding overtime) per week plus health benefits. Provides intern with opportunity to gain editorial experience at leading opinion magazine. Must have excellent organizational skills, research ability, and experience writing news and opinion. Deadline in late February. No calls or snail mail.

Number of awards:	3
Number of applicants:	100

Contact:
The New Republic
1331 H Street NW
Suite 700
Washington, DC 20005
Phone: 202-508-4444
Web: www.tnr.com

New York State Assembly

New York State Assembly Session Internship Program

Type of award: Internship, renewable.
Intended use: For full-time junior, senior or graduate study at accredited postsecondary institution in United States.
Basis for selection: Applicant must demonstrate high academic achievement.
Application requirements: Recommendations, essay, transcript, proof of eligibility. Writing sample. Letter from college endorsing candidate and outlining course credit arrangements.
Additional information: All majors eligible. Interns assigned to work with assembly members or assembly staff. Program runs from January to May. Undergraduate interns receive $4,140 stipend. Applications accepted on an ongoing basis until deadline. Extensions granted upon request. Housing not provided, but offers assistance in finding apartments and roommates. Visit Website for deadline information.

Amount of award:	$4,140-$11,500
Number of awards:	150
Number of applicants:	200
Application deadline:	November 1

Contact:
Kathleen McCarty, Director New York State Assembly
Assembly Intern Committee
Legislative Office Building, Room 104A
Albany, NY 12248
Phone: 518-455-4704
Fax: 518-455-4705
Web: www.assembly.state.ny.us/internship/

New York Times

New York Times James Reston Reporting Fellowships

Type of award: Internship.
Intended use: For senior, graduate or non-degree study at postsecondary institution.
Basis for selection: Major/career interest in journalism. Applicant must demonstrate seriousness of purpose.
Application requirements: Portfolio. Cover letter, resume, eight to ten writing samples.
Additional information: All applicants must have had at least one previous internship, preferably on a daily newspaper. Visit Website for internship descriptions and more information.
  Application deadline: November 15
Contact:
The New York Times
Dana Canedy
620 8th Avenue
New York, NY 10018
Web: www.nytco.com/careers/internships/summer.html

Oak Ridge Institute for Science and Education

Department of Commerce Internship for Postsecondary Students

Type of award: Internship.
Intended use: For undergraduate or graduate study at 4-year or graduate institution in United States. Designated institutions: Department of Commerce headquarters, division offices and field centers.
Eligibility: Applicant must be U.S. citizen.
Basis for selection: Major/career interest in business; communications; computer/information sciences; engineering; graphic arts/design; health sciences; life sciences; mathematics or physical sciences.
Application requirements: Recommendations, transcript.
Additional information: Provides opportunities to participate in hands-on education and training related to Department of Commerce. Minimum 2.5 GPA. Ten-week internship in summer; 15-week internship for fall or spring semesters. Weekly stipend of $500 for undergraduates, $600 for graduate students; housing allowance of $150 per week based on appointment location; limited travel reimbursement; accidental medical expense coverage provided. Summer deadline is January 31. Number of awards varies. See Website for application.
  Application deadline: July 1, December 1
Contact:
Web: see.orau.org

DOE Pre-Service Teacher Internships

Type of award: Internship.

Intended use: For undergraduate or graduate study. Designated institutions: Oak Ridge National Laboratory (Oak Ridge, TN).
Eligibility: Applicant must be at least 18. Applicant must be U.S. citizen or permanent resident.
Basis for selection: Major/career interest in science, general; mathematics or education. Applicant must demonstrate high academic achievement.
Application requirements: Recommendations, transcript. List of courses, research paper, proof of health insurance.
Additional information: Provides opportunities to participate in educational training and research relating to preparation for teaching K-12 science, math, and technology. Ten-week summer program. Bi-weekly stipend with limited travel reimbursement and limited housing allowance. Minimum 3.0 GPA and must have completed a minimum of two math classes above college algebra or at least two laboratory science classes. Application available online. Visit www.scied.science.doe.gov for deadline.
Contact:
Web: www.orau.gov/orise/edu/ornl/doeprog or http://www.scied.science.doe.gov

Global Change Education Program

Type of award: Internship, renewable.
Intended use: For junior, senior or graduate study at 4-year or graduate institution in United States.
Eligibility: Applicant must be U.S. citizen.
Basis for selection: Major/career interest in physical sciences; geology/earth sciences; environmental science; computer/information sciences; engineering; mathematics; life sciences; health sciences; social/behavioral sciences or ecology.
Additional information: Program offers opportunities to participate in research areas related to global change in various U.S Department of Energy facilities (undergraduates) and U.S. Department of Energy facilities and universities (graduates) across the U.S. Undergraduates are awarded a $475/week stipend, plus travel. Graduates are awarded a $1,500/month stipend. Tuition and fees not to exceed $10,000 per academic year. Duration is 10 to 12 weeks in the summer for undergraduates, and three years for graduates, with the option to renew annually. Number of awards varies. For more information, visit www.atmos.anl.gov/GCEP/.
  Application deadline: December 31
Contact:
Phone: 865-576-7009
Web: see.orau.org or www.atmost.anl.gov/GCEP/

Great Lakes Colleges Association/ Associated Colleges of the Midwest Oak Ridge Science Semester

Type of award: Internship.
Intended use: For full-time undergraduate study at accredited 4-year institution in United States. Designated institutions: Oak Ridge National Laboratory (Oak Ridge, TN).
Basis for selection: Major/career interest in astronomy; computer/information sciences; engineering; environmental science; health sciences; life sciences; physical sciences; geology/earth sciences; mathematics or medicine.
Application requirements: Recommendations, transcript.
Additional information: Applicant must be undergraduate at institutions belonging to the Great Lakes Colleges Association or the Associated Colleges of the Midwest. Provides opportunities to participate in research in a broad range of science and engineering activities related to basic sciences, energy, and the environment. Program is 16 weeks in the fall (late August through mid-December). Weekly stipend; limited

travel reimbursement; housing; academic credit offered for combination of research, coursework, and seminar series. Minimum 3.0 GPA. Visit Website for application deadline.

Notification begins: April 1
Total amount awarded: $7,800
Contact:
Web: see.orau.org or www.denison.edu/oakridge

Internship Program for Laboratory Technology

Type of award: Internship, renewable.
Intended use: For undergraduate or graduate study at postsecondary institution. Designated institutions: Oak Ridge National Laboratory (Oak Ridge, TN).
Eligibility: Applicant must be U.S. citizen or permanent resident residing in Tennessee.
Basis for selection: Major/career interest in engineering; engineering, electrical/electronic; engineering, mechanical; computer/information sciences or physical sciences.
Application requirements: Recommendations, transcript.
Additional information: Provides opportunity to receive hands-on experience in technical areas via long-term assignment. Minimum 2.5 GPA. Internship duration varies with academic level; full-time or part-time appointments of up to one year, renewable up to two additional years. Applications accepted year-round. Stipend available; amount based on academic level or degree. Interns also receive benefits of full-time or part-time employees. This program is limited to indiviuals attending colleges and universities in close proximity to Oak Ridge, TN.

Number of awards: 15
Number of applicants: 35
Total amount awarded: $18,000
Contact:
Oak Ridge Institute for Science and Education
Attn: Marie Woodby
P.O. Box 117
Oak Ridge, TN 37831-0117
Phone: 865-576-9934
Web: see.orau.org

National Oceanic and Atmospheric Administration Hollings Undergraduate Scholarship

Type of award: Internship.
Intended use: For junior or senior study at accredited 4-year institution in United States.
Eligibility: Applicant must be U.S. citizen.
Basis for selection: Major/career interest in agriculture; biology; computer/information sciences; education; engineering; hydrology; physical sciences; mathematics or social/behavioral sciences.
Application requirements: Recommendations, transcript.
Additional information: Provides scholarships and internships for students pursuing degrees in fields related to the National Oceanic and Atmospheric Administration. Minimum 3.0 GPA. Ten-week internship required during summer between junior and senior year. Internship pays weekly stipend of $650 plus housing allowance. See Website for application and more information.

Amount of award: $8,000
Number of awards: 112
Number of applicants: 112
Application deadline: January 30
Total amount awarded: $1,792,000
Contact:
Oak Ridge Institute for Science and Education
Attn: M. Carl Wheeler
P.O. Box 117
Oak Ridge, TN 37831-0117
Phone: 865-241-6704
Web: see.orau.org or www.orau.gov/NOAA/HollingsScholarship

ORISE Department of Energy Community College Institute

Type of award: Internship.
Intended use: For full-time undergraduate study at accredited 2-year institution in United States. Designated institutions: Oak Ridge National Laboratory (Oak Ridge, TN).
Eligibility: Applicant must be at least 18. Applicant must be U.S. citizen or permanent resident.
Basis for selection: Major/career interest in computer/information sciences; science, general; engineering; environmental science; life sciences; mathematics or physical sciences.
Application requirements: Recommendations, transcript. Proof of health insurance.
Additional information: Applicant must be student at community college. Provides opportunities to participate in research in a broad range of science and engineering activities related to basic sciences, energy, and the environment. Applicant must have passed at least 12 credit hours of coursework toward a degree (with at least six credit hours in science, math, engineering, or technology courses) at community college. Ten-week summer internship. Bi-weekly stipend. Limited travel reimbursement and limited housing allowance. Visit Website for application and deadlines.
Contact:
Web: see.orau.org or www.orau.gov/orise/edu/ornl/doeprog

ORISE Higher Education Research Experiences at Oak Ridge National Laboratory for Students

Type of award: Internship.
Intended use: For undergraduate or graduate study in United States. Designated institutions: Oak Ridge National Laboratory (Oak Ridge, TN).
Eligibility: Applicant must be at least 18. Applicant must be U.S. citizen or permanent resident.
Basis for selection: Major/career interest in computer/information sciences; environmental science; engineering, environmental; health sciences; life sciences; medicine; physical sciences or mathematics.
Application requirements: Recommendations, transcript. Two academic references.
Additional information: Provides opportunities to participate in research in a broad range of science and engineering activities related to basic sciences, energy, and the environment. Terms vary with academic level; full- or part-time positions available. Minimum 2.5 GPA. Weekly stipend varies with academic level. One round-trip travel reimbursement and housing allowance. Number of awards varies. Deadlines for undergraduates: February 1 for summer, June 1 for fall, and

October 1 for spring. Deadline for freshmen is February 1. See Website for application and more information.

Application deadline: February 1, June 1
Contact:
Phone: 865-241-3824
Web: see.orau.org or www.orau.gov/hereatornl

ORISE Nuclear Regulatory Commission Historically Black Colleges and Universities Student Research Participation

Type of award: Internship.
Intended use: For undergraduate or graduate study at accredited postsecondary institution in United States. Designated institutions: Laboratories conducting NRC research; some appointments on HBCU campuses; some appointments at host universities under the guidance of principal investigators who have NRC research grants.
Eligibility: Applicant must be U.S. citizen or permanent resident.
Basis for selection: Major/career interest in computer/information sciences; engineering; biology; mathematics; geophysics; physics; materials science; physical sciences; health sciences or statistics.
Application requirements: Recommendations, transcript. Resume.
Additional information: Provides opportunities for students from historically black colleges to participate in ongoing NRC research and development. Minimum 2.5 GPA. Ten to 12 weeks during the summer; some part-time appointments of one year. Weekly stipend of $500 to $600. Limited travel reimbursement (round-trip transportation expenses between facility and home or campus). Funded by U.S. Nuclear Regulatory Commission. Visit Website for application.
Contact:
Phone: 865-576-3409
Fax: 865-241-5220
Web: see.orau.org

ORISE Professional Internship Program for National Energy Technology Laboratory

Type of award: Internship, renewable.
Intended use: For undergraduate or graduate study at accredited 2-year, 4-year or graduate institution in United States. Designated institutions: National Energy Technology Laboratory (Pittsburgh, PA, Albany, OR, and Morgantown, WV).
Eligibility: Applicant must be at least 18.
Basis for selection: Major/career interest in chemistry; computer/information sciences; engineering; environmental science; geology/earth sciences; mathematics; physics; physical sciences or statistics.
Application requirements: Transcript. Proof of health insurance. Two references; at least one academic reference.
Additional information: Provides opportunities to participate in fossil energy-related research. Three to 24 consecutive months, full-time or part-time appointments. Weekly stipend. Limited travel reimbursement (round-trip transportation expenses between facility and home or campus). Off-campus tuition and fees may be paid. Deadline for summer is February 15. Number of awards varies. Minimum 2.5 GPA. Visit Website for application.

Number of awards: 20
Number of applicants: 80
Application deadline: June 1, October 1
Contact:
Web: see.orau.org

ORISE Research Participation Program at the U.S. Army Center for Health Promotion and Preventive Medicine

Type of award: Internship, renewable.
Intended use: For undergraduate or graduate study at postsecondary institution in United States. Designated institutions: U.S. Army Center for Health Promotion and Preventive Medicine (Aberdeen Proving Ground, MD) and other approved locations.
Eligibility: Applicant must be U.S. citizen.
Basis for selection: Major/career interest in biology; chemistry; entomology; engineering; environmental science; physical sciences; science, general or health sciences.
Application requirements: Recommendations, transcript. Resume, proof of insurance.
Additional information: Provides opportunities to participate in applied clinical research in areas such as occupational and environmental health engineering, entomology, ionizing and nonionizing radiation, health promotion, industrial hygiene and worksite hazards, ergonomics, environmental sanitation and hygiene, laboratory science, chemistry, biology, toxicology, health physics, environmental health risk assessment and risk communication, and related projects. Up to one year; full-time or part-time appointments. Minimum 2.5 GPA. Stipend based on research area and academic classification. Number of awards varies. Applications accepted year-round. Visit Website for application.
Contact:
Web: see.orau.org

ORISE Student Environmental Management Participation at the U.S. Army Environmental Center

Type of award: Internship, renewable.
Intended use: For undergraduate or graduate study at 2-year, 4-year or graduate institution. Designated institutions: U.S. Army Environmental Center (Aberdeen Proving Ground, MD) and other approved locations.
Eligibility: Applicant must be U.S. citizen.
Basis for selection: Major/career interest in archaeology; biology; chemistry; computer/information sciences; ecology; engineering; entomology; environmental science; forestry or zoology.
Application requirements: Recommendations, transcript. Resume, proof of health insurance.
Additional information: Provides opportunities to participate in research in environmental programs involving cultural and natural resources, restoration, compliance, conservation, pollution prevention, validation, demonstration, technology transfer, quality assurance and quality control, training, information management and reporting, and related programs. Up to one year; full-time or part-time appointments. Stipend based on research area and academic classification. Minimum 2.5 GPA. Applications accepted year-round. Number of awards varies. Visit Website for application.

Contact:
Oak Ridge Institute for Science and Education (ORISE Maryland)
4692 Millennium Drive
Suite 101
Belcamp, MD 21017
Phone: 410-306-9200
Web: see.orau.org

ORISE Student Research - National Center for Toxicological Research

Type of award: Internship, renewable.
Intended use: For undergraduate or graduate study at accredited 2-year, 4-year or graduate institution in United States. Designated institutions: National Center for Toxicological Research (Jefferson, AK).
Eligibility: Applicant must be U.S. citizen.
Basis for selection: Major/career interest in biology; chemistry; computer/information sciences; mathematics; pharmacy/pharmaceutics/pharmacology; science, general or medicine.
Application requirements: Recommendations, transcript. Resume, proof of health insurance.
Additional information: Provides opportunities to participate in research on biological effects of potentially toxic chemicals and solutions to toxicology problems that have a major impact on human health and the environment. One month to one year; full-time or part-time appointments. Stipend based on research area and academic classification. Summer deadline is mid-March; applications accepted year-round for academic year appointments. Number of awards varies. Visit Website for application.

Number of awards:	40
Number of applicants:	100

Contact:
Web: see.orau.org

ORISE Student Research at the Centers for Disease Control and Prevention/Agency for Toxic Substances and Disease Registry

Type of award: Internship.
Intended use: For undergraduate or graduate study at accredited 2-year, 4-year or graduate institution in United States. Designated institutions: Centers for Disease Control and Prevention (Atlanta, GA and other domestic and international locations) and Agency for Toxic Substances and Disease Registry (Atlanta, GA).
Basis for selection: Major/career interest in communications; economics; environmental science; epidemiology; graphic arts/design; health sciences; life sciences; medicine; physical sciences or science, general.
Application requirements: Recommendations, transcript. Resume, proof of health insurance.
Additional information: Provides opportunities to participate in research on infectious diseases, environmental health, epidemiology, or occupational safety and health. Minimum 2.5 GPA. One month to one year; full-time or part-time appointments. Stipend based on research area(s) and academic classification. Applications accepted year-round. See Website for application.
Contact:
Phone: 867-576-9241
Web: see.orau.org or www.orau.gov/cdc

ORISE Student Research Participation at the U.S. Army Medical Research Institute of Chemical Defense

Type of award: Internship, renewable.
Intended use: For undergraduate or graduate study at 2-year, 4-year or graduate institution in United States. Designated institutions: U.S. Army Medical Research Institute of Chemical Defense (Aberdeen Proving Ground, MD).
Eligibility: Applicant must be U.S. citizen.
Basis for selection: Major/career interest in biochemistry; biology; medicine or physical sciences.
Application requirements: Recommendations, transcript. Resume.
Additional information: Provides opportunities to participate in development of medical countermeasures to chemical warfare agents. Internship lasts up to one year; full- and part-time appointments available. Stipend based on research area and academic classification. Number of awards varies. Minimum 2.5 GPA. Applications accepted year-round. Visit Website for application and details.
Contact:
Web: see.orau.org or www.orau.org/maryland

ORISE Student Research Participation at U.S. Army Research Laboratory

Type of award: Internship.
Intended use: For undergraduate or graduate study at 2-year, 4-year or graduate institution in United States. Designated institutions: U.S. Army Research Laboratory (Adelphi and Aberdeen Proving Ground, MD) and other approved locations.
Eligibility: Applicant must be U.S. citizen.
Basis for selection: Major/career interest in biology; medicine; physical sciences; computer/information sciences; materials science or engineering.
Application requirements: Recommendations, transcript.
Additional information: Provides opportunities to participate in research and technology development in areas such as engineering, mechanics, chemistry, computational modeling, science, and materials research related to enhancing the lethality and survivability of America's ground forces. Internship lasts up to one year; up to a total of four years; full- or part-time appointments available. Stipend based on research area and classification. Number of awards varies. Minimum 2.5 GPA. Applications accepted year-round. Visit Website for application.
Contact:
Web: see.orau.org

Savannah River Site Professional Internship Program

Type of award: Internship.
Intended use: For undergraduate or graduate study at 2-year, 4-year or graduate institution in United States. Designated institutions: Savannah River Site (Aiken, SC).
Eligibility: Applicant must be U.S. citizen.
Basis for selection: Major/career interest in business; chemistry; computer/information sciences; engineering; environmental science; geology/earth sciences; mathematics or physics.
Application requirements: Recommendations, transcript. Proof of health insurance.

Additional information: Provides opportunities to participate in energy-related and environmental research. Three to 24 consecutive months; full-time or part-time appointments. Weekly stipend; limited travel reimbursement (round-trip transportation expenses between facility and home or campus). Minimum 2.5 GPA. Summer deadline February 15. Funded by Savannah River Site. Visit Website for application.

   Application deadline: June 1, October 1

Contact:

Web: see.orau.org

Science Undergraduate Laboratory Internships

Type of award: Internship.
Intended use: For undergraduate study at postsecondary institution. Designated institutions: Oak Ridge National Laboratory (Oak Ridge, TN).
Eligibility: Applicant must be U.S. citizen or permanent resident.
Basis for selection: Major/career interest in computer/information sciences; physical sciences; mathematics; life sciences; engineering; science, general or environmental science.
Application requirements: Recommendations, transcript. Proof of health insurance.
Additional information: Internship program provides opportunity to participate in research in a broad range of science and engineering activities related to basic sciences, energy, and the environment. Bi-weekly stipend; limited travel reimbursement and housing allowance. Internship lasts ten weeks in the summer; 16 weeks during semester. See Website for more information and deadlines.

Contact:

Web: see.orau.org or www.orau.gov/orise/edu/ornl/doeprog/

Student Research Participation at the Federal Bureau of Investigation

Type of award: Internship.
Intended use: For undergraduate or graduate study at accredited 2-year or 4-year institution in United States. Designated institutions: FBI Academy (Quantico, VA).
Eligibility: Applicant must be U.S. citizen.
Basis for selection: Major/career interest in forensics; chemistry; biology; physical sciences; health sciences or life sciences.
Application requirements: Recommendations, transcript. Resume.
Additional information: Opportunities to participate in advancement of forensic science for the FBI Laboratory as well as federal, state, and local law enforcement agencies. Award number varies. Applications accepted on year-round basis. Stipend based on academic classification. Appointments are full- or part-time and range from ten weeks to one year. Minimum 2.5 GPA. Visit Website for application.

Contact:

Web: see.orau.org

U.S. Department of Homeland Security Scholarship and Fellowship Program

Type of award: Internship.
Intended use: For sophomore or junior study at accredited 4-year or graduate institution in United States.

Eligibility: Applicant must be U.S. citizen.
Basis for selection: Major/career interest in biology; engineering; social/behavioral sciences; physical sciences; mathematics; computer/information sciences; life sciences; physical sciences or agriculture. Applicant must demonstrate high academic achievement.
Application requirements: Recommendations, transcript.
Additional information: Opportunity to participate in educational program intended to ensure diverse and highly talented science and technology human resource base to meet mission, goals, and objectives of U.S. Department of Homeland Security. Appointments are two years for undergraduates and three years for graduate students, given satisfactory progress. Successful applicants will receive full-tuition scholarship and monthly stipend. Summer internship required following first year of award. Minimum 3.3 GPA. Visit Website for application and more information.

   Amount of award: Full tuition
   Number of applicants: 157

Contact:

Web: www.orau.gov/dhsed

Ohio Newspapers Foundation

AdOhio Advertising Internship

Type of award: Internship.
Intended use: For junior or senior study at postsecondary institution. Designated institutions: Ohio institutions.
Eligibility: Applicant must be residing in Ohio.
Basis for selection: Major/career interest in journalism or advertising.
Application requirements: Resume, writing samples, and cover letter.
Additional information: Ten-week internship in Columbus office of this trade association, which represents 83 daily newspapers, more than 180 weekly newspapers, and more than 150 Websites in Ohio. Duties include writing and layout for sales presentation sheets and client mailings, assistance with newspaper ad bid sheets, newspaper tear sheets, and research. Negotiable start date after June 1. Salary is $350 per week. Finalists will be contacted for interviews.

   Application deadline: March 31
   Notification begins: May 1

Contact:

Ohio Newspapers Foundation
Mark Henry, Manager
1335 Dublin Road, Suite 216-B
Columbus, OH 43215
Web: www.ohionews.org

Ohio Newspaper Association Publications/Public Relations Internship

Type of award: Internship.
Intended use: For sophomore, junior or senior study at postsecondary institution. Designated institutions: Ohio institutions.
Eligibility: Applicant must be residing in Ohio.
Basis for selection: Major/career interest in communications or journalism.

Internships

Application requirements: Resume, writing samples, and cover letter.

Additional information: Ten-week internship at this trade association, which represents 83 daily newspapers, more than 180 weekly newspapers, and more than 150 Websites in Ohio. Duties include writing and assisting in production of newsletter, miscellaneous flyers and mailings, meeting planning, and research. Negotiable start date after June 1. Salary of $350 per week. Finalists will be contacted for interviews.

Application deadline:	March 31
Notification begins:	May 1

Contact:
Ohio Newspapers Foundation
Frank Deaner, Executive Director
1335 Dublin Road, Suite 216-B
Columbus, OH 43215
Web: www.ohionews.org

Oracle Corporation

Product Development Summer Internship Program

Type of award: Internship.
Intended use: For full-time sophomore, junior, senior or graduate study at accredited 4-year or graduate institution in United States.
Basis for selection: Major/career interest in computer/information sciences. Applicant must demonstrate high academic achievement.
Application requirements: Resume.
Additional information: Foreign student must have unrestricted permission to work in United States. Interns are offered excellent compensation and fully furnished corporate apartments are provided. Car/bike rentals and round-trip travel expenses are paid for, as well as a helicopter ride under the Golden Gate Bridge. Visit Website to submit resume and sign up to search for current openings.

Application deadline:	January 1
Notification begins:	February 28

Contact:
Oracle Corporation
500 Oracle Parkway
M/S UPAL01-471
Redwood Shores, CA 94065
Phone: 800-633-0738
Web: www.oracle.com/us/corporate/careers/college/internships/index.html

Owens Corning

Owens Corning Internships

Type of award: Internship.
Intended use: For full-time junior or senior study at accredited 4-year institution.
Eligibility: Applicant must be U.S. citizen or permanent resident.
Basis for selection: Major/career interest in engineering; accounting; human resources; information systems; marketing; materials science; communications or finance/banking.

Applicant must demonstrate high academic achievement and leadership.
Application requirements: Proof of eligibility.
Additional information: Summer internship with housing assistance, competitive salary. Summer program lasts ten to twelve weeks. Most positions in Toledo, Ohio. See Website for more information.
Contact:
Owens Corning
One Owens Corning Parkway
Toledo, OH 43659
Web: www.owenscorningcareers.com

Pacific Gas and Electric Company

Pacific Gas and Electric Summer Intern Program

Type of award: Internship.
Intended use: For full-time undergraduate or graduate study in United States.
Eligibility: Applicant must be U.S. citizen or permanent resident.
Basis for selection: Major/career interest in business; chemistry; communications; computer/information sciences; economics; engineering; geology/earth sciences; marketing; engineering, mechanical or public administration/service. Applicant must demonstrate high academic achievement and seriousness of purpose.
Application requirements: Interview. Resume, cover letter.
Additional information: Paid internships available throughout northern and central California, including company headquarters in San Francisco. Deadline is rolling, but early applications are encouraged. Resume may be submitted online; format specifications available online. Visit Website or call sponsor for openings and campus recruitment dates. Must be eligible to work in the United States. Number and amount of awards vary. Most internships are summer only and typically last 10-12 weeks. Internships include a competitive salary and paid company holidays.
Contact:
Pacific Gas and Electric Company
College Relations/CHP
P.O. Box 770000, Mail Code N14G
San Francisco, CA 94177
Phone: 415-817-8237
Web: www.pge.com/about/careers/college/intern

PBS

PBS Internships

Type of award: Internship.
Intended use: For undergraduate or graduate study at postsecondary institution.
Application requirements: Resume and cover letter.
Additional information: Various internships are available in different departments. All paid, except for internship in General Counsel's office. Internships also offered for graduated students

seeking an MBA. Internships change on a semester basis. Visit Website for internship listings, application forms, and more information.

Contact:
PBS Internship Program
2100 Crystal Dr.
Arlington, VA 22202
Phone: 703-739-5088
Web: www.pbs.org/jobs

PGA Tour

PGA Tour Diversity Intern Program

Type of award: Internship.
Intended use: For sophomore, junior, senior or master's study at postsecondary institution.
Eligibility: Applicant must be U.S. citizen.
Basis for selection: Major/career interest in marketing; business/management/administration; communications; information systems; journalism; radio/television/film; sports/sports administration or public relations. Applicant must demonstrate high academic achievement, depth of character, leadership, seriousness of purpose and service orientation.
Application requirements: Interview, recommendations, essay, transcript.
Additional information: Internship lasts ten weeks at $440 per week with $200 per month deducted for housing (if needed). Site locations include Arizona, California, Florida, Georgia, Maryland, Ohio, and New York. Minimum 2.8 GPA. Visit Website to apply.

Amount of award:	$4,400
Number of awards:	30
Number of applicants:	1,450
Application deadline:	February 28
Notification begins:	May 1
Total amount awarded:	$132,000

Contact:
PGA Tour Diversity Intern Program
Attn: Mike Cooney
100 PGA Tour Boulevard
Ponte Vedra Beach, FL 32082
Phone: 904-273-3520
Fax: 904-273-3588
Web: www.pgatour.com/company/internships.html

Phipps Conservatory and Botanical Gardens

Phipps Conservatory and Botanical Gardens Internships

Type of award: Internship.
Intended use: For junior, senior or graduate study at accredited 2-year or 4-year institution.
Eligibility: Applicant must be U.S. citizen.
Basis for selection: Major/career interest in horticulture; landscape architecture; environmental science or botany. Applicant must demonstrate high academic achievement.

Application requirements: Recommendations. Resume and cover letter.
Additional information: Interns paid $8 per hour. Related majors, such as environmental education, also eligible. Internships may be full- or part-time. Four to six positions available in summer; one to two positions available during academic year. Application deadline is rolling. Contact sponsor or visit Website for more information.

Number of awards:	8

Contact:
Phipps Conservatory and Botanical Gardens Human Resources
1059 Shady Avenue
Pittsburgh, PA 15232
Phone: 412-441-4442
Fax: 412-665-2368
Web: www.phipps.conservatory.org

Princeton Plasma Physics Laboratory

Plasma Physics National Undergraduate Fellowship Program

Type of award: Internship.
Intended use: For junior study at 4-year institution in United States.
Eligibility: Applicant must be U.S. citizen or permanent resident.
Basis for selection: Major/career interest in engineering; physics; mathematics or computer/information sciences. Applicant must demonstrate high academic achievement, depth of character, leadership, seriousness of purpose and service orientation.
Application requirements: Recommendations, essay, transcript.
Additional information: Minimum 3.5 GPA. Internship paid and lasts ten weeks in the summer. Application due in mid-February.

Amount of award:	$4,800
Number of awards:	25
Number of applicants:	100
Application deadline:	February 18
Notification begins:	March 15

Contact:
Princeton Plasma Physics Laboratory
P.O. Box 451, MS-40
Princeton, NJ 08543-0451
Phone: 609-243-2116
Web: www.pppl.gov

Random House

Random House Summer Internship Program

Type of award: Internship.
Intended use: For undergraduate study at 4-year institution.
Basis for selection: Major/career interest in publishing. Applicant must demonstrate seriousness of purpose.

Application requirements: Resume, cover letter expressing interest in specific publishing group.

Additional information: Ten-week internship beginning in early June open to rising college seniors for New York program; Westminster program open to all undergrads. All majors encouraged to apply. Internships are for college credit and unpaid. If invited, applicant must travel to New York City or Westminster, Maryland, at own expense for interview in late February through mid-April. See Website for application, deadline, and more information.

Number of awards:	40
Number of applicants:	2,400

Contact:
Random House Internship Coordinator
Human Resources, 25th Floor
1745 Broadway
New York, NY 10019
Web: www.careers.randomhouse.com

Rhode Island State Government

Rhode Island State Government Internship Program

Type of award: Internship, renewable.

Intended use: For undergraduate or postgraduate study at postsecondary institution.

Eligibility: Applicant must be residing in Rhode Island.

Basis for selection: Major/career interest in governmental public relations or public administration/service. Applicant must demonstrate high academic achievement, depth of character, leadership, seriousness of purpose and service orientation.

Application requirements: Interview, recommendations, transcript, proof of eligibility. Writing sample (for law students only).

Additional information: Minimum 2.5 GPA. Summer program lasts eight weeks; spring and fall programs last entire semester. Fall application deadline is rolling. Compensation for summer interns only, at $100 per week. Spring and fall interns earn academic credit or work-study, if eligible. All placements in Rhode Island.

Number of awards:	243
Number of applicants:	450
Application deadline:	May 15

Contact:
Rhode Island State Government
State Capitol, Room 8AA
Providence, RI 02903
Phone: 401-222-6782
Fax: 401-222-4447
Web: www.rilin.state.ri.us

Simon and Schuster Inc.

Simon and Schuster Summer Internship Program

Type of award: Internship, renewable.

Intended use: For full-time undergraduate study at accredited vocational or 4-year institution.

Basis for selection: Major/career interest in publishing. Applicant must demonstrate high academic achievement.

Application requirements: Interview. Resume. Cover letter. Letter of interest.

Additional information: Internship program is designed to train and recruit a diverse group of students interested in exploring careers in publishing. Summer, spring, fall, and year-round programs are available. Student must register for academic credit with their college or university and provide official documentation confirming this information. Applicants must have well-rounded extracurricular interests and work experience. Visit Website for application.

Application deadline:	April 1

Contact:
Simon and Schuster, Inc.
HR Department/Internship Program
1230 Avenue of the Americas
New York, NY 10020
Web: www.simonandschuster.biz/careers/internships

Smithsonian Environmental Research Center

Smithsonian Environmental Research Center Internship Program

Type of award: Internship, renewable.

Intended use: For undergraduate or master's study at 4-year or graduate institution.

Basis for selection: Major/career interest in biology; chemistry; environmental science; physics; mathematics or education. Applicant must demonstrate seriousness of purpose.

Application requirements: Recommendations, essay, transcript.

Additional information: Projects are 40 hours per week, lasting from 10 to 16 weeks. Stipend is $425 per week and available winter/spring, summer, and fall. Dorm space is available for $75 per week on limited basis. Several application deadlines: spring, November 15; summer, February 1; fall, June 1. Applicants should demonstrate academic credentials, relevant experience, and the congruence of expressed goals with those of internship program. Open to all undergraduates, recent college graduates, and beginning Master's students.

Number of awards:	30
Number of applicants:	250
Application deadline:	November 15, February 1
Notification begins:	December 15, March 15
Total amount awarded:	$144,000

Contact:
Smithsonian Environmental Research Center
Internship Program
647 Contees Wharf Road
Edgewater, MD 21037
Phone: 443-428-2217
Fax: 443-428-2380
Web: www.serc.si.edu/pro_training/internships.aspx

Smithsonian Institution

James E. Webb Internship Program for Minority Undergraduate Seniors and Graduate Students in Business and Public Administration

Type of award: Internship.
Intended use: For senior or graduate study at 4-year or graduate institution. Designated institutions: Smithsonian Institution.
Eligibility: Applicant must be Alaskan native, Asian American, African American, Mexican American, Hispanic American, Puerto Rican, American Indian or Native Hawaiian/Pacific Islander. Applicant must be U.S. citizen or permanent resident.
Basis for selection: Major/career interest in business/management/administration or public administration/service. Applicant must demonstrate high academic achievement.
Application requirements: Recommendations, essay, transcript. Resume.
Additional information: Minimum 3.0 GPA. Applicant must be minority student enrolled as undergraduate senior or graduate student in business or public administration program. Selection based on relevance of internship at the Smithsonian to student's academic and career goals. Internships are full-time, 40 hours per week for ten weeks. Stipend is $500 per week, with additional travel allowances offered in some cases. Deadlines: February 1 for summer and fall; October 1 for spring. Contact sponsor or visit Website for more information and application.

    Application deadline: February 1, October 1
Contact:
Smithsonian Institution Office of Fellowships
470 L'Enfant Plaza, SW, Suite 7102, MRC 902
P.O. Box 37012
Washington, DC 20013-7012
Phone: 202-633-7070
Web: www.si.edu/ofg

Smithsonian Minority Internship

Type of award: Internship.
Intended use: For undergraduate or graduate study at postsecondary institution. Designated institutions: Smithsonian Institution.
Basis for selection: Major/career interest in anthropology; archaeology; ecology; environmental science; art/art history; museum studies; zoology or natural sciences.
Application requirements: Recommendations, essay, transcript. Resume.
Additional information: Research internships at Smithsonian Institution in anthropology/archaeology; astrophysics and astronomy; earth sciences/paleontology; ecology; environmental, behavioral (tropical animals), evolutionary, and systematic biology; history of science and technology; history of art (including American contemporary, African, Asian); 20th-century American crafts; social and cultural history and folk life of America. Applicants must have major/career interest in research or museum-related activity pursued by the Smithsonian Institution. Stipend of $500 per week for ten weeks. February 1 deadline for summer session and for fall; October 1 deadline for spring. Intended for U.S. minority groups under-represented in Smithsonian scholarly programs. Contact sponsor for minority requirements. Minimum 3.0 GPA. Visit Website for more information.

    Application deadline: February 1, October 1
Contact:
Smithsonian Institution Office of Fellowships
470 L'Enfant Plaza, SW, Suite 7102, MRC 902
P.O. Box 37012
Washington, DC 20013-7012
Phone: 202-633-7070
Web: www.si.edu/ofg

Smithsonian Native American Internship

Type of award: Internship.
Intended use: For undergraduate or graduate study at postsecondary institution. Designated institutions: Smithsonian Institution.
Eligibility: Applicant must be Alaskan native or American Indian.
Basis for selection: Major/career interest in Native American studies.
Application requirements: Recommendations, essay, transcript. Resume.
Additional information: Internship at Smithsonian Institution in research or museum activities related to Native American studies. Stipend of $500 a week for ten weeks. Deadline for summer and fall is February 1; spring is October 1. American Indian students encouraged to apply. Contact Office of Fellowships for application procedures or visit Website.

    Application deadline: February 1, October 1
Contact:
Smithsonian Institution Office of Fellowships
470 L'Enfant Plaza, SW, Suite 7102, MRC 902
P.O. Box 37012
Washington, DC 20013-7012
Phone: 202-633-7070
Web: www.si.edu/ofg

Society of Physics Students

Society of Physics Students Summer Internship Program

Type of award: Internship.
Intended use: For full-time undergraduate study.
Eligibility: Applicant or parent must be member/participant of Society of Physics Students.
Basis for selection: Major/career interest in physics. Applicant must demonstrate high academic achievement.
Application requirements: Transcript. Resume and cover letter. Two letters of recommendation (one should be written by SPS advisor).
Additional information: Offers nine-and-a-half-week internships in science policy and research for undergraduate physics majors. Internships include $3,750 stipend, paid housing, and transportation supplement. Internships are based in Washington, DC. Applicants must be active SPS members with excellent scholastic record and experience in science outreach events or science research. See Website for application and deadline.

Amount of award: $3,750
Number of awards: 12
Number of applicants: 483
Application deadline: February 1
Notification begins: March 15
Total amount awarded: $33,300
Contact:
SPS Summer Internship Program
One Physics Ellipse
College Park, MD 20740
Phone: 301-209-3007
Fax: 301-209-0839
Web: www.spsnational.org/programs/internships

Solomon R. Guggenheim Museum

Guggenheim Museum Internship

Type of award: Internship.
Intended use: For junior, senior or graduate study at postsecondary institution.
Basis for selection: Major/career interest in art/art history; arts, general; arts management; communications; education; finance/banking; graphic arts/design; library science; museum studies or museum studies/administration. Applicant must demonstrate high academic achievement.
Application requirements: Interview, recommendations. Cover letter, resume, writing sample.
Additional information: Potential internships available in Conservation, Curatorial, Education, Development, Director's Office, Exhibition Development, Exhibition Management, Finance, Graphic Design, Human Resources, Information Technology, Legal, Library Archives, Marketing, Photography, Public Affairs, Publications, Registrar, Special Events, Special Projects, and Visitor Services. International students must have J-1 visa. Internships during academic year are for college credit; some stipends available in summer. Application deadlines are January 18 for summer, May 3 for fall and academic year, November 1 for spring. Spring, fall, and academic year internships are full- or part-time, with minimum commitment of 16 hours/week for three months. Summer internships are full-time.
Number of awards: 40
Number of applicants: 300
Application deadline: January 18, May 3
Contact:
Solomon R. Guggenheim Museum
Education Coordinator-- Internship Program
1071 Fifth Avenue
New York, NY 10128-0173
Phone: 212-360-4287
Web: www.guggenheim.org

Peggy Guggenheim Internship

Type of award: Internship.
Intended use: For undergraduate or graduate study at postsecondary institution.
Basis for selection: Major/career interest in arts, general; art/art history; education; museum studies or museum studies/administration. Applicant must demonstrate high academic achievement, depth of character, leadership and seriousness of purpose.

Application requirements: Recommendations, essay, transcript. Resume.
Additional information: One- to three-month internship at Peggy Guggenheim Collection in Venice, Italy. Two deadlines: October 15 for internships in January-April; December 1 for internships in May-December. Must be fluent in English with knowledge of spoken Italian. Interns receive a monthly stipend. Request further information and application forms from the Peggy Guggenheim Collection. Visit Website for details.
Number of applicants: 1,400
Application deadline: October 15, December 1
Notification begins: December 1, February 15
Contact:
Peggy Guggenheim Collection Internship Coodinator
Palazzo Venier dei Leoni
701 Dorsoduro, 30123 Venice, Italy
Phone: 39-041-240-5401
Web: www.guggenheim.org or www.guggenheim-venice.it

Sony Music Entertainment

Sony Credited Internship

Type of award: Internship.
Intended use: For undergraduate or graduate study at accredited postsecondary institution.
Eligibility: Applicant must be U.S. citizen or permanent resident.
Basis for selection: Major/career interest in accounting; business; finance/banking; communications; computer/information sciences; law; music; music management or marketing.
Application requirements: Interview, transcript, proof of eligibility. Resume and cover letter.
Additional information: Unpaid internship. Applicant must be available to work at least 16-20 hours a week. Internships are available in various departments throughout company. Deadlines for spring and fall are rolling. When applying, specify which semester you are applying for. Applicant must be enrolled at accredited university and provide verification of course credit. Visit Website for details and application.
Number of awards: 60
Number of applicants: 200
Contact:
Sony Music Entertainment
550 Madison Avenue, 2nd Floor
New York, NY 10022-3211
Phone: 212-833-8000
Web: www.sonymusic.com

Southface Energy Institute

Southface Internship

Type of award: Internship.
Intended use: For undergraduate or graduate study at accredited 2-year, 4-year or graduate institution in United States.
Eligibility: Applicant must be U.S. citizen, permanent resident or international student.
Basis for selection: Major/career interest in architecture; business/management/administration; engineering, civil;

engineering, environmental; engineering, mechanical; environmental science; graphic arts/design; landscape architecture; public relations or urban planning. Applicant must demonstrate high academic achievement.

Application requirements: Statement of intent. Names of references with contact information.

Additional information: Internships cover variety of interests: sustainable building, community design, water-efficient landscaping, smart growth, environmental event planning, energy policy and tech assistance, non-profit marketing, and public relations. Six- to twelve-month positions available. Students work 40 hours per week; weekly stipend of $100. Shared housing available if space permits. Transportation assistance available. Applications accepted year-round. International students must have work authorization.

Contact:
Southface Energy Institute
Internship Coordinator
241 Pine Street, NE
Atlanta, GA 30308
Phone: 404-604-3595
Fax: 404-872-5009
Web: www.southface.org

Spoleto Festival USA

Spoleto Festival Apprenticeship Program

Type of award: Internship, renewable.

Intended use: For undergraduate, graduate or non-degree study in United States.

Basis for selection: Major/career interest in arts management; arts, general; music; public relations or theater/production/technical. Applicant must demonstrate seriousness of purpose.

Application requirements: Recommendations. Three writing samples (media applicants only). Resume, cover letter.

Additional information: Four-week full-time apprenticeship with arts professionals producing and operating international arts festival. Posts available in media relations, development, box office, production, orchestra management, artist services, and office administration. Weekly stipend may be provided; housing and travel allowance provided. See Website for details and deadlines.

Number of awards:	50

Contact:
Spoleto Festival USA
Apprentice Program
14 George Street
Charleston, SC 29401
Web: www.spoletousa.org

Sports Journalism Institute

Aspiring Sports Journalist Internship

Type of award: Internship.

Intended use: For sophomore or junior study at postsecondary institution.

Basis for selection: Major/career interest in journalism; communications; publishing; English or sports/sports administration. Applicant must demonstrate high academic achievement and seriousness of purpose.

Application requirements: Recommendations, essay, transcript. Professional-style photo, up to seven writing samples.

Additional information: The Sports Journalism Institute is a nine-week, paid summer training and internship program for undergraduates interested in sports journalism. Applicants need not be journalism majors. Scholarship available for students returning to college upon successful completion of program. Visit Website for more information, application, and deadline.

Amount of award:	$500
Number of awards:	10

Contact:
Gregory Lee
The Boston Globe
135 Morrissey Blvd.
Boston, MA 02125
Web: www.sportsjournalisminstitute.org

Staples

Staples Summer Internship Program

Type of award: Internship.

Intended use: For undergraduate study at 4-year institution in United States.

Basis for selection: Major/career interest in advertising; marketing; accounting; technology; information systems or finance/banking.

Application requirements: Resume.

Additional information: Internships located at corporate headquarters in Framingham, MA. Other eligible majors include supply chain, corporate strategy, customer service, merchandising/brand management, and sale. Visit Website to see openings and apply online.

Contact:
Staples
500 Staples Drive
Framingham, MA 01702
Web: www.staples.com

Student Conservation Association

SCA Conservation Internships

Type of award: Internship, renewable.

Intended use: For undergraduate or graduate study at accredited postsecondary institution in United States.

Basis for selection: Major/career interest in archaeology; ecology; forestry; natural resources/conservation; history; education; wildlife/fisheries; biology or communications.

Application requirements: Resume.

Additional information: Travel and housing is provided, and a weekly stipend is given for food. Positions at various locations in United States. Applicants are advised to apply three months prior to position start date. Rolling admissions process -- seven application deadlines per year. Applicants with interest

Internships

in environmental education, interpretation, marine biology, and wilderness preservation also eligible. See Website for application.

Amount of award: $1,000-$4,725
Contact:
Admissions Department Student Conservation Association
P.O. Box 550
Charlestown, NH 03603
Phone: 603-543-1700
Fax: 603-543-1828
Web: www.thesca.org

Texas Historical Commission

Preservation Fellows Program

Type of award: Internship.
Intended use: For sophomore, junior, senior or graduate study at 2-year, 4-year or graduate institution in United States.
Eligibility: Applicant must be Alaskan native, Asian American, African American, Mexican American, Hispanic American, Puerto Rican, American Indian or Native Hawaiian/Pacific Islander. Applicant must be U.S. citizen.
Basis for selection: Applicant must demonstrate high academic achievement.
Application requirements: Recommendations, transcript. Resume or CV, list of previous experience with the Texas Historical Commission.
Additional information: Minimum 3.0 GPA. Applicants must either attend institutions in Texas, or be Texas residents attending school out-of-state are eligible to apply. Preservation Fellows receive a $5,000 stipend for eight weeks of 40-hour-week employment under the supervision of the THC, either at its headquarters in Austin or "in the field" with an associated preservation organization.

Amount of award: $5,000
Application deadline: December 31
Contact:
Preservation Fellows c/o Friends of the Texas Historical Commission
P.O. Box 13497
Austin, TX 78711-3497
Phone: 512-463-6100
Fax: 512-475-4872
Web: www.thc.state.tx.us

Time Inc.

Time Inc. Internship Program

Type of award: Internship.
Intended use: For undergraduate or graduate study at accredited 4-year or graduate institution.
Basis for selection: Major/career interest in finance/banking; advertising; communications; graphic arts/design; information systems; journalism or marketing.
Application requirements: Cover letter and resume.
Additional information: Spring and fall academic year internships are offered on an as-needed basis, with available positions and magazines/Websites varying each semester. Most

positions require a minimum of 14 hours per week and are based in NYC. Nine- to ten-week paid summer internship programs include the Consumer Marketing and Sales Internship Program, the Corporate Program, the Editorial Internship Program, the Essence Internship Program and the Finance Internship Program.
Contact:
Time Inc.
1271 Avenue of the Americas
New York, NY 10020
Phone: 212-522-1212
Web: www.timeinc.com/careers/campusrecruiting.php

Tourism Cares

David J. Hallissey Memorial Internship

Type of award: Internship.
Intended use: For sophomore, junior, senior or graduate study at accredited 4-year or graduate institution in United States.
Eligibility: Applicant must be U.S. citizen, permanent resident or international student.
Basis for selection: Major/career interest in tourism/travel or marketing.
Application requirements: Recommendations, transcript. Copy of driver's license or passport, resume. Two-page essay describing what segment of the industry you are focusing on, and how your academic and extracurricular activities tie in to future goals.
Additional information: Minimum 3.0 GPA. Applicant must have strong written and verbal communication skills as well as interpersonal skills and a basic understanding of Microsoft Excel. Preference given to applicants with a knowledge of Microsoft Access and SBSS software. The intern will be working in the American Society of Travel Agents Research Department in the Washington, D.C. area. The intern's basic duties will be assisting in conducting surveys with a research panel using Internet-based software, and research and analysis of issues affecting the travel industry. The intern must submit a report about the intership experience at the end of the period worked. Submit all items in electronic form except transcript, which should be sent directly from school. Visit Website for deadline.

Amount of award: $2,000
Number of awards: 1
Contact:
Tourism Cares
275 Turnpike Street
Suite 307
Canton, MA 02021
Web: www.tourismcares.org/scholarships

Mayflower Tours Patrick Murphy Internship

Type of award: Internship.
Intended use: For sophomore, junior, senior or graduate study in United States or Canada.
Basis for selection: Major/career interest in tourism/travel or hospitality administration/management. Applicant must demonstrate high academic achievement.
Application requirements: Transcript. Resume. Essay detailing work/internship experience in travel and tourism

industry. Should include volunteer/extracurricular activities. Also answer the following question, "What is your sense of the future of the packaged travel industry in North America over the next 10 years?"

Additional information: Minimum 3.0 GPA. Must have an interest in political science. Intern will be assigned to work at office of Stephen Richer, National Tour Association Public Affairs Advocate, in Washington, D.C. area (Alexandria, VA) during fall semester. Primary duties will be researching issues affecting travel and tourism industry. No lobbying. Must have excellent written, oral, and interpersonal skills. All application materials must be scanned to PDF and submitted electronically (except transcript). Visit Website for application and deadline.

Number of awards: 1
Total amount awarded: $2,000
Contact:
Tourism Cares
275 Turnpike Street
Suite 307
Canton, MA 02021
Phone: 781-821-5990
Fax: 781-821-8949
Web: www.tourismcares.org/scholarships

Tyson Foods, Inc.

Tyson Foods Intern Program

Type of award: Internship.
Intended use: For full-time undergraduate study at accredited vocational, 2-year or 4-year institution.
Basis for selection: Major/career interest in agribusiness; agriculture; computer/information sciences; engineering; food production/management/services; food science/technology; health-related professions; law; marketing or science, general. Applicant must demonstrate high academic achievement.
Application requirements: Proof of eligibility. Resume and cover letter.
Additional information: Various paid internships include but not limited to computer programming, industrial engineering, livestock procurement, quality assurance, carcass sales, and production. Program locations across the United States. Must be eligible to work in the U.S. Visit Website for job descriptions and list of campus recruiting events, or to submit resume and cover letter. Summer and academic-year internships available.
Number of awards: 50
Contact:
Tyson Foods, Inc.
Web: www.tyson.com/Corporate/Careers

United Negro College Fund

Oracle Scholars Internship Program

Type of award: Internship.
Intended use: For junior or senior study at 4-year institution in United States. Designated institutions: UNCF member institutions; Historically Black Colleges and Universities.
Basis for selection: Major/career interest in business; marketing; finance/banking; engineering; human resources; computer/information sciences or accounting. Applicant must demonstrate high academic achievement.

Application requirements: Recommendations, transcript. Resume, statement of career interests, and financial need statement.
Additional information: Minimum 3.0 GPA. Eight-week paid summer internship at an Oracle location in either Redwood Shores, CA, or Reston, VA. Includes monthly salary, housing accommodations or monthly housing allowance, and round-trip transportation from school to internship location and local transportation to and from internship site. $10,000 scholarship available upon successful completion of the internship. Visit Website for application, deadlines, and list of eligible schools.
Contact:
UNCF/Oracle Scholarship Interns Program
8260 Willow Oaks Corporate Drive
P.O. Box 1044
Fairfax, VA 22031-8044
Phone: 800-331-2244
Web: www.uncf.org

United States Holocaust Memorial Museum

United States Holocaust Memorial Museum Internship

Type of award: Internship, renewable.
Intended use: For sophomore, junior, senior or graduate study at postsecondary institution.
Eligibility: Applicant must be U.S. citizen, permanent resident or international student.
Basis for selection: Major/career interest in museum studies/administration; history; English; foreign languages; communications; geography; graphic arts/design or communications.
Additional information: Semester-long internships available during summer, fall, and spring in Holocaust research and museum studies. Phone interviews conducted with top qualified candidates. Not all positions paid. Applicants interested in German or Eastern European studies also eligible. Application deadline is March 15 for summer; July 1 for fall; October 15 for spring. Apply online. All applicants subject to criminal background check. International students must have work authorization. Award notification begins at the end of March.
Number of awards: 37
Number of applicants: 526
Application deadline: March 15
Contact:
Internship Coordinator, Office of Volunteer and Intern Services
United States Holocaust Memorial Museum
100 Raoul Wallenburg Place, SW
Washington, DC 20024-2150
Phone: 202-479-9737
Fax: 202-488-6568
Web: www.ushmm.org

United States Senate

U.S. Senate Member Internships

Type of award: Internship.

Intended use: For full-time undergraduate study at accredited 4-year institution.
Eligibility: Applicant must be U.S. citizen or permanent resident.
Basis for selection: Major/career interest in political science/ government; law; communications; public relations; public administration/service or economics. Applicant must demonstrate high academic achievement.
Application requirements: Resume, cover letter, writing sample.
Additional information: Senate member interns generally reside or attend college in senator's state. Positions available in Washington, D.C., or member's state. Internships may be unpaid or paid (less common), but generally offer assistance obtaining college credit. Term of service, eligibility vary. Some internships restricted to upper-level undergraduates. Senators administer their own internship programs. Contact individual senator's office directly. Visit Website for links to member sites, e-mail addresses, and telephone numbers.
Contact:
Office of (name of senator)
United States Senate
Washington, DC 20510
Web: www.senate.gov

U.S. Department of Agriculture

USDA Summer Intern Program

Type of award: Internship.
Intended use: For undergraduate or graduate study at postsecondary institution.
Eligibility: Applicant must be U.S. citizen.
Application requirements: Transcript. Resume, U.S. government forms.
Additional information: Internships last approximately four months (May to August). Stipends are based on level of education, prior experience, and position. Various internships available at different agencies. Also open to high school graduates entering college. Applications available in late December. All majors encouraged to apply. Deadline varies. See Website for more information.
Contact:
Contact individual agencies or see Website.
Web: www.usda.gov

U.S. Department of Energy

Student Research at the U.S. Army Edgewood Chemical Biological Center

Type of award: Internship, renewable.
Intended use: For undergraduate or graduate study at accredited 4-year or graduate institution in United States. Designated institutions: U.S. Army Edgewood Chemical Biological Center (Aberdeen Proving Ground, MD) and other approved locations.
Eligibility: Applicant must be U.S. citizen.

Basis for selection: Major/career interest in biology; computer/information sciences; engineering; environmental science; physical sciences; science, general or mathematics.
Application requirements: Transcript. Resume.
Additional information: Provides opportunities to participate in research and development in support of military missions. Three months to one year; full-time or part-time appointments. Stipend based on research area and academic classification. Applications accepted year-round. Award amount and number vary. Visit Website for application.
Contact:
Phone: 410-306-9205 or 410-306-9204
Web: see.orau.gov

U.S. Department of State

U.S. Department of State Internship

Type of award: Internship.
Intended use: For junior, senior or graduate study at accredited 4-year or graduate institution.
Eligibility: Applicant must be U.S. citizen.
Basis for selection: Major/career interest in political science/ government; foreign languages; governmental public relations; business; public administration/service; social work; economics; information systems; journalism or science, general. Applicant must demonstrate high academic achievement.
Application requirements: Transcript. Statement of interest.
Additional information: Provides opportunities working in varied administrative branches of the Department of State, both abroad and in Washington, D.C. Internships are generally unpaid, but many institutions provide academic credit and/or financial assistance for overseas assignments. Paid internships primarily granted to students in financial need. Must be able to work a minimum of ten weeks. Selected students must undergo background investigation to receive security clearance. Random drug testing performed. Internships available year-round. Deadlines: November 1 for summer, March 4 for fall, July 1 for spring. Visit Website for more information.
Application deadline: March 4, July 1
Contact:
Student Programs Office
U.S. Department of State HR/REE/REC
2401 E Street, NW, Ste. 518
Washington, DC 20522
Phone: 202-261-8888
Web: www.careers.state.gov/students

U.S. House of Representatives

House Member Internships

Type of award: Internship, renewable.
Intended use: For full-time undergraduate study.
Eligibility: Applicant must be U.S. citizen or permanent resident.
Basis for selection: Major/career interest in political science/ government; public administration/service; public relations or communications. Applicant must demonstrate high academic achievement.

Additional information: Members of the United Stated House of Representatives use undergraduate interns for a variety of jobs including constituent contact, research, and correspondence. Positions are based in Congressional District Offices and in Washington, DC. Internships generally facilitate course credit, but offer no stipend. Some paid internships are funded through private nonprofit organizations. Information about the individual House member intern programs can usually be found online. A complete set of links to representatives' sites is available at www.house.gov. In general, applicants residing in the member's home district and enrolled in the same political party are favored. Typically, many Washington, D.C.-based internships are filled by students from outside the member district. Applicants may also be interested in working for congressperson serving on committee (i.e. Agriculture, Financial Services) relevant to their major. Interested parties should contact the representative with whom they are interested in working.
Contact:
Contact individual congressman/congresswoman's office
Phone: 202-224-3121
Web: www.house.gov

U.S. National Arboretum

Part-Time Horticultural Internship

Type of award: Internship.
Intended use: For undergraduate or graduate study at postsecondary institution.
Basis for selection: Major/career interest in botany; horticulture or landscape architecture.
Application requirements: Transcript. Resume, cover letter.
Additional information: Interns work on independent projects supervised by arboretum staff. Pay is $11.91 per hour. Must work two days per week or 16 hours, usually between 7 a.m. and 3:30 p.m. College credit available. Must have completed course work or have acquired practical experience in horticulture or related field. Must have basic gardening or laboratory skills, interest in plants, and ability to work independently. Apply by February 1 to receive first consideration. Visit Website for more information and application.
Contact:
Internship Coordinator
U.S. National Arboretum
3501 New York Avenue, NE
Washington, DC 20002-1958
Phone: 202-245-4563
Fax: 202-245-4575
Web: www.usna.usda.gov

U.S. National Arboretum Summer Internship

Type of award: Internship.
Intended use: For undergraduate or graduate study at postsecondary institution.
Eligibility: Applicant must be U.S. citizen.
Basis for selection: Major/career interest in agriculture; botany; education; forestry; horticulture or public administration/service.
Application requirements: Transcript. Resume and cover letter.

Additional information: Internships pay stipend of $11.91 per hour. Average workday for most interns: Monday through Friday, 7 a.m. to 3:30 p.m. Provides opportunity to gain experience in plant research in premier horticultural collection. Applicants need to have completed coursework or have acquired practical experience in horticulture or related field. Basic gardening or laboratory skills, interest in plants, strong communication skills, and ability to work independently preferred. Course credit may be arranged. See Website for deadline, application, and more information.
Contact:
Internship Coordinator
U.S. National Arboretum
3501 New York Avenue, NE
Washington, DC 20002-1958
Phone: 202-245-4563
Fax: 202-245-4575
Web: www.usna.usda.gov

Year-Long Horticultural Internship

Type of award: Internship.
Intended use: For undergraduate or graduate study at postsecondary institution.
Basis for selection: Major/career interest in botany; horticulture or landscape architecture.
Additional information: Interns participate in educational programs and field trips and work on independent projects supervised by arboretum staff. Pay is $16.33 per hour. Most interns work Monday through Friday, 7 a.m. to 3:30 p.m. College credit is available. Must have completed 24 hours of relevant course work or have one year practical working experience in horticulture or related field. Must have basic gardening or laboratory skills, interest in plants, and ability to work independently. Visit Website for deadline, application, and more information.
Contact:
U.S. National Arboretum
3501 New York Avenue, NE
Washington, DC 20002-1958
Phone: 202-245-4563
Fax: 202-245-4575
Web: www.usna.usda.gov

Wachovia

Finance Undergraduate Internships

Type of award: Internship.
Intended use: For full-time junior or senior study at accredited 4-year institution.
Eligibility: Applicant must be U.S. citizen or permanent resident.
Basis for selection: Major/career interest in finance/banking; accounting; business/management/administration; economics or real estate. Applicant must demonstrate high academic achievement and leadership.
Application requirements: Resume and cover letter.
Additional information: Ten- to twelve-week program consists of work assignments and professional development opportunities related to corporate and investment banking. Number of awards varies. Locations in major cities throughout the U.S. Visit Website to search for internship and to create a profile and apply online. Minimum 3.0 GPA.

The Wall Street Journal

The Wall Street Journal Asia Internship

Type of award: Internship.
Intended use: For undergraduate or graduate study at postsecondary institution.
Basis for selection: Major/career interest in journalism.
Application requirements: Cover letter, resume and 12 bylined clips (letter- or legal-sized).
Additional information: Internships available in the U.S., Europe, and Asia. Selection process strongly emphasizes submitted clips and journalistic experience. Roundtrip airfare allowance included. Pay is $700 per week. Include email address and expected month and year of graduation at top of cover letter.

Number of awards:	1
Application deadline:	November 2

Contact:
The Wall Street Journal
Deborah Brewster, Dep. Managing Editor
1211 Avenue of the Americas
New York, NY 10036
Web: www.dowjones.com/careers-interns.asp

The Wall Street Journal Europe Internship

Type of award: Internship.
Intended use: For undergraduate or graduate study at postsecondary institution.
Basis for selection: Major/career interest in journalism.
Application requirements: Cover letter, resume and 12 bylined clips (letter- or legal-sized). Proof of health insurance.
Additional information: Reporting interns will work in WSJ news bureau in Europe. Must be fluent in one or more of the following languages: French, German, Dutch, or Russian. Must demonstrate interest in Europe and willingness and ability to work in overseas environment. Selection process strongly emphasizes submitted clips and journalistic experience. Successful applicants must pay own roundtrip airfare. Pay is $700 per week. Include email address and expected month and year of graduation at top of cover letter.

Number of awards:	2
Application deadline:	November 2

Contact:
The Wall Street Journal Europe
Attn: Jesse Lewis, Managing Editor
10 Fleet Place
London, EC4M 7QN
Web: www.dowjones.com/careers-interns.asp

The Wall Street Journal Journalism Internship

Type of award: Internship.
Intended use: For undergraduate or graduate study at postsecondary institution.
Basis for selection: Major/career interest in journalism.

Application requirements: Cover letter, resume, and 12 bylined clips (letter- or legal-sized).
Additional information: Full-time summer internship lasts ten weeks. Interns work in one of news bureaus. Previous journalism or college newspaper experience required. Interns paid $700 a week. All majors encouraged to apply. Currently enrolled students only.

Amount of award:	$7,000
Number of awards:	10
Number of applicants:	335
Application deadline:	November 2
Notification begins:	February 28
Total amount awarded:	$70,000

Contact:
The Wall Street Journal, WSJ Intern Application (U.S.)
Deborah Brewster Dep. Managing Editor
1211 Avenue of the Americas
New York, NY 10036
Web: www.dowjones.com/careers-interns.asp

The Walt Disney Company

Disney Theme Parks & Resorts Professional Internships

Type of award: Internship.
Intended use: For junior or senior study at 2-year or 4-year institution in United States.
Basis for selection: Major/career interest in animal sciences; architecture; construction management; engineering; finance/banking; food production/management/services; human resources; hospitality administration/management; marketing or computer/information sciences. Applicant must demonstrate high academic achievement, seriousness of purpose and service orientation.
Application requirements: Interview. Resume and cover letter.
Additional information: Roles available in a variety of fields. Offerings vary by season. Certain roles only open to alumni participants of the Disney College Program. Internships also available to college graduates within 48 months of graduation. Pay rates and schedules vary by location. Must have valid driver's license. Housing may be available, with the exception of management internships. Visit Website for more information, application deadline, and to search for openings.

Contact:
Disney Professional Recruiting
P.O. Box 10000
Lake Buena Vista, FL 32830
Phone: 800-722-2930
Web: www.disneyinterns.com

Walt Disney World and Disneyland

Disney College Program

Type of award: Internship.
Intended use: For undergraduate study at postsecondary institution.

Contact:
Wachovia Corporation
Web: www.wachovia.com

Eligibility: Applicant must be U.S. citizen or permanent resident.
Application requirements: Interview, recommendations. Online application and Web-based interview required.
Additional information: Applicant must have completed one semester at college or university. Must view Disney College Program presentation (online or on campus) to interview for program. Students participate in college-level coursework, and may be able to earn college credit. Students placed at Walt Disney World Resort (near Orlando, FL) are guaranteed a minimum of 30 hours per week with additional hours during peak periods. Pay range varies. Company-sponsored housing is available. Minimal company-sponsored housing is available for students placed at Disneyland Resort (Anaheim, CA). Schedules and pay rates vary by role. Must have strong communication skills, understanding of Guest Service principles, ability to work independently and/or with a large team. Program length varies. See Website for application and more information.

    Number of awards: 10,000

Contact:
Walt Disney World College Recruiting
P.O. Box 10090
Lake Buena Vista, FL 32830
Phone: 800-722-2930
Web: www.disneycollegeprogram.com

Washington Internships for Students of Engineering

Washington Internships for Students of Engineering

Type of award: Internship.
Intended use: For junior, senior or graduate study at postsecondary institution.
Eligibility: Applicant must be U.S. citizen or permanent resident.
Basis for selection: Major/career interest in computer/ information sciences; engineering; engineering, chemical; engineering, electrical/electronic or engineering, mechanical.
Application requirements: Recommendations, essay, transcript. Reference forms.
Additional information: Nine-week summer internship learning about technological issues and public policy available to students who have completed three years of study. Internship located in Washington, D.C. Interns write required research paper as part of process. Lodging expenses covered. Must be member of and sponsored by ANS, ASCE, ASME, IEEE, or SAE. IEEE will sponsor computer science majors. Graduate students beginning Masters study in technology policy-related degree also eligible. $2,100 stipend provided to assist with intern's living and travel expenses. Apply directly to sponsoring organization; application forms and sponsor contact information available on Website.

    Amount of award: $2,100
    Number of awards: 12
    Total amount awarded: $25,200

Contact:
Washington Internships for Students of Engineering
c/o IEEE - USA
2001 L Street, N.W. Suite 700
Washington, DC 20036-4910
Phone: 202-785-0017
Fax: 202-785-0835
Web: www.wise-intern.org

Wolf Trap Foundation for the Performing Arts

Wolf Trap Foundation for the Performing Arts Internship

Type of award: Internship.
Intended use: For sophomore, junior, senior or graduate study in United States.
Eligibility: Applicant must be U.S. citizen, permanent resident or international student.
Basis for selection: Major/career interest in performing arts or arts management. Applicant must demonstrate seriousness of purpose.
Application requirements: Recommendations. Cover letter outlining career goals and specifying internship desired; resume. Two writing samples (except technical, scenic painting, costuming, stage management, accounting, graphic design, photography, or information systems applicants). Graphic design applicants must submit three design samples. Refer to individual internship descriptions for additional required materials.
Additional information: Deadline for full-time summer internships is March 1; deadline for part-time fall internships is July 1; deadline for part-time spring internships is November 1. Stipend provided to help offset housing and travel expenses. College credit available. Applicant must have own transportation. Internships available in the following areas: opera (directing, administrative, stage management, technical, costume, scenic/prop painting); education; development; communications and marketing (advertising, marketing, graphic design, publications, public relations, photography, Web design, multimedia); human resources; ticket services; information systems; planning and initiatives; accounting; and production and sound. International students must meet INS I-9 requirement. Internships vary by season; visit Website for details. Also available to recent college graduates.

    Application deadline: March 1, July 1
Contact:
Wolf Trap Foundation for the Performing Arts
Internship Program
1645 Trap Road
Vienna, VA 22182
Phone: 800-404-8461
Fax: 703-255-1924
Web: www.wolftrap.org

Internships

Women's Sports Foundation

Women's Sports Foundation Internship

Type of award: Internship, renewable.
Intended use: For undergraduate or graduate study in United States.
Basis for selection: Major/career interest in communications; humanities/liberal arts; public relations; publishing or sports/sports administration. Applicant must demonstrate high academic achievement.
Application requirements: Interview. Resume and two letters of recommendation.
Additional information: Internship set up to provide sports management students with exposure to sports industry. Open to students or women in career change. Stipend is $900 to $1000 per month, with minimum six-month term and a maximum length of one year. Internships available in two sessions: January to June and June to December. Most internships located at headquarters in East Meadow, NY, or Manhattan office. Writing samples required for some positions. Visit Website for application.

Number of awards:	20
Number of applicants:	50

Contact:
Women's Sports Foundation
1899 Hempstead Turnpike
Suite 400
East Meadow, NY 11554
Phone: 800-227-3988
Fax: 516-542-4716
Web: www.womenssportsfoundation.org

World Security Institute

World Security Institute Internship

Type of award: Internship.
Intended use: For undergraduate or graduate study at postsecondary institution.
Basis for selection: Major/career interest in political science/government; military science; international relations; communications or computer/information sciences. Applicant must demonstrate high academic achievement, depth of character, leadership, seriousness of purpose and service orientation.
Application requirements: Recommendations, transcript. Resume, cover letter stating interest and reasons for wanting to work at WSI. Three- to five-page writing sample.
Additional information: Intended for graduates and highly-qualified undergraduates. Students must work full-time for internship's duration (three to five months) to receive monthly stipend of $1,300. Deadlines are April 1, July 1, and November 1 for the summer, fall, and spring semesters, respectively. Notification begins on May 1, August 1, and December 1. Transcripts must be submitted for all attended institutions. Check Website for latest information.

Number of awards:	12
Number of applicants:	100
Application deadline:	April 1, July 1
Notification begins:	May 1, August 1

Contact:
World Security Institute
1779 Massachusetts Avenue, NW
Washington, DC 20036
Phone: 202-332-0600
Fax: 202-462-4559
Web: www.worldsecurityinstitute.org/jobs.cfm

Internships

Loans

Alaska Commission on Postsecondary Education

Alaska Family Education Loan

Type of award: Loan, renewable.
Intended use: For full-time undergraduate or graduate study at vocational, 4-year or graduate institution.
Eligibility: Applicant must be U.S. citizen or permanent resident residing in Alaska.
Application requirements: Proof of eligibility.
Additional information: Borrower may apply for 7.3 percent interest rate loan on behalf of family member if the borrower is an AK resident of at least one year, is credit-worthy or has a cosigner, and does not have status at time of loan that would prevent repayment. Both borrower and student must not be past due on child support, must comply with selective service, may not have had student loan written off unless discharged in bankruptcy in the last five years, and may not have been delinquent or defaulted on prior student loans. Must apply annually. Award amounts: $6,500/year for career training program; $8,500 for undergraduate; $9,500 for graduate. Maximum for undergraduate is $42,500; graduate student, $47,500; total per student, $60,000; total per borrower, $102,000.

> **Amount of award:** $6,500-$9,500

Contact:
Alaska Commission on Postsecondary Education
Alaska Family Education Loan
P.O. Box 110505
Juneau, AK 99811-0505
Phone: 907-465-2962
Fax: 907-465-5316
Web: www.alaskadvantage.state.ak.us

Alaska Teacher Education Loan

Type of award: Loan, renewable.
Intended use: For full-time undergraduate or post-bachelor's certificate study at accredited 4-year institution.
Eligibility: Applicant must be U.S. citizen or permanent resident residing in Alaska.
Basis for selection: Major/career interest in education. Applicant must demonstrate high academic achievement.
Application requirements: Recommendations, proof of eligibility, nomination by rural school district. Statement of intent for teaching career.
Additional information: Must be enrolled in program in elementary or secondary school teacher education. May borrow up to $37,500 in total. Must reapply each year. Applicant must meet requirements for teachers set by student's local school board. Must be graduate of AK high school. May not have past-due child support or status at application that will prevent repayment. Must be credit-worthy or have cosigner. Must comply with selective service. Eligible for forgiveness of percentage of loan and interest in each of first five years borrower teaches in rural AK elementary or secondary school:

15 percent for years one to three; 25 percent for year four; and 30 percent for five years and beyond.

> **Amount of award:** $7,500
> **Application deadline:** July 1

Contact:
Alaska Commission on Postsecondary Education
Alaska Teacher Education Loan
P.O. Box 110505
Juneau, AK 99811-0505
Phone: 800-441-2962
Fax: 907-465-5316
Web: www.alaskadvantage.state.ak.us

A.W. "Winn" Brindle Memorial Education Loan

Type of award: Loan, renewable.
Intended use: For full-time undergraduate or graduate study at accredited postsecondary institution.
Eligibility: Applicant must be U.S. citizen or permanent resident residing in Alaska.
Basis for selection: Major/career interest in wildlife/fisheries.
Application requirements: Proof of eligibility.
Additional information: Five percent-interest loan may not exceed cost of tuition, fees, books and supplies, room and board, and limited transportation. Loan may not be for more than eight years of undergraduate/graduate study. Availability of loans is subject to annual funding levels. Preference to applicants nominated by private donors to memorial education loan account. Recipients qualify for forgiveness up to ten percent of loan for each of first five years employed in fishery-related field. Must be current in repayment. No past-due child support. Must be creditworthy or have cosigner. Must comply with selective service.

Contact:
Alaska Commission on Postsecondary Education
Winn Brindle Loan Program
P.O. Box 110505
Juneau, AK 99811-0505
Phone: 907-465-6741
Fax: 907-465-5316
Web: www.alaskadvantage.state.ak.us

American Legion Kentucky Auxiliary

Mary Barrett Marshall Student Loan Fund

Type of award: Loan, renewable.
Intended use: For undergraduate study at vocational, 2-year or 4-year institution. Designated institutions: Eligible postsecondary institutions in Kentucky.
Eligibility: Applicant or parent must be member/participant of American Legion Auxiliary. Applicant must be female. Applicant must be residing in Kentucky. Applicant must be

descendant of veteran; or dependent of veteran; or spouse of veteran or deceased veteran during Grenada conflict, Korean War, Lebanon conflict, Panama conflict, Persian Gulf War, WW I, WW II or Vietnam.
Basis for selection: Applicant must demonstrate financial need.
Application requirements: SASE.
Additional information: Maximum $800 per year, payable monthly without interest after graduation or upon securing employment; 6% interest after five years.
   Amount of award: $800
   Application deadline: April 1
Contact:
American Legion Auxiliary, Department of Kentucky
Chairman Lois Smith
812 Madison Street
Rockport, IN 47635
Phone: 812-649-2163
Web: www.kyamlegionaux.org

American Legion South Dakota

American Legion South Dakota Educational Loan

Type of award: Loan, renewable.
Intended use: For undergraduate study at vocational, 2-year or 4-year institution.
Eligibility: Applicant must be residing in South Dakota. Applicant must be veteran or descendant of veteran; or dependent of veteran.
Additional information: Up to $1,500 per year; $3,000 maximum; 3% interest on unpaid balance.
   Amount of award: $1,500-$3,000
   Application deadline: November 1, May 1
Contact:
American Legion South Dakota
Department Adjutant
P.O. Box 67
Watertown, SD 57201-0067
Phone: 605-886-3604

ASME Auxiliary, Inc.

ASME Auxiliary Student Loan Fund

Type of award: Loan.
Intended use: For junior, senior or graduate study at accredited 4-year or graduate institution in United States. Designated institutions: Schools with ABET-accredited mechanical engineering or engineering technology curricula.
Eligibility: Applicant must be U.S. citizen.
Basis for selection: Major/career interest in engineering, mechanical. Applicant must demonstrate financial need.
Application requirements: Recommendations.
Additional information: Loans are interest-free until graduation. No application deadline. Must be American Society of Mechanical Engineers member. Number of loans available

varies. Visit Website for more information application or send SASE to address.
   Amount of award: $5,000
Contact:
Susan Hawthorne
White Horse Village, S#121
535 Gradyville Road
Newtown Square, PA 19073-2814
Web: www.asme.org/Education/College/FinancialAid/

ASME Foundation

ASME Student Loan Program

Type of award: Loan, renewable.
Intended use: For full-time undergraduate or graduate study. Designated institutions: North American institutions.
Basis for selection: Major/career interest in engineering, mechanical. Applicant must demonstrate financial need.
Additional information: Applicant must be student member of American Society of Mechanical Engineers in United States, Canada or Mexico, and enrolled in mechanical engineering or mechanical engineering technology program/courses. Minimum 2.2 GPA for undergraduates; minimum 3.2 GPA for graduates. Award is up to $3,000 per year with $9,000 maximum for undergraduate degree and additional $3,000 for graduate students. Visit Website for application.
   Amount of award: $3,000
   Application deadline: April 15, October 15
Contact:
ASME
Ann-Marie Beck
22 Law Drive, MS: NO1
Fairfield, NJ 07007-2900
Phone: 973-244-2319
Web: www.asme.org/education/college/financialaid/
Student_Loan_Funds.cfm

California Student Aid Commission

Assumption Program of Loans for Education (APLE)

Type of award: Loan, renewable.
Intended use: For junior or senior study at accredited 4-year institution. Designated institutions: California postsecondary institutions with Commission on Teacher Credential-approved programs.
Eligibility: Applicant must be U.S. citizen or permanent resident residing in California.
Basis for selection: Major/career interest in education; education, early childhood; education, special or education, teacher. Applicant must demonstrate financial need and high academic achievement.
Application requirements: Proof of eligibility, nomination by participating institution.
Additional information: June 30 is priority deadline. Must have received educational loan and not be in default of said loan. Must agree to teach in California public school in teacher

shortage area for at least four years. Loans assumed up to $2,000 for first year, and up to $3,000 for second, third, and fourth years of consecutive service. Those who agree to teach math, science, or special education may receive up to $1,000 of additional loan assumption benefits each year. Another annual $1,000 of benefits may be received by those teaching math, science, or education specialist instruction in schools ranked in API lowest 20 percentile, for a maximum of $19,000. Applicants must be pursuing teaching credentials for K-12.

Amount of award:	$19,000
Number of awards:	7,400
Number of applicants:	50,000
Application deadline:	June 30

Contact:
California Student Aid Commission
Specialized Programs Operations Branch
P.O. Box 419029
Rancho Cordova, CA 95741-9029
Phone: 888-224-7268 opt. 3
Fax: 916-464-7977
Web: www.csac.ca.gov

Connecticut Higher Education Supplemental Loan Authority

CHESLA Loan Program

Type of award: Loan.
Intended use: For undergraduate or graduate study in United States. Designated institutions: Non-profit institutions (non-residents must attend Connecticut non-profit institutions to be eligible).
Application requirements: Alien registration receipt card (I-151 or I-551) for non-citizens.
Additional information: Applicant must be a resident of or attending school in Connecticut. Award amount ranges from $2,000 to full tuition cost. Visit Website for application.

Amount of award:	$2,000
Number of applicants:	2,308
Total amount awarded:	$26,527,184

Contact:
Connecticut Higher Education Supplemental Loan Authority (CHESLA)
21 Talcott Notch Road
Suite 1
Farmington, CT 06032
Phone: 800-252-FELP (CT) or 860-678-7788 (out of state)
Web: www.chesla.org

Delaware Higher Education Commission

Christa McAuliffe Teacher Incentive Program

Type of award: Loan, renewable.
Intended use: For undergraduate study at accredited 4-year institution.

Eligibility: Applicant must be U.S. citizen or permanent resident residing in Delaware.
Basis for selection: Major/career interest in education. Applicant must demonstrate high academic achievement.
Application requirements: Essay, transcript. SAT scores.
Additional information: Applicant must be high school senior with combined score of 1570 on the SAT and rank in top half of class, or undergraduate with minimum 2.75 GPA. Preference given to applicants planning to teach in critical need area as defined by DE Department of Education. Though award is for full-time students, it may be prorated for part-time students in a qualifying program. Loan not to exceed cost of tuition, fees, and other direct educational expenses. Loan forgiveness provision at rate of one year of teaching in a DE public school for one year of loan. Visit Website for deadline information.

Number of applicants:	69

Contact:
Delaware Higher Education Commission
820 North French Street
Wilmington, DE 19801
Phone: 302-577-5240
Fax: 302-577-6765
Web: www.doe.k12.de.us/programs/dhec/how_to_apply/financial_aid

Delaware Nursing Incentive Program

Type of award: Loan, renewable.
Intended use: For undergraduate study at accredited vocational, 2-year or 4-year institution in United States. Designated institutions: Colleges with accredited nursing programs that lead to RN, LPN, or BSN certification.
Eligibility: Applicant must be U.S. citizen or permanent resident residing in Delaware.
Basis for selection: Major/career interest in nursing. Applicant must demonstrate high academic achievement.
Application requirements: Essay, transcript.
Additional information: Loan-forgiveness for practicing nursing at state-owned hospital or clinic, one year for each year of loan. High school seniors must rank in top half of class and have at least 2.5 GPA. Though award generally for full-time students who are residents of DE, current state employees do not have to be DE residents and may be considered for part-time enrollment. RNs with five or more years of state service may enroll in BSN program full or part time. Loan not to exceed cost of tuition, fees, and other direct educational expenses. Visit Website for deadline information.

Number of applicants:	84
Total amount awarded:	$35,000

Contact:
Delaware Higher Education Commission
820 North French Street
Wilmington, DE 19801
Phone: 302-577-5240
Fax: 302-577-6765
Web: www.doe.k12.de.us/programs/dhec/how_to_apply/financial_aid

Loans

Florida Department of Education

Critical Teacher Shortage Student Loan Forgiveness Program

Type of award: Loan, renewable.
Intended use: For undergraduate or graduate study at 4-year or graduate institution in United States.
Eligibility: Applicant must be U.S. citizen or permanent resident residing in Florida.
Basis for selection: Major/career interest in education or education, special.
Application requirements: Transcript.
Additional information: Must be full-time teacher certified and teaching in critical teacher shortage subject area in Florida publicly-funded school. Must apply within first year of certification and teach in CTS subject area for at least 90 days. Visit Website for application and more information.

    Amount of award: $10,000
    Application deadline: July 15
Contact:
Office of Student Financial Assistance
325 West Gaines Street
Tallahassee, FL 32399-0400
Phone: 888-827-2004
Web: www.floridastudentfinancialaid.org

Franklin Lindsay Student Aid Fund

Franklin Lindsay Student Aid Loan

Type of award: Loan, renewable.
Intended use: For full-time sophomore, junior, senior or graduate study at accredited 4-year or graduate institution in United States. Designated institutions: Texas colleges accredited by the Southern Association of Colleges and Schools Commission on Colleges.
Eligibility: Applicant must be U.S. citizen.
Basis for selection: Applicant must demonstrate financial need.
Application requirements: Interview.
Additional information: Minimum 2.0 GPA for undergraduates and 3.0 for graduates. Must have co-signer who is U.S. citizen. Upon graduation or termination from school, loan goes to repayment structure at four percent, with maximum payment term of seven years. Visit Website for application and more information.

    Amount of award: $7,000
    Number of applicants: 97
    Application deadline: June 1
    Total amount awarded: $673,600
Contact:
The Franklin Lindsay Student Aid Fund
c/o JPMorgan Chase Bank, N.A.
P.O. Box 227237
Dallas, TX 75222-7237
Phone: 866-300-6222
Web: www.franklinlindsay.org

Georgia Student Finance Commission

Georgia Promise Teacher Scholarship

Type of award: Loan, renewable.
Intended use: For junior or senior study at accredited 4-year institution. Designated institutions: Colleges/universities in Georgia offering teacher-education programs approved by Georgia Professional Standards Commission.
Eligibility: Applicant must be U.S. citizen or permanent resident residing in Georgia.
Basis for selection: Major/career interest in education, teacher or education. Applicant must demonstrate high academic achievement and seriousness of purpose.
Application requirements: Transcript, proof of eligibility.
Additional information: Provides cancelable loans. Out-of-state residents attending accredited Georgia teacher-education programs also eligible. Recipient must commit to teach one year in Georgia public school for every $1,500 awarded. May teach at preschool, elementary, or secondary level. Applicant must have minimum 3.0 GPA, be academically classified as junior, have declared education as major and/or be accepted for enrollment into teacher-education program leading to initial certification. Must obtain signatures from institution's Department of Education teacher-certification official and financial aid office.

    Amount of award: $1,500-$6,000
    Number of awards: 1,626
    Total amount awarded: $4,435,823
Contact:
Georgia Student Finance Commission Scholarship Committee
2082 East Exchange Place
Suite 100
Tucker, GA 30084
Phone: 800-505-4732
Fax: 770-724-9004
Web: www.gacollege411.org

Grand Encampment of Knights Templar of the USA

Knights Templar Educational Foundation Loan

Type of award: Loan, renewable.
Intended use: For junior, senior or first professional study at accredited vocational, 4-year or graduate institution in United States.
Basis for selection: Applicant must demonstrate high academic achievement and depth of character.
Application requirements: Recommendations.
Additional information: Student should request application from Grand Encampment of Knights Templar in state of residence. Available loan amount varies by state division.

Loans

Contact:
Grand Encampment of Knights Templar of the USA
5909 West Loop South
Suite 495
Belaire, TX 77401-2402
Phone: 713-349-8700
Fax: 713-349-8710
Web: www.knightstemplar.org

Idaho State Board of Education

Idaho Education Incentive Loan Forgiveness Program

Type of award: Loan, renewable.
Intended use: For full-time undergraduate study at postsecondary institution. Designated institutions: Idaho public colleges and universities.
Eligibility: Applicant must be residing in Idaho.
Basis for selection: Major/career interest in education; education, early childhood; education, special; education, teacher or nursing.
Additional information: Loan forgiveness for teaching or nursing service in Idaho. Minimum 3.0 GPA. Must pursue license for teaching or nursing and pursue career within Idaho for a minimum of two years. Contact financial aid office of postsecondary Idaho public institutions for application materials and information.
Contact:
Financial aid office at designated institution.
Phone: 208-332-1574
Web: www.boardofed.idaho.gov/scholarships

Jewish Family and Children's Services (JFCS)

JFCS Scholarship Fund

Type of award: Scholarship.
Intended use: For undergraduate or graduate study at postsecondary institution.
Eligibility: Applicant must be Jewish. Applicant must be residing in California.
Basis for selection: Applicant must demonstrate financial need and high academic achievement.
Additional information: Minimum 2.75 GPA for grants. Applicants must demonstrate connection to Jewish community. High school seniors, undergraduates, and graduate students may apply. Applicants may also be high school students traveling to Israel. Grants available for residents of Sonoma, Marin, San Francisco, San Mateo, or Santa Clara counties; loans available for all nine Bay area counties. Deadline is for consideration for school year; applicants for Israel travel, Holocaust study, and vocational study may apply any time. Organization has several scholarships and loans; see Website for more details.

Amount of award:	$1,000-$1,500
Number of awards:	100
Application deadline:	September 1

Contact:
Jewish Family and Children's Services
Attn: Eric Singer
2150 Post Street
San Francisco, CA 94115
Phone: 415-449-1226
Fax: 415-449-1229
Web: www.jfcs.org

Maine Educational Loan Authority

The Maine Loan

Type of award: Loan.
Intended use: For undergraduate or graduate study at accredited vocational, 2-year, 4-year or graduate institution in United States or Canada.
Eligibility: Applicant must be residing in Maine.
Application requirements: Proof of eligibility. Income information/credit analysis.
Additional information: Loans available to Maine residents attending approved schools and out-of-state students attending Maine schools. May borrow full cost of education minus other financial aid. May be used to pay prior balance up to one academic year. Applicant has 4-20 years to repay, depending on amount owed. See Website for interest rates, payment options, and additional information. Applications accepted year round. Minimum loan amount is $1,000.

Number of applicants:	2,510
Total amount awarded:	$30,000,000

Contact:
Maine Educational Loan Authority
131 Presumpscot Street
Portland, ME 04103
Phone: 800-922-6352
Fax: 207-791-3616
Web: www.mela.net

Massachusetts Board of Higher Education

Massachusetts No Interest Loan

Type of award: Loan.
Intended use: For full-time undergraduate study at accredited vocational, 2-year or 4-year institution.
Eligibility: Applicant must be U.S. citizen or permanent resident residing in Massachusetts.
Basis for selection: Applicant must demonstrate financial need.
Application requirements: FAFSA.
Additional information: No Interest Loan (NIL) Program offers no interest loans to those who meet requirements; students have 10 years to repay NIL loans and a borrowing limit of $20,000 ($4,000/year). Must not have received prior bachelor's degree.

Amount of award:	$1,000-$4,000
Number of applicants:	2,200
Total amount awarded:	$6,000,000

577

Contact:
Office of Student Financial Assistance
Massachusetts Board of Higher Education
454 Broadway, Suite 200
Revere, MA 02151
Phone: 617-727-9420
Fax: 617-727-0667
Web: www.osfa.mass.edu

Military Officers Association of America

MOAA Interest-Free Loan and Grant Program

Type of award: Loan, renewable.
Intended use: For full-time undergraduate study at accredited 2-year or 4-year institution in United States.
Eligibility: Applicant must be no older than 23. Applicant must be U.S. citizen. Applicant must be dependent of active service person, veteran or deceased veteran who serves or served in the Army, Air Force, Marines, Navy, Coast Guard or Reserves/National Guard. Applicant must be child of MOAA member or active-duty, Reserve, National Guard, or retired enlisted military personnel.
Basis for selection: Applicant must demonstrate financial need, high academic achievement, depth of character, leadership, patriotism, seriousness of purpose and service orientation.
Application requirements: Essay, transcript, proof of eligibility. SAT/ACT score. Parent or sponsor's military status and/or MOAA number.
Additional information: Minimum 3.0 GPA. Applicant must be child of active-duty or retired enlisted personnel. Must be under 24; however, if applicant served in Uniformed Service before completing college, maximum age for eligibility increases by number of years served, up to five years. Parent must sign promissory note before funds can be disbursed. Military academy cadets not eligible. Application available on Website.

Amount of award:	$5,500
Number of awards:	1,600
Number of applicants:	2,000
Application deadline:	March 1
Notification begins:	June 1
Total amount awarded:	$8,800,000

Contact:
MOAA Scholarship Fund
Educational Assistance Program
201 North Washington Street
Alexandria, VA 22314-2529
Phone: 800-234-6622
Web: www.moaa.org/education

Minnesota Office of Higher Education

Minnesota Student Educational Loan Fund (SELF)

Type of award: Loan.
Intended use: For undergraduate or graduate study at vocational, 2-year, 4-year or graduate institution. Designated institutions: Minnesota and eligible out-of-state institutions.
Additional information: Applicant must be enrolled at least half-time in eligible Minnesota school, or be Minnesota resident enrolled in eligible school outside Minnesota. Must seek aid from certain other sources before applying, except federal unsubsidized and subsidized Stafford loans, National Direct Student loans, HEAL loans, and other private loans. Institution must approve application. Maximum award for undergraduates is $7,500; graduate students, $9,000. Must have a creditworthy cosigner.

Amount of award:	$500-$9,000
Number of applicants:	24,756
Total amount awarded:	$125,227,808

Contact:
Minnesota Office of Higher Education
1450 Energy Park Drive, Suite 350
St. Paul, MN 55108-5227
Phone: 800-657-3866
Web: www.selfloan.org

Mississippi Office of Student Financial Aid

Critical Needs Alternative Route Teacher Loan/Scholarship

Type of award: Loan, renewable.
Intended use: For junior or senior study at 4-year institution in United States. Designated institutions: Mississippi institutions.
Eligibility: Applicant must be U.S. citizen residing in Mississippi.
Basis for selection: Major/career interest in education; education, early childhood; education, special or education, teacher.
Application requirements: Signed CNTP Rules and Regulations.
Additional information: Minimum 2.5 GPA or must rank in top 50 percent of class. Must be enrolled in program of study leading to Class "A" teacher educator license. Must agree to full-time employment in Mississippi public school located in critical teacher shortage or subject area. Must participate in Entrance Counseling. Award covers tuition, fees, and housing plus book allowance. Students at private institutions receive award equivalent to costs at nearest comparable public institution. Interested non-Mississippi residents may apply if they have been accepted to Mississippi school. See Website for application and more information.

Amount of award:	$4,000
Application deadline:	March 31

Contact:
Mississippi Office of Student Financial Aid
3825 Ridgewood Road
Jackson, MS 39211-6453
Phone: 800-327-2980
Web: www.mississippi.edu/riseupms

Mississippi Health Care Professions Loan/Scholarship

Type of award: Loan, renewable.
Intended use: For full-time junior or senior study at accredited 4-year or graduate institution. Designated institutions: Mississippi institutions.
Eligibility: Applicant must be residing in Mississippi.
Basis for selection: Major/career interest in physical therapy; occupational therapy; speech pathology/audiology or psychology. Applicant must demonstrate high academic achievement.
Application requirements: Transcript, proof of eligibility. Mississippi tax return.
Additional information: Loan forgiveness for service in Mississippi health care institution: one year for each year of financial assistance, with a maximum of two years. Undergraduates must major in speech pathology/audiology, psychology, or occupational therapy; graduates must major in physical therapy or occupational therapy at University of Mississippi Medical Center. Visit Website for application and further information.

Amount of award:	$1,500-$6,000
Number of awards:	3
Application deadline:	March 31
Notification begins:	August 1
Total amount awarded:	$7,500

Contact:
Susan Eckels, Program Manager
Mississippi Office of Student Financial Aid
3825 Ridgewood Road
Jackson, MS 39211-6453
Phone: 800-327-2980
Fax: 601-432-6527
Web: www.mississippi.edu/riseupms

Mississippi Nursing Education Loan/Scholarship

Type of award: Loan, renewable.
Intended use: For junior or senior study at accredited 4-year or graduate institution. Designated institutions: Mississippi institutions.
Eligibility: Applicant must be U.S. citizen residing in Mississippi.
Basis for selection: Major/career interest in nursing; nurse practitioner; pediatric nurse practitioner; health education or health-related professions. Applicant must demonstrate financial need and high academic achievement.
Application requirements: Recommendations, transcript, proof of eligibility. State of Mississippi tax return.
Additional information: Loan forgiveness for nursing service in Mississippi, one year for each year of financial assistance, for a maximum of two years. Minimum 2.5 GPA or must rank in top 50 percent of class. Undergraduate awards for RN to BSN and BSN study. Apply online.

Amount of award:	$4,000-$8,000
Number of awards:	577
Application deadline:	March 31
Notification begins:	August 1
Total amount awarded:	$1,962,560

Contact:
Mississippi Office of Student Financial Aid
3825 Ridgewood Road
Jackson, MS 39211-6453
Phone: 800-327-2980
Web: www.mississippi.edu/riseupms

Mississippi William Winter Teacher Scholar Loan Program

Type of award: Loan, renewable.
Intended use: For full-time junior or senior study at 4-year institution. Designated institutions: Mississippi institutions.
Eligibility: Applicant must be U.S. citizen residing in Mississippi.
Basis for selection: Major/career interest in education; education, early childhood; education, special or education, teacher. Applicant must demonstrate high academic achievement.
Application requirements: Proof of eligibility.
Additional information: Must be studying towards a Class A teacher educator license. Minimum 2.5 GPA or must rank in top 50 percent of class. Loan forgiveness for teaching service in Mississippi public school or public school district: one year for each year of financial assistance, for a maximum of two years. Apply online.

Amount of award:	$4,000
Application deadline:	March 31
Notification begins:	August 1
Total amount awarded:	$1,921,658

Contact:
Mississippi Office of Student Financial Aid
3825 Ridgewood Road
Jackson, MS 39211-6453
Phone: 800-327-2980
Fax: 601-432-6527
Web: www.mississippi.edu/riseupms

Navy-Marine Corps Relief Society

Vice Admiral E.P. Travers Loan

Type of award: Loan, renewable.
Intended use: For full-time undergraduate study.
Eligibility: Applicant must be U.S. citizen. Applicant must be dependent of active service person; or spouse of active service person in the Marines or Navy.
Basis for selection: Applicant must demonstrate financial need.
Application requirements: Proof of eligibility. Current military ID of service member.
Additional information: Minimum 2.0 GPA. Applicant must be dependent child of an active duty service member of Navy or Marine Corp (including Reservists on active duty) or a spouse of active duty or retired service member. Loan must be repaid in allotments over 24-month period (minimum monthly repayment is $50). Must reapply to renew.

Amount of award: $500-$3,000
Number of applicants: 1,200
Application deadline: March 1
Total amount awarded: $800,000
Contact:
Navy-Marine Corps Relief Society
875 North Randolph Street, Suite 225
Arlington, VA 22203
Phone: 703-696-4960
Web: www.nmcrs.org/education

New Hampshire Higher Education Assistance Foundation (NHHEAF)

Leaf Loan Program

Type of award: Loan, renewable.
Intended use: For undergraduate or graduate study at postsecondary institution.
Eligibility: Applicant must be at least 18. Applicant must be U.S. citizen or permanent resident residing in New Hampshire.
Additional information: Must be New Hampshire resident enrolled in U.S. institution or non-resident enrolled in New Hampshire institution. Fee of up to eight percent of principal borrowed charged upon disbursement. Interest rate adjusted monthly. Award ranges from $500 to entire cost less financial aid received. Visit Website for more information.
Amount of award: $500-$10,000
Contact:
New Hampshire Higher Education Loan Corporation
4 Barrell Court
P.O. Box 877
Concord, NH 03302
Phone: 800-525-2577
Fax: 603-224-2581
Web: www.nhheaf.org

New Hampshire Postsecondary Education Commission

Workforce Incentive Program

Type of award: Loan, renewable.
Intended use: For full-time undergraduate or graduate study at accredited 2-year, 4-year or graduate institution.
Eligibility: Applicant must be U.S. citizen or permanent resident residing in New Hampshire.
Basis for selection: Major/career interest in education, special; foreign languages or nursing. Applicant must demonstrate financial need.
Additional information: Program assists in loan repayment. Contact financial aid office at New Hampshire institution or Melanie Deshaies at New Hampshire Postsecondary Education Commission. Maximum $10,000 over five years. Number of awards varies. Visit Website for more information.

Amount of award: $1,500-$10,000
Number of applicants: 139
Application deadline: September 30
Total amount awarded: $210,018
Contact:
Postsecondary Education Commission
WIP Repayment Program
3 Barrell Court, Suite 300
Concord, NH 03301-8543
Phone: 603-271-2555 ext. 360
Fax: 603-271-2696
Web: www.nh.gov/postsecondary

New Jersey Higher Education Student Assistance Authority

New Jersey Class Loan Program

Type of award: Loan.
Intended use: For undergraduate or graduate study at accredited vocational, 2-year, 4-year or graduate institution in United States. Designated institutions: Approved institutions. Proprietary institutions also eligible.
Eligibility: Applicant must be U.S. citizen or permanent resident.
Application requirements: Proof of eligibility. Income and credit history; FAFSA.
Additional information: All New Jersey residents may apply, as may out-of-state students attending school in New Jersey. Must demonstrate credit-worthiness or provide co-signer. Parent or other eligible family member may borrow on behalf of student. Maximum loan amount may not exceed education cost less all other financial aid. Minimum loan amount $500. Low fixed interest rate loans available for both undergraduate and graduate students. Two percent administrative fee deducted from approved loan amount. Apply online for instant credit approval.
Contact:
New Jersey Higher Education Student Assistance Authority
4 Quakerbridge Plaza
P.O. Box 538
Trenton, NJ 08625-0538
Phone: 800-792-8670
Web: www.hesaa.org

New Mexico Commission on Higher Education

New Mexico Allied Health Student Loan-for-Service Program

Type of award: Loan, renewable.
Intended use: For undergraduate or graduate study at accredited postsecondary institution. Designated institutions: Public postsecondary institutions in New Mexico.
Eligibility: Applicant must be U.S. citizen or permanent resident residing in New Mexico.

Loans

Basis for selection: Major/career interest in health-related professions; occupational therapy; mental health/therapy; physical therapy; pharmacy/pharmaceutics/pharmacology; dietetics/nutrition or speech pathology/audiology. Applicant must demonstrate financial need.
Application requirements: FAFSA.
Additional information: Loan forgiveness offered to those who practice in medically underserved areas in New Mexico. Must be accepted by or enrolled in approved programs at accredited New Mexico public postsecondary institution. Call sponsor number or visit Website for application and more information.

Amount of award:	$12,000
Application deadline:	July 1

Contact:
New Mexico Higher Education Department
Financial Aid and Student Services
2048 Galisteo Street
Santa Fe, NM 87505
Phone: 505-476-8400
Web: www.hed.state.nm.us

New Mexico Nursing Student Loan-for-Service

Type of award: Loan, renewable.
Intended use: For undergraduate or graduate study at accredited 2-year or 4-year institution. Designated institutions: New Mexico public colleges and universities.
Eligibility: Applicant must be U.S. citizen or permanent resident residing in New Mexico.
Basis for selection: Major/career interest in nursing. Applicant must demonstrate financial need.
Application requirements: FAFSA.
Additional information: Loan forgiveness for New Mexico resident to practice in medically underserved areas in New Mexico. Part-time students eligible for prorated awards.

Amount of award:	$12,000
Application deadline:	July 1

Contact:
New Mexico Commission on Higher Education
Financial Aid and Student Services
2048 Galisteo Street
Santa Fe, NM 87505
Phone: 505-476-8400
Web: www.hed.state.nm.us

New Mexico Teacher's Loan-for-Service

Type of award: Loan.
Intended use: For undergraduate or post-bachelor's certificate study at accredited postsecondary institution. Designated institutions: Public college or university.
Eligibility: Applicant must be physically challenged. Applicant must be U.S. citizen or permanent resident residing in New Mexico.
Basis for selection: Major/career interest in education, teacher. Applicant must demonstrate financial need.
Application requirements: FAFSA.
Additional information: Must be accepted by undergraduate, graduate, or alternative licensure teacher preparation program approved by State Board of Education. Must provide one year of teaching service for each year of award at a public school in New Mexico.

Amount of award:	$4,000
Application deadline:	July 1

Contact:
New Mexico Commission on Higher Education
Financial Aid and Student Services
2048 Galisteo Street
Santa Fe, NM 87505
Phone: 505-476-8400
Web: www.hed.state.nm.us

New York State Grange

Grange Student Loan Fund

Type of award: Loan, renewable.
Intended use: For full-time undergraduate or graduate study at postsecondary institution.
Eligibility: Applicant must be residing in New York.
Basis for selection: Applicant must demonstrate financial need.
Additional information: Must have been member of New York State Grange for at least 6 months at time of application. Must send SASE for application. Loanee may borrow a maximum of $10,000. May apply for less than the maximum award. Loan repayment at five percent annual interest.

Amount of award:	$2,000
Number of awards:	11
Number of applicants:	11
Application deadline:	April 15
Notification begins:	June 15
Total amount awarded:	$22,000

Contact:
New York State Grange
100 Grange Place
Cortland, NY 13045
Phone: 607-756-7553
Fax: 607-756-7757
Web: www.nysgrange.org

North Carolina Community Colleges Foundation

Community College Grant & Loan

Type of award: Loan.
Intended use: For undergraduate study at 2-year institution.
Eligibility: Applicant must be residing in North Carolina.
Basis for selection: Applicant must demonstrate financial need.
Application requirements: FAFSA.
Additional information: Value of grants and loans vary. Applicant must qualify for Federal Pell Grant. Provides financial assistance to credit and occupational extension students who enroll in low-enrollment programs that prepare students for high-demand occupations.

Total amount awarded:	$762,806

Contact:
North Carolina Community Colleges Foundation
200 West Jones Street
Raleigh, NC 27603
Phone: 919-807-7106
Fax: 919-807-7173
Web: www.ncccs.cc.nc.us

Loans

North Carolina State Education Assistance Authority

North Carolina Nurse Scholars Program

Type of award: Loan, renewable.
Intended use: For full-time undergraduate study at accredited postsecondary institution. Designated institutions: North Carolina institutions.
Eligibility: Applicant must be U.S. citizen residing in North Carolina.
Basis for selection: Major/career interest in nursing. Applicant must demonstrate high academic achievement, leadership and service orientation.
Application requirements: Recommendations, essay, transcript, proof of eligibility.
Additional information: Minimum 3.0 GPA. Candidates for associate's degree in nursing and hospital diploma in nursing will receive $3,000. Candidates for bachelor's in nursing will receive $5,000 or $3,000 per year. Also, $2,500 per year scholarship/loan is available for an RN seeking a BSN degree. Recipient agrees to work full-time as RN in North Carolina; 12 months of work results in forgiveness of one year of loan support. Visit Website for more information.

    Amount of award: $2,500-$5,000
    Number of awards: 450
    Application deadline: February 28, May 3
Contact:
North Carolina Nurse Scholars Program
P.O. Box 14223
Research Triangle Park, NC 27709-4223
Phone: 800-700-1775 ext. 313
Web: www.cfnc.org

North Carolina Student Loans for Health/Science/Mathematics

Type of award: Loan, renewable.
Intended use: For full-time undergraduate or graduate study at accredited postsecondary institution in United States. Designated institutions: North Carolina postsecondary institutions and eligible out-of-state schools.
Eligibility: Applicant must be U.S. citizen residing in North Carolina.
Basis for selection: Major/career interest in health-related professions; mathematics; science, general; dentistry; optometry/ophthalmology; social work or nursing. Applicant must demonstrate financial need.
Application requirements: Transcript, proof of eligibility. FAFSA.
Additional information: Loan obligation may be forgiven through approved employment within the state of North Carolina, provided the recipient works in the field for which he/she was funded. May not be used for religion or theology studies. Application available on Website.

    Amount of award: $3,000-$34,000
    Application deadline: May 1

Contact:
North Carolina Student Loan Program
Health, Science and Mathematics
P.O. Box 14223
Research Triangle Park, NC 27709-4223
Phone: 800-700-1775
Web: www.cfnc.org

Ohio Board of Regents

Ohio Nurse Education Assistance Loan Program

Type of award: Loan, renewable.
Intended use: For undergraduate, post-bachelor's certificate or master's study at 4-year or graduate institution. Designated institutions: Eligible Ohio institutions.
Eligibility: Applicant must be U.S. citizen or permanent resident residing in Ohio.
Basis for selection: Major/career interest in nursing. Applicant must demonstrate financial need.
Application requirements: Proof of eligibility. FAFSA.
Additional information: Future nurse applicants must demonstrate financial need. Future nurse instructor applicants awarded on first-come, first-served basis. Award amount varies; up to $3,000 for future nurses, and at least $5,000 for future nurse instructors. Up to 100% loan cancellation if borrower meets cancellation requirements and practices nursing in Ohio after graduation. Debt cancellation rate of 20% per year for maximum of five years for future nurse recipients; 25% per year for maximum of four years for future nurse instructor recipients. Must not be in default or owe refund to any federal financial aid programs. Visit Website for application and more information.

    Number of awards: 139
    Application deadline: July 15
    Total amount awarded: $215,188
Contact:
Ohio Board of Regents
30 E. Broad Street
36th Floor
Columbus, OH 43215-3414
Phone: 888-833-1133
Fax: 614-752-5903
Web: www.regents.ohio.gov/

Pickett and Hatcher Educational Fund, Inc.

Pickett and Hatcher Educational Loan

Type of award: Loan, renewable.
Intended use: For full-time undergraduate study at 4-year institution.
Eligibility: Applicant must be U.S. citizen.
Basis for selection: Applicant must demonstrate financial need and high academic achievement.

Additional information: Not available to law, medicine, or ministry students. Loans renewed up to $40,000. Applications accepted year-round.

Amount of award:	$1,000-$10,000
Number of awards:	550
Number of applicants:	539
Total amount awarded:	$2,869,434

Contact:
Pickett and Hatcher Educational Fund, Inc.
Loan Program
P.O. Box 8169
Columbus, GA 31908-8169
Phone: 706-327-6586
Fax: 706-324-6788
Web: www.phef.org

Presbyterian Church (USA)

Presbyterian Undergraduate and Graduate Loan

Type of award: Loan, renewable.
Intended use: For full-time undergraduate or graduate study at accredited 2-year, 4-year or graduate institution in United States.
Eligibility: Applicant must be Presbyterian. Applicant must be U.S. citizen or permanent resident.
Basis for selection: Applicant must demonstrate financial need and high academic achievement.
Additional information: Must establish and maintain minimum 2.0 GPA. Contact office for current interest rates and deferment policies. Must give evidence of financial reliability. Undergraduates and graduates can apply for up to $15,000, spread out over length of undergraduate and graduate studies.

Amount of award:	$200-$15,000
Number of awards:	100
Number of applicants:	112
Application deadline:	July 30
Notification begins:	August 15
Total amount awarded:	$400,000

Contact:
Presbyterian Church (USA)
Financial Aid for Studies
100 Witherspoon Street
Louisville, KY 40202-1396
Phone: 888-728-7228 ext. 5735
Fax: 502-569-8766
Web: www.pcusa.org/financialaid

South Carolina Student Loan Corporation

South Carolina Teacher Loans

Type of award: Loan, renewable.
Intended use: For undergraduate or graduate study at accredited 2-year, 4-year or graduate institution.
Eligibility: Applicant must be U.S. citizen residing in South Carolina.

Basis for selection: Major/career interest in education; education, early childhood; education, special or education, teacher. Applicant must demonstrate high academic achievement.
Additional information: Freshmen and sophomores may borrow up to $2,500 per year; juniors, seniors, and graduate students may borrow up to $5,000 per year. Graduate study eligible only if required for initial teacher certification. Entering freshmen must have SAT score equal to South Carolina state average for year of high school graduation, and rank in top 40 percent of high school class. Undergraduate and entering graduate applicants must have 2.75 GPA and have passed PRAXIS 1 Examination. Graduate applicants who have completed at least one semester must have 3.5 GPA. Applicants with SAT score of 1100 or greater (1650 or greater for exams taken on or after March 1, 2005) or ACT score of 24 or greater are exempt from PRAXIS 1 requirement. Loan forgiveness for service in teacher shortage area in South Carolina public schools: 20 percent or $3,000, whichever is greater, for each year of service, 33 percent or $5,000, whichever is greater, if service in geographic and subject shortage area.

Amount of award:	$2,500-$5,000
Application deadline:	April 15
Notification begins:	July 15
Total amount awarded:	$5,000,000

Contact:
South Carolina Student Loan Corporation
P.O. Box 21487
Columbia, SC 29221
Phone: 803-798-0916 or 800-347-2752
Web: www.scstudentloan.org

Student Aid Foundation

Student Aid Foundation Loan

Type of award: Loan, renewable.
Intended use: For full-time undergraduate, master's, doctoral or first professional study at accredited vocational, 2-year, 4-year or graduate institution in United States.
Eligibility: Applicant must be female. Applicant must be U.S. citizen residing in Georgia.
Basis for selection: Applicant must demonstrate financial need, high academic achievement and seriousness of purpose.
Application requirements: Recommendations, essay, transcript.
Additional information: Non-Georgia residents attending Georgia institutions can qualify. Loan not forgivable. Must have financially responsible endorser. Minimum 2.5 GPA. Send SASE with request for application, or download it from Website.

Amount of award:	$3,500-$7,500
Number of awards:	40
Number of applicants:	89
Application deadline:	May 1
Notification begins:	June 1

Contact:
Student Aid Foundation
#312
2550 Sandy Plains Road, Suite 225
Marietta, GA 30066
Phone: 770-973-7077
Fax: 770-973-2220
Web: www.studentaidfoundation.org

Loans

Tennessee Student Assistance Corporation

Tennessee Minority Teaching Fellows Program

Type of award: Loan, renewable.
Intended use: For full-time undergraduate study at accredited 2-year or 4-year institution.
Eligibility: Applicant must be Alaskan native, Asian American, African American, Hispanic American, American Indian or Native Hawaiian/Pacific Islander. Applicant must be U.S. citizen residing in Tennessee.
Basis for selection: Major/career interest in education. Applicant must demonstrate high academic achievement.
Application requirements: Recommendations, essay, transcript. List of extracurricular activities.
Additional information: Entering freshmen applicants have priority and must have minimum 2.75 GPA, rank in top 25 percent of class, or score at least 18 on ACT (860 SAT). Undergraduate applicants must have minimum 2.5 GPA. Must make commitment to teaching. Loan can be forgiven by teaching in Tennessee public pre K-12 schools, one year for each year of funding.

Amount of award:	$5,000
Number of awards:	115
Number of applicants:	276
Application deadline:	April 15
Total amount awarded:	$538,516

Contact:
Tennessee Student Assistance Corporation
404 James Robertson Parkway
Parkway Towers, Suite 1510
Nashville, TN 37243-0820
Phone: 800-342-1663
Fax: 615-741-6101
Web: www.tn.gov/collegepays

Tennessee Student Assistance Corporation/Math And Science Teachers Loan Forgiveness Program

Type of award: Loan, renewable.
Intended use: For undergraduate certificate, graduate or postgraduate study at postsecondary institution.
Eligibility: Applicant must be residing in Tennessee.
Basis for selection: Major/career interest in mathematics; science, general or education.
Additional information: Must be admitted to post-secondary institution seeking advanced degree in math/science, or a certificate to teach math/science, and be a tenured Tennessee public school teacher. Application deadline is September 1 for students beginning the academic year in the fall, February 1 for spring, and May 1 for summer.

Amount of award:	$2,000
Number of awards:	27
Application deadline:	September 1, February 1
Total amount awarded:	$54,000

Contact:
Tennessee Student Assistance Corporation
404 James Robertson Parkway
Suite 1510, Parkway Towers
Nashville, TN 37243-0820
Phone: 800-342-1663
Web: www.tn.gov/collegepays

Tennessee Teaching Scholars Program

Type of award: Loan, renewable.
Intended use: For junior, senior, post-bachelor's certificate or master's study at accredited 4-year or graduate institution.
Eligibility: Applicant must be U.S. citizen residing in Tennessee.
Basis for selection: Major/career interest in education; education, teacher; education, special or education, early childhood. Applicant must demonstrate high academic achievement.
Application requirements: Recommendations, transcript, proof of eligibility. Verification of standardized test score and acceptance into Teacher Licensure Program.
Additional information: Loan can be forgiven for teaching in Tennessee public schools, K-12. Minimum 2.75 cumulative GPA and a standardized test score adequate for admission to the Teacher Education Program in Tennessee schools. Amount of award based on funding.

Amount of award:	$4,500
Number of awards:	177
Number of applicants:	392
Application deadline:	April 15
Total amount awarded:	$706,499

Contact:
Tennessee Student Assistance Corporation
404 James Robertson Parkway
Parkway Towers, Suite 1510
Nashville, TN 37243-0820
Phone: 800-342-1663
Fax: 615-741-6101
Web: www.tn.gov/collegepays

Texas Higher Education Coordinating Board

College Access Loan (CAL)

Type of award: Loan.
Intended use: For undergraduate or graduate study at 2-year, 4-year or graduate institution in United States.
Eligibility: Applicant must be U.S. citizen or permanent resident residing in Texas.
Additional information: Texas colleges and universities have a limited number of CAL loans. Applicants need not show financial need. The loan may be used to cover the family's expected contribution (EFC). Co-signers must have good credit and meet other program criteria. Loans will not be sold to another lender and will be serviced by the THECB until paid in full. Apply online.

Contact:
Texas Higher Education Coordinating Board
Student Services Division
P.O. Box 12788
Austin, TX 12788-2788
Phone: 800-242-3062
Fax: 512-427-6420
Web: www.collegeforalltexans.com and www.hhloans.com

United Methodist Church

United Methodist Loan Program

Type of award: Loan, renewable.
Intended use: For undergraduate or graduate study at accredited postsecondary institution in United States.
Eligibility: Applicant must be United Methodist.
Additional information: Must be active member of United Methodist Church one year prior to application. Must maintain "C" average. May reapply for loan to maximum of $30,000. Interest rate 5 percent; cosigner required. Ten years permitted to repay loan after graduation or withdrawal from school. Qualified applicants are chosen on a first-come, first-served basis.
   Amount of award: $5,000
Contact:
United Methodist Church/Board of Higher Education and Ministry
Office of Loans and Scholarships
P.O. Box 340007
Nashville, TN 37203-0007
Phone: 615-340-7346
Web: www.gbhem.org

UPS

United Parcel Service Earn & Learn Program Loans

Type of award: Loan.
Intended use: For undergraduate study at accredited vocational, 2-year or 4-year institution in United States.
Application requirements: Proof of eligibility.
Additional information: Must be UPS employee. Award for part-time employees is $3,000 per year in student loans with $15,000 lifetime maximum. Award for part-time management employees is $4,000 per year with a $20,000 lifetime maximum. Visit Website for participating locations and job listings.
   Amount of award: $3,000-$20,000
Contact:
Visit www.upsjobs.com for more information.
Phone: 888-WORK-UPS
Web: www.upsjobs.com

U.S. Department of Education

Federal Direct Stafford Loans

Type of award: Loan, renewable.
Intended use: For undergraduate or graduate study at postsecondary institution.
Eligibility: Applicant must be U.S. citizen or permanent resident.
Basis for selection: Applicant must demonstrate financial need.
Application requirements: Proof of eligibility. FAFSA and promissory note.
Additional information: Some loans subsidized, based on need eligibility. Loan amount depends on grade level in school and student type. Telecommunications Device for the Deaf at 800-730-8913. FAFSA available online. Visit Website for interest rates.
   Amount of award: $5,500-$20,500
Contact:
Phone: 800-4-FED-AID
Web: www.studentaid.ed.gov

Federal Family Education Loan Program (FFEL)

Type of award: Loan, renewable.
Intended use: For undergraduate or graduate study at accredited postsecondary institution in or outside United States or Canada.
Eligibility: Applicant must be U.S. citizen or permanent resident.
Basis for selection: Applicant must demonstrate financial need.
Application requirements: Proof of eligibility. FAFSA.
Additional information: Subsidized and unsubsidized loans. First-year dependent undergraduates eligible for up to $5,500; independent first-year undergraduates eligible for $9,500. Visit Website for interest rates and more information.
   Application deadline: June 30
Contact:
Federal Student Aid Information Center
P.O. Box 84
Washington, DC 20044-0084
Phone: 800-4-FED-AID
Web: www.studentaid.ed.gov

Federal Perkins Loan

Type of award: Loan, renewable.
Intended use: For undergraduate or graduate study at accredited postsecondary institution in United States.
Eligibility: Applicant must be U.S. citizen or permanent resident.
Basis for selection: Applicant must demonstrate financial need.
Application requirements: Proof of eligibility. FAFSA.
Additional information: Maximum annual loan amount: $5,500 for undergraduates, $8,000 for graduates. Five percent interest rate. Applicant must demonstrate exceptional financial need. Repayment begins nine months after graduation, leaving school, or dropping below half-time status. Visit Website for more information.
   Application deadline: June 30

Contact:
Federal Student Aid Information Center
P.O. Box 84
Washington, DC 20044-0084
Phone: 800-4-FED AID
Web: www.studentaid.ed.gov

Federal Plus Loan

Type of award: Loan.
Intended use: For undergraduate or graduate study at accredited postsecondary institution in or outside United States or Canada.
Eligibility: Applicant must be U.S. citizen or permanent resident.
Basis for selection: Applicant must demonstrate financial need.
Application requirements: PLUS loan application and promissory note. FAFSA.
Additional information: Unsubsidized loans for parents of undergraduate students, or for graduate students. Must pass credit check. Interest rate is 8.5 percent. Award amount varies. Loan is equal to cost of attendance minus any other financial aid. Generally, repayment must begin 60 days after the loan is fully disbursed. Visit Website for more information.

   Application deadline: June 30
Contact:
Federal Student Aid Information Center
P.O. Box 84
Washington, DC 20044-0084
Phone: 800-4-FED-AID
Web: www.studentaid.ed.gov

Utah State Office of Education

Utah Career Teaching Scholarship/ T.H. Bell Teaching Incentive Loan

Type of award: Loan, renewable.
Intended use: For full-time undergraduate study at accredited 4-year institution. Designated institutions: Utah institutions.
Eligibility: Applicant must be high school junior or senior. Applicant must be U.S. citizen residing in Utah.
Basis for selection: Major/career interest in education, teacher; education; education, early childhood or education, special.
Application requirements: Transcript. SAT/ACT scores.
Additional information: Must have completed requirements for Early Graduation Program (including ACT). Awardees must teach in Utah public school for term equal to number of years loan was received in order to have loans forgiven. Visit Website for application.

   Amount of award: Full tuition
   Number of awards: 25
   Number of applicants: 320
   Application deadline: March 26
Contact:
Linda Adler, Educator Quality and Licensing
Utah State Office of Education
250 East 500 South/P.O. Box 144200
Salt Lake City, UT 84114-4200
Web: www.schools.utah.gov/cert/scholarships/scholars.htm

Virgin Islands Board of Education

Virgin Islands Territorial Grants/ Loans Program

Type of award: Loan, renewable.
Intended use: For full-time undergraduate or graduate study at accredited postsecondary institution.
Eligibility: Applicant must be U.S. citizen or permanent resident residing in Virgin Islands.
Basis for selection: Applicant must demonstrate financial need.
Application requirements: Transcript. Acceptance letter from institution for first-time applicants or transfer students.
Additional information: Minimum 2.0 GPA. Must agree to accept one year of employment in Virgin Islands government for every year of award upon completion of studies. Number and amount of awards vary. Six percent interest on repayment, additional 2 percent if delinquent. Number and amount of award varies.

   Number of applicants: 625
   Application deadline: May 1
Contact:
Virgin Islands Board of Education
Scholarship Committee
P.O. Box 11900
St. Thomas, VI 00801
Phone: 340-774-4546

Wisconsin Department of Veterans Affairs

Wisconsin Veterans Affairs Personal Loan Program

Type of award: Loan.
Intended use: For undergraduate or graduate study at postsecondary institution in United States.
Eligibility: Applicant must be residing in Wisconsin. Applicant must be veteran; or dependent of veteran or deceased veteran; or spouse of veteran or deceased veteran. Must meet WDVA service requirements. Must have 90 days of active duty during wartime and/or two years of continuous active duty.
Application requirements: Proof of eligibility. Credit report.
Additional information: Applicant must have been resident of Wisconsin upon entry into military service or a continuous resident of Wisconsin for at least one year immediately preceding the application date. Maximum loan of $25,000 available. Loan must be secured by a mortgage on the applicant's property or with a guarantor. Subsidized annual interest rate varies; loan term varies depending on amount borrowed. Apply to local county veterans service officer to establish eligibility. Adult children of veterans must be under 26 years old and attending school full-time.

Loans

Wisconsin Higher Educational Aids Board

Wisconsin Minority Teacher Loan Program

Type of award: Loan, renewable.
Intended use: For junior, senior or graduate study at accredited 4-year institution. Designated institutions: Wisconsin colleges and universities offering teaching degree.
Eligibility: Applicant must be Asian American, African American, Mexican American, Hispanic American, Puerto Rican or American Indian. Asian American applicants must be either former citizens or descendants of former citizens of Laos, Vietnam, or Cambodia admitted to the U.S. after 12/31/1975. Applicant must be residing in Wisconsin.
Basis for selection: Major/career interest in education; education, special or education, teacher. Applicant must demonstrate financial need.
Application requirements: Nomination by financial aid office. FAFSA.
Additional information: Recipient must agree to teach in Wisconsin school district where minority students constitute at least 29 percent of enrollment or in school district participating in the inter-district pupil transfer (Chapter 220) program. For each year student teaches in eligible district, 25 percent of loan is forgiven; otherwise loan must be repaid at interest rate of 5 percent.

Amount of award:	$250-$2,500
Number of awards:	109
Total amount awarded:	$238,662

Contact:
Higher Educational Aids Board
Attn: Mary Lou Kuzdas
P.O. Box 7885
Madison, WI 53707-7885
Phone: 608-267-2212
Web: www.heab.state.wi.us

Loans

Sponsor Index

1199 SEIU Benefit Funds, 73
Abbie Sargent Memorial Scholarship
  Fund, 73
Academy of Television Arts &
  Sciences Foundation, 73
Academy of Television Arts &
  Sciences Foundation, 525
Accuracy in Media/American
  Journalism Center, 525
ACFE Foundation, 74
The Actuarial Foundation, 74
ADHA Institute for Oral Health, 75
AFSA Scholarship Programs, 78
AHIMA Foundation, 79
Air Force Aid Society, 79
Air Force/ROTC, 79
Air Traffic Control Association,
  Inc., 79
Aircraft Electronics Association
  Educational Foundation, 80
Aircraft Owners and Pilots
  Association (AOPA), 83
Alabama Commission on Higher
  Education, 83
Alabama Department of Education, 84
Alabama Department of
  Postsecondary Education, 84
Alabama Department of Veterans
  Affairs, 84
Alaska Commission on Postsecondary
  Education, 573
Alcoa Foundation, 85
Alexander Graham Bell Association
  for the Deaf and Hard of
  Hearing, 85
Alexia Foundation, 85
Alliance for Young Artists and
  Writers, 86
Allstate, 525
Alpha Beta Gamma International
  Business Honor Society, 87
Alpha Mu Gamma, the National
  Collegiate Foreign Language Honor
  Society, 87
Alumnae Panhellenic Association of
  Washington, D.C., 87
AMBUCS, 88
American Alpine Club, 88
American Association for Cancer
  Research, 88
American Association of Advertising
  Agencies, 525
American Bar Foundation, 526
American Board of Funeral Service
  Education, 89
American Cancer Society Great Lakes
  Division Foundation, 89
American Center of Oriental
  Research, 90
American Chemical Society, 90

American Classical League, 90
American College of Musicians, 91
American Congress on Surveying and
  Mapping, 91
American Conservatory Theater, 526
American Council of Engineering
  Companies, 94
American Council of the Blind, 94
American Dental Assistants
  Association, 94
American Dietetic Association
  Foundation, 94
American Federation of State, County
  and Municipal Employees, 95
American Federation of State, County
  and Municipal Employees, 527
American Floral Endowment, 95
American Foundation for Aging
  Research, 97
American Foundation for
  Pharmaceutical Education, 97
American Foundation for the
  Blind, 98
American Ground Water Trust, 99
American Helicopter Society, 100
American Hellenic Educational
  Progressive Association Educational
  Foundation, 100
American Hotel & Lodging
  Educational Foundation, 100
American Indian College Fund, 101
American Indian Science &
  Engineering Society, 104
American Institute For Foreign
  Study, 104
American Institute of Aeronautics and
  Astronautics, 105
American Institute of Architects, 105
American Institute of Architects New
  Jersey, 106
American Institute of Certified Public
  Accountants, 106
American Institute of Polish
  Culture, 106
American Legion Alabama, 106
American Legion Alabama
  Auxiliary, 107
American Legion Alaska, 107
American Legion Alaska
  Auxiliary, 108
American Legion Arizona, 108
American Legion Arizona
  Auxiliary, 108
American Legion Arkansas, 109
American Legion Arkansas
  Auxiliary, 110
American Legion Auxiliary,
  Department of Illinois, 110
American Legion Auxiliary,
  Department of Maryland, 110

American Legion California, 110
American Legion California
  Auxiliary, 111
American Legion Colorado, 112
American Legion Colorado
  Auxiliary, 112
American Legion Connecticut, 112
American Legion Connecticut
  Auxiliary, 113
American Legion Delaware
  Auxiliary, 113
American Legion District of
  Columbia, 113
American Legion Florida, 114
American Legion Florida
  Auxiliary, 114
American Legion Georgia
  Auxiliary, 115
American Legion Hawaii, 115
American Legion Idaho, 115
American Legion Idaho Auxiliary, 116
American Legion Illinois, 116
American Legion Illinois
  Auxiliary, 117
American Legion Indiana, 118
American Legion Indiana
  Auxiliary, 118
American Legion Iowa, 119
American Legion Iowa Auxiliary, 119
American Legion Kansas, 120
American Legion Kansas
  Auxiliary, 122
American Legion Kentucky, 122
American Legion Kentucky
  Auxiliary, 122
American Legion Kentucky
  Auxiliary, 573
American Legion Maine, 123
American Legion Maine
  Auxiliary, 124
American Legion Maryland, 124
American Legion Maryland
  Auxiliary, 125
American Legion Massachusetts, 125
American Legion Massachusetts
  Auxiliary, 126
American Legion Michigan, 126
American Legion Michigan
  Auxiliary, 127
American Legion Minnesota, 127
American Legion Minnesota
  Auxiliary, 128
American Legion Mississippi
  Auxiliary, 128
American Legion Missouri, 129
American Legion Missouri
  Auxiliary, 131
American Legion Montana
  Auxiliary, 131

American Legion National Headquarters, 132
American Legion Nebraska, 133
American Legion Nebraska Auxiliary, 134
American Legion Nevada, 135
American Legion Nevada Auxiliary, 136
American Legion New Hampshire, 136
American Legion New Hampshire Auxiliary, 138
American Legion New Jersey, 139
American Legion New Jersey Auxiliary, 139
American Legion New Mexico Auxiliary, 140
American Legion New York, 140
American Legion New York Auxiliary, 141
American Legion North Carolina, 141
American Legion North Carolina Auxiliary, 142
American Legion North Dakota, 142
American Legion North Dakota Auxiliary, 142
American Legion Ohio, 143
American Legion Ohio Auxiliary, 143
American Legion Oregon, 144
American Legion Oregon Auxiliary, 144
American Legion Pennsylvania, 145
American Legion Pennsylvania Auxiliary, 145
American Legion Press Club of New Jersey, 146
American Legion Puerto Rico Auxiliary, 146
American Legion Rhode Island, 146
American Legion Rhode Island Auxiliary, 146
American Legion South Carolina, 147
American Legion South Carolina Auxiliary, 147
American Legion South Dakota, 147
American Legion South Dakota, 574
American Legion South Dakota Auxiliary, 147
American Legion Tennessee, 148
American Legion Tennessee Auxiliary, 149
American Legion Texas, 149
American Legion Texas Auxiliary, 149
American Legion Utah Auxiliary, 150
American Legion Vermont, 150
American Legion Virginia, 151
American Legion Virginia Auxiliary, 151
American Legion Washington, 151
American Legion Washington Auxiliary, 152
American Legion West Virginia, 153
American Legion West Virginia Auxiliary, 153
American Legion Wisconsin, 153

American Legion Wisconsin Auxiliary, 154
American Legion Wyoming, 155
American Legion Wyoming Auxiliary, 156
American Medical Technologists, 156
American Meteorological Society, 156
American Morgan Horse Institute, 157
American Museum of Natural History, 158
American Museum of Natural History, 527
American Nuclear Society, 158
American Physical Society, 161
American Public Power Association, 161
American Quarter Horse Foundation, 161
American Radio Relay League (ARRL) Foundation, Inc., 162
American Respiratory Care Foundation, 169
American Society for Enology and Viticulture, 170
American Society for Microbiology, 170
American Society of Civil Engineers, 171
American Society of Heating, Refrigerating, and Air-Conditioning Engineers, Inc., 172
American Society of Interior Designers Foundation, Inc., 174
American Society of International Law, 528
American Society of Naval Engineers, 175
American Water Ski Educational Foundation, 175
American Welding Society Foundation, Inc., 175
Americans for the Arts, 528
America's Junior Miss, Inc., 88
Annie's Homegrown, 180
AOPA Air Safety Foundation, 180
AP Los Angeles, 181
Appaloosa Youth Foundation, 181
Applied Arts, 530
Applied Materials, Global College Programs, 530
Arizona Board of Regents, 181
Arkansas Department of Higher Education, 182
Armed Forces Communications and Electronics Association, 183
Armenian General Benevolent Union (AGBU), 186
ARMY Emergency Relief, 187
The Art Institutes, 187
Arthur and Doreen Parrett Scholarship Trust Fund, 187
Arts and Business Council of New York, 531
The ASCAP Foundation, 188
ASCO Numatics, 188
Asian American Journalists Association, 188

Asian American Journalists Association, Texas Chapter, 189
ASM Materials Education Foundation, 189
ASME Auxiliary, Inc., 191
ASME Auxiliary, Inc., 574
ASME Foundation, 192
ASME Foundation, 574
Associated Builders and Contractors, Inc., 195
Associated General Contractors Education and Research Foundation, 195
Associated General Contractors of Maine Education Foundation, 196
Associated Press, 196
Association for Library and Information Science Education, 196
Association for Women in Architecture Foundation, 197
Association for Women in Communications, 197
Association of American Geographers, 198
The Association of Insurance Compliance Professionals, 198
Association of State Dam Safety Officials, 199
Astraea Lesbian Foundation for Justice, 199
Automotive Hall of Fame, 199
AXA Achievement Scholarship, 200
Ayn Rand Institute, 200
Barry M. Goldwater Scholarship and Excellence In Education Foundation, 201
Bay Area Family of Funds, 201
Bernstein-Rein Advertising, 531
Best Buy, 201
Bethesda Lutheran Communities, 202
BioCommunications Association, Inc., 202
Black & Veatch Corporation, 531
BlackNews.com, 202
Blinded Veterans Association, 202
BMI Foundation, Inc., 203
BMI Foundation, Inc., 531
Board of Governors of the Federal Reserve System, 532
Boeing Company, 203
Boeing Company, 532
Boston Globe, 532
Boy Scouts of America Patriots' Path Council, 204
Boys and Girls Clubs of Greater San Diego, 204
Broadcast Education Association, 204
Brown and Caldwell, 206
Brown Foundation, 206
Building Industry Association, 206
Bureau of Indian Affairs-Oklahoma Area Education Office, 207
Bureau of Indian Education, 207
Butler Manufacturing Company Foundation, 207
California Association of Realtors Scholarship Foundation, 207

California Farm Bureau
Federation, 208
California Masonic Foundation, 208
California Student Aid
Commission, 209
California Student Aid
Commission, 574
California Teachers Association, 210
California's Junior Miss, 208
CAP Charitable Foundation, 211
Carl's Jr. Restaurants, 212
Catching the Dream, 212
Catholic Aid Association, 213
CCNMA, 213
Center for Architecture, 213
Center for Education Solutions, 214
Central Intelligence Agency, 214
C.G. Fuller Foundation c/o Bank of
America, 215
ChairScholars Foundation, Inc., 215
Charles & Lucille King Family
Foundation, Inc., 215
The Charles A. and Anne Morrow
Lindbergh Foundation, 215
Charleston Women in International
Trade, 216
Chevron Corporation, 532
Chicago Scholars Foundation, 216
Choctaw Nation of Oklahoma, 216
Christian Record Services, 217
Citizens for Global Solutions, 533
City University of New York, 217
The Coca-Cola Foundation, 217
The College Board, 218
Colorado Commission on Higher
Education, 218
Colorado Masons Benevolent Fund
Association, 219
Colorado Society of CPAs Educational
Foundation, 219
Columbus Citizens Foundation, 219
Congressional Black Caucus
Foundation, Inc., 220
Congressional Hispanic Caucus
Institute, 220
Congressional Hispanic Caucus
Institute, 533
Congressional Institute, Inc., 533
Connecticut Building Congress,
Inc., 221
Connecticut Department of Higher
Education, 221
Connecticut Higher Education
Supplemental Loan Authority, 575
Connecticut League for Nursing, 223
Consortium of Information and
Telecommunication Executives, 223
Costume Society of America, 224
Council on International Educational
Exchange, 224
Courage Center, 226
Creede Repertory Theatre, 533
Cushman School, 533
The Cynthia E. Morgan Memorial
Scholarship Fund, 226
Cystic Fibrosis Foundation, 226
The Dallas Foundation, 226

Data Processing Management
Association/Portland Chapter, 228
Datatel Scholars Foundation, 229
Daughters of Union Veterans of the
Civil War 1861-1865, 229
Davidson Institute, 229
Davis-Roberts Scholarship Fund, 229
Delaware Higher Education
Commission, 230
Delaware Higher Education
Commission, 575
Denver Rescue Mission, 534
Discover Financial Services, 231
District of Columbia Higher
Education Financial Services, 232
Dolphin Scholarship Foundation, 232
Dow Jones News Fund, 534
DuPont Company, 535
Eastern Orthodox Committee on
Scouting, 233
Eastman Kodak Company, 535
Edmund F. Maxwell Foundation, 233
Elie Wiesel Foundation for
Humanity, 233
Elizabeth Greenshields
Foundation, 233
Elks National Foundation, 234
Engineers Foundation of Ohio, 234
Entergy, 536
Entertainment Weekly, 536
The Entomological Foundation, 234
The Environmental Institute for
Golf, 235
The Environmental Institute for
Golf, 536
Epilepsy Foundation, 236
Epilepsy Foundation of San Diego
County, 236
EqualityMaine Foundation, 236
ESA Foundation, 236
ESPN Inc., 536
Essence Magazine, 537
Executive Women International, 237
Experimental Aircraft
Association, 237
Explorers Club, 238
Federal Employee Education and
Assistance Fund, 238
Federal Reserve Bank of New
York, 537
Feminist Majority Foundation, 537
Filoli Center, 538
Finance Authority of Maine, 239
Financial Service Centers of New
York, 239
First Catholic Slovak Ladies
Association, 239
First Marine Division
Association, 239
Fisher Communications, Inc., 240
Florida Department of Education, 240
Florida Department of Education, 538
Florida Department of Education, 576
Florida Power & Light Company, 538
Foundation for Surgical
Technology, 242

Foundation of the National Student
Nurses Association, Inc., 243
Fox Group, 538
Francis Ouimet Scholarship Fund, 243
Franklin D. Roosevelt Library, 538
Franklin Lindsay Student Aid
Fund, 576
Fred G. Zahn Foundation, 243
Freedom From Religion
Foundation, 243
Garden Club of America, 244
Garden Club of America, 539
Genentech, Inc., 539
Georgia Student Finance
Commission, 246
Georgia Student Finance
Commission, 576
Georgia-Pacific, LLC, 539
Glamour Magazine, 248
The Global Challenge Award, 248
Golden Apple, 248
Golden Key International Honour
Society, 249
Grand Encampment of Knights
Templar of the USA, 576
Grange Insurance Association, 251
Great Minds in Stem, 251
Greater Kanawha Valley
Foundation, 251
Greenhouse Partners, 251
Hannaford Bros Co., 539
Harness Tracks of America, 252
Havana National Bank, 252
Hawaii Community Foundation, 252
Helicopter Association
International, 274
Herschel C. Price Educational
Foundation, 274
Higher Education Services
Corporation (HESC), 274
Hispanic Association of Colleges and
Universities, 540
Hispanic College Fund, 275
Hispanic Heritage Foundation, 276
Hispanic Scholarship Fund, 276
Hoffman-La Roche Inc., 540
Hopi Tribe Grants and Scholarship
Program, 279
Horatio Alger Association, 280
Horticultural Research Institute, 284
Houston Livestock Show and
Rodeo, 286
IBM, 540
ICMA Retirement Corporation, 287
Idaho State Board of Education, 287
Idaho State Board of Education, 577
Illinois Department of Veterans'
Affairs, 288
Illinois State Board of Education, 289
Illinois Student Assistance
Commission, 289
The Indianapolis Star, 540
INROADS, Inc., 541
Institute for Humane Studies, 292
Institute of Food Technologists, 292
Institute of Real Estate Management
Foundation, 293

Insurance Scholarship Foundation of America, 293
International Association of Fire Fighters, 294
International Buckskin Horse Association, Inc., 294
International Executive Housekeepers Association, 294
International Foodservice Editorial Council, 294
International Furnishings and Design Association Educational Foundation, 295
International Order of the King's Daughters and Sons, 296
International Radio and Television Society Foundation, 541
Intertribal Timber Council, 296
Iowa College Student Aid Commission, 297
Italian Catholic Federation, 299
IUE-CWA, 299
J. Paul Getty Trust, 541
Jackie Robinson Foundation, 300
James Beard Foundation, 301
James F. Byrnes Foundation, 304
Japanese American Association of New York, 305
Jaycee War Memorial Fund, 305
Jeannette Rankin Foundation, 306
Jewish Family and Children's Services (JFCS), 577
Jewish Vocational Service, 306
Jewish War Veterans of the United States of America, 306
John Deere, 542
The John F. Kennedy Center for the Performing Arts, 542
John F. Kennedy Library Foundation, 542
John Wiley and Sons, Inc., 543
Johnson Controls, 543
J.W. Saxe Memorial Fund, 543
Kansas Board of Regents, 307
Kappa Kappa Gamma Foundation, 309
KarMel Scholarship Committee, 309
Kentucky Higher Education Assistance Authority (KHEAA), 310
Kentucky Higher Education Assistance Authority (KHEAA), 543
The Kim and Harold Louie Family Foundation, 311
KIMT, 544
Knights of Columbus, 312
Kosciuszko Foundation, 312
The Lagrant Foundation, 314
Lambda Alpha National Collegiate Honors Society for Anthropology, 314
Landscape Architecture Foundation, 314
Latin American Educational Foundation, 316

League of United Latin American Citizens, 316
Learning for Life, 317
Library of Congress, 544
Life and Health Insurance Foundation for Education, 318
Liggett-Stashower, Inc., 318
Lighthouse International, 318
Los Padres Foundation, 319
Louis Carr Internship Foundation (LCIF), 544
Louisiana Department of Veterans Affairs, 320
Louisiana Office of Student Financial Assistance, 320
Louisiana State Department of Education, 321
Macy's, Inc., 544
Maine Division of Veterans Services, 321
Maine Educational Loan Authority, 577
Maine Innkeepers Association, 321
Maine Metal Products Association Education Fund, 322
Maine Restaurant Association, 322
Maine Society of Professional Engineers, 322
Maine State Society of Washington, DC, 323
Makovsky & Company Inc., 545
Manomet Center for Conservation Sciences, 323
Marin Community Foundation, 323
Marin Education Fund, 324
Marine Corps Scholarship Foundation, 324
Maryland Higher Education Commission Office of Student Financial Assistance, 324
Massachusetts Board of Higher Education, 328
Massachusetts Board of Higher Education, 577
Massachusetts Democratic Party, 329
Massachusetts Democratic Party, 545
Massachusetts Department of Education, 329
MCC Theater, 545
McKee Scholars, 329
Menominee Indian Tribe of Wisconsin, 330
The Merchants Exchange, 330
Metropolitan Museum of Art, 545
Michigan Higher Education Assistance Authority, 330
Michigan Society of Professional Engineers, 331
Microscopy Society of America, 332
Microsoft Corporation, 332
Midwestern Higher Education Compact, 332
Military Officers Association of America, 332
Military Officers Association of America, 578

Military Order of the Purple Heart, 333
Milk Processor's Education Program, 333
Minnesota Department of Veterans Affairs, 333
Minnesota Office of Higher Education, 334
Minnesota Office of Higher Education, 546
Minnesota Office of Higher Education, 578
Miss America Organization, 335
Mississippi Office of Student Financial Aid, 336
Mississippi Office of Student Financial Aid, 578
Missouri Department of Elementary and Secondary Education, 337
Missouri Department of Higher Education, 337
Missouri League for Nursing, 339
Montana Board of Regents, 339
Montana Trappers Association, 341
The Moody's Foundation, 341
Morris Arboretum of the University of Pennsylvania, 547
Mother Jones, 548
Museum of Modern Art, 548
NAACP, 341
NAACP Legal Defense and Education Fund, Inc., 343
NASA Alabama Space Grant Consortium, 343
NASA Arizona Space Grant Consortium, 549
NASA Connecticut Space Grant Consortium, 343
NASA Delaware Space Grant Consortium, 344
NASA Delaware Space Grant Consortium, 549
NASA District of Columbia Space Grant Consortium, 344
NASA Georgia Space Grant Consortium, 344
NASA Hawaii Space Grant Consortium, 344
NASA Hawaii Space Grant Consortium, 549
NASA Idaho Space Grant Consortium, 345
NASA Illinois Space Grant Consortium, 345
NASA Kentucky Space Grant Consortium, 345
NASA Maine Space Grant Consortium, 346
NASA Michigan Space Grant Consortium, 346
NASA Minnesota Space Grant Consortium, 347
NASA Missouri Space Grant Consortium, 347
NASA Montana Space Grant Consortium, 347

NASA Nevada Space Grant Consortium, 348
NASA New Jersey Space Grant Consortium, 550
NASA New Mexico Space Grant Consortium, 348
NASA North Carolina Space Grant Consortium, 348
NASA North Dakota Space Grant Consortium, 349
NASA Ohio Space Grant Consortium, 350
NASA Oregon Space Grant Consortium, 350
NASA Pennsylvania Space Grant Consortium, 350
NASA Pennsylvania Space Grant Consortium, 550
NASA Rhode Island Space Grant Consortium, 350
NASA Rocky Mountain Space Grant Consortium, 351
NASA South Carolina Space Grant Consortium, 351
NASA Texas Space Grant Consortium, 352
NASA Vermont Space Grant Consortium, 352
NASA Virginia Space Grant Consortium, 353
NASA West Virginia Space Grant Consortium, 353
NASA Wisconsin Space Grant Consortium, 354
National Academy for Nuclear Training, 354
National Amateur Baseball Federation, Inc., 355
National Art Materials Trade Association, 355
National Association of Black Accountants Inc., 356
National Association of Black Journalists, 356
National Association of Black Journalists, 550
National Association of Letter Carriers, 357
National Association of Water Companies (NJ Chapter), 357
National Association of Women in Construction, 358
National Athletic Trainers' Association Research & Education Foundation, 358
National Basketball Association, 551
National Black Nurses Association, 358
National Black Police Association, 359
National Center For Learning Disabilities, 359
National Commission for Cooperative Education, 359
National Dairy Shrine, 360
National Eagle Scout Association, 361

National Environmental Health Association/ American Academy of Sanitarians, 362
National Federation of the Blind, 362
National FFA, 365
National Geographic Society, 551
National Ground Water Research and Education Foundation, 365
National Inventors Hall of Fame, 365
National Italian American Foundation, 365
National Jewish Committee on Scouting, 366
National Jewish Committee on Scouting, Boy Scouts of America, 366
National Junior Classical League, 367
National Merit Scholarship Corporation, 367
National Museum of the American Indian, 551
National Museum of Women in the Arts, 551
National Poultry & Food Distributors Association, 368
National Press Photographers Foundation, 368
National Restaurant Association Educational Foundation, 370
National Rifle Association, 371
National Science Foundation, 552
National Science Teachers Association, 371
National Sculpture Society, 371
National Security Agency, 372
National Society of Accountants, 372
National Society of Accountants Scholarship Foundation, 372
National Society of Black Engineers, 373
National Society of the Sons of the American Revolution, 377
National Speakers Association, 377
National Stone, Sand & Gravel Association, 377
Native Daughters of the Golden West, 378
Navy Supply Corps Foundation, 378
Navy-Marine Corps Relief Society, 378
Navy-Marine Corps Relief Society, 579
NCAA, 379
NCR Corporation, 552
Nebraska Coordinating Commission for Postsecondary Education, 379
Nebraska State Department of Education, 379
Nevada Department of Education, 379
New Dramatists, 552
New England Board of Higher Education, 380
New England Employee Benefits Council, 380
New Hampshire Higher Education Assistance Foundation (NHHEAF), 580

New Hampshire Postsecondary Education Commission, 380
New Hampshire Postsecondary Education Commission, 580
New Jersey Commission on Higher Education, 381
New Jersey Department of Military and Veterans Affairs, 381
New Jersey Higher Education Student Assistance Authority, 382
New Jersey Higher Education Student Assistance Authority, 580
New Jersey State Golf Association, 384
New Mexico Commission on Higher Education, 384
New Mexico Commission on Higher Education, 553
New Mexico Commission on Higher Education, 580
The New Republic, 553
New York State Assembly, 553
New York State Education Department, 385
New York State Grange, 386
New York State Grange, 581
New York State Higher Education Services Corporation, 387
New York State Native American Education Unit, 389
New York Times, 554
New York Women in Communications Foundation, 389
Nisei Student Relocation Commemorative Fund, 390
NMIA Ohio, 390
Non Commissioned Officers Association, 390
North American Limousin Foundation, 391
North Carolina Community Colleges Foundation, 391
North Carolina Community Colleges Foundation, 581
North Carolina Division of Veterans Affairs, 392
North Carolina Division of Vocational Rehabilitation Services, 392
North Carolina State Board of Refrigeration Examiners, 392
North Carolina State Education Assistance Authority, 392
North Carolina State Education Assistance Authority, 582
North Dakota University System, 395
Northern Cheyenne Tribal Education Department, 396
Northwest Danish Association, 396
Oak Ridge Institute for Science and Education, 554
OCA, 397
Office of Vocational and Educational Services for Individuals with Disabilities, 397
Ohio Board of Regents, 397
Ohio Board of Regents, 582
Ohio National Guard, 398

Ohio Newspapers Foundation, 398
Ohio Newspapers Foundation, 558
Oklahoma Engineering
 Foundation, 399
Oklahoma State Department of
 Education Professional Services
 Division, 400
Oklahoma State Regents for Higher
 Education, 400
OMNE/Nursing Leaders of
 Maine, 402
ONS Foundation, 402
OP Loftbed, 402
Oracle Corporation, 559
Oregon Collectors Association, 402
Oregon Student Assistance
 Commission, 403
The Orthotic and Prosthetic Education
 and Development Fund, 412
Osage Tribal Education
 Committee, 413
Owens Corning, 559
Pacific Gas and Electric
 Company, 559
Papercheck.com, 413
Par Aide, 413
Patient Advocate Foundation, 414
PBS, 559
Peacock Productions, Inc., 414
Penguin Putnam, Inc., 414
Pennsylvania Higher Education
 Assistance Agency, 415
Pennsylvania State System of Higher
 Education Foundation, Inc., 417
The Persian Scholarship
 Foundation, 418
PFLAG National Office, 418
PGA Tour, 560
The Phillips Foundation, 419
Phipps Conservatory and Botanical
 Gardens, 560
Pickett and Hatcher Educational Fund,
 Inc., 582
Plumbing-Heating-Cooling
 Contractors - National Assoc.
 Educational Foundation, 419
Point Foundation, 420
Presbyterian Church (USA), 421
Presbyterian Church (USA), 583
Press Club of Houston Educational
 Foundation, 422
Pride of the Greater Lehigh
 Valley, 422
The Princess Grace Foundation
 USA, 422
Princeton Plasma Physics
 Laboratory, 560
Print and Graphics Scholarship
 Foundation, 423
Professional Association of Georgia
 Educators Foundation, Inc., 423
Quill and Scroll Foundation, 424
Radio-Television News Director
 Foundation (RTNDF), 424
Random House, 560
Recording for the Blind and
 Dyslexic, 425

Red River Valley Fighter Pilots
 Association, 426
Reserve Officers Association, 426
Restaurant Association of Maryland
 Education Foundation, 427
Rhode Island Higher Education
 Assistance Authority, 427
Rhode Island State Government, 561
Rocky Mountain Coal Mining
 Institute, 428
Ronald McDonald House
 Charities, 428
The Rotary Foundation, 428
ROTC/Air Force, 429
ROTC/United States Army, 429
Sachs Foundation, 430
SAE International, 430
Sallie Mae Fund, 433
Salute to Education, Inc., 433
Scarlett Family Foundation
 Scholarship Program, 434
Screen Actors Guild Foundation, 434
Seabee Memorial Scholarship
 Association, Inc., 434
Seattle Jaycees, 435
Second Marine Division
 Association, 435
Senator George J. Mitchell
 Scholarship Research Institute, 435
Seneca Nation and BIA, 436
Sertoma, 436
Service Employees International
 Union, 436
Shoshone Tribe, 436
Sid Richardson Memorial Fund, 437
Siemens Foundation, 437
Simon and Schuster Inc., 561
Slovak Gymnastic Union Sokol,
 USA, 438
Slovenian Women's Union of
 America, 438
Smithsonian Environmental Research
 Center, 561
Smithsonian Institution, 562
SNM, 439
SNM Technologist Section, 439
Sociedad Honoraria Hispanica, 439
Society for Range Management, 440
Society for Science & the Public, 440
Society of Daughters of the United
 States Army, 440
Society of Exploration
 Geophysicists, 441
Society of Manufacturing Engineers
 Education Foundation, 441
Society of Physics Students, 448
Society of Physics Students, 562
Society of Plastics Engineers, 448
The Society of the Descendants of the
 Signers of the Declaration of
 Independence, 451
Society of Women Engineers, 451
Soil and Water Conservation
 Society, 463
Solomon R. Guggenheim
 Museum, 563
Sons of Italy Foundation, 464

Sons of Norway Foundation, 465
Sony Music Entertainment, 563
South Carolina Commission on
 Higher Education, 466
South Carolina Higher Education
 Tuition Grants Commission, 467
South Carolina Student Loan
 Corporation, 583
South Dakota Board of Regents, 468
South Dakota Department of
 Education, 469
Southern Nursery Organization, 469
Southern Scholarship Foundation, 470
Southface Energy Institute, 563
SPIE - The International Society for
 Optical Engineering, 470
Spina Bifida Association, 470
Spoleto Festival USA, 564
Sports Journalism Institute, 564
Staples, 470
Staples, 564
State Council of Higher Education for
 Virginia, 471
State of Alabama, 471
State Student Assistance Commission
 of Indiana, 471
Stephen T. Marchello Scholarship
 Foundation, 473
Student Aid Foundation, 583
Student Conservation
 Association, 564
Studio Art Centers International, 473
Sunkist Growers, 475
Supreme Guardian Council,
 International Order of Job's
 Daughters, 475
Swiss Benevolent Society of New
 York, 476
TAG Education Collaborative, 476
Taglit-Birthright Israel, 477
Tennessee Student Assistance
 Corporation, 477
Tennessee Student Assistance
 Corporation, 584
Texas 4-H Club, 479
Texas Association, Family Career and
 Community Leaders of
 America, 480
Texas Future Farmers of America, 481
Texas Higher Coordinating Board, 481
Texas Higher Education Coordinating
 Board, 481
Texas Higher Education Coordinating
 Board, 584
Texas Historical Commission, 565
Third Marine Division
 Association, 486
Thurgood Marshall College Fund, 486
Time Inc., 565
Tourism Cares, 487
Tourism Cares, 565
Transportation Clubs
 International, 493
Treacy Company, 495
Trinity Episcopal Church, 495
Two Ten Footwear Foundation, 495
Tyson Foods, Inc., 566

UCB Pharma Inc., 496
Unico Foundation, Inc., 496
Union Plus, 497
Unitarian Universalist Association, 497
United Food and Commercial Workers International Union, 497
United Methodist Church, 585
United Methodist Church General Board of Higher Education and Ministry, 497
United Methodist Communications, 498
United Negro College Fund, 498
United Negro College Fund, 566
United States Association of Blind Athletes, 500
United States Holocaust Memorial Museum, 566
United States Institute of Peace, 500
United States Senate, 566
United Transportation Union Insurance Association, 501
University Film and Video Association, 501
Upakar, 501
UPS, 585
U.S. Army Recruiting Command, 501
U.S. Department of Agriculture, 502
U.S. Department of Agriculture, 567
U.S. Department of Education, 502
U.S. Department of Education, 585
U.S. Department of Education Rehabilitation Services Administration, 503
U.S. Department of Energy, 567
U.S. Department of Health and Human Services, 503
U.S. Department of State, 567
U.S. Environmental Protection Agency, 503
U.S. House of Representatives, 567
U.S. National Arboretum, 568
U.S. Navy/Marine NROTC College Scholarship Program, 504
USTA Tennis and Education Foundation, 505
Utah Higher Education Assistance Authority (UHEAA), 505
Utah State Office of Education, 506
Utah State Office of Education, 586
The Vegetarian Resource Group, 506
Ventura County Japanese-American Citizens League, 506
Vermont Golf Association Scholarship Fund, Inc., 506
Vermont Student Assistance Corporation, 507
Veterans of Foreign Wars, 511
Virgin Islands Board of Education, 511
Virgin Islands Board of Education, 586
Virginia Department of Education, 512
Virginia Department of Health, 512

Virginia Department of Rehabilitative Services, 513
Virginia Museum of Fine Arts, 513
Wachovia, 568
The Wall Street Journal, 569
Wal-Mart Foundation, 513
The Walt Disney Company, 569
Walt Disney World and Disneyland, 569
Washington Crossing Foundation, 514
Washington Internships for Students of Engineering, 570
Washington State Higher Education Coordinating Board, 515
Washington State PTA, 515
Wells Fargo, 516
Welsh Society of Philadelphia, 516
West Pharmaceutical Services, Inc., 516
West Virginia Division of Veterans Affairs, 517
West Virginia Higher Education Policy Commission, 517
Western European Architecture Foundation, 519
Western Golf Association/Evans Scholars Foundation, 519
William Randolph Hearst Foundation, 519
Wilson Ornithological Society, 520
Wisconsin Department of Veterans Affairs, 520
Wisconsin Department of Veterans Affairs, 586
Wisconsin Higher Educational Aids Board, 521
Wisconsin Higher Educational Aids Board, 587
Wolf Trap Foundation for the Performing Arts, 570
Women Grocers of America, 522
Women in Defense, A National Security Organization, 522
Women's Sports Foundation, 571
Women's Western Golf Foundation, 523
Woodrow Wilson National Fellowship Foundation, 523
World Security Institute, 571
Worldstudio Foundation, 523
Xerox, 524
Yakama Nation Higher Education Program, 524

Program Index

100th Infantry Battalion Memorial Scholarship Fund, 252

911 Education Fund Scholarship Program, 433

A. Patrick Charnon Memorial Scholarship, 214

AAGS Joseph F. Dracup Scholarship Award, 91

AAJA Texas Student Scholarship, 189

Abbie Sargent Memorial Scholarship, 73

ABC Stores Jumpstart Scholarship, 252

Abe Voron Scholarship, 204

Academic Challenge Scholarship, 182

Academic Scholars Program, 400

Academic Scholarship for High School Seniors and GED Graduates, 370

Academic Scholarship for Undergraduate Students, 370

Academic-Year Ambassadorial Scholarship, 428

Accel Program Grant, 246

Access Missouri Financial Assistance Program, 337

Access to Better Learning and Education (ABLE) Grant Program, 240

Accuracy in Media Internships, 525

ACEC Scholarship, 94

ACSM Fellows Scholarship, 91

Actuarial Diversity Scholarships, 74

Actuary of Tomorrow Stuart A. Robertson Memorial Scholarship, 74

Ada I. Pressman Memorial Scholarship, 451

Ada Mucklestone Memorial Scholarship, 117

Adele Filene Student Presenter Grant, 224

ADHA Institute General Scholarships, 75

ADHA Institute Merit Scholarships, 75

ADHA Institute Part-Time Scholarship, 75

Adler Science and Math Scholarship, 124

Admiral Grace Murray Hopper Scholarship, 451

AdOhio Advertising Internship, 558

Adrienne Alix Scholarship, 138

Advertising Internship, 531

Aerospace Undergraduate Research Scholarship Program, 353

AFCEA General Emmett Paige Scholarship, 183

AFCEA General John A. Wickham Scholarship, 184

AFCEA ROTC Scholarship, 184

AFCEA Scholarship for Working Professionals, 184

AFPE Gateway to Research Scholarships, 97

AFSCMA/UNCF Union Scholars Program, 527

AFSCME Family Scholarship, 95

AG Bell College Scholarship Awards, 85

AGC Education and Research Undergraduate Scholarship, 195

AGC of Maine Scholarship Program, 196

Agnes Jones Jackson Scholarship, 341

Agnes Malakate Kezios Scholarship, 191

AHEPA Educational Foundation Scholarships, 100

Ahmad-Sehar Saleha Ahmad and Abrahim Ekramullah Zafar Foundation, 403

AIA New Jersey Scholarship Foundation, 106

AIAA Foundation Undergraduate Scholarship, 105

AIA/AAF Minority/Disadvantaged Scholarship, 105

AICP Heartland Chapter Scholarship, 198

AICP Scholarship, 199

Aiea General Hospital Association Scholarship, 253

Air Force Aid Society Education Grant, 79

Air Force Sergeants Association Scholarship, Airmen Memorial Foundation, and Chief Master Sergeants of the Air Force Scholarship Programs, 78

Air Traffic Control Full-Time Employee Student Scholarship, 79

Airgas-Jerry Baker Scholarship, 175

Airgas-Terry Jarvis Memorial Scholarship, 176

AIWF Culinary Scholarship, 507

A.J. Spielman Scholarship, 487

Alabama Junior/Community College Athletic Scholarship, 84

Alabama National Guard Educational Assistance Program, 83

Alabama Scholarship for Dependents of Blind Parents, 471

Alabama Student Assistance Program, 83

Alabama Student Grant Program, 83

Alaska Airlines Scholarship, 487

Alaska Family Education Loan, 573

Alaska Teacher Education Loan, 573

Albert E. Wischmeyer Memorial Scholarship Award, 441

Albert M. Lappin Scholarship, 120

Albert T. Marcoux Memorial Scholarship, 136

Albina Fuel Company Scholarship, 403

Albuquerque ARC/Toby Cross Scholarship, 162

Alcoa Foundation Sons and Daughters Scholarship Program, 85

Alexander Harris Scholarship, 487

Alexander M. Tanger Scholarship, 204

Alexia Foundation Grant and Scholarship, 85

Alfred T. Granger Student Art Fund, 507

Alice Glaisyer Warfield Memorial Scholarship, 493

ALISE Bohdan S. Wynar Research Paper Competition, 196

ALISE Research Grant, 197

ALISE/Dialog Methodology Paper Competition, 197

All Iowa Opportunity Scholarship, 297

Allan Eldin & Agnes Sutorik Geiger Scholarship Fund, 253

All-Arizona Academic Team, 181

Allcott/Hunt Share It Now II Scholarship, 403

Allen J. Baldwin Scholarship, 191

Allison E. Fisher Scholarship, 356

Allman Medical Scholarships, 335

Allstate Internships, 525

Alma White-Delta Kappa Gamma Scholarship, 253

Aloha Scholarship, 131

Alpha Beta Gamma National Scholarship, 87

Alpha Delta Kappa/Harriet Simmons Scholarship, 403

Alpha Mu Gamma Scholarships, 87

Alphonse A. Miele Scholarship, 496

Alphonso Deal Scholarship, 359

Alumnae Panhellenic Association Women's Scholarship, 87

Alwin B. Newton Scholarship, 172

AMBUCS Scholars-Scholarship for Therapists, 88

American Board of Funeral Service Education National Scholarship, 89

American Chemical Society Scholars Program, 90

American Conservatory Theater Production Internships, 526

American Council of Engineering Companies of Oregon Scholarship, 403

American Electric Power
Scholarship, 192

American Express Scholarship
Competition, 100

American Express Travel
Scholarship, 487

American Ex-Prisoner of War, Peter
Connacher Memorial
Scholarship, 404

American Federation of State, County,
and Municipal Employees
(AFSCME) Oregon Council
#75, 404

American Foundation for Aging
Research Fellowship, 97

American Hotel & Lodging
Educational Foundation Incoming
Freshman Scholarship
Competition, 101

American Legion Alabama Auxiliary
Scholarship, 107

American Legion Alabama Oratorical
Contest, 106

American Legion Alabama
Scholarship, 107

American Legion Alaska Auxiliary
Scholarship, 108

American Legion Alaska Auxiliary
Western District Scholarship, 108

American Legion Alaska Oratorical
Contest, 107

American Legion Americanism and
Government Test, 118

American Legion Arizona Auxiliary
Health Care Occupation
Scholarship, 108

American Legion Arizona Auxiliary
Nurses' Scholarship, 109

American Legion Arizona Oratorical
Contest, 108

American Legion Arkansas Auxiliary
Scholarships, 110

American Legion Arkansas Oratorical
Contest, 109

American Legion Arkansas
Scholarship, 109

American Legion Auxiliary
Department of Oregon
Scholarship, 144

American Legion Auxiliary National
President's Scholarship, 132

American Legion California Auxiliary
General Scholarships, 111

American Legion California
Oratorical Contest, 110

American Legion Department
Oratorical Awards, 122

American Legion Department
Oratorical Contest, 144

American Legion Department
Oratorical Contest, 151

American Legion Eagle Scout of the
Year, 132

American Legion Eagle Scout of the
Year, 150

American Legion Family
Scholarship, 118

American Legion Florida Auxiliary
Memorial Scholarship, 114

American Legion Florida Auxiliary
Scholarships, 115

American Legion Florida General
Scholarship, 114

American Legion Georgia Auxiliary
Scholarship, 115

American Legion High School
Oratorical Contest, 145

American Legion Idaho Auxiliary
Nurse's Scholarship, 116

American Legion Idaho
Scholarships, 115

American Legion Illinois Boy Scout
Scholarship, 116

American Legion Illinois Oratorical
Contest, 116

American Legion Illinois
Scholarships, 116

American Legion Indiana Oratorical
Contest, 118

American Legion Iowa Oratorical
Contest, 119

American Legion Kansas Auxiliary
Department Scholarships, 122

American Legion Kentucky Auxiliary
Mary Barrett Marshall
Scholarship, 122

American Legion Legacy
Scholarship, 132

American Legion Maine Auxiliary
Scholarship, 124

American Legion Maryland Auxiliary
Scholarship, 125

American Legion Maryland Boys
State Scholarship, 124

American Legion Maryland Oratorical
Contest, 124

American Legion Maryland
Scholarship, 125

American Legion Massachusetts
Auxiliary Scholarship, 126

American Legion Massachusetts
General and Nursing
Scholarships, 125

American Legion Michigan Auxiliary
Memorial Scholarship, 127

American Legion Michigan Oratorical
Contest, 126

American Legion Minnesota Auxiliary
Department Scholarship, 128

American Legion Minnesota
Legionnaire Insurance Trust
Scholarship, 127

American Legion Minnesota
Oratorical Contest, 128

American Legion Mississippi
Auxiliary Scholarship, 128

American Legion Missouri Auxiliary
Scholarship, 131

American Legion Montana Auxiliary
Scholarships (1), 131

American Legion Montana Auxiliary
Scholarships (2), 131

American Legion Music
Scholarship, 120

American Legion National High
School Oratorical Contest, 132

American Legion Nebraska Oratorical
Contest, 133

American Legion Nebraska
President's Scholarship, 134

American Legion Nevada Oratorical
Contest, 135

American Legion New Hampshire
Boys State Scholarship, 136

American Legion New Hampshire
Oratorical Contest, 136

American Legion New Jersey
Auxiliary Department
Scholarships, 139

American Legion New Jersey
Oratorical Contest, 139

American Legion New York Auxiliary
Scholarship, 141

American Legion New York
Oratorical Contest, 140

American Legion North Dakota
Auxiliary Scholarships, 142

American Legion North Dakota
Oratorical Contest, 142

American Legion Ohio Auxiliary Past
President's Parley Nurse's
Scholarship, 143

American Legion Ohio Auxiliary
Scholarship, 143

American Legion Ohio
Scholarships, 143

American Legion Oratorical
Contest, 115

American Legion Oratorical
Contest, 120

American Legion Oratorical
Contest, 141

American Legion Oregon Auxiliary
Department Nurses
Scholarship, 144

American Legion Press Club of New
Jersey and Post 170--Arthur
Dehardt Memorial Scholarship, 146

American Legion Puerto Rico
Auxiliary Nursing
Scholarships, 146

American Legion Rhode Island
Auxiliary Book Award, 146

American Legion Rhode Island
Oratorical Contest, 146

American Legion South Carolina
Auxiliary Scholarship, 147

American Legion South Carolina
Department Oratorical Contest, 147

American Legion South Dakota
Auxiliary Nurse's Scholarship, 147

American Legion South Dakota
Auxiliary Scholarships, 147

American Legion South Dakota
Educational Loan, 574

American Legion South Dakota
Oratorical Contest, 147

American Legion Tennessee
Oratorical Contest, 148

American Legion Texas Auxiliary
General Education Scholarship, 149

American Legion Texas Auxiliary Medical Scholarship, 149

American Legion Utah Auxiliary National President's Scholarship, 150

American Legion Vermont Scholarship, 150

American Legion Virginia Oratorical Contest, 151

American Legion Washington Auxiliary Scholarships, 152

American Legion Washington Scholarships, 151

American Legion West Virginia Auxiliary Scholarship, 153

American Legion West Virginia Oratorical Contest, 153

American Legion Western District Postsecondary Scholarship, 107

American Legion Wisconsin Auxiliary Department President's Scholarship, 154

American Legion Wisconsin Auxiliary H.S. and Angeline Lewis Scholarships, 154

American Legion Wisconsin Auxiliary Merit and Memorial Scholarship, 154

American Legion Wisconsin Auxiliary Past Presidents Parley Scholarship, 155

American Legion Wisconsin Eagle Scout of the Year Scholarship, 153

American Legion Wyoming Auxiliary Past Presidents' Parley Scholarship, 156

American Legion Wyoming E.A. Blackmore Memorial Scholarship, 155

American Legion Wyoming Oratorical Contest, 155

American Meteorological Society Undergraduate Scholarships, 156

American Meteorological Society/Industry Minority Scholarship, 157

American Quarter Horse Foundation Scholarships, 161

American Restaurant Scholarship, 301

American Society for Enology and Viticulture Scholarship Program, 170

American Society of International Law Internships, 528

American Water Ski Educational Foundation Scholarship, 175

American Welding Society District Scholarship Program, 176

Americanism Essay Contest Scholarship, 110

AMHI Educational Scholarships, 157

AMHI van Schaik Dressage Scholarship, 158

Amtrol Scholarship, 99

Angelo S. Bisesti Scholarship, 158

Anna Gear Junior Scholarship, 151

Anna K. Meredith Fund Scholarship, 473

Anne Ford and Allegra Ford Scholarship, 359

Anne Maureen Whitney Barrow Memorial, 452

Anne U. White Fund, 198

Annie's Homegrown Sustainable Agriculture Scholarships, 180

Annual Scholarship, 451

ANS Undergraduate Scholarships, 158

"Anthem" Essay Contest, 200

Anthropology Internship Program, 527

A.O. Smith Water Heaters Scholarship, 419

AOPA Air Safety Foundation/McAllister Memorial Scholarship, 83

Appaloosa Youth Foundation Educational Scholarships, 181

Applied Arts Internships, 530

Arboriculture Internship, 547

Area Go Texan Scholarships, 286

Arizona Chapter Dependent Scholarship, 487

Arizona Chapter Vertical Flight Engineering Scholarship, 100

Arizona Scholarship, 488

Arizona Tuition Scholarships for Children/Spouses of Slain Public Servants, 181

ARRL Earl I. Anderson Scholarship, 162

ARRL Scholarship Honoring Barry Goldwater, K7UGA, 162

Arsham Amirikian Engineering Scholarship, 176

Arthur and Doreen Parrett Scholarship, 187

Arthur and Gladys Cervenka Scholarship, 441

Arthur and Helen Copeland Scholarship for Females, 500

Arthur E. Copeland Scholarship, 500

Arthur K. Gilkey Memorial/William Putnam/Bedayn Research Grants, 88

Arthur M. and Berdena King Eagle Scout Scholarship, 377

Arthur Patch McKinlay Scholarship, 90

Artistic and Administrative Internships, 526

Arts & Business Council of New York Internship, 528

Arts Action Fund Internship, 528

Arts Policy Internship, 528

ASDSO Undergraduate Scholarship, 199

ASHRAE General Scholarships, 172

ASHRAE Memorial Scholarship, 172

ASHRAE Region IV Benny Bootle Scholarship, 172

ASHRAE Region VIII Scholarship, 173

ASLA Council of Fellows Scholarship, 314

ASM Outstanding Scholars Awards, 189

ASME Auxiliary Student Loan Fund, 574

ASME Auxiliary/FIRST Clarke Scholarship, 192

The ASME Foundation Hanley Scholarship, 192

ASME Foundation Scholarships, 192

ASME Power Division Scholarship, 192

ASME Student Loan Program, 574

ASNE Scholarship, 175

Aspiring Sports Journalist Internship, 564

Associated Press/APTRA-Clete Roberts Memorial Journalism Scholarship, 181

Assumption Program of Loans for Education (APLE), 574

Astrid G. Cates Scholarship Fund and Myrtle Beinhauer Scholarship, 465

A.T. Anderson Memorial Scholarship, 104

Athletic Trainers' Entry Level Scholarship, 358

Atlas Shrugged Essay Contest, 200

Atrisco Heritage Foundation Scholarship, 276

Audria M. Edwards Scholarship Fund, 414

Austin Family Scholarship Endowment, 101

Automotive Educational Fund Scholarship, 199

Averyl Elaine Keriakedes Memorial Scholarship, 134

Aviation Maintenance Technician Scholarship Award, 274

A.W. Bodine Sunkist Memorial Scholarship, 475

A.W. "Winn" Brindle Memorial Education Loan, 573

Award in Desert Studies, 244

AXA Achievement Scholarship in Association with U.S. News & World Report, 200

B. Bradford Barnes Scholarship, 230

B. K. Krenzer Re-entry Scholarship, 452

Bachelor's Scholarships, 402

Baker Hughes Scholarship, 452

Bal Dasa Scholarship Fund, 253

Ball Horticultural Company Scholarship, 95

Bandon Submarine Cable Council Scholarship, 404

Bank of the Cascades Scholarship, 404

Baroid Scholarship, 99

Barry K. Wendt Commitment Award and Scholarship, 377

Barry M. Goldwater Scholarship, 201

Batttelle Collegiate Scholarship, 373

Bay Area Council Scholarship Program, 201

BB&T Charitable Scholarship Program, 276

Bechtel Foundation Scholarship, 452

Bechtel Group Foundation Scholarship, 373

Behavioral Sciences Student Fellowship, 236

Ben Selling Scholarship, 404

Benjamin Franklin/Edith Green Scholarship, 405

Bern Laxer Memorial Scholarship, 301

Berna Lou Cartwright Scholarship, 191

Bernard B. Jacobs Internship Program, 552

Berntsen International Scholarship in Surveying, 91

Berntsen International Scholarship in Surveying Technology, 92

Bertha Lamme Memorial Scholarship, 453

Bertha P. Singer Scholarship, 405

Best Buy @15 Scholarship Program, 201

Best Teen Chef Culinary Scholarship Competition, 187

BIA San Diego Scholarship, 206

B.J. Harrod Scholarships, 453

Black Nurses Scholarship, 358

The BlackNews.com Scholarship Essay Contest, 202

Blossom Kalama Evans Memorial Scholarship, 253

Blue Bell Scholarship, 480

BMI Student Composer Awards, 203

BMW/SAE Engineering Scholarships, 430

Bob Baxter Scholarship, 368

Bob East Scholarship Fund, 368

Bob Hasson Memorial Scholarship Fund Essay, 402

Bob Zappatelli Memorial Scholarship, 301

Boeing Internships, 532

Bonus Incentive Grant (BIG), 289

Boston Globe Summer Internship, 532

Boston Scientific Scholarship, 453

Boy and Girl Scouts Scholarship, 233

Boy Scout of the Year Scholarship, 119

BP Corporate Scholarship, 373

Bradford White Scholarship, 419

Brill Family Scholarship, 453

Broadcast News Grants, 188

Bruce van Ess Scholarship, 299

Buckingham Memorial Scholarship, 80

Buckskin Horse Association Scholarship, 294

Bud Glover Memorial Scholarship, 80

Burlington Northern Santa Fe Foundation Scholarship, 104

Business Achievement Awards, 249

Business Reporting Intern Program, 534

Butler Manufacturing Company Foundation Scholarship, 207

C. J. Davidson Scholarship, 480

Cadbury Community Outreach Scholarships, 75

Caddie Scholarship, 384

Cady McDonnell Memorial Scholarship, 92

Cal Grant A & B Entitlement Award Program, 209

Cal Grant A and B Competitive Awards, 209

Cal Grant C Award, 209

California Chafee Grant Program, 209

California Child Development Grant Program, 210

California Farm Bureau Scholarship, 208

California Masonic Foundation Scholarship, 208

California Robert C. Byrd Honors Scholarship, 210

California Teachers Association Martin Luther King, Jr., Memorial Scholarship, 210

California's Junior Miss Competition, 208

Calvin Coolidge Memorial Foundation Scholarship, 507

Camille C. Chidiac Fund, 254

Canada Scholarship, 488

Candon, Todd, & Seabolt Scholarship Fund, 254

Captain James J. Regan Memorial Scholarship, 317

C.A.R. Scholarship, 207

Cargill Scholarship Program, 498

Carl N. & Margaret Karcher Founders' Scholarship, 212

Carole Fielding Video Grant, 501

Carole Simpson Scholarship, 356

Carole Simpson Scholarship, 424

Caroline Kark Scholarship, 386

Caroline Thorn Kissel Summer Environmental Studies Scholarship, 244

Carville M. Akehurst Memorial Scholarship, 284

Castle & Cooke Mililani Technology Park Scholarship Fund, 254

Castle & Cooke W. Y. Yim Scholarship Fund, 254

Caterpillar Corporate Scholarship, 373

Caterpillar Inc. Scholarship, 454

Caterpillar Scholars Award, 442

Cayetano Foundation Scholarship, 255

CBC Scholarship, 221

The CBC Spouses Cheerios Brand Health Initiative Scholarship, 220

The CBC Spouses Education Scholarship, 220

The CBC Spouses Performing Arts Scholarship Program, 220

The CBC Spouses Visual Arts Scholarship, 220

CCNMA Scholarship, 213

Center for Architecture Design Scholarship, 213

Central New Mexico Scholarship, 454

C.G. Fuller Foundation Scholarship, 215

Chafee Education and Training Grant (ETG) Program, 415

Chafee Education and Training Scholarship, 405

Challenge Met Scholarship, 162

Champlain Valley Kennel Club Scholarship, 507

Chapter 17 St. Louis Scholarship, 442

Chapter 198 - Downriver Detroit Scholarship, 442

Chapter 4 - Lawrence A. Wacker Memorial Scholarship, 442

Chapter 52 - Wichita Scholarship, 443

Chapter 56 - Fort Wayne Scholarship, 443

Chapter 6 - Fairfield County Scholarship, 443

Chapter 67 - Phoenix Scholarship, 443

Charles & Lucille King Family Foundation Scholarships, 215

Charles and Annette Hill Scholarship, 121

Charles and Melva T. Owen Memorial Scholarship, 362

Charles B. Scharp Scholarship, 191

Charles Clarke Cordle Memorial Scholarship, 162

Charles E. Leonard Memorial Scholarship, 508

Charles Evans Scholarship, 464

Charles Hardy Memorial Scholarship, 436

Charles L. Bacon Memorial Scholarship, 129

Charles L. Hebner Memorial Scholarship, 230

Charles N. Fisher Memorial Scholarship, 163

Charles R. Ford Scholarship, 305

Charles (Tommy) Thomas Memorial Scholarship, 158

Charles W. Riley Fire and Emergency Medical Services Tuition Reimbursement Program, 324

Charleston Women in International Trade Scholarship, 216

Charlotte Woods Memorial Scholarship, 494

CHCI Congressional Internship, 533

Chefs of Louisiana Cookery Scholarship, 301

CHESLA Loan Program, 575

Chester Haddan Scholarship Program, 412

Chester M. Vernon Memorial Eagle Scout Scholarship, 366

Chevron Corporation Scholarships, 454

Chevron Internship Program, 532

Chicago FM Club Scholarship, 163

Chicago Scholars Program, 216

Chick Evans Caddie Scholarship, 519
Children and Youth Scholarships, 123
Children of Veterans Tuition
  Grant, 330
Chittenden Bank Scholarship, 508
Choctaw Nation Higher Education
  Program, 216
Christa McAuliffe Memorial
  Scholarship, 137
Christa McAuliffe Teacher Incentive
  Program, 575
Christian Record Services
  Scholarship, 217
Christian Wolffer Scholarship, 301
Christine H. Eidie Memorial
  Scholarship, 318
Chrysler Foundation Scholarship, 454
CIA Undergraduate Scholarship
  Program, 214
CIEE International Study Programs
  (CIEE-ISP) Scholarships, 224
CITE Scholarship, 223
Citizens for Global Solutions
  Internship, 533
City University SEEK/College
  Discovery Program, 387
Claire Oliphant Memorial
  Scholarship, 139
Clare Brett Smith Scholarship, 473
The Clarence & Josephine Myers
  Scholarship, 443
Clark-Phelps Scholarship, 405
Clat Triplette Scholarship, 302
Clinton J. Helton Manufacturing
  Scholarship Award, 444
CLN Scholarships, 223
The Cloisters Summer Internship
  Program, 545
Coca-Cola All-State Community
  Colleges Academic Team
  Scholarship, 217
Coca-Cola Scholars Program, 217
Colgate "Bright Smiles, Bright
  Futures" Minority Scholarships, 76
College Access Loan (CAL), 584
College Bound Fund Academic
  Promise Scholarship, 427
College Photographer of the Year
  Competition, 369
College Scholarship Program, 219
College Television Awards, 73
CollegeSTEPS Program, 516
Collegiate Inventors Competition, 365
Colon Furr Scholarship, 141
Colorado Masons Scholarship, 219
Colorado Student Grant, 218
Colorado Supplemental Leveraging
  Educational Assistance Partnership
  (SLEAP), 218
Colorado Work-Study Program, 218
Commander's Scholarship Fund, 129
Community College Grant &
  Loan, 581
Community Scholarship Fund, 255
Community Service Award, 249
Computer Science Scholarship, 362

Concurrent Enrollment Waiver
  (Enrollment in Two Texas
  Community Colleges), 481
Congressional Hispanic Caucus
  Institute Scholarship Awards, 220
Congressional Institute
  Internships, 533
Connecticut Aid for Public College
  Students, 221
Connecticut Aid to Dependents of
  Deceased/POW/MIA Veterans, 221
Connecticut Capitol Scholarship
  Program, 221
Connecticut Independent College
  Student Grant, 222
Connecticut Minority Teacher
  Incentive Grant, 222
Connecticut Robert C. Byrd Honors
  Scholarship, 222
Connecticut Scholarship, 488
Connecticut Tuition Waiver for Senior
  Citizens, 222
Connecticut Tuition Waiver for
  Veterans, 222
Connecticut Tuition Waiver for
  Vietnam MIA/POW
  Dependents, 223
Connie and Robert T. Gunter
  Scholarship, 444
Construction Trades Scholarship, 358
Contiki Vacations Scholarship, 488
Continuing or Re-entry Student
  Scholarship, 111
Cooperative Internship Programs, 535
Cora Aguda Manayan Fund, 255
Core Scholarship, 360
Costas G. Lemonopoulos
  Scholarship, 357
Courtland Paul Scholarship, 314
Crest Oral-B Dental Hygiene
  Scholarship, 76
Critical Needs Alternative Route
  Teacher Loan/Scholarship, 578
Critical Teacher Shortage Student
  Loan Forgiveness Program, 576
CRT Internship Program, 533
CTA Scholarship for Dependent
  Children, 211
CTA Scholarships for Members, 211
Cummins Inc. Corporate
  Scholarship, 373
Cummins Scholarship, 455
Cushman School Internship, 533
The Cynthia E. Morgan Memorial
  Scholarship Fund, 226
Cystic Fibrosis Student
  Traineeship, 226
D. Fred and Mariam L. Bovie
  Scholarship, 176
D. Fred and Mariam L. Bovie
  Technical Scholarship, 177
Dairy Student Recognition
  Program, 360
Dallas Architectural Foundation -
  Humphries/HKS Scholarship, 226
Dallas Architectural Foundation -
  Swank Travelling Fellowship, 227

Dan McKeever Scholarship
  Program, 412
Dana Christmas Scholarship for
  Heroism, 382
Daniel E. Lambert Memorial
  Scholarship, 123
Darfur Humanitarian Essay, 405
Darlene Hooley for Oregon Veterans
  Scholarship, 405
Darrel Hess Community College
  Geography Scholarship, 198
Datatel Scholars Foundation
  Scholarship, 229
Dave Herren Memorial
  Scholarship, 489
David Alan Quick Scholarship, 237
David Arver Memorial
  Scholarship, 80
David Family Scholarship, 406
David J. Fitzmaurice Scholarship, 299
David J. Hallissey Memorial
  Internship, 565
David L. Irons Memorial Scholarship
  Fund, 255
David L. Stashower Scholarship, 318
David T. Woolsey Scholarship, 315
Davidson Fellows Scholarship, 229
Davis-Roberts Scholarship, 229
Dayco Scholarship Program, 466
The Dayton Amateur Radio
  Association Scholarships, 163
DC Adoption Scholarship, 232
DC Tuition Assistance Grant Program
  (DCTAG), 232
Decommissioning, Decontamination
  and Reutilization Scholarship, 159
DEED Student Research Grants, 161
Delaware Nursing Incentive
  Program, 575
Delaware Scholarship Incentive
  Program, 230
Delaware Space Grant Undergraduate
  Research Internship, 549
Delaware Space Grant Undergraduate
  Tuition Scholarship, 344
Delayed Education Scholarship for
  Women, 159
Dell Inc. Scholarship, 455
Della Van Deuren Memorial
  Scholarship, 155
Delta Faucet Company
  Scholarship, 419
Delta Gamma Foundation Florence
  Margaret Harvey Memorial
  Scholarship, 98
Denny Lydic Scholarship, 494
Denver Rescue Mission Center for
  Mission Studies Internships, 534
Department of Commerce Internship
  for Postsecondary Students, 554
Department of Iowa Scholarships, 119
Department of Massachusetts
  Oratorical Contest, 125
Department of New Hampshire
  Scholarship, 137
Department Oratorical Awards, 143

Department President's Scholarship, 112

Department President's Scholarship for Junior Auxiliary Members, 112

Department Vocational Scholarship, 137

Deseo at the Westin Scholarship, 302

Detroit Chapter One - Founding Chapter Scholarship Award, 444

Developmental Disability Scholastic Achievement Scholarship, 202

Diamond State Scholarship, 230

Directors Scholarship, 444

Disabled War Veterans Scholarship, 184

Discover Scholarship Program, 231

Disney College Program, 569

Disney Theme Parks & Resorts Professional Internships, 569

Distance Learning/Online Scholarship, 185

District of Columbia Leveraging Educational Assistance Partnership Program, 232

DMI Milk Marketing Scholarships, 360

DOE Pre-Service Teacher Internships, 554

Dolly Ching Scholarship Fund, 255

Dolphin Scholarship, 232

Donald A. Williams Soil Conservation Scholarship, 463

Donald and Shirley Hastings National Scholarship, 177

Donald Burnside Memorial Scholarship, 180

Donald F. Hastings Scholarship, 177

Donald Riebhoff Memorial Scholarship, 163

Doris & Clarence Glick Classical Music Scholarship, 256

Dorothy Campbell Memorial Scholarship, 406

Dorothy Lemke Howarth Scholarships, 455

Dorothy M. & Earl S. Hoffman Scholarships, 455

Dorothy P. Morris Scholarship, 456

DPMA/PC Scholarship, 228

Dr. & Mrs. Arthur William Phillips Scholarship, 417

Dr. Alfred C. Fones Scholarship, 76

Dr. Alvin and Monica Saake Scholarship, 256

Dr. and Mrs. Moon Park Scholarship, 256

Dr. Click Cowger Scholarship, 121

Dr. Dan J. and Patricia S. Pickard Scholarship, 227

Dr. Don and Rose Marie Benton Scholarship, 227

Dr. Hannah K. Vuolo Memorial Scholarship, 140

Dr. Hans & Clara Zimmerman Foundation Education Scholarship, 256

Dr. Hans and Clara Zimmerman Foundation Health Scholarship, 257

Dr. Harold Hillenbrand Scholarship, 76

Dr. James L. Lawson Memorial Scholarship, 163

Dr. Kate Waller Barrett Grant, 151

Dr. W. Wes Eckenfelder Jr. Scholarship, 206

Dual Enrollment Grant, 477

Duane Hanson Scholarship, 173

DuPont Company Scholarship, 456

DuPont Co-ops, 535

DuPont Internships, 535

Dutch and Ginger Arver Scholarship, 80

E. Wayne Kay Community College Scholarship, 445

E. Wayne Kay Co-op Scholarship, 445

E. Wayne Kay High School Scholarship, 445

E. Wayne Kay Scholarship, 445

Eagle Scout of the Year, 114

Eagle Scout of the Year Scholarship, 148

Earl & Patricia Armstrong Scholarship, 498

Earl Dedman Memorial Scholarship, 95

Earl G. Graves Scholarship, 342

Early Childhood Development Scholarship, 310

Eastside & Northshore Kauai Scholarship Fund, 257

Ecolab Scholarship Competition, 101

Economic Research Division Project Internships, 532

Ed Bradley Scholarship, 424

Ed Markham International Scholarship, 96

Edgar J. Boschult Memorial Scholarship, 134

Edmond A. Metzger Scholarship, 164

Edmund F. Maxwell Foundation Scholarship, 233

Edna M. Barcus Memorial Scholarship and Hoosier Scholarship, 118

The EDSA Minority Scholarship, 315

Education Achievement Awards, 249

Education and Leadership Development Program, 300

Educational Aide Exemption, 481

Educational Benefits for Children of Deceased Veterans and Others, 231

Edward D. Hendrickson/SAE Engineering Scholarship, 430

Edward J. Brady Memorial Scholarship, 177

Edward J. Dulis Scholarship, 189

Edward J. Nell Memorial Scholarship, 424

Edward Payson and Bernice Pi'ilani Irwin Scholarship Trust Fund, 257

Edward S. Roth Manufacturing Engineering, 446

E.E. Black Scholarship, 257

Eight and Forty Lung and Respiratory Nursing Scholarship Fund, 132

Eizo & Toyo Sakumoto Trust Scholarship, 257

Eleanor Allwork Scholarship, 213

Electronics for Imaging Scholarship, 456

Elena Albano "Maka'alohilohi" Scholarship Fund, 258

Elie Wiesel Prize in Ethics, 233

Elizabeth A. Sackler Museum Educational Trust, 473

Elizabeth Dow Ltd. Internships, 530

The Elizabeth Greenshields Grant, 233

Elizabeth McLean Memorial Scholarship, 456

Elks Most Valuable Student Scholarship, 234

Elks National Foundation Legacy Awards, 234

Ellison Onizuka Memorial Scholarship, 258

Elsie B. Brown Scholarship Fund, 138

Emanuele and Emilia Inglese Memorial Scholarship, 365

Emily Lester Vermont Opportunity Scholarship, 508

Endowment Fund For Education (EFFE), 202

Engineering Scholarship Program, 481

Engineering Technology Scholarships, 173

Engineering/Technology Achievement Awards, 249

Engineers Foundation of Ohio Scholarships, 234

Entergy Jumpstart Co-ops and Internships, 536

Entertainment Weekly Internship Program, 536

The Entomological Foundation BioQuip Undergraduate Scholarship, 234

EPA National Network for Environmental Management Studies Fellowship, 503

Epilepsy Foundation of San Diego County Scholarship, 236

Erman W. Taylor Memorial Scholarship, 129

ESA Foundation Scholarship Program, 236

ESPN Internship, 536

Essence Summer Internship, 537

Esther Kanagawa Memorial Art Scholarship, 258

E.U. Parker Memorial Scholarship, 362

Eugene Bennet Visual Arts Scholarship, 406

Eugene C. Figg Jr. Civil Engineering Scholarship, 171

Eugene "Gene" Sallee, W4YFR Memorial Scholarship, 164

Eugenia Vellner Fischer Award for the Performing Arts, 336

Executive Women International Scholarship, 237
Exelon Scholarship, 457
Exemption for Peace Officers Disabled in the Line of Duty, 482
Exemption for the Surviving Spouse and Dependent Children of Certain Deceased Public Servants (Employees), 482
Explorers Club Youth Activity Fund, 238
Extrusion Division/Lew Erwin Memorial Scholarship, 448
ExxonMobil Corporate Scholarship, 374
F. Koehnen Ltd. Scholarship Fund, 258
Fashion Group International of Portland Scholarship, 406
Father James B. Macelwane Annual Award, 157
Federal Direct Stafford Loans, 585
Federal Employee Education and Assistance Fund Scholarship, 238
Federal Family Education Loan Program (FFEL), 585
Federal Pell Grant Program, 502
Federal Perkins Loan, 585
Federal Plus Loan, 586
Federal Supplemental Educational Opportunity Grant Program, 502
Federal Work-Study Program, 502
Feminism & Leadership Internship, 537
Ferdinand Torres Scholarship, 98
FFA Scholarships, 481
FFRF Student/Youth Activist Award, 243
Field Aviation Co. Inc. Scholarship, 81
Field Botany Scholarships, 245
Fifth Floor Restaurant Scholarship, 302
The Filipino Nurses' Organization of Hawaii Scholarship, 259
Filoli Center Garden Internships and Apprenticeships, 538
Finance Undergraduate Internships, 568
Financial Women International Scholarship, 259
First Catholic Slovak Ladies Association Scholarship Program, 239
First Marine Division Association Scholarship, 239
Fisher Broadcasting Company Scholarship for Minorities, 240
Fitz Dixon Memorial Scholarship, 417
Fleming/Blaszcak Scholarship, 448
Fletcher & Fritzi Hoffmann Education Fund, 259
Flight 587 Memorial Scholarships, 387
Florence Lemcke Memorial Scholarship, 152

Florida Academic Scholars Award, 240
Florida Gold Seal Vocational Scholars Award, 240
Florida Medallion Scholars Award, 241
Florida Power & Light Internship Program, 538
Florida Scholarship, 489
Florida Student Assistance Grant Program, 241
Florida Work Experience Program, 538
Floyd Qualls Memorial Scholarship, 94
Fontainebleau Prize, 214
Foodservice Communicators Scholarship, 294
Ford Motor Company Scholarship, 457
Ford Motor Company/American Indian College Fund Corporate Scholars Program, 102
Ford Opportunity Program, 406
Ford Scholars Program, 407
Foundation Scholarship, 102
Foundation Student Scholarship, 242
The Fountainhead Essay Contest, 200
Four-Year Nursing Scholarship, 429
Four-Year Scholarship, 429
Fox Internship, 538
Fran Johnson Non-Traditional Scholarship, 96
Francis M. Peacock Native Bird Habitat Scholarship, 245
Frank and Dorothy Miller ASME Auxiliary Scholarships, 193
Frank D. Visceglia Memorial Scholarship, 204
Frank L. Weil Memorial Eagle Scout Scholarship, 367
Frank M. Coda Scholarship, 173
Frank O'Bannon Grant, 471
Frank Stenzel M.D. and Kathryn Stenzel II Scholarship, 407
Franklin Lindsay Student Aid Loan, 576
Fred G. Zahn Foundation Scholarship, 243
Fred M. Young, Sr./SAE Engineering Scholarship, 430
Fred R. McDaniel Memorial Scholarship, 164
The Fred Rogers Memorial Scholarship, 73
Freeman Fellowship, 171
Freshman Undergraduate Scholarship Program, 157
Friends of Hawaii Public Housing Scholarship, 259
Fulfilling the Legacy Scholarship, 374
Future Leaders of Manufacturing Scholarships, 446
Future Teachers Scholarship, 400
F.W. "Beich" Beichley Scholarship, 193
Gabe A. Hartl Scholarship, 80

Gabriel Prize, 519
Gaining Early Awareness and Readiness for Undergraduate Programs (GEAR UP) Scholarship, 415
Garden Club of America Summer Environmental Awards, 245
Garland Duncan Scholarships, 193
Garmin Scholarship, 81
Gary J. Miller Undergraduate Prizes for Cancer and Cancer-Related Biomedical Research, 88
Gates Millennium Scholars Program, 498
GCA Internship in Garden History and Design, 539
GCSAA Legacy Awards, 235
GCSAA Scholars Competition, 235
GCSAA Student Essay Contest, 235
GE Business/Engineering Scholarship for Minority Students, 316
GEICO Life Scholarship, 249
Genentech, Inc. Internship Program, 539
General College Scholarship, 276
General Electric Foundation Scholarship, 457
General Electric Women's Network Scholarship, 457
General Fund Scholarship, 164
General John Paul Ratay Educational Fund Grants, 332
General Motors Foundation Scholarships, 457
General Scholarship, 219
General Scholarship, 464
Geography Students Internship, 551
George A. Hall/Harold F. Mayfield Award, 520
George A. Roberts Scholarships, 190
The George Foreman Tribute to Lyndon B. Johnson Scholarship, 424
George M. Brooker Collegiate Scholarship for Minorities, 293
George Mason Business Scholarship Fund, 259
George Reinke Scholarship, 489
Georgia Hope Grant - GED Recipient, 246
Georgia Hope Grant - Public Technical Institution, 246
Georgia Hope Scholarship - Private Institution, 246
Georgia Hope Scholarship - Public College or University, 247
Georgia Law Enforcement Personnel Dependents Grant, 247
Georgia LEAP Grant, 247
Georgia Promise Teacher Scholarship, 576
Georgia Robert C. Byrd Scholarship, 247
Georgia Tuition Equalization Grant, 247
Georgia-Pacific Internship and Co-op Programs, 539

Gerrit R. Ludwig Scholarship, 260
G.I. Dependents' Scholarship
    Program, 84
Ginger and Fred Deines Canada
    Scholarship, 494
Ginger and Fred Deines Mexico
    Scholarship, 494
Girl Scout Achievement Award, 133
Giuliano Mazzetti Scholarship, 446
GlaxoSmithKline Opportunity
    Scholarship, 392
Glenn Jackson Scholars, 407
Global Challenge Awards, 248
Global Change Education
    Program, 554
Go Higher Grant, 310
Gold Star Scholarship Program, 378
Golden Apple Scholars of Illinois
    Program, 248
Golden LEAF Scholars Program -
    Two-Year Colleges, 393
Golden LEAF Scholarship - Four-Year
    University Program, 393
Goldman Family Fund: New Leader
    Scholarship, 323
Goldman, Sachs and Co.
    Scholarship, 458
Good Eats Scholarship Fund, 260
Google Hispanic College Fund
    Scholarship Program, 275
Government and Public Affairs
    Internship, 528
Governor Terry E. Branstad Iowa
    State Fair Scholarship, 297
Governor's High School Merit
    Scholarship, 339
Governor's Merit-at-Large
    Scholarship, 340
Governor's Need Based
    Scholarship, 340
Governor's Scholars Program, 182
Grace Pacific Outstanding Scholars
    Fund, 260
Grace S. High Memorial Child
    Welfare Scholarship Fund, 138
Graduate, Baccalaureate or
    Coordinated Program
    Scholarships, 94
Grand Army of the Republic Living
    Memorial Scholarship, 229
Grange Denise Scholarship, 386
Grange Insurance Scholarship, 251
Grange Student Loan Fund, 581
Grange Susan W. Freestone Education
    Award, 386
Grant Program for Dependents of
    Correctional Officers, 289
Grant Program for Dependents of
    Police or Fire Officers, 289
Great Lakes Colleges
    Association/Associated Colleges of
    the Midwest Oak Ridge Science
    Semester, 554
Great Minds in Stem Scholars
    Program, 251
Greater Kanawha Valley Scholarship
    Program, 251

Greater Research Opportunities
    Undergraduate Student
    Fellowships, 504
Greenhouse Scholars, 251
The Grotto Scholarships, 475
Grow Your Own Teacher Scholarship
    Program, 287
Guggenheim Museum Internship, 563
Gulf Coast Hurricane
    Scholarships, 449
Guy M. Wilson Scholarship, 126
Guy Marshall Scholarship Fund, 260
HACU (Hispanic Association of
    Colleges and Universities)
    Scholarships, 104
HACU National Internship
    Program, 540
Hall/McElwain Merit
    Scholarship, 361
Hank LeBonne Scholarship, 363
Hannaford Internships, 539
Hansen Scholarship, 237
Harness Tracks of America
    Scholarship Fund, 252
Harold Bettinger Memorial
    Scholarship, 96
Harold K. Douthit Scholarship, 398
Harriet Hoffman Memorial
    Scholarship, 120
Harriet Irsay Scholarship, 106
Harry & Lorraine Ausprich Endowed
    Scholarship for the Arts, 417
Hattie Tedrow Memorial Fund
    Scholarship, 142
Hawaii Chuck Yim Gee
    Scholarship, 489
Hawaii Pacific Gerontological Society
    Nursing Scholarship Fund, 260
Hawaii Pizza Hut Scholarship
    Fund, 261
Hawaii Society of Certified Public
    Accountants Scholarship Fund, 261
Hawaiian Homes Commission
    Scholarship, 261
HCF Scholarship Program, 275
Health Career Scholarship, 296
Healthy Waters Institute of the
    Freshwater Trust, 407
Hearst Journalism Award, 519
Heartland Scholarship Fund, 400
Helen J. Sioussat/Fay Wells
    Scholarship, 204
Helping Heroes Grant, 477
Henry A. Zuberano Scholarship, 261
Henry Adams Scholarship, 174
Henry Broughton, K2AE Memorial
    Scholarship, 165
Henry Buschong Scholarship, 244
Henry J. Reilly Memorial College
    Scholarship, 426
Henry Salvatori Scholarship, 464
Herbert & Ollie Brook Fund, 261
Herbert Lehman Educational
    Fund, 343
Herman M. Holloway, Sr. Memorial
    Scholarship, 231

Herman O. West Foundation
    Scholarship Program, 516
Hermione Grant Calhoun
    Scholarship, 363
Herschel C. Price Educational
    Scholarship, 274
Hideko & Zenzo Matsuyama
    Scholarship Fund, 262
High Honors Endorsement Tuition
    Scholarship, 182
High School Oratorical Contest, 114
Higher Education Grant Program, 207
Higher Education License Plate
    (HELP) Program, 290
Higher REACH Scholarship, 513
Highmark Scholarship, 417
Hilo Chinese School Scholarship, 262
Hirsch Family Scholarship, 227
Hispanic Division Huntington
    Fellowship, 544
Hispanic Heritage Youth Awards
    Program, 276
Historically Black Colleges and
    Minority Institutions
    Scholarships, 203
Hoffman-La Roche Inc. Student
    Internship, 540
Hokuli'a Foundation Scholarship
    Fund, 262
Homestead Capital Housing
    Scholarship, 408
Hon Chew Hee Scholarship Fund, 262
Honeywell Avionics Scholarship, 81
Honeywell International Inc.
    Scholarship, 458
Ho'omaka Hou Scholarship, 262
Hooper Memorial Scholarship, 494
Hope Foster Child Tuition Grant, 477
HOPE-Aspire Award, 477
Hope-General Assembly Merit
    Scholarship, 478
Hopi BIA Higher Education
    Grant, 279
Hopi Education Award, 279
Hopi Tribal Priority Award, 279
Horatio Alger Ak-Sar-Ben Scholarship
    Program, 280
Horatio Alger Arizona
    Scholarship, 280
Horatio Alger California Scholarship
    Program, 280
Horatio Alger Delaware Scholarship
    Program, 280
Horatio Alger District of Columbia,
    Maryland and Virginia Scholarship
    Program, 281
Horatio Alger Franklin
    Scholarship, 281
Horatio Alger Georgia Scholarship
    Program, 281
Horatio Alger Idaho Scholarship
    Program, 281
Horatio Alger Illinois Scholarship
    Program, 282
Horatio Alger Louisiana Scholarship
    Program, 282

Horatio Alger Minnesota Scholarship
Program, 282
Horatio Alger Missouri Scholarship
Program, 282
Horatio Alger Montana Scholarship
Program, 282
Horatio Alger National
Scholarship, 283
Horatio Alger North Dakota
Scholarship Program, 283
Horatio Alger Pennsylvania
Scholarship Program, 283
Horatio Alger South Dakota
Scholarship Program, 283
Horatio Alger Texas Ft. Worth
Scholarship Program, 284
Horatio Alger Texas Scholarship
Program, 284
Horatio Alger Utah Scholarship
Program, 284
Horatio Alger Wyoming Scholarship
Program, 284
Horizons Scholarship, 522
Horticultural Research Institute Spring
Meadow Scholarship, 285
House Member Internships, 567
Houston Livestock Show and Rodeo
Scholarships, 480
Howard Brown Rickard
Scholarship, 363
Howard E. and Wilma J. Adkins
Memorial Scholarship, 177
Howard P. Rawlings Guaranteed
Access Grant, 324
H.P. "Bud" Milligan Aviation
Scholarship, 237
HSBC-North America Scholarship
Program, 277
Hubertus W.V. Wellems Scholarship
for Male Students, 342
Hudner Medal of Honor
Scholarship, 238
Hu-Friedy/Esther Wilkins Instrument
Scholarships, 77
Hugh A. Smith Scholarship, 121
Humane Studies Fellowship, 292
The Hyatt Hotels Fund for Minority
Lodging Management Students
Competition, 101
Iager Dairy Scholarship, 360
Ian Doane Smith Scholarship
Fund, 263
IBM Co-op and Intern Program, 540
IBM Corporation Scholarship, 458
Ida M. Crawford Scholarship, 408
Ida M. Pope Memorial
Scholarship, 263
Idaho Education Incentive Loan
Forgiveness Program, 577
Idaho Governor's Cup
Scholarship, 287
Idaho Minority/"At-Risk"
Scholarship, 287
Idaho Robert C. Byrd
Scholarship, 288
IEHA Educational Foundation
Scholarship, 294

Illinois Future Teacher Corps, 290
Illinois General Assembly Legislative
Scholarships, 289
Illinois National Guard Grant, 290
Illinois Veteran Grant (IVG)
Program, 290
Independent Living Act (Department
of Human Services Tuition
Waiver), 401
Indian American Scholarship, 501
Indiana Minority Teacher & Special
Education Services
Scholarship, 472
Indiana National Guard Supplemental
Grant, 472
Indiana Nursing Scholarship, 472
Indiana Robert C. Byrd Honors
Scholarship, 472
Indiana Twenty-First Century Scholars
Program, 472
Industrial Automation Engineering
College Scholarships, 188
Inn at Blackberry Farm
Scholarship, 302
INROADS Internship, 541
Institute of Food Technologists
Freshman Scholarship, 292
Institute of Food Technologists
Junior/Senior Scholarship, 292
Institute of Food Technologists
Sophomore Scholarship, 293
Institutional Scholarship Waivers, 84
Intel International Science and
Engineering Fair, 440
Intel Science Talent Search, 440
Intelligence Scholarships, 185
International Furnishings and Design
Association Educational Foundation
Leaders Commemorative
Scholarship, 295
International Furnishings and Design
Association Student Member
Scholarships, 295
International Gas Turbine Institute
(IGTI) Scholarship, 193
International Incentive Awards, 474
International Radio and Television
Society Foundation Summer
Fellowship Program, 541
International Semester
Scholarship, 104
International Studies Scholarship, 374
Internship and Co-op Program, 530
Internship Program for Laboratory
Technology, 555
Internships at Macy's and
Bloomingdale's, 544
Iowa Farm Bureau Federation
Scholarship, 297
Iowa Grant, 297
Iowa National Guard Educational
Assistance Program, 298
Iowa Robert C. Byrd Honor
Scholarship, 298
Iowa Tuition Grant, 298
Iowa Vocational-Technical Tuition
Grant, 298

Irene E. Newman Scholarship, 77
Irving W. Cook WA0CGS
Scholarship, 165
Isemoto Contracting Co., Ltd.
Scholarship Fund, 263
ISFA Education Foundation College
Scholarship, 293
Italian Catholic Federation
Scholarship, 299
Italian Language Scholarship, 464
ITT Scholarship, 458
Ivy Parker Memorial Scholarship, 459
J. Richard Mehalick Scholarship, 174
Jack A. & Marilyn MacAllister
Foundation, 102
Jack R. Barckhoff Welding
Management Scholarship, 178
Jackson Foundation Journalism
Scholarship, 408
Jacob Van Namen Marketing
Scholarship, 96
Jagannathan Scholarship, 393
James A. Turner, Jr. Memorial
Scholarship, 178
James B. Carey Scholarship, 299
James Bridenbaugh Memorial
Scholarship, 96
James Carlson Memorial
Scholarship, 408
James E. Webb Internship Program for
Minority Undergraduate Seniors
and Graduate Students in Business
and Public Administration, 562
James F. Byrnes Scholarship, 304
James Hughes Memorial Scholarship
Fund, 417
James L. Allhands Essay
Competition, 195
James V. Day Scholarship, 123
Janet Jackson Rhythm Nation
Scholarships, 499
Japanese American General
Scholarship, 305
Japanese American Music Scholarship
Competition, 305
Jaycee War Memorial
Scholarship, 305
Jean Fitzgerald Scholarship Fund, 263
Jeanette Rankin Foundation
Scholarship, 306
Jeanne E. Bray Law Enforcement
Dependents Scholarship, 371
Jeannette C. Eyerly Memorial
Scholarship, 363
Jedidiah Zabrosky Scholarship, 508
Jeffrey Alan Scoggins Memorial
Scholarship, 408
Jennifer C. Groot Fellowship, 90
Jennifer Curtis Byler Scholarship
Fund for the Study of Public
Affairs, 378
Jennifer Ritzmann Scholarship for
Studies in Tropical Biology, 224
Jere W. Thompson, Jr. Scholarship
Fund, 227
Jerome B. Steinbach Scholarship, 409
Jerry Clark Memorial Scholarship, 95

Jewish Vocational Service Scholarship Fund, 306

Jewish War Veterans of the United States of America Bernard Rotberg Memorial Scholarship, 306

Jewish War Veterans of the United States of America JWV Grant, 306

Jewish War Veterans of the United States of America XX Olympiad Memorial Award, 307

JFCS Scholarship Fund, 577

Jill S. Tietjen P.E. Scholarship, 459

Jimi Lott Scholarship, 369

Jimmy A. Young Memorial Education Recognition Award, 169

J.K. Rathmell, Jr. Memorial Scholarship for Work/Study Abroad, 97

The Joel Abromson Memorial Scholarship, 236

Joel Polsky Academic Achievement Award, 174

John & Elsa Gracik Scholarships, 194

John A. High Child Welfare Scholarship, 137

John and Geraldine Hobble Licensed Practical Nursing Scholarship, 121

John and Muriel Landis Scholarship, 159

John C. Lincoln Memorial Scholarship, 178

John Dawe Dental Education Fund, 263

John Deere Student Training Programs, 542

John E. Bowman Travel Grants, 225

John F. Kennedy Scholars Award, 329

John Joseph Moakely Democratic Internship, 545

John L. Dales Standard Scholarship, 434

John L. Dales Transitional Scholarship, 434

John Lennon Scholarships, 203

John M. Haniak Scholarship, 190

John McKee Scholarship, 329

John R. Lamarsh Scholarship, 159

John W. Anderson Foundation Scholarship, 499

John Wiley and Sons, Inc. Internship Program, 543

Johnny Davis Memorial Scholarship, 81

Johnson & Johnson Scholarships, 77

Johnson Controls Co-op and Internship Programs, 543

Jose D. Garcia Migrant Education Scholarship, 409

Jose Marti Scholarship Challenge Grant Fund, 241

Joseph & Alice Duarte Memorial Fund, 264

Joseph J. Frank Scholarship, 129

Joseph P. Gavenonis Scholarship, 145

Joseph R. Dietrich Scholarship, 159

Joseph S. Adams Scholarship, 439

Joseph Tauber Scholarship, 73

Jospeh L. Bracone Memorial Scholarship, 464

Judith Resnik Memorial Scholarship, 459

Jules Maidoff Scholarship, 474

Juliette A. Southard/Oral-B Laboratories Scholarship, 94

June Gill Nursing Scholarship, 387

Junior Member Scholarship, 134

Junior Miss Scholarship, 88

J.W. Saxe Memorial Prize for Public Service, 543

K. K. Wang Scholarship, 449

The K2TEO Martin J. Green, Sr. Memorial Scholarship, 165

Ka'a'awa Community Fund, 264

Kahala Nui Residents Scholarship Fund, 264

Kahiau Scholarship Fund, 264

Ka'iulani Home for Girls Trust Scholarship, 264

The Kaj Christensen Scholarship for Vocational Training, 396

Kansas Comprehensive Grant, 307

Kansas Ethnic Minority Scholarship, 307

Kansas Nursing Service Scholarship, 308

Kansas ROTC Service Scholarship, 308

Kansas State Scholarship, 308

Kansas Teacher Service Scholarship, 308

Kansas Vocational Education Scholarship, 309

Kapolei Community & Business Scholarship, 265

Kappa Kappa Gamma Scholarship, 309

Karla Girts Memorial Community Outreach Scholarship, 77

KarMel Scholarship, 309

Katharine M. Grosscup Scholarship, 245

Katherine F. Gruber Scholarship Program, 202

Kathleen S. Anderson Award, 323

Kathryn D. Sullivan Science and Engineering Fellowship, 351

Kathryn Dettman Memorial Journalism Scholarship, 196

Kathy LeTarte Scholarship, 489

Kawasaki-McGaha Scholarship Fund, 265

Kazuma and Ichiko Hisanaga Scholarship Fund, 265

Ken Chagnon Scholarship, 413

Ken Kashiwahara Scholarship, 425

Kennedy Center Arts Management Internship, 542

Kennedy Library Archival Internship, 542

Kenneth Andrew Roe Mechanical Engineering Scholarship, 194

Kenneth Jernigan Memorial Scholarship, 364

Kentucky College Access Program Grant (CAP), 310

Kentucky Educational Excellence Scholarship (KEES), 310

Kentucky Teacher Scholarship, 310

Kentucky Tuition Grant, 311

Kentucky Work-Study Program, 543

Keppra Family Epilepsy Scholarship Program, 496

KIMT Weather/News Internships, 544

King Kekaulike High School Scholarship, 265

King Olav V Norwegian-American Heritage Fund, 465

Kittredge Coddington Memorial Scholarship, 508

Klussendorf Scholarship, 360

K.M. Hatano Scholarship, 265

Knights Templar Educational Foundation Loan, 576

Kohala Ditch Education Fund, 266

Koloa Scholarship, 266

Korean University Club Scholarship Fund, 266

Kosciuszko Foundation Year Abroad Program, 312

Kuchler-Killian Memorial Scholarship, 364

Kurt W. Schneider Memorial Scholarship Fund, 266

L. Gordon Bittle Memorial Scholarship for SCTA, 211

L. Phil Wicker Scholarship, 165

L-3 Avionics Systems Scholarship, 81

La Toque Scholarship in Wine Studies, 302

Lagrant Scholarships, 314

Laheenae Rebecca Hart Gay Scholarship, 267

LaMacchia Family Scholarship, 490

Landscape Forms Design for People Scholarship, 315

Larry Whiteside Scholarship, 356

Latin American Educational Scholarship, 316

Latin Honor Society Scholarship, 367

Latino Diamante Scholarship Fund, 393

Laura Blackburn Memorial Scholarship, 123

Laura N. Dowsett Fund, 267

Laura Rowe Burdick Scholarship Fund, 267

Laurence R. Foster Memorial Scholarship, 409

Law Enforcement Officer Memorial Scholarship, 382

Law Enforcement Officers' Dependents Scholarship, 182

Law Enforcement Personnel Dependents (LEPD) Grant Program, 210

Lawrence Luterman Memorial Scholarships, 139

The L.B. Cebik, W4RNL, and Jean Cebik, N4TZP, Memorial Scholarship, 165

Leaf Loan Program, 580
Lee A. Lyman Memorial Music
    Scholarship, 509
Lee Tarbox Memorial Scholarship, 82
Legacy of Hope, 473
Lehman Scholarship, 459
Lele Cassin Scholarship, 474
Leonard Bettinger Memorial
    Vocational Scholarship, 97
Leonard M. Perryman
    Communications Scholarship for
    Ethnic Minority Students, 498
Letitia B. Carter Scholarship, 427
Leveraging Educational Assistance
    Partnership (LEAP), 505
Leveraging Educational Assistance
    Partnership Program (LEAP), 336
Leveraging Educational Assistance
    State Partnership Program
    (LEAP), 288
LIFE Lessons Essay Contest, 318
LIFE Scholarship Program, 466
Lighthouse College-Bound
    Award, 319
Lighthouse Undergraduate Award, 319
Lillian and Samuel Sutton Education
    Scholarship, 342
Lillian Moller Gilbreth
    Scholarship, 460
Lillie Lois Ford Boys'
    Scholarship, 130
Lillie Lois Ford Girls'
    Scholarship, 130
Limi Boosters National Educational
    Grant, 391
Limi Boosters Scholarship, 391
Lindbergh Grant, 215
Literary Achievement Awards, 249
Local Arts Agency Services
    Intern, 529
Lockheed Martin Aeronautics
    Company Scholarships, 460
Lockheed Martin Corporate
    Scholarship, 374
Lockheed Martin Foundation
    Scholarships, 460
Los Padres Foundation College
    Tuition Assistance Program, 319
Lottery Tuition Assistance
    Program, 466
Lou and Carole Prato Sports
    Reporting Scholarship, 425
The Louie Foundation
    Scholarship, 311
Louis and Fannie Sager Memorial
    Scholarship, 372
Louis Carr Summer Internship, 544
Louis S. Silvey Grant, 307
Louisiana Go Grants, 320
Louisiana Memorial Scholarship, 166
Louisiana Rockefeller Wildlife
    Scholarship, 320
Louisiana Taylor Opportunity
    Program for Students (TOPS)
    Award, 321

Louisiana Veterans Affairs
    Educational Assistance for
    Dependent Children, 320
Louisiana Veterans Affairs
    Educational Assistance for
    Surviving Spouse, 320
Lowell Gaylor Memorial
    Scholarship, 82
The Lowell H. and Dorothy Loving
    Undergraduate Scholarship, 92
The Loy McCandless Marks
    Scholarship, 245
Lucile B. Kaufman Women's
    Scholarship, 446
Lucille & Charles A. Wert
    Scholarship, 190
LULAC National Scholarship Fund
    Honors Awards, 317
LULAC National Scholarship Fund
    National Scholastic Achievement
    Awards, 317
LULAC National Scholarshp Fund
    General Awards, 317
Lydia I. Pickup Memorial
    Scholarship, 460
Macy's College Scholarship
    Program, 277
Maine Innkeepers Association
    Scholarship, 321
The Maine Loan, 577
Maine Metal Products Association
    Scholarship, 322
Maine Robert C. Byrd Honors
    Scholarship, 239
Maine Society of Professional
    Engineers Scholarship
    Program, 322
Maine State Society of Washington,
    DC, Foundation Scholarship
    Program, 323
Maine Veterans Services Dependents
    Educational Benefits, 321
Major Don S. Gentile
    Scholarship, 496
Malcolm X Scholarship for
    Exceptional Courage, 499
ManageFirst Program
    Scholarship, 370
Marathon Oil Corporation College
    Scholarship, 277
Marble-Boyle Award, 198
Marcia S. Harris Legacy Fund
    Scholarship, 427
Margaret E. Swanson Scholarship, 77
Margaret Jones Memorial Nursing
    Scholarship, 267
Margarite McAlpin Nurse's
    Scholarship, 152
Margo Ballard and Vivian Meinecke
    Memorial Scholarship, 339
Margot Karle Scholarship Fund, 199
Marguerite Ross Barnett Memorial
    Scholarship, 338
Maria C. Jackson-General George A.
    White Scholarship, 409
Marie Sheehe Trade School
    Scholarship, 117

Marin Education Undergraduate
    Scholarships, 324
Marine Corps Scholarship, 324
Marine Corps Sgt. Jeannette L.
    Winters Memorial Scholarship, 185
Marion Huber Learning Through
    Listening Award, 425
Marion J. Bagley Scholarship, 138
Marion Maccarrell Scott
    Scholarship, 267
Mark J. Smith Scholarship, 219
Marketing and Communications
    Internship, 529
Marketing Internship Scholarship, 295
Marriott Scholars Program, 275
Marshall E. McCullough
    Undergraduate Scholarship, 361
Mary Barrett Marshall Student Loan
    Fund, 573
Mary Jo Young Scholarship, 311
Mary Josephine Bloder
    Scholarship, 268
Mary Lou Brown Scholarship, 166
Mary Macey Scholarship, 522
Mary Marshall Nursing LPN
    Scholarship, 512
Mary McLeod Bethune
    Scholarship, 241
Mary P. Oenslager Scholastic
    Achievement Award, 426
Mary V. Munger Scholarship, 461
Mary Virginia Macrea Memorial
    Scholarship, 120
Maryland Delegate Scholarship, 325
Maryland Distinguished Scholar:
    Achievement, 325
Maryland Distinguished Scholar:
    National Merit and National
    Achievement Finalists, 325
Maryland Distinguished Scholar:
    Talent in the Arts, 325
Maryland Educational Assistance
    Grant, 326
Maryland Edward T. Conroy
    Memorial Scholarship Program, 326
Maryland Jack F. Tolbert Memorial
    Grant, 326
Maryland Part-Time Grant
    Program, 327
Maryland Senatorial Scholarship, 327
Maryland Tuition Reduction for
    Non-Resident Nursing
    Students, 327
Masonic Range Science
    Scholarship, 440
Massachusetts Christian A. Herter
    Memorial Scholarship Program, 328
Massachusetts Federation of Polish
    Women's Clubs Scholarships, 313
Massachusetts Gilbert Matching
    Student Grant, 328
Massachusetts MASSgrant
    Program, 328
Massachusetts No Interest Loan, 577
Massachusetts Public Service Grant
    Program, 328

Massachusetts Robert C. Byrd Honors Scholarship, 329
Massachusetts Scholarship, 490
MassMutual Multicultural College Scholarship, 277
MASWE Scholarships, 461
Matsuo Bridge Company Ltd of Japan Scholarship, 178
Matthews/Swift Educational Trust - Military Dependants, 312
Matthews/Swift Educational Trust - Police/Firefighters, 312
Maureen V. O'Donnell/Eunice C. Kraft Teacher Training Scholarships, 90
Maya Angelou/Vivian Baxter Scholarship, 499
Mayflower Tours Patrick Murphy Internship, 565
Maynard Jensen American Legion Memorial Scholarship, 134
The Mayor's Chesapeake Energy Scholarship, 228
MCC Theater Internships, 545
McFarland Charitable Foundation Scholarship, 252
McNamara Family Creative Arts Project Grant, 278
M.D. "Jack" Murphy Memorial Nurses Training Fund, 130
Medical Career Scholarships, 127
Medical Technologists Student Scholarship, 156
Meetings and Events/Executive Office Internship, 529
Melvin R. Green Scholarships, 194
Membership Internship, 529
Memorial Education Grant, 113
Memorial Scholarship Fund, 486
Menominee Adult Vocational Training Grant, 330
Menominee Higher Education Grant, 330
Mentoring Program for College Juniors, 546
The Merchants Exhange Scholarship Fund, 330
Meridith Thoms Memorial Scholarships, 461
MESBEC Scholarships, 212
Metropolitan Scholarships, 286
MG Eugene C. Renzi/ManTech International Corporation Scholarship for Math and Science Teachers, 185
MG James Ursano Scholarship Program, 187
MIA/POW Scholarship, 288
Michael Hakeem Memorial Award, 244
Michigan Competitive Scholarship, 330
Michigan Robert C. Byrd Honors Scholarship, 331
Michigan Scholarship, 490

Michigan Society of Professional Engineers Scholarships for High School Seniors, 331
Michigan Tuition Grant, 331
Microbiology Undergraduate Research Fellowship (MURF), 170
Microscopy Society of America Undergraduate Research Scholarship, 332
Microsoft Corporation Scholarships, 461
Microsoft General Scholarship, 332
Mid-Continent Instrument Scholarship, 82
Midwest Student Exchange Program, 332
Milan Getting Scholarship, 438
Mildred R. Knoles Opportunity Scholarship, 117
Mildred Towle Scholarship - Study Abroad, 268
Mildred Towle Scholarship for African-Americans, 268
Military Dependents Scholarship Program, 183
Military Order of the Purple Heart Scholarship, 333
Military Service Recognition Scholarship (MSRS), 387
Miller Electric Manufacturing Company Ivic Scholarship, 179
Miller Electric Mfg. Co. Scholarship, 179
Minnesota Achieve Scholarship, 334
The Minnesota American Legion Memorial Scholarship, 128
Minnesota Educational Assistance for Surviving Spouse or Dependent, 333
Minnesota Educational Assistance for Veterans, 334
Minnesota GI Bill, 334
Minnesota Indian Scholarship Program, 334
Minnesota Post-Secondary Child Care Grant, 335
Minnesota Public Safety Officers Survivors Program, 335
Minnesota State Grant Program, 335
Minnesota Student Educational Loan Fund (SELF), 578
Minnesota Work-Study Program, 546
Minority Scholarship Program, 206
Minority School Scholarships, 79
Minority Teachers of Illinois Scholarship, 290
Miss America Competition Awards, 336
Mississippi Eminent Scholars Grant, 336
Mississippi Health Care Professions Loan/Scholarship, 579
Mississippi Higher Education Legislative Plan, 336
Mississippi Nursing Education Loan/Scholarship, 579
Mississippi Scholarship, 166

Mississippi Tuition Assistance Grant, 337
Mississippi William Winter Teacher Scholar Loan Program, 579
Missouri Department of Higher Education Vietnam Veteran's Survivor Grant Program, 338
Missouri Higher Education "Bright Flight" Academic Scholarship, 338
Missouri League for Nursing Scholarship, 339
Missouri Minority Teaching Scholarship, 338
Missouri Public Safety Officer or Employee's Child Survivor Grant, 339
Missouri Robert C. Byrd Honors Scholarship, 337
MOAA American Patriot Scholarship Program, 333
MOAA Interest-Free Loan and Grant Program, 578
Monetary Award Program (MAP), 291
Montana Higher Education Grant, 340
Montana Tuition Fee Waiver for Veterans, 340
Montana University System Community College Honor Scholarship, 340
Montana University System Honor Scholarship, 341
Monte R. Mitchell Global Scholarship, 82
Montgomery GI Bill (MGIB), 501
Moody's Mega Math "M3" Challenge, 341
Morgan Stanley Scholars Program, 102
Morris Arboretum Education Internship, 547
Morris Arboretum Horticulture Internship, 547
Morton B. Duggan, Jr. Memorial Education Recognition Award, 169
Morton Gould Young Composer Awards, 188
Mother Jones Ben Bagdikian Fellowship Program, 548
MSGC Undergraduate Underrepresented Minority Fellowship Program, 346
MTA Doug Slifka Memorial Scholarship, 341
Muggets Scholarship, 285
Multicultural Advertising Intern Program, 525
Multicultural Arts Management Internship Program, 531
Multicultural Undergraduate Summer Internships at the Getty Center, 541
Multimedia Intern Program, 534
Museum Coca-Cola Internship, 551
Museum of Modern Art Internship, 548
Myrtle and Earl Walker Scholarship, 447

NABA National Scholarship Program, 356

NABJ Internships, 550

NAFEO (National Association for Equal Opportunity in Higher Education) Scholarships, 105

NAMTA Educational Scholarship, 355

NAMTA Foundation Visual Arts Major Scholarship, 355

Nancy Lorraine Jensen Memorial Scholarship, 466

Nannie W. Norfleet Scholarship, 142

NASA Academy Internship, 550

NASA Connecticut Space Grant Undergraduate Fellowship, 343

NASA District of Columbia Undergraduate Scholarship, 344

NASA Hawaii Undergraduate Student Research Program, 549

NASA Idaho Space Grant Undergraduate Scholarship, 345

NASA Minnesota Space Grant Consortium Wide Scholarship, 347

NASA Missouri State Space Grant Undergraduate Scholarship, 347

NASA Ohio Space Grant Junior/Senior Scholarship Program, 350

NASA Pennsylvania Space Grant Sylvia Stein Memorial Scholarship, 350

NASA Rocky Mountain Space Grant Consortium Undergraduate Scholarship, 351

NASA Space Grant Arizona Undergraduate Research Internship, 549

NASA Space Grant Georgia Fellowship Program, 344

NASA Space Grant Hawaii Undergraduate Fellowship, 344

NASA Space Grant Illinois Undergraduate Scholarship, 345

NASA Space Grant Kentucky Undergraduate Scholarship, 345

NASA Space Grant Maine Consortium Annual Scholarship and Fellowship Program, 346

NASA Space Grant Michigan Undergraduate Fellowship, 346

NASA Space Grant Montana Undergraduate Scholarship Program, 347

NASA Space Grant Nevada Undergraduate Scholarship, 348

NASA Space Grant New Mexico Undergraduate Scholarship, 348

NASA Space Grant North Dakota Consortium Lillian Goettler Scholarship, 349

NASA Space Grant North Dakota Undergraduate Scholarship, 349

NASA Space Grant Oregon Undergraduate Scholarship, 350

NASA Space Grant Rhode Island Undergraduate Research Scholarship, 350

NASA Space Grant South Carolina Undergraduate Student Research Fellowship, 352

NASA Space Grant Teacher Education Scholarship, 353

NASA Space Grant Texas Columbia Crew Memorial Undergraduate Scholarships, 352

NASA Space Grant Undergraduate Scholarship, 343

NASA Space Grant Vermont Consortium Undergraduate Scholarships, 352

NASA Space Grant Virginia Community College Scholarship, 353

NASA Space Grant Wisconsin Consortium Undergraduate Research Program, 354

NASA Space Grant Wisconsin Consortium Undergraduate Scholarship, 354

NASA West Virginia Space Grant Undergraduate Research Fellowship, 353

National Achievement Scholarships, 367

National Amateur Baseball Federation Scholarship, 355

National Association of Women in Construction Founders' Scholarship, 358

National ChairScholars Scholarship, 215

National Co-op Scholarship, 359

National Dairy Shrine Kildee Scholarship, 361

National Federation of the Blind Educator of Tomorrow Award, 364

National Federation of the Blind Scholarships, 364

National FFA Collegiate Scholarship Program, 365

National Guard Educational Assistance Program, 309

National Guard Tuition Waiver, 401

National Guild of Piano Teachers $200 Scholarship, 91

National Guild of Piano Teachers Composition Contest, 91

National Health Service Corps Scholarship, 503

National High School Oratorical Contest, 112

National High School Oratorical Contest, 112

National High School Oratorical Contest, 113

National High School Oratorical Contest, 150

National Italian American Foundation Scholarship Program, 366

National Junior Classical League Scholarship, 367

National Leadership Grant, 465

National Merit Scholarships, 368

National Museum of the American Indian Internship, 551

National Oceanic and Atmospheric Administration Hollings Undergraduate Scholarship, 555

National Peace Essay Contest, 500

National Presbyterian Scholarship, 421

National President's Scholarship, 127

National President's Scholarship, 140

National President's Scholarship, 144

National Press Photographers Foundation Still and Multimedia Scholarship, 369

National Press Photographers Foundation Television News Scholarship, 369

National Security Agency Stokes Educational Scholarship Program, 372

National Society of Accountants Scholarship, 372

National Society of Black Engineers Golden Torch Awards, 375

National Society of Black Engineers Leroy Callendar PCI Award Program, 375

National Speakers Association Scholarship, 377

National Student Nurses Association Scholarship, 243

National Tour Association State Scholarship, 490

Native American Education Grant, 421

Native American Leadership in Education Scholarship, 212

Native Daughters of the Golden West Scholarship, 378

Navy Supply Corps Foundation Scholarship, 378

NBA Internship Program, 551

NBRC/AMP Robert M. Lawrence, MD Education Recognition Award, 170

NBRC/AMP William W. Burgin, Jr. MD Education Recognition Award, 170

NC Sheriff's Association Criminal Justice Scholarship, 394

NCAA Division I Degree-Completion Award Program, 379

NCR Summer Internships, 552

NEBHE's Tuition Break Regional Student Program, 380

Nebraska Robert C. Byrd Honors Scholarship, 379

Nebraska State Grant, 379

NEEBC Scholarship, 380

NEHA/AAS Scholarship, 362

Neil Hamilton Memorial Scholarship, 409

NEMAL Electronics Scholarship, 166

NESA Academic Scholarships, 361

Nettie Dracup Memorial Scholarship, 92

Nevada Robert C. Byrd Honors Scholarship, 379
Nevada Student Incentive Grant, 380
New England FEMARA Scholarship, 166
New Hampshire Incentive Program, 380
New Hampshire Scholarship for Orphans of Veterans, 381
New Horizons Rene Campbell Memorial Scholarship, 490
New Jeresy Student Tuition Assistance Reward Scholarship (NJSTARS), 382
New Jersey Class Loan Program, 580
New Jersey Educational Opportunity Fund Grant, 381
New Jersey Edward J. Bloustein Distinguished Scholars, 382
New Jersey POW/MIA Tuition Benefit Program, 381
New Jersey Scholarship, 462
New Jersey Scholarship, 491
New Jersey STARS II, 382
New Jersey Survivor Tuition Benefits Program, 383
New Jersey Tuition Aid Grants (TAG), 383
New Jersey Urban Scholars, 383
New Jersey War Orphans Tuition Assistance Program, 381
New Jersey World Trade Center Scholarship, 383
New Mexico Allied Health Student Loan-for-Service Program, 580
New Mexico Competitive Scholarships, 384
New Mexico Legislative Endowment Program, 384
New Mexico Legislative Lottery Scholarship, 384
New Mexico Nursing Student Loan-for-Service, 581
New Mexico Scholars Program, 384
New Mexico Student Choice Grant, 385
New Mexico Student Incentive Grant, 385
New Mexico Teacher's Loan-for-Service, 581
New Mexico Vietnam Veteran's Scholarship, 385
New Mexico Work-Study Program, 553
The New Republic Internship, 553
New York American Legion Press Association Scholarship, 141
New York Scholarship, 491
New York State Aid for Part-time Study Program, 388
New York State Arthur O. Eve Higher Education Opportunity Program (HEOP), 385
New York State Assembly Session Internship Program, 553

New York State Memorial Scholarship for Families of Deceased Police/Volunteer Firefighters/Peace Officers and Emergency Medical Service Workers, 388
New York State Native American Student Aid Program, 389
New York State Readers Aid Program, 397
New York State Regents Awards for Children of Deceased and Disabled Veterans, 388
New York State Robert C. Byrd Federal Honors Scholarship, 386
New York State Scholarships for Academic Excellence, 386
New York State Tuition Assistance Program, 388
New York State Veterans Tuition Award, 389
New York State World Trade Center Memorial Scholarship, 389
New York Times James Reston Reporting Fellowships, 554
New York Women in Communications Foundation Scholarship, 389
Newhouse Foundation Scholarship, 550
News Copy Editing Intern Program, 535
NGWREF Len Assante Scholarship Fund, 365
Nick Van Pernis Scholarship, 268
Nisei Student Relocation Commemorative Fund, 390
Nissan Community College Transfer Scholarship, 278
Nissan North America, Inc. Scholarship, 103
Nissan Scholarship, 337
NMIA Ohio Scholarship Program, 390
Non Commissioned Officers Association Scholarship for Children of Members, 390
Non Commissioned Officers Association Scholarship for Spouses, 390
North American Indian Scholarship, 296
North Carolina Aubrey Lee Brooks Scholarship, 394
North Carolina Community Colleges Wachovia Technical Scholarship, 391
North Carolina Legislative Tuition Grant, 394
North Carolina Nurse Scholars Program, 582
North Carolina Scholarships for Children of War Veterans, 392
North Carolina State Board of Refrigeration Examiners Scholarship, 392
North Carolina Student Incentive Grant, 394
North Carolina Student Loans for Health/Science/Mathematics, 582

North Carolina Vocational Rehabilitation Award, 392
North Central Region Scholarship, 447
North Dakota Indian Scholarship Program, 395
North Dakota Scholars Program, 395
North Dakota State Student Incentive Grant, 395
Northern California Chapter - Richard Epping Scholarship, 491
Northern California DX Foundation Scholarship, 167
Northern Cheyenne Higher Education Program, 396
Northrop Grumman Corporate Scholarship, 375
Northrop Grumman Corporation Scholarship, 462
Northwest Danish Association Scholarship, 396
NPFDA Scholarship, 368
NSBE Fellows Scholarship, 375
NSPS Board of Governors Scholarship, 93
NSPS Scholarships, 93
Nuclear Medicine Student Fellowship Award, 439
Nurse Gift Tuition Scholarships, 134
Nurse Pracitioner Nurse Midwife Scholarship, 512
NYC World Trade Center Memorial Scholarship, 274
OCA-AXA Achievement Scholarships, 397
OCA/UPS Foundation Gold Mountain College Scholarship, 397
OCA/Verizon Foundation College Scholarship, 397
Office of Hawaiian Affairs Scholarship Fund, 268
Ohio College Opportunity Grant, 397
Ohio National Guard Scholarship Program, 398
Ohio Newspaper Association Publications/Public Relations Internship, 558
Ohio Newspapers Minority Scholarship, 399
Ohio Newspapers Women's Scholarship, 399
Ohio Nurse Education Assistance Loan Program, 582
Ohio Safety Officers College Memorial Fund, 398
Ohio Scholarship, 491
Ohio War Orphans Scholarship, 398
Oklahoma Engineering Foundation Scholarship, 399
Oklahoma Tuition Aid Grant, 401
Oklahoma's Promise - Oklahoma Higher Learning Access Program, 401
Olive Lynn Salembier Re-entry Scholarship, 462
OMNE/Nursing Leaders of Maine Scholarship, 402

OP Loftbed $500 Scholarship Award, 402
Operation Enduring Freedom and Operation Iraqi Freedom Scholarship, 509
Operations and Power Division Scholarship, 160
Opportunity Scholarship, 286
Oracle Scholars Internship Program, 566
Oratorical Contest, 116
Oratorical Contest Scholarships, 153
Oregon Dungeness Crab Commission, 410
Oregon Foundation for Blacktail Deer Outdoor & Wildlife Scholarship, 410
Oregon Occupational Safety and Health Division Workers Memorial Scholarship, 410
Oregon Robert C. Byrd Honors Scholarship, 410
Oregon Scholarship Fund Community College Student Award Programs, 410
ORISE Department of Energy Community College Institute, 555
ORISE Higher Education Research Experiences at Oak Ridge National Laboratory for Students, 555
ORISE Nuclear Regulatory Commission Historically Black Colleges and Universities Student Research Participation, 556
ORISE Professional Internship Program for National Energy Technology Laboratory, 556
ORISE Research Participation Program at the U.S. Army Center for Health Promotion and Preventive Medicine, 556
ORISE Student Environmental Management Participation at the U.S. Army Environmental Center, 556
ORISE Student Research - National Center for Toxicological Research, 557
ORISE Student Research at the Centers for Disease Control and Prevention/Agency for Toxic Substances and Disease Registry, 557
ORISE Student Research Participation at the U.S. Army Medical Research Institute of Chemical Defense, 557
ORISE Student Research Participation at U.S. Army Research Laboratory, 557
Osage Tribal Education Committee Award, 207
Osage Tribal Education Scholarship, 413
Oscar and Rosetta Fish Fund, 269
The Ouimet Scholarship, 243
Owens Corning Internships, 559

Pacific Gas and Electric Summer Intern Program, 559
Pacific Northwest Chapter/William Hunt Scholarship, 492
PAGE Foundation Scholarships, 423
Palmetto Fellows Scholarship Program, 467
Papercheck.com Charles Shafae' Scholarship Fund, 413
Par Aide's Joseph S. Garske Collegiate Grant Program, 413
Partnership for Access to Higher Education (PATH), 415
Part-Time Horticultural Internship, 568
Part-Time Student Scholarship, 296
Part-Time Tuition Aid Grant for County Colleges, 383
Past Department Presidents' Junior Scholarship, 111
Past President's Parley Education Grant, 113
Past President's Parley Health Care Scholarship, 128
Past President's Parley Nurse's Scholarship, 112
Past President's Parley Nurses Scholarship, 115
Past President's Parley Nurses' Scholarship, 136
Past President's Parley Nurses' Scholarship, 138
Past President's Parley Nurses' Scholarship, 140
Past Presidents' Parley Nursing Scholarship, 111
Past President's Parley Nursing Scholarship, 113
Past President's Parley Nursing Scholarship, 119
Past President's Parley Scholarship, 110
Past President's Parley Scholarship, 126
Past President's Parley Scholarship, 131
Past President's Parley Scholarship, 142
Past President's Parley Scholarship for Nurses, 140
Past President's Parley Student Scholarship in Medical Field, 141
Past President's Scholarship, 120
Past Presidents Scholarship, 179
Past Presidents Scholarships, 462
Pat & Jim Host Scholarship, 492
Patrick and Judith McHugh Scholarship, 509
Paul A. Stewart Award, 520
Paul and Helen L. Grauer Scholarship, 167
Paul and Helen Ruckes Scholarship, 98
Paul Cole Scholarship, 439
Paul Jennings Scholarship, 300
Paul Tsongas Scholarship Program, 328

Paulina L. Sorg Scholarship, 269
Payzer Scholarship, 238
PBS Internships, 559
PBS&J Corporate Scholarship, 375
Pearl I. Young Scholarship, 349
peermusic Latin Scholarship, 203
Peggy Guggenheim Internship, 563
Pennsylvania Robert C. Byrd Honors Scholarship, 415
Pennsylvania State Grant Program, 415
Pennsylvania Work-Study Program, 416
Performing Arts Fellowships, 186
Peridian International Inc./Rae L. Price FASLA Scholarship, 315
Perry & Sally Sorenson Scholarship for Dependents of Hospitality Workers, 269
Perry & Sally Sorenson Scholarship for Foster Youth, 269
The Persian Scholarship Recognition Award, 418
Pete Carpenter Fellowship, 531
Pete Wilson Journalism Scholarship, 425
The Peter Cameron/Housewares Charity Foundation Scholarship, 303
Peter F. Vallone Academic Scholarship, 217
Peter Kump Memorial Scholarship, 303
Peter Papworth Scholarship, 269
Peter Wollitzer Scholarships for Study in Asia, 225
Peters Scholarship, 228
PFLAG National Scholarship Program, 418
PGA Tour Diversity Intern Program, 560
PGSF Annual Scholarship Competition, 423
PHCC Auxiliary of Massachusetts Scholarship, 420
PHCC Educational Foundation Need-Based Scholarship, 420
PHD Amateur Radio Association Scholarship, 167
Philip and Alice Angell Eastern Star Scholarship, 509
Phipps Conservatory and Botanical Gardens Internships, 560
Phoenix Section Scholarship, 463
Pickett and Hatcher Educational Loan, 582
Pittsburgh Local Section Scholarship, 160
Pittsburgh Scholarship, 449
Plane & Pilot Magazine/Garmin Scholarship, 83
Plant Propagation Internship, 547
Plant Protection Internship, 547
Plasma Physics National Undergraduate Fellowship Program, 560
Plastics Pioneers Scholarships, 449

Plumbing-Heating-Cooling Contractors - National Association Educational Foundation Scholarship, 420

Poggio Scholarship, 303

Point Scholarship, 420

Police/Firefighters' Survivors Educational Assistance Program, 84

The Polish American Club of North Jersey Scholarships, 313

The Polish National Alliance of Brooklyn, USA, Inc. Scholarships, 313

Post-High School Tuition Scholarship, 213

Postsecondary Educational Gratuity Program, 416

Practical Nursing Scholarship, 135

Praxair International Scholarship, 179

Presbyterian Student Opportunity Scholarship, 421

Presbyterian Undergraduate and Graduate Loan, 583

Preservation Fellows Program, 565

Presidents' $2,500 Scholarships, 425

President's Parley Nursing Scholarship, 124

President's Scholarship, 136

Press Club of Houston Scholarship, 422

Princess Cruises Scholarship, 492

Princess Grace Award for Dance, 422

Princess Grace Award For Film, 422

Princess Grace Award For Playwriting, 422

Princess Grace Award For Theater, 423

Print & Online News Grants, 188

Private-Sector Initiatives Internship, 529

Pro Deo/Pro Patria Scholarship, 312

Procter & Gamble Scholarship, 278

Product Development Summer Internship Program, 559

Professional Land Surveyors of Oregon Scholarship, 411

PROMISE Scholarship, 517

ProStart National Certificate of Achievement Scholarship, 371

PRSA-Hawaii/Roy Leffingwell Public Relations Scholarship, 270

Public Relations Internship, 545

The Publican Scholarship, 303

Puckemin Inn Scholarship, 303

Pulliam Journalism Fellowship, 540

Quebec Scholarship, 492

Rain Bird Intelligent Use of Water Company Scholarship, 315

Rainbow Scholarship, 422

Ralph K. Hillquist Honorary SAE Scholarship, 431

Random House Summer Internship Program, 560

Ray Yoshida Kauai Fine Arts Scholarship, 270

Raymond DiSalvo Scholarship, 160

Raymond F. Cain Scholarship Fund, 270

Raymond K. Conley Memorial Scholarship, 137

RCMI Technical/Trade School Scholarship, 428

Red River Valley Fighter Pilots Association (RRVA) Scholarship Program, 426

Reduction in Tuition Charges for Students Taking 15 or More Semester Credit Hours Per Term, 482

Regional Student Leader of the Year Award, 250

Regional University Baccalaureate Scholarship, 401

RehabGYM Scholarship, 509

Reid Blackburn Scholarship, 369

Research Experiences for Undergraduates - Maria Mitchell Observatory, 552

Research Experiences for Undergraduates in Systematics and Evolutionary Biology, 527

Research Experiences for Undergraduates in the Physical Sciences, 527

Research Services Internship, 530

Reuben Trane Scholarship, 174

Rewarding Young Leaders in Our Community Scholarship, 239

Rhode Island State Government Internship Program, 561

Rhode Island State Grant, 427

Rich Meiers Health Administration Fund, 270

Richard Eaton Foundation Award, 205

Richard F. Brentano Memorial Scholarship, 411

Richard Lee Vernon Aviation Scholarship, 238

Richard W. Bendicksen Memorial Scholarship, 167

Richie Gregory Fund, 270

Rick Arkans Eagle Scout Scholarship, 366

Ritchie-Jennings Memorial Scholarship, 74

R.L. Gillette Scholarship, 98

RMHC Scholarship Programs, 428

Robanna Fund, 271

Robert B. Bailey Scholarship, 225

Robert C. Byrd Honors Scholarship, 84

Robert C. Byrd Honors Scholarship, 231

Robert C. Byrd Honors Scholarship, 311

Robert C. Byrd Honors Scholarship, 321

Robert C. Byrd Honors Scholarship, 482

Robert C. Byrd Honors Scholarship Program, 241

Robert C. Byrd Honors Scholarship Program, 291

Robert C. Byrd Honors Scholarship Program, 400

Robert C. Byrd Honors Scholarship Program, 503

Robert D. Blue Scholarship, 298

Robert G. Lacy Scholarship, 160

Robert L. Livingston Scholarship, 300

Robert L. Peaslee-Detroit Brazing and Soldering Division Scholarship, 179

Robert Noyce Scholarship Program, 418

Robert R. Lee Promise Category A Scholarship, 288

Robert R. Lee Promise Category B Scholarship, 288

Robert T. (Bob) Liner Scholarship, 160

Robert W. Valimont Endowment Fund Scholarship, 145

Roberta Marie Stretch Memorial Scholarship, 135

Rockwell Automation Scholarships, 463

Rocky Mountain Coal Mining Institute Scholarship, 428

Rodney E. Powell Memorial Scholarship, 391

Roger W. Emmons Memorial Scholarship, 411

Ron Bright Scholarship, 271

Ron Brown Scholar Program, 211

Ronald Reagan College Leaders Scholarship Program, 419

Roosevelt Archival Internships, 538

Rose and Flower Garden Internship, 548

Rosedale Post 346 Scholarship, 121

Rosemary & Nellie Ebrie Fund, 271

Rosewood Family Scholarship Program, 242

ROTC/Air Force Four-Year Scholarship (Types 1, 2, and 7), 429

ROTC/Navy Nurse Corps Scholarship Program, 504

ROTC/Navy/Marine Four-Year Scholarship, 504

ROTC/Navy/Marine Two-Year Scholarship, 505

Roy Wilkins Scholarship, 342

Ruby Paul Campaign Fund Scholarship, 135

Rudolf Nissim Prize, 188

Rudolph Dillman Memorial Scholarship, 98

Russ Casey Scholarship, 322

Ruth Clark Furniture Design Scholarship, 296

RWMA Scholarship, 180

Sachs Foundation Undergraduate Grant, 430

SACI Consortium Scholarship, 474

SAE Detroit Section Technical Scholarship, 431

SAE Long-Term Member Sponsored Scholarship, 431

SAE Women Engineers Committee Scholarship, 431

SAE/David Hermance Hybird Technologies Scholarship, 431

SAE/Ford Partnership for Advanced Studies Scholarship, 432

Safeway Foundation Hawaii Scholarship Fund, 271

Sal Ingrassia Scholarship, 300

Salute to Education Scholarship, 433

Sam Walton Community Scholarship, 514

Samara Foundation of Vermont Scholarship, 510

Samsung American Legion Scholarship, 133

Samuel Fletcher Tapman ASCE Student Chapter Scholarship, 171

Samuel Robinson Award, 421

Savannah River Site Professional Internship Program, 557

SCA Conservation Internships, 564

Scan/Design Foundation by Inger and Jens Bruun Scholarship for Study in Denmark, 396

Scarlett Family Foundation Scholarship, 434

Schneider-Emanuel American Legion Scholarships, 154

Scholar Athlete Milk Mustache of the Year Awards, 333

Scholarship Educational Assistance Program, 354

Scholarship for Children of Deceased or Totally Disabled Veterans, 145

Scholarship for Children of Living Veterans, 145

Scholarship for College or Vocational, 148

Scholarship for Minority Accounting Students, 106

Scholarship for Minority Undergraduate Physics Majors, 161

Scholarship for People with Disabilities, 226

Scholarships for Children and Spouses of Deceased or Disabled Veterans and Servicemembers, 242

Scholarships for Children of SACI Alumni, 474

Scholarships for Students of Puerto Rican Descent, 275

Scholarships for Survivors, 414

Scholastic Art Portfolio Gold Award, 86

Scholastic Art Portfolio Silver Award, 86

Scholastic Photography Portfolio Gold Award, 86

Scholastic Photography Portfolio Silver Award, 86

Scholastic Writing Portfolio Gold Award, 86

Schonstedt Scholarships in Surveying, 93

School Art Scholarships, 286

Science Undergraduate Laboratory Internships, 558

SciTech Scholarship, 416

The Scotts Company Scholars Program, 536

Sculpture Society Scholarship, 371

Seabee Memorial Scholarship, 434

Seattle Jaycees Scholarship, 435

Seattle Professional Chapter Scholarship, 197

Second Chance Program, 319

Second Effort Scholarship, 183

Second Marine Division Association Scholarship Fund, 435

SEG Foundation Scholarship, 441

Selected Reserve Montgomery GI Bill, 501

Senator George J. Mitchell Scholarship, 435

Senator Richard M. & Dr. Ruth Matsuura Scholarship Fund, 271

Seneca Nation Higher Education Program, 436

Senior Citizen, 65 or Older, Free Tuition for Up to 6 Credit Hours, 482

Senior Scholarship, 314

Sertoma Scholarships for Students Who are Hard of Hearing or Deaf, 436

Seth Horen, K1LOM Memorial Scholarship, 167

Shane Dean Voyles Memorial Scholarship, 130

Shannon Scholarship, 495

Sheryl A. Horak Law Enforcement Explorer Scholarship, 318

Shirley McKown Scholarship Fund, 272

Shoshone Tribal Scholarship, 436

Shuichi, Katsu and Itsuyo Suga Scholarship, 272

Sid Richardson Scholarship, 437

Siegel Service Technology Scholarships, 432

Siemens Awards for Advanced Placement, 437

Siemens Competition in Math, Science and Technology, 437

Siemens Merit Scholarship, 438

Sigma Phi Alpha Undergraduate Scholarship, 78

Signet Classic Student Scholarship Essay Contest, 414

Silas Purnell Illinois Incentive for Access, 291

Silver Eagle Indian Scholarship, 136

Simon and Schuster Summer Internship Program, 561

Six Meter Club of Chicago Scholarship, 168

Six-Month Internship, 546

Slovenian Women's Union Scholarship For Returning Adults, 438

Slovenian Women's Union Scholarship Foundation, 438

SME Education Foundation Family Scholarship, 447

Smithsonian Environmental Research Center Internship Program, 561

Smithsonian Minority Internship, 562

Smithsonian Native American Internship, 562

Society of Daughters of United States Army Scholarship Program, 440

Society of Exploration Geophysicists Scholarship, 441

Society of Physics Students Leadership Scholarship, 448

Society of Physics Students Summer Internship Program, 562

Society of Plastics Engineers General Scholarships, 450

Sonia Streuli Maguire Outstanding Scholastic Achievement Award, 476

Sony Credited Internship, 563

Sorrento Lingue Scholarship, 465

South Carolina HOPE Scholarships, 467

South Carolina Need-Based Grants Program, 467

South Carolina Teacher Loans, 583

South Carolina Tuition Grants, 467

South Dakota Annis I. Fowler/Kaden Scholarship, 468

South Dakota Ardell Bjugstad Scholarship, 468

South Dakota Haines Memorial Scholarship, 468

South Dakota Marlin R. Scarborough Memorial Scholarship, 468

South Dakota Opportunity Scholarship Program, 469

South Dakota Robert C. Byrd Honors Scholarship, 469

Southern California Chapter - Pleasant Holidays Scholarship, 493

Southern California Council Endowed Internship, 552

Southern Nursery Organization Sidney B. Meadows Scholarship, 469

Southern Scholarship Foundation Scholarships, 470

Southface Internship, 563

Sovereign Nations Scholarship Fund, 103

The SPE Foundation Blow Molding Division Memorial Scholarships, 450

Special Education Teacher Tuition Waiver, 291

Special Education Teaching Scholarships, 117

Spence Reese Scholarship, 204

Spencer's Scholarship, 304

SPIE Educational Scholarship in Optical Science and Engineering, 470

Spina Bifida Association One-Year Scholarship, 470

Spirit of Youth Scholarship, 144

Spirit of Youth Scholarship for Junior Members, 133

Spoleto Festival Apprenticeship Program, 564

Sports Copy Editing Intern Program, 535

Sports Illustrated Scholarship, 356

Stan and Leone Pollard Scholarship, 493

Stan Beck Fellowship, 235

Stanfield and D'Orlando Art Scholarship, 497

Stanford Chen Internship Grant, 189

Stanley H. Stearman Award, 372

Staples Associates Annual Scholarships Plan, 470

Staples Summer Internship Program, 564

State Contractual Scholarship Fund, 394

Stella Blum Student Research Grant, 224

STEM Scholarship, 352

STEM Teacher Scholarships, 186

Stephen T. Kugle Scholarship, 194

Steven G. King Play Environments Scholarship, 316

Student Aid Foundation Loan, 583

Student Aid Grant or Vocational Technical Scholarship, 135

Student Internship Program, 525

Student Merit Scholarships, 79

Student Nurse Scholarship, 118

Student Research at the U.S. Army Edgewood Chemical Biological Center, 567

Student Research Participation at the Federal Bureau of Investigation, 558

Students With Disabilities Endowed Scholarship Honoring Elizabeth Daley Jeffords, 510

Student-to-Student (STS) Program, 292

Studio at the Montage Resort & Spa Scholarship, 304

Study Abroad Scholarships, 250

Stutz Memorial Scholarship, 139

Summer Internship Program, 531

Summer Internship Program, 546

Summer Research Diversity Fellowships in Law and Social Sciences for Undergraduate Students, 526

Summer Undergraduate Scholarship, 351

Supreme Guardian Council, International Order of Job's Daughters Scholarship, 475

Susan Burdett Scholarship, 152

Susan Miszkowitz Memorial Scholarship, 463

Susie Holmes Memorial Scholarship, 475

Swiss Benevolent Society Medicus Student Exchange, 476

Swiss Benevolent Society Pellegrini Scholarship, 476

Sylvia W. Farny Scholarship, 191

Taglit-Birthright Israel Gift, 477

Takehiko Hasegawa Academic Scholarship, 272

TANF (Temporary Assistance to Needy Families) Exemption, 483

Tau Beta Pi/SAE Engineering Scholarship, 432

Teacher Assistant Scholarship Fund, 395

Teacher Quest Scholarship Program, 206

Teamsters Clyde C. Crosby/Joseph M. Edgar Memorial Scholarship, 411

Teamsters Council #37 Federal Credit Union Scholarship, 411

Teamsters Local 305 Scholarship, 412

Technical Minority Scholarship, 524

Technology Scholarship, 416

Ted and Nora Anderson Scholarship, 122

Tennessee Dependent Children Scholarship Program, 478

Tennessee HOPE Access Grant, 478

Tennessee HOPE Scholarship, 478

Tennessee Minority Teaching Fellows Program, 584

Tennessee Ned McWherter Scholars Program, 479

Tennessee Robert C. Byrd Honors Scholarship Program, 479

Tennessee Student Assistance Award Program, 479

Tennessee Student Assistance Corporation/Math And Science Teachers Loan Forgiveness Program, 584

Tennessee Teaching Scholars Program, 584

Texas 4-H Opportunity Scholarships, 479

Texas Early High School Graduation Scholarship, 483

Texas Farm Bureau Scholarship, 480

Texas Fifth-Year Accounting Student Scholarship Program, 483

Texas Foster Care Students Exemption, 483

Texas Good Neighbor Scholarship, 483

TEXAS Grant (Toward Excellence, Access, and Success), 484

Texas Hazlewood Act Tuition Exemption: Veterans, 484

Texas Highest Ranking High School Graduate Tuition Exemption, 484

Texas Legion Oratorical Contest, 149

Texas National Guard Tuition Assistance Program, 484

Texas Public Educational Grant, 484

Texas Scholarships for Nursing Students, 485

Texas Transportation Scholarship, 494

Texas Tuition Exemption for Blind or Deaf Students, 485

Thelma Foster Junior American Legion Auxiliary Members Scholarship, 148

Thelma Foster Senior American Legion Auxiliary Member Scholarship, 148

Theodore Mazza Scholarship, 496

Thermoforming Division Memorial Scholarships, 450

Thermoset Division/James I. MacKenzie Memorial Scholarship, 450

Thomas J. Bardos Science Education Awards for Undergraduate Students, 89

Thomas M. Stetson Scholarship, 99

Thomas R. Pickering Foreign Affairs Fellowship, 523

Thomas Wood Baldridge Scholarship, 305

Thurgood Marshall Scholarship Award, 486

Thz Fo Farm Fund, 272

Time Inc. Internship Program, 565

Timothy S. and Palmer W. Bigelow Scholarship, 285

TMC/SAE Donald D. Dawson Technical Scholarship, 432

Tom and Judith Comstock Scholarship, 168

Tommy Lee Memorial Scholarship Fund, 272

The Tommy Tranchin Award, 228

The Tongan Cultural Society Scholarship, 273

Top 10 College Women Competition, 248

Toraji & Toki Yoshinaga Scholarship, 273

Toshiba/NSTA ExploraVision Award, 371

Toyota Corporate Scholarship, 376

Toyota Motor Sales U.S.A., Inc. Scholarship, 278

Travelers Foundation, 103

Treacy Company Scholarship, 495

Tribal Business Management Scholarship, 212

Trimmer Education Foundation Student Scholarships, 195

Tri-State Surveying & Photogrammetry Kris M. Kunze Scholarship, 93

Truman D. Picard Scholarship, 296

Tuition Equalization Grant (TEG), 485

Tuition Exemption for Children of Disabled or Deceased Firefighters, Peace Officers, Game Wardens, and Employees of Correctional Institutions, 485

Tuition Exemption for Children of U.S. Military POW/MIAs from Texas, 485

Tuition Incentive Program, 331

Tuition Rebate for Certain Undergraduates, 486

Tuition Waiver for Foster Care Recipients, 327

Two Ten Footwear Design Scholarship, 495

Two Ten Footwear Foundation Scholarship, 495

Two Year Community College BEA Award, 205

Tyson Foods Intern Program, 566

UBS/PaineWebber Scholarships, 499

UHEAA Grant, 505

Undergraduate Research Fellowship (URF), 171

Undergraduate Research Grants, 250

Undergraduate Research Scholarship, 348

Undergraduate Scholarship, 516

Undergraduate Scholarship Program, 349

Undergraduate Summer Fellowships in Engineering and Science, 550

Undergraduate Summer Internship, 537

Union Plus Scholarship, 497

United Food and Commercial Workers International Union Scholarship Program, 497

United Health Foundation Scholarship, 103

United Methodist Loan Program, 585

United Methodist Scholarships, 497

United Parcel Service Earn & Learn Program Loans, 585

United States Holocaust Memorial Museum Internship, 566

United States Senate Youth Program, 519

United Transportation Union Insurance Association Scholarship, 501

University Journalism Scholarship, 399

Unmet Need Scholarship Program, 433

Urban Forestry Internship, 548

U.S. Department of Education Fulbright-Hays Project Abroad Scholarship for Programs in China, 225

U.S. Department of Homeland Security Scholarship and Fellowship Program, 558

U.S. Department of State Internship, 567

U.S. National Arboretum Summer Internship, 568

U.S. Senate Member Internships, 566

U.S. Steel NSBE Academic Scholarship, 376

USDA Summer Intern Program, 567

USDA/1890 National Scholars Program, 502

USTA Scholarships, 505

Utah Career Teaching Scholarship/T.H. Bell Teaching Incentive Loan, 586

Utah Centennial Opportunity Program for Education (UCOPE), 505

Utah Keith Griffall Scholarship, 493

Utah Robert C. Byrd Honors Scholarship, 506

VADM Samuel L. Gravely Jr. USN (Ret.) Memorial Scholarship, 186

Vantagepoint Public Employee Memorial Scholarship Fund, 287

Vara Gray Scholarship Fund, 149

The Vegetarian Resource Group College Scholarships, 506

Ventura County Japanese-American Citizens League Scholarships, 506

Verizon Corporate Scholarship, 376

Vermont Alliance for Arts Education (VAEE) Scholarship, 510

Vermont Golf Association Scholarship, 506

Vermont Incentive Grant, 510

Vermont John H. Chafee Education and Training Scholarship, 510

Vermont Non-Degree Program, 511

Vermont Part-Time Grant, 511

Vertical Flight Foundation Scholarship, 100

Vice Admiral E.P. Travers Loan, 579

Vice Admiral Jerry O. Tuttle, USN (Ret.) and Mrs. Barbara A. Tuttle Science and Technology Scholarship, 186

Vicki Willder Scholarship Fund, 273

Virgin Islands Leveraging Educational Assistance Partnership Program, 511

Virgin Islands Music Scholarship, 511

Virgin Islands Territorial Grants/Loans Program, 586

Virginia Academic Common Market, 471

Virginia Lee-Jackson Scholarship, 512

Virginia Museum of Fine Arts Fellowship, 513

Virginia Rehabilitative Services College Program, 513

Virginia Robert C. Byrd Honors Scholarship, 512

Virginia Tuition Assistance Grant, 471

Vision Award, 205

Visual and Performing Arts Achievement Awards, 250

Visual Task Force (VTF) Scholarship, 357

Vocational Rehabilitation Assistance, 503

Vogt Radiochemistry Scholarship, 161

Voice of Democracy Scholarship, 511

The Wall Street Journal Asia Internship, 569

The Wall Street Journal Europe Internship, 569

The Wall Street Journal Journalism Internship, 569

Wal-Mart Associate Scholarship, 514

Wal-Mart Stores Inc. Corporate Scholarship, 376

Wal-Mart Stores, Inc. High School Scholarship, 278

Walt Bartram Memorial Education Award (Region 12 and Chapter 119), 447

Walter and Marie Schmidt Scholarship, 412

Walter H. Kupau Memorial Fund, 273

Walter S. Patterson Scholarship, 205

Walton Family Foundation Scholarship, 514

Washington Crossing Foundation Scholarship, 514

Washington Internships for Students of Engineering, 570

Washington State American Indian Endowed Scholarship, 515

Washington State Need Grant, 515

Washington State Scholars Program, 515

Washington State Scholarship Program, 515

Water Companies (NJ Chapter) Scholarship, 357

Wayne G. Failor Scholarship, 418

Web Challenge Contest, 476

Weisman Scholarship, 223

Wells Fargo Scholarship, 279

Welsh Heritage Scholarship, 516

West Virginia Engineering, Science, and Technology Scholarship, 517

West Virginia Higher Education Adult Part-time Student (HEAPS) Grant Program, 517

West Virginia Higher Education Grant, 518

West Virginia Robert C. Byrd Honors Scholarship, 518

West Virginia Underwood-Smith Teacher Scholarship, 518

West Virginia War Orphans Educational Assistance, 517

Western Plastics Pioneers Scholarship, 451

W.H. McClennan Scholarship, 294

Wild Bill Fogle Memorial Scholarship, 412

Wilder-Naifeh Technical Skills Grant, 479

Will J. Henderson Scholarship Fund in Hawaii, 273

William A. and Ann M. Brothers Scholarship, 180

William B. Howell Memorial Scholarship, 180

William C. Davini Scholarship, 496

William C. Doherty - John T. Donelon Scholarships, 357

William D. & Jewell W. Brewer Scholarship Trusts, 126

William E. "Buck" Bragunier Scholarship for Outstanding Leadership, 186

William E. Weisel Scholarship, 447

William F. Johnson Memorial Scholarship, 153

William J. and Marijane E. Adams, Jr. Scholarship, 194

William James & Dorothy Bading
Lanquist Fund, 274
William L. Boyd, IV, Florida Resident
Access Grant Program, 242
William Park Woodside Founder's
Scholarship, 190
William R. Goldfarb Memorial
Scholarship, 168
Willie Rudd Scholarship, 300
Willis F. Thompson Memorial
Scholarship, 195
Willis H. Carrier Scholarship, 174
Wilma D. Hoyal/Maxine Chilton
Memorial Scholarship, 109
Wilma Motley Memorial California
Merit Scholarship, 78
Wisconsin Academic Excellence
Scholarship, 521
Wisconsin Hearing & Visually
Handicapped Student Grant, 521
Wisconsin Higher Education
Grant, 521
Wisconsin Indian Student Assistance
Grant, 521
Wisconsin Minority Teacher Loan
Program, 587
Wisconsin Minority Undergraduate
Retention Grant, 522
Wisconsin Talent Incentive Program
Grant, 522
Wisconsin Tuition Grant, 522
Wisconsin Veterans Affairs Personal
Loan Program, 586
Wisconsin Veterans Affairs Retraining
Grant, 520
Wisconsin Veterans Education GI Bill
Tuition Remission Program, 520
Wolf Trap Foundation for the
Performing Arts Internship, 570
Women in Architecture
Scholarship, 197
Women's Sports Foundation
Internship, 571
Women's Western Golf Foundation
Scholarship, 523
Wooddy Scholarship, 74
Workforce Improvement Grant, 183
Workforce Incentive Program, 580
World Security Institute
Internship, 571
Worldstudio AIGA Scholarship, 523
Yakama Nation Tribal
Scholarship, 524
Yale R. Burge Competition, 175
Yankee Clipper Contest Club, Inc.
Youth Scholarship, 168
Yanmar/SAE Scholarship, 433
Yasme Foundation Scholarship, 168
Y.C. Yang Civil Engineering
Scholarship, 172
Year-Long Horticultural
Internship, 568
Yellow Ribbon Scholarship, 493
Young Epidemiology Scholars Student
Competition, 218
Young Naturalist Awards, 158
Young Survivor Scholarship, 89

You've Got a Friend in Pennsylvania
Scholarship, 169
Zachary Taylor Stevens Memorial
Scholarship, 169
Zeller Summer Scholarship in
Medicinal Botany, 246
Zov's Bistro Scholarship, 304